Gun Digest

36th Anniversary
1982 Deluxe Edition

EDITED BY KEN WARNER

DBI BOOKS, INC., NORTHFIELD, ILL.

OUR COVER GUNS

There are two, an HK93A3 rifle in 223 caliber and an HKP9S competition sport handgun in 9mm, plus a drawing that explains just how any number of firearms made by Heckler & Koch work—with roller bearings in carefully calculated seats to lock the guns as long as they need be, whether they are handguns or full-size infantry machineguns in 7.62mm NATO caliber. Battle rifle types like the HK91 and HK93 are among the fastest selling rifles in the United States today. For more on the H-K designs, see the catalog entries and page 44. Cover photo by John Hanusin.

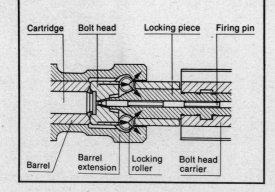

Cartridge | Bolt head | Locking piece | Firing pin

Barrel | Barrel extension | Locking roller | Bolt head carrier

GUN DIGEST STAFF

EDITOR-IN-CHIEF
  Ken Warner
ASSISTANT TO THE EDITOR
  Lilo Anderson
SENIOR STAFF EDITOR
  Harold A. Murtz
ASSOCIATE EDITOR
  Bob Anderson
PRODUCTION MANAGER
  Pamela J. Johnson
CONTRIBUTING EDITORS
  Bob Bell
  Dean A. Grennell
  Larry S. Sterett
  Hal Swiggett
  Ken Waters
  J.B. Wood
EUROPEAN CORRESPONDENT
  Raymond Caranta
EDITOR EMERITUS
  John T. Amber
PUBLISHER
  Sheldon L. Factor

DBI BOOKS INC.

PRESIDENT
  Charles T. Hartigan
VICE PRESIDENT & PUBLISHER
  Sheldon L. Factor
VICE PRESIDENT — SALES
  John G. Strauss
TREASURER
  Frank R. Serpone

ISBN 0-910676-26-7   Library of Congress Catalog #44-3588

IN THE BLACK ◉

The Presidential View

Shooters got who they wanted into the White House in 1981, and it took only a few weeks before their faith in President Ronald Reagan was tragically tested. In a two-second splatter of 22 rimfire bullets, he and three others hit the ground, victims of a peculiarly American breed of nut assassin.

As soon as he could get to the subject, and that was thankfully soon, President Reagan took the wind out of the anti-gun sails by affirming that his experience was no reason to believe more gun laws were needed. The hue and cry continues, but without presidential backing is unlikely to get far, considering relative party strength in the Congress.

Auctioning Toward Class

Larry Wilson tells us Colt's and Christies, the great auction house, are partnering to put on what they hope will be a $2,000,000-plus auction of fine firearms and other collectibles right in New York City on Park Avenue October 7, 1981.

Money aside, the gun people see such occasions as excellent public relations on behalf of firearms ownership since virtually every item sold will be of merit, either artistically or historically. A catalog by Wilson should be out when you read this.

Bigelow On The Bounce

Peripatetic Bill Bigelow, editor and buckskinner for everyman, is trying once again with "All About Antique Arms" an annual with, he says, a dozen staffers, a price of $5.95, and offices at P.O. Box 190, Big Timber, MT 59011.

We wish him, as in the past, luck.

Milestones

● The Third Annual SHOT Show by the National Shooting Sports Foundation was just as good as they said it was going to be and Number Four is supposed to be something like 20% better again. Number Three nicely filled the Superdome in New Orleans one week before the Superbowl. It will be January 11, 12 and 13 in Atlanta's World Congress Center for Number Four for which over 500 companies had signed up six months before the show.

NSSF keeps on rolling in its PR and conservation efforts. The slogan for Hunting and Fishing Day 1981 is "A Day For Years To Come," which is good writing. NSSF's success at getting high recognition sports figures and other celebrities to go public is most admirable. And the "Unendangered Species" film strip mentioned here last year is 8,000 copies strong in the nation's schools and more thousands on order. There's a 50¢ bumper sticker that says "Hunters pay for conservation" probably worth displaying.

● Steve Herrett became the 9th Outstanding American Handgunner at the O.A.H.A. banquet held during the NRA Annual Meetings in Denver. Herrett's contributions, of course, are attached to handguns everywhere in the world and he has lately been doing a lot to make handgun hunting go.

● The National Rifle Association went around and around with itself in political and parliamentary infighting, but the way it worked out was Harlon Carter is Executive Vice President for five years and it can be expected he'll get the rest of it sorted out. It is hard to tell the players without a scorecard, and there are no scorecards, but the membership numbers and the sound and solid shooters programs and the nicely managed legislative and political effort are still all in line.

● Winchester-Western did not create an Outdoorsman of the Year in 1981, but they did introduce and produce the John Wayne Commemorative Model 94 and the Model 70 Featherweight, both of which are moneymakers. If they go out, they'll go out in style from the marketing point of view.

Recalls

● Remington pulled back some 38 Special + 158-gr. loads, Index R38S12 and Lots P28A and P29A. These rounds, manufactured in July 1980, may separate at the cannelure on firing. Rounds will be replaced at no cost.

● Beeman's sent out a warning on the possibility of accidental discharge associated with the safety on the Beeman 250, Hy Score 828 and similar rifles. The safety involved is a large plastic unit with spring metal trigger block. Beeman's will replace it free on guns they sold; charges for others.

● Sturm, Ruger & Co., Inc. found three cracked stainless steel Mini-14 receivers in guns fired with bore obstructions or high-pressure loads and has decided to call back all stainless Mini-14's below serial number 182-51929 for reproofing. Program is at no charge to owners. Call 603-863-3300, Ext. Mini-14 for details.

**JOYCE W. HORNADY
1907-1981**

This is Joyce Hornady as thousands saw him, a big man in a big industry, who talked to anybody interested in guns. He died in a plane crash en route to the 1981 SHOT Show, together with Edward A. Heers and James W. Garber, his employees and friends. All three will be missed.

**James F. Davis, Jr.
1929-1980**

This is Fred Davis of Falls Church, VA, shooting the 8-bore double rifle he once took to Africa. Fred was an accomplisher, considering what a dreamer he was, and a friend to the Editor from our first meeting, and a great shot, and it's tragic when a mistake in traffic loses us one like him.

CONTENTS

DEPARTMENTS

Remington's 721-722:

This is Remington Model 721 rifle No. 0000001.

THE STORY OF A SUCCESS

by STUART OTTESON

REMINGTON today stands well out front as the leading maker of sporting long arms in the world. Their Model 700 bolt action enjoys the same position among high power rifles. It's been that way for so long we sometimes take it for granted.

Matters were once far different. Between the World Wars, Remington's gunmaking operations came perilously close to following the likes of Newton, Standard, Lefever, and Ross into the history books. Impressive physical facilities existed at Ilion, thanks largely to their World War I activities, but not many guns were being shipped, and those that were often as not sold at a loss to the factory. Remington kept going during those years mostly on profits from the cartridge division in Bridgeport.

When DuPont took over in 1933, Remington was running a poor third in gun sales behind Winchester and Savage. DuPont's Board of Directors

planned to close down the firearms end of the business, but as a matter of routine they first dispatched a team of DuPont engineers headed by a Mr. George Read to Ilion to determine what if anything was worth salvaging. In the course of his survey, Mr. Read fortunately became a convert. On his return to Wilmington he made such a strong appeal on Ilion's behalf that he is now credited with almost single-handedly saving the factory.

Despite new DuPont investment which followed, things didn't really turn around at Ilion for some time. New machinery and processes were set up, but DuPont encountered a lot of resistance to attempts to modernize the design of the guns themselves. The problem was mostly how the guns were made, not how well they shot.

Remington's product line had evolved without much continuity over the years, a situation which can play havoc in volume arms manufacture.

Each gun was an individual, and while most worked well enough, their manufacture was slow and inefficient.

An example was the Model 720, the immediate predecessor to the 721 and 722 rifles. It listed at $97.40 just before the war, certainly no bargain basement price. Though put together from a lot of leftover military parts, it was costing more than that to make and sell. The extremely fine Model 37 target rifle was known around the plant as the Model $37 because that was roughly what Remington was losing on each one.

Under such circumstances, morale throughout the organization was understandably very low, and even with DuPont's help, Ilion's future continued to look dim. The Second War reversed things almost completely. This was not because of the enormous arms contracts, because profits on these were relatively meager. In fact, overbuilding and overexpansion could easily leave a company like Remington in worse shape than it started. The First War certainly hadn't yielded any lasting economic benefits.

World War II created an opportunity, or excuse, if you will, to "clean house" and modernize at Remington that didn't exist during normal times. DuPont instituted a far-reaching program in anticipation of post-war conditions. Officially titled *Reconversion and Modernization,* it was known around the plant as simply R & M. The 721 and 722 rifles were slated as the vanguard project of this R & M program, and were expected to pave the way for what was to eventually be a whole series of successful new Remington firearms. They were thus extremely critical to Remington's future in the DuPont corporate structure. In turn, success or failure of the new bolt rifles became in large measure the responsibility of one man, Merle (Mike) Walker.

Walker is a native of Iowa, and got an engineering degree from Iowa State in 1934. This was the depth of the Depression, and so almost any job was a welcome blessing. Thus, Walker was more than happy to be working for Dow Chemical in the late 1930s, although he had little desire to finish out his career there.

One might wonder how a person makes the transition from organic chemist to one of the world's top firearm designers working for Remington. Surprisingly enough, Walker simply answered an ad in *The American Rifleman* magazine. He went to Ilion for an interview in April, 1942, and came on board as part of Remington's Research Department three months later. There were a lot of new faces then, as DuPont was assembling a large engineering staff to meet their massive wartime arms commitments.

The new centerfire rifle project officially began on August 12, 1942, with an authorization of $200 to prepare a project outline, the first "paperwork," so to speak. Later that year, the head of the Research Department, a Dr. R. Hentchel, used another $11,500 for some preliminary background research. That was as far as things got until Walker took over the project two years later.

During 1942 and 1943 Walker was busy on war jobs, ranging from the development of buttoned rifle barrels manufactured (for Springfield rifles, but later, of course, with industry-wide application) to an optical sighting-in device for the Springfield rifle (which bore some resemblance to the collimators now used by gunsmiths). He even worked up a 4,250 feet-per-second artillery round capable of defeating the Nazi Tiger tank, though some other method was found and used by the military. Regularly producing 15-inch groups at 1,000 yards, performance of this last item was something even today's long-range target shooters don't scoff at.

In August of 1944, with the Springfield rifle contracts completed, Walker was given $35,000 to begin making drawings and building prototypes of a new rifle. While designers from other projects were to make important contributions, the actual 721-722 "team" consisted of only three other men; Dana McNally, Leon Rix, and Knute Reed. McNally was an engineer; the other two men assisting Walker working strictly on the boards as draftsmen. While you won't hear them mentioned again, these three in fact bore the yeoman's share of work in getting the new design drawn up and into prototype form.

The paper studies done in 1942 pretty well established what was desired: a light fast-handling rifle which could be made at low enough cost to market successfully and make some money for Remington. Volume would be the key to success. Thus, the new rifles were not primarily targeted to compete with Winchester's Model 70, the leading bolt action of the day, but rather with the Winchester Model 94, Marlin Model 36, and Savage Model 40, which together represented the biggest market for centerfire rifles. Remington gambled that if they could offer a stronger and more powerful rifle, which still handled as well and sold as cheaply, it would cut deeply into that market.

What makes the 721-722 story worth recounting now in some detail is not simply the fact that the rifles became a commercial success and met the specifications, but that they exceeded them to such an extent that the rifle design remains a leader today, more than 30 years later, and seems to grow stronger each year in the marketplace. It thus, I believe, deserves special recognition alongside other enduring firearms such as the Model 1898 rifle of Paul Mauser, the Colt single-action revolver, and John M. Browning's lever-actions.

Walker's crew had the first drawings of the rifle ready by the end of 1944. They pretty accurately depicted what was to become the production 721, except at the breech. Walker's "counterbore" pattern was one of the last elements of the design to fall into place, and the rifle was originally drawn up with a 35-degree cone breech. Considering that Remington had used a cone pattern since at least 1920, and Winchester still used one, and would in fact for another twenty years, that's not surprising. The 722, when it was later drawn up, differed from the 721 only in length, measuring exactly 0.85 inches less through the magazine and loading port.

Design

It might be useful at this point to examine some of the principal mechanical features of the 721-722.

Mike Walker in 1951 with 722 rifle chambered in the then new 222 cartridge.

The most costly single component of a bolt action is its receiver. Thus in cutting costs and production times, Walker had to get away from the traditional forging with its intricate machine work. He was not the first to build a high power rifle from barstock. Savage had done so for many years. His contribution instead lay in utilizing a very simple round receiver which did not finish to look like an overgrown rimfire rifle.

The receiver was carefully proportioned for a trim 1.355-inch diameter, thus making use of standard 1⅜-inch barstock. Instead of special grooves or slots, the tooling jigs and fixtures indexed directly in the boltway. Much effort also went into multiple tooling cuts. Those underneath the tang and bridge, for example, were made on a single pass with three cutters bolted together. A simple bracket blanked from steel plate and clamped between the receiver ring and barrel served as the recoil lug.

The bolt was also "modernized." Besides very large and solid locking lugs, and a bolt handle shaped for low-mounted scopes, its construction was carefully planned for volume manufacture. The "standards" at the time for quality high power bolt action rifles definitely called for a one-piece forged assembly. But such parts were not only very slow and costly to make, the end result wasn't necessarily precise. Walker fabricated his bolt, induction brazing the bolt handle in place with silver solder, and also making the bolt head separate. With the head and body of the bolt machined from barstock, extreme precision and concentricity was possible, while the furnace-brazed joint between them used a copper alloy that for practical purposes yielded one solid piece of steel. As extra insurance, a sturdy steel dowel fits cross ways through the joint.

Besides barstock and screw-machine parts, stampings were used where strength and wear weren't critical. This included the magazine and much of the "fire control unit." To avoid the need for inserts, adjusting screws in this latter assembly threaded directly into the sheet metal by means of 90 degree bends and partial threads cut into opposing interior walls of the trigger housing.

In writing up an incentive award for Walker in 1948, his supervisors noted that whereas the Model 720 bolt and receiver had required a combined total of more than 250 machine operations, the Model 721 required approximately 60. Beyond pure numbers, perhaps a more accurate gauge of Walker's contribution is the fact that his design allowed the Ilion workforce to produce truly precision parts in volume, and without the high degree of individual skill and workmanship that previously would have been needed.

Cartridges in the new rifle were extracted after firing by a small circular spring inside the bolt head. If any single part played a key role in the 721/722, it was this extractor. Not until it was certain that it worked in a high power rifle, and equally important that it could be successfully mass-produced, could Remington proceed with the final pattern of the bolt and barrel, and the all-important breech formed between them.

When developed by John Howell in 1945 for an unsuccessful autoloading rifle, the extractor's object was not so much a safer and stronger breech, but

ABOUT THE AUTHOR
Stuart Otteson once nearly withdrew from human society when, through no personal fault, he lost access to 1500 acres of Virginia groundhog pasture that had been his private preserve. He is a rifle nut. He is also 42, a mechanical engineer, and the writer of **The Bolt Action,** *just about the best book done on rifle actions. If Otteson still could shoot that 1500 acres, we probably wouldn't have the work he does for* **Rifle** *magazine, or this piece.   K.W.*

rather a cheaper part capable of a surer grip than conventional extractors. It was a crescent-shaped spring with a claw formed in its middle. Instead of being pivoted or collared to the bolt, it snapped into a peripheral groove milled inside the bolt face. Being thus trapped and contained within the counterbore itself, rather than fastened externally, it was less disposed to slippage, and enormous extracting power was potentially possible. Remington later ran advertising claims of double normal strength , based on tear-away tests in which the new extractor held up to around 300 pounds, compared to 150 pounds with conventional types.

But forming the necessary claw on this springy little part very nearly proved its undoing. The machined prototype versions were far too expensive for mass production. The problem was well known throughout the Research Department, and it wasn't until one of the toolmakers, Homer Young, devised a method for coining the claw that this novel extractor could be safely counted as part of the new rifle.

The ejector also occupied the bolt face rather than penetrating from outside. But here the way was shown by our World War II combat rifles, and Walker simply adopted the spring-loaded pins used in the M-1 rifles and carbines.

With everything nestled within the bolt face, it was now possible to ring the cartridge with a solid and unbroken belt of steel. The breech devised and patented by Mike Walker went further than this by also closely counterboring the end of the barrel to accept the bolt nose. Thus the cartridge was not only enshrouded by the bolt, but both were then enshrouded by a barrel flange. If a cartridge tried to rupture, pressure could expand the belt on the front of the bolt only far enough to fill the recess in the barrel.

Attached to the opposite end of the receiver is the fire control unit, more commonly known as the trigger and safety. For the Models 30 and 720, Remington had merely dressed up the existing military triggers. When Winchester introduced a superb new trigger in the Model 70, Remington had little choice but to follow suit. They had fortunately by then acquired a first rate trigger design of their own from a California inventor named John Sweany, and had experience with using it in the Model 37 rimfire target rifles since shortly before World War II.

Walker took the somewhat bulky Sweany layout and reshaped it into a slimmer easy to manufacture unit. It is fully adjustable and has a special spring loaded "connector" piece between the trigger and sear to allow a cleaner pull and the virtual absence of overtravel or "slap."

Hinged to the trigger housing is a two position side-mounted safety. It uses a cam to block the sear, a fact that caused the Research Department some unanticipated grief shortly before the rifles were to be released.

The patent attorneys in Bridgeport discovered during a final check of the rifle that this arrangement might in-

The rifle's bolt stop also underwent last minute revision. It originally consisted of a stop lever only, so that like the units fitted many years later to Remington's economy-line Model 600 rifles, something like a small screwdriver or jacknife was needed to get the bolt out. This was generally recognized to be a pretty cheesy arrangement by most Remington employees who handled the early pilot rifles. One of them, Charles Morse, volunteered to devise a linkage release system fitted to the trigger housing (ironically enough, it was

Barrels and Sights

The 721 and 722 rifles were fitted with six-groove barrels, rifled by the button system developed by Walker during the war. The standard outside contour was a double taper of medium weight, closely resembling the barrels in the Winchester Model 70. A short distance forward of the receiver ring a swell was formed to serve as the base for the rear sight assembly. Behind this swell, the barrel tapered 0.110 inches per inch, while forward to the muzzle the taper was only one-tenth as steep, 0.011 inches per inch.

The 721 (top) and 722 (bottom) rifles were trim but plain. These are two of original prototype rifles.

fringe the safety in Winchester's Model 52 target rifle, and thus a redesign was ordered. Phil Haskell, a young engineer from the Aberdeen Proving Grounds, got the last-minute assignment. Like Walker, he had arrived via an ad in *The American Rifleman,* although about four years later. After several weeks of pondering the subtleties of such an infringement problem, Haskell split the sear into two side-by-side stampings, one for the trigger and the other for the safety cam.

No one today can fully explain why this change satisfied the attorneys, or even if they originally had that much of a problem. The only sure thing is that a lot of gunsmiths through the years have puzzled over what Remington was up to. In any event, once this "solution" was accepted, the thousands of guns already in the warehouse were uncrated and returned to the factory for refit with two-piece sears.

Morse who would later develop the Model 600). This proved a very auspicious change, as the "new convenient bolt stop" became a major marketing feature of the new rifles.

While, according to Walker, there were literally "thousands" of problems and delays getting the rifles finished up and into production, the only other one he clearly recalls now involved heat treatment. Both to speed production and reduce warpage, the receivers in the first pilot rifles were hardened at the front only. But a color line appeared in the blueing, forcing Remington to start heat treating the entire part. Too much warpage then occurred, however, to allow using close fitting precision bolts. The problem was only solved by going to chrome moly steel and an *austempering* process where a hot salt quench subjects the final machined receiver blank to much less temperature shock and thus less warpage than conventional oil or water quenches.

Although the original 721-722 drawings show four barrel lengths, ranging from 20 to 26 inches, the rifles were introduced in 24 and 26-inch lengths only. The 26-inch length was reserved for 300 H&H (at least until the 222 Remington version was added a couple years later). The magnum barrel was also heavier than the standard contour, the combination increasing the rifle's over-all weight by about one pound. In later years, 22-inch barrels were offered in some calibers.

The receiver was drilled and tapped for scope bases and receiver sights. Some of the very first production rifles lacked holes on top of the bridge for a rear scope base, but this was very quickly corrected after complaints from the gun writers who tried to use them.

Each rifle had a white metal bead front sight dovetailed into a matted ramp brazed to the front of the barrel, and a step adjustable V-notch rear sight dovetailed into the integral swell near the rear of the barrel. Unlike the Winchester Model 70, this swell did not also serve as the base for a barrel screw, for the 721-722 rifles had semi-floating barrels screwed only to the receiver.

Weight and Handling

While action strength perhaps made the 721-722 rifles famous, their light weight and good handling also drew praise. The 721 and 722 weighed 7¼ and 7 pounds, respectively, very favorable figures for a high power rifle at that time. In comparison, Winchester's Model 70 listed at 7¾ pounds, at least until 1952 when their 6½ pound "Featherweight" version came along. And the custom rifles being put together at that time on surplus military actions often tipped the scales at 8 pounds or more.

The stock, although very plain and lacking either checkering or sling swivels, generally met with favor also. Cut from American walnut, it had a good pistol grip and a full semi-beavertail forearm. A shotgun type metal buttplate fitted to the back was nicely checkered to prevent slippage. While normally coming in an iron sight version (dropping 1⅞ inches at the comb and 2⅞ inches at the heel), a high comb stock (drop at comb of 1⅜ inches, and at heel 2³/₁₆ inches) more suitable for scope use accompanied the 222 rifle and was optional at no extra cost in other calibers.

Cartridges

After culling out a few "oddballs" suggested by marketing, such as the 30 Remington, Walker ended up with a lineup of six cartridges for the new rifles. The 721 was slated for 30-06, 270 Winchester, and the 300 H&H Magnum, while in the 722, 220 Swift, 257 Roberts, and 300 Savage chamberings were planned.

During some test firings in 1946, a defective Swift cartridge let go in a 721 rifle Walker was using. While no real damage or injury resulted, the experience nonetheless left a strong impression. Since Walker hadn't been all that anxious about tooling for a special slanted magazine for the Swift anyway, it took only a couple days to decide to kick it from the lineup, leaving only five chamberings at the time the rifles were introduced.

In 1950 a brand new varmint cartridge was developed. Labeled the 222 Remington, it is sometimes assumed to have been developed part and parcel

with the new 722 rifle. According to Walker, however, that wasn't the case and there was no tie-in with his earlier decision to drop the 220 Swift.

The 222 modified earlier experimental cartridges developed at Bridgeport to utilize .30 Carbine cup blanks. The original cartridges, while suitable for single shot rifles, were too short to feed in the 722. Walker put a steeper shoulder on the cartridge, lengthened the neck, and then stretched the whole thing out by about ³/₁₀ of an inch so it could better bridge the gap between the magazine and chamber. In the process, velocity was boosted from 2800 to 3200 feet per sec-

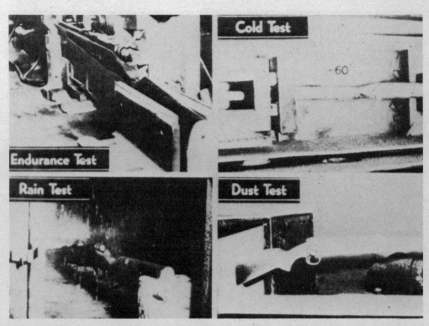

Excerpt from Remington literature shows stress marketers laid on factory tests of the new rifles.

ond with a 50-grain bullet.

Even lengthened, feed with the 222 was less than ideal. But instead of giving up, or going to a different type of magazine and feed system altogether, as Winchester had done for the 22 Hornet, Remington (more specifically, Phil Haskell) kept tinkering with the angles and dimensions of the 722 magazine until it finally digested this little cartridge with some reliability. Also of concern was whether the bullets were too solid for small varmints. After spending a good part of his summer shooting woodchucks with the new cartridge, Walker convinced Bridgeport to swage the bullets from thinner jackets. Thereafter, the cartridge quickly gained popularity, still universal today, and greatly complemented sales of the 722 rifles.

Cartridges were, of course, added, and dropped, from the rifles' chamberings in subsequent years. For the 721, the 280 Remington and 264 Winchester Magnum became available, while the 308 Winchester, 244 Remington, 222 Remington Magnum, and 243 Winchester appeared in the lineup for the shorter rifle.

Tests

The 721 was probably subjected to a more grueling series of tests than any commercial firearm before or since. Wayne Leek, another Aberdeen recruit, ran Ilion's newly formed Test Department. He introduced a lot of military methods, applying them with a vengeance to his first victim, the new 721 rifle.

These included a dust test, ice test, rain test, and blow-up test. An automatic fixture was built which put the rifles through 50,000 cycles to check wear of the bolt and firing system. Leek also placed the 721 prototypes in an "iron lung" for gas-leak tests using white blotter paper and cartridges filed down to the point that their heads would open up and spill gas upon firing. The rifle came through this latter test pretty well, except that the cocking piece was somewhat disposed to blow back through the unshrouded bolt sleeve. While it never got completely away, it did exhibit a nasty habit of cocking on the receiver.

When loaded with dust, a perhaps unrealistic criterion for a non-military arm, the cocking piece also tended to bind with the sear. To overcome this, the flat area of contact between these two pieces was relieved by cutting serrations into the top of the sear. For production, the same result was gained with less expense by simply lathe-turning the cocking piece to yield a radiused contact surface with the sear below.

The blow-up tests were the big thing, and the most publicized. They were run on two 721 rifles chambered for 30-06, which Walker considered the worst cartridge from a blow-up

standpoint. Starting with a proof cartridge, 220-grain bullets were progressively lodged in front for each shot until the rifles no longer functioned. By the fifth extra bullet, the bolt head had expanded into the barrel counterbore so tightly in both rifles that the bolt handles were broken off trying to open them. But because the enshrouded cartridge heads remained intact through it all, no further damage occurred and the only gas to escape came through the primer.

Such conditions far exceeded anything that a brass cartridge head could withstand alone. According to Remington, the two 721 pilot rifles were subject to pressures estimated as high as 300,000 pounds per square inch. Conventional rifles tested alongside them for comparison all turned to

scrap at much lower pressures.

Patents

Besides the button rifling patent (no. 2,383,356 issued August 21, 1945), three others related specifically to the 721-722 rifles. Number 2,473,373, covering John Howell's extractor, was filed on January 30, 1946 and issued a little over three years later on June 14, 1949. The next (no. 2,514,981), for Walker's redesign of the Sweany trigger, plus Haskell's work on the safety, was filed on February 12, 1948 and issued July 11, 1950.

The last, number 2,585,195 covering Mike Walker's *counterbore* breeching mechanism, wasn't filed until January 8, 1949, almost a full year after official announcement of the new rifles, and at a time when many thousands were already in circulation.

Thus there was great difficulty with the application. Remington's attorneys and the Patent Office went around and around on the invention, the Patent Office seemingly determined to throw just about every patent they could lay their hands on against it, particularly the just-issued Howell patent.

Remington not only had to come up with depositions establishing when, where, and who did what on the new rifle, they pulled out all stops to convince the people in Washington of its overwhelming technical merits. Copies of the many favorable gun reviews were furnished. Twice the Remington attorneys lugged down all the rifle specimens used in the blow-up tests, the wrecked Mausers, Springfields, Winchesters, etc., as well as the unscathed 721s. They once even took the head examiner over to the Arlington Rifle Club for an afternoon's shooting with the new rifles.

By going back and blowing up a 721 rifle with the barrel flange machined away, Remington finally convinced the Patent Office that it was not Howell's bolt face alone that accounted for the new breech's remarkable strength, but that in fact the barrel flange was the real key which allowed continued support of the cartridge under the most extreme pressure conditions. The Patent Office thereupon relented, and issued Walker's patent on February 12, 1952.

Introduction and Delivery

While development of the 721-722 was a well kept secret at the factory, a select group of gun writers examined pilot rifles in the spring of 1947, and soon rumors of a new Remington rifle were surfacing. Those actually shown rifles probably didn't do too much talking, however, at least in specifics, because rumors centered on a commercialized version of the Springfield.

Considering the million-plus

Mike Walker around 1952 testing one of first 222 benchrest rifles. Mike and his wife Olive were among leading stool shooters in the '50s and '60s.

Remington 721/722 Specifications

Caliber	Rifle	Magazine capacity	Over-all length	Weight	Barrel length
30-06	721	4	44¼	7¼	24
270	721	4	44¼	7¼	24
300 H & H	721	3	46¼	8¼	26
300 Savage	722	4	43¼	7	24
257 Roberts	722	4	43¼	7	24
222 Remington	722	5	45¼	7½	26

The 1962 Model 700, a major facelift of the 721-722, came in two grades. The 700BDL (at top in short action) featured fancy-pattern pressed checkering, tips on forearm and pistol grip, white line spacers, hinged floorplate, and sling assembly. Standard grade 700ADL (bottom in long action) had simpler checkering pattern and blind magazine.

Springfield rifles Remington had just finished cranking out for the Army, such a conclusion wasn't irrational. In fact, there were those at Remington who had originally leaned strongly in that direction. But once Mike Walker took charge, there was no further hesitation about going to a completely new rifle. He had carefully studied Remington's pre-war experiences, and well knew that even though development costs might be much lower, making converted military rifles was not profitable in the long run.

Marketing had originally scheduled announcement of the new rifles for January, 1947. Since that committed them to a wholly impractical timetable, Walker and the rest of the Research staff got a little stirred up, to put it mildly. Even 1948 presented a lot of problems, but an announcement date of January 21, 1948 was finally agreed on.

The 721 and 722 were cataloged at $79.95 and $74.95 respectively, compared to $59.50 for Winchester's Model 94, $58.75 for the Marlin Model 36, and $52.40 for the Savage Model 40. While thus falling a little short of the original pricing goals, they were still comfortably below the $106.00 that the Model 70 was commanding at the time. To their advantage, the 722 offered U.S. shooters the first true short-actioned production bolt rifle in some 20 years.

It was also very helpful that deliveries of Model 70 rifles following the war were so slow that it was often dif-

ficult to lay hands on one at almost any price. Many shooters were turning in desperation to custom rifles built on surplus military actions, running $175 and up for decent specimens. The market was ripe for an eighty-dollar rifle with state-of-the-art performance.

The first small lot of production guns was distributed to writers for evaluation in the fall of 1947. Deliveries to wholesalers were scheduled to begin by caliber as follows:

30-06 Springfield .. March 1948
300 Savage .... May 1948
270 Winchester and 257 Roberts .... July 1948
300 H&H Magnum ....
September 1948

The rifles were officially designated the 721A and 722A to denote a "standard" grade. "Fancy" grades were also offered, the B (Special) with a checkered stock of selected walnut and sling swivels, and D (Peerless) and F (Premier) grades which featured even better wood, plus engraving. There were also later designations such as the 721AC-722AC and 721BDL-722BDL, but in practice even Remington marketing seldom used suffixes, and the guns were invariably referred to simply as Models 721 and 722.

Sales

Sales of the Model 30 and 720 rifles which preceded the 721-722 had totalled a scant 25,000, roughly 1,000 rifles a year. Thus DuPont knew that the new rifle had nowhere to go but up.

The big question, of course, was how far? Development of the rifles cost $175,000, and tooling roughly another million. New high-volume guns coming out today routinely cost a lot more, but that was an unprecedented investment for the time, and an enormous pile of pre-1950 dollars.

DuPont gambled that the low retail price made possible by the new machinery and processes would generate enough sales volume in the post-war market to recover the investment. The break-even point was figured to be approximately 15,000 rifles per year. Considering Remington's dismal pre-war sales record, the whole thing obviously required some confidence on management's part.

An opportune juxtaposition of a good rifle, low retail price, and booming post-war demand for high power hunting rifles brought an acceptance and sales volume that took even Remington by surprise. Favorable articles and evaluations began pouring in so fast that the Marketing Department compiled a 23-page booklet entitled "What The Experts Say About the New Remington Models 721 & 722 Big Game Rifles." It contained twenty writeups which appeared in print during the first four months of 1948, ranging all the way from a brief announcement in the *New York Times*, to an exhaustive dual evaluation in *The American Rifleman* by the esteemed team of Julian Hatcher and Al Barr.

The following summary of the "experts" reactions shows they liked a lot more things about Remington's new rifles than they disliked:

Features acclaimed:

1. Light weight and good balance.
2. Strength.
3. Safety.
4. Speed and smoothness of operation.
5. Good stock lines and proportions.
6. Convenient and noiseless safety.
7. Convenient bolt stop.
8. Extractor strength.
9. Low selling price.
10. "Miracle" trigger.
11. Bolt handle shape and safety location for low-mounted scopes.
12. Smooth and clean receiver lines.

Most of the complaints about "austerity" were tempered by a recognition that the very favorable retail price of the new rifles forced Remington to keep some things basic. The lack of checkering on the stock was a good example. Even at the labor rates then, hand checkering would have boosted the rifles' retail price by between $10 and $15, bringing it up closer than Remington wanted to be to the Model 70.

The first full year's production (1949) was approximately 42,000 rifles, and that was more a manufacturing limitation than anything else, because for the first couple years the factory was working day and night and Remington was selling everything they could ship from Ilion. Sales in 1950 topped 50,000.

But the rifle's engineering virtues could sustain this level of sales only so long. Very plain and unexciting lines limited its ultimate sales potential.

at Remington very happy, but they didn't satisfy Walker, and he had a completely restyled rifle ready for 1952. Remington's management, loth to tamper with success, vetoed the change. The same thing occurred in 1960.

Meanwhile, in 1958 another rifle with obviously close ties was briefly added to the Remington product line alongside the 721 and 722. The Model 725 originated on "the other side of the house" insofar as Remington's engineering organization was concerned, being designed under Wayne Leek, who had by then come up from the testing department to become a design supervisor, mostly for shotguns and rimfire rifles.

While the 725 had a slightly swept back bolt handle, releasable floorplate, and checkered stock, it also tended to harken back to Remington's pre-war rifles, in the process requiring some expensive extra machining cuts. Sales were poor, about 10,000 rifles total, and it was discontinued after three years.

The commercial failure of this rifle obviously helped persuade management finally to approve Walker's redesign of the 721-722. In 1962 the Remington Model 700 came into being, superseding the 721 and 722. At the same time sales began to take off, climbing back into the 50,000 to 60,000 category in the first year of production. They have been on the rise ever since, eventually surpassing 100,000 per year and making the Model 700 (which is really still just a prettied up 721/722) easily the best bolt-action seller in the world, today pursued seriously only by Ruger's Model 77. •

Two men who actively contributed to 721-722 project: Wayne Leek (left) tested the rifles; Homer Young figured out how to manufacture the little spring clip extractors.

Features criticized:

1. Lack of scope base holes on bridge (immediately corrected).
2. Non-detachable sheet metal floorplate and trigger guard.
3. Plain uncheckered varnish-finished stock.
4. Lack of sling swivels.

While it certainly wasn't ugly, neither could anyone ever accuse it of winning any beauty contests against the Model 70, or even the many custom-built Mausers, Springfields, and Enfields, for that matter. In 1951 sales began to cool off, thereafter settling down into the 30,000 range, although there were one or two more 50,000-rifle years.

Such sales continued to make many

ACKNOWLEDGEMENTS

Several current and former Remington employees helped gather material for this article. I want to thank Ted McCawley, Clark Workman, Mike Walker, Larry Goodstal, Phil Haskel and, most particularly, Sam Alvis, former Chief Engineer at Ilion and, in retirement, Ilion's untiring historian and archivist. Stuart Otteson

IT MAY dumbfound those fascinated by the glamorous age of American pioneering to learn that many fabulous long rifles never were rifles at all. Technically they were smoothbores, smoothbores of special kinds, not oddities or rebores or rarities. We speak of traditional firearms created as far back as early colonial times. Ancestrally, these long American smoothbores deserve a place of distinction akin to that of their far more famous relatives, the long rifles.

As a class, surviving long smoothbores have come down to us through the years as unnoticed as wallflowers at a dance. Much of their obscurity may be blamed on mistaken identity. They look like long rifles; they often served as shotguns; they were not exactly either. Because of this ambiguity, they never had a real name all their own.

For nearly two centuries now, the few people who recognized these guns as a distinct type have groped for a satisfactory name for them. Most tries went wide of the mark. For example: Everyone knows that a rifle has rifling and a smoothbore hasn't, yet these long guns were dubbed with such contradictions as "smoothbore rifles," a misnomer adopted by the U.S. Army before 1800. The phrase that best describes their function would be "ball-or-shot guns," but that is cumbersome. For our purposes here, then, let us christen them American *long smoothbores*. All the early ones were flintlocks, but the type continued well

Look Again At...
Long Rifles With
Smooth Bores

by ASHLEY HALSEY, JR.

Author with his probable favorite smoothbored rifle: a 1780 Jacobus Schuler.

into the percussion period.

To arrive at a clearer understanding of the long smoothbores and their correct status among American firearms, consider their salient features and how they came into being:

At the start of gunsmithing in the 13 American colonies, there were two basic kinds of civilian shoulder arms: The light smoothbore fowling piece or bird gun, principally English in origin, and the heavy hunting rifle of Germanic derivation. The two stood extremes apart in both appearance and performance. The fowling piece, graceful and thin if not frail, threw shot. In the flintlock period, it served as the predecessor of the modern shotgun. The rifle, stubby and weighty by comparison, fired a substantial round ball. Rifle fodder ran as big as 60 to 70 caliber. Several colonial American versions of English fowlers that I have examined, by contrast, gauged the smoothbore equivalent of less than half that caliber.

In the inevitable American process of change and progress, the rifles stretched out very nearly to fowling piece length and slimness without surrendering their rifling. Some indigenous fowlers also appeared, notably the Hudson River type with their extra-long smoothbore barrels suitable for pass shooting in that majestic valley. Largely lost to sight in the transition period, however, was the development of a combination-purpose long smoothbore.

Like all new things in the New World, the long smoothbore was invented in response to a need and a demand. In this instance the cry was for a hard-hitting large caliber gun that could be loaded with a choice of shot or unpatched balls faster than a patched-ball rifle could swallow its single projectile. The new arm offered this versatility and what passed in muzzle-loading days for speedy loading. It fit neatly into its time and place.

Look backward a moment to that time and place. Most Americans today harbor a tidy notion that the frontier advanced almost in a line from east to west over all obstacles, climbing mountains and fording rivers. Actually it was a wavering process. It began on the brink of the Atlantic in the 1600's. From there it marched "by the left flank, right flank" and in grim times such as Indian massacres, "double-to-the-rear." It flowed through the gaps and valleys, bypassing the highlands. In those areas—Adirondacks, Poconos, Alleghenies, Appalachians, Ozarks, in turn—the larger

game lurked in the fastnesses and forayed around the settlements. Wildlife biologists tell of elk and bison roving east of the Mississippi and infiltrating the Atlantic coastal plain. Wolves prowled in plenty. Bears in their deceptively lumbering way wandered widely in the East and some still do. Hunting in the settled areas, however, gradually turned more to mixed bags including squirrels, rabbits and fowl.

During the period from the late 1600's through the mid 1700's, meanwhile, the rifle underwent its transformation from Germanic short hunting arm to the legendary American long rifle, although it kept such jaeger features as the octagon barrel and patchbox. Essentially it emerged as the "big game" rifle of its time. As such, it lacked the capability of a shotgun in taking small game. To overcome this, some 18th and 19th century gunsmiths produced over-and-under muzzleloaders with one barrel rifled, one smooth. These proved relatively heavy in the field and expensive to make. They obviously were not the best answer.

Meanwhile, enter quietly the long smoothbore. It is impossible to say just when it established itself. Probably it was known by word-of-mouth by the third quarter of the 1700's. The Verner long smoothbore illustrated herewith may have been one of the first of its kind fabricated in America.

To fulfill the double need for a ball-or-shot gun, the new firearm had to be more than a lightweight fowling piece and it was. For one thing, its octagon breech section was usually heavier and stronger than most fowlers and some rifles. To save weight and simplify barrel production, however, its barrel was round for most of its length from breech section to muzzle. In this respect the barrel followed the pattern of the fowler barrel. Some other characteristics are typical of the long rifle.

The veil over the identity of the new gun was due in part to its birthplace.

Like the famous long rifles, the long smoothbores came first from the hands and forges of the Teutonic immigrants who settled in eastern Pennsylvania before 1750. In creating the long smoothbores they naturally utilized many proven features of the rifles. This is highly visible in at least three respects. In a half-dozen other ways, they fashioned the new arms with differences, some evident and some not.

Nearly all of the dozens of long smoothbores that I have owned or examined over some 50 years shared these features in common with the long rifles:

• Front and rear open sights, Kentucky rifle style.
• Cheekpieces, also usually found only on rifled arms.
• Patchboxes, many of them as elaborate as on the long rifles.

The differences were more numerous though sometimes less noticeable. The smoothbores featured:

• Broader, less curved butts than

Nary a groove infects the barrels of these four original rifle-styled smoothbores, all with half-octagon, half-round barrels and none of them re-bored.

rifles as a rule.
• Plain triggers, not double-set or "hair" triggers such as appeared particularly on the later Kentucky rifles.
• Barrels not over one-third octagonal and the rest round, instead of being entirely octagonal.
• Bores almost invariably above 50 caliber where the rifles, with early exceptions, ranged around 45 caliber or below.
• Barrels averaging several inches longer than rifles.
• Lighter over-all weight than rifles despite the longer barrels.

Each of these points deserves discussion. Let us take up first what an old Pennsylvania Dutch gunsmith might have called "the alikes":

The smoothbores' rifle sights and cheekpieces played useful roles in firing ball instead of shot. They surely helped in aiming and holding. Antique fowlers and modern shotguns alike carry only bead front sights. The long

Early long smoothbore, about 1770, identified by carving as work of Andrew Verner, Bucks Co., Pa. Serpentine sideplate and wrist escutcheon are early characteristics. Length 58½"; barrel 42"; two-thirds round: rudimentary front and rear sights; present bore 72-cal.; maple stock; 6 lbs.; no patchbox.

Circa 1780, this unsigned long smoothbore is attributed to Jacobus Shuler, Quakertown, Pa. Length 62½"; 47" barrel; two-thirds round; front and rear rifle-style sights; 52-cal. smoothbore; striped maple stock; wt. 6½ lbs.; minimum fittings; no patchbox, buttplate or tailpipe.

The long smoothbore in its prime, this unsigned but identifiable product of Nicholas Beyer, Lebanon, Pa., was made circa 1805. Length 59"; barrel 44½"; over two-thirds round barrel; rifle-style front and rear sights; cal. 68; wt. 6¾ lbs.; striped maple stock; engraved brass furniture and elaborate patchbox with bird finial recognized as Beyer design.

The ultimate in percussion long smoothbores, circa 1840. It is an original percussion; has back-action lock signed "Henry Parker," barrel signed "Deeds," but stock workmanship that of Boyer of Orwigsburg, Pa. Length 63"; barrel 48"; almost three-fourths round; front and rear rifle sights; 56-cal.; large brass patchbox; musket-type trigger guard; fine striped maple stock; wt. 8½ lbs.

smoothbores, however, mounted lengthy blade front sights like the rifles—what else?

The predilection for patchboxes on long smoothbores is harder to explain in retrospect. Part of it could have been traditional appearance. Quality rifles sported patchboxes, so . . . Even today, Kentucky rifle experts, of whom there are many and more a-making, dispute the purpose of these ornate brass creations. But it is fair to assume that if they were handy in loading patched-ball rifles, as their widespread acceptance suggests, they no doubt helped in fitting a patched ball snugly into a smoothbore.

Aside from personal experience, my own evidence on that score is slight but affirmative. I just once found aged cloth patches, but to the correct caliber, in the box of a long percussion smoothbore from Pennsylvania. I have detected smears and remnants of grease in other boxes. But more often, some collectors now theorize, the patchboxes held bullets, vent picks, spare flints or percussion caps.

"They were like a lady's handbag," one said.

So much for the characteristics that the long smoothbore shared with the long rifle. Now let us review the differences between the two types.

Colonial American gun butts were thick with little in-curve. Some measured as much as two inches across, leading certain advanced collectors to describe them as "clubby." As American rifles grew elongated, their butts became thinner and more crescent-shaped. These changes were far less pronounced in the smoothbores. Their butts retained a slight curve but more nearly resembled those of modern shotguns.

As for double-set or hair triggers, never have I seen them either in fact or in photograph on a long muzzleloader manufactured as a smoothbore. They would serve no purpose on such a gun and in truth could prove a handicap. Some remained on long rifles that were bored out smooth, but that is another story. Modern set triggers are found mainly on European hunting rifles fired from stands or on target handguns and rifles. They simply do not go with shotgunning techniques, old or new.

The four remaining differences all have to do with barrels and can be discussed together:

The preference for the octagon-to-round barrels arose from several advantages. They were easier to make. Barrels of the period were hammered out of long flat strips of iron called skelps. These were laboriously turned and welded around rod-like mandrels to create bores. In making barrels round for most of their length, the smoothbore manufacturers eliminated beating out and finishing the eight full-length flats required for octagonal rifle barrels. And, of course, the slow, painstaking process of rifling the smoothbore by hand became unnecessary. All this added up to a sizeable labor saving.

To function as shotguns, the long smoothbores were given larger bores than their contemporary rifles. That left less metal in the barrel and enabled the gunsmiths to lengthen barrels without adding weight. Employment of mostly round barrels further reduced the weight. The resulting long smoothbore could reach out well with shot or ball without overburdening its shooter in the field.

The earlier musket-like smoothbores weighed six to six and a half pounds, not heavy even by today's aluminized standards. Later ones reached above seven pounds. But they still must have seemed as feathery light as fairy wands in a day when true long rifles often weighed in at eight to ten pounds or more.

As for comparative calibers, a few early Pennsylvania rifles revealed their Germanic jaeger descent in having bores of .50-in. or more. Nearly all of the more typical ones made, say, from 1790 to 1820, gauged 45 caliber or under. Compare that with my statistical sampling of 26 old guns of the period which can be indisputably classified as original long smoothbores. All except one measured above 50 caliber and that exception gauged 48. Four of the others were 60 or above and one reached 70.

From its inception the long smoothbore must have been a joy to the frontiersmen and others who carried it. An outstanding advantage was that the proper size of round ball gave fair accuracy without patching. This happily bypassed the bothersome and time-consuming chore of greasing or spit-moistening a patch, placing it on the muzzle, centering the bullet on it, patch-cutting or trimming off the excess cloth, and starting it down the bore usually with a special short starter. While an experienced rifleman could do this faster than it takes to tell, patching nevertheless consumed precious time. In extremes of desperation, beset by a charging bear or rampaging Indians, it remained possible to fire an unpatched ball from a rifle bore. At close range in a crisis, the loss of velocity due to the deep open rifling scarcely mattered.

But the long smoothbores afforded shooters a better option in firing round bullets. Circumstances permitting, their users probably preferred to patch the balls. This increased obturation—perhaps saving a little powder—and improved accuracy. If a shooter did not want to pause to patch, the absence of rifling assured a better bullet fit and less waste of pressure.

There is reason to believe that some devotees of the long smoothbore carried two sizes of balls for the same gun: One for use with patches and a slightly fatter one to be slipped down the bore bare. If so, that would answer questions as to a minor mystery in antique arms collecting. There exist a number of old double-cavity round ball moulds with only a slight difference in the calibers they cast. One of these moulds

would throw, say, one ball of 535 caliber and another miking .54″ or .545″. Collectors have conjectured over these moulds for years. A theory that they were for over-and-under muzzleloaders with two rifled barrels of nearly identical caliber fails to hold up well. With such close calibers in a rifle, it has been pointed out, a thicker patch on the smaller ball almost certainly would turn the trick. But with the long smoothbore, the larger ball cast by these double moulds would be ideal for loading bare. The other, of course, would be reserved to be put down patched. It's an interesting speculation.

The long smoothbore possessed another virtue that was even more valuable at times. It could be quickly charged with two round bullets, loaded bare one on top of the other. Capt. John G.W. Dillin, the pioneer writer on long rifles, reported coming upon an old hunter in the Pennsylvania hills in 1891 who had just shot a good buck with a smoothbore heavily loaded with two balls. Both passed through the neck. Dillin testified that such double loads were frequently used. A latter-day authority and master maker of long flintlock rifles, Carl Pippert, a Marylander, told this writer the same thing recently. There is ample testimony to back up the custom.

Anyone unfamiliar with muzzleloader shooting may reasonably ask: Why wouldn't the regular, deepgroove Kentucky rifle, or at least a shallow-groove version of it, serve equally well when double-loading is desired?

To most who have fired muzzleloader rifles, either antique or reproduction, the answer should be fairly evident. It takes long enough to load and ram down a single patched ball under most conditions, especially in a foul bore. To double that loading time and more than double the risk of balls jamming on their way down the bore invites a plight. Certainly it must have been highly undesirable within range of a fleeting deer or disgruntled bear. By contrast, I have seen experienced muzzleloader shooters literally pop two balls into a smoothbore in an instant. One, in fact, got the nickname "Bullfrog" because he carried (for short periods) several balls bulging in his mouth and spat them into the muzzle.

Back in the prime of the long smoothbores, moreover, "doubleshotted" arms were in common use. To appreciate this fully, it is essential to know the military smallarms and

ordnance of the muzzleloader period. At one time, say 1750-1825, all artillery and standard-issue muskets consisted of smoothbores. A recognized U.S. Infantry load from the Revolutionary War into the Civil War consisted of "buck and ball," three buckshot and a large ball packaged for the 69 caliber musket. Cannon, especially naval ones, were crammed on occasion with a weird assortment of projectiles. That mention refers not to fiction writers' fanciful assertions that such guns were loaded with a "keg of nails"—a precious commodity back then—but to carefully-designed multiple projectiles.

The armies used grapeshot and canister to mow down advancing ranks of infantry and bombshells to explode inside fortifications and enemy ships. Naval ammunition in the square-rigger days was even more exotic. U.S. warships fired chain shot (two big balls linked by chain), bar shot (two balls connected by a bar), expanding bar shot (two balls each on a bar, the bars linked by chain) and an anti-personnel load called langrage, a fancy name for a canvas bag of scrap iron. British Navy variations included star, faggot and three-piece chain shot calculated to lash out in every direction.

So it took no stretch of the imagination to charge a long smoothbore hunting arm with two or more balls or any one of several combinations of buckshot and smaller shot. I have several times in past years pried combinations of No. 6 and No. 9 shot, or the like, from the reluctant chambers of old muzzleloaders. Other mixtures were even stranger, suggesting that shooters might have run out of one size of shot and topped off the load with another.

While the versatility of the long smoothbore passed proof beyond question, what did remain in question was its true identity—a situation that continues to this day. The slow passage of the years further obscured this distinctive American arm. Another simple and logical firearms evolution almost sank it from sight.

Guns a century and more ago were too prized to be casually discarded. Due to hard and long use, many octagon-barrel long rifles eroded their bores. These "rocky roads" became pitted traps for bullets. Patched balls hung up in them. Ramrods snapped. So, no doubt, did tempers.

Hence the worn rifle barrels were reamed out smooth to facilitate further use of the arms. Where the barrel walls remained thick enough,

In not much external contrast to the smoothbores, here is a true Kentucky rifle, circa 1790-1800. Length 59"; full octagon barrel 43" long; wt. 11 lbs. Signed only "H.B." on barrel but clearly a product of the Lebanon, Pa., school. It has deep 7-groove rifling in 42-cal.

rifling could be recut to a larger caliber. But that took time and money and not everyone wanted to expend these on old rifles. To judge by the considerable number of fine flintlock rifles that have turned up in original form—with the significant exception of smoothbored barrels—many gun owners must have said, "Don't bother with rerifling it" after reboring. What's more, the altered rifles could perform smoothbore tricks such as readily accepting double-shotted loads.

The alterations confront collectors and historians today with not two but three variations in American long muzzleloaders. We have:

1. The long rifle in its pristine form, say, deeply rifled with seven grooves in 45 caliber and with a full-octagon barrel—currently regarded as the most desirable by collectors.

2. The smoothbore conversion of the long rifle by reaming and possibly reboring it into a gun that would ungrudgingly take shot or ball and which otherwise looked identical to an original rifle.

3. The increasingly obscured long smoothbore, built as such from the start but displaying the rifle features discussed here.

To what extent, then, were original long smoothbores produced? Like most such questions, there is no pat answer. There are some clear indications.

The Kentucky Rifle Association, certainly the foremost organization in the world specializing in this firearm, published books in 1967 and 1976. These reveal considerable progress in recent years in assembling hard facts on Kentucky rifles and stand as milestones in the collecting field.

The first volume presented photographs and details of 100 long arms. Of the 100 that I counted there, 13 are smoothbores, but ten of these very likely began life rifled. Only three displayed the distinguishable features of the long smoothbore. These, then, would represent 3% of the whole.

Publication of the 1976 KRA volume with data and photographs of some 279 fine representative long arms enabled me to make a study on a larger scale. Of the total in that volume, no fewer than 26 met my strict definition of original smoothbores. That, then, would amount to nearly 10% as compared with 3% detected in the previous volume.

What emerges between those lines appears to be a growing perception of the status of the smoothbore. They've been there all along, but more have come to light and won the attention of advanced collectors.

The long smoothbore has received occasional recognition in a growing bibliography on Kentuckies. Included are such basic books as John Dillin's volume, first issued in 1920; Joe Kindig, Jr.'s monumental meditation in print over his personal collection of 500 of these firearms, not one of which did he ever shoot; the Kentucky Rifle Association's aforementioned definitive works of love on the subject, and the scholarly perceptions published by George Shumway, Roy F. Chandler, James R. Johnston, Henry J. Kauffman, Merrill Lindsay and others.

Dillin (pages 39-40), 1946 edition) reports that his exhaustive research of "several hundred" smoothbore long guns revealed only six which could be classified as original smoothbores with certainty. The rest presumably were bored-out rifles. At least one "old man" in the Lehigh County area of Pennsylvania, Dillin recalled, was said to have specialized in converting aged rifles to smoothbores in the mid-1800's. That, be it noted, is just about when many of the fine old long rifles would have worn out.

The same source reveals that an original smoothbore by a Pennsylvania maker of the 1780's named Reading was "called a smoothbore rifle" and that such guns were uncommon then. The term "smooth rifle" also crops up in a U.S. Army Ordnance report of arms repaired at West Point, N.Y., in 1783-92, as quoted by William Guthman in his "March to Massacre." Among some 15,000 firearms of all kinds repaired, the report lists "smooth rifles" as a separate category.

In his massive book *Thoughts on the Kentucky Rifle in Its Golden Age*, Joe Kindig, Jr., dismisses the smoothbore in rifle form with a paragraph on page 36. Joe, long preeminent in the Kentucky or Pennsylvania rifle field, comments that guns with part octagon and part round barrels "are generally smoothbore" although he found about one in ten of this type rifled. He explains that the smoothbores were made "to shoot shot or a ball" and lets it go at that.

A fuller definition appears in "Longrifles of Note, Pennsylvania," a monograph by author-publisher George Shumway, of York, Pa. In discussing a long smoothbore made by John Noll, who worked in Pennsylvania about 1780 to 1820, Shumway comments that the gun was not a "true rifle" but "rather a smoothbore rifle with a barrel part octagon and part round." He adds that the phrase "smooth rifle" came into currency to designate flintlocks with rifle front and rear sights, cheekpieces, patchboxes, and "rifle-type trigger guards." Shumway also attempted to rescue the long smoothbore from anonymity by coining a one-word name for it. After referring to "longrifles"—one word—he terms the lengthy smoothbores "longfowlers," also one word. A capacity for discharging several 50-plus-caliber balls at a time, however, would seem to lift them out of the bird-hunting fowler category.

In a scholarly introduction to the second KRA volume, Member George H. Carroll points out that the Allentown-Bethlehem gunsmiths of Pennsylvania, who contributed importantly to long arm evolution, produced relatively few rifles. So many were smoothbores that Carroll comments: "A preference of smoothbore weapons was probably more in evidence throughout Pennsylvania than popular imagination now concedes."

As for myself, as author and long-time collector and shooter, let me make clear that I no more claim to have discovered the long smoothbore than Columbus laid claim to having discovered North America. The firearm, like the continent, has been there all along. Others have glimpsed it and reported on it as I have noted. Here I only attempt to amplify, analyze and publicize the facts of its existence. It is time to bring this distinctive firearm out of the shadows and into the campfire light as a proudly American arm in its own—the American long smoothbore. ●

Advices To Young Collectors

by JOHN T. AMBER
Editor Emeritus

Stroking a pet Lancaster double rifle, Amber's hands reveal his motivation: love for fine guns, all kinds, nearly, from all eras. (Photo by R.S.L. Anderson.)

AS I SIT HERE, thinking back on a near-lifetime of arms collecting, I've been tempted to tell you—the beginning collectors and those about to wet their feet—to forget about it. We're living in a parlous dangerous time, small and not-so-small wars raging all over the globe. Our economy is in tatters, like the rest of the world generally, and inflation worsens day by day. Many, if not most, economists agree, as do political pundits, that a severe recession, if not a full-blown depression, will soon hit us all. As I write this, late in March of 1980, the stock market has fallen to its lowest level in several years.

But there is a saving grace. In fact, there are two of them. First, inflation, now running at near-20% annually in the U.S., shows no sign of diminishing appreciably. If that is true—and I believe it to be—then the subsequent prices of antique and collectors firearms (not to mention modern or semi-modern arms) bought today will almost keep pace with inflation. In many instances the future will see certain types and classes of arms bringing prices beyond the inflation rate—if it does not go too high. This situation will be commented on later.

The second factor—and one I consider much more important than merely contending with inflation—is the genuine enjoyment to be found by the serious collector, the student of firearms; their lore and history, their technological advances over the centuries, their economic impact. Let the gun "investor" worry about inflation, about protecting his equity. I've never thought of such money men as being genuine collectors; they often know little or nothing about the background of the things they amass.

If that sounds arrogant, so be it. I hope to reach here men or women with a real interest in firearms, those with a desire to enrich their lives, to expand their horizons. I have found the study of firearms to be an endlessly fascinating field, an area of research that has shown me, time and again, that the more I learn the more there is to learn. It is my fond hope that some of you, at least, will come to love firearms as I have.

Now let's talk about gun collecting itself and how to go about it with the least depletion of your bank account. To save you money—and some heartache—I'm going to suggest a course of action that, I'm quite certain, many of you will *not* observe—human nature and rash acquisitiveness being what they are. Still, you will do much better off financially and ego-wise, if

A prize for Amber is this notable gold-inlaid Billinghurst buggy rifle—rarity and condition and quality all at once.

you abide by hard earned and often costly-to-me experiences.

First, don't buy another gun until you have read and digested a dozen or more books on gun collecting in general and taken in a like number of antique arms shows. By that time you may well have decided to specialize, selecting some maker or models or types to concentrate on. You don't have to do that, of course, though most mature collectors eventually specialize. However, I've known some fine collections that had no particular theme—apart from quality. You should, certainly, join one or more collectors' groups, then get to know some of their veteran members and talk over your plans and ambitions with them.

To demonstrate the advantages of being cautious and conservative in your early efforts, I'll tell you something about my beginning days as a gun collector—back in the second and third decades of this century. It is not true that my experiences go back to the Mexican War.

In those far off days there was little guidance for the budding gun collector—I was bitten early on when an indulgent uncle gave me, when I was about 10 or so, a Winchester Model 1890 pump-action 22. Always an omnivorous reader since I'd been long confined to a wheelchair when I was about 5, I turned my attention to gun publications, which were then—1920 and later—scarce indeed. The only gun magazine available was Arms and the Man and its successor, The American Rifleman. Hardbound books (nothing was paperback then, as I recall), were equally scarce, and new gun books were introduced at quite in-

frequent intervals. I read all of the Tom Samworth-published books I could lay hands on, and, because my interest had grown to include centerfire arms, a particular favorite was Captain E.C. Crossman's Book of the Springfield, first published in 1932. I must have read that work a half-dozen times, both for its entrancing meat and for Ned's caustic and cutting style. I also devoured the books of Col. Townsend Whelen, Major Julian Hatcher, Clyde Baker (Modern Gunsmithing, 1933), and others.

During these years—the period just before the Great Depression—I was slowly putting together a small collection of, mostly, handguns. I had very little money and, for that reason, I bought cheap stuff, mostly of low quality and, often enough, in rough condition. Gun collecting associations were virtually unknown in those times, at least in the Midwest, and collectors were scattered and unorganized. As did others, I visited the local sports stores, the gunsmith shops and the pawnshops periodically (when I had a few dollars to spare), buying or "trading up"—or so I told myself.

A rude awakening, to coin a phrase, came in the early 1930s. Out of work, all but busted, I had to sell my small collection, some 30 pieces—all but one of which were—as I know now—junk. I don't think I realized 40¢ on the dollar invested. Yes, I know, the panic of the 1930s was on, but the one good piece I had—a virtually mint 1860 Colt Army in commercial style, not military—brought me $25, and I had to plead for that.

That unhappy experience taught me a well-deserved lesson—and a realization that two basic tenets apply to gun

collecting: Buy quality and buy condition. By "quality" I mean the higher versions in a given line or make, the deluxe, the semi-fancy, the engraved specimens; by "condition" I mean the best possible state for the gun in question—new or nearly so, as free of defects, surface or otherwise, as you can find. A third precept applies here—don't hesitate to pay more than you'd like, or more than the market indicates at the moment of buying. Any excess cost will soon, say within a year or so, become the going, standard price—inflation will take care of that. It always has.

The injunctions—quality and conditions—are not entirely inviolate. Guns will come along (at least they used to!) that, because of their rarity—coupled with a high demand for the make or model—should be snapped up regardless of condition.

I'll illustrate: I bought gladly the only specimen I ever saw for sale of the 1st Model Sharps rifle, despite its quite rough exterior. However, it was reasonably sound, it worked well, and it was intact except for a missing cap wheel. Another time, for the same reasons, I bought a Browning-made and so-marked single-shot rifle, the forerunner of the later Winchester high-wall actioned rifle. This was a well-working, shootable rifle, but its condition was hardly more than fair to good.

At the other extreme I paid what I felt was, at the time, a hell of a high price for a Remington-Walker offhand-style rifle in 32-40 caliber. Only a handful of these superb target rifles were made, less than 20, I think. I got what I'd long wanted, and it met all of my criteria—it was in near-new condition, its quality impossible to fault (extra-fancy walnut in buttstock and fore-end), and very scarce indeed.

Admittedly, the opportunities for buying top condition and high grade quality firearms are much fewer than they were in the 1930s and 1940s, even in the 1950s. Much of the stuff offered in those years—and there was a great lot of it—has now disappeared, swallowed up in museum collections or almost as unattainable in near-permanent private collections. Happily, now and then a fine private collection comes on the market after the death of the owner, usually sold by auction. Watch for these sales and attend if you can. You'll likely see pieces of quality and condition long absent from the gun show tables.

What, then, to collect today? Lots of things, certainly, and I don't mean barbed wire specimens, Indian artifacts or Nazi memorabilia! You may have to lower your sights a bit, settling for lesser-known, smaller-demand firearms, perhaps those not in the most desirable condition, though anything you buy should be presentable, at least. You might want to look into semi-modern arms, too, those made, roughly, post-1900. There are, to be sure, many collectors of more recently made firearms—Colt and S&W cartridge guns, various makes and types of autoloading pistols.

I've digressed. The depression ended

Even 17th century guns can retain great condition as this Pietro Manani pistol shows. One of a pair, this is another Amber prize.

for me in 1933, when I found a good job. I had to work seven days a week, from about 10 A.M. to 10 in the evening, but I made—for that day—pretty good money and, because of the long hours, had little chance to spend it. A seasonal, summer-only job, I wound up at the end of September with a new Ford automobile and $1750 in my pocket. I was rich.

I was soon on the prowl for another collection—a more balanced one this time in that I bought a fair number of rifles, too. My reading had acquainted me with the numerous rifles and carbines used in the Civil War, and with the tremendous variety of weird and wonderful action design that came— and went—during the transition years, the late 1860s on, when the breechloader rapidly replaced the muzzle-loading caplock mechanism. I was fascinated by some of the odd designs so many inventors offered in attempting to make their fortunes. Most of them didn't.

At the end of 1935, I went to work in Marshall Field & Company's Gun Shop. Only modern firearms were

handled, but I was in an excellent position to learn about a great variety of such guns, and also to meet most of the shooters and hunters in the area, not to mention many collectors.

When the war came in 1942, I felt I should sell most of my small collection—some 60 pieces now, including a dozen or so competition guns, for I was into casual target shooting with handgun and centerfire rifle. I also had a few Sharps, Ballards, Winchesters, and other long guns—most of those I put in storage, hoping I'd return from the Navy to use them once again. The modern arms I could eventually replace—or so I thought.

I lost very little on those I sold, and that only because I had to dispose of them hurriedly. By this time I knew better. Every piece I had was in very good to excellent condition, and those I tucked away were desirable collectors items, if not of fancy or engraved grade.

The war over, I came back to Field's and, because sporting arms were all but non-existent, I suggested we open an antique arms department. Field's did that, and in short order we were flourishing. I went here and there buying collections, attending auctions and gun shows, searching for sources. One of the latter was the White Brothers in New York City, their old quarters near the Battery loaded with Civil War guns and accouterments in quantities! Sharps rifles and carbines, gleaming brass-mounted 1841 Mississippi and 1863 Remington Zouave rifles, Plymouth Navy and Colt 1863 rifled muskets. I bought many cases of these, 20 units per case, all in

new condition. We sold the Colts, if memory serves, for about $30, each supplied with bayonet, bayonet scabbard, sling strap, cartridge belt, cap and cartridge boxes—all in prime condition! Ah, happy days.

Our biggest buy was a lot of over 1,000 pieces—very mixed but almost everything in fine condition—from W. Keith Neal, then and now a well-known English collector-dealer and author of several books. Most of the firearms in this great lot were of English origin, but there was a goodly number of European arms. Many were flintlocks, plus a fair number of wheel-locks and snaphaunces. A dozen or so Scottish all-metal flint pistols were in the lot, all genuine fighting pistols of the 1750s. Dozens of cased duellers went on sale—John and Joe Mantons, Mortimers, et al. A grand collection, which we did well with.

During this brief period—the antique arms department lasted for only a few years—I gained much valuable experience, of course. At the same time I was forming my third collection, but now with a different thrust. I would concentrate on fine rifles of all types and periods; more particularly, I was interested in single-shot rifles of all periods, from flintlock and caplock to such cartridge rifles as Sharps, Ballards, Winchesters, Peabody and Peabody-Martinis, to name only a few. I bought repeating rifles too, as long as they were prime-condition pieces— and preferably engraved or in otherwise deluxe form. I had learned— quality and top condition were the watchwords. I have not, since those years, deviated from those criteria. Go, thou, and do likewise!

As noted earlier, certain makes or models of firearms—or individual specimens—will, over a period of time, advance in value beyond the rise in the inflation rate. Scarcity or rarity, plus increasingly heavy demand, account for this situation. In general, however, average prices will advance apace with inflation, though certain categories may lag behind. Your obligation is to study the trends, the field and your chosen area. That's far more easily done today than it was in the past; the market offers various gun-value guides, notably *Flayderman's Guide to Antique Firearms . . . and their values*. However, don't depend entirely on such printed prices—books take time to reach the public, therefore the prices current when you read the book may well be different. Use your knowledge and other price sources to check any book of values. Good luck!

BALLISTIC COEFFICIENTS FOR SELECTED 22 LONG RIFLE CARTRIDGES

Here is how serious experimental work is accomplished

by **W. WAYNE BLACKWELL**
and **M. H. KITANO**

THE 22 RIMFIRE is undoubtedly one of the more popular cartridges ever offered to the general public and because of this popularity there exists an almost mind-boggling array of manufacturers' brands from which to choose. This variety coupled with a lack of readily available bullet performance data for many of today's brands makes it difficult for the average shooter to judge the relative merits of a particular manufacturer's offerings. Many times this leads to purchases based solely on packaging, brand name, or box labeling rather than on what's in the box itself. Lacking actual test data the ballistic coefficient of a bullet can be a valuable aid in helping a shooter to make a more intelligent cartridge selection. Generally, the greater the bullet ballistic coefficient, the less velocity a bullet will shed as it travels downrange. In practical terms this translates into a flatter trajectory and higher kinetic energy levels for the bullet at all ranges. For this article we calculated the ballistic coefficients for fifteen

Kitano preparing to fire 22 Long Rifle bullet over the two sets of chronograph screens. The rear screens were placed about 25 yards downrange for these tests.

brands of 22 Long Rifle ammo. These data are given in Table I. Table II lists bullet drop, kinetic energy and remaining velocity data calculated at 25, 50 and 100 yards for the bullets tested.

The ballistic coefficient is basically a number associated with an actual bullet and is used to estimate the performance of that bullet when compared to a standard bullet. The Russian army colonel Mayevski developed mathematical correlations for a standard bullet based on firing tests conducted by the Krupp Company in Germany near the turn of the century. Mayevski's correlations and the standard bullet they describe form the basis for methods in use today which successfully estimate the in-flight performance of bullets used by both the hunter and target shooter. The famous Ingalls' Ballistics Tables, developed by Colonel James M. Ingalls of the U.S. Army, are based upon Mayevski's correlations. Most of the major bullet companies presently use the Ingalls' or similar tables in conjunction with test firing data to compute ballistic coefficients for production bullets.

There are essentially two methods which may be used to determine the ballistic coefficient of a bullet today. The easiest and least accurate method uses a chart first published in 1936 by Wallace H. Coxe and Edgar Beugless. In this method the ballistic coefficient is calculated from a form factor, which is obtained by visual comparison of a bullet with bullet shapes given on a chart. The Coxe-Beugless point-shape chart is not easy to use because the change in bullet shape on the chart is so gradual that it becomes difficult to determine which chart shape best matches a given bullet. Also, the chart only treats simple point shapes and the more complex shapes can only be roughly approximated. This method also does not account for the variation in ballistic coefficient with a change in velocity.

The other method of determining ballistic coefficients is by experimental measurement using a series of firing tests. This method is considered the more accurate method of the two and was used for the ballistic coefficients presented in this article. This method, however, does require instrumentation (two chronographs in this case).

Only two measurements are re-

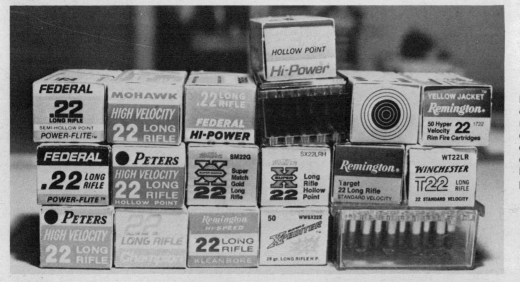

Fifteen different brands of 22 Long Rifle ammo used for these tests, conducted—according to other experts GUN DIGEST consulted—with scrupulous attention to correct procedure.

The Oehler Model 33 chronograph is the small, compact unit shown on the left and was connected to the photoelectric screens located near the muzzle. The Schmidt-Weston chronograph is shown on the right and was connected to the rear screens.

quired during test firings to calculate a ballistic coefficient. Exactly which two measurements are made can vary. Either (1) initial velocity (usually muzzle or near muzzle velocity) and time of flight over a known distance or (2) initial velocity and remaining velocity at a known distance or (3) initial velocity and bullet drop at measured distance can be used. We chose to measure the initial velocity and remaining downrange velocity at a measured distance to determine ballistic coefficients for this article.

For these tests an Oehler Model 33 Chronograph was used to measure initial velocity and a Schmidt-Weston Standard Chronograph was used for downrange velocity measurement. Both chronographs use photoelectric screens for bullet detection and give direct velocity readouts. The Schmidt-Weston screens are powered internally and are capable of relaying an impulse signal over a considerable distance. This allowed both chronographs to be placed on the shooting bench for taking readings even though the downrange screens were located some distance away.

As you can imagine, long distance chronographing is not the easiest thing in the world to do. Bullet placement is critical with photoelectric screens, since the bullet must pass through an area roughly 6 inches by 6 inches to trigger both screens. There is always the chance that a stray bullet will find its way into the hardware of one or both screens, putting the unit out of commission. We used two old circular saw blades as a deflector shield in front of the downrange set of chronograph screens. On one occasion, however, a bullet just cleared our deflector shield and crashed into the rear downrange screen. We sat at the shooting bench transfixed at the sight of our downrange screen support tripod toppling over from the impact of the bullet. Needless to say, that ended that day's shooting! Fortunately, no major damage was done.

For these tests the Oehler sky-screens were placed about four feet in front of the shooting bench. The Schmidt-Weston screens were placed directly in line with the Oehler screens and were located about 25 yards downrange. The distance between each set of screens was measured to the nearest sixteenth of an inch. We also measured the distance from the muzzle of our test firearm to the first set of screens for calculation of the bullet muzzle velocity. Both chronographs were standardized against each other before each series

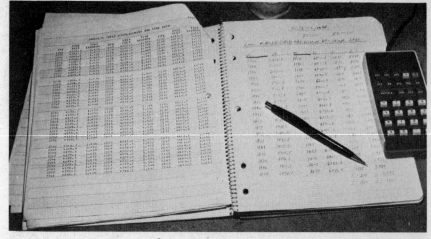

Once the initial and downrange velocities were obtained, the data were used to calculate ballistic coefficients using Ingalls' Tables as outlined in the test. Ballistic coefficients can readily be determined with the help of a hand calculator.

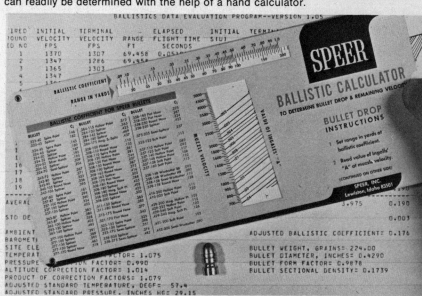

Ballistic coefficients may also be calculated from initial and downrange velocities by use of the Speer Ballistic Calculator. This is an inexpensive slide rule device produced by the Speer people of Lewiston, Idaho.

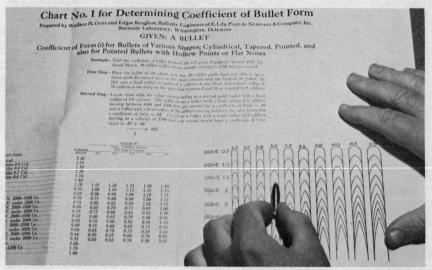

An alternate method of calculating ballistic coefficients by use of the Coxe-Beugless Chart is illustrated. The bullet is matched to a shape found on the chart and a form factor is determined from which the ballistic coefficient can be obtained.

TABLE I

Ballistic Coefficients Calculated From Firing Tests

22 Long Rifle Brand	Bullet Weight Grains	Initial Velocity fps	Downrange Velocity fps	Ballistic-Coefficient @ Site Condition	@ Standard Condition
CCI Stinger	30.5	1645	1464	0.088	0.086
Eley	39.8	1065	1024	0.147	0.140
Federal:					
Hi-Power HP	38.5	1214	1119	0.096	0.093
Power-Flite Semi-HP	38.0	1236	1141	0.102	0.098
Hi-Power	40.0	1262	1138	0.086	0.082
Peters High Velocity	39.3	1282	1191	0.124	0.120
Remington:					
Standard Velocity	39.8	1143	1072	0.106	0.102
Target Standard Velocity	40.0	1166	1085	0.098	0.093
Hi-Speed	39.5	1237	1150	0.115	0.110
Mohawk High Velocity	40.0	1257	1148	0.097	0.093
Yellow Jacket HP	32.5	1454	1288	0.083	0.081
Winchester:					
Super Match Gold	40.0	1085	1036	0.129	0.123
T22	40.0	1136	1071	0.121	0.117
Super X Extra Power HP	37.8	1243	1128	0.090	0.086
XPediter	29.0	1554	1363	0.079	0.076

NOTE: TABLE I velocities are instrumental values.

TABLE II

Calculated Muzzle, 25, 50 and 100 Yard Data

22 Long Rifle Brand Yards From Muzzle	Velocity fps				Kinetic Energy foot-pounds				Bullet Drop* Inches		
	0	25	50	100	0	25	50	100	25	50	100
CCI Stinger	1663	1481	1321	1096	187	149	118	81	0.4	1.8	8.7
Eley	1070	1028	993	933	101	93	87	77	1.0	4.0	17.1
Federal:											
Hi-Power HP	1225	1128	1056	953	128	109	95	78	0.8	3.3	14.3
Power-Flite Semi-HP	1247	1147	1074	969	131	111	97	79	0.8	3.1	13.8
Hi-Power	1276	1153	1066	948	145	118	101	80	0.7	3.1	13.8
Peters High Velocity	1292	1200	1127	1022	146	126	111	91	0.7	2.9	12.7
Remington:											
Standard Velocity	1151	1078	1022	935	117	103	92	77	0.9	3.6	15.6
Target Standard Velocity	1175	1091	1027	932	123	106	94	77	0.8	3.5	15.3
Hi-Speed	1247	1157	1089	989	136	117	104	86	0.7	3.1	13.6
Mohawk High Velocity	1269	1160	1080	968	143	119	104	83	0.7	3.1	13.7
Yellow Jacket HP	1471	1303	1170	1007	156	123	99	73	0.5	2.4	11.1
Winchester:											
Super Match Gold	1091	1041	999	931	106	96	89	77	0.9	3.9	16.5
T22	1143	1081	1030	952	116	104	94	81	0.9	3.7	15.4
Super X Extra Power HP	1256	1143	1062	950	132	110	95	76	0.7	3.2	14.0
XPediter	1573	1381	1222	1027	159	123	96	68	0.5	2.1	10.1

*From horizontal line of departure. Drop—0 inches at the muzzle.

of firings by alternately placing the two sets of screens in tandem near the shooting bench and firing over both pairs of screens. The readings of both chronographs checked within one foot per second of each other for the range of velocities used in this series of tests.

After the chronograph screens had been properly positioned, each bullet tested was fired across both sets of screens to obtain both initial and downrange velocities. A Winchester Model 320 rifle with four-power scope was used for all cartridges tested.

Once initial and downrange velocities had been obtained, the ballistic coefficient was calculated by use of the Ingalls' Tables, as they appear on pages 590-616 of *Hatcher's Notebook* (Stackpole Books, 1966). For further details on the calculation methods used, the reader is referred to *Hatcher's Notebook*.)

In view of the fairly large amount of firing data gathered for this article, we found it convenient to computerize the Ingalls' Tables and print a new table with space functions in one foot per second increments. This eliminated the need for the time consuming interpolations required by the Ingalls' Tables as they appear in Hatcher's Notebook. A Hewlett-Packard Model 29C programmable calculator was programmed for calculation of ballistics coefficients. The hand calculator along with the computerized Ingalls' Tables allowed quick and relatively easy calculation of ballistics coefficients at the range. To aid in the calculation of statistical data and bullet drop, kinetic energy, and remaining velocity for the 25, 50, and 100 yard data given in this article, we also developed programs for use on larger computers. All calculated data reported in this article have been verified by computational checks via these computer programs.

It should be pointed out, however, that the hand calculator derived ballistic coefficients proved to be as accurate as any calculated by the larger computers, and that all data for this article could have been calculated fairly easily by a determined man with a hand calculator. We just chose not to do all our computations by hand, since we had ready access to a larger computer. As an aid to anyone interested in performing hand calculations based on the Ingalls' Tables, we plan to market in the near future our computerized Ingalls' Table which features one foot per second velocity increments, thus eliminating the need for interpolation of table data.

A minimum of twenty shots were fired for each brand of 22 Long Rifle cartridge tested. The ballistic coefficients in most instances proved to be surprisingly consistent, usually showing a standard deviation of less than five percent.

Ballistic data obtained at one set of conditions must be corrected to standard conditions if it is to provide meaningful information to a large number of shooters. The data for this article were obtained at the Winchester Rifle and Pistol Range, located near Dallas, Texas. The elevation of this range is

Close-up of Schmidt-Weston chronograph screens showing a deflector shield used in front of the first screen unit to protect the screen from a possible stray bullet.

430 feet above sea level. Ballistic coefficients calculated for the conditions at this location were corrected to the standard conditions used by the U.S. Army Ballistic Research Laboratories at the Aberdeen Proving Ground in Maryland. These standard conditions are:

Altitude	Sea Level
Barometric Pressure	29.51 Inches of Mercury
Temperature	59 Degrees Fahrenheit
Relative Humidity	78 Percent

Sierra in their latest loading manual, pages 381-383, outlines the procedure for correcting bullet ballistic coefficients to standard conditions and the reader is referred to that manual for more complete calculation details. The corrected ballistic coefficients, reported in this article, can be adapted to any area by following the same procedure as outlined by Sierra.

In order to calculate the kinetic energy of bullets the weight of the bullets must be known. To determine this we took five cartridges randomly from each box of cartridges to be tested and pulled and weighed the bullets from the selected cartridges. The average weight of the weighed bullets was used for each cartridge tested from the box.

As a check on our method of calculating ballistic coefficients we tested three of Sierra's jacketed bullets and compared our calculated coefficients against those reported by Sierra in the second edition of their loading manual. Comparison results are summarized in a chart.

The ballistic coefficient when used in conjunction with other factors such as muzzle velocity, bullet weight, and bullet shape (solid nose, hollow point, etc.) can give a shooter a pretty good picture of what he is buying before he makes a purchase. In the final analysis, however, the purchased cartridges must be fired to confirm their performance in the shooter's firearm. As useful as the ballistic coefficient is it cannot be used to determine the accuracy of a bullet fired from a given firearm. The Eley, Winchester Super Match Gold and Peters High Velocity cartridges had the highest calculated ballistic coefficients based on our test data, however, in our test firearm they did not show better accuracy than cartridges, such as the Federal Hi-Power or Winchester Super X Extra Power hollow point, which had considerably lower coefficients.

Hopefully, the information presented in this article can be of assistance to 22 rimfire shooters who are still searching for their favorite Long Rifle brand.   •

Typical output page generated by the computer program used by the authors to verify ballistic coefficients calculated for this article.

CALCULATIONS COMPARED

Bullet/grain	Velocity feet per second	Sierra Coefficient	Calculated Coefficient
224/53 HP	3300	.235	
	2900	—	.229
	2500	.223	
257/75 HP	3300	.240	
	2600	—	.243
4295/240 HP	1200	.172	
	1175	—	.171
	800	.171	

The above ballistic coefficients have been corrected to the standard conditions discussed in this article. The good comparison of calculated coefficients against these published coefficients should give confidence that these methods of testing and calculation are accurate.

A Fresh Look At The Old Standards

Author's Standard Model G autoloading slide-action rifle.

by LAYNE SIMPSON

THE SUN HAD just torn away from the horizon's grip, its warm rays chasing away a bit of October crispness. Other than a single alarm sounded just at daybreak by that accursed jaybird, the hunter sitting with his back to the rough bark of a red oak remained undetected.

Woods ants are most often big, black and nosey. This one was no exception. He (possibly she) studied the boot string but a moment before scurrying up the pants leg, over the wool mitten and out onto a rifle laying across the hunter's legs. Watching the insect make its way out to the muzzle, the hunter read the barrel inscription as tiny legs passed over it—"M. F. Smith's Patents-Patented Mar. 6, Apr. 10, Apr. 24, 1906-Man'f'd By Standard Arms Co., Wilmington, Delaware, USA-.25 Caliber."

And then this buck, running late from an all-night lovefest, had one last scrape to check before vanishing from daylight as all mature bucks are likely to do. It was one of few mistakes he had made since losing his spots over four years ago and it proved quite costly. As he paused at the message place, a tiny hundred-grain bullet smacked him just back of his shoulder which prompted a whirl and beeline toward yon thick swamp. But he didn't make it as a second Core-Lokt turned out the few remaining lights.

Retrieving two spent shells from among fallen leaves, the successful deer hunter smiled while thinking of all the criticism leveled against this little woods cartridge, mostly by those that had merely sat behind a typewriter and judged it on size alone. The headstamps read: REM-UMC .25 REM.

The field dressing chore proved easy enough but the three-mile drag back to old faithful CJ-5 took awhile. Leaning back against cool pine needles for a breather, the hunter watched a jet airliner leave its contrail against a blue sky and chuckled at the possibility of it being the presidential jet headed farther south to check out this year's peanut crop.

And what are a CJ-5 Jeep, a jet airliner and a President who grows goobers doing in the same story with a rifle that few hunters still kicking have ever seen and a cartridge that didn't see daylight after World War Two?

Those shots weren't fired during the revolutionary 'teens, roaring twenties, difficult thirties, or even as far back as the trying forties. That trigger was pulled about a month before I write this, more precisely October of 1980. I was that hunter, the buck is now frozen in neat little packages, and the star performer in that particular production now rests under a thin film of oil in my gun cabinet—a Standard Model G, autoloading/slide action rifle. If the name is confusing, don't be embarrassed because it is an autoloading rifle that can, with a twist of the wrist, be made to function as a slide action—and vice versa.

The aforedescribed deer hunt culminated several months of research, study and testing of a rifle that failed miserably as a commercial venture yet it is one of the most interesting that I have ever worked with. Not only is this rifle fascinating but it holds two unique distinctions. Firstly, the Standard Model G is the first sporting rifle manufactured in the United States that employed expanding powder gases to operate the action. This credit

has on occasion been given to Remington for their Model 740 autoloader but it was late by forty-five years. Secondly, the Model G has to hold the all-time record as the most criticized hunting rifle ever available to the American hunter.

Let's spin the clock back to 1909. Patents were on file in Washington and it was clear sailing for a sporting arm to revolutionize the hunting world. The designers and investors were convinced of it.

An early hangup had been the development of a cartridge that would feed smoothly through the action since with the exception of Winchester's 351 autoloader pipsqueak, domestic hunting rounds were rimmed. But Remington solved that problem in 1906 by introducing a line of rimless cartridges with their new recoil-operated Model 8 autoloader. So in 1910, the Standard Arms Company introduced two new rifles designated Model G and Model M, both chambered for the 25, 30 and 35 Remington rimless cartridges.

The Model M (manual operated) listed for $30.00 and was the first new centerfire pump or slide action rifle introduced since Colt's Lightning in 1885. For an additional $7.50, you could have more firepower in the Model G (gas operated) which would spit out bullets with little more effort than the mere twitching of the trigger finger. The two models were identical except the Model M had no gas handling apparatus.

One thing is certain, the Standard Arms advertising folks were ambitious in their claims. Those describing the gas-operated principle weren't too far from being factual. And, although

During an age of horse buggies and trains, takedown rifles were extremely popular. The three rifles shown from top — Remington Model 81, Standard Model G, Remington Model 14-C— can be quickly taken down for stowage in a duffle bag or suitcase.

they called no names, it's easy to recognize a few jabs at Winchester's blowback-operated autoloader and the sliding barrel and "clumsy, ugly" magazine of Remington's fast-shooter.

A few claims were simply ridiculous. Like: the 35 recoils about like a 25-20 loaded with black powder or muzzle blast is reduced by part of the excess gas pressure being relieved to operate the action. The rifle did represent a major departure from the norm and with this knowledge, no doubt enthusiasm was tough to rein back.

Two years later, in 1912, Remington announced their Model 14 pump action rifle. I mention this because the Model 14, along with the Remington Model 8 were Standard's competition among those hunters who opted for a pump or auto in lieu of the various lever actions that practically ruled the hunting roost during that period.

The Remington Model 8 proved extremely successful and was in production in original and slightly revised form until 1954. By a similar token, the Model 14 enjoyed great success, being modified a bit as the Model 141 in 1935 and surviving the ever escalating cost of labor until 1950. But in 1914, less than five years after its optimistic unveiling, the Standard rifle was as dead as a possum on a hard road.

My conservative and only slightly

educated guesstimate is that fewer than 8000 of these rifles left the production line. That doesn't sound like many until we consider that Remington, a much larger company, averaged just over 2000 Model 8's and around 5500 Model 14's each year they were in production.

By modern standards, my 25-caliber Model G is quite heavy at eight pounds, nine ounces. A 35 Remington Model G that I worked with quite briefly weighed four ounces less due to its larger bore, but that's still pretty hefty. My specimen has a plain, uncheckered buttstock of varnished walnut although higher grades were offered with pistol-grip stock, fancy wood, checkering, various sight combinations and engraving on the receiver.

The most striking features of these rifles are buttplates and fore-ends cast of bronze. The buttplate glitters with the company logo surrounded by oak leaves while the fore-end has a similar treatment with a woods scene and a moose head on one side and what was probably meant to be a bear on the other. Striking though it may be, that bronze is cold in winter hunting. Walnut would have been much more practical and comfortable, not to mention more conservatively attractive, leastwise to modern eyes.

The nickel steel barrel is 22½ inches

long and tapers nicely from 0.995-inch, where it screws into the receiver, down to .520-inch at the muzzle. The bore in my rifle slugs at .250-inch while the six grooves are .0035-inch deep. The rate of twist is one turn in ten inches. Sighting is simple enough, with a Marble Sheard dovetailed into the front ramp-barrel band assembly and a leaf sight at the rear with a unique sliding, stepped elevator cast of bronze. At first glance the elevator appears to be in the shape of a dragon but closer examination proves it to be a mate to the bear on the fore-end. Rather than the more common dovetail cut atop the barrel, the rear sight is dovetailed into the front of the receiver. I suppose this was done to prevent weakening the barrel at the chamber area.

In studying the innards of this rifle, it's easy to find ideas years ahead of their time, at least for this type of firearm. The Standard is bottom loaded through a hinged floorplate which is opened by sliding a release button toward the trigger guard. The magazine box is milled into the receiver and holds five 25- or 30-caliber cartridges or four 35's. The follower is powered by a coil spring which also serves to keep tension on the floorplate when it is closed. The rifle contains a total of six springs, all of which are coil-type.

Cartridges are staggered in the magazine a la Model 1898 Mauser with the top cartridge resting against the bottom of a rail milled into the receiver, again quite like the '98 Mauser. The Standard's magazine, however, positions the top cartridge more directly in line with the chamber than does the Mauser's.

To chamber the first round, a button on the bottom of the fore-end releases it. When it is pulled to the rear and returned, the rifle is ready to fire, assuming that the safety lever is moved forward. The safety lever exits the receiver bottom into the trigger bow, which is not a bad place for it to be, in my opinion. John Garand, who designed one of our most successful military rifles, thought likewise. The Standard's safety locks both sear and trigger.

With the rifle set on semi-auto, it takes five pulls on the trigger to be ready to reload again. The Standard Arms brochure claimed six shots in one second but my trigger finger is not quite so agile.

Think of the gas handling system of the Model G as an M1 Garand which came 22 years early or maybe a spinoff from Ferdinand von Mannlicher's military autoloader of 1895. All three rifles employ a fixed cylinder, enclosing a reciprocating piston to drive a connecting rod, or as often called, an operating rod, to the rear. On the Standard rifle, a large metal tube extends from the receiver out beneath the barrel, serving as a raceway for the sliding fore-end and for housing the twin action bars. These action bars are attached to the bolt on one end and the piston connecting rod at the other.

Forward of this housing is a smaller tube, in this case a cylinder, that extends out to the gas port assembly near the muzzle. Inside this cylinder the connecting rod is surrounded by a coiled return spring. Three and a half inches back of the muzzle, a small hole, serving as a gas port, is drilled through the barrel wall. Modern gas-operated autoloaders such as Remington's Model 742 and the Winchester Model 100 have this port located much closer to the receiver but again, note the similarity between the Standard rifle and the highly successful M1 Garand.

As a bullet traveling down the bore passes the port, gases under pressure travel the path of least resistance, which momentarily is this tiny hole in the barrel wall. The gas impinges on the piston face which, via the connecting rod and action bars, unlocks the bolt, ejects the empty cartridge case

and compresses the bolt return spring. The gas pressure is relieved as the bullet exits the barrel and via a bleed-off port located in the cylinder wall about three and a half inches back of the gas inlet. Once the pressure is relieved, the return spring draws the bolt forward, strips a fresh cartridge from the magazine into the chamber and cams the breech block into its locked position. Of course, another pull on the trigger repeats the cycle.

The gas valve is a simple affair and could be described in principle as a plug cock such as one sees in an old wine cask. In the "on" position, the cock is rotated so the gas channel is located directly beneath the port. Rotating the gas cock 180 degrees seals off the port for manual or pump operation.

For autoloading operation, the fore-end is locked in its extreme forward position but the designers realized that some hunters would, without thinking, fire the rifle with the fore-end in the incorrect position. They designed the fore-end/action bar connector as a ratchet affair that disconnects the two should the forearm be

From left: Remington-UMC 87-gr. Hi-Speed Mushroom bullet; Western Super-X 117-gr. round-nose boattail; Remington 117-gr. round nose. Western ammo was loaded hotter or Remington had weakened with age. Standard rifles were also chambered for 30 and 35-cal. Remington cartriges on right.

held stationary while in this position. Ingenious to say the least and it probably saved a few broken fingers as well.

After putting over four hundred rounds of factory loads and handloads through my Model G, I believe these rifles are as strong as most others available to the hunter in the U.S. during the first two decades of this century, excepting of course, the Newton rifles and the few 1903 Springfield sporters that were available. Possibly not as rigid as the Remington Model 8, but more so than the blowback Model 07 Winchester, and certainly equal to the Remington Model 14 and the various Winchester lever actions.

In point of fact, the Standard's breech lockup is similar in principle to

the familiar 99 Savage with its reciprocating, tipping bolt. The Standard bolt proper does not tip down at its rear for unlocking as does the Savage—only the locking block tips. In both rifles, when the bolt is locked it is in compression between breech face and an abutment in the receiver with backthrust being transferred directly to the receiver.

Actually, the Standard bolt more closely resembles that of the gas-operated Browning Automatic Rifle, designed during World War I, although they differ slightly as well. Where the BAR employs hinged links between operating rod and locking member, the Standard utilizes a sliding cam block that serves the same purpose. In the Standard's favor, the cam block seems less likely to break than connecting links. Additionally, the BAR's locking block is attached to the bolt proper by a pin that probably, through eventual wear, bears a portion of the shear load. The Standard design required no such pin. Unlike the Model 99 Savage with its locking abutment milled through the receiver roof, both the BAR and Standard rifles

have a locking recess milled into the bottom of the roof thus requiring a "humpback" shape to the receiver.

Such a close comparison of these rifles adds a bit of mystery to why the Standard rifle failed so early in its career.

The Standard bolt face is recessed, enclosing a portion of the cartridge head like most of our modern bolt action rifles. Should gas pressures from a particular load be high enough to slam the bolt back into the receiver's back wall, two coil springs cushion the blow and prevent metal from battering against metal. There's nothing exotic about the extractor except to say that it is of the spring-loaded claw type and works. The ejector is fixed, sliding through a groove in the bolt's bottom and propels cases skyward with great authority.

Since the bolt proper remains horizontal and concentric with the chamber during operation and the top cartridge lies in the magazine almost directly in line with the chamber, feeding is smooth and reliable. When the bolt is locked, its face fits closely into a recess milled into the receiver thus adding another ring of steel enclosing the cartridge head. Sounds rather familiar, doesn't it?

To prevent the rifle from firing until the bolt is fully locked, a lever riding against the locking block disconnects trigger from sear until the block is seated snug in its abutment. This sear disconnect also prevents the rifle from firing in the full-automatic mode and from being fired by holding down the trigger while operating the action manually.

The Wright brothers made their first flight only seven years before this rifle was introduced and Henry Ford's Model T hit the road a mere two years before. Most traveling big game hunters traveled by train. So, as was common with big game rifles during that era, the Standard features a quick takedown system for easy stowing in duffle bag or grip. It's quick, all right, and unique in its method of compensating for wear, plus it can be further stripped down for thorough cleaning in just a jiffy.

Just aft of the trigger guard is a recess that extends up inside the receiver. The takedown tool or a loaded cartridge is inserted and pushed against a spring-loaded lever. This allows separation of the bottom or inner frame from the receiver shell. The former contains the safety, trigger and ejector components while the latter hangs on to everything else. A tapered pin at the receiver front mates with a cavity in the inner frame. The spring-loaded lever presses the inner frame forward and since the pin doesn't bottom out, any slack due to wear is taken up.

Further disassembly is accomplished by removing the fore-end and a screw concealed by a sight slot blank just behind the front sight. The gas cylinder is pulled forward, the connecting rod unscrewed from the action bar joint and that's all she wrote. All of this can be done with a loaded cartridge. Neat.

My Model G has a fine bore and I never cease to be amazed at rifles of this vintage surviving the ravages of time. This one was born 13 years before Remington came forth with J. E. Burns' Kleanbore primer. And my rifle shows evidence of seeing much use. A bit of Sherlocking reveals that the previous owner or owners who carried the rifle were right-handed and basement-analyzing seven decades of accumulated, greasy gunk cleaned from the innards indicates it was used for more than a wall hanger or door stop.

Other than the Remington Model 14, I doubt that any other hunting rifle manufactured in the U.S. required machine work so intricately complex as the Model G. The hand fitting and workmanship bestowed on the inner works of these rifles that I have examined rivals the best from any arms company. A friend in the industry who should know such things figures that even with today's advanced technology it would cost upwards of six hundred dollars to mass produce the Model G. Add a bit of profit and some overhead to that figure and it's not difficult to see why they don't hardly make 'em like they used to.

Due to the terrible press that Standard has received over the years and to satisfy my own curiosity, I decided their rifle deserved a thorough testing and a comparison with their competitor's goods. Now don't get me wrong. I believe constructive criticism has been, is now and always will be healthy. I believe in it so long as both sides of the rock are turned over in the process.

Like all such tests, mine can be shot plumb full of holes by those so inclined simply because of the limited number of Standard rifles at my disposal. I would like nothing better than to report that my test results came from firing trainloads of ammunition in a multitude of Model G's, but these things are kind of tough to come by. So I had to make do with my old 25-caliber rifle.

The other two rifles are also in my using battery—a Remington Model 14-C in 35 Remington and a Remington Model 81 which is nothing more than the 1906-vintage Model 8 with modified wood, except mine is in 300 Savage which didn't happen in

TEST RIFLE COMPARISON

	Model G	Model G[1]	Model 81	Model 14
Date Test Rifle Manufactured	1911	—	1947	1928
Caliber	25 Rem.	25 Rem.	300 Sav.	35 Rem.
Price When Introduced	$37.50	$30.00[2]	$30.00	$20.00
Weight Of Test Rifles	8 lb. 9 oz.	—	8 lb. 12 oz.	7 lb. 4 oz.
Overall Length	41¾"	—	41"	40¾"
Average Accuracy, Factory Loads[3]	4.20 moa	4.15 moa	3.45 moa	3.60 moa
Average Accuracy, Best Handloads	2.75 moa	2.65 moa	2.55 moa	2.89 moa
Functioning Tests				
Factory Loads, 80 Degrees F[3]	98%	100%	100%	100%
Factory Loads, 25 Degrees F[3]	37%	100%	100%	100%
Fact. Equivalent Handloads, 80 Degrees F[4]	100%	100%	100%	100%
Fact. Equivalent Handloads, 25 Degrees F[4]	93%	100%	100%	100%
105% Fact. Equivalent Handloads, 25 Degrees F	100%	100%	100%	100%
90% Fact. Equivalent Handloads, 80 Degrees F	97%	100%	100%	100%
90% Fact. Equivalent Handloads, 25 Degrees F	86%	100%	100%	100%
80% Fact. Equivalent Handloads, 80 Degrees F	23%	100%	100%	100%
80% Fact. Equivalent Handloads, 25 Degrees F	0%	100%	100%	100%

Notes:
[1] Model G set on manual operation
[2] Model M listed for $30.00 in 1910
[3] 25-cal. Remington factory ammunition was 1930's and 1940's vintage, 300 Savage and 35 Remington, fresh
[4] Equivalent to Western brand ammunition which clocked higher velocities than Remington

Exploded shot of Model G, from top to bottom: receiver shell and barrel; slot blank and set screw which secures gas port housing and cylinder to barrel; return spring; breech bolt in locked mode; twin action bars; connecting rod with piston on end; fore-end raceway and action bar housing; housing end cap; bronze fore-end; fore-end release and ratchet lever and pin. Gas handling system is of the same principal as the highly successful M1 Garand, i.e., fixed cylinder with captive, reciprocating piston.

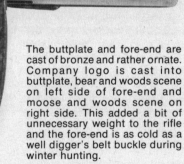

The buttplate and fore-end are cast of bronze and rather ornate. Company logo is cast into buttplate, bear and woods scene on left side of fore-end and moose and woods scene on right side. This added a bit of unnecessary weight to the rifle and the fore-end is as cold as a well digger's belt buckle during winter hunting.

Safety lever exits the frame into the trigger bow. Rather a handy place for it. Hinged floorplate is released by sliding button located just forward of the trigger bow, to the rear. Rifle is loaded and of course unloaded from the bottom. Button shown above trigger inside of frame is for holding the bolt open. When thumb pressure is removed from this button the return spring pushes the bolt forward and locks it. I suppose this was for single loading of cartridges. It's backward from most rifles which have a bolt *release* button or lever.

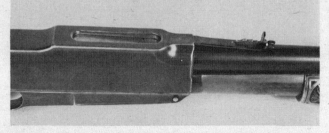

Shown is the ejection port and rear sight dovetailed into the receiver front. The stepped elevator is cast of bronze, in the profile of a bear's head. At first glance it appears to be in the form of a dragon. Note the hump-back receiver. This serves as a locking abutment from the bolt's tipping block.

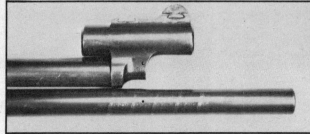

Gas assembly at top with barrel below turned 90 degrees to illustrate the gas port. Valve cock controls gas flow from the barrel to the piston and can be turned to the "off" position for manual operation of the rifle. Slot just aft of the front sight blade takes a blank which conceals the takedown setscrew. Rifle can be taken completely down for cleaning in a matter of seconds with nothing more than a loaded cartridge.

this rifle until 1940. The three rifles have fine bores and their mechanical condition is up to snuff. All tests were performed with the original, iron sights and an Oehler Model 33 Chronotach verified velocities.

First came accuracy and functioning tests with factory ammunition which at the outset put the Model G at a disadvantage. Where all other factory loads were relatively fresh, the 25 Remington cartridge has long been discontinued. I had no choice but to use fodder loaded during the 1930's and 1940's. You don't just walk into the local gun shop and gather this stuff off the shelf. Three boxes set me back 75¢ per trigger squeeze, but fortunately shopping around turned up several more boxes at a third the price.

Most of my factory 25 Remingtons were Remington-UMC 87-grain hollow point and 117-grain soft point loadings, with a few rounds of Western Super-X loaded with, interestingly enough, a 117 grain round nose, boattail bullet. These loads chronographed an average of 2689, 2217 and 2312 feet per second respectively from the 22½-inch barrel. It seemed the 117-grain Remington cartridges were loaded to lower pressures than the Western and rounds from the same box showed an extreme velocity spread of just over 200 feet per second. Doubtless, a large part of this can be attributed to age but I suspect quality control among ammunition manufacturers left a bit to be desired as compared to today.

These spreads in velocity with the Remington ammunition didn't seem to affect accuracy greatly, they did affect the Model G's functioning. Anytime a particular load indicated a drastic drop in velocity and thus pressure, functioning became a sometime thing. When using the Western loads and handloads loaded to equal pressures, the Model G hummed like a well-oiled machine. Taking handloads down to about a 20 percent reduction in pressures resulted in practically zero functioning.

What did I prove? Actually several things. The Model G was designed to operate at maximum factory load pressures and anything less clogs up the machinery. Across the street, Remington's autoloader gobbled up anything that faintly resembled a cartridge until handloads were reduced by twenty percent. No problems here with factory loads but I must mention that they were Federal's finest and latest.

So, Act One revealed that the Model G is what it eats. Feed it good stuff and it chatters away like a popcorn machine at the Saturday matinee. Poor or underloaded ammunition pains it greatly and, I might add, the hunter using it. In defense of the rifle though, is the fact that anytime a weak load failed to operate the system, it was a bit quicker to clear than the Remington autoloader since all it takes is a quick stroke of the fore-end. Without doubt, the Standard Arms engineers were aware of the variations in factory ammunition since their brochure states that the gas inlet valve can be adjusted for both gas pressure and ambient temperature variations. It appears they just couldn't whip the former problem.

My test results also indicate that due to a decrease in chamber pressures, cold weather tends to compound the Model G's tendency to stutter. Load this rifle with ammunition already marginal or slightly below what appears to be about a 35,000 psi operating pressure and you'd best switch to the manual mode of operation before taking to the woods. When handloads that maintained adequate pressures during such conditions are used, I found the Model G about as reliable as any other autoloader, including the latest now available. This discovery wouldn't have helped a lot back in 1910 since handloading was practiced by only a very few.

Three other gremlins also haunt these rifles. The two that I have worked with have absolutely minimum chambers and dirty ammunition or cartridges that are only slightly corroded will gum up the works. Secondly, due to the close fitting of the action bars and breech bolt within the receiver, the rifle must be kept sparkling clean inside and it must be lubricated. My Model G malfunctioned terribly until I tore it down and cleaned out the gunk and coated all moving parts with Dri-Slide. Finally, carbon builds up quite rapidly in the gas port and around the piston when I use the old 25 factory ammunition. Though I did not fire enough of these loads through the rifle to become a factor in its operation, I expect it would become a problem with continued use if I failed to clean out the carbon.

So what we have here is a rifle that required at least annual maintenance if it were fired and hunted with a great deal in the hands of average citizens who spent very little or, in many cases, no time in such activity. The tool kit supplied with at least some of these rifles contained two brass brushes, one for cleaning the bore and another for removing carbon from the piston and cylinder, along with a small pick for cleaning out the gas port. I wonder how many of these tools were actually used by the owners.

After shaking everything out of the bag, I believe that with a few minor refinements the Model G would have been as successful as its competitor. Why this did not come to pass, I do not know. Maybe they ran out of money. Or perhaps straight razors and blivet bags proved more profitable.

The slide action Model M's demise is more of a mystery. In comparing my Remington Model 14 with this rifle, it's obvious that both are well made, reliable and equally accurate. I prefer the Model M's safety and box magazine but the Model 14 is better balanced and lighter. Its shape is more proportionate too. Possibly, the poor reputation quickly established by the Model M's gas-powered mate doomed them both. Or price may have scuttled the ship. The Standard Model M sold for a third more than Remington's prize pump gun and ten dollars was a lot of money back when Joe Average Factory Worker made about five bucks a week.

And finally, what was the Standard Arms Company's reasoning behind such a rifle as the Model G? No doubt that's a question that may never be correctly answered. One source of long ago has it that the original intent was to produce a pure autoloading rifle but with development capital exhausted before all bugs were worked out the owners added the slide action mechanism "just in case." I doubt it.

I'm only guessing, too, but rather I believe the intent was to offer the hunter what was considered to be the best of two worlds, so to speak. Pump action shotguns had really caught on with hunters while the autoloading big game rifle was new on the scene. The Winchester and Remington autoloaders were still young and unproven so it was a bit early to predict their future. So what to do? You give a man accustomed to the trombone scattergun a big game rifle that operates in a familiar manner yet with the twist of a valve becomes one of them new-fangled "automatics." And of course if the old sugar jar was short by $7.50, the Model M could be had.

Regardless of the reason or intent that produced these interesting relics of gunmaking history, my hat is off to its creators for having enough guts to give it a try. And M.F. Smith, wherever you are, rest easy. Somebody finally said something good about your rifle. ●

HANDGUNS evolve slowly. Before there were automobiles, radios, or airplanes men carried sidearms that served their purpose just about as well as anything we have today, and while the pistol on my belt is indeed better than that used by Alvin York it is very similar to his, differing only in refinements that make it somewhat easier to shoot but hardly more efficient.

This is remarkable, but may be explained by analysis of the problem a sidearm is meant to solve. As a reactive instrument for decisive short-range action without advance notice, the pistol has had no real *need* to evolve, since its purpose has not changed and our technology has not come up with anything better able to accomplish that purpose.

Thus it is that significant improvements have been few and widely spaced for more than a century. The self-contained metallic cartridge was probably the single most important forward step, coming into common use just about 100 years ago. When this was combined with smokeless powder and the development of reliable self-loading mechanisms, we arrived at the modern "automatic pistol," just in time for World War I. Since then we have seen only the addition of the double-action feature in the self-loader; an advance which, while very exciting at the time of its announcement back in the '30s, proved to be essentially illusory—an answer in search of a question. Some very powerful new cartridges have appeared which make the handgun suitable—in highly skilled hands—for taking game up to about 400 pounds in weight, and quite a bit more in special circumstances. This use of the pistol, however, is a bit esoteric. It is very interesting to those who specialize in it, but not really relevant to the primary mission of the weapon type.

Is there, then, no way to improve upon what we have had for three generations? With the U.S. government now going backward from one antique but highly effective pistol cartridge to another which is even more antique and about half as effective, it would seem that further progress is held to be impossible. But we know that should not be so. Progress is *always* possible, given the will and the wit.

In the magnificent Browning/Colt 45 auto pistol of 1911 we have a superb balance of stopping power and controllability, augmented by simplicity, durability, reliability, and compactness. Can we do better than that? Yes, we can. Until some entirely different principle is discovered, we cannot build a handgun that departs in any single radical characteristic from what we now have, but we can combine all the best features of the weapons we now have into one design, under the guidance of the people who

THE BREN TEN: INTENDED TO BE BETTER

This may be one of the guns of the future, by Dornaus & Dixon, out of Cooper, Petter, SIG and Browning, and designed for a cartridge of the future in 10mm.

know the most about practical shooting, and produce it by the most modern methods so that it is ready to go "out of the box."

This has been done. We shall have the Bren Ten if present plans mature. Here we have a very powerful, medium-sized, easily controlled, high capacity, selective action pistol utilizing thoroughly proven mechanical systems and enhanced by a number of unique features found in no other piece. Its heart is a new cartridge that offers the stopping power of the illustrious 45 in a more compact package together with increased kinetic energy, range, and (if desired) penetration. Its durability, reliability and accuracy have yet to be put to the test of time, but since the relevant materials and systems have been individually time-tested in antecedent weapons we can safely predict their success in combination.

Any smallarm must be considered as a composition of two elements: weapon and cartridge. The Bren Ten is unusual in that it is the only pistol taking the new 10mm auto pistol cartridge, and that it will take no other. You can't have the one without the other. If it is indeed a great leap forward, it is because the design doesn't drag any leftovers along.

The action is of the Browning tilt-lock type and derives from Browning through Petter to SIG 210 to Cz 75. The latter piece is admittedly the inspiration for the new gun, as shown in the name. The Czech arsenal at Brno is the parent of both the renowned English Bren gun (Brno plus Enfield came out "Bren") and the Cz 75 9mm pistol. The 75 is the best of the 9's and it seemed to me that if it could be had in 45 caliber it might eventually supersede the 1911. That idea was expanded to include the experimental 10mm cartridge originally pioneered by Whit Collins and Irving Stone, and wound up as a prototype built by Tom Dornaus, late of the Pachmayr organization. This prototype can fire either the 45 or the 10 since a barrel and slide for either cartridge has been made, plus one 45 magazine. This was done to permit us to shoot the weapon, since the 10mm ammunition is not in production and must be made by hand at this time.

The original 10mm cartridge was made by cutting off the 30 Remington rifle case and fitting it with the 180-grain bullet of the 38-40 (which is of 40 caliber). This combination gave astonishing performance—well up toward 1200 f/s with fairly modest charges of Unique—in a test barrel. We felt that more mass was in order and settled on a 200-grain JTC bullet which, when loaded to an overall length of 1.3", still leaves enough case volume to break 1100 f/s without excessive pressure or recoil. A 40-caliber, 200-grain, flatpoint starting at 1100 fps gives us a pretty balance of mass, velocity, impact area, and Hatcher "k." It also shows more energy at 100 yards than the 45 does at the muzzle.

Power is easy—look at the big-bore magnums. How about recoil? Well, if we take the momentum of the two loads we find that the 10 is to the 45 as 22 is to 19.5. It kicks a little more, but not quite as much as a really hot 45, such as the old Western Super X load. When we fired the 10 out of the prototype, we found that the advanced butt design borrowed from the Cz 75 made up for the difference, and that the Bren, despite its increased power, was every bit as "soft" as the Colt, easily managed with thumb and forefinger alone by a trained person.

Unlike almost all other handguns, the Bren Ten was designed by shooters for shooters. It incorporates all sorts of nifty features that only serious shooters would think of. It is, for example, de-horned, with no sharp corners or edges rearward to abrade hands or clothing. Its fully adjustable rear sight is revetted in a solid steel cup to protect it from hard knocks. Its front sight, though stronger than those on most autos, is instantly replaceable by field stripping. Its recoil-spring guide doubles as a combination tool. Its magazine release of the Browning type can be set two ways by half-turning a detent screw. The magazine may either fly free as with a Colt or be held half-ejected for those who fear magazine loss or damage. Magazine capacity is 11 rounds.

The trigger-cocking (double-action) mechanism is another system borrowed from the Cz 75, and is the smoothest and lightest of its type. It is offered only to please the unenlightened, however, for the selective action allows the pistol to be properly carried in Condition One on the belt. The thumb safety is positioned forward under the swell of the thumb for comfortable operation. It is *reversible,* and may be quickly plugged-in on the right side for a lefthander. This feature is unique with the Bren Ten, and far better than ambidextrous safeties seen on modified Colts—stronger, more comfortable, and not to be rubbed off inadvertently in the holster. It is easily

Jeff Cooper draws nicknames (Chairman Jeff, Dr. Death) and respect alike in his role and posture as a handgunner for all seasons: His mark is on the Bren Ten.

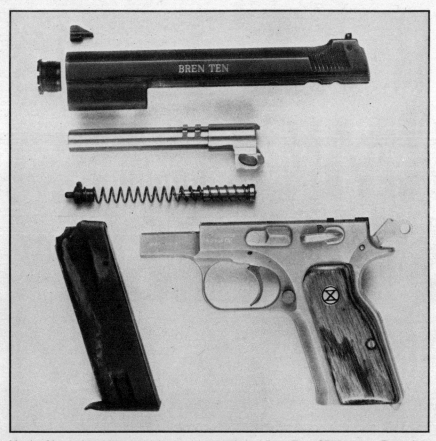

Much of its antecedents can be seen in the stripped Bren Ten: CZ75 shape; Browning lock; SIG slide-inside-frame. It's meant to be the compleat defensive arm, out of the box.

operable with the trigger finger of the weak hand in case of strong-hand disability.

The pistol is very similar to the 1911 in size, and weighs two ounces less when unloaded. It is very similar in "feel" to the Cz 75. Barrel, frame, and springs are of stainless steel, but not the slide. Stocks, the only parts that the customer may want to modify to his individual taste, are of maple on the prototype but will be black plastic on the production guns. The Patridge sights are illuminated by the three-dot system as on the H-K P-7, but can easily be filled in by shooters who stick to black-on-black. Any sort of trick front sight can be plugged in in seconds, without tools.

It would be economically unsound to produce an instrument as advanced as the Bren Ten by old-fashioned methods. I was told in Germany that the Cz 75 was marketable at a competitive price only because the commissars can set any price they fancy, and that the piece would have to go for at least $1200 if it were made by conventional methods and free labor. Such is not the intention with the Bren Ten. Tom Dornaus has set up his brain-child to be run off on pro-

grammed automatic cutters which dispense with operators and need only directors and trouble-shooters. The machines have been checked out and they work. By this means the pistol can be produced for something like $450 retail, which is a bargain considering that it comes across the counter ready to go with no sights to install, no trigger job, no dehorning.

Ammunition plans have been made, and the manufacturer stands ready to throw the production line switch on the day the cutters are ordered.

The Bren Ten is not just another new pistol design. We have plenty of

The 10mm cartridge may be thought of as a rimless 38-40, or just something sort of halfway from 9mm to 45, but not like either one.

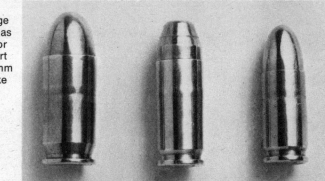

those. We do not need another big, cumbersome, expensive 9. Those who can live with that power level are best advised to go to the Heckler & Koch P-7 (PSP), which is the right size and weight for a second-line cartridge. Neither do we need a giant pistol suitable for hunting moose and elk. But we armed citizens do need something with which to replace the grand old 1911 45, not because it won't do but rather because it is due for phase-out. Colt Industries has long indicated that it is not happy in the gun business and would get out if it could do so comfortably. With the Pentagon about to replace a really good pistol with a mediocre one at huge cost to the taxpayers we cannot look to the new service pistol as an adequate replacement for our own use. The Bren Ten, if it works, is the obvious answer.

Will it work? The prototype sure does. Not being a machinist, my reservation is that I do not know whether or not the programmed cutters can mass-produce triggers like the one in the prototype. Tom assures me that they can, and he ought to know, but until I have personally tested a respectable number of production guns I cannot swear to this. I do know that production triggers can be excellent, so where there is a will there is apparently a way.

As I write this the financing of the project is still not ready, though there have been a lot of nibbles and a couple of hard strikes. Quite a lot of money is involved, and if it is to be raised by public subscription the situation will be complicated. At least one foreign government has bid to back the whole show at one stroke, but with governments there are always strings attached. As long as anyone listens to me, for instance, there will *not* be a "Bren Nine."

In the absence of some evidence to the contrary I am going to go out on a limb and assert that the Bren Ten is indeed the better mousetrap. ●

CARMICHEL ON RIFLES

by JIM CARMICHEL

Respected writer and shooter Jim
Carmichel of *Outdoor Life* here casts a
critical eye on a Scandinavian rifle.

Bolt-Action Rifles

THE BOLT-ACTION rifle has recently come to dominate
the North American hunting scene, especially among
sportsmen who own, or intend to own, two or more centerfire rifles. One of the reasons is the modern emphasis on
cartridge performance, most of all of Magnum cartridges.
With the exception of the Browning BAR autoloader, the
choice of a rifle firing a belted Magnum cartridge is limited
to bolt-action guns.

Though most game in North America, as in all other
parts of the world, is shot at ranges of under 100 yards
(90m), North American hunters like to be prepared for
longer shots. This is most usual among hunters in the
western states, where shots at pronghorn, elk, and mule
deer may be at ranges as great as 300 yards (270m) or more.
This type of shot does not call for a high rate of fire, but it
does require cartridges that deliver plenty of punch at long
range, and a rifle capable of better-than-average accuracy.
Thus, the appeal of bolt-action rifles is their combination of
an excellent range of calibers and the inherent accuracy of
the bolt mechanism. Added to that, some bolt-action rifles
are extemely handsome and distinctive, and have a considerable appeal to today's shooters.

Though the basic bolt-action design has been updated and improved over the years, it has really not changed much since the days of Paul Mauser, who refined the turnbolt concept into a working reality a century ago. Its simplicity of design and operation, together with its high strength, makes it the safest and most reliable repeating action available.

Nothing quite matches the accuracy of a bolt-action gun. During the last hundred years, various falling-bolt, single-shot actions were considered the most accurate, but the bolt gun has ruled supreme for the past few decades. This is marked with current target rifles, both rimfire and centerfire, which are all based on bolt-action designs. The one exception, the British BSA rimfire match rifle, is notable just because it is the exception.

There are several reasons for this intrinsic accuracy. First among them is the inherent stiffness of the action. Any flexing or bending of a rifle action when it fires lessens accuracy, and the symmetrical locking arrangement of most bolt guns helps in resisting such flexing; so does the one-piece stock, which is (usually) rigidly attached to the action. The more modern bolt-actions are also capable of extremely fast lock times and have triggers that can be finely adjusted, two features which aid accuracy and performance.

Although the bolt-action is considered to be the slowest mechanism in operation of all repeating-rifle mechanisms, it can be fired at a surprisingly high rate. The American Match Course of Fire includes a 200-yard (183m) phase which calls for ten shots to be aimed and fired within sixty seconds: the shooter begins in the standing position, must then get into the sitting position, fire five shots, reload the magazine, and fire five more shots. A good bolt-action rifle marksman can easily do this with seconds to spare and place all his shots into an area smaller than that of his hand.

Americans were introduced to the bolt-action rifle in a big way only during World War I, when hundreds of thousands of Doughboys were issued with 1903 Springfield rifles. Up until then, experiments with bolt designs had met with only limited success. In 1879, for example, Winchester began manufacturing the Hotchkiss bolt gun, and some 85,000 were made during the next twenty years. Remington made the Lee-designed bolt-action rifle from 1886 until 1906. A more successful rifle was the Krag-Jorgensen bolt gun, built under license by Springfield Armory and chambered for the 30-40 Krag round. This was the standard United States Service rifle from 1894 until 1904, the Army's first bolt-action rifle, and its standard arm during the Spanish-American War.

Since then, dozens of American-made and -designed bolt-action rifles have come and gone, and dozens of European models have been used by North American hunters. Most popular of the European makes have been the Sakos and various Mausers. At present, the most popular American centerfire bolt guns are the Remington M-700, Winchester M-70, Ruger M 77, and Savage M-110. Another popular bolt gun is the Weatherby Mark-V; this is the product of an American company whose guns have been built in West Germany and are now being built in Japan. There are, of course, other bolt-action guns, too numerous to mention here, but the target-type centerfire guns should not be forgotten; smaller makers, such as Shilen and Wichita, produce guns that are among the most accurate in the world and are truly remarkable pieces of design.

The Winchester Model 52 rifle had been North America's most respected rimfire bolt-action gun when it was discontinued in 1979; for many years, it had been the leading target rifle in the United States and the one that had established a number of national records. The sportier version of the M52 is considered to be the best of its type ever built in the United States, and collectors now pay several hundred dollars for a good specimen. At present, the German-made Anschütz Rimfire, another bolt design, is the overwhelming favorite among North American target shooters.

One of the goals of every American rifle-lover is to acquire one of the beautiful custom-made rifles built by one of the top American stockmakers. The demand exceeds the supply, prices are several hundred dollars at least, and, with very few exceptions, these superb rifles are all bolt-action guns.

Lever-Action Rifles

The lever-action rifle, more than any other, has come to symbolize American hunting and the traditional American concept of arms design. This is so thanks to the tremendous publicity or image-making of popular literature, motion pictures, and television epics that consistently link the lever-action rifle with the "taming" of the American West.

It is fascinating to note that attempts to improve, refine, or streamline the basic nineteenth-century lever-action rifle have almost universally failed. Examples of this are the modern-looking Winchester Model 88 centerfire (1955-1973) and Model 150 rimfire (1967-1973), Sako's Finnwolfe (1963-1972) and Model 73 (1973-1975), Marlin's "Levermatic" rimfire Model 56 and Model 57, and centerfire Model 62 (1955-1965), and Remington's Model 76 (1962-1964). All were improved designs of the hammerless type, with short-throw mechanisms and greater strength and accuracy, but, despite their obvious improvements over lever-action designs dating from the nineteenth century, all were commercial failures within only a few years.

The most modern mechanical lever-action currently being produced, Browning's BLR, is carefully wrapped up in 1890s trappings to give it a distinctively "Western" flair. The only exception to the rule of Western appearance is the Savage Model 99, which, though dating back to 1899, has a hammerless profile, It has been constantly updated since its introduction; even so, Savage recently "reintroduced" the old Model 99A in an effort to lure shooters captivated by its "Gay 90s" configuration.

Historians of firearms seldom note that the lever-action was an early commercial disappointment, despite its place in American history. Oliver Winchester saw it as a military arm and promoted it as such in the war ministries of Europe, Asia, and South America. "Where," he asked, "is the military genius who will grasp the significance of this machine of war and thereby rule the capitals of the world?" The world's military genii remained skeptical and, except for sporadic orders for lever-action muskets, Winchester had to make do with a relatively small but steady civilian demand for his wares. Nevertheless, his Model 94 carbine has become the symbol of all lever-action guns and exemplifies them in discussions of their uses, virtues, and faults.

The lever-action gun in North America is most commonly classified as a "brush gun;" its use is in brushy or wooded areas where most shots are fired at less than 80 yards (75m), and shots of over 100 yards (90m) are an exception. For these conditions, a short, light, easily carried carbine capable of a relatively high rate of fire is needed.

Lever-action rifles have never been considered to be especially accurate, and certainly not when compared with bolt-action rifles and some types of single-shot rifle. This relative lack of accuracy is due to the two-piece stock design, the light barrel, and the comparatively non-rigid action (receiver) which flexes considerably on firing. Nor have lever-action rifles been chambered, until recently, for notably accurate cartridges.

Fine accuracy has, however, never been essential to the purposes of the lever-action rifle, although some models are capable of surprising accuracy. With selected ammunition, some guns can group five shots inside a circle of 2 inches (5cm) diameter at 110 yards (100m); even if this is an exception, virtually any modern lever-action rifle can group its shots within a circle of twice that diameter.

The first lever-action rifles were chambered for the early self-contained cartridges, which were also used in pistols. The Winchester Model 73 (1873-1919) fired 44-40 and similar pistol-type cartridges, which were barely adequate for deer and not adequate at all for bear, elk, and bison. Bigger, more powerful cartridges called for bigger, more massive rifles; a succession of lever-action rifles was designed for the 45-70 and larger cartridges. Winchester and Marlin made rifles to fire these bison-class cartridges, a development that culminated with the Winchester Model 1895 (1895-1931), which fired such high-powered cartridges as the 30-06 and the giant 405 Winchester round, which had a muzzle energy of 3,220 ft/lbs (444kgm).

Lever-action guns might have been designed for bigger and bigger cartridges but for the advent of the bolt-action rifle; the surviving lever-action rifles are the light, fast-handling carbines used for hunting deer and black bear. An exception is the lever-action rifles made by Marlin, the 45-70 and the 444, which take Marlin cartridges made to a nineteenth-century pattern; these cartridges do not expand the practical use of the lever-action gun, and the combination appeals almost entirely to shooters who have a sentimental attachment to such old-fashioned styles.

The leading feature of lever-action rifles has been said to be their speed of action, but, in practice, this is seldom realized: to maintain a high rate of fire, the butt must remain against the shoulder and the sights be kept steadily on the target while the lever is operated and the trigger pulled. The typical hunter, however, is more likely than not to remove the rifle from his shoulder while he deliberately operates the mechanism between shots; this gives an operational speed about the same as that of a bolt-action.

The external hammer of most lever-actions has long been considered an important safety feature, but, in practice, this is not quite what it seems. To lower the hammer to the "safe" position, the trigger must be pulled; occasionally, the hammer slips from under the thumb and fires the rifle. To obviate this, Mossberg has recently introduced a modification to the Model 479 lever-action rifle; this takes the form of a manually operated cross bolt which blocks the hammer even if it falls by accident.

Lever-action rifles are usually sighted by means of open "V-sights" fitted in the factory; up until recently, this sighting arrangement could be refined by an adjustable "peep" sight fitted to the receiver or tang. While such peep (or aperture) sights are still manufactured by a few sight makers and are available for all current makes of lever-action rifle, today's buyer is most likely to choose a telescopic sight. However, this can lead to problems.

The popular Winchester 94 ejects its fired cases out of the top of the receiver, on which there is no solid place to mount a scope sight. Even if a scope sight can be mounted over the receiver, the ejected shells may strike it, fall back into the mechanism, and cause a stoppage. This problem is usually got around by attaching the scope mounting to the left of the receiver and positioning the scope off-center to the left, so that ejected cases do not strike it. Another solution, developed by the Leupold Optical Company, is to attach the scope to the barrel forward of the receiver; this calls for a scope with unusually long eye relief, such as Leupold's specially designed eye-relief scopes. They have 2X or 4X magnification and offer 10- to 24-inch (25 to 60cm) eye relief. Some other lever-action models, for example those by Browning, Marlin, and Mossberg, feature side ejection and solid receiver tops, which permit conventional scope mountings.

The cartridge that is almost synonymous with the lever-action rifle is the 30-30 WCF and, indeed, the 30-30 caliber is one of the favorites for the lever-action rifles made by Winchester, Marlin, Mossberg, and Savage. While certainly adequate for deer and smaller bear, in terms of performance it is overshadowed by almost all other calibers for which lever-action rifles are currently chambered.

The Savage Model 99, for example, is currently available in 22-250 Remington, 250 Savage, 243 Winchester, 300 Savage, 308 Winchester, 358 Winchester, and 375 Winchester. The 22-250, a purely varmint cartridge, is not suitable for big game, but any one of the other cartridges is good for deer. The Browning BLR is available in 243, 308, and 358, all calibers of modern, high-intensity cartridges suitable for deer-sized game.

The Marlin rifles have not been adapted to high-intensity cartridges. They take medium-to-low pressure cartridges such as the 357 and the 44 Magnum pistol, the 30-30, the 35 Remington, and the 45-70. The Mossberg rifles are similar to the Marlin guns and take either the 30-30 or the 35 Remington.

"Carmichel on Rifles" is excerpted from this massive $49.95 book now available from Abbeville Press. Edited by Robert Elman, *The Complete Book of Hunting* collects, in 140,000 words and over 700 photos, the observations of nearly 20 worldwide experts. We print the excerpt by permission of the publisher.

It seems safe to say that lever-action centerfire rifles will remain popular for many years to come and they will not vary very much from their present conventional configurations. The same can be said of the lever-action rimfires in the 22 caliber; their appeal is based on their "Old West" styling, for their accuracy is about the same as most other rimfire rifles. In speed and ease of operation, they rank ahead of bolt-action rimfires. In one respect, they may be slightly superior to most other American rimfire hunting rifles, and that is that they are of an unusually high quality. The rimfire, lever-action rifles by Browning, Marlin, and Winchester are all markedly better made than most other rimfires, and if they are among the most expensive rimfires made in the United States, this is partly because they are made of the best materials.

Pump and Autoloading Rifles

No less a manufacturer than Colt made a pump-action rifle way back in 1885: the "Lightning." It was not especially successful and was discontinued after the turn of the century, even though it was well made. While the pump action is very popular in North American shotguns, it has never been really favored for rifles. The appeal of the pump-action rifle is mainly to those hunters who use pump- (or slide-) action shotguns and have become accustomed to ejecting shells by pumping the forestock.

Current centerfire pump-action rifles are pretty well summed up by Remington's Model 760 Gamemaster (in 243, 6mm Remington, 270, 308, and 30-06 calibers) and Savage's Model 170 (in either the 30-30 or 35 Remington calibers). In skilled hands, the pump-action rifle is second only to the autoloader in operating speed.

After firing, the forestock is pulled fully to the rear by the forward hand, then moved forward again until the action locks into battery position. This back-and-forth motion extracts and ejects the fired case, cocks the firing mechanism, and feeds a fresh cartridge into the chamber. It is a smooth, natural movement and offers the advantage of allowing the shooter's hands to remain in their firing positions. The main disadvantage in operation is the small mechanical leverage exerted during the extraction phase: if spent cases tend to stick in the chamber, extraction may become difficult and may even cause a temporary stoppage.

Accuracy of pump-action centerfire rifles is on a par with that of lever-action and autoloading rifles. There can be considerable variation of accuracy, however, among rifles of the same make, model, and caliber, and even if blanket condemnations of the accuracy of pump-action rifles are sometimes heard, they are not necessarily justified.

Pump-action rimfires are somewhat more popular than the larger bores. Models are made by Browning and Remington, while the Brazilian firm of Rossi currently produces a replica of the discontinued Winchester Model 62, which was in production from 1932 to 1959.

No development of pump-action rifles seems to have occurred recently, if one excepts that incorporated in Browning's BPR rimfire, a pump rifle made possible simply because it has so many parts in common with the similar Browning rimfire BAR-22 autoloader.

Autoloaders, or semiautomatics, in centerfire and rimfire forms, are much more popular in the United States than pump-action rifles. At this writing, half-a-dozen or so American-made or -designed sporting-type centerfire autoloaders are on the market, together with another dozen or more copies of military-type rifles that should be classed as "junk guns." Browning, Harrington & Richardson, Ruger, and Remington all have centerfire sporting rifles available in many calibers, ranging from the 223 Remington and the 44 Magnum, up to the 300 Winchester Magnum. Experimental autoloaders have been made in the 458 Winchester Magnum caliber.

The obvious advantage of an autoloading rifle is its speed and ease of fire. The shooter needs only to pull the trigger and the extraction, ejection, and feeding operations are performed automatically. It is wrong to call these guns automatics, for an automatic is, correctly speaking, a machine gun which continues to fire as long as the trigger is depressed. "Semiautomatic" is more correct. On an autoloader, the trigger must be pulled for each shot. In the United States, private ownership of full automatics, or machine guns, is prohibited except under special license, and nowhere in the United States or Canada are automatics permitted for sport hunting. Autoloaders, by contrast, may be legally used for hunting, subject to the restrictions in force in some states, which limit magazine capacity to only a few rounds.

The objection to autoloaders that is most often heard is their alleged tendency to jam. The usual cause of stoppages is hand-loaded ammunition that has been improperly prepared, but apart from this, autoloaders are surprisingly trouble-free and reliable.

The mechanisms in current production are either the gas-operated or the straight-blowback. The latter is extremely simple: the rearward thrust of the fired cartridge pushes the bolt backward and thereby begins the new cycle of operation. The combination of simplicity and ease of manufacture has made this mechanism the logical choice for rimfire rifles, but it does not adapt well to use with higher-powered cartridges, which require an increasingly heavy breechblock to balance the rearward thrust. At one time, Winchester, for example, made centerfire sporting autoloaders that had simple blowback mechanisms—the Models 07 and 10—but they weighed up to 8½ lb (4kg) with their massive breechblocks; they fired relatively low-energy rounds, the 351 and the 401 Winchester.

With rifles firing high-intensity cartridges, a more practical method is to use some of the gases from the fired cartridge to actuate the mechanism, the same system as that used for semiautomatic shotguns. This system is used, for instance, in the Browning BAR Sporter, the Remington 742, and the Ruger Mini-14.

Remington once built some autoloading rifles using the Browning long-recoil system, but they have long since been discontinued; this type of action is complicated to make and less efficient than the gas system, and it will probably not be used again for rifles.

Though the accuracy of autoloading rifles is often belittled, there is no reason to expect them to be less accurate than pump-action or lever-action guns, or, for that matter, many bolt-action rifles. Highly refined National Match versions of two United States Service autoloading rifles, the M-1 Garand and the M-14, are capable of astonishingly fine accuracy, sometimes grouping ten shots inside a 3-inch (7.5cm) circle at 200 yards (190m). However, many autoloaders suffer from hard, creepy trigger pulls and thoughtless stock designs, and these faults make for a lack of accuracy that has nothing to do with the actual firing mechanism.

Though autoloading big-game rifles are most common in the northeast of the United States, where close-range fast-firing is more desirable than long-range precision, they are widely used all over North America for every type of big game, while the rimfire versions are popular among those who shoot small game such as squirrels and rabbits. ●

COLT
SHOTGUNS

by DON HARDIN

Straight grip hammer double at the top is 10 gauge #13662. Lower gun an early hammer model 12 gauge #110.

Colt hammerless guns, upper gun is 10 gauge #2 grade #2238 merchandised by Kennedy & Curtis of Philadelphia in 1892. Lower gun is 12 gauge #1 grade #6465.

In 13 years, over 30,000 doubles came out of Hartford

ONE USUALLY associates the Colt Firearms Co. of Hartford, Conn. with the production of pistols ranging from before the Civil War to the present. However, Colt produced several long arms, and probably the finest of these were their shotguns. Although only offered for a short period, these prestigious doubles were among the finest obtainable from an American maker. Until 1881, English shotguns were generally used by the affluent American sportsman. At this time, a tariff of 35% on imported breech-loading shotguns to protect the American arms makers was passed by Congress and made the production of better quality American shotguns a more feasible enterprise.

Colt introduced a hammer double in 1878 and a hammerless model in 1883; both of which were discontinued in 1891. Approximately 22,700 of the hammer guns and 8,366 hammerless doubles were manufactured during the thirteen years of production.

The hammer guns were built with two locking lugs plus a dolls head rib extension. (About 400 of the early hammer guns and the unusually rare Colt double rifles did not have the dolls head extension rib, and a few Colt hammer guns show a rather rectangular extension rib). The hammer guns were equipped with rebounding locks so that, upon opening, the firing pins were withdrawn from the breech face and could not cause a loaded shell to fire accidentally when the gun was closed. Colt doubles were produced with barrels joined by brazing instead of the commonly used method of soldering them together.

Four grades of hammer guns graced the Colt line, varying in engraving, quality and figure of wood, as well as in the checkering.

The Colt Hammer double grades of 1885 were listed as:

Twist Barrels with no engraving, a small amount of checkering offered at $55.

Fine Twist Barrels with no engraving, well checkered, offered at $60.

Laminated Barrels line engraved, checkered offered at $65.

Damascus Barrels engraved with game scenes, well checkered, offered at $75.

Guns with straight grip stocks were $5 less than the stated prices which were for guns with half-grip stock style 12 gauge guns. Ten gauge guns were $10 more in each model. The price list also indicated that 12 gauge guns priced at over $75 and 10 gauge guns priced over $85 would be furnished to order.

If the buyer wished, these custom made guns could be provided with more engraving, finer wood or special features as well as cards indicating how each barrel had patterned.

The Colt double rifles were made on the hammer gun frame. This rifle, made in four 45-caliber options (45-70, 45-80, 45-90, 45-100), is one of the most collectable of Colt firearms as only around 40 guns were produced. The rifles were equipped with 28-inch barrels and carried ornamentation comparable to their shotgun counterparts.

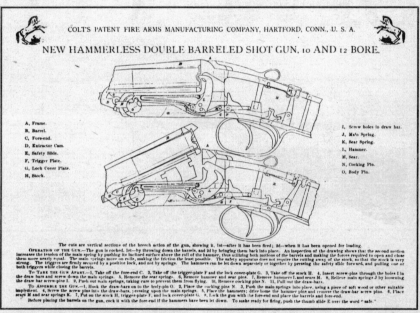

After developing both sidelock and boxlock experimental models; the Colt Firearms Co. introduced a boxlock top lever opening gun of an Anson and Deeley outward appearance, but the Colt hammerless was partially cocked by the lowering of the barrels timed so that the closing of the barrels completed the cocking via the cocking rolls. This method was advertised to be more uniform and to take less force in the process than was common in similar doubles.

At the time of its introduction (1883), a hammerless gun was somewhat of a novelty and the shooter was not familiar with a safety. Detailed assurances and instruction as to the effective design of the safety were therefore included in Colt advertising.

The hammerless line of the Colt double was produced in three grades and higher grades were additionally available at special order. In 1883, the grade #1 gun was sold for $80, the grade #1½ at around $100 and the grade #2 gun at $125.00. The guns

were more ornate in each ascending grade. However, Great Western Gun Works Catalogue of 1888-89 offered the #1 grade at $64 and the #2 at $100.00, indicating that they were commonly discounted in price.

The #1 grade gun was lightly engraved with line engraving around the frame, hinge pin and fences. The gun was stocked with high quality English Walnut and provided with Damascus barrels. Stock dimensions were provided to order within stated limits, and variation from the limits cost $7.50 as an extra charge.

Well supplied with high quality engraving, the #2 grade gun usually sported game scenes on each side of the breech. The action plate, fences and trigger guard were also elaborately covered with scroll and game scene engraving. Finest Damascus barrels and finest English walnut stocks were advertised on the Colt flyer for the #2 grade double.

The #1½ grade gun, as one would expect, was between the #1 and #2 grades in terms of ornamentation and price. (The grade designation of Colt hammerless guns can be found on the underside of the barrels beside the extension cam slot.) Extra barrels could be purchased at $50 for the grade #1 guns and $60 for the grade #2 gun.

It is interesting to note the popularity of the 10 gauge gun at this time in our sporting history (1880s) in contrast to their rarity today. A Colt #2 grade 10 gauge in this writer's collection has 28-inch barrels and is choked improved cylinder and modified indicating use for upland game. Recoil is quite mild when loaded with 1¼ oz. of

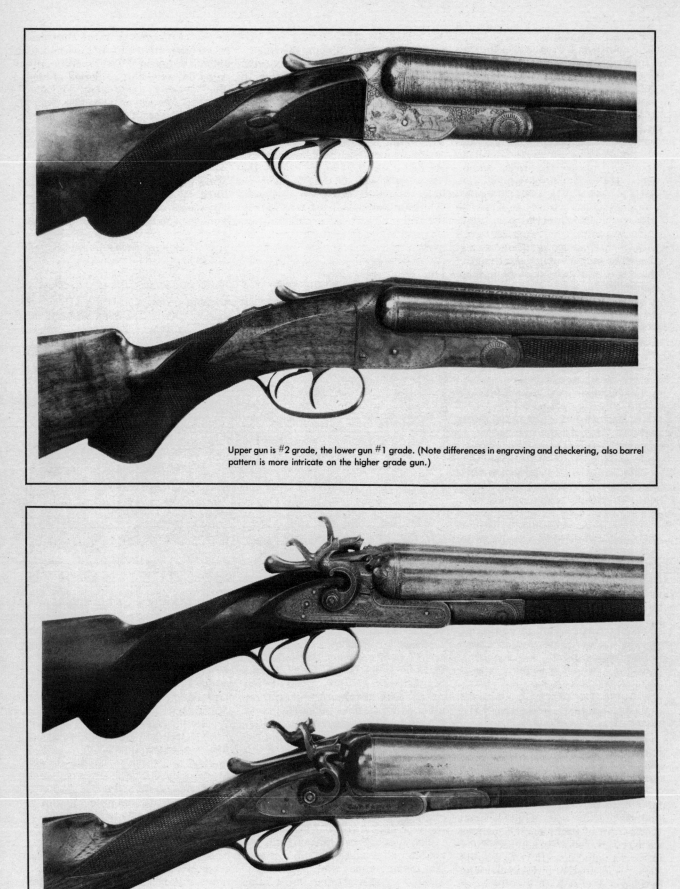

Upper gun is #2 grade, the lower gun #1 grade. (Note differences in engraving and checkering, also barrel pattern is more intricate on the higher grade gun.)

Colt hammer guns. The upper gun is a well engraved early model, serial #110. The lower gun is a late model hammer gun — 10 gauge #13662.

shot in the black powder loading popular at that time. (The typical black powder 12 gauge load was 1⅛ oz. of shot.)

A tag was attached to each gun attesting to the patterning of the barrels. (Gun #6660, a 12 gauge, threw 355 pellets with the left barrel and 375 with the right using 1¼ oz. of #8 shot.)

The Colt shotguns were all available on special order with extra engraving or varied stock dimensions. Many of the Colts were stocked with less drop than the typical stocking of that period. One gun, an 8 gauge specially produced for President Cleveland with 34-inch barrels weighing in at 12 lbs. 3 oz., was a good example of the degree of special attention given to preferred sportsmen. Several hammerless doubles were known to have been gold inlayed in different degrees on ornate detail.

Colt engraving would have to be considered as good as any in the industry. Under the direction of Cuno A. Helfricht, head engraver, the hammerless guns in the higher grades exhibit some of the best English style engraving, yet showed the Germanic training of most of the immigrant engravers of that time. The game scenes, particularly, are unique in their balance and lack of clutter, complemented by the clean lines indicative of skilled engravers.

The beautiful Damascus barrels used on the shotguns were purchased from Liege barrelmakers, where the Belgian barrel guild produced the Damascus barrels used by most of the makers of high quality American double guns. (The import tax on barrels in the rough was only 10%.) One gun in the Colt Firearms Collection in Hartford showed the legend "Colt" built in the Damascus pattern. The fancier patterns were used on the more expensive grades. There were no Colt doubles built with fluid steel barrels at the time production ended (1891). During this period all-steel barrels were being accepted by gunmakers but on a basis of a lower priced grade of shotgun than one having Damascus steel.

The Colt doubles were not produced for a long period, probably because Colt pistol sales were going well and the margin of profit on the doubles wasn't as good per man hour expended in their production. (Harrington and Richardson, another pistol maker who developed a very high quality hammerless double during the same period, also gave up the production of the prestige double and stayed with

pistol production.)

For a brief period during the 1950s, a double imported from France and produced by "Manufrance" (appearing to be identical to their Robust model), was sold with Colt markings.

Currently, the high grade Colt doubles represent a good value in the collecting of antique arms, as they are priced lower than some of the competing makers' guns of lesser quality produced during the same period of history. The guns, consequently, should be a good investment as well as pleasing possessions. •

Picture shows Germanic style of engraving so prevalent on Colt arms. Gun is #2 grade.

Early model Colt hammer gun. Damascus grade. Although heavily engraved, quality is not as good as found on comparable hammer guns.

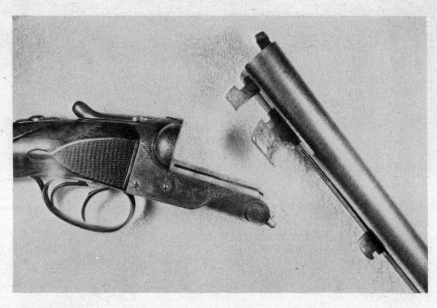

Action assembly of #2 grade Colt hammerless. Note dolls head in addition to barrel lump locking.

HK

ONE GOOD IDEA . . .

LEADS TO MANY OTHERS.

by KEN WARNER

It's a shut-and-open case: The H-K roller locks are controllable—with fluted chambers—to serve many kinds of firearms, and form the technical base for much H-K output. Above: Before firing. Below: As it opens.

The P7 9mm pistol is a technical breakthrough in another direction—squeeze-cocking, gas-unlocked, light in weight—and has become a police standard. High-priced, it still sells fast.

YOU CAN READ it all in the H-K literature: The company began in 1949 to produce precision parts for others and then to make fixtures and tools to make such parts for others, and then got the chance to develop the roller-locked CETME into the G3 Automatic rifle for the West German military. And they've never looked back.

The key to the H-K success is as much the successful adaptation of a single idea—the roller-locked hesitation breech—as to any other factor. That is what they have sold successfully; that is what they make successfully; that is what they have adapted to firearms use in everything from a 30-ounce 9mm pistol to a full-rated infantry machine gun in 7.62mm NATO, and have now adapted to the 940mm length cartridge, such as the 9.3x62mm, the 30-06 and the 7x64. The lock is the key to the whole thing. There can be management processes, industrial knowhow, marketing powers, other kinds of firearm designs, but any and all of the ingredients of industrial success stem back to that single technical achievement.

There has been much technical controversy over the precise nature of this roller-lock. The argument by some is that it is no lock at all; others believe it to be a hesitation lock; at Heckler & Koch they believe it to be a true lock, but a temporary one. Since they are

Every firearm in an infantry platoon could have H-K's roller locks from P9S pistols as sidearms through the MP5 submachine gun and G3 assault rifle to the heavy-duty belt-fed HK21 machine gun. Choices: 223 or 308 in everything but the handgun, where the choice is 9mm or 45.

able to make it work to a variety of purposes by varying the angle at which the roller bearings must climb, and by varying the size of the whole assembly, one ought to give weight to the H-K opinion.

Undeniably, much of the H-K technical approach is outside the mainstream. That does not necessarily make it unrealistic. It might be said, on the other side, that H-K bends its technology to suit its central achievement—the roller block. That is probably also true.

Heckler & Koch make guns as they would make carburetors or automobile suspension systems. Given that the receiver of an H-K G3 is a complicated assemblage of stamped and machined parts, welded; and given that the barrel is hammer forged and subsequently turned and ground in exemplary fashion; and given that the associated assemblies are carefully manufactured, particularly including the bolt and bolt head; still, the final assembly is more like shock absorber manufacture than old ideas of assembling quality firearms.

From one simplified point of view, H-K shoulder arms are merely complicated Sten guns: There is a receiver body into which is welded or pinned a barrel and through which a reciprocating bolt functions.

Since in fact H-K firearms are expected to perform quite well in terms of accuracy and grouping, it is obvious

they are not really Sten guns. Barrels are hammer forged, and fit into very precisely made parts, though the assembly of a barrel to a receiver is complicated by the fact that welding under production conditions and at production rates introduces problems. Each barrel and receiver are straightened together; that is, the welded-in barrel is tested for runout and, in the same fixture, the assembly is bent until the barrel will point within the limits of the standard sight adjustment. That is military production.

Commercial or sporting receivers are very different. H-K welds a very complicated milled part to the standard G3 barrel shroud and then mills a top cover and within this combination the G3-type bolt operates. Barrels for this commercial assembly are not welded, but are ground on centers to fit the shroud and are press-fit from the front and then pinned. Barrel straightening is not necessary and the units are not even gauged for straightness in the factory because there is no requirement. Any minor maladjustment that might occur is amply taken up by the flexibility inherent in the roller locks.

In the sporting guns, as we have said, the barrel enters a shroud from one side and the bolt head enters from the other side to achieve the center of the firearm. These parts are very carefully made. The shroud is machined and case-hardened to precise dimen-

sion and strength; the bolt head is very carefully machined and assembled of parts heat-treated to a high strength; the barrels are center ground to a tight fit. It is not a system calculated to make life easy for the private gunsmith nor to permit easy barrel swapping, but it works. There are other controversies:

The fluted chamber has a precise function in aiding easy and rapid extraction and providing an impulse to the bolt head. It is a reliable method. The fact that the cartridge cases are somewhat disfigured is not a factor to H-K.

The location of the safety lock on the left side of the receiver, midway in the stock, is a point of controversy within the H&K organization when it comes to sporting arms. In defense of the engineers, this lock is very reliable. Until there is a near-equal device, it is unlikely H-K will change this safety to suit the needs of the sporting shooter.

The ungainly outline of most H-K shoulder arms meant for sporting purposes does not concern H-K. The company feeling is that they are not making traditional sporting arms, but better sporting arms, and these must seek their own shape.

This technical arrogance, if one wishes to call it that, does have a basis in fact. That is, the devices do function as H-K says they function. Certainly, the worldwide experience of the same

Straight blowback works, too, in H-K-4's and the VP70—the original "volks pistole"—and the VP70Z, marketed here. The HK4 can be converted to handle 22 Long Rifle, 25 ACP, 32 ACP and 380 Auto. The original VP70 offered a shoulder stock and 3-shot bursts and was intended to arm whole peoples. The VP70Z is semi-auto only, and is admired as a basic sort of pistol.

Sporting shoulder arms include blowback rimfire and three lengths of centerfire actions—640mm (223), 770mm (308) and 940mm (30-06). They share the technology with military arms, but are made entirely differently.

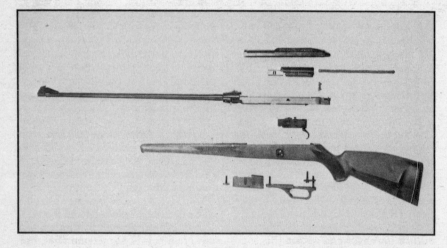

Editor at work with H-K 770, scoped. On this memorable day, he hit 3 out of 5 200-meter iron chickens twice running, offhand, with this rifle.

devices in military arms would have uncovered serious weaknesses if they existed. And the technical approach is often ingenious.

Take, for instance, the flash hiders now built into all the sporting centerfire rifles. In an extension of the barrel, there are three elliptical apertures, quite large, one on the bottom, and one on each side. These apertures are much wider at the outside of the tube than they are at the bore, and they minimize the apparent flash by injecting air into the gases to speed their burning. They burn intensely in a small ball immediately in front of the muzzle instead of in a big fireball some inches away. The net result is a considerable reduction in the intensity of flash for the firer.

I have fired three shots under sporting conditions in near-darkness with an H-K rifle so equipped. On one of those occasions I had to try a second shot at a second target immediately. I was concerned with making the shot and not with the observation of any flash. The rifle was a 30-06 and it was near full dark and I simply cannot remember seeing any flash.

There are plants building H-K's in 12 countries from Malaysia to Columbia and Mexico to Norway. In 1982 they'll start production in a plant in Chantilly, Virginia. Apart from its technical excellence, you see, the system travels very well.

•

Cheaper then and cheaper now, many guns are....

Author finds Tennessee Valley Arms' "Poor Boy" as authentic in appearance as a Hawken type.

AS AUTHENTIC AS A HAWKEN

by RICK HACKER

SINCE THE 20th Century black powder "boom" began in 1954, a special phenomenon has been evolving, an overwhelming wave that has every front-stuffer, from bearded buckskinner to nimrod and neophyte, involved. I call this malady *Hawkenitis,* and it is reaching epidemic proportions.

Not since the 1850's has there been such a variety of muzzle-loading rifles produced for contemporary black powder shooters. The decade of the '80's, rather than the first half of the 19th Century, should go down in history as the Golden Age of Muzzleloaders. Yet, with total indifference to stock shape, barrel length and over-all rifle design, it seems every other charcoal burner is christened with the cherished name of Hawken. That, I know, sets the stage for potential sales and acceptance by the nation's growing ranks of pseudo- and semi-, as well as staunchly, dedicated Mountain Men, those shooters who emulate the fur trade and Rocky Mountain exploration era of our nation's history. Further, the majority of black powder shooters encountered on the firing line or in the hunting field pack "Hawken" styled-or-stamped rifles.

Individuals new to the sport refer to any half-stocked muzzle-loading rifle as a Hawken, just as writers of a century ago referred to all repeating rifles as Winchesters. They, at least, had an excuse, for in the 1880's, there were more Winchesters around than Marlins or Ballards. In the case of the muzzleloaders, there are more "Hawken" rifles in existence today than old Sam or Jake ever dreamed of making in their combined lifetimes.

It seems ironic that in a sport as individualistic as muzzle-loading, every other pilgrim carries the same-styled rifle. Go to any blanket shoot, club gathering or rendezvous, and you'll rarely, if ever, see two Mountain Men wearing the same hat, shirt, or pants. But most of them will be carrying a Hawken rifle, secure in the knowledge that "it's authentic for the period."

The reason behind this commonality of firepower is the hallowed belief that the Hawken rifle was *the* chosen gun of every Mountain Man who ventured West of St. Louis, and that in the hands of pathfinders like Jim Bridger, Kit Carson and Bill Sublette, it killed more Blackfeet and "made

more meat," than any other rifle of the fur trade era. In fact, to hear some otherwise knowledgeable members of the black powder fraternity tout the name of the big mountain rifle, I'm surprised that the campaign slogan of Andrew Jackson in 1828 wasn't "Two Hawkens in Every House."

But such was not the case; a careful look at the facts, firearms and the men of the 1810-1860 era tells us a completely different story, one that has been distorted and overshadowed by the illustrious illusion of the Hawken rifle—an illusion, I might add, that has been largely created in our own century.

Don't get me wrong. I am not out to taint the Hawken image as a rugged and reliable hunting rifle; I have nothing but first-hand respect for the mighty plains gun; one of my favorite black powder arms is a half-stock 54-caliber Hawken rifle that I often take on hunting trips, either as my primary weapon, or as a tried-and-true backup gun, for I know the Hawken will never fail me in wind, rain or snow. Its workhorse design will take weeks of pounding in a saddle scabbard and its thick octagon barrel can handle heavy

Dixie Gun Works' Tennessee Mountain Rifle has "grease hole" in the butt, as did the originals. This is the only fur-trade era replica offered in either right or left-hand versions.

Navy Arms' Harpers Ferry is reminiscent of one of the first flintlocks to be carried into the Rocky Mountains by early day explorers.

Western Arms Trade Musket, a rugged and versatile tool for large and small game, fills the fusil role completely.

duty charges capable of dropping the largest of North American game.

But today—just as 130 years ago—there are other muzzle-loading rifles of the fur trade period that will do the job just as efficiently, and in some cases, even better than the famous Hawken. Blasphemy, you may say, but bear with me, Hawken lovers, and we'll discuss those rifles, one by one. What makes these alternate mountain rifles so appealing? They were used more than the Hawken ever was, and their replica counterparts are available today.

To fully appreciate the role that the Hawken rifle played—or didn't play, in this case—in the saga of the American Mountain Man, it is helpful to analyze a few facts: The Rocky Mountain fur trade era, the period in our history generally credited with giving birth to the trapper, explorer and Hawken rifles, began in 1810, reached its zenith by the 1830's, and had generally died out by 1840. Jacob Hawken did not start his gunsmithing business (as opposed to gunmaking) in St. Louis until 1820, and was not joined by his younger brother Sam until 1825, according to American Fur Trade accounts, so the era of the beaver trappers was 25% over before the famed "J&S Hawken" stamp was ever put on a barrel flat. After reviewing scores of documents from the original Hawken Shop in St. Louis, Charles Hanson, in his excellent book *The Hawken Rifle: Its Place in History,* estimates that all told, there were less than 3,000 Hawken rifles made

through 1854, when the shop was sold to J. P. Gemmer.

The height of Hawken production occurred in the early 1840's, after the fur trade era had closed, but just prior to the mass migration West and the discovery of gold in California in 1849. This, in part, explains why many Hawken rifles are discovered in regions of the Far West, as Gemmer continued making the big-bored mountain rifle and variations of the famed gun up through the 1880's.

Thus we see that by the time the fur trade saga was ending, the era of the Hawken was just beginning, and lasted up through the waning days of the buffalo hunter, when the self-contained metallic cartridge guns were finally made strong enough to handle the bone-crushing charges that the muzzleloader had become so famous for.

The question remains: if the Mountain Man era began in 1810 and lasted until 1840, and the Hawken rifle did not reach its zenith until 1840 and lasted until the 1880's, just what did men like Joe Meek, Tom Fitzpatrick, Jed Smith and their contemporaries use to blaze their legends into American history? It is true that documented evidence shows Kit Carson and Jim Bridger owned Hawken rifles, but contemporary accounts tell us those rifles were acquired well *after* the close of the fur trade years, and were used during the time both men served as guides along the Santa Fe and Oregon Trails. Mountain Man Joe Meek, who trapped in the Rocky

Mountains with Bridger and Sublette, is known to have purchased a Hawken during the fur trade period, but he soon sold it, as he felt it was too heavy! Evidently, in those years the Hawken mystique had not yet been perfected.

Furthermore, the relatively scant recorded number of Hawken rifles made (far more than those known to exist) could not have begun to grace the pommels and scabbards of the thousands of trappers, hunters and explorers who ventured into the Rocky Mountains and the Far West during the first half of the 19th Century.

I intertwine several of my hobbies, and as a collector of early American literature I have been blessed with a better-than-average opportunity to read firsthand accounts of the rifles used by our 19th Century forefathers. The first printed reference to a "Hawken rifle" does not occur in any book I've seen until 1847, well after the close of the fur trade era. Mentions gain momentum around the turn of the century, when a few gun writers of the time became fascinated with the shooting qualities of what were then called the "old buffalo guns"—a hint in itself. The real literary peak of "Hawkenitis" did not reach a crescendo until the 1970's. It should be noted that rarely from the early to mid-1800's is any rifle ever mentioned by its maker's name, a testimony to the fact that no one rifle ever enjoyed universal popularity at any one time. References are usually to a "rifle-gun," or more simply, just a "gun," which could, in fact, have been a shotgun,

Lyman's Trade Rifle is a rugged, simply designed representative rifle of the 1825-1840 period, but not a Hawken.

Mowrey's duplication of the Ethan Allen rifle, which was noted for simplicity and accuracy during the late 1830s.

The double-barreled shotgun, as reproduced today by Dixie, Navy Arms, Euroarms and Trail Guns Armory was one of the most popular, yet least heralded long guns of the Mountain Man era.

musket or rifle. Actually, all three types of firearms were in vogue, as we shall see.

The indisputable fact is that the initial "plains rifle" to venture into the Shining Mountains was unquestionably a flintlock, and flint undoubtedly remained the most popular ignition system for most of the fur trade era. The caplock made its appearance in 1820, but that does not mean that every man west of the Missouri River miraculously acquired one. Distances were long and both supplies and "new product announcements" had a slow and difficult time making their way West. Even when the percussion rifle did enter the camp of the Mountain Man, it was not always welcomed as a better idea.

Caplock prices were higher than flinters, a reversal of today's manufacturing costs, and there was a notable amount of prejudice against this "new-fangled" ignition system: percussion caps were costly to buy and difficult to obtain. Moreoover, if a trapper lost his capbox, his percussion rifle was a club, whereas flints for a firelock were inexpensive, easily obtainable and could even be found on the ground, free for the knapping! The flintlock also served double duty as a tinder lighter, but the percussion rifle had no such dual capacity. Small wonder, then, that the flintlock rifle was being made in this country as late as the 1850's, well after the acceptance of the percussion arm. What the caplock did offer, however, was faster ignition and more positive firepower, rela-

tively free from effects of wind and moisture which might render a flintlock inoperable during a crucial moment in a mountain man's life.

Jim Colter, a member of the Lewis & Clark Expedition of 1803-06, is generally credited with being the first of the mountain men and the individual whose exploits launched the beginning of that era. When he left the expedition on its return to the States, he was most probably armed with the new Harper's Ferry Model 1803 rifle, the official weapon of the Lewis & Clark sojourn and the gun that, quite naturally, is credited with being the forerunner of all Mountain Rifles. With its short-for-the-period 32-inch barrel, half-stock configuration and relatively small 54 caliber, it was a revolutionary new design for flintlocks, but it proved itself admirably during the highly publicized three-year trek by the Corps of Engineers into the uncharted North American wilderness. Backed by a standard powder charge of 75 grains of FFg, it made a notably accurate and substantially powerful weapon. It would have seemed to have been a logical and highly desirable choice of any adventurer heading into the Far West.

With approximately 4,300 of the 1803 Harper's Ferry rifles produced between 1803 and 1820, the gun was in far greater supply than the total production of all Hawkens during the entire lifespan of the Hawken shop. Today, a fine replica of the 1803 Harper's Ferry, which bridges the design gap between the Kentucky and plains

rifles, is available from Navy Arms. The only deviation from the original is the rifled bore, which has been enlarged to 58 caliber, making it even more effective as a hunting weapon than the original. It would be an ideal "early period" mountain gun for the 1810 to 1830 years.

Another early period rifle that has been largely ignored by many in the mountain man fraternity, although not by other groups, is the American-bred Kentucky rifle. By far the most popular long gun on the American frontier, we tend to think of the "Kaintuck" as primarily an Eastern arm, but such was not the case. On the aforementioned Lewis & Clark expedition, many of the non-government men took their Kentuckies with them as the only friends they could trust in the face of unknown danger. A few individuals had their barrels freshened out to larger calibers in anticipation of the unknown, but bore sizes generally were .40 to .60, depending on the gun.

During the fur trade era, flintlock Kentucky rifles are prominent throughout, with percussion long guns proper anywhere from 1825 on through the end of the trapper era. It should be pointed out, however, that Kentucky rifles were popular and still being manufactured in this country in the 1850's and many were still in use by Western hunters through the 1920's! It was probably the ultimate mountain man's rifle, and the one most likely to be found in the free trapper's camp of the 1810-1835 period. Kit Carson is known to have carried a Kentucky rifle from his native state during at least part of his Rocky Mountain years.

Obviously, the Kentucky rifle of the Rocky Mountains was not the brass and silver exhibition piece that hung over a better-dressed colonial fireplace. The Kentucky of the fur trader was of the plainer variety, the type usually associated with the Appalachians and often called a Poor Boy, due to its lack of ornamentation. It was a working tool, carrying no reflective metal that might alert Indians or spook game, sported browned iron furniture and boasted a relatively sturdy, one-piece stock, considering the barrels on some guns were over 40 inches long. Many barrels were often cut down to 30 inches or less, making them handier to use on horseback or to carry through dense forest.

Today, there are two excellent examples of the Rocky Mountain long rifle, with both of which I have hunted and which will stand up under the hardest of use, to which I sometimes unintentionally subject my guns, as a few individuals can testify. One is the Tennessee Mountain Rifle, made by Dixie Gun Works and one of the best values for the money available to the trapper or hunter of today. The TMR is available in either left or right handed versions—the only mass-produced muzzle-loading rifle able to claim this distinction—and can be had in flintlock or percussion persuasion, depending upon which of the pros or cons make you feel comfortable. Remember, it was only flintlocks up until the 1820's, after which both ignition systems were in vogue for Rocky Mountain inhabitants. The rifle sports a 41½-inch barrel, one-piece cherry stock—yes, it's proper for the period—browned furniture and double set triggers with fixed sights.

The other version of the fur trade long gun (although they don't call it that) is the Tennessee Rifle assembled by Tennessee Valley Arms. The rifle follows the standard "Poor Boy" pattern of long rifle (browned iron furniture and no fancy embellishments), and its 41-inch barrel comes in a standard caliber of 45. The TVA gun is made on a semi-custom basis; that is, no gun is started until an order is received. Therefore, a number of desirable and personalized options may be obtained for an additional charge. For example, any caliber is available, up to 62, making this a true Rocky Mountain bear gun and fancy maple may be ordered for the stock. In addition, a variety of locks, sights and patchboxes may be had.

Trappers, brigade leaders and St. Louis merchants venturing into the Rockies all found the short shotgun ideal in "close encounters of an unknown kind."

The TVA rifle is higher in price than the Dixie product and the wait is longer, but the workmanship and shootability are excellent; for those having very definite ideas on what their mountain long rifle should be, the TVA is an excellent investment.

Both the Dixie Gun Works and Tennessee Valley rifles can be ordered with convertible locks. Thus, you can switch from flintlock to percussion in a matter of minutes, depending on which side of the 1820's you feel like shooting from, and whether or not you want to spend some extra money for the privilege. True to their ancestors, both Poor Boys are rifled with slow twists for the patched round ball. In 50 caliber they handle 75-85 grains of FFg extremely well.

However, the rifled gun was not the only shoulder weapon that made its way into the Rockies. The mountain wilderness saw smoothbore flintlocks, early highly practical arms with well-documented benefits. Smoothbores,

though, have seen surprisingly little use by the modern-day Hawken-era buckskinners.

Called a fusil by 19th and 20th Century writers (and by some early accounts a "fusee") the earliest gun also became known as a "trade gun," due to its popularity with Indians. The trade gun terminology first appeared in 1761 and eventually was applied to any gun that was popular with both Indians and the white man. There are even some accounts of Hawkens and fancier rifles made by Dimick and Tryon being referred to as Trade Guns, so the name does not always imply an inferior weapon. By 1820, a Trade Gun among trappers was worth about 16 beaver pelts each, or in actual currency, approximately $4. In those days, pelts were worth more than cash on the frontier, for they could be traded in St. Louis for many times their Far West value.

As might be suspected from the name "fusil," the first trade guns had a

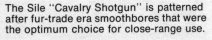
The Sile "Cavalry Shotgun" is patterned after fur-trade era smoothbores that were the optimum choice for close-range use.

French origin. The French military early on adopted a light—usually 16-bore—short musket for special troops, and when this design got to North America, it was immensely preferred over heavier and longer muskets for woods-running. Once the market—the Indians—knew what it wanted, everybody supplied it.

So smoothbores had their uses, and the rifled bore came later in trade terms. And many made do with fusils, and some, no doubt, preferred them.

The earliest trade gun available to today's buckskinner is a shortened military-style flintlock Western Arms/Allen Arms is planning to import. I have one. This fusil is actually a 1762-styled English Brown Bess musket of Revolutionary War fame, which has had the barrel cut down to a more manageable 30 inches, a common practice among the trappers and Indians. The caliber is a whopping 75, which translates into 12 gauge, so the gun can double as either a short range big game getter, firing a .715" patched round ball behind 75 to 90 grains of FFg powder, or can be loaded with 1½ drams of #6 shot in front of 3 drams (82½ grains) of FFg to serve as an effective bird and rabbit gun. In times of trouble, it was and can be stoked with "buck and ball." For defense needs, reloading was made easier and faster by the unrifled bore, which did not always require a patch

around the ball. All in all, it was (and still is) a handy all-purpose gun, a fact borne out by the fusil's longevity, which lasted throughout the mountain man period. The gun changed little in design over the years—its most noticeable addition being a "dragon" sideplate.

The fusil's only limitation, now as then, is the fact that its smoothbore limited the effective shooting range to 50 yards when loaded with round ball. As well, extensive patterning to get good shot loads may be necessary, and the long hammer fall is noticeable. However, the Western Arms Trade Gun is a versatile black powder weapon sporting an unbreakable metal ramrod as did the originals and an etched brass serpentine sideplate reminiscent of the earlier fusils. It is an authentically-copied fur-trade version of the gun that played havoc with both Indian and trapper alike.

While on the topic of trade guns, a somewhat more refined version of the trade *rifle* is put out by Lyman, patterned after the popular 1830's trade rifles of Henry Leman, John Krider and J. Henry & Sons. The Lyman Trade Rifle is a relatively plain, rugged half-stock mountain rifle, the type that would have found its way into the saddle scabbards and camps of many a wilderness adventurer. The gun is only available in percussion, and its design places it in the 1830 to '40

period, at least externally. The interior contains 20th Century improvements which make it a better shooting piece. For example, the 28-inch barrel is rifled with 1 turn in 48 inches—faster than the old-timers—so that it may be used for both round or conical ball. In actual fact, the conical slug did not come into widespread use until the 1850's, but it is a far more effective hunting projectile and was used in certain Hawkens of the latter-day period. The Lyman rifle also sports a coil mainspring, which makes for a more reliable lock. Buttplate, trigger guard and barrel fixtures are of polished brass, a desirable attraction for trade purposes. Available in either 50 or 54 caliber, it is a well made alternative for the Voyageur who wants to escape Hawkenitis.

Another commonly used firearm of the mountain men that has been neglected by today's shooters, is the double-barreled percussion shotgun, which was a true "working gun" of the mountain man. Kit Carson carried one along with his rifle and favored it for close skirmishes with Indians. Loaded with a .75" to .90" ball in each barrel (depending on gauge) the shotgun also gained favor for short range running of buffalo. First brought across the plains in the 1830's and reaching a height of fur-era popularity by the 40's, the smoothbore percussion double was produced in substantial amounts by the Hudson Bay Company (which continued to sell them up until the 1900's) as well as a few American manufacturers like Dimick. Throughout the latter half of the fur trading era, the double-barreled shotgun remained a highly desirable and saleable item for frontier outfitters.

The shotgun was a secondary arm for most, being carried by companies of traders or trappers in wagons, or in separate scabbards to augment the hunting rifle's prowess. Shooting elk or grizzly with a large-caliber rifle was one thing, but using these same guns for grouse or migrating geese was quite another. That's when the scattergun helped fill the cooking kettle. The shotgun had another, sometimes more valuable, use to the mountain man: it could be a devastating short-range weapon. Many night guards around fur company camps preferred a fully-charged shotgun to their own rifles. Aiming in the dark was not a problem; you merely pointed and pulled.

There are three excellent fur trade era shotguns available to buckskinners today. The first is the classic 12-

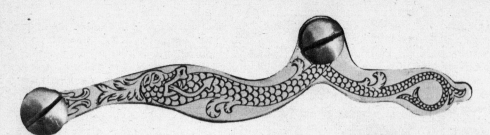

The "Spirit Dragon" or Serpent was a popular item for the sideplate of trade guns.

The smoothbore fusil could dispense this lethal load of "buck" and ball."

Trail Guns Armory produces the only double rifle currently made that is reminiscent of the European-styled muzzleloaders carried by some better-heeled Rocky Mountain adventurers.

gauge side-by-side double. Navy Arms, Dixie Gun Works and Euroarms (14 W. Monmouth St., Winchester, VA 22601) all can deliver excellent versions of this scattergun, one which I have taken hunting on numerous occasions and have never found it to be lacking in function, pointability or performance. Loaded with 1½ oz. of #6 shot and 3 drams (82½ grains) of FFg, it is an excellent bird and rabbit gun out to 40 yards.

If you decide to limit your shotgunning to closer-in targets, or desire a wider pattern, I heartily recommend a unique 12-gauge sawed-off percussion shotgun imported by Sile Distributors. With 14-inch twin tubes—legal on muzzleloaders—this percussion hand cannon is just the thing for a wilderness trader desiring an efficient backup weapon. Barrels are cylinder choked, and because of the chopped-down tubes, the Sile gun weighs a scant five pounds. It has sling swivels and a sturdy brass ramrod, both desirable features. I speak from experience when I tell you this scattergun is a definite conversation-starter when carried into a wilderness encampment. It is definitely not a gun for introverts.

For Rocky Mountain adventurers who think bigger is better, I can endorse the new 10-gauge double being put out by Dixie Gun Works. It has thicker barrels and stock than its 12-gauge counterpart and its browned tubes and buttplate give it authenticity. The polished locks and metalwork are etched with a tasteful design, which is all the embellishment any mountain man should stand. Stoked up with 4 drams (110 grains) of FFg under 1½ to 2 oz. of shot this 10-bore produces devastating patterns out to 50 yards, but be sure to put some padding between your shoulder and your buckskins because you *do* know when it goes off.

In contrast to the commonality of the double barreled shotgun, double rifles were exceedingly scarce on the American frontier of the early 1800's. Part of the reason was their relatively high cost, combined with the fact that most mountain men were just not used to the double rifle. But these two factors were more than offset by the double's ability to fire two successive shots. Thus, in spite of their high cost, doubles were used by a few notable early explorers, including Joe Meek and Jim Bridger. George Fredrick Ruxton, the English adventurer whose mid-19th Century books on his earlier exploits with the American Mountain Men created a surge of interest in our country, carried a double rifle throughout his journeys in the West. It is interesting to note that Ruxton was the first author to mention the Hawken rifle by name (*Life in the Far West - 1847*.) Thus, even though he knew about the Hawken, and had the money and means to travel to St. Louis to get one if he wished, he chose to use his double when traveling through the Rockies and Great Plains of our uncharted continent.

Today, there is only one firm making a black powder percussion double rifle of the mountain man era. Trail Guns Armory (1634 E. Main, League City, TX 77573) imports a well-made side-by-side rifle available in 50 or 58 caliber. The gun sports folding rear sights, hooked breech for easy cleaning, and sling swivels, in true European fashion. In the larger caliber version it has proven itself in Africa, and should therefore be a perfect choice for the well-to-do hunter or adventurer facing the challenges of the mountains beyond the Platte. The gun can easily digest loads of 110 to 150 grains of FFg behind a patched round ball. The 1 in

Hunting with an early 19th Century styled fusil can be challenging, but author proved versatility of the gun by taking this pheasant with it.

48 inch twist of the rifling can also take conical slugs when going after thicker-skinned game such as elk.

One of the most reliable rifles at the close of the fur trade era was also the least known. Ethan Allen was famous for manufacturing his multi-shot pepperbox pistols, but in 1835, working out of his Grafton, Massachusetts plant, he created a single shot percussion rifle that was the epitome of simplicity.

Very few went West, for production of Allen's firm was strained, and he never could meet total demand for his rifle. Yet, a few did make their way into the Rockies and today, the Ethan Allen Plains Rifle is re-created by Mowrey Gun Works. Available in either brass or browned steel (the browned version being more authentic for the period), the rifle sports a 32-inch barrel and is available in either 50 or 54 caliber. This Mowrey rifle stock is available in either cherry or an exquisitely-grained hand-rubbed curly maple stock and anyone who doesn't order this deluxe wood is crazy. For the 20th Century free trapper wanting something a little bit different, yet of authentic quality, this rifle is it.

Most of the guns here can be found in the catalog section of this book. They can be "Indian-ized," much as the fur traders or coureurs de bois did: brass tacks available from Dixie Gun Works can be pressed into various geometric shapes in the wooden stocks, and Tennessee Valley Arms sells a nicely detailed serpent sideplate, which can be inletted into the Dixie, Lyman, TVA or Navy Arms rifles we

have reviewed. Scrap leather darkened with the oil can be laced around the forestock or grip of any shoulder arm to simulate a rawhide-repaired break, for further authenticizing.

In reviewing the variety of early 19th Century shotguns and rifles discussed in this article, it is obvious that the mountain man of the early 1800's had much more to choose from than only Hawken rifles, which were not that abundant nor in the forefront until at least 20 years after the last rendezvous. Moreover, with the exception of the double rifle, the original prototype of every rifle in this article cost less than a Hawken. Good Hawkens cost $16 to $24—more than an 1830's frontiersman's monthly salary, if he had any salary at all. The majority of trappers of the fur trade period made very little in actual wages—most of their "salary" being bartered for whiskey, tobacco, and other necessities spawned by their life in the Rockies. Splurging on an expensive Hawken plains rifle was not only foolhardy, it was often downright impossible! Plain Kentucky rifles brought about $10 each and the lesser grade trade guns could be purchased in the States for as little as $4 apiece. During this time, Hawken rifles were selling for $20 and as high as $35.

Even with inflation, it still costs *less* to be authentic. That's good news for the voyageurs, long hunters, and outfitters of the 1980's and it must certainly be a refreshing revelation for the spirits of the mountain men we emulate. Even the ghosts of Sam and Jake probably feel relieved, for they must have known the truth all along.

●

It's legal in France, and fun anywhere, so our European Correspondent can tell all about...

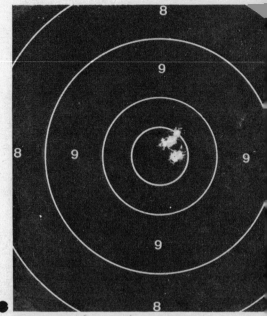

The Kintzmann rifles do not suffer from accuracy deficiency, though highly silenced.

SHOOTING SILENCED RIFLES

by RAYMOND CARANTA

Raymond Caranta at play in his yard, shooting standard 22 LR without alarming anyone.

AT THE Bastille 1979 European Hunting and Fishing Show, I saw an enigmatic, limited production, silenced rifle with a typically German extra-long name—Kintzmann Spezialwaffen. This development gun was built on a Kriegeskorte self-loading rifle action chambered in 22 Long Rifle.

This selfloader is quite clever. The receiver and bolt are essentially cylindrical lathe turnings while the action is mostly made of stampings. The stock is a single piece of nice French walnut; the bolt is chrome-plated with dual extractors; and field stripping for cleaning from the rear requires no tools. Five or 10-shot magazines are of the beautiful pre-war Mauser style.

When Kintzmann designed his silencer, he was probably attracted by this action because the side-cocking lever, a transverse pin, provides a simple way of locking the bolt, readily converting this self-loader into an efficient repeater. The original barrel is free-floating, with no protrusions

The repeater option looks like any good grade heavy-barreled semi-auto 22. All the visible barrel is sound baffle—actual bore is under 12 ″ long.

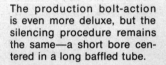

The production bolt-action is even more deluxe, but the silencing procedure remains the same—a short bore centered in a long baffled tube.

The silencer's guts look like this, are held in place with a threaded cap.

hampering the fitting of the silencer tube.

To reduce the noise level while using standard velocity rounds, Kintzmann cut off the barrel to 10.8 inches (275mm) and fitted around it a 23-inch light alloy tube, screwed onto the receiver's front end. This sleeve contains, from the muzzle, a spring expansion chamber and 9 plastic gas-catching baffles. It is closed by a threaded end fitting knurled on the outside.

The over-all length of the gun is 42 inches and it weighs 5.67 pounds. There are no metal sights, but the receiver is grooved for fitting a scope. As the pictures show, it does not present any unusual appearance.

The sale of silencers or sound moderators is free in France, and I was able to buy the prototype. I fitted it first with a 1.5x Japanese scope, as shown on the over-all view, and then with a Weaver "Qwik-Point" non-magnifying sight.

The privilege of small-bore rifles fit-

ted with silencers is that it is possible to use them readily everywhere, without driving to a shooting range, and without disturbing the neighbors. One has the same safety responsibility as with any firearm, of course. I use mine on my lawn; at 25 meters, the length of my front garden, the gun loaded with R.W.S. target ammunition is highly accurate.

Shooting with my elbows on the edge of a window, I obtained at 25 meters a five-shot grouping at .35x.27 inches with the 1.5x scope and .55x.75 inches with the Quik-Point sight. The best of these two groupings has roughly a 1.27 minute of angle value. The silencer has absolutely no detrimental effect on accuracy, it seems to me.

I had just performed a noise level measurement of all the silencers available on the French market, so it was easy to compare the Kintzmann with its competition.

All these commercial silencers are either screwed onto the muzzle or

provided with a bayonet fitting using the front sight as a lock. The longest is 9 inches and the shortest 5.5 inches. This length adds to the rifle's length. They weigh from 7 oz. to 3.4 oz.

As the full barrel length provides the maximum muzzle velocity, special rounds made by Eley and Winchester (for the European market only) called "Subsonic" are required in order to avoid the characteristic "crack" of supersonic projectiles. For my testing of commercial silencers, I had used the British Eley "Subsonic" and two French rifles, a bolt action Gaucher "Colibri" featuring a 21.65-inch barrel and a self-loading Unique "X 51 bis" with a 20-inch barrel.

The lowest noise levels recorded for three-round strings at ten feet from the shooter, at a 45° angle, in still air, all shooting performed the same day at exactly the same place, were 63.5 db (decibels) for the bolt action and 65 db for the self-loader. Silencer test results may significantly vary in relation to atmospheric conditions at the moment

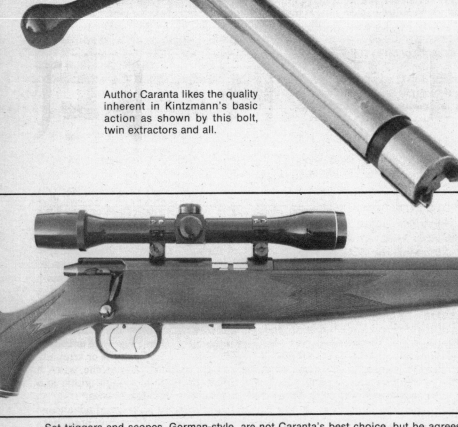

Author Caranta likes the quality inherent in Kintzmann's basic action as shown by this bolt, twin extractors and all.

Set triggers and scopes, German-style, are not Caranta's best choice, but he agrees they really work when handled right.

For some purposes, the Weaver Kwik-point suits 22 rifles, Caranta feels. He tried his first Kintzmann with one, liked it.

of shooting, so I repeated the commercial silencer test the day I measured the Kintzmann performance. The noise level is roughly 2 db lower than that of the best separate commercial silencers previously tested. All are quiet, but the Kintzmann is much the quietest, and with standard ammunition.

Using plain target ammunition of various makes, the muzzle velocity varies from 920 to 1020 f.p.s. The solid target bullets penetrate two dry fir boards 1 inch thick and 1 inch apart at 10 feet.

In July, 1980, the production Kintzmann was ready. The self-loading option was renounced and the silencer was fitted on a bolt action repeating 22, a good one. It is fitted with cheekpiece and set trigger and offers five and ten-round magazines.

The silencing device is identical to that of the pre-production gun but the barrel has been shortened to 10.63 inches (270mm). The external sleeve is 23.23 inches long and the over-all length is 42.24 inches. The weight is 6.5 pounds, including the sling and 4x Japanese scope delivered with it by the importer.

I am not too fond of these German set-triggers as the let-off is too light for me. However, I must admit, after a box of ammunition and some wild shots, accuracy is supreme. At 25 meters, my best five-shot grouping, always firing R.W.S. standard velocity, measured .118x.236 inches, less than one minute of angle. The noise level was identical to that of the pre-production gun fired as a repeater.

Now that I own this brace of fine silenced rifles, what do I do with them, besides displaying them to the other gun bugs? I must show some embarrassment: I hate to kill animals, even pests, when I can, so the only purpose of these small wonders, as far as I am concerned, is target shooting and practice. Accurate and easy to maintain as they are, both guns are perfectly fitted to that task. Why use powerful and relatively expensive 22 Long Rifle ammunition for shooting on my lawn when good air rifles provide a very similar accuracy at that range without any danger and no maintenance at all? Well, I like my Kintzmann Spezialwaffens because they are nicely designed and made and represent, at least to my eyes, the acme of the modern sporting rimfire rifle technology. And if I was a farmer or gamekeeper with pests to control—they'd be the perfect tools. ●

If you think a repeater is too bulky, and can't afford a good double, you might...
TRY A SINGLE

by KEN WARNER

I GAVE UP my search for the good moderately priced double gun when the dealer cost on the cheapest new gun I could find that came anywhere near the ideal rose above $1000. You—you, the hunter and reader—cannot get what us "experts" think is a good new double for less than $1500.00 to $2000.00.

There are cheaper doubles to be had, of course. They are sturdy, heavy, and often clubby tools, by and large, that offer the *procedural* benefits of double guns, but not what the printed wisdom of the years has perceived as *shooting* benefits. For a time I contemplated altering such guns into the state of balance and weight needed, and that is possible, but not really practical.

So, a couple of years ago, at about the same time as a colleague, Gough Thomas of the British *Shooting Times,* I came to contemplate the single barrel gun as a viable route to the highly-touted shooting graces of the fine double gun. He has discussed the matter in a couple of his trenchant columns, but he operates in the United Kingdom, where brief dalliance with numbers of guns is not simple, and his standards are indubitably higher than mine.

I simply acquired a couple dozen cheap and not so cheap single barrel guns and looked them over, tried them out, lived with them. I tried to confine all my personal shooting to singles for a couple of seasons, but that wasn't wholly possible, and had it been, it wouldn't have made much sense because they were not great seasons.

The idea was to discover if the single barrel gun, suitably employed, offered the procedural and shooting advantages of the fine double without sacrificing too much. I believe it does. That is, unless you are an unusually fine shot you may be disappointed on any single day, but you'll probably bring as many birds to bag over a mixed season with a single gun as any other; after a season or so, your cartridge-to-bird ratio will improve greatly; you will all the while enjoy some other advantages over cheap doubles or expensive repeaters.

And those are the ideal gun advantages you have read of in this and other journals for 30 years or so: the easy management, light weight and simple handling to a quick and hitting shot long considered the sole province of the good double. You don't get the second shot and you can't pay more than $100 or so for one here in the States, so they don't run to refinement in fit and finish. All the rest of it is there when time comes for the shot—a six-pound 12-bore, say, lofting 1⅛ oz. of shot at standard velocities, with much of the weight between your hands.

It's a dead-straight gun, of course, with cast neither on nor off, but that's not much of a trial to American shooters who shoot dead straight guns their whole lives. Pitch and pull length and other buttstock dimension and proportion start as average and can be adjusted to suit as with any gun, perhaps most easily by installing a recoil pad.

There is almost universally a hammer to manage, but that's not the worst of systems, really. The top snap may be a thumb button instead, or even the trigger guard pulled to the rear. And, generally speaking, whatever is in the chamber is ejected when the gun is opened, fired or not. Triggers are, in most current models, crisper than they used to be, and manageable. There may be zinc or sintered or even nylon parts, but what will you? These are the 1980's.

And then, inescapably, there's the look of the currently available singles. They are not ugly, not in a world which includes pump guns and autoloaders. In the main, though, they're ordinary. They are not really sleek or trim, except to the hands. Handsome, when it comes to available single guns, just has to be as handsome does.

My notion of procedural advantage distinct from shooting advantage concerns all that time when one has the gun in hand but is not shooting: one is walking, preparing to shoot, travelling or has arrived home with a gun to clean and store. I have been accustomed to repeating shotguns for 40 years, but find them procedurally far more difficult than the break-open gun.

That is, one pushes or pulls or levers some reasonably obvious appurtenance and the break-open gun breaks open, revealing all—it is either loaded or unloaded, and either way it is out of action. One pops a cartridge (cartridges) into the only fitting place (places) in sight, and shuts the gun.

One soon discovers whether or not one must subsequently unlatch some other mechanism called a "safety" or cock an exposed hammer in order to shoot. Having shot, one need only repeat the process to shoot again. When it's all over, the break-open gun is easily separated into three pieces, which are easy to clean and pack and store.

These are procedural advantages and all the U.S. single guns discussed here have them.

Over the months and years I have been acquainting myself with single-barrels, I have acquired some rather broad opinions of the various brand names and models. Throughout here, when required, I have examined the details, but I do have a general opinion of each sort of shotgun:

First, there is little functional choice among them. The strength of one model is counterbalanced always by a weakness and so on. For me, the realities of weight and gauge and feel are more important than brand name, construction detail or basic design.

The Winchester guns are all sturdy guns of full weight. They are more comfortable to shoot in cold blood than all the rest. They are done up nicely and present a good appearance, but there are some anomalies. For instance, the Model 37 Winchester in 28 gauge furnished to me is built on a full 20-gauge frame, it seems, and the barrel has very thick walls. The gun weighs 7¼ pounds and really does not make a lot of practical sense.

The Winchester Model 37 Youth gun is the choice for the sturdy young-ster with good shoulders and arms. It is heavier by 19 ounces at 6 lb., 7 oz., than its Stevens counterpart. The standard Model 37 12-bore, with 30-inch barrel, makes the most immediate pick-it-up-and-go-hunting gun, although obviously it is not suitable for all shooting. It weighs 6 lb., 7 oz., carries very nicely, and delivers a genuine full choke pattern to the point of aim.

Most typical current single-barrel is probably the Savage Model 94, with top-lever, case-hardened receiver, relatively light weight, in choice of four gauges.

On balance, the Winchesters are the most conservative in most respects of the generally available single shots; certainly, a great many people would consider them the most handsome.

The Stevens-Savage guns seem more to be to be built for hunters who walk a lot and carry guns more than they shoot. They seem in general to be quicker to the shot; obviously, because of their lighter weight recoil is more of a factor. Their checkering is pressed checkering; the stock finishes over hardwoods are somewhat syrupy looking; but the guns really do perform.

The Savage Model 94 Youth gun has the right dimension and the right weight for even a relatively small kid, but any parent who tried to teach a child to shoot using this gun without using very light-recoil handloads would be doing both the child and the sport a disservice. Once that hurdle is passed, the Savage Youth gun for an accomplished youth shooter would provide an excellent field companion.

The shape and balance and the stock measurements of the Savage-Stevens line, which has several different breech and opening mechanisms, seem to be right down the center line of American need. Comb drop and drop at heel and pitch are all esoterica, to be sure, but they really count in gun feel; the Savage-Stevens guns have good gun feel.

The Harrington & Richardson guns strip away all the non-essentials and deliver handy working guns in all of the right combinations. A Harrington & Richardson 28-bore, for instance,

weighs just five pounds, and is as lively a shotgun as one could find, no matter the price. The Topper 12 and 20-bore slug specials are particularly well suited to the utility role. In practice, the functioning of the H&R guns in the hands—the mechanics of loading, cocking, firing, unloading and reloading—are very straightforward and people learn them easily.

One day a friend came by my place about 2:30 and suggested we run about an hour down-country and shoot some doves. I grabbed the most recently shot single-barrel and a box of shells and a stool and left. It came on to rain, but I got seven legitimate shots and picked up five birds. The gun was an H&R 20-ga. Buck Special with rifle sights and cylinder bore and the loads were Skeet 9's and I was left with hardly a thing to say.

Those are the three mainstream American brands. Possibly equal to at least two of them in sales are the guns imported from Brazil by F.I.E. These guns are made in two factories and are two very different guns. One of them, called the CBC by people who know, is made by the Remington subsidiary in Brazil, and we are told, in fact, that it is marketed outside the U.S. as a Remington. The other is the ERA, which is very much a Brazilian-style utility gun, but it has some specific virtue. Certainly, for the money, these guns represent very good value, although their construction details and general design are distinctly imported. Where money is important—even though where we're talking just about a very few dollars—the imports are functional guns. Where extreme light weight is likely to be useful, one or two of them are very good choices. In general, their chokes are exceedingly tight. Galef brings in a familiar pattern of gun—the folding shotgun—and it has much to recommend it. including its being a true hammerless design. And there are a number of Russian models around also.

One British single gun that has received a certain amount of American attention in print is the Greener GP gun, GP meaning General Purpose, no doubt. This is a sturdy mechanism, a large Martini action, that yet permits a six-pound gun. Gotten up with British ideas in stocking, it has long—decades and decades and decades—been touted in the U.K. as the useful expedition gun for rough service and as sound enough for use by the lower echelons of overseas British wherever there is shooting.

Getting one was not so simple in 1979 and in the end I had to prevail on a friend to import three and pay a stiff price. When it arrived it proved to be a Mark I, not a GP, and quite a bit different in manufacturing detail from the GP I knew of, but the same gun in broad general terms. It was fun to shoot and I shot it well, but really it's a different story—its management, though no problem at all, seems to me enough different from the rest to take it out of consideration here.

For the record, the gun weighs 6¼ pounds, has a 27½" barrel with full choke. It never even hiccuped. Once you learn to manage this underlever action, its manners are very good indeed. I did get it onto the wrong dove field and can tell you it is not the right machine for 20-yard doves because that choke is really tight and my reputation in southern Arizona will never recover, but it was all in the interest of science. (Ordinarily, I have little compunction about reaming out unnecessary choke, but in the case of this Greener, it is so extraordinarily tight I thought I'd wait and examine that separately.)

It offers, unconventionally, the shooting advantages of the good game gun. The weight is between the hands, the dimensions correct, the trigger pull clean, and it points well. So I expect all those advertisements to the non-pukka or expeditionary British were sound enough. The Greener GP —or Mark I—itself certainly is.

Taking the general availabilities into account, it ought to be obvious in this short description that any man with access to a full display of the commonly available single shots can, within the limit of the single shotgun idea, suit himself. He will have barrel work to do, of course, if he wants anything but a full choke or modified, and he might want to spend a little money or time getting a recoil pad, not so much because a recoil pad is required, but that it affords the opportunity to give the gun the proper length and pitch, but all that aside, there is a single gun in the United States to suit any pocketbook and most sporting uses.

There is one unmitigated joy to the American single-barrel shotgun. One can go to the field with his tested choice, and can leave in the car a second gun, identical or different, as a back-up without undue concern over its physical safety or the investment involved. These days, investment in an entirely suitable second single does not amount to two or three days' pay for a laboring man. They offer, therefore, peace of mind on money, at least, and surcease of worry in the rain.

One ought not buy a single-shot gun and head merrily out to hunt. I recommend shooting at least 100 rounds quickly so one can detect incipient or actual malfunctions while the gun dealer still remembers his name. It has not been my experience that singles malfunction or are mis-manufactured anymore than ordinary American factory arms. They are made for the mass market, however, and they are not all perfect.

Beyond that, the firing of 100 rounds does a great deal to smooth out the inevitable burrs, relieve the crankiness of new parts, and familiarize the new owner with his new possession. That first 100 rounds, by the way, does more to accomplish this than all the subsequent firing, although with use and in the hands of the man that knows it, almost any single barrel becomes a rapidly worked and comfortable shooting tool. The experience of those of my colleagues who do a great deal of testing is that the bulk of malfunctions to be discovered in any firearm are found in that first 100 rounds.

In the current case, I left all but one of my 25 or so single shots just as they came from the box and shot them that way. There is not world enough or time to work over a dozen guns to suit. I did do that one, though.

In pursuit of knowledge and a good gun, I took a standard 28-inch barreled $70 (at the time) Savage Model 94 12-gauge and spent $55 in gunsmithing on it. (Well, that is what it would cost to have the same work done by a fellow of equal talent to the fellow who did my work.) I didn't do much. I had a first-class recoil pad installation accomplished to put the pull length at 15 inches, which is an eighth-inch longer than I am told is perfect for me, but I intended this gun for a shirt-sleeve gun anyway. The other work involved removing all but .006-inch of choke.

At that point, ready for the woods, I had a 5¾-pound, very fast, very positive slim shoulder arm that proved to be very efficient in the harvesting of feathered game. It was a great pleasure also to carry, was about as safe a mechanism as a firearm can be in the hands of a man in the field, and its management and manipulation was at no time, even the end of the day, difficult. I don't even think the gun is bad-looking, although it is not anything like my Churchill-style AyA, a handsome Brescian hammer 20 I own, or a Westley Richards that has my allegiance. Perhaps handsome really is as handsome does. And more certainly, alongside those excellent repeaters and doubles I own, this Savage 94 will always have its place.

I found a number of things using it and about three other singles extensively over a period of time. Except when I missed, I found little to fault with any of them, and some things to praise.

One hidden benefit of single-barrel guns is the considerably reduced load of ammunition one need carry. For instance, in a hard day of Pennsylvania pheasant hunting, one is really unlikely to get fair shots at more than 10 birds. If one carries a single-barrel gun, he therefore need carry no more than 10 shells. A confident marksman might carry no more than three or four shells where the limit is three birds, but I have never—not to remember—seen a marksman so confident.

Most fellows who straggle off away from their cars in the uplands carry, if they intend to be gone for the morning, the best part of a box of shotshells if they shoot magazine guns. The single-gun gunner would be planning glorious sport indeed were he to load his pockets with more than 10 cartridges.

Quite naturally, then, some of the other accoutrements of sport become unnecessary. You certainly do not need a shell vest, and if you claim you need it to carry the game, then that is because you have too heavy a gun. The veteran single-gun shooter knows very well that he can carry two-thirds of a pheasant limit in one hand and his gun in the other and be none the worse for it. In all, as these things are added up, the single shooter may leave pounds and pounds of gear at the gate, compared to his multi-shot brethren.

When the time comes to shoot, it is marvelous how uncluttered the mind is for the single-shooter. It isn't so much a deadly grim determination to succeed in spite of having only one shot, nor is it a fear of failure, but rather a calm realization that what is happening right now is what has to be dealt with, because what happens next is not going to happen for five or fifteen seconds.

I know because I have enjoyed playing a little game with a couple of friends which we call "single-barrel Skeet." It is played just as we shoot regular Skeet, except for the doubles. The doubles are thrown as singles just five seconds apart. That is, the shooter calls for the first bird and, willy-nilly, hit or not, ready or not, five counts later the other birds comes out of the other house. One learns with this game how to load a single barrel quickly and I have been treated to watching a good friend break 24 birds in a single-barrel Skeet round. He had, I might add, the full and complete attention of all the other members of the squad throughout the entire performance.

Concerning technique, we found no single way to success in the quick-loading of a single-barrel gun. That is, one fellow gets along with an extra shell tucked in his hatband; the next must carry the shells he intends to

load in his left hand out along the forend; and the third does better with one shell between the fingers of his right or trigger hand. There are probably 16 other ways to get the job done, so, as so much in shooting, it all depends.

If the doves or ducks or geese are flying well, the single gun is no bad handicap whatever so long as you're only going to shoot one limit. If that's three geese, or six assorted ducks or 12 doves, you'll get them all with a single gun if you're shooting well and they're flighting well.

The same is true on good days in good pheasant country with a three or four-bird limit, and the circumstances of most good grouse and woodcock cover mean there's really only one good shot per flush. On called turkeys, the single works fine.

The fellow who can double on the flush of a quail covey—well, the single puts him out of it. The joy of the right and left is gone wherever it existed. After a time, it might be replaced by long strings of days with, say, six or seven birds in bag for each ten shells, which has its own satisfactions, particularly on the days when it's eight birds.

To a degree, perhaps, we choose our guns and enjoy them on the basis of the identities carried with them. It would be easily possible to carry this thought to a ridiculous degree, since functionality and price and many other factors also enter into the selection of a gun for purchase or a gun for use on a given day.

Nevertheless, I am just as happy setting off to the hedges for, say, pheasants with a single-barrel shotgun that costs maybe $80 even in these inflation-ridden times as I am with a Westley Richards ejector double. And I own both guns. Maybe that means the day in the field is what counts with me; it may also be that I care just as much about the stereotype of a farm boy kicking out the home brush rows with a hammer single as I do for the stereotype of the tweedy connoisseur of fine guns, dogs and fast automobiles who shoots the expensive double.

Your reporter, and a colleague overseas, and doubtless some other people, would like to see a very nicely done single barrel gun for sporting use. It would have a selective ejector, a hammerless top-snap action, some grace of line, and a suitable choice of barrels and chokes and ribs and the like. It would be light for gauge and, as all of us collectively see it in our minds' eyes, it would be altogether a thing of grace and beauty. And it would cost

lots less than an equivalent double gun.

Now that I have acquired this shallow experience with a great many single guns in a number of different situations, I agree wholeheartedly that perhaps as many as 15 or 20 of us would buy such a gun each year, were it available. After a very long time, I am sure, the quality single would find its place in the market, but it is unlikely anyone but a pioneer and venturesome capitalist would invest what it takes to put one there.

That capitalist would have, for a while, that market to himself and could make a mark in it, but I am not looking for it any time soon. In barefaced honesty, I have to say there is no real need for such a gun. The guns I have been shooting have few of the desired graces, but they do have the virtues of the elegant sporting gun—they are easy to carry, quick to swing, reliable in function and they shoot where aimed.

The fellow who would take the trouble to acquire one of these, alter its choking and barrel length and stock dimension to suit him, and use it in the field with the success I know he can reach has something else entirely in mind if he insists on a hammerless top-snap action, perhaps with a little engraving, and some high-priced touches including excellent walnut, rust blueing, perhaps a chaste little rib to glance his eye along. That man is looking for some form of social acceptance.

Oh, perhaps that is unfair. There is no doubt that such a gun would be handsomer and therefore nicer to own than even a much refurbished American hammer single. And a fellow who is really looking for that, in my mind, could probably get it by taking some extra time and trouble working with knowledgeable gunmakers somewhere. However, it would cost a lot more than seems sensible. For not much more, he could have a rather nice double, and nothing here says that a good single beats a good double.

I don't think the nice single is in the cards.

As in choosing a partner for life, one cannot always expect to get passion, good looks and competence in the same package, but two out of three ain't bad. So me and my Savage Model 94 12-gauge and some other singles will still, each year, travel to the bushes together and enjoy the experience. I shall acquire the social acceptance I deserve, no doubt, by my bearing. And what I don't hit, I'll miss, same as with any gun I ever fired. •

The author with his ideal plinker—a good combination of rifle, scope, carrying strap and accurate ammo.

MY IDEAL PLINKER

by ED PARK

Editor's Note: This is a ten-year-old article. I tell you that because author Park says he was right in the first place, and this same Ruger 10/22 is his most-shot firearm today.

BEFORE purchasing a new big game rifle, a fellow probably reads many articles by respected gun editors to find the "best" type of rifle action, the "best" caliber, the grade of stock he wanted, the "best" sights, and all the other many variables that must be considered. He'll carefully study the ballistics tables in his GUN DIGEST, comparing bullet weights, velocities, energies and trajectories. If he's a handloader he'll look at the bullets made by his favorite manufacturers.

He'll leaf through the many pages, admiring them all. He may be thinking mainly of really big game in Alaska or Africa, maybe a fast-handling brush gun for deer, a long-range outfit for antelope or mountain sheep, or possibly a rifle that is good for both big game and varmints. Whatever his desires, he'll compare the various features and come up with *his* ideal rifle.

Unfortunately most sportsmen do not give that kind of thought to 22 rimfire rifles. I say *unfortunately* because if a person took advantage of all the hunting and plinking opportunities, he'd find the 22 would be used much more often than any other firearm. Something can always be found that makes a logical target for the 22 rimfire.

In recent years, the need to obtain a better 22 has been growing. My old single shot with iron sights, in use for 30 years, is still in good shape, still accurate, but just not enough gun for the plinking that I'd come to enjoy. Finally, I decided to purchase a really excellent 22 rifle, not just one I could get by with. I intended to come up with what I could honestly consider *my* ideal plinker.

I intended to use the new 22 for small game such as squirrels and cottontails, varmints like magpies and jackrabbits, a fair amount of target work to help me keep my shooting eye in shape for other types of hunting, some night hunting of jackrabbits at the ranch of some friends who are overrun with jackrabbits, some ground squirrel hunting in which we often will shoot many hundreds of ground squirrels in one day, and general tin-can plinking just for fun.

Basically I'm a bolt-action rifle man. I feel strongly it's the first shot that is the most important, and that, in most cases, a second shot won't be needed if that first one is correctly placed. The bolt action is also our strongest and most accurate repeating action.

But is the bolt action the best type of action for a 22 rimfire? If target work is important, then the bolt action must definitely be considered. But the lever action or pump is faster if rapid-fire hunting or plinking is anticipated, and tops in this category is the semi-automatic.

Some persons will lean toward the lever action for they like the classic western flavor such an action suggests. Others pick the pump because it matches the action of their favorite shotgun. If cost is a critical factor, a good single-shot should not be ignored.

I settled on a semi-auto. I figured my many years with a single-shot and with a bolt-action big game rifle, combined with my belief that the first shot is the most important, would keep me from using a semi-automatic like a machine gun. I was sure I'd use the auto-loader correctly—making each shot count.

Modern rimfire rifles of any type are plenty accurate enough for all uses except target competition. Some of my hunting, such as for cottontails or jackrabbits, often requires that fast second shot. At times we'll get into jackrabbits so thick several will be running before us.

My next consideration was type of magazine. In semi-auto, as with other repeaters, I had the choice of box or tubular magazine.

At first thought, I favored the tubular magazines. There are many more makes and models available, and the magazines may be had to handle up to 18 Long Rifle cartridges or up to 21 Shorts. I weighed a 10-shot clip versus the 18 shot tubular magazine, and the choice seemed logical. And one feature I didn't like about most 10-shot boxes is that they protrude below the general lines of the rifles. I don't like their looks.

Before I purchased my own rifle, I had two interesting experiences that changed my mind. One showed two definite problems with tubular magazines, and the other showed advantages in clip magazines.

In the first instance I was shooting ground squirrels with a friend who has a slick little semi-automatic with a tubular magazine. In fact, it is the particular rifle I was strongly leaning toward as the ideal plinker.

The shooting was in a pasture riddled with ground squirrel holes. The pests were draining off valuable irrigation water and eating tons of pasture. Targets were plentiful, if we remained motionless and in a low prone position, but show much motion and the squirrels would go below ground for awhile.

The first problem with a tubular

Extra magazines make reloading quick and inconspicuous, a major reason Park prefers the box magazine to the tubular.

Hundreds of silver-gray squirrels and other small game have fallen to Park's plinker in their ten years together.

magazine, then, is it is hard to reload without a lot of motion. Remove the plunger, hold the rifle up at enough of an angle for the bullets to slide in easily, then replace the plunger. These motions often spooked the ground squirrels, and I began to have second thoughts on this type of magazine.

Also, it seemed inevitable a squirrel would pop up while the plunger was out and the loading was in progress. The rifle is out of action for the long seconds it takes to reload.

A few days later I was again hunting the same ground squirrels with another friend who was using a clip-fed semi-auto. Here I quickly found that the spent clip could be removed and a loaded one slipped in the rifle with a minimum of motion, and the rifle could be kept in position, on

target. With two or more clips, the shooter can reload one during the pauses in the action, or, with two of us taking turns shooting with one rifle, the observer could be kept busy loading the spare clips. Two box magazines of 10 shots more than equals the continuous shooting of an 18-shot tubular magazine. There's also nothing to prevent the shooter from having 3, 4, 5 or more clips.

Those two experiences convinced me the clip-fed semi-automatic, with at least two clips, was a better choice than a tubular magazine rifle.

Besides, there is safety. With the magazine out and the action open and empty, that gun is safe. With a tubular magazine model it is easier to leave an unseen cartridge in the magazine. That rifle is then not safe.

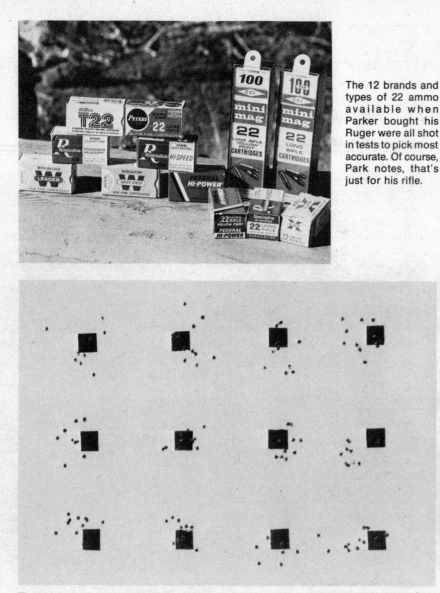

The 12 brands and types of 22 ammo available when Parker bought his Ruger were all shot in tests to pick most accurate. Of course, Park notes, that's just for his rifle.

The original 12 groups with 12 different brands and types of ammo. The variation in group size and location is normal, and would differ, brand by brand, for each 22 rifle tried.

money for a high quality rifle, I was not going to ruin the whole thing with a cheap scope.

My choice was a Weaver K-4, the same model I use on my 30-06.

The other addition was a carrying strap. I do not use a rifle sling for shooting, so need only a strap for carrying.

As I stopped to get some 22 shells, I recalled an article I'd read, talking of how accuracy in 22 rimfires varied considerably with the particular brand of ammunition in each gun. I decided that since I'd spent considerable time, effort and money in getting my ideal plinker together, I'd be ruining it all if I didn't give an equal consideration to brands of ammunition, and I bought one box each of all the different brands I could find readily, one each of standard velocity, high velocity and hollow point. I stayed with only those brands and types I could easily buy locally, and came up with 12 different boxes of ammunition.

Then to the shooting bench:

I fired 10-shot groups to begin with, all at 50 yards. The first group was centered a half-inch below my point of aim. The second group was tighter but the center of that group was an inch below and a half-inch to the right. I was already getting a difference, both in spread of group, and in point of impact.

After all 12 groups had been shot, I had quite a variation. The largest group measured 2⅞"; the smallest 1⅝". Group centers were all over the place, high, low, right, left. Some spread out horizontally, others vertically. A composite grouping would measure about four inches.

Which brands or types of cartridges did the best for me isn't important. The brand I chose *might* also be the best in your rifle, but it also might shoot the worst. The only way you can choose which ammunition to use in your rifle is to try them all out, as I did.

A friend also has a Ruger 10/22, and we also shot his rifle with all 12 types of 22 ammunition that I'd used. In some cases, results were similar to mine but in some other cases the results were far different. The ammunition that shot best in my friend's Ruger did not shoot best in mine.

So now I have my rifle, my scope and my choice of ammunition. I have *my* ideal plinker, a rifle that will do what I want a 22 to do, will serve me well for many years, and will best suit the needs to which I'll put it. I hope when you decide to buy your own 22 you'll be as satisfied with your choice as I am with mine. ●

I still had a hang-up on those long clips. It was then I found one excellent semi-automatic on the market that has a ten-shot clip that fits flush with the profile of the rifle. This is the Ruger 10/22 with its unique rotary magazine.

There were other considerations, of course. The gun had to be of excellent quality, good looks, rugged construction, able to hold a scope solidly, accurate, short in overall length, good safety features, and made by a reputable company that will stand back of their product and be in business if and when I needed repairs. The Ruger 10/22 fits all of these.

So the Ruger 10/22 it was, and I had more than one choice of style to select from. A few years back Ruger made the Carbine, Sporter and Interna-

tional models. The carbine model has a stock similar to the .30 M-1 carbine, with a metal band on the end of the forearm. The sporter has a Monte Carlo style stock and differently shaped forearm. The International, now discontinued, had a Mannlicher style stock. I chose the sporter model because I liked the looks better and I wanted the raised Monte Carlo for use with a scope.

Then I began to add accessories.

First came a scope sight. I've always had a scope on my pet big game rifle, have never seen the need for iron sights in the types of shooting I do, and hence wanted a scope on my new 22. Since I do a lot of night shooting (safely) on jackrabbits in the car headlights, a bright scope is important. I figured that if I was going to spend the

THE CASE FOR PAPER CARTRIDGES

**Some work at the loading bench speeds
up shooting muzzleloaders in the field**

by Bill Bennington

By THE SIMPLE EXPEDIENT of using paper cartridges, I have found that I can load and fire a Sharps breechloading, caplock rifle almost as quickly as I can a modern, falling block cartridge rifle; get off a second shot from a muzzleloading rifle much faster; and speed up the tedious process of loading a cap and ball revolver. That is plenty, but there is more.

There are other justifications for using paper cartridges rather than mere speed in loadings. Consider the consistency of beforehand powder metering of charges. No matter how careful your loading procedure, in the case of these three guns some powder spillage is bound to occur, sooner or later, with the use of a flask, horn, powder measure or other metering device.

If you prefer to travel lightly, there is additional justification in being able to leave behind these same metering devices, stashing the powder-filled, paper tubes in a simple belt pouch, perhaps wrapped in plastic or common wax paper if bad weather is imminent. The saving in weight is nominal, depending on the size of the flask or horn, but dispensing with a few of the items on the usual black powder shooter's checklist is certainly worth some additional effort.

Just how much time is consumed in the preparation of paper cartridges depends, to a certain extent, on the problems facing you in their preparation. For instance, I recently acquired one of Shiloh Rifle Company's new sporting, percussion Sharps made to handle a paper cartridge containing 100 grains of FFg powder. Shiloh offers a paper cartridge kit for their other guns but no nitrated paper to assemble this size tube. This left me with the realization that in order to fire the load the gun was designed to use, I had to prepare my own paper from the nitrating right down to determining the overall size of the long tubes. So I did it.

I first purchased some bond paper from a stationery store and then prepared a nitrating solution, a necessary step to insure proper combustion of the paper during firing. To one cup of ordinary tap water, I added three heaping tablespoons of saltpeter (available at almost any pharmacy or hardware store where it is usually spelled, *saltpetre*) and thoroughly dissolved it in a pan large enough to contain both the mixture and the 8½ x 11-inch sheets. Some dozen or more sheets were soaked for at least 15 minutes and then air dried.

Measurement of the Sharps' chamber had shown that the tubes needed to be 2¼ inches long in the finished state and I added to this an additional ½ inch for the necessary front overlap to be twisted in effecting closures, or to give the necessary length if I decided at some future date to enclose the bullet within the cartridge. The paper was cut into strips 2¾ inches in width and then into rectangles sufficient to give me approximately one and a half turns around the forming stick.

The paper tubes were formed around the aluminum rod from the Shiloh kit, glued lengthwise with a combustible glue, the front overlap twisted to close, and then the assembly was slid from the dowel. Next, the 100-grain charge was measured and poured into the tube, and the back end "pleated" on the sides with the fingers and glued, forming a tail. This tail was then clamped with a clothes pin and allowed to dry thoroughly. It is clipped off by the rising breechblock of the Sharps when actually loading the gun. The entire process was somewhat lengthy, but actual preparation of the cartridges from the paper rectangles required only a short time. Not considering drying time for the glue, actual assembly time spent on each cartridge was approximately one and one half minutes. You might prefer to assemble them by steps, i.e. forming the tubes, charging them in another step and closing them to complete the process.

A much faster method was developed for those cartridges used in the percussion revolver and the ones for the muzzleloading rifle. It was first determined that an ordinary cigarette paper was very close to the proper size for the revolver. A smaller wooden dowel was used to form the tubes, the paper rolled around it lengthwise and glued, forming containers that would enter the chambers of the cylinder, easily. Again, the front overlap was twisted as tightly as possible while the tube was still on the dowel, then removed, a Pyrodex charge added and the rear then twisted to close. Any additional twist that I felt was unnecessary at the rear was clipped off with a pair of scissors.

The cartridges for the frontloading rifle were made using the same dowel as used for the sixgun since I wanted the tube small enough in diameter to literally fall down the barrel, fouled or not, and in the 50 caliber Hawken this was possible since it was a ⅜" dowel. I substituted extra wide cigarette papers for the smaller ones (drawing some speculative glances from the young sales person who apparently remembered my earlier purchase), rolled them lengthwise around the dowel and glued. Other procedures were identical to those for the sixgun and I wound up with a cartridge three inches long containing a 70-grain equivalent of Pyrodex. It was strong enough to hold together until firing time, yet easily burst from pressure in seating the patched, round ball. Pyrodex was used in this instance to prove that paper cartridges could be ignited with normal procedures usually reserved for black powder, and without being tied exclusively to the older propellant.

Why not use this same paper in preparing cartridges for the breechloading Sharps? The tubes for the breechloader must be considerably stronger for they must be forced into the chamber so that only the tail protrudes and stiff enough so that the breechblock cuts off this same tail. A few granules of powder find their way to the top of the breechblock, usually, along with the paper tail and this is good if the amount of powder is not excessive. It proves that the rear of the tube is open and exposed to the percussion cap's flame.

Reason two: by virtue of the same type, stiff, bond paper, you have the option of enclosing the bullet within the cartridge for even faster loading and firing. There is a slight loss in accuracy using this type cartridge, for with the front of the paper cartridge encircling the bullet, it becomes impossible to seat the bullet past its midpoint; thus it's impossible to seat the bullet as concentrically and in as good a firing position. You use a bullet seater when loading separately, but only the fingers are used to seat the cartridge. The complete package is excellent for a fast follow-up shot, about as close to a modern cartridge as it is possible to come using breechloading, percussion guns.

Of course, there is an option with the muzzleloading rifle, too. For a strictly combustible cartridge, thin paper is essential for good burning characteristics, with closures at each end either twisted or tied with thread but if you prefer, these cartridges may be

The breechloading Sharps for loose ammunition is a prime candidate for paper cartridges. Bennington found he got greatly increased speed of fire, convenience, together with sufficient accuracy as this target shows.

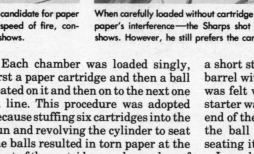

When carefully loaded without cartridge paper—bullet seated forward without paper's interference—the Sharps shot better for Bennington, as this group shows. However, he still prefers the cartridge convenience.

made from heavier stock, the end torn off with the teeth or fingers in loading, the powder simply poured down the barrel and the tube thrown away. I prefer the combustible type for speed and ease of loading. For the revolver, the thinner the better for these should burst easily in the ball or bullet seating process, yet hang together readily with only both ends twisted. Cigarette papers burn very cleanly in either gun while unconsumed bits of paper may occasionally be seen in the Sharps' barrel, leading to my practice of blowing down the barrel after every shot to clear away any debris remaining.

In actual shooting, the percussion revolver performed no differently than with loose powder loadings, but it was possible to reload a bit speedier, dispensing with the powder flask usually used with the attendant spillage of powder. My test gun was an 1860 Army replica from Western Arms, with a shoulder stock attachment that I used only to shoot groups at fifty yards. Groups at this distance, fired over sandbags, were not spectacular (they seldom are with c&b revolvers) but I was able to keep all six shots in the black of the Dixie Standing Bear target. Normal 25-yard groups ran approximately 2½ inches, comparable to those shot with loose powder.

My load was a 28-grain equivalent of Pyrodex with the .451″ round ball. Caps were the usual Italian ones that seemed to be adequately hot and fitted the nipples of the 1860s cylinder very well. Only one chamber failed to fire on schedule after several rounds had gone through the big sixgun and the second capping of that particular nipple brought a reassuring boom from the revolver.

Each chamber was loaded singly, first a paper cartridge and then a ball seated on it and then on to the next one in line. This procedure was adopted because stuffing six cartridges into the gun and revolving the cylinder to seat the balls resulted in torn paper at the front of the cartridges and some loss of powder. An industrial-type clear grease was applied over the front of each chamber and then each was capped, completing the loading ritual.

For testing combustible cartridges in a muzzleloading rifle, I chose one of the most popular rifles on the market, the known and respected Thompson/Center Hawken in 50 caliber. CCI non-corrosive caps were used to ignite the charges and no hangfires or misfires resulted. Two types of cartridges were fired in the Hawken, ones made from nitrated onionskin stationery and those made from the extra wide cigarette papers. The onionskin tubes were not completely consumed on firing and I soon discarded them, fearing that a smoldering bit of paper might ignite the following cartridge with unpleasant results. With cigarette papers, consumption was complete in every instance.

Again, Pyrodex was used with both 60 and 70-grain equivalent charges for two reasons. With the use of this great replica powder, it is not so necessary to clean the barrel after every few shots and its harder-to-ignite trait would prove the adaptability of paper cartridges to the muzzle-loader. I chose the Speer swaged round ball in size .490″ and a pre-cut patch of .015″ thickness and my loading procedure was simple. A paper cartridge was dropped down the barrel, the patched round ball was started down the muzzle with

a short starter and rammed down the barrel with the ramrod. When contact was felt with the cartridge, the short starter was again employed to give the end of the ramrod a quick rap, forcing the ball to burst the cartridge and seating it at the same time.

I marked the ramrod with a ball point pen to be certain each ball was fully seated, compressing the Pyrodex for sure ignition. Ordinary capping and firing produced reliable groups at 50 yards running 2 to 2½ inches, the big rifle fired from a temporary rest at that distance. Cleaning the gun after the firing sessions produced no unburned remnants of paper and only ordinary fouling in the bore and nipple from the Pyrodex. I was completely satisfied with these results.

Actually I used two Sharps in testing those cartridges for the breechloading guns; one the 1863 New Model Rifle/Musket from Shiloh and their newest, the big, Model 100 (#2 Sporting Rifle), firing a 100-grain, FFg-loaded cartridge. Both guns were in 54 caliber and the 425 grain Buffalo Slug was used in both.

The cartridges for the military gun were made from materials in the Shiloh kit and contained a 60-grain charge of the same black powder while those for the sporting gun were prepared as described at the beginning of this piece. Shiloh musket caps were used in firing both guns and both proved to be excellent performers. Pyrodex was not used because of the impracticality of attempting to compress it in a breechloader.

The military version showed signs of being exceptionally accurate with both the Shiloh cartridges and those by the C.W. Cartridge Company con-

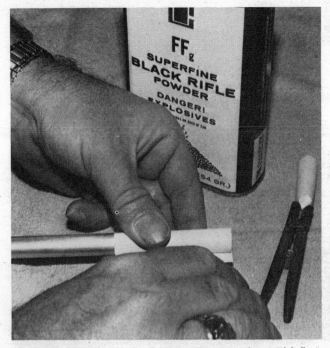
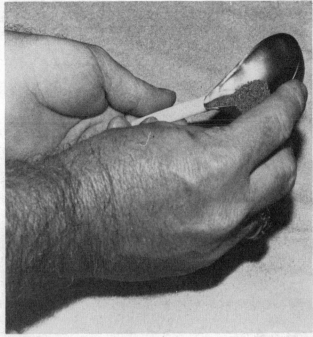

A big aluminum dowel forms tubes for Sharps 100-gr cartridges. With bullet in one end, the other end is glued into a tail—using clothespin for a clamp—which the breechblock clips off as the action is closed after loading.

Bench-weighed powder charges are one benefit of the use of cartridges in any of the blackpowder arms, Bennington thinks. This consistency of charge goes far toward counterbalancing the problems of bullet seating over paper.

taining the bullet within the cartridge. I benchrested this gun with both types and it produced some amazingly small groups at 50 yards. Accuracy was excellent with the big, sporting rifle, but perhaps the recoil of the 100-grain charge kept me from doing quite as well with it.

Following is a list of items needed to prepare paper cartridges of any form mentioned:

1. Proper size dowel depending on caliber and fit desired. A wood dowel should be waxed to keep freshly glued paper from sticking to it.
2. Eight or ten clothes pins for the Sharps cartridges. These hold the tail until the drying process is completed and this many will allow you to process them faster.
3. A small, plastic funnel is invaluable for charging the paper tubes, keeping down spillage of powder.
4. A small powder measure is good for metering charges if you do not want to weigh each charge.
5. A tube of combustible glue is a must. I have found Elmer's Glue-All to be excellent and fairly fast drying.
6. A goodly supply of paper, the type depending on the cartridge you plan to use, properly sized and nitrated, if necessary.

Paper cartridges are fragile, but I am for their use in the three types of percussion guns mentioned. I find that I shoot my c&b revolvers more with their use and make more frequent trips to the range with both my muzzleloaders and breechloaders, too. There are some drawbacks, I will quickly admit. Occasionally, one is going to come apart before you get to the range and you will encounter a situation with the Sharps in which the bullet has been seated too far forward in the chamber, allowing the cartridge to go in too far, requiring fishing around with the fingers to pull it back to the point that the tail will be severed by the breechblock. Too, the rear end closure is a bit tedious for the Sharps tubes, sometimes requiring a second gluing and setting with the clothes pin.

The process of manufacturing your own cartridges may be a bit tiresome at first but as with most things, practice makes, if not perfect, at least faster. You may not like being confined to specific charges, dictated by the size and capacity of the cartridges, but continued use will show that they are, indeed, both practical and easy to use; capable of very good results. That next hunt might be a good place to prove them, once and for all. •

Results equal to cartridges made with the commercial paper cartridge kit, like this box of Buffalo Slug loads, can be obtained with bond paper and drugstore chemicals—the powder, lube and ball are the same, of course.

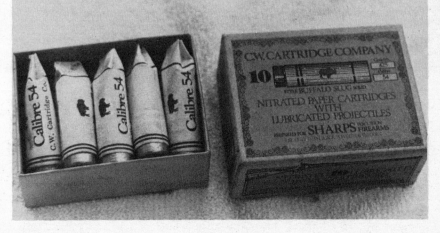

SWIVEL GUNS

OF SOUTHEAST ASIA

by JOHN W. SANDERS

Lelas and lantakas are the same thing, only different.

THROUGHOUT THE GREATER part of the age of firearms, Asia has played a relatively inconspicuous role in weapons development. During the past several centuries the countries of this politically turbulent region have constituted a ready market for both modern and obsolete military arms of European and American manufacture, but, with the notable exception of 20th Century Japan, have had little success in either firearms design or production. It is almost a truism that there are no distinctly Asiatic firearms, in contrast with the amazing variety and sophistication of Asian edged weapons.

The small swivel cannon of the islands and coastal regions of Southeast Asia are a significant exception to the above assertion. These weapons, known as *lela* or *meriam ketchil* in the Indonesian archipelago, Malaysia and Borneo, and usually known as *lantaka* in the Philippines, were once in widespread use over a large portion of Southeast Asia and the countries bordering on the South China Sea. Present in prodigious numbers prior to the present century, they are still often encountered in backwoods villages and river settlements of the islands and peninsulas of the historic East Indies.

Gunpowder was known to the Chinese, and was used in the manufacture of fireworks and pyrotechnical devices, long prior to the invention of firearms. Literary evidence suggests that the propulsive powers of a charcoal-sulphur-saltpeter mixture were employed in rockets and incendiary contrivances in the Orient perhaps as early as the 11th Century, but it is generally accepted that firearms as an effective form of weapon were a European development of the early 14th Century. These first firearms, crude muzzleloading devices severely limited in size and strength by the rudimentary metallurgic knowledge and mechanical skills of that era, used the uncorned or nongranular type of powder originated by the Chinese. The formula for this weak but potentially revolutionary propellent, and a knowledge of its use,

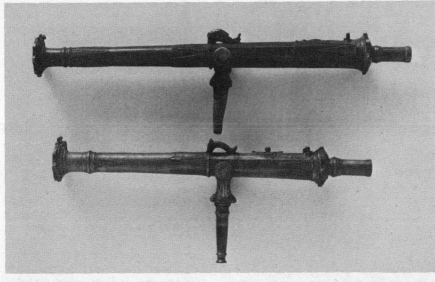

Two small lelas from Sumatra; note diminutive dolphins above swivels. Upper gun 39 inches; lower 32 inches; calibers just over 1".

appears to have been carried to Europe by Arab scholars and traders, those indefatigable travellers and middlemen of the pre-Renaissance period.[1]

Commerce is not a one-way proposition, of course. The Arab trading class responsible for introducing gunpowder to the Western World were probably among the first to appreciate the significance of the invention of firearms, and were not dilatory in bringing news of this remarkable development back to the Far East. Samples of early European firearms soon followed, also brought by the Arab merchants, and by the early 16th Century small cannon were apparently in extensive use over the maritime regions of the Orient. During the first circumnavigation of the Globe by the crew of Ferdinand Magellan, the great navigator and explorer, such cannon were encountered in the islands of the Indies in 1521, a time when guns were still somewhat of a novelty in Europe. A decade prior to this date a large number of small cannon were said to have been used against the Portuguese by Malays at the siege of Malacca, further evidence that firearms preceded rather than followed European expansion into Asia.

Descriptions of early Oriental artillery suggest that the cannon observed by, and often used against, the first European merchants and explorers were close copies of the small ship's guns of contemporary Europe. Arms of this type could have originated almost anywhere in Europe or the Middle East, and would have been a convenient cargo for the small Arab trading vessels of that time, being reasonably portable, functional, and of considerable merchandise value in a region of almost constant internecine warfare and piracy.

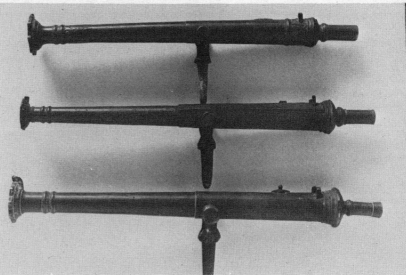

Three typical Sumatran lelas. Lengths range from 38 to 41 inches, calibers from .95 to 1.12 inches.

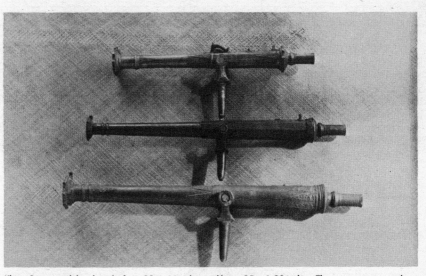

Three Sumatran lelas; lengths from 32 to 44 inches, calibers .95 to 1.38 inches. These same guns are shown on schematic diagram.

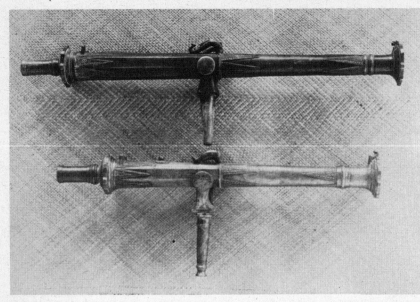

Right side of guns at top of page preceding. The decorative theme of the pointed panels is carried out fore and aft on both guns.

Mindanao, in the Phillippines; and a large gun foundry, operated during the greater part of the 17th Century by the Portuguese, was located in Macao and produced some of the finest bronze guns in the Far East.

Perhaps because of an inadequate industrial base, or perhaps simply because of traditional Oriental conservatism, cannon design did not change appreciably over the centuries following the introduction of firearms to the East. Muzzleloading cannon of simple design and limited size continued to be made up until fairly recent times. Until made strikingly obsolete by the colonial wars of the late 19th Century and the contemporaneous suppression of piracy by the British and Dutch navies, such cannon were the standard fighting arms of the freebooters, merchant seamen and native potentates of Malaya and the islands of the East Indies. During the 16th through 19th

Demand for, and satisfaction with, this form of trade goods must have been great. Within a short time of the introduction of these arms, the casting of similar small cannon was begun in various parts of the East, and the cheaper locally-made products soon displaced the European imports. Large quantities of both swivel guns and larger cannon were manufactured in the East Indies islands and on the Asian mainland. Major cannon foundries were situated in the Palembang, Meningkabau and Atcheh districts of Sumatra, at Trengganu on the Malay Peninsula, and in Brunei, on the island of Borneo. Important cannon manufacturing establishments were also present in the Lake Lanao area of

This highly ornate little lela, found in Borneo, is only 26 inches in length.

A handsome lela from the J. L. Fish Collection; 39 inches long, caliber 1.12 inches.

Centuries the bulwarks of the small seagoing craft of the region were often lined with swivel guns of small to moderate size; used for both offense and defense, such easily handled and relatively inexpensive weapons were popular with both honest mariners and pirates alike. Although probably not highly effective when used to batter the hull or rigging of an opponent, they were doubtless quite lethal when directed against the crew of an enemy ship at close quarters and would serve as an impressive deterrent to a gang of pirates bent on boarding a merchant vessel. Small swivel cannon of this type would also be of use to small craft travelling up the broad jungle rivers, where the small forts and stockades erected by the petty sultans and rajahs of the river towns

This magnificent lela, probably a product of Brunei, has a dragon muzzle; length 61 inches; bore about 2 inches. From the Singapore National Museum.

might represent a hindrance to legitimate traffic. As land-based armament, swivel guns also served as the basic artillery of the small coastal or jungle fortresses, being sufficiently deadly to discourage attack and having the valuable attributes of easy maintenance and longevity in a humid tropical climate.

Cast of brass or bronze, rarely of iron, these cannon were essentially indestructible if not overloaded. The typical swivel guns of the *lela* or *lantaka* variety ranged in length from three to six feet, with a relatively small caliber of one to two inches and rather thick barrel walls because of the limitations in tensile strength of non-ferrous material. Weights rarely exceeded a few hundred pounds, and many of the smaller swivel cannon were not much heavier than a musket. All known examples are smooth-bores, although a few rifled specimens

could have been made in recent times. Most swivel guns were slender and gracefully proportioned, with considerable integrally cast ornamentation in the form of bands and rings, lozenges, elongate triangles, and fanciful scrollwork and floral designs in typical Moro-Malayan style. Markings and inscriptions are rarely present. The muzzles of these guns are invariably expanded to a conical or discoidal form, a common characteristic of the early European cannon from which these arms were derived. The barrels normally exhibit a gentle taper, and although most are round, octagonal and half-octagonal barrels are not uncommon, and magnificent fluted barrels, some with the fluting in the form of a spiral, are sometimes seen. Less commonly encountered are cannon in the form of a dragon, crocodile or mythical monster; such types, usually products of the Brunei

foundries, are true works of art, grotesque but strangely attractive and of well-balanced design. Most of the more ornate specimens, regardless of size, are provided with small carrying rings or semicircular loops in the shape of dolphins or serpents above the trunnions. Almost all of these cannon are fitted with open sights, usually in the form of a small chunky blade or squarish knob on the muzzle ring and two projecting ears or an egg-shaped bulge at or just in front of the touch-hole. The trunnions are rather short, and are positioned near the center of balance but slightly below the centerline of the barrel, as typical of the 15th-16th Century predecessors of these arms. The swivel yokes, or *chagaks*, are formed with a sturdy U-shaped upper portion with holes or cups to fit the trunnions; the lower portion of the yoke is in the shape of a tapered spike suitable to fit

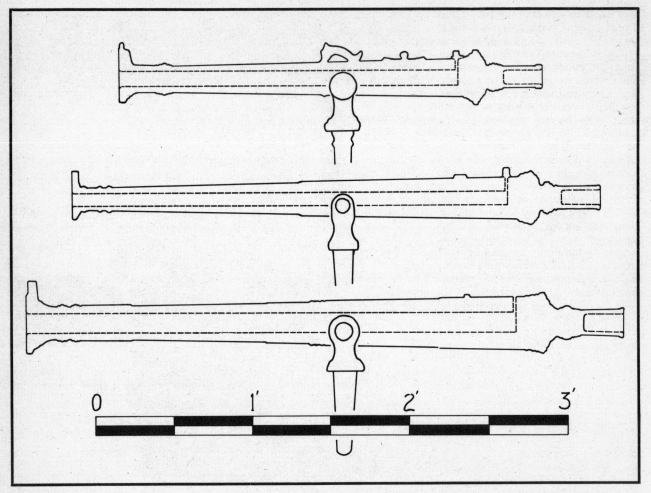

This schematic of three Sumatran lelas and lantakas represent the same guns shown three pages ahead. Author finds these dimensions and proportions to be approximately typical of the broad range of these fascinating little guns that have been weapons, symbols and money to their maker.

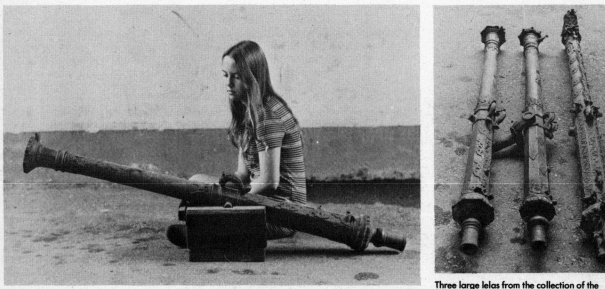

Another ornate lela from the collection of the Singapore National Museum. Length 58 inches, caliber about 1.50 inches.

Three large lelas from the collection of the Singapore National Museum. Lengths from 57 to 61 inches, calibers 1.50 to 2.00 inches.

into a hole or socket in the gunwale of a boat or on a beam along a wall. It should be noted that wheeled gun carriages of European design were a rarity in Southeast Asia; when the swivel pieces could not be fired from a ship or fort with previously prepared sockets, the guns were apparently fired with their swivel spikes jammed into the ground, or the guns were merely propped against some convenient brace. In place of a bulbous cascabel or knob at the breech, as typical of the muzzleloading cannon of the West, the Oriental swivel guns were characterized by an integral tubular projection, approaching bore size in inner diameter; after loading the piece and prepatory to firing, the gunner could insert the butt of the rammer into this hollow projection or socket so as to facilitate manipulating the gun.

A rare variation of these swivel cannon is the *rentaka*, made of cast iron and usually smaller than the more common brass or bronze models.

Breech detail of small lela, probably from Borneo, with elaborate ornamentation on both the gun and the swivel mounting.

Typical swivel mount, or *chagak*, with small dolphins or carrying handles on barrel.

The three large lelas of the Singapore National Museum shown on previous page range from almost simple to extremely ornate.

Breech details of three medium-sized lelas, showing typical sockets at rear and characteristic rear sight lugs. Gun at rear shows small crocodile in front of touch-hole.

Muzzle details of three typical lelas. Chunky front sights and flared muzzle are a common characteristic of these arms.

Also rare were the *ekor lontong* or "monkey tail" guns, brass swivel pieces with a curved metal handle rather than a socket at the breech end. Double-barrel cannon, cast in one piece, have been reported, and a bell-mouthed blunderbuss variety of swivel gun was also made in small quantities.

An intriguing if somewhat puzzling variant of these swivel cannon is in the form of a miniature copy, essentially identical to the larger guns but typically 6 to 12 inches in length and with a bore diameter of ¾ inches or less. Such guns are also commonly provided with a tiny swivel yoke, although

Miniature lela, only 7½ inches long; caliber approximately .65. Note tiny swivel mount.

Collection of miniature cannon of both lela and European pattern, from Sumatra. Lengths from 6½ to 11½ inches, calibers from .45 to .70.

loaded with a stiff charge of powder and banana leaf wadding, should propel a lead ball or slug with as much force as a conventional muzzleloading pistol of similar caliber, and would be equally hazardous to an intruder or opponent armed with only a sword or dagger. Until fairly modern times, handguns were not often seen in Southeast Asia; in the absence of widespread familiarity with conventional pistols or revolvers, a scaled-down cannon might seem the logical answer to the need for a compact and easily portable personal weapon.

As we have seen, swivel guns of all sizes were abundant and saw much service in both war and defense throughout the maritime portions of the Far East. Apart from their use as weapons, however, both those of the large and miniature variety served an added purpose—they provided a sub-

examples lacking the swivel and constructed with a European-style cascabel rather than the characteristic Malayan socket-breech are also frequently seen. These small guns, still found in respectable numbers in Indonesia, are of questionable utility as weapons and most probably were made as toys or for firing salutes. According to a magazine article by H.L. Baron,[2] however, in parts of the Philippines and adjacent islands these diminutive cannon were actually used as handguns, carried in the waistband of the pantaloons and mounted in tree-crotches or rested on a forked stick when ready to fire. Ignition would be by pushing a burning twig, or possibly a glowing cigar tip, against the touch-hole—hardly convenient for ambuscades or a battle on a rainy day! Despite the unwieldy nature of such a throwback to the original handcannon, these small weapons, when

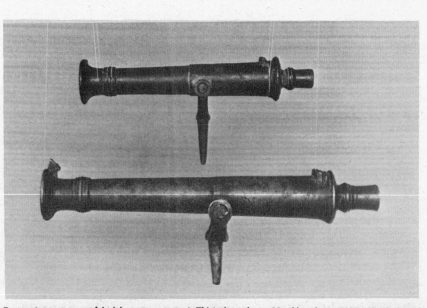
Two miniature cannon of the lela pattern; upper is 7½ inches, about .65 caliber, lower 11½ inches long and .75 caliber. Swivels are typical of many of these tiny guns.

Miniature cannon from Indonesia; upper and middle specimens of European pattern and lower of lela pattern. Lengths 6½ to 10 inches, calibers .45 to .55.

stitute for money in the currency-poor island of Borneo and parts of the Indonesian-Phillippine archipelago. To quote from G.C. Wooley,[3] in a discussion of Borneo cannon:

"Cannon, apart from use in war, had in Borneo at least a value as currency. The ordinary gun, with normal decoration, was valued at approximately $25-$30 [Straits dollars] a pikul [approximately 180 pounds]. Fines for the more serious offenses could be expressed as 'so many pikuls', and one or more cannon to make up the weight specified would be paid. Cannon also formed a regular item [in a bride's dowry]. Differences in workmanship, apart from exceptional cases, would not alter to any large extent the intrinsic value of the gun as so much metal, and this value would not fluctuate much, so cannon made a fairly stable currency. A cannon was not difficult to store, stood up on end and lashed to a house post, as they can be seen today; it would not deteriorate by rust, whereas buffaloes or cattle might die instead of multiplying, and in case of a raid or on feast days when a loud noise was called for, it might even be positively useful."

The enigmatic miniature cannon as previously described can perhaps best be interpreted as a currency substitute, or token money. Although of dubious value as weapons, they might well have served as "small change," the larger swivel guns being retained for only the more momentous financial transactions.

Further to the monetary use of cannon, over much of Southeast Asia Chinese *cash*, the small brass coins with the square hole through the center, were an accepted medium of exchange until the establishment of the modern national states of Indonesia, Malaysia and the Philippine Republic and their colonial predecessors. Quantities of such coins, as brass of excellent quality, provided the metal from which many of the swivel guns were cast. In many sections of the Orient such cannons had a cash value equivalent to their weight in brass coins, and served as a convenient substitute for currency in dealings where the exchange of large numbers of small coins would have been awkward. One or more cannon, in obvious display at the house of the owner, would also provide a certain psychic satisfaction as a status symbol, not unlike the Cadillac or Mercedes-Benz parked in the drive of a member of our affluent society today.

Aside from any military or monetary importance, many Asian cannon were believed to possess certain consequential supernatural qualities. C.A. Gibson-Hill[4] has described an interesting Malayan cannon locally regarded as a help in attaining fertility; ladies desiring children would lay flowers on the barrel of the piece to obtain its favor. Similar beliefs are said to have been held in regard to certain Javanese cannon, which would be presented with offerings by supplicants who, to obtain the maximum magical benefits, would also sit astride

the barrel for a short time. Another example of superstitious reverence for a particular cannon has been described by Dennis Bloodworth:[5]

"Kramats [spirits] are common throughout Indonesia and Malaysia, and when a few years ago the Malayan Railway Administration wanted to move an old brass cannon that was holding up the construction of a terminal near Penang, the matter had to be referred to the State Religious Affairs Department. For many believed that the cannon had healing powers, and its caretakers demanded that a medium first obtain [the cannon's] permission for the move."

The *lelas* and *lantakas* of Southeast Asia, no longer practical military weapons or valid currency substitutes, are still in use in limited numbers in jungle villages and settlements as signal guns, fired to announce visitors or celebrate holidays and important social occasions, and to mark the beginning and the end of the daily fasting periods during the Moslem holy month of Ramadan. No longer being made, they are slowly but inexorably declining in number as the soft metal of the touch-holes erode away from repeated firings, and as breeches burst when modern smokeless powder salvaged from rifle cartridges is unwisely substituted for low-pressure black powder. Many cannon were stolen, destroyed or converted to scrap during the Japanese Occupation of WW II. But appreciable numbers have found a haven in museums and in the collections of appreciative antiquarians, preserved for posterity as tangible reminders of the romantic days of piracy and brigandage in far-off corners of the South Seas. •

References

1. Howard L. Blackmore, 1965: *Guns and Rifles of the World*, Viking Press, New York
2. H.L. Baron, 1971: "Moro Mini-Cannon," *Guns and Ammo*, Petersen Publishing Co., Los Angeles
3. G.C. Wooley, 1947: "Malay Cannon," *Journal of the Malayan Branch, Royal Asiatic Society*, Vol. XX, Pt. II, Singapore
4. C.A. Gibson-Hill, 1953: "Notes on the Old Cannon Found in Malaya," *Journal of the Malayan Branch, Royal Asiatic Society*, Vol. XXVI, Pt. I
5. Dennis Bloodworth, 1970: *An Eye for the Dragon*, Farrar, Strauss and Giroux, New York

Some make it; some don't; and nobody knows why

MODERN CARTRIDGE FAILURE AND SUCCESS

by BOB HAGEL

The 243 Winchester, left, became a best-seller overnight, but the 244 Remington needed a new headstamp and a faster twist before it gained its well-deserved share of the sales.

EVER SINCE the first metallic cartridge was invented, those who love guns, target shooting, hunting or just experimenting with firearms and ammunition, have been trying to improve it to better fit their needs. Some of these wanderings in cartridge design have proven hugely successful, and a real improvement to anything offered previously. Other ideas really didn't contain any great gems of wisdom, and were marginal improvements on existing cartridges, but for some unknown reason they grasped the imagination of the shooting public and became immediately popular numbers. On the other hand, other cartridges with almost identical dimensions and ballistic performance never gained even modest popularity, and became obsolete before most shooters even knew they existed.

There are a great many reasons for this, but the whims, fancies and trends of the American shooter almost defy rational analysis. Many shooters, especially hunters, are inclined to believe many of the unfounded and unproven tales about the performance of certain cartridges that are handed down from generation to generation. I well remember the arguments that waxed hot and heavy between the older hunters when I was a boy, as to

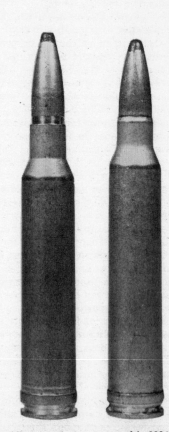

The difference in the success story of the 308 Norma Magnum, at left, and the 300 Winchester Magnum is due more to lack of domestic factory ammunition and rifles for the 308 than to cartridge efficiency. Both are excellent big game cartridges.

the merits of the 30-30 and 32 Special cartridges as deer-slayers. They never stopped to consider that except for .012" difference in bullet diameter, cartridge dimensions and performance were almost identical.

The same group of hunters were also split in their opinions—and biases—between the 30-40 Krag and the 30-06 Springfield. Many claiming that the 30-40 was a better cartridge than the '06 for heavy game like elk and moose—the old 30-40 just plain killed better. They failed to take note of the fact that they used 220-gr. bullets in the 30-40, and 150-gr. in the 30-06. When the light, fragile 150-gr. blew up and failed to penetrate to the vitals, it was the cartridge that failed, not the bullet, in their minds.

This is a sample of the thinking of yesteryear, and some of these notions persist today. But there are many other reasons why cartridges fail or succeed in popularity and sales appeal. Then, as well as now, shooting editors and gun writers can make or break the sales appeal of a cartridge. Living proof of this is visible in the promotion the late Jack O'Connor gave the 270 Winchester, and the down-grading the 220 Swift received from a number of writers. The 270 is still going very strong after 55 years of successful sales, and the Swift, that came along ten years later, is an obsolete round with American ammunition manufacturers. But there are other more tangible reasons why certain cartridges have either failed to become popular or have taken a place beside the best sellers of all time.

It would take a book to cover them all, so let's start with the post-war period of World War II that triggered the greatest boom in cartridge development the shooting world has ever known.

Very little varmint hunting had been done during the war years, and when the fighting stopped there was a shortage of guns, ammunition and reloading components that prohibited much shooting in the quantities used by varmint hunters. So when Remington unveiled the 222 Remington cartridge in 1950 it became an overnight success. There were several reasons for this: First, the ammunition was available at a price that allowed considerable shooting by nearly everyone that was serious about varmint hunting. Accuracy was top-rate, and the new round proved to be a small but potent package. It also had something going for it that none of its predecessors had ever enjoyed: a supply of excellent varmint bullets by new bullet

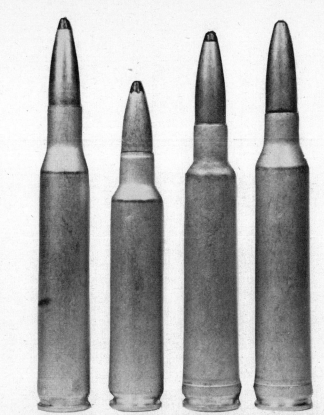

These 7mm cartridges are all efficient in their class, but only the 7mm Remington Magnum made the best-seller list. From left is 280 Remington; 284 Winchester; 7x61 Sharpe & Hart, and 7mm Remington Magnum.

making firms like Speer and Hornady that were reasonably priced and readily available.

Where the 220 Swift had received the reputation of being extremely hard on barrels, the small powder charge and much lower velocity of the 222 increased barrel life by many thousands of rounds. It was also soon discovered that the 222 Remington was capable of even greater accuracy for the new accuracy bug's game of benchrest shooting than such former standbys as the wildcat 22-250 and 219 Donaldson Wasp. Again, it was easier on barrels, was more economical, and was even more pleasant to shoot.

All of this makes sense and is easy to understand, but when Remington introduced the 222 Remington Magnum in 1958, there was nothing like the positive response kicked off by the 222. I find it a rather strange state of affairs, considering that the two cartridges were built on the same basic case, but with the 222 Magnum being a bit longer to afford slightly more powder capacity that gave a 55-gr. bullet 100 fps higher velocity than the 222 developed with the 50-gr. With good handloads the 222 Magnum will produce 200 fps more velocity than the standard 222 with all bullet weights.

The 222 Magnum also won its share of benchrest matches, so accuracy was not a great factor. There wasn't a nickle's worth of difference in reloading a box of ammo, and the two cartridges were used in the same rifle models. Anyone who has ever used the two cartridges extensively for any kind of varmint hunting knows the 222 Magnum delivers superior performance, especially with good handloads. The magnum round not only dropped far behind the standard 222, but there are very few rifles chambered for it today. Apparently the 222 Remington had become so firmly entrenched in shooters' minds that they didn't feel the difference was worthwhile.

The 223 Remington, which was the final outcome of an experimental round based on the 222 Rem. Mag., and standardized for military use in 1964, and released by Remington as a sporting cartridge at about the same time, has fared, so far, little better than the 222 Magnum. A military cartridge is usually an instant success when chambered in sporter rifles, but this did not hold true with the 223 Remington.

Of course there was a good deal of activity and competition in the 22 centerfire cartridge field at about the

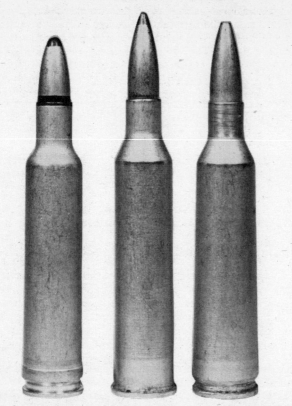

These three cartridges are quite similar in velocity, yet the 224 Weatherby at left, and 225 Winchester, center, are very slow on the market, while the old wildcat 22-250 sold like cold beer at an August rodeo when it went commercial, as at right, in the 22-250 Remington.

same time. Roy Weatherby unveiled the cute little belted 224 Weatherby Magnum, and Winchester sought to replace the good old 220 Swift with the 225 Winchester. Both of these larger cartridges outclassed the 222 Remington Magnum and the 223 Remington as long range varmint cartridges, which probably didn't do the smaller cartridges much good, but neither the 225 nor the 224 caught on either.

Both the Winchester and Weatherby offerings were great performers on all varmints from ground squirrels to coyotes, and with no American commercial rifle being chambered for the Swift, and with W-W phasing out 220 Swift ammunition, they were the most potent of the 22 magnum capacity cartridges.

The 225 Winchester case is almost a direct copy of the Donaldson Wasp. Winchester advertised it as a semirimmed case, but unlike the 220 Swift, it is actually a rimmed case. To function perfectly through Mauser-type staggered column magazines, a filler plate in the rear was slanted back from top to bottom so the rim of each cartridge loaded was *forward* of the one below. This situation probably did not appeal to other rifle manufacturers, and few of them chambered the 225.

Then, too, when shooters learned that W-W had a new 224 cartridge in the works, they looked for something to fully replace the Swift, and maybe they weren't prepared to accept a poor substitute. Anyway, the 225 never got off the ground, and when Remington at last saw the potential of the wildcat 22-250, and started loading ammunition and chambering the M-700 for it in 1965, the 225 became obsolete before it really matured.

The 224 Weatherby has done little better, but the reasons are more obvious. The excellent Weatherby Varmintmaster, a miniature Mark V, is pretty expensive and not found in every hardware store. Factory ammunition is also expensive and is even harder to find. Very few other rifles, either commercial or custom, are chambered for it, which doesn't help cartridge sales. After all, anything the 224 will do the 22-250 will do better, so why chamber for a loser.

As to the great success of the 22-250, it was one of the most popular wildcats ever dreamed up, and it carried that success along with it when it went commercial. Why it took the big arms companies and ammunition manufacturers so long to see the potential of the 22-250 is difficult to understand. Could it be that they are reluctant to

make a case and chamber a cartridge that did not originate on their own drawing boards?

A good deal of experimenting had been going on with wildcat 17-caliber cartridges long before Remington announced the 17 Remington in 1971. Some 17-cal. cartridges were based on cases as small as the 221 Fireball, and some as large as the full-size 222 Remington Magnum. The 17 Remington is based on the 223 Remington case, but slightly longer and with a longer neck than the 17/223.

Some pretty giddy claims were made for these midget cartridges. One fellow told of killing an Alaskan brown bear with one—which, of course, is not impossible—but he intimated that the 17 was capable of taking on any game in North America.

When the 17 Remington appeared in factory loaded ammunition and chambered in the good M-700 Remington, the little cartridge staged a popularity surge for a short time, but soon leveled off. Today it appears sales are rather low.

The main reason for this is probably due to the fact that when varmint hunters really got serious about using it they soon found it had very definite limitations that were not nearly as high as they had been led to believe by some writings on the subject. Neither is the cartridge in the same class as the larger 224 cartridges. The quoted muzzle velocity of 4040 fps with the 25-gr. factory load, fell nearly 100 fps short in the M-700 test rifle I did load development work with. It is possible to handload the 25-gr. bullet to that velocity with a few powders, and I have loaded 20- and 22-gr. bullets at over 4300 fps, but even then they are not effective at long range. I found that they were reliably explosive out to 150 yards on chucks, but beyond that range one bullet would expand while the next would drill a 17-caliber hole in and out. I dug some of those chucks out of rockpiles to find out what had happened.

The problem probably lies with the very small cavity in the point of the tiny bullet. A cavity point bullet depends on trapped fluid or other soft substance to expand it, and there is room for very little fluid in the cavity of a 17 bullet!

I also found that at ranges of over 250 yards, the 17 certainly is not in the same class as the 22-250. It performs more like the 222 Remington. And at 300 yards or over, the 22-250 outclasses it so badly for both accuracy and trajectory it isn't even in the running.

It doesn't seem likely that the 17 will ever challenge the 22 cartridges in a popularity contest, but this market reaction is based on the facts.

One of the most classic examples of cartridge success and failure of a pair of cartridges that deliver very similar ballistic performance is the 243 Winchester and 244 Remington that arrived on the scene almost simultaneously in 1955. There were three reasons for this situation. The first one was in the way Winchester and Remington viewed their new 6mm cartridges in performance in the hunting field, which in turn governed bullet weights and the rifling twist. Second, the shooting press over-reacted to the situation. And third, shooters became convinced that the 243 outclassed the 244 in performance, passed the story along, magnifying it en route.

The problem originated with the fact that Winchester looked at the 243 as a *big game/varmint* cartridge, so gave their barrels a 1-10 twist to stabilize the 100-gr. bullet for shooting deer-size game. Then loaded it with varmint-weight bullets that were also highly accurate in the 1-10 twist. Remington viewed the 244 as a *varmint/big game* cartridge with emphasis placed on accuracy with short, light varmint bullets, and gave their barrels a twist of one turn in twelve inches. For shooting big game they loaded a 90-gr. bullet, for which the 1-12 twist is adequate.

A couple of points here don't add up quite right, not if you're interested in facts. To start with, few of the shooters who yelled long and loud about the poor accuracy of the 244 with 100-gr bullets ever did extensive accuracy testing with 90- and 100-gr. bullets; they simply repeated what they had been told. The fact is, many 100-gr. bullets shot just as well in 244 Remington rifles as the 90-gr. I also know a number of hunters who own 244 rifles with 1-12 twists that shoot factory 6mm Remington ammunition loaded with pointed 100-gr. Core-Lokt bullets. The second point is that if bullets are of the same brand and design, there isn't all that much difference in killing efficiency between the 90- and 100-gr. I've killed a lot of deer-size game with various 6mm caliber cartridges, and my favorite bullet is the 95-gr. Nosler spitzer partition jacket.

Anyway, the 244 had almost become obsolete when in 1963 Remington gave it a headstamp that read 6mm Remington, chambered it in the M-700 with a barrel cut with a 1-9 twist, and poured on the publicity. The result was instant success!

There are also cartridges that met with marginal success, then gradually faded away. The 264 Winchester Magnum is an example. The 264 was hailed with a good deal of enthusiasm by most gun writers. Some of this enthusiasm bubbled over in print in glowing terms that portrayed the big 6.5mm as the ultimate for everything from ground squirrels to Cape buffalo, with a trajectory as flat as a sunbeam. Flat shooting it was, but it was soon found that it had definite limitations for game that was big and tough. It was also soon discovered that the 140-gr. bullet fell far short of the advertised 3200 fps in sporter barrels—even those 26" long. And with the 22" tube of the M-70 Featherweight, velocity of the 140-gr. factory load was only slightly over 2900 fps. This led to some writers saying the 264 was mostly noise and smoke, and actually no better—if as good—as the 270 Winchester. Handloaders also found that only with the slowest powders was it possible to reach the advertised velocity with any bullet weight with 26" barrels, and pressures were very high. The small bore and heavy powder charge made the 264 very touchy to load at full-throttle because of high pressure variation These things had

started the 264 on a downward popularity slide when Remington expanded the case to take .284" diameter bullets and dubbed it the 7mm Remington Magnum. There was enough difference in bore capacity of the two cases that the 7mm would do anything the 264 would do, and do it a lot better. It also had the advantage of using heavy bullets better suited for large animals.

Remington made even a bigger .264" error when they produced the 6.5 Remington Magnum and released it in the short-action Model 600 with its stubby 18½" barrel. The short belted case has similar powder capacity to the 30-06, but that is before you seat the bullet deep enough to function through the short M-600 action. In fact, the 140-gr. bullets had to be seated so deeply that the excessively short neck failed to grip most of them, rendering them useless. Some of the lighter bullets would not hold either, the 125-gr. Nosler then made being one. The 6.5 Remington Magnum is a good cartridge if chambered in a longer action with a 22"-24" barrel and handloaded with the bullets seated out so the short neck will hold them, and where they don't take a big bite of case powder capacity. But it fell flat on its

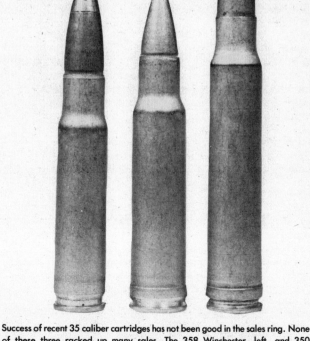

Success of recent 35 caliber cartridges has not been good in the sales ring. None of these three racked up many sales. The 358 Winchester, left, and 350 Remington Magnum, center, both lacked the power one expects from that bore, and the 358 Norma at right suffered from lack of domestic factory ammunition.

belted head when it was born, and never got up.

The 7mm success story is about as mixed as cartridge popularity can get. Remington made a classic failure and a huge success, and Winchester tried without succeeding. Back in 1957 Remington unveiled their 280, which was a kissin' cousin of the German 7x64 Brenneke and wildcat 7mm/06. The Remington 280 is a tad longer from head to shoulder than the 270 and standard '06 case, but otherwise identical except for bullet diameter. The 280 Remington is a very good cartridge, but the big mistake was to chamber it initially in the Remington 740 autoloader. There is nothing wrong with the 740, but pressures must be held below bolt action levels, and Remington saw fit to hold them to around 47,000 psi. When they did chamber the 280 in the M-721 and M-725 bolt actions, they were stuck with an underloaded cartridge that was on a par with the 270 Winchester that was already strongly entrenched. The greatest advantage the 280 holds over the 270 is that it is capable of handling heavier bullets. But R-P failed to load anything spectacular in factory ammunition, and handloaders didn't seem to feel the new cartridge was that much better than the 270.

Consequently, the sales of 280 rifles and ammunition were pretty thin.

In 1963 Winchester came along with the 284 Winchester in a short, fat case with a rebated rim and near-magnum size body. This gave it roughly the same powder capacity as the 280 Remington, but when the heavier 7mm bullets were seated to function through the short magazines for which it was designed, that capacity was reduced considerably. The 284 was designed for lever and autoloading actions, but was loaded to reasonably high pressures by the factory. It made a much better cartridge when loaded in a standard length bolt action so that the full powder capacity of the case could be used, but few bolt action rifles were ever chambered for it. The 284 was not a complete dud, but neither was it a good seller.

Of course the big blow to the 280 and the 284 came when Remington finally decided a 7mm magnum cartridge would pack a hefty wallop—both on the side of assorted game animals and in rifle and ammunition sales. This time they were right, and few cartridges have ever known quicker and greater success. The advent of the 7mm Remington Magnum in 1962 probably had a good deal of influence in damping the sales of other 7mm's.

One wonders why it took so long for the American arms and munition manufacturers to bring forth a 7mm magnum round when there were so many big wildcat sevens being chambered. Maybe it was the limited success of the 7mm Weatherby Magnum and the 7x61 Sharpe & Hart cartridges that had been around since 1944 and 1953 respectively. However, that lack of sales and popularity had little to do with cartridge performance, but with the fact that they were available in few rifles, those rifles were expensive, and ammunition was hard to find. The 7mm Weatherby was a good deal more popular than the 7x61, and is superior in performance because of more powder capacity. The Schultz & Larsen rifle was never overly popular here, and had a history of being hard to come by, with importers changing with the seasons. The 7x61 was a good cartridge, but is obsolete today.

There is little to say about the 30-caliber cartridges that doesn't spell success in capital letters. Ever since the 30-40 Krag cartridge was adopted as the first small bore smokeless powder cartridge for American military use in 1892, the American hunter and target shooter has leaned strongly toward the 30 caliber. There is little doubt that the 30 caliber is about ideal as an all-round bullet diameter for hunting American big game, but there is much more to the success story than that.

First, we used three 30-caliber cartridges in a row as the standard military rifle round; the 30-40, 30-06 and 308 (U.S. T-65). These cartridges were all hugely successful where sales are concerned, and also proved to be good big game cartridges. They also won more than their shares of target shooting tropics. With the American shooter turned on by the .308 diameter bullet, it was natural that the 300 H&H caught on quite well here, and that the 300 Weatherby Magnum is the best seller of the Weatherby line. But neither of those cartridges have come close to approaching the sales of either ammunition or rifles for the 300 Winchester Magnum. Ammunition is available almost anywhere, and nearly all rifle manufacturers, both foreign and domestic, chamber rifles for it. It could have been an even better cartridge if Winchester had given it a bit longer neck and seated the bullets out to utilize the full powder capacity of the case, then chambered it in their magnum length M-70 action. They were probably thinking more of ammunition sales than of efficiency, and if they were, that thinking was good.

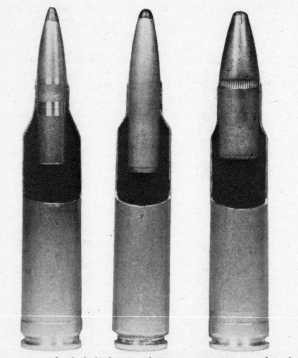

A major reason for the lack of success of these three cartridges stems from the fact that for use in the short actions they were designed for, bullets had to be seated far down in the powder space of the case. The 6.5 Remington Magnum at left would not hold bullets like the old style 140-gr. Nosler (the bearing surface is behind the relief groove). The 175-gr. Nosler (new style) protrudes one fourth of the way into the powder space of the 284 Winchester, center, and the 250-gr. Remington Core-Lokt takes a big bite of powder space from the chubby 350 Remington Magnum.

Everyone who makes a standard length bolt action can chamber it, and most do. Browning even adapted it successfully to their BAR.

And regardless of the disadvantages of the 300 Winchester, it is one of the best 30-caliber big game cartridge ever designed.

Strangely enough, the 308 Norma Magnum, which preceded the 300 Winchester by several years, never really caught on here. A few American-made rifles were chambered for it—mostly custom—and several imports, but few are chambered for it today. There is absolutely nothing wrong with the cartridge, but the lack of rifles, and the fact that no American company made 308 Norma ammunition, has made the cartridge an obsolete item on the American market.

There isn't much to be said about the 338 Winchester Magnum except that it has been very successful for a cartridge of that bore. It is one of the most reliable cartridges ever developed for shooting the heavy American game under all conditions, and it has gained a great deal of popularity for hunting most African game as well. In fact, it and the 340 Weatherby have taken over a good share of the sales that formerly went to the venerable old 375 H&H. Most of this success is due to the bullets available in .338 diameter. Weights ranging from 200-250 grains are available from most bullet firms, and in both pointed and roundnose styles. Sierra even makes a 250-gr. spitzer boat tail, W-W loads a 300-gr., and Barnes Bullets make a heavyweight 300-gr. roundnose in both soft point and F.M.J. Hornady also makes an excellent solid for use on the heaviest African game. Premium quality bullets like Nosler and Bitterroot are also made in .338 diameter.

Cartridges in 35 caliber were quite popular back around the turn of the century, but they have never gained much popularity in recent years. For many years the 35 Remington was the only cartridge in that caliber chambered in American commercial rifles, and it would seem that when Winchester released the 358 in their M-70 and M-88 rifles in 1955, it would have caught on. The 35 bullet is a very good killer on heavy game if given a good jacket design, but it has a pretty high trajectory curve unless it is fired at high velocity. The 358 Winchester on the small capacity 308 Winchester case is a low velocity number that shoots anything but flat, and while it is a good cartridge at fairly close

range, it leaves a lot to be desired for all-round big game shooting. It did gain some popularity with whitetail deer hunters for close range timber shooting, but set no sales records. The American hunter apparently viewed the 358 Winchester as not packing enough punch for the larger game, and too slow to be ideal for any kind of shooting at anything but close range. This cartridge just didn't have what it takes to make the grade among today's high velocity, flat shooting cartridges.

By the time Remington brought out their 350 Remington Magnum ten years later, they should have foreseen its lack of sales appeal. Again, there is nothing wrong with the cartridge for certain kinds of hunting, but it is far from an all-round cartridge. Remington apparently felt that with the trend toward short actions and barrels, the Model 600 would be the answer to the American hunter's prayer, but they failed to realize anything can be carried too far. Both the M-600 and the 350 Remington Magnum fell flat on the market. The cartridge was actually a better cartridge than the 600 action allowed it to be. Its performance can be greatly improved by chambering it in longer actions with throats that allow seating the 250-gr. bullets so they do not protrude far into the powder space of the short case. I also believe that most shooters expected Remington to come forth with a true magnum 35 similar to the 358 Norma, and a first glance at the stubby little 350 case turned them off completely.

And speaking of the 350 Norma Magnum, that cartridge never received anything like the popularity it should have, or that one would expect, on the American market. The big problem here, as with the 308 Norma, was that American commercial rifles were not chambered for it, and all ammunition and cases had to be imported. Another point that held it back, was the fact that the bullets made in 35 caliber were made for cartridges like the 35 Remington and 358 Winchester, and would not hold up under the increased velocity of the big belted case. Anyone who has killed much heavy game knows that if the bullet blows up it will not penetrate deeply enough to be of value, no matter what the diameter is. And if it doesn't penetrate well enough to break up heavy bones and plow through big, tough muscles to reach the vitals, it is of little value on big animals when the going gets rough.

Another blow to the 358 Norma is

the fact that the 338 Winchester will do anything it will do and, due to the much better bullet selection, do it better. The only really good heavy game bullet ever made for the 358 Norma is the Bitterroot Bonded Core, and that bullet has never been readily available. If an American arms and ammunition manufacturer were to develop a big 35 similar to the 358 Norma, load it with bullets made for a magnum velocity cartridge, and chamber it in a good rifle, it just might make the grade. The 458 Winchester did.

New cartridges have been rather scarce during the past few years, but Remington is trying to drum up new business with the 8mm Remington Magnum and the 7mm Express Remington. To date, no one can say for sure how far or how fast they will go, they haven't been around long enough yet. The best we can do is advance an educated guess based on past experience.

I've done a good deal of load development and other testing with the new 8mm Magnum cartridge, and while it is certainly impressive to look at, performance of factory ammunition is disappointing. The ballistics given by Remington are not overly impressive for a case the size of the new 8mm, and factory ammunition chronographed in the Remington M-700 is even less impressive. The full potential of the cartridge can be realized only by handloading. Also, in making comparison tests for expansion and penetration in the recovery box, I found no bullet that did not blow up under the impact of full-throttle handloads. Considering the popularity of the 338 Winchester and 340 Weatherby cartridges, and the much better bullets available in 338 caliber, it is doubtful if the big Remington 8mm cartridge will grab much of the market.

As to the 7mm Express Remington, it is the old 280 Remington case with a new headstamp. And that new headstamp is the only point that can possibly affect sales over the 280 Remington. Factory ammunition chronographed in the Remington Model 700 with the 7mm Express lettering showed no velocity improvement over 280 Remington ammunition. The switch of headstamps from inches to millimeters worked with the 244/6mm Remington, but there was the question of correct rifling twist to consider there. Twist is not a factor with the 280/7mm Express Remington cartridges. I'll be a little surprised if the new version of the 280 Remington sells any better than the old   •

Shotgun

Without choke-bored barrels our shotgun games and sports would be different or non-existent, this author thinks.

Versatility is the foremost advantage offered by the variable choke devices. By simply changing the setting or switching tubes, as this shotgunner is doing, the pellet pattern can be tailored to handle everything from close range woodcock to far out honkers.

by WALLACE LABISKY

JUST AS THE percussion cap was a large improvement over flint ignition, and the breechloader over the muzzleloader, so was the choked barrel another milestone development that pumped fresh life into shotgunning. Think what the smoothbore sports would be like today if we had nothing but cylinder-bored, 30-yard guns. The Skeet shooter would be doing business as usual, as would some upland gunners, but trapshooting as we know it wouldn't exist. Much open-cover bird hunting on the Great Plains and in the West would be almost impossible. Lacking a highly seductive decoy spread, waterfowlers would spend most of their marshland hours swapping lies.

Choke boring of shotguns was quite limited in practice before 1870 or so.

Choke

Its History and Mystery

It was almost non-existent, in fact, but the idea goes back at least a century earlier.

According to early writings some experiments in pattern tightening were carried out in Europe as early as the 1780s.[1] One method left the gun's muzzle two gauge sizes smaller than the bore. Another was to circumferentially roughen the bore for a short distance, just behind the muzzle, the purpose apparently being to slow the wadding and prevent it from slamming into the base of the shot charge—an occurrence which can—and does—disrupt the pattern. But these early efforts died on the vine. The idea, however, remained very much alive.

Roper and Pape

It is a matter of record that the world's first patent for a shotgun choke was granted to S. H. Roper, an American gunsmith, in April of 1866. This was for a short, taper-constricted tube that screwed onto the muzzle of single-barrel guns. W. W. Greener, the well-known English gunmaker of that period, wrote that he had tried one of Roper's tubes but had found it less effective than a good modified choke.[2] Nonetheless, Roper's device was clearly an improvement over the straight cylinder-bored barrel and certainly it stands as the forerunner of the modern-day variable choke.

William Pape, a gunmaker of considerable note in Newcastle, England was, within weeks (May, 1866) also granted a patent for choke-boring,

[1] W. W. Greener, *The Gun and its development* (London, 1910).

[2] Greener, *op cit.*

this being in conjunction with a breech-loading action of his design.

Some years later a British sportsman offered a cash prize that was to be awarded to the person adjudged to be the originator of choke boring. Accordingly a London sporting weekly, *The Field,* formed a committee and Pape was so recognized. Some historians question whether the committee had all the evidence in hand.

It appears as fact that choke-boring saw practical application long before 1866. For example, J. W. Long wrote in his *American Wild Fowl Shooting*[3] that a Rhode Island gunsmith, one Jeremiah Smith, was successfully choking shotguns as early as 1827. Pape, incidentally, did very little to further and perfect choke-boring during his patent's first decade.

[3] New York, 1879, 2nd ed.

Fred Kimble

Shortly after the Roper and Pape achievements Fred Kimble, the legendary Illinois waterfowler and all-round shotgun great, began to put his ideas on choke into motion. Kimble chronicled these efforts in a two-part article published in *The American Rifleman* (Nov. and Dec. 1936)— every word absolutely fascinating reading for any shotgunner.

In this report Kimble did not specifically state that he had no knowledge of the Roper and Pape efforts; only that he had never heard of any of the very early experiments in choke-boring. He said that one day he simply had the thought that if he could constrict the muzzle of a gun the spread of the shot pattern would be reduced.

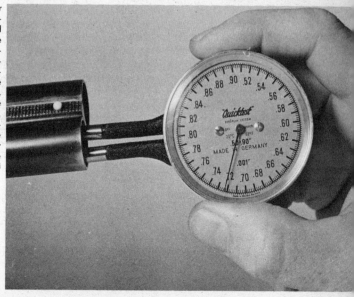

A TMI inside dial caliper gauge, calibrated in increments of .001", is used here to determine the amount of choke constriction in the right barrell of a 12-gauge side-by side gun. Muzzle diameter alone, however, tells nothing about the actual amount of choke. Bore or "cylinder" diameter must also be known. This particular tool will "read" the bore to a depth of about 5 inches.

Kimble attributed his success as much to accident and luck as anything else. He began with a heavy musket barrel which he bored out to true cylinder, the gun producing 5-foot-wide patterns at 40 yards. Having heard that some English gunmakers were relieving the muzzle slightly to reduce pattern size, he tried this narrowing the spread to 4 feet. Seeking greater improvement he rebored the barrel to within an inch of the muzzle. This resulted in a very heavy constriction, but the results were worse—the patterns opened to 7 feet!

Disappointed, and convinced he was on the wrong track, Kimble began reaming out the muzzle constriction, intending to return the barrel to true cylinder. But, unknowingly, he didn't entirely remove the constriction and, when he again shot the gun for pattern, it delivered the entire shot charge into a 30″ circle at 40 yards!

Shortly thereafter Kimble wrote to his good friend J. W. Long (the writer), telling him of the patterns he was getting. Long immediately had Tonks of Boston build a 10-gauge muzzleloader choked according to Kimble's instructions. This gun shot an even tighter pattern than Kimble's. This was about 1871.

Kimble then had Tonks build for him a 9-gauge muzzleloader, a gun which printed such tight patterns that it took months and months of shooting before Kimble finally mastered its use. The charge Kimble used in this gun was 1¼ ozs. of shot, and he claimed it gave 30 yards more effective range than any other gun in Illinois at that time. In a duck-shooting match (one of many) with a fellow named Knapp, who loaded 2½ ozs. of shot in a 4-bore single barrel, Kimble came out far ahead—he shot 128 birds to his competitor's 27.

Kimble's 6-Bore

About 1875 Kimble obtained an unfinished barrel from Thomas Kilby and Son of Birmingham, England, which he made into a 6-bore muzzleloader. He bored and choked it so carefully that this gun would place the entire charge into 24″ at 40 yards. With 1½ ozs. of No. 3 shot, Kimble said, it was consistently effective on ducks to 80 yards.

If there has ever been another shotgun the equal of Kimble's 6-bore for pattern efficiency it has been kept a closely-guarded secret. Even today the big gun companies, with vast expertise at their command, cannot seem to choke a barrel that will print

An example of screw-in type choke tubes is seen in the Breda Quick-Choke system. The barrel muzzle is precisely machined and threaded to accept interchangeable tubes offering a full range of constriction. At right are the ½, ¾ and Full-choke tubes, all of them of the true conical type.

tighter than about 85%, and most current max-choke barrels fall at least 5% short of that. When used with special shot-buffered loads, however, it is usually no strain to reach a 90% to 95% performance level with our current crop of full-choke barrels. Such loads contain, usually, a granulated plastic which helps to cushion the pellets against deformation.

The muzzle-loading gun, of course, holds an inherent advantage over the breechloader—it has no chamber *per se,* and therefore no forcing cone. In the muzzleloader the shot charge starts its journey at bore diameter and remains that way until it reaches the choke. Individual pellets certainly must suffer some damage as they are jammed against one another during initial acceleration, but they are spared the further deformation caused by a chamber cone. This surely accounts, at least in part, for the phenomenal pattern performance of Kimble's guns. Another possible explanation is this: Kimble used a coarse-grained black powder which he made himself, and which burned very slowly and evenly, propelling the shot charge in a way that apparently produced a minimum of shot deformation.

In 1872 an Illinois gunsmith, one J. L. Johnson, claimed to have the "secret" of choke-boring, and he adver-

tised that he could guarantee his barrels (muzzleloaders) to put the entire shot charge inside a 30″ circle at 40 yards. Then, so goes the story[4], a chap named Faburn visited Johnson's shop for the purpose of gaining all the information he possibly could. Johnson, understandably, was reluctant to divulge his knowledge but somehow Faburn managed to discover that Johnson's method was to cut a recess just behing the muzzle. Faburn then designed an expanding bit to cut this recess in cylinder-bored barrels and, on June 25, 1872, obtained a patent on it. Faburn's boring bit, it has been reported, immediately enjoyed a tremendous sale among gunsmiths throughout the country.

Meanwhile W. W. Greener was about ready to add his several pages to the annals of shotgunning. In his considerable and respected writings about chokes and choking he made it abundantly clear that he never asserted that he was the originator of choke, though he was sometimes accorded that distinction by others. But he did insist, perhaps somewhat immodestly, that he was in large part instrumental in furthering the acceptance of choke-boring and in bringing it to a near state of perfection in terms of design.

[4]Greener, *op cit.*

Greener's choke-boring efforts grew more intense early in 1874; he speaks of "numberless experiments, rendered doubly difficult by the lack of suitable tools" being necessary "before regular shooting could be relied upon." By December of that year *The Field* carried a Greener advertisement which offered choke-bored 12-gauge breechloaders, of 7½ pounds or less, that would deliver a 40-yard pattern of 210 pellets (69%) indside a 30" circle using 3 drams of powder and 1⅛ ozs. of No. 6 shot. These were English 6s, about like U.S. 7s.

Trial of 1875

J. H. Walsh, then editor of *The Field,* commented favorably on Greener's achievement. This editorial support, along with the advertisement itself, was immediately questioned by numerous readers—these holding the opinion that their cylinder-bored doubles were the finest shooting guns in existence. As a result the Gun Trial of 1875 was arranged to settle the issue.

Of the several public gun trials staged by our English cousins, that of 1875 is generally regarded as the greatest. Thirty-three competitors entered a total of 114 shotguns, 68 in the 12-gauge choke-bore class. The rules governing 12-bore guns restricted the shot charge to 1⅛ ozs. of English No. 6s. Chilled shot, still relatively new then, was used exclusively for the choke-bore competition. This was black powder shooting only, with a choice of Pigou or Curtiss & Harvey brands. Charges ranged from 3 to 3½ drams in the 12-bore event, there apparently being no rules governing load velocity.

The guns were scored for pattern and penetration at 40 and 60 yards, measured from the butt of the stock. Six shots were fired from each barrel in each of three different relays—two at 40 yards, one at 60 yards—for 36 rounds in all.

Greener swept the 12-gauge event with a 7½-pound breech-loading double having 30" tubes, his powder charge 3¼ drams of Pigou No. 4. His combined 40-yard pattern average (both barrels) was 199 pellet hits (65%), and 214 (70%) in the second relay. At 60 yards his winning gun (one of two he had entered) averaged a 92-count pattern. Thus Greener walked off with the prized 40-guinea silver cup, and those who had loudly disputed his claim limped home to lick their wounds. This victory was all the sweeter for Greener because his guns had finished second to Pape's in the trial of 1866.

The performance, according to Greener[5], surpassed what was attained at the New York Gun Trials of 1873, and also at the Chicago Trials of 1874. The best 12-bore at New York delivered an average pattern of 150; the best at Chicago was 166. Then, at the Chicago Trial of 1879, the best 12-gauge gave a 170 pattern with a 3-dram 1⅛-oz. loading running 20 pellets more to the ounce than English 6s. So it was Greener's opinion that the Americans at this time had not yet perfected the "choke-boring system." Probably so, but obviously only in regard to breech-loading guns.

At the 1875 Gun Trial Greener also took first place in the large-bore category (8- and 10-bore), and in the small-bore class with a 20-gauge choke bore. After that, nobody dared question its value. But now his opponents, not having enjoyed their dish of crow, began to question the life of a choke-bored barrel. The muzzle constriction, they ventured, would probably shoot out after a few hundred rounds.

Accordingly the Wear and Tear Trial of 1875 was quickly arranged—2,500 rounds were to be fired over 6 weeks. Again it was a Greener gun (but another) that took the pattern and penetration honors.

Modern Choke Systems

In terms of basic design shotgun choke hasn't changed significantly since the days of Kimble. Today's integral and basic chokes include *conical-parallel, true conical* and *recess.* Conical-parallel is probably the most widely favored among gunmakers, recess chokes being a rarity in factory barrels. There are, too, special chokes for Skeet barrels.

Conical-parallel choke usually starts 2-4 inches behind the muzzle, a tapering reduction in bore diameter being followed by a parallel (same diameter) section extending to the muzzle. This type of choke is sometimes referred to as English choke, probably in deference to W. W. Greener's efforts, but also because most British gunmakers seem to be steadfast proponents of the design.

True conical choke lacks muzzle parallelism, being simply a tapering reduction in bore diameter out to the very muzzle. Like C-P chokes, conical choke varies considerably in length, for each maker has his own ideas as to what is best. But generally speaking, the greater the constriction the

longer the choke.

Adjustable chokes of the collet type, such as Poly-Choke and Cyclone, fit within the conical category, as do those systems with changeable, screw-on tubes such as the Lyman Choke. However, the screw-in tubes of Winchester's Winchoke system are of the conical parallel type—or they were when the system was first introduced. The Ithaca/Perazzi MT-6 over-under trap gun also has screw-in choke tubes, again of conical-parallel design, as does their new single barrel trap gun.

As the term implies, the recess-type choke (sometimes called a jug choke) is simply an enlargement of the bore about a half-inch or so behind the muzzle. Their total length will vary, but as a rule it will be somewhat longer than the heaviest shot charge likely to be used. This recess permits the shot charge to expand slightly in the jug, the choking

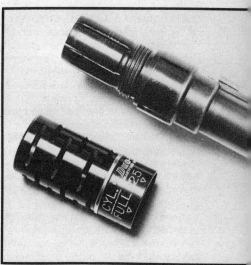

The collet-type chokes, such as this Cyclone with a ventilated sleeve shown on a Winchester M12 barrel, are somewhat more convenient than the interchangeable-tube type chokes. Muzzle constriction is increased or decreased by simply rotating the sleeve one way or the other. A ventilated sleeve offers some reduction in recoil but, more importantly, it helps reduce powder gas turbulence at the muzzle, which can have a disrupting effect on patterns.

[5]*op cit.*

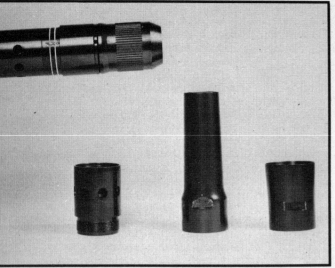

The Lyman choke system is offered in 12, 16 and 20 gauge. Seen on the barrel is the adjustable collet-type choke in conjunction with the optional recoil chamber. Below, from left— the recoil chamber, all-purpose (Mod) tube and the Upland tube. The latter is flared at the muzzle end. Not shown is the long-range (Full) tube, same over-all length as the AP tube.

effect realized when the charge is again constricted to bore diameter.

Recess choke is sometimes used to tighten up muzzleloader patterns and to restore choke to those barrels shortened after suffering muzzle damage. The thickness of the barrel walls dictate how much choke can be restored. Usually the thickness is such that the recess cannot be cut deeply enough to produce much more than modified-choke performance.

Jug choking is also used to tighten patterns from barrels only lightly to moderately choked. Let's say that we have a conical or a conical-parallel choke of .020″ constriction in a 12-gauge barrel which is throwing a 60% pattern. Cutting a recess immediately behind the choke cone, thereby increasing bore diameter by .008″, say, would boost pattern efficiency about 5%.

A high-grade over-under trap gun I recently tested has true conical chokes, but both barrels also had a shallow, yet measurable, recess immediately preceding the choke cone. Apparently this was the result of a final "regulating" attempt at the factory to improve the pattern.

Some changeable-tube chokes show elements of both conical and recess designs. The Cutts Compensator and the now-discontinued Weaver Choke are examples. Both have a ventilated "cage" through which the shot charge must pass before it enters the full-taper, conical-type tube.

The final category of choke design includes those special configurations intended for Skeet shooting, where it's advantageous to have very wide, even patterns at ranges of 20/25 yards. Some manufacturers work for a 40-yard efficiency of 30/35%, which

is actually a bit more open than true cylinder-bore patterns.

Some Skeet chokes are nothing more than a short conical section offering an extremely light constriction, often about .002″ to .003″. Some combine a conical section with a slightly flared muzzle, others simply stick with a straight cylinder bore and bell the muzzle.

What must surely rank as the most complex of all Skeet chokes are those examined on a pair of West German over-under guns—the Rottweil Olympia and the Mauser Model 620, both adaptations of the chokes of the Tula (Russian) competition Skeet 12, the Model MU-8.* This system involves a deep recess or jug plus a short muzzle belling. Their muzzle diameters are big enough to take a 12-gauge cartridge! These three are the only factory usages of recess choke known to me.

Methodologies Examined

Although, as noted, choke design has changed little since the 1870-'80 period, manufacturing methods have. This is not to say that reamer-boring from the breech has been totally abandoned for more sophisticated methods, but there is a strong trend in that direction.

William Pape's method of choking, as described in his patent, is typical of a practice that was traditional for many, many years. Pape began by boring the barrel to true cylinder dimensions, breech through muzzle,

*See GUN DIGEST 31/77 for J. M. Taylor's "The Tula Choke." p. 237.

but to one "size" smaller than the intended gauge. He then rebored to the intended gauge, but stopped about an inch from the muzzle. This last inch was then taper-reamed to the muzzle extremity.

This description strongly suggests that Pape's system produced the type of choke we now classify as conical. We can further speculate that one "size" smaller meant a 13-gauge in the case of a 12-bore barrel. Since a 13-gauge tube has a nominal bore diameter of .710″, the constriction would have amounted to about .020″, which probably produced a modified pattern.

Even in W. W. Greener's day gunmakers searched for labor-saving shortcuts, one of which was to swage-choke the barrel, that is, by applying external pressure at the muzzle. Greener frowned on this method, his disapproval probably related more to craftsmanship than anything else. At any rate his opinion seems to have been shared far and wide for a good many decades.

But today swage choking is a fairly common practice, and one not necessarily confined to economy-priced guns. Several of the biggest names in the firearms field have turned to swage-choking for production-line guns. However, in nearly every instance, if not all, the posh, custom-

Winchester's Winchoke system, used in their Models 1200 and 1400 in 12 and 20 gauge, is another example of the screw in approach to choking. Three degrees of choke are offered— IC, Mod and Full. This efficient and low cost system adds no unsightly "glob" at the muzzle, inasmuch as the muzzle end of the choke tube matches the outside diameter of the barrel.

built scatterguns on which much hand labor is lavished, are still being reamer-choked in the traditional way. Perhaps the reason is a matter of policy rather than one of better performance, for the swaged chokes seem to easily keep performance pace.

Present-day manufacturing techniques are so advanced that it is virtually impossible to eyeball a choke and say with absolute certainty whether it was reamer-bored or swaged. The exception is a rough choke visually or to the touch—in this case one can assume the choke to be reamer-bored; the manufacturer overlooked final polishing or didn't bother with it.

Barrels intended to receive a swaged choke are finish reamed to true cylinder from breech to muzzle and are then usually honed to a mirror-bright finish. A lubricated mandrel with negative choke configuration is positioned in the muzzle and external radial pressure is applied against the barrel walls, thus forming the constriction. Barrel-to-barrel variations in choke dimensions are minimal with this method. External taper at the muzzle—which might be visible—is avoided by leaving extra metal there and then finish-profiling the tube after swaging.

Fiction and Fact

The old and once-widespread practice of using a dime coin to determine the choke of a 12-gauge barrel rates as pure bunk. Even an accurate measurement with an inside micrometer tells nothing, because choke is the *difference* between bore diameter and the point of greatest constriction at or near the muzzle. In the parlance of shotgunners this difference is usually expressed as so many "points" of choke—a point having a value of $1/1000''$.

If every shotgun bore in a given gauge was of precisely the same diameter, then muzzle measurements alone would be meaningful. But bore diameters can, and do, vary considerably. For example, the 12-gauge bore has long been standardized at .729", but this is a nominal figure only. It is not unusual for some bores to run as much as .010" larger, and for some to be undersized by the same amount. An autoloading 12 in my gun rack has a bore of just .715", the tightest I've ever encountered.

These variations, by the way, are one of the reasons why a variable choke device doesn's always deliver a pattern percentage that agrees with the selected choke setting. The set-

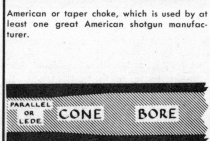

Choke drawings shown are greatly exaggerated for purposes of illustration.

American or taper choke, which is used by at least one great American shotgun manufacturer.

Standard choke, which is used by the English and by some of the largest American manufacturers.

Swaged choke brought about by forcing the barrel into a die, is chiefly used on cheap shotguns, but it works.

Jug or recess choking can put constriction in a sawed-off barrel.

Bell choking is used to open up patterns for short-range shooting.

Combination of recess and bell chokes on a 20-gauge upland gun. Barrels are supposed to be improved cylinder and modified and *both* barrels are so bored. Recess is about 2½ inches long. On Imp. Cyl. barrel the bell flares from .623" to .632".

tings are geared to a nominal bore diameter, but in extreme cases of "loose" or "tight" bores the pattern results can easily be 10% off base.

Standard or nominal bore diameters for the other gauges are .775" for the 10; .670" for the 16; .615" for the 20; .550" for the 28; and .410" for the 410. As this shows, the 410 represents caliber, not "bore."

A rule of choke as valid today as it was in the 1870s is this: the larger the bore, the greater the constriction must be to deliver a pattern of matching efficiency. Starting with the 410 there is roughly a 4- to 5-point difference in choke constriction between each gauge. Assuming a full-choke performance of 70 to 75%, the 410 will have a constriction of about .020", the 10-gauge about .040".

As Kimble soon discovered, too much muzzle constriction can be disastrous. Excessive "squeeze-down" accelerates the rate of dispersion, resulting in patterns that are likely to be far more open than the barrel marking indicates. Called an "over-choke condition," it usually results when a 12-bore barrel has more than 40 points of constriction; a 16 more than 35; a 20 more than 30; a 28 more than 25 and a 410 more than 20 points.

Further, as a general rule, the smaller the shot size the more the constriction must be to meet a certain efficiency level. A 12-gauge trap gun, for example, that throws 75% to 80% patterns with No. 7½ or 8 shot will rarely do that well with, say, No. 4 or 5 shot, an over-choke condition existing with these larger pellets.

Because coarse shot "over-reacts" to heavy chokes, magnum barrels usually benefit from less muzzle constriction than standard-chambered field models. In my experience a 12-gauge magnum (with a standard .729" bore diameter) seems to reach peak patterning with about .034" choke when using No. 4 shot, but about .030" choke seems best with 2s. In such cases—when a choke is matched to the larger shot sizes—pattern efficiences can be expected to drop off a few percentage points with each decrease in pellet diameter.

Improvements in shotshells have somewhat altered the choke picture in terms of the constriction necessary to attain a given pattern efficiency. The combination of pie or fold crimp, plastic shotcup wad columns and harder shot (higher antimony content) makes a given degree of choke more efficient than it was in grandad's day. As likely as not an improved-cylinder barrel becomes a weak modified (55%); a modified tube becomes an improved modified (65); and the full-choke tubes becomes an extra-full (75)) or even an super-choke (80%). Some gun companies now seem to be compensating for this to some extent by dropping a few points of choke.

Many, perhaps most, older full-choke barrels, particularly those made pre-WWI, were heavily constricted at the muzzle. With modern loads and small shot these guns often throw wickedly-tight patterns. But with coarse shot they tend to be over-choked and, in general, their patterns benefit considerably when the choke is relieved or opened several thousandths of an inch.

The British traditionally slice the choke pie into smaller pieces than we Americans do. Major Burrard* assigns pattern percentages thus: cylinder, 40%; improved cylinder, 50%; quarter choke, 55%; modified or half choke, 60%; improved modified or ¾ choke, 65%; full choke, 70%. Robert Churchill* was in close agreement, except that he rated improved cylinder and quarter choke as one and the same at 50%. He also included a ⅛ choke at 45% and a super choke at 75%.

Aside from an improved-modified boring and Skeet chokes, U.S. gun companies feel that three chokes—improved cylinder, modified and full—provide the shooter with everything he needs. They're probably right, too, because pattern *averages* vary considerably from the same barrel because of such variables as shot size, velocity, weight of charge, type of wadding, shot hardness and filler material, if any.

Because of this our gunmakers don't paint themselves into a tight corner when assigning pattern percentage values to the different choke designations. An improved-cylinder tube is usually catalog rated at 35/45%, modified at 45/55% and a full choke at 65/75%. Pattern tests, however, usually prove these ratings quite conservative, for with modern cartridges the higher value is more the rule than the exception.

Choke values for the 410 are based on 25-yard shooting, not 40-yard tests. Regardless of gauge or choke, all catalog values are a sea-level figure; each 1,000-foot increase in elevation can be expected to produce about a 2.5% gain in efficiency.

Most discussions of choke performance dwell primarily on constriction, but choke lengths and contours are believed to also be an important factor. Oberfell and Thompson (O&T), those two shotgun-loving Oklahomans who poured a vast amount of time and work into a book called *The Mysteries of Shotgun Patterns,* came up with some interesting findings in this respect.

With long conical-type 12-bore chokes they concluded that full-choke patterns required greater constrictions than short ones, but that in general any length exceeding 2½" offered little or no advantage. In O&T's tests with conical-parallel chokes they found that the highest

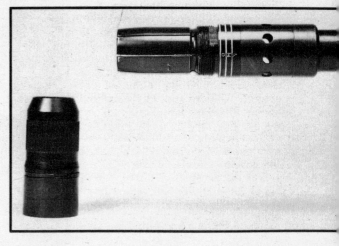

The Lyman adjustable choke pictured here with the adjusting sleeve removed is an example of the collet-type choke device. The choke element is comprised of 7 segments, these being forced together to produce greater muzzle constriction as the sleeve is tightened. Three white bands on the choke body serve as reference points, and there are 40 click-stop settings possible between the Full and Cylinder markings. The holes seen reduce felt recoil.

pattern efficiency was with ½" of parallel (77%), and that extremely short parallels (⅛" and ¼") gave tighter patterns than parallels of one to 2½".

In the appended table it will be noted that with full chokes the muzzle parallel is always substantially shorter than the conical section. Although the sampling is by no means large, slightly longer parallels appear to be favored for improved-cylinder and modified borings. All guns listed were made after 1960.

The Mystery

The real mystery of choke is not a matter of dimensions and contours. Nor is it a matter of effect. We know full well what choke is, and we likewise know what its function is. But much less understood is *why* choke produces the effect it does.

A number of theories have come to light over the years. Some have been wildly cockeyed, a few quite plausible. General Journee* offered an explanation worth noting. He conjectured that the outer pellets in the

shot column, upon striking the choke's cone, are given a component velocity at right angles to the surface of the cone. This imparts a final directional travel that parallels the angle of the cone and which, in turn, counters the tendency for the shot mass to spread.

If it were possible to use some type of X-ray at a very high speed and examine the shot charge while it is in the choke section, we would not be forced to theorize. We do, however, have solid proof, through high-speed photography, that when leaving a chokeless barrel the shot column emerges as a compact, cylindrical mass having a diameter that matches the bore. On the other hand, when leaving the muzzle of a full-choke barrel, the shot column considerably exceeds its in-bore length and the shot pellets are much more loosely grouped than when leaving a cylinder bore. The choke has altered their directional travel, and it may very well be that all this comes about in precisely the way Journee theorized in 1902.

Often cited as a secondary choke action is that the constriction delays or slows the wadding, however infinitesimally. Here again high-speed photography has shown that, as the shot charge leaves a cylinder bore the under-shot wad is still in direct contact with the base pellets; and, because of the suddenly-released and outrushing powder gases, the wad is actually forced into the now-unconfined shot mass, causing the latter to spread laterally. This, of course, increases the rate of dispersion, making for more fliers.

Conversely, photos of a full-choke barrel do not show this same close-contact relationship between the wadding and the shot mass. The

*See bibliography attached.

*See bibliography attached.

usual explanation is that the shot charge, because of its high momentum and low coefficient of friction in comparison with the wadding, is not slowed as much by the choke. This gives it a chance to outrun the wadding. Although the gain is tiny, it appears to be adequate in largely eliminating the lateral spreading induced by gas-and-wad pressure against the base of the shot charge. It also appears, however, that an excess velocity could easily negate the choke's delaying action on the wads.

This theory of wad delay seems sound in regard to a conventional, multi-wad column, but much less so when a plastic shotcup wad is involved. High-speed photography shows that, when leaving the muzzle of even a tightly-choked barrel the shot charge is still contained by its protective pouch. There is no apparent wad delay until air resistance occurs.

This brings us around to another interesting series of tests carried out by Oberfell and Thompson, one which led them to believe that a smooth, mirror-like finish in the choke area does not produce the highest percentage patterns. O&T obtained several full-choke barrels through regular trade channels and shot them for patterns as received; they were again shot after the tubes were given a slick polish, during which, care was taken not to change the constriction. After polishing, pattern efficiency dropped off about 5%.

In other O&T tests full-choke tubes of the conical-parallel type were put through the same course, but then were also tested after being roughened—circumferential grooves were cut near the muzzle, these grooves being .003″ deep and 1/8″ wide. The parallel sections for these tubes were of varying lengths. Pattern improvement after grooving ranged from 2.6% to 4.8%, but in one test, in which the 1/2″ parallel was known to be of optimum length, the smooth tube bettered its grooved counterpart by 7.2%!

It appears that O&T's main purpose in presenting these findings was to counter the widely-held belief that a highly polished choke is always superior. But it also appears that in doing so they unintentionally lent support to the theory of wad delay. The tests, however, were quantitatively limited and, in summing up their findings, the authors said that it was *not* to be inferred that grooving a choke will always give increased pattern efficiency. Plastic shotcup wads did not yet exist when O&T carried out these tests, but if they had been available it is unlikely that the grooved tubes would have shown any advantage at all.

Choke has now played a vital role in shotgunning for roughly 100 years, during which long time there have been virtually no changes in basic design. Over the past decade or so we have seen a small increase in pattern efficiency for a given amount of muzzle constriction, but chiefly because of improvements on the shotshell side. It is unlikely that the next 100 years will be any different, for choke development seemingly reached its apex during the infancy years. ●

Bibliography

The Gun and Its Development, W. W. Greener, 9th ed. London, 1910.

The Mysteries of Shotgun Patterns, George C. Oberfell and Charles E. Thompson, Stillwater, Okla. 1960.

Churchill's Shotgun Book, Robert Churchill, New York, 1955.

The Modern Shotgun, Major Sir Gerald Burrard, London, 1931-1932 (Vols. 1, 2 and 3). 1st U.S. ed. 1961, A. S. Barnes and Co., Inc., New Yrok.

The Shotgun Book, Jack O'Connor, New York, 1965

Shotguns By Keith, Elmer Keith, Harrisburg, Pa., 1950.

The American Shotgunner, Francis E. Sell, Harrisburg, Pa., 1962.

Tir des Fusils de Chasse, F. A. Journee, Paris, 1902.

12-Gauge Choke Constrictions and Types

Make and Model	Bore Diameter	Choke Marking	Choke Constriction	Choke Type*
Winchester 1200 Trap Pump	.730″	FULL	.030″	C-P (1 7/8″/1/2″)
High Standard S'matic Auto	.728″	MOD	.020″	C-P (1 3/4″/3/4″)
Savage Fox BSE	.729″	IMP CYL	.009″	C-P
Double	.729″	MOD	.019″	C-P
Browning B-SS	.726″	MOD	.014″	C-P (2 1/2″/5/8″)
Double	.726″	FULL	.036″	C-P (2 3/4″/1″)
Browning O/U	.726″	MOD	.020″	C-P (parallel 1″)
Superlight	.726″	FULL	.038″	C-P (parallel 1/2″)
Tikka Combo O/U	.724″	FULL	.037″	C-P (2 1/8″/7/8″)
Chas. Daly O/U	.726″	MOD	.021″	C-P
Hunter Grade	.726″	FULL	.038″	C-P
Ithaca/SKB O/U	.724″	IMP CYL	.004″	C-P (2″/1 3/4″)
M500 Field	.722″	MOD	.018″	C-P (2″/1 1/8″)
Dakin Double	.722″	MOD	.014″	C-P
M140 S/S	.724″	FULL	.029″	C-P
Brno Super O/U	.718″	FULL	.025″	C (2 3/4″)
M 12/12	.718″	FULL	.030″	C (2 3/4″)
Weatherby Centurion Auto	.728″	FULL	.027″	C (1″)
Weatherby Patrician Pump	.728″	IMP CYL	.007″	C
Nikko 5000 O/U	.727″	IMP MOD	.023″	Rec + C (4″/taper 2 1/2″)
Grade II, Trap	.726″	FULL	.036″	Rec + C (4 1/2″/taper 2 1/2″)
Nikko 5000 O/U	.729″	MOD	.013″	C (2 1/4″)
Grade II, Field	.729″	FULL	.033″	C (2 3/4″)
Marlin M-120 Magnum Pump	.727	FULL	.034″	C-P (3″/5/8″)
Browning Citori	.724″	FULL	.034″	C-P (3 1/2″/1/2″)
Magnum O/U	.726″	FULL	.034″	C-P (3 3/4″/1/2″)
Browning Liege	.724″	MOD	.020″	C-P (2 5/8″/1 5/8″)
O/U	.724″	FULL	.042″	C-P (2 5/8″/5/8″)
Savage	.724″	IMP CYL	.012″	C-P (1 3/4″/5/8″)
444 O/U	.722″	MOD	.019″	C-P (1 3/4″/5/8″)
Savage	.724″	IMP CYL	.009″	C-P (7/8″)
330 O/U	.724″	MOD	.019″	C-P (1 1/4″)
Beretta GR-2	.725″	MOD	.021″	C-P (2 3/8″/1 5/16″)
S/S Double	.725″	FULL	.037″	C-P (2 3/8″/1 1/16″)
Browning 2000 Magnum Auto	.728″	FULL	.045″	C-P (3″)
Browning 2000 Standard Auto	.725″	FULL	.034″	C-P (3″/1 1/8″)
Ithaca/Perazzi	.735″	IMP CYL	.715″	C-P (1″/3/4″)
Model MT-6 Tubes	.735″	FULL	.694″	C-P (7/8″/7/8″)

*For the conical-parallel type chokes, the first figure given indicates the total length of the choke section, and the second figure (where included) is the length of the muzzle parallel. For the conical-type chokes, the figure given represents the total length of the choke section. All guns listed were manufactured after 1960.

ELK RIFLES:

NO SIMPLE FORMULA

The time and money a modern elk hunter puts in dictates more effort in picking the right rifle

by Pete Nelson

THE ELK CAMP in the clearing would have made a purist wince. Black plastic had been draped over an A-frame of hacked-up fir poles. The interior was dim as a cave. A decrepit kerosene lantern swung from the ridge pole, and the gear strewn inside looked like salvage yard outcasts. It was not a scene for a calendar picture.

The camp's owner was a genial old man, who obviously hunted elk on a financial shoestring. I stopped for a brief chat, and before I could pull away, he insisted on showing off his elk rifle. He stooped down to a cot and snatched a rifle from under the blankets, then brought it into sunlight.

It was a gleaming 340 Weatherby. Quite an elk rifle, he said, though he had to underload it by several grains to take the "viciousness" out of the recoil.

Although the logic of buying a magnum rifle and drastically underloading it left me scratching my head, the old guy at least demonstrated what I have long contended: Elk hunters don't scrimp on their firearms. Say what you want about the usefulness of a given model and caliber as an all-purpose big game gun, but today's typical elk hunter spends heavily for a license, transportation by pack train or four-wheel-drive, and possibly guide fees. He isn't about to settle for less than a serious elk rifle. Nor is he interested in being a one-gun hunter.

The capabilities of deer rifles and elk rifles overlap substantially, of course. But ardent elk men think in terms of "elk rifles that will also work for deer hunting," not the reverse.

At the outset, it must be realized that this hunting, itself, is as diverse as the other hunting sports. Elk are quarry for September bugle seasons and frostbitten December hunts. They may be hunted in alpine country or brushy lowlands. They thrive in rain forests of the coastal mountains and in the semi-arid interior West.

Obviously, then, no single formula can dictate the ideal rifle. The horseback hunter may value a light, small gun that can be quickly snatched from a scabbard. The man who reaches his area by four-wheel-drive or other vehicle may opt for a heavier rifle with a longer barrel.

But, despite the diversity of elk hunting, there is one universal requirement—reliability. On an expensive, ten-day elk hunt, a balky rifle spells disaster. Shots at elk are rare enough; you want them without malfunctions. Far from the main population areas, quick service for a faulty gun may be impossible, so the stakes prohibit trusting a rifle that isn't thoroughly reliable.

Any rifle and ammo combination should be exhaustively tested long before season. If you have a proven deer load for your rifle, use it rather than a wonder-load you cook up at the last minute. Get to know your rifle at the range. Beware of the rifle, new or used, that you acquire just before season. Without a shakedown at the range, you're gambling heavily to take it elk hunting.

What goes for the rifle applies with equal force to the sighting system. Anything but best-quality scopes and mounts can't be risked. The reason? A sighting system takes more punishment on an elk hunt than it might in several seasons of deer or bear hunting, yet the shots can be longer. On horseback hunts, the scope and mount take a pounding inside the scabbard. Riding through alpine meadows looks nice in pictures, but horseback hunting often entails bucking brush. It's tough on a rifle's finish, and it's sure to bump the zero off kilter for anything but a first-class sighting system. I've seen the tube visibly bent on a bargain-price scope. On the other hand, hunting Roosevelts in the coastal mountains presents its own problems. Torrential rains there are guaranteed to fog any but a good scope.

Even with good equipment, things can go wrong. The premium scope on my Remington 760 has always held zero during a given hunt. It bred confidence, maybe a little too much. Prior to last year's elk season, I took the rifle to the range for sighting in. The first two shots touched each other, an inch and a half above the ten-ring. With a smile, I cleaned the rifle and cased it for the hunt.

Opening day proved my confidence was misplaced. Not until then did I notice the scope was so loose that it would turn or slide back and forth within the mounts. I had forgotten one essential part of the sighting-in process—checking the hex screws on the mounts for tightness. Fortunately, I was able to borrow the right-size allen wrench from a well-equipped partner and tighten things down. Then I rezeroed the rifle.

Don't overlook the quality swing-out mounts for your elk rifle. These are reliable, and they give you something the typical rigid mounts won't—the option to switch to iron sights in seconds. No scope can be perfect, so this is a sensible backup. An eight-pound 36 Whelen with a Pachmayr swing-over is one of the most accurate hunting rifles I've used.

Like it or not, rain and snow are often on the elk hunter's menu. This is an argument for free-floating barrels. The expert stockmakers recommend fancy systems of pressure bedding to give better accuracy. But remember that for elk rifles, reliability far outweighs ultimate accuracy in importance. After all, the heart-lung vital area on an elk is a nine minute-of-angle target at 150 yards. Any incremental accuracy gained with pressure-bedded systems is more than offset by their vulnerability to wet weather. Moisture-swelled wood can quickly change point of impact for these rifles. Free-floated barrels, especially those with ample channel clearance, are more reliable in soggy weather. They shoot well enough that you'll never miss that pressure-bedded system on game the size of deer, much less elk.

Reliability overshadows the choice of caliber, often a favorite jousting ground of gun writers and hunters, and next to reliability in importance, in fact, is not the choice of cartridge, but instead the rifle's configuration. This includes the type of action, weight, length, balance, and similar features.

The bolt action is the runaway favorite among elk hunters. Making the admittedly arbitrary assumption that the 30-30, the 35 Remington, and the 44 Magnum are *deer* cartridges, you'll get an idea of this country's bolt-action bias with respect to what we call elk cartridges. About 30 different bolt guns beckon the elk hunter. Eliminating the single shots, military models, and black powder weapons leaves the forlorn sum of eight alternatives—three automatics, four lever guns, and one slide action.

Despite bolt action bias, these eight "unbolt" rifles present superb credentials for elk hunting. In no case should you be compelled to join the bolt action stampede without first considering the requirements of your own hunting.

Typical view of a bull elk — in the jackpoles and covering ground fast. Today's elk are smarter than ever, so the gunner and his rifle must be prepared for these conditions.

This is the view on an elk — here a cow — that you will get more than half of the time. Devotees of the .277 tube beware: this is no picnic!

The Remington 760 is the sole slide-action rifle available in elk calibers. It's solid and reliable, and accuracy is acceptable. Scope is a Redfield 2-7x.

The well-established Browning automatic is available in calibers 308, 270, 30-06, 7mm Remington Magnum and 300 Winchester Magnum, all proven elk killers. The Harrington and Richardson 360 in 308 caliber and the Remington 742 in 280 Remington, 308, or 30-06 complete the lineup of elk-competent automatics.

The underpublicized Remington 760 has popularity where it counts—with hunters. This accurate slide-action in 270, 308, or 30-06 is an elk rifle that needs no apology.

Lever guns? The handy Savage 99 in 300 Savage or 308 has a following among rough-country elk hunters.

There is little reason to pick the 300 Savage if you instead can get the more popular 308 chambering, however. The 99 was formerly chambered in 284 Winchester. It gave ballistics approaching the 270. If you can find one of these, it will make an able elk rifle in any part of the country The 99 is now once again chambered for the 358 Winchester, the fat-bore brother of the 308.

The Browning lever gun is a newcomer, at least relative to the Savage. The choice of either 308 or 358 Winchester makes a happy dilemma The resurrection of the once-dead 358 in this rifle has gratified those elk hunt-

One good way to sit out a snowstorm is covering the clearcuts, which can be productive under these conditions. A heavy magnum rifle is just the ticket. This one is an 11-lb. 800 Winchester Magnum.

Even while on horseback, it pays to be alert to spot elk. Many times have mounted hunters come around a bend to meet elk face to face. The lead hunter has his 300 Weatherby at the ready, a good policy.

roars of righteous rage from the bolt gun people. One well placed shot, they sniff, puts meat on the table far better than a fusillade of hasty rounds.

True, but a fast second shot is better, nonetheless, than a slow second shot, everything else being equal. Modern hunting pressure has made elk shy and fleet. In the heavy cover where they seek refuge, you deserve a slap on the back just for getting a round off, let alone this business about making a surgically perfect shot. And, big as they are, elk running through brush are easy to miss.

This is not to imply that rate of fire can make up for poor marksmanship. On the other hand, armchair theorizing about one-shot kills often breaks down in the helter-skelter of real-world elk hunting.

My hunting partner, Gene Fasano, is a conscientious, hard-working elk hunter. He has won some measure of immortality by killing 10 elk during the last ten seasons, in a state where the average success rate is only 10 to 12 percent. A couple of those were cows, for which he had special tags.

The important thing about this accomplishment is that it shows Gene has adapted to hunting elk *in this decade,* with its problems of crowding and spooky, brush-happy elk. He is a superb game shot and patient tactician. Of those elk, half were one-shot kills, three were two-shot kills, and two were three-shot kills, giving an average of 1.7 shots per elk. This includes only shots at upright elk, not close-range finishers on prostrate animals.

This may be the lowest shots-per-elk average a successful hunter can hope for. Realistically, you don't hear a high proportion of solitary shots in elk country these days. Revere the one-shot creed if you will. Gene, too, values that first shot, but his favorite elk rifle is a Browning automatic in 7mm Remington Magnum.

The levers, slides, and automatics have other advantages, too. All except the Browning Magnum are light and reasonably compact, so they carry well in rugged elk terrain. The lever guns and the Remington 760 are narrow and slab-sided, so they fit snugly in scabbards.

The weak point in the design of many of these rifles is in the wood. Apparently designed for iron sights, the stocks have excessive drop, almost evocative of gun design from the last century. This style stock, though attractive in silhouette, is obsolete in rifles chambered for elk-competent cartridges. Besides being needlessly punishing, they're too low for scopes.

ers who want a big punch in a small package for rough country hunting.

More specialized among the current lever guns is the Marlin 444. It shoots a cartridge with the same name and spits more than 3000 foot-pounds of energy from a 22-inch barrel. Unfortunately, the fat, .429-inch diameter bullet doesn't range well. Also, many question the thin jacket of the factory bullet for performance on heavy-boned game. Handloaded with tougher and heavier bullets, the 444 shows ample authority as a woods rifle, and Remington now loads a 265-grainer.

Finally, for heavy-bullet buffs, there is the Marlin 1895 in caliber 45-70. Hunters willing to check the second-hand market may also want to consider other lever actions, the Winchester 88 in 308, and the Winchester 71 in 348. The 71's have long had favor with veteran elk hunters. Today they fetch good prices, but current lever guns, featuring side-ejection and spitzer bullets, offer more utility.

The obvious virtue of the automatics, slide guns, and (to a lesser extent) the lever guns is a fast second shot. That simple statement always draws

The standard stock on the Savage 99, for instance, is a real cheek-creaser, having lots of drop and a mean, narrow comb. Shooting the ordinarily amiable 284 Winchester in one of these brought tears to my eyes. The 99 deserves a better stock.

Several of these rifles can be obtained in the more expensive grades with Monte Carlo stocks. The alternative is to restock one of the common grades with a modern piece of wood. I had good success with two such jobs—one on the Savage 99 and one on a Remington 760.

In detailing the merits of the alternatives, however, we never fully escape the shadow of the bolt action. That action's capabilities earn it favor with the majority of elk hunters. Bolt guns are chambered for more different cartridges, and most are available in the powerful magnum calibers. Though there is no compelling need for magnums in timber hunting, their clout in open country gives the hunter an extra measure of flexibility. Bolt actions are reliable—more so, certainly, than automatics, anyway. Field maintenance is simple.

Bolt action rifles also give unsurpassed accuracy. (Actually, the importance of this is overrated for much elk hunting. When you spot a bull ripping through the jack fir at 75 yards, the last thing you'll worry about is whether your pet cannon shoots minute-of-angle groups.)

The bolt action's capacity to digest high-pressure loads is no secret. Its extraction power is formidable. Handloaders, whose ranks include many elk hunters, demand top performance from a rifle. Nearly to a man, they shoot bolt actions. Triggers on bolt guns are often excellent.

Finally, the clean lines, the sturdy, one-piece stock and the marvelous simplicity of the action appeal to the purists among us. Ignoring those intangibles leaves little to value in a firearm apart from sheer destructiveness, a dismal outlook.

Many bolt guns are also light and compact, a fact that can't be overlooked. Today's successful elk hunters are penetrating farther into the woods and scrounging in thicker cover. The game department in my state continually admonishes that hunters who want bulls, particularly big bulls, should hunt the brush. I don't know what cartridge, if any, works best in brush, but I defy anyone to say that a short, light rifle doesn't carry easier through the thick stuff. Twelve or 14 ounces and a couple inches are profoundly significant in hellish elk country.

Under appropriate conditions, scouting for elk on horseback is an unbeatable system that gives a rifle more punishment than just about anything else. A solid, reliable piece is vital and scope mounts must be first class.

Though actually less important than reliability and configuration in rifles, the choice of cartridges excites passions. The debate about cartridges points up one fact: elk are tough to kill.

Actually, we overrate the importance of differences like an inch of trajectory or 100 foot-pounds of muzzle energy. Our modern cartridges are more similar than we like to admit. With comparable bullets, the 270, the 30-06, and many others perform similarly, at least in sporter-length barrels. One hunter I know does well with a 30-06 but he is currently drooling over ballistics for the 7mm Remington and barking at the moon on clear nights. With that rifle added to his arsenal, he figures he'll be able to indulge in some long-range elk slaughter. Given the similarity of the ballistics, I'd guess that an elk safe from one cartridge may well be safe from the other.

It is virtually impossible to referee a mud-slinging match over elk cartridges. The reason is that we all judge cartridges by the rather emotional yardstick of our personal success with them. The man who has killed three

Big country like western Montana requires horses to cover the territory and flat-shooting rifles to hit elk at ranges that don't get any shorter as the elk get smarter. Rifles shown here are 300 Weatherbys. Leaving slings attached while rifle is in scabbard is an invitation for trouble.

elk with a 30-06 wouldn't have a 308 in camp for driving tent pegs. He who accidentally gets a one-inch group with a 308 would sooner use birdshot than an 270. And so on.

Not all differences in cartridges are trivial, of course. Overlooked in many editorial duels on the subject is that cartridge choice depends on the rifle's configuration. If you want a light, compact gun for running those formidable elk ridges, the most powerful cartridges should be ruled out. They kick too much in light rifles.

On the other hand, some smaller bores, particularly the small-bore magnums, are inefficient in short barrels. Velocity loss in shorter barrels doesn't always show up as you expect, but it's a definite trend in the small bores.

By way of illustration, the 350 Remington Magnum is a cartridge that performs well in short barrels. It generates about 3350 ft.-lbs. of muzzle energy from 24-inch barrels and around 3170 ft.-lbs. from 18½-inch barrels. That's an average loss of only 31 ft.-lbs. of energy per inch of shortened barrel.

Now examine the numbers for the 6.5 mm Remington Magnum. This cartridge is identical to the 350, except for the smaller caliber. In 24-inch barrels it lets go with about 2550 ft.-lbs. of muzzle energy. The value for the 18½-inch barrel is 2280 ft.-lbs., a loss of 49 ft.-lbs. per inch of barrel. Yet many hunters would opt for the milder recoil of the 6.5 over the 350 Remington Magnum in a light rifle. Trade-offs like that make it difficult to make categorical statements about elk rifles.

For an extreme example of the effect of barrel-shortening on the small bores, look at the 264 Winchester Magnum. In 26-inch barrels, this cartridge spews out around 3060 ft.-lbs. of muzzle energy. From 22-inch barrels, however, comes a not-so-glittering 2650 ft.-lbs. That's a loss of 102 ft.-lbs. for each inch of shortened barrel. What you gain in portability you lose in oomph and reap in ringing ears.

Fair-sized Roosevelt bull taken in thick cover. The rifle used was a Winchester Model 70 Featherweight in caliber 358 Winchester. Though never very popular, that caliber is a superb choice for hunting the dense cover where bulls are found today.

Short barrels, like everything in firearms, have trade-offs. They punish the ears. (Noise is of little consequence when you shoot at elk, however.) Short barrels also make rifles muzzle-light, which hampers a shooter's natural rhythm, impairing accuracy.

Other drawbacks of short barrels that concern us are ballistic in character. What cartridges work well in these? Generally cartridges with smaller powder capacities, relative to bullet diameter, are best.

Here is where the medium bores, those bigger than 30 caliber, have advantages. Their greater bore capacities mean that short barrels can be used while still sustaining good velocities. The 358 Winchester and 350 Remington Magnum cartridges are good candidates for short rifles. Remington recognized the peculiar virtues of the 350 by offering it in a homely, but handy, 18½-inch barreled carbine. These are no longer made, but used ones sell quickly.

The 35's, of course, have fizzled pathetically in popularity with the shooting public. As far as I know, no one chambers a rifle for the 350, and Winchester's 358 was a blue baby from its first day at the sales counter.

The 35's bellyflop puzzles many. Some say that if the country had more elk and moose, and fewer whitetails and mulies, the 35's would gain proportionally on the 30 calibers and others. No doubt the 338 Winchester Magnum killed a lot of 35 Whelens on the drawing boards of custom gun shops before it accounted for a single head of game. That outfit has ballistics to make the other potent medium bores seem like rabbit guns. The 8mm Remington Magnum may be yet another horse to pull the hearse.

In spite of the flashy statistics, the big magnums offer comparatively little extra utility in timber hunting. Case capacity is large enough to make them bellow in short barrels, and recoil would be distracting in light rifles. Furthermore, 4000 ft.-lb. muzzle energies are not essential for killing elk at close ranges.

Considering the sluggishness of some small bores in short barrels, the poor availability of mild medium-bore cartridges, and the rude manners of the medium-bore magnums, perhaps a logical choice is the faithful 30-06. That cartridge had probably accounted for more elk than any other. It's proven itself in rifles of many configurations. And a choice of configuration is important, once reliability is established. Remember, though, reliability of gun and sights comes first. ●

As a general rule, the fat-case, small-bullet cartridges need long barrels to be at their best ballistically and to be somewhat civil in report. Long barrels are not always bad. A little muzzle-heaviness makes for steadier shooting, many find.

Elk rifles must have detachable slings that allow the sling's removal for hunts in dense cover. The rifle is quieter without the sling and doesn't hang up in brush, a crucial virtue for horseback hunting. Many hunters have had guns silently snatched from scabbards as they rode through brush. The rifle is left hanging by its sling in an anonymous sapling. It takes a lucky hunter to find it again.

A plain, narrow, carry-type sling is best. It rolls up easily to fit in a pocket, and it weighs little. Rigged as a hasty sling, it is adequate for long range shooting. Time is too short for rigging more elborate slings when a bull breaks cover on a distant ridge.

Actually, for some types of elk hunting, barrels up to 26 inches are not inconvenient. Many hunters like to stump-hunt under certain conditions, covering open crossings or clearcuts and waiting for elk movement. For these hunters, long barrels and weight up to 10 pounds have little penalty.

Usually elk feed in clearcuts or other open areas only under protection of darkness. Dark nights, stormy weather, or even fog may sometimes cause them to linger in these feeding areas until shooting light. Sometimes pressure from hunters in heavier cover will make a herd cut quickly through a more open crossing. Under the right conditions, some hunters trundle big, heavy, powerful rifles into position overlooking these areas. Sometimes they take extra cushions and set the rifles atop stumps, ready to go.

Beware of the heavy, powerful rifle that is specialized only for this type of hunting. During midday or fair weather, the best stump hunters know that waiting for elk to ramble out in the open is a thin reed to lean on. They then hunt the brush. Their rifles are apt to be compromises, reflecting the conflicting demands of the sport. Some have two elk rifles, one a long range, thunder-and-lightning piece, the other a handy job for running ridges. Generally, the light rifle sees more use and is recommended by experienced elk men.

One of the most basic ways of making a rifle lighter and handier is to shorten the barrel. Twenty-two inches is a practical maximum for rough country hunting. Twenty inches is handier. Even shorter-barreled carbines are okay if they're not too muzzle-light for good balance. Regardless of weight, a gun that doesn't balance in the hand will tire a wide-ranging hunter.

HEAVIER ARTILLERY

by JOHN BRINDLE

Dr. Brindle scores on two important counts. He makes a strong case for a weightier American-style trap gun, and another for a unified all-gauge Skeet set—that each of the four gauges, when mounted, should be identical in every respect, with all of them tipping the scale at 9 pounds or so.

John Brindle holds the International Skeet "ready" position.

A SUBSTANTIAL profit, and the gratitude of many shooters, awaits the first manufacturer who dares to get away from tradition in fixing the weight of trap and Skeet guns he puts on the North American market. Don't get me wrong, these guns will still require the other elements desired by the competition claybirder—sharp, durable trigger pulls, barrels patterning as needed, suitable rib-pitches, stocks capable of being used successfully by most shooters (and of being altered to fit virtually all), and have a weight distribution suited to the job in hand. Right now we have a selection of guns excellent in all these respects but, I venture to suggest, virtually none having the right weights shown to be desirable by those shooters at the forefront of American clay target games.

This is not true of guns for Skeet and trap under International (ISU) rules. At 7½ to 7¾ lbs., over-and-under guns built for ISU Skeet shooting are probably of the correct weight. Going above this weight range by adding more mass in various ways to existing guns raises Skeet scores for very few people. Indeed, for most such shooters, being asked to chase these fast targets with a 9- or 10- lb. gun would result in lower

scores. Recoil is not a problem in ISU Skeet. It is not a game of long shootoffs, as American (NSSA) 12-gauge Skeet certainly is at present.

International trap, too, is a game of fast targets and a limited number of shells fired in a day. Over-and-under trap guns intended for this game go from 7½ to 8¼ lbs., many Europeans going for the lighter guns (and 28- and 29-inch barrels) while we North Americans often pick the heavier models and hesitate between 30- and 32-inch barrels. It is possible to see the effects of experience in American-style (ATA) trap in this. However, like the 12-gauge ISU Skeet gun, the gun for International trap, though perhaps not quite perfect in any of its models, is probably right as regards weight at least.

Having said all of which, that's about all the wholly good things that can be said!

NSSA Skeet Guns

Let's return first to Skeet guns for American, NSSA, rules. One of the most interesting phenomena in Skeet in recent years has been the upsurge in using full-length 20- and 28-gauge and 410 insert tubes in 12-gauge over-and-under guns for shooting Skeet in these smaller-gauge classes.

The use of such tubes seems to have had its origin in a desire to use the same gun, with its familiar trigger-pulls, and the same appearance to the eye when shooting, in all 4 gauge-classes of American Skeet. The more expensive alternative is three extra pairs of barrels for a 12-gauge over-and-under gun, all 4 pairs having the same weight, weight-distribution and length. The price differential of these alternatives is great. Whereas an excellent set of tubes runs around $550 to $600, three extra barrel sets will set one back between $2000 and $4000, depending whether they are custom-built or come from the factory, fitted to an already expensive European Skeet gun.

Surprisingly this is one of those rare cases in the world in which a cheap alternative turns out to have an advantage, and a lesson to teach too. It is gradually becoming apparent that the best equipment currently available for all-gauge Skeet is a 12-bore o-u with suitably-choked, full-length tubes in the smaller gauges. So much so that the names of a couple of insert-tube makers are fast becoming household words around the Skeet circuit, and it remains to ask why.

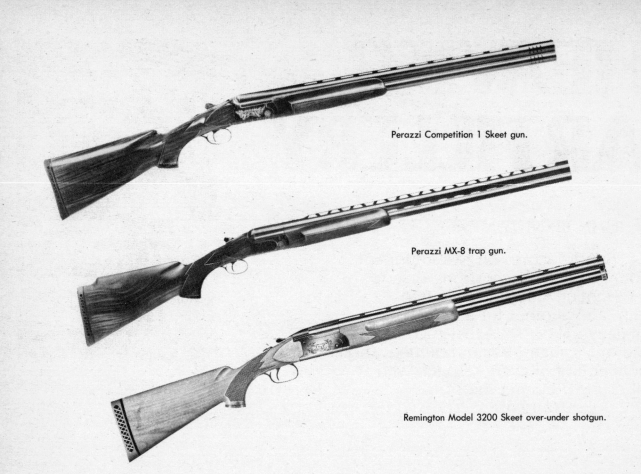

Perazzi Competition 1 Skeet gun.

Perazzi MX-8 trap gun.

Remington Model 3200 Skeet over-under shotgun.

The makers of such insert Skeet tubes have put a lot of study into the way they choke them, but equally good patterns are produced by regular barrels in these gauges: some of them custom bored and choked by the very people who make the insert tubes. Where is the difference? The answer is simple. It is a matter of over-all gun weight and of forward balance. A 12-gauge o-u carrying a pair of these tubes generally weighs between $8^{1}/_{2}$ and $9^{1}/_{4}$ lbs. The tubes (aluminum alloy or aluminum alloy and steel) go about a pound the pair, give or take a couple of ounces. This extra weight, note, is spread along the full length of the barrels. This suggests that the ordinary 20/28 gauge and 410 Skeet guns, of whatever type are usually of some $6^{3}/_{4}$ to $7^{1}/_{2}$ lbs. That's far too light and, with their relatively light barrels, of insufficient inertia up front.

Too Light

It further suggests that even 12-gauge guns weighing as much as $7^{1}/_{2}$ to $8^{1}/_{4}$ lbs. are too light for best results at American Skeet, particularly in view of the recoil of the 12-gauge load; and that those NSSA Skeet shooters who have been adding weight in various ways to the barrels and forearms of their 12-gauge guns,

mainly autoloaders and o-u guns, have been on the right track.

There is no reason from the shooter's viewpoint why a 20/28/410 Skeet gun should show *any* differences in weight, balance, or in appearance to the shooter's eye when the gun is at the shoulder, from a 12-gauge Skeet gun of the same make and model. Logically, they should all be built on 12-gauge frames, they should have barrels of exactly the same total weight, weight distribution and length as the 12-gauge barrels (which simply means progressively thicker walls for the smaller gauges) topped off with a rib identical in all 4 gauges. Too, all should weigh about 9 lbs., eliminating the use of lead plugs, lead tape or lead bars.

No doubt there's room on the market for a class of Skeet guns for the casual "weekend skeeter." That's who's buying and shooting "as is" the $6^{1}/_{2}$ to 7 lb. smaller-gauge guns right now, not the guy who is winning competitions. The irony is that the serious Skeet competitor finds it easier to outfit himself at the moment, by means of insert tubes, with an o-u gun in gauges smaller than 12, than in 12 gauge. A set of tubes gives him the weight and balance he needs. The obvious solution is a pair of custom 12-gauge Skeet barrels for the same

gun, a pound or so heavier than the original barrels, the latter being simply regarded as "holders" for the insert tubes in the three smaller gauges. Ironic indeed, for the competition American Skeet shooter should be able to buy a 9 lb. o-u with matched sets of barrels in all 4 gauges. Currently he often shoots a 12-gauge gas-operated autoloader which, though weighing around 8 lbs., has its weight more forward and so feels like an o-u a pound heavier. Being an autoloader, a lot of the recoil is soaked up by the mechanism. But a 9 lb. stackbarrel recoils gently with the same load, and it would have the advantage of being the same type of gun so many champions use in the other three gauges.

The ATA Trap Gun

Added weight is the first thing most expert U.S. trapshooters apply to guns they buy. The manufacturers are still stuck at around $8^{1}/_{4}$ lbs. for these guns whether single shots, o-u's, pumps or autoloaders. Depending on the person and the purpose, the guys on the firing line have left the manufacturers behind by $1^{1}/_{2}$ to $3^{1}/_{2}$ lbs.! There has been a great refinement in ATA trapshooting techniques in recent years—scores are so high that the only way to land near the top

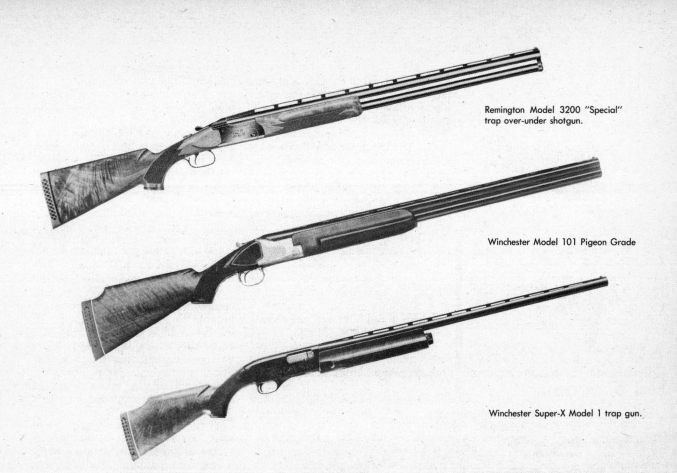

Remington Model 3200 "Special" trap over-under shotgun.

Winchester Model 101 Pigeon Grade

Winchester Super-X Model 1 trap gun.

of the list is to overcome tension at all times, which means staying as physically relaxed as possible right through the shoot, shot after shot. This alone calls for guns heavier than those in vogue 10 and 20 years ago, for the cumulative effects of recoil begin to chip away at performance after a very short time. Far more shells are fired in a given time in American trap, note, than in any other clay target game except in the very similar games shot in various parts of the British Commonwealth. Too, there is a tendency in both 16-yard singles and in handicap for high holds with high-shooting guns, and with this style but a short movement is needed to cover the target. A heavy gun is ideal for this style. It can be moved the requisite distance in the time available, and its very weight smooths the movement (and we all know how important *that* is).

Trap guns intended solely or primarily for singles, meaning single shots and pumps, would better meet the needs of today's trapshooter if they weighed 10 to 10¼ lbs. rather than 2 lbs. less. The extra weight should be *integral* weight, in a more massive receiver, stock bolt, and barrel (in its breechward third at least). Some shooters would still add a pound or so by installing a couple of recoil

reducers, which is legitimate. Guns intended for singles and doubles, but nowadays bought mainly for doubles—over-and-unders and autoloaders—probably should be around 9½ lbs. from the factory box if they are to reflect the trend increasingly apparent among expert doubles shooters (longer barrelled, wider-ribbed, higher-stocked versions of the 12-gauge Skeet guns of 9 lbs. I was wishing for above).

New Dimensions

Most imported superposed trap guns are a demonstration of the needs of the trapshooter in most of the rest of the world and, apart from the United Kingdom, Australia and New Zealand, that means the ISU shooter. Such guns, as delivered, no longer meet the needs of the trapshooter under American rules—if they ever did. Nor can they be made to do so by the mere provision of higher ribs, higher stocks, and so on, desirable as these things are for American trap. Added massiveness of the gun as a whole is also required: *a complete new dimensioning.* The single-shot trap guns based on these over-and-under guns are in the same weight area at 8 to 8¼ lbs. Their makers should not be content to add "passenger weight" to these o-u guns and single shots.

Added weight should be used to give extra strength, and in particular greater durability in the hinging and bolting systems, so that those surfaces subject to wear become so large they last as long as the rest of the gun. That weight can be added in such a way that the manner in which the gun balances in the hands, via its weight distribution, can be left undisturbed. That is, assuming that weight distribution in today's trap guns is correct! Expert trapshooters should be listened to carefully in regard to this, as in all else in the design of such guns.

The clay target is an American invention. After 97 years of clay target shooting in North America surely it has achieved such status, respectability and importance that the guns we use to shoot it under our native rules should be designed right—designed with both eyes on the clay target as it flies in these games, rather than with continuing sidewise glances at hunting and ISU shooting. Having been a hunter for 40 years (on both sides of the Atlantic) and having shot only two rounds of Skeet in my entire life without dropping the butt before calling for the target (never again!) I feel I have a right to say that, free of accusations of bias.

●

HANDGUNS TODAY:

AUTOLOADERS

by J. B. WOOD

BY THE TIME you read this, we certainly will not have the answer to the Big Question—which 9mm pistol will eventually be chosen by the Joint Services Program to replace the old 45 U.S. Service automatic? After the testing process was well under way, there were nine serious entries:

• From Browning, there were three—the well-known Model 1935 High Power, a double action version of the same gun, and a model called the "Fast Action," with a sort of abbreviated double action system.

• Heckler & Koch entered two pistols, the P9S, and the detachable-stock VP-70, the latter with selective full-auto capability.

• Star of Spain offered a sleek new double action, the Model 28.

• Beretta of Italy entered a modified version of their Model 92S.

• Colt's contestant was all in stainless steel, designated the SSP.

• The Smith & Wesson entry was practically identical to the new Model 459.

All of the guns have staggered magazines, with capacities ranging from 18 rounds in the VP-70 to 9 rounds in the P9S, with the average in the 14-15 round range. All of the pistols, with the exception of the Browning HP, had some form of double action.

After extensive testing, the field was narrowed to three: The Beretta, the Smith & Wesson, and the double action version of the Browning HP. According to an unofficial source, the Beretta had a slight edge. If it's the one chosen, there are plans to produce it here in the U.S., rather than importing the pistols from Italy. It should be noted that at the time this is being written there had been no final report. The winner might even be one of the other guns from the original nine, or the tests could be extended to include one or more of the new pistols developed since the program began. There seem, at this writing, to be plans to review all the tests, so all bets are off.

Regardless, any major military test program spurs the development of new designs, and modifications of existing designs, to the benefit of all shooters. At this point, it is not known whether Browning will commercially produce the DA or FA versions of the High Power. The production of the SSP by Colt is also a question mark. Star will definitely market the Model 28, and the other pistols in the tests are already commercially available. Now, let's look at what's new this year:

American Derringer Corp.

The inclusion of this company in the Auto Pistol Section is no mistake. In addition to Remington-style two-shot derringers, they have also resurrected the 25 stainless steel auto pistols that were originally offered by the American Firearms Manufacturing Company of San Antonio between 1966 and 1974. In addition to the standard 8-shot model, they're also making a "baby" model, with a shorter grip frame and a 6-round capacity. Another special version is one called the ".250 Magnum," to be chambered for a special 25 Auto cartridge that has a case length 3/32 of an inch longer than the standard round, and is loaded somewhat hotter. The gun will also function with regular 25 Auto cartridges. I have examined the new guns, and in comparison with an original-production gun that I own, the new company does it better. The pistols are

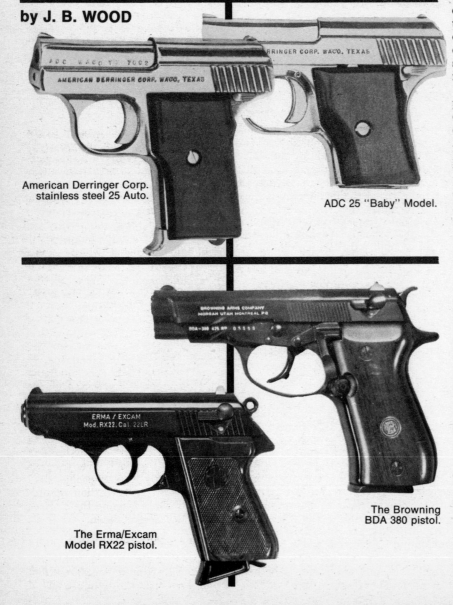

American Derringer Corp. stainless steel 25 Auto.

ADC 25 "Baby" Model.

The Browning BDA 380 pistol.

The Erma/Excam Model RX22 pistol.

available in regular 4140 steel as well as stainless, and in either case they are all-steel, with no major alloy parts. Also, the prices are very reasonable.

AMT, Incorporated

The makers of the Hardballer and the 380 Back-Up are about to add another pistol to the line. Externally, it will be a twin brother to the Back-Up. The difference will be in the chambering—22 Long Rifle. The 22 version will also be in stainless, and this should be a fine gun for campers, fishermen, and survivalists. Also, for those who already own a 380 Back-Up, it will be great for lower-cost practice shooting. I've had a 380 Back-Up for some time, and have long appreciated its quality and dependability.

Beretta

The changes made for the U.S. Test Program have been incorporated into the design of the Model 92S, mainly moving the magazine release to a more conventional position, at the rear of the trigger guard. It will be reversible for left-handed shooters. Called the 92S-1 in the tests, the new version has been designated Model 92SB, and it also includes an ambidextrous safety.

The big news from Beretta, though, is the introduction of a compact Model 92SB, with a shortened slide, barrel, and grip frame. The over-all length is 7^{11}/$_{16}$ inches, height is 5 inches, width 1.36 inches, and it weighs 32 ounces. The 92SB-Compact also has the ambidextrous safety and relocated magazine catch of the larger gun. The prototype is now making the rounds of U.S. government agencies for testing, and commercial availability is at least several months away.

Browning

Along with the venerable High Power and the excellent 22 Challenger II, Browning will continue to offer the fine BDA 380 pistol, their special version of the Beretta 84. The 45 BDA, though, made by SIG/Sauer, is going the way of the briefly-imported 9mm and 38 Super versions—it's being dropped. When the present supply is sold, there will be no more of these with the Browning name. No official explanation for this was given, but I think the gun just didn't sell because not enough people knew about it. It's a beautifully engineered pistol, and everyone who shoots mine rushes out to buy one. If you decide now, you'd best hurry, as only a total of about five thousand in 45 caliber were imported by Browning.

CB Arms

With importation of the Walther TPH restricted to police, there's a need for a small double action 22 pistol having similar features. The first gun I've actually handled that fits this description is the "Double Deuce" by CB Arms. Of all-steel construction, the gun has an external resemblance to the Walther, but there are differences, inside and outside. The two guns I examined, in blue and hard chrome, appeared to be well-made and nicely finished. Price of the blued version will be around the $200 level, with the hard chrome optional and somewhat higher.

Charter Arms

This company is more noted for revolvers of high quality and medium price, but last year they entered the auto pistol field, with a handgun version of their AR-7 Carbine. The new pistol, called the Explorer II, calls to mind the general shape of the old Mauser 1896, and has several interesting features. There are three barrel lengths available, and the pistol's quick-takedown makes changing barrels easy. The bottom of the grip has storage space for a spare magazine. The adjustable rear sight was recently improved, and there is an optional scope mount which attaches by simple replacement of the sideplate screw.

I've been shooting the Explorer II recently, and its performance and accuracy are beyond reproach. I can see that it would be a perfect choice for survival applications, and it would also make a fine field gun for handgun hunting. Its size and length call for a two-hand hold, but I had no difficulty in hitting plinking targets with one hand, as the gun is very lightweight, only 28 ounces. The quality and dependability are up to Charter standards, and the price is reasonable.

Detonics

I've had a stainless Mark V Detonics pistol for some time now, and can't seem to find anything about it to criticize. Early in 1981, I examined a new Detonics in 9mm Parabellum, made even more carrying-compact by the absence of sights. Speaking of sights, Detonics now has available a new rear sight called the Combat Selector which is adaptable to other guns, as well as the Detonics series. Elevation adjustments are accomplished by changing blades of differing heights, and once locked in place the entire assembly is solid and secure. Another new separate accessory from Detonics

is not for their pistols at all—it's a buffered competition recoil spring system for the Colt-pattern guns, with a full-length guide and two counter-wound springs.

Dornaus & Dixon

A California firm, Dornaus & Dixon Enterprises, has relied heavily on the advice of Jeff Cooper in designing a new double action combat pistol called the Bren Ten. The general features and appearance of the gun lean toward the Czech Model 75 pistol, with a touch of the Swiss SIG P-210. The "Ten" in the name refers to a new 10mm cartridge, which will be introduced along with the pistol.

I have handled the prototype pistol, but there was no opportunity to shoot it at the time. I was impressed by the quality and features, and the gun has a good "feel" in the hand, very much like the Czech Model 75. Actual production is about a year away, and I'm looking forward to trying this one when it's ready. In the meantime, for those who want to inquire further, here's the address: Dornaus & Dixon Enterprises, 16718 Judy Way, Cerritos, CA 90701.

Excam, Inc.

Two new pistols were recently added to the Excam line, one designed by Erma of Germany, and the other from Tanfoglio Giuseppe of Italy. The Erma/Excam RX22 is externally almost an exact model of the Walther PPK, with pronounced internal differences. The most important of these is a patented firing pin block automatic safety that is cleared only when the trigger is fully depressed to the rear. The pistol has an 8-round magazine, and weighs just 17 ounces. The chambering is for 22 Long Rifle.

The other pistol is the Targa GT32XE, an all-steel 32 Auto with a 12-round magazine and an external hammer. There are two manual safety levers, blocking the trigger and firing pin, and nicely-finished wood grips are standard. There's also a 380 version, the GT380XE, with the same features and an 11-round magazine.

I've fired both the RX22 and the GT32XE, and their performance and accuracy are excellent. Over the past three years the Excam people have progressively upgraded their quality standards while keeping their prices reasonable, in my opinion.

FTL Marketing Corp.

In the time since I first mentioned the FTL Auto Nine in the 1980 edition, I've had an opportunity to use one of these nice little 22 autos a lot, and it has worked like all of John Raymond Wilkinson's designs—perfectly. Just as with any small 22 pistol, there are certain brands of ammo it likes best, but it's worth noting that my gun will handle CCI Stingers. This tiny 8¼-ounce gun has an 8-round magazine and a cross-bolt push-button safety that blocks the sear, and the slide is finished in hard chrome. There is one catch—because it's a high-quality piece, it's not inexpensive. See Testfire, page 238.

Heckler & Koch

In the design department, Heckler & Koch seems unable to do anything wrong. Their P9S and HK4 pistols are renowned for innovative features and complete reliability. The VP 70Z, the semi-auto version of the detachable-stock VP 70, is now generally available, and its double action trigger system and 18-round magazine capacity make it an attractive choice for special police units and for home defense.

Speaking of innovation, Heckler & Koch can probably claim the grand prize for their PSP pistol, now known as the P7. The smallest 9mm Parabellum pistol now being made, it utilizes a unique locking system, with a fixed barrel and gas ported into a special cylinder to keep the slide closed during the instant of high pressure.

Its most outstanding feature, though, is a squeeze-cocking lever which forms the frontstrap of the grip frame. Unless the lever is depressed—and it requires little effort—the pistol is not cocked. Each shot is single action, but the gun has the safe-carrying advantage of a double action.

For those accustomed to conventional autos, it takes some getting used to. Once you've mastered it, though, it's just as easy as any other gun. After being compressed, the lever requires practically no effort to hold it in position, so accurate aimed fire is also possible.

In the time just before writing this, I've been range-testing a P7, and there's a lot that I like about it. The sights are particularly good, with white dots framing the rear notch, and a white dot on the rear face of the front blade. The pistol is very flat and compact, with excellent balance and handling qualities. I tried it with several loads, including JSP and JHP types, and it fed them all flawlessly.

Interarms

The Star Model 28 will be available commercially, along with a 22 conversion unit and an optional single action

The Targa Model GT32XE pistol.

The Heckler & Koch P7 pistol, previously known as the PSP.

The Bersa Model 644 pistol.

Navy Arms "Mamba".

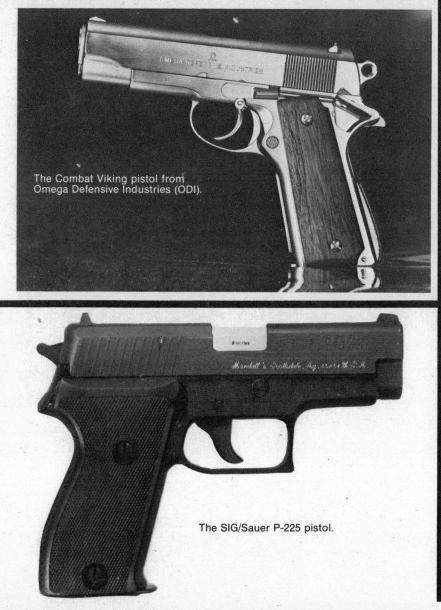

The Combat Viking pistol from Omega Defensive Industries (ODI).

The SIG/Sauer P-225 pistol.

trigger system. Before we see it, though, the Star factory must fill a sizeable order from the Spanish military. Available sooner will be a new double action pistol from Astra. Designated the Model A-80, it will be made in 9mm Parabellum, 38 Super, and 45 Auto. A prototype pistol seen early in 1981 was impressive, with outstanding handling qualities.

Quantity deliveries of the new American-made Walther PPK/S in 380 are well under way, and we can watch for the next nice surprise from Interarms/Walther. The original tentative sequence was a stainless steel 380 next, then regular steel 32 and 22 chamberings. Things may or may not proceed in that exact pattern. Walther is phasing out German PPK/S production, and in the future will buy them from America for sales in the rest of the world. The elegant new P5 may eventually eclipse the three models of the P-38 in popularity.

I recently asked Interarms was there any chance that the little TPH will be made in America. The answer: A good possibility, but not in the immediate future.

Interarms imports the Bernardelli 22 and 380 pistols, so it's a good bet that they will soon have the new double action 9mm Bernardelli. With all-steel construction and a double-column 14-round magazine, the new gun weighs 35 ounces, and measures 8½ inches over-all. The barrel length is 4¾ inches, and the rear sight is adjustable. It's too soon to predict the availability and price range, as the gun is just now beginning production. I've always had high regard for Bernardelli pistols, so I'm really interested in this one.

I recently tried the Argentine-made 22 Bersa Model 644 pistol. The gun is single action, with an external hammer, and its appearance shows both Walther and Beretta influence. There are two manual safety systems, one blocking the hammer, the other a cross-bolt push-button that blocks the trigger. The magazine capacity is ten rounds, and the quality of workmanship is excellent. The pistol sits well in the hand, and my gun is outstandingly accurate for a medium-frame automatic.

Iver Johnson

For a while, production of the neat little X300 "Pony" 380 was interrupted, but they are now available again. Iver Johnson will soon add another small auto to the line, and this one is double action. Of all-steel construction, it bears a strong resemblance to the Walther pattern, and chambering will be for 25 Auto and 22 Long Rifle. At this time, the price range and the date for commercial availability are not known.

Jennings Arms

One of the newest small 22-cal. pistols on the market is the Jennings J-22, a hammerless striker-fired single action gun with a six-round magazine. It's of mostly alloy construction, but all parts under particular stress or subject to wear are of steel, and this includes the internal breechblock, which is a separate insert in the slide. This is one of the new pistols that I've been able to test-fire extensively, and its performance is excellent with several brands of 22 Long Rifle. Another bit of good news is the price—it's under $90. It's a nice-looking little gun that feels good in the hand, and it *works*. See Testfire, page 239.

M & N Distributors

The neat little Budischowsky TP-70 pistol has had a checkered career. First, it was made by Norarmco in Michigan, and then by a Florida firm. Neither of these efforts lasted long, but the fault was not in this well-designed little gun. Now, I'm glad to report that the TP-70 has found a home, and quantity production seems assured with M & N Distributors. When the huge backlog of orders for the 25 version is filled, the factory will turn to the 22 Long Rifle chambering, perhaps by late 1981.

Navy Arms

After a year's wait while important overseas contracts were filled, the 9mm Mamba pistol is now beginning to be available on the commercial market. The big stainless steel pistol is designed for practical military and police use, and leans toward utilitarian good looks rather than sleek beauty. There are several really fine points in the design, including an ambidextrous safety that locks the hammer while leaving the slide free, and an ultra-smooth double action trigger pull.

The gun is heavy at 42 ounces, and this weight keeps it rock-steady in the hand, giving good accuracy from its 5-inch barrel. The stated magazine capacity is 15 rounds, but my Mamba comfortably holds 16, and the shallow delivery angle and good factory throating allow the use of JSP and JHP loads. The flat, vertically-ribbed frontstrap and comfortable grips give a good hold, and all parts of the gun are heavy, with ample allowance for

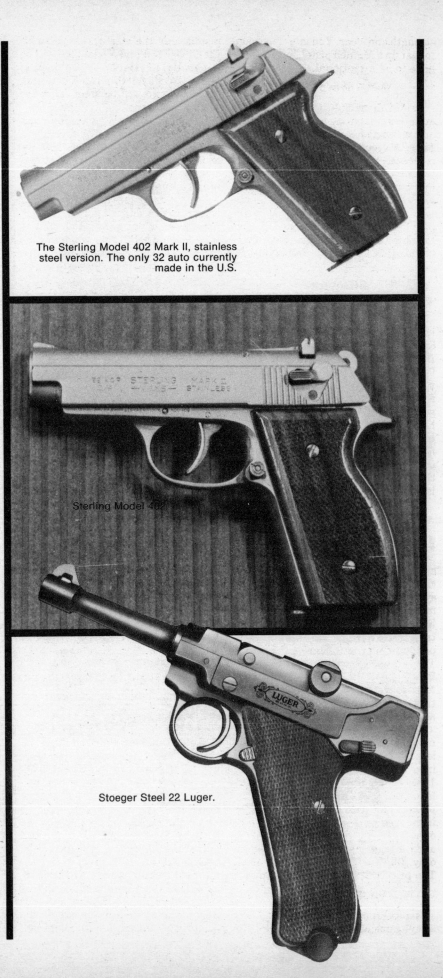

The Sterling Model 402 Mark II, stainless steel version. The only 32 auto currently made in the U.S.

Sterling Model 402.

Stoeger Steel 22 Luger.

strength and wear. You might manage to tear up a Mamba pistol, but it would have to be intentional.

ODI, Incorporated

Imagine a Colt Commander in stainless steel, with a Seecamp double action trigger system and teakwood grips. A super-expensive custom gun, reverently received after a year's wait, right? Wrong. ODI Incorporated is marketing this pistol, called the Combat Viking, and the price will be in the medium-expensive category. A "regular" Viking will also be available, in full-size, and the caliber option for both will be 45 Auto or 9mm Parabellum.

SIG/Sauer

The SIG/Sauer Model P-220, is still available in all three chamberings, imported by Mandall Shooting Supplies of Scottsdale, Arizona. Browning imported this as their BDA. Of even more interest is the new short version, the 9mm P-225, also available from the same source. I was also pleased to learn that Mandall's will have the P-230 as well, the beautiful lightweight 380 that was unavailable for a while. I have tested all three of the SIG/Sauer pistols extensively, and their quality, reliability, and accuracy is absolutely top-grade.

Sile

Over the past two years, the Benelli B-76, one of my favorite 9mm double action pistols, has undergone some small but significant internal changes. The recoil spring and buffer system have been improved, and the magazines are now tempered and hard-chromed. The lower edges of the trigger are bevelled, to eliminate any possibility of friction inside the guard. These items were not causing any difficulty; Benelli Armi is just continuing to improve the pistol. There is now a target version of the Benelli, with an adjustable rear sight.

The important news from Sile is the new Seecamp-designed 25 ACP stainless steel double action pistol. I examined one of the prototypes early in 1981, at the SHOT Show in New Orleans, and it's really a well-engineered piece. The gun is small—just 4⅛ inches over-all—and weighs only 10 ounces. It has an 8-round magazine and the trigger system is double action only, like the Czech Model 45 pistol. The price will be in the $150 range.

Smith & Wesson

It now appears that both the new alloy-frame Model 439 and Model 459 pistols, and the steel-frame versions, the Model 539 and Model 559, will be generally available by October of 1981. Except for the frame material, the latter two will be identical to the alloy-frame guns.

In all four of these guns, the main internal change is in the safety system. As originally designed, this incorporated a firing pin block that was cleared only with the final trigger movement, and eliminated the hammer-drop feature. The latter change didn't set well with several official users of the guns, so production was delayed while the hammer-drop feature was restored to the safety system. The firing pin block was retained, so when the safety is applied, the firing pin will be *double* locked.

A shielded, fully adjustable rear sight and an improved extractor are other features of the redesigned pistols.

Sterling Arms

I'd like to report the all-steel 45 double action pistol from Sterling is ready, but we'll have to wait a bit longer. I imagine we'll see production pieces in about a year, if all goes well.

Meanwhile, Sterling has introduced the first 32 automatic made in the U.S. since 1945, their Model 402, in regular and stainless steel. When paired with the Winchester Silvertip 32 Auto round, the new pistol is an excellent substitute for the 380 pistols, offering lighter recoil and improved accuracy. The Model 402 is one of the guns I've tried extensively, and its performance was perfect. It feeds the hollow-point rounds without alteration, and it has the fully-adjustable rear sight of the other Sterling DA pistol, the 380 Model 400 Mark II. Also, the price is very reasonable, in comparison with other pocket pistols having similar features.

Steyr

Steyr Daimler Puch of Austria, through their American corporation, will be offering two significant automatic pistols soon. The 9mm Parabellum double action, designated the Steyr GB80, is the original gun on which the Rogak P-18 was based. As built by Steyr, there will be several important differences in features and construction. The original gas-retarded locking system will be used, as well as the 18-round magazine.

The other pistol, while imported by Steyr, is being made by famed rifle and shotgun producer Renato Gamba of Italy, and is called the Gamba RGP81. In 32 and 380 Auto chambering, it is double action, with a 12-round magazine. The manual safety blocks the firing pin, and there is a combat-style finger rest at the front of the trigger guard.

I haven't yet seen actual samples of either gun, but from the illustrations in the factory brochure they are both handsome pieces.

Stoeger

The 22 Luger, designed a few years ago by Gary Wilhelm, now has all-steel construction. For those who prefer the weight and other attributes of steel, this is a welcome touch. There's other news from the Stoeger people, but we still must wait a while to see the gun: The new 45 double action pistol from Llama has now reached final design stage.

The new gun is a handsome piece, and has several interesting design touches. Among these are a ball-bearing hammer spring system, separate trigger bars for double and single action, and a two-section articulated firing pin. Externally, there have been some slight changes in appearance from the gun shown two years ago when it was first announced, but the general outline and placement of controls are the same. This pistol has had four years of design work and three years of testing, so they're obviously trying to get everything right before production begins, which will be soon.

Another new offering from Stoeger, which we may see even before the arrival of the double action Llama, is a Luger pistol in 9mm chambering, with traditional looks and a modern mechanical approach.

Wildey

It's Murphy's Third Law, I think, that says "Everything takes longer than you think it will." By now, Wildey Moore probably feels he should have this dictum framed on his office wall. The production finally got into full swing in March, 1981, and deliveries to dealers should be happening at the time you're reading this. There were two good reasons for the long delay—some small elements of redesign, and Wildey's idea that the gun should not be put on the market until everything was exactly right. This big gas-operated 45 Magnum and 9mm Magnum will be popular with handgun hunters and metallic silhouette shooters, and I'm looking forward to trying one out. ●

HANDGUNS TODAY:
SIXGUNS AND OTHERS

by HAL SWIGGETT

THERE IS much to tell this year: new guns, even from one of the real biggies, a line discontinued; a line reintroduced; an old line company back on its feet; two or three new companies established. It's been a good year with all indications the next one will be even better.

Derringers are looked upon askance by some, and only two were submitted of six asked for at the SHOT show. Those two were willing to show their guns to someone whose stated purpose was to fire them before they would be mentioned. All weren't derringers as a pair were of the mini revolver design, but all were little guns intended for concealment. One of the minis did show up but was recalled before I had a chance to try it, and I honored their request to return it unfired.

This year's review even includes a pair of pneumatic pistols, things left out in the past, and you will see why as you come to them—in alphabetical order:

American Derringer Corp.

The American Derringer is U.S.-made in stainless steel, has an over-all length of a fraction more than 4¾ inches, 3-inch barrels and weighs 15.5 ounces in 38 Special. It is single action, and there is a safety which the manufacturer says must be engaged to make the gun safe to carry loaded. This safety is automatically disengaged when the hammer is cocked.

The test gun was in 38 Special. I fired it 24 times with Remington 38 Special +P loads. That's probably more times than most derringers are fired over an entire service life. The gun is still intact. I still have four fingers and a thumb on my right hand. If I had use for a derringer I wouldn't be afraid to trust this one.

American Derringer chambers, on special order, 45 Colt, 45 Auto, 45 Auto Rim, 44 Special, 44-40, 41 Magnum, 357 Magnum, 9mm Luger, 38 Super, 380 Auto, 30-30 Win. and 223 Rem. Their sales sheet also stated "*WARNING: SEVERE RECOIL IN THIS CALIBER" and all of those special order calibers wear the asterisk except the 380 Auto.

I have never been known as recoil conscious—my pet at the moment is a 45-70 custom T/C—but, friends and neighbors, 15 ounces of 3-inch gun with a tiny derringer handle just don't do much for me in more than plain old-fashioned 38 Special.

Barami Corp.

Hip-Grip has been around a baker's dozen years and only minor changes have been made. Simply put it is a pistol handle holster. Plastic-looking, smooth black grips replace those already on the revolver. The right side fits higher on the frame than an ordinary grip with the upper three-quarters of an inch set about half an inch out from the frame. It fits over a belt or trouser waistband so the gun can be worn against the body, under trousers and hence completely concealed; it works; with any smooth revolver it is very comfortable, but target sights can gouge.

Recommended for off-duty police, plain clothesmen, bank tellers, store clerks, most anybody who has reason to legally carry a hide-away, the Hip-Grip is made for J and K frame S&W's, Detective Special, Cobra, Agent and Diamondback Colts and

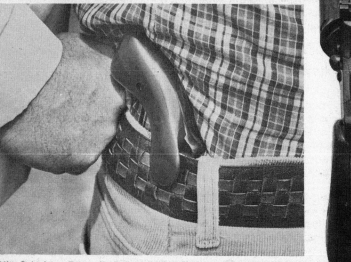

American Derringer Corp. 38 Special stainless steel derringer.

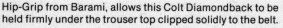

Hip-Grip from Barami, allows this Colt Diamondback to be held firmly under the trouser top clipped solidly to the belt.

Charter Arms Undercover, Uncercov- erette, Pathfinder and Bulldog Spe- cial.

Charter Arms

The Bulldog is loose again. Every year Charter Arms adds a new one to the line. This time it is the Police Bulldog in two models. Both are 38 Special, wear a 4-inch barrel, fixed sights, square butt, checkered walnut grips and high lustre service blue. Both are 5-inches high and 9-inches in length over-all. So what is the differ- ence, you ask? One weighs in at 21- ounces and the other, dressed in a bull barrel, tops it by an ounce.

Charter's little 2-inch Undercover that first saw the light of day more than 15 years ago is now available in stainless steel at a trifling 17-ounces. The popular Pathfinder 22 LR in the 3-inch barrel version is also available in stainless steel at 20-ounces. The 6-inch edition is still to be had in serv- ice blue.

Colt

A new Sheriff's Model Single Action Army revolver was shown by Colt at the SHOT show. The same changes peculiar to the 19th Century original have been made: a special frame with no aperture cut for the ejector rod and a special 3-inch barrel.

There is to be a single cylinder 44-40 version with standard Single Action Army eagle stocks. A dual cylinder edition—a few will be made with both 44-40 and 44 Special cylinders—will be Royal Blue and Nickel and have American walnut stocks with no medallion. The single cylinder version is blued with color case-hardened frame.

And from Colt, some bad news: Colt Single Action Armies will be discon- tinued on or about December, 1981. Some models have already been dis- continued. The phase-out will occur model by model each month. There is no anticipated plan to reintroduce the line, however, should conditions war- rant, 1983 would be the earliest target date.

COP

The left side reads: "COP INC, TORRANCE, CA. U.S.A.," and "CAL. 38SP/357MAG." On the right side above the grip is the serial number, in this case 009731. M&N Distributors market what I am at a loss to define. I consider it a derringer because of the size, but it shoots four times. The four barrels are 3⅛-inches in length and the little gun measures only 5½- inches over-all with a height of barely

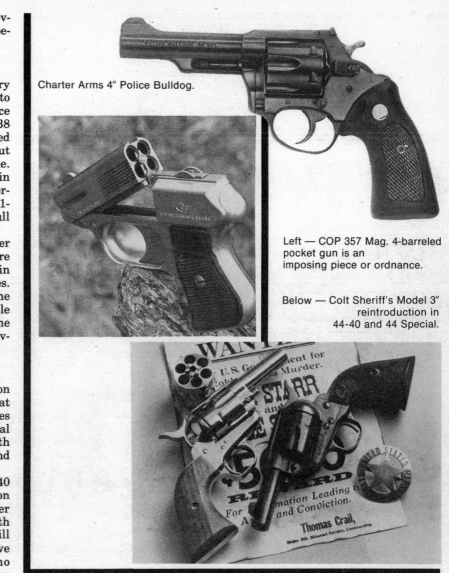

Charter Arms 4" Police Bulldog.

Left — COP 357 Mag. 4-barreled pocket gun is an imposing piece or ordnance.

Below — Colt Sheriff's Model 3" reintroduction in 44-40 and 44 Special.

4⅛-inches. It is just one inch wide and tipped my postal scales at 27-ounces.

The barrels are rifled only suffi- ciently to make it legal. A gun such as this isn't intended for more than across-a-small-room use, so what dif- ference could that make? The gun opens shotgun style by sliding the knurled rear sight humps back. The extractor raises the cases enough to slip a thumbnail in.

I found no way to determine which of the four barrels would fire first so as- sume it isn't a gun to carry if only two or three rounds were available. Since literature with the gun describes it as designed specifically for law enforce- ment professionals, I doubt that was ever a considered point.

Fired by double action only, the hammerless gun has no safety and doesn't need one. The trigger pull is 17-pounds and covers ¹¹/₁₆-inch. The first half-inch of this takes 12-14

pounds then the ³/₁₆-inch breaks with the additional 3 to 5 pounds. It was surprisingly easy to fire.

When the gun arrived Jim Pacheco —I use his gun shop FFL—had to try it. He stuffed four magnum loads in it and shoved his hand through the rubber opening in his test rig. It went bang. Jim came up slowly, changed his grip and repeated the performance. With the second bang, he came up a bit slower still and carefully unwrapped his hand from the grip.

Opening the gun I threw out the question, "Aren't you going to shoot all four?"

His replay was classic: "It don't take me four shots to see how it's going to handle."

It wasn't all that bad. I shot twelve Remington 110-grain SJHP's through it fast as I could pull the trigger on four and reload. Twelve more Federal 125-grain JHP's likewise. For dessert

Above — Daisy Power Line
Model 717 pneumatic handgun.

El Dorado all stainless steel
44 Magnum with 7″ barrel.

The High Standard High Sierra 9-shot
22 LR-22 Magnum convertible. It's single
action in looks and double-action.

mostly from the barrels made by El Dorado themselves from 17-4 PH steel.

The test gun was a 44 Magnum. It was given a thorough workout with Federal 180-grain JHP's, Frontier 240-grain JHP's and Remington's 240-grain SJHP's plus a goodly supply of handloads by Swiggett concocted with 23.5 grains of H110 under 240-grain jacketed bullets. It shot them all well.

Except for the rear sight blade the gun is entirely corrosion resistant. All parts requiring high strength are 17-4 stainless steel, the most corrosion-resistant of all heat treatable stainless steels. All small parts including springs are either stainless steel or beryllium copper. Calibers available include 357 Magnum, 44 Magnum, 45 Colt and 45 Win. Mag. Barrel lengths are 4⅝-inches in 357 and 45 Colt; 7½-inches in 44 Magnum and 9½ and 10½-inches in all calibers. The front sight is a serrated ramp. The rear is fully adjustable for windage and elevation.

El Dorado is a registered trade mark. The guns are manufactured and assembled entirely in the United States.

Harrington & Richardson

A pair of new Swing Outs, as H&R refers to them, are target grade 22 rimfire revolvers. Fully adjustable rear sights and heavier barrels make these relatively inexpensive revolvers prime candidates for the serious rimfire shooter.

The Model 904 is available with a 6-inch barrel in Crown Lustre blue or a 4-inch barrel with the blue satin finish. The Model 905 is available only in the 4-inch length and it wears a durable protective nickel finish.

High Standard

Isn't it great when an "old line" company can hit upon hard times yet survive and make a comeback? High Standard has done just that. Determination, possibly, or maybe simply faith in the American way but I think probably a little of both. (And maybe some smarts: Editor).

Long famous for fine 22 pistols of top target quality, H-S had a line of western look-alike 22 revolvers and a single derringer thrown in, then a 357 Magnum double action added for flavor. Frosting on the cake was to come in the form of the Crusader—a big double action in two frame sizes— one for the 357 Magnum and a still more hefty one for the 44 Magnum and 45 Colt.

another dozen Federal 158-grain JHP's were fired as fast as I could pull the trigger and reload. All were full magnum loads.

The intended purpose is personal protection for law enforcement professionals. There isn't the slightest doubt in my mind about its ability to handle its assignment well.

Daisy

These past several years have seen me change many of my habits. I now get a good deal of handgun practice in the house. I started with a Walther match target pistol; then decided to switch to more realistically priced airguns. About a year ago I acquired a Daisy Power Line Model 717. It weighs 46-ounces, has a crisp trigger pull of 64-ounces and a barrel length of 9½-inches. The sights are, for visibility, equal to any high-priced centerfire. The rear is fully adjustable. The pistol

is pumped a single stroke with a side lever operating at close to 16-pounds. The sight radius is 12¾-inches.

This outfit offers amazing accuracy for anyone not familiar with pneumatic guns. I use a little bullet trap and can shoot at 23 feet as I watch television. Using Daisy match pellets, nickel-sized 10-shot groups are common and more than a few could be easily covered with a dime.

It helps me. Maybe a little living room shooting will make longer range hits easier for you too. Be careful. It's not a toy.

El Dorado Arms

The El Dorado Arms single action tested had seven inches of barrel, all stainless steel, weighed 46-ounces and had a trigger pull of 51-ounces. The manufacturer claims its better than average accuracy comes from the careful lineup of cylinder and barrel, but

Then the bottom dropped out. It is firmly sealed now and the base is solid. Clem Confessore is president and heads up a group of private investors. The company was moved from Hamden to East Hartford. In only three years, High Standard moved from loser status to a profitability under this new ownership.

Currently marketed are the four target pistols—Victor, Trophy, Citation and Sharpshooter—along with the Sport King for the plinker, and three double action western-style revolvers, the Double Nine, Longhorn and High Sierra. Rounding out the line for the moment is the little Derringer in 22 Magnum.

I have had considerable experience with one of the fine target pistols and the little Derringer in 22 LR. That little two-holer has finished off several deer even though not designed for or thought of in that sense. Recently, one of the High Sierras has received a rather thorough workout.

Wearing a 7-inch octagonal barrel the convertible western-style revolver weighs 33-ounces with the LR cylinder and one-half ounce less with the Mag cylinder. Double action trigger pull is right at 20-pounds. The single action pull is a clean 4½-pounds. The long hammer spur makes it easy to thumb back. The ejector rod housing is for looks only as the swing-out cylinder ejects with the usual push of the cylinder pin latch. For good looks the trigger guard and backstrap are brass. The rear sight is adjustable.

The gun shoots good. Putting 100 rounds each of Federal, CCI and Remington high velocity through the LR cylinder proved it more than adequate as a small game hunting revolver. One hundred 22 Mags were put through that cylinder, half CCI and half Winchester. It shot equally well, though much too hot for cottontails and squirrels if eating is the goal. Jackrabbits are fair targets out to as far as we ought to shoot at them and I wouldn't hesitate to use those rimfire Magnums on called coyotes out to thirty yards or so.

Interarms

The fine Virginian single action revolver is now in full production according to Bob Magee. He tells me it is being turned out in 357, 41, and 44 Magnums and 45 Colt in barrel lengths from 5-inches to 12-inches, not each in all calibers however, and also in stainless steel in 44 Magnum.

And now there is a new Astra. Chambered for the 45 ACP cartridge this double action revolver should find favor with lovers of the 45 ACP cartridge but dislikers of brass hunting. Wearing a 6-inch barrel it will also handle, without those little half-moon clips, 45 Auto rim ammo. For a whole lot of years I have used a S&W Model 1950 chambered for this cartridge. Handloaded with Keith-style bullets it does a mighty fine job on small to medium-sized game.

I seldom use those little clips. The cartridge chambers on the case mouth. All the clip does is make extraction easier. A short pencil shoves out any stubborn empties.

Lawman Leather, Inc.

Lawman has another great shoulder holster, the Trophy-Hunt. This one is designed for big hunting handguns, specifically the Thompson/Center Contender and 10- to 14-inch barrels —plain or bull; scopes or iron sights; over-size grips and fore-ends or the issue variety. In other words, if it comes on or fits a T/C Contender it will fit in the "Trophy-Hunt."

The firm's "Big-Hawk" is designed specifically for Ruger's hefty Super Blackhawk. It, too, can be used for open sighted revolvers or, with the snap-on hood, for scope-sighted handguns. The rigging isn't all that much different than other shoulder holsters but I've found those subtle differences do make them extremely comfortable.

Merrill Sportsman

The Merrill Sportsman single shot pistol continues to grow. Now available in 22 S, L, LR; 22 Mag RF; 22 Hornet; 256 Win. Mag.; 7mm Merrill; 30 Herrett; 30-30 Win.; 30 Merrill; 357 Mag-38 Spl; 357 Herrett; 375 Win.; 41 Rem. Mag. and 44 Rem. Mag.

Barrel lengths come in 10¾- and 14-inch except for a special 22 Silhouette barrel which measures 9-inches.

Mitchell Arms

Made in Italy by Aldo Uberti & Co. these single action revolvers are "spittin' images" of the original Colt designs. All the characteristics of the fine old Single Action Army are present and made from modern steels.

The Mitchell single actions are imported in both 44 Magnum and 45 Colt calibers and in barrel lengths of 4¾-inches, 5½-inches, 6-inches, 7½-inches, then 10, 12 and 18-inches. The 18-inch version is available with a shoulder stock.

The color case-hardened forged steel frame is downright handsome, especially on the test 44. A solid brass backstrap and trigger guard add to the beauty as do the one-piece solid walnut grips. A special safety device is built into the hammer assembly which catches the hammer at half cock should it slip from the thumb in cocking. The safety, for carrying, is about one-quarter cocked though I'd encourage any shooter of this or any other single action to disregard *all* safety devices and leave an empty chamber under the hammer. If more than five rounds are needed, you either need more practice or another profession/ hobby.

The test Mitchell SA's provided were a 44 Magnum with a 6-inch barrel and fixed sights and a 7½-inch barrel 45 Colt with an adjustable rear sight.

Since I can see little reason for a fixed sight 44 Magnum it was gone over first. Weighing 42.5-ounces the gun had a mean 7½-pound trigger pull, which ruled out serious accuracy testing. The grip is ¼-inch longer than on the 45, 1/16-inch longer at the top and ⅛-inch larger at the bottom, which made easy holding. Forty rounds of 23.5 grains of H110 under a 240-grain jacketed bullet were fired with no slipups. It seemed to shoot fairly close to the fixed sights, but the trigger weight made it hard to be sure.

The 45 Colt was more fun. Weighing 39½-ounces with its 7½-inch barrel, the trigger pulled an even five pounds. The only factory amo on hand was a box of Hirtenberg (Austria) with 255-grain lead bullets. Half, 25 rounds, was shot up; then my personal loads of 10 grains of Unique under a 454424 bullet went to work. That load shoots good in every 45 Colt I've shot and this one was no exception. Sighted in to hit the point of aim at 50-yards, three jackrabbits fell victim to its accuracy. All told, 263 rounds went through the 45 without a miscue.

Loading the Mitchell is traditional Colt—half cock and rotate the cylinder. Both calibers are available with fixed or adjustable sights.

Mossberg

Like many others, Mossberg's Abilene single-action took a bit longer to get out than planned. I had the privilege of fondling one of the 45 Colt versions some time back and, with only slight insistence, fired it a few times—not enough to call it a test but sufficient to decide whether or not I liked the gun.

In 357 Magnum the Abilene offers 4⅝, 6 or 7½-inch barrels. The 45 Colt comes only in the 6-inch length. The 44 Magnum is to be had in all three of those, plus a 10-inch barrel.

Mitchell Arms two Italian-made single actions. Available with fixed or adjustable sights and in most popular barrel lengths.

Mossberg's 4⅝" 44 Magnum Abilene.

Right — Ruger Speed Six 9mm stainless steel revolver. Above — Ruger's fine new Redhawk 7½" double action 44 Magnum.

The rear sight is adjustable and the front a ramp. The hammer is wide with a deeply serrated spur. The finish is mirror blue or Magnaloy brushed chrome.

The Abilene Silhouette Model sports a 10-inch bull barrel and is fitted with an Elliason adjustable rear sight. Oversize grips top off this "iron animal" model.

To finish what I was talking about in the first paragraph—I liked the Abilene 45 Colt. It shot well with Federal factory ammo. Unfortunately, so well did it go that I'm afraid it, too, will become one of those items I find I must have in my work, and I'll end up missing another house payment.

Ruger

The long awaited Redhawk 44 Magnum worked its way into a few hands this past season. It's 51-ounces and 13-inches over-all, with 7⁷/₁₆-inch barrel. The trigger pull on mine breaks clean at 66-ounces. The sights are excellent, the front is a red inserted ramp, the rear fully adjustable and both are blue, making them easier to see than if they were stainless steel.

Mine arrived with three weeks of hunting season left so I carried it daily, in a Bianchi #X15 Large shoulder holster that seems to be designed to take most anything. Sighted in to hit my point of aim at 75-yards with Federal 180-grain JHP's the Redhawk first finished off a whitetail buck that had earlier been shot by a rifle hunter. This was at 55 steps.

One of the chores for guides on at least one of the biggest exotic game ranches is thinning out does of the exotic deer species. Thus employed, the Redhawk brought down three—one at 65 steps, another at 57 steps and the closest at 43 steps.

It is very comfortable to shoot. The grip design doesn't seem to be all that different but it does not cause any discomfort at all with whatever is shot in it. I know at least four hundred assorted rounds have been fired, most of which were handloads consisting of 23.5 grains of H110 under a 240-grain jacketed bullet, the only load I build in 44 Magnum.

I try to use factory ammo when hunting because that is what most shooters use and this gives me data I can pass on to them. The Federal 180-grain JHP is deadly. All four of those deer were dropped with a single shot.

The Ruger Redhawk is worth the wait.

Last year, when the 9mm chambering in the Speed-Six and Police Service-Six was announced, I belittled the idea. Since then I have tried one out, a Speed-Six with a 2¾-inch barrel that weighs an even two pounds. The double action trigger pull is 13-pounds, plus or minus a fraction. The single action pull is crisp at 70-ounces. With fixed sights, both 95-grain Federal JSP and 90-grain S&W JSP shot to the sights so close I wouldn't have made an adjustment had it been possible.

Long a fan of the little 9mm Parabellum cartridge in sporting versions, I have shot thousands in four autoloaders. It has been my spring and summer carry gun for the past dozen or so years. And, needless to say, being a Baptist hasn't hurt because I've also spent a lot of time on my knees searching for factory brass. The military surplus stuff I left to nature.

With the Speed-Six this is not necessary because you can dump the empties out in the hand. Delivered with a dozen half-moon clips—9mm cartridges head space on the case mouth same as does the 45 ACP—the gun is easily fired without their use but the clips make extraction easier. Loaded three at a time—you will find it easier with a twisting motion that comes with practice—clips allow the ejector rod to push out those empties. Without clips, a pencil will get out any stubborn cases that can't be lifted with a fingernail.

The stainless steel Speed-Six wears checkered walnut grips. And it could well be I was wrong in my appraisal last year. The 9mm Federal 115-grain JHP starts off at 1160 fps and thumps, at the muzzle, with 345 ft/lbs of energy. Federal's most potent 38 Special +P load travels out the muzzle at 915 fps and hits, again at the muzzle, with 294 ft/lbs of energy.

Smith & Wesson

An "L" frame S&W?

Smith & Wesson takes top honors in the new gun department this year as they announced their new "L" frame revolver, the Model 586 Distinguished Combat Magnum. Chambered for the popular 357 Magnum, it's a new profile, a new frame size, a new gun.

At 46-ounces with a 6-inch barrel, the Model 586 is also available with a 4-inch tube weighing 42-ounces. It has 6-shot capacity, a wide semi-target hammer and a wide smooth combat trigger. The test gun has a ⅛ Baughman front sight with the S&W Red Ramp. The adjustable rear sight has the white outline notch. The grips are checkered Goncalo Alves Target with a speed loader cutaway. These grips are the same size as the "K" frame.

The heavy straight barrel has a full-length extractor shroud which makes it almost a clone to the Colt Python. From the side it looks like a Python without a vent rib. From the bottom it looks like a Python, period. It weighs exactly the same as the Python and feels in the hand exactly like a Python. I have here on my desk one of each—both 6-inch barrels—and they balance and feel identical.

Three finishes are available: S&W bright blue or nickel for the Model 586 and S&W satin stainless for the Model 686. If this hasn't been enough to whet your appetite, the price is $247 for the 586 and $21 more for the stainless 686. These are the suggested prices and delivery was to have started in May for the 586 and June for the 686.

The trigger on our test gun is clean and crisp at 66-ounces and accuracy appears to be in keeping with its looks. A smattering of assorted 357 Magnum ammo has been put through the 586 including 110, 125, 158-grain jacketed bullets and a full box of 158-grain semi wadcutters, about 150 rounds in all. That's not enough to tell much about the gun, except I don't believe anyone is going to be disappointed.

There is still more. There will be, in September and October of 1981, Models 581 and 681. Basically, these are the same guns with 4-inch barrels only and fixed sights, at suggested prices of $178 for the blue, $187 for nickel and $198 for the stainless.

Don't go away: there is still a "K" frame Model 547 9mm Luger and Parabellum with two barrel lengths, 4⅛ and 3-inches both with fixed sights. Weight of the short one is 32-ounces. Available in S&W blue only and suggested at $246 with a June, 1981, delivery date.

The 4-inch will have the square butt; the 3-inch the round butt. See Testfire, page 225.

SSK Industries

Home of the "loud-n-boomers" SSK builds custom barrels bored from 17 Remington to 50-70. J.D. Jones, the impresario behind this action, thrives on lots of noise and sturdy thumps to his wrist, forearm and shoulder. His 375 JDJ has taken game all over this continent and numerous African trophies.

New this year is a hefty scope mount base made to handle heavy recoiling handguns. Using three Bushnell rings none of his calibers has budged a scope yet. I have one on a 35 Remington with a 2½x Redfield so firmly tagged the scope hasn't moved in three to four hundred shots.

The new Model 586 Smith & Wesson Distinguished Combat Magnum is in 357 Magnum and built on an all new "L" frame.

A new mount designed and marketed by SSK. It uses three Bushnell rings and has held up under all of the heavy calibers chambered by them.

Sterling

Sterling Arms Corp is well known for autoloading pistols in 22, 25, 32 and 380 calibers but now they have a new dimension. Called the X-Caliber, it is a single shot hunting and target pistol of break-open type. Interchangeable barrels in 22 S, L, or LR; 22 Rimfire Magnum; 357 Magnum and 44 Magnum are available in both 8 and 10-inch versions. With the 8-inch barrel the pistol weighs 52 ounces. The rear sight is fully adjustable and the wood, both forearm and grip, is cocobolo. The gun isn't out at this writing but I have been assured it will be in dealers hands in 22 by publication. The bigger borings will be following soon.

Thompson/Center

The Contender pistol set off a phenomenon unprecedented in handgunning circles. When they made good guns available at reasonable prices T/C opened the serious handgunning field to thousands of shooters, chambering all of the known handgun calibers of any importance and a good many rifle cartridges.

There is nothing new from T/C this year except that they have dropped the 45 ACP, 22 K-Hornet and 25-35 Winchester. I've shot neither of the first two but one of the most accurate barrels I own is my 25-35. I hate to see it go but I doubt they have sold a double handful of them.

The T/C "Recoil Proof" long eye relief handgun scopes are available in 1.5, 2.5, 3 and 4 power. There is a T/C mount to fit these scopes to the Contender plus Buehler, B-Square, Conetrol, Leupold and Redfield all make mounts for the Contender.

United Sporting Arms

United is in full production of their Seville single action. Different from the myriad other single actions, the Seville is multi-caliber. It can be had in about as many calibers as a heart could desire, all on the same frame. Barrels and cylinders change with the twist of two screws.

My test gun (guns?) is (are?) 44 Magnum and 45 Colt. On arrival, the 44 barrel and cylinder were in place so it became the first to be fired, even before I looked into how to make the change.

There are a lot of things I like about the Seville. And a couple to the contrary.

The finish is good. The plain walnut grips are carefully fitted. The ramp

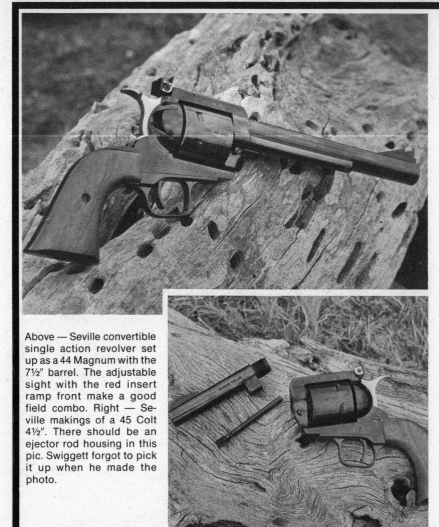

Above — Seville convertible single action revolver set up as a 44 Magnum with the 7½" barrel. The adjustable sight with the red insert ramp front make a good field combo. Right — Seville makings of a 45 Colt 4½". There should be an ejector rod housing in this pic. Swiggett forgot to pick it up when he made the photo.

front sight has a red insert (the only thing I like better is yellow). The rear sight is good, very good. The sight itself is either stainless or satin finished something or other, but the adjustment screws are blue as is the blade which is also deeply serrated crossways to do away with any possible reflection.

So what's to dislike?

The sight elevation screw can be seen in the notch. And the front sight is the same width on both barrels. On the shorter 45 barrel it fills the notch. I like to see daylight on both sides. Minor problems.

Another complaint which touches a sore spot with me because there is no such critter: the 45 barrel reads, on the left side, Seville Cal .45, which is fine, but the cylinder reads Cal .45 L.C. There is a 45 ACP cartridge and there is a 45 Colt cartridge. There is not a 45 Long Colt cartridge.

The hammer comes back a long way. Or you could say the hammer has a

long way to fall to hit the firing pin. No problem for an experienced single action shooter except I use a high hold on the grip. It is impossible to get that hold without touching the hammer spur. If the gun was mine I would have the last three serrations ground off.

The 44 barrel didn't get much of a workout. Forty rounds told me if I missed it was my fault. This was Remington's 240-grain SJHP ammo. The 45 Colt 4½-incher is another matter. It didn't take long to run 100 rounds of Federal 225-grain SWCHP through the slick handling Seville. Switching over to my handloads proved to be sheer shooting pleasure. Grapefruit-sized rocks are easy to hit at 40 to 50 steps. I'm a field shooter. Paper is for those who don't have full outdoor privileges.

I don't know about the durability of the interchangeable barrel system but accomplishing the fact is simplicity itself. It takes about as long to do it as it does to tell how it is done. Of course the

The Tempest by Webley.

Wichita MK-40 Silhouette pistol.

The Y.O. Ranch
Centennial Commemorative.

gun does have to be sighted in after each barrel change.

The Seville is available in 357 Magnum, 41 Magnum, 44-40, 44 Magnum, 45 ACP, 45 Colt and 45 Winchester Magnum and in about any barrel length you might dream up.

Webley

The Webley Tempest feels like a real gun. In caliber 177 the one I have been shooting has a 6¹³/₁₆-inch barrel and a sight radius of 7½-inches. The rear sight is adjustable by trial and error. To pump the single stroke needed to fire, the rear of the barrel is released with a thumb catch and raised to the front. It takes, give or take a little, about 28-pounds of push to cock the pistol. I have fired it extensively with their Silver Jet Magnum Pellets, Precision Wadcutter Match pellets and Silver Bear SWCHP pellets.

My living room range is twenty-three feet and I shoot into a small bul-

let trap. Nickel-sized 10-shot groups came rather often with Silver Jets. Match WC's do best though not all that much in my hands. The trigger is adjustable. Mine is at an even four pounds which is as light as I can set it in spite of the instructions. The let-off is crisp.

I'm convinced that the use of a pneumatic pistol around the home or shop will help any handgunner. In no way is the Tempest a toy.

Dan Wesson 44

Barely, but definitely, in production is the new Dan Wesson 44. The immediate push is towards those two n.iddle lengths, 6-inch and 8-inch. This 44 Magnum is more exciting than the current 357 Wesson.

Outward appearance is much the same, but the big 44 is a new gun. Interchangeable barrels are, of course, the big feature.

The "Power Control" system, the brain-child of Paul Brothers, vents

gases in an entirely different way, first through holes near the muzzle, then through slots in the shroud. This is efficient without a doubt, but word has it that lead bullets can be a problem, and company officials are recommending plain unvented barrels for lead bullet shooters. Jacketed bullets, too, require occasional attention to the shroud and barrel vents beyond that usually given a handgun.

Offered in the customary Dan Wesson Pistol Pac the 44 comes fitted with the 8-inch barrel, an extra 6-inch barrel, an extra grip, two additional sights blades, a Dan Wesson belt buckle and emblem—all in a handsome carrying case. Such class—all the way—has become a Dan Wesson tradition.

Wichita

Single shot pistols are all the rage among silhouette shooters and also mighty popular with some of the handgun hunting fraternity. Wichita makes fine bolt action single shot pistols.

The Classic features 11¼-inches of octagon barrel, Micro sights, soft satin blue finish and American walnut. The Wichita MK-40 Silhouette Pistol wears a 13-inch heavy barrel and a fiberthane stock, metallic gray in color. At 4½-pounds the MK-40 meets all IHMSA and NRA competition standards.

Y.O. Commemorative

The Y.O. Ranch celebrated their 100th anniversary in 1980 and as part of the celebration turned out commemorative six-shooters. Colt 45 SAA revolvers were turned into pieces of art by master engraver Frank Hendricks. Like so many things in the gun industry these didn't get out until after the year of celebration. Two hundred were made. Fifty are Premier models 80% covered with engraving, with bands of gold inlaid near the muzzle, just in front of the frame and on the back of the cylinder, along with a gold eagle head on the hammer. The Y.O. escutcheon is gold and fitted to the left ivory grip. There is a smaller Y.O. escutcheon on the upper backstrap. The legend "1880 — Y.O. Centennial — 1980" is engraved on the left side of the barrel. The other side reads "A Century of Ranching in Texas."

There are 150 Deluxe models. These have 60% engraving coverage and the escutcheons are silver. Both editions are silver plated and fitted with ivory grips. From the Y.O. Ranch, Box 200, Mountain Home, TX 78058.   •

by **ROBERT KEFFER**

ONE MAN'S FANCY

It's a Krieghoff double rifle, with a lot of extra touches

DOUBLE RIFLES are not only useful as heavy caliber guns for dangerous African game. Many European hunters prefer the double for use on drive hunts where wild boar, red stag and roe deer are driven past hunters on stands. Since the double is short and has excellent handling qualities, it is the best design for quick shots and quick second shots. With ejectors, reloading is very fast, also.

The double rifle is not, of course, designed as a long range hunting arm, but hunting accuracy out to 200 meters is very good, as I had a chance to discover with John Petitt's rifle.

Petitt, a USAF sergeant then stationed at Rhine-Main Air Base in West Germany, saved up his pennies and bought a Krieghoff Model Teck over-under rifle in 300 Winchester Magnum. He scoped it with a 3x9 Kahles in German claw mounts. That was only the start.

He decided he wanted one of a kind, so he took it to Rolf Peter, one of Germany's master firearms engravers, to have his personal touch added. Peter,

in his 40's, was born in Suhl, now in East Germany, but in 1947 followed his work to Münnerstadt in West Germany. He worked there as an apprentice until 1961 when he received a Master Engraver Certificate and went into business for himself. Peter spends most of his engraving time working for Waffen Frankonia, a large German mail order firm that specializes in guns and hunting gear, and for Pachmayr. But, as we can see, he does take individual commissions.

The engraving he did for John Petitt makes the Teck a masterpiece, in my opinion. John himself carefully planned the engraving, relief carving, the inlays, and was able to tell Rolf Peter just what he wanted. To go along with the rest, he had the stock carved with a relief pattern of oak leaves and acorns.

On the Teck, the left and right lockplates are provided with richly detailed heads of roe deer and wild boar. The bottom of the action shows the head of a regal red stag. The top lever is adorned with a gold-inlaid crown

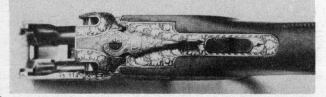

Fancy's owner, John Petitt, scopes his double rifle when posted on stand. He uses his prize rain or shine and has killed his share with it.

The German style of lavish embellishment does not disappear when the rifle is shouldered. This tang and top lever treatment remains in sight.

With a German rifle and hunting in Germany, American John Petitt blends into the local scene, with German clothes and the typical rifle carrying style of his companions.

and on the pistol grip cap are John Petitt's initials. The job took a year.

The rifle is a showpiece, but Petitt hunts with it frequently in Germany. He has taken numerous roe deer, red stag (*hirsch*) and wild boar with the gun.

It was at a range I found out why John Petitt—and by extension many others who hunt in Germany—like doubles for hunting. On a clear day with no wind, we fired 20 shots using Federal 200-grain factory loads at 100 meters.

The rifle was easy to shoot. The trigger pull is crisp without creep, and pulls off at about 3½ pounds. When you set the front trigger, you get a pull just over one pound.

I said "hunting accuracy" and that is what we got. The largest group we fired measured under 3″ and the smallest just under 2″. At 80 meters, the factory targets show, the rifle does better.

Compared to good magazine rifles, the one disadvantage of the double rifle is long range accuracy. For one thing, the barrels shift as they heat up. Something any double rifle owner should know is that Krieghoff sights in their doubles permitting only an 8 to 10 second interval between shots from the first and second barrel.

In practice, under hunting conditions, this is not so much of a disadvantage, as Petitt's trophies show. This showpiece works for him. Krieghoff builds good rifles, particularly for hunters. In fact, H. U. Krieghoff's motto is "Guns built by hunters for hunters." He has hunted the world wide with Krieghoff guns.

Sempert & Krieghoff was founded in Suhl in 1885 by Ludwig Krieghoff. The firm was the first to provide a method of custom stocking to fit the shooter and the first to use Duralumin for action bodies. Engineers and gunsmiths at Krieghoff are accustomed to significant innovation in firearms technology.

Their Model Teck over-under is built on an extra-strong shotgun frame, with a Kersten double cross bolt and double under lugs. Petitt's rifle has 25″ barrels and a length over-all of 42½″. The rifle, with its scope, weighs about 8½ pounds.

John Petitt might, of course, have gotten a fancy job straight from the factory. Krieghoff provides a wide selection of options, including engraving and wood carving. With Rolf Peter's help, however, Petitt got his very own gun. It is one man's fancy. •

A specific advantage of the double rifle for much hunting and travel to hunting is easy takedown, which makes it compact for packing and easy to clean.

Deeply cut pistol grip cap, with properly timed screws, displays Petitt's initials, also cut, not inlaid.

At the bench, Petitt finds his 300 Winchester Magnum's ability to deliver the shot satisfactory, as well he should, since it goes under 3″ consistently, using factory ammunition.

WHITETAILS:
North America's Real Challenge

BY DAN L. FLORES

Anyone who hunts whitetail deer knows he's been hunting. They are not easy if the goal is a good buck.

This is a good buck in any territory, though he'll be better later, both in antlers and in smarts. The sizes of whitetails vary greatly; their character, however, is the same everywhere.

HIGH IN A scarred pine, on the edge of an evergreen-blanketed hill which thrusts up from hardwood bottoms, a deer hunter waited. His ears told him dawn was approaching, but as yet no hint of light had come creeping through the forest. Nevertheless, fresh, early-morning sounds were beginning to fill the motionless air. A brown thrush had been the first to break the silence, setting up an awesome, rasping racket in a brushtop near the tree where the hunter perched so uncomfortably, and from somewhere deep in the hardwood bottoms came the excited chattering of a gray squirrel.

The hunter shifted his position to relieve cramped muscles and looked to the east. A grayish-red line ran along the horizon. He hoped shooting light would come soon.

Dawn broke. Somewhere, far back toward the highway, a rifle boomed. The grinding of truck gears floated faintly through the morning air, and a tiny breeze stirred the pine's uppermost limbs. The hunter peered through his scope to see if the crosshairs were visible. They were, and he was glad. He was positive the deer would be coming soon.

Minutes later a movement at the far edge of the pine thicket snapped him to attention. Motionless, he spent long moments studying the scene.

The movement had been made by a whitetailed deer—a doe. She had stepped cautiously from behind a brushpile, testing the wind with her

marvelous nose. Had the wind been just right, the doe may well have smelled the hunter in his perch high in the pine. But this morning there was no telltale whiff of human scent and, after a minute the doe began to move through the thick evergreens.

The hunter ignored her. With bated breath he scrutinized every inch of the forest the doe had just left. The rut was in full swing and he expected the big buck he was after to be right behind her. But 5 minutes passed, then 10, and the hunter began to feel sweat running down his temples. Then, just as he had begun to despair, he caught a glimpse of dark antlers moving against the shadowy backdrop. Eyes narrowed, he made out the form of a heavy-horned whitetail buck moving slowly along the series of scrapes, pausing at each one to sniff and then paw with a forefoot, massive neck

bulging and the weight of the heavy, wide antlers rocking his head up and down with each step.

The hunter was already in position, his 270 rested across a limb for added support. The buck, totally unaware of the drama in which he was a part, turned in the direction the doe had taken, stepping quickly, head down, through the pinestraw. The hunter sucked in a ragged breath and steadied the crosshairs a bit forward of the point of the deer's shoulder. The thrush was setting up an awful racket in the brush at the base of the tree, but for the hunter there was nothing in the whole universe but his rifle and that deer. His index finger began its smooth crush, and the still air was shattered as the 270 bucked against his shoulder.

Recoil blacked out the sight picture, but the hunter didn't need the scope to

their maturity, though the number of points is apt to vary widely from one year to the next. In old age the quality and size of the antlers usually deteriorates.

Traditionally, the size of the antlers has determined whether a whitetail is of trophy proportions. Number, length and evenness of points, spread, and heaviness of beam are all taken into consideration in evaluating trophy animals. Naturally, because of the great variations in size in the different locales in which whitetails are found, criteria for determining a trophy vary widely from one area to the next. In some regions a buck with a 12-inch

confirm the results of the shot. Out of the tail of his eye he had seen the heavy whitetail slump down in the tall, yellow grass between the pines and the hardwoods. The hunt was over.

The fine eight-point I nailed that morning in mid-November, 1973, was the 26th whitetailed deer I'd taken since I began hunting that species in the middle 1960s. Though not the best deer I've shot, he was nonetheless a beautiful representative of what many hunters regard as the grandest big game animal in North America. For me, that deer and that hunt epitomize what whitetail hunting is all about.

Whitetail Deer Habitat and Habits

It is a reiteration of the obvious to note that the whitetail is still our most wide-ranging and popular game animal. Except for a smattering of states in the far and middle West, subspecies of whitetails are found in every state of the Union, from Maine to Arizona, to say nothing of Canada, Mexico and points south. The average mature Eastern or Southern buck usually weighs less than 150 lbs. Some whitetails, particularly in the upper Midwest, grow much larger, however, with exceptional animals reaching a live weight of 300 lbs. On the other end of the scale, the two subspecies known as the Key deer and the Coues or Sonoran whitetail weigh less than 100 lbs. Small whitetails are also found in the "hill country" of central Texas. Mature bucks in this area seldom exceed 90-100 lbs., and does and young bucks of 60-75 lbs. are frequent.

A clean long-range shot is not the usual fare the Virginia white-tail serves, but croplands and powerline cuts sometimes give a good rifleman a chance. This wide-branching eight-pointer was worth some effort.

The whitetail has a number of characteristics which serve to distinguish it from other deer. For one thing, the hooves are thinner and much daintier than those of either mule deer or blacktails. Secondly, the whitetail has a large, flaglike tail which is cottonwhite underneath. In males, the points on the antlers project from a single beam. During its first fall, when a buck is 6-8 months old, it usually carries "buttons" with little or no projecting antler bone. One-and-a-half year old bucks commonly carry antlers totaling anywhere from 2 to 10 points, depending upon conditions of feed and heredity. Under normal conditions, bucks will grow heavier and often larger antlers each year throughout

antler spread is considered an excellent one, while in others a buck would not be given a second glance by a trophy hunter unless the inside spread exceeded 18 inches.

The difficulty of taking a whitetail buck is due to several habits of the species. Except under unusual conditions the whitetail is a nocturnal feeder and the great proportion of its activity takes place at night. The whitetail is also a browser, which means it normally is found in heavy cover or, at best, edge country where clearings meet with timber. Consequently, whitetails are simply hard to find; they move but little during the day, and what movement there is takes place in relatively heavy cover where seeing or approaching the animals is difficult.

To complicate the situation, whitetails are among the most nervous and wary of game animals. Their remarkable sense of smell is used to its fullest extent. Whitetails also have superb hearing, much better than a man's, and their eyesight, while weaker than the other senses, is still good. They spot horizontal movement against the vertical forest growth instantly, and often make out a motionless hunter, though they may not recognize him for what he is.

Once it identifies something as dangerous, the whitetail rarely panics, but seems to make a calculated decision as to the best method of escape. Often it will choose to remain motionless and depend upon its natural camouflage to render it undetectable. On other occasions it will skulk out of the area. Bucks are particularly adept at this. I once watched incredulously as a young whitetail buck used a fire lane scarcely 16-18 inches deep to escape my approach. The buck managed to move along it with only antlers and ears showing.

Sometimes the whitetail escapes danger by running, and I know of no other animal that can explode from cover and put distance between itself and a hunter more quickly. When in flight, the whitetail moves through the woods with exceptional grace and agility. Commonly it bounds away from danger, changing direction often, so that hitting it with a rifle seems impossible. In more open country the whitetail can run flat out in the manner of a racehorse, attaining a speed of 45 m.p.h. over short stretches. It is a habit of the whitetail, however, to run in wide circles, and rarely will it leave its home territory even when being pursued.

Much of the charm of whitetail hunting lies in the fact that these deer are so wary, and in the difficulty which normally accompanies the taking of a good animal. The whitetail has been called the only trophy which cannot be bought, and that's a pretty apt description. Once, at the famous YO Ranch in Texas, I saw two veteran hunters finally give up after three days of trying to take whitetail bucks—and whitetails are no more numerous anywhere in the world than they are on the YO. To my thinking, this says a lot for the whitetail.

I was fortunate enough to grow up in a region which was just being repopulated by whitetails as I became old enough to hunt them. The deer population in northwestern Louisiana was small in the early and mid '60s, and for a while sightings of deer were historic events. My brother had grown up in the same area a decade earlier, and though he spent every spare moment roaming the woods around home, he *never* saw a deer. It was in 1963 that I saw my first deer track in the woods. For three days I was so excited I couldn't sleep.

This unusual high rack would be penalized in Boone & Crockett scoring, but very few whitetail hunters could resist putting it on a wall.

First Deer

I killed my first whitetail—a doe—in 1964, when I was 15. At that time whitetails were still so scarce in my area that one would often hunt an entire season and see only two or three animals. The chief advantage of this—and I really believe it was an advantage—was that if you ever expected to kill a good whitetail, you damn well had to learn their habits and how to hunt them! Plenty of people became disgusted with the whole business, but I was one of those who stuck it out. In 1965 and 1966 I dropped two of the best bucks ever taken out of my area—a fine, dark-horned 8-pointer with an exceptionally heavy rack, and a beautiful 12-pointer which scored 148 on the Boone & Crockett scale. In 1968, Louisiana initiated its liberal 5-deer-a-season limit, and in the three years following I collected an even dozen fine Louisiana whitetails. The hunting was difficult (in fact, it still is exceptionally tough in that region), but to a dedicated young hunter that only heightened the satisfaction.

Since those halcyon days of the late '60s, I've had the privilege of hunting, studying, and photographing whitetailed deer in a good many areas of the country. Regardless of location, however, the whitetail is essentially the same animal, and hunting techniques which work well in one area will usually perform suitably in others provided the terrain and climate are not markedly dissimilar.

It has always been my feeling that matching wits with a whitetailed buck should be a solitary endeavor. I love companionship on a deer hunt, and some of my best memories are of isolated deer camps where three or four of us got away from it all for a few days. When the *hunting* started, however, we were on our own. It follows that I have never gone in much for the community-type hunts, two of the most common of which are drives and dog-hunting as it is conducted in the South. I don't deny that these methods work well and account for plenty of deer, but on the couple of occasions when I have bagged a deer in front of dogs or during a drive, I never experienced the exhilaration which comes from taking on an old buck on a one-to-one basis. Added to this is the inherent danger of community hunts, with standers sometimes lining roads and rights-of-way virtually elbow to elbow for a mile or more.

Almost as good as a fingerprint, this track tells of a large and heavy deer and the dewclaw imprints say "Buck!" Few old-timers could resist trying to follow this one.

A beat-up sapling and a smelly scrape will add up to horns if the hunter will give the project enough time.

The Lone Hunter

The solitary, or woodsman's, approach to deer hunting can be handled in a number of ways, all of which work well within their limitations. A common method in the Northwest and upper Midwest, where snow often accompanies the opening of deer season, is tracking—a technique now immortalized by Larry Benoit, who tracks high-country whitetails in the snowy mountains of Vermont. Tracking deer in snow is almost a science, but it's a science which can devolve into a marathon of endurance between deer and hunter.

Once the hunter has determined that a fresh set of tracks is that of a buck (difficult with medium-size tracks, but not impossible; a buck's hooves are usually more rounded than a doe's, and buck tracks tend to toe out slightly rather than pointing directly forward), he must attempt to come up on the animal from an unexpected direction, as older deer watch their backtrack carefully. Rarely can the hunter expect success by following doggedly directly on the tracks. Instead he must establish a general direction for the tracks and then use whatever knowledge he has of the country in attempting to come up on

the deer from other than behind it. It's hard, difficult work, but highly satisfying when it works.

In the central and southern portions of the whitetail's range, the relative absence of snow calls for a change in technique for the solitary hunter. Here the hunter must make a choice: should he engage in stalking, or still-hunting, and go after deer, or should he take a stand and hope that hunting pressure, or the deer's natural routine, if undisturbed, will bring the buck to him?

Of the two methods, still-hunting calls for more skill and woodsmanship, and for this reason I've always regarded it as more rewarding than stand-hunting. In crowded deer woods it can be dangerous, however, so it is best confined to private lands or middle-of-the-week forays when fewer hunters are in the woods. If conditions are right—especially when there is a heavy dew or light rain—the skillful still-hunter can sometimes take his pick of bucks.

Scrapes are where the deer make them, but the pattern is always clear. Look for more scrapes, Flores says, and then choose your stand accordingly and wait him out. He'll be along.

The still-hunter is taking the game to a whitetail on its home ground, where the deer has every advantage. It knows the country infinitely better, and its ability to detect the hunter is much superior to the hunter's ability to locate the deer. To offset these advantages the hunter must be adaptable. To counter the deer's acute sense of hearing, for example, the hunter must make every step with consummate care, avoid crunching leaves and snapping twigs, and he should wear soft clothing which does not rasp against brush. Camouflage will help

negate the deer's ability to spot foreign objects in its territory, but even more important is moving with infinite slowness, as deer spot movement readily. Two or three steps and a *long* pause—a minute or more—is none too slow. The hunter can reduce the deer's ability to spot him by moving with the sun at his back, and of course he always moves inside the edge of timber—never across openings. Perhaps most importantly, to counter the deer's superb nose, the hunter tries always to move *into* the wind.

Good still-hunters generally concentrate on feeding areas early and late. In my area of the country, deer feed primarily on acorns during the early part of the season, and still-hunting through an acorn flat just at the crack of dawn is an excellent method for getting action. Except during periods of a full moon (when deer feed all night, bed down before dawn, and then feed again for a short period around noon), or in exceptionally cold weather, whitetails bed down shortly

after sunup. Once the day begins to warm, then, the still-hunter must concentrate on finding bedded deer. Favored bedding locations vary widely in different parts of the country. In the South, deer generally bed higher up; prevailing breezes on the hills and ridgetops help cool them and drive away annoying insects. During cold weather, whitetails in both North and South move into heavy cover—canebrakes, thickets, swamps and brushy draws—which offer protection from the wind and good concealment. If the day is sunny, deer will move to the sunny side of a draw or thicket for warmth. During very warm weather, however, Northern whitetails bed in the low bottoms near cold streams which cool the air near them.

To spot deer, the still-hunter should kneel down at frequent intervals to peer under brush and the lower limbs of trees. He should look for moving legs, the flick of an ear or tail, in short, any *piece* of a deer, and he should listen carefully for the tiny sounds which characterize feeding or moving deer. The careful still-hunter will also check his backtrack occasionally for the curious whitetail that may circle around behind him.

Still-hunters commonly see more deer than hunters employing other methods, but unless one is skilled it can be frustrating, as most of the deer spotted will already have detected the hunter and will be making an escape. In the 5 or 6 years I've been still-hunting, I can recall only three whitetail bucks which were totally unaware of my presence when I squeezed off the shot. One, taken just outside an upland pine thicket, was so intent on trailing doe that he passed within 15 feet without seeing or smelling me. About 30 yards from me he paused to get his bearings and I drove a 130-gr. Nosler from my 270 through his lungs. He was only a forkhorn, but an exceptionally heavy one.

Stand Hunting

Probably the best method of deer hunting for the majority of hunters is stand-hunting. This is the most popular approach in the South and lower Midwest, and is in fact a fine method in any pole-and-timber whitetail cover. A tree stand is the most effective type, as deer seldom look up and the hunter's scent is carried on air currents which often pass over the animal's head. Tree standing also enables the hunter to see over intervening brush and cover a larger area. Taking a stand on the ground—preferably against a tree trunk or a brushpile to break your outline—is not ineffective, but the hunter must remain motionless.

Taking a good buck from a stand requires two things: patience and the ability to recognize and interpret deer sign. The location of the stand is all-important, and reading sign is the key to finding good stand locations. For stand-hunters, two types of sign are of paramount importance. These are runways (deer trails) and "scrapes."

Deer are creatures of habit, and they regularly follow the same trails

Good fit, light weight and a short barrel add up to the ideal deer rifle, Flores says, if the hunter can hit with it. Here he demonstrates his Model 70 Featherweight in the thick cover he finds typical.

through their range. Some runways, particularly those connecting feeding and bedding areas, are traveled more than others. These are the ones which are most productive in undisturbed woods. Runways can be hunted most successfully when 1) they are located in isolated areas, 2) tracks on them indicate two-way movement, and 3) they are used by a rutting buck and are flanked by scrapes. Runways are likewise productive when deer use them as prime routes to escape dogs or other hunters.

Deer Scrapes

The most important sign the hunter can locate, particularly if the weather has turned brisk, is a series of scrapes. I believe I was the first contemporary writer to point out the significance of scrape hunting for whitetailed deer, but since my first articles on the sub-ject appeared a few years ago, other writers have lifted my ideas, alas, without giving me credit.

At any rate, the presence of scrapes can be directly attributed to the onset of the rut. During the rut, a whitetail yields to two strong biological urges—the urge to mark off and defend a home territory from rivals, and the stronger urge to reproduce. A scrape is a pawed-out spot on the ground; usually fan-shaped, it may measure up to 5 or 6 feet across. Scrapes are made in series, serving the double function of marking off the buck's territory and as a rendezvous point for the buck and the does that are in season (does come in heat for only three days at a time, so timing is of utmost importance).

For the hunter, the most important thing to remember is that during the rut the buck will constantly be making the rounds of his scrapes, checking

This Model 70 standard rifle in 270 Winchester and a 4X scope makes a fine deer rifle, Flores thinks. He'll go with aperture sights, too, but not with scope magnification over 4X.

them over and over again to see if they are being visited by a receptive doe. During these hectic times the buck eats very little and spends a great deal of time dashing about its territory wild-eyed, with tongue lolling, or wallowing in his scrapes (and often grunting like a pig while doing so). To keep the scrapes "hot" he will re-paw them and urinate and defecate in them frequently. Build a stand over such a series of scrapes, have the patience to sit it out for two or three days, and you're virtually guaranteed a buck. Scrape hunting is that effective.*

Choice of Calibers

Suitable guns for whitetailed deer constitute the largest selection in sporting arms, so what is "best" for whitetails is a touchy subject. I have never felt that the type or caliber of the whitetail rifle was especially important. The average whitetail is a small animal, and it is usually taken at fairly close range, so neither worlds of power nor great accuracy are required. That is why such cartridges as the 250-3000 and the 30-30 have always been viewed as excellent whitetail rounds.

Actually, what is required is a rifle which shoots a bullet that will expand quickly on a soft-skinned, light-framed animal, and preferably will punch through and leave a blood trail in case the deer runs off. Incidentally, many whitetails do not drop in their tracks even when hit well with a suitable cartridge/bullet combo. Out of my 28 deer, only 7 dropped in their tracks; most ran from 10 to 150 yards before dropping, and practically every deer I've shot was hit either through the lungs or the shoulder. That's why a blood trail is important.

Minimum deer cartridges begin with the 6mms. In fact, in Texas, where more deer are taken every year than in any other state in the country, the 243 is one of the most favored deer cartridges. My own experience with the 243 has been fairly extensive. I've taken 7 whitetails with my M70 Featherweight in this caliber. Six of these were one-shot kills, but of the 3 whitetails I've wounded and lost, 1 was hit through the back ribs with a 243 and a light varmint bullet. In the 6mms I prefer 95- and 100-gr. bullets for deer—specifically the 95-gr. Nosler (which can be driven to 3,281 fps with 47/IMR-4831 in my rifle), and the

100-gr. Hornady. I've chronographed the latter bullet at 3,135 fps when backed by 47/N-205. That seems astounding from the 243 case, but that's what I got. Performance of both these bullets on deer is superb, by the way, with quick expansion and quarter-size exit holes.

I've taken 12 deer with the 270 and my favorite load is the 130-gr. Nosler in front of 55/4350 (about 3,100), and a couple apiece with the 25-06 (120-gr. Hornady and 54/IMR-4831 for 3,213) and the 30-06 (150-gr. Nosler or Hornady and 60/4350 for about 3,000 fps). Each of these cartridges, plus dozens more in the same power range, is excellent for deer with good bullets and correct shot placement. Medium weight bullets work best on deer regardless of caliber, as most of the heavier weights are designed for bigger game and tend to punch through whitetails without imparting as much shock.

In addition to the one mentioned, I like 100-gr. bullets in the smaller 25s such as the 250-3000 and the 257 Roberts; 125-gr. in 6.5; 140- and 150-gr. in the 7mms; and 150-gr. bullets for such 30-cal. rounds as the 30-30, 30-40, 300 Savage, 308, and 30-06. In the 35 Remington and 358, I prefer a 180-gr. such as the Speer flat point for whitetails. I base my choices here on killing ability rather than the old worn-out brush-busting theory, for regardless of bullet weight I've never seen a dependable and consistent brush bucker.

Action type is relatively unimportant in most whitetail hunting. Pumps and semi-autos often get the nod because of their speed of fire, but in reality, there isn't a great deal of difference in speed among the various action types in getting off *aimed* second and third shots. Keep in mind, also, that the best shot at a buck is usually the first shot. Regardless of action, the ideal whitetail rifle should be light, fit well, and quick to get into action. I like rifles of 8 lbs. or less with scope and sling, and for timber hunting the barrel shouldn't exceed 22 inches. My current favorite whitetail rifle is a pre-'64 M70 Featherweight 30-06 with a 4x Redfield in Redfield JR mounts. This rifle weighs less than 7½ lbs. and handles like lightning in thick cover, yet is accurate enough for the occasional long shot down a right-of-way or across a cutover pasture.

There are only two *good* choices in sighting equipment for deer hunting, in my opinion. One is the large aperture receiver sight, which is comparatively inexpensive and the best type

of iron sight ever devised. The other —and the better choice— is a low-powered, low-mounted scope of from 1½x to a maximum of 4x or 5x. Aside from the obvious advantages of light-gathering ability and a clearer sight picture for added safety, the most important quality of a scope for whitetails is that it makes it possible to pick a hole through intervening brush so the bullet won't be deflected. The scope also performs better on running game. The correct procedure for using a scope on running deer, by the way, is to throw the rifle up like a shotgun, pointing it with both eyes open before looking through the scope.

Lure of The Whitetail

In closing, I can't help feeling the futility of trying to depict with written script the fascination and appeal of whitetail hunting. I'm reminded of all the magic moments that are integral with deer hunting: the hours and days of early fall spent roaming reddened forest, scouting for sign and attempting to pin down a particular old buck's routine; the pleasant labor of constructing a stand over scrapes that only you and the deer know about, or of poring over topographical maps in an effort to anticipate what a buck will do as you follow his tracks through a sparkling landscape of fresh snow; a forest coming to life in that pre-dawn dimness when you can barely see the eyelets of your boots; the magical materialization from limbs, brush, and branches of a seer's leg, or ear, or its body outline; the glint of first sunlight on white tines as a heavy-antlered buck steps cautiously between the trees; the oily snick of the safety being flicked off, the first rush of buck fever, and then the reverberating *boom!* of your rifle echoing through a suddenly still forest; the drumming of hooves as the buck bounds down the hill, and then, just at the edge of hearing, the crash as it runs headlong into a sapling in a shower of leaves, one antler tine digging a long furrow in the black earth, and the long span of belly-hair shining white against the brown woodland floor; the smell of good, honest sweat as you and your partner toil to drag your buck (or his) back to camp; and finally, a glittering canopy of stars, and a frosty night, and the dance of fire-cast shadows on the tent as you and your companions laugh softly and talk and dream secret dreams of other deer and other wilderness deer camps.

That, as well as I can portray it, is the fascination of the whitetailed deer. ●

*This presupposes that the rutting period and the hunting season coincide. There are many whitetail regions in the U.S. where this is not the case.   Ed.

Airgun Accessories: A Review

A brief guide to those
important gadgets that make
the sport more enjoyable

by J. I. GALAN

A fully-accessorized FWB-80 match pistol
sporting a Bushnell 74-2911-X (2.5x) pistol
scope with special mount. Also, a Custom
air pistol holster, small accessory pouch
and a large, zippered accessory pouch for
carrying pellet tins, etc.

As AIRGUN technology approaches an unprecedented plateau of refinement and popularity, airgun accessories have arrived at a rate hardly thinkable just a few years ago. And the end of this accessory boom is nowhere in sight. Each passing month, more gadgets specifically designed or modified for airguns are reaching the market. Many of the available accessories are in great demand—telesights, for instance—while some are so esoteric they interest only a small group of airgun purists.

Even the most casual airgunner will, sooner or later, decide to "accessorize" the airgun by adding better sights or a sling. The fundamental idea, of course, is to improve or further develop the over-all performance and handling characteristics of the gun, and in turn enhance the shooter's enjoyment of the sport. Airgun accessories don't necessarily have to mount on guns, either. A great deal of shooting enjoyment can be derived from a basic air rifle or pistol simply by

having a fun and safe target to shoot at. This brings us to the first category of accessories that we will cover in this dissertation: targets and target traps.

I remember, growing up in the late fifties, that when I wanted backyard target practice with any of my airguns, all I could do was stuff an empty cardboard box full of old magazines and newspapers. There were perhaps a couple of BB or pellet traps available commercially, but they were hardly ever seen on dealers' shelves. The situation is quite different today! There are at least a dozen different pellet trap models available now, some of which incorporate their own spinning or flip-down targets.

Airgun targets themselves have also evolved and diversified. The current metallic silhouette shooting craze has also jumped into the field of airguns, properly scaled down, of course. Paper targets have also multiplied and added new variety to the more formalized sport of paper-punching.

The virtually silent traps sold by Air Rifle Headquarters (247 Court Street, Grantsville, WV 26147), and by Beeman Precision Airguns (47 Paul Drive, San Rafael, CA 94903), are among the most popular. ARH offers three different sizes, starting at $13.95 for the Lambert model, which measures just 6⅝"x6⅝"x2½" deep, on up to the large Executive model, selling for $34.50. Beeman sells two versions of these silent traps, the DeLuxe and the Compact Wall-Hung model. Both have the same frontal dimensions and retail for around $34. All utilize thick layers of ballistic putty in order to soak up pellets and BB's safely, in almost total silence. Paper targets are simply pinned to the cardboard face sheet. Apartment dwellers will find any of these compact traps an extremely useful accessory for airgun practice right at home, without the slightest chance of disturbing the neighbors.

Another trap which has become available in recent months comes from

Action Target Products, Inc. (3895 West 2nd. Avenue, Hialeah, FL 33012). The Action Target trap is made of thin but tough synthetic material that is virtually indestructible. Although much larger than the aforementioned silent models, it offers some unusual design features that make it extremely useful. Light weight is one, so it may be hung from a nail as well as placed free-standing. The most unusual feature is the way this trap traps. As the synthetic walls deflect the projectile toward the rear, an ordinary roll of paper towels catches them, quietly and without ricochet! Every hundred shots or so, the roll of paper towels should be rotated slightly to expose a fresh section. When the entire roll is pretty well shot up, a new one is dropped in and you're ready for several hundred more shots. This trap retails for around $45.

Action Target Products also sells a novel line of airgun and 22 rimfire silhouette targets that fall down when hit and can be reset from the firing line by means of a string. These silhouettes are made of a self-sealing plastic that can be used through hundreds of hits from any high-power pellet rifle, as well as 22 rimfires. They come complete with bases, which are made of the same material and can be placed almost anywhere. The silhouettes are bright orange, while the bases are white and never need repainting. Besides the regular line of standard "metallic" silhouettes, Action Target Products informed me recently that rat and rabbit silhouettes may be added soon in order to make the sport of silhouette shooting more meaningful to airgunners. I have tested several of the current production silhouettes as well as some of the experimental models for months and can vouch for the fact that they're loads of fun and a real challenge to shoot at. Priced at only $11 each, they are just what the doctor ordered for informal plinking.

Daisy offers a pellet trap complete with the four different animal silhouettes, that spin when hit. Intended basically for shooting at 10-meters, it can be moved much farther away for greater challenge to one's shooting skills. Beeman also sells a metallic silhouette pellet trap in which the four basic metal silhouettes flip back when hit. It comes complete with its own cord that resets all four silhouettes right from the firing line with just one tug. Also available from Beeman is a complete set of 20 metallic silhouettes (5 of each animal) scaled down exactly to meet NRA specifications for the new airgun

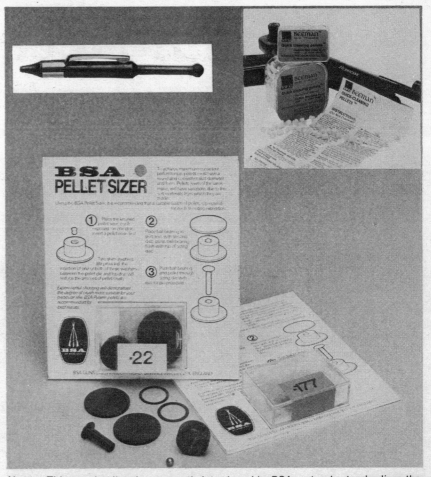

Above—This novel pellet sizer, recently introduced by BSA, not only standardizes the outside diameter of the pellet skirt, but the *inside diameter* as well. Suggested retail price should be approximately $10. The Beeman Pell-Seat (Inset, top left) is a handy little device that helps to place pellets correctly in the breech of most spring-piston guns. VFG quick-cleaning felt pellets (Inset, top right) are an important accessory to have. You can shoot your airgun clean with them!

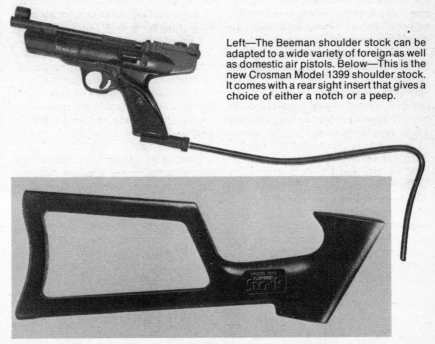

Left—The Beeman shoulder stock can be adapted to a wide variety of foreign as well as domestic air pistols. Below—This is the new Crosman Model 1399 shoulder stock. It comes with a rear sight insert that gives a choice of either a notch or a peep.

The Beeman Model 66 features parallax correction dial, graduated in yards and meters, plus pellet drop dials set on the w&e knobs.

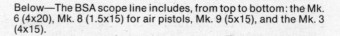

Below—The Beeman Model 30 (4x20) air rifle scope. Inexpensive and yet, rugged.

Below—The BSA scope line includes, from top to bottom: the Mk. 6 (4x20), Mk. 8 (1.5x15) for air pistols, Mk. 9 (5x15), and the Mk. 3 (4x15).

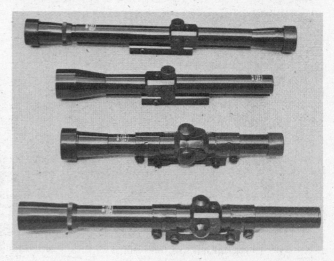

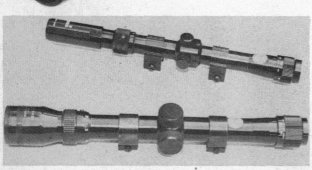

Above—Also available from ARH, The Tasco 630V-FM (top) and the Tasco 611V-FM. Both feature variable power and parallax correction dials.

metallic silhouette course. The entire set retails for approximately $50. Crosman Air Guns is also likely to have sets of metallic silhouettes for airguns available by the time you read this.

Beeman sells the Johannsen electric target carrier, complete with back plate. This superb European unit is one of those exotic accessories for serious shooters who must have and can afford the very best. It is ideal for those who are fortunate enough to have a permanent airgun range built right in their homes. Priced just shy of $400, the basic Johannsen unit is definitely one of the most expensive accessories available at the present time. An even more expensive model is also available, which is intended for a special 10-meter crossbow, as well as for airguns.

There are a couple of traps available commercially for use with BB guns. One of these comes from Daisy and consists simply of a cardboard box with a front cutout and a sheet of a rubbery material that stops BB's safely and without ricochet after they have gone through the paper target in front. These Daisy BB traps can also be used safely with pellet guns having muzzle velocities *under* 400 fps, which immediately makes them attractive

for use with several popular domestic and a few foreign air pistol models. The Daisy BB trap is available at most gun shops and department stores, and it retails for approximately $4.

Marksman Products, Inc. also produces an attractive BB and low-velocity pellet trap of the same general type as the Daisy model. The Marksman trap, however, comes complete with its own roll-up target, having seven different and colorful scenes, from Dinosaurs to Space Wars. It has a double safety inner trap made of urethane-treated ballistic cloth that will withstand pellets and BB's up to 450 fps. A nylon safety netting safely controls rebounds. This Marksman unit is also widely available, retailing for around $6.

Having any of the aforementioned targets and traps, however, is only part of the fun of shooting at them with airguns. If you can't hit the target because of lack of skill, then practice and more practice will make you a better shot. If you are already a decent shot and yet feel that your shooting can be improved with the use of better sights, then another vast area of airgun accessories awaits you.

It's no secret that most adult air rifles are capable of far more precise shooting than that possible with iron

sights. In the case of some domestic air rifle models, in particular, the sights that come with the guns can't be described as anything but rudimentary. Since most of those rifles also have receiver grooves for telesight use, why not take full advantage of their intrinsic accuracy? Telescopic sights greatly simplify the process of aiming by placing both the target and the sight—in this case some sort of crosshairs—on the same plane, while at the same time magnifying the target image itself for even better shot placement.

(EDITOR'S NOTE: Writer Galan here seems to coin a new word for telescopic sight—telesight. No doubt it's been done before, but this incarnation is Galan's, not mine. It makes, I might observe, as much sense as the widely used "scope sight" and offers more euphony. K.W.)

The only problem encountered with the mating of airguns and telesights stems from the fact that airguns are relatively short-range instruments, while regular telesights—even those used on rimfire rifles—are intended for much longer distances. As a result, if you clamp just any ol' scope on your pet air rifle, the results may be quite discouraging. Parallax is the apparent shift of the target image and the reticle, relative to each other, when

This Johannsen electric target carrier with pellet plate is ideal for indoor airgun ranges.

Right—Lightweight pellet trap is from Action Target Products. The trap is a roll of paper towels.

Right—Action Target Products offers all four of the regular animal silhouettes in self-sealing plastic.

Below—The Marksman BB/pellet trap with roll-up targets offers lots of fun for young and grownups alike.

Left—ARH sells these extremely efficient Silent pellet traps. They're filled with ballistic putty and come in three different sizes.

the shooter's eye is not perfectly centered on the scope axis and is especially evident at very short ranges. In order to obtain good results *consistently* from a scoped air rifle, the scope itself should be parallax-adjusted for short distance, say 20 to 30 yards. Fortunately, there are now quite a few telesights available that meet that requirement. In addition, some of the newest models incorporate parallax-adjustment controls, so that the shooter can quickly and easily set his scope for any given range.

Air Rifle Headquarters currently offers thirteen different telesights especially selected for airgun use. Two of those models are pistol scopes by Bushnell, while the remaining eleven models are for air rifles, made by both Bushnell and Tasco. From the latter, ARH carries eight different models, from the inexpensive 601 T-X (4x with ¾″ tube and ring mounts) at around $30, to the superb model 611V-FM (2x-6x), retailing for around $150 plus mounts. The Tasco 611V-FM, as well as the 630V-FM (3x-7x) come with parallax adjustment rings, graduated in distance from 25 to 300 ft. (630) and from 33 to 300 ft. (611). These rings also act as a range-finder, which makes these scopes ideal for field use. Should the shooter forget to dial the

correct setting for a given range, the target will appear fuzzy, a reminder to adjust parallax. The rest of the Tasco models sold by ARH are parallax-corrected.

The three Bushnell air rifle scopes sold by ARH are the 72-3003-X (4x), which goes for $52, including standard mount; the model 72-3103-X (3x-7x), selling for just under $60, with standard mount; and the petite but excellent model 70-2545 (1½x-4½x), which costs $149.95, plus mounts.

Air pistol shooters may also squeeze out more of their pistols' built-in precision by installing telesights. ARH carries the Bushnell model 74-2910-X (1.3x) at $116.90, including installation fee; and the Bushnell 74-2911-X (2.5x), which retails for $121.90, including installation.

Beeman carries a total of five air rifle scopes, plus two air pistol scopes in their Blue-Ribbon/Blue-Ring line. The top of the line is the Model 66. This telesight features 2 to 7x zoom, parallax adjustment ring similar to the aforementioned Tasco 611V-FM model and so-called "silhouette" click windage elevation knobs. The latter incorporate graduated scales that allow the shooter to compensate for pellet drop at various distances. This telesight costs approximately $140,

without mounts. A special version of this same model, adapted for Running Target, has a dot set on each side of a special thin-line horizontal crosshair. This model costs about $25 more than the standard Model 66.

The Beeman scope Models 60 and 50, like the 66, also have a 1″ tube and 32mm objective. The 60 has a 2-7x zoom (about $100), while the 50 is a fixed 2.5x sight (about $60). Both of these come without mounts. Next in line come the Model 40 and the Model 30. The Model 40 is a really compact (only 9¾″ long) and useful ⅞″ tube, with a 1.5 to 4x zoom capability. It comes with its own milled mounts and, for about $60, is a truly outstanding telesight to have on just about *any* fine air rifle. The Model 30 (4x) is the least expensive Beeman scope, retailing for just under $20; however, it is still a superb value when one considers that it comes with all glass coated lenses and milled mounts.

The Beeman air pistol scopes include the elegant Model 25 Blue Ribbon and the economical but tough Model 20 Blue Ring. The Model 25 (2x, 20mm objective), features a 1″ tube and the aforementioned silhouette elevation scales set on the w&e knobs. It sells for around $120, sans mounts. The Model 20 (1.5x) features all glass coated lenses and milled mounts. It retails for just under $40. *All* of the preceding Beeman scopes have the practical 5-point (or dual X) reticle.

Beeman also distributes the truly superb—and expensive—Nickel Running Boar Scope. This state-of-the-art glass is, as its name implies, used by shooters who participate in running target events and who want the best that money can buy. At around $500, the Nickel scope definitely seems to be a frivolous and exotic accessory, unless you happen to be a dedicated shooter going after some *real* gold at the international level.

There is yet another line of airgun telesights available in the U.S. The BSA line is distributed by General Sporting Goods Corp. (798 Cascadilla Street, Ithaca, NY 14850). Of the six airgun scopes sold under the BSA label, at least four are available to American airgunners at the time of this writing. These are the models: Mk. 3 (4x, 15mm), Mk. 6 (4x, 20mm), Mk. 8 air pistol scope (1.5x, 15mm), and the Mk. 9 (5x, 15mm). Both the Mk. 3 and the Mk. 9 come with regular fine crosshair reticles, while the Mk. 6 and the Mk. 8 feature the European-style 3-post reticle. The latter I find quite handy, especially for targets in dim light or even for quick-shooting situations. All of these models are competitively priced and include mounts.

In addition to regular telesights, there are a variety of point-on-target, non-magnifying sights currently available, which can add quite a bit of pizzazz to your airgunning. Since there is no magnification of the image, there is no parallax problem either. They are excellent primarily for quick-shooting situations or for moving targets but can do a creditable job on regular, deliberate shooting situations as well. These sights have no critical eye relief or restricted pupil exits and permit bi-ocular vision, which translates into a field of view close to 180° wide.

The most expensive of these sights is the Aimpoint, made in Sweden. This sight utilizes a battery-operated diode that creates a bright red point of light. The latter can be controlled in intensity to suit any ambient light condition. After sighting in, just place the bright point of light on the target and shoot. The Aimpoint comes supplied with two polarizing filters—one for the front lens and one for the rear lens—and a set of mercury batteries. Special mounts that fit the receiver grooves of different European air rifles are available as well from Aimpoint at

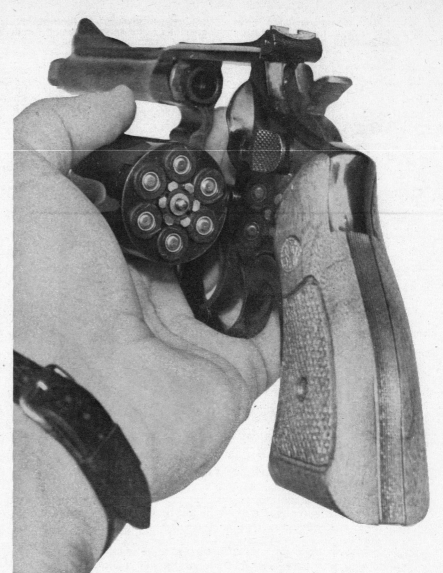

Above—The Impac kit from Taurus International allows a 38 Spl. revolver, such as this S&W Model 15, to fire 177-cal. pellets at approximately 400 fps.

Below—These are the major components of the Impact Handgun Conversion Kit, from top to bottom: 6″ and 4″ barrel inserts in 177-cal., 9mm P and 38 Spl. plastic casings (loaded). Below that, the components of each cartridge: the pellet, pyrotechnic tube and casing.

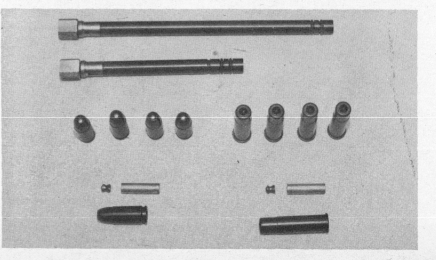

Designed especially for the Webley "Hurricane" air pistol, this Beeman holster is made of California latigo leather with a tough oil finish. About $20.

Below—This breathable expanded vinyl zip-up case from Beeman allows moisture to evaporate while shedding water externally.

This Deluxe Leather zip-up pistol rug can protect your valuable air pistol, in style. Available from Beeman in medium and extra-large sizes, about $17 and $19 respectively.

Below—The Beeman Professional Pistol Case can fit two large air pistols and accessories easily and securely.

Right—This leather holster for large spring-piston air pistols is available from Air Rifle Headquarters for $12.50.

extra cost. This sight sells for around $160, available from Aimpoint U.S.A., Inc. (201 Elden Street, Herndon, VA 22070).

Tasco offers the Tasco Rama, which has an electronically illuminated red aiming point. While in some aspects similar to the Aimpoint sight, the Tasco Rama retails for a bit less and the #758 is available with mounts that fit grooved receivers.

Weaver's Quick-Point Model R-22, designed primarily for 22 rimfire rifles, can be used readily and successfully on most air rifles with receiver grooves. It utilizes available light to illuminate its bright orange dot and is sighted in just like a regular telescopic sight. As with the two aforementioned models, the shooter looks right through the sight at his target, placing the dot on it. Retailing for around $60, this is a straightforward and economical sight to have on any adult air rifle intended for plinking and pest-control chores.

A slightly different point-on-target sight which is now available in the U.S. is the Single-Point. While the shooter can't see through this sight, it nevertheless still places a red aiming point on the target by utilizing the combined effect of both eyes. One eye looks at the red point in the tube as the other eye sees the target. Both views are then combined as one with the result that the red point is seen superimposed on the target. It is definitely a peculiar sight and some people never get used to it. Adjustments are similar to those of a standard scope. Beeman sells it for around $150, plus mounts.

A dandy little sight that I have been using for some time on a few of my pet air pistols is the relatively new Insta-Sight from Thompson/Center. This tiny one-power sight is only 2¾" long and it adapts easily to air pistols that have receiver grooves or those that can be fitted with special grooved bases. The Insta-Sight utilizes a reticle consisting of four tapered posts that don't touch each other at the center. The posts are light green, while the rest of the optics has a pinkish hue. Such colors certainly give this sight a unique slant that may appeal to those who would like to add a futuristic feel to their air pistol plinking. Available from Thompson/Center Arms (Farmington Road, Rochester, NH 03767).

Shooters who prefer the traditional aperture or peep sights can also pick and choose from among the wide variety of such sights currently available. ARH and Beeman sell several different European models for certain specific models and brands of air rifles. Also available from those outfits are Williams peep sights specially adapted to fit the receiver grooves of most European air rifles currently available in the U.S. These same firms can provide a staggering array of front and rear sight accessories—such as inserts, filters, shades, etc.—to please even veteran Olympic shooters!

You don't have to be a member of that select group, of course, in order to reap the benefits of some of the gadgets that help those lofty marksmen attain world titles. Nor do you need to spend a lot of money for some of those accessories, either. Take pellet sizers, for instance. These nifty little items can make a dramatic difference in group size, even when run-of-the-mill bulk-packed pellets are used. They do away with differences among pellet skirt diameters, which automatically reduces group size, sometimes by as much as 40 percent. Domestic pellets, notorious for their often astronomical variances, can be made to shoot almost as well as many of the better foreign-made pellets after being run through one of these sizing dies.

At the present time there are three pellet sizers on the market. One model, the Giles Sizing Die, is available from ARH. It comes in three inside diameters: .178″, .179″ and .180″, each going for $8.50, plus $9.50 for the plunger, which fits all three dies. The other pellet sizer model is available from Precision Pistols (6278 Hamilton Lane, La Crescenta, CA 91214). It sizes all pellets to a uniform .179″ diameter and consists also of the die itself and a plunger. This particular pellet sizer, which retails for $20 postpaid, was developed by Don Nygord, Pan American Gold Medalist in air pistol and U.S. Air Pistol Champion. The third model comes from BSA and is available in the U.S. through Precision Sports (P.O. Box 30-06, Ithaca, NY 14850). This sizer *appears* to be more complicated to use than the two previous models, simply because it consists of seven parts. While a bit slower to use than the others, the BSA Pellet Sizer offers the added bonus of re-forming the *inside* diameter of the pellet skirt as well as the outside diameter. This is an important consideration that can make a world of difference when using low-cost bulk pellets. The BSA sizer should retail for approximately $10.

One of the most useful and simple devices to appear in a long time has been marketed recently by Beeman. It is a pell-seat that enables the shooter to load spring-piston airguns, especially barrel cockers, easily and *without* damaging the pellets in the process. The Beeman Pell-Seat is shaped like a small ballpoint pen, with pocket clip and all. One end is shaped into a hard ball, for smoothing out irregularities in pellet skirts during loading. The other end has a rounded point, which can be used to push the pellet right into the rifling. This accessory retails for $4.95 and is a virtual must.

Speaking of pellets. Where do you carry your pellets when you go hunting or plinking? One of the most common places is the good ol' shirt pocket. This method can lead to an awful lot of damaged or lost pellets, though. Leather belt pouches, originally designed to carry 22 rimfire ammo, are now the perfect way to carry a large quantity of pellets, securely, afield. ARH and Beeman both sell these pouches for around $14. They are plastic-lined inside and have a spring-loaded top that is easily activated for opening or closing.

Carrying your airgun(s) properly also calls for some special accessories, such as holsters, cases and slings. In the case of imported air pistols, both ARH and Beeman offer a variety of custom holsters, designed specifically to fit most of the air pistols sold by those two companies. They also offer a number of rifle and pistol cases, as well as slings. Crosman also markets an entire line of air pistol holsters tailored to fit Crosman pistols, of course. These particular holsters are all made from top-grade cowhide and are very reasonably priced at around $7 each.

Crosman has also launched a novel accessory for one of their pistol models in recent months. The 1399 Custom Shoulder Stock fits the Crosman 1322 and 1377 pneumatic pistols, as well as the discontinued Crosman pistol models 1300, 130, 137, 150, 157, and 105. This handy accessory is made of high-impact plastic with a pebble black finish and can be installed in seconds, using the same two grip screws that come with the pistol. In addition, the Stock comes with a reversible rear sight element that can be used as an open sight or as a peep sight. The Stock turns any of the aforementioned pistol models into compact, yet superbly efficient mini-rifles, since the steady support gained with the stock means superior accuracy. In these days of runaway inflation, the Crosman Shoulder Stock sells for an incredibly low $10 to $13 at most gun shops and department stores that carry the Crosman line.

Beeman can equip most of the air pistols sold by them with detachable skeletonized shoulder stocks. Prices vary somewhat, depending on the type of adapter socket needed for each specific model but generally the entire setup can be had for around $23.

There is one more accessory that I'd like to include here, although it relates to airguns in a roundabout way only. This particular accessory is, in fact, intended for powder-burning handguns, more specifically 357 Magnum/38 Special revolvers and 9mm semi-autos. It comes in kit form, complete with all the necessary components to turn most of the above caliber handguns into quiet pellet-firing training weapons. The kit is imported by Taurus International, Ltd. (59 Ann Drive South, Freeport, NY 11520). It consists of two 177-cal. barrel inserts, one for guns with a 4″ barrel and the other for a 6″ barrel. In addition, there are several plastic 38/357 and 9mm casings. Each casing is prepared with a pyrotechnic tube, a box of which is supplied with the kit. These tubes have small pistol primers set at one end. A 177-cal. pellet (a box of about 100 is included also) is dropped nose first into the primer hole, then pushed forward with a pyrotechnic tube. The latter is seated flush with the base of the casing, exposing the primer.

Both revolvers and automatics are loaded in the normal manner. Very realistic combat-style practice can be had right at home with revolvers. Automatics must have the slide manually operated after each shot, for obvious reasons. The muzzle velocity attained by pellets used with this kit out of a 4″ barrel is around 400 fps. At 10 meters, most shots group within 2 inches and the noise level is comparable to that made by a CO_2 or pneumatic gun. The Impac Handgun Training Conversion Kit retails for around $40 and truly adds a new perspective to firearms training or plinking, with the tremendous convenience of a pellet gun.

Trying to cover each and every available airgun accessory would demand the writing of an entire book. The accessories seem to be the most important or the most popular with airgunners. By the time this is published, some of the prices given may be somewhat higher.

An airgun that by itself might rate as mediocre may be upgraded by adding the right accessories. This dissertation will hopefully serve as a handy guide to those who wish to get more out of their airguns. ●

BOOTS
in the uplands

Duffey wears rubber bottom pacs as Pumpkin, an English Springer Spaniel, puts a cock bird into flight. Bauer photo.

If you hunt birds and small game, just one pair of boots won't do.

by DAVE DUFFEY

A FAMILIAR shotgun, a willing gun dog and a comfortable pair of boots make a triangular base to support the most enjoyable days hunters spend in the uplands. This is about boots.

There is no all-around boot, as most of us who hunt have discovered; certainly no perfect boot any more than there is an ideal gun or the all-purpose hunting dog that can most effectively deal with all of the situations encountered during a given hunting season. Furthermore, no two people possess the same feet and legs, endurance, strength, tone and pain threshold.

Thus, a wiry trapper I hiked with in the Ontario bush wore cheap tennis shoes and stayed happy. Maybe that type of footgear, jogging shoes or what have you suits you too. For most, only boots qualify as footgear for the serious hunter.

Every hunter has favorite boots. If they are his *only* boots, a hunter handicaps himself and his day is literally and figuratively dampened any time another type of boot would have kept him dry, comfortable and going strong at the day's end.

Four types of boots standing at attention in your closet will ready you for virtually anything and enable you to go to the limits of your personal endurance: all-leather (except for sole and/or heel) of the type epitomized by such brands as Red Wing, Irish Setter and Russell Birdshooter; rubber bottom/leather top shoe pacs of the L. L. Bean prototype; all rubber, calf-high boots styled like Uniroyal's Red Ball Calhoun; hip boots from any of several manufacturers of good quality rubber products.

On idyllic hunting days, when the air is crisp and you can smell the wine in the breezes that bring game scent to a dog's nose, the leather birdshooting boot is the only "right" footgear. So let's begin from that end:

All-Leather Boots

Proper fit is important, but you are the only judge of "feeling good." Well-made boots of proper size *and width* should feel okay when first pulled on over the weight of sock you customarily wear and, if worn around the yard or downtown for a few days, will break in by the end of their first hunt without laming their occupants. Too tight is terrible but, while feet will enlarge after long hours of walking, buying boots larger than your other comfortable shoes will cause slippage resulting in foot and toe cramps as you unconsciously try to compensate for a boot not molded to the foot.

If you insist on anticipating foot spread or frequently want to accommodate extra or heavy sock bulk, get a wider width or at most a half-size larger than ordinary shoes.

For anyone in a masochistic mood: putting on new boots, standing in water until they soak through and then walking them dry will mold them to individual feet. For me, that's a lot of unnecessary bother when wet grass, wet snow, fording a shallow creek and other day to day hunting experiences accomplish the same thing. Of course, this masochism will produce any problem there is right at home, which is a benefit.

Other than in a desert, leather soles are slippery and impractical; hobnails and logger's "corks" are only for those who never walk into a house or drive a car without pulling off their boots; and crepe rubber or composition soles of cord and rubber are as good as anything. "Vibram" soles with large, open lugs are essentially for specialty boots, best used in mountainous and rocky hunting. They grip good, but are heavy, hard and interfere with "ground feel" which is important to a man on foot just as "road feel" contributes to safe and proper handling of an automobile. And they haul all sorts of crud into a house or car. If boot soles, and particularly heels, are extremely hard they can give their wearer a headache or back, shoulder and leg pain as surely as a straight-pasterned horse's jarring gait will distress its rider.

Every hunting boot should have a definite heel with sharp corners and front edge. It will save serious slips going down inclines, on hillsides and when oak leaves, pine needles or light snow makes footing treacherous. A good heel will properly pitch the foot to avoid calf muscle and Achilles tendon strains, as well.

Because they are comfortable for standing and walking on hard surfaces, men who work in factories and garages have made wedge soles popular. They are dangerous for outdoorsmen. When the tread design, which provides the only grip on the walking surface, wears, the soles assume ski-like qualities on snow and other smooth, slippery surfaces.

Boot vamps and uppers should be oil-tanned leather, preserved, kept supple and, to some extent, waterproofed by application of inexpensive neatsfoot oil or good commercial boot dressings that come in paste or liquid form, like Snow-Proof, Pecard and Red Wing. If you decide to "make your own," ingredients like mink oil,

beeswax and beef tallow are effective. Avoid petroleum base oils. Silicone treatment may be recommended for some non-oil tanned leathers, but it is costly and offers no advantages over conventional "boot greases" when it is required.

Blame it on tradition or perception of that tradition, but too many hunting boots feature "moccasin toes" that are cosmetic frauds and less practical than smooth-toed boots. Because it had no hard sole, the Indian's moccasin was, of necessity, seamed and sewed on top rather than nailed and stitched to a formed sole. A day afield

Leather uppers without moc toes, like these Dunhams, get Duffey's vote on most nice days.

in true moccasins would put most modern nimrods into the hospital, but the idea of moccasin comfort has become so ingrained that faking the real thing sells boots.

In true moccasin construction, some firms, like Russell Moccasin Co., have added soles and heels to the basic natural "foot cradle." Most simply adorn their boots with stitched instep-to-toe ridges.

That moccasin-top ridge forms a dam, holding water and wet snow on the top of the boot foot; the stitching permits penetration, accelerating wet foot discomfort; and the prominent ridge is subject to premature wear. Smooth insteps and toes allow moisture to drain off an unpunctured surface and keep feet dry longer.

Boots with stiff counters which prevent over-running at the heel are recommended for most sportsmen.

Without that support, in old boots, a hunter may find himself walking on a sharp edge as his heel pushes the upper's leather out over the edge of the boot heel. That's tiring, uncomfortable, even painful.

Lace-up boots are generally preferable to pull-on types for long, hard walking. They can be snugged up or loosened to accommodate foot expansion and will keep out weed seeds and other chaff that can work down and irritate feet. Lacing hooks and speed lacer loops are quicker than eyes and their chances of snagging or ripping out are minimal.

The better-made pull-on types, properly fitted, don't slip excessively, do provide better bruise protection when hunting in blow-downs and other cover containing below-knee obstacles, and are satisfactory for off-and-on walking, as when motor vehicles and horses are utilized.

Proper boot height is a matter of individual choice. Lace boots up to 18 inches high once were the choice of outdoorsmen and do provide added protection. Like other small town lads in the 1930s my first "High-cuts" (with a sewed-on jack knife pocket) encased my leg to the knee. Boots of this height are heavy and binding, however.

If there is a near-universal "right height" for leather hunting boots it would be 10 inches, with six-footers perhaps preferring 12 inches, shorter-legged men 8 inches. With 10 inches almost the standard, many hunters assume that's the height of their upland boots. But manufacturers have been skimping for some years now. Actual measurements show nine or even 8-inch heights pawned off as 10-inch boots. For most this is acceptable; providing the necessary support to prevent sprains and breaks when an ankle twists, keeping out debris and permitting fast, tip-toe fording of shallow streams. But 7-inch boots are a rip-off. Better to buy much less expensive work shoes.

Rubber Bottom/Leather Top Boots

If I were restricted to a single pair of hunting boots they would have to be the rubber bottom/leather top shoe pacs. These rank as the most versatile of all hunting footgear, except in the arid southwest.

Like all general purpose items, these boots are a compromise; a most practical and comfortable one, as are shotgun barrels choked improved cylinder or modified, Springer Spaniels and German Shorthaired Pointers.

They're not for extremes, like wading or hot, dry hikes. But they do well in the variable weather and terrain conditions so often encountered during day-in, day-out hunting. When early morning grass is dew-damp or frosted, the bean and corn fields muddy, in snow, drizzle and slush they've kept me happy on upland hunts on foot and off horseback for small and big game; field trailing, snowshoeing and working in the slop of kennels and stables.

They are light, have excellent "ground feel", a heel and a sole tread design that grips as well as anything short of caulks or lugs so they are comfortable and safe for all day use, don't hang up in a stirrup, are easily cleansed of muck and mire and require minimum maintenance.

Detractors complain rubber bottom-leather tops are sloppy, don't provide enough arch support or foot protection on stony going. I can sympathize but don't identify with the need for soles and supports found only in the firmer soled leather boots, since shoe pacs are somewhat moccasin-like. Besides you can remedy or alleviate any shortcomings by what you put into these boots along with your feet.

On a stand, in an auto or in the house they *will* give you clammy feet. They are for a man on the move and while being walked in seem to pump air and do not restrict circulation. They should be pulled off upon coming inside or exchanged for another set of footgear and dry socks for the drive home.

Traded off with all-leather boots on decent hunting days they ensure the maximum in dry feet and comfortable walking. In damp and snow, they make sticking it out endurable and productive. It is good practice on all-day hunts to change boots—and socks—at lunch break. Wear the rubber bottoms in the morning chill and in the boggy woodcock and grouse bottoms; switch to the all leather when everything dries off.

Because of their roomy, noncritical fit, the rubber bottoms are ideally suited to the insole use. Leather and sheepskin ones, with steel arch supports, are available, but wool or papermill felt insoles are cheaper and don't conduct cold. Removed at night to dry out, insoles will start you out the next morning with warm, dry boots.

There is an ideal sock for this type of boot, the most popular brand name being Wick-Dry. The soft loft of these cotton, terrycloth-like socks fills up the boot without being tight and they wear like iron and launder without shrinkage. Heavy wool socks are tops, but rubber bottom boots chew them up like a squirrel cutting nuts.

The terrycloth socks are good year around. Wear "young ones" in the wet and cold. When age compresses their loft they work fine in all-leather boots in mild and hot weather. Mail order outfitters and sporting goods stores stock them and, because they once were issued to infantrymen to wear with shoe pacs, they may be found in army surplus stores.

All-Rubber, Calf High Boots

When a truly waterproof boot is called for, this style is a necessity. Well-treated leather will shed water and a quick stepper can with impunity wade a shallow puddle or hop-skip a small creek. Leather will not keep feet dry when steadily soaked by wet grass, snow, slush and mud. Only rubber does that and all-rubber boots, 12 to 14

About The Author
Dave Duffey hasn't had a pair of shoes in over 30 years. He just stayed in boots after getting out of the Army in 1947 and still wears them every day of the year as he trains gun dogs, hunts, guides, writes his *Outdoor Life* dog column, and manages a hunting club in Wisconsin; even on rare trips cityside he's in boots.

"It never made sense," Duffey explains, "to wear good boots on natural terrain and then get shin splints from pounding pavement for a few days in flimsy shoes just to be in style."

inches high, permit deeper wading than with the rubber/leather combination and prevent soaked, chilled ankles where the saturated cuffs of hunting pants hit the leather.

Rubber boots come in a wide selection, including full lace to the instep, three-eye laces at the top or no-lace pull-ons like cannery and dairy industry workers wear. Not many are really suitable for a great deal of walking over variable terrain.

For a walking rubber boot, the Red Ball Calhoun manufactured by Uniroyal, is the best choice. When a hunter prefers the support and comfort of leather whenever possible, requiring waterproof rubber only when the weather is inclement, the Calhoun is a sensible and occasionally superior alternative to the rubber bottom/leather top.

Light, with a heel and an excellent tread design, the elasticity of its high quality rubber (which resists snags and punctures) allows wearing heavy socks, snugging it to the foot for safe, comfortable walking. Insoles, however, will crowd the foot in a properly sized boot. The tread design is a set of protrusions best described as rubber caulks which grip well in soft, slick going. It wears rapidly, however, on hard surfaces.

Calhouns come in regular and snug ankle variations. Avoid the latter unless you always have someone available to pull them off. If damp on the inside, they may be impossible to remove by yourself. One night in grouse camp, it was touch and go as to whether a 6' 3", 215-pound game warden friend was going to get me out of them.

Even when the laces are drawn tight in the three eyelets, skinny-shanked hunters may find pants tucking necessary to fill out the upper rim. Thus, debris working down into the boot can be a nuisance. When pants cuffs are kept outside boots, as they should be to allow free leg swing and keep dampness outside instead of running down into the boot, high heavy socks will prevent chafing from the loose boot tops.

A combination of the essentially comfortable Calhoun boots and a pair of naugahyde or nylon chaps beats even hip boots in wet upland going. Light pants or jeans should be tucked into the ample boot tops and the bottoms of the chaps swinging free and draining the water down the outside of the boots. This is easier to move around in, and the chaps can be taken off and carried in a game bag once the weather clears or the cover dries.

All Rubber Hip Boots

Hippers are the style an upland hunter will get the least use out of and may even avoid when he should be donning them, but they're great to have when needed to stay dry in rain, wet snow or soaking cover and, more important, to wade into hard to reach places, the high ground and hummocks in marshes where pheasants take refuge, flooded bottom land on squirrel hunts, driving a swamp for deer or on a sideline foray jump-shooting mallard and wood duck.

Hippers are harder to walk in than other boots. It is work to stick it out for the better part of a day. Regular hip boots are heavy and binding as is, so insulated hippers are out of the question for me.

If weather or hunting situation dictates starting out in hip boots, but it changes later on and a great deal of walking is required, rolling them down and snapping the tops to the calf-straps will make it easier going until a change can be made. But you'll want to get out of them when you can because they'll still be awkward, will collect debris and are vulnerable to rips and tears from brush, briars and fences.

No pull-on boot, rubber or leather, gives the ankle support of laced leather boots and, because some nimbleness is lost in hip boots, they are most likely to cause accident or injury where the footing is tricky. Hip boots are also the exception to the size selection rule. Consider getting them a size larger than your other boots which permits wearing two pair of socks, filling out the boot and reducing slippage at the heel, or wear wool socks with some booties called Bama Sokkets.

These Austrian-made foot warmers do what the advertising claims they do—wick off perspiration—thereby "insulating" regular waders and hip boots with a minimum of bulk and weight. I find them one of the few gimmicks continually foisted on outdoorsmen that really work. When I pull off hip boots after a day in the kennel and marsh caring for and training dogs, the outside of the Sokkets are wet, but the socks inside them dry as if they just came out of the drawer.

A home-made gimmick for use with lace boots, a sort of double tongue, is also worth consideration. Cut tongues from worn out boots and fashion an extra tongue for each boot that will cover the instep, sticking out beyond the bottom lace. Fringe the bottom of this half-tongue and punch two lace

holes in it to fasten it by running the lace through them before starting on the bottom eyelets. This protects insteps constantly flexing and straining against boot lace pressure and carries water off a vulnerable leak area.

Insulated Boots

Because they are great for standing around in damp and bitter cold situations, insulated boots have their place in many outdoor situations. But upland hunting is a game of movement,

The full boot wardrobe includes all-rubber boots like these Red Ball Oneidas and hip boots, too.

normally abandoned in sub-zero situations and walking keeps feet comfortable in regular footwear without bulk and weight penalties.

If standing is more a part of your hunting endeavor than walking or if, for whatever reason, cold feet cause problems, the rubber bottom boots with leather or nylon tops, epitomized by the Sorels or snowmobile types that have removable felt liners are best bets. But they are clumsy, tiring, uncomfortable and therefore risky to wear when lots of walking is the order of the day.

This type of boot has taken the out-

door market by storm, particularly for ice fishermen, deer hunters and other stand around types. But for generations farmers, stockmen, loggers and other cold weather workers have kept warm and mobile wearing felt shoes with a rubber heel inside four-buckle galoshes or low work rubbers. You may also find this combination practical and less expensive.

If you move around a great deal, prize being able to feel your footing and would like to use the same style boot for a wide variety of conditions, you might go off the deep end, as I have, and own three pair of L. L. Bean rubber bottom/leather top boots at the same time.

Pair One, for bare ground hunting, is size 10, *medium* width to wear with one pair of medium weight socks. Pair Two, for snow time, is size 10, *wide* width to accommodate two pairs of socks. Pair Three, for really bitter weather and stand-and-walk deer hunting, is size 12, *wide* width and handles well when filled up with heavy socks and Bama Sokkets.

Leather-lined boots are comfortable

and expensive, and practical for up-landers. They are slightly warmer than unlined leather. Insulated leather boots, however, are a laugh or a tragedy, depending on whether they're on someone else's feet or yours. No leather boot is waterproof and once the insulation that is an integral part of the boot gets sodden it is difficult to dry out and may keep your feet damp and cold for days.

Rubber insulated boots are only a shade better, unless they are of very high quality which means the integral insulation is housed between the outer skin and a full rubber inner liner. Otherwise, while they are waterproof, when you go in over the tops or sweat excessively you'll have the same problems as with soaked insulated leather boots, the sensation of walking around on a wet sponge after you've poured out the water, for long periods of time.

Boot Socks

The right socks can compensate for a slightly poor boot fit, giving glove-like comfort rather than putting up with nagging little problems that don't disable or ruin a day but are distracting when you should be concentrating on the game you are hunting, handling your dog and getting off a killing shot. Boots come in standard sizes and feet do not. It's up to you to adjust to production boots when you can't afford handmade jobs, just as you can do well with a standard shotgun or rifle when a customized, personally fitted one isn't feasible or is more than you need. Proper weight socks fill out space or give you needed room, while cushioning and preventing chafing, blisters or interference with blood circulation.

Early season and dry condition hunting can be done in "sweat socks" like athletes wear; or some GI wool socks with double bottoms from a surplus store. They are comfortable in snug boots, cushioning the foot with no bulk in the rest of the sock.

Good bulky wool socks and so-called ragg socks, which approach the raw wool stockings grandmas and elderly aunts used to knit, are made by firms like Wigwam and featured by mail order outfitters like Eddie Bauer and Norm Thompson. They are expensive but worth the money.

One solution, when rubber-bottom shoe pacs are worn, is to pull cheap cotton socks, like Rockford work socks, over the vulnerable wool stockings. The pacs should accommodate this moneysaver with no pain or strain. In leather boots, where fit is more critical, wear the two pairs of socks when trying on new boots.

Or, don't wear wool. Use the terry-cloth cotton socks described in the section on shoe pacs. They're comfortable in leather boots, too, and as warm as anything but heavy all wool socks.

Snake Boots

If a lot of time is spent afield in snake infested hunting country, serious consideration should be given these specialized boots, a pull-on, 18-inch high item made of heavy bullhide that will turn the fangs of a poisonous reptile.

Laceless, they are snugged to the foot with an instep strap and buckle and at the top by another. When well-fitted they can be walked in, make good riding boots, give better protection from bruises and cuts than the lower, tight to leg, lace boots and are ideal for plantation type quail hunting where horses and jeeps are used.

When snakes are out, in warm weather, these boots are hot and heavy. Wetted by dew or perspiration they can be real bears to pull off, particularly if you have a high instep. I once got a pair in the mail that actually gave me leg cramps and a pulled muscle when I tried them on with *dry* socks and struggled to get out of them. It was a matter of cut them off or sleep in them until a sturdy friend risked a hernia dragging them off while I lay on the floor hanging onto a door jamb.

Russell and Gokey are the best known makers of these boots. Since they cost double or triple what other upland boots do and are supposed to be handcrafted, the safe thing to do is have them fitted rather than order out of stock. Boots of lighter leather and lower height of the same style are available from many bootmakers for hunters who don't want to be bothered with lacing and unlacing their boots.

For most sportsmen, who wear them only during the hunting seasons, boots are a good, long term investment that will last long with proper care. Minimum care for leather boots would be an annual "greasing," but oft-worn, water-soaked and brush-scuffed favorites might have to be tended every week during the hunting season.

Late summer, just prior to the season opener is a good time to "oil 'em up." Set the boots out on the stoop in the bright sun, which will work on possible mold or mildew caused by improper storage and warm the leather so it will readily absorb application of one of the leather preservatives previously mentioned.

They are best hand-rubbed into dry, warm, clean leather. Brush off the

boots or wipe them with a rag. Old tooth-brushes work well to clean boots and to work grease into hard to get at places, like around the welt and into seams. After you've greased them let them stay in the sun until most of the application has soaked in. Then put them away, ready for the first outing.

During the season, they can be greased when dry at room temperature and the warmth of your hands will help work in the oil. Running your fingernails on a bar of soap will keep the grease from getting up under the nails. The Snow Proof stuff doesn't stain hands, stockings or pants cuffs and boots "waterproofed" with it can also be polished.

Drying wet leather boots should be a gradual process. Do not put them into an oven, next to a hot stove or before a fireplace or hot campfire. Stuffing them with crumpled newspaper will make them wearable by morning and your foot heat can dry them as you walk. For a fast job, a blow dryer for hair should be judiciously used so it won't overheat.

Wearing different pairs of boots on alternate days will be good for your feet and the boots, or so the infantry teaches. In basic training, embryo foot soldiers were issued two pairs of high shoes and required to bar-lace one pair and cross-lace the other. Then a quick visual check by the platoon sergeant at morning inspection ascertained whether the shoes were being alternated each day—and it was extra duty if you happened to pull on your bar-laces on a cross-lace day.

Whether this made any more sense than the frequent rubbing of "Dubbin" into rough-out finish boots I don't know, but it was never forgotten. But even with 14 pair of boots, at last count, cluttering the basement and closets, I wear out a couple pairs of those most used annually. Hanging rubber boots in a basement or cool closet when they're not in use will stretch their working days. Bright light and extremes of heat and cold cause rubber deterioration.

Whether your boots last you six months or 20 seasons, whatever their quality and however they are maintained or neglected, the important thing is having the right pair on hand for the job you want done.

If you have to get by with just one pair, you'll be able to do more things in relative comfort with the rubber bottom/leather tops. Two pairs, one all-leather, one all-rubber, both calf high, will be a shade better. Adding hip boots to that ensemble gets you some bonus hunting. ●

GUNS FOR THE TWENTY PERCENT

Better off than before, this lefty says it's NOT as nice as it could be.

by JAMES T. FENDER

THOUGH 20 percent of Americans are left-handed, bolt-action centerfire rifles specifically adapted for left-handers were not offered in production form until the introduction of the Savage 110L in 1959. A number of alterations, one hand-made action, and several left-handed 22 rimfire rifles were made before that time, but such rifles were expensive, prone to malfunctions or hard to find.

The problems of a left-handed shooter in a predominantly right-handed world antedate the cartridge era. I have examined one 19th century percussion rifle which had its lock and hammer on the left side and a cheekpiece on the stock's right side. One early shooter, at least, accommodated his rifle to his needs rather than adjusting himself to an awkward-to-manipulate rifle. However, as rifles evolved into bolt actions, they were designed to accommodate most shooters—the right-handers. The modern southpaw was left to improvise as best he could for a long time.

Now, however, he has available a wide variety of arms designed for his use. In addition, he's able to use with facility numerous other arms which, though not intended for exclusive LH use, lend themselves to ambidexterity.

Not every southpaw bolt-action or other type introduced in the past decade remains in production. Some, though heavily advertised before their introduction, never reached the distribution stage. However, never again need a lefty settle for less than a firearm designed and produced exclusively for his or her use. A rundown of the currently available production or custom firearms, as well as notes on those formerly produced, may be useful:

It is not clear who made the *first* modern left-handed conversions, but N. B. Fashingbauer of Lac du Flambeau, Wisconsin, Bob West of Littleton, Colorado, and Dale Guise of Gardners, Pennsylvania, altered certain bolt actions to left-handed operation long before commercial portside actions were offered. These actions, however, were custom made only, were not widely distributed—and they were expensive. Mostly modified right-handed actions, ejection was not normally altered. It remained for Mathieu Arms of Oakland, California, to produce the first true left-handed centerfire action. (Mossberg Arms produced several 22 rimfire rifles with true LH actions during 1937-1940, but production was never resumed after WW II.)

The Mathieu Action

The Mathieu action was a superb one, though evidently produced one at a time. It wasn't truly a production item though Roy Weatherby for one saw its advantages, and bought a number for his magnum rifles. Mathieu Arms apparently went out of business in the mid-1950s, but anyone who has a left-hand Mathieu action has an exceptionally fine and historically significant action.

Parker Ackley, now located in Salt Lake City, Utah, contracted with a Japanese firm to produce a very close copy of the Mauser 98 action in right- and left-hand versions. The Japanese firm, however, failed after producing

just 100 right-hand and 50 left-hand actions.

It remained for Savage Arms to introduce the first production left-handed rifle. In 1959, Savage announced that two different action lengths would be available in the 110L. This rifle was, of course, the famous Model 110, a Mauser-type action with dual opposed locking lugs on the bolt and a staggered column box magazine. Its designer, the late Nicholas Brewer, exercised a great deal of ingenuity in developing an action which could be readily and inexpensively made in left- and right-hand versions. The 110 may not appeal to some because of the number of stamped parts, as opposed to smooth milled parts, but others have welcomed such refinements as the sliding shotgun-style tang safety. The 110L enjoyed immediate success—the left-handed shooter could, at long last, buy a rifle which would suit him with the same exactitude right-handers had always enjoyed.

The Weatherby and Others

The success of the left-hand Savage 110 prompted others to offer true LH rifles. Roy Weatherby introduced his innovative Mark V action in a left-hand version, currently offered in 9 calibers—cost about $500-$700. Left-hand Weatherby barreled actions are also offered.

Remington introduced a true left-hand rifle in its 700 BDL model, and later made a limited number of barreled actions available. The Remington 700 lines are, perhaps, more pleasing to some than those of the Savage 110, and the 700 BDL has a detachable floorplate, which the Savage lacks. However, the 110 may be had with a *detachable* box magazine, in right- or left-hand versions, and for some, that's a useful option. The left-hand 700 BDL is currently produced in only 3 calibers—270, 30-06 and 7mm Remington Magnum; the right-hand version is made in 2 action lengths and 16 different calibers. Neither Remington nor Savage now offer actions alone, but one can buy a barreled action and fit another barrel in the desired caliber, and many do.

Ranger Arms of Texas produced rifles in left-hand and right-hand versions. A fair number of LH Texas Magnum rifles were sold, but the company had problems and ceased production.

Custom Left-Handers

Champlin Firearms continues to produce their custom action (and

rifles) in right- and left-hand versions, chambered for virtually any centerfire rifle cartridge, though they are rather more suited to big calibers. Champlin offers a wide variety of custom features—tapered octagon barrels, folding-leaf rear sights, and a squared-off "dragoon" style trigger guard, among others. Only the Champlin action is pre-built; metal and wood work begins only after placement of a firm order.

Custom gunmaker Fred Wells makes a 98 Mauser-style action with square bridge and receiver, as well as various other 98-derived actions. These actions, virtually handmade, can be furnished in any centerfire rifle cartridge desired. His LH custom made action starts at about $2,000, a complete rifle selling for $5,000, or thereabouts. Delivery time is about 18 months. Materials, workmanship and finished products are on a par with the finest rifles made anywhere—superb craftsmanship.

From time to time other LH actions have been imported. Around 1973, F.F.V. Sports of Billings, N.Y., imported left-hand Carl Gustav rifles and actions made in Sweden. Mauser of West Germany for a time offered their Model 3000 action in a left-hand version, and some were sold in the United States. Sales of Mauser right- and left-hand versions were disappointing and the manufacturers withdrew, at least temporarily, from the American market. Currently no European arms company has publicly announced plans to introduce LH rifles in the U.S.

The Outlook

As far as can be learned no major armsmaker (Remington, Winchester, Savage or Ruger) has any plans to offer other LH centerfire rifles, or to introduce one. However, two smaller firms—Wichita Engineering & Supply and Du Biel Arms are offering LH actions or complete rifles. The Du Biel rifle, offered only as a complete firearm, is available in 3 action lengths. Firm prices have not been established for the left-hand rifles as of this writing. Wichita produces a variety of actions and completed rifles. Their Bench Rest Action, a single shot design, is available in 4 different models. A varmint rifle and a classic rifle are also available in LH models and in a variety of calibers.

The 22 Rimfires

Browning Arms marketed a Belgian-made 22 rimfire rifle with a rather unusual straight-pull "T-bolt" method of operation. These were available in right- and left-hand versions, but were only on the American market for about 3 years. Increasing production costs plus poor sales, did the rifle in. Today, these rifles are selling at several times their original cost.

The only LH 22 rimfire rifle left is the Remington 581 clip repeater which, even though it has its operating bolt on the left side, ejects fired cases to the right. Some southpaw small game hunters have used the 581 as the basis for a custom gun, though most of them would prefer LH ejection as well.

The Single Barrels

The left-hander can easily fire any of the available 22 rimfire semi-automatic, pump or lever-action rifles. Two are particularly well suited—the Browning semi-automatic with its downward ejection, and the Ruger 10/22. The sturdy little Ruger ejects its empties well to the right and front of the shooter, thus preventing his being struck by a hot case. Some other 22 autos, such as the Weatherby, sometimes pepper the left-hander with ejected cases.

Al Freeland offers a true left-hand version of the famous BSA Martini-International single shot 22 match rifle. Roughly 15% of his BSA rifles sales are left-hand versions.

Savage Arms has long imported the Anschutz 22 rimfire target rifles from West Germany. Though it is available only with the standard right-hand bolt, it can be had with a LH stock. It has found a ready market with smallbore competition shooters here. Gary Anderson used one in winning many of his smallbore championships at the national and international levels. The Walther 22 target rifles, imported by Interarms Ltd., can also be had with left-hand stocks but with right-hand bolts.

The southpaw has always been able to handle the lever-action, pump and semi-auto centerfire rifles offered by the various American armsmakers. Some of these, notably Remington, offer such rifles with LH stocks and reversed safeties. In fact, because of the earlier scarcity of good LH bolt-action rifles, many or our portsiders long ago became happy with such rifles. Many of these shooters are quite content with them, for few have bothered to obtain LH bolt actions.

The Single Shots

Single shot rifles have also cut deeply into the number of potential customers for true LH bolt rifles. Years before introduction of the Ruger No. 1 single shot rifle, southpaw varmint shooters had bought and used satisfactorily such single shots as the Winchester Hi-Wall, the 44½ Stevens or various Remington Rolling Blocks. My first varmint rifle was a Winchester Hi-Wall chambered in 219 Improved Zipper, and was bought as much for the ease of operating it from the left shoulder as for its considerable accuracy. The Ruger SS and Browning SS rifles have been highly popular with LH shooters.

Among shotguns, of course, single and double barrels can be used equally well by everyone, southpaws or not. This also holds true for the drillings or rifle/shotgun combinations, though in many cases either type may have a right-hand cheekpiece, which could be annoying.

Several years ago Remington introduced the 1100 semi-autos and 870 pumps in true LH versions. Both offer left-side ejection and reversed safeties. However, Remington does not offer a slug barrel with rifle sights for any of their LH pump or semi-auto shotguns. Winchester made their 1400 shotgun in a true LH version from 1970 until the end of 1972, but they don't plan to reintroduce it.

Other pump shotguns offer ambidextrous qualities. The Ithaca 37, which loads and ejects at the bottom, has long been a favorite of portsiders. Browning's new pump shotgun, the BPS, also has bottom loading and ejection. Having the left-hander in mind, the BPS has a sliding tang safety. The BPS barrel types will include a slug barrel with rifle sights.

Handguns

Any revolver or semi-auto pistol can be used by left-handers unless it carries elaborate right-hand target grips. The revolver cylinder, which swings open to the left, adapts to the LH shooter; it can be easily and securely held with the right thumb through the yoke while the left thumb and forefinger load fresh cartridges into the cylinder. The little and ring fingers of the right hand meanwhile can rotate the cylinder. Unlatching the left-side cylinder lock remains a problem, of course.

The semi-auto pistol is equally shootable by the left-hander except that the manual safety, the slide lock and magazine release call for release by the right thumb. This situation can be corrected, at least on the 1911 Colt auto and other big-bores by adding an ambidextrous safety. It's a catalog item from several sources and custom gunsmiths, and Colt's custom shop will have a factory version. Some LH shooters have complained that the various Colt Government models eject the fired cases up and back, striking the shooter. A competent pistolsmith can fix that, however, insuring that ejected cases fly off at about a 45-degree angle.

The Failed Ones

It is interesting to speculate why some southpaw rifles did not survive here. I believe that the left-hand Carl Gustav and Mauser actions were not aggressively marketed. The same holds true today for the Savage and Remington LH actions. After Carl Gustav spent some three years attempting to penetrate the U.S. market (with RH and LH rifles), they sold all stocks on hand to a distributor. The available LH rifles were sold out within a few weeks via an advertisement in a national arms publication. The same was true of the Mauser action; in reviewing the pertinent factory literature I located only one ad which mentioned—and in a footnote at that—that the Carl Gustav action was available in a LH version.

A late Remington catalog, despite numerous written references to their LH arms, pictures not a single LH rifle or shotgun. The latest Savage catalog has two illustrations of LH arms. The 19th edition of the *Weatherby Guide* illustrates only one southpaw version of the Mark V rifle.

In short, after showing an initial awareness of the potential market for LH bolt-action rifles, most manufacturers have been content to merely list such rifles. There has been no aggressive marketing. I've talked to many LH shooters during my years as a firearms safety instructor, but only a few were aware that LH bolt rifles were available!

Clearly the manufacturers are not making their southpaw wares widely known and until more of such guns are sold, there's little likelihood that other makers will offer them. It's a Catch-22 situation—the gunmakers won't spend more money on ads until they see an increase in sales, while LH shooters, still unaware of the wide range of firearms designed for them, fail to buy what they don't know exists.   •

See our Directory of the Arms Trade for locations of the firms mentioned here.

The $4000 Spike

by BOB BELL

I EXPECT MEN have been sitting around campfires telling hunting stories for about five million years now, give or take a century or so. One result of this seems to be that almost everyone knows every story. Oh, not the precise details insofar as names, places and stuff like that go, but the general sound of things. When you meet a stranger somewhere and it turns out he's a hunter just back from northwestern Colorado with a nice mule deer, you've already got a picture in your mind of the vast sweeps of that country, the mountains beyond, the smell of the junipers. You even have a fair idea of what his buck's rack looks like. Or maybe his trophy was a bull elk from Chamberlain Basin, a bear from Ontario's black spruce and lake country . . . whatever. Doesn't matter much, you've heard a lot of similar stories before, probably told a fair number yourself.

But once in a great while, something different comes along—a story you never heard before. The kind I got from this guy quite a few years back. Maybe you've heard it, but I've never heard it from anyone else. That's probably why I never passed it on. I've sort of saved it for myself, savoring it from time to time when I needed some reassurance about the role of the indi-

vidual in this over-regulated society of ours. Then I got to thinking—maybe this is the time to tell it, maybe there are some others like me out there who will appreciate it. I also expect there are some it will offend. But so what, nobody can please everybody.

I should tell you right off I don't know if this story is true or not. I've wondered about it off and on through the years, but never decided one way or the other. The man who told it to me seemed like the truthful type, but who knows these things for sure? No matter.. Some things it's better not to know.

I'm not certain of the year. I think it was 1947. Dick and his younger brother Bob and I were camped in a fair-size clearing about a dozen miles north of Elk City, Idaho. That was just a village then—a few houses, a store, a gas station—and maybe still is. I hope so.

Bob had killed a six-point bull but Dick and I were still looking. We didn't hunt cooperatively, which might have increased the odds of success, but I liked knowing he was somewhere in the same country with me. We'd met in basic training a few years earlier, at Camp Sibert, Alabama, and then gone the route together—England, France, Belgium, Holland, Luxembourg, to

VE Day beyond the Elbe River in Germany—and I still count him the best friend I ever had though he's been gone a long time now.

Anyway, coming back to camp one evening, I got to the meadow a bit after dark, and came out of the woods near another camp, perhaps a half-mile from ours. We'd seen the tent previously but hadn't met the hunters. The cheese-clothed quarters of an eating-size bull were hanging from a nearby tree now, and it turned out there was only one hunter, a man probably in his mid-40s.

He was only of medium height, but he looked bigger, wide and solid—thighs that bulged his Levis, shoulders and arms that wanted to bust out of his heavy gray shirt, square thick hands and a broad, ruddy, full-featured face. He looked like a Slavic Indian, if there ever was such a thing, and I remember thinking that tangling with him would be like trying to shove over a ponderosa stump with my bare hands. I had no intention to do any such thing, but anyone's first reaction to him had to be physical. He just gave off an aura of power.

He'd started a fire for company, but he had coffee going on a two-burner Coleman. We talked a minute, but I never asked his name; you didn't do that in Idaho in those days. By then the coffee was hot and he offered me a cup. So we sat on a couple of chunks and sipped it, talking some more. The usual stuff. What directions we'd hunted, what sign we'd seen, what tomorrow's weather might be. I was getting ready to leave when I spotted his rifle. It was on a sleeping bag back inside his small tent, but I could see well enough, and its lines looked familiar.

"Is that a Linden stock?" I said.

He looked at me speculatively a moment, as if I'd said something more intelligent than he expected. Then his gaze shifted to my 348, as if anyone lugging a big lever action around would hardly know any more about rifles than which end the bullet came out of.

"Yeah," he said finally. And then, quietly, as if he read the question in my face that I didn't have the nerve to ask: "Would you like to look at it?"

I just nodded, and he reached inside the tent, lifted it out, and then handed me the first honest-to-God, Alvin Linden-stocked rifle I ever had in my hands. Or even had seen in the flesh. The nearest I'd ever come previously was the pictures in Jack O'Connor's articles.

To say it was beautiful seems inadequate, but that's really the only word that fits. The wood—it was walnut, fairly dark—must have been beautiful in the blank and it was even better now, the firelight rippling on the fiddleback grain in the butt, each stock line and curve perfectly proportioned, the joints where wood and metal met almost invisible. There was no separate forearm tip, just a modified schnabel. The buttplate and grip cap were Niedner's checkered steel. The checkering went all the way around the grip, harmonizing with the bottom line of the cheekpiece, and there was plenty up front. The action was a Springfield, much slicked up, the bolt handle and safety gracefully altered. The bolt body and follower

L. REEDSTROM

were damascened, the action corners radiused differently, the tang had been slimmed, and there was a touch of simple, but flawless, engraving. The scope was an early Lyman Alaskan All-Weather in a Stith Streamline mount, still the nicest looking rig ever

designed to latch a glass sight onto a rifle.

"What caliber is it?" I asked. I knew the action had worn an '06 barrel originally, but this one had a different contour and was a couple of inches shorter than issue.

"It's a 270."

"That's a great cartridge. I've shot a couple of deer with 270s belonging to friends. The results were truly impressive." I was still looking at his rifle. There was enough wear on the bluing and tiny marks on the stock to show it wasn't new, but it had never been abused in any way. It looked like a tested outfit in its prime of life. About like the man who owned it. Reluctantly, I handed it back. "I'm

sure you've had good luck with it," I said.

He shoved the bolt forward but didn't turn it closed, slid it slowly back, then forward again. "Yeah." He sat down, the rifle across his lap, refilled the coffee cups and motioned me

to sit again. "Care for some stew? It's still hot."

"Thanks, but my pals are expecting me back soon. They'll have supper ready."

He nodded disinterestedly. Then, "A lot of hunters think the 270 is only a deer cartridge. This one has taken lots bigger stuff for me. Sheep, elk, moose . . ."

"I didn't mean it was only a deer load. But that's all I've had the chance to hunt with it."

"I know that's what you meant. But your remark reminded me of something. A hunt a while back. You might find it interesting 'cause I was using this gun which you seem to have taken a shine to."

"Did you get a nice trophy?"

A smile flashed across his face, then vanished.

"An unusual one, I guess you'd say." He took a sip of coffee, sat there staring into the flames of the fire. "It was season before last, my first one home in five years, and I took my daughter hunting. She hadn't even been in her teens when I left, and now she was old enough to hunt with me. Hell of a big hunk of her life I missed. But that's how it was, you probably know something about those things. Anyway, we were having a fine time. Ginny's mother was along too, enjoying camp life, cooking over a fire and all that. She doesn't hunt, but she's a good claybird shot and she'd taught Ginny more than most hunters know about gun handling.

"We'd been out four-five days and hadn't had a shot. I saw one nice buck but passed it up 'cause I wanted Ginny to score first. Then one afternoon I left her to watch a sidehill while I went back to the tent for my forgotten binoculars. Coming back, I met her on her way to camp, so mad she was crying. Took her a couple minutes to settle down enough to tell me what had happened. Seems a little whitetail buck, a spike, came out on that sidehill and she dropped him. I'd put a little 257 together for her—a Mauser action I'd brought back, a light short Buhmiller barrel, Mannlicher stock, K2.5 scope—and she was good with it. One shot did it, she said. She was so happy she just hopped up and down like a twelve-year-old. Got him on her own, couldn't wait to show me when I got back.

"Well, before I got there, two strangers came along. They offered to clean the buck for her, but before they were done they'd not only cleaned it but also taken it—and her little 257."

"I'll be damned!"

"Yeah. And told her to bug off if she didn't want to get hurt."

"What'd you do?" I'd never seen this man till a short time before, I still didn't know his name and probably never would, but I just couldn't imagine him letting things end that way. Anyone could tell he wasn't the type to do that.

heard, the sound that engine made after that Silvertip hit. Just a weird clunkin' and clankin'."

"What happened then?"

"Well, the car had already lost power, like an old bull elk that's taken one through the lungs, so a second shot wasn't necessary. But I'd learned over the previous few years not to take any

But the gas had been running out on the road from the previous shot, and this bullet apparently hit a rock or hunk of metal or something and made a spark, and . . ."

I stared at him, speechless. "It didn't . . . ?"

That big grin flashed across his face, stayed this time. "It sure did."

"Oh, I told Ginny to go on back to camp, then I hightailed it for the sidehill. It was easy to see where they'd cleaned the spike, just as easy to follow their drag marks. They had to go uphill a ways before crossing a ridge and angling down through some open ponderosa to the hardtop road in the bottom. So I wasn't really far behind them. Fact is, they were just loading the deer in the trunk of their car when I came down the ridge."

"What'd they do when they saw you?"

"They were just getting in the car and didn't see me till I hollered. Then they took a quick look, yelled something at each other, and dove into the car. Took off like an ol' red turpentined cat, leavin' black streaks of rubber on the road."

"They got away." I felt deflated at the thought.

"Well, no." He finished his coffee, offered to refill my cup, then replenished his own. "Fact is, I hadn't expected 'em to stick around and talk, so even as I yelled at 'em I was thumbin' the safety off on this old 270, and they hadn't made more than 20 yards or so in low gear when I put a 130-gr. Silvertip into the engine."

"Hot damn!"

"Yeah. Craziest thing you ever

unnecessary chances and I sure as blazes didn't want this one gettin' away, so I put another bullet right alongside the first."

"Lord Almighty!"

"Right. I'd like to have seen what they did to the block. Anyway, that ol' car sort of drifted to a stop and those two guys piled out, screaming like a couple of inbred idiots, wavin' their arms and doing all sorts of dance steps. I guess they wanted me to know they were there, but of course I already knew that. And to tell the truth, I was still in a miserable mood about the whole thing, so . . . "

"You didn't shoot 'em!"

"No, of course not. Though I gotta admit the thought went through my mind. What I really did was put the third shot into the gas tank. I suppose it still seemed vaguely possible that they'd get the thing running again, and I didn't want that to happen. When that one cracked down there, those two guys just squirted into the bush like the devil himself was jabbin' them. I watched till they went out of sight. It didn't take 'em long."

"So you went down then and got the deer back?"

"No. You see, I still had one round left in the rifle and I figured, why save it? So I sent it down at the tank too.

"It blew?"

"Like a 155 hit it."

"Omigod." I just stared at him some more, picturing it. Then I felt a grin building, and then we were both roaring together. It seemed poetic justice somehow. "That's one way to teach a couple of game thieves a lesson," I gasped, clutching my aching sides. "A real expensive way for them."

"More expensive than you think," he said.

"How's that?"

"Fact is, that big old maroon car of theirs was actually a new Cadillac. I figger that spike buck cost 'em maybe four-five thousand dollars, everything considered, and they didn't get to eat him."

The idea flabbergasted me for a minute. Then I went off into another fit of laughter.

"I've never really regretted it," the man said, after I'd quieted down, "but I've never taken much pride in it either. Truth is, I'd much rather have had those little spike horns on a plaque in our den, and Ginny's 257 back, than to have wiped out a new Caddie."

Then he grinned again. "But you gotta admit, this old 270 has what it takes, no matter what the target is." ●

Gun Digest Discussion No. 1

The Question: Do some shoot well on game, but can't hit targets? The answers, out of nearly 400 years of experience, from:

Roger Barlow
Bob Bell
Dwain Bland
Tom Brakefield
Frank Marshall, Jr.
Norm Nelson
Hal Swiggett
Stuart Williams
Jim Woods

IT WAS A fine restaurant and had been a splendid meal, with that added sauce chefs don't make—good conversation. The talk had ranged widely from delicious industry gossip to technical news and game conversation, cartridges and wine, the proper behavior in a *hochsitz* and next year's hunt.

And then my host, a hunter bred, with the experience of hundreds of trophies in his own hands, a cosmopolitan executive, a man of both decision and distinction, a man who runs a useful portion of the firearms industry, leaned toward me and said it, said it confidentially:

"I'm not so good at targets, you know, but on game I hardly ever miss."

Out of my own experience in this matter, I summoned the ability to nod gravely, and say, "It is often so among hunters."

Thankfully, the moment passed. It was not, in the context of that dinner, or of that friendship, important. My host is a fine companion on a hunt, in adversity and out, and he does indeed do his full share of hitting when the game is on the move.

I had been, however, surprised to hear him say that. Perhaps I should not have been, because one often hears it. Generally, it's a young man or an old one, a person you can figure has not the leisure for much practice, nor the money, either. Mostly, they're just average performers on game. There have been, of course, those exceptions I have considered rare—grizzled fellows, sometimes—who connect every pop.

This time, a new thought struck me: Suppose there's something to it?

Conventionally, all us experts discount such a statement about 100 percent. We know that success on game is not so difficult if for this shot at hand a man can merely shoot up to his own standard. Properly directed, even decrepit centerfire rifles are well up to the task of hits on game out to 200 yards and beyond. So when a fellow says he can hit hair and not paper, we expect he's just a consistent below-average shot.

Maybe, it occurred to me this time, there's more to it than that. Could it be that some of us do well only when it counts? Could it be that shooting well is really simple, that inside any of us that have learned how to discharge a firearm are the eyes and coordination of Natty Bumppo, and that some of us tap those talents whenever game is on the rise and not otherwise?

It is my hope some learned fellow can figure it out on some scientific basis. For now, however, I present here the views of nine writing men I know to be widely experienced, thinking hunters and shooters.

I have no sound opinion myself, not since that dinner, but my friends here are answering this question: Can some shooters do well on game but not on targets?

Kw

Barlow: Yes

I believe many shooters can hit game birds with fair or even remarkable consistency when they cannot do equally well on clay targets because I myself have this problem and have often observed others in the same fix.

My friend Vladimir V. Vladimirov was head of INTOURIST here for the U.S.S.R. in the 1960's. Back home, Vladimir was an ardent and effective waterfowl hunter but had done no hunting in the U.S. during his several years tour of duty in New York City. He had been absolutely fascinated by my photographs and pheasant and grouse shooting stories, so I persuaded him to get the needed State Department clearance to come to Virginia to shoot pheasants with me on a nearby preserve before he left the United States permanently.

The afternoon before, I set up a practice trap so he could familiarize himself with my 2-shot Browning. A box of shells later, he was almost heartbroken and greatly embarrassed as he had not broken a *single* clay target though that's a gun I've found everyone shoots well.

"Look", he said, "I'll just take movies of you shooting tomorrow, then I'll have something on pheasant hunting I can take home with me and always enjoy".

The next morning when the Brittany went on point 40 yards into the first strip of cover, I handed him the Browning saying, "Let me have the camera so at least you'll have a little actual footage of yourself with a pheasant coming up".

He reluctantly handed over his

type of target apparently tightens us up, destroys our timing, makes us "poke" our targets. Once we *know* we can hit both clay and feathered targets we will generally do so. Confidence is one of the most important aspects of successful shotgun shooting. If you can consistently hit one kind of target you can certainly hit the other type just as easily—if only you believe you can.

Roger Barlow likes hammer guns and has used them in the uplands for 25 years.

camera and walked forward to make the flush. The Super-8 whirred, two magnificent cock pheasants blasted off, the Browning bellowed twice . . . and there were two solid thuds as the roosters, cleanly killed in the air, hit the ground!

Vladimir was unquestionably the happiest Russian alive at that moment for he considered pheasants the world's most spectacular game birds and to have bagged a *pair* of them after the previous day's fiasco was almost beyond belief. Had he and I been in positions of authority that morning we could easily, right then and there, have amicably settled every U.S.-Soviet dispute and problem that existed!

He went on to shoot nine more pheasants without a miss and the next day connected with the only ruffed grouse he had a shot at.

So why *does* a shooter miss 25 relatively easy clays one day and the next hit eleven straight pheasants—topping it off with a very difficult grouse?

Of course, there are some shooters who rarely miss clays and have little success with live game.

It is clear basic shooting skill is really there. For many of us, the "wrong"

Bob Bell shoots everything well and has done so since the '30's—the 1930's.

Bell: Yes and No

The world is divided into two kinds of shooters: those who can hit game but not targets and those who can hit targets but not game. Individuals who can do both are so rare they require no comment. This split is so because the hair-and-feathers guys, hereinafter referred to as the Hairy Ones, can't shoot too well, while the artificial target decimators, commonly called Claybird Busters or Paper Punchers, simply can't shoot as well as they'd like.

Let's look at 'em:

The Hairy Ones are basically happy-go-lucky kooks. They don't know they don't shoot well; in fact, they think they're pretty good, simply because they kill a lot of game. The game they kill, however, actually re-

quires little shooting ability. Typically, a Hairy One will doze on a deer crossing until a like-minded compatriot who got too cold to sit any longer unintentionally shoves a deer whose time has run out down the path. Our hero then ambushes it and thinks his 40-yard lung shot was worthy of song and legend. How much ability does it take to hit a basketball-size target at putting green distance? More than it takes to drill an elk's boiler room at similar distance, maybe, which Ol' Hairy will be doing a week later, but not much.

Similarly, the same fella managed to clobber a pheasant at 22 yards as it cleared the standing corn at all of 20 mph, and thought that too was a magnificent performance. Well, a clean kill is always admirable, but it doesn't always require outstanding gun skill.

Such hits make a lot of Hairy Ones believe they're genuine hellbenders with a gun when most are mediocre at best. However, they never forget a good shot, never remember a miss. It never occurs to them that the hit might have been due to good luck, and bad luck always causes the miss. Hairy Ones always hunt with like-minded friends and all gladly ignore each other's misses. All of which means that this group doesn't take shooting too seriously.

The Claybird Busters and Paper Punchers are unfortunates whose minds drive them to score-keeping, statistical analyses, scientific investigation of all factors influencing or affected by hits and misses—in other words, they have masochistic tendencies. Such individuals are drawn to the competitive powder-burning sports. CB/PP's enjoy suffering, and since suffering derives from imperfection and few human endeavors are less amenable to perfection than claybird busting, they obviously have found a home here. No matter how many consecutive hits are made, no one can go forever without a miss. Nor can anyone put every bullet into the same hole. The CB/PP's are doomed to ultimate frustration, which is why they continue these "sports" to the doddering age, suffering all the way, though rarely in silence. You'd think Fate might just once relent a whisper and allow someone a caliber-size group, but it won't. All-knowing Fate fully understands that it's a sadistic thing to be kind to a masochist.

I don't mean to be unkind to either the Hairy Ones or the CB/PP's. I tell it the way it is because in addition to all my other problems I have this compulsion to be honest. And I know each group so well because, somehow, I'm a member of both.

Tom Brakefield likes 7mm Remington Magnums, 338's, and any kind of big game.

Dwain Bland has hunted nearly 50 years, is hooked on turkeys and muzzleloaders.

Bland: No

I don't believe in a shooter who can hit game, but not a target, because the man who is a pretty fair wing shot with a shotgun, is apt to be much the same with clay birds, whether they be skittering from a trap layout, or winging from the high and low houses on a Skeet range.

Take the goose hunter: 'Course, there's not the test of abilities with goose killing as with, say, knocking down doves, but he must be an excellent judge of range, have a fine sense of calculating lead, and he learned in the beginning about a smooth follow-through.

Duck hunting has even more of all those, plus, the angles are more evi-

dent, and the speed of target increases. 'Course, due to the shooting of many waterfowl over decoys, both ducks and geese, I don't think the waterfowler will be as good at targets as the upland gunner, at least not in the beginning.

Now, the man who hunts all sorts of upland birds will ordinarily have no trouble on targets. Oh, he might not be an instant Dead-Eye Dick, but he'll take to it pretty quick, particularly if he's hunted many quailbirds in heavy cover or if he's spent part of his lifetime in the "patridge" woods.

Quail and grouse hunting are known for the tremendous varying kinds of shots a gunner can face in a day's time. Birds exploding underfoot, back of the hunter, near and far, and all leaving the county in every direction on the compass. Folks who would pass up dinner for a tromp in a wet bog for timberdoodles or a late afternoon try for doves on a high wind pass shoot won't have any trouble clay birdin', either.

Much game shooting is very much like shooting trap. Range, trajectory of bird, angles, all these lean towards a clay pigeon's way of leaving the box. Skeet was originated by men who hunted "patridge," and quail men, woodcock hunters, dove hunters, all should do well on a Skeet range.

Among the men I've known in almost half a century of hunting, those who were considered good game shots also were good on clay targets. The lousy shots did likewise on targets. And, it works pretty well the other way round. Good trap or Skeet shots I've known seemed to have little trouble afield.

Brakefield: Yes

I believe in shooters who can hit game, but not targets, because we are all of us strange, quivery, quaky batches of emotions housed in undependable, all-too yielding protoplasm. In a word, people aren't automatons

(especially people hyped up by adrenalin).

One of the late Jack O'Connor's inimitable articles went on at some length on this very point. True to the O'Connor style, one "citizen" after another "stoutly proclaimed" that though they weren't paper punchers they were four hells on laying down haired game two sections away. The article, as with all of Jack's writing, was a delight to read. Sadly, I didn't and don't agree with the venerated gentleman on his point that a good game shot is almost always a good target shot (however informal) and (as they say) vice versa.

It isn't a black/white equation. Usually a fairly decent shot on the range can hit his share of game and a consistently decent game shot has no trouble sighting in his own rifle. But I have noticed over the years that some men shoot *consistently* and *considerably* better at game rather than paper or, conversely, score much better at the butts than on living, breathing animated targets that don't want to be 10-ringed.

Why? I suspect there is a complex mix of reasons stretching from to how the individual learned to shoot, on through his own personal emotional make-up and up to and including his priorities. There are so many fascinating vagaries to the shooting game.

Sometimes a hunter (or shooter) is dead on and can do no wrong. My first trip to Africa I shot 13 head of game in 14 shots and the zebra really didn't need the second. The professional hunter was extolling my greatness to one and all by the fifth day indicating that only one Texan had ever shot better with him. By the end of the hunt when I had dropped a running bushbuck about 70 meters out in high elephant grass and a fast moving impala twice that far away within two hours of each other, my friend rose to new (and embarrassing) heights of ballistic adoration.

I accepted all with a measure of good grace and enjoyment and waited for the inevitable pendulum-swing. Three months later, it came, half a world away in Montana, when I missed two successive standing whitetails within 200 meters, one of them the largest I've ever had a crosshair on! So it goes.

My second trip to Africa I brought along a buddy who I like in spite of the fact that various rifled mechanisms are natural third appendages for him. He can shoot better at 300-meter targets than I can from a bench half the time. On any rifle *that he is familiar with* he can consistently hit tin cans thrown into the air by others, two times out of three and sometimes better on a particular string. Alas, dear friends, that is simply and forevermore out of yours truly's shooting range. I can hit them but only occasionally and *never* when I really want to.

This was his first trip to Africa. He had bad luck on his first two shots—a kudu he missed with the help of a small branch that deflected the shot and a standing bushbuck well out— and things just seemed to go wrong after that. By the end of the trip, I thought he and his wife were ready for a do-it-yourself divorce and he had not shot truly or well the whole time. The simple truth is that if you shoot much, sometimes you shoot far better than other times and, with most folks I know anyway, there generally *does* seem to be a bi-level variance between paper punching and game shooting.

ten ring. This proposition never fails to raise eyebrows, because in my prowl area the best game shots in camp are, quite ironically, notable match shooters or have been.

Norm Nelson is a pump shotgun freak and shoots a rifle now and then, too.

Nelson: No

I don't believe in shooters who can hit game, but not targets, because . . . the Three Great American Lies are: (1) "Your check is in the mail;" (2) "Hi . . . I'm from the government and I'm here to help you;" (3) "Maybe I'm no good at targets and clay birds, but I sure can hit 'em dead when I'm out hunting."

Most of the many rifle and shotgun hunters I've known were self-taught. Some good hunters are not very good shooters. They get game but largely because they're clever enough to do it close where it's almost impossible to miss. Our most important "big game" is the whitetail deer, a forest dweller usually shot at 50 yards or less— generally less. A short-sighted Wyoming ranch hand literally couldn't see a running antelope at 125 yards on

Frank Marshall's life with good guns has been interrupted only by WW II.

Marshall: No

I don't believe in shooters who can hit game, but not targets, because I've been convinced after a half century watching fine game shots who decided to take up the match target game, and thereafter, easily tuned to the fundamentals, beat a path to the trophy table regularly.

That fur and feathers finesse might create a negative psychosis in such experts exposed to the comparatively comfortable and calm environs of the target range is in every area contrary to common sense logic. Hitting a mark with a gun is still the primary objective; it requires the same talents; and the fellow who is good afield may be even better at the targets.

I have never yet, under the decreased duress of the target range, observed a game shot convert to this easy going routine who failed the test. Target tyros, new in camp, sometimes find to their dismay that they can't hit a herd "even with a shotgun" this year. To ease the pain, shame or whatever, they then dig out the old garbage about the nimrod who puts venison on poles as he pleases but would be lost to the cause on the target shooter's tiny open, short-grass range, but he could get within 25 yards of bedded-down mule deer. He couldn't see (let alone hit) them much farther than that!

Hunters I've known who were *good* game shots also were competent on clays or paper targets on occasion. In his 50's, my father "hadn't popped a paper target since my teenage YMCA rifle team days" as, from a sitting position, no sling, he nearly clover-leafed three bullets in a 100-yard target's 10-ring.

"Pretty easy when the target's standing still," he remarked. handing the scoped 30-06 back to me to case up for the trip.

Shooting fundamentals are pretty constant laws, whether the target is a V-ring or venison, clay pigeon or cock pheasant. The skilled rifleman uses breathing control, trigger squeeze, and cold-blooded target concentration whether he's on the target range or picking off distant game. The wingshooter uses his fast swing and

follow through whether he's busting blue rocks or feathering a ruffed grouse.

There's no particular magic in fur or feathers that will make a consistently good shot out of a shooter who cannot readily score well in moving target games or paper targets. Perforating paper targets won't teach a guy how to hit a muley bounding up the rimrocks, but his learned (misnamed "instinctive") shooting ability will serve him well in automatically assuring that his breathing control and trigger squeeze will come into play at the moment of truth without his consciously thinking of it. That leaves his brain free to concentrate on the problem of predicting where that erratically moving target is going to be when the bullet arrives. And the guy who can do a reasonable job of powdering clay birds on the Skeet or trap range will find that most waterfowl and upland bird gunning is actually easy by comparison.

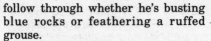

Swiggett: Yes

I believe in shooters who can hit game, but not targets, because that's me. The reason, I will concede, is undoubtedly between my ears.

I grew up shooting cottontails, squirrels and crows with a 22 rifle and 22 shorts. I started this at six, and graduated to a single-shot 410 and then a 20-gauge a couple of years later. I stuck to that little 22 for serious hunting, because I could kill just as much and a lot cheaper, there in the 1920's.

I was never interested in targets. Cans were fun if they could be kept rolling. Knots on trees or fence posts were great for checking rifle sights. Along with other youngsters of my era, I learned to shoot by shooting at game.

I miss at least my share of shots right along with the next guy, but I think I can qualify as a better than average pasture rifle shooter, pasture handgunner and pasture shotgunner. From a bench, testing rifles and handguns and ammo, I can hold groups about as tight as is possible out of a vise with hunting scopes. This—tests—I take seriously.

Shotguns and clay targets leave me way out in left field. I look at Skeet as a regimented game and not worthy of anyone's time other than the person with nothing else to do who wants to

become a mechanical shooter. To be a good Skeet shooter one has to become a mechanical shooter, and I'm simply not that dedicated. Trap is a bit different, and more often than not a good field shooter will also do rather well at trap.

Games, well, that's something different. Crazy Quail and that great "Aw Shucks" at Remington Farms, where heckling while shooting along with anything else to distract the shooter is part of the action, are target games that interest field shooters. And they usually do well.

I remember a particular instance when one of the leading gun writers of today offered to show me that "Aw Shucks" at Remington Farms. We shot by ourselves, just the two of us. He had shot it many times, and it was my first try. He broke 17. I broke 18. He hasn't shot that course with me since. Over the years, I've improved to a pair of 23's and one 24 but never all 25 in a round.

My best at a top "Crazy Quail" set-up, thinking specifically of the one at Winchester's Nilo Farms, is nine out of ten which I've squeaked out three times. More often than not my score is three to five or six, out of ten.

These are games, played for fun. Target shooting is deadly serious business and I shoot for pleasure.

Yes, there are also untold numbers of target shooters who can't hit hair or feathers, not even if it was tied down—just because it isn't made of clay or doesn't have a bullseye on it. It's between their ears, too.

Williams: Yes

I believe in shooters who can hit game, but not targets, because Skeet and trap are highly artificial, *learned* games. Skeet is—or is supposed to be—absolutely consistent and repeatable, shot after shot, round after round. To master the game of Skeet means essentially mastering 16 different problems of lead and angle, or 16 different sight pictures, whichever way you prefer to express it. Shooting in the field requires much more adaptability. If one shoots a variety of game under a variety of circumstances— bob-whites and pheasants over dogs, flushing chukas or ruffed grouse, decoying teal and mallards, high passing doves and geese, driven Scottish grouse or pheasants or Spanish red-

Hal Swiggett has pulled triggers for over 50 years, and is good with all guns.

duds at the other is that one will shoot well at what he *practices*. He can't expect to become deadly on live birds by practicing on Skeet, although there is a good amount of carry-over, and the Skeet will certainly not harm his field shooting. Neither can he expect to master clay targets by practicing on feathered ones.

I remember quite well a discussion I had several years ago down in Colombia with Bill Farfan, probably their greatest wingshot. Bill was, in his heyday, also one of the world's finest Skeet shooters, having placed 6th at the World Shooting Championship in Phoenix in 1970 and won the gold medal at the Bolivarian Games at about the same time. He told me that when he was preparing for a major competition he had to quit shooting live birds completely for at least six weeks before the competition. As he explained it, the problems of speed, distance, and angle were totally different, and any field shooting he might do in that period would only serve to hurt his Skeet game.

Stuart Williams has hunted over 30 years and likes custom rifles and fine shotguns.

legged partridge—he will encounter an infinite variety of problems of lead and angle. That is why no field shooter—not even the best—can shoot the very high percentages of a merely good Skeet or trap shooter.

Another reason why an outstanding field shooter may be a total dud at Skeet, particularly the international version, is that that clay bird is travelling a lot faster than almost any bird he will ever encounter in the field, and it's a smaller target than virtually any game bird. Remember, the clay target is presented to the shooter in its smallest dimension—*in profile*. That profile measures just about 4"x1¼", for a total area of about 5 square inches.

Another reason why some very good field shooters are duds on clay birds is that the typical field shot is presented at accelerating birds, whereas all shots at clay targets are at decelerating birds. That clay target begins to lose velocity from the very instant it departs the trap, but a pheasant or quail or sharptail rising in front of dogs, or a mallard or pintail jumping off a pothole is gaining velocity rapidly.

Ultimately, the reason why some people are dazzlers at one game and

Jim Woods has shot for 40 years, favors the 700 Remington and 20-gauge doubles.

Woods: No

I don't believe in shooters who can hit game, but not targets, because really good game shots have no trouble shooting targets, and that applies equally to big game hunters and bird hunters I have known.

Big-game hunters must shoot their game under the most adverse of conditions. Game is often at long and varying ranges, oftentimes on the move, sometimes partially obscured in cover, and sometimes in poor light. Most big game hunters would agree that two or more of these single handicaps generally work together to thwart the hunter's best efforts. Remove those handicaps, and put the hunter at a shooting bench or amid the other controlled conditions of a target range, even shooting offhand at a moving animal target, and the good field shot will shoot tight clusters into the vitals of the paper targets to the point that it gets boring.

Upland bird shooters also see their quarry in the worst possible of hunting situations, with birds flushing from underfoot, to over the shoulder, to through a lacework of briars and brush. Dove shooters may have the toughest job of all the bird hunters in bringing down the aerial acrobats they pursue. The good hunters, though, the ones who fill their bag almost every time out, are conditioned to snap the gun to the shoulder and come on target, and fire quickly. The predictable flight of clay birds, either from a Skeet house or trap, cannot be as unnerving to a shooter as the wingbeat whirr and flutter of a flushing quail, or the darting flight of a whitewing dove.

This is not to suggest that a good field shot would beat out a disciplined benchrest shooter or a dedicated trap or Skeet shooter at his own game. In just the target games, the target shooting specialist would probably take the visiting hunter nearly every time. However, if a tournament was devised that included a round of clay birds plus a bag of game birds; or a session at the bench, and then an actual big game hunt, the good field shot should have the aggregate edge over the strictly target shooter every time. ●

SPORTING ARMS OF THE WORLD

by LARRY S. STERETT

The Leader MK 5 rifle is chambered for the 223 cartridge, is manufactured in Australia, and is shown without magazine here. "Sporter" versions are planned also.

Introduction

There have been changes other than price increases in the sporting arms of the world. In 1980, SKB of Japan was to celebrate its 125th Anniversary. By early spring, the SKB outlet in the U.S. was down the tube, and the parent company in Japan was in difficulty, though SKB shotguns are excellent in design, and craftsmanship. By mid-year, Golden Eagle Firearms, the Houston, Texas, distributor of the Nikko over-under shotguns and bolt action centerfire rifle, had folded. Prior to Ithacagun closing in 1979, the firm had distributed both the SKB and Perazzi shotguns, in addition to Finnish Tikka sporting arms. Ithacagun is operating again, manufacturing their own line of shotguns; SKB went on its own, and has folded; Tikka guns are available from at least two sources, including Armsport, Inc.; Winchester picked up the Perazzi line, but effective May 1, 1981, the connection was severed; and as you read this, Perazzi shotguns may be available from Perazzi, R. D. No. 1, Lee Center, NY 13363.

Another noted change has been the increase in sporter versions of military small arms designs, such as the semiautomatic USI and the Leader rifle. Maybe it's a sign of the times. Still, there are a number of new chamberings available in rifles, new barrel lengths and chokes in shotguns, and enough modifications in tested designs to keep shooters happy, and there are even a few new models available.

Above — The Steyr Daimler Puch "Aug" rifle is a bullpup design in synthetics, with a built-in 1.5x scope, folding forward hand grip, peekaboo magazine, various barrels. Chambered for the 223 cartridge.

Below — Bingham Ltd.'s new drum-fed autoloading rimfire carbine is unique in appearance for a 22, but looks like a lot of early submachine guns did.

Armsport

Last year, Armsport introduced a new 12 gauge Unsingle Trap gun, with high ventilated rib, detachable trigger assembly, and palm swell on the pistol grip. This year the Unsingle is available with the ventilated rib adjustable for changing the impact point. The other features have been retained, making the Unsingle one of the excellent designs available to trap shooters. See Testfire, p. 232.

Baikal International

The Baikal line of shotguns remains the same as in the past editions, consisting of single barrel, side/side, and over-under models, plus an autoloader; the total is 18 variations in all. Prices on the lower end of the scale have increased slightly (hasn't everything?), but prices on the upper end have remained the same, or were early in '81. The top quality over-under and side/side models feature excellent quality engraving, and range in price from just under $2300.00 to $5400.00 at the retail level.

Beretta U.S.A. Corp.

The Beretta A301 is available in 12 and 20 gauges, and in field, Skeet, trap and magnum versions. Now a modified version has been added to the line. Tabbed the Model A302, it features a Mag-Action system which permits the shotgun to handle regular length or magnum length 12- or 20-gauge shells by simply changing barrels. Thus, a shotgunner with a new A302 could install a 30-inch 12 gauge barrel chambered for 3-inch shells for waterfowl shooting, and replace it with a 26-inch 12 gauge improved cylinder barrel chambered for standard length (2¾ inches) shells for quail hunting. In addition, the same barrels will fit either the A301 or the new A302, and the 28-inch Multichoke barrel (4 choke tubes) is now available chambered for 3-inch 12 gauge shells.

The excellent Model 680 over-under Trap shotgun is now available as an Unsingle Mono-Trap with choice of 32 or 34-inch full choke barrel, or a Trap Combo with 30-inch over-under barrels and a choice of 32 or 34-inch Unsingle barrel. At $2100.00 for the Combo, it's a bargain when compared to some other trap-grade shotguns on the market.

Bingham Ltd.

One of the most interesting plinking guns to hit the pike in a long time is the new semi-automatic carbine being distributed by this Georgia firm. Resembling the 1940 Soviet PPD submachine gun, it is chambered for the rimfire 22 Long Rifle cartridge, and features a straight blow-back action, one-piece walnut stock with finger grooves on the forearm, a pivoting side safety, ventilated barrel jacket, and a drum magazine. With this gem, you can load the drum, and go through a box of cartridges in a hurry; in fact, it will take you longer to load the drum than it will to empty it, and it won't be half as much fun. The carbine examined was a beauty, well-proportioned, and definitely an eye catcher. It should be a barrel of fun to shoot.

Dynamit Nobel of America

The Rottweil American Trap line has been trimmed a bit, but not really in a noticeable way. The AAT Single and AAT Combination guns are the big movers, and as a result the regular Combination, consisting of the AT over-under with a conventional 34-inch single barrel has been discontinued, as has the conventional over-under alone and the regular single barrel. Otherwise the line remains basically the same.

Heckler & Koch, Inc.

About the time you read this H & K should have two new autoloading sporting rifle models available—the Model HK630 chambered for the 223 cartridge, and the HK940 chambered in a choice of 30-06 or 7x64mm. Both rifles will feature a choice of standard rifled or polygonal rifled barrels, European walnut stock with Monte Carlo cheekpiece, adjustable sights, and a single stage trigger. The HK630 measures 42 inches in over-all length, and has a weight of approximately 7 pounds with a 4-round detachable magazine. (A 10-round magazine will be available as an option for both the HK630 and HK940 rifles.) The HK940 rifle measures 47 inches over-all, and has a weight of approximately 8.8 pounds with a 3-round detachable magazine. Scopes and scope mounts are available for both rifles as options, and the rifles with open sights are priced at $640.00 and $770.00 each, respectively.

In the Benelli shotgun line, three new 12 gauge grades are available—the 121-M1 Police/Military, Model Special Trap, and Model Special 80 Skeet. Prices on the new grades are $421.00, and $699.00, and $740.00 each, respectively, and all Benelli shotguns are guaranteed for two years.

Interarms

Spanish-manufactured AYA shotguns have been available through various firms from time to time in the U.S., but never in large quantities. Now, Interarms has selected four side/side models—4A, 117, 1, and 53—of classic English styling for the American market. These four models resemble the Churchill design, and each has a splinter-type forearm, and straight English grip stock with checkered butts, without pad or plate, in true English tradition. The barrels are of the demi-block design, and the receivers are case-hardened in color, with scroll and floral engraving depending on the model. The Model 4A is a boxlock design, available in a choice of 12 or 20 gauge, or .410 bore, while the other three models are true sidelock designs. The Models 117 and 53 are available in a choice of 12 or 20 gauge, with 26 or 28-inch barrels, while the Model 2 is available only in .410 bore with 26-inch barrels. Double triggers and automatic ejectors are standard on all models, and the prices in early 1981 range from $750.00 (4A) to $2200.00 (53).

The Rossi rifles and shotguns are still available, as is the Manufrance autoloading shotgun, but the Manufrance Falcor over-under shotgun has been dropped from the Interarms line. The Mark X Mauser rifle line remains unchanged, as does the Walther line of rifles, pistols, air rifles, and pistols.

Kassnar Imports

This firm has the Parker-Hale 1200 Series of rifles from England in Super, Super Magnum, and Varmint grades. Based on the Mauser action, these rifles feature 24-inch barrels, chambered for cartridges ranging from the 22-250 Remington to the 300 Winchester Magnum, depending on the grade. In addition, there is a cheaper rifle labeled the Midland 2100. It also features a 24-inch barrel, and is available in six chamberings from the 243 Winchester to the 300 Winchester Magnum. The Midland action is a combination of Mauser/Springfield features, including a Mauser-type non-rotating claw extractor, and the receiver is drilled and tapped for scope mount bases which are provided with the rifle. A hand checkered walnut stock and a hinged magazine floorplate are other features of the 2100. Kassnar also imports the Squires Bingham line of arms and ammunition from the Philippines, including the Model 30D pump action 12 gauge shotgun, and the M16, Model

The Mannlicher Oxford boxlock side/side comes in 12 and 20 gauge. With the lines of a classic English double, it features an Anson and Deeley action and Purdey locking.

The K.F.C. Deluxe M-250 gas-operated 12 gauge autoloader offers only vent rib barrels, has shallow forend design.

This IJ-27 over-under 12 gauge shotgun is one of the most popular of the Baikal line of shotguns, offers good value.

20, and Model 1500 rimfire rifles. The Squires Bingham arms are manufactured by the Arms Corporation of the Philippines, which took over the original SB firm.

Kawaguchiya Firearms/ La Paloma Marketing

Japanese shotguns are not exactly new to U.S. shooters, but the latest K.F.C. model is something different. Labeled the M-250, it is a gas-operated 12 gauge autoloader with a two-piece bolt and an off-set gas mechanism. Instead of being wrapped around the tubular magazine, the gas mechanism is off-set to the left in the depression between the magazine and the barrel; this allows a shallower forearm. The action bar is not connected to the breech bolt, and does not move when the bolt is retracted manually. Barrel lengths include 26, 28, and 30-inch models with standard chokes, in addition to a version with detachable choke tubes. (The barrels all have ventilated ribs.) Available in Standard and Deluxe grades at under $500.00, the M-250 will handle all standard-length 12 gauge shotshells.

La Paloma also imports the K.F.C.

boxlock over-under shotguns in OT-E1 and OT-E3 trap and Skeet grades, and FG field grade, all chambered for standard length (2¾ inches) shells. The target models feature chrome-lined barrels topped with 13mm wide ventilated ribs. Other features include single selective trigger, non-automatic safety, selective automatic ejectors, and high grade French walnut stock and beavertail forearm; oil finish on the target guns and polyurethane on the field grade.

Kodensha Co., Ltd.

As this is written early in 1981, the Nikko line of centerfire rifles and over-under shotguns is in need of a distributor in the United States and may have such a distributor by the time you read this. The line was previously imported by the Golden Eagle Firearms firm in Texas. In the over-under shotgun line, available versions include the Model 5000, 5000-I, 5000-II, and 5000-III Grandee, in field, Skeet, and trap grades, and as the Model 199 in trap and Skeet grades. All the grades are available in 12 gauge, and the 5000-I and 5000-II versions are also available in 20 gauge chambered for 3-inch shells. The cen-

terfire Model 7000 rifle is currently available only in Grade I, in a choice of chamberings from 22-250 Remington to the 458 Winchester Magnum, including a couple of Weatherby calibers.

Wm. Larkin Moore Co.

This firm handles new high grade Italian and Spanish-manufactured side/side shotguns, in addition to some quality "used" shotguns, such as Purdey, Greener, Parker, Holland & Holland, Westley Richards, and Woodward models. Currently, one boxlock and four Italian Piotti sidelock models are available, in a choice of .410 bore, or 28, 20, 16, and 12 gauge versions, with a host of options. Six sidelock Spanish Garbi models are available in a choice of 20, 16, and 12 gauge versions, all built to have the characteristic feel of a "best" London side/side. Two Anson & Deeley design boxlock ejector and four Holland & Holland sidelock design AYA models are available in the same gauges as the Piotti models, including the .410 bore. Aquirre y Aranzabal (AYA) is Spain's largest gunmaker, and the top grade AYA shotguns are considered by many shooters to be the equal of any of the English guns of yesteryear. Three of the AYA models have hand detachable lockplates, and the stock type and dimensions, barrel lengths and chokes, and action finish are to the customer's specifications. As with the other shotguns, many options are available, but considering the Model XXV SL with 25-inch barrels, Churchill rib, and single trigger retails for under $2500.00, it's a bargain, especially when the Piotti models range from $4000.00 to $14,000.00 at the retail level, as this is written. The Moore Company also has new Ferlib and Vincenzo Bernardelli shotguns in popular gauges.

Puccinelli Co.

The latest Puccinelli-IAB shotguns have engraved receivers with black chrome finish, now designed to permit quick buttstock changing, plus a trim semi-beavertail forearm. The stock and forearm are of exhibition grade walnut, and the buttstock has a palm swell on the pistol grip. A sliding trigger option is available, as it was previously, but a new "switch" trigger mechanism allows the single trigger to be changed from a pull-pull to a release-pull, simply by moving a small selector. Also available is the new adjustable ventilated rib on the Unsingle; this adjustment permits the pattern center to be moved from dead center up to 15 inches high at 40 yards, in 1-inch intervals. Prices on the new IAB 400 range from $4800.00 for the S400 over-under with barrels measuring 29½ inches in length, to $7785.00 for the SCA 400 Supercombo with 32-inch over-under barrels and two 34-inch Unsingle barrels having adjustable ventilated ribs, but different chokes. Other new over-under IAB models include the 12 gauge Record in trap, Skeet, and pigeon grades, with barrel lengths ranging from 28 inches to 32 inches, depending on the grade. The Record features a coin-finish receiver, and separated barrels connected only at the breech, and free to expand independently at the muzzle via a supporting ring around the under barrel. For hunting, the more conventional Parcours and Fly over-unders, with barrel lengths of 26¾ or 28 inches, are available. In addition, the Puccinelli firm has a number of investment-grade sidelock and boxlock shotguns of English side/side styling. These shotguns in 12 or 28 gauge, or .410 bore, feature hand detachable sidelocks, relief or banknote engraving, 24 kt inlaid lettering, and exhibition grade French walnut stocks with straight grip. Prices for these side/

sides start at $10,000.00 and proceed upward, with at least one such gun starting at $40,000.00.

Savana Canada Sports Ltd/Ltee

The Italian line of Fabarm shotguns is available to North American shooters through this Canadian firm. There's the gas-operated Ellegi 12 gauge autoloader, which features interchangeable barrels for standard or magnum-length shotshells, on the same receiver without adjustment. The Ellegi is said to have fewer parts than other autoloaders, and a unique gas recovery system which is self-cleaning. The breech bolt, barrel extension, and link assembly are of stainless steel, with a special chrome plating. A variety of barrel lengths and chokes are available, including a Multichoke barrel with five interchangeable screw-on choke tubes from cylinder to full choke. Also available are three over-under shotguns—the Alfa 1, Alfa 2, and Gamma—and a side/side—the Beta—all in 12 gauge. The Beta has a one-piece forged receiver, and the two barrel lumps on the monobloc are divided and spaced to provide four bearing surfaces, practically eliminating any barrel movement. Available with double triggers, or a single selective design, and a choice of pistol grip or straight English stock and splinter forearm of French walnut, the Beta is a classic design. Barrel lengths and chokes are conventional.

The Alfa 1 and 2 shotguns are considered hunting models, with ventilated rib barrels, and double or single selective trigger, respectively. Various barrel lengths and chokes are available, and the weight of the Alfa is dependent on the barrel lengths, and the density of the walnut stock and schnabel forearm. The Gamma is available in Trap, Skeet, STL, STL Deluxe, and L.G. 3 grades. Barrel lengths and chokes are dependent on the grade, and select French walnut is used for the buttstock and schnabel forearm. Selective automatic ejectors, ventilated side ribs, and a 10mm wide ventilated top rib are standard features of the trap and Skeet guns, and all grades are available with single selective triggers. The trap model has a Monte Carlo stock.

Shotguns of Ulm

The K80 over-under shotgun was introduced early in 1980, in trap and Skeet grades, with a ventilated rib of uniform width. For 1981 an optional tapered ventilated rib with a ramp was introduced on the standard grade

trap gun, in addition to four more grades with different engraving patterns. The new grades are the II Bavaria and III Danube, featuring engraved coin-finished receivers, and the IV Gold Target and V Crown Grade with engraved blued receiver and gold inlays. (The V Crown Grade has an inlaid gold crown on the bottom of the receiver, plus pheasants and a dog on the receiver side panels.) Also new for 1981 is the KS2, a true sidelock side/side featuring the same coin-finish receiver and sideplates, engraved with hunting scenes with gold inlays; the engraving is in the banknote style, outlined with fine English scrollwork, and the gold inlays are on the sideplates and on the bottom of the receiver. The KS2 is available in 20 gauge, with 28-inch barrels chambered for 3-inch shells. The right barrel is choked modified and the left full, and a narrow tapered top rib separates the barrels. The English-style straight grip stock and semi-beavertail forearm are of "Exhibition Grade" English walnut, with an oil finish. Deluxe checkering without a border graces the grip and forearm, and drop points are featured to the rear of the sideplates. A single nonselective trigger is standard, and the approximate weight of the KS2 is 6 pounds, depending on the density of the walnut.

The K80 four-barrel Skeet set is now available, so an identical weight and sight picture is presented to the shooters, regardless of the gauge being used. The barrels are all 28 inches in length, and the 12 gauge barrels now feature the Russian-type Tula choke on both the over and under barrels; the under barrel of the 12 gauge gun has four narrow vents on each side to exit gases, minimizing muzzle jump and reducing recoil. Except for the barrels, and the different buttstock and interchangeable forearms, the K80 Skeet guns are basically the same as the regular K80 models.

Steyr Daimler Puch of America Corp. Mannlicher Division

There have been a number of changes in the Mannlicher line from Steyr Daimler Puch, particularly in the shotgun portion. The Ambassador, London, and Oxford side/side models remain the same, and some of the originally-introduced Edinburgh target model over-under and mono guns may be seen, but the latest 12 gauge Edinburgh models are manufactured by Franchi, for Renato

The Beretta Model 680 Trap gun has the word "Trap" inlaid into the bottom of the trigger guard to avoid mixups, no doubt.

Above—The Valmet 412 KE series of shotguns features selective automatic ejection, while the 412 K features positive cam-operated extraction, in same basic action.

On this Puccinelli-IAB over-under shotgun note the beveled wood at the receiver join and at the forearm iron; it's a sign of quality.

Gamba, to be distributed by the Mannlicher Division of S.D.P. While the Renato Gamba version of the Franchi over-under is not exactly the same as the Franchi version sold by Franchi through Stoeger Industries, the family resemblance is very evident. The receiver of the new Edinburgh has a coin finish with some engraving, and the one-piece steel ventilated top rib, with ramp, has been redesigned, as has shape of the buttstock and forearm. The barrel selector button is on the trigger, as it is on regular Franchi models, and the shape of the trigger is considerably different from what it was on the original Renato Gamba Edinburgh design. The Edinburgh is available in Skeet grade, with a choice of 26 or 28-inch barrels, as a trap grade over-under with choice of 30 or 32-inch barrels, a Mono-trap with choice of 32 or 34-inch over barrel, or a Trap Combo with a set of over-under barrels and one mono barrel, with barrel lengths and chokes as on the individual models. A fitted leather case is available as an option for the Edinburgh.

Looking for something different in rifles? The "Aug" should be available shortly after you read this. The "Aug" is Steyr Daimler Puch's "Army Universal gun," and the first version will be full automatic, designed for military or law enforcement, with the semi-automatic sporter version by late 1981. Featuring a "bullpup" design with stock, see-thru magazine and pistol grip assembly of high quality synthetic materials, the "Aug" is virtually maintenance free and practically indestructible. The barrel is cold-forged, with a chrome-lined bore, and it is interchangeable; barrel lengths of 16, 20, and 24 inches are available. Chambered for the 223 cartridge, the "Aug" holds 30 rounds of ammunition in a double staggered column, detachable see-thru box magazine. Built into the hand or carrying grip is a 1.5x scope with windage and elevation settings. Priced at $1500.00, the "Aug" contains five basic groups—barrel, hammer assembly, bolt, receiver, and stock—and can be field stripped and reassembled without tools, in addition to allowing interchangeability of parts.

In the regular Steyr Mannlicher rifle line, the models available include the L, SL, M, S. S/T, SSG in Marksman and Match grades, and the ML 79 "Luxus" in L and M versions. The ML 79 rifle is supplied with a 3-round detachable box magazine, while the other models have 5-round detachable rotary magazines, except in the Magnum versions which feature 4-round magazines. Single or double triggers are available on all models, except the ML 79, which comes with a single set trigger. Calibers range from the 222 Remington to the 458 Winchester Magnum, depending on the model. Two often overlooked models in the Steyr line are the SSG Marksman and the Model M Professional; both with ABS "Cycolac" stocks and a Parkerized metal finish on all parts to reduce glare and wear. The Professional features a barrel length of just under 24 inches, and is available chambered for the 7x57, 7x64, 270 Winchester, or 30-06 cartridges, with several metric calibers available as options, including the 9.3x62. The SSG Marksman has a 26-inch barrel and is available chambered for the 243 or 308 Winchester cartridges, with no options.

The Marksman comes with a folding rear sight, while the Professional may be obtained with or without sights. Double triggers are standard, but a single trigger is available. Both rifles are ideal working rifles.

The Mannlicher Division has four other rifles available—the Safari 77 over-under rifle in calibers 7x65R, 375 H&H, and 458 Winchester Magnum, at over $9,000.00, the Mustang single shot rifle in calibers 222 Remington, 243 and 270 Winchester, and 30-06, for under $11,000.00, plus the Fabrique Nationale LAR and FNC autoloaders, at approximately $2,000.00, depending on the model. The Safari and Mustang are break action rifles, and both come with fitted leather cases. (The Mustang comes with a Zeiss scope in claw mounts.) The Mustang has a Holland & Holland type sidelock, with fully engraved lockplate, while the Safari uses a Greener design.

The F.N. LAR is chambered only for the 308 cartridge, but is available in four versions—Competition, Paratrooper, Heavy Barrel with wood stock and bipod, and Heavy Barrel with synthetic stock and bipod. The FNC model is chambered for the 223 cartridge, and is available in standard or paratrooper version for under $1,800.00. No accessories are available for the FNC, but there's a long list available for the LAR, including a Hensoldt scope for $1,056.00, in addition to the Hensoldt scope mount for $328.00. If you want a LAR rifle, with accessories, be prepared to pay . . . dearly.

Stoeger Industries

The Franchi Standard, Model 500, and 520 autoloading shotguns are not cataloged for 1981, although the 530 Trap gun is available in limited quantities, and there's a new 530 European (without choke tubes) Trap autoloader scheduled about the time you read this. In the Sako rifle line, the Model 78 bolt action chambered for the rimfire 22 Long Rifle cartridge in standard and heavy barrel grades is not cataloged. The 7mm Remington Magnum chambering has been dropped from the Safari Grade centerfire rifle line, leaving only the 300 and 338 Winchester Magnum chamberings, plus the 375 H&H, while the price of the Safari rifle has increased $260.00 over what it was last year. Stoeger has also taken on the distribution of the El Gamo line of Spanish-manufactured precision air rifles and air pistols in the United States.

Toledo Arms

This is a new organization of Spanish arms manufacturers who have set up an outlet in the U.S. to supply American shooters with the finest in Spanish shotguns and shooting accessories. In addition to stocking many of the standard models of 18 different Spanish manufacturers, the firm will also have a service/repair station in Miami with sufficient parts in stock to handle any repair situation which might occur. Among some of the firms represented by Toledo Arms are Armas Garbi, Union Armera, Jose Uriguen, Zabala Hnos. S.A., Francisco Sarrigarte, Industrias Danok, El Caballo, and Empresa Nac. Sta. Barbara.

Valmet

The Valmet "shooting system" was introduced in 1980, and there have been some additions. Originally, all shotgun models were chambered for the 12 gauge cartridge, except for two 20 gauge options in the 412 KE version. Chambered for the 3-inch cartridges, these 20 gauge versions were available in a choice of 26-inch barrels choked improved cylinder/modified or 28-inch choke modified/full. Now the 412 Skeet is available in 20 gauge with 26-inch barrels choked skeet/skeet. The regular 12 gauge Skeet gun has another barrel length added—28-inch choked skeet/skeet—and the 26-inch barrels have been changed from skeet/skeet choking to cylinder/improved cylinder choking. In the 412 Shotgun/Rifle Combination gun, two new chamberings have been added—243 Winchester and 223 Remington— to go with the other three —222, 308, and 30-06—already available. The barrel lengths—24 inches—and the choking on the 12 gauge barrel—improved modified—remains the same. In the 412 Double Rifle line two additional chamberings—243 Winchester and 375 Winchester—are available. The only other changes in the Valmet line include price increases of from $50.00 to $160.00, with lesser increases on the optional barrels.

The "shooting system" from Finland is just that. Introduced originally in the 1960's, the latest Valmet design allows interchangeability of barrels on a basic receiver unit without costly custom fitting. In other words, with an over-under Valmet shotgun, and a couple of optional barrel units, the U.S. shooter is set for hunting almost every type of game found on the North American continent, and with a couple of additional units, for trap and Skeet.

Waidmanns Guns International Incorporated

The Heym line of German-manufactured drillings, rifles, combination guns, and shotguns are available through U.S. and Canadian distributors in most popular calibers and gauges. New for 1981, to commemorate the 135th anniversary of the Heym is a side/side rifle in a choice of engraved sidelock or boxlock versions. Available in a wide variety of calibers, U.S. and metric, each double rifle will be furnished with a leather-covered trunk-type case. Top of the new side/side rifle line will be a super-deluxe grade, featuring hand detachable sidelocks, extra choice walnut, and high relief engraving with gold and silver inlays of the customer's choice. Canadians contact Waidmannsheil Ltd., P.O. Box 861, Bolton, Ont., Canada LOP 1A0.

World Public Safety Inc.

Shooters are long familiar with the Colt AR-15, AR-180, and more recently with the Ruger Mini-14 rifles, all chambered for the 223 cartridge. Heckler & Koch's M93 design is less well known, but equally as reliable. Now there's another design that appears to be up and coming. Manufactured in Smithfield, NSW Australia, by Leader Dynamics Pty. Limited, the Leader "T2" Series rifle is a gas-operated, locked breech, semi-automatic rifle constructed of chrome-moly steel. Featuring a barrel length of just over 16 inches, and an overall length of just under 36 inches, the Leader weighs approximately 7½ pounds, depending on the particular model. The receiver hinges at the lower front, and stripping the action is particularly easy, as the breech mechanism components remain in one compact unit when removed from the rifle. The MK 5 version features a reinforced fiberglass stock, forearm, and pistol grip, protected front and rear sights, sling swivels, and a carrying handle, and resembles a para-military design. The Sporter version is available in two grades; the MK1, which is the same as the MK5, except for having a wood buttstock and forearm, plus a base on the carrying handle to accept a scope mount, and the MK2, which has a forearm and a special stylized wooden buttstock/pistol grip unit. All three models have flash suppressors on the barrel muzzle, and 20-round detachable box magazines are standard. ●

I HUNT TIMBER: I VOTE VARIABLE

The notoriously thick coastal Washington forest offers a 150-yard possibility down a natural "tunnel" in timber.

Power changes make sense in timber shooting.

by NORM NELSON

DRIFTING THROUGH the woods, my deer radar was turned on all the way, looking for Columbia blacktails in the wet, Pacific coastal forest. And then there was movement ahead. Through a natural tunnel in the timber, I spotted a large deer about 80 yards away, walking slowly at right angles to me on a grass-overgrown logging trail.

By this time, my Savage 99 in 358 caliber was at my shoulder, duplex crosshairs of the 3x Leupold scope on the slowly moving animal.

My only problem was a big one: I could not tell if this was a buck. The deer's nose stayed down at ground level, and the frost-killed grass was still high enough to block any view of the critter's headgear, if any.

I'm 95% sure it was a buck. It was too heavy-bodied for a doe. The head was down, because the animal was apparently sniffing other deer tracks on the old skid road—typical buck behavior in the rut. But I could not fire without seeing legal antlers; and that was the last I saw of this deer, despite careful, upwind stalking of the whole area.

That 3x scope, theoretically a good magnification choice for timber, just wasn't enough to do the job here, despite the excellent optical quality.

How about another hard luck story? This one involves too much scope magnification for forest hunting. Years ago in my native northern Minnesota forests, I jumped a bedded whitetail buck at very close range. After a couple of bounds, he stopped in thick brush to see what I'd do next.

Did I proceed to blow away that amazingly dimwitted buck in easy archery range? Hell, no. Why not? Because I couldn't find him—or sort him out from the melange of gray alder brush—in time to get off a shot before he took off for good.

In both cases, I needed the versatility of a good variable-power riflescope. With the Headless Hessian blacktail, a quick crank-up to 5 or 6x just might have shown me antler tips in the grass where the deer's head was hidden. With the too-close whitetail, a wide field of view and low power might have let me see him.

And now for an experience with a happier ending which drives home the point of how a variable can save the day. In dim daybreak, I was walking a Pacific Northwest logging road with a 300 Winchester BAR mounting a Redfield 2-7x. The scope was set at 2x for maximum, fast field of view in case an elk suddenly clattered across the narrow road at close range. Where the road approached a low-brushed clearcut, I spotted a small herd of elk at about 200 yards. It was legal shooting time, but visibility was terrible be-

152 THE GUN DIGEST

cause of driving rain and mountain-hugging clouds.

Flopping down on the road shoulder, I quickly scoped the elk, looking for antlers. Ordinarily, you spot bulls first by their lighter, taffy color even before you see antlers. All the sopping wet elk were the same shade in the gloom and rain, and the 2x setting couldn't tell me a thing about antlers. I flipped the power setting to 7x and could then see the skinny spikes of a young Roosevelt bull. A spike bull was good enough—I wanted tender winter meat more than big antlers that season. Just then, the milling elk broke into a run for timber, but one shot put the bull in the bracken ferns and kept the Nelson tribe eating well for months.

That last incident underlines the practical, hunting field importance of a little-understood factor cited by Bob Bell in his article, "Why Is A Scope?" in the 1981 edition of GUN DIGEST. Relative brightness ratings are highest in low-powered scopes and lowest in high-powered scopes, but Bell points out that European shooters have been more sophisticated in understanding that high-powered scopes may well have an edge in supplying a better target image under poor light conditions.

This is measured by what's well-named the "twilight factor." As formulated by Europeans, this rating is based on multiplying the unobstructed diameter of the objective lens (in millimeters) by the magnification (4x or whatever), then taking the square root of that product. With the Redfield I was using, the twilight factor at the 2x setting (when I couldn't pick out any antlers) was 7.75. At the 7x setting, the twilight factor was 14.5. As Bell pointed out, twilight factors become important in dim light, and in my elk incident, it was downright crucial.

(This doesn't make an argument automatically for using, say, a 6x scope all the time for forest hunting's often poor lighting, even though the twilight factor of a 6x could be almost double that of a 2½x scope. The 19-20 ft. field (at 100 yards) of a typical 6x big game scope is much too small for timber hunting's typically close ranges. You have to fit the power to the circumstance.)

The modern variable scope is here to stay. It offers versatility a forest hunter really needs. Sure, you may spend years in the timber and never see game beyond the 40-yard mark. But then comes the time when you do get a longer range chance, possibly under adverse light, and you need the extra magnification and perhaps its twilight factor very badly, right now.

Naturally, this presupposes that the variable is going to be mounted on a rifle of sufficiently flat trajectory and practical killing power to be useful at longer ranges. Putting 2-7x variables on 30-30's, 35 Remington's and 45-70's won't make dual-purpose outfits for close range timber use and to also burn down game across big clearcuts. You'd have single-purpose rifles with dual-purpose glassware, but that could be good on a purely timber gun when you need more magnification at modest range (e.g., my head-down blacktail "buck") or a better look at an animal in the forest's often dim light. Now we're talking about a variable scope making a good timber rifle into an even better timber hunting outfit.

Excluding those designed only for 22 rimfires, there are at the time of this writing some 82 variable scopes being sold in this country. How do you pick a winner from that hodge-podge?

First be prepared to spend a fair amount to increase the likelihood of getting a reliable scope. Compared to fixed power scopes, variables are complicated, both optically and mechanically. The lower-priced makes compromise in both departments, and the results can be grim. For example, in a top-line variable, the mechanical camming systems are precision-machined, not just stamped out and press-fit like cheaper makes. When variables first appeared in the 1950's, they got a lot of bad press due to problems like changing zero when power was shifted. Some of the cheapos still do this. If you're up against a really tight scope purchase budget, you're better off to get a good-quality fixed-power scope than invest in a dubious variable.

I still recall the Oriental war idol expression on partner George Hess's face when he cranked up the power on his discount variable hunting in Montana. As he turned the power shift ring, the scope reticules revolved, too. Good thing there was a spare rifle in the party for him to use the rest of that hunt.

No doubt, my expression was equally interesting when after hours of trans-mountain driving, I reached my hunting area, pulled my rifle out of its nice, padded, protective case and heard the glassy tinkle of lenses falling out of my new American variable. Unlike lucky George, my closest spare rifle was 200 miles away.

Second, what type of variable? They come in roughly three categories, based on range of power. First are the lower-range jobs of, say, 1.5-5x. The major lines like Bushnell, Leupold, Lyman, Redfield and Weaver all have models in this approximate power-range category. So do some of the lesser-knowns. This is a highly useful breed of variable scope. At low ranges, fields of view are relatively huge—up to 70-plus feet at 100 yards. Even at much closer ranges, that provides lots of field to instantly find a fast-bounding buck. Also important to the timber snapshooter, these lower-range variables provide plenty of eye relief.

The middle-ground range of variables is typified by the highly popular 2-7x (roughly) models. Almost every scope line on the market offers a goodie here. At the lowest settings, fields of view aren't quite as huge—the Redfield 2-7x typical of this breed provides a 42-ft. field at 2x. That's still plenty for timber hunting. Naturally, field of view starts shrinking fast at the upper ranges of these scopes. Eye relief then, although usually somewhat reduced, is still very good for quick, clear sighting.

The third category covers the biggest variable scopes ranging from 3-4x on up to 9, 10 or even 12x. Here, the added power is getting to be too much for most timber use. The lower range setting of a standard (non-widefield) variable can be down to 30 feet at 4x or only about 34-35 ft. at 3x. The widefield models with rectangular optics come out somewhat better here and could be chosen if you must have this much scope.

One caveat here. Widefield scopes may be more prone to hermetic leakage that results eventually in fogging. The spline-fit system used to keep the rectangular optical lens assembly on its properly level axis is far more difficult to seal than a conventional round optical assembly. At the time of this writing, I am told by an industry source that no maker has yet satisfactorily solved this problem. I'm not at liberty to quote directly here but can only add that the source is both an expert and reliable one. In my own experience (too much) with fogging scopes, 80% of them were indeed widefield models.

Overall, my rule of thumb based on some hard experience plus the counsel of better, wiser men is that 38-40 feet of field (at 100 yards) is the practical minimum for timber hunting. Remember, even that big a field translates into only 11-12 feet at 30 yards in the tag alders, doghair maple or young, thick piney woods where a lot of fast deer hunting action takes place all over the U.S. Remember, too, that at close-in timber ranges, the game is very likely to be aware of your presence and thus probably broken-field running or bounding to beat hell by the time you're aware of *its* presence. That's when you need all the field of view your glass can give you.

The big, Category 3 variables pose some problems. Added cost, extra size and shorter eye relief are among these. Worse, they can be tough to mount on many rifles, impossible on some. Many of the big variables have oversized front lenses that must be mounted higher than normal simply to clear the barrel. Unless the rifle is custom-stocked with an unusually high comb, these tall-mounted scopes leave you "cheeking" the rifle not with your cheek but your jawbone. That's not as steady, nor does it feel very good with fairly high-powered recoil.

How much more weight the big variables add depends on brands and models. The 2-10x version of Leupold's superb Vari-X III models weighs only 1¼ oz. more than the companion 2½-8x Vari-X III. In other makes, the difference between medium and top-powered variables can be up to 3 to 4 oz. The spread between the smallest 1.5-5x variables and the largest hunting variables is even greater. A few ounces extra weight is not going to founder you on a hard day's hunt. But the added heft of the largest variables adversely affects the handling and steadiness of many hunting rifles—the top-heaviness involved makes canting all too easy. Finally, the top-power, big variables are generally longer and simply don't look as good when mounted on rifles of somewhat slender, short lines, for whatever esthetics are worth.

What about reticules? Not long ago, American hunting scopes came in three reticule models—standard crosshairs, post plus horizontal crosshair, or the dot. All three have drawbacks for the forest hunter. Typical crosshairs can pull a vanishing act in poor light against dark backdrops. The post combo is excellent in bad light and very fast for snapshooting, but it has limitations for fine aiming on a distant target, particularly when some holdover is needed. The dot reticle can be the biggest booby trap of all for timber use.

Years ago, I scoped a 35 Whelen '03 Springfield with a 2½x Bear Cub wearing a special order Lee 6-min. dot. That's a very big one. Once when I had to take a moose across a sedge bog at about 300 yards, I found the dot, swollen to an 18-inch blob at that range, was like trying to draw a bead with a

basketball. I got the moose but only after a barrage of sloppy shooting caused by my sloppy aiming point and despite a good, prone position with hasty sling, no less. Yet at 25-50 yards in the puckerbrush, the 6-min. dot was still too small to find easily against dark evergreens early or late in the day. The standard 4-min. dots, a third smaller, are even worse here.

But there is a solution to the timber reticule problem. The Europeans got there long before us. Shortly after

A variable scope's choice of wide field or more magnification can be vital in hunting forest game like this big buck whitetail, hard to see either near or far.

World War II, I saw my first duplex crosshairs in a pre-war German Supra 4x that a chum had liberated. We snickered at the fence post-thick crosshairs that in the middle abruptly transformed into normal or even somewhat fine crosshairs. Then I grew thoughtful. I took that weirdo scope out into the gloaming and sighted through it at logs, stumps and other objects in the forest edges already very dim before sundown. Even when I couldn't see the center crosshairs very well, it was apparent that the gross, peripheral crosshairs were still letting me center on poorly seen objects. For shooting under poor light conditions, this was a very dandy reticule indeed.

The American version of the duplex crosshairs does the business here. Your eye is quickly led to the center of the reticule by the thicker crosshairs. Zap, you're looking at the intersection

even when bad light or dark background almost erases the finer crosshairs at actual center. Problem solved.

If you think that selecting a scope from 82 variable models is tough, wait until you start the tricky job of matching an appropriate mount.

On the face of it, you'd think the problem would be too many choices. In addition to the 82 scope choices, there are about 60 big game rifles on the market. This does not count combinations of the same action (example: dif-ferent versions of the Model 70 Winchester), nor single-shots which 99 out of 100 hunters would agree are not logical timber rifle choices, nor double rifles, which 199 out of 200 hunters cannot afford, nor specialty rifles like 44-40 replicas or military-target jobs. As a third factor, there are also about 61 basic big game scope mounts available. Some of these come in different combinations themselves, but let's stick with those 61.

Theoretically, that's 300,120 possible scope-mount-rifle combinations! But don't scream. Actually, for a given rifle, the number of available mounts may be drastically reduced. For some rare birds, such as certain imported rifles, you may find only one or two mounts on the market. Of course, for something pretty standard, like a Remington 700, you can find 20 or more different makes of mounts, many of them available with three choices of ring height (fortunately).

The surprising thing is how many mount-scope combos don't work together for certain rifles. Case in point: My afore-mentioned 35 Whelen Springfield has an excellent Pachmayr Lo-Swing side mount. This provides quick reversion to iron sights if anything is haywire with the scope. I'm paranoid on this point, because no less than five scopes have fogged on me in the hunting field, not counting a

This whitetail buck was downed by Al Nelson, using a Redfield 2-7x variable and a short-barreled bolt action carbine, in thick Minnesota swamp country.

couple that failed mechanically. There's also the fact that in a heavy rain or driving snowstorm (both good times to hunt dense timber, incidentally), you simply can't keep scope lenses *or* see-through scope caps dry enough for a clear and safe view of the target. Rubber-tensioned, instant snap-off scope caps are one answer. But they can fail to pop off and are always brush-catchers.

However, my Bushnell ScopeChief 1½-4½x variable on this rifle barely fits. The between-rings span of the Pachmayr is just not great enough to let me put that ScopeChief as far forward as I'd like. The scope turret is in the way, even though I file-notched some extra clearance into the front ring of the mount.

That's not a rare case. Many good scopes and many good mounts simply won't mate on many good rifles. With

fairly common rifles, the rational way to approach this is to pick a scope for your rifle, then take both of them to a gunsmith or a sporting goods store with competent clerks to select a mount that actually fits both scope and rifle in combination.

However, if your rifle is not a common model, your choice of mounts may be very limited. In that case, you'd better hold off picking a scope until you have the mount, *then* choose a scope for the rifle-mount combo. You're

almost sure to find scopes that won't fit. Either the turret is in the wrong place, or the objective lens lacks barrel clearance with the height of available rings, or there may even be a clearance problem involving the power-shifting ring back by the scope's ocular lens.

What makes a good scope mount to begin with? I'm partial to swing-out or quick-detachable mounts, because I've had more trouble with scopes than the Flying Dutchman had with weather and navigation. Properly installed and adjusted, a quality swing-out mount like the Pachmayr is utterly reliable. Years ago, I had one on a .243 that doubled in brass as a summertime crow rifle; and the whole rig held zero admirably.

Another way to go here is a simple detachable mount. A number of these are available, ranging from low-priced Weaver top mounts that can be coin-

loosened to slip off the scope if weather or scope failure so requires, up to stout and expensive old-timers like the Griffin & Howe or Jaeger lever-locking side mounts. Even the camming stud mounts like the well-known Redfield Jr. are quick-detachable in this sense. Remounted, they should be reasonably still zeroed where you had it before removal. Well, maybe not enough for varmint hunting but okay for big game. It might be very smart to run a few tests of your rig at the range to see how well it does hold zero after removal and replacement.

See-through or tunnel mounts have revived in recent years. However, with a decent variable, you shouldn't need a rig like this. They put a scope far too high for reasonable use. Years ago in the pre-variable Dark Ages, I built a nifty 25-06 varminter that had target-scope blocks for a Unertl 10x Vulture. This was a great prairie dog rifle in Wyoming. However, I also wanted it available on the same trips for open country mule deer and antelope hunting with a 4x scope in place of the 10x glass.

Thinking myself very clever, I installed a tall Echo side mount that would put the 4x scope high enough to clear the permanently mounted target scope block on the receiver bridge. The whole idea stank. Even though this rifle had an unusually high comb, I still had a terrible time using that high-mounted 4x scope, despite my long neck. Also, the vulnerably high mount seemed susceptible to zero changes, even though mounted with two sizable screws and a couple of expansion pins in the receiver wall. The whole set-up defied one of rifle shooting's great rules—the lower you can mount a scope, the better. And see-through mounts violate this rule.

Summed up, the better breeds of variables on the scope market today are the answer to a serious forest hunter's prayers, present or incipient. Stick, however, with the 1-5x or 2-7x (approximate) categories. These provide the ideal combinations of great field at low settings, all the magnification you're ever likely to need, and enough eye relief for fast work. The duplex crosshairs offered by most makers are the only way to go. Solidly mount the whole thing in a good mount, preferably one that will give you the chance to revert to iron sights if the scope ever fails out on the boondocks. Sight the whole rig in well, and think good thoughts. Then go forth prepared for just about any shooting contingency that forest big game hunting throws at you. ●

HAND-LOADING TO DATE

by DEAN A. GRENNELL

For those who favor the taper crimp, Redding-Hunter has them in 32 S&W Long, 380 Auto, 9mm Luger, 38 Super, 38-357, 45 ACP and 30 M-1.

Hand held adjustable powder measure from Quinetics, Inc. Trigger is thumb actuated and metering chamber does not shear powder granules. Delivery tube fits case necks from .22 up.

New three-die sets from RCBS are designed for straight-sided cartridges and certain bottleneck numbers. Sets for 357 and 44 Magnum have spacer rings so they can be used for 38 and 44 Special without further adjustment.

NUMEROUS new items have appeared since last year and we'll review them by manufacturers, in no special order:

Hornady/Pacific/Frontier: Despite the tragic loss of the organization's founder and president, Joyce W. Hornady, as well as project engineer Ed Heers and customer service manager Jim Garber in an aircraft crash on January 15, 1981, this enterprise will continue under the direction of Hornady's son Steve and his widow, Mrs. Marvel Hornady.

Pacific's latest reloading press for rifle/handgun combines the O-frame Model O-7, introduced a year ago, with the compound-toggle linkage that has been a feature of their Multi-Power C. The result is known as the Double O-7; a remarkably husky and powerful machine, indeed. Suggested retail, less dies and shell holder, is $93.95, plus an additional $11 for the automatic primer feed, if desired.

Several recommended shotshell loads are listed in the final pages of the Pacific catalog as a handy reference for users of Pacific's shotshell reloading equipment. A third edition of the *Hornady Handbook* is fresh off the press, considerably revised and expanded to 688 pages, with several new cartridge listings, a section on reloading for silhouette competition in both rifles and handguns, and a copious listing of ballistic data, to distances up to 1000 yards for those bullets apt to be used at such ranges. Suggested retail is $9.95 per copy, at your local dealer or direct from Hornady.

New bullets in the Hornady line include three in .224-inch diameter: a 52-grain boat-tail hollow point; 55-grain soft point with cannelure; and a 55-grain full metal jacket boat tail, likewise cannelured. There's a new .277-inch boat-tail soft point at 140 grains, and a .284-inch 162-grain and .308-inch 190-grain to the same design. A 190-grain BTHP match bullet rounds out new Hornady rifle additions.

In handgun bullets, Hornady has added a 50-grain FMJ-RN at .251-inch diameter for use in the 25 ACP, adding

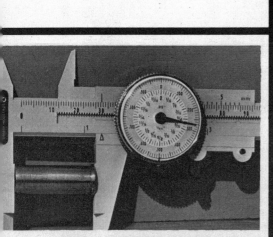

RCBS case length gauge has dial readout, is made of high-strength superpolyamid plastic; reads from zero to 5.177" by .001" increments. Can measure inside or outside diameter, and depth as well.

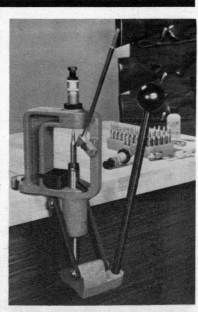

Pacific's Double 0-7, a new "angled" frame reloading press, provides extra power in case resizing and bullet swaging, also includes Pacific's unique PPS Priming System for fully automatic priming.

that caliber to their line of Frontier Cartridges. Also new are the 124-grain FMJ-FP in .355-inch and 230-grain FMJ-FP in .451-inch. The FP designation is a flat point rather than the usual round nose (RN). Besides the 25 ACP, Frontier now offers the 220 Swift as a factory load.

The combined catalog covering the lines of **CCI, Speer and RCBS** is priced at $1.50 from **Omark Industries** but it's a colorful production, well worth buying and adding to your archives for future reference, down the years. The newest Speer bullet is a 55-grain, .224-inch Spitzer soft point with cannelure, for those rifles that require crimped loads.

RCBS is reported to be once more well along on the final touches to their Green Machine, which we reported and illustrated last year. It's a progressive and automated design for reloading handgun cartridges such as the 38 Special or 357 Magnum. Also new is the RCBS Pistol Ammo-Crafter kit, including their Little Dandy powder measure; a copy of the tenth *Speer Reloading Manual;* resizing lubricant and case lube pad; a Model 5-0-5 scale and two rotors for the Little Dandy measure, numbers 2 and 18. The vernier scaled case length gauge previously offered has been joined by one

with a direct dial readout, thereby avoiding a considerable amount of eyestrain for the user.

In the RCBS competition reloading dies, they've added the 223 Remington, 7mm-08 and 7mm Remington Magnum. Meanwhile, the finish on these has been changed from hard chrome to a black oxide with white markings for easier visibility.

RCBS also has added three-die reloading sets for straight-sided handgun cases and a few bottleneck numbers, as well. The sets for 357 and 44 Magnums include a spacer ring to put beneath the die collar so that, by removing it, you're correctly adjusted to reload the 38 and 44 Special. I've been using these and find that they work extremely well. I don't know if RCBS plans to offer an optional version of these with tungsten carbide sizing dies, but I'd certainly hope they will.

Over at **Sierra Bullets** they've been working up several new numbers. In their MatchKing line, they've added a .284-inch, 150-grain HPBT and a matching .308-inch 150-grain. New to their GameKing line is a 55-grain, .224-inch FMJBT with cannelure. Sierra's Tournament Master line now consists of six different FMJ numbers for handgun silhouette competition,

with a .357-inch 125-grain and a .410-inch 220-grain as the most recent entries. They also have a new bullet display board this year, with the sample bullets affixed to a slab of solid redwood. The current catalog should be available from your dealer, or request one direct from Sierra.

Texan Reloaders, Inc. has been transplanted, to Illinois and is back in active business again. Their complete catalog of presses and equipment for reloading metallics and shotshells is $1, postpaid.

Dynamit Nobel of America, Inc. now offers the noted Brenneke shotgun slugs in 12, 16 and 20-gauge as a reloading component, along with tenpacks of the Brenneke slug loads by Rottweil, as well as various shotshell loads from Rottweil. A descriptive brochure is free on request.

Hodgdon Powder Co., Inc. is back in full production with their Pyrodex replica black powder. It's available in three grades: RS for rifles and shotguns; P for pistols and CTG for black powder cartridge arms. The Hodgdon line of smokeless powders remains much as before, except that they've discontinued their HS5 and H-205 numbers. A descriptive brochure on the Hodgdon line is free on request.

Norma-Precision has redesignated their No. 19119 38 Special factory load as Plus-P. Load specifications remain the same, with its 110-grain JHP bullet rated at 1225 fps/367 fpe. Earlier production was marked as "Not Plus-P," due to differences between European pressure measuring techniques and those used in this country. Greg Pogson, their vice president, notes that some of the earlier lots remain on display in U.S. gun shops, and urges that they be treated as Plus-P, regardless of the labeling. These can be identified by the lot code numbers stamped on the side of the inner carrier of the box, and include those numbers beginning with the following sets of three digits: 016, 048, 057, 086, 117, 118, and 127.

Pogson notes their supply of Norma powders is excellent, including the highly popular MRP (magnum rifle powder). Since many U.S. dealers have reported difficulties in obtaining Norma powders, Pogson says that Norma is willing to make direct sales to dealers. Interested dealers can request details from him.

Winchester-Western has developed a new 45-grain bullet for the 25 ACP that, they say, is designed to increase the stopping power of the petite cartridge, meanwhile retaining functional reliability in autoloading pis-

Hodgdon has discontinued H205, which was an excellent performer in 22-250 Remington and many similar cartridges. Readers may wish to purchase any cans of these they encounter, before the hoarders snap them up.

Third edition of the *Hornady Handbook* has grown to 688 hardbound pages, gives dope on over 100 Hornady bullets for use in 117 different cartridges, including popular European catridges and wildcat and obsolete loads.

These new Hornady boat-tail spire points are for hunters, hence special features to assure performance at 200 yards and beyond: match-type accuracy; dependable expansion; Hornady's special Interlock.

Case-Gard P100 cartridge boxes from MTM in two sizes, both at $2.95. Smaller size works with 380 auto (*if* you have long fingernails!), and, of course, for 9mm, 38 Special/357 Magnum. Larger size handles 41, 44 and 45 cartridges.

tols. The bullet has a small steel ball embedded in the tip, with a shallow cavity beneath it. In years past, we might have expected that the new bullet might be made available as a separate reloading component, but W-W has discontinued sales of their bullets as a component.

The Alberts Corporation now offers a brochure of recommended load data for their line of Alberts swaged lead handgun bullets formerly called Taurus bullets. The brochure is free on request, a self-addressed stamped envelope would be appreciated. Sales to dealers only, though.

MTM Molded Products Com-pany has their No. 81 catalog ready, copies free on request. New this year are the Mag 100 Case-Gard ammo boxes in two sizes: 38 Special/357 Magnum, and 41/44/45 ACP. If you were about to ask, yes, the larger size will also handle the 45 Long Colt. Suggested retail on these is $2.95 for either size, and they should prove extremely convenient and popular with handloaders. Top and bottom surfaces are designed to facilitate solid stacking. Also new from MTM, at the same price, is a Case-Gard bolt concealer box, designed for storing rifle bolts at a point remote from the rest of the rifle, as a measure to discourage theft and unsafe handling.

Corbin Manufacturing & Supply has redesigned their Mity-Mite bullet swaging press to incorporate an integral upper crosspiece that converts it from a C-frame to the much stronger O-frame. They now offer swaging dies for home production of bullets for the 223 Remington cartridge from spent 22 LR brass. Die sets are available for use with conventional reloading presses having 7/8-14 thread, or for the Mity-Mite. The Mity-Mite designation, by the way, is being phased out in favor of referring to it as the Corbin Swaging Press. Dies for the .223 bullet have a 5-caliber ogive, leaving a gen-

New Rainel de P.R. shotshell cases offer advantages in both manufacture and reloading, but not until an original ammunition plant starts loading them.

erous length of parallel shank for a longer bearing surface with the case neck, so as to resist being pushed rearward during the feed cycle in auto-loading rifles. The bullet design is a full jacketed open tip, with a point opening of .081-inch. The dies have been designed so that there is no pressure ring at the base so as to avoid the tendency of such rings to expand the case neck during seating, thereby loosening the grip on the bullet. Bullet weight with this die set can be varied between 52-55 grains. The set for the 7/8-14 presses is $100, or $278 for the Corbin Swaging Press, complete with the set of dies for it. Current backlog on delivery is about one year for the CSP and dies, but sets for the reloading presses are reported to be in stock and available for immediate shipment at this time.

C-H Tool & Die Corporation has a new catalog of their reloading presses and equipment that's free on request. Tony Sailer reports that he's working up the design for a power case trimmer, and hopes to have it in production soon. Their Heavyweight Champion press has been given minor design changes and the list on that one is now up to $199, which may seem a substantial sum, but it's probably the all-out brawniest reloading press on today's

market, with its 1.185-inch diameter ram that has an opening drilled down the center to deposit the spent primers in a container, and the ram is hardened to an advanced state of toughness so as to resist deformation, even when swaging the largest bullets.

Quinetics Corporation has a new hand-held powder measure with a thumb-actuated dispensing trigger. It's adjustable as to drop weight and can be used with rifle or handgun cases from 22 to 45 calibers. The measuring chamber is designed to eliminate the shearing of powder granules during use.

NorthEast Industrial, Inc. is a recent newcomer to the ranks of bullet mould makers. Their catalog, illustrating over 160 mould designs in the complete range of calibers is available for two stamps of the current denomination to carry a one-ounce first class letter. NEI does not offer handles, but their one and two-cavity blocks can be used with RCBS mould handles and their four-cavity blocks are for use with the Lyman four-cavity mould handles. All of their blocks are machined from high-grade aluminum bar stock to an excellent level of workmanship. Two other NEI products are of interest to bullet casters: NEI flux, for improving the quality and castabil-

ity of molten alloy and NEI Mold-Prep, an all-weather gun lubricant and thermal barrier used as a substitute for smoking the inner surface of mould cavities.

Rainel de P. R., Inc. is now in production on the Reiwelin Process plastic shotshell case, in 12-gauge for the present. The head, rim and primer pocket area is reinforced with steel to eliminate the problems that have plagued previous all-plastic shotshell cases. The cases are said to perform well across the extreme range of temperature variation and are excellent as to reloadability, accepting either folded or rolled crimps with equal ease. Their generous internal capacity makes them highly versatile for specialized applications such as waterfowl loads. The cost factor is said to compare favorably with contemporary designs and they can be produced in any desired color, with decorative graphics to the user's taste. Inquiries are invited from manufacturers and other large-quantity purchasers.

Taracorp Industries, is the current producer of Lawrence Brand lead shot, and they also offer bars of bullet casting alloy in various specifications through their dealer network.

The Oster Group makes and markets seven different alloys for casting bullets, as well as highly purified straight lead for muzzleloading projectiles and straight tin or antimony. Custom alloys can be made up to specifications, in minimum orders of 500 pounds or more. The firm has an extensive amount of background and experience in the specialized field of centrifugal rubber mould casting and they are prepared to discuss the application of that technique to the casting of bullets. Jerome Gonicberg, their vice president, is the man to whom inquiries should be directed.

DBI Books, Inc., (One Northfield Plaza, Northfield, Illinois 60093) publishers of GUN DIGEST, have also brought out a second edition of *ABC's of Reloading* to update the first edition that appeared in 1974. This is a book intended to be used in conjunction with one or more of the many excellent handbooks and manuals of load data on the market. It is designed to provide the untutored would-be reloading beginner with the knowledge and familiarity needed for a satisfactory entry into the field of reloading. Profusely illustrated with photos and drawings, it's precisely the book I wish I'd had, back about 1950 when I was just getting started. That's hardly surprising, because I wrote both editions with exactly that objective in mind. •

PYRODEX:
Five Years Down The Road

by JOHN BIVINS

I FIRST HEARD about Pyrodex in the fall of 1974. The product hadn't received its familiar trade name at that time, but it didn't need any catchy appellations to excite the imagination about the possibilities.

Ironically, most of the personnel involved in the development and early production of Pyrodex weren't exactly flowing over with experience in the muzzle-loading field. Dan Pawlak himself had done very little black powder shooting, and was the first to admit that. However, he possessed an extensive knowledge of pyrotechnics and understood full well that the sport of muzzle-loading was growing at an astounding rate.

Black powder was in trouble in the marketplace, largely due to the heavy restrictions placed upon it by its classification as a Class A explosive, and it didn't take an Einstein to see that an alternative muzzle-loading propellant was needed. The surprising thing was the fact that none of the old-time powder manufacturers had marketed such a thing, though it's known that at least one had been working on such a replacement.

Aside from Pyrodex, however, black powder has had no competition since the early 1940's when King's Semi-Smokeless was last made. King's was a fine, consistent and strong powder; according to some, it was partially a nitrocellulose base, though it could be loaded bulk for bulk with black powder. Its demise has been mourned by veteran shooters, and there are still a few jealously-guarded hoards of the stuff about, ample acknowledgment of the esteem held for it.

The one central thing that impressed me most about the development of Pyrodex, I think, was Dan Pawlak's absolutely consummate desire to make the finest product he

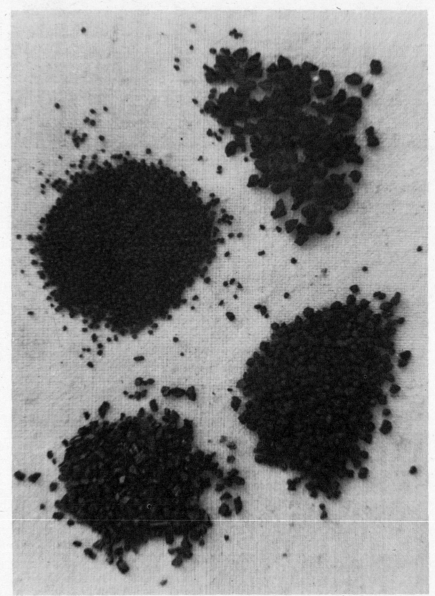

Pyrodex is shown here for visual comparison with black powder. Clockwise from upper left is Pyrodex P, GOEX FFg, Pyrodex RS, and GOEX FFFg. The differential in grain sizes between various comparable grades of Pyrodex and black powder has nothing to do with the burning rates of Pyrodex, due to the different chemical makeup of the latter.

possibly could. I have never known anyone with a more keenly honed sense of integrity and motivation to seek the best avenues of approach to problems. Dan and I spoke long and often on the needs of the muzzle-loading community, and I never ceased to be astounded about how deeply the man *cared* about what he was doing. There is little question that in Dan's loss we have been deprived of valuable products of one of the most fertile minds in the propellant field.

Pyrodex has survived Dan, however, and continues to improve under the capable hands of its co-inventor, Mike Levenson. After the disaster at the Issaquah plant, production of the powder was nonexistent to slow as the manufacturing shift was made to Kansas. The Issaquah plant produced over a quarter-million pounds of Pyrodex, and was heavily back-ordered. The new Kansas facility, however, has more than doubled the production of the first plant, and Pyrodex has been in steady supply since the spring of 1980.

Its use is widespread, assisted, no doubt, by its early approval by the National Muzzle Loading Rifle Association for use on the National ranges, and hence by all Charter clubs. It has been declared legal in all state primitive weapons seasons that I am aware of, and it's a popular product. Despite a flurry of press reviews of Pyrodex shortly after its 1976 introduction, though, little has been mentioned of it by writers since. Perhaps it's time to review some of its characteristics, and just how it's best used by shooters.

Dan's initial goal with Pyrodex was to produce a powder that could be transported under the Class B designation which smokeless powders have long enjoyed. Attaining safe transportation by common carrier would ensure a ready supply of powder to shooters; the "Class A" designation of black powder by the Department of Transportation had caused both short supply and regional prices that were nothing short of Black Market. Providing a new propellant with the properties needed to classify it as a "Class B" explosive or "flammable solid" would, of course, render it far safer to use by the shooter.

In formulating Pyrodex, Dan far exceeded D.O.T. regulations, in fact, since Pyrodex has a laboratory cook-off ignition temperature of over 600 degrees Fahrenheit, quite a contrast to the 357 degree ignition of black powder in that test. Even smokeless powders have a lower ignition than Pyrodex, as low as 375 degrees in a

heated pan. Needless to say, no question remains about safety in transporting or storing Pyrodex. It is *so* safe, due to its high ignition temperature, that shooters have had to cope with certain limitations of the powder, as we'll discuss.

A second attribute which Dan sought in Pyrodex was a lower component of solids left in the products of combustion—less fouling, in other words. That was one of the fine things about King's, yet, if anything, Dan was able to best King's in the fouling department. Using Pyrodex, I have fired upward of 50 consecutive shots in muzzle-loading rifles with no noticeable increase in bore fouling.

Needless to say, that's a most welcomed contrast to sticking a patched ball in a bore fouled by no more than a half-dozen charges of black powder. Some of the creative cussing I've resorted to in a few such cases over the past thirty years of shooting would melt down my writing machine if I dared to reconstruct it.

For those who couldn't bring themselves to believe the clean-burning properties of Pyrodex, Dan would grin and quietly hand them photographs of transducer-measured breech pressure curves read on an oscilloscope screen. One photograph depicted five shots in a .50 round-ball test barrel, using an 80-grain charge of FFFg black powder without cleaning. The curves were peaking all over the screen. A second photo illustrated ten shots of an 80-grain charge of Pyrodex in the same barrel, also without cleaning; the 'scope trace was one fat curve. Those original traces may be seen here, and our comparative tables listing velocities and pressures clearly show that Pyrodex ballistic figures don't fluctuate from shot to shot when the bore isn't swabbed out.

Pyrodex does in fact have burning characteristics very slightly different from black powder, largely due to the chemical retardants that serve to make the product safer. The time-to-peak-pressure curve is longer than black powder; tests have shown that it tends to peak a half millisecond *later* than black powder, which is not especially significant. More important is that the pressure peak for Pyrodex tends to be lower than that of black. That is, for a given weight of charge, Pyrodex equals, and often betters, the velocity of a black powder load at *lower* pressure, which becomes especially important to those inclined to move heavy projectiles at velocities which would be considered high by earlier standards. Such characteristics will be

discussed in greater detail later. I asked Pyrodex Corporation's ballistician, Richard McMahon, to provide me with fresh data on the powder, and on black powder as well, for comparative purposes, and we'll examine those.

It might seem that I'm suggesting that Pyrodex is a panacea for all ills including gout, herniated trigger finger, and bent barrels on rifles. It's not; Pyrodex has a whole personality of its own that must be dealt with, just as we learned to live with black powder.

Just what, you might well ask, *is* Pyrodex? Dan shook me up a bit five years ago by grinning slyly and retorting that the stuff is just black powder. Somewhat *modified* black powder, that is. It contains potassium nitrate, charcoal, and sulfur just as black powder does, but in different and significantly smaller proportions. To promote more thorough combustion and to raise ignition temperature, other compounds are important ingredients in Pyrodex. They provide the powder with its more agreeable attributes, but they *can* also bring forth somewhat disagreeable situations, too, as we'll see.

One of these is, of course, the ignition problems which tend to plague Pyrodex users. Right from the first Hodgdon Powder Co., the sole supplier of Pyrodex, made it known in their literature that the product was unsuitable for use in flintlocks. Being largely a flintlock round-ball shooter, I wasn't exactly delighted with such pronouncements. Pyrodex must be stoutly compressed in loading, and it's difficult to ignite, as we've seen; even hot sparks from a good flintlock often won't even light the stuff, and when it does ignite in the pan it burns in a rather leisurely way. Add to this the problem that in a flintlock you effectively have zero charge compression in the area of the vent, and the result is a long, though interesting, fuse effect. It's particularly interesting if you're bent on making so-called primitive weapons *truly* primitive; I'd rather have a good spear.

Various conversations with Dan Pawlak shed no great enlightenment upon what a flint shooter must do to be able to enjoy trying an alternative to the old "coal," for Dan hadn't found the time to work with flintlocks. I was determined, however, and after trying to coax one particularly stubborn charge of Pyrodex to light, I finally gave up and picked what might have been three or four grains of FFFFg black through the vent. Priming with the FFFF, I touched the piece off, and the ignition went with all the speed I was used to with black powder. Aha, said I, duplex charging is the answer.

Not wanting to slow my time in loading, for I am a devoted out-of-the-bag shooter and don't like to fuss about with things, I made myself a priming horn which utilized the spout and valve from a Colt .31 pocket pistol. This tiny flask head was readily restyled to give it the appearance of an 18th century flask head; the spout threw 9 gr. of FFFFg, more than enough to provide a boost for Pyrodex. This little charge precedes the main charge of Pyrodex down the bore, of course, and since I normally load with greased patches, I suspect that no more than half that tiny charge reaches the breech since much of it sticks to the bore walls. Whatever the case, this does the trick admirably, for ignition is instantaneous and the Pyrodex consumes the nasties that the black powder would have otherwise left behind. I can shoot all day without cleaning, except for the lock, which fouls up just as nicely as ever.

Important to efficient ignition with any sort of powder in a flintlock is the vent. It must bisect the line formed by the top of the pan. That is, the vent should lie half in and half out of the pan, so that the first burning grains of the priming ignite the charge. Also, the vent must be counterbored, and this is best done inside the vent. I use stainless vents counterbored with a No. 29 drill, leaving only 1/16″ of vent wall at the outside. The actual vent hole can then be drilled with a No. 53 drill for minimum gas loss. In loading, care should be taken to see that powder has entered the vent counterbore by lightly slapping the stock opposite the lock before seating the ball.

This is a very successful system in a flintlock, and using the duplex charge I've shot away more rounds than I'd care to count, and have been successful in competition with it.

But what about Pyrodex in caplocks? Certainly, most Pyrodex shooting is confined to percussion guns, since most shooters don't know that it can be used in flintlocks. One might think that the ignition problems can be licked quite handily just by using hot caps, but 'taint necessarily so. Hot caps *are* a necessary adjunct to using Pyrodex successfully, but there are other bugs in the soup as well.

Dan Pawlak found that Pyrodex ignites more consistently when the charge is heavily compressed, and he experimented with measured ramrod pressures even as high as 100 pounds. Now, this is somewhat counter to one

of the sacred tenets of black powder, which is Thou Shalt Not Crush Thy Charge, which robs oxygen and causes erratic burning—or so it goes. I tend to have my doubts, for that's one area of black powder interior ballistics which hasn't seen much research. In any event, Pyrodex *must* be compressed.

But what happens if you're shooting a "patent" breech rifle or shotgun with a long counterbore that's smaller than bore size? Right! There's a bridging effect in the counterbore, and the charge can't be compressed near the nipple, and you are presented with a nice hangfire. This can be overcome by using *really* hot ignition, such as centerfire primers in one of the "sealed" ignition devices, namely Anderson's "Flam-in-Go," which uses pistol primers. These devices give consistent igni-

tion this principle, though various arms manufacturers still seem to insist on using the less efficient counterbored breech.

One product which Dan worked on with Michael's of Oregon, and which is now readily available, is Michael's "Hot Shot" nipple, specifically designed to assist the ignition of Pyrodex. This curious little nipple has two vents on the sides, which tend to reduce air pressure in the flash channel and provide more oxygen, providing a much fatter spark from the cap. I rather suspect that the vented breech often seen on English percussion sporting rifles and guns has somewhat the same effect, though the old boys likely didn't know that. They were more interested in venting a bit of gas to keep the flash channel cleaner. In

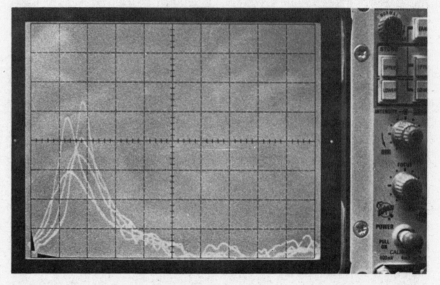

An oscilloscope pressure/time trace showing the erratic pressure curves of five rounds of 80 gr. FFFg black powder behind a .490 round ball, without cleaning between shots.

with Pyrodex and increased velocity as much as 200 fps in my own tests, but they aren't practical for anything other than competition rifles, particularly heavy slug rifles. They're just too slow to use in the field.

A better solution for pieces that will be stoked with Pyrodex is a breech constructed like they should be, and were on both Hawkens and English sporting rifles. The thread shank is kept short, no longer than ½″ except for the really big bores, and the flash channel is angled from the vent right to the front of the plug, not dog-legged as many modern breeches are. The angled channel obviates any need for a counterbore in the breech, making it stronger, and eliminating an area where the charge isn't uniformly compressed. There are several breeches on the market that are constructed on

fact, such vents may have been used initially because gunmakers were reluctant to confine a charge after years of building vented weapons. They worried about excessive recoil with a caplock, but that of course was a bit naive.

There are other caplock breech systems which tend to defy the use of Pyrodex. At the top of this list is the breechloading percussion Sharps, which has a long and torturous flash channel in the breechblock, combined with a cone-shaped cavity in the block. The result is a loose charge that will hangfire almost every shot when Pyrodex is used, though not usually as badly as a counterbored breech in a muzzleloader, probably due to those huge musket caps. Hangfiring with Pyrodex can be cured in any muzzleloader by duplex charging as I outlined in regard to flintlocks, but that does little or no good in a breech-loader since the priming charge of black isn't held in position against the breech.

Getting consistent ignition with Pyrodex, then, is a matter of both snappy caps and well-designed breeching in a muzzleloader. Without the latter, you can resort to duplex loading with perfect success and clean shooting, but I don't think we should have to resort to that in a caplock. That isn't the *only* area that muzzle-loading manufacturers need to examine traditional systems a little more closely. We seem at times to ignore the high state of the art as it existed in the last century, and are content to live with design compromises, even when the *correct* design would cost no more

fact I've heard a number of serious complaints of pitted bores after using Pyrodex. I've experienced it myself. Now, one of the most disastrous things a shooter can do with a muzzleloader, no matter the powder used, is to clean it *partially* and set it aside. If this is done with Pyrodex, particularly in humid weather, serious pitting can develop within 24 hours, usually at the muzzle. If a rifle has been shot with Pyrodex and *not cleaned at all*, then set aside, there is far less tendency for this to happen.

I tried this last deliberately, leaving two (inexpensive!) rifles sitting in the corner for a week in humid weather. I found light surface rusting, but no pitting—but *don't* take that as a recommendation that you can get away with it.

black powder will cause rusting just as Pyrodex will, probably even to the same degree judging from my own experince. The fact of the matter is that some of the by-products of burning black powder are enormously hygroscopic, namely potassium sulfite and potassium carbonate; the latter is a very virile salt and will "doe great mischief" as they might have said in the 18th century. Further, there is a synergistic effect when the various salts are present together; they are stronger as a *group* of salts than they might be singly.

I discovered the possible corrosion potential of Pyrodex early on, probably because I live in a part of the country where all metal things grow beards in the summer, and called Dan about it. He promptly sent me a two-part bore cleaning compound that he formulated to leave the bore chemically clean of all salts left in the fouling of either Pyrodex or black powder. That formula absolutely stopped any tendency for oxides to form, but unfortunately Dan died before he could put it into production. Hodgdon's indicates that Dan's formula contains mineral spirits as a vehicle, which could easily cause spontaneous combustion in discarded cleaning patches and rags, so Dan's cleaner hasn't been produced yet. To my knowledge, there is *no* bore cleaner on the market for muzzleloaders that is designed to neutralize salts and acids, and for the life of me I can't understand why. It's badly needed. Until we have it, though, clean your piece carefully when you shoot Pyrodex, especially in damp weather.

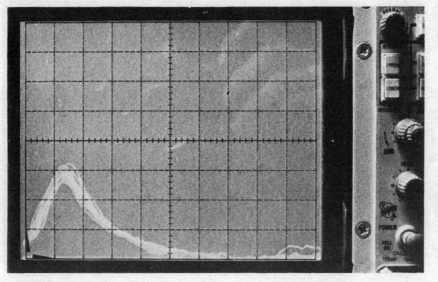

A similar trace showing ten rounds of Pyrodex RS, also in the 80 gr. charge and a .490 ball, and again without cleaning.

to produce. Of course, all this is academic with centerfires, where no ignition problems exist even with coarser-grained Pyrodex CTG.

One of the finest attributes of Pyrodex, of course, is the relatively small amount of fouling left in the bore. Even after a good deal of shooting, there's not much crud to wash out of the bore, in great contrast to the black, reeking muck which one must dredge out after shooting black powder. But where the rose blooms, there must perforce be thorns as well. Let's go back to that formulation of Pyrodex that we spoke of before. There are chemicals present other than those in black powder.

So what? Well, those, gentlemen, produce rather virile *salts*. Add water, and we have the potential to do some rather rapid eating of metal, and in

When using Pyrodex, I clean my pieces as soon as I return home, using warm water with a mild liquid detergent added, only a drop. I swab until the patches are clean, dry, then swab the bore out vigorously with alcohol, to absorb any moisture left. After setting the piece aside for a half-hour, I then oil. Don't be tempted to think that you can just swab out the bore with a water-displacing oil such as WD-40; no such oil has miraculous properties, and if you haven't washed all the salts out, they will happily eat away on barrel steel under the film of oil.

What of black powder in regard to corrosion? In my estimation, it is far less active than Pyrodex. It has fewer salts, and though partial cleaning is dangerous even with black powder, serious pitting is much less likely to result. If a bore isn't cleaned at all,

For competitive shooters, one of the plus features of black powder is the very consistent velocities that it provides, often no more than plus or minus 30 fps with careful loading. When I first tested Pyrodex five years ago, most loads were not as consistent as black powder, especially with heavier charges. Dan Pawlak spoke of producing a "match" grade of RS with very low velocity dispersion, but current production of Pyrodex is so consistent that there seems little need for such a thing. For example, even the heaviest charges we tried in preparing our charts here seldom showed more than 40 fps of velocity dispersion in tests, while equal measures of black powder provides as much as 110 fps of dispersion between high and low shots. The Pyrodex figures are remarkable for such heavy loadings as we tried, but this should not be construed as a recommendation for heavy charges.

There is a tendency in this country

INSTRUMENTAL COMPARISONS: BLACK POWDER VS. PYRODEX
(in incremental loadings)

TABLE A
Speer .490 Round Ball, GOEX FFg Black Powder. (Cleaning between each shot)

Powder Charge (Grains Wt.)	Lead Crusher (L.U.P.)	Transducer (P.S.I.)	Time to Peak (milliseconds)	Velocity (fps)
40	8,900	10,500	0.2	1331
60	9,300	11,000	0.3	1543
80	11,500	13,500	0.4	1771
100	12,500	14,300	0.4	1941

TABLE B
Speer .490 Round Ball, Pyrodex RS. (No cleaning between each shot)

Lead Crusher (L.U.P.)	Transducer (P.S.I.)	Time to Peak (milliseconds)	Velocity (fps)
5,400	5,900	0.5	1210
7,000	7,300	0.7	1502
9,200	9,300	0.9	1763
12,000	13,000	0.9	2011

TABLE C
Thompson/Center .50 Maxi-Balls, GOEX FFg Black Powder. (Cleaning between each shot)

Powder Charge (Grains Wt.)	Lead Crusher (L.U.P.)	Transducer (P.S.I.)	Time to Peak (milliseconds)	Velocity (fps)
40	12,800	14,400	0.4	1074
60	—	19,100	0.5	1307
80	—	21,500	0.5	1425

TABLE D
Thompson/Center .50 Maxi-Balls, Pyrodex RS. (No cleaning between each shot)

Lead Crusher (L.U.P.)	Transducer (P.S.I.)	Time to Peak (milliseconds)	Velocity (fps)
9,100	10,500	0.6	1073
13,100	14,800	0.8	1320
—	16,900	1.0	1532

CAUTION: All loads listed are by grains **weight,** not volume measure.

EDITOR'S NOTE: Bivins furnished test results of much heavier loads. I chose not to print them. *KW*

Notes to Tables A, B, C, D

1. Each reading listed in the tables represents an average of five shots fired with each powder charge and projectile.

2. Equipment: 28"Thompson/Center .50 barrel, fitted with both a lead-crusher unit and a PCB Pieztronics, Inc. Model 188A Ballistic Transducer linked with PCB Model 462B52 Charge Amplifier; pressure-time curves were read on a Tektronix oscilloscope, yielding peak pressure in psi and time-to-peak-pressure in milliseconds. Velocity was read on an Oehler Model 34 Chronotach, using Oehler Model 51 screens with a 10-foot spacing.

3. Propellants: GOEX FFg black powder, Lot No. 800C16C; Pyrodex RS, Lot No. 5551.

4. Ignition: Remington No. 11 percussion caps.

5. Projectiles: Speer .490 swaged round balls averaging 177.30 grains weight, used with Thompson/Center No. 703 patches, .015" thick, lubricated with Hodgdon Spit Patch; Thompson/Center .50 Maxi Balls averaging 369.0 grains weight, lubricated with Thompson/Center Maxi-Lube.

INSTRUMENTAL COMPARISONS: BLACK POWDER VS. PYRODEX,
WITH AND WITHOUT CLEANING

TABLE E
.490 Round Ball, 80 Gr. weight GOEX FFg. (Cleaning after each shot)

Round No.	Lead Crusher (L.U.P.)	Transducer (P.S.I.)	Time to Peak (milliseconds)	Velocity (fps)
1	10,500	12,200	0.4	1768
2	11,700	14,000	0.4	1807
3	11,400	14,000	0.4	1775
4	13,500	15,900	0.3	1818
5	12,700	15,100	0.4	1798
6	11,600	12,800	0.4	1756
7	13,500	15,000	0.4	1803
8	12,100	12,900	0.4	1778
9	13,500	15,100	0.4	1778
10	13,000	12,500	0.5	1820
11	12,700	13,100	0.5	1796
12	13,500	15,000	0.4	1800
Average	12,700	14,000	0.4	1792
Std. Deviation	—	—	—	20
Extreme variation	3000	3700	—	47

TABLE F
.490 Round Ball, 80 Gr. weight GOEX FFg. (No cleaning after each shot)

Lead Crusher (L.U.P.)	Transducer (P.S.I.)	Time to Peak (milliseconds)	Velocity (fps)
13,100	14,000	0.4	1811
12,800	14,000	0.5	1724
13,500	14,500	0.4	1739
13,500	17,900	0.4	1602
12,800	13,000	0.5	1782
13,500	19,500	0.4	1613
13,500	18,900	0.4	1624
—	3,900	1.0	1288
—	18,900	0.4	1613
—	22,000	0.4	1661
—	19,000	0.4	1611
—	19,000	0.4	1450
—	16,200	0.4	1626
—	—	—	144
9,000	—	332

TABLE G
.490 Round Ball, 80 Gr. weight Pyrodex RS, (No cleaning after each shot)

Round No.	Lead Crusher (L.U.P.)	Transducer (P.S.I.)	Time to Peak (milliseconds)	Velocity (fps)
1	7,600	7,100	1.0	1709
2	7,900	8,800	1.0	1726
3	7,800	8,400	1.0	1722
4	8,500	9,300	1.0	1754
5	9,200	9,600	1.0	1762
6	8,500	9,200	1.0	1747
7	8,900	9,200	1.0	1747
8	8,500	9,000	1.0	1748
9	9,000	9,000	1.0	1732
10	8,000	8,200	1.1	1726
11	8,900	9,100	1.1	1755
12	8,000	7,900	1.1	1720
Average	8,400	8,800	1.0	1737
Std. deviation	—	—	—	17
Extreme deviation	1600	2500	—	53

TABLE H
.50 Maxi-Ball, 80 Gr. weight Pyrodex RS, (No cleaning after each shot)

Lead Crusher (L.U.P.)	Transducer (P.S.I.)	Time to Peak (milliseconds)	Velocity (fps)
—	15,100	0.9	1494
—	16,200	1.0	1500
—	16,900	1.0	1510
—	16,900	1.0	1505
—	15,500	1.1	1488
—	17,700	1.0	1516
—	15,000	1.1	1481
—	15,700	1.1	1494
—	15,700	1.1	1499
—	16,200	1.1	1498
—	15,100	1.1	1496
—	15,800	1.0	1499
—	16,000	1.0	1498
—	—	—	9
2600	—	35

Notes to Tables E, F, G, H

1. Round number 8 in Table F was not used in calculating extreme variations due to the abnormally low values.

2. Equipment, propellants (including powder lot numbers), ignition, and projectiles were identical to those in Tables A, B, C, D.

today to "magnumize" muzzleloaders by overcharging, but a point of diminishing returns is quickly reached in such practices, not to mention the possibility of damage to a muzzle-loader, or worse, the shooter. There is ample evidence that shooters in centuries past were conservative in their loading, often using little more than a charge equal in weight to the size of the projectile, say 55 gr. for a 50-caliber rifle. We can certainly use heavier loads than that with perfect safety, but there is little valid reason for attempting to get 2000 fps out of a rifle that is most effective with an 1800 fps load.

I, for one, am not an exponent of Minie-Ball type slugs in anything other than Civil War replicas and the like. In sporting rifles, they afford less accuracy and a rainbow trajectory, and I do not believe that they have truly been proven more effective in hunting use. I have not been able to fault the round ball on deer-sized game if an adequate caliber is used; I prefer a .50 for such use.

The fact is that just about no one is prepared to say what pressure levels should be considered safe in muzzle-loaders. Even if barrels were heavy, and made of high tensile-strength chrome-moly steel, the breeches still constitute a weak point. It is known that some of the big benchrest slug rifles are digesting 20,000 psi and more, using sealed ignitions, but such readings are far and away above what any sporting gun or rifle should be expected to handle.

The test data we've provided here was measured on Pyrodex Corporation's test rig, which is constructed around a 28" Thompson/Center 50-cal. barrel. The equipment used simultaneously reads pressure through both lead crusher (yielding lead units of pressure, or LUP) and transducer, which provides both a psi and a time-to-peak-pressure trace on an oscilloscope. Velocity is read on an Oehler Model 34 chronograph. The lead crusher system is used to back up readings by transducer. LUP readings above 13,000 are not shown, due to the fact that lead crushers can't be read accurately over that figure. (Copper crushers are usually substituted over that level, but it must be realized that lead units of pressure, copper units of pressure—CUP—and pounds-per-square-inch read by a transducer are not equal values in any sense.)

The tables shown indicate no abnormal pressure excursions with either black powder or Pyrodex, though in heavier loadings Pyrodex

exhibits a steadier rise in velocity than does black powder. Both powders definitely reach a point of diminishing returns for a given length of barrel, however, where velocity rises taper off or even drop as more and more unburned powder is blown out the muzzle.

Among the tests which Richard McMahon's staff ran for me were four strings of 12 shots using the same weights of charges, to demonstrate what the effect of cleaning the bore after each shot was—and the effect of *not* cleaning. The results in Tables E to G, were predictable enough to those familiar with both black powder and Pyrodex.

Using a .490 round ball and a charge of 80 grains weight of black powder, the instruments revealed black powder's usual fine consistency from shot to shot, when the bore was kept clean, with an extreme variation in velocity of only 47 fps in 12 shots. Pressure showed more variation, perhaps since the tests weren't necessarily completed on the same day.

In Table F, where the same load was shot without cleaning after each shot, the extreme variation in velocity for the black powder zoomed to 332 fps, even after throwing out one low reading that was likely caused by an unseated ball. The standard deviation of the velocity readings jumped from 20 fps in the clean bore to 144 fps in the no-cleaning series, and the extreme variation in pressure was a full 9000 psi on the oscilloscope.

Twelve shots of Pyrodex fired without cleaning, however, showed the same consistency as black powder in a clean bore, (comparing Table G with Table E) and in fact the pressure readings were lower and more consistent than those of black powder, showing an extreme variation of 1600 LUP versus the 3000 LUP of black powder.

We included a dozen shots of the same charge of Pyrodex, still without cleaning, but using a 370-gr. maxiball. The extreme variation in velocity in this series (Table H) was only 28 fps, showing the slight preference Pyrodex has for greater mass in the loading.

The results of such careful tests indicate that Pyrodex has lost nothing during the five years of its young life, and if anything is more consistent. It is a product that is not without its own eccentricities which must be respected, just as we have learned to correctly adapt to any modern propellant. Ideally, I'd like to see the ignition temperature of Pyrodex lowered somewhat, and I'd like to see something done to lessen the effect of per-

chlorates and the like left in products of combustion. In this regard, I'd particularly like to see a commercial bore cleaner produced that will chemically remove harmful salts in the fouling of either black powder or Pyrodex.

On the positive side, Pyrodex is a better propellant than black powder in several instances, and equals its older cousin in others:

• Pyrodex is far safer to transport in either bulk or powder horn, and therefore should be more readily available than black powder in some areas.

• Pyrodex is less easily ignitable than black powder, which is an especial boon to safety at the firing line in competitive shooting, though it is an explosive and if mishandled can be dangerous.

• It is more fun to shoot, since between-shot cleaning isn't needed in the least, and that in itself will extend the life of many muzzle-loading barrels.

• Pyrodex is far easier to clean up after extended shooting, in terms of fouling left in the bore.

• Pyrodex has proven itself exceedingly consistent in shot-to-shot velocity and pressure readings, while often giving both lower pressure readings and higher velocity than black powder for the same given weight of charge and projectile. I have personally shot my best benchrest groups with Pyrodex, and in a flintlock at that.

I believe Pyrodex remains a credit to Dan Pawlak. It is suitable for use in all muzzle-loading guns, given a willingness on the part of the shooter to adapt to the characteristics of the powder.

Will it, or should it, replace black powder? Emphatically, no. Pyrodex couldn't be made to equal the low ignition temperatures of black powder while still retaining its rating as a Class B explosive.

The fact is that the muzzle-loading game has benefited from the existence of *both* powders, and I hope it remains that way for a long time to come. •

EDITOR'S NOTE:
We welcome John Bivins' point of view on the merits of Pyrodex, but we must tell you that Pyrodex, Inc. commissioned this article after the firm took exception to some material in last year's GUN DIGEST. Solely in the interest of fairness, we chose this way to get their position into the record and we believe it does that. KW

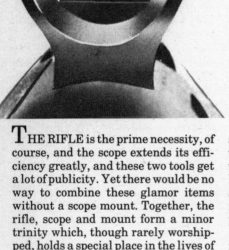

SCOPES AND MOUNTS

What's in a mount?

by BOB BELL

6.5-20x Leupold proved to be an excellent varmint scope, giving minute-of-angle groups on 700 Remington Varmint model 22-250, firing groups at different power settings throughout entire magnification range. Its wide choice of power makes it easy to adapt to different shooting ranges, mirage conditions, and ambient light.

THE RIFLE is the prime necessity, of course, and the scope extends its efficiency greatly, and these two tools get a lot of publicity. Yet there would be no way to combine these glamor items without a scope mount. Together, the rifle, scope and mount form a minor trinity which, though rarely worshipped, holds a special place in the lives of riflemen.

We'd like to discuss mounts this year, as a follow-up to last year's general comments on scopes. We're interested here in mounts for big game rifles, action-mounted varmint scopes, and rigs for rimfire rifles, not the comparatively simple blocks used for traditional long target scopes.

Certain characteristics are necessary in a mount if it is to serve satisfactorily over a period of years. A first-time buyer perhaps doesn't think enough about such things—most seem to make their selections on the basis of appearance or what a friend tells them—but anyone who used scopes

awhile tends to have definite ideas on the subject. I happened to bring this up while talking with Don Burris, who has been involved in the engineering and manufacture of scopes and mounts for a long time. His summary is to the point and worth quoting:

"Mounts should have the following functional priorities: (1) ruggedness: they must support the scope against heavy and repeated recoil, and against a sharp blow such as might occur if the hunter falls, and not lose the scope's zero; (2) they should be precision machined to align properly on the rifle and be easily positioned to provide the proper eye relief and height for the broadest range of scopes and shooters; (3) they should have a balanced weight-to-ruggedness ratio: a minimum amount of material to provide the maximum support; (4) appearance should be aesthetically pleasing to provide a pride-of-ownership benefit."

Some of Don's comments are primarily from a manufacturer's

viewpoint, but overall they're points all buyers should consider seriously. He gives ruggedness the highest priority and few experienced riflemen would dispute that. When even a light-recoiling rifle is fired, significant forces are exerted on the scope and mount; when a magnum goes off, the effect can be devastating.

Consider what happens every time a shot is fired: From a position of rest, the rifle is suddenly propelled backward with a force of many gravities. Yet within a tiny fraction of a second, due to its own weight, the resistance of the shooter's body and the dissipation of energy in various ways, its rearward movement comes to a stop—and to some extent is essentially reversed.

While this is happening, a weight of up to a pound (the scope) is perched above the rifle, attached to it by a mount that's normally secured by only a few tiny screws. In that overhead position, with the recoil forces working beneath it, the scope's inertia tends to make it stand still while the gun jerks away. The tendency is to shear the screws and leave the scope sitting momentarily free in thin air.

All that keeps the scope and rifle together is the mount. And it's not enough simply to keep them together. The mount has to keep all parts in their original relationship to each other. If there is any slippage, any permanent movement between the scope and mount or mount and rifle, the outfit is out of zero. I say "permanent" movement because I have a hunch there must be some temporary misalignments due to the forces involved, though the elasticity of the material probably corrects these, at least within our normal ability to detect by shooting. Regardless, the importance of the mount is obvious.

I don't know how many makes of mounts have come and gone through the years—scores at least, maybe hundreds. There are a couple dozen American manufacturers at the moment and I don't know how many others around the world. In a sense, all are similar: they all hold the scope on the gun. Some probably do it better than others—in the theoretical sense that has to be true—yet in ordinary use there seems to be little difference. Maybe that's because few shooters shoot enough to push a unit to its limit. Or maybe those which have survived in the marketplace have all reached about the same stage of efficiency, insofar as holding things together goes.

European scopes often have dovetails sweated to the bottom of the tube instead of separate rings. These engage female dovetails on the action. Others have claw feet, on rings or sweated fast, that rotate into specially machined blocks when the scope is arced through a vertical plane. Spring-loaded slides lock them into place. The dovetail type is usually easily adjusted for eye relief, but the claw foot design, if sweated fast, cannot be. Therefore, to be properly used the scope must be perfectly positioned when originally mounted. Then, of course, it will not fit anyone else of a different build, or even the same person if he shoots in shirt sleeves during the summer and in heavy clothing in winter.

Back in the '30s, when scopes were beginning to interest American hunters, even many users did not completely trust them. Quite a few wanted to have iron sights available at the same time, so scope mounts often were high, side-mounted affairs which made that possible. The only thing

was, the scopes were slow to use because they didn't naturally align with the aiming eye—especially with the low-combed stocks of those days—and they were hard to keep in zero because the added height acted as a lever to increase the force exerted on the scope by recoil.

It took countless articles by knowledgeable gunwriters to convince most hunters that a scope should be installed as low as possible and centrally over the action. This, plus the development of high-combed stocks which supported the cheekbone solidly when the eye was lined up with the scope's exit pupil, made telescopes fully as fast to use as the best iron sights.

Many hunters liked side mounts for another reason. When designed for quick removal of the scope, as with the Griffin & Howe, Jaeger, Echo and others, they left the top of the action uncluttered, so conventional open sights or perhaps cocking-piece mounted peeps could be used.

Most American mounts today sit atop the action, one block on the receiver ring, the other on the bridge, or a single base that bridges the loading/ejection port of a bolt action. I believe the Redfield Jr. was the first of these. Current nearly identical ones include the Leupold STD, and Burris, and the Buehler is similar in many respects.

A dovetail stud on the bottom of the front Redfield-type ring fits into a tightly fitting hole in the base when the scope is at a right angle to the bore, and locks securely when rotated 90 degrees. At the rear of the base, opposing screws engage a semi-circular cut in each side of the rear ring and lock the scope solidly. By loosening one and tightening the other, windage adjustments can be made—a necessity when using scopes which have no internal windage adjustment. It's helpful even in this time of constantly centered reticles, for it's always a good idea to keep the reticle as near to the true optical center of the scope as possible.

Bridge-type bases are easily installed by means of three or four screws and seem to guarantee alignment for the mount rings. However, it's not uncommon for rifle actions, especially the older military types, to vary considerably in dimensions, so a long base will not necessarily fit perfectly. This often escapes notice because the screws snug everything tight, but in such cases the base is being bent. Then when the scope is attached, it too is bent when the mount's windage screws pull everything together. This might not be a

serious problem, but it certainly can't help anything, especially with a variable power scope where internal mechanical movement is required for magnification change.

Making a bridge-type base into a two-piece design by removing the center portion doesn't eliminate the problem, unless you make certain that after installation the tops of the two bases are level to each other, and at the same height where that is needed. Since factory-drilled holes are normally used for mounting, the user has little control over this, but he should be aware that such holes are not always perfectly placed. Also, many two-piece designs do not have integral recoil shoulders. Neither do all one-piece bases, but some do, and that's an advantage, assuming contact is made with the action. Again, that's not always the case due to variations in finished dimensions.

Weaver-type bases do not have a recoil shoulder and at least one nationally renowned gunsmith has said that because of this they should not be used on rifles with more recoil than a 30-06. However, a friend who built a 475 Atkinson & Marquart Magnum, which delivers over 9000 foot-pounds of energy and only God knows how much recoil, used Weaver mounts with perfect satisfaction. I doubt that he fired many rounds through this cannon, though. But he may have. He's the same guy who built a rifle to handle the 50-caliber machine gun cartridge (750-gr. bullet ahead of 200+ grains of powder) and routinely fired groups with it off the bench. (My total experience with that monster was a single one-shot group; I wouldn't fire it again, nohow, unless a 5-ton elephant was within a dozen steps and charging flat-out.)

Weaver bases have the virtue of closely returning the scope to zero after removal. They're essentially dovetails, and the transverse screw which locks a ring to a base also fits snugly into a groove, thus prevents fore and aft movement of the scope in relation to the blocks.

However, the fear in regard to this kind of bases is not that the scope will move on them but that the screws securing them to the action will shear under recoil. I've never had that happen on a rifle, but did on a handgun. Shortly after the 44 Magnum came out, we tried to put a K4 on one with conventional blocks. Factory ammo routinely sheared the four mounting screws and sent the scope flying.

To get around the problem, Sako decades ago began making their actions with integral tapered dovetail bases. This was perhaps the biggest modern-day improvement in scope mounting. Not only did it eliminte those dinky screws but the mounts, because of their taper, got tighter the more you shot them. When Ruger began making the M77, he also offered integral bases—one of the outstanding features on this fine rifle. However, the demand of buyers who apparently didn't see the virtue in this design, or perhaps wanted to use other mounts

Redfield tip-up aperture sight installed on rear of Pachmayr Lo-Swing mount on Bob Bell's 338.

Holden Ironsighter Widefield Mount.

Conetrol mounts are now available for all Steyr guns.

for some reason, forced him to supply the 77 in round-top version also. This doesn't really reflect well on the common sense of a lot of shooters.

Shooters have long debated the relative merits of the bridge-type base vs. the two-piece type, those favoring the former claiming it is stronger and more stable, the two-piece fans pointing to a savings in weight and a more accessible loading port. Those are obvious differences, but when I brought up the subject with Don Burris he got a bit more technical. He pointed out that most scope mounts have about a 4-inch span between ring centers, and that an 80° temperature increase of the rifle's receiver—not unusual when a number of shots are fired—will increase its length .002 inches. Because the scope is above the receiver it does not become as warm. Don raised the question of where this length increase is absorbed in the sighting system. He feels that with two-piece bases and tight rings, the receiver will try to stretch the scope tube as it heats, while the one-piece bridge will absorb

some of the expansion and decrease the effect on the scope.

In recent years, in the constant circling of life which makes old things seem new, a number of manufacturers have returned to high mount systems which permit instant choice between the scope and iron sights. Today's designs essentially mount the scope on top of hollow metal ovals through which the open sights can be used. These have attracted considerable followings, particularly where snow and rain are normal during hunting season.

Jerry Holden, of Ironsighter See-Thru mount fame, tells me that one out of every six of his mounts is sold in my home state of Pennsylvania. Anyone who has hunted deer here in December can understand the Ironsighter's popularity.

Another approach to this problem is the QD (Quick Detachable) mount. It's been mentioned in regard to side mounts, but various top mounts also serve this way. The screw-locked Weaver type is probably semi-QD, maybe even less if you don't have some kind of tool handy to turn those big screws, the Burris Zee rings require at least a coin (penny or dime) to remove, and Bushnell's need an allen wrench. However, Phil Pilkington's recent modification of the Redfield-type base substitutes a lever for one of the windage screws to make this kind of mount a QD unit. (See details later on.) Len Brownell also makes available his own double lever QD top mount which can be instantly re-

moved using only the fingers.

For those who prefer a different type of access to the irons, the Pachmayr Lo-Swing is the way to go. It's probably even faster than the double lever QD unit. You simply grasp the scope and rotate it out of the way, exposing the iron sights for use. It's been a favorite of some back-country hunters for decades. Weaver also has made a Pivot mount for years, though they don't seem to push it, at least in my part of the country.

Through the years various exotic mounts have been created to solve specific problems. For instance, Redfield once built a swing-away job (I don't know if it ever had a name, or if more than one unit was built) to use on top-ejecting Winchester lever actions. It mounted low and centrally and when the rifle's lever was pushed down a series of cams, gears, levers or whatever swung the scope aside to let the ejected empty case fly out; when the gun's lever was raised, the scope arched back to its normal aiming position. It was quite a contraption, according to the late Ed Hilliard. He didn't say how consistently it positioned itself. Anything this complicated would probably have too much inherent slop to be highly accurate, but on the other hand, is extreme accuracy needed to stay on a deer's shoulder at 80 yards?

For a mount, as for the scopes discussed last year, pick one that will do the kind of job you're going to put it to. As Burris said, ruggedness is of paramount importance, particularly on a magnum, but most of today's mounts are strong enough. Some have useful features missing on others—windage adjustment, QD capability, eye relief adaptability, no-drill installation, etc. So make your choice first on the basis of genuinely needed features, then for subjective reasons such as appearance. If you'd like to pay $20 for a mount but the one you really want costs $50, pay the $50. Or $250. You won't be happy with the less expensive one, even if it performs well, and after awhile the "saved" money will be gone anyhow, so you might as well have the rig you want.

However, it's important to recognize that some mounts and scopes just don't go together. The most important thing a mount must do, actually, is position the scope where it's in perfect relation to the eye when the gun is thrown to the shoulder as a big buck or elk jumps for cover. The scope's height must be perfect, the eye relief must be perfect, for shots like this. Getting it that way should be attended to long before the hunt, through careful fitting and adjustment based on actual shooting.

And the thing is, some mounts just won't accept some scopes, at least for some shooters. It's not so much the diameter of the scope as its length—particularly its length between the enlarged sections of the objective and the ocular, and the distances between these sections and the adjustment turret. Mount manufacturers long ago recognized this problem and some offer extensions on the bottom halves of the rings to accommodate for such things. But these might not be available with the mount you want, or you might not like the looks, so consider all the problems before you commit yourself.

We've got damn good scopes and

B-Square has a new no-gunsmithing mount for the Ruger Mini-14. It is installed by replacing the bolt stop cover plate with B-Square's cover plate, a minor chore. The mount, which attaches with a single knob, has both windage and elevation adjustments and can be quickly removed and replaced. $49.95, or $10 more for stainless finish to match the stainless Ruger.

Also new this year is a B-Square mount for the Heckler and Koch 91/93 rifles. It slides on the clamps to the receiver with two thumb screws. No drilling or tapping required, and the iron sights can be used beneath the scope. Rings fit 1-inch scopes, and glass and mount can be removed as a unit. $49.95.

ing or tapping is required for installation.

Also available by the time you read this will be dovetail bases for the short, medium and long Sako actions. These are two-piece bases designed to provide about four-inch ring centers on all actions, thus will accommodate the short-tube scopes such as Leupold's Vari-X III's. Besides being a tight fit on the Sako dovetails, four set screws provide additional locking. Bases, $33.25 per set.

Buehler bases are also made for numerous handguns. An interesting one is the Code DW, which is installed on the barrel shroud of the Dan Wesson revolvers. Even with a scope and mount in place, the shroud can be easily exchanged.

B-square *no-gunsmithing* mount for the Ruger Mini-14.

S&K style for Mini-14

mounts these days, but none are perfect. Maybe one of these days, what with investment castings, etc., it will be possible to buy a rifle which has not only integral bases but at least the bottom halves of the rings as part of the action. Many years ago a well-to-do rifleman named Ralph Packard had a built-from-scratch outfit in which the scope mount was part of the action (it used to be in the Smithsonian . . . maybe still is), so it's not impossible. Maybe we can even go whole hog and suggest that the scope tube also be one piece with the mount and action. That would probably make things solid enough for even me. Sort of the ultimate scope mount.

Here's the year's changes in the scope business, company by company:

American Imports currently offers seven rimfire scopes, both straight and variable powers, on ¾- and ⅞-inch tubes, with an assortment of mounts to fit grooved receivers. Ten big game models are available, six in the conventional straight powers and four variables, two of the latter being wide angles. All big game models except the 2½x20 and 4x20 have enlarged objectives. Top of the line is a 4-12x40 variable. A 1½x pistol scope also is offered. The 4x32 super Wide Angle mentioned last year has been discontinued.

Leonard M. Brownell is internationally reknowned as a stockmaker. Some years back he designed and began producing a double lever quick-detachable scope mount to complement his custom rifles. He wanted a design that would be both esthetically pleasing and mechanically strong, and which would return to zero when removed and replaced. The dovetail system seemed the logical choice as it can be accurately machined, is strong, and provides larger areas of contact between the rings and bases than various other designs.

Bases are made for most popular bolt actions ($25-$35) and can be custom built. Rings, which are handsomely contoured and deeply blued, are $85 per set.

Buehler, as always, continues to expand their mount line to accommodate new firearms introduced during the year. New since the last GD are one-piece bases for Remington's recently introduced Model Four autoloader and Model Six slide action (which replace the M742 and M760), and their less-expensive versions, the 7400 and 7600 Remingtons. These bases are Code 4-6 and Code 74.

For the increasingly popular Ruger Mini-14, Buehler has a one-piece base that's machined from high tensile aluminum and hand finished. No drill-

Burris, though one of the newest scopemakers, has an extensive line of top quality glasses, including straight powers of 2.7x to 12x, variables in the conventional combinations from 1.7-5x through the big 6-18x, Mini fixed powers in 4x, 6x and 8x, a couple of Mini variables, and four LER (Long Eye Relief) models, two of which are new, for handguns or whatever. As if that weren't enough, two new 3-9x's with unique reticles have been introduced this year, along with an assortment of new mounts to extend their line. The Burris Fullfield scopes have larger-than-normal fields in the vertical as well as the horizontal dimension—in other words, they're round as well as big—with multiple layers of Hi-Lume coating. Doubtless, Don Burris deserves most of the credit for the scope line that bears his name; though he might not be known to every backwoods hunter, Burris is an optical engineer who had many years of experience in another top scope company's employ before beginning his own, so he's not new in this field.

The new 3-9x ARC (Automatic Range Compensating) scope has both a fixed crosshair reticle which is conventionally zeroed at 200 yards and a variable dot reticle which can be independently adjusted out to a 500-yard zero. This is not a bullet drop compensator which requires that you make an elevation adjustment for drop. Rather, the dot moves down automatically as you increase the magnification for a long shot. The crosshair reticle does not move during the change, so it remains at the 200-yard zero. The dot's movement is optical, not mechanical.

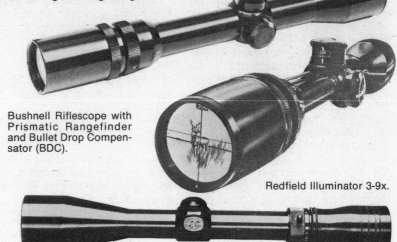

Swift Mark I 1.5-4.5, 32mm; Designed for brush to middle range shooting, the 658 complements slug-shooting shotguns.

Bushnell Riflescope with Prismatic Rangefinder and Bullet Drop Compensator (BDC).

Redfield Illuminator 3-9x.

Bell shooting the M788 7mm/08 with Redfield 1½-5x variable.

It is placed in the rear focal plane, behind the zoom system, and moves in a calibrated fashion as the scope's power is changed. The crosshair, however, is installed in the first focal plane, ahead of the zoom system, so is not affected by the zoom action and thus maintains its position—and zero—throughout all power settings. Price, $236.95.

The second new 3-9x is the RAC (Rangefinder with Automatic Compensator reticle). Similar to the previous model, it also has stadia wires in the bottom of the field which work on the 18-inch withers-to-brisket measurement of a large deer. Again, you zero the crosshair at 200 yards to begin with. When a distant deer is seen, you turn the power ring until the stadia wires bracket it; this change simultaneously lowers the dot into zero at the proper distance; you use the dot as your aiming point and shoot.

Currently, this RAC scope is calibrated for various factory loads in calibers 270, 308, 30-06, 300 Winchester Magnum, 8mm Remington Magnum and 338 Magnum, at ranges up to 500 yards. Price $239.95.

Bushnell lists 15 basic big game scopes this year, four in their top line Scopechief VI models, six variable power Banners, and five fixed power Banners. The catalog listing looks longer, as variations featuring the Bullet Drop Compensator and/or the Prismatic Rangefinder are listed separately. Nevertheless, the number is still impressive. And of course there are several ⅞-inch 22 scopes and a couple of handgun models.

Top of the line is the 3-9x Scopechief VI 3-9x, which features a 40mm objective for good light transmission even at 9x. With BDC and PRF it retails at $219.95, which might come as a bit of a

shock to older shooters who remember the good old days when the most expensive Bushnell sold for $59.50. (They forget what salaries were, back then.) No matter. This 3-9x is a fine glass, and $33 of the price quoted is due to the Prismatic Rangefinger unit. To use this, the game is bracketed between a stadia line and the horizontal crosshair by turning the power adjusting ring. The target's apparent size changes while the recticle lines remain stationary, and the range in yards appears at the top of the field of view. You then dial the BDC knob to the distance shown, hold right on and fire.

Newest Bushnells are the 4-12x40mm and 3-9x38mm Banner variables, the latter a wide angle design, and the straight 10x Metallic Silhouette scope, with 40mm objective. This scope has the power many MS shooters have come to depend on, offering about the ideal compromise between magnification and field for this demanding sport. It features the BDC unit, which allows quick dialing of the range desired (you can read it visually rather than having to count clicks), a decided advantage when the pressure's on and a counting error could be costly.

Clear View Mfg. Co. has four basic styles of raised mounts. Jerry Weast says that one or another will fit 95 percent of the rifles manufactured today, accommodating scopes with up to 40mm objectives. They are made of heat-treated aluminum, with kidney-shaped openings the full width of the ring cap to get a large field for iron sight use. Mount walls are heavy and radiused inside to add strength, and alloy-steel socket-head screws are used throughout.

Conetrol's DapTar base for the long Sako action with integral dovetail has been modified to permit use with the growing number of mini and variable power scopes having short tube sections. The accommodation was made by reversing the female dovetail of the front base so that the scope ring will be situated over the rear of the receiver ring instead of the front, thus bringing the scope rings closer together.

DapTar bases are machined to fit integral mechanisms or cuts provided on many guns, without drilling or tapping. Recent additions to this line are for the Ruger M77 flat-tops, DuBiel, Ruger No. 1s with quarter ribs, BSA, Ithacagun, LSA, Brno with large and small dovetails, Krico, Heckler & Koch, Steyr, Sako and the grooved receivers of rimfire rifles and air guns designed to accept Tip-Off mounts.

Fontaine Industries is now supplying a line of Japanese-built optical goods that includes both wide angle and standard field waterproof hunting scopes in 4x and 3-9x, with either 32mm or 40mm objectives. All have round eyepieces. A Trajectory Compensating System (TCS) is offered in most models. After zeroing in at 100 yards, it allows the shooter to compensate for bullet drop by dialing for other ranges. The TCS reportedly differs from other bullet-drop systems by being calibrated for individual bullet weights and types. For instance, one turret drum is calibrated specifically for the 150-gr. Winchester Silvertip and the similarly shaped 150-gr. Remington PSP loads in the 30-06. Various drums are available and interchangeable.

Prices range from $79.15 to $230.95. Several standard field, non-waterproof scopes are available at $85.80 to $131.95.

Griffin & Howe's double lever mount is something of a legend. It's been around so long and its quality is so high that it almost seems unreal. Of course, its price is up there, too—some $245 for the side mount version—so maybe that helps account for the feeling many hunters have about it. They just haven't seen enough of them in the field to be convinced they're real. They are, though. And they can be had to fit 1-inch, 26mm and 30mm scope tubes, in several heights and offset if desired.

Habicht hunting scopes in 1.5x20, 4x32 and 6x42 sizes and several versions, now are available in this country from Strieter Corp. Built in Austria by Swarovski Optik, these scopes have internal adjustments for windage and elevation and constantly centered reticles, which isn't always the case with European scopes. They also have movable spring-loaded ocular lenses, to reduce the chance of injury if a poor shooting position results in a whacked eyebrow. An integral spirit level to eliminate canting is available at extra cost. Prices of the various models run $435 to $625.

J.B. Holden Co. has an Ironsighter See-Thru mount to fit most popular American rifles—centerfires, rimfires with grooved receivers, some muzzle-loaders—and assorted handguns. New this year is a modified version called the Widefield. No sample was available at this writing, but a photo indicates the riser sections which lift the scope high enough to make the iron sights visible have been widened to give a larger field of view than previous models. This could be a useful mount for some of the new large-objective scopes that are coming on the market. Price $16.75.

Kahles scopes of various kinds have been produced in Austria since before the turn of the century. Currently they are being imported into America by Del Sports, in four straight power basic models, the Helia-Super 2.5x20, 4x31, 6x42 and 8x56, and three variables, the 1.5-4.5x, 2.3-7x and 3-9x. These are made in both steel and lightweight versions, the former now available in 1-inch diameter to fit American mounts. This is a recent change in response to demand here. Optionally, 26mm diameter also is available for those who want it, and the light alloy models come with 26mm tubes only.

Kahles scopes are made with a choice of 18 different reticles, most of them conbinations of posts and cross-

hairs. Knowing the distance subtended by opposing posts of course lets such a unit serve as a rangefinder when the approximate size of the target is known. Several reticles include center dots and the No. 3 is a center dot on CH—comaratively simple by European standards.

Kassnar Imports has been selling scopes under their own name for fourteen years now, in both fixed and variable powers, standard and wide angle big game models, plus several rimfire glasses. This year they have added a new line, the Kassnar Beta 3s. It consists of only three models, a 4x32, 6x42 and 8x56, but these obviously will cover the needs of almost all big game hunters. These Beta 3s are built in Japan to Paul Kassnar's specifications, and he says his goal was to offer scopes equal in quality to the top German and American models.

Tubes are aircraft quality aluminum alloy, to eliminate rusting and reduce weight, matte finished to reduce light reflection. Lenses are camera quality and each unit is secured by alloy locking rings. Three different coatings are used on the lenses—magenta, ultra-violet and amber—to provide maximum light levels and top quality images under extreme variations in light quality. The ultra-violet reduces haze and the amber cancels the yellow cast of the UV coating.

The reticle system is different than in many other scopes today. It is constantly centered by means of a reticle-moving system rather than the image-moving system so common nowadays. Kassnar feels that his system is more impervious to recoil than the other.

Incorporated within the optical system is a small spirit level. It's visible in the bottom of the field and immediately indicates any canting of the rifle, assuming the scope is mounted level to begin with. Many aren't, if only eyeballed in to begin with, but it's comparatively easy to do with the integral spirit level.

Adjustments are by clicks which can be both felt and heard. Their value is given as a 7mm movement per click at 100 meters, which for all practical purposes translates into quarter-minutes. Directions of impact movements are marked on the dials.

Focusing is of the binocular system, by rotating the ocular lens unit. Plus and minus diopters are marked on the eyepiece, which also has a neoprene shock absorber.

A choice of four reticles is available in the Betas: 3 posts, 3 posts with CH, 4

posts with CH (Duplex), and plain CH. The 6x42 I've been using has the 3 post/CH type (no post at top). It's conspicuous under any light conditions in which I'd be hunting, and after a bit of familiarization I've come to like the absence of that top post. It results in a noticeably less cluttered field of view.

Kesselring quick detachable mounts are made for many popular rifles, with rings to accept ¾″, ⅞″, 1″ and 1.023″ (26mm) scope tubes, plus various large-diameter German models. Both windage and elevation adjustments can be made in the mount. Split rings are made for use with enlarged-tube scopes, and standard rings for straight-tube models. There is also a "See'Em-Under" base which is grooved on top so the open iron sights can be used in an emergency. All Kesselring mounts are now the same price, $39.50.

Kuharsky Brothers line of scope mounts has been sold to Pem's Distributing, 5063 Waterloo Road, Atwater, Ohio 44201.

Lee Tackhole Dot no longer is installed in the Weaver T models. According to Dan Glenn, when changing reticles in this model, tiny particles from inside the tube often fell on the inverter lens, where they were highly magnified and showed up as shadows, so he felt it was best to discontinue dot installation in this scope. There are other models by various manufacturers in which Lee Dots are not installed for one reason or another; however, most scopes can be fitted with the reticle and it's an efficient design that I've liked and used for many years.

Leupold, we said last year, would have a hard time finding an unfilled slot in their line—or lines, because they've actually got three, all of top quality. But they did it this year. Not within any line but by extending two of them, the M8 straight power and the Vari-X III, with a new scope in each.

The new Leupold variable is a 6.5-20x (actually 6.5-19.2x for the nitpickers). The maker sees this as a highly adaptable varmint model, and that's undoubtedly where it will find most use. With a power spread like this, it can be used for walking up chucks with a Hornet or taking them at a quarter-mile with a 25-06.

The 6.5-20x is only 14.2 inches long and weighs but 16 oz. Unobstructed diameter of the objective lens is 41mm, which is big enough to give plenty of light under most conditions at the higher powers, under all conditions at lower powers. There's a choice of Duplex, converging Post and Crosshair, and Dot reticles, the latter subtending

Bushnell 1.3x-2.5x "Power Booster" 1" pistol scope, Model 74-2800.

Buehler mount for Dan Wesson revolver; base is installed on the barrel shroud.

Bushnell Centurion handgun ring mounts, Models 76-3401, 76-3501, 76-3601.

1 moa at 6.5x, 0.33 at 20x. This is about perfect for all kinds of use. Adjustment divisions are 1/2 moa. This scope has an adjustable objective, of course—necessary at the higher powers for precise focusing to avoid eyestrain and obtain a perfect image. Eye relief is 3.5-4.5 inches, which makes it usable even on a magnum.

Besides its use on varmints, this variable will find favor with many target shooters who will like the way its magnification can be adapted to prevailing mirage conditions. Price, $332.75, plus $19.40 for dot.

The second addition is the M8-36x, a high power target model doubtless intended for use under specialized conditions. This scope is quite an engineering accomplishment. Not for the high power alone, but the fact that it's presented in a scope which is less than 14 inches long and which weighs less than 16 ounces.

Lyman has announced that a new 35x Lightweight Benchrest scope will be available by the time this GD appears, but we've not seen it at this writing. As with the 20x and 25x LWBR models, it is to be 17 inches long, built on a 1-inch tube, with ⅛-inch internal adjustments. Total

adjustment range, 60 moa. Outside diameter of the objective lens unit is listed as 2.165 inches, weight 19 oz., eye relief 3 inches, and field of view 3 feet 8 inches. Price, $399.95. The earlier Lyman LWBR scopes have proven very popular and dependable, so the outlook for this new 35x seems bright.

Lyman also makes silhouette target scopes in 6x, 8x and 10x, at prices ranging from $229.95 to $249.95, a 4x hunting scope at $149.95 and 2-7x and 3-9x variables at $169.95 and $179.95. Crosshairs, dots and duplex reticles are available.

Pachmayr doesn't have an extensive mount line, but their Lo-Swing model has long been popular with hunters wanting to install a scope low and centrally, yet with the option for iron sight use if necessary. A while back I used one for my second 338, for the above reasons. This is a rough-country rig, and I thought it a pious idea in case the little Redfield variable somehow got discombobulated. I've never had that happen on a hunt, but it sure would be a problem if it did. I don't like open sights, though, so on this one I installed the little tip-up aperture from an Old Redfield Jr. base on the rear face of the Pachmayr base. Don't know how this combination will strike the two manufacturers, but it works well from a shooting standpoint.

Phil Pilkington is another custom gun builder who has given thought to detachable scope mounts. Recognizing the popularity of the bridge types such as the Redfield (or the 2-piece-base variations thereof), and the fact that opposing windage screws at the rear lock the scope into position, Pilington saw these could be adapted to quick removal and consistent replacement. Essentially, the Pilkington QD Conversion replaces one of the windage screws with a finger-operated lever which is retained in the mount base by a threaded stud. In closed position the lever holds the scope ring solid as the original screw did. Turning the lever through approximately a half-circle moves the locking area away and makes it possible to rotate the

scope across a flattened section of the lever and off the base.

Precise Imports stopped handling scopes in 1980 and has disposed of their inventory.

Redfield will have a new 3-9x big game scope by the time you read this. They call it the Illuminator, because of its brighter-than-normal optics. The objective lens system is a new air-spaced triplet design which is claimed to give optimum resolution, color correction and flatness of field. I put it that way because at this writing the scope is not available for testing. Hopefully, we'll have one to use extensively before next year.

The Illuminator will also have a 5-element erector lens system intended to transmit an image of highest fidelity and maintain the purity of light ray transmission. The designers' goal was to capture all available light and deliver it to the shooter's eye as clearly as possible throughout the entire field of view. As many riflemen know, there is often a difference between image quality and brightness at the center of the field and at its edge, so the stated objectives for this new scope are worthwhile.

In the mount line, a new Redfield item is the SR (Senior) Special unit. This is essentially an unfinished set of mount blocks—unfinished in the sense that the final machining on the bottom surface is left for the gunsmith to do. The front block is machined to accept the familiar Redfield rotary dovetail and the rear block has the windage screws installed. Otherwise, the blocks (nicely blued) are merely solid steel units. By proper machining, a good gunsmith can fit them to actions for which no standard mounts are available, to barrels of various diameters, or whatever. Screw holes for attaching must be drilled and countersunk, also. Price of bases, $20.50.

S & K Mfg. Co.'s big sellers continue to be their Insta Mounts for Ruger's Mini-14 and the M-1A (M-14). The Insta Mounts are best known for the fact that they require no drilling or tapping, of course. Sid Haight tells me they are putting windage adjustments in the S&K style bases, and several bases, without windage, are also made of the Weaver style. A new mount scheduled for release this year will fit the HK 91 and 93. Price is expected to be $70 complete.

Swift Instruments Inc. has been importing and producing high-quality optical goods for half a century, including an 8-unit line of riflescopes, one for rimfires, the others for big game. All of the latter are built on 1-inch tubes with enlarged objectives, even the 1.5-4.5x. This is a bit unusual. Most variables in this power range have straight tubes. This Swift, Model 658, has a 32mm objective, which is normal for a 4x, thus transmits as much light as most conventional 4x's. We've been using this particular model for some months now, with excellent results. One useful quality is an unusually long eye relief, some 4½ inches by actual measurement at bottom power, 3½ at top. This means it's easily mounted on a heavy recoiling rifle without worrying about getting your eyebrow belted.

The Swift line includes wide angle glasses in 4x and 3-9x and conventional versions in 4x, 6x and 3-9x. The WA scopes have round oculars, not the TV-shape so common now and either CH or Quadraplex (Duplex) reticle.

Thompson/Center's popular Contender pistol, which has been chambered for many strange and wonderful magnum loads as well as the more prosaic factory cartridges, doubtless had something to do with T/C's line of Recoil Proof handgun scopes, which now numbers six. Actually, there are four, with a choice of target type turrets on two to differentiate them from the basic models. Powers are 1.5x, 2.5x, 3x and 4x, the 2.5x and 4x having integral mounting rails. All have duplex reticles, and fields vary from 28 feet for the bottom power to 10 feet for the 4x. Eye relief on all of them is about 11 to 20+ inches.

Physically, these RP scopes are built on 1-inch hardened aluminum tubes with enlarged oculars (the 4x has an enlarged objective), lengths run from 7.5 to 9.2 inches, and weights from 5.1 to 10.4 oz., the mounting rail accounting for a significant part of this on the two scopes.

Handguns, particularly with hopped-up loads like the Contender handles, exert a tremendous force on a scope. In years past, before special scopes and mounts were developed for handguns, it was not unusual to have scopes come apart rather quickly—or at least leave the gun when the mounting screws sheared. T/C has dealt with this problem by beefing up their glasses and testing every one by clamping it to a steel trundle which is struck by a swinging weight which creates a force of approximately 32 G's. The result of such testing is their line of Recoil Proof scopes—which they state is the only scope design ever submitted to the U.S. Patent Office purely on the merits of its recoil proof design.

Weaver has such an extensive scope line—one of the biggest anywhere—that it can't be easy to add any. Yet the El Paso company has done it this year, with four new models, one so recent that it isn't even in their 1981 catalog.

This newest addition is a big, medium-power, Germanic-looking glass called the K856. The "K" of course means it's part of the long-popular round-eyepiece Weaver line introduced just after WW II (and much improved and updated in the decades since). The "8" refers to the magnification, and the "56" is the unobstructed diameter, in millimeters, of the objective lens.

The K856 is built on a 1-inch steel tube, is 15 inches overall, weighs 18.7 oz., has a front end diameter of 2.46 inches and eyepiece diameter of 1.48 inches. Eye relief is 3.5 inches, field is 15 feet at 100 yards, adjustments are internal and of quarter-minute value. Either the Dual-X or German Post reticle ($18 extra) is available. The latter, long popular in Europe where much dim-light shooting is done, consists of three posts, the horizontal ones being flat-ended, the bottom one pointed. Such a design subtends more target than most Americans are used to, but it can be seen in any light that anyone would be shooting in and at normal range is no problem on big game.

We haven't been able to try it on game yet, but have been shooting a sample on a M700 Remington 7mm Magnum, and it works. The adjustments are the highly consistent Micro-Trac design and our reticle is a Dual-X, which can act as a range-finder and also provides a long-range aiming point if you determine just where bullet drop coincides with the top of the bottom post.

Also new from Weaver are a pair of Auto-Comp scopes, the FX4 and VX9, the former a straight 4x, the latter a 3-9x. These have a pair of knobs in the top turret, the upper one used to determine range by adjusting horizontal stadia wires to bracket the target, the lower one to adjust for bullet drop. Interestingly, both the range determination and the trajectory compensation features work independently of all magnification changes in the VX9. Rings are furnished for three trajectory groupings, plus a blank one which can be calibrated precisely for your own handload.

Weaver's other new scope this year is the T30, which gives benchresters a choice among six action-mounted, internally adjusted target models. At 30x, I believe this is the highest-power scope Weaver has ever offered. At 19.4 inches and 20.3 oz. it's a bit bigger than the 25x we tested and wrote up last year, but is essentially the same. Power is probably too high and field too small for varmint use, but increasing numbers of benchrest shooters are demanding ultra-high magnification, so this T30 should be welcome. Price $324, dot or fine crosshair $18 extra.

In response to the constantly increasing use of scopes on handguns, Weaver has also come up with three new mounts this year. All are no-drill, no-tap designs, and they fit the Ruger Mark I 22 auto and 357 Blackhawk, and the Colt Python 357. To install, you remove the rear sight, slip on a barrel yoke and attach the base with two screws. Detachable top mount rings (included) fit as on a rifle mount. The same system also is available for Ruger's Mini-14. Price, $39.95.

Williams Gun Sight Co. is now manufacturing a side mount that will fit either the old or new style receiver of Ruger's Mini-14. Called the SM-MINI-14, it has positive locks which in effect make it a one-piece mount, is quickly detachable, and an eccentric bushing in the base of the Williams QC mount provides extra windage adjustment. The scope can be positioned over the bore with HCO rings, or offset with split rings. With either setup, the iron sights are simultaneously available. Base only, $16.65; HCO rings, $36; split rings, $29.55.

Zeiss scopes have long been rated among the world's best. Unfortunately, they are not available in the U.S. at this time, partly because they do not have some of the specific features required by American hunters. However, it is expected that this company soon will be producing a line of rifle scopes combining the high quality optical characteristics Zeiss is known for with the features American hunters want.   •

FOR SURE SHOTS ON ANTELOPE:

HUNT THE WATERHOLES

by
CHARLES J. FARMER

ANTELOPE HUNTING can and should be a precise sport. The animal, the terrain in which he is found, and the distances at which most shots occur lend themselves to precision marksmanship. This is not often the case in deer, elk or bighorn sheep hunting, where heavy cover, rugged mountain terrain and physical conditioning add variables to the basic skill of good shooting. In other words, there can be some good excuses for a missed shot.

Despite the fact that all the ingredients of antelope hunting tend to emphasize the importance of rifle accuracy, rather than other factors involved in sport hunting, common shooting methods rarely reflect this. The manner in which too many antelope are hunted sickens good sportsmen. Little emphasis is placed on shooting accuracy. Rather, most so-called hunters seem to feel that "there is always another buck to shoot at."

For example, in Wyoming, the leading antelope hunting state, the pronghorn hunt is usually a one-day affair conducted primarily from a four-wheel-drive vehicle. Once an animal is spotted from a road, the driver cuts down the distance as much as he can and the rest is a matter of bailing out of the vehicle and trying a shot. There is no stalking involved and running shots are the rule. Herd shooting is common despite frequent pleas from the Wyoming Game and Fish Department not to shoot into groups of antelope. The pleas from game officials largely go unheeded. The pronghorn has been taken for granted in the past and today's common method of hunting this great game animal reflects this attitude.

There is a method of hunting antelope, though, that hones both shooting and skills. It is not a new method by any means, but it is a technique employed by only a few. I call it "waterhole hunting." It's simple in many ways, but more complex than meets the eye.

Waterhole hunting puts the emphasis exactly where it belongs—on knowledge of the game and its habits, patience, ballistic know-how and rifle skill. The rewards of hunting waterholes exceed the demands. The hunter can be more selective, thus his chances for a trophy antelope are better than by the random scouting method. His shooting position is far better than by most other methods, and he normally has far more time to make his shot—at a range that is comparatively short on an animal that's moving slowly if at all—thus cleaner

kills and sweeter meat will result.

In no way can a hunter bailing out of a vehicle be concentrating on marksmanship. Sure, some fine heads are taken in this manner every season, but an abundance of shooting opportunities, rather than accuracy, is the reason for such success.

From a waterhole blind, the rifle becomes an accurate, one-shot hunting piece of primary importance—not a scattergun. There is no need to hurry when the rules of waterhole hunting are followed.

The principle behind the method of waterhole hunting is based on the natural instinct of the antelope to water daily—sometimes twice a day. Game will be coming *to the hunter* almost as regular as clockwork. There can be no comparison to still-hunting other species of game such as deer or elk—sometimes erratic in their watering and feeding schedules. Antelope are dependable drinkers. Choose the right location and get ready.

The Waterhole

Water is relatively scarce on the sagebrush prairies of western antelope country. In most parts of central and western Wyoming, for example, it is at a premium during the fall hunting seasons. Spring runoff ponds and streams have long since dried up and only those "wet" throughout the year remain. Antelope favor reliable water sources and vary little in their drinking habits from year to year.

The "waterhole" you choose could be a river. There are places along its course that pronghorns favor. Game trails, fresh tracks and droppings will help you pinpoint such a spot. Sagebrush usually grows high and thick along a river, providing ideal locations for a strategic blind.

In the mountain states bands of antelope often congregate around windmills. This is a common sight in Wyoming. Watering or stock tanks, sometimes-ponds, are created by the action of the windmill. Such water is a product of man's actions, not nature's, yet antelope have learned to depend on it. Windmills are rarely plentiful in natural cover, but blinds can be constructed to blend in with their surroundings. Permission, of course, must be obtained first from the landowner.

Finally, there is the prairie pond. In most cases where these exist, an underwater spring supplies a constant source of water. Spring ponds are favored by all forms of wildlife, and those supporting shore birds, waterfowl, muskrats and coyotes are fa-

vored by antelope. Pronghorns have learned to depend on these ponds. If you discover such a waterhole in the spring or summer and it is used by wildlife of all varieties, then: it is a good bet for antelope in the fall.

Ponds created especially for stock by ranchers also fit into this category. New ponds rarely attract large numbers of antelope, but as the pond ages, provided it is a consistent supplier of water, it will gain popularity. Look for mature vegetation—prairie grass, sagebrush or trees—around the pond. This will give you an indication of the pond's age. A new farm pond will ordinarily show freshly graded topsoil on or near the dam.

Pre-season scouting trips best determine productive waterholes, but chances are that any mature pond which holds water during hunting season and is located on the sage prairie will be used by antelope. Many such ponds are located on public Bureau of Land Management (BLM) holdings. Others are situated on private land where permission to hunt should be obtained.

The Waterhole Blind

Choosing a blind site is important. Construction of your hiding spot is equally important. Make it natural. This means that nine times out of ten you will be concealed in a pen of sagebrush.

A buck antelope is a wary customer when it comes to visiting his favorite drinking spot. I have watched pronghorns from a distance in the off-season. Their approach to a waterhole is cautious. A blowing piece of tumbleweed or sagebrush will send them off like bullets. One time I set up a camera on a tripod and photographed waterhole wildlife by means of a remote control unit that cocked and released the shutter. The setup had little effect on ducks, geese or a visiting coyote, but antelope kept their distance. Although the tripod was camouflaged and the camera fairly well hidden, the pronghorns never took their gaze off it. And every time the shutter clicked, they bolted. This may give you an idea of what's necessary for proper blind construction.

Keep the blind's profile low—about four feet high at maximum. It can be long enough to lie down in. Try to build it some time before the season opens. If it is natural looking and blends into the rest of the scenery, chances are it will not spook watering pronghorns at all. It might be helpful or necessary to dig a shallow pit for more comfort or possibly to add more depth for a small,

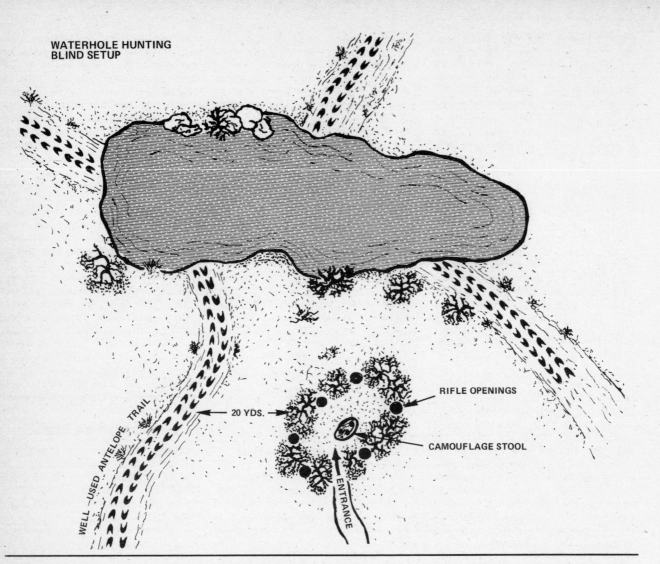

WELL-USED ANTELOPE TRAIL

20 YDS.

RIFLE OPENINGS

CAMOUFLAGE STOOL

ENTRANCE

camouflaged stool.

Tie bundles of sage or other appropriate materials together with olive-drab nylon cord. The kind used to anchor duck decoys is excellent. High wooden or metal stakes spook antelope. Their eyes are extremely keen. Stake the sagebrush down in the manner that a tent is staked. Secure pegs to the rope holding the sage together and pound them into the ground. This will keep the gusty prairie wind from blowing your blind away. There is nothing particularly complicated about this blind's construction—just keep it natural, of a size and shape to break your outline and give you room to move into shooting position.

Allow one or several small openings in the sagebrush to shoot through, especially if you intend to shoot from a prone position from within the blind. If you move slowly inside the blind, the openings normally will not give you away, and prone shooting from some sort of rest should be possible. This is my choice. I usually know from which

direction most antelope will approach. You can learn this by observation or by checking the direction of tracks. Position the blind off main waterhole trails at least 20 yards or so to avoid being in direct line of pronghorn movement. And place it where you can see the entire waterhole. There have been times, during hunting and photography trips, when bucks have "snuck" into water without my knowing it. One minute nothing, the next minute a big buck is drinking down there. Chances are you will shoot your buck on his approach to the waterhole, but do not rule out the possibility of a waterside shot. When necessary, you want to be able to make it.

As an extra precaution, take some sage tips (buds) and rub them into your clothing. If the wind is not in your favor, this trick helps. Otherwise, position your blind so that the wind will be blowing toward you when shooting. I have not found antelope particularly keen nosed, but the extra effort might help.

If you do not plan for observation

ports in your blind, your only alternative will be shooting over the top of the sage wall—not the best method. You may spook antelope when you rise, and you will not have an adequate rest for a clean shot. By staying low inside the blind, you have time to glass the animals, determine if there is a suitable buck, adjust scope power if necessary, get into good shooting position and fire.

All of the bucks I have killed from a waterhole blind have been well within 200 yards and standing still when I fired. This is the reason for the "waterhole technique." It allows for clean kills at sensible shooting ranges—and you had better believe there is a powerful element of excitement when you sight a buck 500 yards out and he finally moves into sure-kill shooting range. Then you realize you have challenged the pronghorn with sportsmanlike terms. And he's yours.

The Rifle

Because the hunter plays a waiting game with this waterhole technique and most shots will range from 100 to 200 yards, almost any rifle/cartridge combination which will group in an average-size Stetson from a distance of two football fields will do the job. In my opinion, three calibers fill the bill nicely for this type of gunning—the 243, 270 and 30-06. I could be dogmatic and say that the 243 is the best choice for antelope. It's a favorite, no doubt, but the 270 and '06 have performed equally well under my observation, and I haven't the slightest doubt that similar loads such as the 6mm Remington, 280, 284, 7x57mm and the like will do equally well. But because my experience has been largely with the first three loads mentioned, they're the ones I'll cover here.

The 243 Winchester cartridge with a bullet weight of 100 grains is fine. Many experts call this a flat-shooting bullet, ideal for antelope, and I agree. At the muzzle, the bullet has a velocity of 3070 feet per second and at 100 yards it's still moving at 2790 fps. Plenty of speed. In the energy department, it has 2090 ft. lbs. at the muzzle and 1730 at 100 yards. A buck antelope hit in the heart or lungs with this bullet will not travel far, if at all.

Another flat shooter is the 270 Winchester. This cartridge made its reputation with the 130-gr. bullet, and for long-range shooting it's probably the best, but for waterhole hunting I've had good luck with the 150-gr. combination, which I like for heavier game. It shoots plenty flat over the ranges we're talking about here and I don't believe it's as destructive as the lighter bullet. I've heard many stories about the pronghorn's ability to pack a lot of lead. This they will do if a vital spot is missed. Gut-shot or butt-shot antelope go a long ways on occasion, as do those with "swinging-gate" leg hits. But such results usually come from long-range running shooting—the kind we're trying to avoid by hunting the waterholes. At the distances normally encountered here, the 150-gr. 270 load with some 2400 fps remaining velocity at 100 yards has better than 1900 fp of energy there, and that's more than plenty for any pronghorn you are likely to encounter.

Much the same thinking applies to my choice of the 180-gr. bullet in the 30-06. The 150-gr. spitzer is the projectile normally recommended for antelope when the '06 is the chosen cartridge. Again, for ultra-long range shooting it would be hard to fault this selection. But up to 200 yards the 180-gr. load is for all practical purposes just as flat, and this bullet has less tendency to ruin the forequarters if it happens to land there.

Some gun experts tend to downgrade the 30-06 because it cannot be called a specialty caliber. The truth of the matter is that it does most things well. When matched with the right bullet weight, its versatility is remarkable. It is not "too much gun" for pronghorns when properly used. Heart or lung shots ruin little meat, regardless of the caliber. Shoulder and spine shots do their share of meat damage. It's best not to take them.

The 30-06, 180-gr. bullet has a muzzle velocity of 2700 fps, which decreases to 2470 at 100 yards. Energy-

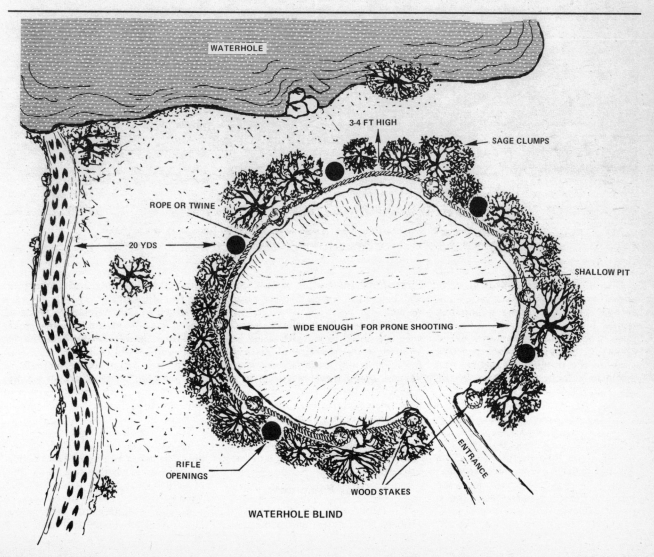

WATERHOLE BLIND

wise, at the muzzle it packs 2910 fp, with 2440 at 100 yards.

Scopes and Sight-In

There are iron-sight men and there are telescopic-sight men. Antelope hunting luck seems to favor shooters who use scopes, and I believe the variable models, 3-9x or 2½-8x, are best. The rule to follow in choosing a good scope for antelope hunting is not to skimp. Buy the best name-brand model you can afford. To get on the paper quickly, bore-sight it yourself or have your sporting goods dealer do it for you. Most own an optical bore-sighter and usually provide the service free of charge.

ting (on the ground or from a stool); prone, provided you built the blind in such a manner; squatting or kneeling. Unless you miss your first chance and want to gamble on a running shot, it is doubtful whether you will shoot standing.

In pre-season practice sessions, fire several rounds from each position. And, *most important*, use the same rifle and load you will be using on the antelope hunt. Lighter or heavier loads, off-brand bargain loads, "free bullets" or whatever, will defeat the purpose of these practice sessions. If you load your own, make sure you know what you are practicing with and stick with the same load for the

items add comfort to the wait and, at the same time, increase your chances of big buck success. In the clothing department there is nothing special except garments that feel good in weather that normally will range from 50 to 65 degrees. You will have to wear bright colors of some sort—that's a state law. As long as these colors are broken up by a good blind you won't be detected.

A small wood-and-canvas stool painted in green, brown and black is handy. You can use it while spotting game and fold it up when getting into shooting position. A canteen of water is a good idea. A small shovel or army entrenching tool for constructing the

My wife Kathy sets sights on good buck at right. Actually at this point, buck had been hit with lung shot after watering at pond below. Seconds later, it dropped; Kathy hadn't needed to scramble out of blind.

During pre-season sight-in visits to the range, remember that average antelope specimens are common but trophy bucks are rare. If you want a good head, take the guesswork out of shooting. Spend whatever practice time on the range is necessary, and settle only for a tight group in the black at 200 yards.

Chances are your waterhole blind shooting will offer a choice of four shooting positions. At the time you sight your trophy, hopefully you can choose your favorite position. This isn't always the case, but even so you'll have more time to get ready from the blind than in any other antelope shooting situation.

The four basic positions will be sit-

hunt. Experimentation should come well before the season if you're a handloader.

Several practice sessions after the rifle is sighted in will definitely help your chances. Practice at distances from 100 to 200 yards—shooting from various scope power settings to see which gives you the best results. Know how much of the animal will be in the scope at what ranges. Find the range or power best for you at 100 and 200 yards, and stick to it—some variables change point of impact as the power is altered.

Other Equipment

The most important tools have already been noted, but some other

blind (chopping sage and pit digging) fits the bill. Candy bars or snacks are worthwhile. An adjustable shooting tripod has advantages. A folded jacket also works as a rest. You should have a knife and possibly a hatchet for cleaning game. After taking pictures of your trophy, dress it out, wash the body cavity thoroughly, skin and quarter it, pack into the game sacks you brought and let cool in shade.

There are easier ways to shoot antelope than the method I've described, but none is any better. The extra effort makes the hunt more satisfying. Waterhole hunting will strengthen the bond between you and your rifle, make you a better hunter, and deepen your admiration for a beautiful animal. ●

Single-Action Safety

There's more to it than anybody planned.

by DONALD M. SIMMONS

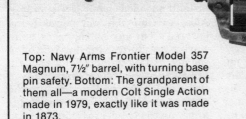

Top: Navy Arms Frontier Model 357 Magnum, 7½" barrel, with turning base pin safety. Bottom: The grandparent of them all—a modern Colt Single Action made in 1979, exactly like it was made in 1873.

Top: RG 88 single-action 22 Long Rifle, steel frame with wood grips. Some parts are imported from West Germany, but the revolvers are assembled in Florida and avoid the Factoring Criteria and the "Hammer Drop test." Bottom: Italian-made "Buffalo" type 22 Long Rifle with a manually applied hammer block safety, zinc die case frame.

SOME YEARS ago I wrote of the advent of some safeties being added to the copies of the old Colt Single Action Army. At that time I pointed out that because of our government's jurisdiction over the qualifications for imported handguns, we had a potentially dangerous situation. Each overseas manufacturer was dependent on his own ingenuity to devise a single action revolver that could pass our government's hammer drop test.

What is the history of our government's entry into the field of firearms safety?

In the early '70's, Treasury got H.P. White, a firearms testing laboratory, to devise and execute a series of endurance tests on a group of contemporary handguns. White was told to include a hammer-drop test for revolvers: with the hammer set in whatever position the manufacturer recommended for safety, a weight equal to the loaded revolver was dropped from 36" on the revolver's hammer spur. This very tough test was to be repeated five times and if the revolver hammer did not fire the under-the-hammer cartridge, the gun passed the test. All good modern double action revolvers could pass this test, but no exact copy of the old Colt Single Action revolver could do so. Treasury, armed with H.P. White's report and bolstered by a committee which included some apparently short-sighted people from the firearms manufacturing industries, proceeded to set up standards for the importation of handguns. Basically, this "factoring criteria" was a point system giving so much for caliber, over-all length, weight and whether the arm had target grips or adjustable sights. As far as revolvers were concerned, they could have all the points they needed and they still wouldn't pass unless they could get through the hammer drop test.

At this point all imported copies of Colt's Single Action were in trouble, but as the smoke cleared, J.P. Sauer (Hawes) of West Germany, Uberti (Cattleman) of Italy, Dakota (EMF) of Italy and Hammerli (Interarms/Virginian) of Switzerland all found an answer to beat the hammer drop test. They all found a different answer and since this initial list of acceptability, there have been many more foreign makers who have subsequently come up with their own fixes—again none of which are like any of the others.

The Single Action Colt was launched in 1873 and discontinued in 1940. The total production was 357,859 revolvers including the Bisley and the target models of each line. By 1956, Colt, goaded by both domestic and foreign manufacturers, resurrected the Colt S.A. just as it had been put in mothballs in 1940—no changes. To date, Colt has made about 150,000 of these revolvers counting a great many so-called commemorative issues. Added to this is the new line of 22 rimfire Colt Single Actions which were made from 1957-1977 in a quantity of about 575,000 revolvers.

We find that since 1956, Colt has turned out almost 3/4 of a million single action pistols, all pretty much like the first Colt Single Action made in 1873. The quantity of post-war single actions has more than doubled the entire output of 67 years of pre-war production. Why did not Colt change their old design? Others like Ruger had overhauled the Colt design and brought it up to date with coil springs and investment castings, yet Colt clung to their fragile leaf springs and their expensive machined forgings. I feel the basic reason for Colt's inertia was that the buying public wanted the Colt S.A. as it had been, not modernized. Colt, more than any other maker was producing nostalgia—they were making a replica and they were doing it the way they had done it for over a hundred years.

The Colt Single Action has four hammer positions: down or fired position; quarter safety notch or safe position; half-safety notch or loading and unloading position; and finally full cock or firing position. Sounds simple and it was, but you don't carry a Colt S.A. in the quarter-safety position. You carry it either with the hammer down on an empty chamber or, in the case of centerfire cartridges, with the downed hammer resting between cartridge rims in adjacent chambers. These are the only safe ways to carry a Colt and for a rimfire model, the empty chamber is the only safe answer.

If the cylinder of the revolver has

Top: Ruger New Model Blackhawk 357 Magnum with a complete safety system which includes a transfer bar and hammer down loading. Bottom: Ruger Blackhawk Old Model 357 Magnum can be recognized by the three screw frame.

rebated chambers, (counterbored at the rear so that the rim of the cartridge is flush with the cylinder), it can be hard to find which chamber has been left unloaded. This can be done very easily during loading by inserting the first cartridge and skipping the next chamber and then loading the next four chambers. When this is complete, draw the hammer fully to the rear and lower it all the way and it is on the empty chamber.

This, then, was a way of life if you wanted to carry a Single Action Colt. It was insurance against dropping the gun and having it land on its hammer and discharging, and it was partial insurance against snagging the hammer on some object and having it drawn back partially and then suddenly released. In this case, the hammer might over-ride the notches and fire if there were an under-the-hammer cartridge. However, there were still other dangers. The gun could be dropped from the hand during loading and, shearing the half-cock notch, fire the

pistol if a loaded chamber was in line. Also, anytime the hammer is being lowered from any notch, there is always a possibility of losing control of the descending hammer and accidentally firing the revolver. And finally, if the user lowers the hammer into the quarter or half-cock notches with his finger on the trigger, he might end up with the revolver's sear on the lip of the notch and not in the notch itself. This is called the phantom notch situation and is very dangerous since a light touch on the trigger will fire the revolver. The phantom notch is avoided by entering the quarter or half-cock notches only by pulling back on the hammer with one's finger completely off the trigger. The last

Harrington & Richardson Model 676 22 Long Rifle looks like a single action with rod ejection but it actually is a double action pistol with a transfer bar safety.

Seville Sheriff Model made by United Sporting Arms. This is the author's, one-of-a-kind gun assembled in Tombstone, AZ, and is the only one ever made in 45 ACP only. Transfer bar safety; loads in the half cock notch.

Ruger Single Six, 22 Long Rifle, a very early model. Ruger's sales of these acted as a lever to bring Colt back into production of both centerfire and 22 rimfire single action revolvers.

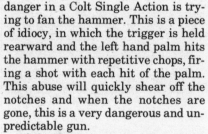

Dug-up Remington New Model Army showing the hammer rest notch on the cylinder and the hammer rest nose on the hammer. Cap and ball revolvers used the between chamber positions as a safe way to carry.

danger in a Colt Single Action is trying to fan the hammer. This is a piece of idiocy, in which the trigger is held rearward and the left hand palm hits the hammer with repetitive chops, firing a shot with each hit of the palm. This abuse will quickly shear off the notches and when the notches are gone, this is a very dangerous and unpredictable gun.

While the imported copies of the Colt could now all pass the drop test if their particular safety system was applied, they really did not solve any of the other problems inherent with a Single Action Colt.

The Uberti/Cattleman, imported for a while by Iver Johnson, and now imported by Mitchell Arms Corp. of Costa Mesa, CA, has an ingenious automatic hammerblock. This is operative when the revolver's hammer is in the quarter safety notch.

The Italian-made single action "Frontier" imported by Navy Arms Co., has a rotating base pin which has a stud on the end toward the shooter. When the base pin is to the left, the hammer has a relief cut which allows it to fall and fire. However, if the base pin is to the right, the hammer can't reach the primer. The change in base pin position requires the depression of the base pin lock.

Navy Arms also for some years, has imported an Uberti-made copy of the Remington Model 1875 Single Action revolver. These have the Uberti quarter safety block and are safe in this position. The Italian-made "Dakota" line, imported by EMF, has a small wheel-like eccentric cam mounted on the top of the hammer, when rolled one way, it blocks the hammer in the quarter-cock notch.

Next, we come to the Hammerli/Virginian revolver, imported by Interarms for several years. It is equipped with a device called "Swiss safe," To lock a Hammerli, the revolver is half cocked and the base pin is pushed inward to its second notch and in this position, it protrudes from the frame, blocking the hammer. So, a Virginian is carried with the base pin pushed in at half cock as is the current Virginia Dragoon.

Excam Inc. imports a line of 22-caliber reduced-size Colt look-a-likes. These inexpensive revolvers have a manually applied block mounted on the left side of the frame at the swell for the cylinder. This Italian copy, according to its brief instruction manual, suggests use of the safety block in all hammer positions.

F.I.E. Corporation of Miami, Florida, both assembles foreign-made parts into revolvers and also imports some Arminius S.A. revolvers, which use the transfer bar system if assembled in the States. This covers most of today's imports.

Domestic S.A. Revolvers

After World War II, there was a great demand for all handguns and the price of Colt Single Action revolvers made before the war went to $200 and even $300 for an excellent one. The first copy was made by Great Western and it had a line of "like Colt" revolvers in all calibers and barrel lengths. Being a copy, Great Western didn't change anything basic about their product and they only lasted a short while. Ruger came out with a Single Six revolver 22-caliber with an aluminum frame. Bill Ruger, however, completely redesigned the Colt S.A. internally, replacing all flat springs with long life coil springs and many other good changes. However, they still had Colt's four position hammer and could only be safely carried with five rounds in the cylinder and the hammer down on the empty sixth chamber. Ruger in 1955 came out with their Blackhawk line of center-fire single action revolvers which were internally like the earlier Single-Six. In 1958, Ruger introduced a small 22 single action revolver, the Bearcat. These resembled the old Remington line of converted cap and ball, but did not have a hammer rest position between the chambers.

After 1968, Ruger started working on a really safe single action revolver. They borrowed Iver Johnson's transfer bar system, for years sloganed by "Hammer the Hammer;" then Ruger went one step, and it was a giant step, further. They eliminated all intermediary hammer notches, just leaving the hammer down position and the full cock position. The New Model Ruger loads with its hammer full down by simply opening the loading gate at which time, the cylinder bolt drops and the cylinder is free to spin as when a Colt S.A. is in half-cock.

New Model Rugers can be carried with six rounds in the cylinder and the hammer down because the transfer bar which transmits the energy from the hammer to the frame mounted firing pin, has dropped below the fir-

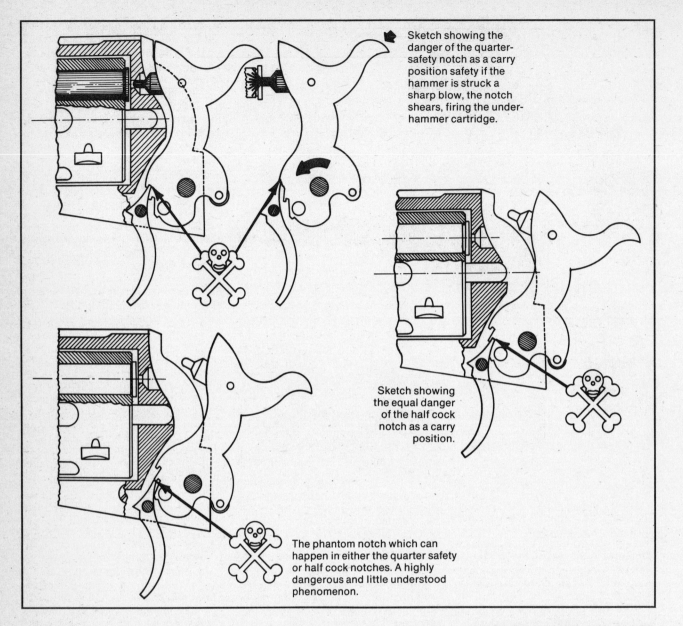

Sketch showing the danger of the quarter-safety notch as a carry position safety if the hammer is struck a sharp blow, the notch shears, firing the under-hammer cartridge.

Sketch showing the equal danger of the half cock notch as a carry position.

The phantom notch which can happen in either the quarter safety or half cock notches. A highly dangerous and little understood phenomenon.

ing pin. Because there are no notches between down and full back, there can be no phantom notches. If the New Model Ruger were dropped when loading the last cartridge, it still wouldn't discharge.

The Seville/United Sporting Arms and its look-a-like, the Abilene/United States Arms Corp., now being sold by Mossberg, both use the transfer bar like Ruger, but they have retained one intermediate notch—the half-cock—and load and unload at this position.

Today's Problem

So we find on the market today, guns in the single action class, running from Colt's four-position, three-click hammer with no safety, to the completely safe Ruger New Model with its two-position, one-click ham-

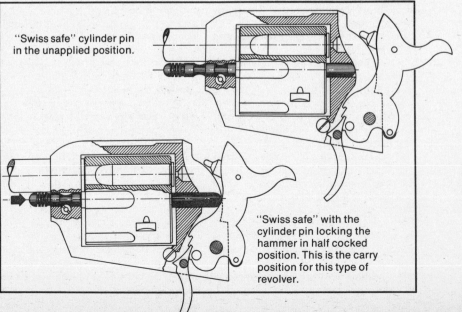

"Swiss safe" cylinder pin in the unapplied position.

"Swiss safe" with the cylinder pin locking the hammer in half cocked position. This is the carry position for this type of revolver.

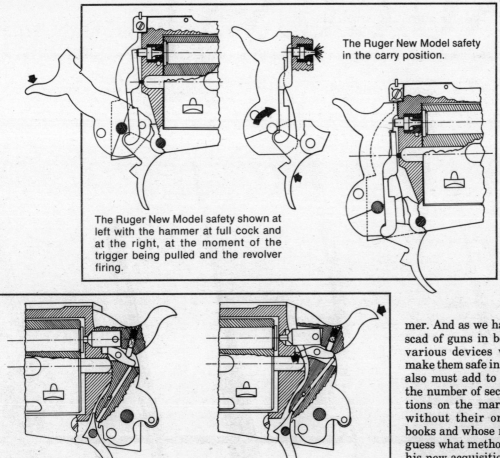

The Ruger New Model safety in the carry position.

The Ruger New Model safety shown at left with the hammer at full cock and at the right, at the moment of the trigger being pulled and the revolver firing.

Uberti type safety which is shown here in the unapplied condition at the moment of firing the revolver.

Uberti safety in the locked up quarter safety notch position. The Uberti safety functions automatically in this notch.

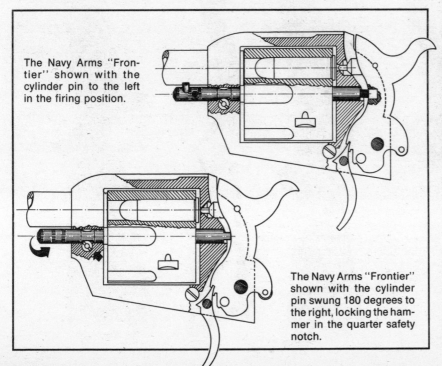

The Navy Arms "Frontier" shown with the cylinder pin to the left in the firing position.

The Navy Arms "Frontier" shown with the cylinder pin swung 180 degrees to the right, locking the hammer in the quarter safety notch.

mer. And as we have seen, we have a scad of guns in between which have various devices which *if used* will make them safe in most situations. We also must add to the above problem, the number of second hand single actions on the market which are sold without their original instruction books and whose new owner can only guess what method of safety exists on his new acquisition.

In a nutshell, if you have any single action revolver and you are not sure how to carry it, lower the hammer on an *empty* chamber and even if it has a safety you don't understand, you will be safe this way. Use a holster with a flap if available, if not get one with a tight fitting hammer thong or strap and don't use a cheap unfitted holster. This is because a great deal of safety is provided from the thickness of the leather which gives rigidity to the walls of the holster. This in turn will keep the cylinder from turning and the hammer down and safe. If you buy a secondhand single action without an instruction manual, send to the manufacturer, giving the model and serial number. He will see that you get the proper manual for he is out to keep future customers unharmed.

Let's all make a conscientious effort to improve our safety habits when handling and using a single action revolver. If you are allowing someone else to shoot your revolver, explain the safety on your particular gun. Don't take it for granted that someone who knows one type of Single Action knows all types. Even at the risk of antagonizing your friends, preach safety; think safety and some day you may save a life and it might be your own. ●

LONG GUNS

by LARRY S. STERETT

Ljutic's new "Space Rifle" (left) is available in a variety of calibers, while the "Space Gun" (second from left) is available only in 12 gauge with a 30-inch barrel and screw-in choke tubes. Winchester's Model 70 XTR Featherweight rifle (center) is a blend of modern technology and classic styling. The Bauer Rabbit (sec-ond from right) will handle any 410-bore shotshell and 22 rimfire L.R. cartridge, and disassembles into a com-pact unit just over 20" long. Harrington & Richardson's new Model 5200 single shot 22 rimfire bolt action target rifle (right) is capable of better than minute-of-angle accuracy.

THE BIG NEWS in the U.S. long gun field has to be the Olin Corporation's decision to sell the domestic portion of Winchester sporting arms, but to retain the ammunition line and the Japanese-manufactured line of shotguns. What this means isn't exactly clear, but according to some Winchester sources contacted, if the sporting arm is manufactured in Japan with the Winchester name on it, it will be retained. If it is manufactured in the U.S. the manufacturing rights, facilities, patents, etc., will be sold, along with the use of the Winchester name for five years. Sound a bit complicated! What actually happens remains to be seen. Winchester did sever the Perazzi connection, by mutual consent it is understood, and the Winchester future should be interesting to watch. Regardless, Winchester has introduced a number of new high grade

over-under guns—manufactured in Japan.

Browning has also introduced some high grade shotguns, but sadly the excellent Model 2000 autoloader has been dropped, due to increasing manufacturing costs. Replacing the 2000 will be a Beretta-manufactured Model 80 with Browning's name on it. Ljutic has the most unusual of the new long arms, with their "Space Gun and Rifle," while Harrington & Richardson has a winner in their new precision Model 5200 bolt action target rifle. Other firms have trimmed their lines a bit, but there are plenty of new models being introduced by such firms as Savage, Sceptre, and Weatherby, to provide something for everyone.

Bauer Firearms Corp.

Remember the old F.I. Bronco 22/410 over-under combination gun? Basically the same gun is now available as the Bauer Rabbit. Measuring 38½ inches in over-all length, when assembled, it takes down into a compact length of just over 20 inches for stowing in a backpack or survival pack. Chambered for the 22 rimfire Long Rifle cartridge in the over barrel, and 3-inch .410 shells in the under barrel, the Rabbit tips the scales at 4¾ pounds, and features a special rust and wear resistant finish on the stock, barrels, and receiver.

Browning

There are three new Browning shotguns, in addition to a new 4-barrel Citori Skeet set. In tribute to the Mallard duck, there's a special 12-gauge Limited Edition Waterfowl Superposed available. There will be 500 Belgium-manufactured guns, based on the Lightning model. An engraved grey steel receiver inlaid—sides and bottom—with 24 carat gold drake and

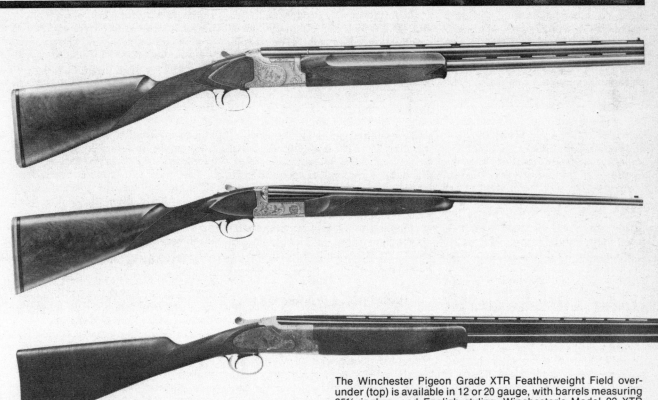

The Winchester Pigeon Grade XTR Featherweight Field over-under (top) is available in 12 or 20 gauge, with barrels measuring 25½ inches, and English styling. Winchester's Model 23 XTR Lightweight Pigeon Grade side/side (center) follows the traditional English styling with straight grip stock. The Grade V Sideplate Citori 20 gauge over-under (bottom) features deluxe etching, a straight grip stock and a forearm with a slight Schnabel.

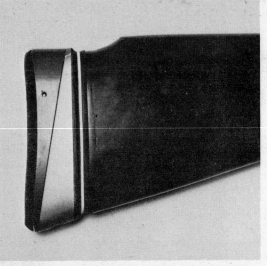

Above—The Griggs Recoil Redirector replaces the regular recoil pad. Additional spacers can be added, if desired, as shown. Right—The B.M.F. Activator attaches quickly, via two nylon screws, and is adjustable to fit any 22 rimfire autoloading rifle.

hen mallards in flight, in addition to a golden drake head on the bottom of the trigger guard, is coupled with 28-inch barrels choked modified/full. The select, figured French walnut stock and forearm have an oil finish, and are hand checkered at 24 lines-per-inch; the butt is checkered, without a recoil pad or plate. Priced at $7000.00, the Waterfowl Superposed is provided with a form-fitted, velvet lined, hand-crafted black walnut case with brass fittings.

The second new shotgun is a 20-gauge Grade V Sideplate Citori over-under. Carrying a price of $1800.00, it features 26-inch blued barrels choked improved cylinder/modified or modified/full, and a satin steel finished receiver with false sideplates etched with upland game scenes. The long tang trigger guard has a similar finish, but is etched with floral motifs, and the head of a quail. The barrel selector is built into the safety mechanism on the upper tang, in the Browning tradition, and the single trigger is gold plated. The American walnut stock has a straight grip, and it and the slim schnabel forearm have an oil finish, in addition to hand checkering.

New to the Citori line is a 4-barrel Grade I Skeet set, complete with fitted luggage case, all for $2500.00. Consisting of the regular 12 gauge receiver/buttstock assembly and one forearm, it comes with 12, 20, and 28 gauge barrels, plus a .410 bore barrel. (All Citori target barrels have a high post floating target rib.)

A number of the Grade I, II, and V Citori models are to be discontinued as soon as present inventories are exhausted. These include mainly the hunting versions, with 28-inch barrels in 12, 20, and 28 gauge, plus .410 bore, choked improved cylinder/modified, and the 26-inch barrels in the same gauges, including the .410, choked modified/full, in addition to the 30- and 32-inch trap barrels choked full/full.

The final new shotgun is the B-80, an autoloader manufactured by Beretta for Browning, and based on Beretta's excellent gas-operated design, which replaces the B-200. Available in both 12 and 20 gauge versions, including a Buck Special grade with rifle sights, the B-80's forged steel receiver, with its squared-off shape, will handle standard length and magnum length shotshells simply by changing to the appropriate barrel. In Field grade the B-80 lists at $509.95; a ventilated rib barrel is standard, as is a recoil pad on the pistol grip buttstock.

Harrington & Richardson

The firm with the largest line of single shot break action shotguns has two excellent new rifles. The first is the Model 340, a bolt action centerfire design based on the Mauser action with a 22-inch barrel chambered for the 30-06 cartridge. The American walnut stock has hand checkering, a metal pistol grip cap, a contrasting wood forearm tip, and a "classic" comb, without Monte Carlo. Resembling an

early M70 styling, the Model 340 lists for under $300.00. The second new rifle is the Model 5200, a single shot rimfire match rifle design originally requested for U.S. military use. Weighing approximately 11 pounds, without sights, the Model 5200 features a 28-inch match quality barrel which will produce m.o.a. accuracy. The massive walnut stock has a full length rail on the forearm, straight comb, and a full pistol grip. The trigger pull on the rifle is adjustable from 1 to 3½ pounds, and the hand stop on the forearm is adjustable the entire length of the rail. Priced at $325.00, the Model 5200 may become the standard by which other rimfire match rifles are judged.

The Model 172 Trapdoor Springfield rifle and the two over-under shotguns have dropped from the H & R line. However, there have been a number of additions to the revolver line, covered elsewhere in this issue.

Ithaca Gun Company

The Ithacagun Centennial was in 1980, and in keeping with this milestone the firm brought out two special limited edition series shotguns for collectors. The Presentation Series features the 12-gauge Model 37 pump and Model 51 semi-automatic shotguns, and the 10-gauge Mag-10 autoloader, in a special Supreme Grade, with gold-mounted blued receiver and extra fancy walnut stock and forearm. Available individually or in 3-gun matched sets, the Presentation guns come in compartmentalized leather-

Harrington & Richardson's Model 340 centerfire bolt action rifle (left) features a classic-style walnut stock. Weatherby's latest is the Lazermark Magnum (second from left). The laser-carved stock is available as an option on all Weatherby Mark V rifles in all nine calibers. The top of the new Savage rimfire line is the bolt Fox Model FB-1 (second from right), which features a flush-mounting, detachable box magazine having a release button on the right side of the stock. The Wichita Arms Varmint rifle (right)—the new stainless steel Magnum is very similar, except for having a brushed stainless steel finish and a slightly longer barrel.

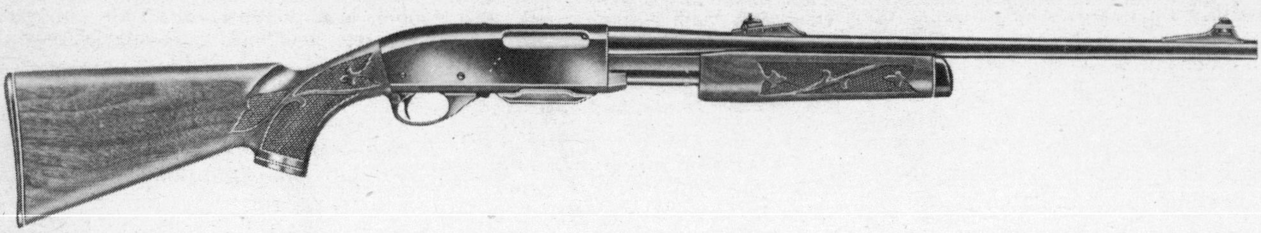

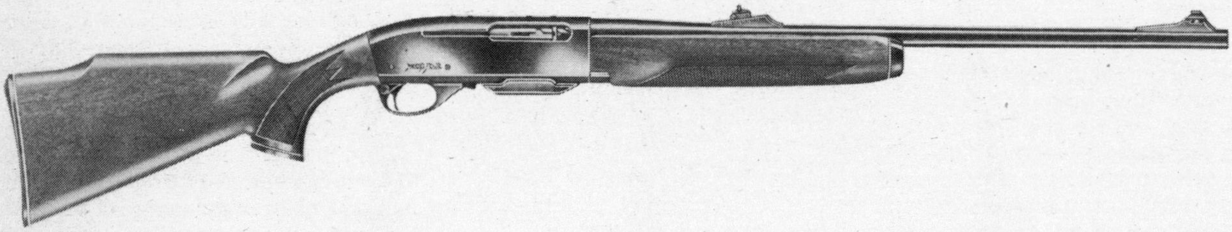

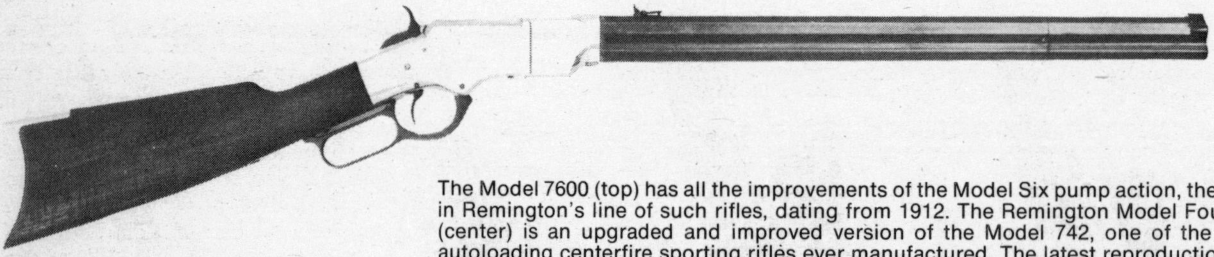

The Model 7600 (top) has all the improvements of the Model Six pump action, the latest in Remington's line of such rifles, dating from 1912. The Remington Model Four rifle (center) is an upgraded and improved version of the Model 742, one of the finest autoloading centerfire sporting rifles ever manufactured. The latest reproduction iron frame Henry rifle (bottom) joins a Navy Arms line which previously included brass frame rifle and carbine reproductions of the Henry, as shown here.

covered take-down cases. The 2500 Series consists of the popular 12-gauge Model 37 pump action shotgun with a semi-fancy walnut stock and an etched, silver-plated antique finished receiver. Only 2500 guns in this series will be built, and each comes in a special full length, leather-covered hard case. The 12-gauge shotguns have 28-inch modified choke, ventilated rib barrels, while the Mag-10 has a 32-inch full choke barrel. Only 200 each of the Presentation Series shotguns will be manufactured. Prices on the Centennial shotguns range from $795.00 to $1495.00, depending on the series and model.

The other shotguns in the Ithaca line include the Model 5E and "Dollar" Grade Single Barrel Trap guns, the latter known as the "Knick," and the Model 37 in Ultra Featherlight, Featherlight (Plain, Standard, Deluxe, and Supreme grades), Basic Featherlight, Magnum, and Deerslayer, plus the Model 51 autoloader in Standard, Deluxe, and Deerslayer grades, and the Mag-10 in

Standard, Deluxe, and Supreme grades. The Models 37 and 51 are available in a choice of 12- or 20-gauge versions, and the Mag-10 and Model 37 are also available in special law enforcement versions. Finally, shortly after you read this there may be another Ithaca autoloader, a 12-gauge Trap grade version of the Mag-10—scaled down.

Kimber of Oregon, Inc.

Last year the Model 82 bolt action rimfire rifle was introduced. Featuring a classic stock design, and chambered for the 22 Long Rifle cartridge, the Model 82 immediately became a hit. Now, the Model 82 is available chambered for the 22 WRM cartridge, in addition to the 22 Long Rifle, and another style stock has been added to the line. The 82 Magnum rifle has a 4-round detachable box magazine which fits flush with the stock, while the regular rimfire magazine holds five cartridges. Otherwise, except for the changes necessary for the longer cartridge, the latest Model 82 is the

same as the regular Model 82 Sporter.

The new stock is called the Cascade. Of California Claro walnut, the Cascade stock features a Monte Carlo comb, with cheekpiece, but has the same checkered steel buttplate and steel grip cap as the regular classic stock, including checkering at 20 lines-per-inch. (Available on either of the Model 82 rifles, the Cascade stock option costs an additional $7.00.) Both Model 82 rifles are available as complete rifles, without sights, for under $450.00, with open sights as an option, with the more expensive Leupold 4x scope installed, or as a barreled action without sights.

Ljutic Industries, Inc.

There's no doubt the award for the long arms with the most unorthodox appearance has to go to the Ljutic "Space" guns—shotgun, rifle, and pistol. Known for a line of winning 12-gauge trap gun designs, including the Mono-Gun, Dyna Trap, and Bi-Matic single barrel models, and the Bi-Gun over-under, the Ljutic firm has introduced a new design that resembles a gas pipe with a handle on it, or possibly even an old-fashioned crutch with a hand grip. All three versions—shotgun, handgun, and rifle—are single shot, bolt action designs, with a straight bolt handle on the bottom of the tubular receiver. (The barrel, receiver, and tubular buttstock, are in a straight line on the shotgun and rifle.) The "Space Gun" shotgun is available only in 12 gauge with a 30-inch barrel, two screw-in choke tubes, and a high mounted muzzle bead, while the "Space Rifle" is available in popular calibers from the 222 Remington to the 300 Winchester Magnum, and comes with a high-mounted scope. Production models of either gun retailed for under $1000 in mid-1981, while the "Space Pistol" was approximately $200 less in price. All the "Space . . ." models feature a button trigger, and specially shaped forearm and pistol grip.

Marlin Firearms

Since the last edition, Marlin has discontinued the lever action Model 336A, the only rifle in the Marlin line with a 24-inch barrel. Also discontinued in the centerfire rifle line has been the Glenfield Model 30GT, a handy, straight-grip carbine with a barrel length of 18½ inches. The shotgun line remains the same, and the only changes in the rimfire line consist of dropping the barrel band/swivel assembly and the lower swivel on the Glenfield 70 autoloader. Otherwise, except for slight price increases, the Marlin line remains the same solidly constructed line of lever action centerfire rifles, autoloading and bolt action rimfire rifles, and pump and bolt action shotguns, as were covered last year.

Michigan Arms Corp.

Looking for a black powder rifle that has the appearance of a modern rifle? MAC is manufacturing such a new rifle in two models—the Wolverine and the Friendship Special Match—which use battery cup 209-size shotshell primers for ignition. Featuring a stainless steel breech plug, choice of walnut, cherry, or maple pistol grip stock with Monte Carlo, and a bolt action in-line receiver, the MAC rifles are available in a choice of 45, 50, or 54 caliber. The rifles measure 44 inches in over-all length with a 26-inch octagonal barrel measuring 1-inch across the flats. Weight per rifle is approximately 7¾ pounds, depending on the caliber, and the rifles come with sights and a ramrod.

Mossberg

In the last edition, the new Mossberg autoloading Model 5600 shotgun was mentioned. It has been temporarily shelved, as has the bolt action RM-7 rifle. A number of production RM-7 rifles reached the market, prior to the decision to put it on the back burner for awhile, but the Model 5600 autoloader is still under development. Look for both models in mid-1982. The Model 500 pump action shotgun is available in various grades, including the Hi-Rib Trap version, and the economy New Haven 600 versions. One of the sleepers in the Mossberg rimfire rifle line is the Model 380 autoloader, which features an adult-size hardwood stock and a 15-round buttstock-housed, tubular magazine; it's a handy plinking or small game hunting rifle.

Navy Arms

Val Forgett's firm is known for its replica black powder arms, and there are several new arms in this line, including two 75-caliber Brown Bess muskets, three 58-caliber Enfields, as originally manufactured by the London Armory Company, a 58-caliber M1863 Springfield rifle, and a 12 gauge side/side shotgun. Not as well known are the breechloading centerfire rifles and carbines. The latest of the breechloaders is a limited edition of 500 iron frame Henry rifles in a choice of 44/40 Winchester centerfire or 44 rimfire calibers. Featuring a 24-inch octagonal barrel, an over-all length of 43 inches, and a weight of approximately 9¼ pounds, the Henry has a 13-round magazine capacity. The receiver and buttplate are case-hardened in color, and the walnut buttstock has an oil finish; the Henry rifle does not have a forearm. In either caliber, the new Henry rifle goes for $750.00 in its limited edition.

Remington

The Limited Edition Model 1100 "One of Three Thousand" 12 gauge shotgun mentioned last year is now available, and the 7mm-08 cartridge has been added to the list of cartridges for which the Model 700 BDL rifle is chambered. The Model 870 "Competition" pump action, gas-operated, recoil-reduction single shot trap shotgun mentioned in the last edition, has been temporarily shelved until a minor problem is solved. The big news this year is the introduction of redesigned versions of the pump and autoloading centerfire rifles. The new models include the Model Four and 7400 autoloaders, and the Model Six and 7600

pump action designs. Top of the line are the Model Four and Six, which list for $449.95 and $399.95 each, respectively. (The Models 7400 and 7600 are more economical by $50.00 each, and are chambered for the same cartridges.) The Model Six is available chambered for five popular cartridges—6mm Remington, 243 Winchester, 270 Winchester, 30-06, and 308 Winchester—while the Model Four is chambered for the same cartridges, plus the 7mm Remington Express. The bolts on both rifles have been redesigned, with additional bearing surfaces and locking lugs similar to those on bolt action rifles, while the gas-metering system on the autoloader has been redesigned, as have the action bars on the pump action. The detachable box magazines have been built of heavier gauge steel, and redesigned for faster feeding of the cartridges into the chamber; the magazine release had been beefed-up and made more accessible for use with or without gloves. Other noticeable changes include contouring the receiver top to match the contours on the old Model 742 and 760, and the imbedding of a brass cartridge case head of the appropriate caliber into the blued steel just forward of the receiver on the bottom. (The caliber is also stamped on the left side of the barrel.) The Model Four and Six rifles have walnut Monte Carlo stocks, with fluted comb and full cheekpieces, full pistol grips with black plastic caps and white spacers, and flared forearms with black tip and white spacer. The squarish shape of the forearms on past Deluxe models of the 742 and 760 rifles has been changed to a more pleasing rounded shape. Simple patterns of positive-cut checkering grace the sides of the pistol grip and the bottom of the forearms, replacing the basketweave patterns of past years. On the Model 7400 and 7600 rifles the buttstocks do not have the Monte Carlo with cheekpiece found on the Model Four and Six rifles, or the same forearm shape, but mechanically they are the same; the checkering patterns on the 7400 and 7600 are also new, and much more elaborate than on the Four and Six rifles, but it is impressed checkering, and not positive-cut. Barrel length on the new rifles is 22 inches, giving an over-all length of 42 inches, and the approximate weight is 7½ pounds, regardless of the model. See Testfire, p. 230.

Savage Arms

New from Westfield this year is an entirely new Fox line of sporting arms,

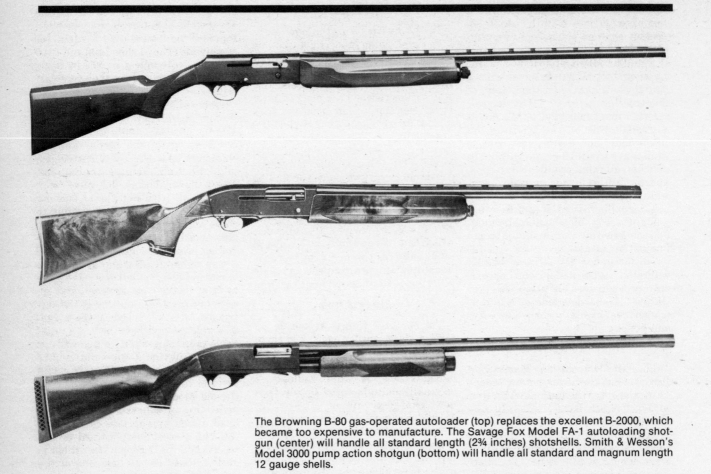

The Browning B-80 gas-operated autoloader (top) replaces the excellent B-2000, which became too expensive to manufacture. The Savage Fox Model FA-1 autoloading shotgun (center) will handle all standard length (2¾ inches) shotshells. Smith & Wesson's Model 3000 pump action shotgun (bottom) will handle all standard and magnum length 12 gauge shells.

starting with a pair of Japanese-manufactured 12 gauge shotguns. These shotguns—the Model FA-1 autoloader and the Model FP-1 pump action—are modified versions of similar shotguns distributed as the Weatherby Centurion and Patrician designs. Stocks are of select walnut with checkering and a rosewood cap on the pistol grip. The barrels have ventilated ribs, and the lengths and chokes include 28-inch modified, and 30-inch full; the pump gun will handle magnum-length (3-inch) shells.

The new rimfire rifle line includes seven models—the Savage 980-DL and Stevens 987 autoloaders, with tubular magazines for the 22 Long Rifle cartridge; the Savage 982-DL and Stevens 982 and 982-T (with 4x scope) bolt action repeaters with detachable box magazine for the 22 Long Rifle cartridge; the 982-MDL bolt action repeater chambered for the 22 WRM cartridge, and the Fox FB-1 22 Long Rifle bolt action repeater with detachable box magazine. (The box magazines have a 5-round capacity, although 10-round magazines are

available.) Prices range from under $100.00 for the Model 987, to under $300.00 for the FB-1 with select walnut stock having a rosewood forearm tip and pistol grip cap, rollover Monte Carlo cheekpiece, and Wundhammer swell on the pistol grip. There is also a "special order" Savage/Anschutz Model 54-MS rifle for metallic silhouette shooting. Featuring a special silhouette stock and 2-stage trigger, it listed for just under $650.00 in early 1981.

In the centerfire rifle line the 7mm/08 chambering has been added to the bolt action Savage Model 110-S metallic silhouette line, and to the lever action Model 99-C, while the 375 Winchester is now chambered for in the Model 99-A rifle. The 110-E is now available for the 308 Winchester cartridge, while the 110-ES with 4x scope can now be obtained chambered for the 243 Winchester cartridge.

Other changes in the Savage line include the dropping of the Model 99-CD and 99-375 rifles, in addition to the Model 112-R, and the handy Model 242 over-under 410-bore shotgun. The

various older rimfire rifles, except for the 72, 89, and 125 and 125-Y, have been replaced by the new line mentioned previously.

Smith & Wesson

A few years back this Bangor Punta firm introduced the 12 gauge Model 1000 autoloading shotgun in a field style. It has since expanded the line to include both 12 and 20 gauge models in field, slug, Skeet, and magnum grades, in addition to a 12 gauge Model 1000S Super Skeet model with special ventilated Skeet choke. The 1000S and 1000 Magnum grades have steel receivers, while the other grades have aluminum alloy receivers. A pump action version was introduced as the 1000P, with a steel receiver designed to accept either standard or magnum length 12 gauge shotshells. Available only in field grade with a choice of plain or ventilated rib barrel, the 1000P could be obtained with a barrel length of 26, 28, or 30 inches, choked improved cylinder, modified, or full, respectively, or a 22-inch model with rifle sights for slug shooting. Apparently the 1000P designation caused some confusion, since the autoloader also has the 1000 label. In 1981, the pump gun was reintroduced as the Model 3000. It's the same shotgun as before in all features and specifications—only the name has been changed.

Other long arms in the S&W stable include the excellent Model 1500 rifles in Standard and Deluxe grades. Both grades are available in seven popular calibers, ranging from the 243 Winchester to the 300 Winchester Magnum.

Spectre, Inc.

Over a decade went into the development of the Atchisson 12 gauge Assault Shotgun. Although intended for military and police use, in a selective fire version it also has merit for home defense or even personal protection in some areas, such as the Alaskan bush. The original prototype never made it to the production state, and was built from a hybrid of parts, some from the BAR, the M16, and the Thompson. Now, a Georgia firm has undertaken to manufacture a redesigned version of the shotgun, which will be listed as the Atchisson Assault 12.

Using high strength injection moldings, and flat steel stampings to reduce cost, the new design will use a clamshell type of construction. Measuring 38 inches in over-all length, with a barrel length of 18 inches, the semi-automatic version will fire from a closed bolt, and will feature a 7-round detachable box magazine, with a 20-round drum magazine available as an option. The new shotgun will handle any standard length (2¾ inches) 12 gauge shell—shot, buck, or rifled slug—and will weigh approximately ten pounds.

Universal Firearms

Universal's M-1 carbine is well known in its various models, including the latest variation with the Schmeisser-type folding, paratrooper stock. New is a Limited Edition Commemorative version. Limited to a production run of 999 carbines, commemorating the 40th Anniversary of the M-1 (1941-1981), the Limited Edition has a glass bead military-type finish on all metal parts, and a hand-rubbed high luster finish on the select walnut stock. Inletted into the right side of the stock butt is a solid brass "war and peace" commemorative medallion. Each LE carbine is supplied in a Gun Guard hard case, along with a detachable 2½x Weaver scope and mount, barrel band with bayonet lug, bayonet

and scabbard, 5, 15, and 30-round magazines, sling and oiler, a commemorative solid brass belt buckle with scaled-down M-1 carbine on the face, and a registration certificate suitable for framing. The tab for the Commemorative M-1 is $598.00, complete.

Weatherby

New from South Gate is the "Limited State Series" consisting of 100 custom grade Mark V rifles—two for each of the 50 states—in 300 Weatherby Magnum caliber. Each rifle has exclusive custom carving on the forearm, pistol grip, and below and to the rear of the cheekpiece, plus gold fill lettering on the barrel and receiver, gold fill engraving on the floorplate, and gold plated trigger and sling swivels, in addition to a custom hand-honed action and a multi-color ceramic buttstock inlay for each state. Each rifle comes in an aluminum Weatherby single rifle case with a matching ceramic state plate on the outside.

Also available in all nine calibers for $125.00 above the regular Mark V rifle price, is the Lazermark Weatherby. The Lazermark Magnum features laser carved patterns on the forearm, pistol grip, and below and to the rear of the cheekpiece, thus presenting an unique appearance.

Wichita Arms

Looking for a "classic" custom designed bolt action rifle? Wichita Arms' WC-100 single shot is available chambered for such cartridges as the 17-222, 222 Remington, 6x47, 6mm PPC, and 308 Winchester, for $1295, or with a blind magazine for $100.00 additional. Featuring an oil-finished AAA grade Claro or American walnut stock, with hand checkering, and a octagon receiver and barrel, the "Classic" is capable of shooting groups measuring under 1 m.o.a. The WV-1200 Varmint rifle is chambered for the same calibers, and is a bit heavier, but more economical at $895.00 for the single shot version. The difference is the round receiver and the round, straight tapered 20-inch barrel, which requires less machine work. The craftsmanship is still the same, including the AAA grade hand finished stock. A Silhouette rifle in the same calibers, including the 7mm-08 Remington, is priced the same as the Varmint rifle, but features a match grade 24-inch barrel, fluted bolt, and 2-oz. trigger, with the same high quality AAA grade walnut stock.

The newest arrival to the Wichita

line is the stainless steel Magnum WM-1250. Chambered for standard rifle calibers from the 270 Winchester to the 458 Winchester Magnum, the WM-1250 is available with a blind magazine, or as a single shot, complete with hard case, for $1750.00. The receiver and bolt are of 17-4 Ph stainless steel, heat treated to 207,000 psi tensile strength, and the stainless steel, target grade barrel is available in a choice of 22 or 24-inch lengths. The bolt features three locking lugs, and a diameter of ⅞-inch; the rear of the bolt has a shroud, and there are three ports in the body for gas venting. The barreled action is glass bedded in the oil-finished AAA grade American walnut stock, and the pistol grip and forearm are hand checkered at 20 lines-per-inch. Weight of the Magnum is approximately 8½ pounds.

Wichita Arms also manufactures left and right hand bench rest actions and barreled actions, including right hand/left port and left hand/right port versions, such as the WBR-1375 and WBR-1200, in addition to silhouette pistol actions, mini rifle actions for bench rest shooting, complete silhouette pistols, accessories for the Ruger Mini-14, rifle rests, and Multi-Range sights for silhouette pistols. All of the rifles and pistols examined have been of excellent design and craftsmanship, and the same comment goes for the accessories, including the sights.

Winchester

The Models 70A XTR and 70A XTR Magnum rifles have been discontinued, but new is the Model 70 XTR Featherweight. Featuring a 22-inch barrel, available chambered for six popular cartridges, including the time-tested 257 Roberts and 7x57 Mauser, the Featherweight weighs approximately 6¾ pounds. The American walnut stock is a "classic" in design, with deluxe cut checkering patterns, a Schnabel forearm tip, red rubber butt pad, and a blued steel pistol grip cap. It's a beauty, and only $433.00; Winchester may have difficulty producing enough of these Featherweights.

New is a Model 1300 XTR Waterfowl grade pump action, with 30-inch ventilated rib barrel and three Winchoke tubes—modified, full, and extra full. The Model 1300 XTR with the 26-inch improved cylinder barrel has been discontinued in both 20 and 12 gauge versions, and so have the Model 1500 XTR versions in the same barrel lengths. The Model 1500 XTR autoloader is now available in Field grade in 12 gauge only with a 28 or 30-inch ventilated rib barrel; the 20 gauge plain and ventilated rib barrel Field guns have been discontinued, except for the Winchoke version, which is available with or without the ventilated rib. Also discontinued is the 12 gauge Super-X Model 1 STR in Field grade; only the Trap and Skeet grade Super-X autoloaders are still being built. Returning to the Winchester catalog are the Field grade Model 1200 slide action and Model 1400 autoloader in 12 and 20 gauge, with 28-inch Winchoke barrel chambered for 3-inch, magnum length shotshells. Magazine capacity on the 1200 and 1400 is 5 rounds; a Defender Model 1200 is available with 18-inch cylinder bore barrel and a magazine capacity of 7 rounds.

New is a Model 23 XTR Lightweight Pigeon Grade side/side in 12 gauge, with barrels measuring 25½ inches, choked improved cylinder/improved modified, and in 20 gauge with the same barrel lengths, but choked improved cylinder/modified. A English-style straight stock, with red rubber butt pad, and a semi-beavertail forearm of American walnut, add to the styling. The barrels are chambered for 3-inch cartridges, and a single trigger is standard, with the selector incorporated into the safety mechanism. Weight of the Lightweight is approximately 6¼ to 6¾ pounds, and the price tag is $1175.00, complete with a Deluxe gun case. Also new is the Pigeon Grade XTR Featherweight Field over-under, with the same barrel lengths as the side/side, and in the same gauges and chokes. The Featherweight over-under weighs approximately 6½ to 6¾ pounds, and has a tapered ventilated top rib, ventilated side ribs, a straight grip stock with red rubber butt pad, a trim forearm with finger grooves along the upper edge, and a price tag of $1400.00, complete with a Deluxe gun case.

The Model 101 and Xpert Model 96 over-under shotguns are no longer cataloged, although selected models in 12 and 20 gauge Field, Skeet, and Trap versions are available on a limited basis. New is the 12 gauge Model 101 XTR Waterfowl Winchoke version with 32-inch barrels chambered for 3-inch shells, ventilated top rib and ventilated side ribs, and four Winchoke tubes—modified, improved modified, full and extra full—all for $1125.00. Also new is the 12 gauge Model 101 XTR Winchester with 28-inch barrels chambered for standard length cartridges, and the Model 101 XTR Lightweight Field and Pigeon Grade XTR Lightweight Field in 12 or 20 gauge, with 27-inch barrels chambered for 3-inch cartridges, and featuring ventilated top ribs and ventilated side ribs. Each of the last five over-unders comes with six Winchoke tubes—two each, improved cylinder, modified, and full. The Model 101 XTR Featherweight carries a $1150.00 price tag, while the Pigeon Grade goes at $1450.00, complete with Deluxe gun case. The Pigeon Grade over-under trap and Skeet guns have been upgraded to Pigeon Grade XTR, and there's a new Pigeon Grade XTR Winchoke Trap, which is basically the same shotgun, but with interchangeable choke tubes, four of which are provided—modified, improved modified, full, and extra full. The regular Pigeon Grade XTR Trap, with or without Monte Carlo stock, lists for $1300.00, while the Winchoke version lists for $1425.00; a Deluxe gun case comes with either version.

One of the most interesting over-under shotguns introduced by Winchester is the 12 gauge Model 501 Grand European in Trap and Skeet grades. Both models feature ventilated side ribs between the barrels and a tapered ventilated top rib. The Trap grade has a choice of 30 or 32-inch barrels, choked improved modified/full, while the Skeet gun comes with 27-inch barrels choked Skeet/Skeet. The barrel bores are chromed to resist corrosion and fouling, and selective automatic ejectors are standard, as is a single trigger, with the barrel selector incorporated into the safety mechanism. The semi-fancy grade American walnut stock and Schnabel forearm are hand checkered at 22 lines-per-inch, and the Trap gun is offered with a regular or Monte Carlo configuration buttstock. Weight of the Trap gun is approximately 8 pounds, and the price tag for either version is $1800.00, complete with custom-crafted, leather-trimmed, canvas-covered case, with brass-plated hardware and combination lock.

Special Order

On a special-order basis, and with great emphasis on the European market, Winchester is going to produce virtually any combination of rifled and smoothbore gun that can fit a Japanese over-under frame. This will include over-under rifles, small and large in bore; combination rifle-shotguns in 12 and 20-ga. and several rifle calibers; and combinations with two or more sets of barrels. The samples all looked good and the prices were competitive.

B.M.F. Activator, Inc.

Like to burn up rimfire cartridges in your favorite autoloading rifle? The B.M.F. Activator is a manually operated cranking device which mounts on the trigger guard, and can empty a rimfire rifle magazine in seconds—up to 1200 rounds per minute. Costing $19.95, and constructed of space-age plastics, the Activator attaches via two nylon screws. As the cranking handle is rotated, an internal mechanism repeatedly trips and releases the trigger, once the proper adjustment is made. Designed to work right- or left-handed, the Activator is entirely legal, and the handle can be removed, allowing the device to act as a safety when the rifle is not being used.

Meadow Industries

Have a rifle or shotgun with a stock that's too low? The Variable "Convert-A-Stock" pad attached to your stock will raise your cheek so your shotgun will center its patterns a bit higher—up to 23½ inches—or place your eye in the proper alignment with the riflescope. Two models are available—the VCS-6 which provides six height adjustments, and the VCS-11 which provides 11 changes of height, up to ⅝-inch. The adhesive backed Velcro fasteners do not damage the stock finish, the Velcro spacers can be attached in any position to change the cheek position, and the Naugahyde pad will hold up in any weather. Instructions come with each unit, which lists for under $15.00; it's a lot cheaper than a new stock.

Griggs Recreational Prods.

Many shooters, especially trap and Skeet shooters, are bothered by recoil during long shooting sessions. Often this recoil could be reduced, if the stock could simply move away from the face or cheek surface during the rearward movement. Now it will, if the shotgun or rifle is fitted with a Griggs Recoil Redirector. This Redirector, which replaces the regular recoil pad or butt pad, consists of a sliding aluminum unit with internal spring tension. As the fired rifle or shotgun moves to the rear, the unit causes the butt of the stock to slide down and away from the facial area, thus reducing felt recoil. The Redirector costs $79.95, and is adjustable for different shooters. Five different colors are available. It weighs just over 11 ounces, and comes with illustrated mounting instructions. If the stock needs lengthening, spacers are available at a slight added cost. ●

HENRY HARRINGTON:
A Cutler Who Made Guns

by JAMES E. SERVEN

He didn't make many, but there is no mistaking the ones he did make.

The grim look is at least as much characteristic of early photo technique as it is of the personality, but there is little doubt Henry Harrington was a man of purpose.

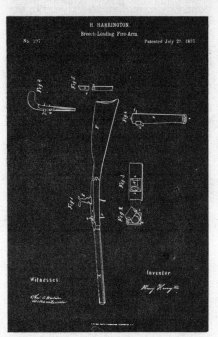

Dated 1837, Harrington's breechloader patent tried to cover all the bases. Under it he made handguns and long arms alike, but one at a time.

NOT LONG AFTER this country became a nation, Henry Harrington was born in Shrewsbury, Massachusetts, on September 10, 1796. At 22 years of age he had saved a little money and constructed a 14' × 16' wooden building to house a forge and workshop in Southbridge, Massachusetts. In that same year (1818) he married 18-year old Anna Oaks. They started off in the business of making cutlery and children. Evidently they succeeded in both endeavors.

Six sons and two daughters lived to be more than eighty. The youngest son, John, died in Southbridge in 1936 at the age of ninety-three. It was indeed a hardy clan!

The Henry Harrington endeavors prospered. He eventually produced some of the finest knives, razors and other edged instruments available anywhere. With a great knowledge of cutlery, he yet had a strong urge to create something different. Thus it is not strange that he turned his inventive thoughts to firearms.

Today the Henry Harrington pistols and rifles that came from his shop are among the rarest of American weapons and a great prize for those who may own one. Relatively few are known in collections. The most extensive group is in the Wells collection at Old Sturbridge Village, where there is a regional museum of early New England life in Sturbridge, Massachusetts.

Harrington was a contemporary of Samuel Colt, whose multi-shot pistols were patented in 1836. The Harrington multi-shot arms were patented just one year later in 1837. These two Yankee armsmakers worked in a period when New England had begun to wrest armsmaking prominence from Pennsylvania whose industry had flourished in the earlier "Kentucky" or long rifle days.

While Colt and Harrington shared a common zeal for making successful guns, here the similarity in character ended. Colt had a keen eye for business

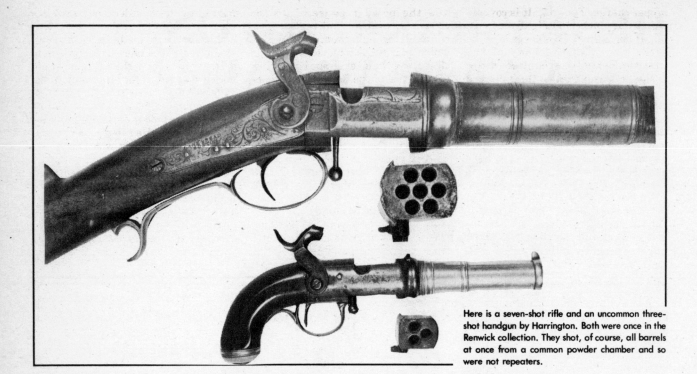

Here is a seven-shot rifle and an uncommon three-shot handgun by Harrington. Both were once in the Renwick collection. They shot, of course, all barrels at once from a common powder chamber and so were not repeaters.

promotion and profit. On the other hand, Harrington had no great ambition for fame and fortune. Mass production was distasteful to Harrington; his greatest satisfaction came in producing arms that were individually styled, although the principle of his patented arms was almost always the same.

Harrington's application for his United States letters patent (granted as No. 297 and dated July 29, 1837) is quoted in part as follows:

"I, Henry Harrington, of Southbridge, in the county of Worcester and Commonwealth of Massachusetts, cutler, have invented a new and useful Improvement in Fire-arms, called 'Harrington's improvement in Guns, Pistols, and Cannon', the following is a full and exact description thereof:

"The exterior barrel, of convenient bore and length, resembles the gunbarrel in common use. The interior is filled with several small barrels or tubes. . . . These small barrels, extending in length from the muzzle downward to a powder chamber sliding into the lower end at the breech. . . . The tubes or small barrels may be made also by drilling through a solid barrel or bar of metal.

"In the breech or lower end of the barrel is a mortise, made through the same from the upper side, to receive a powder chamber. This chamber is made nearly square, is exactly fitted to the space made by the mortise, and slides therein. Holes in the front plate of the chamber are made slightly tapering, so that the opening into the chamber is smaller than that into the barrels, against which they rest or slide. The chamber itself contains a cavity sufficiently large to hold a

Here are the Renwick Harringtons from the other side. They are slightly unusual in appearance but do not reveal their truly unusual character when seen in profile, loading chambers properly in place. Note the wire-wrapping of the rifle barrels ahead of the breech area.

proper charge of powder. It is covered with a flat plate of metal, turning on a pin at one corner. This cover is of the same size with the body of the chamber. Behind this chamber a screw is placed, turning into a thick piece of metal. The head of the screw is large enough to admit receiving a small handle or pin, which projects under the barrel so far as to admit of being moved with ease by the finger. By this means the screw is made to press hard against the chamber, or to leave the chamber so that it can slide out easily.

"In loading the gun above described the chamber is slipped out. The shot or balls are poured or placed in the holes and pressed into the chamber by the finger. The cover is then turned open and the powder poured into the chamber, which is prevented from running through them by the shot which fills them. The cover is again closed, the chamber slipped down into the mortise of the barrel, the percussion cap placed on the tube, the screw turned up so that the head presses the chamber hard against the lower ends of the small barrels, and the gun is ready to be discharged.

"Any number of sliding chambers may be fitted to the same gun. When it is desired to fire rapidly they may be previously charged and slipped into the gun in quick succession."

The surviving examples of Henry Harrington's work examined for this study, with one possible exception, have either been multi-shot arms with the removable breechblock or a few single-shot arms made along the general lines of the more common Allen system. It is said that Ethan Allen once worked for Henry Harrington. To support this, Allen started out, like Harrington, to make cutlery. And it has been claimed that one of the Wessons worked for Harrington, although it is not clear if this was Daniel or Edwin.

One of the theoretical advantages claimed for Harrington's breech-loading, multi-shot weapons was their ability to produce a broadly-placed and rapid firepower. As in the claims similarly made for carrying extra loaded chambers for other weapons,

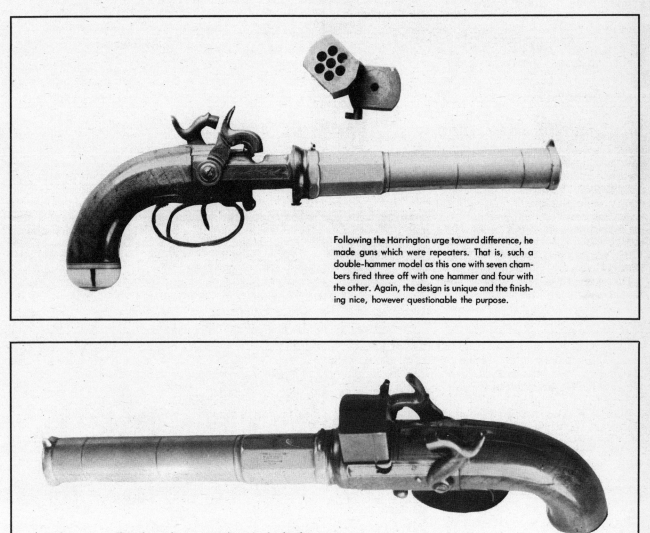

Following the Harrington urge toward difference, he made guns which were repeaters. That is, such a double-hammer model as this one with seven chambers fired three off with one hammer and four with the other. Again, the design is unique and the finishing nice, however questionable the purpose.

This is the two-hammer gun, showing its loading from the top. The end-on or culprit's view of such a gun must have been alarming. Harrington talked of spare sets of loading chambers, but apparently never produced any. Once separated from the gun, of course, such an assembly would be a quite anonymous piece of ironmongery.

this proved unconvincing. The weight and bulk of extra chambers made such a system disliked and very seldom employed.

While the same principles of operation appear in both the multi-shot rifles and pistols made by Harrington, there are major differences in the number of chambers, etc. One interesting variation is to be found in the seven-shot arms that have two cocks

forms of stars, an eagle, or other decorative symbols.

A gun owned by Major Renwick bore a lockplate marked *Lane & Read-Boston*. Lane and Read were prominent old-time dealers in guns, and may have acted as Boston agent for the Southbridge gunmaker. Alternately, Harrington may have purchased the lock from them.

Shoulder arms of this design have

not been seen by the writer with barrels longer than 24″ and most are some shorter. The clustered barrels are finally encased for about six inches at the breech by a metal collar and a short collar at the muzzle. They are brazed together, spirally wrapped with wire and painted black.

Seven clustered barrels and the accompanying seven-shot breechblock appear to have been as near to stan-

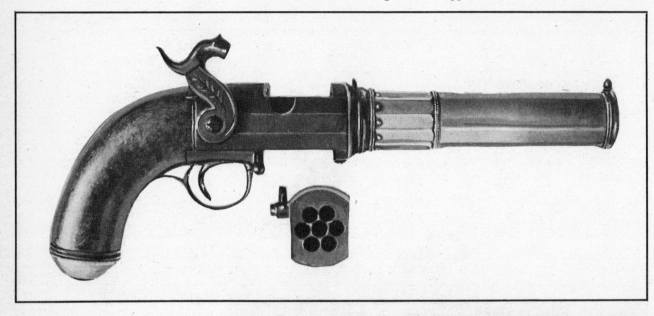

or hammers. In such arms the chamber is divided so that the right-hand hammer will fire the first three charges and the left-hand hammer will fire the final four charges. The rifle of this type in the Wells collection at Old Sturbridge Village is 40-caliber. A two-hammer pistol in the Horner collection is of 25-caliber.

At the time Harrington was first in business, he found it advantageous to stamp his blades with an approximation of English proofmarks or seals. This was for the same reasons the American H. E. Leman had found it good business to place a proofmark on his trade guns to assure their acceptance by those accustomed to proofmarked English-made muskets.

However, soon the Harrington-made blades were recognized to be fully equal or in some cases superior to the products made in Sheffield, England. Thereafter he applied his own name and mark. The practice was carried over to the firearms made by Harrington. Markings to be found may include *Henry Harrington, Patent 1837, Southbridge, Mass.* and some kind of small mark such as the heart and asterisk marks shown on the Horner pistol. There may be other marks in the

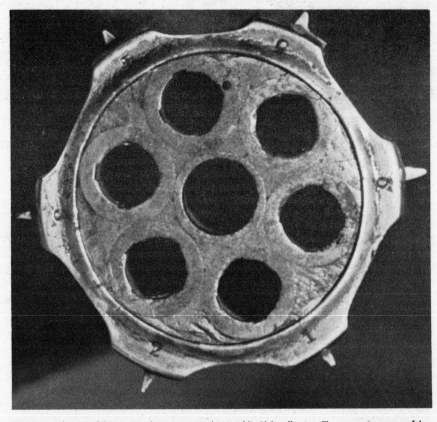

This is a muzzle view of the suspected Harrington in the Harold's Club collection. The composite nature of the barrel assembly can be seen, as can the four-groove rifling.

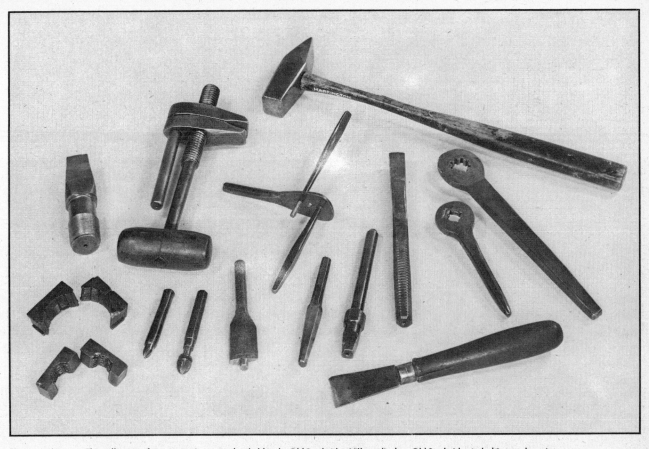

This collection of Harrington's own tools is held in the Old Sturbridge Village display. Old Sturbridge is the biggest depository of Harrington lore and remnant record. The cutlery business, of course, accounts for most of Henry Harrington's importance.

dardization as any firearms models that Harrington designed. However, a rare three-shot pistol was found in the Renwick collection, assembled primarily when the owner resided near Boston. This rather odd pistol bears out somewhat our earlier statement that Harrington had a strong urge to produce something different!

Although none has been turned up in this study, there are rumors that Harrington made some cutlass pistols. It appears logical that a cutler might undertake to combine a blade with a pistol as had two other early Massachusetts gunmakers, C. B. Allen and Morrill, Mossman & Blair.

The nearest thing to a multi-shot cannon, such as mentioned in the patent application is a 25-pound gun which discharges seven 48-caliber balls at one crack. This gun is said to have been designed for military use, but the U. S. Ordnance Department took a look at it and turned it down.

What is believed to be one of Henry Harrington's caplock experimental attempts, because of the similarity in the workmanship, was noted in the famous gun collection at Harold's Club in Reno, Nevada. This gun is unlike the usual Harrington breech-loading gun but is made with six straight bores in one muzzle-loading barrel. It has an underhammer action reminiscent of the early "bootleg" arms, and the only marks on it are the 1 to 6 markings around the muzzle of the barrels, which are revolved by hand.

A feature that tends to indicate this gun may have been made by Harrington is the treatment of the barrels. It has his unique system of brazing the six tubes together, binding them by steel collars at the muzzle and breech and wrapping the midsection of the barrel tightly with wire.

We can assume that the multi-barrel arms of Henry Harrington patented in 1837 exerted some influence on the manufacture of the early "pepperbox" arms that soon sprouted thereafter, manufactured by many New England makers.

At times in the gunmaking trade, the personal background of the individual under study may be as interesting as the surviving examples of his genius and skills. In the years following the War for Independence, Harrington had learned the cutlers trade. He had decided to go in business for himself at age of 22, becoming the first industry started in Southbridge.

Dexter Harrington, one of Henry's sons, joined his father at an early age, showing a keen interest in the business. Henry Harrington died in 1876, one day before his 80th birthday. A couple years before his death they say he could jump in the air and click his heels together twice before landing. Some of our pioneer gunmakers were made of stern stuff.

After his father's death, Dexter Harrington carried on the business, changing the name to Dexter Harrington & Son when joined by his son Charles. Under their guidance the Harrington cutlery business was expanded. Today they are incorporated under the name Russell-Harrington Cutlery Company.

Thus it turned out that the founder of a successful cutlery dynasty, who briefly turned to armsmaking, may be remembered more for the quality of his blades than his production of guns. But gunmaking had been the field which provided an outlet for Henry Harrington's inventive mind and doubtless gave him much pleasure—perhaps the kind of exhilaration which comes today when a collector may obtain one of the very rare Harrington firearms! •

I TOOK CAREFUL aim with the Llama, squeezed off five shots, and was relieved to see the bullets grouping satisfyingly in the black. Considering the first time I shot the pistol only half struck the 25 yard target and many of those hit sideways, I thought this relatively tight group something of an accomplishment. It was not so much the fault of the pistol that it shot the hot plus-P 38 Super loads so badly nor was this poor performance due to any lack of accuracy of the Remington factory ammunition. The problem was

the pistol's barrel was so pitted it had more than passing resemblance to a rusted sewer pipe with barely discernible rifling.

After writing the Llama factory in Spain for a new barrel, I was informed they had no replacement parts for the 50-year-old pistol. This disappointing news prompted me to work up some handloads that would enable me to use the pistol which was in relatively good condition except for the bad barrel.

Several years before I reloaded for a 45-60 '76 Winchester with a pitted

bore and found reduced velocity loads with jacketed bullets gave best accuracy. I decided to use the same approach to see if I could concoct some reasonably good loads for the Llama and an old Star military.

Both the Llama and Star might be called the 1911's cousins because they have more than passing resemblance to the Government Auto. Certainly, the Llama Extra and Colt 45 Auto are very similar. The Llama incorporates the shorter trigger, milled frame, and arched housing of the Model 1911 A-1,

A little pitting doesn't really hurt

Shooting The M1911's Spanish Cousins

by WM. HOVEY SMITH

The author testing loads with the 38 Super Llama Extra. One hundred percent reliability was easily obtained with the Llama, but the Star balked with soft point and some jacketed hollow point bullets.

but has a longer barrel, frame, and slide. Because of the similarity of size, shape, and function of Colt and Llama parts, they might be thought to be interchangeable. Most are not. The Llama was designed in 1931 and introduced in 38 Super Auto-9mm Largo. Later it was offered in 45 ACP, 9mm Luger, and in scaled down versions for 380 ACP, 32 ACP, and 22 Long Rifle.

Star pistols differ from the Llama and Colt in that several simplifications have been made. The most obvious is that the various Stars have no grip safety and the trigger is pinned at the top and pivots rather than slides.

The present Stars even more closely resemble the Colt Government Auto than does the old Star military featured in this article. Besides offering smaller versions in 380 and 32 ACP, Star chose to produce two frame sizes for the 38 Super. This caliber is available in the same size frame as the 45 ACP, which was the method chosen by Colt, and also in a slightly smaller version chambered for the 9mm Luger and 38 Super. The Star military was designed for the 9mm Largo cartridge which resulted in its being slimmer and lighter than the 45 Colt Auto. The Star proved to be a good military handgun and was used by the Spanish Civil Guard. When this pistol was replaced by the present Star Super large numbers were sold as surplus.

Thousands of Star and lesser numbers of Llama pistols were sold by mail order (then quite legal) during the 1950s. These guns were priced at between twenty and forty dollars. Along with these guns large quantities of 9mm Luger, 9mm Bergmann-Bayard (9mm Largo), and 9mm Steyr ammunition were imported. Most of this ammunition was corrosively primed, and resulted in many of these pistols developing badly pitted barrels.

In addition to these military surplus arms, new Llama and Star pistols were sold by Stoeger and other importers. The smaller versions in 380, 32, and 22 Long Rifle proved quite popular. The fact that these pistols closely resembled the Government Auto, and that most disassembled in exactly the same manner added no small amount to their sales appeal. The larger 9mm Luger, 38 Super, and 45 ACP versions did not sell as well. At the time, GI 45s were selling in good to excellent condition for about forty dollars, and many potential customers chose to buy one of these rather than the Spanish imports.

This sales resistance was because decades ago many shoddy copies of

The Llama is chambered for the 38 Super-9mm Largo and is marked on the slide "CAL 9 m/m 38" to distinguish it from similar pistols chambered for the shorter 9mm Luger. It has a slightly longer barrel, slide, and frame than the M1911.

The Star is designed for the 9mm Largo and is slimmer and shorter than either the Colt or Llama. It is also simpler, without, for instance, a grip safety.

This is the original, but good 45's aren't cheap anymore, which is why Smith took up with its Spanish cousins. The M1911 is the standard, but not the only pistol worth shooting.

Colt and Smith & Wesson guns were made in Spanish workshops. Some were downright dangerous, and cast doubts on the safety of any Spanish-made handgun. However, pistols made by Bonifacio Echeverria (Star) and Gabilondo Y. Cia (Llama) have been of at least fair quality and many good to excellent models have been produced since 1930. Some feature hand-fitted actions and target sights.

Llama and Star handguns are becoming increasingly desirable as the price of new and used Colts continues to climb. The possibility of buying a

From left—9mm Luger, 38 Super, and 45 ACP. The 38 Super when loaded to full velocity has more muzzle energy than the other two cartridges. The reduced velocity loads developed by the author to use in pistols with worn barrels are accurate and reliable, but do not compare with factory 38 Super loads.

powerful well-made handgun for less than half the price of a comparable Colt is appealing to many potential buyers. The only reservation many people have is that these pistols are often chambered for the 9mm Largo cartridge.

The 9mm Largo is the Spanish name for the 9mm Bergmann-Bayard cartridge which was introduced into Spain with the Bergmann pistol. It is quite similar and will interchange with the 38 Super. At one time it was thought almost any 9mm, including the 9mm Luger and 380 ACP, would work in guns chambered for the 9mm Largo. This issue was definitively put to rest by the late George C. Nonte Jr. in his article in the 1971 GUN DIGEST. In brief, he found these shorter cartridges would fire and sometimes function the mechanism if they were caught and held against the firing pin by the extractor. If they were pushed into the chamber ahead of the extractor and fired, case heads often separated. He concluded that using these shorter cartridges, particularly the powerful 9mm Luger, in 9mm Largo chambered guns was foolhardy and dangerous.

For the American shooter, the most reasonable substitute for the 9mm Largo is the 38 Super Auto. This cartridge is among the most powerful of pistol cartridges. In comparison with the shorter 9mm Luger it uses a bullet that is four grains heavier at a higher velocity (130-grain bullet at 1280 feet per second vs. a 124-grain bullet at 1110 feet per second for the Luger). This difference gives the 38 Super a muzzle energy of 475 foot pounds which is 136 foot pounds more than the 9mm Luger, and a 140 foot pound advantage over the 45 Auto.

The 38 Super uses the same case and bullet as the older 38 ACP, but is loaded to higher pressure. The warning that the Super 38 is not to be used in the 1900, 1902, and 1903 model Colt automatics is valid as this cartridge is intended for a slight modification of the much stronger 1911 Colt 45 Auto.

Despite the impressive ballistics of the 38 Super it is not outstandingly popular. This lack of interest is no fault of the cartridge's ballistics, but lies squarely with the fact that, except for a period prior to World War II, only full jacketed bullets were available in this caliber. While such bullets give good penetration they do not have the killing power of soft or hollow pointed projectiles. This reduced the popularity of the 38 Super for sporting use.

The answer for increasing the effectiveness of the 38 Super is not by increasing its velocity, but by loading more effective bullets. This need has now been met by Remington who markets a 125-grain jacketed hollow point loading, and by independent bullet makers like Speer, Sierra, and Hornady who offer hollow and soft point bullets in weights of from 88 to 130 grains. These developments con-

siderably enhance the usefulness of pistols chambered for the 38 Super—particularly for the reloader.

Since these pistols might be described as "poor man's Colts," I decided to work up some handloads as cheaply as possible. I purchased a box of 125-grain Speer soft points for $6.50, a Lee Loader in 38 Super for $11.25, a box of primers for $1.10, and used some Unique I had left over. Excluding the cost of the powder and a powder scale I already owned, I reloaded 100 rounds for $18.60 compared to the cost of 100 factory cartridges at $22.10. I realized a savings of $3.50 for the first 100 rounds including the cost of the new reloading equipment.

I had never used a Lee Loader, but quickly became resigned to the fact that patience is a virtue. The Lee is slow, slow, slow; but it gets the job done. The first step is decapping which consists of knocking out the fired primer with a rod. The next is resizing where the lubricated case is driven into the sizing die with a plastic mallet. This was where the work started, and after I sized 100 cases that was all I cared to do that night. Unlike revolver cartridges which are often only neck sized for target loads the 38 Super must be full-length resized to insure positive function.

The next evening I reprimed the sized cases. Lee would have the user reprime as he is knocking the case out of the resizing die, but I found a better feel is obtained if repriming is done separately.

Bullet seating proved to be the most exasperating operation. To seat the bullet, the primed and powder-filled case is placed back into the sizing die, the die placed on the decapping base, and the bullet pounded into the case using the mallet and bullet seating rod. This rod is attached to the priming chamber and is adjustable for bullet seating depth. The three pieces have to be held and aligned with one hand while pounding with the other. The problem is to keep the base aligned with the sizing die to prevent bullets from canting. Canted bullets could be pounded until the soft lead nose resembled a wadcutter, but they would not enter the case. Even when the bullet seated easily, the cone-shaped end of the seating rod deformed the bullet nose into a spire point.

Of the first 50 rounds, three were so deformed they were discarded, 16 had off-center bullets, and 31 were sufficiently uniform to expect some sort of accuracy. Some sort of accuracy—damn poor—was all I did achieve, and I realized I would have to make some

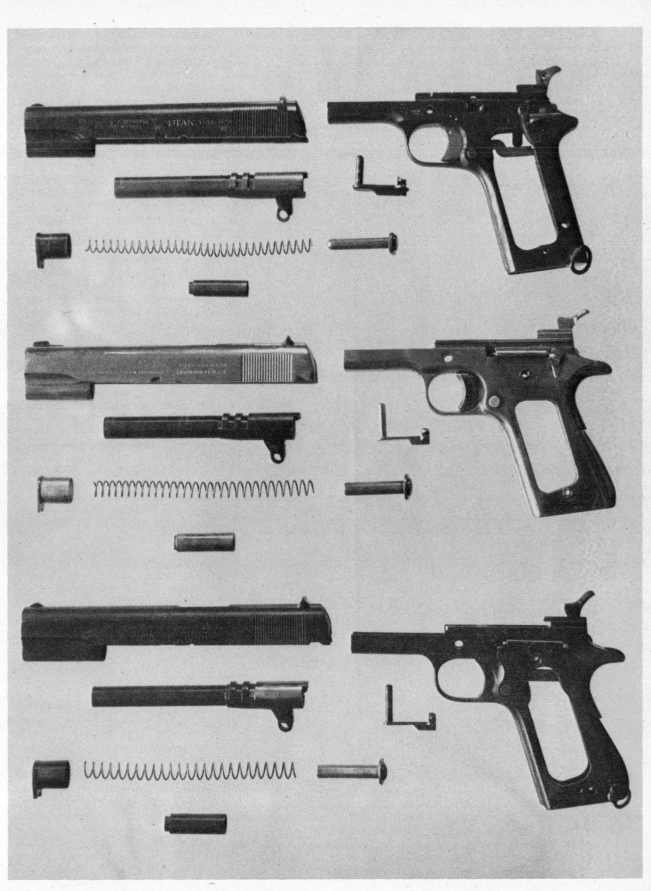

Star military (top), Colt 45 Automatic (middle), and Llama Extra (bottom) field stripped. The similarity of the three pistols is apparent. All use the basic Browning design. The Star differs from the Colt and Llama in that its hammer spring is directly below the hammer instead of being housed lower in the grip. The Star also uses all coil springs, has a simplified thumb safety, and does not have a grip safety.

From left—Colt 45 magazine, Llama magazine, and plated magazine of the Star. The Llama's magazine has indentations on both sides to adapt it to the 38 Super, the same method used by Colt. The modified magazine and modifications to the frame and slide gave Colt a new cartridge and pistol at a fraction of the cost of an entirely new design. The Star's magazine was designed for the 9mm Largo and did not require modification.

From left—88-gr. Speer jacketed hollow point, 100-gr. Speer jacketed hollow point, 115-gr. Sierra jacketed hollow point, 124-gr. full metal cased Remington 9mm Luger bullet, 125-gr. Speer jacketed hollow point, and 125-gr. Speer jacketed soft point.

Resizing with the Lee Loader. A woodworker's vise made full-length resizing the 38 Super cases much easier. The vise is attached to a four inch thick block of wood about a foot square which is braced between the feet when cases are resized.

changes in loading techniques and bullets to obtain reasonable results.

I bought a box of Remington 124-grain metal cased bullets which would resist deformation during reloading. I would have preferred the 130-grain bullet Remington loads in 38 Super, but had to settle for the lighter 124- and 100-grain 9mm Luger bullets because they were the only full metal cased 9mms carried by the distributor. If I could obtain reasonable results with these, there was some possibility of developing good hollow point loadings using a variety of available bullets.

To solve the bullet seating problem, I purchased a woodworker's vise to use as a press and mounted it on a heavy plank. Better bullet seating was obtained, but I still had bullet alignment problems. At the start, I chamfered the case mouths with a pocket knife, but found that a $7.50 deburring tool gave much better results.

Using the vise, the deburring tool, and the metal cased bullets helped tremendously, and both the Llama and Star shot the new loads reasonably well. After some experimentation with different charges of Unique, I found 5.4 grains gave good accuracy and functioned well in both pistols. This load is 1.1 grain less than the 6.5 grains Speer recommends as the starting load for the 38 Super in their manual. The historic tendency with reloading the 38 Super has been to concentrate on loads at the high velocity end of the scale, but for worn barrels reduced velocity loads gave much better accuracy.

This is one case where less definitely gives more.

Reduced velocity loads, target loads, and small game loads are often considered one and the same. They are usually assembled with lead bullets, have velocities between 700 and 800 feet per second, and have as their chief virtues high accuracy and low recoil. The loads listed below differ in that full jacketed or nearly full jacketed bullets are used and many are hollow pointed. This approach was used to reduce leading which would have otherwise been a serious problem in the badly pitted barrels, to promote better feeding, and to make the loads as effective as possible on small game. There is no hope of obtaining reliable expansion at these velocities, but the jacketed hollow points did promise to be non-leading and better killers than jacketed round nose bullets.

Unique and 700-X powders were chosen because they represent a fast and moderately fast powder commonly used in shotgun and pistol reloading. Unique is an extremely versatile powder that works well with heavier bullets in many pistol calibers, and 700-X does nicely with lighter bullets.

A selection of bullets ranging in weight from 88 to 125 grains was obtained. Most of the bullets are made by Speer, and the jackets on the 88- and 100-grain bullets extend very slightly beyond the edge of a large hollow point cavity. These proved to feed better, particularly in the Star, than heavier bullets where lead extended beyond the jacket.

Starting loads were selected by reducing the powder in increments from the lowest charge listed in the Speer tables. When the lightest loading was reached that would reliably function the guns the charge was increased until best accuracy was obtained.

Loads were considered accurate when they would group within the 5½-inch 9 ring of the 25-yard pistol target. Pistols designed for target use are expected to group within the 1¾-inch X-ring at 25 yards, but for issue pistols with bad barrels consistent 5½-inch groups are acceptable. The Llama with the 124-grain Remington bullet often produced 4-inch five-shot groups at this range with occasional clusters of three shots grouping within 1½ inches.

The Llama proved to be an easy pistol to work with, and digested soft point and hollow pointed bullets without a hitch. The Star was another story. It would only function reliably with the 100- and 124-grain full metal cased round nose bullets and the long jacketed Speer hollow points.

Although the loads charted are low velocity loads, some cautions need to be observed. All of the listed loads have a total length of 1.280 inches. If bullets are seated deeper the charges of 700-X need to be reduced to prevent potentially dangerous pressures.

While loads ranging from 5.1 to 5.7 grains of Unique gave no indications of high pressures when used with the 124- and 125-grain bullets, changes of a few tenths of a grain of 700-X are significant. This powder, like Bullseye, should only be used with reduced velocity loads, and no attempt should be made to use 700-X with bullets heavier than 100 grains in 38 Super or to assemble high velocity loads. Excessive pressures may well be reached before the 1200 feet per second velocity level is obtained. No indications of high pressures were seen in the loads listed in the table.

Reduced velocity loads, rough bores, and jacketed bullets can theoretically lead to bullets sticking in the barrel or jackets separating from bullet cores. Neither problem was observed during testing, but charges should not be reduced to the point that the pistol fails to function.

After shooting 1000 rounds through the Llama Extra and perhaps half that number through the Star, I had some definite opinions about the pistols. The Llama was easier to shoot because of its larger grip, wide Patridge sights, heavier weight, and longer sight radius. The smooth backstrap of the Star became slippery when my hand sweated in the 95 degree temperatures of the summer shooting sessions. I found myself doing most of the load testing with the Llama not only because it was easier to load for, but simply because it felt better to shoot.

I have little doubt that Star introduced the present Star Super, which even more closely resembles the Colt 45 Auto, to overcome this handicap. That they succeeded in significantly improving the pistol is attested by the fact that the new Star Super was adopted by Spain's military forces.

Even though both pistols were made some 50 years ago, there were no mechanical failures. Considering that they digested loads ranging from the hot Remington plus-P ammunition, which exceeds the 9mm Largo's ballistics by a considerable margin, to reduced velocity loads without any problems proved they are not the worthless pieces of Spanish junk some think them to be.

During all this, half a dozen cottontails, one red fox, and a feral house cat have been taken with the Llama using reduced velocity loads. All were killed with a single shot, and confirmed that I had restored a pistol to useful life by crafting some handloads that would shoot well in its badly pitted barrel. ●

Reduced Velocity Loads For 38 Super

Bullet	Bull. Weight grains	Powder	Charge grains	Notes
Remington FMC .354	124	Unique	5.4	Best functioning and most accurate load.
Hornady FMC .355	100	Unique 700-X	6.0 4.2	Functions well, but not as accurate as FMC.
Speer JHP .355	125			Bullet nose deformed so much during reloading loads could not be developed.
Speer JSP .355	125	Unique	5.4	Bullet nose deformed during reloading and when being fed from magazine. If bullet bases were lubricated during reloading better loads resulted.
Sierra JHP .355	115	Unique	5.8	Functioned well in Llama, but often failed to feed from Star's magazine.
Speer JHP .355	100	Unique 700-X	6.0 4.2	Best JHP loading in Star and Llama. Difficult to seat bullet without canting in Lee Loader.
Speer JHP .355	88	700-X	4.5	Almost impossible to reload without canting these short bullets. Load functioned well in Llama and Star.

FMC—Full metal cased bullets. JSP—Jacketed soft point. JHP—Jacketed hollow point.
    All loads have an over-all length of 1.280 inches.
    All loads assembled in Remington plus-P cases and used CCI 500 small pistol primers.
    Base of hollow point and soft point bullets lightly lubricated with Lyman bullet lubricant to promote easier bullet seating.
    These loads worked safely in the author's pistols; however, no responibility can be accepted for handloads assembled by others.

Target and Short Range Shooting Devices

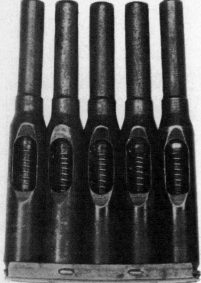

Fig. 7—Hoffer-Thompson chambers in service clip.

Low level cartridges were introduced in 1869 for the 50-70 rifled musket. Since that time a wide variety of reduced load devices have appeared for military and sporting arms. One, in fact, is offered today, made in various caliber/subcaliber combinations.

by PAUL KLATT

FROM THE EARLIEST days of the breechloader attempts have been made to provide the soldier and sportsman with a handy means of converting his high-powered firearms for short range shooting or target practice. There were two primary directions to this effort: cut costs and reduce noise and recoil. Over the years many systems were devised in an effort to achieve these goals. This brief profile presents the diversity of ideas that have been brought forward and attempts to explain the reasons for their success or failure.

The first approach to reducing cost, noise, and recoil was the gallery practice cartridge. This was simply a standard cartridge case loaded with a lightweight bullet and/or a light powder charge. The effective range of such ammunition was considerably less than that of regular ball loads, but effective target practice could be conducted and the trainee was able to get the "feel" of the weapon.

"Reduced-load" ammunition was introduced experimentally by Frankford Arsenal about 1869. Standard service 50-70-450s were loaded with 16, 19, 21 and 23 grains of black powder. The reduced charges, of course, did not fill the 70-gr. case, so varying numbers of fiber wads were placed under the ball to keep the loads against the priming. There is no official record of this ammunition having been produced specifically for gallery practice, but such cartridges were made, and 16 grains of black powder acting on a 450-gr. bullet would seem to have no other use.

Wads were no doubt a problem, especially when one would remain in the barrel, nonetheless wads were used again a few years later in the service 45-70-405 cartridge to reduce the case capacity to 20 grains. Like

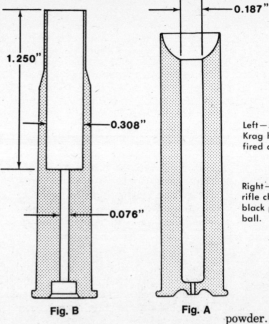

Fig. B **Fig. A**

Left—All-brass case made for the 30-40 Krag held 5 grains of black powder, fired a round lead .308" ball.

Right—Steel case made for Sharps rifle chambers held 12 grains of black powder, fired a round lead ball.

the 50-70 there is no official record of this technique being used to produce a gallery practice cartridge as such, but a 20-gr. powder load is too light for use in the field.

45-70 Round Ball

In 1896 Frankford Arsenal eliminated the wad approach when it produced a 45-cal. musket cartridge loaded with 20 grains of black powder and a 140-gr. round ball seated on the powder (well down into the case). This cartridge was designed specifically as a gallery practice cartridge but saw little use, probably because it was developed about the time of the adoption of the 30-40 Krag rifle and cartridge.

Another technique for containing a light charge of black powder in a standard full-size cartridge case was to machine the case from solid stock and bore a small diameter hole through its length. The Sharps Rifle Co. manufactured a small number of solid steel cases in 45-2¹⁄₁₀" and 40-2½" lengths for use with round balls (Figure A). The 0.187" diameter center hole of the 45-cal. case held 12 grains of black

powder. Frankford Arsenal also used this technique in 1895 when it produced a solid-brass-cased 30-40 Krag cartridge for gallery practice (Figure B). This round contained 5 grains of black powder and a 40-gr. round ball. A variation of the solid-case gallery cartridge was manufactured by the

United States Cartridge Co. Standard 45-cal. musket cases were modified by inserting a lead cylinder with an 0.189" hole bored through the center. The hole was then filled with 15 grains of black powder. These cases were used with a special 176-gr. round-nose cylindrical bullet.

With the advent of smokeless powder there was no longer a need to fill the space above the powder charge and therefore no need to modify the volume of gallery practice cases. Many standard-size cases were loaded with lightweight bullets (Figures 1 through 4) and millions of rounds have been produced, especially for military small arms.

We should not leave the subject of gallery practice ammunition, without at least mentioning the Rabbeth patent cartridge. Produced by Winchester "for all rifles chambered for the 45-70 U.S. Govt. cartridge," this unique round used a wood sabot that contained a 26-cal., 60-gr. conical projectile. The charge consisted of 3 grains of black powder and 7 grains of smokeless. From an 1896 label, they were made "for short range target use especially adapted to indoor practice".

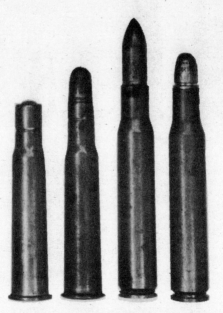

Left to right—Figs. 1—4
Gallery Practice Cartridge for 30-40 U.S. Krag, 42-gr. round ball.

Gallery Practice Cartridge for 30-40 U.S. Krag, 107-gr. bullet.

Gallery Practice Cartridge for 30-06 U.S. Springfield, 198-gr. bullet.

Gallery Practice Cartridge for 30-06 U.S. Springfield, 107-gr. bullet.

Below, Fig. 5—Morris Tube device for 30-40 U.S. Krag.

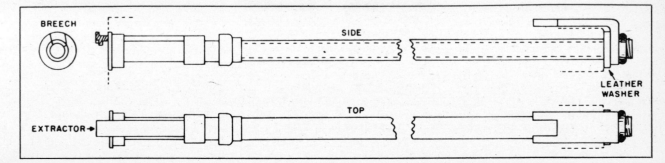

Fig. 6
Hoffer-Thompson
Auxiliary Chamber for 30-06
U.S. Springfield.

Fig. 8
Rifled Auxiliary
Chamber for 30-
40 U.S. Krag,
firing pin (block)
removed.

Fig. 10
Marble Auxiliary
Cartridge for 30-30
Winchester, used
32 S&W Short.

Fig. 11
30-30 Winchester
for comparison
with Fig. 10.

Fig 9, left
Rifled Auxiliary
Chamber for 7.5-
mm Swiss Service
rifle, shown dis-
assembled.

Fig. 12
Marble device, for
303 British, used
32 ACP.

Subcaliber Systems

Although gallery practice cartridges were often made from salvaged cases and inexpensive loads were used, over-all cost was still considerable and further economies were sought. In addition, the noise and recoil from this ammunition was still signifi-cant. Attempts were therefore made to reduce the caliber of the arm so that cartridges of even less magnitude could be used.

The Morris Tube The first attempt to reduce the caliber of a small arm for gallery practice was made about 1895 by the Morris Tube Ammunition and Safety Range Co., Ltd., London (England). This company produced a rifled sleeve or tube that ran the full length of the barrel and chamber (Fig-ure 5). It was inserted from the breech and secured at the muzzle with a knurled nut. The device fired a spe-cial 23-cal. necked centerfire cartridge produced by the same company that

made the tube. The extractor for the special cartridge case was part of the tube, and was operated by the extrac-tor of the gun, with which it was aligned. The Morris tube was pro-duced for Martini-Henry, Snider, and Krag rifles and carbines, but their scarcity today leads this writer to the conclusion that they had a rather short life. The special Morris tube car-tridge was reloadable, used a 36-gr. bullet with three grains of powder, was less expensive to manufacture than such cartridges as the 30-40 Krag, and produced little noise and recoil; however, the cost of the tubes, which had to be made with some pre-cision, precluded their success.

Springfield 1903/22 Conversion Similar to the Morris tube, but even more complicated, was a finely-manufactured system that converted the Model 1903 Springfield to 22 rim-fire. Conversion required the replace-ment of the bolt and trigger assembly, which included the magazine, and the insertion of a rifled sleeve into the barrel. Again a beautiful precision system, which achieved all desired ends, but it required that the gun be practically rebuilt, and the conver-sion kit cost as much as the gun.

Hoffer/Thompson System From about 1907 to 1913 Springfield Armory manufactured a modification of the Model 1903 service rifle with a 22-cal. barrel chambered for a special device known as the Hoffer/Thompson auxil-iary chamber. These chambers (Figure 6) had the general aspect of the ser-vice ammunition and could be loaded into the gun from regulation clips (Figure 7), but they were used to fire the inexpensive 22 short rimfire.

The Hoffer/Thompson auxiliary chamber was machined from steel and used a smooth bore throat or neck to direct the 22-cal. ball into the spe-cial barrel. The rimfire cartridge was loaded through an opening in the side of the auxiliary chamber and fired by a spring-loaded pin which passed through the base. Extraction of the chamber from the gun was accom-plished with the standard M1903 bolt and the spent 22 case was removed from the chamber by use of a special hand tool.

A similar system was developed for the 45 Colt automatic, but specimens are so rare that it appears as though this modification was never more than an experiment.

Rifled Auxiliary Chambers Cost savings were certainly achieved using 22 rimfire ammunition, but the Hoffer/Thompson system was still costly and notoriously inaccurate. What was needed was a means by which small caliber ammunition could be fired in a big bore arm without any modification being made to the rifle. This was accomplished by simply rifling the neck of an auxiliary chamber that matched the dimensions of the standard round. The subcaliber projectile was thus stabilized within the chamber, and the whole system functioned like a short-barreled gun whithin a gun. This type of chamber was manufactured in a variety of sizes from 30 caliber (Figure 8) to at least 3 inch and was used with some success (especially for artillery practice) from about 1898 through WWI.

An interesting variation of the rifled auxiliary chamber was produced by the Swiss for both sporting and military small arms. A 17-cal. BB was fired with the propellant force provided by a No. 2 Berdan primer (Figure 9). The basic difference here was the fact that the subcaliber barrel was made as a separate part of the device.

Marble's Auxiliary Cartridge

Another approach to the auxiliary chamber idea was conceived by the Marble Arms Corp. of Gladstone, Mich. The Marble system adapted a center-fire pistol cartridge for use in a rifle of the same caliber. For example, by using this adapter a 32-cal. revolver round could be fired in a Winchester 30-30 or 32 Special rifle. The pistol cartridge was secured by spring clips to the end of a steel base piece that was shaped to match the rifle cartridge from the shoulder back to the head (Figures 10 and 12). A floating firing pin through the center of the base transmitted the blow of the hammer. These adapters were produced in a variety of sizes and apparently achieved a measure of popularity, but they were limited by the dimensions of the pistol cartridge, which did not always precisely match the necked portion of the rifle cartridge. This allowed gas leaks with some calibers and probably contributed to their eventual disappearance from the market.

Winchester's Supplemental Chamber

Similar to Marble's system but simpler in construction was the Winchester Supplemental Chamber. An excerpt from an old advertisement describes them as follows: "This handy and simple device permits the use of popular pistol cartridges in high power rifles chambered for 30 Win-

Fig. 17 — Zip Chamber reloading components.

Fig. 16 — Packaging for 7mm Zip Chamber reloading components, shown at top.

Fig. 15 — Packaging for 7mm Zip Chamber.

Fig. 14 — Zip Reload Chamber, for 7mm Mauser.

Fig. 13 — Zip Reload Chamber for 30-06, shown disassembled; note 22-cal rimfire charger.

chester; 30 Army; 303 Savage: 303 British; 32-40; 32 Winchester Special; 35 and 405 Winchester cartridges without change or readjustment of the rifle, except the sights. The Winchester Supplemental Chamber is inserted in the rifle, the same as a cartridge, and, as it is extracted from the gun in the same manner as an empty shell, it does not interfere with the instant use of regular ammunition. For short range shooting or indoor target practice it gives excellent results, which makes it a valuable addition to every sportsman's equipment. It is also an aid to attaining proficiency in the use of a regular hunting rifle at a minimum expenditure for ammunition."
Patented August 22, 1899, these chambers were smoothbored sleeves externally shaped to match the chamber of the gun. The head end was counterbored to accept a rimmed pistol cartridge, which was selected for being as close to the rifle caliber as possible. Any mismatch between the diameter of the pistol bullet and the

bore of the rifle barrel would degrade accuracy and/or allow gas leaks. These problems, plus the fact that in some of the chambers the bullet had to jump a considerable distance to get into the barrel, placed them in the same unfavorable situation as the Marble cartridge.

The Zip Reload Chamber

The most exotic of the auxiliary chambers was the "Zip Reload Chamber." Manufactured by National Arms Co., San Francisco, Calif., these interesting devices fired a lightweight bullet with a specially made 22-cal. rimfire blank containing 8 grains of smokeless powder. The steel chambers disassembled for loading the blank charge (Figure 13) and included a spring-loaded firing pin that converted from centerfire ignition to rimfire. They were produced in 30-06 (Figure 13), 7mm Mauser (Figures 14 thru 17), 8mm Mauser 30-40 Krag and 300 Savage. They certainly made low-cost target practice possible, but the initial expense of these precision devices prohibited their coming into general use.

Hollifield Rod Indicator or Dotter

Without doubt the "last word" in target practice devices was the "Hollifield Dotter." Manufactured by the Hollifield Target Practice Rod Co. Inc., Middletown, New York, under U.S. Patents 882551, 867728, 1008337, 1016150, 1094854 and 1130402, the Dotter consisted primarily of a brass tube containing a spring-loaded sharply-pointed steel rod (Figure 18). This assembly was of such length that, when inserted into the bore of the gun from the muzzle, it would position one end of the rod against or very close to the firing pin or hammer. When the trigger was pulled the movement of the firing pin was transmitted to the rod, propelling it out of the tube (the tube being held against the rifling by friction) to a distance of 4 to 6 inches and, under the action of the spring, immediately returned. If the muzzle of the gun was held within 4 to 6 inches of a target, the rod would produce a small diameter puncture or "dot."

Miniature targets were provided, these scaled down from standard dimensions to their apparent sizes at different ranges. For example, the 100-yard bullseye was 0.062″ on the scaled-down Dotter target (Figure 19). The Dotter rod was packaged in a wooden case which also contained a built-in, rubber target holder (Figures 20 and 21). The case was designed to be secured vertically to a wall or other substantial surface, wherein the target holder could be adjusted up or down to the user's requirements.

The Dotter described thus far was the simplest form of the device; it extended through the barrel and chamber to the firing pin and was made for use with the Model 1903 service rifle and the 45 ACP pistol (Figure 20). Another, perhaps more common version of the Dotter, incorporated a rod that ran just the length of the barrel and operated in conjunction with a dummy cartridge constructed much like the rod assembly. By means of a spring-loaded pin through its axis the cartridge functioned as a link between the firing pin and the Dotter rod in the barrel. Dotter cartridges were made up from standard ball or dummy cases and standard bullets or, in some instances, specially machined brass bullets. They are known in 30-06 (Figures 22, 23 and 24), 30-40 Krag (Figures 25 & 26), 303 British (Figure 27), 38 S&W revolver (Figure 28), 38 Colt revolver, and 45 Colt revolver.

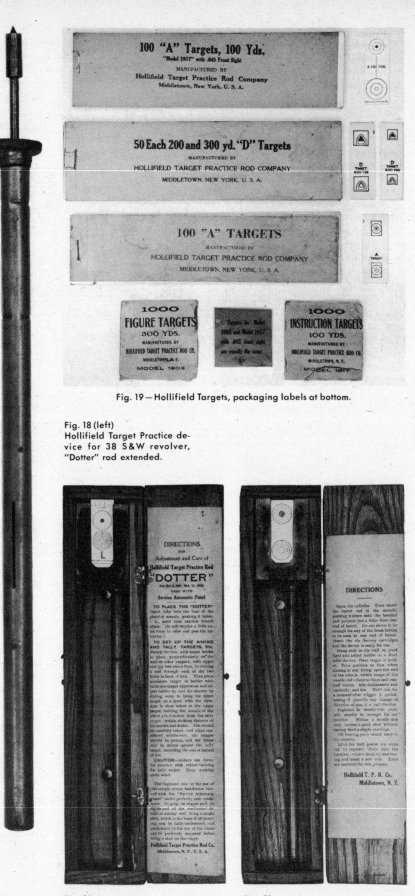

Fig. 19 — Hollifield Targets, packaging labels at bottom.

Fig. 18 (left)
Hollifield Target Practice device for 38 S&W revolver, "Dotter" rod extended.

Fig. 20
Hollifield Device for 45 Colt automatic as packaged with adjustable target holder.

Fig. 21
Hollifield Device for 38 S&W revolver, as packaged.

From time to time throughout the last century the inventor has turned his talent toward developing a means to lessen the cost of target practice and relieve the beginner's trauma with high-powered firearms. There have been other objectives, such as the conversion of big game rifles for use on small game, but the approach has always been to reduce or eliminate the heavy standard loads. Many ingenious systems evolved; some were so crudely designed that they were actually hazardous to use; others required such precision manufacture that cost savings were negated. One of these devices, the Hollifield Dotter, eliminated ammunition altogether and, for a small initial expenditure, made target practice possible and pleasurable for even the timorous. This writer has used the Dotter to introduce a number of people to small arms shooting, and I have been amazed at how effective it is in developing the basic skills. Certainly fine tuning must be done at the range with full loads, but I believe that many of the systems described here could still be used to great advantage. The phenomenon is that they are no longer available*, save one. ●

Fig. 22 (below)
Hollifield Dotter Cartridge, for 30-40 Krag, no bullet configuration. Perhaps an experimental device.

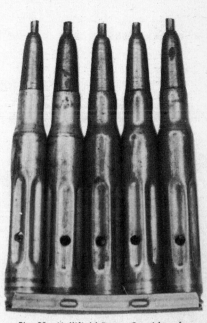

Fig. 23—Hollifield Dotter Cartridges for 30-06 U.S. Springfield in service clip.

---

*One such device, at least, remains. The Lothar Walther auxiliary cartridge is offered in a good range of calibers—rifle and handgun. Made in West Germany, these devices are distributed by Harry Owen, Box 744, Sunnyvale, CA 94088. Various 22 centerfire calibers, from the 222 to the 220 Swift, may be used with these adaptors to shoot 22 L.R. or WMR cartridges, or to shoot 22 Hornet ammunition. Not, of course, using the same adaptor. A Walther adaptor for the 30-06 chamber fires 30 Carbine loads.

Rifled insert barrels, shooting 22 L.R. or WMR rounds, are available for 9mm and 45 ACP auto pistols. The pistol these are to be used for must be specified.

Another form of rifled insert barrel, using a 4mm centerfire, lead bullet cartridge, is made for all auto pistols. Three auxiliary "cartridge" are furnished, along with a knockout rod and cleaning brush, for calibers 32 and 380 ACP, 30 and 9mm Luger. For most other auto pistols, the auxiliary 4mm case is not required.

The 4mm C.F. system, using the auxiliary cases (3 are furnished) is available for all revolvers in calibers 32 S&W Long, 38 S&W or Special, 357 and 44 Magnum, 45 ACP and 45 Colt rimmed.

The same 4mm C.F. cartridge, fired from a Walther insert rifled barrel, is offered for most popular U.S. calibers (22 Hornet to 458 Winchester) and all German (metric) calibers No auxiliary chamber or case is required—the original rifle firing pin functions normally.   Ed.

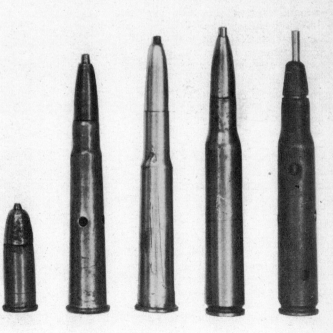

Left to Right—Figs. 24 to 28.
Hollifield Dotter Cartridge for 38 S&W Revolver.
Hollifield Dotter Cartridge for 303 British rifle.
Hollifield Dotter Cartridge for 30-40 U.S. Krag.
Hollifield Dotter Cartridge for 30-06 U.S. Springfield.
Hollifield Dotter Cartridge for 30-06 U.S. Springfield.

Harry Owen/Sport Specialties 22 L.R./222 Remington chamber adaptor sells for $11.95, as do other like devices in several other caliber combinations.

HOW ACCURATE IS YOUR HANDGUN?

by
Claud Hamilton

It helps to get help. Here, friend Martha Penso is setting up Hardballer in the Ransom rest.

Here's what the Hardballer will do at least once. This remarkable one-holer was not repeated, but its existence gives confidence in the gun that made it.

It's work, but a session with a machine rest tells almost all

Have you ever spent a particularly frustrating hour or so at a range when it seemed that you just could not shoot a decent score no matter what? Did you go off home grumbling about "the rotten ammunition they make these days . . . " or the "sorry quality of the guns they make now . . . "? And did you secretly feel a little guilty that maybe you just might have been a part of the problem yourself?

Earlier this year I had such an experience with a fine new target revolver, and it started me thinking. What do we really mean when we say that a handgun is "accurate" or not? Is there a way to quantify this so as to clearly separate those which are accurate from the rest?

For me, the problem has always been one of working to reduce my own rather formidable pointing error. Not ever knowing what part of the final result was attributable to me and what to gun and ammunition always left me never quite sure if I were doing the right thing or even going in the right direction. If I knew what the average gun and average ammunition could be expected to do regularly maybe that might help my confidence.

What is an acceptable standard for handgun accuracy? I had my own ideas about that but asked several friends as well. Lawmen told me that the usual police handgun shooting engagement takes place at 7 to 10 yards range according to the statistics, but that they felt that they needed a sure hit capability on a man-sized target out to 25 yards. Beyond that range they agreed that an officer would be better advised to go to a rifle or shotgun. My one handgun hunter friend sets a rather more demanding standard and says that he wishes to be able, reliably, to place his bullet into a five-inch circle out to 50 or 60 yards.

This last summer I was lucky to have access to a Ransom Rest and I have shot a number of "projects" with it doing things I've never been able to do before. Thinking back over what I have seen it occurred to me that I just might have collected some interesting and usable data, something that might answer my questions.

During the summer I fired a fairly broad range of guns off the rest; fortunately, I saved all the targets for reference. I certainly did not have this thought in mind when I started. I hope that if I had I might have come up with a somewhat better thought out program! I shot 9mm Parabellum, .38 Special, .357 Magnum, .41 Remington Magnum and .45 ACP. I used a spread of all the commercial loads available

and a large number of my own handloads. The guns used included all those for which I had grip adapters: four Colt Government Models and a Gold Cup, a Trooper, a Lawman Mk III, and a Detective Special. Among the Smith & Wessons were a pair of Model 59 9mm pistols, a Model 52 Master, a Model 28 Highway Patrolman, a K-38 and a pair of .41 Magnum Model 57s. Finally there were a pair of Hardballers in .45 ACP stainless, a 9mm Parabellum (Luger), and a Browning P-35.

So, after I had the idea, I sat down with all the targets and ran a home grown analysis to see what sort of information I might be able to find.

The first thing I was reminded of was it just makes no sense to describe a gun as "accurate" or "inaccurate." You have to consider a particular gun and ammunition combination as a team. I really got a graphic lesson on this earlier this year. I fired a Gold Cup National Match .45 against a new .45 ACP target revolver and an old Government Model. The Gold Cup shot beautiful groups using three brands of commercial mid-range FMJ semi-wadcutters, about half the size of the best the other guns could muster. The first use I made of the Ransom Rest this summer was to shoot this fine gun again, but this time against a Hardballer, a new Series 70 Mk IV .45, and an older Government Model that has been worked over some and tightened up. This time I used four new commercial hardball loads and the Gold Cup came in a poor *last*.

My study of the summer's targets showed that the guns I used, and the ammunition, are capable of shooting *2.38-inch* groups *on the average* at 25 yards. The spread between the largest and smallest groups was 4.3 inches; my largest was 4.7 inches (9mm Parabellum) and my smallest was .40 inches (.357 Magnum). I think it important to keep in mind that this is a "worst case" report based always on the largest dimension on centers of each group fired. At least 60 of every 100 shots fired would be closer to the point of aim.

Over the summer I verified over and over again that I can better average group size by taking the time to search for a load that a particular gun "likes" and handles best. Sometimes with pistols this created a problem. One Hardballer, the one that eventually gave me the best .45 group I got, initially would not feed any of the FMJ semi-wadcutters or JHPs. Friend and former gunsmith Haywood Nelms corrected that problem for me by carefully improving and smoothing the

feed ramp area.

Among the interesting data I gathered was the comparative accuracy of the various calibers I shot. Here is how they ranked by average group size:

.38 Special	1.65 inches
9mm Para.	2.24 inches
.357 Magnum	2.25 inches
.45 ACP	2.75 inches
.41 Magnum	2.75 inches

My handloads compared well with the commercial ammunition used. Taken all together, my loads shot groups that averaged 2.17 inches. The commercial ammunition averaged 2.47-inch groups.

There were seven revolvers and twelve pistols involved. Of these, the revolvers managed to shoot average groups of 2.25 inches while the pistols scored 2.48-inch groups on the average. The *three most accurate* guns of the shoot, however, were the K-38 revolver, and the Model 52 Master and 9mm Mauser Parabellum (Luger) pistols. The Luger is a paradox. I cannot shoot that gun well at all by hand, but on the Ransom Rest it is a very different story indeed. These guns did not turn in the best *individual* groups I saw, by the way.

Here is how the guns themselves ranked by caliber:

9 mm Parabellum. The Luger easily outshot the competition. It was never even a race.

.38 Special. The K-38 barely edged the Model 52 Master.

.357 Magnum. My old Model 28 Highway Patrolman Smith was the star.

.41 Magnum. Of course, this involved only the Smith Model 57s.

.45 ACP, the second Hardballer I fired was the champ.

I think that the thing that most impressed me was a phenomenon I encountered that I cannot explain. Three times during the summer I got fantastic, tiny groups consisting of just one hole. Using the same guns and ammunition, I was never able to duplicate these groups. Here's how I stumbled onto this:

Early in the summer while working on another project I loaded a series of .357 Magnum rounds all of which used the same Speer 140-grain JHP bullet. I used AL-7 powder for all, but varied the charge starting with 13 grains and dropping a grain at a time down to 9 grains. What I was *looking* for was any sort of clear trend as to where these loads would print if all were shot to the same aiming point. What I *found* was

Here's the reworked Model 1911, set up in the rest. To operate a Ransom — or any other — rest competently requires the careful repetition of simple steps, the same way every time. On Model 1911's, it also helps to depress the grip safety before locking the gun down.

powder-bullet combination. I also extended my search to the .45 ACP and the .41 Magnum.

I came across only one other handload that gave a group comparable to that first one. It measured .56 inches and was shot also by the Model 28 Smith, this time using a 158-grain Speer bullet ahead of 10.3 grains of 2400 powder. Once again, this was a mild, 70% load in the .357. The only commercial load that turned in a one hole group was in caliber .45 ACP and was made by the Hardballer mentioned before. It measured .92 inches and was shot using Federal 185-grain match FMJ semi-wadcutters. In both instances the same peculiar displacement from the aiming point occurred, the groups centering about two inches right and one inch high.

Do we have to always sacrifice finest accuracy in order to get magnum power? I don't know, but the evidence to that effect seems pretty strong. Of all the guns and calibers that I shot, only the Model 57 in .41 Magnum gave its best performance with a full house magnum load, and this group was far from a "one holer." Speer's 200-grain JHP ahead of 20.0 grains of H110 powder printed in 1.69 inches, but it is *not* a pleasant load to shoot by hand or off the rest!

My records show that by all odds the most inaccurate gun I shot all summer was a Colt Detective Special. I barely managed to keep it on the paper, and never did manage to find out what its problem is. It was so bad that I threw out its targets and did not add them into my results. Next worst was the pair of Model 59 Smiths in 9mm. All the .45 pistols gave good, but not outstanding groups except, of course, for the one sensational group turned in by a Hardballer.

What I gain from all this is the knowledge that, gun for gun, when I look over one of my offhand targets the group will contain probably *no more* than 1.1-inch of gun and ammunition-induced error. This is based on half the average group size of 2.38 inches. All the rest of what I see in the way of pointing error, well, the less said about *that,* the better.

One final comment seems to be in order. The results I have written about apply only to the particular guns and ammunition that I shot. The results were interesting but certainly not statistically conclusive. I don't believe that they form any basis for blanket condemnation or praise of any gun, batch of ammunition, or combination thereof, but they did tell me something about my shooting. ●

that my rather elderly Smith & Wesson Model 28 Highway Patrolman had a definite love affair going with the 9-grain load of AL-7. After turning in an acceptable series of groups with the other loads in the 1½- to 2½-inch range, it suddenly "spun off" two inches to the right and an inch above the aiming point and shot a fantastic, *.40 inch one hole group* with the 9-grain load. The fifth shot touched no paper at all.

This was so strikingly different from everything that I had seen that I contacted Roy Jinks at Smith and Wesson and sent him a Xerox of the group; I asked if he knew what might cause such a group and why it seemed to "spin off" to the right and a little high. Mr. Jinks acknowledged that they have seen this same thing at the factory, but offered no explanation for it or for the displacement of the point of impact.

Thinking more about that load and its remarkable performance, I noted that it was about 69% of the maximum 13-grain load that Speer lists in their

Manual Number 9 for that bullet and powder. This was interesting; I think most of us have read for years that the best, most accurate loads for most any cartridge are not to be found at maximum power but somewhere down near the 70% level. I am sure that Speer's engineers would be the first to admit that their "maximum" loads are not all that precise. I feel pretty sure that different guns from those used in their testing would yield different upper limits. I suspect that there is probably a little "safe-siding" in the Manual, too; I know that there sure would be if I were publishing it.

The .357 Magnum is, after all, a high power cartridge. If one needs all that power, I wondered if it were really axiomatic that accuracy *has* to be sacrificed to get it. With this in mind, I started a deliberate search to see if I could find any more of these phenomenal one hole groups. I made up .357 loads using other bullets and powders and, in each case, put in charges that represented 100%, 90%, 80% and 70% of the listed Speer maximum for that

TO SMITH OR NOT TO SMITH?

by RICHARD ALLEN

It is indeed a question worth asking. And here are some answers.

NO, THE PICTURE is not a joke. I didn't steal it from one of the "Rare Guns" pieces. Don't strain your eyes looking at the back of the topstrap; it's a fixed sight frame, (from a 41 M&P) not an adjustable sight frame with the rear sight removed. I didn't take it back from the gunsmith half done for photographing. This gun was actually returned by a gunsmith, just as photographed, as a completed job.

An isolated instance? Only in that it takes such an obvious and spectacular picture. Gunsmith's errors that bad are all too common.

Some gun writers teach us that an out-of-the-box pistol can be improved by custom work. I've recommended custom touches myself. But what doesn't always get into print is how often gunsmithing goes wrong.

In some cases, you can reasonably say, "So what?" Part of the fun of being interested in guns, for some of us, is putting those little, or big, custom touches on; knowing we have the very best gun for its purpose; selecting what things to do or not to have done to a gun; and winding up with one of a kind. And if the gunsmith occasionally presents you with a very expensive club . . . well, nobody said having guns customized was cheap.

However:

—Customizing is often recommended for self-defense guns. It is important to know if your alterations can affect reliability.

—Trigger jobs on semi-autos can make the pieces unsafe—even for use on target ranges.

—Having a pistol customized costs, in money, time, and frustration. A more realistic appraisal of the chances for failure might make some people wonder if they really need that little bit better than out of the box.

When I was a lot younger, more naive, and more careless with my money, I started shooting pistols. According to all I read on the subject, one could have an out of the box gun improved a good deal. It was just a question of which modifications you consider worth paying for. True, they all might not be *necessary* in a self-defense gun, but making the gun a little better couldn't *hurt*. True, some modifications weren't suitable for weapons, and a few (too tight an accuracy job on an automatic, too light a double action pull on a revolver) could hurt reliability. But no one told me to hold modification of defense guns to a minimum, because everything I had done would be another chance for something to go wrong. I used to think I was particularly unlucky. None of the articles in gun magazines talked about the things that happened to *my* guns in the smith's tender loving hands. Eventually I realized that, while I might be more unlucky than most, it didn't just happen to me. And I live in Los Angeles, center of combat pistol shooting, home of nationally

Same gun as in lead photo, the next time back from the gunsmith. Note the high front sight. In fact, the gun was never done up right. See text.

known gunsmiths. The ones I use are good.

What are your chances of having your gun screwed up by the smith? I don't know. I can't quote odds. What I can do is tell you stories. They may give you something to think about in deciding what work to have done, and some things to look out for when you get the gun back. Names of gunsmiths are left out to protect the innocent . . . to protect the innocent writer from libel suits. Had I known, all the years I was giving guns and money to gunsmiths, that I was going to do this article, I could have prepared. I could have got witnesses to sign statements about the condition of guns before and after, kept copies of my instructions to smiths—and saved up a good deal of money for a lawyer. As it is, I'll just leave out smith's names.

Some particular modifications have their own special problems. Besides, there is no job too routine to be screwed up, sometimes in bizarre ways.

One man had an action job done on his Smith & Wesson. Eventually, the smith handed the gun back to him. Having better gun manners than the smith, the customer pointed the muzzle down and swung the cylinder out. The cylinder-and-crane assembly fell out of the gun. Seems someone had forgotten to tighten that little screw.

One time, I called a gunsmith and asked if my Python was ready.

"Was that gun assembled when you brought it in?" he asked.

"Yes," I replied, with some trepidation.

All he'd lost was the screw and spring that held the cylinder in. Of course, he replaced the parts— eventually. Just because he'd lost a couple of parts out of my gun was no reason to do anything as drastic as buy a few dollars worth of parts retail. He just held my gun until he needed enough from Colt to get his dealer's discount.

The story behind that lead photo starts some years ago. When I first got interested in combat handguns, the Charter 44 Bulldog and the Detonics 45 did not exist. There was the big Colt 45 auto, the small frame 38, and nothing in between. I was fascinated with making more concealable big bore weapons. I had an article published on the subject in 1974.

One big bore weapon is the N frame S&W, hardly a very promising candi-

date for a compact concealment weapon. Never the less, I was interested in seeing what could be done with one and I had a 41 M&P. For what seemed like good reasons at the time, I also wanted it converted to 45 ACP. I won't go into why, because I've since

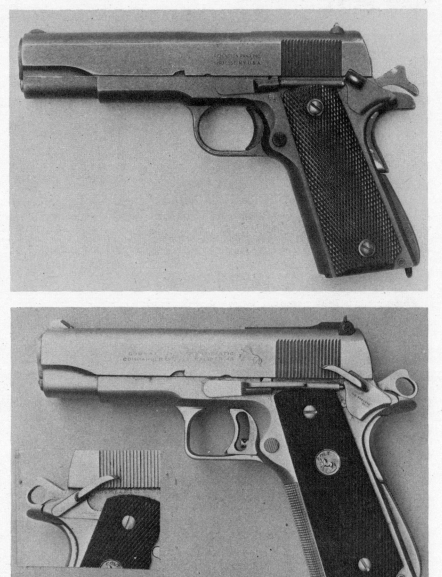

Two extremes in 45 automatics. Top: U.S. Pistol, Model 1911A1, the G.I. 45. This is the gun that gave the 45 automatic its reputation. Safety blade is too small; sights are too small; many people find their grip does not depress the grip safety. Bottom: An elaborate Combat Commander, including accuracy and trigger jobs. Slide stop is higher than mine, so may not have the same problem. I'm told this gun works beautifully, but anything this elaborate is a gamble.

come to doubt my reasoning. At that time, S&W would sell the Model 1955 Target 45 ACP barrel and cylinder. All I had to do was have them put on

the 41 frame. And have the barrel shortened. The smith I used was not one of the giants, but he had been mentioned, favorably, in print. You could reasonably say he had a national reputation.

Unfortunately, I didn't keep a copy of the instructions I gave him, and thus don't know my exact words.

When I got the gun back, as it was in my lead photo, his answer to my protest was simple. I had told him to shorten the barrel and reset the front sight. I hadn't said anything about altering said sight so it could be used to align the gun with the target.

I thought it was funny enough to photograph. Then back it went, with the explanation that I did want to use the front sight for the usual purpose. I suggested he copy the front sight on the 41 barrel. There shouldn't be that much difference, I reasoned, between the 210 grain 41 bullet and the 230 grain 45.

After due delay, I got the gun back again. (Photo.) That front sight looked pretty high, but he was the gunsmith, and he said that was the way it belonged. So I took it to a pistol range, and of course the front sight was too high. As I recall (it was some years ago) the gun sighted 1½ feet low at 20 feet.

Enough was enough. I switched gunsmiths. Besides cutting down the front sight, I asked the second smith to do an action job. He had done a few for me before, and they had worked. But this time I got sticky trigger returns. I bought a new return spring and put it in.

The proper ending to the story would be a final photo, with the front sight the right height, and a few sentences about how it turned out all right in the end. But the project had dragged on for a few years. The Charter Bulldog had made the whole idea obsolete. I had other things to do during my too infrequent range sessions. The fact is, I never did give the gun its next check out. This illustrates another danger of elaborate gunsmithing projects: they can drag on and on until you just don't care any more.

It isn't always the gunsmith's fault. Sometimes, the problem is inherent in the modification. Adjustable sights on combat guns were very "in" in the 1960s. Eventually, combat shooters discovered what Chic Gaylord had said: adjustable sights are more fragile than fixed sights. In the 1970s, Cooper started talking about high visibility fixed sights for combat weapons, and Hoag came out with the protected position for Smith & Wesson sights. What hidden pitfalls are in the modifications popular today? We'll find out—eventually.

Some years ago, I had an extended slide stop made for my house gun. True, the chances of ever having to reload my house gun in a hurry are

very slim. I'm not the kind of iron nerved crack shot who would have any chance of fighting off the SLA single handed anyway; I'm of the anything-I-can't-handle-with-8-shots-I-can't-handle school of thought. But, I reasoned, being able to change magazines without shifting my grip just might

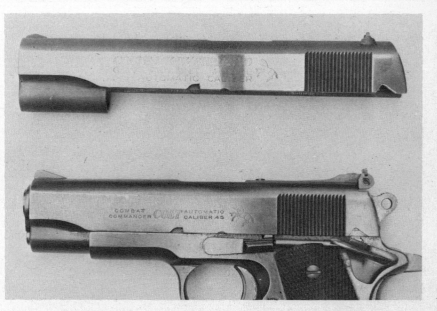

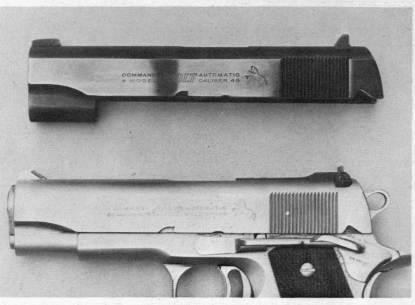

Some sight options, top to bottom: Stock sights on Colt are too small for quick pick-up. One early cure was S&W adjustable sights. In 1960, Chick Gaylord stated adjustable sights were fragile for duty pistols. Fixed sights, larger than stock, are a current custom option, and for those who still prefer S&W sights, some smiths offer the "protected" position.

come in handy, and it couldn't do any harm.

Of course, "It can't do any harm" really means "I don't *see* how it can do any harm."

One day on the pistol range, the slide on my house gun started locking open before the magazine was empty. After a few stoppages, I realized what the problem was. My thumb was pressing up on the slide stop extension.

Oddly enough, I'd had the extended slide stop quite a while before I had the problem. My house gun had a booby trap in something I considered tested and working. Then, for some unknown reason, my grip was a little different one day. Fortunately, it happened on the pistol range.

"It could help and I don't see how it could hurt" is a poor reason for modifying a defense gun.

Trigger jobs on automatics can result in:

—Pistol going full automatic, either when the trigger is pulled or when slide closes or after firing.

—Thumb safety not working. This should also be checked after having a new safety fitted.

The last warrants further discussion. After a trigger job, the hammer will sometimes fall just a little bit when the trigger is pulled while the

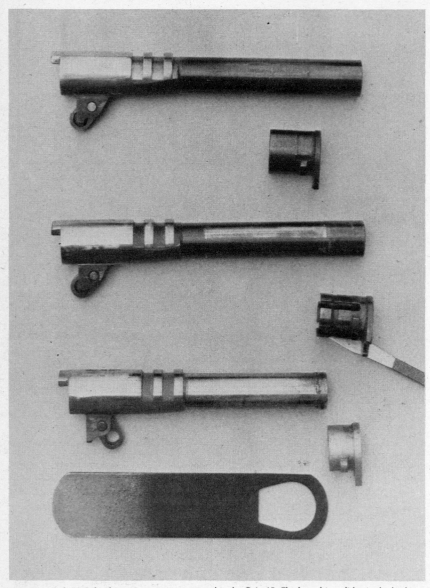

Top: Pre-Mark IV Colt, the same arrangement used in the G.I. 45. The barrel just slides in the bushing. Middle: Mark IV, the current option. The bushing has four spring steel fingers. Bottom: Accuracy jobs have very tight barrel bushings. The one shown here positions the barrel consistently, but it takes a special wrench (shown) to take down the gun. Of all, the original (top) set is the most reliable.

when the slide is slammed closed.

—Hammer sometimes falling only to half cock when trigger is pulled.

—Hammer falling to half cock

thumb safety is on. The hammer moves so little you would never notice unless you were watching closely. The hammer still *looks* full cocked, but when you release the thumb safety the

hammer will fall, sometimes to half cock, sometimes all the way.

But a trigger job on a Government Model is considered essential, isn't it? It depends on what the gun is for. A bad trigger that would make you flinch a shot clear off the target shooting bullseyes at 25 yards wouldn't even be noticed if you shoot a rapist climbing in your bedroom window, or a holdup man across the store counter, or even something as big as a silhouette at 25 yards.

If you have one of those Colts with an 8-pound gritty pull, and you feel you need some chance of hitting beyond point blank range, consider a compromise. Tell the gunsmith you want a 4½-5 pound pull, and aren't interested in seeing just how light the pull can be before something goes wrong. Then check the gun out carefully anyway.

Another "must" for 45 autos is the so-called accuracy job. One gunshop owner, being a serious shooter, naturally needs an accuracy job on the gun he would use if his 20-foot store were held up, or to shoot a burglar across his living room. Well, no harm done . . . so far. His gun works; I've heard of accuracy jobs that didn't.

In an article on 9mm S&Ws, one writer had an interesting comment:

". . . S&W 9mms have an interesting idiosyncrasy: some will jam when the shooting wrist is not locked, just as surely as will an accurized target 45 . . ."*

Oh really? An accurized 45 will do that? Nice that one of the experts we rely on for advice finally got around to telling us. He was discussing a cop who was wounded in the right arm, and managed a couple of shots with his left hand before his 9mm S&W jammed.

A shooter who has been wounded might not have the proper firm, locked wrist grip on his gun. You might have to draw while struggling with an attacker, and thus get the grip wrong. You might just goof. Even with a bad grip, you might still be able to hit a man at point blank range. But it would be nice if the gun didn't jam.

True, all of these things may be unlikely. But how likely is it that you'll ever need more than out-of-the-box accuracy?

An altered gun should be thoroughly checked out before depending

*American Handgunner, July/August, 1978.

on it for anything important. Like most things that should be too obvious to require mention, this can be forgotten by people who should know better. One gun store employee took to wearing a Colt 45, fresh back from a gunsmith with an accuracy job, in the store. His error was brought home to him when he finally tried out the gun on a range. The slide always failed to cycle. He'd been wearing a $750 single shot pistol.

It is time for a digression on how accurate your weapon need be. What you need to make an intelligent decision are the odds. Just how likely is it that you will need more than out-of-the-box accuracy? How likely is it that building more accuracy into the gun will cause a jam at close range, which is where you're more likely to need the gun? Unfortunately, the odds just aren't known. We must guess from what little we do know.

Out of the box is good enough for a man-sized target at 25 yards. You don't need a 3½ pound trigger for that either. Where an accuracy job just might make a difference is in something like a gunfight at 50 yards, or perhaps a man shooting from cover at 25 yards, so all you can see is part of his head. My answer to something like this would be simple: run like hell for cover. You have to be a crack shot with iron nerves to deliver pistol fire accurate enough to be of use under such circumstances. What ever my gun could do, I know I wouldn't be up to it. So my defense gun is set up for close range: no accuracy job, no risky light trigger.

But suppose you are good enough for an accurized pistol to make a difference. Should you have one? I just don't see how it makes sense for a house gun, store gun, or personal defense weapon. The very slim chance of a long range shot doesn't seem to warrant the increased chance of a close range jam.

For a policeman, the question is more complicated. The chances of a mid-range or long range engagement are higher. A policeman isn't always on the defensive. In theory, he should be able to hit a holdup man at some distance. A few have even managed it in practice. Maybe someone knows of statistics a decision can be based on. I just don't have the answer.

We are often told how rugged and basically simple the 1911A1 is. But it is just on the edge of not working in a

few ways. Both trigger and accuracy jobs can push it *very* close to the edge. Often, it falls over. They shouldn't be used unless needed. Unfortunately, they are so fashionable among the competition set a lot of people have lost sight of this, including Colt.

Colt?

Yes, Colt. The pre-Mark IV barrel and bushing were good enough for a civilian self defense gun. The Mark IV barrel and bushing is a sort of built-in accuracy job, prone to an accuracy job's problems.

I bought one when they were new. What the gun magazines didn't bother to mention was that the fancy Mk IV parts sometimes didn't let the slide cycle properly. After a shot, it sometimes didn't quite lock up. It would wind up just far back enough for the disconnector to stop the gun from firing. The increased accuracy would be poor consolation to someone whose gun jammed in a close range fight.

I haven't bought a Mk IV recently. I'm told it still happens on some guns, but a cure has been developed. But again, I am passing on hearsay. I haven't bought a Colt recently.

My cure for the one I did buy was simple. I replaced the Mk IV barrel and bushing with the old kind. If the gun is to be used to shoot a man before he gets close enough to rape you, or to shoot a burglar across the living room, I would recommend replacing the Mk IV with the old barrel and bushing at the first sign of trouble. If you want a more accurate pistol, you might have a smith try to make the Mk IV work.

So, gunsmiths are hard to avoid. In an article advocating holding modifications to a minimum, I am recommending one: a sort of *un*accuracy job.

Automatics have trigger jobs, revolvers have action jobs. Unlike the auto trigger job, the difference between a bad double action and an action job can make a difference even across a room. If you need an action job, you can just tell the smith it is a self-defense gun, that having it go "bang" instead of "click" is more important than a super-slick action, and hope he listens.

When you get an N or K frame S&W back, make sure the mainspring strain screw is all the way in. With any S&W, ask the smith to teach you how to disassemble and reassemble the gun, so you can clean it. While the action job is being done, order a trig-

ger return spring. (Not from your gunsmith. He's apt to keep you waiting long enough without you hurting his feelings.) If the gunsmith does his job properly, you will be out the price of the spring. If the trigger doesn't return every time, you won't have to wait to order the part.

Lightening the single action pull on a revolver can result in the hammer falling when the *hammer* is touched. The hammer block *should* keep the gun from going off, but it is a bit disconcerting. With the hammer cocked, and a high grip on the piece, you could knock the hammer down with the web of your shooting hand. Naturally, the gunsmith won't tell you of the danger when you ask for the job.

What about the "master" gunsmiths? In view of all the stories I've told you, wouldn't it be best to have your work done by a master, and have a better chance of it being done right? Good idea, but that still leaves you with a problem. The masters are booked up very far in advance. If you need a self-defense gun, you need a gun while the master is doing one for you. So you'll still face all the problems I've been talking about with your "meanwhile" gun.

To sum up:

Be very cautious about modifying weapons.

Trigger jobs on automatics require caution even on a target pistol.

Give your gun a good check out after it gets back from the smith. Remember, no job is too simple to screw up.

Having elaborate modifications done is a hobby, not something likely to result in a trustworthy weapon in a reasonable time.

Always give gunsmiths written instructions, and keep a Xerox copy.

Written instructions are a good idea for reasons other than recriminations. They force you to organize your thoughts and decide just what to tell the gunsmith. They eliminate the honest misunderstandings that arise when you ramble on for ten minutes and the smith writes a few words on a tag ●

EDITORIAL NOTE: *This customer point of view backs up the beautifully succinct old-timer who said, "If it ain't broke, don't fix it."*

Any working pistolsmith who would like to discuss customer foibles in print should contact me. K.W.

20th CENTURY

POWDER HORNS

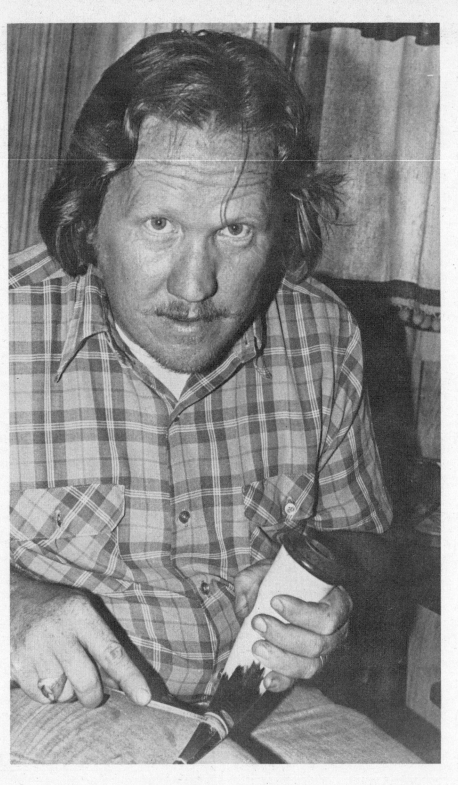

by Rick Jamison

The sentiments and the uses are the same, but the horns of Kirk Olson are different

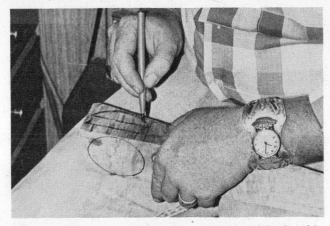

Before cutting the wood from the blank, Olson marks the intended outline of the horn cap.

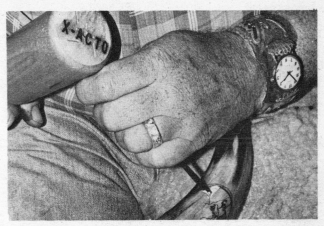

The background is carved away first. Olson uses a mallet and chisels for much of this work.

THE POWDER HORN has been a part of history since long before white men set foot on America's soil. In fact, the horn has been the medium for preserving much of our country's recorded history. They have been scrimshawed, scratched, engraved and carved in every manner imaginable with all sorts of tools, and these inscriptions, preserved in horn, reveal the happenings of the time.

With the return of muzzleloading popularity, shooting accoutrements are likewise in demand. And powder horns are being made, right along with Kentucky rifles, to satisfy nostalgic needs. Like the rifles, some are utilitarian while others are purchased for their artistic value — to repose on a fireplace mantel, never to contain powder. Indeed, some of the horns are fit for an art gallery.

Kirk Olson, working in a back room of his home in Prescott, Arizona, is producing such horns. Although many of his horns are works of art, they're all also functional. Like most with an interest in the old ways, Olson reproduces the old styles to some extent. Some of his horn caps are exact replicas of early ones and like the antiques, his horns are completely hand-worked. In other respects, however, they depart from tradition. Some have said his deep-relief style of carving is

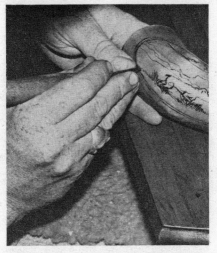

After drawing the scene on the horn, Olson scratches over the lines to make them more permanent.

not in keeping with yesteryear. His scrimshawed maps are another departure. They're not reproductions from early charts. For instance, the map on Olson's own horn is an area of the Prescott National Forest as it appears today.

Olson has quite a reputation for his historical knowledge. In fact, he has restored a number of museum pieces to original condition. Why then, does he not produce his horns in 100% traditional style? Olson's answer reveals an interesting philosophy: "Restoring something to its original condition is one thing, but when someone copies an artifact, he's producing nothing more than a reproduction. By not duplicating traditional carving styles, my horns are original.

"I see no reason to reproduce old maps which are no longer of use to anyone. My horn carries a map of a country hunted by four generations of Olsons, from my grandfather to my son. The cap is made from a piece of cherry wood grown in the same area. I've used old quotations yet only those that fit today. This way, the horn is current and means more to me."

Olson added another reason for his departure from traditional style: "I've seen many fine Kentucky rifles, but

The tip design is done with hand files. Olson uses new files for the rough cutting and worn files for finishing.

Olson is shown here cutting the scallops for the border between the tip and body of the horn.

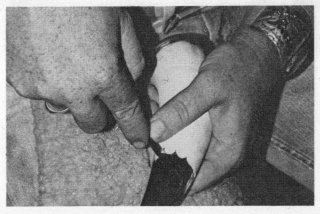

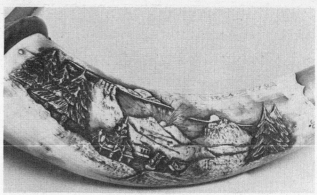

This horn was carved by Olson during the Bicentennial, 1976. It features a York County style cap and proclaims "Liberty or Death," "July 4, 1776."

This horn was carved for Walt Minucci. It features a Prescott scene including the Yavapai County Courthouse, a statue of Bucky O'Neil and Thumb Butte.

the horns of the day simply didn't match the quality of the rifles. I want a horn that's appropriate for the rifle."

By using contemporary designs and quotes, Olson's horns are sometimes quite personal. One fellow wanted Olson to carve a horn with his bird dog on it. Rather than just do the figure of a dog, Olson traveled to the man's home and sketched the surrounding mountains, complete with pheasant habitat. He will apply these sketches to the background on the horn carving and as a result, it will be even more cherished by the owner.

Though some have scoffed at Olson for straying from tradition, few would dispute his craftsmanship. I recently had the opportunity to see Olson at work and talk with him about the steps involved in making the horns. There is more to making a fine horn than meets the eye.

First, a proper horn must be selected. Horns vary in color, texture, thickness and size of the cavity. Some very old horns split and crack and may be unsuitable for carving. If a deep-relief pattern is to be applied to the horn, a thicker horn is selected. For scrimshaw work, a thinner horn may be more desirable. In olden days, horns that were to be scrimshawed were

often scraped even thinner. This allowed the user to determine how much powder remained in the horn by holding it toward a light source and viewing the outline of the powder inside. Scraping the horn thin also made it even more lightweight which was desirable for a hunter.

Not only does horn thickness and cavity size vary, but the large end of the horn varies in terms of roundness. This affects installation of the horn cap. If the horn is quite round, the cap can be turned on a lathe and this was done years ago. If the horn is too far out-of-round, the plug must be hand-fit. If the horn is only slightly out-of-round and the walls not too thick, it can be scraped thinner and softened by boiling. This allows the horn to be shaped to fit the cap. However, altering the shape of a thick horn too much will result in cracking and splitting.

After selecting a proper horn, the tip must be cut to length and the hole bored for powder flow. Olson first uses a wire to determine the depth of the horn cavity and then scribes lines around the outside of the tip to guide the hand drill from the outside tip to the inside peak of the cavity. After drilling the hole, Olson tests it for powder flow. If powder doesn't flow

freely, more horn is removed.

The next step is to fit the cap. Olson's horn caps are made of the finest woods; they are carved from remnants of fine gunstock blanks. The caps provide an air-tight, press fit and Olson verifys this by blowing into the spout to check for air leaks. This tight fit prevents moisture getting into the powder. The plug is then pinned into place with brass or wooden pegs.

After the cap is completed, the tip is shaped. Flats, rings, spirals, or any other design is marked out on the small end of the horn. The flats are draw-filed much like an octagon rifle barrel is draw-filed. New files are used for the roughing out, and worn files are used for finishing. It takes a knack to produce flat flats which follow the natural curve and taper of the horn. It's also difficult for the novice to file round rings without flat spots. After these are cut and smoothed with worn files, Olson uses 400 or 600-grit sandpaper to remove all scratches and file marks.

It appears the smaller, darker tip portion of many Olson horns is made of a separate piece for the color breaks suddenly from a light area to sometimes jet-black. The effect is achieved by cutting more deeply into the horn.

(Left) This horn was carved for NRA life member Art Morrison. It features Morrison's favorite blue tick hound, "Blue," trailing a raccoon during a moonlit night near Prescott. (Right) Olson's signature and quail logo goes onto each of his horns.

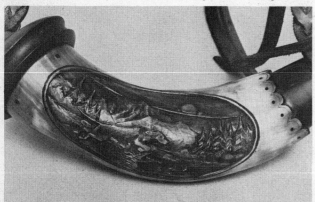

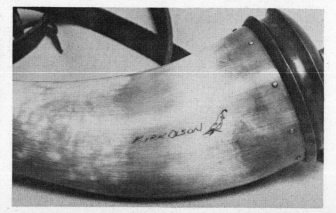

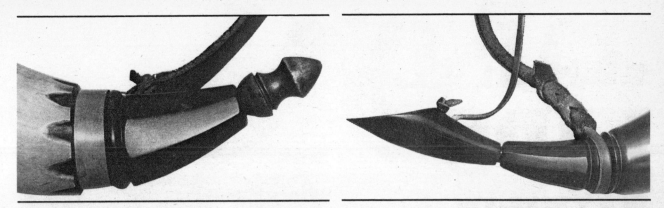

The horn tip is usually dark underneath the lighter outer covering. For this reason, cutting more deeply reveals the solid black underneath portion to contrast sharply with the lighter surface layer.

After cutting through the thin outer sheath, the exposed horn is more porous and susceptible to drying. Olson rubs machine oil into the filed horn tip to bring out the color and to protect it. He then applies a paste wax to prevent drying.

ground is cut away first and then the design is carved. Chisels and knives execute the figure. After the carving is completed, leather dye is swabbed over the entire exterior of the horn and allowed to dry. The excess is then rubbed off with 0000 steel wool until the desired shade and coloring is attained. The cuts take the dye readily and produce the appearance of more depth in the design. In the old days, roots, herbs, walnut hulls, lamp chimney soot and other natural dyes were used to achieve the coloring, rather

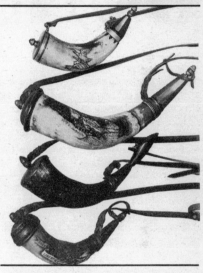

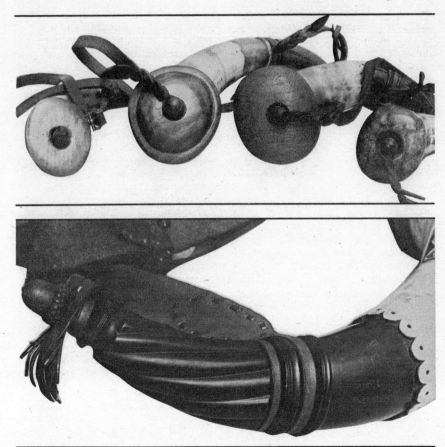

Prior to cutting the design into the side of the horn, Olson first sketches the scene onto the horn in great detail. This way, all proportions are retained after the cutting is begun. The back-

than leather dye. A refined stock finishing oil, such as Casey's Tru-Oil, is then rubbed into the horn and the excess is wiped away with a cloth. This seals the horn and prevents drying.

The horn tip peg is carved of horn or wood; Olson prefers the acorn-shape design. The leather carrying sling is made of ½ to 1½-inch wide leather.

Although Olson is just getting into the horn work seriously, he has been carving them more than 12 years in his spare time. As for prices, the horns start at $75 and go up. Olson would like to keep the price within reach of anyone who seriously wants one. For an elaborate horn like the one Olson made for himself, he charges $550, which, considering the more than 150 hours of hand labor involved, is quite reasonable.

Some have said there are more muzzle-loaders in use today than ever before. For this reason, Olson feels muzzle-loading is today, and his horns reflect current life. Possibly some day historians will be reproducing Olson's horns as originals, representative of this period in time. ●

RAISING KIDS WITH GUNS

Top: Rob figures out a Zouave as part of his education in guns. Left above: Hugh, a lefty, had to handle right-handed guns like this Remington; has since carried big-bores as bear protection. Above: Hugh again, with a favorite utility gun, the M1 Carbine. Below: Liz, for some reason, wasn't happy at this moment with the Nylon 66.

Firearms skills are a useful heritage, whether used or not

by Bill Davidson

REARING FIVE youngsters around guns, hunting and shooting, was one of the few really worthwhile things I've done in life.

The script is supposed to read "A family that shoots together stays together." But in the accelerating social helter-skelter of this last quarter of our century, old maxims mean less and less; like many another 20-year-plus marriage, mine ended in separation. Most of our children were in their 20's and widely scattered across the Mountain West and Gulf South. There was rather little to hold to, and much—sometimes too much—to remember.

But one of the memories worth holding fast is about rearing those five kids in the guns-hunting-shooting lifestyle in which most Americans grew up prior to 1950 or so.

In 26 years together, my wife and I lived, worked and attended college in a bunch of places: Indiana, Gulf-Coast Texas, South Dakota, Pennsylvania, Arizona, Utah, Colorado and Louisiana. Most of that is decent hunting-shooting territory, and during about three-fourths of it we lived in some kind or other of rural surroundings where the everyday use of guns was easy. Most of those years, we had a home shooting range. So it was simple to train our youngsters and others in the safe and reasonable use of firearms.

Simple? Well, nothing worthwhile is ever simple. Hindsight shows it was not always done as well as possible, but it was done with love, thought, patience (most of the time) and tact (usually).

My wife agreed that kids need to learn to handle guns safely and wisely, just as they are better off knowing how to swim, drive and dance. All of these can pass quickly from recreational or social amenities to downright necessities. Whether our kids will ever care to hunt or shoot competitively, they may at some moment need to know how to survive with a firearm.

I was not one of those gun-crank fathers who insists that all the kids grow up to be Lones Wiggers or Margaret Murdocks or Karamojo Bells. As a firearms-hunting writer-editor, I've seen too many young people literally turned off guns and hunting by parents who stridently made these oppressive: People who were so one-way, so hipped on the subject that they crucified their children. Instead, we made guns, the other staples and reasonable training available; each kid received a minimum of what was necessary. Each responded in his or her

own way but evolved differently in each case. The only absolute was that sometime during his or her training, each kid was required to complete and pass a recognized state hunter-safety course.

All that was years ago. But the capper came not long ago, when my far-off middle son, a busy graduate teaching assistant in anthropology in Colorado, told me on the phone how he wished he could join us for a fall deer hunt.

"I wish I had the time to go on a tramp like that," Hugh said. And that expressed for him exactly what his hunting and shooting training meant. He had never been a gun buff, but he loved the outdoors—and hunting was to him a grand tramp. If you feel that is not gung-ho nor orthodox enough, you might like to audit a witch-burning, because any time you can get a young person outdoors, for any decent reason, it is a social boon. In Hugh's case, he enjoys the ritual as well as the emotion of hunting but cares rather little about its consummation. He prefers bird-shooting to big-game hunting but loves both, because they conjure up for him memories which he considers priceless, as he told me to my surprise in our telephone conversation.

And he regards as social lepers those who would crimp your or my or his right to hunt, shoot or defend oneself.

Yet this was the youngster with whom I lost patience. He was at age

eight or nine the one who had real difficulty grasping the sighting-picture concept, and at whom, God forgive me, I swore and fumed on long, hot desert days when nothing seemed to get through to him. But that of course was my fault, not his, for somehow I failed to reach him right at first.

Today he keeps an Ithaca side-by-side double 12 which I gave him (and which he had to learn not to shoot off-balance) and a little Ithaca 22 Magnum single-shot "saddle" carbine. Last summer, working an archaeological dig for the Forest Service in Southeast Alaska, he carried a 375 H&H Magnum rifle to guard work parties against large, mean brown bears. But if he never shoots another quail or bear, he will have learned tolerance and indeed love for an outdoor activity that comes down to us from the dimness of history—and one we still find indispensable at times.

Then there is our older daughter, who at the beginning of her life had some kind of a minor ear problem: Gun reports made her ear hurt, sometimes almost to the screaming point. But as my wife pointed out, it occurred to Margaret that if she wanted to be with her father, she would need to handle the problem—the hurt. And one morning, when I walked down to the firing point, she traipsed behind, holding her ears already before the shooting started—perfectly ready to bear some

An older Liz and her father discuss results on a silhouette during a session on one of the home ranges the Davidson family almost always had and used.

punishment to be with her father.

It was a touching example of what children will do to be with their mothers and fathers at something they believe is important to those parents. We found a doctor who solved the ear problem, and in a little while loud sounds no longer pained Margaret. But I never forgot her following me down to the range, determined to adjust to anything to be with her old man.

Marg never cared for hunting. But we shared a private father-daughter in-joke about my passing through life as "Doctor Killrabbit." This originated when my friends and I used to handgun-hunt for rabbits in the desert flats north of Tucson. Fascinated yet repelled by watching me field-dress rabbits, she made a decision like the one about gun noises: She would adjust to it and like it because her father liked doing it, repugnant as it was. And she came to regard the cleaning of rabbits or other game as a huge joke.

My younger daughter took to it more. She became a star junior rifle pupil for a while; had we remained near good coaching, she might have moved into serious competitive shooting. But she went on deer hunts with first the males in the family and later my friends and I in Arizona and Colorado. She cooked for us but enjoyed the whole scope of such trips, even though I believe she hunted deer only a couple of times. She went happily along on hot desert bird shoots.

Liz never cared much for killing, but she knows what a gun is for. One night when she was 12 or so, my wife in town working and I long gone on a business trip, Liz took a pellet pistol and deliberately laid down two or three well-sent shots to scare away older boys who were trying to burglarize our utility room.

She did them a favor, for the boys were after centerfire-caliber reloads which they had been stealing and trying to detonate off in the desert. Luckily they had not succeeded, but they were back for more cartridges to try again.

The boys' parents indignantly called police, but when the officers sorted it out, the senior cop on the call told my wife: "We can't exactly approve what your daughter did, but there was fair reason. And she really did keep those idiots from hurting themselves."

She was well-enough trained to know precisely what she was doing with the pellet gun. She knew how far off to hold without hurting anyone—and yet to shoot close enough to deliver the message. Today when I'm away, Liz keeps

a Ruger 10/22 22-cal. semiauto rifle with a couple of loaded magazines by her bed. I have more confidence in her with that weapon than I do in most of the adults I've served with in various police agencies in two states. She knows when, how and where—and when not—to use that light, fast-handling rifle. The magazine in the rifle holds hollow-point bullets. Granted any chance at all to react, she will not be easily handled by any intruder.

My youngest son became the most parochial in his gun interests. I trained him on a Savage Model 24 22 Magnum/20-gauge combination gun and a Nylon 66 Remington 22. Later he used a Savage Model 99 lever action in 250 caliber, but he cared little for "modern" guns. Jamie really taught himself to read well on Mountain-Man era books, and we were living in Mountain-Man territory—Southern Colorado, Northern Arizona. He fell in love with muzzle-loading guns. And there he stayed, aside from brief outings with his bolt-action 22 rifle.

But Jamie learned about shooting modern guns, nonetheless. He and his younger sister and I had embryo shooting contests on our home range, usually pitting them with 22 cal. rifles against me with a centerfire handgun. We bet Cokes against beers; Jamie, never exposed to formal competitive rifle training, often beat his well-drilled sister.

His big problem with front-loaders was the one we all share: Remembering to put the powder down-barrel *first*. Once taught how to get out of that predicament, he did pretty well with his 50-cal. Hawken-type Thompson-Center rifle. But he insisted on remaining a fairly-skilled amateur; he wanted no indoctrination beyond the basics. His choice to go it alone thereafter was one I think an intelligent parent should respect. I did.

It was my oldest son, the smallest and coolest of the boys, who became the gun buff. He digested ballistics tables and trajectories and reloading data a great deal faster than his father had done at the same age. He became a very good shot with rifle and shotgun and a fair-to-good one with handguns. He stayed with reloading after the other kids abandoned it. He read everybody's catalogs and brochures. He worked and still works with a high-country geo-physical exploration crew and carries a gun or two wherever he goes with a rig. He wants to complete his college training in Asian studies. He would be a gifted political

scientist. His politics are utterly different from mine, but he shares the feeling his brothers and I have about people who would prevent us from owning guns for reasonable purposes.

And there is this other side to my oldest: Once when I had been away (again) on business and Rob's younger brother Hugh was working at an all-night restaurant to pay tuition bills, three young men were giving the restaurant's woman manager a hard time: A few threats, some abusive language. Hugh told them to get out. They went. Later when two city policemen stopped by for their 3 a.m. coffee break, he told them about the incident. They laughed it off when the woman restaurant manager, not anxious to lose "business," made nothing of it.

But an hour or two later, with the police long gone, the three troublemakers returned. They told Hugh they knew he got off work at 6 a.m.— and they would be waiting outside: With knives, they said.

Hugh phoned his older brother. In 20 minutes, Rob was at the restaurant, sitting halfway in and halfway out of the driver's seat of his pickup, the leftside door ajar and my Ithaca "police" 12-gauge riot gun handily by; its big muzzle was just visible across his lap.

There was no more difficulty at that restaurant. Hugh went peaceably home with his brother. The troublemakers talked about calling the police for themselves, but nothing followed. They had seen the immediate future—a 12-gauge shotgun held by some deft hands and in front of some cool grey eyes. And they had decided on easier options.

Some of you won't like that story. I do. It fits right into a permissive society in which it is all too often up to us to preserve ourselves. People who criticize my example may not be in touch with the real world, which occurs in all-night restaurant parking lots and many other everyday places. People don't often get mugged while out hunting or raped in gun-club ranges. Those social phenomena occur in parking lots and empty office buildings and on side streets.

I hope that during all their lives, my children never need to shoot anything more than big game and birds and predators. But if they do, they know how—and when and when not to do so. I believe that in this uncertain world with its distortions and artificialities, that is a more useful heritage than Kennedys or Rockefellers leave their children. ●

TESTFIRE

S&W Model 586

WHAT LOOKS like a Colt Python, handles like a Colt Python, for openers even shoots like a Colt Python, yet isn't a Colt Python? Would you believe the new S&W Model 586 Distinguished Combat Magnum?

When GD's test revolver serial number AAA0071 arrived I was informed it was a handmade version put together for the announcing seminar at the plant in Springfield and that it was the only one out of S&W's possession. In other words I was to guard it with my life if necessary. I'm dedicated—up to a point—so it never came to that.

I immediately was struck by its similarity to the long established Colt Python. A side view reveals the only real difference is the vent rib on the Python. From the bottom they are almost identical. From the top—well, the ribs are a slightly different width.

My Python is a Jerry Moran customized work of art wearing Herrett's custom grips made for my hand, so to compare the balance and overall feel

the grips were removed from both guns. With one in each hand then switching hands back and forth several times I must admit I can't tell which is in which hand without looking. Since my Python has been dressed with a red insert ramp front sight and the Model 586 comes from the factory with one, they even look alike through the sights.

For commercial reasons, neither firm may like the comparison, but I don't know how better to tell what a S&W Distinguished Combat Magnum Model 586 looks like.

The new revolver is on an all new frame size designated "L" to fit it between the "K" now in use on the 38's and Model 19 and the "N" on which the 44 Magnum and 45 Colt are made. It was determined the Model 19 was in fact too light for the use now given it, particularly by the lawmen for which it was designed. A bit more weight, giving it a bit more strength, but with the feel of the "K" frame seemed to be the ideal. And that is exactly what the "L" frame Model 586 is.

In comparing the "K", "L" and "N" the grip is identical on the "K" and "L" and of course larger on the big "N" frame. Measuring the frame immediately in front of the trigger guard, for depth, I found the "K" to be 2¼

A Visit To Smith & Wesson

The year of 1981 was kicked off with a gun writer's seminar at 129-year-old Smith & Wesson. A dozen writers representing most of the major publications gathered at Springfield, Mass. to hear about an entirely new S&W revolver.

Lee Deters, Executive Vice President, provided a thorough historical review of the 357 Magnum cartridge beginning with the development of what is today called the "K" frame models back in 1894, starting with the 38 U.S. Service cartridge, a black powder 810 ft/sec load. In 1899, the 38 M&P Model was introduced with a new ⅛-inch longer cartridge—the 38 S&W Special. Loads changed, as did pressures, so in 1931 the company brought out a new police revolver built on the "N" frame, the 38/44 Heavy Duty. There was also a model called the 38/44 Outdoorsman with an adjustable sight.

This brought on another problem. The 38/44 cartridge was dimensionally the same as the 38 S&W Special. Shooters were stuffing it in guns not heavy enough for the punishment wrought by the heavier load. Another ⅛-inch was added to the case, and on April 8, 1935, the first S&W 357 Magnum revolver was presented to J. Edgar Hoover of the FBI. The Model 27, a deluxe handgun was Smith's only 357 until 1954 when the Model 28 Highway Patrolman, a no-frills workhorse version came along. That same year Bill Jordan came into the picture. This U.S. Border Patrol shooter convinced S&W hierarchy the ideal law enforcement sidearm would be a "K" frame 4-inch 357 Magnum. His idea bore fruit and the Combat Magnum Model 19 was born.

Loads continued to get hotter with lighter bullets and new powders. Soon officers were training with full magnum loads instead of 38 Specials. The guns were taking a beating. A heavier handgun was indicated, yet it needed to have the feel of the "K" frame.

The Distinguished Combat Magnum Model 586 built on the new "L" frame was born. GUN DIGEST shot one and you can read about it here.

Smith & Wesson Model 586 Distinguished Combat Magnum 357 Magnum revolver.

inches, the "L" to be 2⅞ inches and the "N" to be 2½ inches. All are the same width through the frame across the hammer slot. Without grips my ancient K-38 weighs 34½ ounces, the Model 586 42 ounces and the "N" frame Model 25-5 45 Colt tips the postal scales at 41¼ ounces. I don't own a Model 19 so can't compare those weights. The Colt Python, by the way, also minus grips, weighs 42 ounces—identical to the M586.

Other measurements, further comparing the Model 586 with Colt's Python, reveal the outside diameter of both barrels to be ¹¹⁄₁₆ of an inch. The depth of the barrel and ejector shroud on the M586 is 1³⁄₁₆ inches. The Python measures 1⅜-inch, but remember it has a vent rib. The top strap width on the M586 is ²¹⁄₃₂ inch and the Python ¹¹⁄₁₆ inch. The ejector shroud OD on the M586 is ⁹⁄₁₆ inch and the Python ½ inch.

But let's get specifically to the M586. With grips, which are Goncalo Alves target checkered with speed loader cutaway, the weight is 46 ounces. Sights are S&W micrometer click and Baughman with S&W Red Ramp on the test 6-inch barrel gun but it can also be had with a plain Patridge if desired. The hammer is wide semi-target and the trigger is wide smooth combat. All 4-inch barrel guns furnished with the target hammer and trigger will be equipped with a trigger stop. All 6-inch guns come equipped with a trigger stop.

GD's test M586 is S&W bright blue but it is also available in nickel and as the M686 in S&W satin stainless.

Above—S&W's three frame sizes—"K" frame, 38 Spl; "L" frame, the new M586 357 Mag, and the big "N" frame used with the 44 Mag and 45 Colt. Left to right.

Right—S&W's new "L" frame M586 357 Magnum (left gun), compared to a Colt Python. Real look alikes.

Below—So much does the M586 S&W "L" frame look and measure like the Colt Python that it fits, perfectly, Swiggett's Safariland holster for his 6-inch Colt Python.

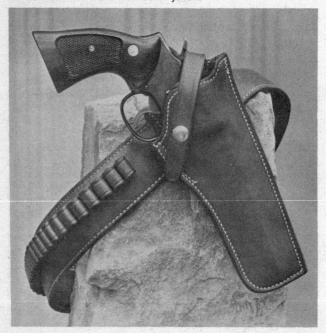

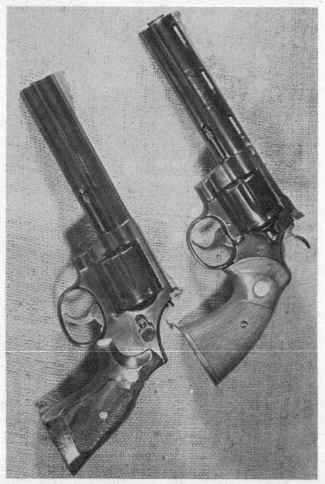

Suggested retail for the M586 in either blue or nickel is $247. The stainless M686 is suggested at $268.

Now that we know what it looks like and what it costs the next question is how does it shoot. "Better than I can," is the answer, to put it bluntly. I used a full assortment of factory loads from Remington, Winchester, Federal and Super Vel including all bullet weights factory loaded. A full day was spent on a range and in the pasture after the review was written for Handguns Today (see page 111). That day saw more than 600 rounds put through the M586 by yours truly and a used-to-be friend. That's the title he put on himself after what he termed "the ordeal."

Most of my shooting takes place on ranches far away from congestion a la city living. Usually it's just me, a few cows, sometimes a herd of sheep or goats and once in a while a horse or two trying out the guns. If a coyote or jack rabbit happens along it immediately becomes a live target. Mostly my targets are baseball to grapefruit-sized rocks and sometimes, when one presents itself broadside, cactus leaves. Knots on fence posts are great for sighting in. I'm not being facetious. That's the way I learned to shoot a long time ago and to this day paper scares me.

As best I could tell the M586 really liked Federal's 158-grain SWC's. This is a lead bullet at 1235 fps. It did almost as well with their same weight JHP at the same listed velocity. As bullet weights went down so did the accuracy—at least in my hands. The high performance at 1400 plus fps 125-grain bullets do not hold as tight for me as heavier slower bullets. In any gun. I know the purpose and for that use they are great but none will ever set any target records. The 110-grain loads: I'd best just say we shot them and they hit some of the targets. Could be my lack of faith in that weight in a 357 causes me to use less care in holding. Lawmen at gun fighting distances will have no trouble hitting their targets with these 110-grain factory loaded cartridges. Jack rabbits at 75 to 100 yards are another matter.

Sighted in at 75 yards, as my Python is, I venture to say it will match the famous Colt shot for shot all day long and maybe even better it—as a hunting/field handgun—for barely more than half the price. As a target gun the M586 S&W "L" frame will have to go through the hands of a few dedicated paper punchers. It won't take them long to find out what it will do—however—I do think they will like what they find.
                                        Hal Swiggett

Marlin Model 1894 - 357 Magnum

In the waning days of the Old West, it was considered advantageous to have a handgun and rifle or carbine which used the same cartridge, so as to

Marlin's Model 1894 carbine chambered for the 357 Magnum cartridge weighs just over six pounds, and measures under three feet in length.

at least have one workable arm in the case of an emergency. Hence, carbines or rifles and revolvers chambered for such cartridges as the 32-20, 44-40 or 38-40 Winchester became popular. Winchester and Marlin were among the rifle and carbine manufacturers, and Colt, S&W, and Merwin Hulbert & Co. (Hopkins & Allen) were among the revolver manufacturers.

Today, such a combination might be handy, but generally the need is more nostalgic. There are carbines available which are chambered for handgun cartridges, such as the autoloading Ruger, but in the tradition of the Old West, only a lever action Winchester or a Marlin will do. Winchester doesn't manufacture them, but modern reproductions of the Model 1892 Winchester are available from Rossi and, more recently, Browning, and Marlin has their Model 1894, introduced in late 1978 for the 357 Magnum cartridge.

Weighing one ounce over six pounds, as it comes from the box, the latest Model 1894 features a barrel length of 18^9/16 inches with an overall length of 35⅝ inches. (The Micro-Groove barrel is rifled with 20 grooves having a right hand twist.) The barrel has a straight taper from breech to the muzzle, which has a slightly concave crown, and the finish is a well polished deep blue, as is the finish on the magazine tube, underlever, hammer, loading gate, and the side of the breech bolt. The top and bottom surfaces of the receiver, including the upper and lower tangs and the fore and aft portion of the sides, have been sand blasted to provide a non-glare satin finish resembling "Parkerizing." Unlike the original Model 1894, the trigger on the modern 1894 is gold plated, and the hammer is fitted with a thumbpiece to permit easier cocking when a scope is mounted.

Sights on the Model 1894 consist of a

The only problem encountered with the Model 1894 was the rim of the 357 Magnum cartridges catching on the front edge of the loading port, as shown here.

dovetailed front having a .084-inch brass bead, and a modified buckhorn open rear having a .064-inch U-shaped notch. The rear sight is dovetailed into the barrel and is adjustable for windage by tapping or drifting, and adjustable for elevation via the stepped elevator. Sight radius on the test carbine measured 14⁵/₁₆ inches.

Marlin still uses American walnut on the lever action carbines and rifles carrying their name, and the forearm and straight grip stock on the 1894 were good quality, well sealed, with a little sapwood showing. The forearm measured 9¹³/₁₆ inches in length, was U-shaped in cross-section, and retained by the receiver at the rear and a barrel band near the forward end. The buttstock on the 1894 is black plastic, with a white spacer, and the stock finish on the test gun was applied after the buttplate was attached, filling the checkered diamonds and distracting from the surfaces usefulness and appearance. (A blued steel buttplate on this particular model would seem more appropriate.)

Wood-to-metal fit on the test carbine was as good as any this writer has seen on any long arm, including rifles and shotguns costing hundreds of dollars more. Wood and metal surfaces were flush, even around the tang areas, and there were no unsightly gaps. (Now, if it just had an oil finish, and a different buttplate.) The length of pull for the stock measured 13½ inches, and for this writer the brass bead fell right into the U-shaped rear sight notch when the carbine was shouldered quickly.

Appearances mean nothing, if an arm isn't accurate or doesn't function reliably. Thus, the next stop was the range, after mounting a Weaver K3-1 scope atop the receiver using Weaver's 63B base and Armsport rings. Accuracy firing was done from the bench, using sandbag forearm and butt rests, with three-shot groups being fired at 25 and 100 yards, using several different brands of ammunition and loads.

The first firing was at the 25-yard range with the scope removed. Using the open sights at this distance, the smallest group obtained measured ⁹/₁₆-inch, produced by Smith & Wesson's factory load with the 125 grain jacketed hollow point bullet. Most of the groups measuring just over one inch were obtained with W-W's Super-X round with the 125 grain jacketed hollow point bullet, and Speer/CCI's load having the 110 grain jacketed hollow point bullet.

Switching to the 100 yard range, with the scope installed, the groups

opened to over four inches for the majority of brands and bullet weights. The smallest group obtained at this distance was with Super Vel cartridges loaded with the 125 grain jacketed hollow point bullet; it measured 3³/₁₆ inches center-to-center, while a couple of other brands produced groups measuring over five inches in size. Such groups are still capable of anchoring a whitetail, and many hunting rifles will not do better, but the 357 Magnum cartridge was designed for handgun use at short ranges.

During the firing of over 300 rounds through the Model 1894, no functioning problems were encountered with feeding or ejecting. (Fired cases were ejected approximately one foot to the right of the receiver.) However, the 7¾ pound letoff of the trigger didn't help the accuracy, and loading of the cartridges through the loading gate into the magazine was difficult. The rim of the case kept catching on the forward edge of the loading port, which was not sloped; a few minutes work with a rotary stone in a Handee tool sloped the inner surface so the cartridges slipped into the magazine without a hitch.

The Model 1894 comes with an extension for the hammer spur, to permit cocking the hammer when a scope is mounted. This extension can be mounted for either left or right hand use, and it definitely speeds up the cocking when the hammer is lowered, regardless of whether the scope is being used.

When the scope is mounted, proper sight alignment for this writer occurred with the cheek just touching the comb of the stock. Tighter cheeking of the stock placed the eye below the level of the scope, or in line with the iron sights for which the Model 1894 is designed. One minor fault on the test gun was noted during the scope mounting; the iron sights on the barrel were tilted to the left.

Overall, the Marlin Model 1894 is a handy carbine, chambered for a cartridge for which many factory loads are available, and handloading is simple. (If handcast bullets are used, a handloader can shoot the Model 1894 almost as cheaply as is possible with a rimfire rifle.) With factory loads, plinking with the Model 1894 is a bit expensive, and the cartridge is a bit light for whitetail-size game at any but very short ranges. For small game at reasonable distances it is more satisfactory, and cartridges loaded with the 110 grain or 125 grain jacketed bullets will improve the trajectory a bit.   *Larry Sterett*

Winchoked 101

The all-around shotgun is always with us, even though it is a myth. Almost every serious shotgunner tries eventually to put together one gun that will serve most uses in most places. It is a nice idea.

An active American gunner, however, who may shoot tiny swishing quail at 20 yards one week and 8-pound Canada honkers at extended range the next, does not easily find an all-around shotgun. Some do, but no one has one that would suit the rest.

And that brings us to Winchester's latest Model 101 over-under, which comes from the factory with a set of three choke tubes for each barrel. The gun is a 12-bore, with 28-inch barrels and with 3-inch chambers. Having tried it, I can say that this gun comes as close to being an all-around shotgun as any I have ever tried or owned.

First, this Winchester is quite a handsome specimen. Done up with the warm brown walnut and the good blue job in the familiar Model 101 pattern, it is quite a package. One hardly notices the choke tubes. In fact, while I was testing this one, I handed it to several groups of knowledgeable shooters and several of those people examined the gun in some detail before they even noticed the choke tubes.

One thing they always looked at was the ventilated spacing between the barrels. It complements the ventilated rib on top, and, while attractive in itself, this venting, it also serves to mask the fact that the barrels are farther separated than is usual with Winchester 101 barrels. That is, of course, a requirement in order to make room for the choke tubes up front. The inevitable corollary is that the Winchoke barrels will fit only on the 101 model for which they were originally designed.

The Winchokes themselves are familiar by now, since they appear on many Winchester's repeaters. The barrels of any gun so-equipped are slightly thickened—very slightly—at the muzzle, and the bore is cleanly bored, reamed and threaded finely from the front. The choke is an equally carefully manufactured tube that screws into this threaded interior of the bore. A small spanner is used to snug it home, and, of course, to remove it. They are available as field chokes in Improved Cylinder, Modified and Full.

Such choke tubes are not magic, of course. The gun is still a shotgun, and the loads one shoots are still shotshells, and the variety of occurrence

Gun comes with six tubes, two each in improved cylinder, modified and full chokes, complete with spanner wrench.

Winchester's Model 101 XTR with Winchoke.

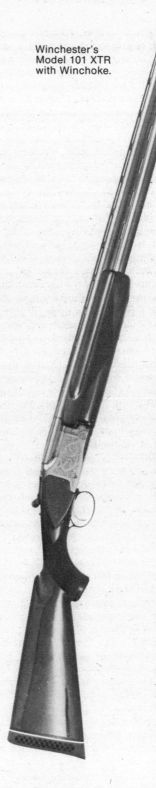

The Winchoked 101 works very well on pheasants, too.

common to any shotgun occurs here. In my experience, the choke markings roughly corresponded to the shooting results.

Shooting, beyond doubt, is the way to find out about a new gun and that is what I did with this Winchester.

First was an informal trap shoot and I fired two rounds, using only the Full chokes. However, I shot one round with the upper barrel, and one round with the under barrel. I shot well up to my standard with field guns—or nearly any gun—in both rounds. I did have to cover the bird a little more to get a clean break than with a trap gun, probably because of the field dimensions of the stock. And it might—I say *might*—have been that I needed to cover the bird a little more with the under barrel than the over barrel.

This impressed me. I came away with the firm belief that at least those two choke tubes shot where they looked, along with the gun, and that for once I had laid hands on a factory gun which was long enough in the stock for me to shoot in shirtsleeves. However, it was the straight and thick stock that worked—it is not a very long stock.

It was quite comfortable. It is not unusual for me to get bitten by a new gun in one way or another. This one was quite comfortable and mannerly throughout that whole fifty rounds.

Set up as the gun is with the 3-inch chamber, and therefore magnum weight and magnum stocking, it is bound to be a very comfortable gun to shoot with any normal 2¾-inch field or target load. The recoil pad, which my tender desk-driver's shoulder appreciates, helps also at clay targets.

The weight of this gun—7½ pounds—is the one fly in an otherwise most handsome all-around ointment. A sturdy and vigorous man would find it no impediment at all. A lot of people think I am reasonably sturdy and reasonably vigorous, but I am also lazy and I have been spoiled for some shooting with normal American guns by the use of lively 6 to 6½ pound double guns. That is a personal note. If I were to use this gun for all my shooting, and I did more than my share of missing, it would be my fault and not the gun's.

I tried, of course, more lively targets. Before I ever got out hunting, I shot a couple of rounds of Skeet, with the Improved Cylinder tubes in place. Again, I shot right up to my usual Skeet standard with field guns. I am not, emphatically not, a competitive shooter, I probably have not fired 100 rounds of Skeet in 20 or 30 years of shooting. I am purely a sociable shooter at this game or at trap and am entirely happy to break 20 birds in a round at either game. I tell you that so that the shooting performance doesn't reflect on the gun. Of course, Improved Cylinder is not Skeet choke—it is enough tighter to require closer holding than Skeet chokes do.

The next thing was a dove shoot. And once again there is only the need to report that things were as usual. I shot better than I usually do, but that was because I had fired a hundred shots at claybirds from this gun with these loads in the 30 days prior to the opening of the dove season. I began the day with a combination of Improved Cylinder and Full chokes. That is not my favored combination, which is Cylinder and Full, but it was as close to that useful arrangement as I could get with the factory Winchokes. In an hour, I saw the Full barrel was more liability than asset, switched to Improved Cylinder, and my stock went up immediately.

The fellow who wants the social and procedural advantages of a nice-looking over-under and wants, at the same time, to own just one 12-gauge shotgun, and shoots a fair sampling of the kind of shooting Americans can get, should try and buy, or buy and try, the Winchester 101 with Winchokes. It is too expensive at $1125 for a knock-around gun, but it is sturdy enough to be a good companion for a long time and versatile enough to be no hindrance in any shotgun hunting.

Technical Data

The Winchester 101 Winchoke model with 28-inch barrels is 45¼ inches long. The sample shot had a length of pull of 14⅛ inches, with drop at comb of 1½ inches, and at heel of 2¾ inches. The recoil pad is a ventilated model, one inch thick, and measuring 5⅛ inches tall and 1⅝ inches wide. The gun, Winchokes in place, and un-

loaded, weighs 7½ pounds; it balances 5½ inches ahead of the trigger. The gun is equipped with the standard Winchester barrel selector-safety combination, which works in the standard fashion.

The Winchokes require some specific management, but nothing onerous. The factory advises they should be turned tightly in place and that seems a good idea since during the first 50 rounds fired, 25 with each barrel, the unused choke tube loosened itself during the firing of 25 shots. This was undoubtedly due to its not being tightened up enough; subsequently this was cured by more attention to detail, although the furnished spanner had to be managed carefully during this chore. It tended to slip if not held tightly in place.

During the press introduction of this gun some time back, an introduction which was made for convenience's sake very early and the press asked to hold the release date, the factory people advised that shooting the gun without any Winchoke in place provided, of course, a Cylinder bore. However, this was not recommended and would be viewed sternly by the factory should any damage occur. Given that careful fitting and fine threads are involved, that is not much of a restriction in average use of the gun.

Personal Notes

If I would keep the gun, and it is a sad fact of life that a gun editor cannot keep every gun, I would get with a friend who had the kind of polishing equipment it takes and I would create a Cylinder choke out of one of the modified tubes; I would open up one of the Full tubes and one of the Improved Cylinders slightly; then I would polish them all, very cleanly. Subsequently, I would probably do almost all of my shooting with a cylinder and an open Improved Cylinder choke in place, and once in a while find a use for the somewhat open Full choke tube.

The rest of them would be there for really special stuff. I would expect the slightly opened Full tube to handle large quantities of large shot very well, for instance; one or the other of the combinations would doubtless be best when it came to buckshot. And if I chose to shoot really cheap handloads, without plastic wads and the like, I could use the chokes of the gun instead of the technology of shotshells to provide myself with good patterns.

These things apart, I would see no reason in the world to alter the Winchoked Winchester 101 in any way.

Ken Warner

Model Six Rifle

It weighs 8 pounds, 10 ounces, topped with a Leupold Vari-X-III 2.5x8 scope in Leupold one-piece mount, and hosting a ⅞-inch leather carrying strap in quick-detachable swivels. The barrel is 22⅛ inches long, and the over-all length an even 42 inches. Chambered for the 30-06 cartridge, with a 4-round detachable box magazine of heavy gauge steel, it's Remington's new Model Six pump action centerfire rifle. Replacing the time-tested Model 760, the Model Six has several redesigned areas, including the upper portion of the receiver, the magazine, magazine latch, forearm shape, checkering on both the forearm and buttstock pistol grip, action bars, and the Monte Carlo buttstock dimensions.

The gracefully tapered barrel on the test gun measured 0.655-inch in diameter at its crowned muzzle. Topping the barrel is a ramp-mounted front sight with a 0.103-inch diameter brass bead, and barrel-mounted open rear sight with U-shaped notch; the rear sight is screw adjustable for windage, and changes elevation via a sliding ramp. The mounted scope prevents use of the open sights, but with the scope removed the open sights are usable over the scope mount base.

The Model Six action features a forged steel receiver, which measured 1.230 inches wide on the test gun. When the action is locked closed, the ejection port on the right hand side is closed with a black plastic ejection port cover to retard the entrance of dust and dirt into the action. The cover slides back and forth with the bolt, via studs located on the interior surface at each end of the cover.

The trigger plate assembly is retained in the lower rear portion of the receiver via two pins, and driving these out will allow the assembly to be pulled downward and removed for cleaning. The crossbolt safety is located in the rear of the trigger guard behind the trigger; on the test gun the safety measured 0.342-inch in diameter, one of the largest currently available on any production sporting arm. When projecting from the right side of the guard, the safety is "on," blocking the trigger; if projecting from the left side a bright red encircling band will be visible, indicating the safety is off, and the rifle is in firing mode.

Located on the forward end of the trigger plate assembly are the action bar lock (left side) and the magazine latch (right side). The trigger guard is constructed of a non-ferrous material,

The Remington Model Six pump action centerfire sporting rifle.

Left—The magazine latch on the Model Six has been redesigned to provide a larger, more positive surface area. Below—The detachable box magazine on the Model Six has been redesigned and constructed of heavier gauge steel.

Right—A decorative feature of the Model Six is the imbedding of a cartridge case head of the appropriate caliber into the steel ahead of the receiver; this feature used to be common on Remington rifles several decades ago.

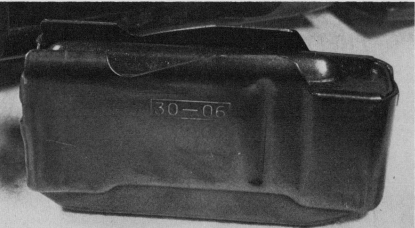

The breech bolt of the Model Six is a rotary design, with bolt action type locking lugs.

while the components of the assembly are of steel. The action bar lock is a steel stamping, grooved on the lower edge to retard finger slippage; pushing up and in on the lock allows the bolt to be retracted by pulling the forearm rearward. (If the rifle has been fired, or the trigger pulled, the action bar lock is automatically dis-engaged, permitting operating of the slide assembly. The magazine latch has been beefed-up a bit; on the test gun it measured 0.463-inch long by 0.094-inch wide, with a grooved surface to reduce finger slippage. The magazine on the test gun weighed 3.18 ounces, empty.

The action of the Model Six utilizes a rotary breech bolt with four lugs toward the forward end, and a fifth lug farther back. As the action bar assembly moves the breech bolt forward, cam pins rotate the bolt until the lugs are locked home. The firing pin protrudes from the rear of the breech bolt for a distance of 0.460-inch, held there by a retractor spring. Pulling the trigger causes the hammer to move forward, striking the firing pin, driving it forward against the spring pressure and into the primer. With the hammer at rest, the firing pin will still protrude a distance of 0.348-inch. Retracting the forearm moves the rear of the slide assembly against a flange on the rear section of the firing pin; movement of the firing pin to the rear starts the primary cocking of the hammer.

The buttstock and forearm on the Model Six are of American walnut, with the durable du Pont "bowling ball" finish. The forearm on the test gun measured 8 9/16 inches long, including the black plastic tip and white spacer. The forearm has been redesigned, is pear-shaped in cross-section with a rounded, palm-fitting bottom, and cut checkering at 20 lines-per-inch. Tapered in width from a maximum of nearly two inches toward the rear to just under 1½ inches at the tip, the forearm is reduced in width along the upper edges for the fingers and thumb. The cut checkering is good, but does have some flat-topped diamonds.

The buttstock on the Model Six is the Monte Carlo type, with a cheekpiece on the left side, and a rounded comb, fluted on each side. A black plastic checkered buttplate, and a black plastic pistol grip cap, both with white spacers, adorn the stock, and cut checkering at 20 lines-per-inch grace the sides of the pistol grip. The pistol grip is a full one, with the distance from the tip of the trigger to the leading edge of the pistol grip cap measuring an even four inches. The circumference of the pistol grip at its smallest measured 4 11/32 inches on the test gun.

All metal surfaces on the Model Six test gun were blued, except for the cross-bolt safety, although the trigger, rear and front sides, and magazine latch did not show the same degree of polish as the barrel and receiver. The finish on the barrel was a deep blue-black, while the box magazine, receiver, action bars, and action tube assembly tended more toward a well polished deep blue. Wood-to-metal fit at the receiver/buttstock junction was satisfactory, with a minimum amount of wood projecting above the metal surfaces.

Regardless of how well a rifle may function, or how good the finish, it's how it shoots that counts. Following the examination, the Model Six was taken to the range, along with an assortment of 30-06 factory loads to see what kind of accuracy it would produce. Since the Model Six is a hunting rifle—it's the first shot that counts, and if you can't do the job in three shots, you've got a problem—three-shot groups were fired from the bench at 100 yards. Sandbags beneath the forearm and buttstock stabilized the rifle, and the Leupold scope was turned to the 8x magnification. The ammunition used consisted of Federal, Frontier, and Remington brands in bullet weights of 125, 150, 165, and 180-grain sizes.

Overall, nearly 200 factory rounds were put through the Model Six. The smallest three-shot group obtained was with Federal's 165-grain boattail soft point round; it measured 1 3/16 inches center-to-center, only 1/16-inch smaller than the smallest group obtained with the 125-grain Federal soft point load. The majority of the groups with the Federal cartridges, and the other two brands, were closer to two inches, which is still satisfactory. But for a comparatively lightweight barrel on a big game rifle, this is definitely satisfactory, and better than many bolt action rifles.

Currently priced at $399.95, the Remington Model Six is a handy pump action hunting rifle for shooters having a preference for this type of action. The craftsmanship was good, accuracy very satisfactory, finish good, and reliability on the test rifle perfect; no misfires, feeding problems, or extraction problems were encountered, although it is possible some bullet shapes might pose a problem, and so might improperly sized handloads. There is also a Remington Model Four, which replaces the Remington 742 similarly.
Larry Sterett

Armsport Unsingle

Armsport's Premier Unsingle Trap gun is manufactured in Brescia, Italy, by Fabbrica Armi Castelli, and "Castellani Gardone-Italy" appears on the lower left side of the receiver in script, with "Armsport Miami Fla." in script on the lower right side of the receiver. The test gun weighed 8 pounds, 10 ounces, and with a barrel length of 33 15/16 inches, it measured 51½ inches over-all.

The Unsingle locks with an under-bolt, which measured 1.228 inches

The Armsport Premier 12 gauge Unsingle Trap gun is chambered for standard length cartridges, and while it may appear a bit unusual, it breaks clay targets with gusto.

Above—The high ventilated steel rib on the Unsingle is free to expand longitudinally as the barrel heats during shooting. Note the one-piece rib has a trestle-style structure.

Above—The Unsingle features a detachable trigger assembly. Note the quality of checkering on the pistol grip, and also the wood-to-metal fit at the receiver/buttstock junction.

Right—The Unsingle has a cylindrical cocking rod which passes between the sides of the divided rear lump. Note the upper portion of the monobloc has a rubber plug to act as a "snap cap" for the upper firing pin, should the trigger be pulled the second time.

wide on the test gun. The lump is divided to permit passage of the cocking lever, and the base sections of the lump project through recesses in the bottom of the receiver, reducing the receiver depth. (The receiver on the test gun measured 1.684 inches wide, and 2.668 inches deep.) Except for the frame-mounted firing pins, the entire firing mechanism on the Unsingle is detachable as a unit. The trigger mechanism is housed in the detachable trigger guard assembly, which is removable or detachable by pushing in on the checkered release on the left side of the guard, at the rear, and pulling down and forward on the rear of the trigger guard. Steel cylinders contain the coil hammer springs, and the large, rounded hammers are drilled with 0.280-inch diameter holes to reduce their weight and shorten lock time. The hammer mechanism is mechanical, so recoil is not a matter of concern for the second shot, when over-under barrels are used in place of the Unsingle barrel.

The trigger on the test gun was 0.303-inch wide. The trigger face was smooth, slightly convex, and the trigger had a slight twist to the right to position the trigger finger. Let-off on the test gun measured 4¼ pounds and 3½ pounds for the first and second pulls, respectively. Only the first pull was used when shooting the Unsingle, but the second pull would be used when firing both barrels of an over-under on the same receiver.

The Unsingle receiver walls measured 0.235-inch thick on the test gun, and decoration consisted of deeply engraved V-shaped grooves which produced a sculptured shadow effect. The areas outlined by the grooving included the trigger plate region, borders of the receiver, top lever, bottom of the trigger guard, forearm iron and latch plate, upper tang, bottom of the lump, etc. Otherwise, there is very little decoration on the Unsingle, although some simple engraving graces the top surface of the top lever shaft, and the outer surface of the trunnions, in addition to stippling on the upper barrel shoulders and the receiver shoulders.

The Unsingle does not use a hinge pin, but hardened steel trunnions on the inside of the receiver walls. This permits a shallower receiver design, since hooks on the sides of the monobloc, on each side of the Unsingle barrel, pivot around the trunnions. By having the bottom surfaces of the divided rear lump of the monobloc project through the bottom of the receiver, and the shoulders on the upper portion of the monobloc wedge against matching shoulders on the receiver walls, the Unsingle is designed to withstand extensive shooting.

As mentioned, the Armsport Unsingle uses a monobloc barrel construction, with the under barrel sleeved into the lower part of the monobloc. Exending forward from 2.690 inches long upper portion of the steel monobloc is a barrel-shaped, 10¼ inches long walnut plug; it fills in the upper part of the forearm where the over barrel would normally be located. (Perazzi uses a similar design, but the walnut section is flat-sided.)

Topping the Unsingle barrel of the test gun was a raised, ventilated steel rib having a slight taper; it measured 0.435-inch wide at the breech, and 0.431-inch wide at the muzzle, with the top surface finely cross-hatched. Attached at the breech, the balance of the rib floats via inverted T-shaped contacts at the muzzle, and just ahead of the forearm; it has a trestle-type construction with a base section, a middle section 0.435-inch above the base section, and the top rib 0.135-inch above the middle section. Five sloping posts support the middle rib, while 21 smaller such posts support the top section. The top section is 1.4185 inches above the center of the barrel at the muzzle; a 0.141-inch diameter cylindrical fluorescent muzzle bead tops the rib, but there is no center bead.

The Unsingle has a selective automatic ejector, located on the right side of the monobloc. Unfired shells are raised 0.343-inch for removal with the finger, but fired casings are tossed two paces to the rear.

On the test gun the metal finish was very good, with the barrel, forearm iron and latch, trigger guard, top lever, and safety slide being a high luster blue-black; the ventilated rib was a less glossy non-glare satin black. The forearm latch plate, trigger, and receiver had a coin finish, with the appearance of buffed nickel. Both sides of the top lever thumb pad were checkered, although the lever will unlock the bolt only when pushed to the right. The thumb pad of the non-automatic safety is also checkered, and it is one of the best shaped safeties seen on any current production shotgun; when pushed to the rear, a large "S" is exposed ahead of the slide to indicate "safe."

The walnut buttstock on the Armsport Unsingle had a length of pull of 14¹¹/₁₆ inches, with drops at the comb, heel of the Monte Carlo, and heel of the stock of 1³/₁₆, 1⁷/₁₆, and 2 inches respectively. The nose of the comb is rounded, and fluted on both sides, while the butt of the test gun was fitted with a ⁹/₁₆-inch thick black rubber recoil pad of Italian manufacture. (A slight amount of cast-off was present at the comb and heel.) At its smallest, the full pistol grip measured 5⅝ inches in circumference; the grip does not have a cap, but it is flared out slightly at the bottom edge, and there's a Wundhammer swell on the right side.

The forearm measured 10³/₁₆ inches in length, and just over two inches in width, with a U-shaped cross-section having a slight flat on the bottom and finger flutes along the upper edge. Both the forearm and buttstock have an oil finish, and were hand checkered at 26 lines-per-inch, with a two line border; the diamonds were sharp, and complete right out to the edge, making it very functional.

Wood-to-metal fit: the wood-to-wood fit on the Unsingle was very good, with the majority of the junctions being flush, and the maximum wood-above-metal projection amounted to a maximum of 0.025-inch at the receiver, and 0.050-inch at the forearm iron. That amount of projection, and more is fairly common on many more expensive shotguns.

Following the examination, the Unsingle was patterned at 40 yards. Starting with Winchester's AA Plus light (2¾, 1⅛, 8) load, the Unsingle produced a five-shot pattern average of 70.1 percent, centered 14½ inches high, and nearly two inches to the right of the point-of-aim. Next, Peters Blue Magic light load of No. 8 shot was tried, and this time the five-shot average was 72.0 percent, centered just over 16 inches high, and nearly an inch to the right of the point-of-aim. Switching to the Peters Blue Magic heavy (3, 1⅛, 7½) load, the Unsingle was checked once more; the five shots averaged 71.8 percent, centered just under 16 inches high, and right at the point-of-aim laterally. With the loads used, the Armsport Unsingle produced good full choke patterns. The centers were a bit high, depending on what a shooter prefers, but not far off the point-of-aim laterally, regardless of the shot size.

The Unsingle test gun handled well, balancing at a point ½-inch ahead of the pivot point for the barrels. After the patterning session, nearly 500 additional rounds of assorted factory loads and handloads were put through the Unsingle, without experiencing any problems, either during firing or with ejection. (The top lever is off-center to the right on the top tang, when the Unsingle is closed; this is to provide for wearing-in of the locking bolt, and the Unsingle should be snapped shut, and not closed by pushing the top lever to the left when locking.) Overall, the Unsingle performed well, producing well-distributed full choke patterns, and really powdering the targets, as long as this shooter did his part, and the fact the gun shot high was an advantage on rising birds.

Priced under $3000.00, the Armsport Premier Unsingle comes complete with an extra detachable trigger assembly, plus a fitted, Italian-leather, luggage-style, custom-crafted carrying case with combination locks, at no extra charge. The case with the test gun weighed 8 pounds, 10 ounces, empty, or the same as the gun. Leather straps around the case are standard.   *Larry Sterett*

Benjamin 347

"A modern classic": That is perhaps one of the most appropriate descriptions of the Benjamin 347 pneumatic rifle, if one is guided by history alone. Indeed, in the field of American pneumatic or pump-up guns, the Benjamin Air Rifle Company stands as *the* pioneer, the first Benjamin air rifle having been manufactured back in 1882. Its pumping mechanism was very similar to that of a common bicycle pump, with the pump itself attached below the barrel, where it still is on all of the multipump pneumatic guns.

Almost one hundred years and several series of guns later (some of which included both pneumatic and CO² rifles and pistols) Benjamin is still going strong with their current models. In pneumatic long guns, these include the model 340, a smoothbore BB caliber, the model 342 in 22 cal., the 347, a 177 cal. and the subject of our test, plus the repeating models 3100 and 3120 in BB and 22-calibers, respectively. Benjamin currently produces only one basic pneumatic air pistol, available as the model 130 (smoothbore BB cal.), 132 (22-cal.) and 137 (177-cal.). Although the above models don't exactly represent a wide selection, they are nevertheless extensively proven after decades of production and continuous upgrading. In recent years, Benjamin has been phasing out a variety of CO² rifles and pistols, devoting all of their efforts to the production of pneumatic guns instead. Generally staying in the background of the current airgun scene, the low profile of the Benjamin Air Rifle Company apparently has not kept it from reaping some of the benefits of the current airgun revolution across the U.S. and abroad. The fact that in 1976 Benjamin purchased Sheridan Products, Inc., manufacturers of the famous Sheridan pneumatic air rifles, can be cited as strong evidence supporting the ongoing success of Benjamin.

The Model 347, in 177-cal., can be regarded as the epitome of the Benjamin line. It is the shortest of the pneumatic rifles for adults produced in the U.S. at this time. Only 34¾ inches long, yet weighing a full 6 pounds, this model has an uncannily solid feel that can add greatly to a shooter's confidence. The 347 could almost be called a carbine, were it not for the fact that it has an 18 ⅝" barrel. The latter is made of brass and is beautifully rifled, having 6 shallow grooves with a right-hand twist.

The latest version of this rifle sports a well-proportioned stock made of American walnut, with an oil finish and checkering on the pistol grip and on the fore-end, which is also the pump lever. The buttstock has a trace of a Monte Carlo cheekpiece and its length of pull is a 12⅞". Over-all, the stock looks very nice and is massive enough (especially the fore-end) to accommodate the biggest pair of hands with ease. My only suggestion in this particular area would be to add a rubber buttplate, since that area of the stock is one of the first to get scratched and dented, especially after a couple of trips afield. This is, after all, a "working" pneumatic rifle, intended primarily for pest control, small-game hunting, and plinking.

The barrel and the pump assembly tube have a tough matte finish that is in keeping with the over-all ruggedness of this gun. The bolt, trigger, trigger guard, rear sight and screws are blued.

Regarding sights, the Benjamin 347 comes with a stout ramp-type front blade and a stepped leaf open rear sight. The latter is screw-adjustable for windage and elevation. The 347 is capable of far better accuracy than that attainable with this open rear sight. Realizing this, Benjamin offers the No. 273 peep sight, for around $5 extra. This peep sight, which is also fully adjustable, increases the shooter's ability to obtain smaller groups. The peep sight slides into a special notch on the left side of the receiver, just behind the pellet-loading track. Also available from Benjamin is a set of bases for telesight use. The set of two, which retails for $10, mounts astride the barrel and accepts most standard tip-off telesight mounts.

Installing a telescopic sight on a pneumatic (pump up) rifle can be a bit

The Benjamin Model 347, a true modern classic.

Above—Only 34¾" long, the 347 is perfect for women or men of small build, yet feels rugged and solid, due to its ample stock. Right—The author's own Model 342 in 22 cal. (left gun), was purchased back in 1968. Notice the older style, slimmer stock and ribbed pump handle, absence of checkering. The 347 sports a more massive, more elegant stock and larger trigger guard.

Below—Ten-meter benchrest accuracy tests produced groups averaging ⁹/₁₆" center-to-center maximum spread with H & N Match pellets.

Above—Benjamin's own No. 273 adjustable peep sight is practically a must for squeezing out all of the inherent precision of this rifle.

sticky for two main reasons. First, the peculiar way in which this type of gun must be grasped during the pumping operation is such that a telesight is then an awkward object that only gets in the way. The second and perhaps the most important reason is that the zero of the scope will be extremely difficult to maintain on this type of rifle. The point of impact will shift vertically not only with the number of pumps, but also with the *pumping cadence for a given string of shots at the same number of pumps!* The shift, admittedly, is not that marked, but it is something to keep in mind when going afield after game. The enthusiast who insists on using a telesight on his pneumatic rifle must be prepared to practice exhaustively and to study his rifle's ballistics closely.

My test 347 came with a trigger letoff weight of 3½ lbs. The single-stage trigger is crisp and, with the aforementioned weight, it contributes greatly to the surprisingly accurate shooting that can be done with this rifle. The trigger is non-adjustable, and I don't recommend any tampering with the sear, either, in order to make it "smoother." Such tampering, especially by amateurs, can easily result in accidental discharges. There is a manual thumb safety located on the tang. It is very effective, blocking the trigger completely when it is applied. It cannot be applied when the bolt is not cocked. The latter is pulled all the way to the rear until it engages the sear with a loud "click." My test rifle had a bolt cocking effort of 22 lbs., which is not difficult at all to handle.

Testing the Benjamin 347 was a sheer pleasure on two counts: the rifle is a darn good shooter and I needed the exercise. Pumping the 347 can be a physically demanding experience to the tyro; however, if a fairly slow, even pumping cadence is adopted, long shooting sessions can be had without feeling unduly tired. The maximum recommended number of pumps is ten. Beyond that, you're running the risk of air-locking the valve. This is a situation in which too much air has been compressed into the storage chamber and the hammer strike on the stem is unable to overcome that air pressure.

Most shooting applications with this rifle, such as plinking, target practice and small pest control can be handled effectively with just 3 to 5 pumps. With five pumps, the average muzzle velocity of my test 347 was 560 fps, using H&N Match pellets. Three pumps produced an average of 460 fps, which is still quite brisk and entirely suitable for all of the aforementioned

applications. With ten pumps, the muzzle velocity climbed up to an average of 743 fps, again using H&N Match pellets. Hobby pellets, which are just about the lightest 177-cal. pellets available (about 7 grains), averaged 762 fps with ten pumps. The new and excellent Beeman Ram Jet heavy weight "silhouette" pellets (9.6 grains) developed an average of 725 fps. Any of the above 10-pump velocities is capable of bowling over most squirrels and cottontails at up to 25 yards with a head shot.

As far as accuracy goes, the Benjamin 347 is capable of grouping all of its shots easily within a ¾" circle at 10 meters (33 ft.), from the bench and using open sights. Most air rifles, foreign and domestic, show an affinity for certain pellets and my test sample was no exception. It seemed to prefer a diet of H&N Match pellets, followed closely by Silver Jet and Ram Jet (the last two turning in almost identical groups). The average over-all group size with H&N was $9/16$", while Silver Jet and Ram Jet averaged $11/16$" each. That was using open sights. After installing a Benjamin peep sight, the average H&N group size shrank down to ½". All accuracy tests were conducted at 5 pumps; group sizes are on centers.

The Benjamin 347 is certainly not a target rifle. It has plenty of power and accuracy for field shooting at medium ranges, which is up to 30 yards or so. The absence of recoil is a definite plus, but some people no doubt will object to its rather loud discharge, which is typical of most multi-pump pneumatics. The fact that this rifle can be pumped up and carried loaded and cocked for those sudden shots is another (and important) consideration for field use. On the other hand, if a second shot must be made, the time and noise of re-pumping will give your quarry ample opportunity to seek safer grounds. In any event, when using air rifles for hunting, the first shot must be the only one!

Retailing for approximately $73, the Benjamin 347 is undoubtedly still a good value, even by today's inflated standards. Its quality and workmanship are in keeping with the fine tradition set by the Benjamin firm over many decades. If treated and used properly, this rifle will last a lifetime with only minimal repairs. I've seen many vintage Benjamin rifles still going strong after 30 years of use. Let's hope that we can continue to enjoy this classic and perhaps newer airguns from America's oldest pneumatic gun producers.   *J.I. Galan*

Four New 22 Mini-Matics

Except for a few limited-production pieces, the very small automatic pistols made before World War Two were chambered for one cartridge—the 6.35mm Browning, known in America as the 25 Auto. These small guns have always been used primarily for personal defense, and in this category the cartridge has one good point: the centerfire semi-rimmed case and jacketed bullet feed well in semi-auto actions. There are several minuses, limited shocking power and expensive ammunition among them.

A much more effective and practical cartridge for small automatics is the 22 rimfire round. Its unjacketed lead bullet will usually deform and stop in the target, transferring all of its energy. Also, it's inexpensive, so you can practice often without straining the finances. The 22 has some minuses. The rimmed case does not stack well in pistol magazines, and the un-jacketed lead bullet sometimes deforms on ramps that are too short or too steep, causing jams. Some early, small 22-cal. pistols were simply reworks of original 25 designs, and frequent malfunctions were the result.

Around 1947, the first of the small 22 automatics began to appear. Vincenzo Bernadelli of Italy introduced a tiny auto in 22 Short and 22 Long chambering. Other Italian makers, Armi Galesi and Rino Galesi, also made small autos for these rounds, and those chambered for the 22 Long are probably the last guns to be made for that practically obsolete cartridge. In Spain, Astra made the Model 2000, chambered for the 22 Short only, and

One of the first of the post-war small 22 pistols, the Astra Model 2000 "Cub," chambered for 22 Short.

The Sterling Model 302 pistol, right side.

Right—The Sterling Model 302, field-stripped.

sold in the U.S. as the "Cub." This gun was later translated into the Colt "Junior" pistol, in 22 and 25 caliber. In 1950, Beretta of Italy introduced the Model 950B in 22 Short as the "Minx," and a companion version in 25 Auto, the "Jetfire." Importation of the European pistols was stopped by Federal regulations in 1968, and the "Junior" was dropped from the Colt line in 1973.

In 1970, Smith & Wesson began production of their Model 61 in 22 Long Rifle chambering, marketed as the "Escort." Based on the 1908 Bayard design, it was not well-received, and was dropped in 1973. Meanwhile, in 1972, Sterling Arms

re-designed and improved the Rino Galesi design, and brought it out as their Model 302 in 22 Long Rifle. Some early Sterlings had a few functioning problems, but these were soon corrected, and the Model 302 is still in production, including a stainless steel version.

Over the past two years, three more small U.S.-made 22 automatics have become available on the market, one appearing just a few months ago. I have tested all four of them extensively, including firing with the new high-performance loads such as the Stinger, Xpediter, and Yellow Jacket. Let's look at each of these pistols, in the order of their appearance.

Sterling Model 302

The Sterling is a true hammerless, striker-fired pistol of all-steel construction, and is heavier and more sturdily built than the original gun on which its design is based. The extractor is thicker, and has better mechanical advantage. The takedown button at the rear is more recessed, almost level with the frame, and less likely to be accidentally depressed. The grips are designed for a good hold, having just a hint of a thumb-rest. The manual safety is positioned for easy operation with the tip of the thumb, and directly blocks movement of the trigger when applied.

Below—The barrel of the Beretta tips up for loading.

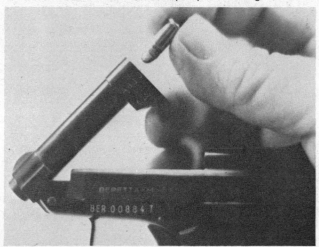

The Beretta Model 950BS pistol, left side.

The magazine is of particularly good design. It's of very strong two-piece construction, with a vertical box folded around the rear and spot-welded to the forward portion. Internally, the rear edges of the front part form a guide for the cartridge rims. In addition to this, there are side lugs on the follower which move in a diagonal track to tilt the follower, adjusting it to keep the cartridge angle right as succeeding rounds are fired.

My own Model 302, of fairly recent manufacture, does not like Stingers or Xpediters, but works perfectly with everything else. In recent years, the Sterling has become very popular with trappers and fishermen, especially the stainless steel version.

Beretta Model 950BS

After being unavailable in the U.S. for more than ten years, the Beretta Minx returned, via the renowned J.L. Galef firm of New York and the Firearms International factory (now Beretta U.S.A. Corporation) in Accokeek, Maryland.

Produced under license from Beretta of Italy, the new Minx has some notable differences, and is now designated Model 950BS. The "S" added to the model letters refers to a manual safety at the left rear of the frame which directly blocks the sear when applied. The firing pin is now an inertia type, allowing a safe chamber-loaded carry with the hammer fully down. This is the only pistol of the new group having an external hammer, and the only one in 22 Short chambering.

Another exclusive feature of the Beretta is a lever on the left side which releases the barrel to swing upward for loading. It's never necessary to cycle the slide by hand, so the grip serrations at the rear of the slide are primarily for looks. As in the original 950B, there is no extractor. Ejection of the fired case relies on residual gas pressure and the low adhesion factor of the 22 Short case. The grips on the new pistol are a little thinner, with more shallow curves at the edges, and the gun feels better in the hand.

There is not a wide variety of 22 Short loads, but I have fired all of the major brands, and mine works perfectly with all of them, including hollow points. In regard to quality, it's as much a Beretta as any of the Italian-made originals, and that's saying a lot.

FTL Auto Nine

John Raymond Wilkinson, father of the OMC Back-Up and the Terry Carbine, designed this neat little pistol for FTL Marketing. The "Nine" in the name is a reference to the pistol's fully loaded capacity. The Auto Nine is a striker-fired true hammerless, and although it is smaller than the others covered here, it is chambered for the 22 Long Rifle round. As with all of Ray's designs, there are several unusual features. At the muzzle, the barrel is surrounded by a screw-in bushing that is well-fitted, keeping the barrel centered and supported. The manual safety, which directly blocks the sear, is a push-button cross-bolt type. When it's pushed toward the right to off-safe position, a red ring is exposed on the right side.

The extractor assembly has no pins or separate springs. It's composed of two spring-leaves retained by slots and circular tabs, the inner leaf bearing the extractor beak. When the striker is cocked, its rear edge is visible at the rear of the slide as an indicator. Internally, the striker has a large sear lug and a very short firing pin point, and breakage should be rare. The frame is of alloy, and the steel slide is finished in hard chrome, giving a two-tone effect that is very attractive.

When firing the Auto Nine, I found that Xpediter rounds often failed to cycle the slide fully, but it worked per-

The Jennings J-22 pistol, left side.

Above—The FTL Auto Nine pistol, right side.

Right—The Auto Nine pistol has an unusual screw-in muzzle bushing.

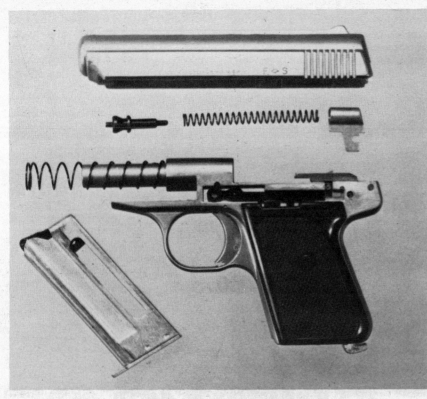

The Jennings pistol, field-stripped. Note the unique shape of the solid striker.

fectly with all other loads, including the Stinger. It should be noted that the company recommends only regular high velocity 22 Long Rifle cartridges.

Jennings Model J-22

Bruce Jennings, whose father produces the Raven P-25 automatic, recently formed his own company to make a sleek little pistol in 22 Long Rifle chambering. While there are some internal similarities to the Raven, the Jennings is quite different. Its external appearance is very Walther-ish, almost like a Model TPH without a hammer. The Jennings is striker-fired, and the striker is of unusual design. It's a solid piece, with a circular collar near the front which contacts the sear, and an extended spring-guide at the rear, the tip visible when the striker is cocked.

The manual safety, perfectly located at the top of the left grip panel, is very efficient. When slid back to the on-safe position, it moves a solid bar of steel beneath a large cross-pin in the sear, blocking any movement. The cartridge feed ramp on the frame is wide and well-shaped, and the delivery angle from the magazine is perfect. Although the slide, like the frame, is of alloy, the breechblock section is a steel insert, to prevent wear in the critical lower rail area.

The Jennings functioned with everything I tried in it, including Stingers and Xpediters, a good performance for the lowest-priced of the guns covered here.

At this point, it would be well to note two important things about the small 22 pistols in general:

With most of them, there will be a particular load that a particular gun will like best, so you should try them with several brands and types. Given the configuration of the 22 cartridge, an occasional malfunction is not unacceptable, and can happen with the best of guns.

The other important thing to remember is to avoid holding the gun loosely. In such small pistols, the slide weight and spring tension are rather critically balanced, and allowing the entire gun to move a fraction within the hand during recoil can be enough to cause a malfunction.

Properly handled, though, and with the right cartridges, today's small 22 automatics are outstandingly reliable, and it's no longer necessary to turn to a 25 auto just for the feeding factor. For personal protection, I wouldn't hesitate to carry any one of the four guns covered here.

I haven't included any target data, as the light weight and tiny fixed sights of these guns make them less than ideal for serious range work. When fired from a rest, though, all of them will group surprisingly well. Fired from a rest at fifteen yards, any of them will group into three or four inches, and this is more than adequate for plinking or personal defense. With a steady one-hand hold and no rest, hits on drink cans at the same range average five out of six.

Now that the small 22 autos have become more reliable, several U.S. gunmakers are working on double action versions, to fill the place of the restricted Walther TPH. Among these are the resurrected TP-70 pistol, and all-new guns that resemble the Walther by CB Arms and Iver Johnson. For details on these, see Handguns Today, pgs. 101 and 103 in this issue.   *J.B. Wood*

Specifications

Sterling Model 302
Length: 4¾ inches
Height: 3⅜ inches
Width: 1 inch
Barrel length: 2⅜ inches
Weight: 13 ounces
Magazine capacity: 6 rounds

Manufacturer:
Sterling Arms Corp., 211 Grand St., Lockport, NY 14094
Price: $104.95

Beretta Model 950BS
Length: 4⅝ inches
Height: 3⁷/₁₆ inches
Width: 1 inch
Barrel length: 2⅜ inches
Weight: 10 ounces
Magazine capacity: 6 rounds

Distributor:
J.L. Galef & Son, Inc., 85 Chambers St., New York, NY 10007
Price: $169.95

FTL Auto Nine
Length: 4⅜ inches
Height: 3 inches
Width: ⅞ inch
Barrel length: 2⅛ inches
Weight: 8¼ ounces
Magazine capacity: 8 rounds

Distributor:
FTL Marketing Corp., 12521-3 Oxnard St., North Hollywood, CA 91601
Price: $199.95

Jennings J-22
Length: 4 15/16 inches
Height: 3⅜ inches
Width: ⅞ inch
Barrel length: 2½ inches
Weight: 13 ounces
Magazine capacity: 6 rounds

Manufacturer:
Jennings Firearms, Inc., 1135 "J" Centre Dr., Industry, CA 91789
Price: $89.95

Model 77 DJV Mauser is made in 243 Winchester, 308 Winchester and 7x64mm, and aimed at the precision field rifle market.

Krico 660S is a sniper rifle of considerable refinement—adjusting comb, ventilated forearm, muzzle device, oversize bolt handle.

The Feinwerkbau CO_2 match pistol shown at Nuremberg offers traditional free pistol configuration.

by RAYMOND CARANTA

THE SHOWS OF

The IWA show in Nuremberg becomes professional right at the entrance.

eyes full of dreams looking at his pets of the year. In spite of the 1974 depression and more restrictive policies of many governments about guns, these shows multiplied and became soon major social events where manufacturers, importers, dealers and writers used to gather to talk around new products.

This year, the two most important European shows for professional visitors were the Brussels "Hunifi-show" organized by M. Christian de Moffarts in Brussels from Februrary 15 to 17 and "IWA 81," held in Nurem-

Tᴇɴ ʏᴇᴀʀꜱ ago, the idea of a large gun show "a l'américaine" would have seemed crazy to the conservative European. In that time, not so remote, guns were treated somewhat like sex, in an atmosphere of relative discretion. Since then, sex and guns have significantly evolved, not so much in the way of practicing but, rather, in the way of displaying them.

The first gun shows, held in Paris, Marseilles and some other places, covering antiques or new stuff were huge successes as business was still booming and everybody went there with

Hunfishow provides much opportunity to talk guns. Here Caranta sees the new double-action Llama Gabilondo.

Astra's A-80 in 9mm has 15-shot magazine, is a contender for Spanish Army adoption.

This 15-round 380 by Gamba is a new version of the Mauser HSc, with a 9mm Police (Ultra) model to come.

EUROPE

berg, from March 13 to 16. A third show, and just as interesting, is Yves de Montais' *"Salon International de l'Arme ancienne et de Collection,"* opened to everybody and mixing up, for the first time, antique guns with modern craftsmanship.

Brussels Hunfishow

This is the "European Hunting and Fishing Equipment Exhibition" (10, rue Achille Fievez, B-1474 Ways, Belgium) which moves each year from one European city to another. In 1973, Hunfishow was in Paris; in 1974 in Milan; in 1975 in Madrid; in 1976 in Copenhagen; in 1977 back in Paris; in 1978 in London; in 1979 Paris again; in 1980, in Milan. The next one will be in Geneva, Switzerland.

This year, there were 310 direct exhibitors and the number of professional visitors was close to 5000 people. At Hunfishow, exhibitors operate every year in a different environment and have to face, therefore, specific problems but the atmosphere is warm, people know each other and the crowd of Italian and Spanish craftsmen ever present contribute to the general climate of sympathy.

There were so many items displayed that it would take a small book to list and describe them. This writer being quite specialized in handguns noted four new selective double-action automatic pistols, all chambered in 9mm Luger.

The new Bernardelli pistol features a steel receiver and a 14-round magazine. The rear sight is adjustable for windage. Over-all length is 8.5 inches, height 5.75 inches, and empty weight 35 oz. The barrel is 4.75 inches long. A 30-cal. Luger variation is also available, mostly for the Italian market as 9mm automatics are classified there as "war material" and cannot be sold commercially.

The second of these pistols is the new Brazilian "Taurus." When Brazil adopted the 15-shot Beretta Model 92 for their army, facilities were erected there for making roughly one-half of the large military order placed with the famous Italian company. Now, these facilities are controlled by the Taurus concern, from Porto Alegre in the Rio Grande do Sul. The new commercial Taurus differs from its elder Italian brother mostly by the magazine catch which is located on the left side of the receiver, behind the trigger guard and by the introduction of a low profile micrometric rear sight.

The third new 9mm automatic is made in Spain by Gabilondo under their Llama trade mark. It is a 13-shot gun fitted with an exceptionally smooth double action. This absolutely nice smoothness results from the fitting of balls along the mainspring travel; I was told that this invention was American. As the people in charge of the booth had no descriptive leaflet and knew not how to field strip the gun, I cannot tell more about this otherwise remarkable achievement. If this pistol is as good as it looks, you will hear from it soon.

The fourth 9 mm Luger automatic pistol is also Spanish. It is the Astra A-80, another contender to the Spanish Army competition for a new service pistol. (There was another, a highly promising Star prototype, but unfortunately it is still confidential.)

The Astra A-80 looks somewhat like a high magazine capacity counterpart of the SIG-Sauer P225 (the new German Police P6 model) with its 15-shot magazine. It is 7.5 inches long, 5.6 inches high and weighs 35 oz. empty. This new Astra pistol looks very compact for the power it represents.

Instead of the high strength sheet-metal slide of its Swiss-German model, the Astra A-80 features a nicely machined solid steel slide. The handy drop-hammer device is very similar.

Among the rifles, I noted a very interesting take-down Mauser action made by a Belgian designer. Among the American exhibitors, Harrington & Richardson, who displayed their new target rifle ordered in large quantities by the U.S. Army, were more dynamic than ever, while Safariland displayed a wide selection of holsters and a choice of body armor. Sturm, Ruger, Inc. attracted a permanent crowd with a Montana cowboy in full array, who performed all day long with playing cards and single action revolvers. The new stainless steel 44 Magnum Redhawk double action revolver, finally available in Europe, was also the subject of much chatter among handgun enthusiasts.

IWA 81

This exhibition started quietly a few years ago as a typically German event among green and olive drab-dressed people trading "drillings" and over-under shotguns nicely carved with high relief and oak-leaves, boars and great grouse and also sophisticated sheet-metal stamped double action pistols with black plastic grips.

The IWA show is held at the same place each year in the suburbs of Nuremberg, certainly one of the most beautiful West German cities. Nuremberg is still surrounded by medi-

At St. Germain-en-Laye, once a year, you can find an all-out American-style gun show in April, which is reported to be a fine time in Paris.

Mayors and governors and generals and buyers all attend the *Salon International*. There were 61 exhibitors from seven countries who saw over 8000 visitors, one of whom paid $32,000 for a pair of French pistols.

eval walls and crowned by an impressive Kaiser's castle called the Burg. Downtown, visitors can enjoy a tremendous "pedestrians only" area full of treasures where a normal lady can easily spend three days walking, lunching and bankrupting her husband. Our hotel was located in a monumental park full of birds, among beautiful small lakes, very close from the "Messezentrum," and we walked up and down every day, together with our excellent friend, Sam Cummings of Interarms.

The show was arranged in a big International Trade Fairs Center. It occupied three very large halls this year. According to the IWA files, 430 companies were represented and among them, 280 exhibited directly, coming from 20 countries. The number of professional visitors exceeded 5000.

Obviously, the small idyllic German world described at the beginning of this section has passed and it has a Common Market atmosphere.

Dynamit Nobel was one of the leading exhibitors. Then, Heckler & Koch were parading with their outstanding "PSP" or "P7" lever locking compact 9mm Luger pistol which is, in my opinion, the most advanced design available today. Walther also had a beautiful booth showing, among a forest of marvellous target rifles, their sophisticated "P5" pistol described in last year's GUN DIGEST. They had also a new CO_2 top-level competition pistol

quite similar to their electronic trigger free pistol but featuring a 300-round capacity rechargeable CO_2 reservoir.

Krico and Heym displayed also some interesting new rifles while Feinwerkbau, the international air gun wizard, revealed a new CO_2 target pistol very low on the hand designed according to requirements very close to those of the Walther program. If both of them are good, as can be expected with such celebrated companies, we will attend quite a nice battle of discounts, during the forthcoming years! Moreover, the Italians, with their new light and compact FAS and Air Match/Domino air pistols seem to have good numbers and, at the Lire rate to the Deutsche Mark, competition may be tougher behind the scenes than on the shooting ranges!

Erma had an interesting electronic rifle for indoor practicing; the Russians disclosed two fine target automatic pistols designed along the FAS/Domino lines for Standard Pistol and Olympic rapid fire I.S.U. events; and Smith & Wesson showed their new three-inch barrel round butt Combat Magnum chambered in 9mm Luger. Among French exhibitors, Verney-Carron displayed reinforced frame over-unders and new double slug guns, while Unique had their now famous Biathlon rifle which obtained a bronze medal at the World championship.

The fourth Salon International de l'Arme ancienne et de collection:

This nice exhibition, mostly of antique guns, is held every year in Saint-Germain-en-Laye, a residential area near Paris, where visitors can admire beautiful monuments and, among them, a wonderful castle. (Applications should be addressed to Mr. Yves de Montais - B.P. 3 - 78110 Le Vesinet - France.)

According to what I have seen, for antiques, it is the very best in France. Moreover, Mr. de Montais, Rossi's agent for Europe, is a perfect gentleman and his show is of the highest level.

This year, he showed a display of fine gun craftsmanship with the best specialists coming from Saint-Etienne and elsewhere in Europe. In view of the success met by the three previous Saint-Germain exhibitions and of the vicinity from Paris, it can easily be forecast that the major problem for the de Montais' staff will be to accommodate the visitors in their however large facilities. •

LENARD M. BROWNELL
Here's what a prototype Ruger looks like. It's a short M-77 in 7-08 Remington made specifically for William B. Ruger, Brownell says.

CUSTOM GUNS

STEPHEN L. BILLEB
Straight-grip style suits lightweight 7x57mm. Unusually, it retains military barrel; has Billeb-rework of military guard. As shown: 6¼ lbs. in New Zealand walnut.

FRANK R. WELLS
All-out silhouetter in Koa wood. A 700 Remington in 308, it carries a Weaver T-10 scope.

BROWN PRECISION
Fiberglass-stocked Remington 700 in 7mm Magnum called High Country. Weighs 7 lb. 2 oz. as shown. Camo paint job is a $65 option.

HAL HARTLEY
This matched pair of Mark X Mausers have 24" barrels, were made up in 340 and 375 Weatherby in Hartley's favorite curly maple, and so alike it takes the ribbon in the checkering to tell one from the other.

ROBERT G. WEST
Lefthand Model 700 in English walnut with Mark X trigger guard fitted has clean, economical lines, though not quite classic.

R. H. DEVEREAUX
Mesquite suits style and purpose of this Model 70 in 375 H&H Magnum. Barrel is 21", with integral muzzle brake.

GARNET D. BRAWLEY
Straight grained English walnut suits this Mauser in 257 Ackley Improved. Has six-point checkering on pistol grip and eight-point on forearm.

PHILIP D. LETIECQ
Classic lefthand stock on Model 70 in 270 Winchester is in English walnut. Brownell quarter-rib and mounts; Biesen and Fisher trim.

BOB EMMONS
Mauser with Lampert metalwork (in the white here) is in California English walnut. Caliber 270; skeleton butt; Brownell grip cap.

JOE BALICKIE
Matched pair of 270's on Mauser 1909 have metal work by Mark Lee, consecutive serial numbers. Wood is English walnut; lines are graceful indeed.

ROBERT G. WEST
Lefthand Model 700 in English walnut with Mark X trigger guard fitted has clean, economical lines, though not quite classic. (Left side.)

R. H. DEVEREAUX
Mesquite suits style and purpose of this Model 70 in 375 H&H Magnum. Barrel is 21", with integral muzzle brake. (Left side.)

DALE W. GOENS
True Russian Circassian, maker says, takes fancy checkering, suits Model 70 in 270 with metal touches like a new guard bow.

VIC OLSON
Straight-grain walnut, clean checkered, suits light sporter on Mauser action.

H. L. "PETE" GRISEL
Model 70 in 280 Remington with Sherer barrel, Blackburn guard and Len Brownell scope mounts, is in English walnut.

JERRY FISHER
Here's the big rifle—375 H&H Magnum in pre-War magnum Mauser—stocked in French walnut and styled to that African look—complete with stock bolts, plain pad, swivel on the barrel, 90° forearm tip.

DAVID MILLER
Model 70 25-06 in California English is ported, has custom scope mount, 23" Marquart barrel, Blackburn bottom metal, weighs 8 lbs.

FRANK R. WELLS
This Model 70 7x57 is slimmed out in English walnut; has Niedner buttplate, Biesen grip cap and classic styling.

KARL GUENTHER
Former Griffin & Howe stockmaker got this Model 70 375 up in Bastogne walnut; note quarter rib; has matted and engraved screws, rib, bolt handle.

MAURICE OTTMAR
Sarasqueta double 9.3x74mm rifle restocked in English walnut and done up with trap grip cap, Silvers pad and claw mounts. Bilal photo.

ROBERT SNAPP
Low-wall Winchester in 22 Hornet makes slim sporter. Ramp, sling lugs, scope bases, sight bases all integral; barrel full octagon. Stock in American walnut by Bob Randall.

C-D MILLER
DeHaas-Miller action holds 30-06 here in 26" Douglas barrel and weighs 7½ lbs. Stock is American walnut.

LARRY AMRINE
This Ojai, California custom gunmaker stocked the Ruger Single Shot rifle in extra-fancy walnut. Bob Swartley did the delicate game-scene engraving. The Leupold scope is held in Len Brownell's quick-detachable double-lever mounts.

AL LIND
GUNS Magazine's 25th Anniversary rifle has crotch English stock. It's in 280 RCBS caliber, wears Viramontez engraving. Bilal photo.

E. C. BISHOP & SON, INC.
Wildcat Model 95 Winchester in 376 Wapiti Express is made to resemble T.R.'s African 405 for Texan to wear on the saddle hunting elk.

TOM McCANN
This is a full-stock 54 caliber Hawken type—Roller lock, Douglas barrel, color case hardened lockplate and hooked breech.

DON KLEIN
Ruger No. 1 mountain rifle weighs 6 lb., 14 oz. as shown. It's a 270 with Shilen barrel, Talley and Biesen cap and butt, and all other metal work by Klein including Henry-style lever lock.

WINSTON CHURCHILL

The Art of The Engraver

We selected for this issue the best photos
of the best engravings we could get
and here try to show each piece to its best advantage.

H. V. GRANT

JOHN WARREN

HEIDEMARIE HIPTMAYER

BYRON BURGESS

JOHN VEST

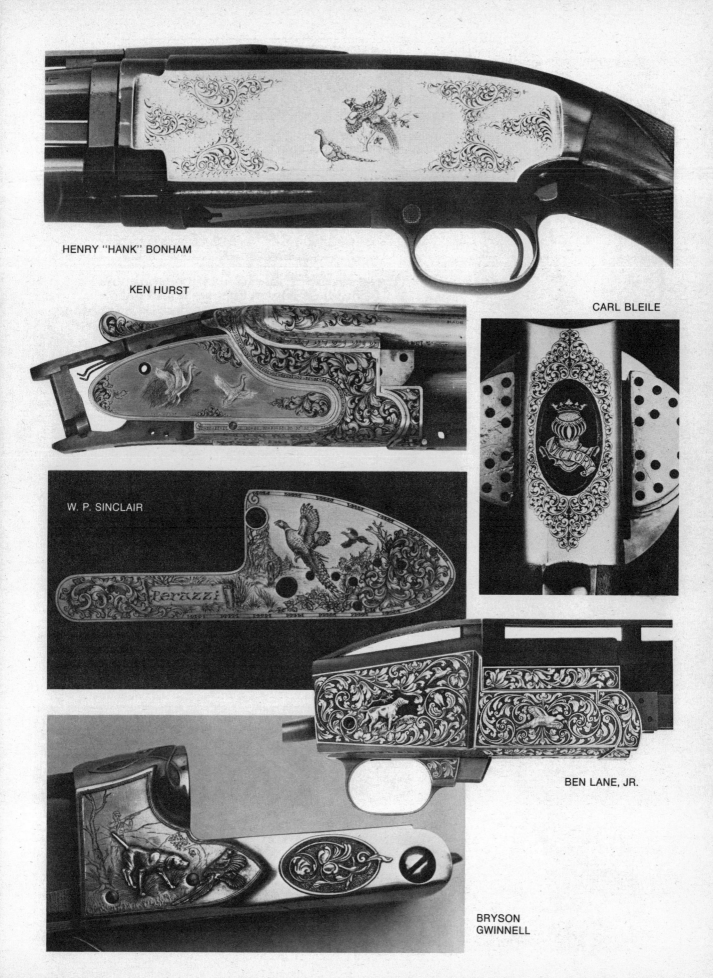

HENRY "HANK" BONHAM

KEN HURST

CARL BLEILE

W. P. SINCLAIR

BEN LANE, JR.

BRYSON
GWINNELL

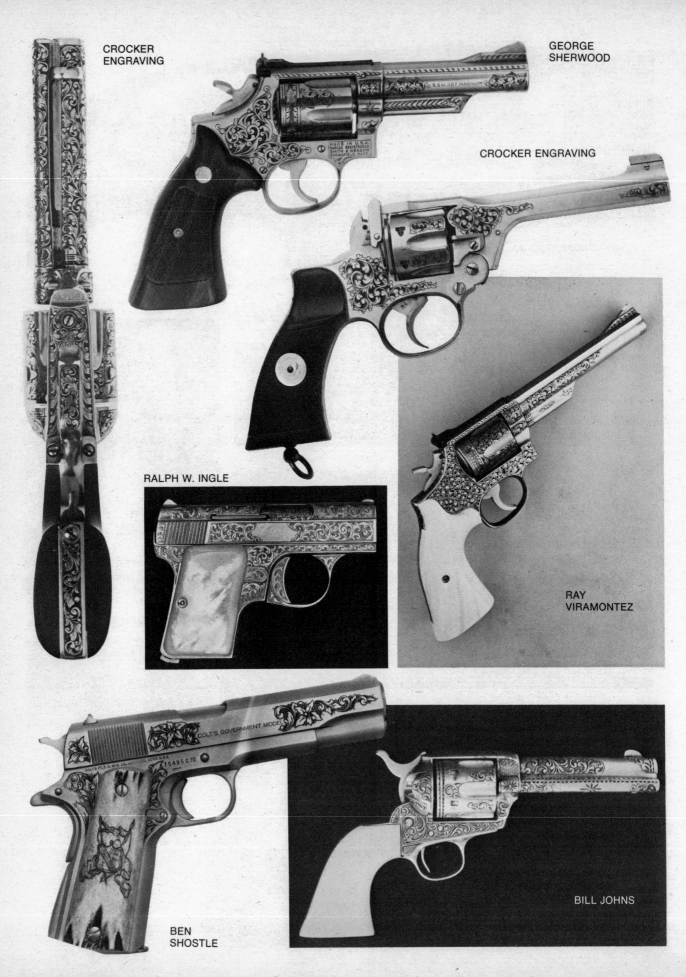

CROCKER ENGRAVING

GEORGE SHERWOOD

CROCKER ENGRAVING

RALPH W. INGLE

RAY VIRAMONTEZ

BEN SHOSTLE

BILL JOHNS

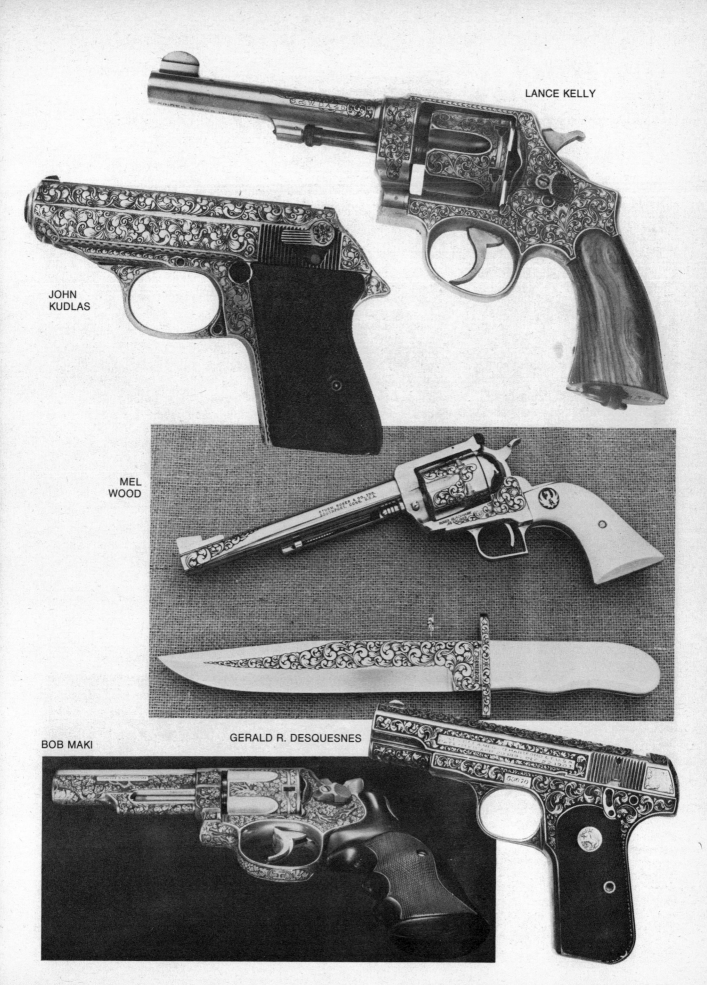

LANCE KELLY

JOHN
KUDLAS

MEL
WOOD

BOB MAKI

GERALD R. DESQUESNES

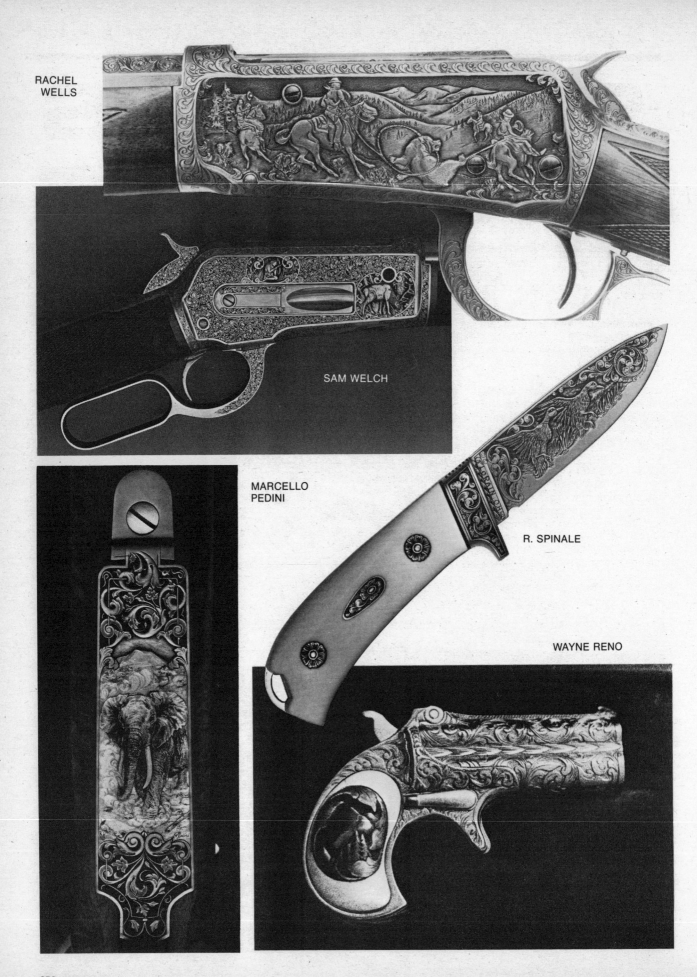

RACHEL WELLS

SAM WELCH

MARCELLO PEDINI

R. SPINALE

WAYNE RENO

SHOOTER'S SHOWCASE

Night Sights That Really Work

Everybody knows that the major problem in using a firearm is to get the bullet or the shot pattern on the target. This task is often complicated enough in the daytime and becomes virtually impossible under some conditions of darkness and is never easy at any time of night.

Gun people have worried about this in many different ways for about as long as there have been guns. The military have spent vast sums of money to create admittedly marvelous and efficient, but very expensive, machinery to permit even long-range pinpoint accuracy at night. For the cop on the beat, however, no one had anything put together that didn't demand some sort of ambient light at the firing position.

Julio A. Santiago has changed all that with the Nite-Sight, a self-luminating system which may be added to most handgun sights and many police-type shoulder arms. It is not cheap, but it is not all that expensive, and it works.

What the user gets is a pair of luminous dots with which he may confidently point his handgun at any

target he can distinguish with his eye. To boot, with the gun in the hand, one has to look carefully to see that it indeed has this sophisticated sighting equipment installed.

The sighting system creates: 1. No change in weight; 2. No change in balance; 3. No change in dimensions; 4. No need for power source; 5. No

change in point of impact; 6. No moving parts.

Further, it has been the experience of some departments and organizations training with this sight that rookies fire their best targets in the night shooting phase, when they use arms with the Nite-Site installed.

There is no such thing as a free lunch, and in this case, the user has to go to some trouble on some gun models to get the sight installed. Some who have concerns might worry over the fact that the system employs radioactive materials, but the whole thing is cleared with the Atomic Energy Commission, and indeed, you get a little tag to put on the gun that says so.

So far, you have learned in this little piece nothing that you could not have gotten from a press release. So let me say this: I have such a system on a personal gun; if I were to lose it, I would buy another. I have tried the system and it works better than anything I could ever envision.   K.W.

PanaVise Work Center

The Model 350 multi-purpose work-center provides tilts, turns and rotation to suit any work attitude and a capacity from nine inches down to very small indeed.

There are a multitude of accessories for this and the standard PanaVise. Write for full literature.

Triple Threat Tree Stand

This outfit from Advanced Hunting Equipment Inc. will take you up into a tree, serve as a lounge chair around any camp with trees in it, and can be used as a litter to haul deer out of the woods.

It weighs about 20 pounds, is furnished with straps for backpacking. Design makes it, designers say, "hard to fall out of" and they also say it will climb a steel pole if it has to.

Sit-Down Rifle Rest

Jim Cravener has been making these for some time and those that use them like not sitting in wet grass and can usually shoot pretty well in the field as well. It weighs just six pounds, adjusts easily to most terrain and angles, sets up and breaks down in about 30 seconds. Cost is something over $100.

Best Quality Boxes

Huey makes boxes to fit nearly any sort of sporting gun (and no doubt others on special order) at prices from $475 up to something over $800 for a big one with some options, but nothing fancy.

Best methods, best materials, most traditional designs are furnished and the cases are built one at a time. And right now, there's a backorder situation—maybe a year. However, for a handgun or a pair of rifles, Huey can and will build it.

Gaudy, Not Gauche, Jacket

This Bob Allen safari print jacket (and pants and hat as well) have to be seen to be appreciated. If one must judge such attire on hoary old tradition, he couldn't stand it—it's zingy.

It is the coat I'd most like to wear to interview Alice Herrington, even if it does cost about $100.

Contour Ground Actions

John's Rifle Shop will custom grind Mauser 98's and similar rifle actions

as shown. Gunsmith John Westrom says he is set up to polish the inside as well.

The result is a clean-lined action set up for use in a custom rifle. Prices depend on the amount of work wanted, but to grind the receiver ring, remove the clip hump and contour the bridge on a 98 is about $65 right now.

One-Man Show In Wood

I. D. Johnson owns his mill, cuts his own blanks, does it all himself. He sells American walnut, wild cherry and butternut, and myrtlewood in blanks for all purposes, including full stock Kentuckies. Prices look low in his current catalog.

He also furnishes pistol grip pieces and knife handle material in a variety of rare woods, and has some inletted stock blanks. Photo shows his best walnut.

Ferguson Rifle Reborn

Steve Sklany is making Ferguson replicas in Kalispell, MT. He's sold two dozen, he says, handling them as custom rifles. He'll sell actions only also, although buyers can expect a wait.

The picture shows a barreled action in the white. Note the quick-turn threads in the breech.

They Are Better When Skinny

Lowell Manley has made a business out of slimming and sharpening factory rifles. For about the cost of a second rifle, vital inches and ounces are removed and a true custom feel sculpted out of the factory wood.

Manley also sells the John Bivins

Express Oil Finish System and a replacement stock escutcheon for Ruger Number Ones.

Big Ten Riot Gun

L. M. French, doing business as Combat Weapons, makes a shortened single-barrel H&R 10-ga. Magnum into a six-pound specialist's gun. It is not a MAG-10 Roadblocker, but it is a lot smaller and a lot cheaper and it handles the same ammunition, its purveyors say.

An added inertia bar makes the recoil bearable, apparently, and the size of the hole in the end of the barrel makes the gun impressive. (1265 Balsam St., Lakewood, CO 80215)

Modern Muzzleloaders

Ten-Ring Precision Inc. makes handguns and shoulder guns designed to win muzzle-loading matches by providing—within any but "traditional only" rules—all the competitive goodies learned in a century of shooting cartridge guns.

Such a match pistol looks like a single-shot Colt automatic, to coin a phrase, and the typical Ten-Ring Match rifle looks like a Free Rifle. Costs are typical for match guns; maybe a little cheap, in fact.

Electronic Green Machines

Franklin Green still makes free pistols and electronic triggers for installation in a variety of guns—the Remington 700, for instance. The handguns take a year to make and cost about $1000; the triggers are something over $100, depending on your rifle.

Either adds a new dimension to competitive shooting, its maker says.

Trigger action reaches a new level of hardly being there at all, and shots are easier to call.

Model 1911 Pieces

Essex now can furnish slides as well as receivers for those who want to build up a 45 Auto more or less from scratch. Receivers are still available in choice of 4140 blued or 416 stainless steel, made to meet or exceed original specs, the makers say, and delivered with stock screw bushings installed.

Essex slides are available in matching steels, and in GI or ribbed-top, ported versions. There is a choice on sight cuts, too.

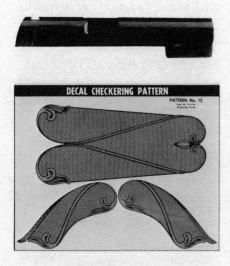

Decal Patterns

For $2.50, Stan de Treville can furnish a decal checkering pattern like this to be easily shifted onto the stock. The makers say the pattern will adapt to the compound curves and tools cut right through it.

In brown on yellow, the de Treville patterns are easy to see and there are dozens of choices, from simple point patterns to carving-checkering combinations. There are also patterns for carving birds and animals on butt-stocks.

Steel for Model 600

Neil Jones (as Custom Products, Meadville, PA) offers this steel trigger guard and floorplate as a bolt-on for any Model 600 series Remington rifle. It replaces the factory nylon unit.

Cost is $31.50. The unit is finished to complement the factory finish.

Bellm Means Ackley

Dennis Bellm is running the old Ackley shop and P.O. Ackley himself is an advisor, the price sheet says. Most of the old services are provided and books are offered as well.

Barrels are now offered, at extra cost, Premium-Lapped. The charge is $25 for new Ackley barrels; $35 for used barrels and other makes, with a $10 recrowning charge.

One-Stop Engraver Shop

Ray Viramontez has started an engraver's supply house, and offers everything from Chinese white to Gravermeister tools.

He ought to know what's needed and offers an unusual catalog for $2.50. It's dedicated, no less, to "those who have chosen to embellish metal."

All-Leather Shoulder Rig

John's Custom Leather has a break-front shoulder outfit for big handguns and small, at from $40 to $60, depending. No elastic is used, but the harness is completely adjustable. John says this rig is for the serious hunter or the lawman who has to wear a shoulder rig all day.

Sensible Tang Sights

S & M means Steinis & Mistretta and these fellows make tang sights for T/C Hawken and Renegade rifles and for Italian-made Hawken type rifles. The sights have elevation adjustment and fold down.

Units are $19.95 and the makers are about to bring out a model for the Winchester Model 94.

Forcing Cone Reamers

Clymer is offering new reamers for fixing up forcing cones. The piloted pistol reamer is $19.50 in five calibers; the shotgun reamer is from $40 to $50 each in six gauges. Most shotgun reamers are 10-fluted and will produce a forcing cone 1⅜" long.

Tasco 6M Vise Mount

This new device is handy for steadying cameras, spotting scopes, long lenses, et al. Fairly compact, the new vise has a rubber-padded pan head, and is quickly attached to a car window, tree limb, fence rail, etc. The clamp faces are rubber padded. It retails at $34.95.

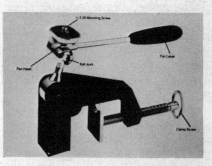

Decoy That Gobbler

Penn's Woods makes it possible to convince that reluctant lover there really is a hen near you with their full-size lady, who comes with a dowel leg and a camo carrying case.

She costs about $25 and she weighs less than a pound, and Penn's Woods, not the editor, says they really work.

Precision Tool Catalog

Perhaps there could be a gun business without Starrett tools, but it's unlikely. They are one of the standard sources for fine machinists implements.

You can get their catalog, their 100th Anniversary catalog, by simply writing in and asking for it. Don't be

surprised if someone named Starrett signs their letter. It's that kind of company.

Cue Card Tells All

Caswell Equipment Co. gives away a card that analyzes handgun targets interestingly. Assuming—which is not always sure—that the gun is zeroed properly and would center the group if properly directed, the actual hits define the shooter's problem.

Consistent hits in the white at between one and two o'clock, for instance, mean a righthanded shooter is "heeling" in anticipation of recoil. It's a neat idea, cards show results for both normal people and southpaws, and they're free for a stamped self-addressed envelope from Caswell.

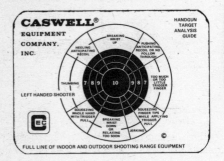

Gun Investor Newsletter

The essence of the newsletter idea is timeliness. The subscriber is willing to pay newsletter prices to get specialized information quicker than he could in magazines or even—sometimes—the daily newspaper.

A fellow named John Matlock runs "Investing In Guns" on that basis, charging $35 for 13 issues. Intelligently, he sends out an issue only

when he has found a buy or some other interesting stuff. How it will go in the future it's hard to say, but he predicted the price rise of the Hi-Standard Model 10 while it was still available. He offers a sample. Write: Investing In Guns, Box 9022, Salt Lake City, UT 84109.

Rests And Pads And Such

Meadow Industries makes a gadget to stick to a trap gun barrel so you can rest the muzzle on the ground instead of your toe, and a stick-on cheekpiece that slips out from under your cheek as the shot goes, and a conversion comb pad that will permit raising the comb as much as 1/2″ in 1/16th″ increments.

It's all done with modern adhesives and Velcro so no harm comes to the gun. See the picture.

High End Accessories for Muzzleloaders

Ken Steggles doesn't fool around. He gets good sterling prices for what they call over there a "range" of goodies for high-class front-stuffers, including anything it might take, besides a gun or a case, to make a cased set complete.

Turnscrews, cleaning rods, patent jags, oil bottles are the least of it. He does bag-type flasks, flinter pocket kits, shot flasks, and cap dispensers as well. And, in fact, he can furnish a rifle case if you want. His catalog is 50p., but send $2.

Shotgun Valet

A'n A Company makes a full-length shotgun cleaner and oiler—about a yard of fleecy dynel and nylon. One pass cleans the bore, they say, and a hook-on oiled bob completes the job on the return stroke.

The fleece is washable; the one size works on 20, 16 and 12-gauges; and it comes in a plastic storage tube.

Nifty Canvas Boot

The Palla, they say, was originally designed for Indo-China. Five armies still wear it, but you can get yours from L.L. Bean and others in the mail-order business, or write to French Dressing, Inc. The Palla is durable, sturdy as a warm weather hiking boot, an alternative to sneakers for everyday wear, and is washable.

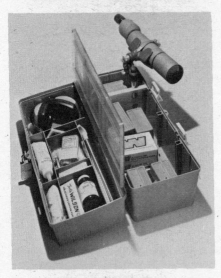

The Biggest Yet

MTM ammo boxes and wallets are known by all, and now they have a new item, the Shooters' Accessory Box, which measures 21x9x9¼ inches and holds more stuff than you can lift if you aren't careful. I have two, one filled with black powder paraphernalia, and the other with items important to handgunning, and they have adjustable dividers which are handy.

1981

Holding steady with not much new to report

by WALLACE LABISKY

STEEL SHOT

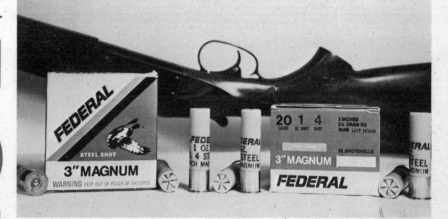

Newest of the steel-shot loads is Federal's 3″ 20-gauge offering which contains one ounce of shot in No. 4 size only. Hardly a goose load, this one, but it will serve nicely for taking ducks over decoys.

Federal's 20-gauge steel-shot wad is similar to those in larger gauges. It fully contains the one-ounce charge of No. 4 shot, and the super-tough, high-density plastic eliminates pellet rub-through and bore contact.

THOSE waterfowlers hoping for news of upgraded steel-shot loads will have to bite the bullet and wait, at least so far as the immediate future is concerned. The big three—Federal, Remington and Winchester—say no new loads will be introduced in 1981, nor will there be any modification of existing loads.

It would be totally wrong, in my estimation, to conclude there is absolutely no developmental work underway, for such activity is usually an on-going thing. But it is obvious that the fast-paced efforts of recent years have been geared way down, perhaps being replaced by a more studied approach.

Last year, in these columns, I reported that Federal was not only toiling mightily on a steel-shot loading in 20 gauge, but that they hoped to perfect the new offering in time for the 1980-81 waterfowling season. That deadline was met with a 1-oz. charge (No. 4 steel only) in the 3″ shell.

For this 20-ga. load, Federal uses a Reifenhauser-type plastic shell with an extra-low paper basewad so as to have sufficient room for the space-eating wad column and relatively bulky payload. The 186 pellets (average count for five loads) are fully contained within a one-piece, shot-cup wad (tough, high-density plastic) which closely follows the design of Federal's 10-ga. steel-shot wad. However, unlike the 10-ga. loads, there

isn't room for a fiber insert wad to be used inside the shot pouch.

The advertised MV (muzzle velocity) of the 1-oz. payload is 1,335 fps (feet per second). While this is roughly 40 fps slower than the fastest 12-ga. steel load (Remington 3″ with 1¼ ozs.), it actually surpasses the velocity of most 2¾″ 12-ga. loads with 1¼-ozs. of steel. Also, it is considerably faster than any 3″ load with either 1⅜ or 1½ ozs. of steel. So, comparatively speaking, the No. 4 steel pellets from this 20-ga. loading really don't suffer in the energy department.

I did not run pattern tests with the 20-ga. steel load, nor did I give it a workout in the field, the reason being that my 20-bores are s/s doubles and over-unders with rather thin barrel-wall thickness at the muzzles. I wasn't the least bit concerned that the plastic wad would fail in preventing pellet rub-through; rather, I simply did not want to risk the starting of any bore expansion at that point where the charge enters the choke.

Last year I also reported on Federal's 3½″ 10-ga. shell which carries 1⅝ ozs. of steel in shot sizes No. 2 and BB. This one is cataloged as having a MV of 1,345 fps, but shells from the lot that I received for test purposes did better than this. For the BB loads, one powder-company lab reported an average MV of 1,387, while another lab came up with a 1,419-fps rating.

Pattern testing was carried out

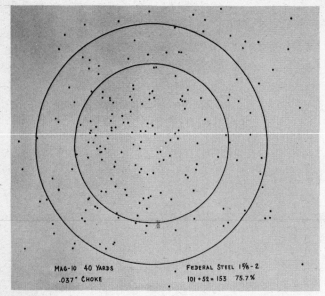

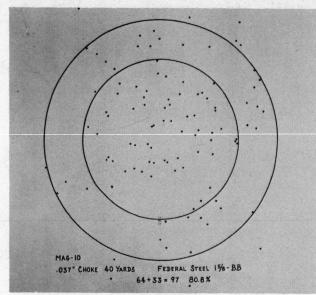

Using Federal's 10-gauge load with 1⅝ ozs. No. 2 steel shot, the author's Ithaca autoloader averaged 73% patterns at 40 yards. This 75% pattern has two-thirds of the 30″ density in the 20″ core, which is typical distribution for steel. The barrel carries .037″ of choke constriction.

Averaging a fraction under 80% at 40 yards, Federal's 1⅝-oz. loading with steel BBs printed tight-cored shot clouds from the Ithaca MAG-10 autoloader. This pattern counts out to a fraction over 80%, with 64 of the 97 pellet hits registering inside the 20″ core.

using an Ithaca MAG-10 autoloader fitted with a choke-relieved barrel (0.037″ constriction). With the steel 2s, the 40-yard efficiencies ranged from 70.7% to 76.2% for five shots. The BBs printed somewhat strong patterns, ranging from 72.5% to 86.6%. In all instances, the 20″ core density was very strong, with thin coverage in the 5″ annular ring. The ambient temperature at the time of firing was 55 degrees F., and there were no malfunctions with the gas-operated Ithaca.

Unfortunately, a rash of malfunctions did crop up later when I was using the same MAG-10 for field-testing the steel 2s on cornfield mallards, this in the face of temperatures that were running some 15 to 20 degrees cooler. Immediately prior to these field sessions the gun's action parts and gas system were thoroughly cleaned, so the 30% malfunction rate that was experienced cannot be attributed to an accumulation of assorted crud.

In every instance, it appeared to be a matter of insufficient gas impulse, with the breech bolt failing to travel rearward with adequate force. Although the empty hull always ejected (albeit in a feeble way), the fresh round failed to properly feed and chamber. Sometimes the bolt slammed home on an empty chamber; at other times it was caught and held by a magazine-released round which occupied various attitudes. With big,

late-season greenheads circling overhead, all this was mighty frustrating, to say the least.

Some weeks later, with the temperature hovering just above the freezing mark, I gave the steel BBs a workout on white-tailed jackrabbits, these hares ranging in weight from six to eight pounds. When I pointed right, any jack that was inside 60 yards was rolled as if poleaxed.

Interestingly, with these BB loads, the MAG-10 displayed no digestive problems at all. Nor were there any malfunctions with 1½-oz. steel-shot handloads that were powered by HS-7 powder in the Federal hull, these generating close to 11,000 lead units of chamber pressure.

All this prompted a close check of the powder charges in the Federal 10-ga. steel loads. Five rounds in each shot size were broken down and the propellant carefully weighed. For the BB loads, the average weight was 54.2 grains, but only 50.9 grains for the 2s. Was this 3.3-grain difference the reason for the malfunctions? I'm inclined to say "yes."

A box each of these 10-ga. steel loads was subsequently returned to Federal's Anoka, Minnesota, facility for lab and functioning tests. It was duly reported that both the BBs and the 2s were producing an average chamber pressure in excess of 10,000 lead units, though it was not disclosed what the actual difference was between the two

shot sizes. It was also reported that the 2s functioned perfectly in Federal's MAG-10 test gun, with the firing likely carried out under a controlled ambient temperature of 68 or 70 degrees F.

Even when fed the very same loads, it is not unusual for functioning differences to occur between individual guns of the same model. As an example, the aforementioned 1½-oz. steel handload flows through my MAG-10 like greased lightning, yet with the same load a friend's MAG-10 becomes a single-shot that refuses to even half-heartedly eject the fired hull. So we cannot justly criticize the Federal steel 2s simply because of the possible idiosyncrasy of one individual gun.

Getting back to that mallard shooting, I did not get to fire enough of those 1⅝-oz. steel 2 loads to fairly judge their effectiveness on hefty, late-season birds. About all I can say is that their performance was middlin' good. I state it in those terms simply because the shocking effect did not seem quite equal to what lead pellets in No. 4 size would produce. Not that adequate pellet penetration was lacking; that part was okay. Rather, it seemed somewhat analogous to shooting a big game animal with a full-jacketed bullet which punches right through with little transfer of energy. But, as I have already indicated, the kill sampling was really too limited to warrant nailing down any solid conclusions. •

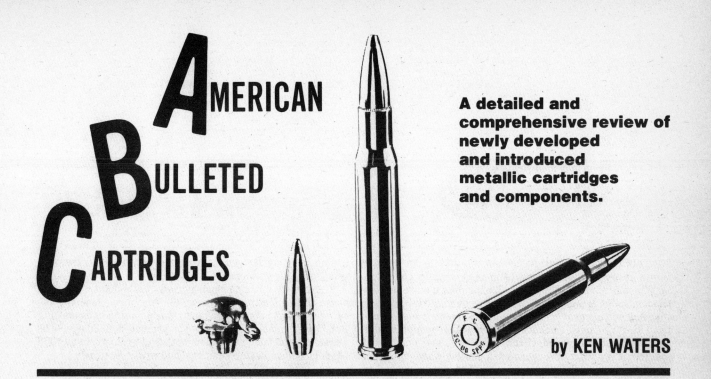

AMERICAN BULLETED CARTRIDGES

A detailed and comprehensive review of newly developed and introduced metallic cartridges and components.

by KEN WATERS

Latest Developments In Metallic Cartridges

A strange year filled with unpredictable events lies behind us. Not even the most confident soothsayer could have been expected to foresee its unusual happenings.

How, for instance, does one react to almost simultaneous announcements of the emergence of an exciting new version of a world famous rifle and an apparent going-out-of-business notice, both from the same company!?

Or that a pair of old cartridges are given new life through improved modern factory loadings, while another of equal merit is discontinued?

This all may be symptomatic of the uncertainty of our times. What seems pretty evident however, despite such news and inflationary high prices, is the continuing vitality of the shooting industry. It's a reassuring spectacle, one segment of which we're about to subject to our annual appraisal:

Winchester-Western

At the most recent Winchester Seminar held at Nilo Farms late in 1980, the key announcement from this writer's point of view was the introduction of a new Featherweight version of the time-honored Winchester Model 70 rifle, and the companion disclosure that the new rifle would be chambered for the 257 Roberts and 7x57 Mauser cartridges in addition to the usual—243, 270, 308 and 30-06. That was distinctly interesting to us since it seemingly heralded a re-birth of popularity for that pair of old but still excellent cartridges.

Actually, the 257 Roberts is not as old as the 270, and the 7x57 is only about ten years older than the 30-03, parent cartridge of the 30-06, so age of origin is obviously irrelevant. What counts here, as with any cartridge, is performance and both these rounds have legitimate claim to plenty of that.

With admirable foresight, Winchester has continued to offer 257 Roberts cartridges in a trio of loadings throughout the years during which no rifles were being chambered in that caliber, with bullet weights of 87-, 100- and 117-grains

at muzzle velocities listed as 3170, 2900 and 2650 fps respectively. Thus, purchasers of the new Model 70 Featherweight in this caliber will have a good selection of available factory ammo from which to choose.

Unfortunately, the same can't be said for the 7x57 where only a single loading with 175-grain bullet is to be had. Badly needed is a factory loading with 139- or 140-grain, or even 150-grain spitzer, bullets at higher velocity with flatter trajectory. In the meantime, Winchester could utilize the 125-grain Power Point or 150-grain 7mm bullets currently being made. Loaded in 7x57 cases, these bullets could readily provide muzzle velocities in excess of 2700 and 2800 fps.

Coupled with that excitingly good news however, came a release that is so astounding I still have trouble believing it. To avoid any chance that I might have misconstrued their intentions, I will quote parts of the Olin public relations release:

"The board of directors of Olin Corporation authorized the disposal of the company's Winchester sporting arms business in the United States, as part of a major restructuring of the Winchester Group to better focus Olin's resources on the Group's successful sporting and defense ammunition business, domestically and internationally. . . . This concentration on our ammunition business insures that those operations will receive the necessary resources and corporate support to be more successful."

It has all the earmarks of a return to the time some of us are old enough to remember when the Winchester Repeating Arms Company of New Haven, Connecticut, and the Western Cartrige Company of East Alton, Illinois, were separate entities. It appears there will be ammunition, and there are even new things this year.

Latest in the Winchester-Western cartridge line-up is an item of importance primarily to owners, present and prospective, of small self-defense pistols. An old favorite due to its compact size has been the 25 Automatic. Increasing numbers of the little pistols are being sold, and Winchester-Western has paid new attention.

Traditionally, the 25 Automatic has been loaded with

Winchester's new 25 caliber Automatic pistol cartridge with 45-grain expanding point bullet is designed to give increased stopping power with functional reliability in autoloading pistols. Sectioned view (center) shows tiny steel ball imbedded in its hollow point nose. Two right views show bullet fired into water from 10 feet.

50-grain round-nose full-metal-cased bullets to insure absolute reliability in feeding from magazine to chamber. W-W's solution to the challenge of providing a more sophisticated bullet is ingenious. Starting with a lead bullet with Lubaloy plating providing a construction with less stiffness than the old metal jackets yet one which would insure dependable feeding and at the same time prevent barrel leading, they next incorporated a hollow nose cavity in which a tiny steel ball is inserted. The entire assembly weighs 45 grains, and this 10% decrease in bullet weight has permitted an increase in muzzle velocity to 835 fps from a 2″ barrel.

As the accompanying photo of one of these bullets that was fired into water at a range of ten feet shows, a significant improvement has been achieved over the old bullets which gave virtually no expansion. While the small increase in velocity may have helped slightly, the new design combining a softer construction with that expanding nose feature is due the major credit for this superior bullet performance.

Interestingly, this construction is very closely similar to that of the old Hoxie bullets which were applied to Winchester cartridges away back in 1907, which likewise utilized a small round ball placed in the nose of a bullet, the ball being driven back into an air-filled cavity to produce increased mushrooming.

Ballistics in 2″ Barrel: Winchester 25 Automatic

Bullet		Velocity (fps)		Energy (ft. lbs.)	
Wt. Grs.	Type	Muzzle	50-yds.	Muzzle	50-yds.
45	Expanding Pt.	835	740	70	55

Another oldie to receive Winchester-Western's revitalizing treatment was the great old 45-70 Government cartridge, introduction of which in a 300-grain bullet loading was reported in this column last year before we'd had an opportunity to try them out. Now we can tell you more about them.

In a modern scope-sighted Marlin Model 1895 these new W-W loads with 300-gr. hollow-point bullets chronographed 1763 fps MV and made five shot groups at 100 yards as small as 1½″. I consider this excellent performance. In an H&R replica of the Officer's Model Springfield Trap Door rifle, the 26″ barrel of this rifle produced increased velocities averaging 1805 fps, yet with case expansion measurements only slightly more than standard 405-grain Winchester loads show in this same rifle. The H&R handled and ejected fired cases without difficulty and with no apparent strain. And an 1886 Winchester 45-70 with 26″ octagon barrel and plain open sights put five rounds of this

ammo in 3″ at 100 yards, chronographing 1808 fps, and producing no problems.

Finally, we want to report briefly on Winchester's 225-grain bullet loading for their 338 Magnum, received too late for a test report last year. Muzzle velocity averaging 2763 fps comes close to W-W's predicted 2780 fps, and accuracy is at least as good as with 250-gr. loads in our 338 Model 70, and better than the 200-grain factories.

Federal

Increasingly, it seems, we look to the Federal Cartridge Corporation for some of the practical and therefore useful metallic cartridge loadings that other ammunition makers pass over or ignore. In recent years they have become particularly adept at bringing out new loadings with superior ballistics in certain of the old but still viable calibers.

Past examples of this were the first modern Express load for the 45-70 wherein bullet weight was decreased to 300-grains and velocity *increased* to 1880 fps, combined with a hollow-point for quicker expansion. And a new load for the venerable 30-30 with 125-grain hollow-point at 2570 fps MV.

Both cartridges have proven excellent as to accuracy in several test rifles of those calibers, and although the 45-70-300 loading requires a barrel longer than 24″ to reach its advertised velocity, the 30-30 125-grain rounds chronographed an average 2551 fps MV from a standard Model 336 Marlin *rifle* barrel.

Now Federal ballisticians have directed their talents toward that old but revered revolver cartridge, the 44 Special. Following the same principles, a 200-grain lead hollow-point semi-waddcutter bullet has been substituted for the traditional 246-grain round-nose lead bullet, enabling muzzle velocities to be increased to a claimed 900 fps from 6½″ barrel revolvers according to the 1981 Federal catalog. The old 246-grain factory standard specifications called for a MV of only 755 fps from 6½″ barrels.

The new ammo arrived just in time for a series of trials over chronograph screens. From our Colt Single Action with 5½″ barrel, velocities averaged 830 fps taken at 10-ft. from the muzzle. In a Ruger "Redhawk" with 7½″ barrel, velocity climbed to an even 900 fps. That's not too different from advertised velocities considering that we used a revolver whereas Federal probably fired them from a closed test barrel; also, that our velocity readings were taken at 10-ft. rather than muzzle.

But increased velocity accounts for only part of the heightened effectiveness of the new round. The square shoulder and hollow nose cavity contribute considerably to an increase in stopping power—something the 44 Special has long needed. It is, in fact, the only *factory* load in this

New Federal cartridge for 44 Smith & Wesson Special revolver has 200-grain semi-wadcutter hollow point bullet.

Federal's new 222 Rem. cartridge features a 55-grain boat-tail bullet with full metal jacket.

caliber from any maker with an expanding bullet, and almost certainly the best of all loads in this caliber.

As always, accuracy is an important consideration, and the new 44 Special rounds are plenty good in that department also, grouping nicely even from a fixed sight gun. I'm happy when an out-of-the-box service revolver will group five consecutive shots in 1½″ at 20 yards and 5″ at 50 yards, and especially on a windy day.

Federal's other addition to the centerfire metallic line in 1981 is a special purpose loading for the 222 Remington, consisting of a 55-grain boat-tail bullet with full metal jacket intended to *prevent* bullet expansion. The primary purpose of these rounds is to provide hunters of fur bearing animals with a flat shooting load that will reach out and yet not damage pelts unduly. Long range shooting must have been contemplated judging from the stress Federal has placed on the boat-tail feature of these bullets. Velocities are listed as 3020 fps at muzzle, 2480 fps at 200 yards, and 1780 fps way out at 500 yards.

Remington-Peters

After last year's blitz, when Remington introduced two new cartridges, a new cartridge case and three new loadings for existing cartridges, they could hardly be expected to make additions to this year's metallic line-up. It appears, rather, there's to be some pruning of old wood.

According to the most recent Remington cartridge chart, four cartridges have been designated "Subject to stock on hand," meaning an end to production. When they're gone, there won't be anymore. Two are old numbers sure to be sorely missed by traditionalists—the 25-35 Winchester and 38-40 Winchester. The other two marked are the 100-grain PSP Corelokt in 264 Winchester Magnum caliber and, surprisingly, the 90-grain PSP Corelokt loading for the 6mm Remington.

Last year, we reported Remington's introduction of a third member of their unique Accelerator family of cartridges, this time in 308 Winchester caliber, and a new higher velocity lighter recoiling load for 44 Magnums with 180-gr. semi-jacketed hollow-point bullet. Now we are able to comment on them.

It seems I have a new varmint rifle; one I didn't plan on. But before I tell about it, readers of this column in past issues may recall that our results with 30-06 and 30-30 Accelerator cartridges were decidedly spotty. If judged by deer rifle standards, their accuracy was probably adequate, but these *aren't* big game cartridges. For varmints—which is what they're intended for—the necessary accuracy just

wasn't there in most of the rifles we tried them in.

Consequently, when it came to test firing the 308 member of the family, my expectations weren't very high. But what a surprise we received. These Accelerators really shoot! The very first five-shot group out of our 308 Winchester Model 70 Target rifle went into 1½″, which was surprising, but to the writer's utter amazement groups got better as we went along, and a best group measuring just ⅝″ shot in gusty wind bordered on the unbelievable. With that sort of consistent accuracy, my 308 has qualified as a first class varmint rifle.

As for velocity those 55-grain pointed soft points in their sabots are traveling an average 3678 fps as they leave the 24″ barrel of this rifle. Right then is when I got into trouble! Let me warn all you chronographers what can happen when these Accelerators are fired over Skyscreens. Twice, to my consternation, the plastic sabots hit and penetrated the Stop screen box leaving star-shaped holes I had to stop and patch. It's a tribute to the ruggedness of Dr. Oehler's Skyscreens that despite this punishment they never once ceased to register. Only those handsome groups stifled my cussing.

R-P's 180-grain high velocity loading of the 44 Magnum was also put through its paces, using Ruger's new "Redhawk" double-action revolver. Rated as having a muzzle velocity of 1610 fps, the Oehler Chronotach gave out readings of 1613, 1625, 1629, 1656 and 1689 for an average of 1652 fps from the 7½″ barrel. This is some 235 fps faster than the standard 240-gr. R-P load from the same gun, and recoil is noticeably less. My guess is that 44 Magnum shooters are going to like this new Remington round.

Super Vel

That old familiar name, Super Vel, is with us again, I'm pleased to report, but from a new location. The H&H Cartridge Corporation, makers of that effective line of revolver and pistol ammunition, has relocated to Hamilton Road, Route 2, Fond du Lac, WI 54935.

Their 1981 brochure lists eighteen handgun cartridges in calibers from 380 ACP to 45 ACP, and some of the quoted velocities are indeed heady numbers. For example, take their 90-gr. JHP loading for the 9mm Luger rated at 1370 fps from a Browning High Power, and a 357 Magnum round with 110-gr. JSP at 1470 fps, or 150-gr. JHP at 1300 from a 6″ barrel Colt Python.

Especially impressive is a 180-gr. JHP loading in 44 Magnum said to develop 1760 fps from a 7½″ Ruger Super Blackhawk.

Left—Norma's 38 Special Magnum cartridges have been redesignated as +P loads. Right—Two 38 caliber cartridges from PMC, at left a 158-grain semi-wadcutter and at right a 148-grain wadcutter, they compliment a previously introduced 158-grain round nose.

We're practically certain to hear more from this outfit in coming months.

Norma

Probably the Norma news of interest to the largest number of U.S. shooters concerns the on-going discussions and testing of their 38 Special Norma Magnum cartridge introduced in 1980, which has resulted in its re-designation as a +P round in the United States.

Norma rated this ammunition, identified as Stock No. 19119, "Magnum" based on its superior ballistic performance, said to develop 20% higher muzzle velocity with 45% more kinetic energy than standard 38 Special rounds. Loaded with 110-grain jacketed hollow-point bullets, an MV of 1225 fps and energy of 367 ft. lbs. from a 4" test barrel was claimed. In 6" test barrels, the comparable figures were 1542 fps and 580 f.p.

Despite these impressive ballistics however, Norma originally didn't identify these cartridges as being "+P;" in fact, early boxes bore a label stating they were "not +P." That decision appears to have been based upon repeated tests in European laboratories, including one or more not connected with the Norma firm, all of which reaffirmed the contention that pressures were at standard rather than +P levels.

Controversy and doubts continued to persist in this country, stemming from American lab results reported as showing average pressures between 18,500 and slightly over 19,500 CUP (Copper Units of Pressure). If so, this would indeed call for a +P rating under U.S. commercial standards which classify as +P 38 Special loads developing between 17,000 and 20,000 CUP, as compared to a limit of 17,000 CUP for standard 38 Special ammunition.

Naturally, the question arrives as to why pressure readings taken from the same ammunition in American and European labs should differ? Several possible answers come to mind, including a European predilection towards free-boring barrels to reduce pressures, but I'm reminded also of something once told me by a noted Scandinavian ballistician. He explained that whereas American pressure barrels are loaded with cartridges having standard brass cases through which a hole may be blown opposite the pressure reading copper (or lead) piston upon firing, European practice calls for the use of pre-drilled cases; that is, with a hole provided in case walls at the piston location.

Apparently this system eliminates any variables due to brass strength, thereby giving a truer picture of actual pressures from the Continental point of view. Whether or not one subscribes to this theory, it is obvious that somewhat different pressure readings can be expected, depending upon which method is used. Any appreciable difference in the throating of test barrels could likewise produce significant variations in pressure readings.

Finally, it should be noted also that where the difference between a +P and standard 38 Special loads may be as little as 1500 to 2000 CUP, a rather fine line is being drawn. Cartridges from the same lot, or even the same box, might conceivably vary by that much in their individual pressure readings.

Norma's solution has been to re-designate these high velocity 38 Special cartridges as +P in observation of U.S. industry standards, simultaneously affirming that although 38 Special Norma Magnum cartridges will henceforth bear a +P headstamp, their ballistics will remain unchanged. This seems an admirable arrangement in that owners of guns approved for use with +P loads will continue to be able to obtain these high performance cartridges, while those with older, light or alloy frame guns are fore-warned against their use.

For 1981, Norma's new offering is in the category of metric rifle calibers, for which they are world famous. Designated the 7.62x39 Short Russian, this is the sporting or commercial version of the Russian military assault cartridge known as the M-43 from its adoption in 1943 as an answer to the German 7.92mm Kurz cartridge.

In recent years, semi-automatic rifles of Finnish manufacture, appearing much like their Russian military counterparts but lacking a full-automatic capability have been sold on the American market. It was necessary either to use imported military Ball ammo with Berdan primers, or to form cases for reloading from 6.5 Mannlicher or 7.35mm Carcano brass in such arms.

That won't be necessary now that Norma has made available a commercial loading in Boxer-primed cases with 125-grain soft point bullet having a rated muzzle velocity of 2385 fps and muzzle energy of 1580 ft. pounds. With ballistics approaching those of a 30-30, this is an effective round for its size. After observing a Valmet semi-auto of this caliber in action on a police range, I'm impressed by its capabilities. From this point on, reloading of the little cartridge will be a whole lot easier.

PMC

A couple of years ago an outfit calling themselves the Poongsan Metal Corporation of South Korea began exporting newly manufactured military ball ammunition to the

U.S. in 30 M-1 Carbine and 5.56mm M-193 (223 Remington) calibers. We tested some rounds in both calibers from an early shipment, finding it somewhat less accurate than American ammo but developing higher velocities and selling for about one-third less. I suspect the exceedingly high velocities of the 5.56mm cartridges may have been at least partly responsible for their lesser accuracy.

Now under the trademark PMC—which also stands for Patton and Morgan Corporation, New York importers of this ammunition—other calibers have been added to the line, including a 147-grain loading for the 308 Winchester with FMC-BT (full metal clad boat-tail) bullet designated M-80, and 150-grain FMC (M-2) issue in 30-06 Springfield caliber.

Additionally, PMC now offers a sporting line with soft point bullets in calibers 223, 308 and 30-06, plus centerfire handgun ammunition in calibers 9mm Luger and 38 Special. Seven American distributors in as many states across the country are equipped to supply local dealers with this ammo, all of which is put up in new brass cases with non-mercuric non-corrosive Boxer (anvil) primers and progressive burning powders.

Smith & Wesson

Last year we told readers about Smith & Wesson's Nyclad ammunition in 38 Special and 357 Magnum calibers. Since then they've added a Nyclad load for the 9mm with 125-gr. SWCHP bullet registering 1102 fps with 339 f.p. muzzle energy from a 4″ barrel S&W Model 39.

The one I particularly want to tell you about though is their new load which they call the "Chief's Special." Specifically designed for use in 2″ barrel snubbies with alloy frames that aren't up to handling +P ammunition, these cartridges are loaded with 125-grain semi-wadcutter hollow-point Nyclad bullets to a muzzle velocity of 825 fps, which is roughly 90% as fast as a +P load with same bullet also from 2″ barrels.

What's more, S&W claims it does this with the low pressure and mild recoil of a conventional wadcutter target load. Add to that bullet expansion to 60-caliber or greater on impact and we have what appears to be an ideal cartridge for plainclothesmen and others dependent upon the little short barrel guns.

The regular line of S&W factory ammo for 380, 9mm, 38 Special, 357 Magnum, 44 Magnum and 45 Auto are, I expect, too well known to require further comment here except to note a point of which readers may or may not be aware, namely that Smith & Wesson make their own bullets to meet rigid requirements and insure desired bullet penetration and expansion performance. I've been seeing increasing numbers of S&W blue boxes on firing ranges the past year or so.

Dynamit Nobel

Good news for owners and handloaders of rifles in the Continental calibers: The big Dynamit Nobel combine of RWS, Rottweil and Geco are actively seeking American business, as a result of which they have established their own jobber's outlet in this country. Now retailers can order directly from Dynamit Nobel of America, Inc., at 105 Stonehurst Court, Northvale, NJ 07647.

First there are RWS centerfire rifle cartridges in thirty-two different calibers from 22 Hornet to the 10.75x73, including such interesting numbers as the 5.6x50 Magnum, 6.5x68, 7x65R, 8x60S, 8x68, 8.15x46R, 9.3x64, 9.3x72R and 9.3x74R. Many are loaded with the world famous Brenneke TIG and TUG bullets, including (believe it or not), a 30-06 loading with 181-gr. Brenneke TUG bullets.

Expensive yes, but really top quality ammunition.

Then there's the Geco line of pistol and revolver cartridges—a total of seventeen different rounds, most interesting of which are a 32 S&W Long target cartridge with 100-grain wadcutter bullet, and a round listed as the 9mm Police or 9mm Ultra with 94-gr. FMJ bullet. The 30 Luger is there also with a 93-gr. FMJ bullet.

Next comes the Rottweil line of Brenneke rifled slugs, and RWS rimfire cartridges which we'll leave for others to tell about. As a confirmed handloader, I found myself engrossed in the listings of RWS bullets for centerfire rifles, unprimed RWS cases, and RWS primers. Of the latter there are six types of anvil (Boxer) primers, and a selection of *nine* Berdan primers. This especially should arouse the interest of a sizeable passel of American handloaders.

For big bore rifle shooters/handloaders, 9.3mm and 10.75mm bullets are sure to attract attention, but there are also excellent selections of 7mm and 8mm bullets. Somewhat disappointing are the 6.5mm bullets, diameters of which are given as .264″. I know I'm not alone in wishing someone would produce a good 160-grain jacketed soft point bullet with a diameter of .267″ for a properly tight fit in 6.5 Mannlicher barrels, most of those I've measured as having .267″ groove diameter. Then the little carbines should show the accuracy of which I've long believed them to be capable.

The RWS unprimed cases in several calibers should also prove popular, especially the 9.3x72R, 9.3x74R and 7x57R. In those calibers with which I've worked, RWS brass has been shown to be of excellent quality with expert annealing.

B.E.L.L.

Speaking of cases for some of the less commonly encountered calibers, here's another outstanding product: cases for English and obsolete rifles from Jim Bell's Brass Extrusion Laboratories. Since we last wrote of BELL cases, Jim has added a pair of additional ones, badly needed like their predecessors.

Now there are gleaming brass hulls for the 425 Westley Richards and that most often seen big British caliber, the 450-3¼″ Express. The latter is being made with two different rim thicknesses—the thin or Standard .040″ rim as used in Purdey double rifles, and a .065″-thick Jeffery rim. While it's possibly coincidence, most all the rifles I've tried them in other than Jefferys, require the thin .040″ rim.

These cases can also be re-formed to fit a pretty fair number of other chambers, including the 450/400, 369 Purdey, 360 No. 2, 333 Rimmed Jeffery, 40-110 Winchester, and several of the old European military rifles such as the 11mm Gras.

Perhaps best of all, they're all pocketed for standard American Large Rifle primers, and have been giving us excellent service in a 450 Purdey double rifle. I'm looking forward to when Jim Bell brings out his indispensable cases for the 405 Winchester and 280 Ross. They will be as warmly received as was his 11mm Mauser brass.

Sierra

Again, as last year, Sierra added five new bullets to their lineup for 1981. In the Game King series of hunting bullets for the longer ranges there is a new .224″ 55-grain FMJ boat-tail with ballistic coefficient of .285.

Competition shooters/handloaders will welcome the addition of a 150-grain 7mm (.284″) hollow-point boat-tail and a similarly contoured 30-caliber HPBT likewise of 150-grain. These should prove especially useful for 200-yard and 300-meter four-position contestants.

And finally for handgun competition shooters, a 220-

grain flat-nose FMJ for 41 Magnums similar to the 44 flat-nose of same weight introduced in 1980, plus a 125-grain round-nose FMJ of .357″ diameter. The new 41 Magnum bullet should find much use on the silhouette ranges.

Other Sierra developments worthy of note are:

(1) Their employment of a system of quality control that requires precision drawing of bullet jackets to tough tolerances: .0006″ for hunting bullets and .0003″ for match bullets, plus weight parameters of ± .3-grain. Much of Sierra's fine reputation for accuracy stems from this exactitude.

(2) Sierra has a new Second Edition of their Reloader's Manual off the press. It's more than just a compendium of load data, having a large Exterior Ballistics section including wind deflection plus explanations on such topics as angular shooting and the effects of altitude. Every serious handloader should have a copy of this book.

(3) Sierra has established a ballistics service to assist shooters with special computations. For a basic price of ten dollars they will also provide complete ballistic data for three different sets of shooting conditions. Sounds like a real service.

CCI-Speer

Comparing 1981 listings with those of 1980, the Speer bullet line doesn't appear to have changed much. Rifle bullet No. 1039, their 22-caliber 52-grain Gold Match hollow-point has disappeared from the catalog, and a new 22-caliber 55-grain spitzer soft point with a cannelure—bullet No. 1049—has been added, I suspect to allow crimping for use in autoloading rifles.

What continues to impress this writer however, is Speer's unique "Lawman" series of centerfire handgun cartridges. Because there are now 23 different cartridges in six calibers comprising this line of factory loaded ammo, its entirely logical that I haven't tested all of them. But those I have tried have proven excellent indeed.

Take Lawman cartridge No. 3965, for instance. It's a 200-grain jacketed hollow-point load for 45 Automatics. In our Colt Gold Cup auto it will group five shots in ¾″ at 50 feet and 4½″ at 50 yards while exiting the muzzle at 908 fps, a fine combination of accuracy, velocity and power. Other favorites are the 357 Magnum and 38 Special with jacketed 140-grain hollow-points.

Emphasis is placed on controlling bullet base upset with this ammo as a means of improving accuracy with what I would judge to be considerable success.

And with police use in mind, Speer ballisticians have selected powders for this series of cartridges which reduce muzzle flash to a minimum. It's easy to see why they're so proud of the Lawman line.

Hornady

Before commenting on the year's doings at Hornady, this writer wishes to express deepest regrets at the passing of Joyce Hornady, talented founder of Hornady Manufacturing Company. Beyond his professional competence, he was a gentleman and our friend. He will be missed.

In May, 1980, Hornady announced that their Frontier Ammunition division had been chosen as the supplier of ammunition for the 1980 International Practical Shooting Confederation U.S. Championships. This honor conferred by the IPSC Match Committee involved the use of Frontier 45 ACP and 9mm cartridges, and optionally 357 Magnum ammo, all of which was loaded with full metal jacket flat-point bullets.

In line with current thinking, Hornady has introduced a 55-grain 22-caliber full metal jacket boat-tail bullet for military shooters as well as hunters of fur bearing animals,

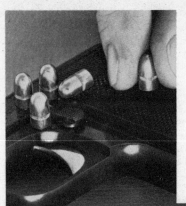

Left—Hornady's newly-introduced 25 caliber, 50-grain full metal jacket round nose bullet. Below —Their new 22 caliber 55-grain full metal jacket boat-tail.

observing that its boat-tail base added to the typical Hornady secant ogive shape increases the ballistic coefficient.

Also in step with what appears to be somewhat of a trend, they've added a new 50-grain FMJ bullet for 25 Automatic pistols. With recent imports of the little pistols and increasing ammunition costs, shooters of this tiny round must be taking up handloading. Join the fraternity.

Certain to meet with wide acceptance are a pair of new boat-tail bullets for 6mm rifles—an 87-grain hollow-point and a 100-grain soft point, increasing the ranging powers of the already flat-shooting Sixes.

A bullet I particularly look forward to taking afield is Hornady's 140-grain BTSP in 270-caliber. This one may be the means of settling all those old disputes about whether a 130- or 150-grain is better. Could be the new 140-grain will out-do both of 'em?

Continuing their expanding list of boat-tail spire point bullets with improved medium-to-long range performance in mind, two of Hornady's most recent developments have been a 7mm 162-gr. BTSP and a 190-gr. BTSP, both beautifully streamlined bullets that will help defy the law of gravity while their special Interlock construction takes care of things on impact. Should be great hunting bullets for the wide-open spaces.

Last but surely not least from the competitive target rifleman's outlook is a new 190-grain hollow-point boat-tail Match bullet in 30-caliber for use clear out to a thousand yards. With a match bullet, consistent accuracy is the whole show, and no effort has been spared to incorporate proven accuracy features. These include a longer bearing surface for better alignment with the bore, a shorter point section to reduce free-bore effect and place the bullet closer to the rifling origin, combined in a shorter over-all length for better stability in flight.

It does seem that handloading components as well as factory loaded metallic cartridges get better every year, both in performance and selection. Let's hope it continues. ●

CENTERFIRE RIFLE CARTRIDGES—BALLISTICS AND PRICES

(R)= REMINGTON; (W) = WINCHESTER-WESTERN); (F) = FEDERAL; (H) = HORNADY-FRONTIER; (PMC) = Patton & Morgan Corp.

Cartridge	— BULLET —		Bbl.	— VELOCITY (fps) —				— ENERGY (ft. lbs.) —				— BULLET PATH† —			Price
	Wt. Grs.	Type	Bbl. (in.)	Muzzle	100 yds.	200 yds.	300 yds.	Muzzle	100 yds.	200 yds.	300 yds.	100 yds.	200 yds.	300 yds.	Per Box
17 Remington (R)	25	HPPL	24	4040	3284	2644	2086	906	599	388	242	+0.5	–1.5	–8.5	**$10.80**
22 Hornet (R) (W)	45	PSP	24	2690	2042	1502	1128	723	417	225	127	0.0	–7.7	–31.3	***19.90**
22 Hornet (R)	45	HP	24	2690	2042	1502	1128	723	417	225	127	0.0	–7.7	–31.3	***19.90**
22 Hornet (W)	46	OPE (HP)	24	2690	2042	1502	1128	739	426	230	130	0.0	–7.7	–31.3	***19.90**
218 Bee (W)	46	OPE (HP)	24	2760	2102	1550	1155	778	451	245	136	0.0	–7.2	–29.4	***29.40**
222 Remington (R) (W) (F) (H)	50	PSP, SX	24	3140	2602	2123	1700	1094	752	500	321	+2.2	0.0	–10.0	**8.50**
222 Remington (R)	50	HPPL	24	3140	2635	2182	1777	1094	771	529	351	+2.1	0.0	–9.5	**9.25**
222 Remington (R)	55	MC	24	3000	2544	2130	1759	1099	790	554	378	+2.3	0.0	–10.0	**8.50**
222 Remington (W)	55	FMC	24	3020	2675	2355	2057	1114	874	677	517	+2.0	0.0	–8.3	**8.50**
222 Remington (F)	55	MC BT	24	3020	2740	2480	2230	1115	915	750	610	+1.9	0.0	–7.7	**8.50**
222 Remington Magnum (R)	55	PSP	24	3240	2748	2305	1906	1282	922	649	444	+1.9	0.0	–8.5	**9.65**
222 Remington Magnum (R)	55	HPPL	24	3240	2773	2352	1969	1282	939	675	473	+1.8	0.0	–8.5	**10.30**
223 Remington (R) (W) (F) (H)	55	PSP	24	3240	2747	2304	1905	1282	921	648	443	+1.9	0.0	–8.5	**9.30**
223 Remington (R)	55	HPPL	24	3240	2773	2352	1969	1282	939	675	473	+1.8	0.0	–8.2	**10.00**
223 Remington (R) (H)	55	MC	24	3240	2759	2326	1933	1282	929	660	456	+1.9	0.0	–8.4	**9.30**
223 Remington (W) (F) (PMC)	55	FMC, MC BT	24	3240	2877	2543	2232	1282	1011	790	608	+1.7	0.0	–7.1	**9.30**
225 Winchester (W)	55	PSP	24	3570	3066	2616	2208	1556	1148	836	595	+1.2	0.0	–6.2	**10.15**
22-250 Remington (R) (W) (F) (H)	55	PSP	24	3730	3180	2695	2257	1699	1235	887	622	+1.0	0.0	–5.7	**9.30**
22-250 Remington (R)	55	HPCL	24	3730	3253	2826	2436	1699	1292	975	725	+0.9	0.0	–5.2	**10.00**
22-250 Remington (F) — Premium	55	BTHP	24	3730	3330	2960	2630	1700	1350	1070	840	+0.8	0.0	–4.8	**10.10**
220 Swift (H)	55	SP	24	3630	3176	2755	2370	1609	1229	927	686	+1.0	0.0	–5.6	**12.95**
220 Swift (H)	60	HP	24	3530	3134	2763	2420	1657	1305	1016	780	+1.1	0.0	–5.7	**12.95**
243 (W) (R) (F) (H)	80	PSP, HPPL, FMJ	24	3350	2955	2593	2259	1993	1551	1194	906	+1.6	0.0	–7.0	**11.60**
243 Winchester (F) — Premium	85	BTHP	24	3320	3070	2830	2600	2080	1770	1510	1280	+1.5	0.0	–6.8	**12.45**
243 Winchester (W) (R) (F) (H)	100	PPSP, PSPCL, SP	24	2960	2697	2449	2215	1945	1615	1332	1089	+1.9	0.0	–7.8	**11.60**
243 Winchester (F) — Premium	100	BTSP	24	2960	2760	2570	2380	1950	1690	1460	1260	+1.4	0.0	–5.8	**12.45**
6mm Remington (R) (W) (Also, .244)	80	PSP, HPPL	24	3470	3064	2694	2352	2139	1667	1289	982	+1.2	0.0	–6.0	**11.60**
6mm Remington (R) (Also, .244)	90	PSPCL	24	3190	2863	2558	2273	2033	1638	1307	1032	+1.7	0.0	–7.0	**11.60**
6mm Remington (R) (W) (F)	100	PSPCL, PPSP	24	3130	2857	2600	2357	2175	1812	1501	1233	+1.7	0.0	–6.8	**11.60**
25-20 Winchester (W) (R)	86	SP, LEAD	24	1460	1194	1030	931	407	272	203	165	0.0	–23.5	–79.6	***18.85**
256 Winchester (W)	60	OPE (HP)	24	2760	2097	1542	1149	1015	586	317	176	0.0	–7.3	–29.6	***23.75**
25-35 Winchester (W)	117	SP	24	2230	1866	1545	1282	1292	904	620	427	0.0	–9.2	–33.1	**12.90**
250 Savage (W)	87	PSP	24	3030	2673	2342	2036	1773	1380	1059	801	+2.0	0.0	–8.4	**11.80**
250 Savage (W)	100	ST	24	2820	2467	2140	1839	1765	1351	1017	751	+2.4	0.0	–10.1	**12.45**
250 Savage (R)	100	PSP	24	2820	2504	2210	1936	1765	1392	1084	832	+2.3	0.0	–9.5	**11.80**
257 Roberts (W)	87	PSP	24	3170	2802	2462	2147	1941	1516	1171	890	+1.8	0.0	–7.5	**10.50**
257 Roberts (W)	100	ST	24	2900	2541	2210	1904	1867	1433	1084	805	+2.3	0.0	–9.4	**13.70**
257 Roberts (W) (R)	117	PPSP, SPCL	24	2650	2291	1961	1663	1824	1363	999	718	+2.9	0.0	–12.0	**13.00**
25-06 Remington (R)	87	HPPL	24	3440	2995	2591	2222	2286	1733	1297	954	+1.2	0.0	–6.3	**12.60**
25-06 Remington (W) (F)	90	PEP, HP	24	3440	3043	2680	2344	2364	1850	1435	1098	+1.2	0.0	–6.1	**12.60**
25-06 Remington (R)	100	PSPCL	24	3230	2893	2580	2287	2316	1858	1478	1161	+1.6	0.0	–6.9	**12.60**
25-06 Remington (F)	117	SP	24	3060	2790	2530	2280	2430	2020	1660	1360	+1.8	0.0	–7.3	**12.60**
25-06 Remington (R) (W)	120	PSPCL, PEP	24	3010	2749	2502	2269	2414	2013	1668	1372	+1.9	0.0	–7.4	**12.60**
6.5mm Remington Magnum (R)	120	PSPCL	24	3210	2905	2621	2353	2745	2248	1830	1475	+1.3	0.0	–6.6	**18.85**
264 Winchester Magnum (W) (R)	100	PSP, PSPCL	24	3320	2926	2565	2231	2447	1901	1461	1105	+1.3	0.0	–6.7	**16.25**
264 Winchester Magnum (W) (R)	140	PPSP, PSPCL	24	3030	2782	2548	2326	2854	2406	2018	1682	+1.8	0.0	–7.2	**16.25**
270 Winchester (W) (R)	100	PSP	24	3480	3067	2690	2343	2689	2088	1606	1219	+1.2	0.0	–6.2	**12.60**
270 Winchester (W) (R) (F)	130	PPSP, BP, SP	24	3110	2849	2604	2371	2791	2343	1957	1622	+1.7	0.0	–6.8	**13.30**
270 Winchester (W) (R) (H)	130	ST, PSPCL	24	3110	2823	2554	2300	2791	2300	1883	1527	+1.7	0.0	–7.1	**12.60**
270 Winchester (F) — Premium	130	BTSP	24	3110	2880	2670	2460	2790	2400	2050	1740	+1.6	0.0	–6.5	**13.55**
270 Winchester (W) (H)	150	PPSP	24	2900	2632	2380	2142	2801	2307	1886	1528	+2.1	0.0	–8.2	**12.60**
270 Winchester (F) — Premium	150	BTSP	24	2900	2710	2520	2350	2800	2440	2120	1830	+1.6	0.0	–7.0	**13.55**
270 Winchester (R) (F)	150	SPCL, SP	24	2900	2550	2225	1926	2801	2165	1649	1235	+2.2	0.0	–9.3	**12.60**
270 Winchester (F) — Premium	150	NP	24	2900	2630	2380	2140	2800	2310	1890	1530	+2.1	0.0	–8.2	**16.60**
7mm Mauser (R) (W)	175	SP	24	2440	2137	1857	1603	2313	1774	1340	998	0.0	–6.8	–23.7	**12.85**
7mm Mauser (F)	175	SP	24	2470	2170	1880	1630	2370	1820	1380	1030	0.0	–6.6	–23.0	**12.85**
7mm-08 Remington (R)	140	PSPCL	24	2860	2625	2402	2189	2542	2142	1793	1490	+2.1	0.0	–8.1	**12.60**
7mm Express Remington (R)	150	SPCL	24	2970	2699	2444	2203	2937	2426	1989	1616	+1.9	0.0	–7.8	**12.60**
280 Remington (R)	165	SPCL	24	2820	2510	2220	1950	2913	2308	1805	1393	+2.3	0.0	–9.4	**12.60**
284 Winchester (W)	125	PPSP	24	3140	2829	2538	2265	2736	2221	1788	1424	+1.7	0.0	–7.2	**13.15**
284 Winchester (W)	150	PPSP	24	2860	2595	2344	2108	2724	2243	1830	1480	+2.1	0.0	–8.5	**14.60**
7mm Remington Magnum (W)	125	PPSP	24	3310	2976	2666	2376	3040	2458	1972	1567	+1.2	0.0	–6.5	**15.65**
7mm Remington Magnum (R) (W) (F)	150	PSPCL, PPSP, SP	24	3110	2830	2568	2320	3221	2667	2196	1792	+1.7	0.0	–7.0	**15.60**
7mm Remington Magnum (F)	150	BTSP-Prem.	24	3110	2920	2750	2580	3220	2850	2510	2210	+1.6	0.0	–6.2	**16.60**
7mm Remington Magnum (F)	165	BTSP-Prem.	24	2860	2710	2560	2420	3000	2690	2410	2150	+1.6	0.0	–6.9	**16.60**
7mm Remington Magnum (R) (W) (F) (H)	175	PSPCL, PPSP	24	2860	2645	2440	2244	3178	2718	2313	1956	+2.0	0.0	–7.9	**15.60**
7mm Remington Magnum (F)	160	NP	24	2950	2730	2520	2320	3090	2650	2250	1910	+1.8	0.0	–7.7	**19.55**
30 Carbine (R) (W) (F) (H)	110	SP, HSP, SP, RN	**20**	1990	1567	1236	1035	967	600	373	262	0.0	–13.5	–49.9	***20.25**
30 Carbine (W) (F) (H) (PMC)	110	FMC, MC, FMJ, FMC	**20**	1990	1596	1278	1070	967	622	399	280	0.0	–13.0	–47.4	**8.10**
30 Remington (R) (W)	170	SPCL, ST	24	2120	1822	1555	1328	1696	1253	913	666	0.0	–9.7	–33.8	**12.75**
30-30 Accelerator (R)	55	SP	24	3400	2693	2085	1570	1412	886	521	301	+2.0	0.0	–10.2	**11.00**
30-30 Winchester (F)	125	HP	24	2570	2090	1660	1320	1830	1210	770	480	0.0	–7.3	–28.1	**9.90**
30-30 Winchester (W) (F)	150	OPE, PPSP, ST, SP	24	2390	2018	1684	1398	1902	1356	944	651	0.0	–7.7	–27.9	**9.90**
30-30 Winchester (R) (H)	150	SPCL	24	2390	1973	1605	1303	1902	1296	858	565	0.0	–8.2	–30.0	**9.90**
30-30 Winchester (W) (R) (F)	170	PPSP, ST, SPCL, SP, HPCL	24	2200	1895	1619	1381	1827	1355	989	720	0.0	–8.9	–31.1	**9.90**
300 Savage (R)	150	SPCL	24	2630	2247	1897	1585	2303	1681	1198	837	0.0	–6.1	–21.9	**12.70**
300 Savage (W)	150	PPSP	24	2630	2311	2015	1743	2303	1779	1352	1012	+2.8	0.0	–11.5	**12.75**
300 Savage (W) (F) (R)	150	ST, SP, PSPCL	24	2630	2354	2095	1853	2303	1845	1462	1143	+2.7	0.0	–10.7	**12.70**
300 Savage (R) (W)	180	SPCL, PPSP	24	2350	2025	1728	1467	2207	1639	1193	860	0.0	–7.7	–27.1	**12.70**
300 Savage (R) (W)	180	PSPCL, ST	24	2350	2137	1935	1745	2207	1825	1496	1217	0.0	–6.7	–22.8	**12.70**
30-40 Krag (R) (W)	180	SPCL, PPSP	24	2430	2098	1795	1525	2360	1761	1288	929	0.0	–7.1	–25.0	**13.25**
30-40 Krag (R) (W)	180	PSPCL, ST	24	2430	2213	2007	1813	2360	1957	1610	1314	0.0	–6.2	–21.1	**13.25**
303 Savage (W)	190	ST	24	1940	1657	1410	1211	1588	1158	839	619	0.0	–11.9	–41.4	**15.00**
308 Accelerator (R)	55	PSP	24	3770	3215	2726	2286	1735	1262	907	638	+1.0	0.0	–5.6	**14.00**
308 Winchester (W)	110	PSP	24	3180	2666	2206	1795	2470	1736	1188	787	+2.0	0.0	–9.3	**12.60**
308 Winchester (W)	125	PSP	24	3050	2697	2370	2067	2582	2019	1559	1186	+2.0	0.0	–8.2	**12.60**
308 Winchester (W)	150	PPSP	24	2820	2488	2179	1893	2648	2061	1581	1193	+2.4	0.0	–9.8	**12.60**
308 Winchester (W) (R) (F) (H) (PMC)	150	ST, PSPCL, SP	24	2820	2533	2263	2009	2648	2137	1705	1344	+2.3	0.0	–9.1	**12.60**
308 Winchester (PMC)	147	FMC-BT	24	2750	2473	2257	2052	2428	2037	1697	1403	+2.3	0.0	–9.1	**8.00**
308 Winchester (F) (H)	165	BTSP, SPBT	24	2700	2520	2330	2160	2670	2310	1990	1700	+2.0	0.0	–8.4	**12.60**
308 Winchester (W) (R)	180	PPSP, SPCL	24	2620	2274	1955	1666	2743	2086	1527	1109	+2.9	0.0	–12.1	**12.60**
308 Winchester (W) (R) (F) (PMC)	180	ST, PSPCL, SP	24	2620	2393	2178	1974	2743	2288	1896	1557	+2.6	0.0	–9.9	**12.60**
308 Winchester (W)	200	ST	24	2450	2208	1980	1767	2665	2165	1741	1386	0.0	–6.3	–21.4	**13.30**
30-06 Springfield (W)	110	PSP	24	3380	2843	2365	1936	2790	1974	1366	915	+1.7	0.0	–8.0	**12.60**
30-06 Springfield (W) (R) (F)	125	PSP, PSP, SP	24	3140	2780	2447	2138	2736	2145	1662	1269	+1.8	0.0	–7.7	**12.60**
30-16 Springfield (W)	150	PPSP	24	2920	2580	2265	1972	2839	2217	1708	1295	+2.2	0.0	–9.0	**12.00**
30-06 Springfield (W) (R) (F) (H) (PMC)	150	ST, PSPCL, SP, SP	24	2910	2617	2342	2083	2820	2281	1827	1445	+2.1	0.0	–8.5	**12.60**
30-06 Springfield (R)	150	BP	24	2910	2656	2416	2189	2820	2349	1944	1596	+2.0	0.0	–8.0	**13.30**
30-06 Springfield (PMC)	150	FMC (M-2)	24	2810	2555	2310	2080	2630	2170	1780	1440	+2.2	0.0	–8.8	**8.00**
30-06 Accelerator	55	PSP	24	4080	3485	2965	2502	2033	1483	1074	764	+1.0	0.0	–5.0	**14.00**
30-06 Springfield (R)	165	PSPCL	24	2800	2534	2283	2047	2872	2352	1909	1534	+2.3	0.0	–9.0	**12.60**
30-06 Springfield (F) (H)	165	BTSP	24	2800	2610	2420	2240	2870	2490	2150	1840	+2.1	0.0	–8.0	**13.15**

CENTERFIRE RIFLE CARTRIDGES—BALLISTICS AND PRICES (continued)

	— BULLET —			— VELOCITY (fps) —				— ENERGY (ft. lbs.) —				— BULLET PATH† —			Price
Cartridge	Wt. Grs.	Type	Bbl. (in.)	Muzzle	100 yds.	200 yds.	300 yds.	Muzzle	100 yds.	200 yds.	300 yds.	100 yds.	200 yds.	300 yds.	Per Box
30-06 Springfield (R) (W)	180	SPCL, PPSP	24	2700	2348	2023	1727	2913	2203	1635	1192	+2.7	0.0	−11.3	**12.60**
30-06 Springfield (R) (W) (F) (H) (PMC)	180	PSPCL, ST, NOSLER	24	2700	2469	2250	2042	2913	2436	2023	1666	+2.4	0.0	−9.3	**12.60**
30-06 Springfield (R)	180	BP	24	2700	2485	2280	2084	2913	2468	2077	1736	+2.4	0.0	−9.1	**13.30**
30-06 Springfield (F)	200	BTSP	24	2550	2400	2260	2120	2890	2560	2270	2000	+2.3	0.0	−9.0	**13.15**
30-06 Springfield (W) (R)	220	PPSP, SPCL	24	2410	2130	1870	1632	2837	2216	1708	1301	0.0	−6.8	−23.6	**12.60**
30-06 Springfield (W)	220	ST	24	2410	2192	1985	1791	2837	2347	1924	1567	0.0	−6.4	−21.6	**13.30**
300 H & H Magnum (W)	150	ST	24	3130	2822	2534	2264	3262	2652	2138	1707	+1.7	0.0	−7.2	**13.30**
300 H & H Magnum (W) (R)	180	ST, PSPCL	24	2880	2640	2412	2196	3315	2785	2325	1927	+2.1	0.0	−8.0	**16.90**
300 H & H Magnum (W)	220	ST	24	2580	2341	2114	1901	3251	2677	2183	1765	+2.7	0.0	−10.5	**16.05**
300 Winchester Magnum (W) (R)	150	PPSP, PSPCL	24	3290	2951	2636	2342	3605	2900	2314	1827	+1.3	0.0	−6.6	**16.45**
300 Winchester Mgnum (W) (R) (F) (H)	180	PPSP, PSPCL, SP	24	2960	2745	2540	2344	3501	3011	2578	2196	+1.9	0.0	−7.3	**16.45**
300 Winchester Magnum (F) Premium	200	BTSP	24	2830	2680	2530	2380	3560	3180	2830	2520	+1.7	0.0	−7.1	**13.55**
303 British (R)	180	SPCL	24	2460	2124	1817	1542	2418	1803	1319	950	0.0	−6.9	−24.4	**12.95**
303 British (W)	180	PPSP	24	2460	2233	2018	1816	2418	1993	1627	1318	0.0	−6.1	−20.8	**12.95**
32-20 Winchester (W) (R)	100	SP	24	1210	1021	913	834	325	231	185	154	0.0	−32.3	−106.3	***18.95**
32-20 Winchester (W) (R)	100	L	24	1210	1021	913	834	325	231	185	154	0.0	−32.3	−106.3	***15.35**
.32 Winchester Special (W)	170	PPSP, ST	24	2250	1870	1537	1267	1911	1320	892	606	0.0	−9.2	−33.2	**11.15**
32 Winchester Special (F) (R)	170	SP	24	2250	1920	1630	1370	1911	1390	1000	710	0.0	−8.6	−30.5	**10.55**
8mm Mauser (R) (W)	170	SPCL, PPSP	24	2360	1969	1622	1333	2102	1463	993	671	0.0	−8.2	−29.8	**13.00**
8mm Mauser (F)	170	SP	24	2510	2110	1740	1430	2380	1670	1140	770	0.0	−7.0	−25.7	**13.00**
8mm Remington Magnum (R)	185	PSPCL	24	3080	2761	2464	2186	3896	3131	2494	1963	+1.8	0.0	−7.6	**18.45**
8mm Remington Magnum (R)	220	PSPCL	24	2830	2581	2346	2123	3912	3254	2688	2201	+2.2	0.0	−8.5	**18.45**
338 Winchester Magnum (W)	200	PPSP	24	2960	2658	2375	2110	3890	3137	2505	1977	+2.0	0.0	−8.2	**19.80**
338 Winchester Magnum (W)	250	ST	24	2660	2395	2145	1910	3927	3184	2554	2025	+2.6	0.0	−10.2	**18.75**
348 Winchester (W)	200	ST	24	2520	2215	1931	1672	2820	2178	1656	1241	0.0	−6.2	−21.9	**24.00**
351 Winchester S.L. (W)	180	SP	**20**	1850	1556	1310	1128	1368	968	686	508	0.0	−13.6	−47.5	***32.25**
35 Remington (R)	150	PSPCL	24	2300	1874	1506	1218	1762	1169	755	494	0.0	−9.2	−33.0	**11.65**
35 Remington (R) (F)	200	SPCL, SP	24	2080	1698	1376	1140	1921	1280	841	577	0.0	−11.3	−41.2	**11.65**
35 Remington (W)	200	PPSP, ST	24	2020	1646	1335	1114	1812	1203	791	551	0.0	−12.1	−43.9	**11.65**
358 Winchester (W)	200	ST	24	2490	2171	1876	1610	2753	2093	1563	1151	0.0	−6.5	−23.0	**18.40**
350 Remington Magnum (R)	200	PSPCL	**20**	2710	2410	2130	1870	3261	2579	2014	1553	+2.6	0.0	−10.3	**18.15**
375 Winchester (W)	200	PPSP	24	2200	1841	1526	1268	2150	1506	1034	714	0.0	−9.5	−33.8	**15.05**
375 Winchester (W)	250	PPSP	24	1900	1647	1424	1239	2005	1506	1126	852	0.0	−12.0	−40.9	**15.05**
38-55 Winchester (W)	255	SP	24	1320	1190	1091	1018	987	802	674	587	0.0	−23.4	−75.2	**14.00**
375 H & H Magnum (R) (W)	270	SP, PPSP	24	2690	2420	2166	1928	4337	3510	2812	2228	+2.5	0.0	−10.0	**19.55**
375 H & H Magnum (W)	300	ST	24	2530	2268	2022	1793	4263	3426	2723	2141	+2.9	0.0	−11.5	**20.65**
375 H & H Magnum (W) (R)	300	FMC, MC	24	2530	2171	1843	1551	4263	3139	2262	1602	0.0	−6.5	−23.4	**19.55**
38-40 Winchester (W)	180	SP	24	1160	999	901	827	538	399	324	273	0.0	−33.9	−110.6	***24.05**
44-40 Winchester (W) (R)	200	SP, SP	24	1190	1006	900	822	629	449	360	300	0.0	−33.3	−109.5	***25.40**
44 Remington Magnum (R)	240	SP, SJHP	**20**	1760	1380	1114	970	1650	1015	661	501	0.0	−17.6	−63.1	**9.60**
44 Remington Magnum (F) (W)	240	HSP	**20**	1760	1380	1090	950	1650	1015	640	485	0.0	−18.1	−65.1	**9.60**
444 Marlin (R)	240	SP	24	2350	1815	1377	1087	2942	1755	1010	630	0.0	−9.9	−38.5	**14.05**
444 Marlin (R)	265	SP	24	2120	1733	1405	1160	2644	1768	1162	791	0.0	−10.8	−39.5	**14.25**
45-70 Government (F)	300	HSP	24	1810	1410	1120	970	2180	1320	840	630	0.0	−17.0	−61.4	**14.35**
45-70 Government (W)	300	JHP	24	1880	1559	1294	1105	2355	1619	1116	814	0.0	−13.5	−47.1	**14.35**
45-70 Government (W) (R)	405	SP	24	1330	1168	1055	977	1590	1227	1001	858	0.0	−24.6	−80.3	**14.35**
458 Winchester Magnum (W) (R)	500	FMC, MC	24	2040	1823	1623	1442	4620	3689	2924	2308	0.0	−9.6	−32.5	**40.05**
458 Winchester Magnum (W) (R)	510	SP, SP	24	2040	1770	1527	1319	4712	3547	2640	1970	0.0	−10.3	−35.6	**26.40**

*Price for 50. †Bullet Path based on line-of-sight 0.9" above center of bore. Bullet type abbreviations: BP—Bronze Point; BT—Boat Tail; CL—Core Lokt; FN—Flat Nose; FMC—Full Metal Case; FMJ—Full Metal Jacket; HP—Hollow Point; HSP—Hollow Soft Point; JHP—Jacketed Hollow Point; L—Lead; Lu—Lubaloy; MAT—Match; MC—Metal Case; NP—Nosler Partition; OPE—Open Point Expanding; PCL—Pointed Core Lokt; PEP—Pointed Expanding Point; PL—Power-Lokt; PP—Power Point; Prem.—Premium; PSP—Pointed Soft Point; SJHP—Semi-Jacketed Hollow Point; SJMP—Semi-Jacketed Metal Point; SP—Soft Point; ST—Silvertip; SX—Super Explosive.

WEATHERBY MAGNUM CARTRIDGES—BALLISTICS AND PRICES

	— Bullet —			— Velocity (fps) —				— Energy (ft. lbs.) —				— Bullet Path† —			Price
Cartridge	Wt. Grs.	Type	Bbl. (in.)	Muzzle	100 Yds.	200 Yds.	300 Yds.	Muzzle	100 Yds.	200 Yds.	300 Yds.	100 Yds.	200 Yds.	300 Yds.	Per Box
224 Weatherby Magnum	50	PE	26	3750	3263	2814	2402	1562	1182	879	640	+2.6	+3.6	0.0	**$21.95**
224 Weatherby Magnum	55	PE	26	3650	3214	2808	2433	1627	1262	963	723	+2.8	+3.6	0.0	**21.95**
240 Weatherby Magnum	70	PE	26	3850	3424	3025	2654	2305	1823	1423	1095	+2.2	+3.0	0.0	**21.95**
240 Weatherby Magnum	87	PE	26	3500	3165	2848	2550	2367	1935	1567	1256	+2.8	+3.6	0.0	**21.95**
240 Weatherby Magnum	100	PE	26	3395	3115	2848	2594	2560	2155	1802	1495	+2.8	+3.5	0.0	**21.95**
240 Weatherby Magnum	100	NP	26	3395	3068	2758	2468	2560	2090	1690	1353	+1.1	0.0	−5.7	**29.95**
257 Weatherby Magnum	87	PE	26	3825	3470	3135	2818	2827	2327	1900	1535	+2.1	+2.9	0.0	**22.95**
257 Weatherby Magnum	100	PE	26	3555	3256	2971	2700	2807	2355	1960	1619	+2.5	+3.2	0.0	**22.95**
257 Weatherby Magnum	100	NP	26	3555	3242	2945	2663	2807	2335	1926	1575	+0.9	0.0	−4.7	**31.95**
257 Weatherby Magnum	117	SPE	26	3300	2853	2443	2074	2830	2115	1551	1118	+3.8	+4.9	0.0	**22.95**
257 Weatherby Magnum	117	NP	26	3300	3027	2767	2520	2830	2381	1990	1650	+1.2	0.0	−5.9	**31.95**
270 Weatherby Magnum	100	PE	26	3760	3341	2949	2585	3140	2479	1932	1484	+2.4	+3.2	0.0	**22.95**
270 Weatherby Magnum	130	PE	26	3375	3110	2856	2615	3289	2793	2355	1974	+2.8	+3.5	0.0	**22.95**
270 Weatherby Magnum	130	NP	26	3375	3113	2862	2624	3289	2798	2365	1988	+1.0	0.0	−5.2	**31.95**
270 Weatherby Magnum	150	PE	26	3245	3012	2789	2575	3508	3022	2592	2209	+3.1	+3.8	0.0	**22.95**
270 Weatherby Magnum	150	NP	26	3245	3022	2809	2604	3508	3043	2629	2259	+1.2	0.0	−5.4	**22.95**
7mm Weatherby Magnum	139	PE	26	3300	3037	2786	2546	3362	2848	2396	2001	+3.0	+3.7	0.0	**22.95**
7mm Weatherby Magnum	140	NP	26	3300	3047	2806	2575	3386	2887	2448	2062	+1.1	0.0	−5.4	**31.95**
7mm Weatherby Magnum	154	PE	26	3160	2928	2706	2494	3415	2932	2504	2127	+3.3	+4.1	0.0	**22.95**
7mm Weatherby Magnum	160	NP	26	3150	2935	2727	2528	3526	3061	2643	2271	+1.3	0.0	−5.8	**31.95**
7mm Weatherby Magnum	175	RN	26	3070	2714	2383	2082	3663	2863	2207	1685	+1.6	0.0	−7.5	**22.95**
300 Weatherby Magnum	110	PE	26	3900	3465	3057	2677	3716	2933	2283	1750	+2.2	+3.0	0.0	**22.95**
300 Weatherby Magnum	150	PE	26	3545	3248	2965	2696	4187	3515	2929	2422	+2.5	+3.2	0.0	**22.95**
300 Weatherby Magnum	150	NP	26	3545	3191	2857	2544	4187	3392	2719	2156	+1.0	0.0	−5.3	**32.95**
300 Weatherby Magnum	180	PE	26	3245	3010	2785	2569	4210	3622	3100	2639	+3.1	+3.8	0.0	**22.95**
300 Weatherby Magnum	180	NP	26	3245	2964	2696	2444	4210	3512	2906	2388	+1.3	0.0	−6.0	**22.95**
300 Weatherby Magnum	200	NP	26	3000	2740	2494	2262	3998	3335	2763	2273	+1.6	0.0	−7.3	**32.95**
300 Weatherby Magnum	220	SPE	26	2905	2578	2276	2000	4123	3248	2531	1955	+1.9	0.0	−8.6	**22.95**
340 Weatherby Magnum	200	PE	26	3210	2947	2696	2458	4577	3857	3228	2683	+3.2	+4.0	0.0	**24.20**
340 Weatherby Magnum	210	NP	26	3180	2927	2686	2457	4717	3996	3365	2816	+1.3	0.0	−6.2	**38.95**
340 Weatherby Magnum	250	SPE	26	2850	2516	2209	1929	4510	3515	2710	2066	+2.0	0.0	−9.2	**24.20**
340 Weatherby Magnum	250	NP	26	2850	2563	2296	2049	4510	3648	2927	2331	+1.8	0.0	−8.2	**24.20**
378 Weatherby Magnum	270	SPE	26	3180	2796	2440	2117	6064	4688	3570	2688	+1.5	0.0	−7.3	**44.95**
378 Weatherby Magnum	270	NP	26	3180	2840	2515	2220	6064	4837	3793	2955	+3.9	+4.9	0.0	**44.95**
378 Weatherby Magnum	300	SPE	26	2925	2564	2234	1935	5700	4380	3325	2495	+1.9	0.0	−9.0	**44.95**
378 Weatherby Magnum	300	NP	26	2925	2620	2340	2080	5700	4574	3649	2883	+4.9	+6.0	0.0	**44.95**
460 Weatherby Magnum	500	RN	26	2700	2395	2115	1858	8095	6370	4968	3834	+2.3	0.0	−10.3	**42.95**
460 Weatherby Magnum	500	FMJ	26	2700	2416	2154	1912	8095	6482	5153	4060	+2.2	0.0	−9.8	**49.95**

Note: 26" barrels used to obtain Weatherby ballistic data. †Bullet Path based on line of sight 1.5" above center of bore. Bullet type abbreviations: FMJ—Full Metal Jacket; NP—Nosler Partition; PE—Pointed Expanding; RN—Round Nose; SPE—Semi-Pointed Expanding.

NORMA C.F. RIFLE CARTRIDGES—BALLISTICS AND PRICES

Cartridge	Wt. Grs.	Bullet Type	Bbl. (in.)	Velocity (fps) Muzzle	100 Yds.	200 Yds.	300 Yds.	Energy(ft. lbs.) Muzzle	100 Yds.	200 Yds.	300 Yds.	Bullet Path† 100 Yds.	200 Yds.	300 Yds.	Price Per Box
222 Remington	50	SP	24	3200	2650	2170	1750	1137	780	520	340	+1.6	0.0	− 8.2	$9.60
222 Remington	50	FJ	24	3200	2610	2080	1630	1137	756	480	295	+1.9	0.0	−10.1	11.70
222 Remington	53	SpPSP	24	3117	2670	2267	1901	1142	838	604	425	+1.7	0.0	− 8.7	9.60
22-250 Remington	53	SpPSP	24	3707	3192	2741	2332	1616	1198	883	639	+1.0	0.0	− 5.7	9.70
220 Swift	50	SP	24	4110	3611	3133	2681	1877	1448	1090	799	+0.6	0.0	− 4.1	18.00
22 Savage Hi-Power (5.6 x 52R)	71	SP	24	2790	2296	1886	1558	1226	831	561	383	+2.4	0.0	−11.4	21.70
22 Savage Hi-Power (5.6 x 52R)	71	FJ	24	2790	2296	1886	1558	1226	831	561	383	+2.4	0.0	−11.4	21.70
243 Winchester	100	SP, FJ	24	3070	2790	2540	2320	2090	1730	1430	1190	+1.4	0.0	− 6.3	13.00
6.5mm Carcano	139	PPDC	24	2576	2379	2192	2012	2046	1745	1481	1249	+2.3	0.0	− 9.6	21.95
6.5mm Carcano	156	SP	24	2430	2208	2000	1800	2046	1689	1386	1123	+2.9	0.0	−11.7	21.00
6.5mm JAP	139	SPBT	24	2430	2280	2130	1990	1820	1605	1401	1223	+2.7	0.0	−10.8	21.00
6.5mm JAP	156	SP	24	2065	1871	1692	1529	1481	1213	992	810	+4.3	0.0	−16.4	21.00
6.5mm Norma (6.5 x 55)	77	SP	29	2725	2362	2030	1811	1271	956	706	562	+2.4	0.0	−10.9	21.00
6.5mm Norma (6.5 x 55)	139	PPDC	29	2790	2630	2470	2320	2402	2136	1883	1662	+1.8	0.0	− 7.8	21.00
6.5mm Norma (6.5 x 55)	156	SP	29	2495	2271	2062	1867	2153	1787	1473	1208	+2.6	0.0	−10.9	21.00
270 Winchester	130	SPBT	24	3140	2884	2639	2404	2847	2401	2011	1669	+1.4	0.0	− 6.6	14.20
270 Winchester	150	SPBT	24	2800	2616	2436	2262	2616	2280	1977	1705	+1.8	0.0	− 7.7	14.20
7mm Mauser (7 x 57)	150	SPBT	24	2755	2539	2331	2133	2530	2148	1810	1516	+2.0	0.0	− 8.4	15.00
7 x 57 R	150	SPBT, FJ BT	24	2690	2476	2270	2077	2411	2042	1717	1437	+2.1	0.0	− 8.9	22.50
7 x 64	150	SPBT	24	2890	2598	2329	2113	2779	2249	1807	1487	+1.7	0.0	− 7.5	22.50
7mm Rem. Express (.280 Rem.)	150	SPBT	24	2900	2683	2475	2277	2802	2398	2041	1727	+1.7	0.0	− 7.4	14.75
7mm Remington Magnum	150	SPBT	26	3250	2960	2638	2440	3519	2919	2318	1983	+1.2	0.0	− 5.8	18.30
30 Carbine U.S.	110	SP	18	1970	1595	1300	1090	948	622	413	290	0.0	−12.4	−45.7	12.60
30-30 Winchester	150	SPFN	20	2410	2075	1790	1550	1934	1433	1066	799	0.0	− 7.0	−26.1	13.30
30-30 Winchester	170	SPFN	20	2220	1890	1630	1410	1860	1350	1000	750	0.0	− 8.1	−29.2	13.30
7.5 x 55 Swiss	180	SPBT	24	2650	2441	2248	2056	2792	2380	2020	1690	+2.1	0.0	− 8.9	22.00
7.62 x 39 Short Russian	125	SP		2385				1580							17.00
7.62 Russian	180	SPBT	24	2625	2415	2222	2030	2749	2326	1970	1644	+2.2	0.0	− 9.1	22.35
308 Winchester	130	SPBT	24	2900	2590	2300	2030	2428	1937	1527	1190	+1.9	0.0	− 8.6	14.15
308 Winchester	150	SPBT	24	2860	2570	2300	2050	2725	2200	1760	1400	+1.9	0.0	− 8.5	14.70
308 Winchester	180	PPDC	24	2610	2400	2210	2020	2725	2303	1952	1631	+2.3	0.0	− 9.4	16.35
30-06	130	SPBT	24	3205	2876	2561	2263	2966	2388	1894	1479	+1.4	0.0	− 6.7	14.15
30-06	150	SPBT	24	2970	2680	2402	2141	2943	2393	1922	1527	+1.7	0.0	− 7.8	14.15
30-06	180	SP	24	2700	2477	2261	2070	2914	2430	2025	1713	+2.1	0.0	− 8.7	14.15
30-06	180	PPDC	24	2700	2494	2296	2109	2914	2487	2107	1778	+2.0	0.0	− 8.6	14.15
303 British	150	SP	24	2720	2440	2170	1930	2465	1983	1569	1241	+2.2	0.0	− 9.7	15.70
303 British	180	SPBT	24	2540	2340	2147	1965	2579	2189	1843	1544	+2.4	0.0	−10.0	15.70
308 Norma Magnum	180	PPDC	26	3020	2798	2585	2382	3646	3130	2671	2268	+1.3	0.0	− 6.1	27.90
7.65mm Argentine	150	SP	24	2920	2630	2355	2105	2841	2304	1848	1476	+1.7	0.0	− 7.8	21.95
7.7mm JAP	130	SP	24	2950	2635	2340	2065	2513	2004	1581	1231	+1.8	0.0	− 8.2	22.50
7.7mm JAP	180	SPBT	24	2495	2292	2101	1922	2484	2100	1765	1477	+2.6	0.0	−10.4	22.50
8 x 57J (.318)	196	SP	24	2525	2195	1894	1627	2778	2097	1562	1152	+2.9	0.0	−12.7	23.00
8mm Mauser (8 x 57JS)	196	SP	24	2525	2195	1894	1627	2778	2097	1562	1152	+2.9	0.0	−12.7	15.50
358 Norma Magnum	250	SP	26	2800	2493	2231	2001	4322	3451	2764	2223	+2.0	0.0	− 8.3	27.95
9.3 x 57 mm	286	PPDC	24	2065	1818	1595	1404	2714	2099	1616	1252	0.0	− 9.1	−32.0	19.75
9.3 x 62 mm	286	PPDC	24	2360	2088	1815	1592	3544	2769	2092	1700	+3.3	0.0	−13.7	19.75

†Bullet Path based on line of sight 1.5″ above center of bore. Bullet type abbreviations: BT—Boat Tail; DC—Dual Core; FJ—Full Jacket; FJBT—Full Jacket Boat Tail; FP—Flat Point; HP—Hollow Point; MC—Metal Case; P—Pointed; PP—Plastic Point; RN—Round Nose; SP—Soft Point; SPFN—Soft Point Flat Nose; SPSBT—Soft Point Semi-Pointed Boat Tail; SPSP—Soft Point Semi-Point; SpPSP—Spire point Soft Point.

RIMFIRE CARTRIDGES—BALLISTICS AND PRICES

Remington-Peters, Winchester-Western, Federal, Omark/CCI

All loads available from all manufacturers except as indicated: R-P (a); W-W (b); Fed. (c); CCI (d). **All prices are approximate.**

CARTRIDGE	WT. GRS.	BULLET TYPE	VELOCITY FT. PER SEC. MUZZLE	100 YDS.	ENERGY FT. LBS. MUZZLE	100 YDS.	MID-RANGE TRAJECTORY 100 YDS	HANDGUN BARREL LENGTH	BALLISTICS M.V. F.P.S	M.E. F.P.	PRICE PER BOX
22 Short T22 (b)	29	C, L*	1045	810	70	42	5.6	6″	865	48	$1.88
22 Short Hi-Vel. (c)	29	C, L	1125	920	81	54	4.3	6″	1035	69	1.88
22 Short HP-Hi-Vel. (a, b, c)	27	C, L	1155	920	80	51	4.2	—	—	—	2.00
22 Short Std. Vel. (a, b, c)	29	L*	1045	870	70	49	8.7	—	1045	870	1.88
22 Short Target (a)	29	L*	1045	872	70	49	4.8	—	—	—	1.88
22 Stinger	32	C, HP	1686	1047	202	78	−2.61	—	—	—	2.85
22 Long Rifle Yellow Jacket	33	HVTCHP	1500	1075	185	85	2.8	—	1500	165	2.63
22 Long Rifle Target (a)	40	L	1150	976	117	85	4.0	—	—	—	2.15
22 Long Rifle Match Rifle (a)	40	L	—	—	—	—	—	—	—	—	7.18
22 Long Rifle Match Pistol (a)	40	L	—	—	—	—	—	—	—	—	7.18
22 Long Hi-Vel. (c)	29	C, L	1045	870	70	49	8.7	—	1045	70	4.30
22 Long Rifle T22 (a, b)†1	40	L*	1145	975	116	84	4.0	6″	950	80	2.15
22 Long Rifle (b)†2	40	L*	1120	950	111	80	4.2	—	—	—	4.30
22 Long Rifle (b)†3	40	L*	—	—	—	—	—	6¾″	1060	100	4.30
22 Long Rifle (d)†4	40	C	1165	980	121	84	4.0	—	—	—	2.15
22 Long Rifle Hi-Vel.	40	C, L	1285	1025	147	93	3.4	6″	1125	112	2.15
22 Long Rifle HP Hi-Vel. (b, d)	37	C, L	131	1020	142	85	3.4	—	1255	140	2.37
22 Long Rifle HP Hi-Vel. (a, c)	38	C, HP	1280	1020	138	88	6.1	—	1280	138	2.37
22 Long Rifle (b, c)		No. 12 Shot	—	—	—	—	—	—	—	—	4.36
22 WMR Mini-Mag Shotshell (d)		No. 11 Shot	1000	—	—	—	—	6″	—	—	2.22
22 LR Mini-Mag Shotshell (d)		No. 12 Shot	950	—	—	—	—	6″	—	—	2.22
22 WMR Mag.	40	HP	2000	1390	355	170	1.6	6½″	1550	213	5.90
22 WMR Mag.	40	MC	2000	1390	355	170	1.6	6½″	1550	213	5.90
5mm Rem. RFM (a)	38	PLHP	2100	1605	372	217		Not Available			13.52

†Target loads of these ballistics available in: (1) Rem. Match; (2) W-W, Super Match Mark III; (3) Super Match Mark IV Pistol Match; (4) CCI MiniGroup.
C—Copper plated L—Lead (Wax Coated) L*—Lead, lubricated D—Disintegrating MC—Metal Case HP—Hollow Point JHP—Jacket Hollow Point PLHP—Power-Lokt Hollow Point HVTCHP—Hyper Velocity Truncated Cone Hollow Point.

CENTER FIRE HANDGUN CARTRIDGES BALLISTICS AND PRICES

Win.-Western, Rem.-Peters, Norma, PMC, and Federal

Most loads are available from W-W and R-P. All available Norma loads are listed. Federal cartridges are marked with an asterisk. Other loads supplied by only one source are indicated by a letter, thus: Norma (a); R-P (b); W-W (c); PMC (d); CCI (e). Prices are approximate.

Cartridge	Bullet Gr.	Bullet Style	Muzzle Velocity	Muzzle Energy	Barrel Inches	Price Per Box
22 Jet (b)	40	SP	2100	390	8⅜	**$21.00**
221 Fireball (b)	50	SP	2650	780	10½	**9.70**
25 (6.35mm) Auto*	50	MC	810	73	2	**12.25**
25 ACP (c)	45	Exp. Pt.	835	70	2	**12.90**
256 Winchester Magnum (c)	60	HP	2350	735	8½	**23.75**
30 (7.65mm) Luger Auto	93	MC	1220	307	4½	**19.70**
32 S&W Blank (b, c)	No bullet		—	—	—	**11.70**
32 S&W Blank, BP (c)	No bullet		—	—	—	**11.70**
32 Short Colt	80	Lead	745	100	4	**11.75**
32 Long Colt IL (c)	82	Lub.	755	104	4	**12.25**
32 Auto (c)	60	STHP	970	125	4	**15.15**
32 (7.65mm) Auto*	71	MC	905	129	4	**14.00**
32 (7.65mm) Auto Pistol (a)	77	MC	900	162	4	**15.15**
32 S&W	88	Lead	680	90	3	**11.85**
32 S&W Long	98	Lead	705	115	4	**12.25**
32-20 Winchester	100	Lead	1030	271	6	**15.35**
32-20 Winchester	100	SP	1030	271	6	**19.00**
357 Magnum	110	JHP	1295	410	4	**18.40**
357 Magnum	110	SJHP	1295	410	4	**18.45**
357 Magnum	125	JHP	1450	583	4	**18.40**
357 Magnum (d)	125	JHC	1450	583	4	**—**
357 Magnum (e)	125	JSP	1900	1001	—	**18.43**
357 Magnum (e)	140	JHP	1775	979	—	**18.43**
357 Magnum (e)	150	FMJ	1600	852	—	**18.43**
357 Magnum*	158	SWC	1235	535	4	**15.60**
357 Magnum (b) (e)	158	JSP	1550	845	8⅜	**18.40**
357 Magnum	158	MP	1410	695	8⅜	**18.15**
357 Magnum	158	Lead	1410	696	8⅜	**15.60**
357 Magnum	158	JHP	1450	735	8⅜	**18.40**
9mm Luger (c)	95	JSP	1355	387	4	**17.45**
9mm Luger (c)	115	FMC	1155	341	4	**17.40**
9mm Luger (c)	115	STHP	1255	383	4	**18.30**
9mm Luger*	115	JHP	1165	349	4	**17.40**
9mm Luger*	125	MC	1120	345	4	**17.40**
9mm Luger (e)	125	JSP	1100	335	—	**17.43**
9mm Winchester Magnum (c)	115	FMC	1475	556	5	**18.65**
38 S&W Blank	No bullet		—	—	—	**14.15**
38 Smith & Wesson	145	Lead	685	150	4	**13.15**
38 S&W	146	Lead	730	172	4	**13.15**
38 Special Blank	No bullet		—	—	—	**14.25**
38 Special (e)	110	JHP	1200	351	—	**16.82**
38 Special, IL +P (c)	150	Lub.	1060	375	6	**14.70**
38 Special IL +P (c)	150	MP	1060	375	6	**16.80**
38 Special	158	Lead	855	256	6	**13.25**
38 Special	200	Lead	730	236	6	**14.15**
38 Special	158	MP	855	256	6	**16.80**
38 Special (b)	125	SJHP	Not available			**16.80**
38 Special WC (b)	148	Lead	770	195	6	**13.80**
38 Special Match, IL	148	Lead	770	195	6	**13.80**
38 Special Match, IL (b)	158	Lead	855	256	6	**13.80**
38 Special*	158	LRN	755	200	4	**13.25**
38 Special	158	RN	900	320	6	**14.85**
38 Special	158	SWC	755	200	4	**13.55**
38 Special Match*	148	WC	710	166	4	**13.80**
38 Special +P (c)	95	STHP	1100	255	4	**17.65**
38 Special +P	95	SJHP	—	—	—	**16.80**
38 Special +P (b)	110	SJHP	1020	254	4	**16.80**
38 Special +P	125	JSP	945	248	4	**16.80**
38 Special +P	158	LRN	915	294	4	**14.70**
38 Special +P (b)	158	LHP	915	294	4	**14.40**
38 Special +P*	158	SWC	915	294	4	**13.55**
38 Special +P*	158	SWCHP	915	294	4	**14.40**
38 Special +P*	158	LSWC	915	294	4	**13.55**
38 Special +P (e)	140	JHP	1275	504	—	**16.82**
38 Special +P (e)	150	FMJ	1175	461	—	**16.82**
38 Special +P*	110	JHP	1020	254	4	**16.80**
38 Special +P*	125	JHP	945	248	4	**16.80**
38 Special Norma +P (a)	110	JHP	1542	580	6	**29.20**
38 Short Colt	125	Lead	730	150	6	**12.90**
38 Short Colt, Greased	130	Lub.	730	155	6	**12.95**
38 Long Colt	150	Lead	730	175	6	**19.45**
38 Super Auto +P (b)	130	MC	1280	475	5	**15.15**
38 Super Auto +P (b)	115	JHP	1300	431	5	**15.75**
38 Auto, for Colt 38 Super (c)	125	JHP	1280	475	5	**15.75**
38 Auto	130	MC	1040	312	4½	**15.65**
38 Auto +P	130	FMC	1280	475	5	**15.15**
380 Auto (c)	85	STHP	1000	189	3¾	**14.35**
380 Auto*	95	MC	955	190	3¾	**10.90**
380 Auto	95	MC	955	192	3¾	**14.35**
380 Auto	88	JHP	990	191	4	**14.35**
380 Auto*	90	JHP	1000	200	3¾	**14.35**
38-40 Winchester	180	SP	975	380	5	**24.05**
41 Remington Magnum	210	Lead	1050	515	8¾	**20.70**
41 Remington Magnum	210	SP	1500	1050	8¾	**24.20**
44 S&W Spec.*	200	LSW	960	410	7½	**18.25**
44 S&W Special	246	Lead	755	311	6½	**18.55**
44 Remington Magnum*	180	JHP	1610	1045	4	**21.80**
44 Remington Magnum (e)	200	JHP	1650	1208	—	**12.02**
44 Remington Magnum (e)	240	JSP	1625	1406	—	**12.02**
44 Remington Magnum (b)	240	SP	1470	1150	6½	**9.60**
44 Remington Magnum	240	Lead	1470	1150	6½	**23.50**
44 Remington Magnum	240	SJHP	1180	741	4	**9.60**
44 Remington Magnum (a)	240	JPC	1533	1253	8½	**14.35**
44 Auto Mag (a)	240	JPC	1350	976	6½	**45.00**
44-40 Winchester	200	SP	975	420	7½	**25.40**
45 Colt*	225	SWCHP	900	405	5½	**17.75**
45 Colt	250	Lead	860	410	5½	**17.80**
45 Colt, IL (c)	255	Lub., L	860	410	5½	**18.85**
45 Auto (c)	185	STHP	1000	411	5	**8.05**
45 Auto (e)	200	JHP	1025	466	—	**9.93**
45 Auto	230	MC	850	369	5	**19.20**
45 ACP	230	JHP	850	370	5	**19.20**
45 Auto WC*	185	MC	775	245	5	**19.85**
45 Auto*	185	JHP	950	370	5	**19.85**
45 Auto MC	230	MC	850	369	5	**19.85**
45 Auto Match (c)	185		775	247	5	**19.85**
45 Auto Match*	230	MC	850	370	5	**19.20**
45 Winchester Magnum (c)	230	FMC	1400	1001	5	**20.55**
45 Auto Rim (b)	230	Lead	810	335	5½	**20.50**

IL—Inside Lub. JSP—Jacketed Soft Point WC—Wad Cutter
RN—Round Nose HP—Hollow Point Lub—Lubricated
MC—Metal Case SP—Soft Point MP—Metal Point
LGC—Lead, Gas Check JHP—Jacketed Hollow Point
SWC—Semi Wad Cutter SJHP—Semi Jacketed Hollow Point

SHOTSHELL LOADS AND PRICES

Winchester-Western, Remington-Peters, Federal

In certain loadings one manufacturer may offer fewer or more shot sizes than another, but in general all makers offer equivalent loadings. Sources are indicated by letters, thus: W-W (a); R-P (b); Fed. (c). *Prices are approximate, list is a random sampling of offerings.*

GAUGE	Length Shell Ins.	Powder Equiv. Drams	Shot Ozs.	Shot Size	PRICE PER BOX
MAGNUM LOADS					
10 (a)	3½	4½	2¼	BB, 2, 4	**$24.65**
10 (a[1], b)	3½	Max	2	BB, 2, 4	**22.95**
12 (a, b, c)	3	Max	1⅞	BB, 2, 4	**15.35**
12 (a[1], b)	3	4	1⅝	2, 4, 6	**14.20**
12 (a[1], b)	2¾	Max	1½	2, 4, 5, 6	**12.85**
16 (a, b, c)	2¾	Max	1¼	2, 4, 6	**12.65**
20 (a, b, c)	3	Max	1¼	2, 4, 6, 7½	**11.90**
20 (a[1])	3	3	1¼	4, 6, 7½	**9.03**
20 (a[1], b, c)	2¾	2¾	1⅛	4, 6, 7½	**10.55**
LONG RANGE LOADS					
10 (a, b)	2⅞	4¾	1⅝	4	**14.15**
12 (a[1], b, c)	2¾	3¾	1¼	BB, 2, 4, 5, 6, 7½, 8, 9	**9.90**
16 (a, b, c)	2¾	3¼	1⅛	4, 5, 6, 7½, 9	**9.50**
20 (a[1], b, c)	2¾	2¾	1	4, 5, 6, 7½, 9	**8.70**
28 (a, b)	2¾	2¼	¾	6, 7½, 8	**8.75**
410 (b)	2½	Max	½	6, 7½	**6.90**
410 (b)	3	Max	11/16	4, 5, 6, 7½, 8	**8.15**
FIELD LOADS					
12 (a, b, c)	2¾	3¼	1¼	7½, 8, 9	**8.75**
12 (a, b, c)	2¾	3¼	1⅛	4, 5, 6, 7½, 8, 9	**8.45**
12 (a, b, c)	2¾	3¼	1⅛	4, 5, 6, 7½, 8	**8.45**
12 (a)	3	4	1⅞	BB, 2, 4, 6	**16.45**
16 (a, b, c)	2¾	2¾	1⅛	4, 5, 6, 7½, 8	**8.45**
16 (a, b, c)	2¾	2¾	1⅛	4, 6, 7½, 8	**8.45**
20 (a, b, c)	2¾	2½	1	4, 5, 6, 7½, 8, 9	**7.65**
20 (a, b, c)	2¾	2½	1	4, 5, 6, 7½, 8, 9	**7.65**
SCATTER LOADS					
12 (b)	2¾	3	1⅛	8	**9.00**
TARGET LOADS					
12 (a)	2¾	3	1⅛	7½, 8	**8.10**
12 (a, b, c)	2¾	2¾	1⅛	7½, 8	**8.10**
20 (a, b, c)	2¾	2½	⅞	9	**7.05**
28 (a, c)	2¾	2	¾	9	**8.55**
410 (a, b, c)	2½	Max	½	9	**6.95**
SKEET & TRAP					
12 (a, b, c)	2¾	3	1⅛	7½, 8	**8.10**
12 (a, b, c)	2¾	2¾	1⅛	7½, 8, 9	**7.85**
20 (a, b, c)	2¾	2½	⅞	9	**7.05**
20 (a)	2¾	2½	⅞	9	**7.05**
28 (a)	2¾	2	¾	9	**8.55**
410 (a)	2½	Max	½	9	**6.95**
BUCKSHOT					
10 (c)	3½	Sup. Mag.	—	4 Buck—54 pellets	**4.70**
12 (a, b, c)	3 Mag.	4½	—	00 Buck—15 pellets	**3.55**
12 (a, b, c)	3 Mag.	4½	—	4 Buck—41 pellets	**3.55**
12 (b)	2¾ Mag.	4	—	1 Buck—20 pellets	**3.10**
12 (a, b, c)	2¾ Mag.	4	—	00 Buck—12 pellets	**3.10**
12 (a, b, c)	2¾	Max	—	00 Buck— 9 pellets	**3.10**
12 (a, b, c)	2¾	3¾	—	0 Buck—12 pellets	**2.80**
12 (a, b, c)	2¾	Max	—	1 Buck—16 pellets	**2.80**
12 (a, b, c)	2¾	Max	—	4 Buck—27 pellets	**2.80**
12 (a)	2¾ Mag.	—	—	000 Buck— 8 pellets	**2.80**
12 (a)	3 Mag.	—	—	000 Buck—10 pellets	**3.55**
16 (a, b, c)	2¾	3	—	1 Buck—12 pellets	**2.80**
20 (a, b, c)	2¾	Max	—	3 Buck—20 pellets	**2.80**
RIFLED SLUGS					
12 (a, b, c)	2¾	Max	1	Slug 5-pack	**3.20**
16 (a, b, c,)	2¾	Max	4/5	Slug	**3.20**
20 (a, b, c)	2¾	Max	⅝	Slug	**2.65**
20 (a)	2¾	Max	¾	Slug	**2.95**
410 (a, b, c)	2½	Max	1/5	Slug	**2.80**
STEEL SHOT LOADS					
10 (c)	3½	Max	1⅝	BB, 2	**20.85**
12 (c)	2¾	3¾	1⅛	1, 2, 4	**9.43**
12 (a, c)	2¾	Max	1¼	BB, 1, 2, 4	**14.90**
12 (b)	3	Max	1¼	1, 2, 4	**16.10**
12 (b)	2¾	Max	1⅛	1, 2, 4	**12.40**
20 (c)	3	3¼	1	4	**11.90**

W-W 410, 28 and 10-ga. Magnum shells available in paper cases only, as are their scatter and target loads; their Skeet and trap loads come in both plastic and paper.

R-P shells are all of plastic with Power Piston wads except; 12 ga. scatter loads have Post Wad: all 10 ga., 410-3" and rifled slug loads have standard wad columns.

Federal magnum, range, buckshot, slug and all 410 loads are made in plastic only. Field loads are available in both paper and plastic.

[1]—These loads available from W-W with Lubaloy shot at higher price.

The Complete Compact Catalog

Nothing is constant but change, it seems. When you are getting together the 36th edition of what is in part a catalog, it is seemly to review the past. We all of us show a great deal of change in the 35 editions of the past, mostly because there is more of everything.

Taken all at once, there is a sameness in Gun Digests until you get down to counting pages and pictures and numbers of models and then you discover all manner of innovations have been successively introduced through the years in this most compact of all firearms catalogs. Some, which proved not to be improvements, were dropped; most persisted and form the nature of these familiar pages, but so quietly nobody noticed.

However, this year we're going to tell you about some of the recent changes. Last year, for instance, we simply had to put a *caveat* about prices on every page. Prices in the sporting goods and firearms business are changing so fast as the industry tries to cope with marketing problems during an inflation we simply had to say "CAUTION: Prices change. Check at gunshop." on every spread. Unfortunately, that hasn't changed and that same warning is there in this issue.

This year, we decided every picture ought to be identified. "About time," you say? Well, that is because you don't know that is about a week's extra work for a number of professionals. However, there they are, intended to make this a better book for you.

We reviewed some of our standard package this time as well. You will find the Arms Library tightened up a little, with some reclassifying so you can find foreign books and catalog reprints and such more easily. And there is, right up front, a list of the significant new titles for the year. And right up front you can find out where to order your reading needs as well.

And we are cleaning up the Directory of the Arms Trade. For instance, DBI Books, Inc., now publishes an annual on knives which lists nearly 2,000 names in that business. That makes it possible, here in Gun Digest, to cut the knives listings down to the factories and mail-order sources.

One important matter has not changed in the slightest: We get no money from advertising nor from the people and products shown in this, the best catalog in the business. That's your best guarantee that these pages are close to pure objective fact as they can be.

Please enjoy it and use it. Our people worked hard on it.

Ken

HANDGUNS—TARGET AUTOLOADERS

BERNARDELLI MODEL 100 PISTOL
Caliber: 22 LR only, 10-shot magazine.
Barrel: 5.9".
Weight: 37¾ oz. **Length:** 9" over-all.
Stocks: Checkered walnut with thumbrest.
Sights: Fixed front, rear adj. for w. and e.
Features: Target barrel weight included. Heavy sighting rib with interchangeable front sight. Accessories include cleaning equipment and assembly tools, case. Imported from Italy by Interarms.
Price: $395.00

Bernardelli 100

BERETTA MODEL 76 PISTOL
Caliber: 22 LR, 10-shot magazine.
Barrel: 6".
Weight: 33 ozs. (empty). **Length:** 8.8" over-all.
Stocks: Checkered plastic.
Sights: Interchangable blade front (3 widths), rear is fully adj. for w. and e.
Features: Built-in, fixed counterweight, raised, matted slide rib, factory adjusted trigger pull from 3 lbs. 5 ozs. to 3 lbs. 12 ozs. Thumb safety. Blue-black finish. Wood grips available at extra cost. Introduced 1977. Imported by Beretta Arms Co.
Price: With plastic grips $370.00
Price: With wood grips $415.00

COLT GOLD CUP NAT'L MATCH MK IV Series 70
Caliber: 45 ACP, 7-shot magazine.
Barrel: 5", with new design bushing.
Length: 8⅜". **Weight:** 38½ oz.
Stocks: Checkered walnut, gold plated medallion.
Sights: Ramp-style front, Colt-Elliason rear adj. for w. and e., sight radius 6¾".
Features: Arched or flat housing; wide, grooved trigger with adj. stop; ribbed-top slide, hand fitted, with improved ejection port.
Price: Colt Royal Blue $470.95

Colt Gold Cup

Domino SP-602

DOMINO MODEL SP-602 MATCH PISTOL
Caliber: 22 LR, 5-shot.
Barrel: 5.5".
Weight: 41 oz. **Length:** 11.02" over-all.
Stocks: Full target stocks; adjustable, one-piece. Left hand style avail.
Sights: Match. Blade front, open notch rear fully adj. for w. and e. Sight radius is 8.66".
Features: Line of sight is only ¹¹⁄₃₂" above centerline of bore; magazine is inserted from top; adjustable and removable trigger mechanism; single lever takedown. Full 5 year warranty. Imported from Italy by Mandall Shooting Supplies.
Price: $1,195.00

DOMINO O.P. 601 MATCH PISTOL
Similar to S.P. 602 except has different match stocks with adj. palm shelf, 22 Short only, weighs 40 oz., 5.6" bbl., has gas ports through top of barrel and slide to reduce recoil, slightly different trigger and sear mechanisms.
Price: $1,195.00

HAMMERLI MODEL 120-1 FREE PISTOL
Caliber: 22 LR.
Barrel: 9.9".
Weight: 44 oz. **Length:** 14¾" over-all.
Stocks: Contoured right-hand (only) thumbrest.
Sights: Fully adjustable rear, blade front. Choice of 14.56" or 9.84" sight radius.
Features: Trigger adjustable for single- or two-stage pull from 1.8 to 12 oz. Adjustable for length of pull. Guaranteed accuracy of .98", 10 shots at 50 meters. From Mandall Shooting Supplies.
Price: Model 120-1 . . . .$995.00
Price: Model 120-2 (same as above except has walnut target grips with adjustable palm-rest. RH or LH; illus.) $1,195.00

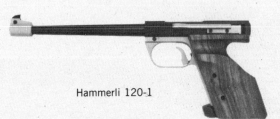

Hammerli 120-1

CAUTION: PRICES CHANGE. CHECK AT GUNSHOP.

HAMMERLI MODEL 150 FREE PISTOL

Caliber: 22LR. Single shot.
Barrel: 11.3".
Weight: 43 ozs. **Length:** 15.35" over-all.
Stock: Walnut with adjustable palm shelf.
Sights: Sight radius of 14.6". Micro rear sight adj. for w. and e.
Features: Single shot Martini action. Cocking lever on left side of action with vertical operation. Set trigger adjustable for length and angle. Trigger pull weight adjustable between 5 and 100 grams. Guaranteed accuracy of .78", 10 shots from machine rest. From Mandall Shooting Supplies.
Price: **$1,500.00**
Price: With electric trigger **$1,695.00**

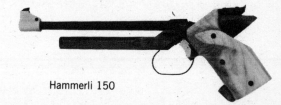

Hammerli 150

HAMMERLI STANDARD, MODELS 208 & 211

Caliber: 22 LR.
Barrel: 5.9", 6-groove.
Weight: 37.6 oz. (45 oz. with extra heavy barrel weight). **Length:** 10".
Stocks: Walnut. Adj. palm rest (208), 211 has thumbrest grip.
Sights: Match sights, fully adj. for w. and e. (click adj.). Interchangeable front and rear blades.
Features: Semi-automatic, recoil operated. 8-shot clip. Slide stop. Fully adj. trigger (2¼ lbs. and 3 lbs.). Extra barrel weight available. Mandall Shooting Supplies, importer.
Price: Model 208, approx. . **$1,295.00**   Model 211 approx. **$1,295.00**

Hammerli 208

HAMMERLI MODEL 230 RAPID FIRE PISTOL

Caliber: 22 Short.
Barrel: 6.3", 6-groove.
Weight: 43.8 oz. **Length:** 11.6".
Stocks: Walnut.
Sights: Match type sights. Sight radius 9.9". Micro rear, click adj. Interchangeable front sight blade.
Features: Semi-automatic. Recoil-operated, 6-shot clip. Gas escape in front of chamber to eliminate muzzle jump. Fully adj. trigger from 5¼ oz. to 10½ oz. with three different lengths available. Designed for International 25 meter Silhouette Program. Mandall Shooting Supplies, importer.
Price: Model 230-1 . . . . **$1,295.00**
Price: Model 230-2 . . . . **$1,295.00**

Hammerli 230

HIGH STANDARD X SERIES CUSTOM 10-X

Caliber: 22 LR, 10-shot magazine.
Barrel: 5½" bull.
Weight: 44½ oz. **Length:** 9¾" over-all.
Stocks: Checkered walnut.
Sights: Undercut ramp front; frame mounted fully adj. rear.
Features: Completely custom made and fitted for best performance. Fully adjustable target trigger, stippled front- and backstraps, slide lock, non-reflective blue finish. Comes with two extra magazines. Unique service policy. Each gun signed by maker.
Price: **$599.50**

Hi-Standard 10-X

HI-STANDARD SUPERMATIC CITATION MILITARY

Caliber: 22 LR, 10-shot magazine.
Barrel: 5½" bull, 7¼" fluted.
Length: 9¾" (5½" bbl.). **Weight:** 46 oz.
Stocks: Checkered walnut with thumbrest.
Sights: Undercut ramp front; frame mounted rear, click adj.
Features: Adjustable trigger pull; over-travel trigger adjustment; double acting safety; rebounding firing pin; military style grip; stippled front- and backstraps; positive magazine latch.
Price: 5½" barrel **$286.00**
Price: 7¼" barrel **$304.00**

Hi-Standard Citation

HI-STANDARD SUPERMATIC TROPHY MILITARY
Caliber: 22 LR, 10-shot magazine.
Barrel: 5½" bull, 7¼" fluted.
Length: 9¾" (5½" bbl.). **Weight:** 44½ oz.
Stocks: Checkered walnut with thumbrest.
Features: Grip duplicates feel of military 45; positive action mag. latch; front- and backstraps stippled. Trigger adj. for pull, over-travel.
Sights: Undercut ramp front; frame mounted rear, click adj.
Price: 5½" barrel $304.00
Price: 7¼" barrel $323.50

Hi-Standard Trophy

HI-STANDARD VICTOR
Caliber: 22 LR, 10-shot magazine.
Barrel: 5½".
Length: 9⅝" over-all. **Weight:** 47 oz.
Stocks: Checkered walnut with thumb rest.
Sights: Undercut ramp front, rib mounted click adj. rear.
Features: Vent. rib, interchangeable barrel, 2 - 2¼ lb. trigger pull, blue finish, back and front straps stippled.
Price: $348.00

Hi-Standard Victor

Ruger Mk. I

RUGER Mark 1 TARGET MODEL AUTO PISTOL
Caliber: 22 LR only, 9-shot magazine.
Barrel: 6⅞" or 5½" bull barrel (6-groove, 14" twist).
Length: 10⅞" (6⅞" bbl.). **Weight:** 42 oz. with 6⅞" bbl.
Stocks: Checkered hard rubber.
Features: Rear sight mounted on receiver, does not move with slide; wide, grooved trigger.
Sights: ⅛" blade front, micro click rear, adjustable for w. and e. Sight radius 9⅜" (with 6⅞" bbl.).
Price: Blued, either barrel length $157.50

SIG P-210-6

SIG P-210-6 AUTO PISTOL
Caliber: 9mm Para., 8-shot magazine.
Barrel: 4¾".
Weight: 37 oz. **Length:** 8½" over-all.
Stocks: Checkered black plastic.
Sights: Blade front, micro. adj. rear for w. & e.
Features: Adjustable trigger stop; ribbed front stap; sandblasted finish. Conversion unit for 22 LR consists of barrel, recoil spring, slide and magazine. Imported by Mandall Shooting Supplies.
Price: P-210-6 ....$1,450.00
Price: 22 Cal. Conversion unit $750.00

SIG P-210-1 AUTO PISTOL
Caliber: 7.65mm or 9mm P., 8-shot magazine.
Barrel: 4¾".
Weight: 31¾ oz. (9mm) **Length:** 8½" over-all.
Stocks: Checkered walnut.
Sights: Blade front, rear adjustable for windage.
Features: Lanyard loop; polished finish. Conversion unit for 22 LR available. Imported by Mandall Shooting Supplies.
Price: P-210-1 ....$1,500.00
Price: 22 Cal. Conversion unit $750.00

SIG/HAMMERLI P-240 TARGET PISTOL
Caliber: 32 S&W Long.
Barrel: 6".
Weight: 4¼ oz. **Length:** 10" over-all.
Stocks: Walnut, target style, unfinished.
Sights: Match sights; ⅛" undercut front, ⅛" notch micro rear click adj. for w. and e.
Features: Semi-automatic, recoil operated; meets I.S.U. and N.R.A. specs for Center Fire Pistol competition; double pull trigger adj. from 2 lbs., 15 ozs. to 3 lbs., 9 ozs.; trigger stop. Comes with extra magazine, special screwdriver, carrying case. From Mandall Shooting Supplies.
Price: $1,500.00
Price: 22 cal. conversion unit $750.00

CAUTION: PRICES CHANGE. CHECK AT GUNSHOP.

SMITH & WESSON 38 MASTER Model 52 AUTO
Caliber: 38 Special (for Mid-range W.C. with flush-seated bullet only). 5-shot magazine.
Barrel: 5″.
Length: 8⅝″. **Weight:** 41 oz. with empty magazine.
Stocks: Checkered walnut.
Sights: ⅛″ Partridge front, S&W micro click rear adj. for w. and e.
Features: Top sighting surfaces matte finished. Locked breech, moving barrel system; checked for 10-ring groups at 50 yards. Coin-adj. sight screws. Dry firing permissible if manual safety on.
Price: S&W Bright Blue **$536.00**

S&W 52

SMITH & WESSON 22 AUTO PISTOL Model 41
Caliber: 22 LR or 22 S, 10-shot clip.
Barrel: 7⅜″, sight radius 9⁵⁄₁₆″ (7⅜″ bbl.).
Length: 12″, incl. detachable muzzle brake, (7⅜″ bbl. only).
Weight: 43½ oz. (7⅜″ bbl.).
Stocks: Checkered walnut with thumbrest, usable with either hand.
Features: ⅜″ wide, grooved trigger with adj. stop; wgts. available to make pistol up to 59 oz.
Sights: Front, ⅛″ Patridge undercut; micro click rear adj. for w. and e.
Price: S&W Bright Blue, satin matted bbl., either caliber **$325.25**

SMITH & WESSON 22 MATCH HEAVY BARREL M-41
Caliber: 22 LR, 10-shot clip.
Barrel: 5½″ heavy. Sight radius, 8″.
Length: 9″. **Weight:** 44½ oz.
Stocks: Checkered walnut with modified thumbrest, usable with either hand.
Features: ⅜″ wide, grooved trigger; adj. trigger stop.
Sights: ⅛″ Patridge on ramp base. S&W micro click rear, adj. for w. and e.
Price: S&W Bright Blue, satin matted top area **$325.25**

UNIQUE DES VO 79 TARGET PISTOL
Caliber: 22 Short.
Barrel: 5.85″, Four gas escape ports, one threaded with plug.
Weight: 44 oz.
Stocks: French walnut, target style with thumb rest and adj. palm shelf. Hand stippled.
Sights: Low, .12″ front, fully adj. rear.
Features: Meets all UIT standards; virtually recoil free. Four-way adj. trigger, dry-firing device, all aluminum frame. Cleaning rod, tools, extra magazine, proof certificate and fitted case. Imported from France by Solersport.
Price: Right hand **$675.00**
Price: Left hand **$705.00**

WALTHER FREE PISTOL
Caliber: 22 LR, single shot.
Barrel: 11.7″.
Weight: 48 ozs. **Length:** 17.2″ over-all.
Stocks: Walnut, special hand-fitting design.
Sights: Fully adjustable match sights.
Features: Special electronic trigger. Matte finish blue. Introduced 1980. Imported by Interarms.
Price: **$1,600.00**

Unique D.E.S. 69

UNIQUE D.E.S. 69 TARGET PISTOL
Caliber: 22 LR.
Barrel: 5.91″.
Weight: Approx. 35 oz. **Length:** 10.63″ over-all.
Stocks: French walnut target style with thumbrest and adjustable shelf; hand checkered panels.
Sights: Ramp front, micro. adj. rear mounted on frame; 8.66″ sight radius.
Features: Meets U.I.T. standards. Comes in a fitted hard case with spare magazine, barrel weight, cleaning rod, tools, proof certificate, test target and two year guarantee. Fully adjustable trigger; dry firing safety device. Imported from France by Solersport.
Price: Right-hand **$675.00**
Price: Left-hand **$705.00**

WALTHER GSP MATCH PISTOL
Caliber: 22 LR, 32 S&W wadcutter (GSP-C), 5-shot.
Barrel: 5¾″.
Weight: 44.8 oz. (22 LR), 49.4 oz. (32). **Length:** 11.8″ over-all.
Stock: Walnut, special hand-fitting design.
Sights: Fixed front, rear adj. for w. & e.
Features: Available with either 2.2 lb. (1000 gm) or 3 lb. (1360 gm) trigger. Spare mag., bbl. weight, tools supplied in Match Pistol Kit. Imported from Germany by Interarms.
Price: GSP **$1,150.00**
Price: GSP-C **$1,200.00**
Price: 22 LR conversion unit for GSP-C **$740.00**
Price: 22 Short conversion unit for GSP-C **$790.00**

Walther GSP

WALTHER OSP RAPID-FIRE PISTOL
Similar to Model GSP except 22 Short only, stock has adj. free-style hand rest.
Price: **$1,150.00**

COLT PYTHON REVOLVER
Caliber: 357 Magnum (handles all 38 Spec.), or 38 Spec. only, 6 shot.
Barrel: 2½", 4", 6" or 8", with ventilated rib.
Length: 9¼"(4" bbl.). **Weight:** 38 oz. (4" bbl.).
Stocks: Checkered walnut, target type.
Sights: ⅛" ramp front, adj. notch rear.
Features: Ventilated rib; grooved, crisp trigger; swing-out cylinder; target hammer.

Price: Colt Blue, 2½" $475.95	Nickeled,4" $506.95
Price: 4" $486.50	6" $508.95
Price: 6" $493.95	8" $519.50
Price: 8" $504.50	8", 38 Spec. $519.50
Price: 8", 38 Spec. $504.50	

Colt Python

SMITH & WESSON COMBAT MASTERPIECE
Caliber: 38 Special (M15) or 22 LR (M18), 6 shot.
Barrel: 2" or 4" (M15) 4" (M18)
Length: 9⅛" (4" bbl.). **Weight:** Loaded, 22 36½ oz, 38 30 oz.
Stocks: Checkered walnut, Magna. Grooved tangs and trigger.
Sights: Front, ⅛" Baugham Quick Draw on ramp, micro click rear, adjustable for w. and e.
Price: Blued, M-15, 2" $196.50
Price: Nickel M-15, 2" $211.50
Price: Blued, M-18, 4" (sq. butt, adj. sights) $241.75

SMITH & WESSON 1955 Model 25, 45 TARGET
Caliber: 45 ACP and 45 AR, 6 shot.
Barrel: 6" (heavy target type).
Length: 11⅞". **Weight:** 45 oz.
Stocks: Checkered walnut target.
Sights: ⅛" Patridge front, micro click rear, adjustable for w. and e.
Features: Tangs and trigger grooved; target trigger and hammer standard, checkered target hammer. Swing-out cylinder revolver. Price includes presentation case.
Price: Blued $399.33

SMITH & WESSON MASTERPIECE TARGET MODELS
Model: K-22 (M17).	K-22 (M48).
Caliber: 22 LR, 6 shot.	22 RF Magnum, 6 shot.
Barrel: 6", 8⅜".	4", 6" or 8⅜".
Length: 11⅛" (6" bbl.).	11⅛" (6" bbl.).
Weight: 38½ oz. (6" bbl.).	39 oz.(6" bbl.).

Model: K-38 (M14).
Caliber: 38 S&W Special, 6 shot.
Barrel: 6", 8⅜".
Length: 11⅛". (6" bbl.)
Weight: 38½ oz. (6", loaded).
Features: All Masterpiece models have: checkered walnut, Magna stocks; grooved tang and trigger; ⅛" Patridge front sight, micro. adj. rear sights. Swing out cylinder revolver. For 8⅜" barrel add **$12.75** for M-48.
Price: Blued, M-17, 6" bbl. sq. butt, adj. sights $257.75
Price: Blued, M-48, 4", 6" bbl. sq. butt, adj. sights $272.00

S&W K-22

Smith & Wesson Accessories
Target hammers with low, broad, deeply-checkered spur, and wide-swaged, grooved target trigger. For all frame sizes, **$10.00** (target hammers not available for small frames). Target stocks: for large-frame guns, **$19.60** to **$22.00**; for med.-frame guns, **$16.55** to **$19.90**; for small-frame guns, **$14.65** to **$19.25**. These prices applicable only when specified on original order. As separately-ordered parts: target hammer assembly **$19.80** and triggers, **$17.00**; stocks, **$21.55** to **$27.90**

> Consult our Directory pages for the location of firms mentioned.

TAURUS MODEL 86 TARGET MASTER REVOLVER
Caliber: 38 Spec., 6-shot.
Barrel: 6" only.
Weight: 41 oz. **Length:** 11¼" over-all.
Stocks: Over size target-type, checkered Brazilian walnut.
Sights: Patridge front, micro. click rear adj. for w. and e.
Features: Blue finish with non-reflective finish on barrel. Imported from Brazil by International Distributors.
Price: About $156.00
Price: Model 96 Scout Master, same except in 22 cal, about $156.00

Taurus 86

   CAUTION: PRICES CHANGE. CHECK AT GUNSHOP.

TP-70

AMERICAN ARMS TP-70
Caliber: 22 LR, 25 ACP
Barrel: 2.6″
Weight: 12.6 oz. **Length:** 4.72″ over-all.
Stocks: Checkered, composition.
Sights: Open, fixed.
Features: Double action, stainless steel. Exposed hammer. Manual and magazine safeties. The 22 cal. version will be available late 1980. From M & N Distributors.
Price: 25 ACP, about $180.00
Price: 22 LR, about $200.00

AMT 45 ACP HARDBALLER
Caliber: 45 ACP.
Barrel: 5″.
Weight: 39 oz. **Length:** 8½″ over-all.
Stocks: Checkered walnut.
Sights: Adjustable combat-type.
Features: Extended combat safety, serrated matte slide rib, loaded chamber indicator, long grip safety, beveled magazine well, grooved front and back straps, adjustable target trigger, custom-fitted barrel bushing. All stainless steel. From AMT.
Price: $450.00

AMT 45 ACP HARDBALLER LONG SLIDE
Caliber: 45 ACP.
Barrel: 7″.
Length: 10½″ over-all.
Stocks: Checkered walnut.
Sights: Fully adjustable Micro rear sight.
Features: Slide and barrel are 2″ longer than the standard 45, giving less recoil, added velocity, longer sight radius. Has extended combat safety, serrated matte rib, loaded chamber indicator, wide adjustable trigger, custom fitted barrel bushing. From AMT.
Price: About $595.00
Price: 45 Skipper (as above except 1″ shorter) $450.00

AMT COMBAT GOVERNMENT
Caliber: 45 ACP.
Barrel: 5″.
Weight: 38 oz. **Length:** 8½″ over-all.
Stocks: Checkered walnut, diamond pattern.
Sights: Combat-style, fixed.
Features: All stainless steel; extended combat safety, loaded chamber indicator, beveled magazine well, adjustable target-type trigger, custom-fitted barrel bushing, flat mainspring housing. From AMT.
Price: $395.00

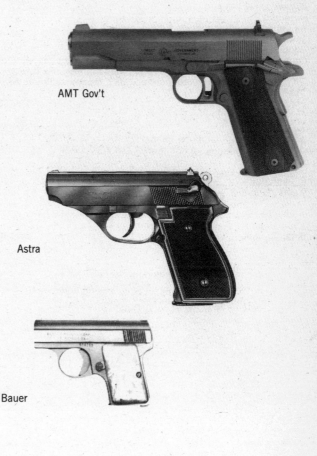

AMT Gov't

Astra

Bauer

ASTRA CONSTABLE AUTO PISTOL
Caliber: 22 LR, 10-shot; 32 ACP, 8-shot; and 380 ACP, 7-shot.
Barrel: 3½″.
Weight: 26 oz.
Stocks: Moulded plastic.
Sights: Adj. rear.
Features: Double action, quick no-tool takedown, non-glare rib on slide. 380 available in blue or chrome finish. Imported from Spain by Interarms.
Price: Blue $320.00
Price: Chrome $350.00

BAUER AUTOMATIC PISTOL
Caliber: 25 ACP, 6-shot.
Barrel: 2⅛″.
Weight: 10 oz. **Length:** 4″.
Stocks: Plastic pearl or checkered walnut.
Sights: Recessed, fixed.
Features: Stainless steel construction, positive manual safety, magazine safety.
Price: Satin stainless steel, 25ACP $122.85

BERETTA JETFIRE AUTO PISTOL
Caliber: 25 ACP
Barrel: 2½″.
Weight: 8 oz. **Length:** 4½″ over-all.
Stocks: Checkered black plastic.
Sights: Fixed.
Features: Thumb safety and half-cock safety; barrel hinged at front to pop up for single loading or cleaning. From J. L. Galef
Price: Blue $169.95
Price: Nickel $199.95

BERETTA MINX M2 AUTO PISTOL
Same basic gun as Jetfire except in 22 Short, weighs 10 oz., 6 shots.
Price: Blue $169.95
Price: Nickel $199.95

Beretta 81/84

BERSA MODEL 644 AUTO PISTOL
Caliber: 22 Long Rifle, 10-shot magazine.
Barrel: 3½".
Weight: 26½ oz. **Length:** 6½" over-all.
Stocks: Contoured black nylon.
Sights: Blade front, rear drift-adj. for windage.
Features: Has three safety devices: firing pin safety, hammer safety and magazine safety. Button release magazine with finger rest. Introduced 1980. Imported from Argentina by Interarms.
Price: $175.00

BERETTA MODEL 70S PISTOL
Caliber: 22 LR, 380 ACP.
Barrel: 3.5".
Weight: 23 ozs. (Steel) **Length:** 6.5" over-all.
Stocks: Checkered black plastic.
Sights: Fixed front and rear.
Features: Steel frame in 32 and 380, light alloy in 22 (wgt. 18 ozs.). Safety lever blocks hammer. Side lever indicates empty magazine. Magazine capacity is 8 rounds (22), 7 rounds in 380. Introduced 1977. Imported by Beretta Arms Co.
Price: $274.00

BERNARDELLI MODEL 80 AUTO PISTOL
Caliber: 22 LR (10-shot); 32 ACP (8-shot); 380 ACP (7-shot).
Barrel: 3½".
Weight: 26½ oz. **Length:** 6½" over-all.
Stocks: Checkered plastic with thumbrest.
Sights: Ramp front, white outline rear adj. for w. & e.
Features: Hammer block slide safety; loaded chamber indicator; dual recoil buffer springs; serrated trigger; inertia type firing pin. Imported from Italy by Interarms.
Price: Model 80 ....$220.00

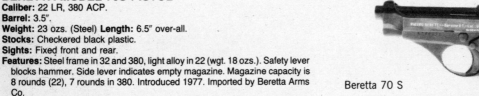

Browning Hi-Power

BERETTA MODEL 81/84 DA PISTOLS
Caliber: 32 ACP (12-shot magazine), 380 ACP (13-shot magazine)
Barrel: 3¾".
Weight: About 23 oz. **Length:** 6½" over-all.
Stocks: Smooth black plastic (wood optional at extra cost).
Sights: Fixed front and rear.
Features: Double action, quick take-down, convenient magazine release. Introduced 1977. Imported by Beretta Arms. Co.
Price: M-81 (32 ACP) $408.00
Price: M-84 (380 ACP) $408.00
Price: Either model with wood grips $425.00
Price: M-82B, 9-shot 32 ACP wood grips, 9-shot mag. $375.00
Price: M-85B, 9-shot 380 ACP wood grips, 9-shot mag. $375.00

BERETTA MODEL 92 DA PISTOL
Caliber: 9mm Parabellum (15-shot magazine).
Barrel: 4.92".
Weight: 33½ ozs. **Length:** 8.54" over-all.
Stocks: Smooth black plastic.
Sights: Blade front, rear adj. for w.
Features: Double-action. Extractor acts as chamber loaded indicator, inertia firing pin. Finished in blue-black. Introduced 1977. Imported by Beretta Arms Co.
Price: $515.00
Price: With wood grips $543.00

Beretta 70 S

Bernardelli Model 100 Target Pistol
Similar to Model 80 except has 5.9" barrel and barrel weight; heavy sighting rib; checkered walnut thumbrest grips; 22 LR only (10-shot). Comes with case, cleaning equipment and tools. $395.00

BROWNING HI-POWER 9mm AUTOMATIC PISTOL
Caliber: 9mm Parabellum (Luger), 13-shot magazine.
Barrel: 4²¹⁄₃₂ inches.
Length: 7¾" over-all. **Weight:** 32 oz.
Stocks: Walnut, hand checkered.
Sights: ⅛" blade front; rear screw-adj. for w. and e. Also available with fixed rear (drift-adj. for w.).
Features: External hammer with half-cock and thumb safeties. A blow on the hammer cannot discharge a cartridge; cannot be fired with magazine removed. Fixed rear sight model available.
Price: Fixed sight model $474.95
Price: 9mm with rear sight adj. for w. and e. $519.95
Price: Nickel, fixed sight $534.95
Price: Nickel, adj. sight $579.95
Price: Silver chrome, adj. sight $539.95

Browning Louis XVI Hi-Power 9mm Auto
Same as Browning Hi-Power 9mm Auto except: fully engraved, silver-gray frame and slide, gold plated trigger, finely checkered walnut grips, with deluxe walnut case.
Price: With adj. sights and walnut case $1,390.00
Price: With fixed sights $1,330.00

> Consult our Directory pages for
> the location of firms mentioned.

CAUTION: PRICES CHANGE. CHECK AT GUNSHOP.

Browning BDA

BROWNING BDA-380 D/A AUTO PISTOL
Caliber: 380 ACP, 13-shot magazine.
Barrel: 3¹³⁄₁₆″.
Weight: 23 ozs. **Length:** 6¾″ over-all.
Stocks: Smooth walnut with inset Browning medallion.
Sights: Blade front, rear drift-adj. for w.
Features: Combination safety and de-cocking lever will automatically lower a cocked hammer to half-cock and can be operated by right or left-hand shooters. Inertia firing pin. Introduced 1978.
Price: Blue $369.50
Price: Nickel $424.95

BROWNING CHALLENGER II AUTO PISTOL
Caliber: 22 LR, 10-shot magazine.
Barrel: 6¾″.
Weight: 38 oz. **Length:** 10⅞″ over-all.
Stocks: Smooth impregnated hardwood.
Sights: ⅛″ blade front on ramp, rear screw adj. for e., drift adj. for w.
Features: All steel, blue finish. Wedge locking system prevents action from loosening. Wide gold-plated trigger; action hold-open. Standard grade only. From Browning.
Price: $224.95

Browning Challenger II

CHARTER EXPLORER II PISTOL
Caliber: 22 LR, 8-shot magazine.
Barrel: 8″.
Weight: 28 oz. **Length:** 15½″ over-all.
Stocks: Serrated simulated walnut.
Sights: Blade front, open rear adj. for elevation.
Features: Action adapted from the semi-auto Explorer carbine. Introduced 1980. From Charter Arms.
Price: $99.00

COLT COMBAT COMMANDER AUTO PISTOL
Caliber: 45 ACP, 7 shot; 38 Super Auto, 9 shot; 9mm Luger, 9 shot.
Barrel: 4¼″.
Length: 8″. **Weight:** 36 oz.
Stocks: Sandblasted walnut.
Sights: Fixed, glare-proofed blade front, square notch rear.
Features: Grooved trigger and hammer spur; arched housing; grip and thumb safeties.
Price: Blue, 9mm $358.95
Price: Blue, 45 ....$352.95
Price: Blue, 38 Super $352.95
Price: Satin nickel, 45 ....$369.95

Colt Commander

COLT SERVICE MODEL ACE
Caliber: 22 LR, 10-shot magazine.
Barrel: 5″.
Weight: 42 ozs. **Length:** 8⅜″ over-all.
Stocks: Checkered walnut.
Sights: Blade front, fully adjustable rear.
Features: The 22-cal. version of the Government Model auto. Based on the Service Model Ace last produced in 1945. Patented floating chamber. Original Ace Markings rolled on left side of slide. Introduced 1978.
Price: Blue only $382.50

Colt Ace

Colt Lightweight Commander
Same as Commander except high strength aluminum alloy frame, wood panel grips, weight 27 oz. 45 ACP only.
Price: Blue $348.95

Colt Conversion Unit
Permits the 45 and 38 Super Automatic pistols to use the economical 22 LR cartridge. No tools needed. Adjustable rear sight; 10-shot magazine. Designed to give recoil effect of the larger calibers. Not adaptable to Commander models. Blue finish $206.50

COLT GOV'T MODEL MK IV/SERIES 70
Caliber: 9mm, 38 Super, 45 ACP, 7-shot.
Barrel: 5″.
Weight: 40 oz. **Length:** 8⅜″ over-all.
Stocks: Sandblasted walnut panels.
Sights: Ramp front, fixed square notch rear.
Features: Grip and thumb safeties, grooved trigger. Accurizor barrel and bushing. Blue finish or nickel in 45 only.
Price: Blue, 45 cal. $352.95
Price: Nickel, 45 cal. $376.50
Price: 9mm, blue only $358.95
Price: 38 Super, blue only $364.95
Price: 45, Satin nickel w/blue, Pachmayr grips $375.50

DETONICS 45 PISTOL
Caliber: 45 ACP, 6-shot clip; 9mm Para., 8-shot clip.
Barrel: 3¼" (2½" of which is rifled).
Weight: 29 ozs. (empty); MK VII is 26 ozs. **Length:** 6¾" over-all, 4½" high.
Stocks: Checkered walnut.
Sights: Combat type, fixed; adj. sights avail.
Features: Has a self-adjusting cone barrel centering system, beveled magazine inlet, "full clip" indicator in base of magazine; standard 7-shot (or more) clip can be used in the 45. Throated barrel and polished feed ramp. Mark V, VI, VII available in 9mm. Introduced 1977. From Detonics.
Price: MK. I, matte blue, fixed sights $497.00
Price: MK. IV, polished blue, adj. sights $539.00
Price: MK. V, matte stainless, fixed sights $580.00
Price: MK. VI, polished stainless, adj. sights $622.00
Price: MK. VII, matte stainless, no sights $622.00

Detonics

ERMA KGP22 AUTO PISTOL
Caliber: 22 LR, 8-shot magazine.
Barrel: 4".
Weight: 29 ozs. **Length:** 7¾" over-all.
Stocks: Checkered plastic.
Sights: Fixed.
Features: Has toggle action similar to original "Luger" pistol. Slide stays open after last shot. Imported from West Germany by Excam. Introduced 1978.
Price: $250.00

Erma KGP 22

ERMA KGP32, KGP38 AUTO PISTOLS
Caliber: 32 ACP (6-shot), 380 ACP (5-shot).
Barrel: 4".
Weight: 22½ ozs. **Length:** 7⅜" over-all.
Stocks: Checkered plastic. Wood optional.
Sights: Rear adjustable for windage.
Features: Toggle action similar to original "Luger" pistol. Slide stays open after last shot. Has magazine and sear disconnect safety systems. Imported from West Germany by Excam. Introduced 1978.
Price: Plastic grips $250.00

ERMA-EXCAM RX 22 AUTO PISTOL
Caliber: 22 LR, 8-shot magazine.
Barrel: 3¼".
Weight: 21 ozs. **Length:** 5.58" over-all.
Stocks: Plastic wrap-around.
Sights: Fixed.
Features: Polished blue finish. Double action. Patented ignition safety system. Thumb safety. Assembled in U.S. Introduced 1980. From Excam.
Price: $169.00

F.I.E. TITAN II PISTOLS
Caliber: 32 ACP, 380 ACP, 6-shot magazine; 22 LR, 10-shot magazine.
Barrel: 3⅞".
Weight: 25¾ ozs. **Length:** 6¾" over-all.
Stocks: Checkered nylon, thumbrest-type; checkered walnut optional.
Sights: Adjustable.
Features: Magazine disconnector, firing pin block. Standard slide safety, available in blue or chrome. Introduced 1978. From F.I.E. Corp.
Price: 32, blue $136.95
Price: 32, chrome $141.95
Price: 380, blue $164.95
Price: 380, chrome $169.95
Price: 22 LR, blue $119.95

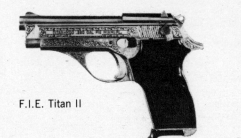

F.I.E. Titan II

F.I.E. "THE BEST" A27B PISTOL
Caliber: 25 ACP, 6-shot magazine.
Barrel: 2½".
Weight: 13 ozs. **Length:** 4⅜" over-all.
Stocks: Checkered walnut.
Sights: Fixed.
Features: All steel construction. Has thumb and magazine safeties, exposed hammer. Blue finish only. Introduced 1978. From F.I.E. Corp.
Price: $154.95

F.I.E. "SUPER TITAN II" PISTOLS
Caliber: 32 ACP, 380 ACP.
Barrel: 3⅞".
Weight: 28 ozs. **Length:** 6¾" over-all.
Stocks: Smooth, polished walnut.
Sights: Adjustable.
Features: Blue finish only; 13 shot (32 ACP), 12 shot (380 ACP). Introduced 1981. From F.I.E. Corp.
Price: $209.95

F.I.E. "TITAN 25" PISTOL
Caliber: 25 ACP, 6-shot magazine.
Barrel: 2⁷⁄₁₆".
Length: 4⅝" over-all. **Weight:** 12 oz.
Stocks: Checkered nylon; checkered walnut optional.
Sights: Fixed.
Features: External hammer; fast simple takedown. Made in U.S.A. by F.I.E. Corp.
Price: Blued ....$64.95   Chromed $74.95

FTL 22 AUTO NINE PISTOL
Caliber: 22 LR, 8-shot magazine.
Barrel: 2¼", 6-groove rifling.
Weight: 8¼ oz. **Length:** 4⅜" over-all.
Stocks: Checkered plastic.
Sights: U-notch in slide.
Features: Alloy frame, rest is ordnance steel. Has barrel support sleeve bushing for better accuracy. Finish is matte hard chrome. Introduced 1978. From FTL Marketing.
Price: $199.95

CAUTION: PRICES CHANGE. CHECK AT GUNSHOP.

RENATO GAMBA RGP81 D.A. AUTO PISTOL

Caliber: 32 ACP, 380 ACP (14-shot magazine); 9 × 18 Ultra (13-shot magazine).
Barrel: 3.34".
Weight: 40 ozs. **Length:** 6.29" over-all.
Stocks: Stippled walnut.
Sights: Open, fixed, with matted sight channel.
Features: Double safety; exposed hammer; combat-type trigger guard; magazine finger extension. Introduced 1981. Imported by Steyr Daimler Puch.
Price: $435.00

Gamba RGP81

HK P9S DOUBLE ACTION AUTO PISTOL

Caliber: 9mm Para., 9-shot magazine.
Barrel: 4".
Weight: 33½ oz. **Length:** 5½" over-all.
Stocks: Checkered black plastic.
Sights: Open combat type.
Features: Double action; polygonal rifling; sliding roller lock action with stationary barrel. Loaded chamber and cocking indicators; un-cocking lever relaxes springs. Imported from Germany by Heckler & Koch, Inc.
Price: P-9S Combat Model $645.00
Price: P-9S Target Model $728.00

H&K P9S

HECKLER & KOCH HK-4 DOUBLE ACTION PISTOL

Caliber: 22 LR, 25 ACP, 32 ACP, 380 ACP, 8-shot magazine (7 in 380).
Barrel: $3^{11}\!/_{32}$".
Weight: 16½ oz. **Length:** $6^3\!/_{16}$" over-all.
Stocks: Black checkered plastic.
Sights: Fixed blade front, rear notched drift-adj. for w.
Features: Gun comes with all parts to shoot above four calibers; polygonal (hexagon) rifling; matte black finish. Imported by Heckler & Koch, Inc.
Price: HK-4 380 with 22 conversion kit $480.00
Price: HK-4 in 380 only $430.00
Price: HK-4 in four cals. $590.00
Price: Conversion units 22, 25 or 32 cal., each $101.00

HECKLER & KOCH P9S DOUBLE ACTION 45

Caliber: 45 ACP, 7-shot magazine.
Barrel: $4^1\!/_{32}$".
Weight: 32½ oz. **Length:** 7½" over-all.
Stocks: Checkered black plastic.
Sights: Open, combat type.
Features: Double action; polygonal rifling; delayed roller-locked bolt system. Imported by Heckler & Koch, Inc.
Price: Combat model $645.00
Price: With adj. trigger, trigger stop, adj. rear sight $728.00

HECKLER & KOCH VP '7OZ DOUBLE ACTION AUTO

Caliber: 9mm Para., 18-shot magazine
Barrel: 4½".
Weight: 32½ oz. **Length:** 8" over-all.
Stocks: Black stippled plastic.
Sights: Ramp front, channeled slide rear.
Features: Recoil operated, double action. Only 4 moving parts. Double column magazine. Imported by Heckler & Koch, Inc.
Price: $489.00

H&K VP70Z

HIGH STANDARD SPORT-KING AUTO PISTOL

Caliber: 22 LR, 10-shot.
Barrel: 4½" or 6¾".
Weight: 39 oz. (4½" bbl.). **Length:** 9" over-all (4½" bbl.).
Stocks: Checkered walnut.
Sights: Blade front, fixed rear.
Features: Takedown barrel. Blue only. Military frame.
Price: Either bbl. length, blue finish $225.00

IVER JOHNSON MODEL X300 PONY

Caliber: 380 ACP, 6-shot magazine.
Barrel: 3".
Weight: 20 oz. **Length:** 6" over-all.
Stocks: Checkered walnut.
Sights: Blade front, rear adj. for w.
Features: Loaded chamber indicator, all steel construction. Inertia firing pin. Thumb safety locks hammer. No magazine safety. Lanyard ring. From Iver Johnson's.
Price: Blue $170.00
Price: Nickel $180.25
Price: Military (matte finish) $170.00

HI-STANDARD SHARPSHOOTER AUTO PISTOL

Caliber: 22 LR, 10-shot magazine.
Barrel: 5½".
Length: 10¼" over-all. **Weight:** 42 oz.
Stocks: Checkered walnut.
Sights: Fixed, ramp front, square notch rear adj. for w. & e.
Features: Military frame. Wide, scored trigger; new hammer-sear design. Slide lock, push-button take down.
Price: Blued $253.00

L.E.S P-18 AUTO PISTOL
Caliber: 9mm Parabellum, 30 Luger, 18-shot magazine; 45 ACP, 10-shot.
Barrel: 5½″, stationary; polygonal rifling.
Weight: About 36 oz.
Stocks: Checkered resin.
Sights: Post front, V-notch rear drift adj. for w.
Features: Gas-assisted action; all stainless steel; inertia firing pin Made in U.S.A. Both single and double action models offered, in two finish grades. From L.E.S.
Price: Std. D.A. (matte finish) 9mm or 45 ....$299.95
Price: Deluxe D.A. (polished) 9mm or 45 ....$389.95
Price: Std. DA, 30 Luger $339.95
Price: Std. S.A. (matte finish) 9mm or 45 ....$279.95
Price: Deluxe S.A. (polished) 9mm or 45 ....$369.95
Price: Std. SA, 30 Luger $319.95

L.E.S. P-18

LLAMA LARGE FRAME AUTO PISTOLS
Caliber: Super 38, 45 ACP.
Barrel: 5″.
Weight: 30 oz. **Length:** 8½″.
Stocks: Checkered walnut.
Sights: Fixed.
Features: Grip and manual safeties, ventilated rib. Engraved, chrome engraved or gold damascened finish available at extra cost. Imported from Spain by Stoeger Industries.
Price: Blue $366.95
Price: Satin chrome, 45 only $424.95
Price: Blue, engraved, 45 only $433.95
Price: Satin chrome, engraved, 45 only $466.95

Llama 45

LLAMA SMALL FRAME AUTO PISTOLS
Caliber: 22 LR, 32 ACP and 380.
Barrel: 3¹¹⁄₁₆″.
Weight: 23 oz. **Length:** 6½″.
Stocks: Checkered plastic, thumb rest.
Sights: Fixed front, adj. notch rear.
Features: Ventilated rib, manual and grip safeties. Model XV is 22 LR, Model XA is 32 ACP, and Model IIIA is 380. Models XA and IIIA have loaded indicator; IIIA is locked breech. Imported from Spain by Stoeger Industries.
Price: Blue $283.95
Price: Satin chrome, 22 & 380 only $349.95
Price: Blue, engraved, 380 only $358.95
Price: Satin chrome, engraved, 380 ....$366.95
Price: Gold damascened, 380 only $1,670.00

Llama 380

LLAMA 9mm LARGE FRAME AUTO PISTOL
Caliber: 9mm Para.
Barrel: 5″.
Weight: 38 oz. **Length:** 8½″.
Stocks: Moulded plastic.
Sights: Fixed front, adj. rear.
Features: Also available with engraved, chrome engraved or gold damascened finish at extra cost. Imported from Spain by Stoeger Industries.
Price: Blue only $366.95

RAVEN P-25 AUTO PISTOL
Caliber: 25 ACP.
Barrel: 3″.
Weight: 12 oz.
Stocks: Smooth walnut or Pearl-O-Lite.
Sights: Ramped front, fixed rear.
Features: Available in blue, nickel or satin nickel finish. From EMF Co.
Price: $55.95

RG 26 AUTO PISTOL
Caliber: 25 ACP, 6-shot magazine.
Barrel: 2½″.
Weight: 12 ozs. **Length:** 4¾″ over-all.
Stocks: Checkered plastic.
Sights: Fixed.
Features: Blue finish. Thumb safety. Imported by RG Industries.
Price: $55.00
Price: Nickel $59.95

> Consult our Directory pages for the location of firms mentioned.

Ruger Standard

RUGER STANDARD MODEL AUTO PISTOL
Caliber: 22 LR, 9-shot magazine.
Barrel: 4¾″ or 6″.
Length: 8¾″ (4¾″ bbl.). **Weight:** 36 oz. (4¾″ bbl.).
Stocks: Checkered hard rubber.
Sights: Fixed, wide blade front, square notch rear adj. for w.
Price: Blued $120.00

CAUTION: PRICES CHANGE. CHECK AT GUNSHOP.

SIG-Sauer P-220

SIG-Sauer P-225

SIG-Sauer P-230

SIG-SAUER P-220 D.A. AUTO PISTOL
Caliber: 9mm or 45 ACP, (9-shot in 9mm, 7 in 45).
Barrel: 4⅜".
Weight: 28¼ oz. (9mm). **Length:** 7¾" over-all.
Stocks: Checkered walnut.
Sights: Blade front, drift adj. rear for w.
Features: Double action. De-cocking lever permits lowering hammer onto locked firing pin. Squared combat-type trigger guard. Slide stays open after last shot. Imported by Mandall Shooting Supplies.
Price: $795.00

SIG-SAUER P-225 D.A. AUTO PISTOL
Caliber: 9mm Parabellum, 8-shot magazine.
Barrel: 3.8".
Weight: 26 ozs. **Length:** 7⁹⁄₃₂" over-all.
Stocks: Checkered black plastic.
Sights: Blade front, rear adjustable for windage.
Features: Double action; decocking lever permits lowering hammer onto locked firing pin. Squared combat-type trigger guard. Shortened lightened version of P-225. From Mandall Shooting Supplies.
Price: $845.00

SIG-SAUER P-230 D.A. AUTO PISTOL
Caliber: 380 ACP, 9mm Police (7 shot).
Barrel: 3¾".
Weight: 16 oz. (380) **length:** 6½" over-all.
Stocks: One piece black plastic.
Sights: Blade front, rear adj. for w.
Features: Double action. Same basic design as P-220. Blowback operation, stationary barrel. Introduced 1977. Imported by Mandall Shooting Supplies.
Price: 380 ....$600.00

SILE-BENELLI B76 DA AUTO PISTOL
Caliber: 9mm Para., 8-shot magazine.
Barrel: 4¼", 6-groove. Chrome-lined bore.
Weight: 34 oz. (empty). **Length:** 8¹⁄₁₆" over-all.
Stocks: Walnut with cut checkering and high gloss finish.
Sights: Blade front with white face, rear adjustable for windage with white bars for increased visibility.
Features: Fixed barrel, locked breech. Exposed hammer can be locked in non-firing mode in either single or double action. Stainless steel inertia firing pin and loaded chamber indicator. All external parts blued, internal parts hard-chrome plated. All steel construction. Introduced 1979. From Sile Dist.
Price: $349.95

Benelli B76

SILE-SEECAMP II STAINLESS DA AUTO
Caliber: 25 ACP, 8-shot magazine.
Barrel: 2", integral with frame.
Weight: About 10 oz. **Length:** 4⅛" over all.
Stocks: Walnut with fine cut checkering.
Sights: Smooth, no-snag, contoured slide and barrel top.
Features: Aircraft quality 17-4 PH stainless steel. Inertia operated firing pin. Hammer fired double action only. Hammer automatically follows slide down to safety rest position after each shot—no manual safety needed. Magazine safety disconnector. Introduced 1980. From Sile Distributors.
Price: $149.95

SMITH & WESSON 9mm MODEL 39 AUTO PISTOL
Caliber: 9mm Luger, 8-shot clip.
Barrel: 4".
Length: 7⁷⁄₁₆". **Weight:** 26½ oz., without magazine.
Stocks: Checkered walnut.
Sights: ⅛" serrated ramp front, adjustable rear.
Features: Magazine disconnector, positive firing pin lock and hammer-release safety; alloy frame with lanyard loop; locked-breech, short-recoil double action; slide locks open on last shot.
Price: Blued ....$284.50 Nickeled $313.50

SMITH & WESSON MODEL 59 DOUBLE ACTION
Caliber: 9mm Luger, 14-shot clip.
Barrel: 4".
Length: 7⁷⁄₁₆" over-all. **Weight:** 27½ oz., without clip.
Stocks: Checkered high impact moulded nylon.
Sights: ⅛" serrated ramp front, square notch rear adj. for w.
Features: Double action automatic. Furnished with two magazines. Blue finish.
Price: Blued $340.75
Price: Nickel $372.00

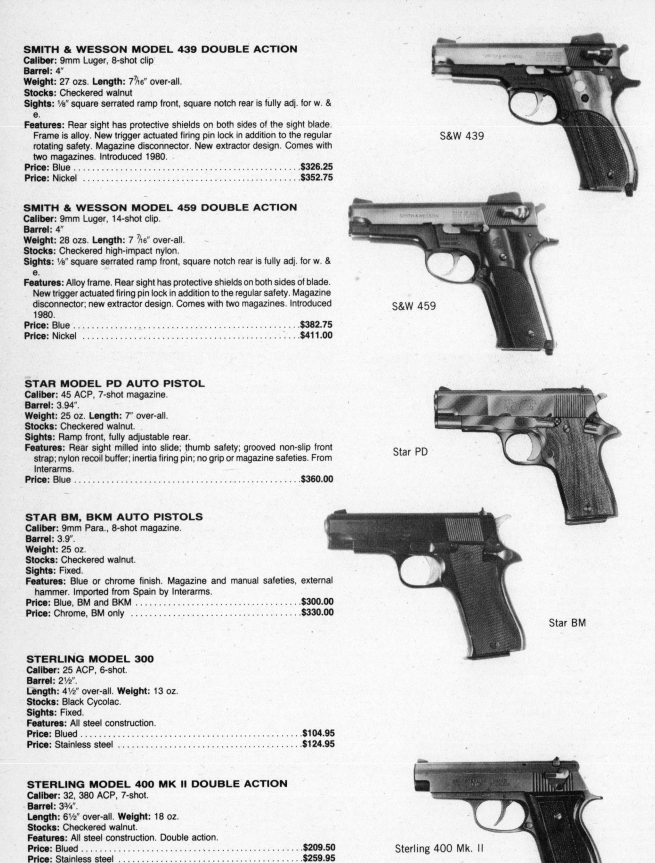

SMITH & WESSON MODEL 439 DOUBLE ACTION
Caliber: 9mm Luger, 8-shot clip
Barrel: 4″
Weight: 27 ozs. **Length:** 7⁷⁄₁₆″ over-all.
Stocks: Checkered walnut
Sights: ⅛″ square serrated ramp front, square notch rear is fully adj. for w. & e.
Features: Rear sight has protective shields on both sides of the sight blade. Frame is alloy. New trigger actuated firing pin lock in addition to the regular rotating safety. Magazine disconnector. New extractor design. Comes with two magazines. Introduced 1980.
Price: Blue $326.25
Price: Nickel $352.75

S&W 439

SMITH & WESSON MODEL 459 DOUBLE ACTION
Caliber: 9mm Luger, 14-shot clip.
Barrel: 4″
Weight: 28 ozs. **Length:** 7⁷⁄₁₆″ over-all.
Stocks: Checkered high-impact nylon.
Sights: ⅛″ square serrated ramp front, square notch rear is fully adj. for w. & e.
Features: Alloy frame. Rear sight has protective shields on both sides of blade. New trigger actuated firing pin lock in addition to the regular safety. Magazine disconnector; new extractor design. Comes with two magazines. Introduced 1980.
Price: Blue $382.75
Price: Nickel $411.00

S&W 459

STAR MODEL PD AUTO PISTOL
Caliber: 45 ACP, 7-shot magazine.
Barrel: 3.94″.
Weight: 25 oz. **Length:** 7″ over-all.
Stocks: Checkered walnut.
Sights: Ramp front, fully adjustable rear.
Features: Rear sight milled into slide; thumb safety; grooved non-slip front strap; nylon recoil buffer; inertia firing pin; no grip or magazine safeties. From Interarms.
Price: Blue $360.00

Star PD

STAR BM, BKM AUTO PISTOLS
Caliber: 9mm Para., 8-shot magazine.
Barrel: 3.9″.
Weight: 25 oz.
Stocks: Checkered walnut.
Sights: Fixed.
Features: Blue or chrome finish. Magazine and manual safeties, external hammer. Imported from Spain by Interarms.
Price: Blue, BM and BKM $300.00
Price: Chrome, BM only $330.00

Star BM

STERLING MODEL 300
Caliber: 25 ACP, 6-shot.
Barrel: 2½″.
Length: 4½″ over-all. **Weight:** 13 oz.
Stocks: Black Cycolac.
Sights: Fixed.
Features: All steel construction.
Price: Blued $104.95
Price: Stainless steel $124.95

STERLING MODEL 400 MK II DOUBLE ACTION
Caliber: 32, 380 ACP, 7-shot.
Barrel: 3¾″.
Length: 6½″ over-all. **Weight:** 18 oz.
Stocks: Checkered walnut.
Features: All steel construction. Double action.
Price: Blued $209.50
Price: Stainless steel $259.95

Sterling 400 Mk. II

CAUTION: PRICES CHANGE. CHECK AT GUNSHOP.

Steyr GB 80

STEYR GB80 DOUBLE ACTION AUTO PISTOL
Caliber: 9mm Parabellum; 18-shot magazine.
Barrel: 5.39″
Weight: 33 oz. **Length:** 8.4″ over-all.
Stocks: Checkered walnut.
Sights: Post front, fixed rear.
Features: Gas-operated, delayed blowback action. Measures 5.7″ high, 1.3″ wide. Introduced 1981. Imported by Steyr Daimler Puch.
Price: **$585.00**

TDE "BACKUP" AUTO PISTOL
Caliber: 380 ACP, 5-shot magazine
Barrel: 2½″.
Weight: 17 oz. **Length:** 5″ over-all.
Stocks: Smooth wood.
Sights: Fixed, open, recessed.
Features: Concealed hammer, blowback operation; manual and grip safeties. All stainless steel construction. Smallest domestically-produced pistol in 380. From AMT.
Price: About **$250.00**

STERLING MODEL 302
Caliber: 22 LR, 6-shot.
Barrel: 2½″.
Length: 4½″ over-all. **Weight:** 13 oz.
Stocks: Black Cycolac.
Sights: Fixed.
Features: All steel construction.
Price: Blue **$104.95**
Price: Stainless steel **$124.95**

STOEGER LUGER 22 AUTO PISTOL
Caliber: 22 LR, 10-shot
Barrel: 4½″
Weight: 30 oz.
Stocks: Checkered walnut.
Features: Action remains open after last shot and as magazine is removed. Grip and balance indentical to P-08.
Price: **$164.95**
Price: Kit includes extra clip, charger, hoister **$204.95**
Price: Combo (includes extra clip, holster, charger and carrying case)**$213.95**

Stoeger Luger

TARGA MODELS GT32, GT380 AUTO PISTOLS
Caliber: 32 ACP or 380 ACP, 6-shot magazine
Barrel: 4⅞″.
Weight: 26 oz. **Length:** 7⅜″ over-all.
Stocks: Checkered nylon with thumb rest. Walnut optional.
Sights: Fixed blade front; rear drift-adj. for w.
Features: Chrome or blue finish; magazine, thumb, and firing pin safeties; external hammer; safety lever take-down. Imported from Italy by Excam, Inc.
Price: 32 cal., blue **$133.00**
Price: 32 cal., chrome **$143.00**
Price: 380 cal., blue **$159.00**
Price: 380 cal., chrome **$167.00**
Price: 380 cal., chrome, engraved, wooden grips **$205.00**
Price: 380 cal., blue, engraved, wooden grips **$214.00**

TARGA MODEL GT27 AUTO PISTOL
Caliber: 25 ACP, 6-shot magazine
Barrel: 2⁷⁄₁₆″.
Weight: 12 oz. **Length:** 4⅝″ over-all.
Stocks: Checkered nylon.
Sights: Fixed.
Features: Safety lever take-down; external hammer with half-cock. Assembled in U.S. by Excam, Inc.
Price: Blue **$58.50**
Price: Chrome **$64.00**

TARGA GT380XE GT32XE PISTOLS
Caliber: 32 ACP or 380 ACP, 12-shot magazine.
Barrel: 3.88″.
Weight: 28 ozs. **Length:** 7.38″ over-all.
Stocks: Smooth hardwood.
Sights: Adj. for windage.
Features: Blue or satin nickel. Ordnance steel. Magazine disconnector, firing pin and thumb safeties. Introduced 1980. Imported by Excam.
Price: 32 cal., blue **$189.00**
Price: 380 cal., blue **$205.00**

TAURUS MODEL PT92 AUTO PISTOL
Caliber: 9mm P, 15-shot magazine.
Barrel: 4.92″.
Weight: 34 oz. **Length:** 8.54″ over-all.
Stocks: Black plastic.
Sights: Fixed notch rear.
Features: Double action, exposed hammer, chamber loaded indicator. Inertia firing pin. Blue finish.
Price: . . . .**N.A.**

VEGA STAINLESS 45 AUTO
Caliber: 45 ACP, 7-shot.
Barrel: 5″.
Weight: 40 oz. **Length:** 8⅜″ over-all.
Stocks: Checkered walnut, diamond pattern.
Sights: Choice of fixed high combat-type or adjustable rear.
Features: Made completely of stainless steel and matches the original 1911A1 Colt almost exactly. Has both grip and thumb safeties. Slide and frame flats are polished, rest sand blasted. From Pacific International Merchandising Corp.
Price: With fixed sights **$349.95**
Price: With Accro-Adjustable sights **$379.95**

Vega Stainless

WALTHER PP AUTO PISTOL
Caliber: 22 LR, 8-shot; 32 ACP, 380 ACP, 7-shot.
Barrel: 3.86".
Weight: 23½ oz. **Length:** 6.7".
Stocks: Checkered plastic.
Sights: Fixed, white markings.
Features: Double action, manual safety blocks firing pin and drops hammer, chamber loaded indicator on 32 and 380, extra finger rest magazine provided. Imported from Germany by Interarms.
Price: (22 LR) $625.00
Price: (32 and 380) $600.00
Price: Engraved models ....On Request

Walther PP

WALTHER AMERICAN PPK/S AUTO PISTOL
Similar to Walther PP except made entirely in the United States. Has 3.27" barrel with 6.1" length over-all.
Price: 380 ACP only...$290.00

WALTHER P-38 AUTO PISTOL
Caliber: 22 LR, 30 Luger or 9mm Luger, 8-shot.
Barrel: 4¹⁵⁄₁₆" (9mm and 30), 5¹⁄₁₆" (22 LR).
Weight: 28 oz. **Length:** 8½".
Stock: Checkered plastic.
Sights: Fixed.
Features: Double action, safety blocks firing pin and drops hammer, chamber loaded indicator. Matte finish standard, polished blue, engraving and/or plating available. Imported from Germany by Interarms.
Price: 22 LR $830.00
Price: 9mm or 30 Luger $750.00
Price: Engraved models ....On Request

Walther P-38

Walther P-38K

Walther P-38K Auto Pistol
Streamlined version of the P-38; 2¾" barrel, 6⅜" over-all, weight 26 ozs. Strengthened slide (no dust cover), recoil bearing cross-bolt. Rear sight adj. for windage, both front and rear sights have white accents. Hammer decocking lever. Non-reflective matte finish. Imported from Germany by Interarms. Introduced 1977.
Price: $750.00

WALTHER P-5 AUTO PISTOL
Latest Walther design that uses the basic P-38 double-action mechanism. Caliber 9mm Luger, barrel length 3½"; weight 28 oz., over-all length 7".
Price: $970.00

Walther P-38IV Auto Pistol
Same as P-38K except has longer barrel (4½"); over-all length is 8", weight is 29 ozs. Sights are non-adjustable. Introduced 1977. Imported by Interarms.
Price: $750.00

> Consult our Directory pages for the location of firms mentioned.

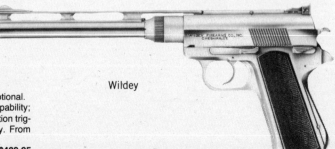

Wildey

WILDEY AUTO PISTOL
Caliber: 9mm Win. Mag. (14 shots), 45 Win. Mag. (8 shots).
Barrel: 5", 6", 7", 8", or 10"; vent. rib.
Weight: About 51 oz. (6" bbl.).
Stocks: Select hardwood, target style optional.
Sights: Adjustable for windage and elevation; red or white inserts optional.
Features: Patented gas operation; selective single or autoloading capability; 5-lug rotary bolt; fixed barrel; stainless steel construction; double-action trigger mechanism. Has positive hammer block and magazine safety. From Wildey Firearms.
Price: 9mm Win. Mag., 5" bbl. $489.95
Price: 45 Win. Mag., 8" bbl. $499.95

CAUTION: PRICES CHANGE. CHECK AT GUNSHOP.

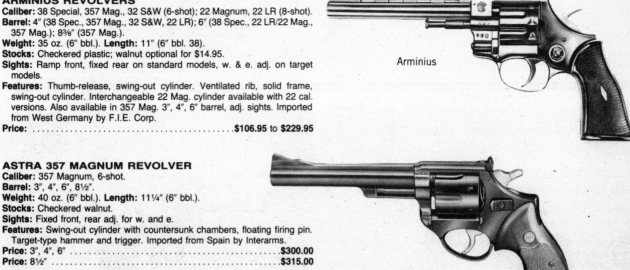

Arminius

Astra 357

ARMINIUS REVOLVERS
Caliber: 38 Special, 357 Mag., 32 S&W (6-shot); 22 Magnum, 22 LR (8-shot).
Barrel: 4" (38 Spec., 357 Mag., 32 S&W, 22 LR); 6" (38 Spec., 22 LR/22 Mag., 357 Mag.); 8⅜" (357 Mag.).
Weight: 35 oz. (6" bbl.). **Length:** 11" (6" bbl. 38).
Stocks: Checkered plastic; walnut optional for $14.95.
Sights: Ramp front, fixed rear on standard models, w. & e. adj. on target models.
Features: Thumb-release, swing-out cylinder. Ventilated rib, solid frame, swing-out cylinder. Interchangeable 22 Mag. cylinder available with 22 cal. versions. Also available in 357 Mag. 3", 4", 6" barrel, adj. sights. Imported from West Germany by F.I.E. Corp.
Price: . . . .$106.95 to $229.95

ASTRA 357 MAGNUM REVOLVER
Caliber: 357 Magnum, 6-shot.
Barrel: 3", 4", 6", 8½".
Weight: 40 oz. (6" bbl.). **Length:** 11¼" (6" bbl.).
Stocks: Checkered walnut.
Sights: Fixed front, rear adj. for w. and e.
Features: Swing-out cylinder with countersunk chambers, floating firing pin. Target-type hammer and trigger. Imported from Spain by Interarms.
Price: 3", 4", 6" $300.00
Price: 8½" $315.00

ASTRA MODEL 41, 44, 45 DOUBLE ACTION REVOLVER
Similar to the 357 Mag. except chambered for the 41 Mag., 44 Mag. or 45 Colt. Barrel length of 6" only, giving over-all length of 11⅜". Weight is 2¾ lbs. Introduced 1980.
Price: $395.00

CHARTER ARMS BULLDOG
Caliber: 44 Special, 5-shot.
Barrel: 3".
Weight: 19 oz. **Length:** 7¾" over-all.
Stocks: Checkered walnut, Bulldog.
Sights: Patridge-type front, square-notch rear.
Features: Wide trigger and hammer; beryllium copper firing pin.
Price: Service Blue $182.50
Price: Stainless steel $244.00

Charter Bulldog

CHARTER TARGET BULLDOG
Caliber: 357 Mag., 44 Spec., 5-shot.
Barrel: 4".
Weight: 20½ oz. **Length:** 8½" over-all.
Stocks: Checkered American walnut, square butt.
Sights: Full-length ramp front, fully adj., milled channel, square notch rear.
Features: Blue finish only. Enclosed ejector rod, full length ejection of fired cases.
Price: 357 Mag., 4" $215.50
Price: 44 Spec., 4" $216.50

CHARTER ARMS POLICE BULLDOG
Caliber: 38 Special, 6-shot.
Barrel: 2", 4", 4" straight taper bull.
Weight: 21 oz. **Length:** 9" over-all.
Stocks: Hand checkered American walnut; square butt.
Sights: Patridge-type ramp front, notched rear.
Features: Accepts both regular and high velocity ammunition; enclosed ejector rod; full length ejection of fired cases.
Price: Blue only, ...$170.00

Charter Arms Pathfinder
Same as Undercover but in 22 LR caliber, and has 3" or 6" bbl. Fitted with adjustable rear sight, ramp front. Weight 18½ oz.
Price: 22 LR, blue, 3" $187.00
Price: 22 LR, square butt, 6" $201.50
Price: 22 Mag., square butt, 3" $196.00
Price: 22 Mag, square butt, 6" $202.00
Price: Stainless, 22 LR, 3" $239.50

CHARTER ARMS UNDERCOVER REVOLVER
Caliber: 38 Special, 5 shot; 32 S & W Long, 6 shot.
Barrel: 2", 3".
Weight: 16 oz. (2"). **Length:** 6¼" (2").
Stocks: Smooth walnut or checkered square butt.
Sights: Patridge-type ramp front, notched rear.
Features: Wide trigger and hammer spur. Steel frame.
Price: Polished Blue $173.00
Price: 32 S & W Long, blue, 2" $173.00
Price: Stainless, 38 Spec. 2" $229.50

COLT LAWMAN MK III REVOLVER
Caliber: 357 Mag., 6 shot.
Barrel: 2" or 4", heavy.
Weight: 33 oz.
Length: 9⅜".
Stocks: Checkered walnut, service style.
Sights: Fixed, glare-proofed ramp front, square notch rear.
Price: Blued $274.95
Price: Nickel $292.50
Price: With Coltguard finish $291.50

COLT PYTHON HUNTER
Caliber: 357 Magnum
Barrel: 8".
Weight: 53 oz.; with scope 63 oz. **Length:** 13¼" over-all.
Stocks: Colt/Pachmayr.
Sights: Luminous orange insert front, Accro adj. rear.
Features: Comes with Colt/Leupold 2x long eye relief scope in Colt/Redfield lightweight mounts, 50 round ammo case, cleaning rod and brush, tool set, aluminum Colt/Halliburton carrying case.
Price: About **$995.00**

Python Hunter

COLT DIAMONDBACK REVOLVER
Caliber: 22 LR or 38 Special, 6 shot.
Barrel: 4" or 6" with ventilated rib.
Length: 9" (4" bbl.). **Weight:** 24 oz. (2½" bbl.), 28½ oz. (4" bbl.).
Stocks: Checkered walnut, target type, square butt.
Sights: Ramp front, adj. notch rear.
Features: Ventilated rib; grooved, crisp trigger; swing-out cylinder; wide hammer spur.
Price: Blue, 4" bbl., 38 Spec. or 22 . . . .**$353.95**
Price: Blue, 6" bbl., 22 or 38 . . . .**$361.95**

Diamondback

COLT DETECTIVE SPECIAL
Caliber: 38 Special, 6 shot.
Barrel: 2".
Length: 6⅝" over-all. **Weight:** 22 oz.
Stocks: Full, checkered walnut, round butt.
Sights: Fixed, ramp front, square notch rear.
Features: Glare-proofed sights, smooth trigger. Nickel finish, hammer shroud available as options.
Price: Blue **$259.95**
Price: Nickel **$279.95**

Colt Det. Spec.

COLT TROOPER MK III REVOLVER
Caliber: 22 LR, 22 WMR, 38 Spec., 357 Magnum, 6-shot.
Barrel: 4" 6" or 8".
Length: 9½" (4" bbl.). **Weight:** 39 oz. (4" bbl.), 42 oz, (6" bbl.).
Stocks: Checkered walnut, square butt. Grooved trigger.
Sights: Fixed ramp front with ⅛" blade, adj. notch rear.
Price: Blued with target hammer and target stocks, 4", 357 . . . . . .**$323.95**
Price: Nickeled 38/357 Mag. 4" **$343.50**
Price: 22 LR, blue, 4" **$323.95**
Price: 22 LR, blue, 8" **$330.50**
Price: 22 WMR, Nickel, 8" **$355.95**
Price: 357, blue, 8" **$330.50**
Price: 357, Coltguard finish, 8" **$354.95**
Price: 22 LR, Coltguard finish, 4" **$342.50**

Colt Trooper Mk. III

F.I.E. MODEL N38 "Titan Tiger" REVOLVER
Caliber: 38 Special.
Barrel: 2" or 4".
Length: 6¼" over-all. (2" bbl.). **Weight:** 27 oz.
Stocks: Checkered plastic, Bulldog style. Walnut optional ($15.95).
Sights: Fixed.
Features: Thumb-release swing-out cylinder, one stroke ejection. Made in U.S.A. by F.I.E. Corp.
Price: Blued 2" or 4" . . . . .**$119.95**   Nickel, 2" or 4" bbl. **$137.95**

F.I.E. N38

H&R MODEL 940 ULTRA "SIDE-KICK" REVOLVER
Caliber: 22 S, L or LR, 9 shot.
Barrel: 6" target weight with ventilated rib.
Weight: 36 oz.
Stocks: Checkered walnut-finished hardwood with thumbrest.
Sights: Ramp front; rear adjustable for w. and e.
Features: Swing-out, safety rim cylinder.
Price: H&R Crown-Lustre Blue **$110.00**

H&R Model 939 Ultra "Side-Kick" Revolver
Like the Model 940 but with a flat-sided barrel.
Price: H&R Crown-Lustre Blue **$110.00**

CAUTION: PRICES CHANGE. CHECK AT GUNSHOP.

H&R 676

HARRINGTON & RICHARDSON M676 REVOLVER
Caliber: 22 LR/22 WMRF, 6-shot.
Barrel: 4½", 5½", 7½" or 12".
Weight: 31 oz. (4½"), 41 oz. (12").
Stocks: One piece smooth walnut-finished hardwood.
Sights: Western type blade front, adj. rear.
Features: Blue barrel and cylinder, "antique" color case-hardened frame, ejector tube and trigger. Comes with extra cylinder.
Price: 4½", 5½", 7½" bbl. $115.00
Price: 12" bbl. $135.00

HARRINGTON & RICHARDSON M622 REVOLVER
Caliber: 22 S, L or LR, 22 WMR, 6 shot.
Barrel: 2½", 4", round bbl.
Weight: 20 oz. (2½" bbl.).
Stocks: Checkered black Cycolac.
Sights: Fixed, blade front, square notch rear.
Features: Solid steel, Bantamweight frame; pull-pin safety rim cylinder; non-glare finish on frame; coil springs.
Price: Blued, 2½", 4", bbl. $69.50
Price: Model 632 (32 cal.) $74.50
Price: Model 642, 22 WMR 79.50

HARRINGTON & RICHARDSON M732 GUARDSMAN
Caliber: 32 S&W or 32 S&W Long, 6 shot.
Barrel: 2½" or 4" round barrel.
Weight: 23½ oz. (2½" bbl.), 26 oz. (4" bbl.).
Stocks: Checkered, black Cycolac.
Sights: Blade front; adjustable rear on 4" model.
Features: Swing-out cylinder with auto. extractor return. Pat. safety rim cylinder. Grooved trigger.
Price: Blued, 2½" bbl. $89.50   Nickel (Model 733), 2½" bbl. $94.50
Price: Blued, 4" bbl. ..$89.50   Nickel, 4" bbl. $94.50

HARRINGTON & RICHARDSON M929 "SIDE-KICK"
Caliber: 22 S, L or LR, 9 shot.
Barrel: 2½", 4" or 6".
Weight: 26 oz. (4" bbl.).
Stocks: Checkered, black Cycolac.
Sights: Blade front; adjustable rear on 4" and 6" models.
Features: Swing-out cylinder with auto. extractor return. Pat. safety rim cylinder. Grooved trigger. Round-grip frame.
Price: Blued, 2½", 4" or 6" bbl. $89.50
Price: Nickel (Model 930), 2½" or 4" bbl. $94.50

HARRINGTON & RICHARDSON M949 FORTY-NINER
Caliber: 22 S, L or LR, 9 shot.
Barrel: 5½" round with ejector rod.
Weight: 31 oz.
Stocks: One-piece, smooth frontier style wrap-around, Walnut-finished hardwood.
Sights: estern-type blade front, rear adj. for w.
Features: Contoured loading gate; wide hmmer spur; single and double action. Western type ejector-housing.
Price: H&R Crown-Luster Blue 89.50
Price: Nickel (Model 950) $94.50

HARRINGTON & RICHARDSON MODELS 604, 904
Caliber: 22 LR, 9-shot (M904), 22 WMR, 6-shot (M604)
Barrel: 6".
Weight: 38 oz.
Stocks: Smooth walnut.
Sights: Blade front, fully adjustable "Wind-Elv" rear.
Features: Swing-out cylinder design with coil spring construction. Single stroke ejection. Tanget-style bull barrel has raised solid rib giving a 7¼" sight radius.
Price: M604 or 904 ....$135.00

Harrington & Richardson Model 686 Revolver
Similar to the Model 676 except has a ramp and blade front sight and fully adjustable "Wind-Elv" rear sight. Same barrel lengths and chamberings.
Price: 4½", 5½", 7½" barrel $135.00
Price: 12" barrel $160.00

Harrington & Richardson Model 649 Revolver
Similar to model 666 except has 5½" or 7½" barrel, one piece wrap around walnut-finished hardwood grips, western-type blade front sight, adjustable rear. Loads and ejects from side. Weighs 32 oz.
Price: $99.50
Price: Model 650—as above except nickel finish $115.00
Price: M649 with 7½" bbl., dual cylinder $110.00

Harrington & Richardson Model 976 Revolver
Similar to the Model 949 except has 7½" barrel, has color case-hardened frame, ejector rod housing and trigger. Has 9-shot cylinder. Standard model has blade front sight and windage-adjustable rear sight; Deluxe model has ramped blade front and fully adjustable "Wind-Elv" rear.
Price: Standard model $105.00
Price: Deluxe model $135.00

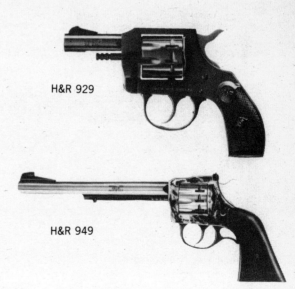

H&R 929

H&R 949

Harrington & Richardson Models 603, 903
Similar to 604-904 except has flat-sided barrel.
Price: $135.00

H&R 999

H&R SPORTSMAN MODEL 999 REVOLVER
Caliber: 22 S, L or LR, 9 shot, 32 S&W Long, 6-shot.
Barrel: 4", 6" top-break (16" twist), integral fluted vent. rib.
Length: 10½". **Weight:** 34 oz. (6", 22 cal.).
Stocks: Checkered walnut-finished hardwood.
Sights: Front adjustable for elevation, rear for windage.
Features: Simultaneous automatic ejection; trigger guard extension. H&R Crown Lustre Blue.
Price: Blued, 4", either caliber $140.00
Price: Blued, 6", either caliber $140.00

HIGH STANDARD DOUBLE-NINE CONVERTIBLE
Caliber: 22 S, L or LR, 9-shot (22 WRM with extra cylinder).
Barrel: 5½", dummy ejector rod fitted.
Length: 11" over-all. **Weight:** 32 oz.
Stocks: Smooth walnut, frontier style.
Sights: Fixed blade front, rear adj. for w. & e.
Features: Western styling; rebounding hammer with auto safety block; spring-loaded ejection. Swing-out cylinder.
Price: Blued $210.50

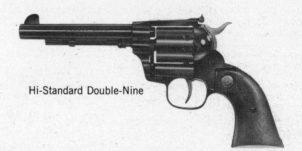

Hi-Standard Double-Nine

High Standard Long Horn Convertible
Same as the Double-Nine convertible but with a 9½" bbl., adjustable sights, blued only, Weight: 38 oz.
Price: With adjustable sights $214.50

HIGH STANDARD HIGH SIERRA DOUBLE ACTION
Caliber: 22 LR and 22 LR/22 Mag., 9-shot.
Barrel: 7" octagonal.
Weight: 36 oz. **Length:** 12½" over-all.
Stocks: Smooth walnut.
Sights: Blade front, adj. rear.
Features: Gold plated backstrap and trigger guard. Swing-out cylinder.
Price: Adj. sights, dual cyl. $214.50

High Sierra

Crusader

HIGH STANDARD CRUSADER COMMEMORATIVE REVOLVER
Caliber: 44 Mag., 45 Long Colt.
Barrel: 6½", 8⅜".
Weight: 48 oz. (6½").
Stocks: Smooth Zebrawood.
Sights: Blade front on ramp, fully adj. rear.
Features: Unique gear-segment mechanism. Smooth, light double-action trigger pull. First production devoted to the commemorative; later guns will be of plain, standard configuration.
Price: ....N.A.

LLAMA COMANCHE REVOLVERS
Caliber: 22 LR, 38 Special, 357 Mag.
Barrel: 6", 4" (except 22 LR, 6" only).
Weight: 22 LR 24 oz., 38 Special 31 oz. **Length:** 9¼" (4" bbl.).
Stocks: Checkered walnut.
Sights: Fixed blade front, rear adj. for w. & e.
Features: Ventilated rib, wide spur hammer. Chrome plating, engraved finishes available. Imported from Spain by Stoeger Industries.
Price: Blue finish...$308.95
Price: Satin chrome, 357 only $391.95

Llama Comanche

CAUTION: PRICES CHANGE. CHECK AT GUNSHOP.

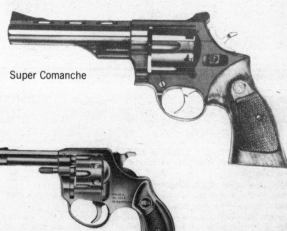

Super Comanche

Llama Super Comanche Revolver
Similar to the Comanche except: 44 Mag., 6″ barrel only; 6-shot cylinder; smooth, extra wide trigger; wide spur hammer; over-size walnut, target-style grips. Weight is 3 lbs., 2 ozs., over-all length is 11¾″. Blue finish only.
Price: $481.95

RG 14 REVOLVER
Caliber: 22 LR, 6-shot.
Barrel: 1¾″ or 3″.
Weight: 15 ozs. (1¾″ bbl.) **Length:** 5½″ over-all.
Stocks: Checkered plastic.
Sights: Fixed.
Features: Blue finish. Cylinder swings out when pin is removed. Imported by RG Industries.
Price: $45.00
Price: Model 23 (central ejector, no pin to remove) $58.00

RG 14

RG 31 REVOLVER
Caliber: 32 S & W (6-shot), 38 Spec. (5-shot).
Barrel: 2″.
Weight: 24 ozs. **Length:** 6¾″ over-all.
Stocks: Checkered plastic.
Sights: Fixed.
Features: Cylinder swings out when pin is removed. Blue finish. Imported by RG Industries.
Price: 32 cal. $75.00
Price: 38 cal. $75.00

RG 40 REVOLVER
Caliber: 38 Spec., 6-shot.
Barrel: 2″.
Weight: 29 ozs. **Length:** 7¼″ over-all.
Stocks: Checkered plastic.
Sights: Fixed.
Features: Swing-out cylinder with spring ejector. Imported by RG Industries.
Price: Plastic grips $95.00
Price: Wood grips $99.95

RG 38S REVOLVER
Caliber: 38 Special, 6-shot.
Barrel: 3″ and 4″.
Weight: 3″, 31 oz.; 4″, 34 oz. **Length:** 3″, 8½″; 4″, 9¼″.
Stocks: Checkered plastic.
Sights: Fixed front, rear adj. for w.
Features: Swing out cylinder with spring ejector. Imported from Germany by RG Industries.
Price: Plastic grips $99.95
Price: Wood grips $109.95

RG MODEL 39 REVOLVER
Caliber: 32 S&W, 38 Spec., 6-shot.
Barrel: 2″.
Weight: 21 oz. **Length:** 7″ over-all.
Stocks: Checkered plastic.
Sights: Fixed.
Features: Swing-out cylinder with spring ejector. Introduced 1980. Imported by RG Industries.
Price: Blue only $99.95

RG MODEL 74 REVOLVER
Caliber: 22 LR, 6-shot
Barrel: 3″.
Weight: 21½ oz. **Length:** 7¾″ over-all.
Stocks: Checkered plastic.
Sights: Fixed.
Features: Swing-out cylinder with spring ejector. Introduced 1980. Imported by RG Industries.
Price: Blue, plastic grips $79.95
Price: Blue, wood grips $89.95

ROSSI MODELS 68, 69 & 70 DA REVOLVERS
Caliber: 22 LR (M 70), 32 S & W (M 69), 38 Spec. (M 68).
Barrel: 3″.
Weight: 22 oz.
Stocks: Checkered wood.
Sights: Ramp front, low profile adj. rear.
Features: All-steel frame. Thumb latch operated swing-out cylinder. Introduced 1978. Imported by Interarms.
Price: 22, 32 or 38, blue $139.00
Price: As above, 38 Spec. only with 4″ bbl. as M 31 ....$144.00
Price: Model 38 (adj. sights) $159.00
Price: Model 51 (6″ bbl., 22 cal.) $159.00
Price: M68, M69, M70 in nickel $144.00

RUGER SECURITY-SIX Model 117
Caliber: 357 Mag. (also fires 38 Spec.), 6-shot.
Barrel: 2¾″, 4″ or 6″, or 4″ heavy barrel.
Weight: 33½ oz. (4″ bbl.) **Length:** 9¼″ (4″ bbl.) over-all.
Stocks: Hand checkered American walnut, semi-target style.
Sights: Patridge-type front on ramp, white outline rear adj. for w. and e.
Features: Music wire coil springs throughout. Hardened steel construction. Integral ejector rod shroud and sighting rib. Can be disassembled using only a coin.
Price: 2¾″, 4″, 6″ and 4″ heavy barrel $211.50
Price: 4″ HB, 6″ with Big Grip stocks $228.00

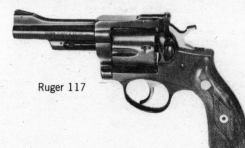

Ruger 117

HANDGUNS—REVOLVERS, SERVICE & SPORT

RUGER POLICE SERVICE-SIX Models 107, 108, 109
Caliber: 357 (Model 107), 38 Spec. (Model 108), 9mm (Model 109), 6-shot.
Barrel: 2¾" or 4" and 4" heavy barrel.
Weight: 33½ oz (4" bbl.). **Length:** 9¼" (4" bbl.) over-all.
Stocks: Checkered American walnut, semi-target style.
Sights: Patridge-type front, square notch rear.
Features: Solid frame with barrel, rib and ejector rod housing combined in one unit. All steel construction. Field strips without tools.
Price: Model 107 (357) $178.00
Price: Model 108 (38) $178.00
Price: Model 109 (9mm) $194.00
Price: Mod. 707 (357), Stainless, 4" & 4" HB $198.00
Price: Mod. 708 (38), Stainless, 4" & 4" HB $198.00

Ruger 707

RUGER SPEED-SIX Models 207, 208, 209
Caliber: 357 (Model 207), 38 Spec. (Model 208), 9mm P (Model 209) 6-shot.
Barrel: 2¾" or 4".
Weight: 31 oz. (2¾" bbl.). **Length:** 7¾" over-all (2¾" bbl.).
Stocks: Round butt design, diamond pattern checkered American walnut.
Sights: Patridge-type front, square-notch rear.
Features: Same basic mechanism as Security-Six. Hammer without spur available on special order. All steel construction. Music wire coil springs used throughout.
Price: Model 207 (357 Mag.) $178.00
Price: Model 208 (38 Spec. only) $178.00
Price: Model 209 (9mmP) $194.00
Price: Mod. 737 (357), Stainless $198.00
Price: Mod. 738 (38), Stainless $198.00
Price: Model 739 (9mm P), Stainless $214.50

RUGER STAINLESS SECURITY-SIX Model 717
Caliber: 357 Mag. (also fires 38 Spec.), 6-shot.
Barrel: 2¾", 4" or 6".
Weight: 33 oz. (4 bbl.). **Length:** 9¼" (4" bbl.) over-all.
Stocks: Hand checkered American walnut.
Sights: Patridge-type front, fully adj. rear.
Features: All metal parts except sights made of stainless steel. Sights are black alloy for maximum visibility. Same mechanism and features found in regular Security-Six.
Price: 2¾", 4", 6" and 4" HB $233.50
Price: 4" HB, 6" with Big Grip stocks. $250.00

RUGER REDHAWK
Caliber: 44 Rem. Mag., 6-shot.
Barrel: 7½".
Weight: About 3¼ lbs. **Length:** 13" over-all.
Stocks: Square butt. American walnut.
Sights: Patridge-type front, rear adj. for w. & e.
Features: Stainless steel, brushed satin finish. Has a 9½" sight radius. Introduced 1979.
Price: $325.00

Ruger Redhawk

SMITH & WESSON M&P Model 10 REVOLVER
Caliber: 38 Special, 6 shot.
Barrel: 2", 4", 5" or 6"
Length: 9¼" (4" bbl.). **Weight:** 30½ oz. (4" bbl.).
Stocks: Checkered walnut, Magna. Round or square butt.
Sights: Fixed, ⅛" ramp front, square notch rear.
Price: Blued ....$171.75   Nickeled $185.50

S&W 10

SMITH & WESSON 38 M&P AIRWEIGHT Model 12
Caliber: 38 Special, 6 shot.
Barrel: 2 or 4 inches.
Length: 6⅞" over-all. **Weight:** 18 oz. (2" bbl.)
Stocks: Checkered walnut, Magna. Round or square butt.
Sights: Fixed, ⅛" serrated ramp front, square notch rear.
Price: Blued ....$218.25   Nickeled $247.50

Smith & Wesson 38 M&P Heavy Barrel Model 10
Same as regular M&P except: 4" ribbed bbl. with ⅛" ramp front sight, square rear, square butt, wgt. 34 oz.
Price: Blued ....$171.75   Nickeled $185.50

SMITH & WESSON Model 13 H.B. M&P
Caliber: 357 and 38 Special, 6 shot.
Barrel: 4".
Weight: 34 oz. **Length:** 9¼" over-all.
Stocks: Checkered walnut, service.
Sights: ⅛" serrated ramp front, fixed square notch rear.
Features: Heavy barrel, K-frame, square butt.
Price: Blue, M-13 ....$176.50
Price: Nickel $192.75
Price: Model 65, as above in stainless steel $196.75

S&W 13

CAUTION: PRICES CHANGE. CHECK AT GUNSHOP.

HANDGUNS — REVOLVERS, SERVICE & SPORT

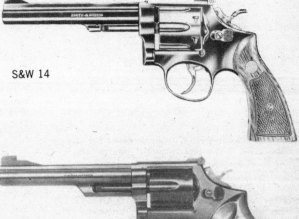

SMITH & WESSON Model 14 K-38 MASTERPIECE
Caliber: 38 Spec., 6-shot.
Barrel: 6″, 8⅜″.
Weight: 38½ oz. (6″ bbl.). **Length:** 11⅛″ over-all (6″ bbl.)
Stock: Checkered walnut, service.
Sights: ⅛″ Patridge front, micro click rear adj. for w. and e.
Price: 6″ bbl. $242.50
Price: 8⅜″ bbl., with target trigger, hammer, stocks $291.00

S&W 14

SMITH & WESSON 357 COMBAT MAGNUM Model 19
Caliber: 357 Magnum and 38 Special, 6 shot.
Barrel: 2½″, 4″, 6″.
Length: 9½″ (4″ bbl.). **Weight:** 35 oz.
Stocks: Checkered Goncala Alves, target. Grooved tangs and trigger.
Sights: Front, ⅛″ Baughman Quick Draw on 2½″ or 4″ bbl., Patridge on 6″ bbl., micro click rear adjustable for w. and e.
Price: S&W Bright Blue or Nickel, round butt, adj. sights $228.00

S&W 19

SMITH & WESSON HIGHWAY PATROLMAN Model 28
Caliber: 357 Magnum and 38 Special, 6 shot.
Barrel: 4″, 6″.
Length: 11¼″ (6″ bbl.). **Weight:** 44 oz. (6″ bbl.).
Stocks: Checkered walnut, Magna. Grooved tangs and trigger.
Sights: Front, ⅛″ Baughman Quick Draw, on plain ramp. micro click rear, adjustable for w. and e.
Price: S&W Satin Blue, sandblasted frame edging and barrel top ..$261.75
Price: With target stocks $282.00

SMITH & WESSON 357 MAGNUM M-27 REVOLVER
Caliber: 357 Magnum and 38 Special, 6 shot.
Barrel: 4″, 6″, 8⅜″.
Length: 11¼″ (6″ bbl.). **Weight:** 44 oz. (6″ bbl.).
Stocks: Checkered walnut, Magna. Grooved tangs and trigger.
Sights: Any S&W target front, micro click rear, adjustable for w. and e.
Price: S&W Bright Blue or Nickel, 4″, 6″ $383.00
Price: 8⅜″ bbl., sq. butt, target hammer, trigger, stocks $398.00

SMITH & WESSON 44 MAGNUM Model 29 REVOLVER
Caliber: 44 Magnum, 44 Special or 44 Russian, 6 shot.
Barrel: 4″, 6″, 8⅜″.
Length: 11⅞″ (6½″ bbl.). **Weight:** 47 oz. (6″ bbl.), 43 oz. (4″ bbl.).
Stocks: Oversize target type, checkered Goncala Alves. Tangs and target trigger grooved, checkered target hammer.
Sights: ⅛″ red ramp-front, micro. click rear, adjustable for w. and e.
Features: Includes presentation case.
Price: S&W Bright Blue or Nickel 4″, 6″ $419.83
Price: 8⅜″ bbl., blue or nickel $433.07
Price: Model 629 (stainless steel) $478.83

S&W 629

SMITH & WESSON 32 REGULATION POLICE Model 31
Caliber: 32 S&W Long, 6 shot.
Barrel: 2″, 3″.
Length: 7½″ (3″ bbl.). **Weight:** 18¾ oz. (3″ bbl.).
Stocks: Checkered walnut, Magna.
Sights: Fixed, ⅒″ serrated ramp front, square notch rear.
Price: Blued $211.25

S&W 31

SMITH & WESSON 1953 Model 34, 22/32 KIT GUN
Caliber: 22 LR, 6 shot.
Barrel: 2″, 4″.
Length: 8″ (4″ bbl. and round butt). **Weight:** 22½ oz. (4″ bbl.).
Stocks: Checkered walnut, round or square butt.
Sights: Front, ⅒″ serrated ramp, micro click rear, adjustable for w. & e.
Price: Blued ....$211.00 Nickeled $229.25
Price: Model 63, as above in stainless, 4″ $243.50

S&W 63

CAUTION: PRICES CHANGE. CHECK AT GUNSHOP.

SMITH & WESSON 38 CHIEFS SPECIAL & AIRWEIGHT
Caliber: 38 Special, 5 shot.
Barrel: 2", 3".
Length: 6½" (2" bbl. and round butt). **Weight:** 19 oz. (2" bbl.); 14 oz. (AIR-WEIGHT).
Stocks: Checkered walnut, Magna. Round or square butt.
Sights: Fixed, ¹/₁₀" serrated ramp front, square notch rear.
Price: Blued std. M-36 .... $194.00   Standard weight Nickel $210.00
Price: Blued AIR'W M-37 .. $215.75   AIRWEIGHT Nickel $244.00

S&W 36

Smith & Wesson 60 Chiefs Special Stainless
Same as Model 36 except: 2" bbl. and round butt only.
Price: Stainless steel $234.00

SMITH & WESSON BODYGUARD MODEL 38
Caliber: 38 Special; 5 shot, double action revolver.
Barrel: 2".
Length: 6⅜". **Weight:** 14½ oz.
Features: Alloy frame; integral hammer shroud.
Stocks: Checkered walnut, Magna.
Sights: Fixed ¹/₁₀" serrated ramp front, square notch rear.
Price: Blued .... $224.75   Nickeled $253.75

S&W 38

Smith & Wesson Bodyguard Model 49 Revolver
Same as Model 38 except steel construction, weight 20½ oz.
Price: Blued .... $208.75   **Price:** Nickeled $227.00

SMITH & WESSON MODEL 64 STAINLESS M&P
Caliber: 38 Special, 6-shot.
Barrel: 4".
Length: 9½" over-all. **Weight:** 30½ oz.
Stocks: Checkered walnut, service style.
Sights: Fixed, ⅛" serrated ramp front, square notch rear.
Features: Satin finished stainless steel, square butt.
Price: $185.00

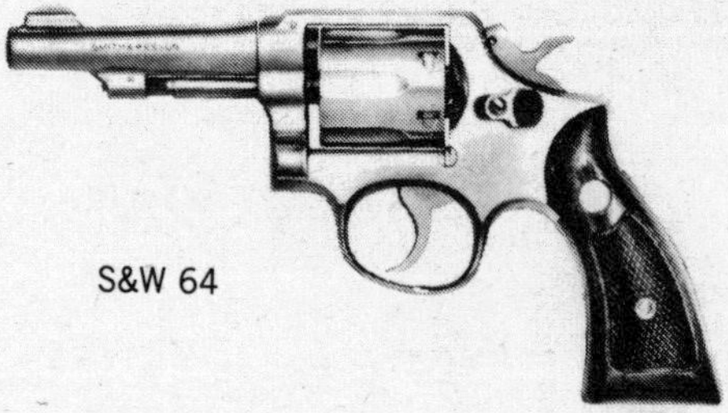

S&W 64

SMITH & WESSON MODEL 67 K-38 STAINLESS COMBAT MASTERPIECE
Caliber: 38 special, 6-shot.
Barrel: 4".
Length: 9⅛" over-all. **Weight:** 34 oz. (loaded).
Stocks: Checkered walnut, service style.
Sights: Front, ⅛" Baughman Quick Draw on ramp, micro click rear adj. for w. and e.
Features: Stainless steel. Square butt frame with grooved tangs, grooved trigger with adj. stop.
Price: $228.75

SMITH & WESSON MODEL 66 STAINLESS COMBAT MAGNUM
Caliber: 357 Magnum and 38 Special, 6-shot.
Barrel: 2½", 4", 6".
Length: 9½" over-all. **Weight:** 35 oz.
Stocks: Checkered Goncala Alves target.
Sights: Front, ⅛" Baughman Quick Draw on plain ramp, micro click rear adj. for w. and e.
Features: Satin finish stainless steel, grooved trigger with adj. stop.
Price: $244.00

S&W 66

SMITH & WESSON 41 MAGNUM Model 57 REVOLVER
Caliber: 41 Magnum, 6 shot.
Barrel: 4", 6" or 8⅜".
Length: 11⅜" (6" bbl.). **Weight:** 48 oz. (6" bbl.).
Stocks: Oversize target type checkered Goncala Alves wood and target hammer. Tang and target trigger grooved.
Sights: ⅛" red ramp front, micro click rear, adj. for w. and e.
Price: S&W Bright Blue or Nickel 4", 6" $419.83
Price: 8⅜" bbl. $433.07

S&W 57

CAUTION: PRICES CHANGE. CHECK AT GUNSHOP.

HANDGUNS—REVOLVERS, SERVICE & SPORT

SMITH & WESSON MODEL 586 Distinguished Combat Magnum
Caliber: 357 Magnum.
Barrel: 4", 6", both heavy.
Weight: 46 oz. (6"), 42 oz. (4").
Stocks: Goncalo Alves target-type with speed loader cutaway.
Sights: Baughman red ramp front, S&W micrometer click rear (or fixed).
Features: Uses new L-frame, but takes all K-frame grips. Full length ejector rod shroud. Smooth combat-type trigger, semi-target type hammer. Trigger stop on 6" models; 4" models factory fitted with target hammer and trigger will have trigger stop. Also available in stainless as Model 686. Introduced 1981.
Price: Model 586 (blue only) $247.00
Price: Model 686 (stainless) $268.00
Price: Model 581 (fixed sight, blue) $178.00
Price: Model 681 (fixed sight, stainless) $198.00

S&W 586

SMITH & WESSON MODEL 547
Caliber: 9mm Parabellum
Barrel: 3" or 4" heavy.
Weight: 34 oz. (4" barrel). **Length:** 9⅛" over-all (4" barrel).
Stocks: Checkered square butt Magna Service (4"), checkered walnut target, round butt (3")
Sights: ⅛" Serrated ramp front, fixed ⅛" square notch rear.
Features: K-frame revolver uses special extractor system—no clips required. Has ¼" half-spur hammer. Introduced 1981.
Price: Blue only $246.00

S&W 547

Taurus 66

TAURUS MODEL 66 REVOLVER
Caliber: 357 Magnum, 6-shot.
Barrel: 3", 4", 6".
Weight: 35 ozs.
Stocks: Checkered walnut, target-type. Standard stocks on 3".
Sights: Serrated ramp front, micro click rear adjustable for w. and e.
Features: Wide target-type hammer spur, floating firing pin, heavy barrel with shrouded ejector rod. Introduced 1978. From International Distributors.
Price: Blue, about $184.00
Price: Satin blue, about $199.00
Price: Model 65 (similar to M66 except has a fixed rear sight and ramp front), blue, about $161.00
Price: Model 65, satin blue, about $175.00

TAURUS MODEL 73 SPORT REVOLVER
Caliber: 32 S&W Long, 6-shot.
Barrel: 3", heavy.
Weight: 22 oz. **Length:** 8¼" over-all.
Stocks: Oversize target-type, checkered Brazilian walnut.
Sights: Ramp front, notch rear.
Features: Imported from Brazil by International Distributers.
Price: Blue, about $122.00
Price: Satin blue, about $141.00

TAURUS MODEL 80 STANDARD REVOLVER
Caliber: 38 Spec., 6-shot.
Barrel: 3" or 4".
Weight: 31 oz. (4" bbl.). **Length:** 9¼" over-all (4" bbl.).
Stocks: Checkered Brazilian walnut.
Sights: Serrated ramp front, square notch rear.
Features: Imported from Brazil by International Distributors.
Price: Blue, about $117.00
Price: Satin blue, about $131.00

TAURUS MODEL 83 REVOLVER
Caliber: 38 Spec., 6-shot.
Barrel: 4" only, heavy.
Weight: 34½ ozs.
Stocks: Over-size checkered walnut.
Sights: Ramp front, micro. click rear adj. for w. & e.
Features: Blue or nickel finish. Introduced 1977. From International Distributors.
Price: Blue, about $125.00
Price: Satin blue, about $138.00

Taurus 83

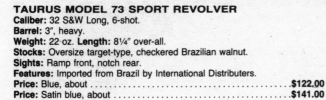

CAUTION: PRICES CHANGE. CHECK AT GUNSHOP.

TAURUS MODEL 82 HEAVY BARREL REVOLVER
Caliber: 38 Spec., 6-shot.
Barrel: 3″ or 4″, heavy.
Weight: 33 oz. (4″ bbl.). **Length:** 9¼″ over-all (4″ bbl.).
Stocks: Checkered Brazilian walnut.
Sights: Serrated ramp front, square notch rear.
Features: Imported from Brazil by International Distributors.
Price: Blue, about $122.00
Price: Satin blue, about $137.00

TAURUS MODEL 84 SPORT REVOLVER
Caliber: 38 Spec., 6-shot.
Barrel: 4″.
Weight: 30 oz. **Length:** 9¼″ over-all.
Stocks: Checkered Brazilian walnut.
Sights: Serrated ramp front, rear adj. for w. and e.
Features: Imported from Brazil by International Distributors.
Price: Blue, about $120.00
Price: Satin blue, about $133.00

Taurus 85

TAURUS MODEL 85 REVOLVER
Caliber: 38 Spec., 5-shot.
Barrel: 3″.
Weight: 21 oz.
Stocks: Smooth walnut.
Sights: Ramp front, square notch rear.
Features: Blue or Satin blue finish. Introduced 1980. From International Distributors.
Price: . . . . N.A.

DAN WESSON 44 MAGNUM REVOLVER
Caliber: 44 Magnum, 6 shots.
Barrel: 4″, 6″, 8″, 10″, interchangeable, with or without "Power Control" gun levelling device.
Weight: 45 oz. (4″ bbl.) **Length:** 12″ (6″ bbl.).
Stocks: Walnut or exotic wood. Two interchangeable styles, Target or Combat.
Sights: Serrated ⅛″ front blade with red insert (yellow and white also available.) White outline rear adj. for w. & e.
Features: Interchangeable barrels, grips, front sight blades. Bright blue finish only. Only 6″ and 8″ guns are shipped from the factory—4″ and 10″ barrel assemblies available separately. Introduced 1981.
Price: 6″, standard weight $348.50
Price: 8″, standard weight $357.50
Price: Pistol Pac, standard weight $506.00
Price: 6″ heavy shroud $368.50
Price: 8″, heavy shroud $377.50
Price: Pistol Pac, heavy shroud $545.00

Dan Wesson 44

DAN WESSON MODEL 9-2, MODEL 15-2 & MODEL 22
Caliber: 22 LR, 38 Special (Model 9-2); 357 (Model 15-2), both 6 shot.
Barrel: 2″, 4″, 6″, 8″, 10″, 12″, 15″. "Quickshift" interchangeable barrels.
Weight: 36 oz. (4″ bbl.), 40 oz. (4″ rimfire). **Length:** 9¼″ over-all (4″ bbl.).
Stocks: "Quickshift" checkered walnut. Interchangeable with eight other styles.
Sights: ⅛″ serrated blade front with red insert (Std.), white or yellow insert optional, as is Patridge. White outline, rear adj. for w. & e.
Features: Interchangeable barrels; four interchangeable grips; few moving parts, easy disassembly; Bright Blue finish only. Contact Dan Wesson for additional models not listed here. 10″, 12″ and 15″ barrels also available with vent. rib. Rimfire specs. essentially the same as 357 models.
Price: 9-2V, 15-2V (vent. rib) 8″ $289.50
Price: 9-2V, 15-2V, 10″ $311.50
Price: 9-2VH, 15-2VH (heavy vent. shroud) 12″ $356.50
Price: Pistol Pac, VH $634.00
Price: 9-2, 15-2 (Std. shroud) 2″ $242.00
Price: 9-2, 15-2, 6″ $257.00
Price: 9-2, 15-2, 8″ $265.00
Price: 9-2, 15-2, 15″ $332.00
Price: 9-2, 15-2, Pistol Pac $471.00
Price: 22-cal. same as 357 models.

Dan Wesson 15-2

DAN WESSON MODEL 8-2 & MODEL 14-2
Caliber: 38 Special (Model 8-2); 357 (Model 14-2), both 6 shot.
Barrel: 2″, 4″, 6″, 8″. "Quickshift" interchangeable barrels.
Weight: 34 oz. (4″ bbl.) **Length:** 9¼″ over-all (4″ bbl.).
Stocks: "Quickshift" checkered walnut. Interchangeable with three other styles.
Sights: ⅛″ serrated ramp front, rear fixed.
Features: Interchangeable barrels; 4 interchangeable grips; few moving s, easy disassembly.
Price: 2″ barrel $187.00
Price: 4″ barrel $193.00
Price: 6″ barrel $199.00
Price: Pistol Pac (cased with all above bbls.) $339.50

CAUTION: PRICES CHANGE. CHECK AT GUNSHOP.

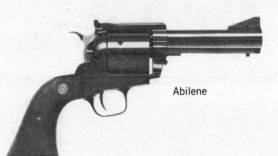

Abilene

ABILENE SINGLE ACTION REVOLVER
Caliber: 357 Mag., 44 Mag., 45 Colt, 6 shot.
Barrel: 4⅝", 6" (all cals.), 7½" (44 Mag. only).
Weight: About 48 oz.
Stocks: Smooth walnut.
Sights: Serrated ramp front, click adj. rear for w. and e.
Features: Wide hammer spur. Blue or stainless steel. From Mossberg.
Price: Blue, 357, 4⅝", 6", 7½" $232.95
Price: Blue, 44 Mag., 7½", ...$274.95
Price: Either cal., Magnaloy (hard chrome) $299.95
Price: 10" barrel, 44 Mag. $356.95
Price: 45 LC, blue $267.95

COLT SINGLE ACTION ARMY REVOLVER
Caliber: 357 Magnum, 44 Spec., 44-40, or 45 Colt, 6 shot.
Barrel: 4¾", 5½", 7½" or 12".
Length: 10⅞" (5½" bbl.). **Weight:** 37 oz. (5½" bbl.).
Stocks: Black composite rubber with eagle and shield crest.
Sights: Fixed. Grooved top strap, blade front.
Features: See Colt catalog for variations and prices. Only basic models and prices listed here.
Price: Blued and case hardened 4¾", 5½" bbl. $479.95
Price: Nickel with walnut stocks $555.95
Price: With 7½" bbl., blue $503.95

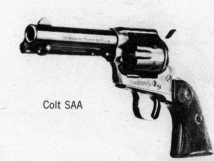

Colt SAA

F.I.E. "HOMBRE" SINGLE ACTION REVOLVER
Caliber: 357 Mag., 44 Mag., 45 LC.
Barrel: 5½" or 7½".
Weight: 45 oz. (5½" bbl.).
Stocks: Smooth walnut with medallion.
Sights: Blade front, grooved topstrap (fixed) rear.
Features: Color case hardened frame. Bright blue finish. Super-smooth action. Introduced 1979. From F.I.E. Corp.
Price: $194.95

F.I.E. "LEGEND" SINGLE ACTION REVOLVER
Caliber: 22 LR/22 Mag.
Barrel: 4¾".
Weight: 32 oz.
Stocks: Smooth walnut or black checkered nylon. Walnut optional ($16.95).
Sights: Blade front, fixed rear.
Features: Positive hammer block system. Brass backstrap and trigger guard. Color case hardened steel frame. From F.I.E. Corp.
Price: 22 LR $104.95
Price: 22 combo $121.95

Colt Single Action Army—New Frontier
Same specifications as standard Single Action Army except: flat-top frame; high polished finish, blue and case colored; ramp front sight and target rear adj. for windage and elevation; smooth walnut stocks with silver medallion, or composition grips.
Price: 45 Colt, 4¾", blue $555.95
Price: Either cal., 7½", blue $571.50
Price: 357 Mag., 7½", nickel $571.50

F.I.E. E15 BUFFALO SCOUT REVOLVER
Caliber: 22 LR/22 Mag., 6-shot.
Barrel: 4¾", 7", 9".
Length: 10" over-all. **Weight:** 32 oz.
Stocks: Black checkered nylon.
Sights: Blade front, fixed rear.
Features: Slide spring ejector. Blue, chrome or blue with brass backstrap and trigger guard models available.
Price: Blued, 22 LR $64.95
Price: Blue, 22 combo $80.95
Price: Chrome, 22 LR $69.95
Price: Chrome, combo $85.95
Price: Blue/brass, combo $89.95

> Consult our Directory pages for the location of firms mentioned.

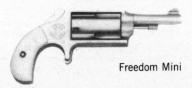

Freedom Mini

FREEDOM ARMS MINI REVOLVER
Caliber: 22 Short, Long, Long Rifle, 5-shot, 22 WMR, 4-shot.
Barrel: 1", 1¾".
Weight: 4 oz. **Length:** 4" over-all.
Stocks: Black ebonite or simulated ivory.
Sights: Blade front, notch rear.
Features: Made of stainless steel, simple take down; half-cock safety; sheathed trigger; cartridge rims recessed in cylinder. Comes in presentation case.
Price: 22 LR, 1" barrel $124.75
Price: 22 LR, 1" bbl., unfluted cyl., matte finish $109.95
Price: 22 LR, 1¾" barrel $129.50
Price: 22WMR, 1" barrel $144.75
Price: 22 WMR, 1¾" barrel $149.50
Price: 22 WMR, 1¾" bbl., unfluted cyl., matte finish $130.00

HANDGUNS—SINGLE ACTION REVOLVERS

Mitchell

MITCHELL SINGLE ACTION REVOLVERS
Caliber: 22 LR/22 Mag., 357 Mag., 44 Mag., 44 Mag./44-40, 45 Colt.
Barrel: 4¾", 5½", 6", 7½", 10", 12", 18".
Weight: About 36 oz.
Stocks: One-piece walnut.
Sights: Ramp front, rear adj. for w. & e.
Features: Color case-hardened frame, grip frame is polished brass. Hammer block safety. Introduced 1980. From Mitchell Arms Corp.
Price: 22/22 Mag., 357, 44, 45, 4¾", 5½", 7½", fixed sights **$189.95**
Price: As above, adj. sights **$199.95**
Price: 44 Mag. 45 Colt, 10", 12", 18" bbl. **$236.95**
Price: Dual cyl., fixed sights **$209.95**
Price: Dual cyl., adj. sights **$226.95**

NAM Mini

Navy 1875

Ruger Super Single Six

Ruger Blackhawk

NAM MINI REVOLVER
Caliber: 22 LR, 5-shot.
Barrel: 1".
Weight: 4.5 oz. **Length:** 3.8" over-all.
Stocks: Smooth plastic.
Sights: Blade front only.
Features: Stainless steel, single action only. Spur trigger. The 22 WMR version will be available late 1980. From M & N Distributors.
Price: About **$119.95**

NAVY ARMS 1875 REMINGTON-STYLE REVOLVER
Caliber: 357, 45 Long Colt, 44-40.
Barrel: 7½".
Weight: 2 lbs., 2 oz. **Length:** 14" over-all.
Stocks: Smooth walnut.
Sights: Fixed.
Features: Color case-hardened frame; fluted cylinder. Originally made 1875 to 1889 by Remington. From Navy Arms.
Price: Blued **$225.00**
Price: Nickel plated **$215.00**

RUGER NEW MODEL SUPER SINGLE-SIX CONVERTI-BLE REVOLVER
Caliber: 22 S, L, LR, 6-shot. 22 WMR in extra cylinder.
Barrel: 4⅝", 5½", 6½" or 9½" (6-groove).
Weight: 34½ oz. (6½" bbl.) **Length:** 11¹³/₁₆" over-all (6½" bbl.).
Stocks: Smooth American walnut.
Sights: Improved patridge front on ramp, fully adj. rear protected by integral frame ribs.
Features: New Ruger "interlocked" mechanism, transfer bar ignition, gate-controlled loading, hardened chrome-moly steel frame, wide trigger, music wire springs throughout, independent firing pin.
Price: 4⅝", 5½", 6½", 9½" barrel **$157.50**
Price: 5½", 6½" bbl., stainless steel **$224.00**

RUGER NEW MODEL BLACKHAWK REVOLVER
Caliber: 357 or 41 Mag., 6-shot.
Barrel: 4⅝" or 6½", either caliber.
Weight: 42 oz. (6½" bbl.). **Length:** 12¼" over-all (6½" bbl.).
Stocks: American walnut.
Sights: ⅛" ramp front, micro click rear adj. for w. and e.
Features: New Ruger interlocked mechanism, independent firing pin, hardened chrome-moly steel frame, music wire springs throughout.
Price: Blued **$197.50**
Price: Stainless steel (357) **$237.50**

RUGER NEW MODEL CONVERTIBLE BLACKHAWK
Caliber: 45 Colt or 45 Colt/45 ACP (extra cylinder).
Barrel: 4⅝" or 7½" (6-groove, 16" twist).
Weight: 40 oz. (7½" bbl.). **Length:** 13⅛" (7½" bbl.).
Stocks: Smooth American walnut.
Sights: ⅛" ramp front, micro click rear adj. for w. and e.
Features: Similar to Super Blackhawk, Ruger interlocked mechanism. Convertible furnished with interchangeable cylinder for 45 ACP.
Price: Blued, 45 Colt **$197.50**
Price: Convertible **$217.00**

Ruger New Model 357/9mm Blackhawk
Same as the 357 Magnum except furnished with interchangeable cylinders for 9mm Parabellum and 357 Magnum cartridges **$217.00**

Ruger New Model 30 Carbine Blackhawk
Specifications similar to 45 Blackhawk. Fluted cylinder, round-back trigger guard. Weight 44 oz., length 13⅛" over-all, 7½" barrel only.
Price: **$197.50**

CAUTION: PRICES CHANGE. CHECK AT GUNSHOP.

HANDGUNS—SINGLE ACTION REVOLVERS

Ruger Super Blackhawk

RUGER NEW MODEL SUPER BLACKHAWK
Caliber: 44 Magnum, 6-shot. Also fires 44 Spec.
Barrel: 7½" (6-groove, 20" twist).
Weight: 48 oz. **Length:** 13⅜" over-all.
Stocks: Genuine American walnut.
Sights: ⅛" ramp front, micro click rear adj. for w. and e.
Features: New Ruger interlocked mechanism, non-fluted cylinder, steel grip and cylinder frame, square back trigger guard, wide serrated trigger and wide spur hammer. Deep Ruger blue.
Price: $228.00

SMITH & WESSON K-38 S.A. M-14
Caliber: 38 Spec., 6-shot.
Barrel: 6".
Length: 11⅛" over-all (6" bbl.). **Weight:** 38½ oz. (6" bbl.).
Stocks: Checkered walnut, service type.
Sights: ⅛" Patridge front, micro click rear adj. for w. and e.
Features: Same as Model 14 except single action only, target hammer and trigger.
Price: 6" bbl. ....**Special Order only**

S&W S.A. M14

TANARMI S.A. REVOLVER MODEL TA22S LM
Caliber: 22 LR/22 Mag., 6-shot.
Barrel: 4¾".
Weight: 32 oz. **Length:** 10" over-all.
Stocks: Walnut.
Sights: Blade front, rear adj. for w. & e.
Features: Manual hammer block safety; color hardened steel frame; brass backstrap and trigger guard. Imported from Italy by Excam.
Price: 22/22 Mag., target sights $105.00

TANARMI SINGLE ACTION MODEL TA76
Same as TA22 models except blue backstrap and trigger guard.
Price: 22 LR, blue $60.00
Price: Combo, blue $75.00
Price: 22 LR, chrome $67.00
Price: Combo, chrome $82.00

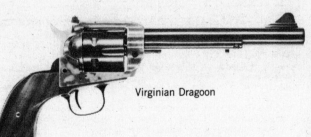

Virginian Dragoon

THE VIRGINIAN DRAGOON REVOLVER
Caliber: 357 Mag., 41 Mag., 44 Mag., 45 Colt.
Barrel: 44 Mag., 6", 7½", 8⅜"; 357 Mag. and 45 Colt, 5", 6", 7½".
Weight: 48 ozs. (6" barrel). **Length:** 11⅞" over-all (6" barrel).
Stocks: Smooth walnut.
Sights: Ramp-type Patridge front blade, micro. adj. target rear.
Features: Color case-hardened frame, spring-loaded floating firing pin, coil main spring. Firing pin is lock-fitted with a steel bushing. Introduced 1977. Made in the U.S. by Interarms Industries, Inc.
Price: 41 Mag., 7½", blue $219.00
Price: 44 Mag., 6", 7½", 8⅜", blue $239.00
Price: 45 Colt, 5", 6", 7½", blue $219.00
Price: 357 Mag., 12", blue $249.00
Price: 41 Mag., 45 Colt, 12", blue $269.00
Price: 44 Mag., 12", blue $289.00
Price: 44 Mag., 45 Colt, 6", 7½", stainless $279.00
Price: 44 Mag., 10½" Sil. model $299.00

HANDGUNS—MISCELLANEOUS

BUSHMASTER AUTO PISTOL
Caliber: 223.
Barrel: 11½".
Weight: 5¼ lbs. **Length:** 20½" over-all.
Stocks: Synthetic pistol grip.
Sights: Post front, open rear.
Features: Comes with 30-shot magazine; changing handle on upper rear of receiver; steel receiver. From Bushmaster Firearms.
Price: $439.95

Bushmaster

CLASSIC ARMS TWISTER

Caliber: 22 LR or 9mm Rimfire.
Barrel: 3¼".
Weight: 18 ozs.
Stocks: Pearlite.
Sights: None.
Features: Over-under barrels rotate on an axis for two separate shots. Spur trigger. 9mm Rimfire ammunition available. Available from Navy Arms.
Price: Either caliber **$79.95**

Classic Twister

C. O. P. 357 MAGNUM

Caliber: 38/357 Mag., 4 shots.
Barrel: 3¼"
Weight: 28 oz. **Length:** 5.5" over-all.
Stocks: Checkered composition
Sights: Open, fixed.
Features: Double-action, 4-barrels, made of stainless steel. Width is only one inch, height 4.1". From M & N Distributors.
Price: About **$250.00**

C.O.P. 357

HI-STANDARD 9194 AND 9306 DERRINGER

Caliber: 22 Rimfire Magnum. 2 shot.
Barrel: 3½", over and under, rifled.
Length: 5" over-all. **Weight:** 11 oz.
Stocks: Smooth plastic.
Sights: Fixed, open.
Features: Hammerless, integral safety hammerblock, all steel unit is encased in a black, anodized alloy housing. Recessed chamber. Dual extraction. Top break, double action.
Price: Blued (M9194) . . . . .**$130.00** Nickel (M9306) **$151.50**

Hi-Standard 9194

F.I.E. D-38

F.I.E. MODEL D-38 DERRINGER

Caliber: 38 Special.
Barrel: 3".
Weight: 14 oz.
Stocks: Checkered white nylon, walnut optional.
Sights: Fixed.
Features: Chrome finish. Spur trigger. Tip-up barrel, extractors. Gun is made in U.S.A.
Price: **$79.95**

LJUTIC LJ 25 PISTOL

Caliber: 25
Barrel: 2¾".
Stocks: Checkered walnut.
Sights: Fixed.
Features: Stainless steel; double action; ventilated rib. Introduced 1981. From Ljutic Industries.
Price: **$149.95**

MERRILL SPORTSMAN'S SINGLE SHOT PISTOL

Caliber: 22 LR Sil., 22 WMR, 22 Hornet, 256 Win. Mag., 357 Mag., 357/44 B & D, 30-30 Win., 30 Herrett, 357 Herrett, 41 Mag., 44 Mag., 7mm Merrill, 30 Merrill.
Barrel: 9" or 10¾", semi-octagonal; .450" wide vent. rib, matted to prevent glare; 14" barrel in all except 22 cals.
Weight: About 54 ozs. **Length:** 10½" over-all (9" bbl.)
Stocks: Smooth walnut with thumb and heel rest.
Sights: Front .125" blade (.080" blade optional); rear adj. for w. and e.
Features: Polished blue finish, hard chrome optional. Barrel is grooved for scope mounting. Cocking indicator visible from rear of gun. Has spring-loaded barrel lock, positive thumb safety. Roller trigger adjustable for weight of pull. From Rock Pistol Mfg.
Price: 9" barrel **$410.00**
Price: 9", 22 Sil. **$425.00**
Price: 10¾" barrel **$445.00**
Price: 14" barrel **$530.00**
Price: Extra barrel, 9" . . . . **$130.00** 10¾" **$165.00**
Price: Extra 14" bbl. **$250.00**

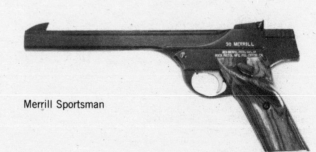

Merrill Sportsman

CAUTION: PRICES CHANGE. CHECK AT GUNSHOP.

Mitchell Derringer

ROLLING BLOCK SINGLE SHOT PISTOL
Caliber: 22 LR, 22 Hornet, 357 mag.
Barrel: 8".
Weight: 2 lbs. **Length:** 12".
Stocks: Walnut.
Sights: Front adj. for w., buckhorn adj. for e.
Features: Polished brass trigger guard. Imported by Navy Arms.
Price: $175.00

XP-100

Remington XP-100 Silhouette Pistol
Similar to standard XP-100 except chambered for 7mm BR Remington caliber; 15" barrel gives 21¼" over-all length; 4⅛ lbs.
Price: $338.95

Semmerling

MITCHELL'S DERRINGER
Caliber: 38 Spec.
Barrel: 2¾"
Weight: 11 oz. **Length:** 5¼" over-all.
Stocks: Walnut, checkered.
Sights: Fixed, ramp front.
Features: Polished blue finish. All steel. Made in U.S. Introduced 1980. From Mitchell Arms Corp.
Price: $129.95

Rolling Block

REMINGTON MODEL XP-100 Bolt Action Pistol
Caliber: 221 Fireball, single shot.
Barrel: 10½ inches, ventilated rib.
Length: 16¾ inches. **Weight:** 60 oz.
Stocks: Brown nylon one-piece, checkered grip with white spacers.
Features: Fits left or right hand, is shaped to fit fingers and heel of hand. Grooved trigger. Rotating thumb safety, cavity in fore-end permits insertion of up to five 38 cal., 130-gr. metal jacketed bullets to adjust weight and balance. Included is a black vinyl, zippered case.
Sights: Fixed front, rear adj. for w. and e. Tapped for scope mount.
Price: Including case $299.95

SEMMERLING LM-4 PISTOL
Caliber: 45 ACP.
Barrel: 3½".
Weight: 24 ozs. **Length:** 5.2" over-all.
Stocks: Checkered black plastic.
Sights: Ramp front, fixed rear.
Features: Manually operated repeater. Over-all dimensions are 5.2" x 3.7" x 1". Has a four-shot magazine capacity. Comes with manual, leather carrying case, spare stock screw and wrench. From Semmerling Corp.
Price: Complete $748.00
Price: Thin Version (blue sideplate instead of grips) $748.00

TANARMI O/U DERRINGER
Caliber: 38 Special.
Barrel: 3".
Weight: 14 oz. **Length:** 4¾" over-all.
Stocks: Checkered white nylon.
Sights: Fixed.
Features: Blue finish; tip-up barrel. Assembled in U.S. by Excam, Inc.
Price: $75.00

STERLING X-CALIBER SINGLE SHOT
Caliber: 22, 22 WMR, 357 Mag., 44 Mag.
Barrel: 8" or 10", interchangeable.
Weight: 52 oz. (8" bbl.). **Length:** 13" over-all (8" bbl.).
Stock: Coco Bolo
Sights: Patridge front, fully adj. rear.
Features: Barrels are dovetailed for scope mounting; hammer is notched for easy cocking with scope mounted. Finger grooved grip.
Price: Any caliber listed $199.95

Sterling X-Caliber

HANDGUNS – MISCELLANEOUS

T/C Contender

Thompson-Center Super 14 Contender
Similar to regular Contender except has 14″ barrel with fully adjustable target-type sights. Available in 30 Herrett, 357 Herrett, 222 Rem., 223 Rem., 7mm TCU, 30-30 Win., 35 Rem., 41 and 44 Mag., and 45 Win. Mag. only. Introduced 1978.
Price: $255.00
Price: Extra barrels $110.00

THOMPSON-CENTER ARMS CONTENDER
Caliber: 221 Rem., 7mm T.C.U., 30-30 Win., 22 S, L, LR, 22 WMR, 22 Hornet, 256 Win., 357 Mag., also 222 Rem., 44 Mag., 45 Long Colt, 45 Win. Mag.
Barrel: 10″, tapered octagon, bull barrel and vent. rib.
Length: 13¼″ (10″ bbl.). **Weight:** 43 oz. (10″ bbl.).
Stocks: Select walnut grip and fore-end, with thumb rest. Right or left hand.
Sights: Under cut blade ramp front, rear adj. for w. & e.
Features: Break open action with auto-safety. Single action only. Interchangeable bbls., both caliber (rim & center fire), and length. Drilled and tapped for scope. Engraved frame. See T/C catalog for exact barrel/caliber availablity.
Price: Blued (rimfire cals.) $235.00
Price: Blued (centerfire cals.) $235.00
Price: Extra bbls. (standard octagon) $95.00
Price: Bushnell Phantom scope base $8.75
Price: 357 and 44 Mag. vent. rib, internal choke bbl. $110.00

WICHITA MK-40 SILHOUETTE PISTOL
Caliber: Available in all calibers, including all IHMSA calibers.
Barrel: 13″, non-glare blue; 700″ dia. muzzle.
Weight: 4½ lbs. **Length:** 19⅜″ over-all.
Stock: Metallic gray fiberthane glass.
Sights: Wichita Multi Range sighting system.
Features: Aluminum receiver with steel insert locking lugs, measures 1.360 O.D.; 3 locking lug bolt, 3 gas ports; flat bolt handle; completely adjustable trigger. Introduced 1981. From Wichita Arms.
Price: $595.00

Wichita MK-40

WICHITA SILHOUETTE PISTOL
Caliber: 7mm PPC, 308x1½, 308 (full length). Other calibers available upon request. Single shot.
Barrel: 14¹⁵⁄₁₆″, (shorter lengths available).
Weight: 4½ lbs. **Length:** 21⅜″ over-all.
Stock: American walnut with oil finish, or fiberglass (yellow or black). Glass bedded.
Sights: Lyman globe front with inserts, Lyman or Williams peep rear.
Features: Comes with either right- or left-hand action with right-hand grip. Fluted bolt, flat bolt handle. Action drilled and tapped for Burris scope mounts. Non-glare satin blue finish. Remington-type trigger (with Canjar set shoe optional at extra charge). Introduced 1979. From Wichita Arms.
Price: $695.00
Price: As above except with Rear Position Stock and target-type Lightpull trigger. (Not illus.) $758.00

Wichita Silhouette

WICHITA CLASSIC PISTOL
Caliber: Any, up to and including 308 Win.
Barrel: 11¼″, octagon.
Weight: About 5 lbs.
Stock: Exhibition grade American black walnut. Checkered 20 lpi. Other woods available on special order.
Sights: Micro open sights standard. Receiver drilled and tapped for scope mount on special order.
Features: Receiver and barrel octagonally shaped, finished in non-glare blue. Bolt has three locking lugs and three gas escape ports. Completely adjustable Wichita trigger. Introduced 1980. From Wichita Arms.
Price: $1,495.00
Price: With fitted case $1,995.00

Wichita Classic

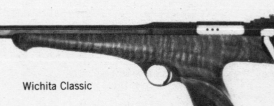

CAUTION: PRICES CHANGE. CHECK AT GUNSHOP.

CENTERFIRE RIFLES—AUTOLOADING & SLIDE ACTION

Armalite AR-180

ARMALITE AR-180 SPORTER CARBINE
Caliber: 223 semi-automatic, gas operated carbine.
Barrel: 18¼" (12" twist).
Weight: 6½ lbs. **Length:** 38" over-all.
Stock: Nylon folding stock, phenolic fiber-glass heat dissipating fore-end.
Sight: Flip-up "L" type sight adj. for w., post front adj. for e.
Features: Safety lever accessible from both sides. Flash hider slotted to prevent muzzle climb.
Price: $547.00
Price: 3x (2.75 x 20mm) scope with quick detachable side-mount. .$139.95
Price: Extra 5-round magazine $9.95
Price: Extra 20-shot magazine $15.95
Price: Extra 40-shot magazine $29.95

Auto-Ordnance 27A-1

AUTO-ORDNANCE MODEL 27 A-1
Caliber: 45 ACP, 30-shot magazine.
Barrel: 16".
Weight: 11½ lbs. **Length:** About 39½" over-all (Deluxe).
Stock: Walnut stock and vertical fore-end.
Sights: Blade front, open rear adj. for w.
Features: Re-creation of Thompson Model 1927. Semi-auto only. Deluxe model has finned barrel, adj. rear sight and compensator; Standard model has plain barrel and military sights. From Auto-Ordnance Corp.
Price: Deluxe $489.95
Price: Standard $469.95
Price: 1927A5 Pistol (M27A1 without stock; wgt. 7 lbs.) $469.95
Price: Lightweight model $469.95

AUTO-ORDNANCE 1927A-3
A 22 caliber version of the 27A-1. Exact look-alike with alloy receiver. Weight is about 7 lbs., 16" finned barrel, 10, 30- and 50-shot magazines and drum. Introduced 1977. From Auto-Ordnance Corp.
Price: $449.65

BERETTA BM 62 AUTO RIFLE
Caliber: 308 (7.62mm), 20-shot magazine.
Barrel: 17.5".
Weight: 9¼ lbs. **Length:** 38.5" over-all.
Stock: Walnut.
Sights: Blade front, peep rear fully adjustable for w. & e.
Features: Civilian sporting version of the BM-59 military rifle used by Italian armed forces. Has a bolt hold-open device, clip guide, rotary bolt, semi-auto only. Folding bipod, sling, 5-shot magazine, cleaning kit, bayonet and scope mount available. Introduced 1980. From Beretta Arms Co.
Price: $985.00

Browning Magnum Auto Rifle
Same as the standard caliber model, except weighs 8⅜ lbs., 45" over-all 24" bbl., 3-round mag., Cals. 7mm Mag., 300 Win. Mag.
Price: Grade I ....$594.95   Grade III $1,060.00
Price: Grade IV $1,960.00

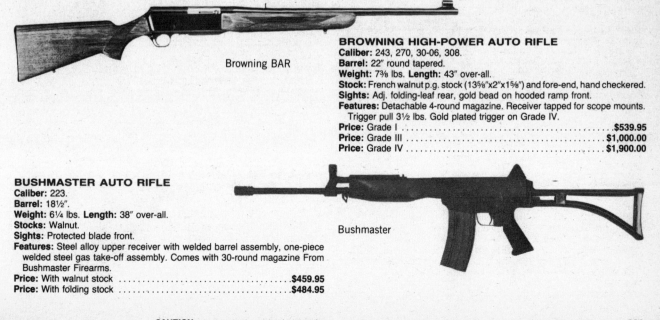

Browning BAR

BROWNING HIGH-POWER AUTO RIFLE
Caliber: 243, 270, 30-06, 308.
Barrel: 22" round tapered.
Weight: 7⅜ lbs. **Length:** 43" over-all.
Stock: French walnut p.g. stock (13⅝"x2"x1⅝") and fore-end, hand checkered.
Sights: Adj. folding-leaf rear, gold bead on hooded ramp front.
Features: Detachable 4-round magazine. Receiver tapped for scope mounts. Trigger pull 3½ lbs. Gold plated trigger on Grade IV.
Price: Grade I $539.95
Price: Grade III $1,000.00
Price: Grade IV $1,900.00

BUSHMASTER AUTO RIFLE
Caliber: 223.
Barrel: 18½".
Weight: 6¼ lbs. **Length:** 38" over-all.
Stocks: Walnut.
Sights: Protected blade front.
Features: Steel alloy upper receiver with welded barrel assembly, one-piece welded steel gas take-off assembly. Comes with 30-round magazine From Bushmaster Firearms.
Price: With walnut stock $459.95
Price: With folding stock $484.95

Bushmaster

CENTERFIRE RIFLES—AUTOLOADING & SLIDE ACTION

COLT AR-15 SPORTER
Caliber: 223 Rem.
Barrel: 20″.
Weight: 7¼ lbs. **Length:** 38⅜″ over-all.
Stock: Reinforced polycarbonate with buttstock stowage compartment.
Sights: Post front, rear adj. for w. and e.
Features: 5-round detachable box magazine, recoil pad, flash suppressor, sling swivels.
Price: **$475.95**
Price: With 3x scope **$621.70**

Colt AR-15

Colt CAR-15

Colt AR-15 Collapsable Stock Model
Same as standard AR-15 except has telescoping nylon-coated aluminum buttstock and redesigned fore-end. Over-all length collapsed is 32″, extended 39″. Barrel length is 16″, weight is 5.8 lbs. Has 14½″ sight radius. Introduced 1978.
Price: **$521.95**
Price: With 3x scope **$667.70**

COMMANDO ARMS CARBINE
Caliber: 9mm or 45 ACP.
Barrel: 16½″.
Weight: 8 lbs. **Length:** 37″ over-all.
Stock: Walnut buttstock.
Sights: Blade front, peep rear.
Features: Semi-auto only. Cocking handle on left side. Choice of magazines— 5, 15, 30 or 90 shot. From Commando Arms.
Price: Mark 9 or Mark 45 .... **$195.00**
Price: Nickel plated **$225.00**

Commando

DEMRO TAC-1 CARBINE
Caliber: 9mm or 45 ACP
Barrel: 16⅞″.
Weight: About 8 lbs. **Length:** 35¾″ over-all.
Stock: American walnut.
Sights: Removeable blade front, open rear adj. for w. & e.
Features: Fires from open bolt. Has a combination-lock safety that can be pre-set by the user.
Price: **$455.00**
Price: With fitted attache case **$485.00**

Demro XF-7 Carbine
Similar to the TAC-1 Carbine except has collapsable buttstock, high impact synthetic fore-end and pistol grip. Does not have combination-lock safety. Has 5, 15 or 30-shot magazine (45 ACP) or 32-shot magazine (9mm).
Price: **$529.00**
Price: With fitted attache case **569.00**

FN-LAR

F.N.-LAR COMPETITION AUTO
Caliber: 308 Win., 20-shot magazine.
Barrel: 21″ (24″ with flash hider).
Weight: 9 lbs., 7 oz. **Length:** 44½″ over-all.
Stock: Black composition butt, fore-end and pistol grip.
Sights: Post front, aperture rear adj. for elevation, 200 to 600 meters.
Features: Has sling swivels, carrying handle, rubber recoil pad. Consecutively numbered pairs available at additional cost. Imported by Steyr Daimler Puch of America.
Price: **$1,975.00**

FNC AUTO RIFLE
Caliber: 223 Rem.
Barrel: 18″.
Weight: 9.61 lbs.
Stock: Synthetic stock.
Sights: Post front; flip-over aperture rear adj. for elevation.
Features: Updated version of FN-FAL in shortened carbine form. Has 30-shot box magazine, synthetic pistol grip, fore-end. Introduced 1981. Imported by Steyr Daimler Puch.
Price: Standard model **$1,695.00**
Price: Paratrooper, with folding stock **$1,798.00**

FN-FNC

CAUTION: PRICES CHANGE. CHECK AT GUNSHOP.

CENTERFIRE RIFLES—AUTOLOADING & SLIDE ACTION

FN-LAR Paratrooper

F.N.-LAR Paratrooper 308 Match
Similar to F.N.-LAR competition except with folding skeleton stock, shorter barrel, modified rear sight. Imported by Steyr Daimler Puch.
Price: **$2,088.00**

F.N.-LAR Heavy Barrel 308 Match
Similar to F.N.-LAR competition except has wooden stock and fore-end, heavy barrel, folding metal bipod. Imported by Steyr Daimler Puch.
Price: With wooden, stock **$2,617.00**
Price: With synthetic stock **$2,418.00**

H&H HK770

HECKLER & KOCH HK770 AUTO RIFLE
Caliber: 308 Win., 3-shot magazine.
Barrel: 19.6".
Weight: 7½ lbs. **Length:** 42.8" over-all.
Stock: European walnut. Checkered p.g. and fore-end.
Sights: Vertically adjustable blade front, open, fold-down rear adj. for w.
Features: Has the delayed roller-locked bolt system and polygonal rifling. Magazine catch located at front of trigger guard. Receiver top is dovetailed to accept clamp-type scope mount. From Heckler & Koch, Inc.
Price: **$640.00**

HECKLER & KOCH HK-91 AUTO RIFLE
Caliber: 308 Win., 5- or 20-shot magazine.
Barrel: 19".
Weight: 9½ lbs. **Length:** 40¼" over-all.
Stock: Black high-impact plastic.
Sights: Post front, aperture rear adj. for w. and e.
Features: Delayed roller lock bolt action. Sporting version of West German service rifle. Takes special H&K clamp scope mount. Shown with light bipod and Zeiss scope. Imported by Heckler & Koch, Inc.
Price: HK-91 with plastic stock **$656.00**
Price: HK-91 with retractable metal stock **$830.00**

HECKLER & KOCH HK-93 AUTO RIFLE
Similar to HK-93 except in 223 cal., 16.13" barrel, over-all length of 35½", weighs 7¾ lbs. Slight differences in stock, fore-end.
Price: HK-93, with plastic stock **$638.00**
Price: HK-93 with retractable metal stock **$812.00**

IVER JOHNSON'S PLAINFIELD CARBINE
Caliber: 30 U.S. Carbine.
Barrel: 18" four-groove.
Weight: 6½ lbs. **Length:** 35½" over-all.
Stock: Glossy finished hard wood.
Sights: Click adj. open rear.
Features: Gas operated semi-auto carbine. 15-shot detachable magazine.
Price: **$149.50**
Price: Paratrooper model—with telescoping wire stock, front vertical hand grip
.... **$181.00**
Price: Super Enforcer (9" bbl., full p.g.) **$193.00**

LEADER MARK SERIES AUTO RIFLE
Caliber: 223 Rem.
Barrel: 16.1".
Weight: 7.5 lbs. **Length:** 35.8" over-all.
Stock: Synthetic stock, pistol grip and fore-end.
Sights: Protected post front, revolving aperture rear adj. for windage.
Features: Gas operated, locked breech system based on a fixed piston, mobile cylinder design. Comes with flash suppressor, 10 or 20 round magazine. Introduced 1981. Imported by World Public Safety.
Price: Mk. 5 (snythetic stock) **$480.00**
Price: Mk. 2 (wooden thumbhole stock), about **$490.00**
Price: Mk. 1 (wooden stock and fore-end) about **$490.00**

Remington Four

Remington 7400

REMINGTON MODEL FOUR AUTO RIFLE
Caliber: 243 Win., 6mm Rem., 7mm Exp. Rem., 308 Win. and 30-06.
Barrel: 22" round tapered.
Weight: 7½ lbs. **Length:** 42" over-all
Stock: Walnut, deluxe cut checkered p.g. and fore-end. Full checkpiece, Monte Carlo.
Sights: Gold bead front sight on ramp; step rear sight with windage adj.
Features: Redesigned and improved version of the Model 742. Positive cross-bolt safety. Receiver tapped for scope mount. 4-shot clip mag. Has cartridge head medallion denoting caliber on bottom of receiver. Introduced 1981.
Price: **$449.95**
Extra 4-shot clip magazine **$9.95**

Remington Model 7400 Auto Rifle
Similar to Model Four except does not have full cheekpiece Monte Carlo stock, has slightly different fore-end design, impressed checkering, no cartridge head medallion. Introduced 1981.
Price: **$399.95**

Remington Six

REMINGTON MODEL SIX SLIDE ACTION
Caliber: 6mm Rem., 243, 270, 308 Win., 30-06.
Barrel: 22″ round tapered.
Weight: 7½ lbs. **Length:** 42″ over-all.
Stock: Cut-checkered walnut p.g. and fore-end, Monte Carlo with full cheek-
  piece.
Sights: Gold bead front sight on matted ramp, open step adj. sporting rear.
Features: Redesigned and improved version of the Model 760. Has cartridge
  head medallion denoting caliber on bottom of receiver. Detachable 4-shot
  clip. Cross-bolt safety. Receiver tapped for scope mount. Introduced 1981.
Price: $399.95
  Extra 4-shot clip $9.25

Remington Model 7600 Slide Action Rifle
Similar to Model Six except does not have Monte Carlo stock or cheekpiece,
no cartridge head medallion. Slightly different fore-end design. Impressed
checkering. Introduced 1981.
Price: $349.95

Ruger Mini-14

RUGER MINI-14 223 CARBINE
Caliber: 223 Rem., 5-shot detachable box magazine.
Barrel: 18½″.
Weight: 6.4 lbs. **Length:** 37¼″ over-all.
Stock: American hardwood, steel reinforced.
Sights: Ramp front, fully adj. rear.
Features: Fixed piston gas-operated, positive primary extraction. 10 and 20-
  shot magazines available from Ruger dealers, 30-shot magazine available
  only to police departments and government agencies.
Price: $269.50
Price: As above except in stainless steel $310.00

Ruger 44

RUGER 44 AUTOLOADING CARBINE
Caliber: 44 Magnum, 4-shot tubular magazine.
Barrel: 18½″ round tapered.
Weight: 5¾ lbs. **Length:** 36¾″ over-all.
Stock: One-piece walnut p.g. stock (13⅜″x1⅝″x2¼″)
Sights: ¹⁄₁₆″ front, folding leaf rear sight adj. for e.
Features: Wide, curved trigger. Sliding cross-bolt safety. Receiver tapped for
  scope mount, unloading button.
Price: $298.00

SIG-AMT

SIG-AMT AUTO RIFLE
Caliber: 308 Win., 20-shot detachable box magazine.
Barrel: 18¾″.
Weight: 9½ lbs. **Length:** 39″ over-all.
Stock: Walnut stock and fore-end, composition vertical p.g.
Sights: Adj. post front, adj. aperture rear.
Features: Roller-lock breech, gas-assisted action; right-side cocking handle;
  loaded chamber indicator; no-tool take-down. Winter trigger (optional) allows
  firing with mittens. Spare parts, magazine, etc. available. From Mandall
  Shooting Supplies.
Price: $2,200.00

Savage 170

SAVAGE MODEL 170 SLIDE ACTION
Caliber: 30-30 or 35 Rem., 3-shot mag.
Barrel: 22″ round tapered.
Weight: 6¾ lbs. **Length:** 41½″ over-all.
Stock: Walnut (14″x1½″x2½″), with checkered p.g. Hard rubber buttplate.
Sights: Hooded ramp front, folding-leaf rear.
Features: Hammerless, solid frame tapped for scope mount. Top tang safety.
Price: $204.45

CAUTION: PRICES CHANGE. CHECK AT GUNSHOP.

CENTERFIRE RIFLES—AUTOLOADING & SLIDE ACTION

Garand Rifle

SPRINGFIELD ARMORY M1 GARAND RIFLE
Caliber: 30-06, 8-shot clip.
Barrel: 24".
Weight: 9½ lbs. **Length:** 43½" over-all.
Stock: Walnut, military.
Sights: Military square blade front, click adjustable peep rear.
Features: Commercially-made M-1 Garand duplicates the original service rifle.
   Introduced 1979. From Springfield Armory.
Price: Standard, about $525.00
Price: National Match, about $625.00
Price: Ultra Match, about $699.00

M1A

SPRINGFIELD ARMORY M1A RIFLE
Caliber: 7.62mm Nato (308), 5-, 10- or 20-round box magazine.
Barrel: 25¹/₁₆" with flash suppressor, 22" without suppressor.
Weight: 8¾ lbs. **Length:** 44¼" over-all.
Stock: American walnut or birch with walnut colored heat-resistant fiberglass
   handguard. Matching walnut handguard available.
Sights: Military, square blade front, full click-adjustable aperture rear.
Features: Commercial equivalent of the U.S. M-14 service rifle with no provi-
   sion for automatic firing. From Springfield Armory. Military accessories avail-
   able including 3x-9x2 ART scope and mount.
Price: Standard M1A Rifle, about $610.00
Price: Match Grade, about $710.00
Price: Super Match (heavy Premium barrel), about $799.00

BM-59

SPRINGFIELD ARMORY BM-59
Caliber: 7.62mm NATO (308 win.); 20-round box magazine.
Barrel: 17.5".
Weight: 9¼ lbs. **Length:** 38.5" over-all.
Stock: Walnut, with trapped rubber butt pad.
Sights: Military square blade front, click adj. peep rear.
Features: Full military-dress Italian service rifle. Available in selective fire or
   semi-auto only. Refined version of the M-1 Garand. Accessories available
   include; folding alpine stock, muzzle brake/flash suppressor/grenade launch-
   er combo, bipod, winter trigger, grenade launcher sights, bayonet, oiler.
   Extremely limited quanties. Introduced 1981.
Price: Standard model $995.00
Price: Alpine model with short barrel $1,125.00
Price: Alpine model with short barrel, folding stock $1,195.00
Price: Nigerian model with pistol grip stock $1,075.00

Enforcer

UNIVERSAL ENFORCER MODEL 3000 AUTO CARBINE
Caliber: 30 M1 Carbine, 5-shot magazine.
Barrel: 10¼" with 12-groove rifling.
Length: 17¾". **Weight:** 4½ lbs.
Stocks: American walnut with handguard.
Sights: Gold bead ramp front. Peep rear.
Features: Accepts 15 or 30-shot magazines. 4½-6 lb. trigger pull.
Price: Blue finish $249.00
Price: Nickel plated finish (Model 3010N) $298.00
Price: Gold plated finish (Model 3015G) $367.00
Price: Black or olive Teflon-S finish (3020TRB, 3025TCO) $311.00

1003 Carbine

UNIVERSAL 1003 AUTOLOADING CARBINE
Caliber: 30 M1, 5-shot magazine.
Barrel: 18"
Weight: 5½ lbs: **Length:** 35½" over-all
Stock: American hardwood stock inletted for "issue" sling and oiler, blued
   metal handguard.
Sights: Blade front with protective wings, adj. rear.
Features: Gas operated, cross lock safety. Receiver tapped for scope mounts.
Price: $199.00
Price: Model 2560 "Ferret" in 256 Win. $229.00

CENTERFIRE RIFLES—AUTOLOADING & SLIDE ACTION

Universal Model 1005 SB Carbine

Same as Model 1003 except has "Super-Mirrored" blue finish, walnut Monte Carlo stock, deluxe barrel band. Also available finished in nickel (Model 1010N), 18K gold (Model 1015G), Raven Black Du Pont Teflon-S (Model 1020TB) or Camouflage Olive Teflon-S (Model 1025TCO).

Price: Model 1005SB **$250.00**
Price: Model 1010N **$266.50**
Price: Model 1015G **$329.00**
Price: Model 1020TB, 1025TCO **$279.00**

Universal Commemorative Model 1981 Carbine

Same basic specs as Model 1003 Carbine except comes with 5, 15 and 30-shot magazines, Weaver scope and mount, bayonet and scabbard, brass belt buckle—all in a foam-fitted case. Stock is of select black walnut with inletted medallion. Metal parts are Parkerized. Introduced 1981.

Price: Complete **$598.00**

5000 PT Carbine

Universal Model 5000PT Carbine

Same as standard Model 1003 except comes with "Schmeisser-type paratrooper" folding stock. Over-all length open 36"; folded 27".

Price: Blue only **$233.00**

UZI CARBINE

Caliber: 9mm Parabellum, 25-round magazine.
Barrel: 16.1".
Weight: 8½ lbs. **Length:** 24.2" (stock folded).
Stock: Folding metal stock.
Sights: Post-type front, "L" flip-type rear adj. for 100 meters and 200 meters.
Features: Adapted by Col. Uzi Gal to meet BATF regulations, this semi-atuo has the same qualities as the famous submachine gun. Made by Israel Military Industries. Comes in molded Styrofoam case with sling, magazine and a short "display only" barrel. Imported by Action Arms Ltd. Introduced 1980.
Price: **$595.00**

UZI Carbine

WILKINSON "TERRY" CARBINE

Caliber: 9mm Para., 30-shot magazine.
Barrel: 16³⁄₁₆".
Weight: 7 lbs. 2 ozs. **Length:** 28½" over-all.
Stock: Black P.V.C. plastic stock, grip and fore-end.
Sights: Williams adjustable.
Features: Closed breech, blow-back action. Bolt-type safety and magazine catch. Ejection port has spring operated cover. Receiver dovetailed for scope mount. Semi-auto only. Introduced 1977. From Wilkinson Arms.
Price: **$315.00**
Price: Extra magazine **$18.95**

Terry Carbine

CENTERFIRE RIFLES—LEVER ACTION

Browning B-92

BROWNING B-92 LEVER ACTION

Caliber: 44 Rem. Mag., 11-shot magazine.
Barrel: 20" round.
Weight: 5 lbs., 8 oz. **Length:** 37½" over-all.
Stock: Straight grip stock and classic fore-end in French walnut with high gloss finish. Steel, modified crescent buttplate. (12¾" x 2" x 2⅞").
Sights: Post front, classic cloverleaf rear with notched elevation ramp. Sight radius 16⅝".
Features: Tubular magazine. Follows design of original Model 92 lever-action. Introduced 1979.
Price: **$299.95**

Browning BLR

BROWNING BLR LEVER ACTION RIFLE

Caliber: 243, 308 Win. or 358 Win. 4-shot detachable mag.
Barrel: 20" round tapered.
Weight: 6 lbs. 15 oz. **Length:** 39¾" over-all.
Stock: Checkered straight grip and fore-end, oil finished walnut (13¾"x1¾"x2⅜").
Sights: Gold bead on hooded ramp front; low profile square notch adj. rear.
Features: Wide, grooved trigger; half-cock hammer safety. Receiver tapped for scope mount. Recoil pad installed.
Price: **$364.95**

CAUTION: PRICES CHANGE. CHECK AT GUNSHOP.

Dixie 1873

DIXIE ENGRAVED MODEL 1873 RIFLE
Caliber: 44-40.
Barrel: 23½", octagon.
Weight: 7¾ lbs. **Length:** 43" over-all.
Stock: Walnut.
Sights: Blade front, adj. rear.
Features: Engraved and case hardened frame. Duplicate of Winchester 1873. Made in Italy. From Dixie Gun Works.
Price: $499.00
Price: Plain, blued carbine $450.00

Marlin 336C

MARLIN 336C LEVER ACTION CARBINE
Caliber: 30-30 or 35 Rem., 6-shot tubular magazine
Barrel: 20" Micro-Groove∗.
Weight: 7 lbs. **Length:** 38½"
Stock: Select American black walnut, capped p.g. with white line spacers. Mar-Shield∗ finish.
Sights: Ramp front with Wide-Scan™ hood, semi-buckhorn folding rear adj. for w. & e.
Features: Gold plated trigger, receiver tapped for scope mount, offset hammer spur, top of receiver sand blasted to prevent glare.
Price: Less scope $220.95

Marlin 336T Lever Action Carbine
 Same as the 336C except: straight stock; cal. 30-30 only. Squared finger lever, 18½" barrel, weight 6¾ lbs. $220.95

Glenfield 30A Lever Action Carbine
 Same as the Marlin 336C except: checkered walnut finished hardwood p.g. stock, 30-30 only, 6-shot. $205.95

Marlin 1894

MARLIN 1894 LEVER ACTION CARBINE
Caliber: 44 Magnum, 10 shot tubular magazine
Barrel: 20" Micro-Groove∗.
Weight: 6 lbs. **Length:** 37½"
Stock: American black walnut, straight grip and fore-end. Mar-Shield∗ finish.
Sights: Hooded ramp front, semi-buckhorn folding rear adj. for w. & e.
Features: Gold plated trigger, receiver tapped for scope mount, offset hammer spur, solid top receiver sand blasted to prevent glare.
Price: $232.95

Marlin 1894C

MARLIN 1894C CARBINE 357
Caliber: 357 Magnum, 9-shot tube magazine.
Barrel: 18½" Micro-Groove∗.
Weight: 6 lbs. **Length:** 35½" over-all.
Stock: American black walnut, straight grip and fore-end.
Sights: Bead front, adjustable semi-buckhorn folding rear.
Features: Solid top receiver tapped for scope mount or receiver sight; offset hammer spur. Gold plated steel trigger; receiver top sandblasted to prevent glare.
Price: About $232.95

Marlin 1894S

MARLIN 1895S LEVER ACTION RIFLE
Caliber: 45-70, 4-shot tubular magazine.
Barrel: 22" round.
Weight: 7½ lbs. **Length:** 40½".
Stock: American black walnut, full pistol grip. Mar-Shield∗ finish; rubber butt-pad; q-d. swivels; leather carrying strap.
Sights: Bead front with Wide-Scan hood, semi-buckhorn folding rear adj. for w. and e.
Features: Solid receiver tapped for scope mounts or receiver sights; offset hammer spur.
Price: $309.95

Marlin 444

MARLIN 444S LEVER ACTION SPORTER
Caliber: 444 Marlin, 4-shot tubular magazine
Barrel: 22″ Micro-Groove®.
Weight: 7½ lbs. **Length:** 40½″
Stock: American black walnut, capped p.g. with white line spacers, rubber rifle butt pad. Mar-Shield® finish; q.d. swivels, leather carrying strap.
Sights: Hooded ramp front, folding semi-buckhorn rear adj. for w. & e.
Features: Gold plated trigger, receiver tapped for scope mount, offset hammer spur, leather sling with detachable swivels.
Price: $250.95

Marlin 375 Rifle
Similar to 444S except chambered for 375 Win., 5-shot magazine; 20″ barrel; over-all length of 38½″; weight of 6¾ lbs. Comes with adj. leather carrying strap and q.d. swivels $250.95

NAVY ARMS HENRY CARBINE
Caliber: 44-40 or 44 rimfire.
Barrel: 21″.
Weight: About 9 lbs. **Length:** About 39″ over-all.
Stock: Oil stained American walnut.
Sights: Blade front, rear adj. for e.
Features: Reproduction of the original Henry carbine with brass frame and buttplate, rest blued. Will be produced in limited edition of 1,000 standard models, plus 50 engraved guns. From Navy Arms.
Price: Standard $500.00
Price: Engraved $1,500.00
Price: Iron frame, standard $750.00
Price: Iron frame, engraved $1,500.00

Navy Henry

Navy 1873

NAVY ARMS "1873" MODEL RIFLE
Caliber: 44-40.
Barrel: 24″ (rifle, octagon); 20″ (carbine, round), 16½″ (trapper).
Weight: 9 lbs. (rifle); 7½ lbs. (carbine).
Stock: Walnut.
Sights: Blade front, step adj. rear.
Features: Available in blue, case-hardened or nickel (44-40 only) finish. Sliding dust cover, lever latch. Imported by Navy Arms Co.
Price: Rifle $375.00
Price: Carbine $235.00
Price: Trapper $235.00

> Consult our Directory pages for the location of firms mentioned.

ROSSI SADDLE-RING CARBINE
Caliber: 38 Spec. (9 rounds), 357 Mag. (8 rounds).
Barrel: 20″.
Weight: 5¾ lbs. **Length:** 37″ over-all.
Stock: Walnut.
Sights: Blade front, Buckhorn rear.
Features: Re-creation of the famous lever-action carbine. Handles 38 and 357 interchangeably. Introduced 1978. Imported by Interarms.
Price: $283.00
Price: Blue, engraved $325.00

NAVY ARMS MODEL 66 LEVER ACTION RIFLE
Caliber: 38 Special, 44-40.
Barrel: 16½″, 19″, 24″.
Weight: 9¼ lbs. **Length:** 39½″.
Stock: Walnut.
Sights: Fixed front, folding rear.
Features: Replica of Winchester Model 1866 "Yellowboy." Available with three grades of engraving, selected stock and fore-end at additional cost. Imported by Navy Arms.
Price: Trapper Carbine $250.00
Price: 24″ octagon bbl. (illus.) $350.00

Savage 99E

SAVAGE 99E LEVER ACTION RIFLE
Caliber: 300 Savage, 243 or 308 Win., 5-shot rotary magazine.
Barrel: 22″, chrome-moly steel.
Weight: 7 lbs. **Length:** 39¾″ over-all.
Stock: Walnut finished with checkered p.g. and fore-end (13½x1½x2½).
Sights: Ramp front with folding leaf sporting rear. Tapped for scope mounts.
Features: Grooved trigger, slide safety locks trigger and lever.
Price: $296.60

CAUTION: PRICES CHANGE. CHECK AT GUNSHOP.

CENTERFIRE RIFLES—LEVER ACTION

Savage 99A

Savage 99A Lever Action Rifle
Similar to the 99E except: straight-grip walnut stock with schnabel fore-end, top tang safety, no magazine window. Folding leaf rear sight. Available in 250-3000 (250 Savage), 243, 308 Win., or 375 Win. $326.10

Savage 99C

Savage 99C Lever Action Clip Rifle
Similar to M99A except: Detachable staggered clip magazine with push-button ejection. Cut checkering on Monte Carlo stock and fore-end. Wgt. about 6¾ lbs., 41¾" over-all with 22" bbl. Available in cals. 243, 308, 7mm-08 Rem. $333.50

Winchester 94 BB

WINCHESTER MODEL 94 BIG BORE XTR
Caliber: 375 Win., 6-shot magazine.
Barrel: 20".
Weight: 6⅛ lbs. **Length:** 37¾" over-all.
Stock: American walnut with fine cut checkering, warm rich color. Satin finish.
Sights: Hooded ramp front, semi-buckhorn rear adjustable for w. & e.
Features: All external metal parts have Winchester's new deep blue high polish finish. Stock measurements are: 13¼" x 1¾" x 2½". Rifling twist 1 in 12". Rubber recoil pad fitted to buttstock. Introduced 1978.
Price: $283.00

Winchester 94

WINCHESTER 94 LEVER ACTION CARBINE
Caliber: 30-30, (12" twist). 6-shot tubular mag.
Barrel: 16", 20"
Weight: 6½ lbs. **Length:** 37¾" over-all.
Stock: Walnut straight grip stock and fore-end (13"x1¾"x2½").
Sights: Bead front sight on ramp with removable cover; open rear. Tapped for receiver sights.
Features: Solid frame, top ejection, half-cock hammer safety.
Price: $223.00
Price: Trapper model, 16" barrel $223.00

Winchester Model 94XTR Carbine
Same as standard Model 94 except has high-grade finish on stock and fore-end with cut checkering on both. Metal has highly polished deep blue finish.
Price: $243.00

Winchester 94 Antique Carbine
Same as M94 except: color case-hardened and scroll-engraved receiver, brass-plated loading gate and saddle ring. 30-30 only $238.00

CENTERFIRE RIFLES—BOLT ACTION

Alpine

ALPINE BOLT ACTION RIFLE
Caliber: 22-250, 243 Win., 264 Win., 270, 30-06, 308, 308 Norma Mag., 7mm Rem. Mag., 8mm, 300 Win. Mag., 5-shot magazine (3 for magnum).
Barrel: 23" (std. cals.), 24" (mag.).
Weight: 7½ lbs.
Stock: European walnut. Full p.g. and Monte Carlo; checkered p.g. and fore-end; rubber recoil pad; white line spacers; sling swivels.
Sights: Ramp front, open rear adj. for w. and e.
Features: Made by Firearms Co. Ltd. in England. Imported by Mandall Shooting Supplies.
Price: Standard Grade $375.00
Price: Custom Grade $395.00

CENTERFIRE RIFLES — BOLT ACTION

BSA CF-2

BSA CF-2 BOLT ACTION RIFLE
Caliber: 222 Rem. 22-250, 243, 6.5x55, 7mm Mauser, 7x64, 270, 308, 30-06, 7mm Rem. Mag., 300 Win. Mag.
Barrel: 24".
Weight: 7¾ lbs. **Length:** 45" over-all.
Stock: European walnut with roll-over Monte Carlo, palm swell on right side of pistol grip, skip-line checkering. High gloss finish.
Sights: Open adjustable rear, hooded ramp front. Removable.
Features: Adjustable single trigger or optional double-set triggers, side safety, visible cocking indicator. Ventilated rubber recoil pad. North American-style stock has high gloss finish, European has oil. Introduced 1980. From Precision Sports.
Price: Standard calibers, North American style $600.00
Price: Magnum calibers, North American style $625.00
Price: Double-set triggers, extra $65.00
Price: Heavy barrel, extra $32.50
Price: Standard calibers, European Style $650.00
Price: Magnum calibers, European style $675.00

Browning BBR

BROWNING BBR BOLT ACTION RIFLE
Caliber: 25-06, 270, 30-06, 7mm Rem. Mag., 300 Win. Mag.
Barrel: 24" medium sporter weight with recessed muzzle.
Weight: 8 lbs. **Length:** 44½" over-all.
Stock: Select American walnut cut to lines of Monte Carlo sporter full p.g. and high cheek piece; 18 l.p.i. checkering. Recoil n magnums.
Features: Short throw (60°) bolt with fluted surface, 9 locking lugs, plunger-type ejector, adjustable trigger is grooved and gold plated. Hinged floorplate with detachable box magazine (4 rounds in standard cals, 3 in mags). Convenient slide safety on tang. Special anti-warp aluminum fore-end insert. Low profile swivel studs. Introduced 1978.
Price: $429.95

CHAMPLIN RIFLE
Caliber: All std. chamberings, including 458 Win. and 460 Wea. Many wildcats on request.
Barrel: Any length up to 26" for octagon. Choice of round, straight taper octagon, or octagon with integral quarter rib, front sight ramp and sling swivel stud.
Length: 45" over-all. **Weight:** About 8 lbs.
Stock: Hand inletted, shaped and finished. Checkered to customer specs. Select French, Circassian or claro walnut. Steel p.g. cap, trap buttplate or recoil pad.
Sights: Bead on ramp front, 3-leaf folding rear.
Features: Right or left hand Champlin action, tang safety or optional shroud safety, Canjar adj. trigger, hinged floorplate.
Price: From $3,200.00

Champlin

COLT SAUER GRAND AFRICAN
Caliber: 458 Win. Mag.
Barrel: 24", round tapered.
Length: 44½" over-all. **Weight:** 10½ lbs.
Stock: Solid African bubinga wood, cast-off M.C. with cheekpiece, contrasting rosewood fore-end and p.g. caps with white spacers. Checkered fore-end and p.g.
Sights: Ivory bead hooded ramp front, adj. sliding rear.
Price: $1,108.95

Colt Sauer

COLT SAUER RIFLE
Caliber: 25-06, 270, 30-06, (std.), 7mm Rem. Mag., 300 Wea. Mag., 300 Win. Mag. (Magnum).
Barrel: 24", round tapered.
Length: 43¾" over-all. **Weight:** 8 lbs. (std.).
Stock: American walnut, cast-off M.C. design with cheekpiece. Fore-end tip and p.g. cap rosewood with white spacers. Hand checkering.
Sights: None furnished. Specially designed scope mounts for any popular make scope furnished.
Features: Unique barrel/receiver union, non-rotating bolt with cam-actuated locking lugs, tang-type safety locks sear. Detachable 3- and 4-shot magazines.
Price: Standard cals. ....$996.95 Magnum cals. $1,030.95
Price: Grand Alaskan, 375 H & H $1,058.00

Colt Sauer Short Action Rifle
Same as standard rifle except chambered for 22-250, 243 and 308 Win. 24" bbl., 43" over-all. Weighs 7½ lbs. 3-shot magazine. $996.95

CAUTION: PRICES CHANGE. CHECK AT GUNSHOP.

DuBiel

Du BIEL ARMS BOLT ACTION RIFLES
Caliber: Standard calibers 22-250 thru 458 Win. Mag. Selected wildcat calibers available.
Barrel: Selected weights and lengths. Douglas Premium.
Weight: About 7½ lbs.
Stock: Five styles. Walnut, maple, laminates. Hand checkered.
Sights: None furnished. Receiver has integral milled bases.
Features: Basically a custom-made rifle. Left or right-hand models available. Five-lug locking mechanism; 36 degree bolt rotation; adjustable Canjar trigger; oil or epoxy stock finish; Presentation recoil pad; jeweled and chromed bolt body; sling swivel studs; lever latch or button floorplate release. All steel action and parts. Introduced 1978. From Du Biel Arms.
Price: Rollover Model, left or right-hand **$2,250.00**
Price: Thumbhole left or right hand **$2,250.00**
Price: Classic, left or right hand **$2,250.00**
Price: Modern Classic, left or right hand **$2,250.00**
Price: Thumbhole Mannlicher, left or right hand **$2,250.00**

H&R 301

H&R Model 301 Bolt Action Carbine
Same as Model 300 except has 18″ barrel, full length Mannlicher-style stock with plain cheekpiece and blued nose cap. Not available in 22-250.
Price: **$495.00**

HARRINGTON & RICHARDSON M-300 BOLT ACTION
Caliber: 22-250, 243, 25-06, 270, 30-06, 308, 7mm Rem. Mag., 300 Win. Mag.
Barrel: 22″ round, tapered.
Weight: 7¾ lbs. **Length:** 42½″ over-all.
Stock: American walnut, hand checkered p.g. and fore-end, Monte Carlo, roll-over cheekpiece.
Sights: Adjustable rear, gold bead ramp front.
Features: Hinged floorplate; sliding side safety; sling swivels, recoil pad. Receiver tapped for scope mount. Commercial Mauser action.
Price: **$395.00**

Heym SR-20N

HEYM MODEL SR-20 BOLT ACTION RIFLES
Caliber: 5.6x57, 243, 6.5x57, 270, 7x57, 7x64, 308, 30-06 (SR-20L); 9.3x62 (SR-20N) plus SR-20L cals.; SR-20G—6.5x68, 7mm Rem. Mag., 300 Win. Mag., 8x68S, 375H&H.
Barrel: 20½″ (SR-20L), 24″ (SR-20N), 26″ (SR-20G).
Weight: 7-8 lbs. depending upon model.
Stock: Dark European walnut, hand-checkered p.g. and fore-end. Oil finish. Recoil pad, rosewood grip cap. Monte Carlo-style. SR-20L has full Mannlicher-style stock, others have sporter-style with schnabel tip.
Sights: Silver bead ramp front, adj. folding leaf rear.
Features: Hinged floorplate, 3-position safety. Receiver drilled and tapped for scope mounts. Adjustable trigger. Options available include double-set triggers, left-hand action and stock, Suhler claw mounts, deluxe engraving and stock carving. Contact Heym for more data.
Price: SR-20L **$899.00**
Price: SR-20N **$829.00**
Price: SR-20-G **$879.00**
Price: Left-hand action and stock, add **$134.00**

KRICO MODEL 400L BOLT ACTION RIFLE
Caliber: 22 Hornet, 5-shot magazine.
Barrel: 24″.
Weight: 6.6 lbs.
Stock: Select French walnut. Ventilated rubber recoil pad.
Sights: Hooded post front, open rear adj. for windage.
Features: Detachable box magazine; checkered pistol grip and fore-end; sling swivels. Available with single or double set trigger. Contact Heym for more data.
Price: **$479.00**

Kleinguenther K-15

KLEINGUENTHER K-15 INSTA-FIRE RIFLE
Caliber: 243, 25-06, 270, 30-06, 308 win. 7x57, 308 Norma Mag., 300 Weath. Mag., 7mm Rem. Mag., 375 H & H, 257-270-300 Weath. Mag.
Barrel: 24″ (Std.), 26″ (Mag.)
Weight: 7 lbs., 12 ozs. **Length:** 43½″ over-all.
Stock: European walnut M.C. with 1″ recoil pad. Left or right hand. Rosewood grip cap. Hand checkered. High luster or satin finish.
Sights: None furnished. Drilled and tapped for scope mounts. Iron sights optional.
Features: Ultra-fast lock/ignition time. Clip, or feed from top of receiver. Guaranteed ½″ 100 yd. groups. Many optional stock features available. Imported from Germany, assembled and accurized by Kleinguenther's.
Price: All calibers **$975.00**

Krico Model 400E Bolt Action Rifle
Same as Model 400L except has straight fore-end, walnut-finished beech stock, no fore-end tip, hard rubber butt plate.
Price: With single trigger **$409.00**
Price: With set trigger **$419.00**

Krico Model 420L Bolt Action Rifle
Same as Model 400L except has full Mannlicher-style stock, 20″ barrel, weighs 6.2 lbs. Solid rubber butt pad.
Price: **$579.00**

CENTERFIRE RIFLES — BOLT ACTION

Mark X

MARK X RIFLE
Caliber: 22-250, 243, 270, 308 Win.; 30-06; 25-06; 7 × 57; 7 mm Rem. Mag; 300 Win. Mag.
Barrel: 24″.
Weight: 7½ lbs. **Length:** 44″.
Stock: Hand checkered walnut, Monte Carlo, white line spacers on p.g. cap, buttplate and fore-end tip.
Sights: Ramp front with removable hood, open rear adj. for w. and e.
Features: Sliding safety, quick detachable sling swivels, hinged floorplate. Also available as actions or bbld. actions. Imported from Europe by Interarms.
Price: With adj. trigger and sights, from $319.00
Price: With adj. trigger, no sights, from $304.00

Mark X Marquis

MARK X CAVALIER RIFLE
Caliber: 22-250; 243; 25-06; 270; 7 × 57; 7mm Rem. Mag.; 308 Win.; 30-06; 300 Win. Mag.
Barrel: 24″.
Weight: 7½ lbs. **Length:** 44″.
Stock: Checkered Walnut with Rosewood fore-end tip and pistol grip cap, Monte Carlo cheek piece and recoil pad.
Sights: Ramp front with removable hood, open rear adjustable for windage and elevation.
Features: Contemporary-styled stock with sculptured accents; roll over cheek piece and flat bottom fore-end. Adjustable trigger and quick detachable sling swivels, standard. Receiver drilled and tapped for receiver sights and scope mounts. Also available without sights. Imported by Interarms.
Price: With adj. trigger and sights $369.00
Price: Adj. trigger, without sights $354.00
Price: 300 Win. Mag., 7mm Rem. Mag., with sights $379.00
Price: As above, without sights $364.00

MARK X MARQUIS MANNLICHER-STYLE CARBINE
Caliber: 270, 7x57, 30-06, 308 Win.
Barrel: 20″.
Weight: 7½ lbs. **Length:** 40″ over-all.
Stock: Hand checkered European walnut.
Sights: Ramp front with removable hood; open rear adj. for w. and e.
Features: Quick detachable sling swivels; fully adj. trigger; blue steel fore-end cap; white line spacers at p.g. cap and buttplate. Mark X Mauser action. Imported by Interarms.
Price: With adj. trigger and sights $369.00

MARK X ALASKAN MAGNUM RIFLE
Caliber: 375 H&H, 458 Win. Mag.; 3-shot magazine.
Barrel: 24″.
Weight: 8¼ lbs. **Length:** 32″ over-all.
Stock: Select walnut with crossbolt; hand checkered p.g. and fore-end; Monte Carlo; sling swivels.
Sights: Hooded ramp front; open rear adj. for w. & e.
Features: Hinged floorplate; right-hand thumb (tang) safety; adj. trigger. From Interarms.
Price: $389.00

MARK X VISCOUNT RIFLE
Caliber: 22-250; 243; 25-06; 270; 7x57; 7mm Rem. Mag.; 308 Win.; 30-06; 300 Win. Mag.
Barrel: 24″.
Weight: 7½ lbs. **Length:** 44″.
Stock: Genuine Walnut stock, hand checkered with 1″ sling swivels.
Sights: Ramp front with removable hood, open rear sight ajustable for windage and elevation.
Features: One piece trigger guard with hinged floor plate, drilled and tapped for scope mounts and receiver sight, hammer-forged chrome vanadium steel barrel. Imported by Interarms.
Price: With adj. trigger, sights, from $279.00
Price: With adj. trigger, no sights, from $267.00

MARK X CONTINENTAL MANNLICHER-STYLE CARBINE
Caliber: 243, 270, 7x57, 308, 30-06.
Barrel: 20″.
Weight: 7½ lbs. **Length:** 40″ over-all.
Stock: Hand checkered European walnut. Straight European-style comb with sculptured cheekpiece.
Sights: Ramp front with removable hood; open rear adj. for w. and e.
Features: Similar to Mannlicher-Style except for stock differences noted above, single adjustable or double-set triggers, classic "butter-knife" bolt handle. Button release hinged floorplate. Imported by Interarms.
Price: Double-set triggers, with sights $389.00
Price: Single adj. trigger, with sights $369.00

Mauser 66

Mauser Model 66SH Magnum Rifle
Similar to Model 66S except has 26″ barrel, weighs about 8¼ lbs., measures 44″ over-all and comes in 7mm Rem. Mag., 6.5x68, 300 Win. Mag., 7mm SE v. H., 300 Weatherby Mag., 9.3x64, 8x68S.
Price: $1,479.00

Mauser Model 66SG Big Game Rifle
Similar to Model 66S except has 26″ barrel, weighs about 9¼ lbs. and is chambered for 375 H & H Mag. and 458 Win. Mag.
Price: $1,819.00

MAUSER MODEL 66 BOLT ACTION RIFLES
Caliber: 5.6x61, 243, 6.5x57, 270, 7x64, 308 Win., 30-06, 9.3x62.
Barrel: 24″.
Weight: About 7½ lbs. **Length:** 41″ over-all.
Stock: European walnut, oil finish, Pachmayr recoil pad, rosewood fore-end and grip cap, sling swivels.
Sights: Hooded ramp front, Williams open adj. rear.
Features: Interchangeable barrels within caliber groups; silent safety locks bolt and firing pin. Double set or single trigger completely interchangeable. For more data contact Heym.
Price: Standard calibers, Model 66S $1,379.00
Price: Standard calibers, full-length stock $1,479.00
Price: Model 66S Ultra (21″ barrel, 7lbs) $1,479.00
Price: Model 66SM (single set trigger, special wood and finish) ..$1,749.00

CAUTION: PRICES CHANGE. CHECK AT GUNSHOP.

CENTERFIRE RIFLES — BOLT ACTION

Mauser 77

Mauser Model 77 Magnum Rifles
Similar to standard Model 77 except has 26″ barrel, 46″ over-all length, weighs about 7½ lbs. Magnum version chambered for 7mm Rem. Mag., 6.5x68, 300 Win. Mag., 9.3x62, 375 H & H Mag., 9.3x64, 8x68S. Big Game version chambered for 375 H & H, 458 Win. Mag.
Price: **$1,339.00**

MAUSER MODEL 77 BOLT ACTION RIFLE
Caliber: 243, 6.5x57, 270, 7x64, 308, 30-06.
Barrel: 24″.
Weight: About 7½ lbs. **Length:** 44″ over-all.
Stock: European walnut with oil finish, rosewood fore-end tip and grip cap. Bavarian checkpiece, recoil pad and palm-swell p.g.
Sights: Ramp front, open rear adj. for w. & e.
Features: Detachable 3-round box magazine; same trigger system as Model 66, single set or double set; patented silent safety. Introduced 1981. Contact Heym for more data.
Price: Half-stock **$1,249.00**
Price: Full length stock **$1,339.00**

Parker-Hale 1200

PARKER-HALE MIDLAND RIFLE
Caliber: 243, 270, 30-06, 308, 7mm Rem. Mag., 300 Win. Mag.
Barrel: 24″.
Weight: 7 lbs. **Length:** 45″ over-all.
Stock: Walnut; hand-checkered p.g. and fore-end.
Sights: Bead on ramp front, folding adjustable rear.
Features: Uses Springfield action; 4-shot magazine; receiver drilled and tapped and comes with Parker-Hale 1″ mounts and rings. Introduced 1981. From Kassnar Imports.
Price: All calibers **$289.95**

PARKER-HALE SUPER 1200 BOLT ACTION RIFLE
Caliber: 22-250, 243 Win., 6mm Rem., 25-06, 270 Win., 30-06, 308 Win., 7mm Rem. Mag., 300 Win. Mag.
Barrel: 24″.
Weight: 7¼ lbs. **Length:** 45″.
Stock: 13.5″ x 1.8″ x 2.3″. Hand checkered walnut, rosewood p.g. and fore-end caps, fitted rubber recoil pad with white line spacers.
Sights: Hooded bead front, folding adj. rear. Receiver tapped for scope mounts.
Features: 3-way side safety, single-stage adj. trigger, hinged mag. floorplate. Varmint Model (1200V) has glass-bedded action, free-floating bbl., avail. in 22-250, 6mm Rem., 25-06, 243 Win., without sights. Imported from England by Kassnar.
Price: .... **$369.95 ($374.95, mag. cals.)**
Price: 1200V **$374.95**

Remington 700 Classic

Remington 700 Safari
Same as the 700 BDL except 375 H&H or 458 Win. Magnum calibers only. Hand checkered, oil finished stock with recoil pad installed. Delivery time is about five months. **$649.95**

REMINGTON 700 "CLASSIC" RIFLE
Caliber: 22-250, 6mm Rem., 243, 270, 30-06, 7mm Rem. Mag.
Barrel: 22″ (6mm, 243, 270, 30-06), 24″ (22-250, 7mm Rem. Mag.).
Weight: About 7 lbs. **Length:** 43½″ over-all (22-250).
Stock: American walnut, 20 l.p.i. checkering on p.g. and fore-end. Classic styling. Satin finish.
Sights: Hooded ramp front with gold bead, sliding-ramp rear adjustable for w. & e.
Features: A "classic" version of the M700ADL with straight comb stock. Fitted with rubber butt pad on all but magnum calibers, which has a full recoil pad. Sling swivel studs installed.
Price: All cals. except 7mm Rem. Mag. **$364.95**
Price: 7mm Rem. Mag. **$379.95**

Remington 700 ADL

Remington 700 C Custom Rifle
Same as the 700 BDL except choice of 20″, 22″ or 24″ bbl. with or without sights. Jewelled bolt, with or without hinged floor plate. Select American walnut stock is hand checkered, rosewood fore-end & grip cap. Hand lapped barrel. 16 weeks for delivery after placing order **$750.00**

Remington 700BDL Left Hand
Same as 700 BDL except: mirror-image left-hand action, stock. Available in 270, 30-06 only.
Price: **$414.95**
Price: 7mm Rem. Mag. **$429.95**

Remington 700 BDL Varmint
Same as 700 BDL, except: 24″ heavy bbl., 43½″ over-all, wgt. 9 lbs. Cals. 222, 223, 22-250, 6mm Rem., 243, 25-06, 7mm-08 Rem. and 308. No Sights.
Price: **$419.95**

REMINGTON 700 ADL BOLT ACTION RIFLE
Caliber: 222, 22-250, 6mm Rem., 243, 25-06, 270, 7mm Exp. Rem., 308 and 30-06.
Barrel: 22″ or 24″ round tapered.
Weight: 7 lbs. **Length:** 41½″ to 43½″
Stock: Walnut, RKW finished p.g. stock with impressed checkering, Monte Carlo (13⅜″x1⅝″x2⅜″).
Sights: Gold bead ramp front; removable, step-adj. rear with windage screw.
Features: Side safety, receiver tapped for scope mounts.
Price: **$334.95**
Price: 7mm Rem. Mag. **$349.95**

Remington 700 BDL Bolt Action Rifle
Same as 700-ADL, except: 7mm-08 Rem; skip-line checkering; black fore-end tip and p.g. cap, white line spacers. Matted receiver top, quick release floorplate. Hooded ramp front sight. Q.D. swivels and 1″ sling
Price: **$399.95**
Available also in 17 Rem., 7mm Rem. Mag. and 300 Win. Mag., 8mm Rem. Mag., caliber. 44½″ over-all, weight 7½ lbs. ....
Price: **$414.95**
Peerless Grade .... **$1,300.00**   Premier Grade **$2,600.00**

CAUTION: PRICES CHANGE. CHECK AT GUNSHOP.

Remington 788

REMINGTON 788 BOLT ACTION RIFLE
Caliber: 22-250, 223 Rem., 7mm-08 Rem., 243, and 308 (4-shot).
Barrel: 18½" round tapered (24" in 223 and 22-250).
Weight: 7-7½ lbs. **Length:** 41⅝" over-all.
Stock: Walnut-finished hardwood with Monte Carlo and p.g. (13⅝"x1⅞"x2⅝").
Sights: Blade ramp front, open rear adj. for w. & e.
Features: Detachable box magazine, thumb safety, receiver tapped for scope mounts.
Price: $239.95
    Sling strap and swivels, installed $16.50
    Model 788 with Universal Model UE 4x scope, mounts and rings in cals. 223 Rem., 243 Win., 7mm-08 Rem., 308 and 22-250 ....$284.95

Ruger 77

RUGER 77 BOLT ACTION RIFLE
Caliber: 22-250, 220 Swift, 243, 6mm, 308, 358 Win. (5-shot).
Barrel: 22" round tapered (24" in 220 Swift).
Weight: 6¾ lbs. **Length:** 42" over-all.
Stock: Hand checkered American walnut (13¾"x1⅝"x2⅛"), p.g. cap, sling swivel studs and recoil pad.
Sights: Optional gold bead ramp front, folding leaf adj. rear, or scope rings.
Features: Integral scope mount bases, diagonal bedding system, hinged floorplate, adj. trigger, tang safety. Scope optional.
Price: With Ruger steel scope rings (77R) $325.00
Price: With rings and open sights (77RS) $341.25
Price: 458 Win. Mag. $429.50
Price: Barreled action, 338, with open sights $279.50
Price: Barreled action only all cals. except 338, 458, open sights ..$262.50
Price: Barreled action, all cals. except 338, 458, no sights $262.50
Price: Bbld. action, 338, no sights $262.50
Price: Bbld. action, 458, with open sights $357.50

Ruger Model 77 Magnum Rifle
Similar to Ruger 77 except: magnum-size action. Calibers 25-06, 270, 280, 7x57, 30-06 (5-shot), 7mm Rem. Mag., 300 Win. Mag., 338 Win. Mag., 458 Win. Mag. (3-shot). 270, 7x57, 280 and 30-06 have 22" bbl., all others have 24". Weight and length vary with caliber.
Price: $325.00

Ruger 77 Varmint

RUGER MODEL 77 VARMINT
Caliber: 22-250, 220 Swift, 243, 6mm, 25-06, 280, 308.
Barrel: 24" heavy straight tapered, 26" in 220 Swift.
Weight: Approx. 9 lbs. **Length:** Approx. 44" over-all.
Stock: American walnut, similar in style to Magnum Rifle.
Sights: Barrel drilled and tapped for target scope blocks. Integral scope mount bases in receiver.
Features: Ruger diagonal bedding system, Ruger steel 1" scope rings supplied. Fully adj. trigger. Barreled actions available in any of the standard calibers and barrel lengths.
Price: $325.00

Ruger Model 77 Magnum Round Top
Same as Model 77 except: round top receiver, drilled and tapped for standard scope mounts. Open sights are standard equipment. Calibers 25-06, 270, 30-06, 7mm Rem. Mag.
Price: All cals. $325.00

Sako Standard

SAKO STANDARD SPORTER
Caliber: 17 Rem., 222, 223 (short action); 22-250, 220 Swift, 243, 308 (medium action); 25-06, 270, 30-06, 7mm Mag., 300 Mag., 338 Mag., 375 H&H Mag. (long action).
Barrel: 23" (222, 223, 243), 24" (other cals.).
Weight: 6¾ lbs. (short); 6¾ lbs. (med.); 8 lbs. (long).
Stock: Hand-checkered European walnut.
Sights: None furnished.
Features: Adj. trigger, hinged floorplate. 222 and 223 have short action, 243 and 22-250 have medium action, others are long action. Imported from Finland by Stoeger.
Price: Short action $659.00
Price: Medium action $659.00
Price: Long action $692.00
Price: Magnum cals. $709.00
Price: 17 Rem. $709.00

Sako Deluxe Sporter
Same action as Standard Sporter except has select wood, Rosewood p.g. cap and fore-end tip. Fine checkering on top surfaces of integral dovetail bases, bolt sleeve, bolt handle root and bolt knob. Vent. recoil pad, skip-line checkering, mirror finish bluing.
Price: 222 or 223 cals. $875.00
Price: 220 Swift, 22-250, 243, 308 ....$875.00
Price: 25-06 270, 30-06 ....$917.00
Price: 7mm Rem. Mag., 300 Win. Mag., 338 Mag., 375 H&H $934.00

Sako Heavy Barrel
Same as std. Super Sporter except has beavertail fore-end; available in 222, 223 (short action); 220 Swift, 22-250, 243, 308 (medium action); 25-06, 7mm Mag. (long action). Weight from 8¼ to 8½ lbs. 5-shot magazine capacity.
Price: 222, 223 (short action) $709.00
Price: 22-250, 243 (medium action) $709.00

Sako Super Deluxe Sporter
Similar to Deluxe Sporter except has select European Walnut with high gloss finish and deep cut oak leaf carving. Metal has super high polish, deep blue finish.
Price: $1,660.00

CAUTION: PRICES CHANGE. CHECK AT GUNSHOP.

Sako Classic

Sako Classic Sporter
Similar to the Standard Sporter except: available in 243 (medium action), 270, 30-06 and 7mm Rem. Mag. (long action) only; straight-comb "classic-style" stock with oil finish; solid rubber recoil pad; recoil lug. No sights furnished—receiver drilled and tapped for scope mounting. Introduced 1980.
Price: 243 ....**$775.00**
Price: 270, 30-06 ....**$809.00**
Price: 7mm Rem. Mag. **$825.00**

Sako Carbine

Sako Carbine
Same action as the Standard Sporter except has full "Mannlicher" style stock, 20" barrel, weighs 7½ lbs. 243, 270 and 30-06 only, medium or long action. Introduced 1977. From Stoeger.
Price: 243, 270, 30-06 only **$825.00**

Sako Safari

Sako Safari Grade Bolt Action
Similar to the Standard Grade Sporter except available in long action, calibers 7mm Rem. Mag., 300 Win. Mag., 338 Win. Mag. or 375 H & H Mag. only. Stocked in European walnut, checkered 20 l.p.i., solid rubber butt pad; grip cap and fore-end tip; quarter-rib "express" rear sight, hooded ramp front. Front sling swivel band-mounted on barrel.
Price: **$1,660.00**

Savage 110S

SAVAGE 110S, SILHOUETTE RIFLE
Caliber: 308 Win., 7mm-08 Rem., 5-shot.
Barrel: 22", heavy tapered.
Weight: 8 lbs., 10 ozs. **Length:** 43" over-all.
Stock: Special Silhouette stock of select walnut. High fluted comb, Wundhammer swell, stippled p.g. and fore-end. Rubber recoil pad.
Sights: None. Receiver drilled and tapped for scope mounting.
Features: Receiver has satin blue finish to reduce glare. Barrel is free-floating. Top tang safety, internal magazine. Available in right-hand only. Introduced 1978.
Price: **$298.45**

Savage 340

SAVAGE 340 CLIP REPEATER
Caliber: 22 Hornet, 222 Rem., 223 (4-shot) and 30-30 (3-shot).
Barrel: 24" and 22" respectively.
Weight: About 6½ lbs. **Length:** 40"-42"
Stock: Walnut, Monte Carlo, checkered p.g. and fore-end white line spacers.
Sights: Hooded ramp front, folding-leaf rear.
Features: Detachable clip magazine, sliding thumb safety, receiver tapped for scope mounts.
Price: **$208.20**

Savage 110C

SAVAGE 110C BOLT ACTION RIFLE
Caliber: 243, 270, 30-06, 4-shot detachable box magazine, 7mm Rem. Mag. (3-shot).
Barrel: 22".
Weight: 7 lbs. **Length:** 43" over-all.
Stock: Select walnut with Monte Carlo, skip-line cut checkered p.g. and fore-end.
Sights: Removeable ramp front, open rear adj. for w. & e.
Features: Tapped for scope mounting, free floating barrel, top tang safety, internal box magazine, hard rubber buttplate. Right hand only in 25-06, 22-250 with 24" barrel.
Price: Right hand 110C **$296.60**
Price: Left hand 110CL **$298.45**
Price: Right hand, mag. cals. **$305.90**
Price: Left hand, mag. cals. **$307.75**

SHILEN DGA RIFLES
Caliber: All calibers.
Barrel: 24" (Sporter, #2 Weight), 25" (Varminter, #5 weight).
Weight: 7½ lbs. (Sporter), 9 lbs., (Varminter).
Stock: Selected Claro walnut. Barrel and action hand bedded to stock with free-floated barrel, bedded action. Swivel studs installed.
Sights: None furnished. Drilled and tapped for scope mounting.
Features: Shilen Model DGA action, fully adjustable trigger with side safety. Stock finish is satin sheen epoxy. Barrel and action non-glare blue-black. From Shilen Rifles, Inc.
Price: Sporter or Varminter rifle **$927.00**

CENTERFIRE RIFLES—BOLT ACTION

S&W 1500

SMITH & WESSON M1500 BOLT ACTION RIFLE
Caliber: 243, 270, 30-06, 7mm Rem. Mag.
Barrel: 22″ (24″ in 7mm Rem. Mag.).
Weight: 7½-7¾ lbs. **Length:** 42″ over-all (42½″ for 270, 30-06, 7mm).
Stock: American walnut with Monte Carlo comb and cheekpiece; 18-line-per-inch checkering on p.g. and fore-end.
Sights: Hooded ramp gold bead front, open round-notch rear adj. for w. & e. Drilled and tapped for scope mounts.
Features: Trigger guard and magazine box are a single unit with a hinged floorplate. Comes with q.d. swivel studs. Composition non-slip buttplate with white spacer. Magnum models have rubber recoil pad. Introduced 1979.
Price: Standard cals $334.95
Price: Magnum cals $349.95

Smith & Wesson Model 1500 Deluxe Rifle
Similar to Standard model except comes without sights, has engine-turned bolt; floorplate has decorative scroll. Stock has skip-line checkering, pistol grip cap with inset S&W seal, white spacers. Sling, swivels and swivel posts are included. Magnum models have vent. recoil pad.
Price: Deluxe, std. cals $379.95
Price: Deluxe, magnum cals $394.95

Stevens 110E

STEVENS 110E BOLT ACTION RIFLE
Caliber: 308, 30-06, 243, 4-shot.
Barrel: 22″ round tapered.
Weight: 6¾ lbs. **Length:** 43″ (22″ barrel).
Stock: Walnut finished hardwood with Monte Carlo, checkered p.g. and fore-end, hard rubber buttplate.
Sights: Gold bead removable ramp front, step adj. rear.
Features: Top tang safety, receiver, tapped for peep or scope sights.
Price: $257.80

Stevens 110E-S

STEVENS MODEL 110-ES BOLT ACTION RIFLE
Caliber: 243, 308, 30-06; 5-shot magazine.
Barrel: 22″.
Weight: 7 lbs. **Length:** 43″ over-all.
Stock: Walnut-finished hardwood with Monte Carlo; checkered p.g. and fore-end.
Sights: Removeable ramp front, removeable adjustable rear.
Features: Comes with 4x scope and mounts; hard rubber buttplate; top tang safety; free-floating barrel. Introduced 1981. From Savage Arms.
Price: Model 110-ES $257.80
Price: Model 110-E (as above, no scope mounts) $217.40

Steyr SL

STEYR-MANNLICHER MODELS SL & L
Caliber: SL—222, 222 Rem. Mag., 223; SL Varmint—222; L—22-250, 6mm, 243, 308 Win.; L Varmint—22-250, 243, 308 Win.; L optional cal.—5.6x57.
Barrel: 20″ (full stock); 23.6″ (half stock).
Weight: 6 lbs. (full stock). **Length:** 38¼″ (full stock).
Stock: Hand checkered walnut. Full Mannlicher or standard half-stock with M.C.
Sights: Ramp front, open U-notch rear.
Features: Choice of interchangeable single or double set triggers. Five-shot detachable "Makrolon" rotary magazine, 6 rear locking lugs. Drilled and tapped for scope mounts. Imported by Steyr Daimler Puch of America.
Price: Full Stock $958.00
Price: Half-stock $893.00
Price: Optional caliber, add $50.00

Steyr-Mannlicher ML79 "Luxus"
Similar to Steyr-Mannlicher models L and M except has single-set trigger and detachable 3-shot steel magazine; 6-shot magazine optional. Same calibers as L and M. Oil finish or high gloss lacquer on stock.
Price: Full stock $1,172.00
Price: Half stock $1,097.00
Price: Optional cals., add $50.00
Price: Extra 3-shot magazine $41.50
Price: Extra 6-shot magazine $78.65

Steyr Varmint

Steyr-Mannlicher Varmint, Models SL and L
Similar to standard SL and L except chambered only for: 222 Rem. (SL), 22-250, 243, 308 and optional 5.6x57 (L). Has 26″ heavy barrel, no sights (drilled and tapped for scope mounts). Choice of single or double-set triggers. Five-shot detachable magazine.
Price: $965.00
Price: Optional caliber, add $50.00
Price: Spare magazine $25.00

CAUTION: PRICES CHANGE. CHECK AT GUNSHOP.

CENTERFIRE RIFLES—BOLT ACTION

Consult our Directory pages for the location of firms mentioned.

Steyr M

STEYR-MANNLICHER MODEL M
Caliber: 7x64, 7x57, 25-06, 270, 30-06. Left-hand action cals.—7x64, 25-06, 270, 30-06. Optional cals.—6.5x57, 8x57JS, 9.3x62, 6.5x55, 7.5x55.
Barrel: 20″ (full stock); 23.6″ (half stock).
Weight: 6.8 lbs. to 7.5 lbs. **Length:** 39″ (full stock); 43″ (half stock).
Stock: Hand checkered walnut. Full Mannlicher or std. half stock with M.C. and rubber recoil pad.
Sights: Ramp front, open U-notch rear.
Features: Choice of interchangeable single or double set triggers. Detachable 5-shot rotary magazine. Drilled and tapped for scope mounting. Available as "Professional" model with parkerized finish and synthetic stock (right hand action only). Imported by Steyr Daimler Puch of America.
Price: Full stock $958.00
Price: Half stock $893.00
Price: For left hand action add $127.00
Price: Professional model with iron sights $715.00
Price: Professional model without sights $690.00

Steyr S/T

STEYR-MANNLICHER MODELS S & S/T
Caliber: Model S—300 Win. Mag., 338 Win. Mag., 7mm Rem. Mag., 300 H&H Mag., 375 H&H Mag. (6.5x68, 8x68S, 9.3x64 optional); S/T—375 H&H Mag., 458 Win. Mag. (9.3x64 optional).
Barrel: 25.6″.
Weight: 8.4 lbs. (Model S). **Length:** 45″ over-all.
Stock: Half stock with M.C. and rubber recoil pad. Hand checkered walnut. Available with optional spare magazine inletted in butt.
Sights: Ramp front, U-notch rear.
Features: Choice of interchangeable single or double set triggers. Detachable 4-shot magazine. Drilled and tapped for scope mounts. Imported by Steyr Daimler Puch of America.
Price: Model S or S/T $962.00
Price: With optional butt magazine (illus.) $1,032.00
Price: Optional cals., add $50.00

Tradewinds 5000

TRADEWINDS HUSKY MODEL 5000 BOLT RIFLE
Caliber: 270, 30-06, 308, 243, 22-250.
Barrel: 23¾″.
Weight: 6 lbs. 11 oz.
Stock: Hand checkered European walnut, Monte Carlo, white line spacers on p.g. cap, fore-end tip and butt plate.
Sights: Fixed hooded front, adj. rear.
Features: Removable mag., fully recessed bolt head, adj. trigger. Imported by Tradewinds.
Price: $395.00

Weatherby Mark V

WEATHERBY MARK V BOLT ACTION RIFLE
Caliber: All Weatherby cals., 22-250 and 30-06.
Barrel: 24″ or 26″ round tapered.
Weight: 6½-10½ lbs. **Length:** 43¼″-46½″
Stock: Walnut, Monte Carlo with cheekpiece, high luster finish, checkered p.g. and fore-end, recoil pad.
Sights: Optional (extra).
Features: Cocking indicator, adj. trigger, hinged floorplate, thumb safety, quick detachable sling swivels.
Price: Cals. 224 and 22-250, std. bbl. $679.95
With 26″ semi-target bbl. $694.95
Cals. 240, 257, 270, 7mm, 30-06 and 300 (24″ bbl.) $699.95
With 26″ No. 2 contour bbl. $714.95
Cal. 340 (26″ bbl.) $714.95
Cal. 378 (26″ bbl.) $859.95
Cal. 460 (26″ bbl.) $989.95

Weatherby Mark V Rifle Left Hand
Available in all Weatherby calibers except 224 and 22-250 (and 26″ No. 2 contour 300WM). Complete left handed action; stock with cheekpiece on right side. Prices are $10 higher than right hand models except the 378 and 460WM are unchanged.

Weatherby Vanguard

WEATHERBY VANGUARD BOLT ACTION RIFLE
Caliber: 25-06, 243, 270, and 30-06 (5-shot), 7mm Rem. and 300 Win. Mag. (3-shot).
Barrel: 24" hammer forged.
Weight: 7⅞ lbs. **Length:** 44½" over-all.
Stock: American walnut, p.g. cap and fore-end tip, hand inletted and checkered, 13½" pull.
Sights: Optional, available at extra cost.
Features: Side safety, adj. trigger, hinged floorplate, receiver tapped for scope mounts.
Price: **$439.95**

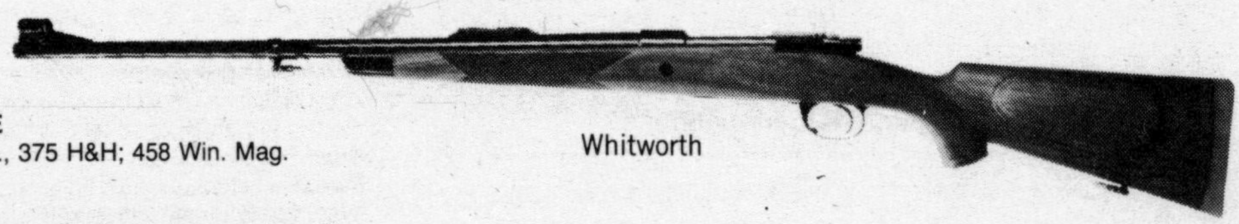

Whitworth

WHITWORTH EXPRESS RIFLE
Caliber: 7mm Rem. Mag., 300 Win. Mag., 375 H&H; 458 Win. Mag.
Barrel: 24".
Weight: 7½-8 lbs. **Length:** 44".
Stock: Classic English Express rifle design of hand checkered, select European Walnut.
Sights: Three leaf open sight calibrated for 100, 200, 300 yards on ¼-rib, ramp front with removable hood.
Features: Solid rubber recoil pad, barrel mounted sling swivel, adjustable trigger, hinged floor plate, solid steel recoil cross bolt. Imported by Interarms.
Price: 7mm Rem. Mag., 300 Win. Mag. **$525.00**
Price: 375, 458 . . . .**$560.00**

Wichita Varmint

WICHITA VARMINT RIFLE
Caliber: 17 Rem. thru 308 Win., including 22 and 6mm PPC.
Barrel: 20⅛", Atkinson chrome-moly.
Weight: 9 lbs. **Length:** 40⅛" over-all.
Stock: AAA Fancy American walnut. Hand-rubbed finish, hand-checkered, 20 l.p.i. pattern. Hand-inletted, glass bedded steel grip cap, Pachmayr rubber recoil pad.
Sights: None. Drilled and tapped for scope mounts.
Features: Right or left-hand Wichita action with three locking lugs. Available as a single shot or repeater with 3-shot detachable magazine. Checkered bolt handle. Bolt is hand fitted, lapped and jeweled. Side thumb safety. Firing pin fall is ³⁄₁₆". Non-glare blue finish. Shipped in hard Protecto case. From Wichita Arms.
Price: **$995.00**

Wichita Classic

WICHITA CLASSIC RIFLE
Caliber: 17 Rem. thru 308 Win., including 22 and 6mm PPC.
Barrel: 21⅛", Atkinson chrome-moly.
Weight: 8 lbs., 2 oz. **Length:** 41" over-all.
Stock: AAA Fancy American walnut. Hand-rubbed and checkered (20 l.p.i.). Hand-inletted, glass bedded, steel grip cap. Pachmayr rubber recoil pad.
Sights: None. Drilled and tapped for scope mounting.
Features: Available as a single shot or repeater. Octagonal barrel and Wichita action, right or left-hand. Checkered bolt handle. Bolt is hand-fitted, lapped and jewelled. Adjustable Canjar trigger is set at 2 lbs. Side thumb safety. Firing pin fall is ³⁄₁₆". Non-glare blue finish. Shipped in hard Protector case. From Wichita Arms.
Price: **$1,595.00**

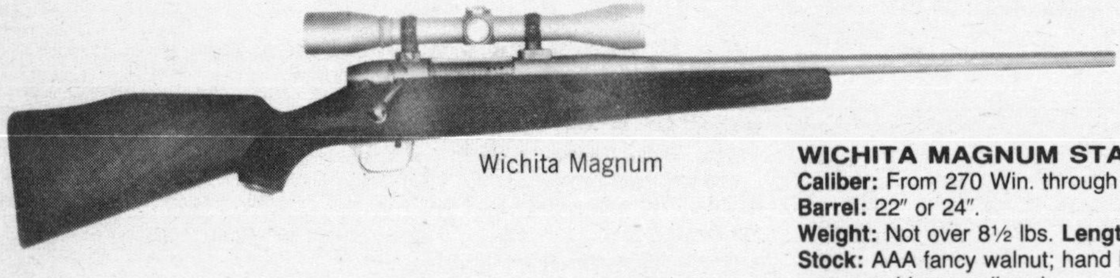

Wichita Magnum

WICHITA MAGNUM STAINLESS RIFLE
Caliber: From 270 Win. through 458 Win. Mag.
Barrel: 22" or 24".
Weight: Not over 8½ lbs. **Length:** 44¾" over-all (24" barrel).
Stock: AAA fancy walnut; hand inletted; glass bedded; steel grip cap; Pachmayr rubber recoil pad.
Sights: None. Drilled and tapped for Burris scope mounts.
Features: Stainless steel barrel and action, round contour. Target grade barrel. Available as a single shot or with a blind magazine. Fully adj. trigger. Bolt is ⅞" in diameter with recessed face. Hand rubbed stock finish, checkered 20 lpi. Shipped in a hard case. Introduced 1980. From Wichita Arms.
Price: **$1,995.00**

CAUTION: PRICES CHANGE. CHECK AT GUNSHOP.

CENTERFIRE RIFLES—BOLT ACTION

Winchester 70XTR

WINCHESTER 70 XTR STANDARD RIFLE
Caliber: 222, 22-250, 25-06, 243, 270, 308 and 30-06, 5-shot.
Barrel: 22" swaged, floating. 10" twist (222 & 22-250 have 14" twist, 308 is 12").
Weight: 7½ lbs. **Length:** 42½" over-all.
Stock: Walnut, Monte Carlo, (13½"x1¾"x1½"x2⅛") checkered p.g. and fore-end.
Sights: Removable hooded bead ramp front, fully adj. open rear flips down for scope mounting.
Features: Sling swivels installed, steel p.g. cap, hinged floorplate, receiver tapped for scope mounts. Has new streamlined rear sight base, new Winchester blue finish. Stock has new color and finish.
Price: **$412.00**

Winchester Featherweight

Winchester Model 70 XTR Featherweight
Similar to standard Model 70 except available only in 243, 257 Roberts, 270, 7x57, 30-06 or 308; 22" barrel; classic-style stock with Schnabel fore-end ribbon-style checkering fashioned after early Model 70 custom rifle patterns. Red rubber butt pad with black spacer, sling swivels included. High polish blue metal surfaces. Tapered featherweight barrel. Weighs 6¾ lbs. Introduced 1981.
Price: **$433.00**

Winchester 70 African

Winchester 70 African
Same as M70 Standard except: 458 Win. Mag. only, 3-shot. 22" non-floating heavy bbl. 14" twist. Stock measures 13½"x1⅜"x1¾"x2⅜", has ebony fore-end tip and grip cap; wgt. 8½ lbs., recoil pad and special rear sight.
Price: **$724.00**

Winchester 70 XTR Magnum Rifle
Same as M70 Standard except with recoil pad and in these magnum cals.: 7 Rem., 264, 300, 338 Win., 375 H&H (not XTR), 3-round mag. capacity. Wgt. 7¾ lbs. (8½ lbs. in 375), 24" bbl., 44½" over-all. R.H. twist: 9" in 264, 9½" in 7mm, 10" in 300, 338. ....**$428.00**
Cal. 375 H&H (not XTR) **$652.00**

Winchester 70 XTR Varmint Rifle
Same as M70 Standard except: 222, 22-250, and 243 only, target scope blocks, no sights, 24" heavy bbl., 14" twist in 22-250, 10" twist in 243. 44½" over-all, 9¾ lbs. Stock measures 13½"x⁹⁄₁₆"x¹⁵⁄₁₆"x⅜" from bore line.
Price: **$433.00**

CENTERFIRE RIFLES—SINGLE SHOT

Browning B-78

BROWNING MODEL '78 SINGLE-SHOT RIFLE
Caliber: 30-06, 25-06, 6mm Rem., 243, 22-250 and 7mm Rem. Mag.
Barrel: 26", tapered octagon or heavy round.
Length: 42" over-all. **Weight:** Oct. bbl. 7¾ lbs. Heavy round bbl. 8½ lbs.
Stock: Select walnut, hand rubbed finish, hand checkered (13⅝"x1⅝"x2⅛"*). Rubber recoil pad. *Bore measurement.
Sights: None. Furnished with scope mount and rings.
Features: Closely resembles M1885 High Wall rifle. Falling block action with exposed hammer, auto. ejector. Adj. trigger (3½ to 4½ lbs.) Half-cock safety.
Price: **$449.95**

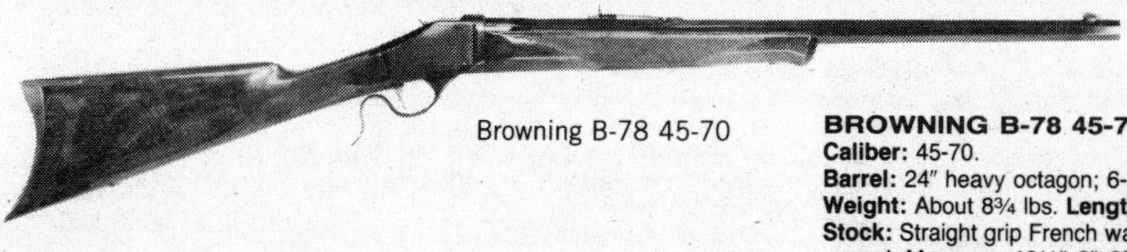

Browning B-78 45-70

BROWNING B-78 45-70 RIFLE
Caliber: 45-70.
Barrel: 24" heavy octagon; 6-groove, 1-in-20" twist.
Weight: About 8¾ lbs. **Length:** 40¾" over-all.
Stock: Straight grip French walnut with semi-schnabel fore-end, hand checkered. Measures 13¼"x2"x2¾".
Sights: Blade front, step-adj. rear. Drilled and tapped for scope mounts.
Features: Curved, blued steel buttplate; low profile recessed swivel studs (swivels provided).
Price: **$449.95**

CENTERFIRE RIFLES—SINGLE SHOT

H&R 155

Harrington & Richardson Model 157 Single Shot Rifle

Same as Model 158 except has pistol grip stock, full length fore-end, and sling swivels. Scope not included; drilled and tapped for mounts. 22 Hornet or 30-30 cals.

Price: $99.50

Harrington & Richardson Model 058 Combo Gun

Same as Model 158, except fitted with accessory 20-ga. barrel (26", Mod.).

Price: 22 Hornet or 30-30 Win. plus 20-ga $99.50

HARRINGTON & RICHARDSON Model 155 "SHIKARI"

Caliber: 44 Rem. Mag. or 45-70, single-shot.
Barrel: 24" or 28" 45-70, 24" (44 Mag.).
Weight: 7-7½ lbs. **Length:** 39" over-all (24" bbl.).
Stock: Walnut finished hardwood.
Sights: Blade front, adj. folding leaf rear.
Features: Blue-black finish with color case hardened frame. Exposed hammer. Solid brass cleaning rod with hardwood handle included.
Price: Either caliber $110.00

HARRINGTON AND RICHARDSON 158 TOPPER RIFLE

Caliber: 30-30 and 22 Hornet.
Barrel: 22" round tapered.
Weight: 6 lbs. **Length:** 37".
Stock: Walnut finished hardwood stock and fore-end.
Sights: Blade front; folding adj. rear.
Features: Side lever break-open action with visible hammer. Easy takedown.
Price: 22 Hornet or 30-30 ....$85.00

HEYM-RUGER Model HR 30/38 RIFLE

Caliber: 243, 6.5x57R, 7x64, 7x65R, 270, 308, 30-06 (standard); 6.5x68R, 300 Win. Mag., 8x68S, 9.3x74R (magnum).
Barrel: 24" (standard cals.), 26" (magnum cals.).
Weight: 6½ to 7 lbs.
Stock: Dark European walnut, hand checkered p.g. and fore-end. Oil finish, recoil pad. Full Mannlicher-type or sporter-style with schnabel fore-end, Bavarian cheekpiece.
Sights: Bead on ramp front, leaf rear.
Features: Ruger No. 1 action and safety, Canjar single-set trigger, hand-engraved animal motif. Options available include deluxe engraving and stock carving. Contact Heym for more data.
Price: HR-30N, round bbl., sporter stock, std. cals. $1,889.00
Price: HR-30G, as above except in mag. cals. $1,949.00
Price: HR-30L, round bbl., full stock, std. cals. $2,099.00
Price: HR-38N, octagon bbl., sporter stock, std. cals. $2,129.00
Price: HR-38G, as above, mag. cals. $2,189.00

Heym-Ruger

> Consult our Directory pages for the location of firms mentioned.

Ruger No.1

RUGER NUMBER ONE SINGLE SHOT

Caliber: 220 Swift, 22-250, 243, 6mm Rem., 25-06, 270, 7x57mm, 30-06, 7mm Rem. Mag., 300 Win., 338 Win. Mag., 45-70, 458 Win. Mag., 375 H&H Mag.
Barrel: 26" round tapered with quarter-rib (also 22" and 24", depending upon model).
Weight: 8 lbs. **Length:** 42" over-all.
Stock: Walnut, two-piece, checkered p.g. and fore-end (either semi-beavertail or Henry style).
Sights: None, 1" scope rings supplied for integral mounts. 3 models have open sights.
Features: Under lever, hammerless falling block design has auto ejector, top tang safety. Standard Rifle 1B illus.
Price: $405.00
Available also as Light Sporter, Medium Sporter, Special Varminter or Tropical Rifle $405.00
Price: Barreled action, blued only $286.50

Ruger No.3

RUGER NO. 3 CARBINE SINGLE SHOT

Caliber: 22 Hornet, 223, 375 Win., 45-70.
Barrel: 22" round.
Weight: 6 lbs. **Length:** 38½".
Stock: American walnut, carbine-type.
Sights: Gold bead front, adj. folding leaf rear.
Features: Same action as No. 1 Rifle except different lever. Has auto ejector, top tang safety, adj. trigger.
Price: $284.00

CAUTION: PRICES CHANGE. CHECK AT GUNSHOP.

H&R 171

HARRINGTON & RICHARDSON Model 171 Cavalry Model Carbine
Caliber: 45-70 single shot.
Barrel: 22".
Weight: 7 lbs. **Length:** 41".
Stock: American walnut with saddle ring and bridle.
Sights: Blade front, barrel mounted leaf rear adj. for e.
Features: Replica of the 1873 Springfield Carbine. Blue-black finish. Deluxe version shown has engraved breech block, side lock & hammer.
Price: $325.00
Springfield Model 172 Silver Plated Carbine $1,500.00

HARRINGTON & RICHARDSON Officers Model 1873
Caliber: 45-70, single shot
Barrel: 26" round.
Weight: About 8 lbs. **Length:** 44" over-all
Stock: Oil finished walnut, checkered at wrist and fore-end white metal tipped.
Sights: Blade front, vernier tang rear adj. for w. & e.
Features: Replica of the 1873 Springfield has engraved breech block, side lock and hammer.
Price: $375.00

HARRINGTON & RICHARDSON Model 174 L.B.H. Commemorative Carbine
Caliber: 45-70, single shot.
Barrel: 22".
Weight: 7 lbs., 4 oz. **Length:** 41".
Stock: American walnut with metal grip adapter.
Sights: Blade front, tang mounted aperature rear adj. for w. and e.
Features: Replica of the 1873 Springfield carbine. Engraved breech block, side lock and hammer. Action color case hardened. Each comes with book entitled "In the Valley of the Little Big Horn".
Price: $325.00

Navy Rolling Block

NAVY ARMS ROLLING BLOCK RIFLE
Caliber: 45-70.
Barrels: 26½".
Stock: Walnut finished.
Sights: Fixed front, adj. rear.
Features: Reproduction of classic rolling block action. Available in Buffalo Rifle (octagonal bbl.) and Creedmore (half round, half octagonal bbl.) models. From Navy Arms.
Price: 18", 26" full octagon barrel $305.00
Price: Creedmore Model, 30" full octagon $330.00
Price: 30", half-round $310.00
Price: 18", 26", half round $305.00
Price: Half-round Creedmore $330.00

ROLLING BLOCK BABY CARBINE
Caliber: 22 LR, 357 Mag.
Barrel: 20", octagon.
Weight: 4¾ lbs. **Length:** Approx. 35" over-all.
Stock: Walnut.
Sights: Blade front, rear adj. for e.
Features: Small rolling block action is color case hardened with blue barrel. Trigger guard and buttplate polished brass. Imported by Navy Arms.
Price: 22 LR $225.00
Price: 357 Mag $225.00

Rolling Block Baby

Sile Sharps

SILE SHARPS "OLD RELIABLE" RIFLE
Caliber: 45-70, 45-120-3¼" Sharps.
Barrel: 28", full octagon, polished blue.
Weight: 9½ lbs. **Length:** 45" over-all.
Stock: Walnut with deluxe checkering at p.g. and fore-end.
Sights: Sporting blade front, folding leaf rear. Globe front, vernier rear optional at extra cost.
Features: Falling block, lever action. Color case-hardened hammer, buttplate and action with Sile's automatic safety. Seven models of the Sharps are available from Sile, two in M/L configuration. All are available with engraved action for **$97.25** extra. From Sile Distributors Inc., Shore.
Price: Old Reliable $377.50
Price: Sporter Rifle $362.50
Price: Military Carbine $345.00
Price: Sporter Carbine $362.50

TARGET, MATCH & SILHOUETTE RIFLES

Anschutz 1411

ANSCHUTZ 1411 MATCH 54 RIFLE
Caliber: 22 LR. Single shot.
Barrel: 27½ round ($^{15}/_{16}$" dia.)
Weight: 11 lbs. **Length:** 46" over-all.
Stock: French walnut, American prone style with Monte Carlo, cast-off cheekpiece, checkered p.g., beavertail fore-end with swivel rail and adj. swivel, adj. rubber buttplate.
Sights: None. Receiver grooved for Anschutz sights (extra). Scope blocks.
Features: Single stage adj. trigger, wing safety, short firing pin travel. Available from Savage Arms.

Anschutz 1407 Match 54 Rifle
Same as the model 1411 except: 26" bbl. (⅞" dia.), weight 10 lbs., 44½" over-all to conform to ISU requirements and also suitable for NRA matches. Available from Savage Arms.
Price: Right hand, no sights $663.75
Price: M1807-L (true left-hand action and stock) $764.60
Price: Int'l sight set $173.00
Price: Match sight set $118.70

Price: Right hand, no sights $746.15
Price: M1811-L (true left-hand action and stock) $913.30
Price: Anschutz Int'l. sight set $173.00

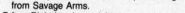

Anschutz 1413

Anschutz 1413 Super Match 54 Rifle
Same as the model 1411 except: International type stock with adj. cheekpiece, adj. aluminum hook buttplate, weight 15½ lbs., 50" over-all. Available from Savage Arms.
Price: Right hand, no sights $1,070.25
Price: M1813-L (left-hand action and stock) $1,225.75

Anschutz 54-MS

Anschutz Model 54-MS Silhouette Rifle
Same basic features as Auschutz 1413 Super Match 54 but with special metallic silhouette stock and two-stage trigger. **Available on special order only from Savage Arms.**

Anschutz 64-MS

ANSCHUTZ MODEL 64-MS
Caliber: 22 LR, single shot.
Barrel: 21¾", medium heavy, ⅞" diameter.
Weight: 8 lbs., 1 oz. **Length:** 39½" over-all.
Stock: Walnut-finished hardwood, silhouette-type.
Sights: None furnished. Receiver drilled and tapped for scope mounting.
Features: Designed for metallic silhouette competition. Stock has stippled checkering, contoured thumb groove with Wundhammer swell. Two-stage trigger is adj. for weight of pull, take-up, and over-travel. Slide safety locks sear and bolt. Introduced 1980. Imported by Savage Arms.
Price: $336.00

BSA Martini

BSA MARTINI ISU MATCH RIFLE
Caliber: 22 LR, single shot.
Barrel: 28".
Weight: 10¾ lbs. **Length:** 43-44" over-all.
Stock: Match type French walnut butt and fore-end; flat cheekpiece, full p.g.; spacers are fitted to allow length adjustment to suit each shooting position; adj. buttplate.
Sights: Modified PH-1 Parker-Hale tunnel front, PH-25 aperture rear with aperture variations from .080" to .030".
Features: Fastest lock time of any commercial target rifle; designed to meet I.S.U. specs. for the Standard Rifle. Fully adjustable trigger (less than ½ lb. to 3½ lbs.). Mark V has heavier barrel, weighs 12¼ lbs. From Freelands Scope Stands.
Price: I.S.U., Standard weight $950.00
Price: Mark V heavy bbl. $1,000.00

CAUTION: PRICES CHANGE. CHECK AT GUNSHOP.

TARGET, MATCH & SILHOUETTE RIFLES

Beeman HW60

BEEMAN/WEIHRAUCH HW60 TARGET RIFLE
Caliber: 22 LR, single shot.
Barrel: 26.8".
Weight: 10.8 lbs. **Length:** 45.7" over-all.
Stock: Walnut with adjustable buttplate. Stippled p.g. and fore-end. Rail with adjustable swivel.
Sights: Hooded ramp front, match-type aperture rear.
Features: Adj. match trigger with push-button safety. Left-hand version also available. Introduced 1981.
Price: Right-hand **$495.00**
Price: Left-hand **$545.00**

Beeman 2000

BEEMAN/FEINWERKBAU 2000 TARGET RIFLE
Caliber: 22 LR.
Barrel: 26¼".
Weight: 9 lbs. 12 oz. **Length:** 43¾" over-all.
Stock: Standard match. Walnut with stippled p.g. and fore-end.
Sights: Globe front with interchangeable inserts; micrometer match aperture rear.
Features: Meets ISU standard rifle specifications. Extremely short lock time. Trigger fully adjustable for weight, release point, length, lateral position, etc. Comes in Junior or Standard form. Introduced 1979. Imported by Beeman's Inc.
Price: About **$795.00**

Finnish Lion

FINNISH LION STANDARD TARGET RIFLE
Caliber: 22 LR, single-shot.
Barrel: 27⅝".
Weight: 10½ lbs. **Length:** 44⁹⁄₁₆" over-all.
Stock: French walnut, target style.
Sights: Globe front, International micrometer rear, p.g. or thumbhole style.
Features: Optional accessories: palm rest, hook buttplate, fore-end stop and swivel assembly, buttplate extension, 5 front sight aperture inserts, 3 rear sight apertures, allen wrench. Adjustable trigger. Imported from Finland by Mandall Shooting Supplies.
Price: **$595.00**
Price: Thumbhole stock model **$695.00**
Price: Heavy barrel model (either stock) **$650.00**

Krico 640S

KRICO MODEL 6405 MATCH SPORTER
Caliber: 17 Rem., 222, 223, 22-250, 243, 308.
Barrel: 20", semi-bull.
Weight: 7.5 lbs.
Stock: French walnut with ventilated fore-end.
Sights: None furnished.
Features: Five-shot repeater with detachable box magazine. Available with single or double-set trigger. Contact Heym for more data.
Price: 17 Rem., 222, 223 cals **$739.00**
Price: 22-250, 243, 308 cals **$759.00**

Krico 430S

KRICO MODEL 430S MATCH RIFLE
Caliber: 22 Hornet.
Barrel: 24".
Weight: 8.6 lbs.
Stock: Walnut. Target style with stippled p.g. and fore-end.
Sights: None furnished. Drilled and tapped for scope mounts.
Features: Comes wtih either double set or match trigger. Has 11mm dovetail rail for scope mounting. Contact Heym for more data.
Price: Single shot, set trigger **$499.00**
Price: Repeater, set trigger **$559.00**

Krico 650S

KRICO MODEL 650 S/2 BENCHRESTER
Caliber: 223, 243, 6mm, 308.
Barrel: 23.6″ bull.
Weight: 11.5 lbs.
Stock: Special benchrest stock of French walnut with adjustable recoil pad.
Sights: Metallic sights on request; drilled and tapped for scope mounts.
Features: Bolt action single shot. Stippled pistol grip area. Standard trigger is 8 oz. single stage, available with double set or pure match trigger. Contact Heym for more data.
Price: $1,049.00

KRICO MODEL 650S SNIPER RIFLE
Caliber: 222, 223, 243, 308.
Barrel: 26″. Specially designed match bull barrel, matte blue finish, with muzzle brake/flash hider.
Weight: 10.6 lbs. **Length:** 46″ over-all.
Stock: Select walnut with oil finish. Spring-loaded, adj. cheekpiece, adjustable recoil pad.
Sights: None furnished. Drilled and tapped for scope mounts.
Features: Match trigger with 10mm wide shoe; single standard or double set trigger available. All metal has matte blue finish. Bolt knob has ¾″ diameter. Scope mounts available for special night-sight devices. Contact Heym for more data.
Price: Without scope, mount $950.00
Price: With Nickel 3-12x56 scope and mount $1,750.00
Price: With Schmid & Bender 1.5-6x42 or 2.5-10x56 sniper scope $2,080.00

Krico 330S

KRICO MODEL 330S MATCH RIFLE
Caliber: 22 LR, single shot.
Barrel: 25.6″, heavy.
Weight: 9.9 lbs.
Stock: Special match stock of walnut finished beech; built-in hand-stop; adjustable recoil pad.
Sights: Hooded front with interchangeable inserts; diopter match rear with rubber eye-cup.
Features: Match trigger set at factory for 4 oz. pull. Stippled pistol grip area. Contact Heym for more data.
Price: $559.00

Mauser 66SP

MAUSER MODEL 66 SP MATCH RIFLE
Caliber: 308 Win.
Barrel: 27.5″ with muzzle brake.
Weight: 12 lbs. (without scope).
Stock: Special walnut match design with broad fore-end, thumbhole pistol grip; spring-loaded cheekpiece, Morgan adj. recoil pad.
Features: Uses the Mauser telescopic short action. Other calibers available upon request. Has 3-shot magazine, match trigger adjustable for pull and travel. Contact Heym for more data.
Price: ....P.O.R.

Mossberg 144

MOSSBERG MODEL 144 TARGET RIFLE
Caliber: 22 LR only. 7-shot clip.
Barrel: 27″ round (¹⁵⁄₁₆″ dia.)
Weight: About 8 lbs. **Length:** 43″ over-all.
Stock: Target-style walnut with high thick comb, cheekpiece, p.g., beavertail fore-end, adj. handstop and sling swivels.
Sights: Lyman 17A hooded front with inserts, Mossberg S331 receiver peep with ¼-minute clicks.
Features: Wide grooved trigger adj. for wgt. of pull, thumb safety, receiver grooved for scope mounting.
Price: $169.95

REMINGTON 40-XB RANGEMASTER TARGET Centerfire
Caliber: 222 Rem., 22-250, 6mm Rem., 243, 25-06, 7mm Rem. Mag., 30-338 (30-7mm Rem. Mag.), 300 Win. Mag., 7.62 NATO (308 Win.), 30-06. Single shot.
Barrel: 27¼″ round (Stand. dia.-¾″, Hvy. dia.-⅞″)
Weight: Std.—9¼ lbs., Hvy.—11¼ **Length:** 47″
Stock: American walnut with high comb and beavertail fore-end stop. Rubber non-slip buttplate.
Sights: None. Scope blocks installed.
Features: Adjustable trigger pull. Receiver drilled and tapped for sights.
Price: Standard s.s., stainless steel $714.95
Price: Repeating model $767.90
Price: Extra for 2 oz. trigger $79.95

REMINGTON 40-XC NAT'L MATCH COURSE RIFLE
Caliber: 7.62 NATO, 5-shot.
Barrel: 23¼″, stainless steel.
Weight: 10 lbs. without sights. **Length:** 42½″ over-all.
Stock: Walnut, position-style, with palm swell.
Sights: None furnished.
Features: Designed to meet the needs of competitive shooters firing the national match courses. Position-style stock, top loading clip slot magazine, anti-bind bolt and receiver, bright stainless steel barrel. Meets all I.S.U. Army Rifle specifications. Adjustable buttplate, adjustable trigger.
Price: $779.95

CAUTION: PRICES CHANGE. CHECK AT GUNSHOP.

TARGET, MATCH & SILHOUETTE RIFLES

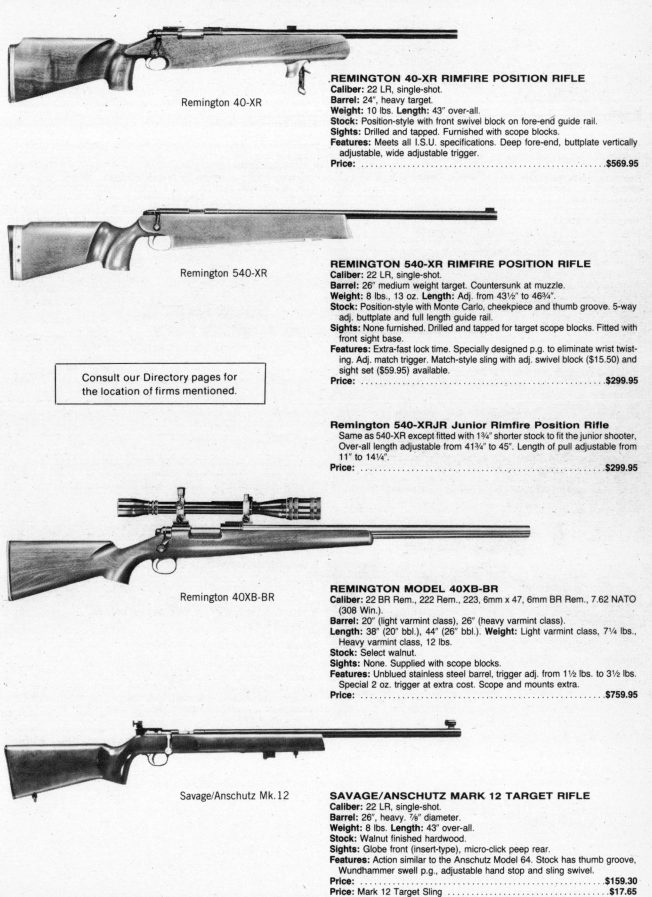

Remington 40-XR

REMINGTON 40-XR RIMFIRE POSITION RIFLE
Caliber: 22 LR, single-shot.
Barrel: 24″, heavy target.
Weight: 10 lbs. **Length:** 43″ over-all.
Stock: Position-style with front swivel block on fore-end guide rail.
Sights: Drilled and tapped. Furnished with scope blocks.
Features: Meets all I.S.U. specifications. Deep fore-end, buttplate vertically adjustable, wide adjustable trigger.
Price: $569.95

Remington 540-XR

REMINGTON 540-XR RIMFIRE POSITION RIFLE
Caliber: 22 LR, single-shot.
Barrel: 26″ medium weight target. Countersunk at muzzle.
Weight: 8 lbs., 13 oz. **Length:** Adj. from 43½″ to 46¾″.
Stock: Position-style with Monte Carlo, cheekpiece and thumb groove. 5-way adj. buttplate and full length guide rail.
Sights: None furnished. Drilled and tapped for target scope blocks. Fitted with front sight base.
Features: Extra-fast lock time. Specially designed p.g. to eliminate wrist twisting. Adj. match trigger. Match-style sling with adj. swivel block ($15.50) and sight set ($59.95) available.
Price: $299.95

Consult our Directory pages for the location of firms mentioned.

Remington 540-XRJR Junior Rimfire Position Rifle
Same as 540-XR except fitted with 1¾″ shorter stock to fit the junior shooter, Over-all length adjustable from 41¾″ to 45″. Length of pull adjustable from 11″ to 14¼″.
Price: $299.95

Remington 40XB-BR

REMINGTON MODEL 40XB-BR
Caliber: 22 BR Rem., 222 Rem., 223, 6mm x 47, 6mm BR Rem., 7.62 NATO (308 Win.).
Barrel: 20″ (light varmint class), 26″ (heavy varmint class).
Length: 38″ (20″ bbl.), 44″ (26″ bbl.). **Weight:** Light varmint class, 7¼ lbs., Heavy varmint class, 12 lbs.
Stock: Select walnut.
Sights: None. Supplied with scope blocks.
Features: Unblued stainless steel barrel, trigger adj. from 1½ lbs. to 3½ lbs. Special 2 oz. trigger at extra cost. Scope and mounts extra.
Price: $759.95

Savage/Anschutz Mk.12

SAVAGE/ANSCHUTZ MARK 12 TARGET RIFLE
Caliber: 22 LR, single-shot.
Barrel: 26″, heavy. ⅞″ diameter.
Weight: 8 lbs. **Length:** 43″ over-all.
Stock: Walnut finished hardwood.
Sights: Globe front (insert-type), micro-click peep rear.
Features: Action similar to the Anschutz Model 64. Stock has thumb groove, Wundhammer swell p.g., adjustable hand stop and sling swivel.
Price: $159.30
Price: Mark 12 Target Sling $17.65

TARGET, MATCH & SILHOUETTE RIFLES

Savage/Anschutz 64

SAVAGE/ANSCHUTZ 64 MATCH RIFLE
Caliber: 22 LR only. Single shot.
Barrel: 26″ round (¹¹/₁₆″ dia.)
Weight: 7¾ lbs. **Length:** 44″ over-all.
Stock: Walnut finished hardwood, cheekpiece, checkered p.g., beavertail fore-end, adj. buttplate.
Sights: None (extra). Scope blocks.
Features: Sliding side safety, adj. single stage trigger, receiver grooved for Anschutz sights.
Price: ....\$343.25   64L (Left hand) \$362.75
    As above but with Anschutz 6723 Match Sight Set:
Price: Model 64S (Right hand) \$431.70
Price: 64SL (Left hand) \$502.20
Price: Anschutz Match sight set \$118.70

SHILEN DGA BENCHREST SINGLE SHOT RIFLES
Caliber: 22, 22-250, 6x47, 308.
Barrel: Select/Match grade stainless. Choice of caliber, twist, chambering, contour or length shown in Shilen's catalog.
Weight: To customer specs.
Stock: Fiberglass. Choice of Classic or thumbhole pattern.
Sights: None furnished. Specify intended scope and mount.
Features: Fiberglass stocks are spray painted with acrylic enamel in choice of basic color. Comes with Benchrest trigger. Basically a custom-made rifle. From Shilen Rifles, Inc.
Price: DGA Benchrest Rifle \$1,060.00

Shilen DGA

SHILEN DGA SILHOUETTE RIFLE
Caliber: 308 Win., 7x308 recommended. Others available. Single shot or magazine.
Barrel: 25″, #5 contour.
Weight: 8 lbs., 11 ozs.
Stock: Select walnut. Competition-developed pattern for Silhouette shooting. Free-floated action, bedded action. Recoil pad installed with 13¾″ pull.
Sights: None furnished. Drilled and tapped for scope mounting.
Features: Shilen DGA action. Fully adjustable trigger with side safety. Available with left-hand cheekpiece. Chrome-moly steel barrel; bore and chamber held to target tolerances. Available with Benchrest trigger (2-6 oz., \$40.00) or Electric trigger (\$150.00). Base and ring options same as Shilen Sporter and Varminter.
Price: Silhouette rifle \$883.00

> Consult our Directory pages for the location of firms mentioned.

Steyr SSG Match

STEYR-MANNLICHER SSG MARKSMAN
Caliber: 308 Win.
Barrel: 25.6″.
Weight: 8.6 lbs. **Length:** 44.5″ over-all.
Stock: Choice of ABS "Cycolac" synthetic half stock or walnut. Removeable spacers in butt adjusts length of pull from 12¾″ to 14″.
Sights: Hooded blade front, folding leaf rear.
Features: Parkerized finish. Choice of interchangeable single or double set triggers. Detachable 5-shot rotary magazine (10-shot optional). Drilled and tapped for scope mounts. Imported by Steyr Daimler Puch of America.
Price: Synthetic half stock \$729.00
Price: Walnut half stock \$845.00
Price: Synthetic half stock with Kahles ZF69 scope \$1,482.00
Price: Optional 10-shot magazine \$66.00

Steyr SSG

Steyr-Mannlicher SSG Match
Same as Model SSG Marksman except has heavy barrel, match bolt, Walther target peep sights and adj. rail in fore-end to adj. sling travel. Weight is 11 lbs.
Price: Synthetic half stock \$996.00
Price: Walnut half stock \$1,106.00

CAUTION: PRICES CHANGE. CHECK AT GUNSHOP.

Swiss K-31

SWISS K-31 TARGET RIFLE
Caliber: 308 Win., 6-shot magazine.
Barrel: 26".
Weight: 9½ lbs. **Length:** 44" over-all.
Stock: Walnut.
Sights: Protected blade front, ladder-type adjustable rear.
Features: Refined version of the Schmidt-Rubin straight-pull rifle. Comes with sling and muzzle cap. From Mandall Shooting Supplies.
Price: **$1,000.00**

Unique T-66

UNIQUE T-66 MATCH RIFLE
Caliber: 22 LR, single shot.
Barrel: 25.6".
Weight: 11 lbs., 6 oz. **Length:** 43.5" over-all.
Stock: Straight grained French walnut, fore-end and p.g. hand stippled.
Sights: Interchangeable globe front; fully adj. Micro-Match rear; 8 inserts for front sight.
Features: Meets both NRA and UIT standards. Extremely fast lock time. Comes with proof certificate, two year guarantee, test target of 10-shot 50 meter group. True left hand model available. Imported from France by Soler-sport.
Price: Right hand **$575.00**
Price: Left hand **$605.00**

Walther U.I.T. Super

WALTHER U.I.T. SUPER
Caliber: 22 LR.
Barrel: 25½".
Weight: 10 lbs., 3 oz. **Length:** 44¾".
Stock: Walnut, adj. for length and drop; fore-end guide rail for sling or palm rest.
Sights: Globe-type front, fully adj. aperture rear.
Features: Conforms to both NRA and U.I.T. requirements. Fully adj. trigger. Left hand stock available on special order. Imported from Germany by Interarms.
Price: **$1,000.00**

Walther GX-1 Match Rifle
Same general specs as U.I.T. except has 25½" barrel, over-all length of 44½", weight of 15½ lbs. Stock is designed to provide every conceivable adjustment for individual preference and anatomical compatibility. Left-hand stock available on special order. From Interarms.
Price: **$1,500.00**

Walther U.I.T. Match
Same specifications and features as standard U.I.T. Super rifle but has scope mount bases. Fore-end has new tapered profile, fully stippled. From Interarms.
Price: **$1,100.00**

Walther Running Boar

WALTHER RUNNING BOAR MATCH RIFLE
Caliber: 22 LR.
Barrel: 23.6".
Weight: 8 lbs. 5 oz. **Length:** 42" over-all.
Stock: Walnut thumb-hole type. Fore-end and p.g. stippled.
Features: Especially designed for running boar competition. Receiver grooved to accept dovetail scope mounts. Adjustable cheekpiece and butt plate. 1.1 lb. trigger pull. Left hand stock available on special order. Imported by Interarms.
Price: **$950.00**

Armsport 4000

ARMSPORT "EMPEROR" 4000 DOUBLE RIFLE
Caliber: 243, 270, 284, 7.65, 308, 30-06, 7mm Rem. Mag., 9.3, 300 H & H, 375 H & H; Shotgun barrels in 12, 16 or 20-ga.
Barrel: Shotgun barrel length and chokes to customer specs.
Stock: Dimensions to customer specs. Stock and fore-end of root walnut.
Sights: Rifle barrels have blade front with bead, leaf rear adj. for w.
Features: Receiver and sideplates engraved. Gun comes with extra set of barrels fitted to action. Packaged in a hand-made, fitted luggage-type leather case lined with Scotch loden cloth. Introduced 1978. From Armsport.
Price: Complete **$16,300.00**

ARMSPORT "EMPEROR" 4010 DOUBLE RIFLE
Side-by-side version of the Model 4000 over-under rifle. Available in 243, 270, 284, 7.65, 308, 30-06, 7mm Rem. Mag., 9.3, 300 H&H, 338 Win. and 375 H&H. Shotgun barrels in 16 or 20 ga., choice of length and choke. Comes in fitted luggage-type case.
Price: **$12,750.00**

Bauer Rabbit

BAUER RABBIT
Caliber/Gauge: 22 LR over 410 (3").
Barrel: 20".
Weight: 4¾ lbs. **Length:** 38½"; disassembled 20".
Stock: Metal skeleton.
Sights: Fixed.
Features: Takes down quickly into two pieces. Single selective trigger. Rust resistant finish on stock, barrel and receiver.
Price: **$80.00**

BROWNING SUPERPOSED CONTINENTAL
Caliber/Gauge: 20 ga. x 20 ga. with extra 30-06x30-06 o/u barrel set.
Barrel: 20 ga.—26½" (Mod. & Full, 3" chambers), vent. rib, with medium raised German nickel silver sight bead. 30-06—24".
Weight: 6 lbs. 14 oz. (rifle barrels) 5 lbs. 14 oz. (shotgun barrels)
Stock: Select high grade American walnut with oil finish. Straight grip stock and schnabel fore-end with 26 l.p.i. hand checkering.
Sights: Rifle barrels have flat face gold bead front on matted ramp, folding leaf rear.
Features: Action is based on a specially engineered Superposed 20-ga. frame. Single selective trigger works on inertia; let-off is about 4½ lbs. Automatic selective ejectors. Manual top tang safety incorporated with barrel selector. Furnished with fitted luggage-type case. Introduced 1979.
Price: **$5,200.00**

Browning Continental

COLT SAUER DRILLING
Caliber: 12 ga., over 30-06, 12 ga. over 243.
Action: Top lever, cross bolt, box lock.
Barrel: 25" (Mod. & Full).
Weight: 8 lbs. **Length:** 41¾" over-all.
Stock: American walnut, oil finish. Checkered p.g. and fore-end. Black p.g. cap, recoil pad. 14¼"x2"x1½".
Sights: Blade front with brass bead, folding leaf rear.
Features: Cocking indicators, tang barrel selector, automatic sight positioner, set rifle trigger, side safety. Blue finish with bright receiver engraved with animal motifs and European-style scrollwork. Imported by Colt.
Price: **$3,355.00**

Colt Sauer

FERLACH DRILLING (FRANZ SODIA)
Caliber/Gauge: Any desired.
Action: Anson & Deeley.
Barrel: Any length, to customer specs.
Weight: To customer specs. **Length:** To customer specs.
Stock: Custom or standard dimensions; best wood on request.
Sights: Any style, to customer specs.
Features: Options include highly figured wood, magnum chambering, scope, fancy disc plates, cartridge trap, etc. Imported by Ferlach (Austria) of North America.
Price: **$3,900.00**

CHAPUIS EXPRESS RIFLE
Caliber: 7x57R, 7x65R, 30-06, 9.3x74R, 444 Marlin, 45-70, 375 H&H. Set of extra 20-ga. barrels optional.
Barrel: 23.6" for rifle except 444 and 45-70 which are 21½"; 26½" or 27½" for shotgun.
Weight: 7¼ to 8½ lbs. **Length:** 44" over-all (std. cals.).
Stock: Select French or American walnut, oil finish. Fine checkering on p.g. and fore-end. Right or left-hand stock. Deluxe wood, accessories optional.
Sights: Express sights; blade on ramp front, fixed shallow-V rear. Optional rear sight with folding leaves available.
Features: Single joining rib between barrels. Auto ejectors standard. Game motif and scroll engraving on receiver and sideplates. Rifle comes with regulation target for 75 meters. Available in three models: RG boxlock; R Deluxe false sideplates, and President with blued sideplates and receiver with gold inlays. From R. Painter Co.
Price: RG boxlock **$2,803.00**
Price: R Deluxe **$3,329.00**
Price: President **$3,860.00**
Price: Extra set of 20-ga. barrels with fitted leather case **$868.89**
Price: Extra set of rifle barrels . . . . **P.O.R.**

CAUTION: PRICES CHANGE. CHECK AT GUNSHOP.

DRILLINGS, COMBINATION GUNS, DOUBLE RIFLES

Ferlach Double

FERLACH DOUBLE RIFLE (FRANZ SODIA)
Caliber: Any caliber desired; metric, English or American.
Action: Boxlock or sidelock, side-by-side or over-under.
Barrels: Any length desired.
Weight: To customer specs. **Length:** To customer specs.
Stock: Best walnut; fine checkering.
Sights: Silver bead front, with folding night sight if specified. Sourdough rear with vertical inlay and 200 yd. folding leaf. Scopes with claw mount available.
Features: Any desired, including highly figured wood, auto ejection, folding sights, extra barrel sets, night sights. Imported by Ferlach (Austria) of North America.
Price: Base, boxlock action **$4,950.00**
Price: Base, sidelock action **$9,500.00**
Price: Base, boxlock action, with ejectors **$5,900.00**

Heym 33

HEYM MODEL 22S SAFETY COMBO GUN
Caliber/Gauge: 16 or 20 ga. (2¾", 3") over 22 Hornet, 22 WMR, 222 Rem., 222 Rem. Mag., 223, 22-250, 243 Win., 5.6x50R, 6.5x57R, 7x57R.
Barrel: 24", solid rib.
Weight: About 5½ lbs.
Stock: Dark European walnut, hand-checkered p.g. and fore-end. Oil finish.
Sights: Silver bead ramp front, folding leaf rear.
Features: Tang mounted cocking slide, separate barrel selector, single set trigger. Base supplied for quick-detachable scope mounts. Patented rocker-weight system automatically uncocks gun if accidently dropped or bumped hard. Contact Heym for more data.
Price: Model 22S **$1,459.00**
Price: Cals. 6.5x57R, 243, and 7x57R **$1,659.00**
Price: Factory fitted scope mounts, add **$123.00**

HEYM MODEL 88B SIDE-BY-SIDE DOUBLE RIFLE
Caliber: 5.6x50R, 222 Rem., 5.6x57R, 243, 6.5x57R, 7x57R, 7x65R, 308, 30-06, 8x57JRS, 9.3x74R, 375 H & H.
Barrel: 25".
Weight: 7½ lbs. (std. cals), 8½ lbs. (mag.) **Length:** 42" over-all.
Stock: Fancy French walnut, classic North American design.
Sights: Silver bead post on ramp front, fixed or 3-leaf express rear.
Features: Action has complete coverage hunting scene engraving. Comes with fitted leather case. Available as boxlock or with q.d. sidelocks. Contact Heym for more data.
Price: Boxlock, from **$4,900.00**
Price: Sidelock, Model 88B-SS, from **$6,900.00**

HEYM MODEL 55B/77B O/U DOUBLE RIFLE
Caliber: 5.6x50R, 222 Rem., 5.6x57R, 243, 6.5x57R, 7x57R, 7x65R, 308, 30-06, 8x57JRS, 300 Win. Mag., 9.3x74R; 375 H&H, 458 Win. Mag.
Barrel: 25".
Weight: About 8 lbs., depending upon caliber. **Length:** 42" over-all.
Stock: Dark European walnut, hand-checkered p.g. and fore-end. Oil finish.
Sights: Silver bead ramp front, open V-type rear.
Features: Boxlock or full sidelock; Kersten double crossbolt, cocking indicators; hand-engraved hunting scenes. Options available include interchangeable barrels, Zeiss scopes in claw mounts, deluxe engravings and stock carving, etc. Contact Heym for more data.
Price: Model 55B boxlock **$4,159.00**
Price: Model 55BSS sidelock **$6,388.00**
Price: Interchangeable shotgun barrels **$1,839.00**

HEYM MODEL 33 BOXLOCK DRILLINGS
Caliber/Gauge: 5.6x50R Mag., 5.6x57R, 6.5x57R, 7x57R, 7x65R, 8x57JRS, 9.3x74R, 243, 270, 308, 30-06; 16x16 (2¾"), 20x20 (3").
Barrel: 25" (Full & Mod.).
Weight: about 6½ lbs. **Length:** 42" over-all.
Stock: Dark European walnut, checkered p.g. and fore-end; oil finish.
Sights: Silver bead front, folding leaf rear. Automatic sight positioner. Available with scope and Suhler claw mounts.
Features: Greener-type crossbolt and safety, double under-lugs. Double set triggers. Plastic or steel trigger guard. Engraving coverage varies with model. Contact Heym for more data.
Price: Model 33, from **$3,979.00**

HEYM MODEL 37 DOUBLE RIFLE DRILLING
Caliber/Gauge: 7x65R, 30-06, 8x57JRS, 9.3x74R; 20 ga. (3").
Barrel: 25" (shotgun barrel choked Full or Mod.).
Weight: About 8½ lbs. **Length:** 42" over-all.
Stock: Dark European walnut, hand-checkered p.g. and fore-end. Oil finish.
Sights: Silver bead front, folding leaf rear. Available with scope and Suhler claw mounts.
Features: Full side-lock construction. Greener-type crossbolt, double under lugs, cocking indicators. Contact Heym for more details.
Price: Model 37 double rifle drilling **$7,159.00**
Price: Model 37 Deluxe (hunting scene engraving) from **$8,169.00**

Heym Model 37 Side Lock Drilling
Similar to Model 37 Double Rifle Drilling except has 12x12, 16x16 or 20x20 over 5.6x50R Mag., 5.6x57R, 6.5x57R, 7x57R, 7x65R, 8x57JRS, 9.3x74R, 243, 270, 308 or 30-06. Rifle barrel is manually cocked and uncocked.
Price: Model 37 with border engraving **$5,269.00**
Price: As above with engraved hunting scenes **$6,269.00**

Heym 55B/77B

Heym Model 55BF/77BF O/U Combo Gun
Similar to Model 77B/55B o-u rifle except chambered for 12, 16 or 20 ga. (2¾" or 3") over 5.6x50R, 222 Rem., 5.6x57R, 243, 6.5x57R, 270, 7x57R, 7x65R, 308, 30-06, 8x57JRS, 9.3x74R, or 375 H&H. Has solid rib barrel. Available as boxlock or sidelock, with interchangeable shotgun and rifle barrels.
Price: Model 55BF boxlock **$3,329.00**
Price: Model 55BFSS sidelock **$5,558.00**

DRILLINGS, COMBINATION GUNS, DOUBLE RIFLES

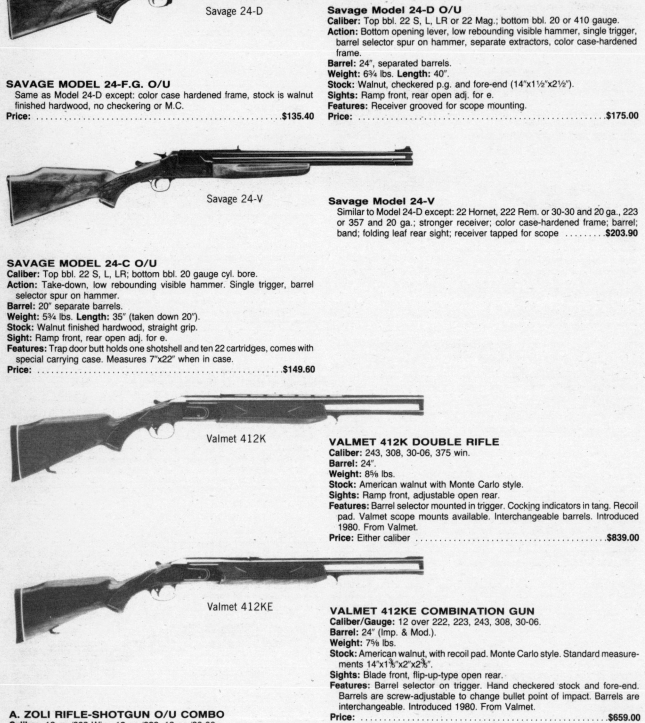

Savage 24-D

Savage Model 24-D O/U
Caliber: Top bbl. 22 S, L, LR or 22 Mag.; bottom bbl. 20 or 410 gauge.
Action: Bottom opening lever, low rebounding visible hammer, single trigger, barrel selector spur on hammer, separate extractors, color case-hardened frame.
Barrel: 24″, separated barrels.
Weight: 6¾ lbs. **Length:** 40″.
Stock: Walnut, checkered p.g. and fore-end (14″x1½″x2½″).
Sights: Ramp front, rear open adj. for e.
Features: Receiver grooved for scope mounting.
Price: $175.00

SAVAGE MODEL 24-F.G. O/U
Same as Model 24-D except: color case hardened frame, stock is walnut finished hardwood, no checkering or M.C.
Price: $135.40

Savage 24-V

Savage Model 24-V
Similar to Model 24-D except: 22 Hornet, 222 Rem. or 30-30 and 20 ga., 223 or 357 and 20 ga.; stronger receiver; color case-hardened frame; barrel; band; folding leaf rear sight; receiver tapped for scope $203.90

SAVAGE MODEL 24-C O/U
Caliber: Top bbl. 22 S, L, LR; bottom bbl. 20 gauge cyl. bore.
Action: Take-down, low rebounding visible hammer. Single trigger, barrel selector spur on hammer.
Barrel: 20″ separate barrels.
Weight: 5¾ lbs. **Length:** 35″ (taken down 20″).
Stock: Walnut finished hardwood, straight grip.
Sight: Ramp front, rear open adj. for e.
Features: Trap door butt holds one shotshell and ten 22 cartridges, comes with special carrying case. Measures 7″x22″ when in case.
Price: $149.60

Valmet 412K

VALMET 412K DOUBLE RIFLE
Caliber: 243, 308, 30-06, 375 win.
Barrel: 24″.
Weight: 8⅝ lbs.
Stock: American walnut with Monte Carlo style.
Sights: Ramp front, adjustable open rear.
Features: Barrel selector mounted in trigger. Cocking indicators in tang. Recoil pad. Valmet scope mounts available. Interchangeable barrels. Introduced 1980. From Valmet.
Price: Either caliber $839.00

Valmet 412KE

VALMET 412KE COMBINATION GUN
Caliber/Gauge: 12 over 222, 223, 243, 308, 30-06.
Barrel: 24″ (Imp. & Mod.).
Weight: 7⅝ lbs.
Stock: American walnut, with recoil pad. Monte Carlo style. Standard measurements 14″x1⅝″x2″x2⅜″.
Sights: Blade front, flip-up-type open rear.
Features: Barrel selector on trigger. Hand checkered stock and fore-end. Barrels are screw-adjustable to change bullet point of impact. Barrels are interchangeable. Introduced 1980. From Valmet.
Price: $659.00

A. ZOLI RIFLE-SHOTGUN O/U COMBO
Caliber: 12 ga./308 Win., 12 ga./222, 12 ga./30-06.
Barrel: Combo—24″; shotgun—28″ (Mod. & Full).
Weight: About 8 lbs. **Length:** 41″ over-all (24″ bbl.).
Stock: European walnut.
Sights: Blade front, flip-up rear.
Features: Available with German claw scope mounts on rifle/shotgun barrels. Comes with set of 12/12 (Mod. & Full) barrels. From Mandall Shooting Supplies.
Price: With two barrel sets, without claw mounts $1,595.00
Price: With two barrel sets, with claw mounts $1,750.00

Consult our Directory pages for the location of firms mentioned.

CAUTION: PRICES CHANGE. CHECK AT GUNSHOP.

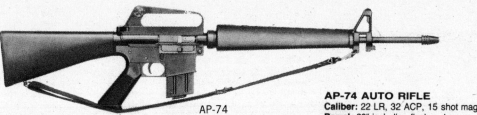

AP-74

AP-74 AUTO RIFLE
Caliber: 22 LR, 32 ACP, 15 shot magazine.
Barrel: 20″ including flash reducer.
Weight: 6½ lbs. **Length:** 38½″ over-all.
Stock: Black plastic.
Sights: Ramp front, adj. peep rear.
Features: Pivotal take-down, easy disassembly. AR-15 look-alike. Sling and sling swivels included. Imported by EMF.
Price: $198.00
Price: With walnut stock and fore-end $220.00
Price: 32 ACP $210.00
Price: With wood stock and fore-end $230.00

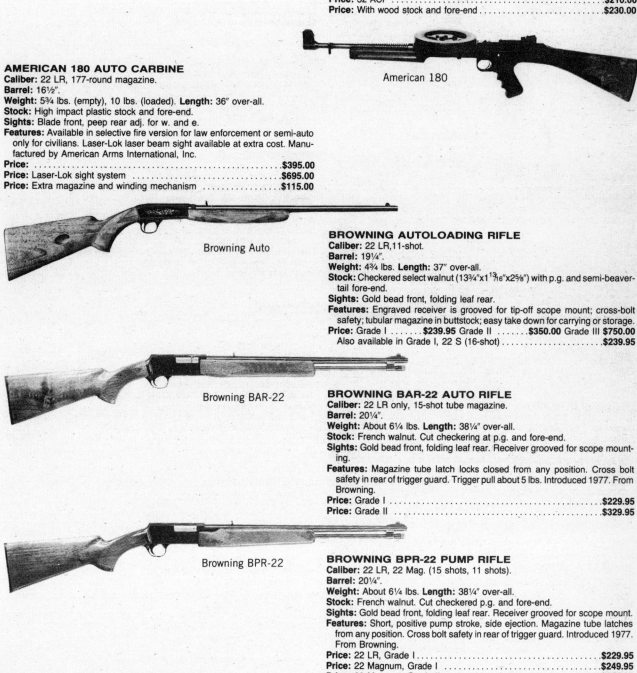

American 180

AMERICAN 180 AUTO CARBINE
Caliber: 22 LR, 177-round magazine.
Barrel: 16½″.
Weight: 5¾ lbs. (empty), 10 lbs. (loaded). **Length:** 36″ over-all.
Stock: High impact plastic stock and fore-end.
Sights: Blade front, peep rear adj. for w. and e.
Features: Available in selective fire version for law enforcement or semi-auto only for civilians. Laser-Lok laser beam sight available at extra cost. Manufactured by American Arms International, Inc.
Price: $395.00
Price: Laser-Lok sight system $695.00
Price: Extra magazine and winding mechanism $115.00

Browning Auto

BROWNING AUTOLOADING RIFLE
Caliber: 22 LR,11-shot.
Barrel: 19¼″.
Weight: 4¾ lbs. **Length:** 37″ over-all.
Stock: Checkered select walnut (13¾″x1¹³⁄₁₆″x2⅝″) with p.g. and semi-beavertail fore-end.
Sights: Gold bead front, folding leaf rear.
Features: Engraved receiver is grooved for tip-off scope mount; cross-bolt safety; tubular magazine in buttstock; easy take down for carrying or storage.
Price: Grade I ....$239.95 Grade II ....$350.00 Grade III $750.00
Also available in Grade I, 22 S (16-shot) $239.95

Browning BAR-22

BROWNING BAR-22 AUTO RIFLE
Caliber: 22 LR only, 15-shot tube magazine.
Barrel: 20¼″.
Weight: About 6¼ lbs. **Length:** 38¼″ over-all.
Stock: French walnut. Cut checkering at p.g. and fore-end.
Sights: Gold bead front, folding leaf rear. Receiver grooved for scope mounting.
Features: Magazine tube latch locks closed from any position. Cross bolt safety in rear of trigger guard. Trigger pull about 5 lbs. Introduced 1977. From Browning.
Price: Grade I $229.95
Price: Grade II $329.95

Browning BPR-22

BROWNING BPR-22 PUMP RIFLE
Caliber: 22 LR, 22 Mag. (15 shots, 11 shots).
Barrel: 20¼″.
Weight: About 6¼ lbs. **Length:** 38¼″ over-all.
Stock: French walnut. Cut checkered p.g. and fore-end.
Sights: Gold bead front, folding leaf rear. Receiver grooved for scope mount.
Features: Short, positive pump stroke, side ejection. Magazine tube latches from any position. Cross bolt safety in rear of trigger guard. Introduced 1977. From Browning.
Price: 22 LR, Grade I $229.95
Price: 22 Magnum, Grade I $249.95
Price: 22 Magnum, Grade II $349.95

RIMFIRE RIFLES—AUTOLOADING & SLIDE ACTION

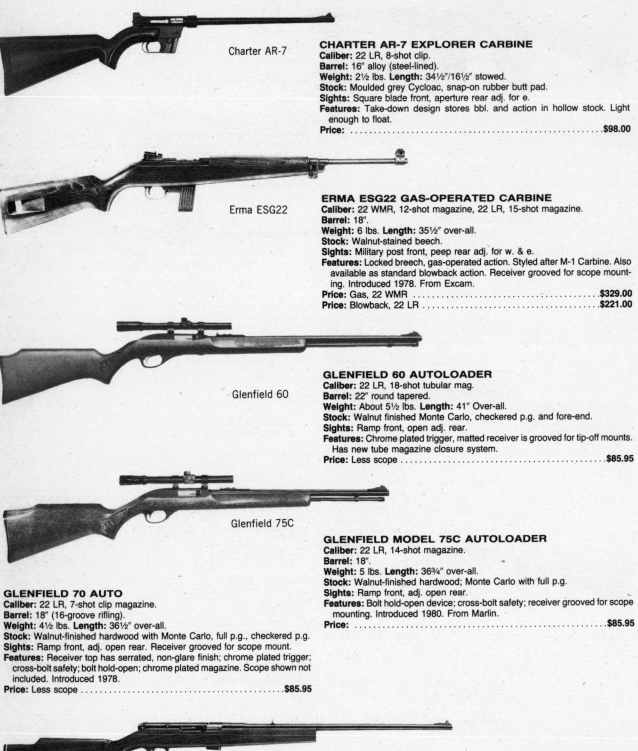

Charter AR-7

CHARTER AR-7 EXPLORER CARBINE
Caliber: 22 LR, 8-shot clip.
Barrel: 16″ alloy (steel-lined).
Weight: 2½ lbs. **Length:** 34½″/16½″ stowed.
Stock: Moulded grey Cycloac, snap-on rubber butt pad.
Sights: Square blade front, aperture rear adj. for e.
Features: Take-down design stores bbl. and action in hollow stock. Light enough to float.
Price: $98.00

Erma ESG22

ERMA ESG22 GAS-OPERATED CARBINE
Caliber: 22 WMR, 12-shot magazine, 22 LR, 15-shot magazine.
Barrel: 18″.
Weight: 6 lbs. **Length:** 35½″ over-all.
Stock: Walnut-stained beech.
Sights: Military post front, peep rear adj. for w. & e.
Features: Locked breech, gas-operated action. Styled after M-1 Carbine. Also available as standard blowback action. Receiver grooved for scope mounting. Introduced 1978. From Excam.
Price: Gas, 22 WMR $329.00
Price: Blowback, 22 LR $221.00

Glenfield 60

GLENFIELD 60 AUTOLOADER
Caliber: 22 LR, 18-shot tubular mag.
Barrel: 22″ round tapered.
Weight: About 5½ lbs. **Length:** 41″ Over-all.
Stock: Walnut finished Monte Carlo, checkered p.g. and fore-end.
Sights: Ramp front, open adj. rear.
Features: Chrome plated trigger, matted receiver is grooved for tip-off mounts. Has new tube magazine closure system.
Price: Less scope $85.95

Glenfield 75C

GLENFIELD MODEL 75C AUTOLOADER
Caliber: 22 LR, 14-shot magazine.
Barrel: 18″.
Weight: 5 lbs. **Length:** 36¾″ over-all.
Stock: Walnut-finished hardwood; Monte Carlo with full p.g.
Sights: Ramp front, adj. open rear.
Features: Bolt hold-open device; cross-bolt safety; receiver grooved for scope mounting. Introduced 1980. From Marlin.
Price: $85.95

GLENFIELD 70 AUTO
Caliber: 22 LR, 7-shot clip magazine.
Barrel: 18″ (16-groove rifling).
Weight: 4½ lbs. **Length:** 36½″ over-all.
Stock: Walnut-finished hardwood with Monte Carlo, full p.g., checkered p.g.
Sights: Ramp front, adj. open rear. Receiver grooved for scope mount.
Features: Receiver top has serrated, non-glare finish; chrome plated trigger; cross-bolt safety; bolt hold-open; chrome plated magazine. Scope shown not included. Introduced 1978.
Price: Less scope $85.95

H&R 700

HARRINGTON & RICHARDSON Model 700 Auto Rifle
Caliber: 22 WMRF, 5-shot clip.
Barrel: 22″.
Weight: 6½ lbs. **Length:** 43¼″ over-all.
Stock: Walnut, Monte Carlo, full p.g., composition buttplate.
Sights: Blade front, folding leaf rear.
Features: Drilled and tapped for scope mounting. 10-shot clip available. Made in U.S. by H&R.
Price: $179.00

H&R Model 700 Deluxe Rifle
Same as Model 700 except has select walnut stock with cheekpiece, checkered grip and fore-end, rubber rifle recoil pad. No iron sights; comes with H&R Model 432 4x, 1″ tube scope, with base and rings.
Price: $295.00

CAUTION: PRICES CHANGE. CHECK AT GUNSHOP.

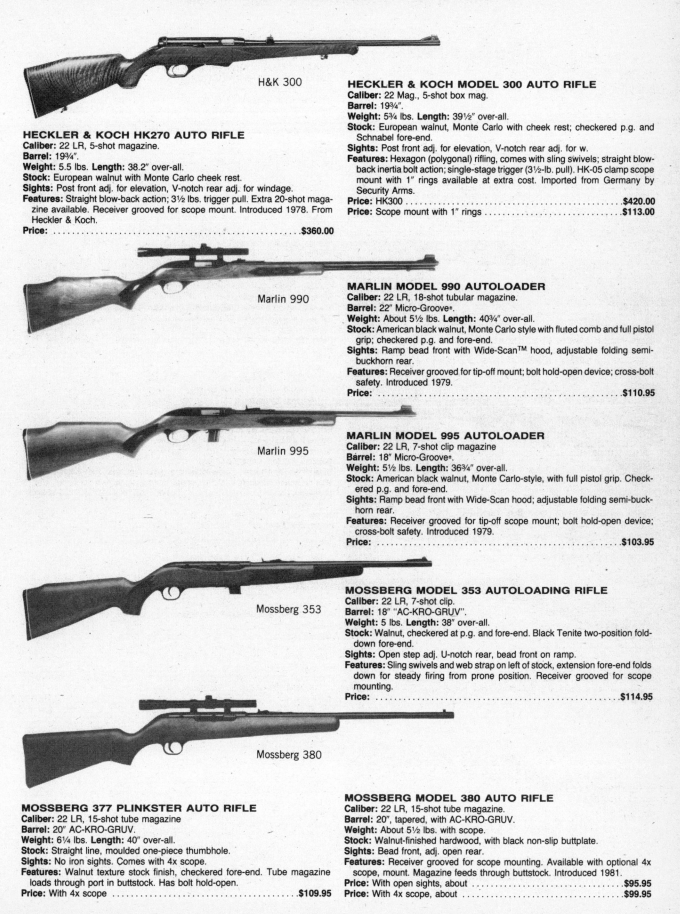

H&K 300

Marlin 990

Marlin 995

Mossberg 353

Mossberg 380

HECKLER & KOCH HK270 AUTO RIFLE

Caliber: 22 LR, 5-shot magazine.
Barrel: 19¾".
Weight: 5.5 lbs. **Length:** 38.2" over-all.
Stock: European walnut with Monte Carlo cheek rest.
Sights: Post front adj. for elevation, V-notch rear adj. for windage.
Features: Straight blow-back action; 3½ lbs. trigger pull. Extra 20-shot magazine available. Receiver grooved for scope mount. Introduced 1978. From Heckler & Koch.
Price: $360.00

HECKLER & KOCH MODEL 300 AUTO RIFLE

Caliber: 22 Mag., 5-shot box mag.
Barrel: 19¾".
Weight: 5¾ lbs. **Length:** 39½" over-all.
Stock: European walnut, Monte Carlo with cheek rest; checkered p.g. and Schnabel fore-end.
Sights: Post front adj. for elevation, V-notch rear adj. for w.
Features: Hexagon (polygonal) rifling, comes with sling swivels; straight blow-back inertia bolt action; single-stage trigger (3½-lb. pull). HK-05 clamp scope mount with 1" rings available at extra cost. Imported from Germany by Security Arms.
Price: HK300 ....$420.00
Price: Scope mount with 1" rings $113.00

MARLIN MODEL 990 AUTOLOADER

Caliber: 22 LR, 18-shot tubular magazine.
Barrel: 22" Micro-Groove*.
Weight: About 5½ lbs. **Length:** 40¾" over-all.
Stock: American black walnut, Monte Carlo style with fluted comb and full pistol grip; checkered p.g. and fore-end.
Sights: Ramp bead front with Wide-Scan™ hood, adjustable folding semi-buckhorn rear.
Features: Receiver grooved for tip-off mount; bolt hold-open device; cross-bolt safety. Introduced 1979.
Price: $110.95

MARLIN MODEL 995 AUTOLOADER

Caliber: 22 LR, 7-shot clip magazine
Barrel: 18" Micro-Groove*.
Weight: 5½ lbs. **Length:** 36¾" over-all.
Stock: American black walnut, Monte Carlo-style, with full pistol grip. Checkered p.g. and fore-end.
Sights: Ramp bead front with Wide-Scan hood; adjustable folding semi-buckhorn rear.
Features: Receiver grooved for tip-off scope mount; bolt hold-open device; cross-bolt safety. Introduced 1979.
Price: $103.95

MOSSBERG MODEL 353 AUTOLOADING RIFLE

Caliber: 22 LR, 7-shot clip.
Barrel: 18" "AC-KRO-GRUV".
Weight: 5 lbs. **Length:** 38" over-all.
Stock: Walnut, checkered at p.g. and fore-end. Black Tenite two-position fold-down fore-end.
Sights: Open step adj. U-notch rear, bead front on ramp.
Features: Sling swivels and web strap on left of stock, extension fore-end folds down for steady firing from prone position. Receiver grooved for scope mounting.
Price: $114.95

MOSSBERG 377 PLINKSTER AUTO RIFLE

Caliber: 22 LR, 15-shot tube magazine
Barrel: 20" AC-KRO-GRUV.
Weight: 6¼ lbs. **Length:** 40" over-all.
Stock: Straight line, moulded one-piece thumbhole.
Sights: No iron sights. Comes with 4x scope.
Features: Walnut texture stock finish, checkered fore-end. Tube magazine loads through port in buttstock. Has bolt hold-open.
Price: With 4x scope $109.95

MOSSBERG MODEL 380 AUTO RIFLE

Caliber: 22 LR, 15-shot tube magazine.
Barrel: 20", tapered, with AC-KRO-GRUV.
Weight: About 5½ lbs. with scope.
Stock: Walnut-finished hardwood, with black non-slip buttplate.
Sights: Bead front, adj. open rear.
Features: Receiver grooved for scope mounting. Available with optional 4x scope, mount. Magazine feeds through buttstock. Introduced 1981.
Price: With open sights, about $95.95
Price: With 4x scope, about $99.95

CAUTION: PRICES CHANGE. CHECK AT GUNSHOP.

RIMFIRE RIFLES—AUTOLOADING & SLIDE ACTION

Nylon 66MB

REMINGTON NYLON 66MB AUTO RIFLE
Caliber: 22 LR, 14-shot tubular mag.
Barrel: 19⅝" round tapered.
Weight: 4 lbs. **Length:** 38½" over-all.
Stock: Moulded Mohawk Brown Nylon, checkered p.g. and fore-end.
Sights: Blade ramp front, adj. open rear.
Features: Top tang safety, double extractors, receiver grooved for tip-off
  mounts.
Price: $114.95
Price: Model 66MB With Universal UA 4x scope $123.95

Remington Nylon 66BD Auto Rifle
Same as the Model 66AB except has black stock, barrel, and receiver cover.
Black diamond-shape inlay in fore-end. Introduced 1978.
Price: $114.95
Price: Model 66 BD with 4x scope $123.95

Remington Nylon 66AB Auto Rifle
Same as the Model 66MB except: Apache Black Nylon stock, chrome plated
  receiver.
Price: $121.95

Remington 552A

REMINGTON 552A AUTOLOADING RIFLE
Caliber: 22 S (20), L (17) or LR (15) tubular mag.
Barrel: 21" round tapered.
Weight: About 5¾ lbs. **Length:** 40" over-all.
Stock: Full-size, walnut-finished hardwood.
Sights: Bead front, step open rear adj. for w. & e.
Features: Positive cross-bolt safety, receiver grooved for tip-off mount.
Price: $148.95

Remington Model 552BDL Auto Rifle
Same as Model 552A except: Du Pont RKW finished walnut stock, checkered
fore-end and capped p.g. stock. Blade ramp front and fully adj. rear sights.
Price: $166.95

Remington 572

REMINGTON 572 FIELDMASTER PUMP RIFLE
Caliber: 22 S(20), L(17) or LR(14). Tubular mag.
Barrel: 21" round tapered.
Weight: 5½ lbs. **Length:** 42" over-all.
Stock: Walnut-finished hardwood with p.g. and grooved slide handle.
Sights: Blade ramp front; sliding ramp rear adj. for w. & e.
Features: Cross-bolt safety, removing inner mag. tube converts rifle to single
  shot, receiver grooved for tip-off scope mount.
Price: $154.95
Price: Sling and swivels installed $15.50

Remington Model 572 BDL Deluxe
Same as the 572 except: p.g. cap, walnut stock with RKW finish, checkered
grip and fore-end, ramp front and fully adj. rear sights.
Price: $171.95
Price: Sling and swivels installed $15.50

Rossi 62

ROSSI 62 SA PUMP RIFLE
Caliber: 22 S, L or LR.
Barrel: 23".
Weight: 5¾ lbs. **Length:** 39¼" over-all.
Stock: Walnut, straight grip, grooved fore-end.
Sights: Fixed front, adj. rear.
Features: Capacity 20 Short, 16 Long or 14 Long Rifle. Quick takedown.
  Imported from Brazil by Interarms.
Price: Blue $152.00
Price: Nickel $166.00

ROSSI 62 SAC CARBINE
Same as standard model except has 16¼" barrel. Magazine holds slightly
fewer cartridges.
Price: Blue $152.00
Price: Nickel $166.00

Ruger 10/22

RUGER 10/22 AUTOLOADING CARBINE
Caliber: 22 LR, 10-shot rotary mag.
Barrel: 18½" round tapered.
Weight: 5 lbs., 12 oz. **Length:** 36¾" over-all.
Stock: Birch with p.g. and bbl. band.
Sights: Gold bead front, folding leaf rear adj. for e.
Features: Detachable rotary magazine fits flush into stock, cross-bolt safety,
  receiver tapped and grooved for scope blocks or tip-off mount. Scope base
  adapter furnished with each rifle.
Price: $111.50

Ruger 10/22 Auto Sporter
Same as 10/22 Carbine except: Walnut stock with hand checkered p.g. and
fore-end with straight buttplate, no bbl. band, has sling swivels.
Price: $139.50

CAUTION: PRICES CHANGE. CHECK AT GUNSHOP.

RIMFIRE RIFLES—AUTOLOADING & SLIDE ACTION

Savage 980-DL

SQUIRES BINGHAM M16 SEMI AUTO RIFLE
Caliber: 22 LR, 15-shot clip.
Barrel: 16½".
Weight: 6 lbs. **Length:** 38½" over-all.
Stock: Black painted mahogany.
Sights: Post front, rear adj. for e.
Features: Box magazine, muzzle brake/flash suppressor. Imported by Kassnar Imports.
Price: $129.95

STEVENS MODEL 987-T AUTO RIFLE
Caliber: 22 LR, 15-shot tube magazine.
Barrel: 20".
Weight: 6 lbs. **Length:** 40½" over-all.
Stock: Walnut-finished hardwood with Monte Carlo; checkered p.g. and fore-end.
Sights: Ramp front, open rear.
Features: Top tang safety; comes with 4x scope and mount. Introduced 1981. From Savage Arms.
Price: Model 987-T $102.80
Price: Model 987 (without scope and mount) $92.70

SAVAGE MODEL 980-DL AUTO RIFLE
Caliber: 22 LR, 15-shot tube magazine.
Barrel: 20".
Weight: 6 lbs. **Length:** 40½" over-all.
Stock: Select walnut with Monte Carlo, checkered p.g. and fore-end.
Sights: Hooded ramp front, folding leaf rear.
Features: Receiver grooved for scope mounting; top tang safety; white line spacer at buttplate. Introduced 1981.
Price: $136.40

SQUIRES BINGHAM M20D SEMI AUTO RIFLE
Caliber: 22 LR, 15-shot clip.
Barrel: 19½".
Weight: 6 lbs. **Length:** 40½" over-all.
Stock: Pulong Dalaga wood with contrasting fore-end tip.
Sights: Blade front, V-notch rear adj. for e.
Features: Positive sliding thumb safety. Receiver grooved for tip-off scope mount. Imported by Kassnar Imports.
Price: $99.95

> Consult our Directory pages for the location of firms mentioned.

Tradewinds 260-A

TRADEWINDS MODEL 260-A AUTO RIFLE
Caliber: 22 LR, 5-shot (10-shot mag. avail.).
Barrel: 22½".
Weight: 5¾ lbs. **Length:** 41½".
Stock: Walnut, with hand checkered p.g. and fore-end.
Sights: Ramp front with hood, 3-leaf folding rear, receiver grooved for scope mt.
Features: Double extractors, sliding safety. Imported by Tradewinds.
Price: $250.00

Universal 2200

UNIVERSAL 2200 LEATHERNECK CARBINE
Caliber: 22 LR, 10-shot.
Barrel: 18".
Weight: 5½ lbs. **Length:** 35¾" over-all.
Stock: Birch hardwood with lacquer finish.
Sights: Blade front, peep rear adj. for w. & e.
Features: Look-alike to the G.I. Carbine except in rimfire. Recoil operated. Metal parts satin-polish blue. Flip-type safety. Optional 30-shot magazine available. Receiver drilled and tapped for scope mounting. Introduced 1979. From Universal Firearms.
Price: $209.00

Weatherby Mk.XXII

WEATHERBY MARK XXII AUTO RIFLE, CLIP MODEL
Caliber: 22 LR only, 5- or 10-shot clip loaded
Barrel: 24" round contoured.
Weight: 6 lbs. **Length:** 42¼" over-all.
Stock: Walnut, Monte Carlo comb and cheekpiece, rosewood p.g. cap and fore-end tip. Skip-line checkering.
Sights: Gold bead ramp front, 3-leaf folding rear.
Features: Thumb operated side safety also acts as single shot selector. Receiver grooved for tip-off scope mount. Single pin release for quick takedown.
Price: $279.95
Extra 5-shot clip ....$6.95   Extra 10-shot clip $7.95

Weatherby Mark XXII Tubular Model
Same as Mark XXII Clip Model except: 15-shot tubular magazine.$289.95

RIMFIRE RIFLES—LEVER ACTION

Browning BL-22

BROWNING BL-22 LEVER ACTION RIFLE
Caliber: 22 S(22), L(17) or LR(15). Tubular mag.
Barrel: 20″ round tapered.
Weight: 5 lbs. **Length:** 36¾″ over-all.
Stock: Walnut, 2-piece straight grip western style.
Sights: Bead post front, folding-leaf rear.
Features: Short throw lever, ½-cock safety, receiver grooved for tip-off scope mounts.
Price: Grade I **$219.95**
Price: Grade II, engraved receiver, checkered grip and fore-end . . .**$249.95**

Erma EG-73

ERMA EG73 LEVER ACTION CARBINE
Caliber: 22 WRM, 12-shot magazine.
Barrel: 19¼″.
Weight: 6 lbs. **Length:** 37⅜″ over-all.
Stock: Walnut-stained beech.
Sights: Hooded ramp front, Buckhorn rear. Receiver grooved for scope mounting.
Features: Tubular magazine, side ejection. Introduced 1978. Imported by Excam.
Price: **$259.00**

Erma Lever Action Carbines
Model EG712. Similar to Magnum model except chambered for 22 S, L, LR with magazine capacity of 21, 17 and 15 respectively. Barrel length is 18½″, weight is 5½ lbs. Introduced 1978 . . . .**$226.00**
Model EG712 L. As above except has European walnut stock, engraved nickel silver receiver, heavy octagonal barrel. Imported by Excam. Introduced 1978 . . . .**$339.00**

Marlin 39A

MARLIN GOLDEN 39A LEVER ACTION RIFLE
Caliber: 22 S(26), L(21), LR(19), tubular magazine.
Barrel: 24″ Micro-Groove®.
Weight: 6½ lbs. **Length:** 40″.
Stock: American black walnut with white line spacers at p.g. cap and buttplate.
Sights: Bead ramp front with detachable "Wide-Scan"™ hood, folding rear semi-buckhorn adj. for w. and e.
Features: Take-down action, receiver tapped for scope mount (supplied), gold plated trigger, sling swivels, offset hammer spur. Mar-Shield® stock finish.
Price: **$214.95**

Marlin 39M

MARLIN GOLDEN 39M CARBINE
Caliber: 22 S(21), L(16), LR(15), tubular magazine.
Barrel: 20″ Micro-Grove®.
Weight: 6 lbs. **Length:** 36″.
Stock: American black walnut, straight grip, white line buttplate spacer. Mar-Shield® finish.
Sights: "Wide-Scan"™ ramp front with hood, folding rear semi-buckhorn adj. for w. and e.
Features: Squared finger lever. Receiver tapped for scope mount (supplied) or receiver sight, gold plated trigger, offset hammer spur, sling swivels, take-down action.
Price: **$214.95**

Winchester 9422 XTR

WINCHESTER 9422 XTR LEVER ACTION RIFLE
Caliber: 22 S(21), L(17), LR(15). Tubular mag.
Barrel: 20½″ (16″ twist).
Length: 37⅛″ over-all. **Weight:** 6½ lbs.
Stock: American walnut, 2-piece, straight grip (no p.g.).
Sights: Hooded ramp front, adj. semi-buckhorn rear.
Features: Side ejection, receiver grooved for scope mounting, takedown action. Has new XTR wood and metal finish.

Winchester 9422M XTR Lever Action Rifle
Same as the 9422 except chambered for 22 WMR cartridge, has 11-round mag. capacity **$283.00**

Price: **$276.00**

CAUTION: PRICES CHANGE. CHECK AT GUNSHOP.

Fox FB-1

FOX MODEL FB-1 BOLT ACTION RIFLE
Caliber: 22 LR, 5-shot clip.
Barrel: 24".
Weight: 6½ lbs. **Length:** 43" over-all.
Stock: Select walnut; rollover cheekpiece. Wundhammer palm swell grip; cut checkering; rosewood fore-end tip and p.g. cap.
Sights: Hooded ramp front, open rear adj. for w. and e.
Features: Receiver grooved for tip-off scope mounting and is drilled and tapped; double extractors; magazine release mounted flush with right side of stock. Introduced 1981. From Savage Arms.
Price: $270.30

Glenfield 15

GLENFIELD MODEL 15 BOLT ACTION RIFLE
Caliber: 22, S, L, LR, single-shot.
Barrel: 22".
Weight: 5½ lbs. **Length:** 41" over-all.
Stock: Walnut-finished hardwood with Monte Carlo and full p.g.
Sights: Ramp front, adjustable open rear.
Features: Receiver grooved for tip-off scope mount; checkering on pistol grip; thumb safety; red cocking indicator. Introduced 1979.
Price: $82.95

H&R 750

HARRINGTON & RICHARDSON MODEL 750 PIONEER
Caliber: 22 S, L or LR. Single-shot.
Barrel: 22" round tapered.
Weight: 5 lbs. **Length:** 39" over-all.
Stock: Walnut finished hardwood with Monte Carlo comb and p.g.
Sights: Blade front, step adj. open rear.
Features: Double extractors, feed platform, cocking indicator. sliding side safety, receiver grooved for tip-off scope mount.
Price: $69.50

H&R 865

HARRINGTON & RICHARDSON 865 PLAINSMAN RIFLE
Caliber: 22 S, L or LR. 5-shot clip mag.
Barrel: 22" round tapered.
Weight: 5 lbs. **Length:** 39" over-all.
Stock: Walnut finished hardwood with Monte Carlo and p.g.
Sights: Blade front, step adj. open rear.
Features: Cocking indicator, sliding side safety, receiver grooved for tip-off scope mounts.
Price: $79.50

KIMBER MODEL 82 BOLT ACTION RIFLE
Caliber: 22 Short, Long, Long Rifle, 22 Mag.; 5-shot detachable magazine.
Barrel: 24", 6-groove.
Weight: About 6¼ lbs. **Length:** 41" over-all.
Stock: Select walnut. "Classic" style stock. Checkered p.g. and fore-end.
Sights: Blade front on ramp, open rear adj. for w. & e.
Features: High quality adult-sized bolt action rifle. All steel construction. Rocker-type silent safety. All metal parts finished in high polish blue. Available with or without sights. Barreled actions available. Made in U.S.A. Introduced 1980. From Kimber of Oregon.
Price: Classic stock without sights $430.00
Price: Classic stock with sights $455.00
Price: Scope mounts and rings $35.00
Price: Cascade sporter stock, no sights $450.00
Price: Cascade sporter stock, with sights $475.00
Price: Classic stock, no sights, 22 Mag. $465.00
Price: Classic stock, with sights, 22 Mag. $490.00
Price: Cascade sporter stock, no sights, 22 Mag. $480.00
Price: Cascade sporter stock, with sights, 22 Mag. $505.00
Price: Extra 5-shot magazine $8.50
Price: Extra 10-shot magazine $10.00

Kimber 82 Cascade

Consult our Directory pages for the location of firms mentioned.

RIMFIRE RIFLES—BOLT ACTION & SINGLE SHOT

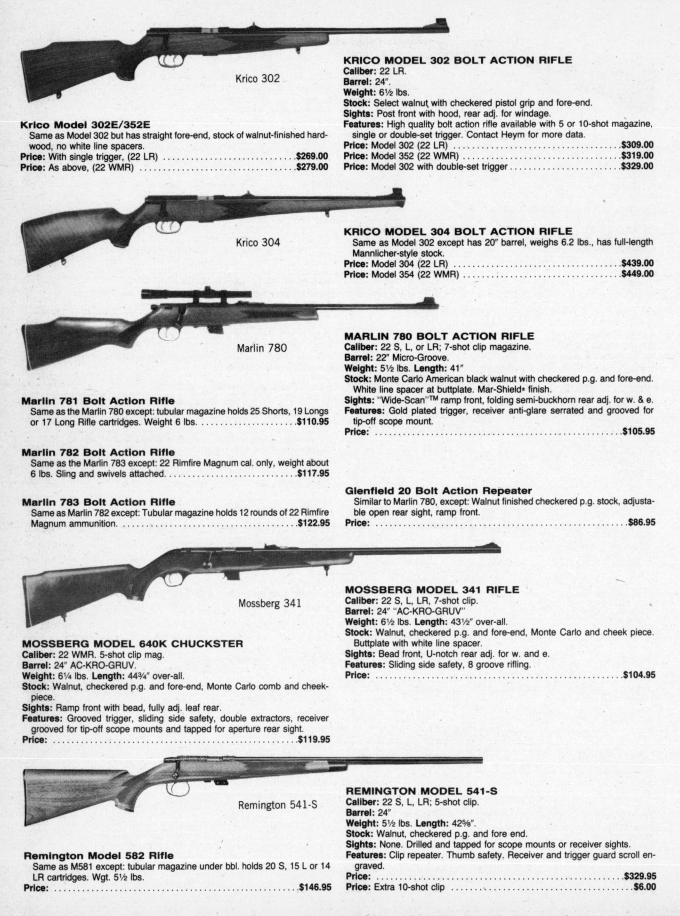

Krico 302

Krico Model 302E/352E
Same as Model 302 but has straight fore-end, stock of walnut-finished hardwood, no white line spacers.
Price: With single trigger, (22 LR) $269.00
Price: As above, (22 WMR) $279.00

KRICO MODEL 302 BOLT ACTION RIFLE
Caliber: 22 LR.
Barrel: 24".
Weight: 6½ lbs.
Stock: Select walnut with checkered pistol grip and fore-end.
Sights: Post front with hood, rear adj. for windage.
Features: High quality bolt action rifle available with 5 or 10-shot magazine, single or double-set trigger. Contact Heym for more data.
Price: Model 302 (22 LR) $309.00
Price: Model 352 (22 WMR) $319.00
Price: Model 302 with double-set trigger $329.00

Krico 304

KRICO MODEL 304 BOLT ACTION RIFLE
Same as Model 302 except has 20" barrel, weighs 6.2 lbs., has full-length Mannlicher-style stock.
Price: Model 304 (22 LR) $439.00
Price: Model 354 (22 WMR) $449.00

Marlin 780

MARLIN 780 BOLT ACTION RIFLE
Caliber: 22 S, L, or LR; 7-shot clip magazine.
Barrel: 22" Micro-Groove.
Weight: 5½ lbs. Length: 41"
Stock: Monte Carlo American black walnut with checkered p.g. and fore-end. White line spacer at buttplate. Mar-Shield® finish.
Sights: "Wide-Scan"™ ramp front, folding semi-buckhorn rear adj. for w. & e.
Features: Gold plated trigger, receiver anti-glare serrated and grooved for tip-off scope mount.
Price: $105.95

Marlin 781 Bolt Action Rifle
Same as the Marlin 780 except: tubular magazine holds 25 Shorts, 19 Longs or 17 Long Rifle cartridges. Weight 6 lbs. $110.95

Marlin 782 Bolt Action Rifle
Same as the Marlin 783 except: 22 Rimfire Magnum cal. only, weight about 6 lbs. Sling and swivels attached. $117.95

Marlin 783 Bolt Action Rifle
Same as Marlin 782 except: Tubular magazine holds 12 rounds of 22 Rimfire Magnum ammunition. $122.95

Glenfield 20 Bolt Action Repeater
Similar to Marlin 780, except: Walnut finished checkered p.g. stock, adjustable open rear sight, ramp front.
Price: $86.95

Mossberg 341

MOSSBERG MODEL 341 RIFLE
Caliber: 22 S, L, LR, 7-shot clip.
Barrel: 24" "AC-KRO-GRUV"
Weight: 6½ lbs. Length: 43½" over-all.
Stock: Walnut, checkered p.g. and fore-end, Monte Carlo and cheek piece. Buttplate with white line spacer.
Sights: Bead front, U-notch rear adj. for w. and e.
Features: Sliding side safety, 8 groove rifling.
Price: $104.95

MOSSBERG MODEL 640K CHUCKSTER
Caliber: 22 WMR. 5-shot clip mag.
Barrel: 24" AC-KRO-GRUV.
Weight: 6¼ lbs. Length: 44¾" over-all.
Stock: Walnut, checkered p.g. and fore-end, Monte Carlo comb and cheekpiece.
Sights: Ramp front with bead, fully adj. leaf rear.
Features: Grooved trigger, sliding side safety, double extractors, receiver grooved for tip-off scope mounts and tapped for aperture rear sight.
Price: $119.95

Remington 541-S

REMINGTON MODEL 541-S
Caliber: 22 S, L, LR; 5-shot clip.
Barrel: 24"
Weight: 5½ lbs. Length: 42⅝".
Stock: Walnut, checkered p.g. and fore end.
Sights: None. Drilled and tapped for scope mounts or receiver sights.
Features: Clip repeater. Thumb safety. Receiver and trigger guard scroll engraved.
Price: $329.95
Price: Extra 10-shot clip $6.00

Remington Model 582 Rifle
Same as M581 except: tubular magazine under bbl. holds 20 S, 15 L or 14 LR cartridges. Wgt. 5½ lbs.
Price: $146.95

CAUTION: PRICES CHANGE. CHECK AT GUNSHOP.

Remington 581

REMINGTON MODEL 581 RIFLE
Caliber: 22 S, L or LR. 5-shot clip mag.
Barrel: 24" round.
Weight: 4¾ lbs. **Length:** 42⅜" over-all.
Stock: Walnut finished Monte Carlo with p.g.
Sights: Bead post front, screw adj. open rear.
Features: Sliding side safety, wide trigger, receiver grooved for tip-off scope mounts. Comes with single-shot adapter.
Price: $125.95
Price: Left hand action and stock $129.95

SAVAGE-STEVENS MODEL 89
Caliber: 22 LR, single-shot.
Barrel: 18½".
Weight: 5 lbs. **Length:** 35" over-all.
Stock: Walnut finished hardwood.
Sights: Blade front, step adj. rear.
Features: Single-shot Martini-type breech block. Hammer must be cocked by hand independent of lever prior to firing. Automatic ejection. Satin black frame finish.
Price: $71.25

Savage/Anschutz Model 1432 Sporter
Same as Model 54 except chambered for 22 Hornet, 24" barrel, 5-shot capacity, over-all length 43⅝" $669.70

SAVAGE STEVENS MODEL 72 CRACKSHOT
Caliber: 22 S, L, LR.
Barrel: 22" octagonal.
Weight: 4½ lbs. **Length:** 37".
Stock: Walnut, straight grip and fore-end.
Sights: Blade front, step adj. rear.
Features: Falling block action, color case hardened frame.
Price: $110.40

SAVAGE/ANSCHUTZ MODEL 54 SPORTER
Caliber: 22 LR. 5-shot clip mag.
Barrel: 23" round tapered.
Weight: 6¾ lbs. **Length:** 42" over-all.
Stock: French walnut, checkered p.g. and fore-end. Monte Carlo roll-over comb, schnabel fore-end tip.
Sights: Hooded ramp gold bead front, folding-leaf rear.
Features: Adj. single stage trigger, wing safety, receiver grooved for tip-off mount, tapped for scope blocks.
Price: $621.30
Price: Model 54M (22 WRM) $628.60

Savage/Anschutz 164

SAVAGE/ANSCHUTZ 1418-1518 SPORTERS
Similar to Model 164 except has European Mannlicher stock with inlays, hand-cut skip-line checkering, double set or single stage trigger.
Price: 1418 (22 LR) $524.85
Price: 1518 (22 Mag.) $534.20

SAVAGE/ANSCHUTZ 164 BOLT ACTION RIFLE
Caliber: 22 LR. 5-shot clip mag.
Barrel: 24" round tapered.
Weight: 6 lbs. **Length:** 40¾" over-all
Stock: Walnut, hand checkered p.g. and fore-end, Monte Carlo comb and cheekpiece, schnabel fore-end.
Sights: Hooded ramp gold bead front, folding-leaf rear.
Features: Fully adj. single stage trigger, sliding side safety, receiver grooved for tip-off mount.
Price: $352.80
Price: Model 164M in 22 WRM (4-shot) $360.45

Savage 982-DL

SAVAGE MODEL 982-DL BOLT ACTION RIFLE
Caliber: 22 LR, 5-shot clip.
Barrel: 22".
Weight: 6 lbs. **Length:** 41" over-all.
Stock: American walnut with Monte Carlo; checkered p.g. and fore-end.
Sights: Ramp front, folding leaf rear.
Features: Flush-fit magazine release; cut checkering; double extractors; receiver grooved for scope mounting; tapered free-floating barrel. Introduced 1981.
Price: Model 982-DL $128.65
Price: Model 982-MDL (22 Mag. version) $123.10

Stevens 982

TRADEWINDS MODEL 311-A BOLT ACTION RIFLE
Caliber: 22 LR, 5-shot (10-shot mag. avail.).
Barrel: 22½".
Weight: 6 lbs. **Length:** 41¼".
Stock: Walnut, Monte Carlo with hand checkered p.g. and fore-end.
Sights: Ramp front with hood, folding leaf rear, receiver grooved for scope mt.
Features: Sliding safety locks trigger and bolt handle. Imported by Tradewinds.
Price: $185.00

STEVENS MODEL 982 BOLT ACTION RIFLE
Caliber: 22 LR, 5-shot clip magazine.
Barrel: 22".
Weight: 5¾ lbs. **Length:** 41" over-all.
Stock: Walnut-finished hardwood with Monte Carlo; checkered p.g. and fore-end.
Sights: Ramp front, open rear.
Features: Double extractors; blued finish; side safety; receiver grooved for scope mounting. Introduced 1981. From Savage Arms.
Price: $103.80
Price: 10-shot clip $6.85

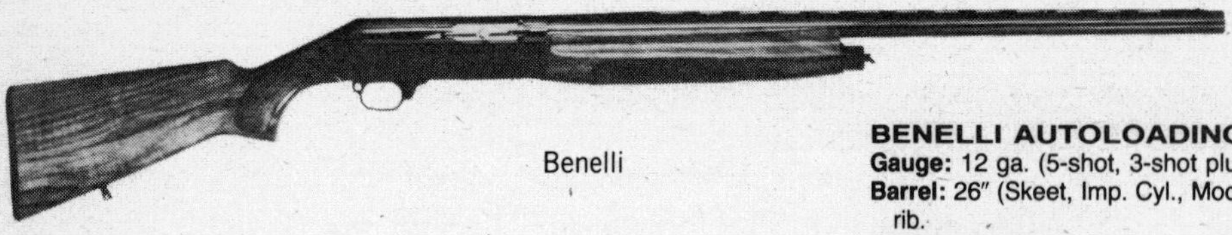

SHOTGUNS—AUTOLOADING

Benelli

BENELLI AUTOLOADING SHOTGUN
Gauge: 12 ga. (5-shot, 3-shot plug furnished).
Barrel: 26″ (Skeet, Imp. Cyl., Mod.); 28″ (Spec., Full, Imp. Mod., Mod.). Vent. rib.
Weight: 6¾ lbs.
Stock: European walnut. 14″x1½″x2½″. Hand checkered p.g. and fore-end.
Sights: Metal bead front.
Features: Quick interchangeable barrels. Cross-bolt safety. Hand engraved on higher grades. Imported from Italy by Heckler & Koch, Inc.
Price: Standard model $418.00
Price: Engraved $489.00
Price: Police model $421.00
Price: Extra barrels $220.00

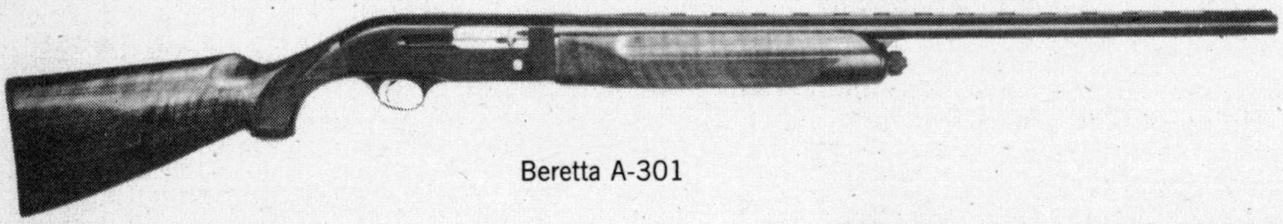

Beretta A-301

Beretta A-301 Skeet and Trap
Same as standard A-301 except: Trap has M.C. stock (14¼″x1⅜″x 1⁹⁄₁₆″x1⅝″) with recoil pad, gold plated trigger, trap choke 30″ bbl. Skeet gun has Skeet choke, gold plated trigger, Skeet stock (14¼″x1⅜″x2⅜″x 2⁹⁄₁₆″) and 26″ barrel. Introduced 1977. Imported by Beretta Arms Co.
Price: Skeet, 12 or 20 ga. $485.00
Price: Trap, 12 ga. only $500.00
Price: Extra barrels $186.00

Beretta A-302 Mag-Action Auto Shotgun
Same basic gun as the A-301 except has improved gas system and requires change of barrel for 2¾″ or 3″ shells. Has lever-operated magazine cut-off. Introduced 1981.
Price: From $565.00

BERETTA A-301 AUTO SHOTGUN
Gauge: 12 or 20
Action: Gas operated.
Barrel: 12 ga.—22″ (slug); 26″ (Imp. Cyl.); 28″ (Mod., Full); 30″ (Full, 3″ chamber); 20 ga.—28″ (Full, Mod.); 26″ (Imp. Cyl.). Vent. rib except slug gun.
Weight: 6 lbs., 5 ozs. (20 ga., 28″).
Stock: 14⅛″x1⅜″x2⅜″, European walnut. Magnum guns have recoil pad.
Features: All gas system parts are of stainless steel. Alloy receiver decorated with scroll pattern engraving. Push button safety in trigger guard. Introduced 1977. Imported by The Beretta Arms Co.
Price: 12 or 20, 2¾″ $485.00
Price: 12 or 20 ga., 3″ Magnum $530.00
Price: Slug gun $485.00
Price: Extra barrels, from $170.00
Price: 12 ga. with four interhangeable choke tubes $590.00

Browning Auto-5

Browning Auto-5 Light Skeet
Same as Light Standard except: 12 and 20 ga. only, 26″ or 28″ bbl. (Skeet). With vent. rib. Wgt. 6⅜-7½ lbs. $534.95

Browning Auto-5 Magnum 12
Same as Std. Auto-5 except: chambered for 3″ magnum shells (also handles 2¾″ magnum and 2¾″ HV loads). 28″ Mod., Full; 30″ and 32″ (Full) bbls. 14″x1⅝″x2½″ stock. Recoil pad. Wgt. 8¾ lbs.
Price: Vent. rib only $544.95

Browning Auto-5 Magnum 20
Same as Magnum 12 except barrels 28″ Full or Mod., or 26″ Full, Mod. or Imp. Cyl. With ventilated rib, 7½ lbs. $544.95

BROWNING AUTO-5 LIGHT 12 and 20
Gauge: 12, 20; 5-shot; 3-shot plug furnished; 2¾″ chamber.
Action: Recoil operated autoloader; takedown.
Barrel: 26″ (Skeet boring in 12 & 20 ga., Cyl., Imp. Cyl., Mod. in 20 ga.); 28″ (Skeet in 12 ga., Mod., Full); 30″ (Full in 12 ga.).
Weight: 12 ga. 7¼ lbs., 20 ga. 6⅜ lbs.
Stock: French walnut, hand checkered half-p.g. and fore-end. 14¼″ x 1⅝″ x 2½″.
Features: Receiver hand engraved with scroll designs and border. Double extractors, extra bbls. interchangeable without factory fitting; mag. cut-off; cross-bolt safety.
Price: Vent. rib only $534.95
Price: Extra barrels, vent. rib only $168.50

Browning A-5 Buck

Browning Auto-5 Light 12, 20, or 12 Buck Special
Same as A-5 Light model except: 24″ bbl. choked for slugs, gold bead front sight on contoured ramp, rear sight adj. for w.&e. Wgt. 12 ga., 7 lbs.; 20 ga., 6 lbs. 2 oz.; 3″ Mag. 12, 8¼ lbs. Illus.
Price: $564.95
Price: 12 or 20 ga. Magnum $579.95
All Buck Specials are available with carrying sling, detachable swivels and swivel attachments for **$10.00** extra.

CAUTION: PRICES CHANGE. CHECK AT GUNSHOP.

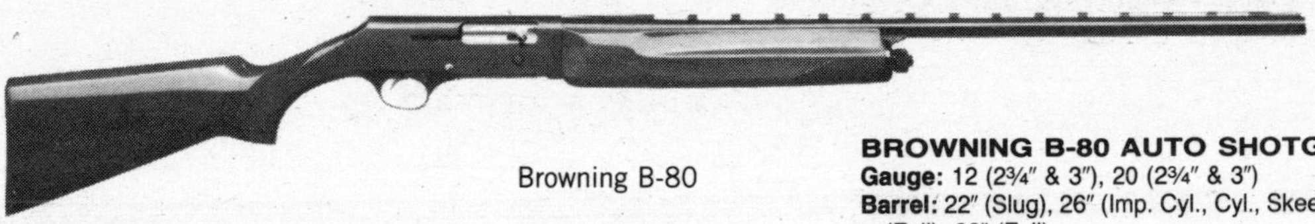

SHOTGUNS—AUTOLOADING

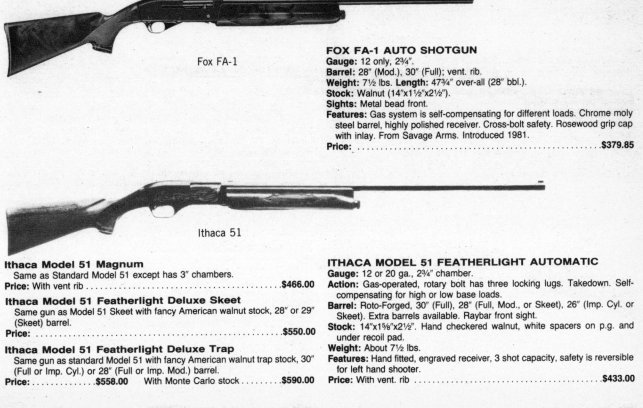

Browning B-80

BROWNING B-80 AUTO SHOTGUN
Gauge: 12 (2¾" & 3"), 20 (2¾" & 3")
Barrel: 22" (Slug), 26" (Imp. Cyl., Cyl., Skeet, Full, Mod.), 28" (Full, Mod.), 30" (Full), 32" (Full).
Weight: About 6½ lbs.
Stock: 14¼ x 1⅝" x 2½". Hand checkered French walnut. Solid black recoil pad.
Features: Vent. rib barrels have non-reflective rib; steel receiver with high-polish blue; cross-bolt safety; interchangeable barrels. Introduced 1981.
Price: 12 or 20 ga., 2¾" or 3", vent. rib $509.95
Price: Buck Special, 12 or 20 ga., 2¾" or 3" $509.95
Price: Buck Special, with accessories (carrying strap, swivels) $529.95
Price: Extra barrels $165.00

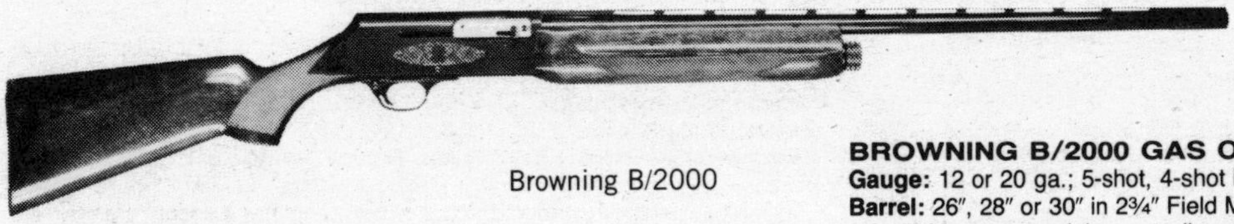

> Consult our Directory pages for the location of firms mentioned.

Browning B/2000

Browning B/2000 12 ga. Trap
Similar to field grade B/2000 except has a special high post floating vent. rib mated to a special receiver rib; front and center ivory beads; special trap recoil pad fitted. Trap model has Monte Carlo stock (14⅜"x1⅜"x1⅜"x2⅛"). Checkered French walnut with semi-beavertail fore-end; 2¾" chamber.
Price: With high post vent. rib $514.95

Browning B/2000 20 ga. Skeet Model
Similar to 12 ga. target guns except 20 ga. only, has conventional vent. rib with front and center ivory beads; does not have the special high post floating rib. Skeet stock and pad, semi-beavertail fore-end; 2¾" chamber.
Price: $474.95

BROWNING B/2000 GAS OPERATED AUTO SHOTGUN
Gauge: 12 or 20 ga.; 5-shot, 4-shot in Magnum.
Barrel: 26", 28" or 30" in 2¾" Field Models, plain or vent. rib; 28", 30" or 32" in 3" Magnum models, vent. rib only.
Weight: 7½ lbs. (26" vent. rib) **Length:** 45⅜" (26" bbl.).
Stock: French walnut, hand checkered, full pistol grip, no recoil pad 14¼"x1⅝"x2½".
Sights: Medium raised bead, German nickel silver.
Features: Internal self-cleaning gas system, soft recoil, speed loading/unloading, extra bbls. interchangeable without factory fitting. No adjustment necessary to gas system for varying loads.
Price: 12 or 20 ga. vent. rib $474.95
Price: Vent. rib, 3" Mag. $474.95
Price: Buck Special $474.95
Price: Buck Special with accessories $494.95
Price: Extra barrels $154.50

Fox FA-1

FOX FA-1 AUTO SHOTGUN
Gauge: 12 only, 2¾".
Barrel: 28" (Mod.), 30" (Full); vent. rib.
Weight: 7½ lbs. **Length:** 47¾" over-all (28" bbl.).
Stock: Walnut (14"x1½"x2½").
Sights: Metal bead front.
Features: Gas system is self-compensating for different loads. Chrome moly steel barrel, highly polished receiver. Cross-bolt safety. Rosewood grip cap with inlay. From Savage Arms. Introduced 1981.
Price: $379.85

Ithaca 51

Ithaca Model 51 Magnum
Same as Standard Model 51 except has 3" chambers.
Price: With vent rib $466.00

Ithaca Model 51 Featherlight Deluxe Skeet
Same gun as Model 51 Skeet with fancy American walnut stock, 28" or 29" (Skeet) barrel.
Price: $550.00

Ithaca Model 51 Featherlight Deluxe Trap
Same gun as standard Model 51 with fancy American walnut trap stock, 30" (Full or Imp. Cyl.) or 28" (Full or Imp. Mod.) barrel.
Price: ....$558.00   With Monte Carlo stock $590.00

ITHACA MODEL 51 FEATHERLIGHT AUTOMATIC
Gauge: 12 or 20 ga., 2¾" chamber.
Action: Gas-operated, rotary bolt has three locking lugs. Takedown. Self-compensating for high or low base loads.
Barrel: Roto-Forged, 30" (Full), 28" (Full, Mod., or Skeet), 26" (Imp. Cyl. or Skeet). Extra barrels available. Raybar front sight.
Stock: 14"x1⅝"x2½". Hand checkered walnut, white spacers on p.g. and under recoil pad.
Weight: About 7½ lbs.
Features: Hand fitted, engraved receiver, 3 shot capacity, safety is reversible for left hand shooter.
Price: With vent. rib $433.00

SHOTGUNS — AUTOLOADING

Ithaca 51 Deer

ITHACA MODEL 51 DEERSLAYER
Gauge: 12 or 20 ga., 2¾″ chamber.
Action: Gas-operated, semi-automatic.
Barrel: 24″, special bore.
Weight: 7½ lbs. (12 ga.), 7¼ lbs. (20 ga.).
Stock: 14″x1½″x2¼″, American walnut. Checkered p.g. and fore-end.
Sights: Raybar front, open rear adj. for w. and e.
Features: Sight base grooved for scope mounts. Easy takedown, reversible safety. Scope optional.
Price: $423.00

Ithaca Mag 10

ITHACA MAG 10 GAS OPERATED SHOTGUN
Gauge: 10, 3½″ chamber, 3-shot.
Barrel: 32″ only. Full choke.
Weight: 11¼ lbs.
Stock: American walnut, checkered p.g. and fore-end (14⅛x2⅜″x1½″), p.g. cap, rubber recoil pad.
Sights: White Bradley.
Features: "Countercoil" gas system. Piston, cylinder, bolt, charging lever, action release and carrier made of stainless steel. ⅜″ vent. rib. Reversible cross-bolt safety. Low recoil force. Deluxe model has full fancy claro American black walnut.
Price: Standard, plain barrel $594.00
Price: Deluxe, vent. rib $759.00
Price: Standard, vent. rib $649.00
Price: Supreme, vent. rib $870.00
Price: Mag 10 Roadblocker (20″ plain barrel) $609.00
Price: Mag 10 Roadblocker with 20″ vent. rib barrel $637.00

> Consult our Directory pages for the location of firms mentioned.

KASSNAR FOX AUTO SHOTGUN
Gauge: 12 only (2¾″ or 3″).
Barrel: 26″ (Imp. Cyl., Mod., Skeet), 28″ (Full, Mod.), 30″ (Full). Vent rib.
Weight: 7¼ lbs.
Stock: American walnut.
Sights: Metal bead front.
Features: Cross bolt safety, interchangeable barrels. From Kassnar Imports.
Price: $329.95

K.F.C. 250

KAWAGUCHIYA K.F.C. M-250 AUTO SHOTGUN
Gauge: 12, 2¾″.
Barrel: 26″, 28″, 30″ (Imp. Cyl. Mod., Full, interchangeable choke tubes).
Weight: 7 lbs. 6 ozs. **Length:** 48″ over-all (28″ barrel).
Stock: 14⅛″x1½″x2½″. French walnut, checkered p.g. and fore-end.
Features: Gas-operated, ventilated barrel rib. Has only 79 parts. Cross-bolt safety is reversible for left-handed shooters. Introduced 1980. From La Paloma Marketing.
Price: Standard Grade $466.00
Price: Deluxe Grade (silvered, etched receiver) $498.00

Manufrance

MANUFRANCE AUTO SHOTGUN
Gauge: 12 ga., (2¾″ or 3″), 3-shot.
Action: Gas operated.
Barrel: 26″ (Imp. Cyl.), 28″ (Mod.), 30″ (Full); vent. rib.
Weight: 6¾ lbs. **Length:** 48″ over-all.
Stock: French walnut, hand checkered p.g. and fore-end.
Features: Magazine cut-off; black matte finish receiver; quick take-down; interchangeable barrels available. Imported by Interarms.
Price: $279.00

CAUTION: PRICES CHANGE. CHECK AT GUNSHOP.

SHOTGUNS—AUTOLOADING

Remington 1100

REMINGTON MODEL 1100 AUTO
Gauge: 12, 3-shot plug furnished.
Action: Gas-operated autoloader.
Barrel: 26″ (Imp. Cyl.), 28″ (Mod., Full), 30″ Full in 12 ga. only.
Stock: 14″x1½″x2½″ American Walnut, checkered p.g. and fore-end.
Weight: 12 ga. 7½ lbs.
Features: Quickly interchangeable barrels within gauge. Matted receiver top with scroll work on both sides of receiver. Crossbolt safety.
Price: ....$391.95   With vent. rib $431.95
Price: Left hand model with vent. rib $457.95

Remington 1100 Collector

Remington 1100 Magnum
Same as 1100 except: chambered for 3″ magnum loads. Available in 12 ga. (30″) or 20 ga. (28″) Mod. or Full, 14″x1½″x2½″ stock with recoil pad, Wgt. 7¾ lbs. $432.95
Price: With vent. rib $472.95
Price: Left hand model with vent. rib $497.95

Remington 1100 Small Gauge
Same as 1100 except: 28 ga. 2¾″ (5-shot) or 410, 3″ (except Skeet, 2½″ 4-shot). 45½″ over-all. Available in 25″ bbl. (Full, Mod., or Imp. Cyl.) only.
Price: With vent. rib $438.95

Remington 1100D Tournament Auto
Same as 1100 Standard except: vent. rib, better wood, more extensive engraving $1,650.00

Remington 1100F Premier Auto
Same as 1100D except: select wood, better engraving $3,300.00
With gold inlay $4,950.00

REMINGTON 1100 Collector's Edition One of Three Thousand
Same as standard 12 ga. Model 1100 except receiver features deep-relief etching, highlighted by gold; richly figured walnut with positive cut checkering; barrel and receiver have matched serial numbers recorded on a framable certificate. Only 3000 will be made. Introduced 1981.
Price: $1,125.00

Remington 1100 LT-20
Basically the same design as Model 1100, but with special weight-saving features that retain strength and dependability of the standard Model 1100.
Barrel: 28″ (Full, Mod.), 26″ (Imp. Cyl.).
Weight: 6½ lbs.
Price: ....$391.95   With vent. rib $431.95
Price: LT-20 magnum (28″ Full) $432.95
Price: With vent. rib $472.95
Price: LT-20 Deer Gun (20″ bbl.) $430.95
Price: LT-20 Ltd. has 23″ (Mod. or Imp. Cyl.) bbl., 1″ shorter stock .$431.95

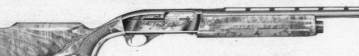

Remington 1000 SA Skeet

Remington 1100 TA Trap
Same as the standard 1100 except: recoil pad. 14⅜″x1⅜″x1¾″ stock. Right- or left-hand models. Wgt. 8¼ lbs. 12 ga. only. 30″ (Mod. Trap, Full) vent. rib bbl. Ivory bead front and white metal middle sight.
Price: ....$456.95   With Monte Carlo stock $466.95
Price: 1100TA Trap, left hand $481.95
Price: With Monte Carlo stock $491.95
Price: Tournament Trap $536.95
Price: Tournament Trap with M.C. stock, better grade wood, different checkering, cut checkering $546.95

Remington 1100 SA Skeet
Same as the 1100 except: 26″ bbl., special Skeet boring, vent. rib (high rib on LT-20), ivory bead front and metal bead middle sights. 14″x1½″x2½″ stock. 12, 20, 28, 410 ga. Wgt. 7½ lbs., cut checkering, walnut, new receiver scroll.
Price: 12 ga., Skeet SA $446.95
Price: 12 ga. Left hand model with vent. rib $471.95
Price: 28 & 410 ga., 25″ bbl. $453.95
Price: 20 ga. LT-20 Skeet SA $446.95
Price: Tournament Skeet (28, 410) $533.95
Price: Tournament Skeet (12 or 20) $526.95

Remington 1100 Deer

Remington 1100 Deer Gun
Same as 1100 except: 12 ga. only, 22″ bbl. (Imp. Cyl.), rifle sights adjustable for w. and e.; recoil pad with white spacer. Weight 7¼ lbs. $430.95

Remington 1100 Extra bbls. 12 and 20 ga.: Plain **$92.95** (20, 28 & 410, **$100.95**). Vent. rib 12 and 20 **$132.95** (20, 28 & 410, **$140.95**). Vent. rib Skeet **$142.95**. Vent. rib Trap **$142.95**. Deer bbl. **$109.95**. Available in the same gauges and chokes as shown on guns. **Prices are approximate.**

Consult our Directory pages for
the location of firms mentioned.

S&W 1000

SMITH & WESSON MODEL 1000 AUTO
Gauge: 12, 2¾" or 3" chamber, 4-shot.
Action: Gas-operated autoloader.
Barrel: 26" (Skeet, Imp. Cyl.), 28" (Mod., Full), 30" (Mod. Full).
Length: 48" over-all (28" bbl.). **Weight:** 7½ lbs. (28" bbl.).
Stock: 14"x1½"x2⅜", American walnut.
Features: Interchangeable crossbolt safety, vent. rib with front and middle beads, engraved alloy receiver, pressure compensator and floating piston for light recoil.
Price: $431.95
Price: Extra barrels (as listed above) $132.95
Price: Extra 22" barrel (Cyl. bore) with rifle sights $109.95
Price: With 3" chamber, 30" (Mod., Full) barrel $472.95

Smith & Wesson Model 1000 20 Gauge & 20 Magnum
Similar to 12 ga. model except slimmed down to weigh only 6½ lbs. Has self-cleaning gas system. Choice of four interchangeable barrels (26", Imp. Cyl. or Skeet, 28" Mod. or Full).
Price: $431.95
Price: Extra barrels $132.95
Price: With 3" chamber, (Mod., Full) $472.95

S&W 1000 Skeet

Smith & Wesson Model 1000S Super Skeet Shotgun
Similar to Model 1000 except has "recessed-type" Skeet choke with a compensator system to soften recoil and reduce muzzle jump. Stock has right-hand palm swell. Trigger is contoured (rounded) on right side; pull is 2½ to 3 lbs. Vent. rib has double sighting beads with a "Bright Point" flourescent red front bead. Fore-end cap weights (included) of 1 and 2 oz. can be used to change balance. Select-grade walnut with oil finish. Barrel length is 25", weight 8¼ lbs., over-all length 45.7". Stock measures 14"x1½"x2½" with .08" cast-off at butt, .16" at toe.
Price: $675.00
Price: Super Skeet interchangeable barrel $220.00

Tradewinds H-170

TRADEWINDS H-170 AUTO SHOTGUN
Gauge: 12 only, 2¾" chamber.
Action: Recoil-operated automatic.
Barrel: 26", 28" (Mod.) and 28" (Full), chrome lined.
Weight: 7 lbs.
Stock: Select European walnut stock, p.g. and fore-end hand checkered.
Features: Light alloy receiver, 5-shot tubular magazine, ventilated rib. Imported by Tradewinds.
Price: $395.00

Weatherby Centurion

WEATHERBY CENTURION AUTO
Gauge: 12 only, 2¾" chamber.
Action: Gas operated autoloader with "Floating Piston."
Barrel: 26" (Mod., Imp. Cyl, Skeet), 28" (Full, Mod.), 30" (Full, Full Trap, Full 3" Mag.), Vent. Rib.
Weight: About 7½ lbs. **Length:** 48¼ (28").
Stock: Walnut, hand checkered p.g. and fore-end, rubber recoil pad with white line spacer.
Features: Cross bolt safety, fluted bolt, gold plated trigger. Imported by Weatherby.
Price: Field or Skeet grade . .$419.95 Trap grade $449.95
Price: Extra interchangeable barrels, from $164.95

Western Field 650

WESTERN FIELD AUTOLOADING SHOTGUN MODEL 650
Gauge: 12 only.
Barrel: 28" (Full, Mod., Imp. Cyl. choke tubes).
Weight: About 7¾ lbs.
Stock: Walnut finished hardwood.
Sights: Metal bead front.
Features: Interchangeable barrel and Accu-Choke tubes; vent. rib; top safety. From Montgomery Ward.
Price: Ward's catalog #10650 ....$249.99

CAUTION: PRICES CHANGE. CHECK AT GUNSHOP.

SHOTGUNS—AUTOLOADING

Super-X Model 1

WINCHESTER SUPER-X MODEL 1 XTR AUTO TRAP & SKEET
Gauge: 12, 5-shot.
Barrel: 26″ (Skeet), 30″ (Full).
Length: 46¼″ over-all (26″ bbl.) **Weight:** About 8½ lbs.
Stock: American walnut with cut-checkered p.g. and fore-end, 14½″x1½″x2″ (Skeet).
Sights: Metal bead front.
Features: Receiver and all metal parts made of machined steel. Straight-line, 3-piece bolt, short-stroke gas system, all steel trigger assembly, steel shell carrier. Trap has 30″ bbl., vent. rib (Full) and regular or Monte Carlo stock. Engraved receiver,
ead front sight, black rubber recoil pad with withe space.

Consult our Directory pages for the location of firms mentioned.

Price: Trap, regular stock $654.00
Extra Barrels:
Price: Field, plain, 26″, 28″, 30″ (Full, Mod., Imp. Cyl.) $121.95
Price: Field, vent. rib, 26″, 28″, 30″ (Full, Mod., Imp. Cyl.) $149.95
Price: Trap or Skeet, 26″, 30″, (Full, Skeet) $163.50
Price: Trap, Monte Carlo stock $669.00
Price: Skeet gun $659.00

Winchester 1500

WINCHESTER 1500 XTR AUTO SHOTGUN
Gauge: 12 and 20, 2¾″ chamber.
Barrel: 26″ (Imp. Cyl.), 28″ (Mod.), 28″ (Full, 20 ga. only), 30″ (Full, 12 ga. only). Plain or vent rib, with or without Winchoke tubes.
Weight: 6½ to 7¼ lbs. **Length:** 46⅝″ to 50⅝″ over-all.
Stock: American walnut, cut-checkered p.g. and fore-end. Field, vent. rib dimensions are 14″x1½″x2½″.
Sights: Metal bead front.
Features: New Winchester XTR fit and finish. Gas-operated auto; self-adjusting system; front locking, rotating bolt. Interchangeable barrels in 3 standard lengths and chokes, or Winchoke system. Engine turned bolt, nickel plated carrier, cross-bolt safety. Introduced 1978.

Price: Vent. rib, 12 or 20 ....$396.00
Price: Plain barrel with Winchoke $381.00
Price: Vent. rib barrel with Winchoke $415.00
Price: Extra barrel, field $98.95
Price: As above, with Winchoke $113.95
Price: Extra barrel, vent. rib $126.95
Price: As above, with Winchoke $141.95

SHOTGUNS—SLIDE ACTION

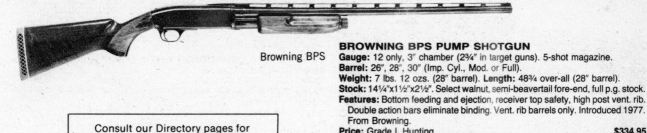

Browning BPS

Consult our Directory pages for the location of firms mentioned.

BROWNING BPS PUMP SHOTGUN
Gauge: 12 only, 3″ chamber (2¾″ in target guns). 5-shot magazine.
Barrel: 26″, 28″, 30″ (Imp. Cyl., Mod. or Full).
Weight: 7 lbs. 12 ozs. (28″ barrel). **Length:** 48¾ over-all (28″ barrel).
Stock: 14¼″x1½″x2½″. Select walnut, semi-beavertail fore-end, full p.g. stock.
Features: Bottom feeding and ejection, receiver top safety, high post vent. rib. Double action bars eliminate binding. Vent. rib barrels only. Introduced 1977. From Browning.
Price: Grade I, Hunting $334.95
Price: Grade I, Trap $349.95
Price: Extra Trap barrel ...$118.50   Extra Hunting barrel $112.50
Price: Buck Special (no accessories) $354.95
Price: Buck Special with accessories $374.95

Fox FP-1

FOX FP-1 PUMP SHOTGUN
Gauge: 12 only, 2¾″ and 3″.
Barrel: 28″ (Mod.), 30″ (Full); vent. rib.
Weight: 7¼ lbs. **Length:** 47¾″ over-all (28″ bbl.).
Stock: Walnut, checkered p.g. and fore-end; (14″x1½″x2½″).
Sights: Metal bead front.
Features: Dual action bars for smooth functioning; handy action release and cross-bolt safety. Rosewood p.g. cap with inlay. From Savage Arms. Introduced 1981.
Price: $347.50

SHOTGUNS—SLIDE ACTION

ITHACA 37 BASIC FEATHERLITE
Gauge: 12 ga; 2¾″ chamber or 3″.
Barrel: 26″ (Imp. Cyl.), 28″ (Mod.) or 30″ (Full).
Weight: 6¾ lbs.
Stock: Walnut, uncheckered and finished with tung oil.
Features: All metal surfaces vapor blasted to a non-glare matte finish. Fore-end is the traditional "Ring tail" style. Plain or vent Rib. Introduced 1980.
Price: Plain barrel $283.00
Price: Vent Rib $327.00
Price: Magnum, Full choke $350.00

ITHACA MODEL 37 FEATHERLIGHT
Gauge: 12, 20 (5-shot; 3-shot plug furnished).
Action: Slide; takedown; bottom ejection.
Barrel: 26″, 28″, 30″ in 12 ga. 26″ or 28″ in 20 ga. (Full, Mod. or Imp. Cyl.).
Stock: 14″x1⅝″x2⅝″. Checkered walnut capped p.g. stock and fore-end.
Weight: 12 ga. 6½ lbs., 20 ga. 5¾ lbs.
Features: Ithaca Raybar front sight: decorated receiver, crossbolt safety; action release for removing shells.
Price: Standard $299.00
Price: Standard Vent Rib $345.00

Ithaca Model 37 De Luxe Featherlight
Same as Model 37 except: checked stock with p.g. cap; beavertail fore-end; recoil pad. Wgt. 12 ga. 6¾ lbs.
Price: With vent. rib $357.00

Ithaca 37 Deer

Ithaca Model 37 Deerslayer
Same as Model 37 except: 26″ or 20″ bbl. designed for rifled slugs; sporting rear sight, Raybar front sight: rear sight ramp grooved for Redfield long eye relief scope mount. 12, or 20 gauge. With checkered stock, beavertail fore-end and recoil pad.
Price: $335.00
Price: As above with special select walnut stock $378.00

Ithaca Model 37 Ultra-Featherlight
Weighs five pounds. Same as standard Model 37 except in 20 ga. only, comes only with 25″ vent. rib barrel choked Full, Mod. or Imp. Cyl. Has recoil pad, gold plated trigger, Sid Bell-designed grip cap. Also available as Ultra-Deerslayer with 20″ barrel.
Price: $378.00

Ithaca Model 37 Magnum
Same as standard Model 37 except chambered for 3″ shells with resulting longer receiver. Stock dimensions are 14″x1⅞″x1½″. Grip cap has a Sid Bell-designed flying mallard on it. Has a recoil pad, vent. rib barrel with Raybar front sight. Available in 12 or 20 ga. with 30″ (Full) or 28″ (Mod.) barrel. Weight about 7¼ lbs. Introduced 1978.
Price: $378.00

Ithaca Model 37 Supreme
Same as Model 37 except: hand checkered beavertail fore-end and p.g. stock, Ithaca recoil pad and vent. rib $525.00
37 Supreme also with Skeet (14″x1½″x2¼″) or Trap (14½″x1½″x1⅞″) stocks at no extra charge.
Other options available at extra charge.

Marlin 120

MARLIN 120 MAGNUM PUMP GUN
Gauge: 12 ga. (2¾″ or 3″ chamber) 5-shot; 3-shot plug furnished.
Action: Hammerless, side ejecting, slide action.
Barrel: 20″ slug, 26″ (Imp. Cyl.), 28″ (Mod.), 30″ (Full), with vent. rib or 38″ MXR plain.
Length: 50½″ over-all (30″ bbl.). **Weight:** About 8¼ lbs.
Stock: 14″x1½″x2⅜″. Checkered walnut, capped p.g., semi-beavertail checkered fore-end. Mar-Shield⁺ finish.
Features: Interchangeable bbls., slide lock release; large button cross-bolt safety.
Price: $297.95
Price: Extra barrels, about $91.95

Glenfield 778

MARLIN GLENFIELD 778 PUMP GUN
Gauge: 12 (2¾″ or 3″ chamber). 5-shot, 3-shot plug furnished.
Barrel: 20″ slug (with sights), 26″ (Imp. Cyl.), 28″ (Mod.), 30″ (Full), all with or without rib; 38″ MXR (Full), no rib.
Weight: 7¾ lbs. **Length:** 48½″ over-all.
Stock: Walnut-finished hardwood. Semi-beavertail fore-end, vent. recoil pad. Checkered p.g.
Features: Machined steel receiver, double action bars, engine-turned bolt, shell carrier and bolt slide. Interchangeable barrel. Introduced 1978.
Price: Plain barrel $216.95
Price: Vent. rib barrel $245.95

Consult our Directory pages for
the location of firms mentioned.

CAUTION: PRICES CHANGE. CHECK AT GUNSHOP.

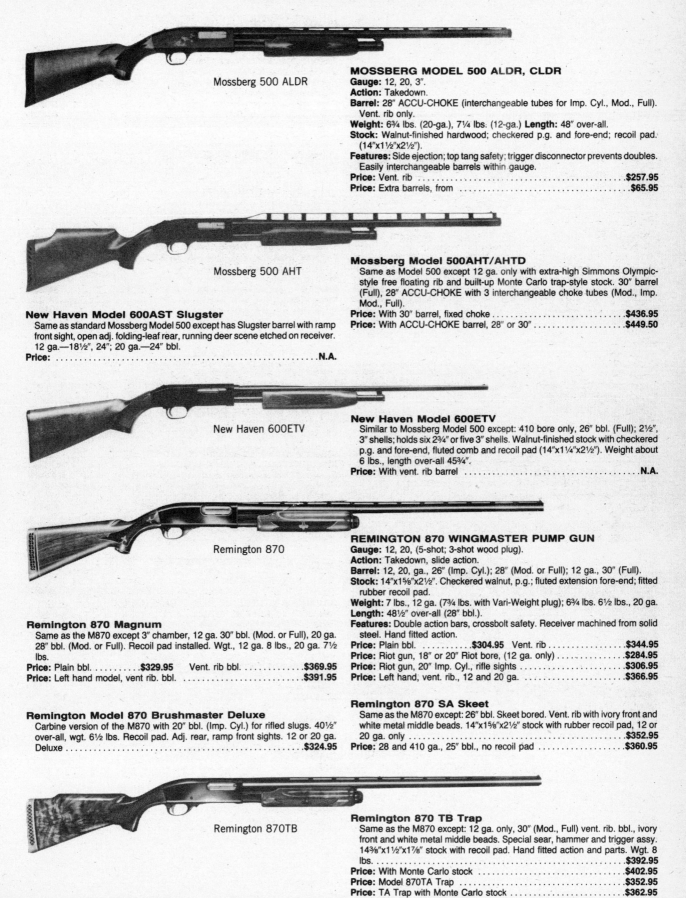

Mossberg 500 ALDR

MOSSBERG MODEL 500 ALDR, CLDR
Gauge: 12, 20, 3″.
Action: Takedown.
Barrel: 28″ ACCU-CHOKE (interchangeable tubes for Imp. Cyl., Mod., Full). Vent. rib only.
Weight: 6¾ lbs. (20-ga.), 7¼ lbs. (12-ga.) **Length:** 48″ over-all.
Stock: Walnut-finished hardwood; checkered p.g. and fore-end; recoil pad. (14″x1½″x2½″).
Features: Side ejection; top tang safety; trigger disconnector prevents doubles. Easily interchangeable barrels within gauge.
Price: Vent. rib $257.95
Price: Extra barrels, from $65.95

Mossberg 500 AHT

Mossberg Model 500AHT/AHTD
Same as Model 500 except 12 ga. only with extra-high Simmons Olympic-style free floating rib and built-up Monte Carlo trap-style stock. 30″ barrel (Full). 28″ ACCU-CHOKE with 3 interchangeable choke tubes (Mod., Imp. Mod., Full).
Price: With 30″ barrel, fixed choke $436.95
Price: With ACCU-CHOKE barrel, 28″ or 30″ $449.50

New Haven Model 600AST Slugster
Same as standard Mossberg Model 500 except has Slugster barrel with ramp front sight, open adj. folding-leaf rear, running deer scene etched on receiver. 12 ga.—18½″, 24″; 20 ga.—24″ bbl.
Price: ....N.A.

New Haven 600ETV

New Haven Model 600ETV
Similar to Mossberg Model 500 except: 410 bore only, 26″ bbl. (Full); 2½″, 3″ shells; holds six 2¾″ or five 3″ shells. Walnut-finished stock with checkered p.g. and fore-end, fluted comb and recoil pad (14″x1¼″x2½″). Weight about 6 lbs., length over-all 45¾″.
Price: With vent. rib barrel ......................................N.A.

Remington 870

REMINGTON 870 WINGMASTER PUMP GUN
Gauge: 12, 20, (5-shot; 3-shot wood plug).
Action: Takedown, slide action.
Barrel: 12, 20, ga., 26″ (Imp. Cyl.); 28″ (Mod. or Full); 12 ga., 30″ (Full).
Stock: 14″x1⅝″x2½″. Checkered walnut, p.g.; fluted extension fore-end; fitted rubber recoil pad.
Weight: 7 lbs., 12 ga. (7¾ lbs. with Vari-Weight plug); 6¾ lbs. 6½ lbs., 20 ga.
Length: 48½″ over-all (28″ bbl.).
Features: Double action bars, crossbolt safety. Receiver machined from solid steel. Hand fitted action.
Price: Plain bbl. ....$304.95 Vent. rib $344.95
Price: Riot gun, 18″ or 20″ Riot bore, (12 ga. only) $284.95
Price: Riot gun, 20″ Imp. Cyl., rifle sights $306.95
Price: Left hand, vent. rib., 12 and 20 ga. $366.95

Remington 870 Magnum
Same as the M870 except 3″ chamber, 12 ga. 30″ bbl. (Mod. or Full), 20 ga. 28″ bbl. (Mod. or Full). Recoil pad installed. Wgt., 12 ga. 8 lbs., 20 ga. 7½ lbs.
Price: Plain bbl. ....$329.95 Vent. rib bbl. $369.95
Price: Left hand model, vent rib. bbl. $391.95

Remington 870 SA Skeet
Same as the M870 except: 26″ bbl. Skeet bored. Vent. rib with ivory front and white metal middle beads. 14″x1⅝″x2½″ stock with rubber recoil pad, 12 or 20 ga. only $352.95
Price: 28 and 410 ga., 25″ bbl., no recoil pad $360.95

Remington Model 870 Brushmaster Deluxe
Carbine version of the M870 with 20″ bbl. (Imp. Cyl.) for rifled slugs. 40½″ over-all, wgt. 6½ lbs. Recoil pad. Adj. rear, ramp front sights. 12 or 20 ga.
Deluxe $324.95

Remington 870TB

Remington 870 TB Trap
Same as the M870 except: 12 ga. only, 30″ (Mod., Full) vent. rib. bbl., ivory front and white metal middle beads. Special sear, hammer and trigger assy. 14⅜″x1½″x1⅞″ stock with recoil pad. Hand fitted action and parts. Wgt. 8 lbs. $392.95
Price: With Monte Carlo stock $402.95
Price: Model 870TA Trap $352.95
Price: TA Trap with Monte Carlo stock $362.95

SHOTGUNS—SLIDE ACTION

Remington 870D Tournament
Same as 870 except: better walnut, hand checkering, Engraved receiver & bbl. Vent.-rib. Stock dimensions to order $1,650.00

Remington 870F Premier
Same as M870, except select walnut, better engraving $3,300.00
Price: With gold inlay $4,950.00

Remington 870 Small Gauges
Exact copies of the large ga. Model 870, except that guns are offered in 28 and 410 ga. 25″ barrel (Full, Mod., Imp. Cyl.). D and F grade prices same as large ga. M870 prices.
Price: With vent. rib barrel $354.95
Price: Lightweight Magnum, 20 ga. plain bbl. (5¾ lbs.) $329.95
Price: Lightweight Magnum, 20 ga., vent. rib bbl. $369.95

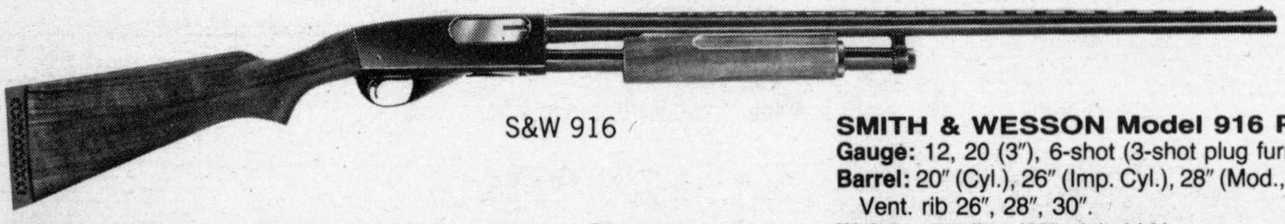

Remington 870 Extra Barrels
Plain $79.95. Vent. rib $119.95. Vent. rib Skeet $129.95. Vent. rib Trap $129.95. 34″ Trap $144.95. With rifle sights $97.95. Available in the same gauges and chokes as shown on guns. **Prices are approximate.**

S&W 916

Smith & Wesson Model 916T Takedown Shotgun
Same as standard Model 916 except has interchangeable barrel capability. Available in 12 or 20 ga. 26″ (Imp. Cyl.), 28″ (Mod., Full) 30″ (Full). Extra barrels available in 20″ (Cyl.) with rifle sights, 26″ (Imp. Cyl.), 28″ (Full or Mod.), 30″ (Full), plain or vent. rib.
Price: 916T, plain barrel $197.95
Price: 916T, vent. rib barrel, recoil pad $234.95
Price: Extra barrel, plain $54.00
Price: Extra barrel, rifle sights $67.50
Price: Extra barrel, vent. rib $100.00

SMITH & WESSON Model 916 Pump Gun
Gauge: 12, 20 (3″), 6-shot (3-shot plug furnished).
Barrel: 20″ (Cyl.), 26″ (Imp. Cyl.), 28″ (Mod., Full or adj. choke) 30″ (Full), plain. Vent. rib 26″, 28″, 30″.
Weight: 7¼ lbs. (28″ plain bbl.).
Stock: 14″x2½″x1⅝″, American walnut, fluted comb, finger-grooved fore-end.
Features: Vent. rib, vent. recoil pad, adj. choke available as options. Satin finish steel receiver with non-glare top.
Price: Plain bbl., no recoil pad $190.95
Price: With vent. rib and recoil pad (illus.) $227.95
Price: With 20″ slug barrel RS $218.95
Price: As above with recoil pad $226.50

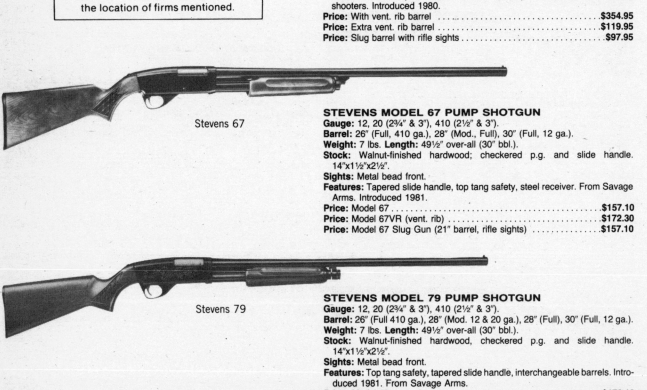

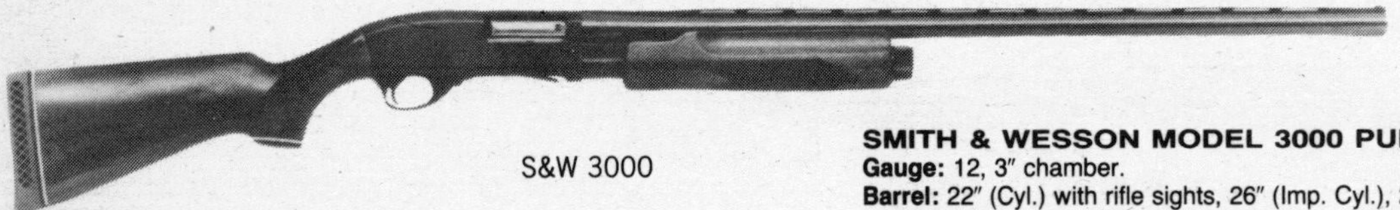

S&W 3000

Consult our Directory pages for the location of firms mentioned.

SMITH & WESSON MODEL 3000 PUMP
Gauge: 12, 3″ chamber.
Barrel: 22″ (Cyl.) with rifle sights, 26″ (Imp. Cyl.), 28″ (Mod.), 30″ (Full), vent. rib or plain.
Weight: About 7½ lbs. **Length:** 48½″ over-all (28″ bbl.).
Stock: 14″x1⅜″x2¼″. American walnut
Features: Dual action bars for smooth functioning. Rubber recoil pad, steel receiver, chrome plated bolt. Cross-bolt safety reversible for left-handed shooters. Introduced 1980.
Price: With vent. rib barrel $354.95
Price: Extra vent. rib barrel $119.95
Price: Slug barrel with rifle sights $97.95

Stevens 67

STEVENS MODEL 67 PUMP SHOTGUN
Gauge: 12, 20 (2¾″ & 3″), 410 (2½″ & 3″).
Barrel: 26″ (Full, 410 ga.), 28″ (Mod., Full), 30″ (Full, 12 ga.).
Weight: 7 lbs. **Length:** 49½″ over-all (30″ bbl.).
Stock: Walnut-finished hardwood; checkered p.g. and slide handle. 14″x1½″x2½″.
Sights: Metal bead front.
Features: Tapered slide handle, top tang safety, steel receiver. From Savage Arms. Introduced 1981.
Price: Model 67 . . . . $157.10
Price: Model 67VR (vent. rib) $172.30
Price: Model 67 Slug Gun (21″ barrel, rifle sights) $157.10

Stevens 79

STEVENS MODEL 79 PUMP SHOTGUN
Gauge: 12, 20 (2¾″ & 3″), 410 (2½″ & 3″).
Barrel: 26″ (Full 410 ga.), 28″ (Mod. 12 & 20 ga.), 28″ (Full), 30″ (Full, 12 ga.).
Weight: 7 lbs. **Length:** 49½″ over-all (30″ bbl.).
Stock: Walnut-finished hardwood, checkered p.g. and slide handle. 14″x1½″x2½″.
Sights: Metal bead front.
Features: Top tang safety, tapered slide handle, interchangeable barrels. Introduced 1981. From Savage Arms.
Price: Model 79 . . . . $170.10
Price: Model 79-VR (vent. rib) $187.90

CAUTION: PRICES CHANGE. CHECK AT GUNSHOP.

SHOTGUNS—SLIDE ACTION

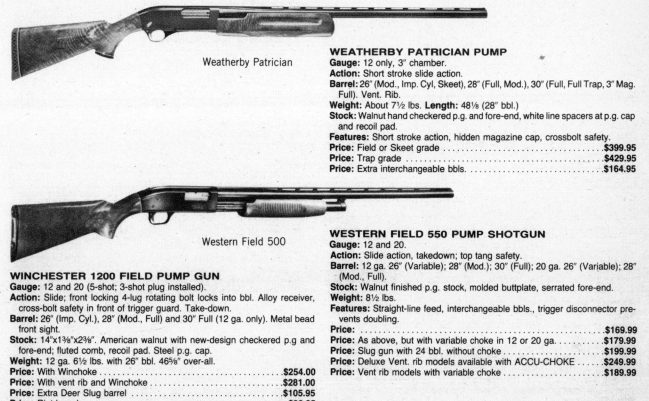

Weatherby Patrician

WEATHERBY PATRICIAN PUMP
Gauge: 12 only, 3″ chamber.
Action: Short stroke slide action.
Barrel: 26″ (Mod., Imp. Cyl, Skeet), 28″ (Full, Mod.), 30″ (Full, Full Trap, 3″ Mag. Full). Vent. Rib.
Weight: About 7½ lbs. **Length:** 48⅛ (28″ bbl.)
Stock: Walnut hand checkered p.g. and fore-end, white line spacers at p.g. cap and recoil pad.
Features: Short stroke action, hidden magazine cap, crossbolt safety.
Price: Field or Skeet grade $399.95
Price: Trap grade $429.95
Price: Extra interchangeable bbls. $164.95

Western Field 500

WINCHESTER 1200 FIELD PUMP GUN
Gauge: 12 and 20 (5-shot; 3-shot plug installed).
Action: Slide; front locking 4-lug rotating bolt locks into bbl. Alloy receiver, cross-bolt safety in front of trigger guard. Take-down.
Barrel: 26″ (Imp. Cyl.), 28″ (Mod., Full) and 30″ Full (12 ga. only). Metal bead front sight.
Stock: 14″x1⅜″x2⅜″. American walnut with new-design checkered p.g and fore-end; fluted comb, recoil pad. Steel p.g. cap.
Weight: 12 ga. 6½ lbs. with 26″ bbl. 46⅝″ over-all.
Price: With Winchoke $254.00
Price: With vent rib and Winchoke $281.00
Price: Extra Deer Slug barrel $105.95
Price: Riot barrel $90.95

WESTERN FIELD 550 PUMP SHOTGUN
Gauge: 12 and 20.
Action: Slide action, takedown; top tang safety.
Barrel: 12 ga. 26″ (Variable); 28″ (Mod.); 30″ (Full); 20 ga. 26″ (Variable); 28″ (Mod., Full).
Stock: Walnut finished p.g. stock, molded buttplate, serrated fore-end.
Weight: 8½ lbs.
Features: Straight-line feed, interchangeable bbls., trigger disconnector prevents doubling.
Price: $169.99
Price: As above, but with variable choke in 12 or 20 ga. $179.99
Price: Slug gun with 24 bbl. without choke $199.99
Price: Deluxe Vent. rib models available with ACCU-CHOKE $249.99
Price: Vent rib models with variable choke $189.99

Winchester 1300

WINCHESTER 1300 XTR PUMP GUN
Gauge: 12 and 20, 3″ chamber, 5-shot.
Barrel: 26″ (Imp. Cyl.), 28″ (Mod.), 28″ (Full, 20-ga. only), 30″ (Full, 12-ga. only). Plain or vent. rib, with or without Winchoke.
Weight: 6½ to 7¼ lbs. **Length:** 46⅝″ to 50⅝″ over-all.
Stock: American walnut, cut-checkered p.g. and fore-end. Field, vent. rib dimensions are 14″x1½″x2½″.
Sights: Metal bead front.
Features: New Winchester XTR fit and finish. Has twin action bars, cross-bolt safety, Alloy receiver and trigger guard. Front-locking, rotating bolt. Nickel plated carrier, engine-turned bolt. Introduced 1978.

Price: Plain barrel $289.00
Price: Vent. rib $323.00
Price: Plain barrel with Winchoke $307.00
Price: Vent. rib with Winchoke $341.00
Price: Extra field barrel $94.95
Price: As above with Winchoke $109.95
Price: Extra field barrel with vent. rib $122.95
Price: As above with Winchoke . . . . $137.95.
Price: Model 1300 Deer Gun $323.00
Price: Waterfowl Winchoke $341.00
Price: 1300 Deer Slug barrel $107.95
Winchester 1200 Extra Barrels: Field w/o sights, 12, 20 ga. $90.95; Field with vent. rib, 12, 20 ga. $116.95
Price: Extra plain Field bbl., Winchoke $105.95
Price: Extra vent rib bbl., Winchoke $131.95

SHOTGUNS—OVER-UNDER

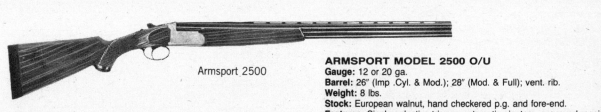

Armsport 2500

ARMSPORT MODEL 2500 O/U
Gauge: 12 or 20 ga.
Barrel: 26″ (Imp .Cyl. & Mod.); 28″ (Mod. & Full); vent. rib.
Weight: 8 lbs.
Stock: European walnut, hand checkered p.g. and fore-end.
Features: Single selective trigger, automatic ejectors, engraved receiver. Imported by Armsport.
Price: $695.00
Price: With extractors only $595.00

ASTRA MODEL 750 O/U SHOT GUN
Gauge: 12 ga., (2¾").
Barrel: 28" (Mod. & Full or Skeet & Skeet), 30" Trap (Mod. & Full)
Weight: 6½ lbs.
Stock: European walnut, hand-checkered p.g. and fore-end.
Features: Single selective trigger, scroll-engraved receiver, selective auto ejectors, vent. rib. Introduced 1980. From L. Joseph Rahn, Inc.
Price: $639.00
Price: With extractors only $562.65
Price: Trap or Skeet (M.C. stock and recoil pad.) $735.72

BAIKAL MC-5-105 O/U
Gauge: 20 ga., 2¾" chambers.
Barrel: 26" (Imp. Cyl. & Mod., Skeet & Skeet).
Weight: 5¾ lbs.
Stock: Fancy hand checkered walnut. Choice of p.g. or straight stock, with or without cheekpiece. Fore-end permanently attached to barrels.
Features: Fully engraved receiver. Double triggers, extractors. Chrome barrels, chambers and internal parts. Hand-fitted solid rib. Hammer interceptors. Comes with case. Imported by Baikal International.
Price: MC-5-105 ....$1,295.00
Price: MC-6-12, as above except in 12 gauge $1,900.00

Astra Model 650 O/U Shotgun
Same as Model 750 except has double triggers.
Price: With extractors $452.04
Price: With ejectors $566.84

BAIKAL MC-7 O/U
Gauge: 12 or 20 ga., 2¾" chambers.
Barrel: 12 ga. 28" (Mod. & Full), 20 ga. 26" (Imp. Cyl. & Mod.).
Weight: 7 lbs. (12 ga.), 6¾ lbs. (20 ga.)
Stock: Fancy walnut. Hand checkered, with or without p.g. and cheekpiece. Beavertail fore-end.
Features: Fully chiseled and engraved receiver. Chrome barrels, chambers and internal parts. Double trigger, selective ejectors. Solid raised rib. Single selective trigger available. Comes with case. Imported by Baikal International.
Price: $2,730.00

BAIKAL MC-8-0 O/U
Gauge: 12 ga., 2¾" chambers.
Barrel: 26" special parabolic Skeet, 28" (Mod. & Full). Available in 2 bbl. sets.
Weight: 7¾ lbs.
Stock: Fancy walnut. Beavertail fore-end permanently attached to barrels. Hand checkered p.g. and fore-end. Monte Carlo.
Features: Handmade competition shotgun. Blued, hand-engraved receiver. Single trigger, extractors. Chrome barrels, chambers and internal parts. Hand fitted vent. rib. Comes with case. Imported by Baikal International.
Price: MC-8-0 Skeet $2,450.00
Price: MC-8-01 Trap $2,450.00

Baikal MC-8-0

Baikal TOZ-34E

BAIKAL TOZ-34E SOUVENIR O/U
Gauge: 12 or 28 ga., 2¾".
Barrel: 12 ga.—28" (Mod. & Full), 28 ga.—26" (Mod. & Full).
Weight: 12 ga.—7¾ lbs.; 28 ga.—6¾ lbs.
Stock: Hand checkered fancy European walnut. Permanently attached fore-end. Rubber recoil pad.
Features: Double triggers, chrome lined barrels and chambers, cocking indicators. Hand engraved receiver. Hammer interceptors. Extractors only. Silvered, hand-engraved receiver. Imported by Baikel International.
Price: $675.00

BAIKAL IJ-27E1C O/U
Gauge: 12 ga., 2¾" chambers, 20 ga., 3" chambers.
Barrel: 26" (Skeet & Skeet), 28" (Mod. & Full).
Weight: 7¾ lbs.
Stock: Hand checkered walnut, rubber recoil pad. Ventilated fore-end. White spacers at p.g. and recoil pad.
Features: Single selective trigger. Chrome barrels, chambers and internal parts. Hand fitted vent. rib. Hand engraved receiver. Selective extractors/ejectors. Imported by Baikal International.
Price: $429.95
Price: With silver receiver inlays $585.95
Price: Skeet or Trap versions $429.95
Price: IJ-27 Super $895.95

> Consult our Directory pages for the location of firms mentioned.

BAIKAL MC-109 O/U
Gauge: 12 ga., 2¾" chambers.
Barrel: 28" (Mod. & Full).
Weight: 7¼ lbs.
Stock: Fancy walnut. Choice of p.g. or straight stock, with or without cheekpiece. Beavertail fore-end. Hand carved and checkered to customer's specs.
Features: Handmade sidelock shotgun. Removable sideplates. Chrome barrels, chambers and internal parts. Single selective trigger, selective ejectors, cocking indicators, hammer interceptors. Hand chiseled scenes on receiver to customer specs. Inlays to customer specs. Comes with case. Imported by Baikal International.
Price: Special order only $5,035.00

BERETTA MODEL 1000 O-U SHOTGUN
Gauge: 12 only.
Barrels: 30".
Weight: About 7 lbs. **Length:** 46½" over-all.
Stock: Walnut; English-style with checkpiece.
Features: Special limited production replica of an early Beretta over-under. Silvered, engraved lockplates, trigger guard, hammers, barrel bands. Ramrod fits on right side of blued barrels. Introduced 1981. From Beretta U.S.A. Corp.
Price: $840.00

CAUTION: PRICES CHANGE. CHECK AT GUNSHOP.

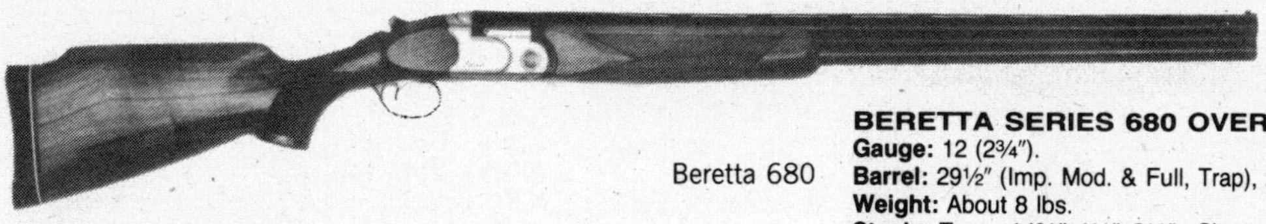

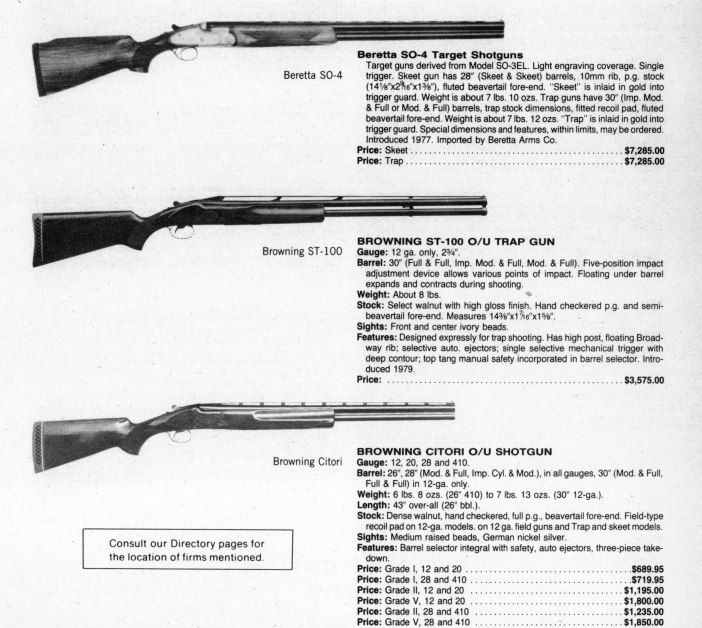

Beretta 680

BERETTA SO-3 O/U SHOTGUN

Gauge: 12 ga. (2¾" chambers).
Action: Back-action sidelock.
Barrel: 26", 27", 28", 29" or 30", chokes to customer specs.
Stock: Standard measurements—14⅛"x1 7/16"x2⅜". Straight "English" or p.g.-style. Hand checkered European walnut.
Features: SO-3—"English scroll" floral engraving on action body, sideplates and trigger guard. Stocked in select walnut. SO-3EL—as above, with full engraving coverage. Hand-detachable sideplates. SO-3EELL—as above with deluxe finish and finest full coverage engraving. Internal parts gold plated. Top lever is pierced and carved in relief with gold inlaid crown. Introduced 1977. Imported by Beretta Arms Co.
Price: SO-3 .... **$6,245.00**
Price: SO-3EL **$7,440.00**
Price: SO-3EELL **$10,000.00**

BERETTA SERIES 680 OVER-UNDER

Gauge: 12 (2¾").
Barrel: 29½" (Imp. Mod. & Full, Trap), 28" (Skeet & Skeet).
Weight: About 8 lbs.
Stock: Trap—14⅜"x1¼"x2⅛"; Skeet—14⅜"x1⅜"x2 7/16". European walnut with hand checkering.
Sights: Luminous front sight and center bead.
Features: Trap Monte Carlo stock has deluxe trap recoil pad, Skeet has smooth pad. From Beretta Arms Co.
Price: Skeet or Trap gun **$1,580.00**
Price: As above with fitted case **$1,580.00**
Price: M686 Field gun **$980.00**
Price: M685 Field gun **$820.00**
Price: M687EL, Field **$2,212.00**
Price: M680 Single bbl. Trap, 32" or 34" **$1,580.00**
Price: M680 Combo Trap O/U, with single bbl. **$2,100.00**

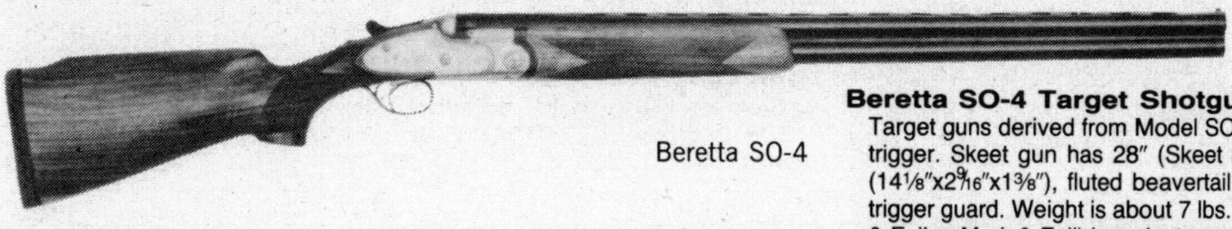

Beretta SO-4

Beretta SO-4 Target Shotguns

Target guns derived from Model SO-3EL. Light engraving coverage. Single trigger. Skeet gun has 28" (Skeet & Skeet) barrels, 10mm rib, p.g. stock (14⅛"x2 3/16"x1⅜"), fluted beavertail fore-end. "Skeet" is inlaid in gold into trigger guard. Weight is about 7 lbs. 10 ozs. Trap guns have 30" (Imp. Mod. & Full or Mod. & Full) barrels, trap stock dimensions, fitted recoil pad, fluted beavertail fore-end. Weight is about 7 lbs. 12 ozs. "Trap" is inlaid in gold into trigger guard. Special dimensions and features, within limits, may be ordered. Introduced 1977. Imported by Beretta Arms Co.
Price: Skeet **$7,285.00**
Price: Trap **$7,285.00**

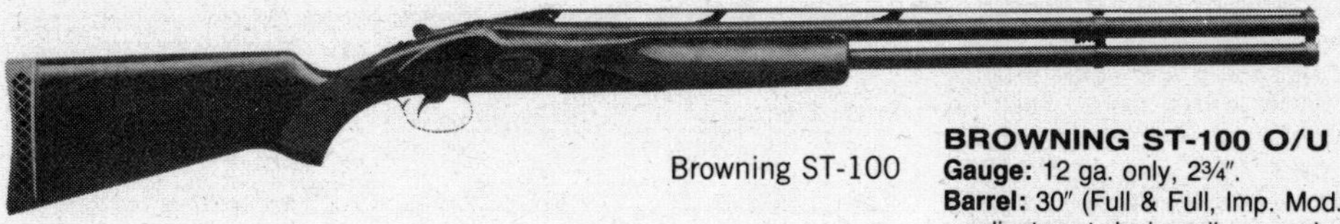

Browning ST-100

BROWNING ST-100 O/U TRAP GUN

Gauge: 12 ga. only, 2¾".
Barrel: 30" (Full & Full, Imp. Mod. & Full, Mod. & Full). Five-position impact adjustment device allows various points of impact. Floating under barrel expands and contracts during shooting.
Weight: About 8 lbs.
Stock: Select walnut with high gloss finish. Hand checkered p.g. and semi-beavertail fore-end. Measures 14⅜"x1 7/16"x1⅝".
Sights: Front and center ivory beads.
Features: Designed expressly for trap shooting. Has high post, floating Broadway rib; selective auto. ejectors; single selective mechanical trigger with deep contour; top tang manual safety incorporated in barrel selector. Introduced 1979.
Price: **$3,575.00**

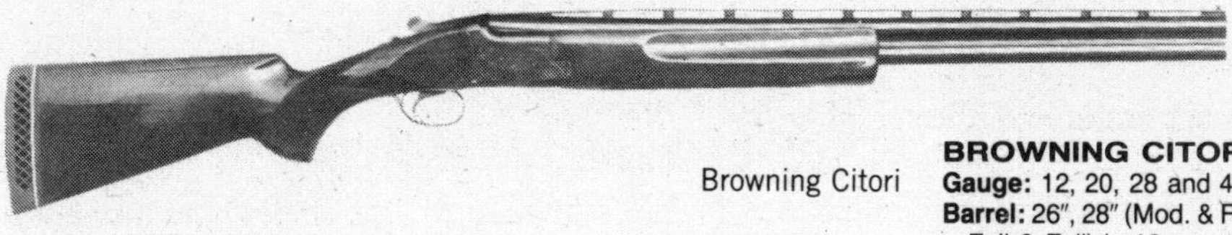

Browning Citori

BROWNING CITORI O/U SHOTGUN

Gauge: 12, 20, 28 and 410.
Barrel: 26", 28" (Mod. & Full, Imp. Cyl. & Mod.), in all gauges, 30" (Mod. & Full, Full & Full) in 12-ga. only.
Weight: 6 lbs. 8 ozs. (26" 410) to 7 lbs. 13 ozs. (30" 12-ga.).
Length: 43" over-all (26" bbl.).
Stock: Dense walnut, hand checkered, full p.g., beavertail fore-end. Field-type recoil pad on 12-ga. models. on 12 ga. field guns and Trap and skeet models.
Sights: Medium raised beads, German nickel silver.
Features: Barrel selector integral with safety, auto ejectors, three-piece take-down.
Price: Grade I, 12 and 20 .... **$689.95**
Price: Grade I, 28 and 410 .... **$719.95**
Price: Grade II, 12 and 20 .... **$1,195.00**
Price: Grade V, 12 and 20 .... **$1,800.00**
Price: Grade II, 28 and 410 .... **$1,235.00**
Price: Grade V, 28 and 410 .... **$1,850.00**

Consult our Directory pages for the location of firms mentioned.

Browning Citori Sporter

Browning Citori O/U Sporter

Similar to standard Citori except; comes with 26″ (Mod. & Full, Imp. Cyl. & Mod.) only; straight grip stock with schnabel fore-end; satin oil finish.

Price: Grade I, 12 and 20 .... $689.95
Price: Grade I, 28 and 410 .... $719.95
Price: Grade II, 12 and 20 .... $1,195.00
Price: Grade V, 12 and 20 .... $1,800.00
Price: Grade II, 28 and 410 .... $1,235.00
Price: Grade V, 28 and 410 .... $1,850.00

BROWNING SUPERPOSED SUPER-LIGHT Presentation Series

Gauge: 12, & 20 2¾″ chamber.
Action: Boxlock, top lever, single selective trigger. Bbl. selector combined with manual tang safety.
Barrels: 26½″ (Mod. & Full, or Imp. Cyl. & Mod.)
Weight: 6⅜ lbs., average
Stock: Straight grip (14¼″ x 1⅝″ x 2½″) hand checkered (fore-end and grip) select walnut.
Features: The Presentation Series is available in four grades and covers the Superposed line. Basically this gives the buyer a wide choice of engraving styles and designs and mechanical options which would place the gun in a "custom" bracket. Options are too numerous to list here and the reader is urged to obtain a copy of the latest Browning catalog for the complete listing. Series introduced 1977.
Price: From $4,190.00

Browning Presentation Superposed Lightning Skeet

Same as Standard Superposed except: Special Skeet stock, fore-end; center and front ivory bead sights. Wgt. 6½-7¾ lbs.
Price: All gauges, from $4,200.00

Browning Limited Edition Waterfowl Superposed

Same specs as the Lightning Superposed. Available in 12 ga. only, 28″ (Mod. & Full). Limited to 500 guns, the edition number at each gun is inscribed in gold on the bottom of the receiver with "American Mallard" and it's scientific name. Sides of receiver have two gold inlayed Mallards, bottom has three. Receiver is completely engraved and grayed. Stock and fore-end are highly figured dark French walnut with 24 lpi checkering, hand-oiled finish, checkered butt. Comes with form fitted, velvet-lined, black walnut case. Introduced 1981.
Price: $7,000.00

Browning Presentation Superposed All-Gauge Skeet Set

Consists of four matched sets of barrels in 12, 20, 28 and 410 ga. Available in either 26½″ or 28″ length. Each bbl. set has a ¼″ wide vent. rib with two ivory sight beads. Grade 1 receiver is hand engraved and stock and fore-end are checkered. Weight 7 lbs., 10 oz. (26½″ bbls.), 7 lbs., 12 oz. (28″ bbls.).
Contact Browning for prices.

Browning Citori O/U Trap Models

Similar to standard Citori except: 12 gauge only; 30″, 32″ (Full & Full, Imp. Mod. & Full, Mod. & Full), 34″ single barrel in Combo Set (Full, Imp. Mod., Mod.); Monte Carlo cheekpiece (14⅜″x1⅜″x1⅜″x2″); fitted with trap-style recoil pad; conventional target rib and high post target rib.
Price: Grade I, (high post rib) $769.95
Price: Grade II (high post rib) $1,295.00
Price: Grade V (high post rib) $1,925.00
Price: Grade I Combo (32″ O/U & 34″ single bbl., high post ribs) incl. luggage case $1,295.00

Browning Citori O/U Skeet Models

Similar to standard Citori except: 26″, 28″ (Skeet & Skeet) only; stock dimensions of 14⅜″x1½″x2″, fitted with Skeet-style recoil pad; conventional target rib and high post target rib.
Price: Grade I, 12 & 20 (high post rib) $769.95
Price: Grade I, 28 & 410 (high post rib) $799.95
Price: Grade II, all gauges (high post rib) $1,295.00
Price: Grade V, all gauges (high post rib) $1,925.00

Browning Presentation Superposed Magnum 12

Browning Superposed 3″ chambers; 30″ (Full and Full or Full and Mod.) barrels, Stock, 14¼″x1⅝″x2½″ with factory fitted recoil pad. Weight 8 lbs.
Price: From $4,140.00

Browning Presentation Superposed Lightning Trap 12

Same as Browning Lightning Superposed except: semi-beavertail fore-end and ivory sights; stock, 14⅜″x1⁷⁄₁₆″x1⅝″. 7¾ lbs. 30″ (Full & Full, Full & Imp. Mod. or Full and Mod.)
Price: From $4,200.00

Superposed Presentation Broadway Trap 12

Same as Browning Lightning Superposed except: ⅝″ wide vent. rib; stock, 14⅜″x1⁷⁄₁₆″x1⅝″. 30″ or 32″ (Imp. Mod, Full; Mod., Full; Full, Full). 8 lbs. with 32″ bbls.
Price: From $4,300.00

Browning Presentation Superposed Lightning

7-7¼ lbs. in 12 ga. 6-6¼ lbs. in 20 ga.
Price: From $4,140.00

Browning Presentation Superposed Combinations

Standard and Lightning models are available with these factory fitted extra barrels: 12 and 20 ga., same gauge bbls.; 12 ga., 20 ga. bbls.; 20 ga., extra sets 28 and/or 410 gauge; 28 ga., extra 410 bbls. Extra barrels may be had in Lightning weights with Standard models and vice versa. Prices range from **$7,450.00** (12, 20 ga., one set extra bbls. same gauge) for the Presentation 1 Standard to about **$16,000.00** for the Presentation 4 grade in a 4-barrel matched set (12, 20, 28 and 410 gauges).

Contento

CONTENTO O/U SHOTGUNS

Gauge: 12 (2¾″) only.
Action: Boxlock, with Woodward side-lugs and double internal bolts for extra low profile.
Barrel: Field 26″, 28″; Skeet 28″; Pigeon 29½″; Trap 32″ Trap models have high post ribs with option of screw-in chokes in both O/U and single barrels. All have vent. side ribs.
Weight: 6.5 to 8.2 lbs.
Stock: Hand checkered European walnut with Monte Carlo. 14½″x1⁷⁄₁₆″. Recoil pad included for individual fitting.
Features: Single selective trigger, auto ejectors. Extra Lusso model has fancy walnut and extensive Florentine engraving. All models in three grades; Standard, Lusso, and Extra Lusso. Introduced 1975. From Ventura Imports.
Price: Grade I. .... $1,195.00 to Extra Lusso Trap $2,725.00

Consult our Directory pages for the location of firms mentioned.

CAUTION: PRICES CHANGE. CHECK AT GUNSHOP.

SHOTGUNS—OVER-UNDER

ERA Full Limit

ERA "THE FULL LIMIT" O/U SHOTGUN
Gauge: 12 or 20 ga., 2¾".
Barrel: 28" (Mod. & Full); vent. top and middle ribs.
Weight: 7¾ lbs.
Stock: Walnut-finished hardwood, hand checkered.
Features: Auto. safety; extractors; double triggers; engraved receiver. Imported from Brazil by F.I.E.
Price: $299.95

Franchi 2003

FRANCHI MODEL 2003 TRAP O/U
Gauge: 12 only (2¾" chambers).
Barrel: 30", 32" (Imp. Mod. & Full, Full & Full).
Weight: 8½ lbs.
Stock: 14½"x1⅞"x1½". Fancy French walnut; checkered p.g. and fore-end. Available in Monte Carlo or straight style; interchangeable. Different dimensions avail.
Features: "Ceiling-Swell" trap trigger with barrel selector; separated barrels; steel muzzle collar to maintain alignment; raised, vent. trap rib. Buttstock drilled and tapped for recoil reducer. Comes with hard luggage-type fitted case. From Stoeger Industries.
Price: $1,550.00

Franchi Model 2005/2 Trap Combo
Same as Model 2003/2004 except comes with two barrel sets—one single, one O/U in same lengths and chokes as specified for those models. Also comes with fitted case.
Price: $2,375.00

Franchi Model 2005/3 Trap Combo
Same as Model 2005/2—two barrel sets in 30" or 32" O/U and 32" or 34" single upper—except custom choking is offered.
Price: $3,125.00

Franchi 3000/2

Franchi 3000/2 Trap Undergun Combo
Same as the Model 2005/2 except comes with 30" or 32" O/U and 32" or 34" underbarrel and three interchangeable choke tubes—Full, Imp. Mod. and Mod. Also comes with fitted case.
Price: $3,295.00

H&R 1212

H&R MODEL 1212 "WATERFOWL" O/U
Gauge: 12 ga. only (3" chambers).
Barrel: 30" (Full & Mod.).
Weight: 7½ lbs. **Length:** 46¾" over-all.
Stock: 14⅜"x1½"x2", hand checkered walnut.
Sights: Gold bead front on vent. rib.
Features: Vent. rib; single selective trigger; engraved action; rubber recoil pad. Imported from Spain by Harrington & Richardson.
Price: $489.00

Harrington & Richarson Model 1212 "Field Gun" o/u
Same as "Waterfowl" except has 2¾" chambers, 28" barrel (Imp. Cyl. & Imp. Mod.), no recoil pad.
Price: $475.00

Heym 55/77

HEYM MODEL 55/77 O/U SHOTGUN
Gauge: 12, 16, 20 ga. (2¾" or 3").
Barrel: 28" (Full & Mod.) standard; other lengths and chokes to customer specs.
Weight: 6¾-7½ lbs.
Stock: European walnut, hand-checkered p.g. and fore-end.
Features: Boxlock or full sidelock action; Kersten double cross bolt, double under lugs; cocking indicators. Arabesque or hunting engraving. Options include interchangeable barrels, front trigger that functions as a single non-selective trigger, deluxe engraving and stock carving. Contact Heym for more data.
Price: Model 55F or 77F boxlock $3,329.00
Price: Model 55FSS or 77FSS sidelock $5,558.00
Price: Interchangeable o/u rifle barrels $2,719.00
Price: Interchangeable rifle-shotgun barrels $1,839.00

> Consult our Directory pages for the location of firms mentioned.

SHOTGUNS—OVER-UNDER

K.F.C. "FG" OVER-UNDER SHOTGUN
Gauge: 12 only (2¾").
Barrel: 26", 28" (Imp. Cyl. & Imp. Mod.); vent. rib.
Weight: About 6.8 lbs.
Stock: 14"x1½"x2⅜". High grade French walnut.
Sights: Sterling silver front bead.
Features: Selective single trigger, selective auto ejectors, non-automatic safety; chrome lined bores, chrome trigger. Introduced 1981. From La Paloma Marketing.
Price: $748.00

K.F.C. FG

K.F.C. OT-Trap-E1 Shotgun
Trap version of FG over-under. Has 30" (Imp. Mod. & Full) barrells, 13mm vent. rib, bone white middle and front beads, scroll-engraved, blued receiver, wide gold-colored trigger. Stock dimensions are 14"x1¼"x1¼"x2"; high grade French walnut; rubber recoil pad; oil finish. Weight is about 7.9 lbs. Introduced 1981. From La Paloma Marketing.
Price: $1,070.00

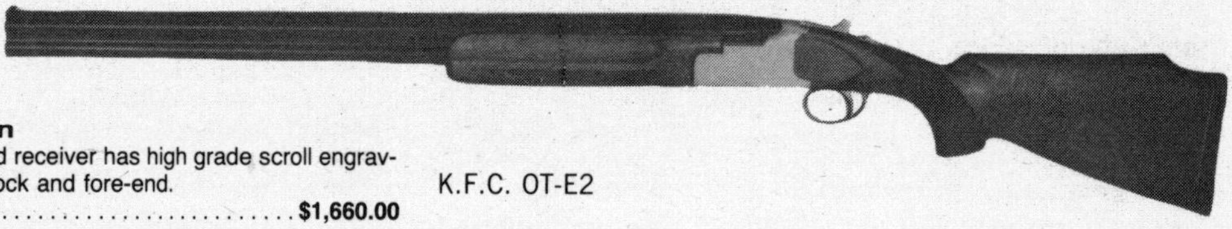

K.F.C. OT-E1

K.F.C. OT-TRAP-E2 Shotgun
Same as E-1 model except chromed receiver has high grade scroll engraving, super deluxe French walnut stock and fore-end.
Price: $1,660.00

K.F.C. OT-E2

K.F.C. OT-SKEET Shotguns
Skeet versions of FG model. Model E-1 has 26" or 28" (Skeet & Skeet) barrels with 13mm vent. rib, middle and front bead sights, gold colored wide trigger. Stock dimensions are: 14"x1½"x2½". Plastic buttplate, push-button fore-end release. Weight is about 7½ lbs.
Price: E-1 ....$1,070.00
Price: E-2 ....$1,660.00

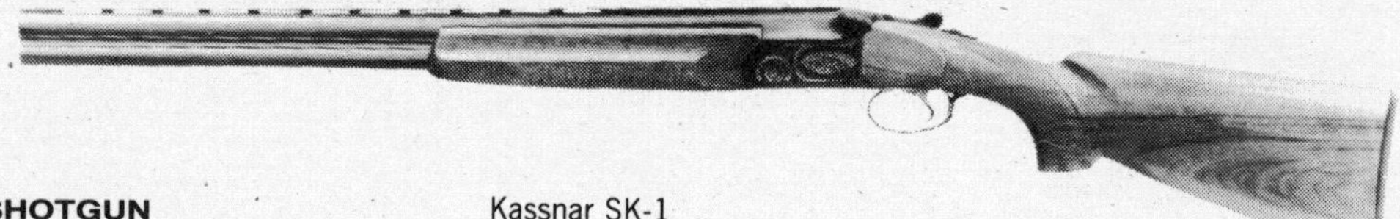

KASSNAR/FIAS SK-1 O/U SHOTGUN
Gauge: 12 or 20 ga. (3" chambers).
Action: Top lever break open, boxlock, Greener cross bolt.
Barrel: 26" (Imp. Cyl. & Mod.), 28" (Mod. & Full), 30" (Mod. & Full), 32" (Full & Full).
Weight: 6-6½ lbs.
Stock: Select European walnut. 14"x2¼"x1¼".
Features: Double triggers and non-automatic extractors. Checkered p.g. and fore-end. Imported by Kassnar Imports.
Price: $449.95

Kassnar SK-1

Kassnar/Fias SK-3 O/U Shotgun
Same as SK-1 except has single selective trigger $469.95

Kassnar/Fias SK-4D O/U Shotgun
Same as SK-4 except has deluxe receiver engraving, sideplates, better wood
....$529.95

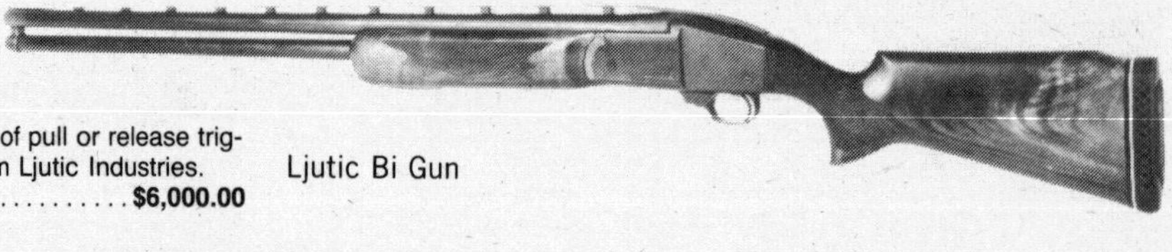

LJUTIC BI GUN O/U SHOTGUN
Gauge: 12 ga only.
Barrel: 28" or 33", choked to customer specs.
Weight: To customers specs.
Stock: To customer specs. Oil finish, hand checkered.
Features: Custom-made gun. Hollow-milled rib, choice of pull or release trigger, pushbutton opener in front of trigger guard. From Ljutic Industries.
Price: $6,000.00

Ljutic Bi Gun

Ljutic Four Barrel Skeet Set
Similar to Bi Gun except comes with matched set of four 28" barrels in 12, 20, 28 and 410. Ljutic Paternator chokes and barrel are integral. Stock is to customer specs, of American or French walnut with fancy checkering.
Price: Four barrel set $16,000.00

CAUTION: PRICES CHANGE. CHECK AT GUNSHOP.

SHOTGUNS—OVER-UNDER

MAUSER MODEL CONTEST O/U SHOTGUN
Gauge: 12 only, 2¾" chambers.
Barrel: 27.5" (Imp. Cyl. & Imp. Mod.).
Weight: About 7 lbs.
Stock: Select European walnut.
Features: Hunting scene engraving on receiver, dummy sideplates; chrome lined barrels, automatic ejectors, single selective trigger. Contact Heym for more data.
Price: Field $1,279.00
Price: Trap $1,949.00

Mauser Contest

MERKEL 201E O/U
Gauge: 12, 16, 20, 28, 3" chambers on request.
Action: Kersten double crossbolt.
Barrel: 26" (Mod. & Imp. Cyl., Cyl. & Imp. Cyl).
Weight: 6¾ lbs.
Stock: Walnut with p.g. or English style. 14¼"x1½"x2¼".
Features: Double, single or single selective trigger, cocking indicators. Fine hunting scene engraving. Imported by J. J. Jenkins.
Price: With single selective trigger $4,468.00

Merkel 201E

Merkel 203E

MERKEL MODEL 203E O/U
Gauge: 12, 16, 20, 28, 3" chambers on request.
Action: Merkel H&H hand-detachable side locks with double sears. Double crossbolt breech.
Barrel: 26" (Mod. & Imp. Cyl.).
Weight: 7 lbs.
Stock: Deluxe walnut with p.g. or English style. 14¼"x1½"x2¼".
Features: Double, single or single selective trigger. Cocking indicators. Choice of arabesque or fine hunting scene engraving. Genuine high-speed lock time sidelock action. Imported by J. J. Jenkins.
Price: With single selective trigger $7,995.00

Gamba Edinburgh

RENATO GAMBA EDINBURGH O/U SHOTGUNS
Gauge: 12 only, 2¾" chambers.
Barrel: Skeet—26.5" (Skeet); Trap—30", 32" (trap chokes); Mono Trap—32", 34" (trap choke).
Weight: 7¼ to 7¾ lbs.
Stock: Trap—14½"x1½"x2"; Skeet—14"x1¼"x2"xN.A. Select walnut with M.C. trap stock. Hand checkered, rubbed European oil finish. Skeet comes with high gloss lacquer finish and Skeet pad.
Features: Chrome lined barrels, double vent. ribs, shaped single trigger (selective available), auto ejectors, silvered receiver with light border scroll engraving. Made by Renato Gamba, Imported by Steyr Daimler Puch of America.
Price: Trap o-u $1,995.00
Price: Skeet o-u $1,995.00
Price: Mono Trap $1,995.00

Remington 3200

REMINGTON 3200 COMPETITION TRAP
Gauge: 12 ga. (2¾" chambers).
Barrel: 30" (Full & Full, Full & Imp. Mod., Full & Mod.), 32" (Full & Imp. Mod.).
Weight: 8¼ lbs. (30" bbl.). **Length:** 48" over-all (30" bbl.).
Stock: Fancy walnut checkered 20 l.p.i. Full beavertail fore-end. Satin finish. 14⅜"x2"x1½". Optional 1⅜" or 1½" drop on Monte Carlo stocks.
Features: Super-fast lock time, separated barrels, engraved receiver. Combination manual safety and barrel selector on top tang. Single selective trigger. Ivory bead front sight, white-metal middle.
Price: Competition Trap with or without M.C. stock $1,525.00
Price: Pigeon (28", Imp. Mod. & Full) $1,525.00

Remington 3200 Competition Skeet
Same as Trap except: 26" or 28" (Skeet & Skeet) barrels, stock measures 14"x2⅛"x1½". Over-all length is 43" with 26" barrels, weight is 7¾ lbs.
Price: Competition Skeet $1,525.00
Price: Competition Skeet 4-bbl. set (with bbls. for 12, 20, 28 and 410 in luggage case $5,725.00

Consult our Directory pages for the location of firms mentioned.

Rottweil 72

ROTTWEIL OLYMPIA '72 SKEET SHOTGUN
Gauge: 12 ga. only.
Action: Boxlock.
Barrel: 27" (special Skeet choke), vent. rib. Chromed lined bores, flared chokes.
Weight: 7¼ lbs. **Length:** 44½" over-all.
Stock: French walnut, hand checkered, modified beavertail fore-end. Oil finish.
Sights: Metal bead front.
Features: Inertia-type trigger, interchangeable for any system. Frame and lock milled from steel block. Retracting firing pins are spring mounted. All coil springs. Selective single trigger. Action engraved. Extra barrels are available. Introduced 1976. Imported from West Germany by Dynamit Nobel.
Price: **$3,325.00**
Price: Trap model (Montreal) is similar to above except has 30" (Imp. Mod. & Full) bbl., weighs 8 lbs., 48½" over-all **$3,325.00**

Rottweil AAT

ROTTWEIL AAT TRAP GUN
Gauge: 12, 2¾".
Barrel: 32" (Imp. Mod. & Full).
Weight: About 8 lbs.
Stock: 14½"x1⅜"x1⅜"x1⅞". Monte Carlo style of selected French walnut with oil finish. Checkered fore-end and p.g.
Features: Has infinitely variable point of impact via special muzzle collar. Extra single lower barrels available—32" (Imp. Mod.) or 34" (Full). Special trigger groups—release/release or release/pull—also available. Introduced 1979. From Dynamit Nobel.
Price: With single lower barrel **$4,062.50**
Price: Combo (single and o/u barrels) **$5,362.50**
Price: Interchangeable trap trigger group **$362.50**

Rottweil American Trap

ROTTWEIL AMERICAN TRAP COMBO
Gauge: 12 ga. only.
Action: Boxlock
Barrel: Separated o/u, 32" (Imp. Mod. & Full); single is 34" (Full), both with high vent. rib.
Weight: 8½ lbs. (o/u and single)
Stock: Monte Carlo style, walnut, hand checkered and rubbed. Unfinished stocks available. Double vent. recoil pad. Choice of two dimensions.
Sights: Plastic front in metal sleeve, center bead.
Features: Interchangeable inertia-type trigger groups. Trigger groups available: single selective; double triggers;, release-pull; release-release selective. Receiver milled from block steel. Chokes are hand honed, test fired and reworked for flawless patterns. All coil springs, engraved action. Introduced 1977. Imported from West Germany by Dynamit Nobel.
Price: **$5,362.00**
Price: American Trap O/U (as above except only with O/U bbls.) **$3,525.00**
Price: American Skeet O/U **$3,325.00**

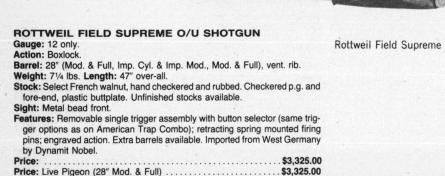

Rottweil Field Supreme

ROTTWEIL FIELD SUPREME O/U SHOTGUN
Gauge: 12 only.
Action: Boxlock.
Barrel: 28" (Mod. & Full, Imp. Cyl. & Imp. Mod., Mod. & Full), vent. rib.
Weight: 7¼ lbs. **Length:** 47" over-all.
Stock: Select French walnut, hand checkered and rubbed. Checkered p.g. and fore-end, plastic buttplate. Unfinished stocks available.
Sight: Metal bead front.
Features: Removable single trigger assembly with button selector (same trigger options as on American Trap Combo); retracting spring mounted firing pins; engraved action. Extra barrels available. Imported from West Germany by Dynamit Nobel.
Price: **$3,325.00**
Price: Live Pigeon (28" Mod. & Full) **$3,325.00**

CAUTION: PRICES CHANGE. CHECK AT GUNSHOP.

SHOTGUNS—OVER-UNDER

Ruger Red Label

RUGER "RED LABEL" O/U SHOTGUN

Gauge: 20 only, 3" chambers.
Barrel: 26", (Skeet & Skeet, Imp. Cyl. & Mod., Full & Mod.).
Weight: About 7 lbs. **Length:** 43" (26" barrels).
Stock: 14"x1½"x2½". Straight grain American walnut. Checkered p.g. and fore-end, rubber recoil pad.
Features: Initial production guns provided with 26" barrels. Premium grade 20 gauge models and 12 gauge guns will be offered later. Patented barrel side spacers may be removed if desired. Introduced 1977.
Price: About **$760.00**

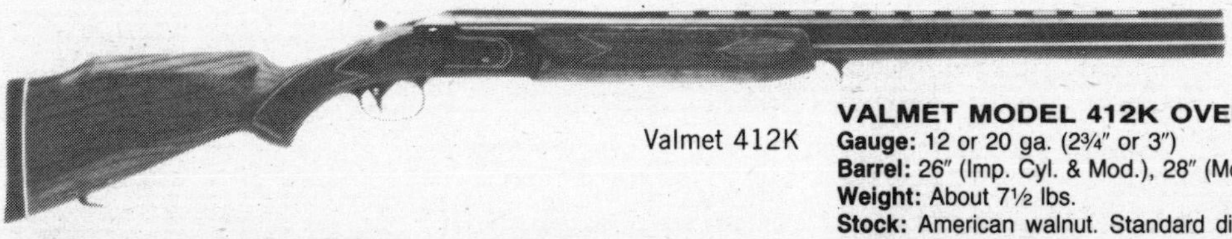

Valmet 412K

VALMET MODEL 412K OVER-UNDER

Gauge: 12 or 20 ga. (2¾" or 3")
Barrel: 26" (Imp. Cyl. & Mod.), 28" (Mod. & Full), 30" (Mod. & Full); vent. rib.
Weight: About 7½ lbs.
Stock: American walnut. Standard dimensions-$13\frac{9}{10}$"x1½"x$2\frac{2}{5}$". Checkered p.g. and fore-end.
Features: Model 412K is extractor (basic) model. Free interchangeability of barrels, stocks and fore-ends into KE (auto. ejector) model, double rifle model, combination gun, etc. Barrel selector in trigger; auto. top tang safety; barrel cocking indicators. Double triggers optional. Introduced 1980. From Valmet.
Price: Model 412K (extractors) **$574.00**
Price: Model 412 KE (ejectors) **$629.00**

Valmet 412KE Target Series

Trap and Skeet versions of 412 gun. Auto. ejectors only; 12 ga., 2¾", 3" chambers, 30" barrels (Imp. & Full.—Trap, Skeet & Skeet—Skeet). 20 ga., 3" chambers. Trap stock measures $14\frac{3}{10}$"x$1\frac{2}{5}$"x$1\frac{3}{5}$"x2½"; Skeet stock measures $13\frac{9}{10}$x$1\frac{4}{5}$"x$2\frac{4}{5}$"x$1\frac{4}{5}$". Trap weight 7⅝ lbs.: Skeet weight 7½ lbs. Non-automatic safety. Introduced 1980. From Valmet.
Price: Trap **$639.00**
Price: Skeet **$634.00**

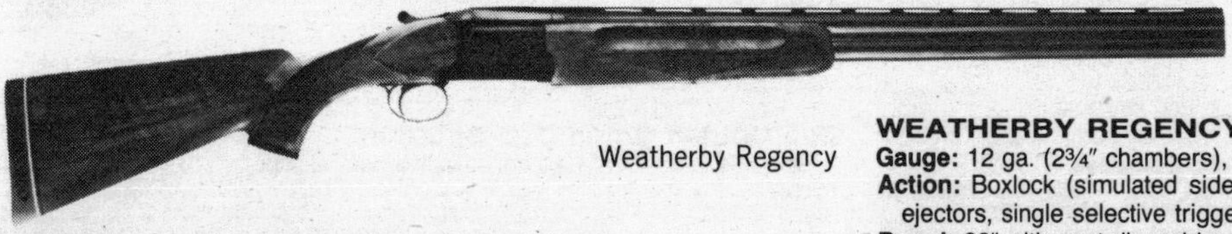

Weatherby Regency

WEATHERBY REGENCY O/U SHOTGUN

Gauge: 12 ga. (2¾" chambers), 20 ga. (3" chambers).
Action: Boxlock (simulated side-lock) top lever break-open. Selective auto ejectors, single selective trigger (selector inside trigger guard).
Barrel: 28" with vent rib and bead front sight, Full & Mod., Mod. & Imp. Cyl. or Skeet & Skeet.
Weight: 12 ga. 7⅜ lbs., 20 ga. 6⅞ lbs.
Stock: American walnut, checkered p.g. and fore-end (14¼"x1½"x2½").
Features: Mechanically operated trigger. Top tang safety, Greener cross-bolt, fully engraved receiver, recoil pad installed.
Price: 12 or 20 ga. Field and Skeet **$1,269.95**
Price: 12 ga. Trap Model **$1,369.95**

WEATHERBY OLYMPIAN O/U SHOTGUN

Gauge: 12 (2¾"; 3" for 30" barrel only), 20 (3").
Action: Boxlock (simulated side-lock).
Barrel: 12 ga. 30" (Full & Mod.), 28EI (Full & Mod., Mod. & Imp. Cyl., Skeet & Skeet); 20 ga. 28", 26" (Full & Mod., Mod. & Imp. Cyl., Skeet & Skeet).
Weight: 7 lbs., 8 ozs. (12 ga. 26").
Stock: American walnut, checkered p.g. and fore-end. Rubber recoil pad. Dimensions for field and Skeet models, 20 ga. 14"x1½"x2½".
Features: Selective auto ejectors, single selective mechanical trigger. Top tang safety, Greener cross-bolt. Introduced 1978. From Weatherby.
Price: 12 or 20, Field and Skeet **$999.95**
Price: 12 ga. Trap **$1,099.95**

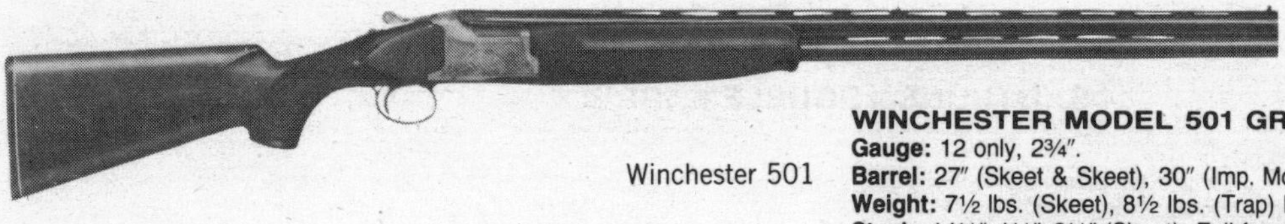

Winchester 501

WINCHESTER MODEL 501 GRAND EUROPEAN O-U

Gauge: 12 only, 2¾".
Barrel: 27" (Skeet & Skeet), 30" (Imp. Mod. & Full), 32" (Imp. Mod. & Full).
Weight: 7½ lbs. (Skeet), 8½ lbs. (Trap) **Length:** 47⅛" over-all (30" barrel).
Stock: 14⅛"x1½"x2½" (Skeet). Full fancy, walnut, hand-rubbed oil finish.
Features: Silvered, engraved receiver; engine-turned breech interior. Slide-button selector/safety, selective auto. ejectors. Chrome bores, tapered vent. rib. Trap gun has Monte Carlo or regular stock, recoil pad; Skeet gun has rosewood buttplate. Introduced 1981.
Price: Trap or Skeet **$1,800.00**

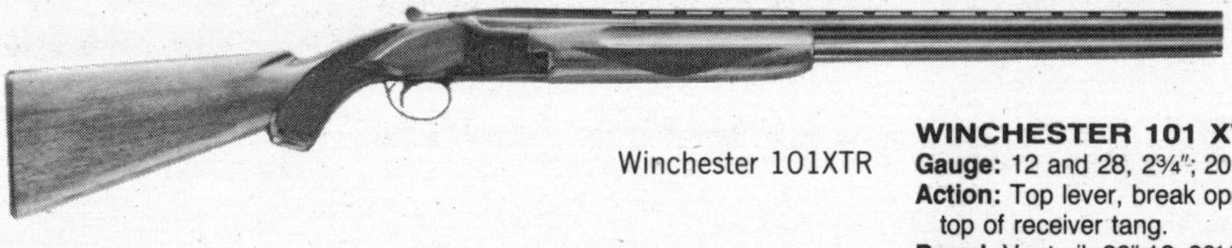

Winchester 101XTR

WINCHESTER 101 XTR O/U FIELD GUN

Gauge: 12 and 28, 2¾"; 20, 3".
Action: Top lever, break open. Manual safety combined with bbl. selector at top of receiver tang.
Barrel: Vent. rib 26" 12, 26½", 20 and 410 (Imp. Cyl., Mod.), 28" (Mod & Full), 30" 12 only (Mod. & Full). Metal bead front sight. Chrome plated chambers and bores.
Stock: 14"x1½"x2½". Checkered walnut p.g. and fore-end; fluted comb.
Weight: 12 ga. 7¾ lbs. Others 6¼ lbs. **Length:** 44¾" over-all (28" bbls.).
Features: Single selective trigger, auto ejectors. Hand engraved receiver.
Price: 101 XTR with Winchoke system, 12 ga. **$1,125.00**
Price: Ltwt., 12 or 20, Winchoke system **$1,150.00**

SHOTGUNS—OVER-UNDER

Winchester 101 Waterfowl

Winchester Model 101 Pigeon Grade
Same as Model 101 Field except has new-design vent. rib with bead front and middle sights, hand-engraved satin finish receiver, knurled, non-slip trigger. Stock and fore-end of fancy French walnut, hand checkered p.g. and fore-end. 12, 20, 28 or 410 ga., 2¾" or 3" chambers. Barrels run from 25½" through 32" with a full range of chokes. Weighs 8¼ lbs.

Price: Standard trap stock, with gun case $1,300.00
Price: Monte Carlo stock $1,300.00
Price: Field grade $1,250.00
Price: 28, 410 skeet $1,300.00
Price: 12, 20 ga. Skeet $1,250.00
Price: Three-gauge Skeet set (20, 28, 410) $3,100.00
Price: Field XTR with Winchoke system $1,450.00
Price: XTR Trap with Winchoke $1,425.00
Price: XTR Featherweight $1,400.00

Winchester Model 101 XTR Waterfowl Winchoke
Same as Model 101 Field Grade except in 12 ga. only, 3" chambers, 32" barrels. Comes with four Winchoke tubes: Mod., Imp. Mod., Full, Extra-Full. Introduced 1981.
Price: $1,125.00

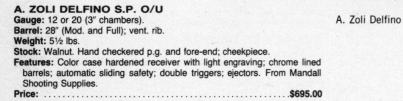

ZOLI SILVER SNIPE O/U SHOTGUN
Gauge: 12, 20 (3" chambers).
Action: Purdey type double boxlock, crossbolt.
Barrel: 26" (I.C.& Mod.), 28" (Mod.&Full), 30", 12 only (Mod.& Full); 26" Skeet (Skeet & Skeet), 30" Trap (Full & Full).
Weight: 6½ lbs. (12 ga.).
Stock: Hand checkered European walnut, p.g. and fore-end.
Features: Auto safety (exc. Trap and Skeet), vent rib, single trigger, chrome bores. Imported from Italy by Mandall Shooting Supplies.
Price: Field $695.00

Zoli Silver Snipe

Zoli Golden Snipe O/U Shotgun
Same as Silver Snipe except selective auto ejectors.
Price: Field $775.00

A. ZOLI DELFINO S.P. O/U
Gauge: 12 or 20 (3" chambers).
Barrel: 28" (Mod. and Full); vent. rib.
Weight: 5½ lbs.
Stock: Walnut. Hand checkered p.g. and fore-end; cheekpiece.
Features: Color case hardened receiver with light engraving; chrome lined barrels; automatic sliding safety; double triggers; ejectors. From Mandall Shooting Supplies.
Price: $695.00

A. Zoli Delfino

SHOTGUNS—DOUBLE BARREL

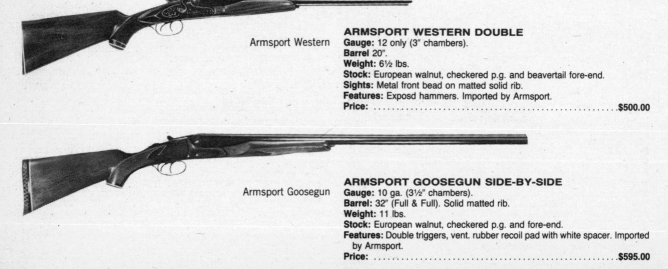

Armsport Western

ARMSPORT WESTERN DOUBLE
Gauge: 12 only (3" chambers).
Barrel 20".
Weight: 6½ lbs.
Stock: European walnut, checkered p.g. and beavertail fore-end.
Sights: Metal front bead on matted solid rib.
Features: Exposd hammers. Imported by Armsport.
Price: $500.00

Armsport Goosegun

ARMSPORT GOOSEGUN SIDE-BY-SIDE
Gauge: 10 ga. (3½" chambers).
Barrel: 32" (Full & Full). Solid matted rib.
Weight: 11 lbs.
Stock: European walnut, checkered p.g. and fore-end.
Features: Double triggers, vent. rubber recoil pad with white spacer. Imported by Armsport.
Price: $595.00

CAUTION: PRICES CHANGE. CHECK AT GUNSHOP.

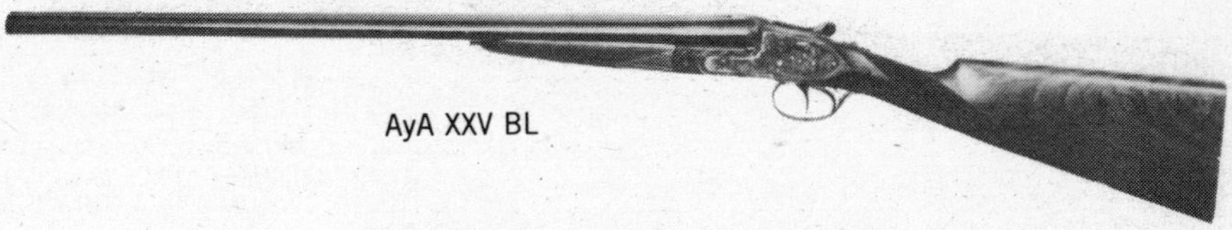

SHOTGUNS—DOUBLE BARREL

AyA XXV BL

AYA MODEL XXV BL, SL DOUBLE
Gauge: 12, 16, 20.
Barrel: 25″, chokes as specified.
Weight: 5 lbs., 15 oz. to 7lbs., 8oz.
Stock: 14½″x2¼″x1½″. European walnut. Straight grip stock with classic pistol grip, checkered butt.
Features: Boxlock (Model BL), sidelock (Model SL). Churchill rib, auto ejectors, double triggers (single available), color case-hardened action (coin-finish available). From Wm. Larkin Moore & Co.
Price: BL, 12 ga. **$1,400.00**
Price: BL, 20 ga. **$1,450.00**
Price: SL, 12 ga. **$2,250.00**
Price: SL, 20 ga. **$2,300.00**

AYA MODEL 117 DOUBLE BARREL SHOTGUN
Gauge: 12 (2¾″), 20 (3″).
Action: Holland & Holland sidelock, Purdey treble bolting.
Barrel: 26″ (Imp. Cyl. & Mod.) 28″ (Mod. & Full).
Stock: 14½″x2⅜″x1½″. Select European walnut, hand checkered p.g. and beavertail fore-end.
Features: Single selective trigger, automatic ejectors, cocking indicators; concave barrel rib; hand-detachable lockplates; hand engraved action. Imported by Interarms.
Price: **$1,050.00**

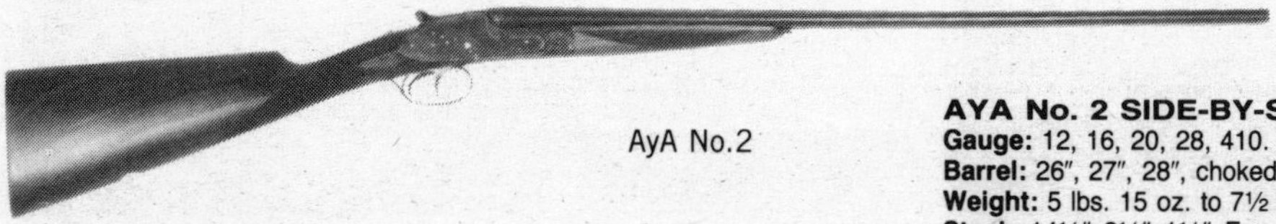

AyA No.2

AYA No. 1 Side-by-Side
Similar to the No. 2 except barrel lengths to customer specifications. Barrels are of chrome-nickel steel.
Price: 12, 16, 20 ga., from **$3,450.00**
Price: 28 ga., from **$3,750.00**
Price: 410 ga., from **$3,850.00**

AYA No. 2 SIDE-BY-SIDE
Gauge: 12, 16, 20, 28, 410.
Barrel: 26″, 27″, 28″, choked to customer specs.
Weight: 5 lbs. 15 oz. to 7½ lbs.
Stock: 14½″x2¼″x1½″. European walnut. Straight grip stock, checkered butt, classic fore-end. Can be made to custom dimensions.
Features: Sidelock action with auto. ejectors, double triggers standard, single trigger optional. Hand-detachable locks. Color case-hardened action. From Wm. Larkin Moure & Co.
Price: 12, 16, 20 ga., from **$1,500.00**
Price: 28 ga., from **$1,650.00**
Price: 410 ga., from **$1,700.00**

AYA Model 56 Side-by-Side
Similar to the No. 1 except in 12, 16 or 20 ga. only, available with raised, level or vent rib. Does not have hand-detachable locks.
Price: **$3,700.00**

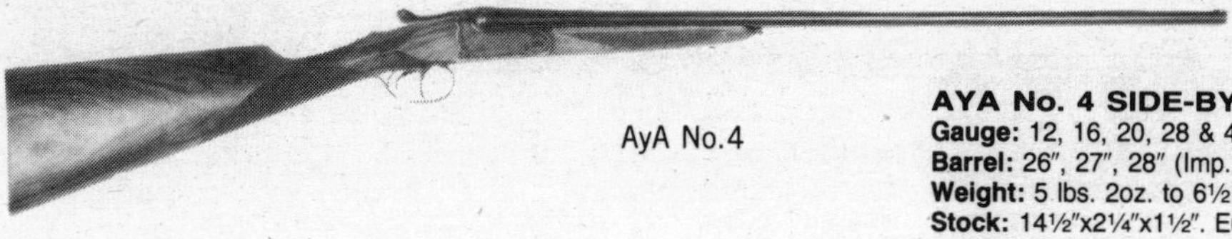

AyA No.4

AYA No. 4 SIDE-BY-SIDE
Gauge: 12, 16, 20, 28 & 410.
Barrel: 26″, 27″, 28″ (Imp. Cyl. & Mod. or Mod. & Full).
Weight: 5 lbs. 2oz. to 6½ lbs.
Stock: 14½″x2¼″x1½″. European walnut. Straight grip with checkered butt, classic fore-end.
Features: Boxlock action, color case-hardened, automatic ejectors, double triggers (single trigger available). From William Larkin Moore & Co.
Price: 12 ga. **$1,400.00**
Price: 20, 28 ga. **$1,450.00**
Price: 410 ga. **$1,500.00**

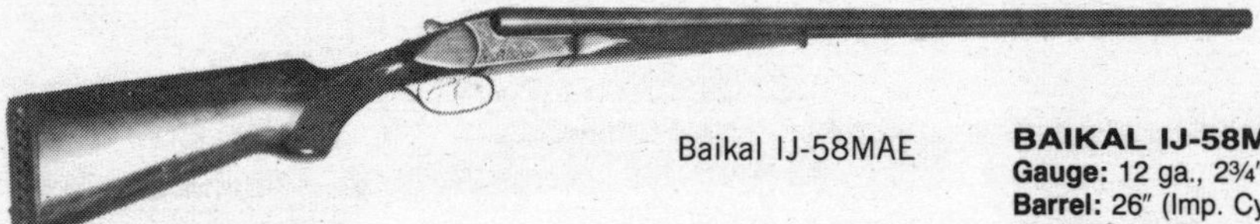

Baikal IJ-58MAE

BAIKAL IJ-58MAE SIDE-BY-SIDE
Gauge: 12 ga., 2¾″ chambers, 20 ga., 3″ chambers.
Barrel: 26″ (Imp. Cyl. & Mod.), 28″ (Mod. & Full).
Weight: 6¾ lbs.
Stock: Walnut. Hand checkered p.g. and beavertail fore-end.
Features: Hinged front double trigger. Chrome barrels and chambers. Hammer interceptors. Fore-end center latch. Hand engraved receiver. Selective ejection or extraction. Imported by Baikal International.
Price: About **$267.95**

BAIKAL MC-110 SIDE-BY-SIDE
Gauge: 12 or 20 ga., 2¾″ chambers.
Barrel: 12 ga. 28″ (Mod. & Full), 20 ga. 26″ (Imp. Cyl. & Mod).
Weight: 6 lbs. (20 ga.), 6¾ lbs. (12 ga.).
Stock: Fancy walnut. Hand checkered p.g. and fore-end. Choice of full p.g. or straight stock. Semi-beavertail fore-end.
Features: Fully engraved receiver with animal and bird scenes. Engraved trigger guard and tang. Double trigger. Chrome barrels, chambers and internal parts. Raised solid rib. Extractors, hammer interceptors. Auto. safety. Comes with case. Imported by Baikal International.
Price: **$3,200.00**

> Consult our Directory pages for the location of firms mentioned.

SHOTGUNS—DOUBLE BARREL

Baikal MC-111

BAIKAL MC-111 SIDE-BY-SIDE
Gauge: 12 ga., 2¾″ chambers.
Barrel: To customer's specifications, choice of chokes.
Weight: 7 lbs.
Stock: Fancy walnut. Choice of p.g. or straight stock. Gold and silver inlays in butt. Semi-beavertail fore-end. Monte Carlo. To customer's specifications.
Features: Handmade sidelock shotgun. Removable sideplates. Chrome barrels, chambers and internal parts. Selective ejectors, single selective trigger, hammer interceptors, cocking indicators. Hand chiseled animal and bird scenes on receiver. Comes with case. Imported by Baikal International.
Price: Special order only **$5,400.00**

BERNARDELLI XXVSL DOUBLE
Gauge: 12.
Action: Holland & Holland-style sidelock with double sears.
Barrel: Demi-block (chopper lump), 25″, choice of choke.
Weight: About 6½ lbs. **Length:** To customer specs.
Stock: Best walnut with dimensions to customer specs.
Features: Firing pins removeable from face of standing breech; manual or auto safety; selective auto ejectors; classic or beavertail fore-end. Imported by Knight & Knight.
Price: With fitted luggage case **$1,865.00**

Bernardelli XXVSL

BERETTA M-424 SIDE-BY-SIDE
Gauge: 12 (2¾″), 20 (3″).
Action: Beretta patent boxlock; double underlugs and bolts.
Barrel: 12 ga.—26″ (Imp. Cyl. & Mod.), 28″ (Mod. & Full); 20 ga.—26″ (Imp. Cyl. & Mod.), 28″ (Mod. & Full).
Weight: 6 lbs. 14 ozs. (20 ga.).
Stock: 14⅛″x1⁹⁄₁₆″x2⁹⁄₁₆″. "English" straight-type; hand checkered European walnut.
Features: Coil springs throughout action; double triggers (front is hinged); automatic safety; extractors. Concave matted barrel rib. Introduced 1977. Imported by Beretta Arms Co.
Price: **$900.00**

Beretta 424

Beretta M-426 Side-By-Side
Same as M-424 except action body is engraved; pistol grip stock; a silver pigeon is inlaid into top lever; single selective trigger; selective automatic ejectors. Introduced 1977. Imported by Beretta Arms Co.
Price: **$1,115.00**

Browning B-SS

Browning BSS Sporter
Similar to standard BSS except has straight-grip stock and full beavertail fore-end with traditional oil finish. Introduced 1977.
Price: Grade I, 12 or 20 ga. **$549.95**
Price: Grade II, 12 or 20 ga. **$975.00**

BROWNING B-SS
Gauge: 12 (2¾″), 20 (3″).
Action: Top lever break-open action, top tang safety; single trigger.
Barrel: 26″ (Mod. and Full or Imp. Cyl. and Mod.), 28″ (Mod. and Full), 30″ (Full & Full or Mod & Full).
Weight: 6¾ lbs. (26″ bbl., 20 ga.); 7½ lbs. (30″ bbl., 12 ga.).
Stock: 14¼″x1⅝″x2½″. French walnut, hand checkered. Full p.g., full beavertail fore-end.
Features: Automatic safety, automatic ejectors. Hand engraved receiver, mechanical single selective trigger with barrel selector in rear of trigger guard.
Price: Grade I, 12 or 20 ga. **$549.95**
Price: Grade II, 12 or 20 ga. **$975.00**

CHAPUIS PROGRESS RBV, R-20 SIDE-BY-SIDE
Gauge: 12 ga. (2¾″), 20 ga. (3″).
Barrel: 26½″ or 27½″ depending on choke (any choke available). Chrome-moly steel with chrome plated bores.
Weight: About 6¼ lbs.
Stock: Select French or American walnut, oil finish. Fine checkering on p.g. and fore-end. Right or left-hand stock available with straight English or p.g. style design. Deluxe wood, grip cap, etc. available as options.
Features: Single barrel joining rib. Auto ejectors are standard. Double triggers. Scroll engraving on frame and sideplates. Extra barrel set available. Introduced 1979. Imported by R. Painter Co.
Price: **$1,415.00**
Price: Extra barrel set **$390.24**
Price: Model Progress-RG (boxlock) **$832.00**
Price: Progress-Hobby (same as RBV/R-20 except profuse engraving, presentation French walnut stock, bbls. browned .... **P.O.R.**
Price: Progress-Slug (boxlock-style with right barrel rifled for slugs) **$954.00**

Chapuis Progress

> Consult our Directory pages for the location of firms mentioned.

CAUTION: PRICES CHANGE. CHECK AT GUNSHOP.

SHOTGUNS—DOUBLE BARREL

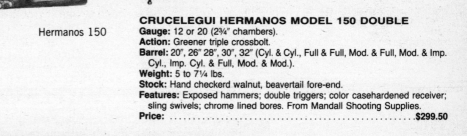

Hermanos 150

CRUCELEGUI HERMANOS MODEL 150 DOUBLE
Gauge: 12 or 20 (2¾" chambers).
Action: Greener triple crossbolt.
Barrel: 20", 26" 28", 30", 32" (Cyl. & Cyl., Full & Full, Mod. & Full, Mod. & Imp. Cyl., Imp. Cyl. & Full, Mod. & Mod.).
Weight: 5 to 7¼ lbs.
Stock: Hand checkerd walnut, beavertail fore-end.
Features: Exposed hammers; double triggers; color casehardened receiver; sling swivels; chrome lined bores. From Mandall Shooting Supplies.
Price: $299.50

ERA Bird Hunter

ERA "Bird Hunter" DOUBLE BARREL SHOTGUN
Gauge: 12, 16, 20, (2¾" chambers), 410 (3" chambers).
Action: Boxlock.
Barrel: 12 (26"), 16 ga. 28" (Mod. & Full); 20 ga. 28" (Mod. & Full); 410 ga. 26" (Mod. & Full).
Stock: Hand checkered walnut, beavertail fore-end, white line spacers on p.g. cap and butt plate.
Features: Raised matted rib, double triggers, engraved receiver. Auto. disconnector. Extractors only. Imported from Brazil by F.I.E. Corp.
Price: $189.95
Price: 12 or 20 ga. Coach Gun, 18" bbl. $199.95

F.I.E. "The BRUTE" DOUBLE BARREL
Gauge: 12, 20 (2¾" chambers), 410 (3" chambers).
Action: Boxlock.
Barrel: 19"
Weight: 5 lbs. 2 ozs. **Length:** 30" over-all.
Stock: Hand checkered walnut with full beavertail fore-end.
Features: The smallest, lightest double barrel shotgun available. Measures only 30" over-all. Introduced 1979. From F.I.E. Corp.
Price: $224.95

Gamba Principessa

RENATO GAMBA PRINCIPESSA SHOTGUN
Gauge: 28 ga., 2¾".
Barrel: 26" (Imp. Cyl. & Mod.), 28" (Mod. & Full).
Weight: About 5½ lbs.
Stock: 14½" x 1¼" x 2". Select European walnut, straight English grip and slim English-style fore-end.
Features: Chrome-lined demi-block barrels; single or double trigger; boxlock action only. Beavertail fore-end available. Fitted with rubber recoil pad. Engraved, color case-hardened receiver. Introduced 1981. Imported by Steyr Daimler Puch.
Price: With double triggers $1,566.00
Price: With single trigger $1,695.00

GALEF'S DOUBLE BARREL SHOTGUN
Gauge: 10 (3½"); 12, 20, 410 (3"); 16, 20 (2¾").
Action: Modified Anson & Deeley boxlock, case hardened.
Barrel: 32" 10, 12 only (Full & Full); 30" 12 only (Mod.& Full); 28" all exc. 410 (Mod.& Full); 26" 12, 20, 28 (I.C.&Mod.); 26" 410 only (Mod.& Full); 22" 12 only (I.C.& I.C.).
Weight: 10½ lbs.(10), 7¾ lbs.(12) to 6 lbs.(410).
Stock: Hand checkered European walnut, p.g., beavertail fore-end, rubber recoil pad. Dimensions vary with gauge.
Features: Auto safety, plain extractors. Imported from Spain by Galef.
Price: 10 ga. ....$439.00   12 - 410 ....$373.80

GIB 10 Gauge

GIB 10 GAUGE MAGNUM SHOTGUN
Gauge: 10 ga. (3½" chambers).
Action: Boxlock.
Barrel: 32" (Full).
Weight: 10 lbs.
Stock: 14½"x1½"x2⅝". European walnut, checkered at p.g. and fore-end.
Features: Double triggers; color hardened action, rest blued. Front and center metal beads on matted rib; ventilated rubber recoil pad. Fore-end release has positive Purdey-type mechanism. Imported by Mandall Shooting Supplies.
Price: $500.00

GARBI MODEL 51 SIDE-BY-SIDE
Gauge: 12, 16, 20 (2¾" chambers).
Barrel: 28" (Mod. & Full).
Weight: 5½ to 6½ lbs.
Stock: Walnut, to customer specs.
Features: Boxlock action; hand-engraved receiver; hand-checkered stock and fore-end; double triggers; extractors. Introduced 1980. Imported by L. Joseph Rahn, Inc.
Price: $490.00

GARBI MODEL 60 SIDE-BY-SIDE
Gauge: 12, 16, 20 (2¾" chambers).
Barrel: 26", 28", 30"; choked to customer specs.
Weight: 5½ to 6½ lbs.
Stock: Select walnut. Dimensions to customer specs.
Features: Sidelock action. Scroll engraving on receiver. Hand checkered stock. Double triggers. Extractors. Imported by L. Joseph Rahn, Inc.
Price: $790.00
Price: With demi-bloc barrels and ejectors $1,085.00

SHOTGUNS—DOUBLE BARREL

Garbi Model 62
Similar to Model 60 except choked Mod. & Full, plain receiver with engraved border, demi-bloc barrels, gas exhaust valves, jointed triggers, extractors. Imported by L. Joseph Rahn.

Price: $790.00
Price: With ejectors $1,064.00

Garbi 71

GARBI MODEL 71 DOUBLE
Gauge: 12, 16, 20
Barrel: 26″, 28″, choked to customer specs.
Weight: 5 lbs., 15 ozs., (20 ga.)
Stock: 14½″x2¼″x1½″. European walnut. Straight grip, checkered butt, classic fore-end.
Features: Sidelock action, automatic ejectors, double triggers standard. Color case-hardened action, coin finish optional. Five other models are available. From Wm. Larkin Moore.
Price: Model 71, from $1,675.00

GARBI MODEL 102 SHOTGUN
Gauge: 12, 16, 20
Barrel: 12 ga.-25″ to 30″; 16 & 20 ga.-25″ to 28″. Chokes as specified.
Weight: 20 ga.-5 lbs., 15 oz. to 6 lbs., 4 oz.
Stock: 14½″ x 2¼″ x 1½″; select walnut.
Features: Holland pattern sidelock ejector with chopper lump barrels, Holland-type large scroll engraving. Double triggers (hinged front) std., non-selective single trigger available. Many options available. From Wm. Larkin Moore.
Price: From $2,850.00

Garbi 102

KASSNAR-ZABALA DOUBLE BARREL SHOTGUN
Gauge: 10 (3½″), 12, 20, 410.
Action: Anson & Deeley-type boxlock with double underlocking lugs.
Barrel: 26″ (Imp. Cyl. & Mod.), 28″, 30″ (Mod. & Full), 32″ (Full & Full). Raised, matted solid rib.
Weight: About 7 lbs. (12 ga.).
Stock: French walnut with plastic finish. Hand checkered p.g. and beavertail fore-end. 14¼″x1⅝″x2¼″.
Features: Hand engraved action, blue finish. Double triggers; front trigger hinged. Metal bead front sight. From Kassnar Imports.
Price: 12, 20 or 410 ga $399.95
Price: 10 gauge $469.95

Gamba London

RENATO GAMBA LONDON DOUBLE
Gauge: 12 or 20 ga., 2¾″ chambers.
Barrel: 26″ (Imp. Cyl. & Mod.), 28″ (Mod. & Full).
Weight: 5¾ to 6½ lbs.
Stock: 14½″x1½″x2½″. Select European walnut with finely cut hand checkered straight grip. Checkered butt. Hand rubbed European oil finish.
Features: Sidelock action based on the Holland & Holland system with double safety and three-lug Purdey locking system. Chrome lined barrels, auto ejectors, single or double triggers. Made by Renato Gamba, imported by Steyr Daimler Puch of America.
Price: Double trigger, either gauge $3,806.00
Price: Single trigger, either gauge $3,978.00

Gamba Oxford

RENATO GAMBA OXFORD DOUBLE
Gauge: 12 (2¾″); 20 (2¾″ or 3″).
Barrel: 26″ (Imp. Cyl. & Mod.), 28″ (Mod. & Full).
Weight: 5¾ to 6½ lbs.
Stock: 14½″x1½″x2½″. Select European walnut, hand checkered straight grip. Checkered butt. Hand rubbed European oil finish.
Features: Boxlock action based on the Anson & Deeley system. Auto ejectors, chrome lined barrels. Single or double trigger (double with articulated front trigger). Made by Renato Gamba, imported by Steyr Daimler Puch of America.
Price: Double trigger, either gauge $1,768.00
Price: Single trigger, either gauge $1,919.40
Price: Optional leather case $185.00

MAUSER BRISTOL SIDELOCK SHOTGUN
Gauge: 12 or 20 ga., 2¾″ chambers.
Barrel: 25″ (Imp. Cyl. & Imp. Mod.), 27.5″ (Mod. & Full).
Weight: About 6½ lbs.
Stock: Classic English design of selected walnut root wood.
Features: Sideplates have arabesque engraving. Barrels have the Churchill sighting plane. Double triggers are standard, single trigger available. Contact Heym or more data.
Price: 12 or 20 ga. $4,999.00

CAUTION: PRICES CHANGE. CHECK AT GUNSHOP.

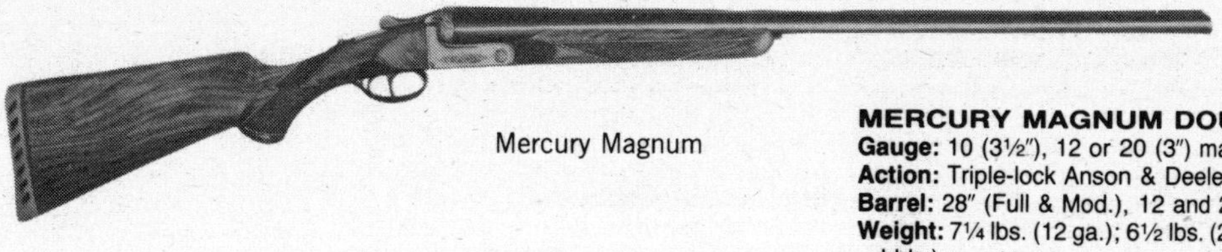

SHOTGUNS — DOUBLE BARREL

Mercury Magnum

MERCURY MAGNUM DOUBLE BARREL SHOTGUN
Gauge: 10 (3½"), 12 or 20 (3") magnums.
Action: Triple-lock Anson & Deeley type.
Barrel: 28" (Full & Mod.), 12 and 20 ga.; 32" (Full & Full), 10 ga.
Weight: 7¼ lbs. (12 ga.); 6½ lbs. (20 ga.); 10⅛ lbs. (10 ga.). **Length:** 45" (28" bbls.).
Stock: 14" x 1⅝" x 2¼" walnut, checkered p.g. stock and beavertail fore-end, recoil pad.
Features: Double triggers, front hinged, auto safety, extractors; safety gas ports, engraved frame. Imported from Spain by Tradewinds.
Price: (12, 20 ga.) $295.00
Price: (10 ga.) $480.00

MERKEL 147E SIDE-BY-SIDE
Gauge: 12, 16, 20, 3" chambers on request.
Action: Anson-Deeley with double hook bolting and Greener breech.
Barrel: 26" (Mod. & Imp. Cyl., Cyl. & Imp. Cyl.).
Weight: 6¼ to 6½ lbs.
Stock: Walnut. English style or p.g., 14¼"x1½"x2¼".
Features: Hunting scene engraving. Double, single or single selective trigger. Imported by J. J. Jenkins.
Price: With single triggers $2,018.00
Price: Model 47E (as above except has scroll engraving) $1,762.00

Merkel 147E

MERKEL 147S SIDE-BY-SIDE
Gauge: 12, 16, 20 ga. with 3" chambers on request.
Action: Sidelock with double hook bolting and Greener breech. Trigger catch bar.
Barrel: 26" (Mod. & Imp. Cyl., Cyl. & Imp. Cyl.).
Weight: 6½ to 6¾ lbs.
Stock: Walnut finish. English style or p.g., 14¼"x1½"x2¼".
Features: 30% faster trigger than conventional lock design. Hunting scene engraving. Highest grade side-by-side Merkel. Double, single or single selective trigger. Imported by J. J. Jenkins.
Price: With single trigger $4,382.00

> Consult our Directory pages for the location of firms mentioned.

Premier Ambassador

PREMIER AMBASSADOR DOUBLE BARREL SHOTGUN
Gauge: 12, 16 (2¾"); 20, 410 (3").
Action: Triple Greener crossbolt, Purdey avail. on 410; side locks.
Barrels: 28" exc. 410; 26" all (Mod. & Full).
Weight: 7¼ lbs. (12) to 6¼ lbs. (410). **Length:** 44½".
Stock: 14" x 1⅝" x 2½": Hand-checkered walnut, p.g., beavertail fore-end. White line spacers at butt and grip cap.
Features: Cocking indicators, double triggers, auto safety. Hand-engraved, color case-hardened action. Imported from Europe by Premier.
Price: $306.00

Premier Continental Double Hammer Shotgun
Same as Ambassador except outside hammers, not avail. in 410.
Price: $278.15

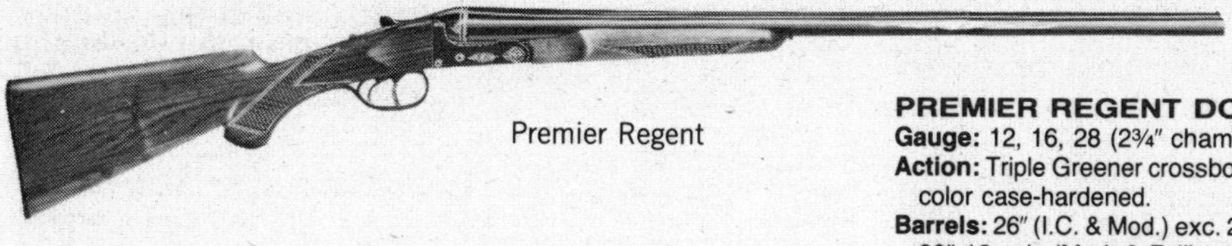

Premier Regent

PREMIER REGENT DOUBLE BARREL SHOTGUN
Gauge: 12, 16, 28 (2¾" chambers); 20, 410 (3" chambers).
Action: Triple Greener crossbolt; Purdey optional on 28, 410. Hand-engraved, color case-hardened.
Barrels: 26" (I.C. & Mod.) exc. 28 and 410 only (Mod. & Full); 28" (Mod. & Full); 30" 12 only (Mod. & Full).
Weight: 7¼ lbs. (12) to 6⅛ lbs. (410). **Length:** 42½" (26" bbls.).
Stock: 14" x 1⅝" x 2½". Hand-checkered walnut, p.g. and fore-end. White line spacers at butt and grip cap.
Features: Matted tapered rib, double triggers, auto safety. Extra bbl. sets avail. Imported from Europe by Premier.
Price: $222.95
Price: With two sets of barrels, 12 ga. ....$423.00 20 ga. $386.75
Price: Extra barrels, fitted $180.00

Premier Brush King Double Barrel Shotgun
Same as Regent except 12 and 20 ga. only, 22" bbls. (I.C. & Mod.), weight 6¼ lbs. (12), 5¾ lbs. (20). Straight English-style stock and fore-end.
Price: $241.45

PREMIER MONARCH DOUBLE BARREL SHOTGUN
Gauge: 12, 16 (2¾"), 20 (2¾" or 3").
Action: Triple Greener crossbolt.
Barrel: 26", 12 and 20 (Mod. & Imp. Cyl.), 28", 12, 16, 20 (Mod. & Full).
Weight: About 7 lbs. **Length:** 44½" over-all (28" barrels).
Stock: 14"x1⅝"x2½". Fancy French walnut, checkered p.g. and fore-end.
Sights: Metal bead, front and middle.
Features: Solid tapered rib; double triggers, auto. ejectors and safety, selective extractors; engraved action. Imported from Europe by Premier.
Price: $449.70

Premier Presentation Double Barrel Shotgun
Same as Monarch except has gold and silver inlayed hunting scenes. Stock style and measurements to customer specs, as well as gauge, barrel length and choking.
Price: With one set of barrels $971.60
Price: Extra barrels $306.00

Premier Magnum Express Double Barrel Shotgun
Similar to Regent except 10 ga. (3½" chambers) 32" or 12 ga. (3" chambers) 30", both Full & Full. Recoil pad, beavertail fore-end.
Price: 12 ga. $251.00
Price: 10 ga. $280.00

SHOTGUNS—DOUBLE BARREL

RICHLAND MODEL 200 DOUBLE BARREL SHOTGUN
Gauge: 12, 16, 20, 28 or 410 (12, 16 and 28 have 2¾" chambers, 20 and 410 3").
Barrel: 22" 20 ga. (Imp. Cyl. & Mod.) 26" (Imp. Cyl. & Mod., Mod. & Full 410 ga.), 28" (Mod. & Full).
Weight: 6¼ to 7¼ lbs.
Stock: 14½"x2⅜"x1½". Spanish walnut, checkered p.g. and fore-end; cheekpiece and rubber vent. recoil pad.
Sights: Metal bead front.
Features: Anson & Deely type action with double under-locking lugs; spring loaded firing pins removeable from front of action. Double triggers blue finish with light engraving. Imported by Richland Arms.
Price: $360.00

Richland Model 711 Magnum Shotgun
Similar to Model 200 except in 12 ga. (3") or 10 ga. (3½") magnums. Choked Full & Full, 12 ga. has 30" barrels, 10 ga. has 32". Weight is 7¾ lbs. (12), 11 lbs. (10.) Uses Purdey triple lock system, auto. safety with double triggers, raised full-length rib with metal beads at front and center.
Price: 12 ga. Magnum $400.00
Price: 10 ga. Magnum $455.00

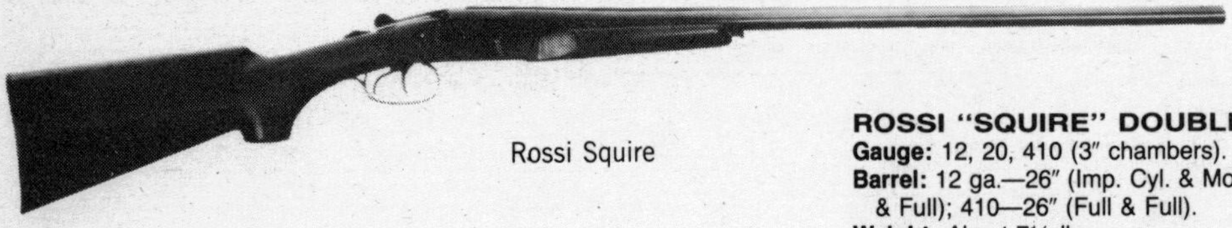

Rossi Squire

ROSSI "SQUIRE" DOUBLE BARREL
Gauge: 12, 20, 410 (3" chambers).
Barrel: 12 ga.—26" (Imp. Cyl. & Mod.), 28" (Mod. & Full); 20 ga.—28" (Mod. & Full); 410—26" (Full & Full).
Weight: About 7½ lbs.
Stock: Walnut finished hardwood.
Features: Double triggers, raised matted rib, beavertail fore-end. Massive twin underlugs mesh with synchronized sliding bolts. Introduced 1978. Imported by Interarms.
Price: 12 ga., 20 ga. $287.00
Price: 410 . . . .$303.00

Rossi Overland

ROSSI OVERLAND DOUBLE BARREL
Gauge: 12, 20, 410 (3" chambers).
Action: Sidelock with external hammers; Greener crossbolt.
Barrel: 12 ga., 20" (Imp. Cyl., Mod.) 28" (Mod. & Full), 20 ga., 20" (Mod., Full), 410 ga., 26" (Full & Full).
Weight: 6½ to 7 lbs.
Stock: Walnut p.g. with beavertail fore-end.
Features: Solid raised matted rib. Exposed hammers. Importerd by Interarms.
Price: 12 or 20 . . . .$273.00
Price: 410 ga. $289.00

Fox B-SE

SAVAGE FOX MODEL B-SE DOUBLE
Gauge: 12, 20, 410 (20, 2¾" and 3"; 410, 2½" and 3" shells).
Action: Hammerless, takedown; non-selective single trigger; auto. safety. Automatic ejectors.
Barrel: 12, 20 ga. 26" (Imp. Cyl., Mod.); 12 ga. (Mod., Full); 410, 26" (Full, Full). Vent. rib on all.
Stock: 14"x1½"x2½". Walnut, checkered p.g. and beavertail fore-end.
Weight: 12 ga. 7 lbs., 16 ga. 6¾ lbs., 20 ga. 6½ lbs., 410 ga. 6¼ lbs.
Features: Decorated, case-hardened frame; white bead front and middle sights.
Price: $338.45
Also available with double triggers, case hardened frame, without white line spacers and auto. ejectors as Model B $296.10

Consult our Directory pages for the location of firms mentioned.

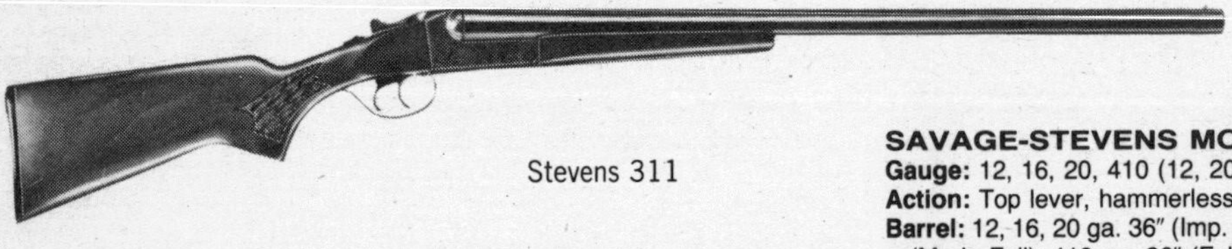

Stevens 311

SAVAGE-STEVENS MODEL 311 DOUBLE
Gauge: 12, 16, 20, 410 (12, 20 and 410, 3" chambers).
Action: Top lever, hammerless; double triggers, auto top tang safety.
Barrel: 12, 16, 20 ga. 36" (Imp. Cyl., Mod.); 12 ga. 28" (Mod., Full); 12 ga. 30" (Mod., Full); 410 ga. 26" (Full, Full).
Length: 45¾" over-all. **Weight:** 7-8 lbs. (30" bbl.).
Stock: 14"x1½"x2½". Walnut finish, p.g., fluted comb.
Features: Box type frame, case-hardened finish.
Price: $214.20

CAUTION: PRICES CHANGE. CHECK AT GUNSHOP.

SHOTGUNS—DOUBLE BARREL

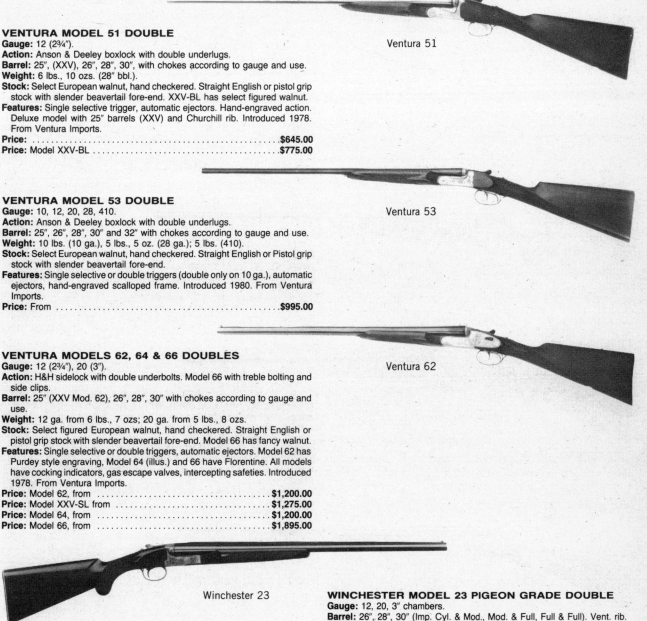

Ventura 51

Ventura 53

Ventura 62

Winchester 23

VENTURA MODEL 51 DOUBLE

Gauge: 12 (2¾").
Action: Anson & Deeley boxlock with double underlugs.
Barrel: 25", (XXV), 26", 28", 30", with chokes according to gauge and use.
Weight: 6 lbs., 10 ozs. (28" bbl.).
Stock: Select European walnut, hand checkered. Straight English or pistol grip stock with slender beavertail fore-end. XXV-BL has select figured walnut.
Features: Single selective trigger, automatic ejectors. Hand-engraved action. Deluxe model with 25" barrels (XXV) and Churchill rib. Introduced 1978. From Ventura Imports.
Price: $645.00
Price: Model XXV-BL $775.00

VENTURA MODEL 53 DOUBLE

Gauge: 10, 12, 20, 28, 410.
Action: Anson & Deeley boxlock with double underlugs.
Barrel: 25", 26", 28", 30" and 32" with chokes according to gauge and use.
Weight: 10 lbs. (10 ga.), 5 lbs., 5 oz. (28 ga.); 5 lbs. (410).
Stock: Select European walnut, hand checkered. Straight English or Pistol grip stock with slender beavertail fore-end.
Features: Single selective or double triggers (double only on 10 ga.), automatic ejectors, hand-engraved scalloped frame. Introduced 1980. From Ventura Imports.
Price: From $995.00

VENTURA MODELS 62, 64 & 66 DOUBLES

Gauge: 12 (2¾"), 20 (3").
Action: H&H sidelock with double underbolts. Model 66 with treble bolting and side clips.
Barrel: 25" (XXV Mod. 62), 26", 28", 30" with chokes according to gauge and use.
Weight: 12 ga. from 6 lbs., 7 ozs; 20 ga. from 5 lbs., 8 ozs.
Stock: Select figured European walnut, hand checkered. Straight English or pistol grip stock with slender beavertail fore-end. Model 66 has fancy walnut.
Features: Single selective or double triggers, automatic ejectors. Model 62 has Purdey style engraving, Model 64 (illus.) and 66 have Florentine. All models have cocking indicators, gas escape valves, intercepting safeties. Introduced 1978. From Ventura Imports.
Price: Model 62, from $1,200.00
Price: Model XXV-SL from $1,275.00
Price: Model 64, from $1,200.00
Price: Model 66, from $1,895.00

WINCHESTER MODEL 23 XTR LIGHTWEIGHT

Similar to standard Pigeon Grade except has 25½" barrel, English-style straight grip stock, thinner semi-beavertail fore-end. Available in 12 or 20 gauge (Imp. Cyl. & Imp. Mod.). Silver-gray frame has engraved bird scenes. Introduced 1981.
Price: $1,175.00

WINCHESTER MODEL 23 PIGEON GRADE DOUBLE

Gauge: 12, 20, 3" chambers.
Barrel: 26", 28", 30" (Imp. Cyl. & Mod., Mod. & Full, Full & Full). Vent. rib.
Weight: 7 lbs.; 6½ lbs. (20 ga.). **Length:** 46¾" over-all (30" bbls.)
Stock: High grade American walnut, beavertail fore-end. Deep cut checkering, new warm, rich color, high-lustre finish. 14"x1½"x2½".
Features: Mechanical trigger; ventilated tapered rib; selective ejectors. Receiver, top lever and trigger guard have silver gray satin finish and fine line scroll engraving. Introduced 1978.
Price: $1,150.00

WINCHESTER 21 CUSTOM DOUBLE GUN

12, 16 or 20 ga. Almost any choke or bbl. length combination. Matted rib, 2¾" chambers, rounded frame, stock of AA-grade full fancy American walnut to customer's dimensions; straight or p.g., cheekpiece, Monte Carlo and/or offset; field. Skeet or trap fore-end. Full fancy checkering, engine-turned receiver parts, gold plated trigger and gold oval name plate (optional) with three initials .... **Price on request from factory.**

Winchester 21 Grand American

Same as Custom and Pigeon grades except: style "B" stock carving, with style "6" engraving, all figures gold inlaid; extra pair of bbls. with beavertail fore-end, engraved and carved to match rest of gun; full leather trunk case or all, with canvas cover .... **Price on request from factory.**

Winchester 21 Pigeon Grade

Same as Custom grade except: 3" chambers, available in 12 and 20 ga.; matted or vent. rib, leather covered pad (optional); style "A" stock carving and style "6" engraving (see Win. catalog); gold inlaid p.g. cap, gold nameplate or 3 gold initials in guard .... **Price on request from factory.**

Consult our Directory pages for the location of firms mentioned.

SHOTGUNS—BOLT ACTION

Marlin 55

MARLIN SUPERGOOSE 10 M5510
Gauge: 10, 3½" Magnum or 2⅞" regular, 2-shot clip.
Barrel: 34" (Full), bead front sight, U-groove rear sight.
Weight: About 10½ lbs. **Length:** 55½" over-all.
Stock: Extra long American black walnut with p.g., Pachmayr vent. pad., white butt spacer.
Features: Bolt action, removable 2-shot clip magazine. Gold plated trigger, positive thumb safety, red cocking indicator. Comes with quick-detachable swivels and leather carrying strap.
Price: **$238.95**

MARLIN MODEL 55 GOOSE GUN BOLT ACTION
Gauge: 12 only, (3" mag. or 2¾").
Action: Bolt action, thumb safety, detachable 2-shot clip. Red cocking indicator.
Barrel: 36", Full choke.
Weight: 8 lbs., 57" over-all.
Stock: Walnut, p.g., ventilated recoil pad, leather strap & swivels. Mar-Shield* finish.
Features: Tapped for receiver sights. Swivels and leather carrying strap. Gold-plated trigger. Brass bead front sight, U-groove rear sight.
Price: **$144.95**

Mossberg 183K

MOSSBERG MODEL 183K BOLT ACTION
Gauge: 410, 3-shot (3" chamber).
Action: Bolt; top-loading mag.; thumb safety.
Barrel: 25" with C-Lect-Choke.
Weight: 5¾ lbs. **Length:** 45¼" over-all.
Stock: Walnut finish, p.g., Monte Carlo comb., rubber recoil pad w/spacer.
Features: Moulded trigger guard with finger grooves, gold bead front sight.
Price: **$111.95**

Mossberg 395K

MOSSBERG MODEL 395K BOLT ACTION
Gauge: 12, 3-shot (3" chamber).
Action: Bolt; takedown; detachable clip.
Barrel: 26" with C-Lect-Choke.
Weight: 7½ lbs. **Length:** 45¾" over-all.
Stock: Walnut finish, p.g. Monte Carlo comb; recoil pad.
Features: Streamlined action; top safety; grooved rear sight.
Price: **$129.95**
   Also available in 20 ga. 3" chamber 28" bbl. 6¼ lbs., as M385K .**$121.95**

Stevens 58

STEVENS SUPER VALUE 58 BOLT ACTION SHOTGUN
Gauge: 410 ga. (2½" and 3" chambers), 3-shot clip.
Action: Self-cocking bolt; double extractors; thumb safety.
Barrel: 24", Full choke.
Weight: 5½ lbs. **Length:** 43" over-all.
Stock: Walnut finish, checkered fore-end and p.g., recoil pad.
Features: Crisp trigger pull, Electro-Cote stock finish.
Price: ....**N.A.**

Western Field Bolt

WESTERN FIELD BOLT ACTION SHOTGUN
Gauge: 12, 20 or 410 (3" chamber).
Action: Self cocking, bolt action. Thumb safety. 3-shot magazine.
Barrel: 24" (Full) 410, 26" (20 ga.), 28" (12 ga.).
Weight: 5½ lbs. **Length:** 44½" over-all (410 ga.).
Stock: Hardwood, Monte Carlo design.
Features: Top safety, grooved rear sight.
Price: 410 ga. **$99.99**
Price: 20 ga. **$99.99**
Price: 12 ga. **$109.99**

CAUTION: PRICES CHANGE. CHECK AT GUNSHOP.

BAIKAL IJ-18E SINGLE BARREL
Gauge: 12 or 20 ga., 2¾" chambers; 410 ga., 3" chamber.
Barrel: 12 ga. 28" (Mod.), 30" (Full), 20 ga. 26" (Mod.), 410 ga. 26" (Full).
Weight: 5¾ lbs.
Stock: Walnut-finished hardwood. Hand checkered p.g. White spacers on buttplate.
Features: Chrome barrel and chamber. Cross-bolt safety in trigger guard. Cocking indicator. Selective ejector-extractor. Imported by Baikal International.
Price: $79.95
Price: IJ-18 (extractor only) $73.50

> Consult our Directory pages for
> the location of firms mentioned.

Beretta Mk.II

BERETTA MARK II SINGLE BARREL
Gauge: 12 only (2¾").
Barrel: 32", 34" (Full).
Weight: About 8 lbs.
Stock: 14⅜"x1⅜"x1⅝". European walnut, checkered p.g. and fore-end.
Features: Action, barrel and stock derive from S58 over-under. Trap rib, two sight beads, chrome lined bores. Ventilated recoil pad. From Beretta Arms Co.
Price: $530.00

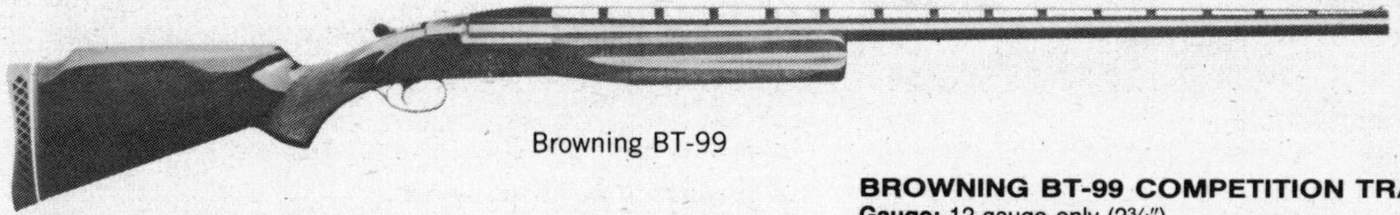

Browning BT-99

CBC "THE GAMEGETTER" DELUXE SINGLE BARREL
Gauge: 12, 20 (2¾"), 410 (3").
Action: Button-break on trigger guard.
Barrel: 12 & 20 ga. 28" (Full); 410 ga. 26" (Full).
Weight: 6½ lbs.
Stock: Walnut finished hardwood, full beavertail fore-end.
Sights: Metal bead front.
Features: Exposed hammer. Automatic ejector. Imported from Brazil by F.I.E. Corp.
Price: $68.95
Price: 20 and 410, Youth Model $69.95
Price: Combo rifle-shotgun (20 ga. or 30-30 interchangeable bbls.) $119.95

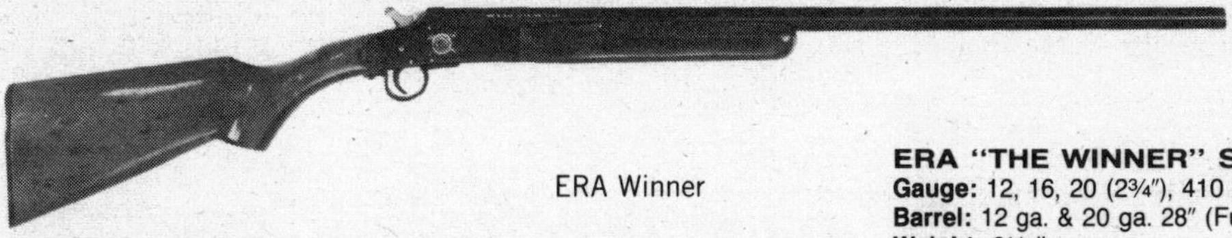

BROWNING BT-99 COMPETITION TRAP SPECIAL
Gauge: 12 gauge only (2¾").
Action: Top lever break-open, hammerless.
Barrel: 32" or 34" (Mod., Imp. Mod. or Full) with ¹¹⁄₃₂" wide high post floating vent. rib.
Weight: 8 lbs. (32" bbl.).
Stock: French walnut; hand checkered, full pistol grip, full beavertail fore-end; recoil pad. Trap dimensions with M.C. 14⅜"x1⅜"x1⅜"x2".
Sights: Ivory front and middle beads.
Features: Gold plated trigger with 3½-lb. pull, deluxe trap-style recoil pad, auto ejector, no safety. Also available in engraved Pigeon Grade.
Price: Grade I Competition $659.95
Price: Grade I Competition with extra bbl. $935.00
Price: Pigeon Grade Competition $1,500.00

ERA Winner

ERA "THE WINNER" SINGLE BARREL SHOTGUN
Gauge: 12, 16, 20 (2¾"), 410 (3").
Barrel: 12 ga. & 20 ga. 28" (Full); 410 ga. (Full).
Weight: 6½ lbs.
Stock: Walnut stained hardwood, beavertail fore-end.
Sights: Metal bead front.
Features: Trigger guard is pulled to open action. Exposed hammer, auto extractor. Imported from Brazil by F.I.E. Corp.
Price: $68.95
Price: 20 and 410 ga. Youth Model $69.95

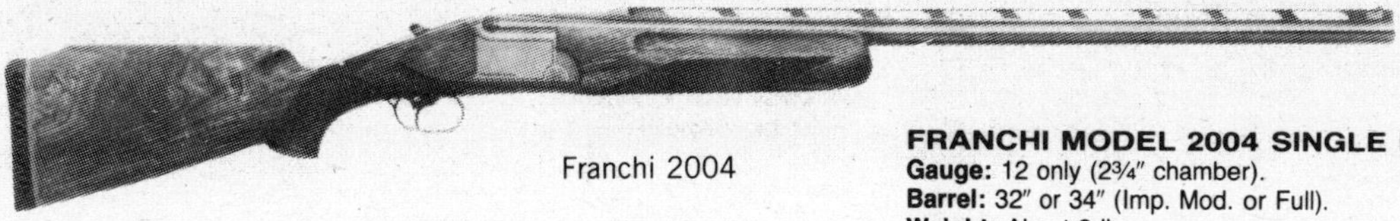

Franchi 2004

FRANCHI MODEL 2004 SINGLE BARREL TRAP
Gauge: 12 only (2¾" chamber).
Barrel: 32" or 34" (Imp. Mod. or Full).
Weight: About 8 lbs.
Stock: 14½"x1⅞"x1½". Fancy French walnut; checkered p.g. and fore-end. Available in Monte Carlo or straight style (interchangeble). Different dimensions avail.
Features: "Ceiling-Sell" trap trigger; raised competition, ventilated, trap rib. Buttstock drilled and tapped for recoil reducer. Comes with fitted luggage-type hard case. From Stoeger Industries.
Price: $1,550.00

GALEF COMPANION SINGLE BARREL SHOTGUN
Gauge: 12, 20, 410 (3"); 16, 28 (2¾").
Action: Folding boxlock.
Barrel: 28" exc. 12 (30") and 410 (26"), all Full.
Weight: 5½ lbs. (12) to 4½ lbs. (410).
Stock: 14"x1½"x2⅝" hand checkered walnut, p.g.
Features: Non-auto safety, folds. Vent. rib $5.00 additional. Imported from Italy by Galef.
Price: Plain bbl. ....$138.00   Vent. rib $167.20

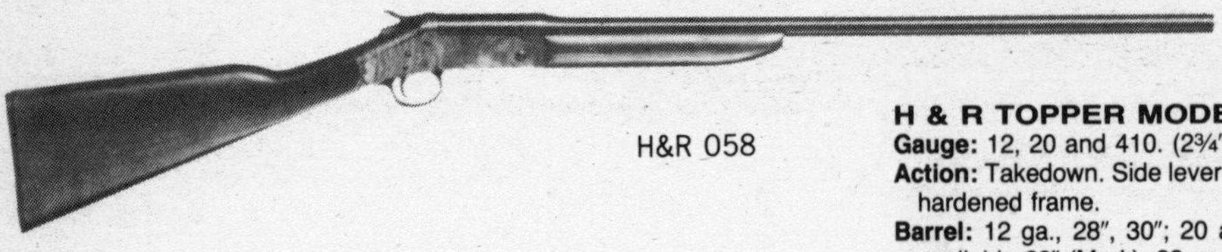

SHOTGUNS — SINGLE BARREL

H&R 058

H & R TOPPER MODELS 058 and 098
Gauge: 12, 20 and 410. (2¾" or 3" chamber), 16, 28 (2¾" only).
Action: Takedown. Side lever opening. External hammer, auto ejection. Case hardened frame.
Barrel: 12 ga., 28", 30"; 20 and 410 ga., 28". (Full choke). 12, 16, 20 ga. available 28" (Mod.), 28 and 410 ga., 26" (Mod., Full).
Stock: Walnut finished hardwood; p.g., (14"x1¾"x2½").
Weight: 5 to 6½ lbs., according to gauge and bbl. length.
Features: Self-adj. bbl. lock; coil springs throughout.
Price: M58 . . . .$79.50
  Model 98, Topper Deluxe Nickel frame, ebony finished stock. 12, 20 and 410 ga., 26" barrel $79.50

H & R Model 088
Same features as Model 058 except has semi-pistol grip stock. Available in most popular gauge and choke combinations, including 12 ga. with 30" or 32" (Full) barrel. Junior model also available (does not have recoil pad).
Price: $68.75

H & R Model 176 Magnums
Same as Model 058 except in 10 gauge (3½" chamber) and 12 gauge (3" chamber) with 36" (Full) barrels. Also available with 32" (Full) barrel in 10, 12, 16 (2¾" chamber) and 20 (3" chamber) gauges. All barrels specially designed for steel shot use. Special long fore-end and recoil pad.
Price: From $84.50

H & R Topper Jr. Model 490
Like M058 except ideally proportioned stock for the smaller shooter. Can be cheaply changed to full size. 20 ga. (Mod.), 28 ga. (Mod.) or 410 (Full) 26" bbl. Weight 5 lbs., 40½" over-all $79.50

H & R Topper Buck Model 162
Same as M58 except 12 or 20 ga. 24" cyl. bored bbl., adj. folding leaf rear sight, blade front, 5½ lbs.; over-all 40". Cross bolt safety: push-button action release $89.50

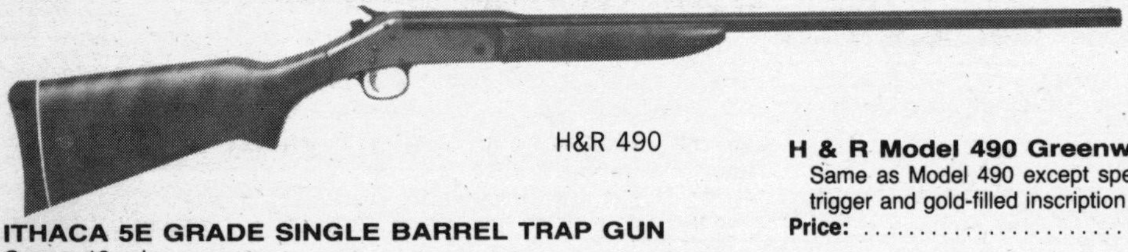

H&R 490

H & R Model 490 Greenwing
Same as Model 490 except specially polished blue finish with gold-finish trigger and gold-filled inscription on frame.
Price: $89.50

ITHACA 5E GRADE SINGLE BARREL TRAP GUN
Gauge: 12 only.
Action: Top lever break open hammerless, dual locking lugs.
Barrel: 30" or 32", rampless vent. rib.
Stock: (14½"x1½"x1⅞"). Select walnut, checkered p.g. and beavertail fore-end, p.g. cap, recoil pad, Monte Carlo comb, cheekpiece, Cast-on, cast-off or extreme deviation from standard stock dimensions $100 extra. Reasonable deviation allowed without extra charge.
Features: Frame, top lever and trigger guard extensively engraved and gold inlaid. Gold name plate in stock.
Price: Custom made $6,500.00
Price: Dollar Grade $9,000.00

> Consult our Directory pages for
> the location of firms mentioned.

Ljutic Mono Gun

LJUTIC MONO GUN SINGLE BARREL
Gauge: 12 ga. only.
Barrel: 34", choked to customer specs; hollow-milled rib, 35½" sight plane.
Weight: Approx. 9 lbs.
Stock: To customer specs. Oil finish, hand checkered.
Features: Pull or release trigger; removeable trigger guard contains trigger and hammer mechanism; Ljutic pushbutton opener on front of trigger guard. From Ljutic Industries.
Price: $3,195.00
Price: With Olympic Rib, custom 32" barrel, 2 screw-in chokes . .$3,495.00

Ljutic Adjustable Barrel Mono Gun
Similar to standard Mono except has micrometer-adjustable choke (allows shooter to adj. the pattern from flat to an elevation of 4 feet), choice of Olympic, step-style or standard rib. Custom stock measurements, fancy wood, etc. $3,495.00

LJUTIC SPACE GUN SHOTGUN
Gauge: 12 only, 2¾" chamber.
Barrel: 30" (Full);
Weight: 8½ lbs.
Stock: 14½" to 15" pull length; universal comb; medium or large p.g.
Sights: Choice of front sight or vent. rib.
Features: Choice of pull or release button trigger; anti-recoil mechanism. Revolutionary new design. Introduced 1981. From Ljutic Industries.
Price: From $995.00

MONTE CARLO SINGLE BARREL SHOTGUN
Gauge: 12 (2¾" chamber).
Action: Monte Carlo, bottom release.
Barrel: 32" (Trap).
Weight: 8¼ lbs.
Stock: 14½"x1⅛"x1⅝" hand checkered walnut, p.g., beavertail fore-end, recoil pad.
Features: Auto ejector, slide safety, gold plated trigger. Imported from Italy by Galef.
Price: $317.00

CAUTION: PRICES CHANGE. CHECK AT GUNSHOP.

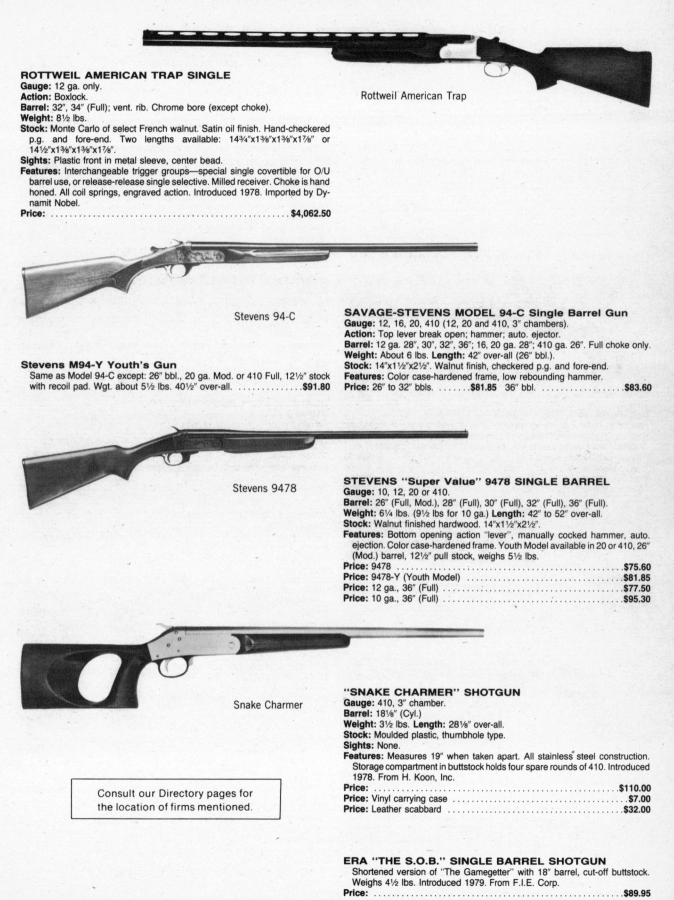

ROTTWEIL AMERICAN TRAP SINGLE

Gauge: 12 ga. only.
Action: Boxlock.
Barrel: 32″, 34″ (Full); vent. rib. Chrome bore (except choke).
Weight: 8½ lbs.
Stock: Monte Carlo of select French walnut. Satin oil finish. Hand-checkered p.g. and fore-end. Two lengths available: 14¾″x1⅜″x1⅜″x1⅞″ or 14½″x1⅜″x1⅜″x1⅞″.
Sights: Plastic front in metal sleeve, center bead.
Features: Interchangeable trigger groups—special single covertible for O/U barrel use, or release-release single selective. Milled receiver. Choke is hand honed. All coil springs, engraved action. Introduced 1978. Imported by Dynamit Nobel.
Price: $4,062.50

Rottweil American Trap

Stevens 94-C

Stevens M94-Y Youth's Gun

Same as Model 94-C except: 26″ bbl., 20 ga. Mod. or 410 Full, 12½″ stock with recoil pad. Wgt. about 5½ lbs. 40½″ over-all. $91.80

SAVAGE-STEVENS MODEL 94-C Single Barrel Gun

Gauge: 12, 16, 20, 410 (12, 20 and 410, 3″ chambers).
Action: Top lever break open; hammer; auto. ejector.
Barrel: 12 ga. 28″, 30″, 32″, 36″; 16, 20 ga. 28″; 410 ga. 26″. Full choke only.
Weight: About 6 lbs. **Length:** 42″ over-all (26″ bbl.).
Stock: 14″x1½″x2½″. Walnut finish, checkered p.g. and fore-end.
Features: Color case-hardened frame, low rebounding hammer.
Price: 26″ to 32″ bbls. . . . .$81.85   36″ bbl. $83.60

Stevens 9478

STEVENS "Super Value" 9478 SINGLE BARREL

Gauge: 10, 12, 20 or 410.
Barrel: 26″ (Full, Mod.), 28″ (Full), 30″ (Full), 32″ (Full), 36″ (Full).
Weight: 6¼ lbs. (9½ lbs for 10 ga.) **Length:** 42″ to 52″ over-all.
Stock: Walnut finished hardwood. 14″x1½″x2½″.
Features: Bottom opening action "lever", manually cocked hammer, auto. ejection. Color case-hardened frame. Youth Model available in 20 or 410, 26″ (Mod.) barrel, 12½″ pull stock, weighs 5½ lbs.
Price: 9478 . . . .$75.60
Price: 9478-Y (Youth Model) $81.85
Price: 12 ga., 36″ (Full) $77.50
Price: 10 ga., 36″ (Full) $95.30

Snake Charmer

"SNAKE CHARMER" SHOTGUN

Gauge: 410, 3″ chamber.
Barrel: 18⅛″ (Cyl.)
Weight: 3½ lbs. **Length:** 28⅛″ over-all.
Stock: Moulded plastic, thumbhole type.
Sights: None.
Features: Measures 19″ when taken apart. All stainless steel construction. Storage compartment in buttstock holds four spare rounds of 410. Introduced 1978. From H. Koon, Inc.
Price: $110.00
Price: Vinyl carrying case $7.00
Price: Leather scabbard $32.00

> Consult our Directory pages for the location of firms mentioned.

ERA "THE S.O.B." SINGLE BARREL SHOTGUN

Shortened version of "The Gamegetter" with 18″ barrel, cut-off buttstock. Weighs 4½ lbs. Introduced 1979. From F.I.E. Corp.
Price: $89.95

BLACK POWDER GUNS

The following pages catalog the black powder arms currently available to U.S. shooters. These range from quite precise replicas of historically significant arms to totally new designs created expressly to give the black powder shooter the benefits of modern technology.

Most of the replicas are imported, and many are available from more than one source. Thus examples of a given model such as the 1860 Army revolver or Zouave rifle purchased from different importers may vary in price, finish and fitting. Most of them bear proof marks, indicating that they have been test fired in the proof house of their country of origin.

A list of the importers and the retail price range are included with the description for each model. Many local dealers handle more than one importer's products, giving the prospective buyer an opportunity to make his own judgment in selecting a black powder gun. Most importers have catalogs available free or at nominal cost, and some are well worth having for the useful information on black powder shooting they provide in addition to their detailed descriptions and specifications of the guns.

A number of special accessories are also available for the black powder shooter. These include replica powder flasks, bullet moulds, cappers and tools, as well as more modern devices to facilitate black powder cleaning and maintenance. Ornate presentation cases and even detachable shoulder stocks are also available for some black powder pistols from their importers. Again, dealers or the importers will have catalogs.

The black powder guns are arranged in four sections: Single Shot Pistols, Revolvers, Muskets & Rifles, and Shotguns. The guns within each section are arranged by date of the original, with the oldest first. Thus the 1847 Walker replica leads off the revolver section, and flintlocks precede percussion arms in the other sections.

BLACK POWDER SINGLE SHOT PISTOLS — FLINT & PERCUSSION

Charleville

CHARLEVILLE FLINTLOCK PISTOL
Caliber: 69.
Barrel: 7½".
Weight: 48 ozs. **Length:** 13½" ovr-all.
Stock: Walnut.
Sights: None.
Features: Brass frame, polished steel barrel, brass buttcap and backstrap. Replica of original 1777 pistol. Imported by Dixie.
Price: $125.00

Traditions, Inc. Tower Pistol
Similar to Tower Flintlock except 45-cal. only, 9" blued barrel, weighs 36 ozs. and is 15¼" over-all. Solid brass furniture, blued ramrod, stainless steel nipple, color case-hardened lock. Imported from Spain by Traditions, Inc.
Price: Assembled, percussion $75.00
Price: Assembled, flint $83.00
Price: Kit, percussion $48.00
Price: Kit, flint $52.00

BLACK WATCH SCOTCH PISTOL
Caliber: 58.
Barrel: 7".
Weight: 1½ lbs. **Length:** 12" over-all.
Stock: Brass.
Sights: None.
Features: Faithful reproduction of this military flintlock. From Dixie, Hopkins & Allen.
Price: ....$99.95 to $125.00

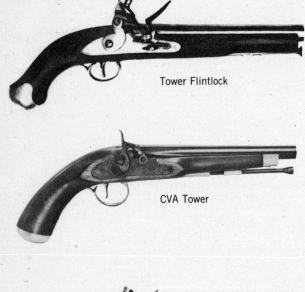

Tower Flintlock

CVA Tower

TOWER FLINTLOCK PISTOL
Caliber: 45, 69.
Barrel: 8¼".
Weight: 40 oz. **Length:** 14" over-all.
Stock: Walnut.
Sights: Fixed.
Features: Engraved lock, brass furniture. Specifications, including caliber, weight and length may vary with importers. Available as flint or percussion. Imported by F.I.E..
Price: ....$59.95.

CVA TOWER PISTOL
Caliber: 45.
Barrel: 9", octagon, rifled.
Weight: 36 oz. **Length:** 15¼" over-all.
Stock: Selected hardwood.
Sights: Brass front, dovetail open fixed rear.
Features: Color case-hardened and engraved lock plate; early-style brass trigger; brass trigger guard, nose cap, thimbles, grip cap; blued barrel and ramrod. Introduced 1981.
Price: Complete, percussion $89.95
Price: Kit form, percussion $69.95
Price: Kit form, flintlock $59.95

Harper's Ferry 1806

HARPER'S FERRY 1806 PISTOL
Caliber: 54.
Barrel: 10".
Weight: 40 oz. **Length:** 16" over-all.
Stock: Walnut.
Sights: Fixed.
Features: Case hardened lock, brass mounted browned bbl. Replica of the first U.S. Gov't.-made flintlock pistol. Imported by Navy Arms.
Price: $150.00

BLACK POWDER SINGLE SHOT PISTOLS—FLINT & PERCUSSION

Kentucky Percussion

KENTUCKY FLINTLOCK PISTOL
Caliber: 44, 45.
Barrel: 10⅛″.
Weight: 32 oz. **Length:** 15½″ over-all.
Stock: Walnut.
Sights: Fixed.
Features: Specifications, including caliber, weight and length may vary with importer. Case hardened lock, blued bbl.; available also as brass bbl. flint Model 1821 ($110.00, Navy). Imported by Navy Arms, The Armoury, F.I.E., CVA (kit only), Hopkins & Allen, Traditions, Inc.
Price: ....$40.95 to $142.00
Price: In kit form, from $112.00
Price: Brass barrel (Navy Arms) $140.00
Price: Single cased set (Navy Arms) $191.00
Price: Brass bbl., single cased set (Navy Arms) $206.00

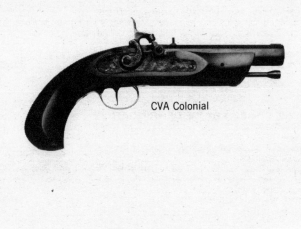

CVA Colonial

CVA Mountain

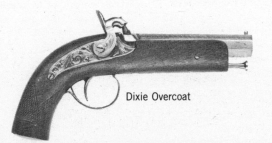

Dixie Overcoat

Kentucky Percussion Pistol
Similar to flint version but percussion lock. Imported by The Armoury, Navy Arms, F.I.E., CVA, Dixie, Century, Armsport, Sile, Hopkins & Allen.
Price: ....$26.95 to $91.80
Price: Brass barrel $132.00
Price: In kit form ....$35.95 to $102.00
Price: Single cased set (Navy Arms) $176.00
Price: Brass bbl. single cased set (Navy Arms) $191.00

Traditions, Inc. Kentucky Percussion Pistol
Similar to Kentucky Percussion except 45-cal. only, 10¼″ blued barrel, 15¼″ over-all. Choice of American walnut or selected hardwood stock. Color case-hardened lock, stainless steel nipple. Imported by Traditions, Inc.
Price: Assembled, hardwood stock $72.00
Price: Assembled, walnut stock $75.00
Price: Kit, hardwood only $47.00

CVA COLONIAL PISTOL
Caliber: 45 (.451″ bore).
Barrel: 6¾″, octagonal, rifled.
Length: 12¾″ over-all.
Stock: Selected hardwood.
Features: Case hardened lock, brass furniture, fixed sights. Steel ramrod. Available in either flint or percussion. Imported by CVA.
Price: Percussion $64.95
Also available in kit form, either flint or percussion. Stock 95% inletted.
Price: Flint $49.95
Price: Percussion $39.95

Traditions, Inc. Colonial Pistol
Similar to CVA Colonial Pistol except has stainless steel nipple, deep groove rifling. Imported by Traditions, Inc.
Price: Assembled, percussion $55.00
Price: Assembled, flint $61.00
Price: Kit, percussion $35.00
Price: Kit, flint $41.00

CVA PERCUSSION MOUNTAIN PISTOL
Caliber: 45 or 50 cal.
Barrel: 9″, octagon. ¹⁵⁄₁₆″ across flats.
Weight: 40 oz. **Length:** 14″ over-all.
Stock: American maple.
Sights: German silver blade front, fixed primitive rear.
Features: Engraved percussion-style lock. Adjustable sear engagement. Fly and bridle. Hooked breech. Browned steel on finished pistol. German silver wedge plates. Stainless steel nipples. Hardwood ramrod. Belt hook. Introduced 1978. From CVA.
Price: $119.95
Price: Kit form $109.95

Traditions, Inc. Mountain Pistol
Similar to CVA Mountain Pistol except stock is selected hardwood, color case-hardened lock. Available in flint or percussion. Imported by Traditions, Inc.
Price: Assembled, percussion $92.00
Price: Assembled, flint $97.00
Price: Kit, percussion $81.00
Price: Kit, flint $86.00

DIXIE OVERCOAT PISTOL
Caliber: 39.
Barrel: 4″, smoothbore.
Weight: 13 oz. **Length:** 8″ over-all.
Stock: Walnut-finished hardwood. Checkered p.g.
Sights: Fixed.
Features: Shoots .380″ balls. Breech plug and engraved lock are burnished steel finish; barrel and trigger guard blued.
Price: Plain model $26.95
Price: Engraved model $34.50

BLACK POWDER SINGLE SHOT PISTOLS—FLINT & PERCUSSION

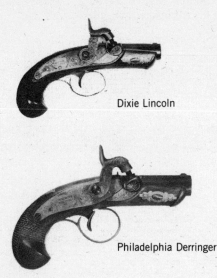
Dixie Lincoln

DIXIE LINCOLN DERRINGER
Caliber: 41.
Barrel: 2″, 8 lands, 8 grooves.
Weight: 7 oz. **Length:** 5½″ over-all.
Stock: Walnut finish, checkered.
Sights: Fixed.
Features: Authentic copy of the "Lincoln Derringer." Shoots .400″ patched ball. German silver furniture includes trigger guard with pineapple finial, wedge plates, nose, wrist, side and teardrop inlays. All furniture, lockplate, hammer, and breech plug engraved. Imported from Italy by Dixie Gun Works.
Price: With wooden case $144.95
Price: Kit (Not engraved) $54.95

Philadelphia Derringer

PHILADELPHIA DERRINGER PERCUSSION PISTOL
Caliber: 41, 45.
Barrel: 3⅛″.
Weight: 14 oz. **Length:** 7″ over-all.
Stock: Walnut, checkered grip.
Sights: Fixed.
Features: Engraved wedge holder and bbl. Also available in flintlock version (Armoury, $29.95). Imported by Sile (45-cal. only), Hawes, CVA (45-cal. percussion only), Hopkins & Allen.
Price: . . . .$18.37 to $120.00
Price: Kit form (CVA) $36.95

Traditions, Inc. Philadelphia Derringer
Similar to standard Derringer except has coil spring back action, brass wedge plates, stainless steel nipple. Selected hardwood stock, brass blade front sight. Imported by Traditions, Inc.
Price: Assembled, percussion $46.00
Price: Kit, percussion $33.00

DIXIE PHILADELPHIA DERRINGER
Caliber: 41.
Barrel: 3½″, octagon.
Weight: 8 oz. **Length:** 5½″ over-all.
Stock: Walnut, checkered p.g.
Sights: Fixed.
Features: Barrel and lock are blued; brass furniture. From Dixie Gun Works.
Price: $39.95

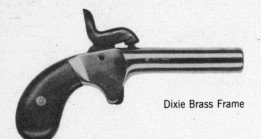
Dixie Brass Frame

DIXIE BRASS FRAME DERRINGER
Caliber: 41.
Barrel: 2½″.
Weight: 7 oz. **Length:** 5½″ over-all.
Stock: Walnut.
Features: Brass frame, color case hardened hammer and trigger. Shoots .395″ round ball. Engraved model available. From Dixie Gun Works.
Price: Plain model $43.95
Price: Engraved model $54.95

BRITISH DRAGOON FLINT PISTOL
Caliber: .615″.
Barrel: 12″, polished steel.
Weight: 3 lbs., 2 oz. **Length:** 19″ over-all.
Stock: Walnut, with brass furniture.
Features: Lockplate marked "Willets 1761." Brass trigger guard and butt cap. From Navy Arms.
Price: $350.00
Price: $295.00

NAVY ARMS LE PAGE DUELING PISTOL
Caliber: 44.
Barrel: 9″, octagon.
Weight: 34 ozs. **Length:** 15″ over-all.
Stock: European walnut.
Sights: Adjustable rear.
Features: Single set trigger. Silvered metal finish. From Navy Arms.
Price: $300.00

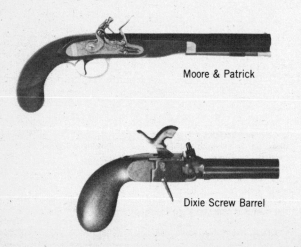
Moore & Patrick

Dixie Screw Barrel

MOORE & PATRICK FLINT DUELING PISTOL
Caliber: 45.
Barrel: 10″, rifled.
Weight: 32 oz. **Length:** 14½″ over-all.
Stock: European walnut, checkered.
Sights: Fixed.
Features: Engraved, silvered lock plate, blue barrel. German silver furniture. From Navy Arms.
Price: $325.00

DIXIE SCREW BARREL PISTOL
Caliber: .445″.
Barrel: 2½″.
Weight: 8 oz. **Length:** 6½″ over-all.
Stock: Walnut.
Features: Trigger folds down when hammer is cocked. Close copy of the originals once made in Belgium. User No. 11 percussion caps.
Price: $69.95

CAUTION: PRICES CHANGE. CHECK AT GUNSHOP.

BLACK POWDER SINGLE SHOT PISTOLS — FLINT & PERCUSSION

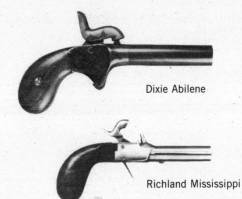

Dixie Abilene

Richland Mississippi

DIXIE ABILENE DERRINGER
Caliber: 41.
Barrel: 2½", 6-groove rifling.
Weight: 8 oz. **Length:** 6½" over-all.
Stocks: Walnut.
Features: All steel version of Dixie's brass-framed derringers. Blued barrel, color case hardened frame and hammer. Shoots .395" patched ball. Comes with wood presentation case.
Price: $44.95

Richland "Mississippi Derringer"
Similar to Dixie Brass Frame Derringer except over-all length is 5⅜". Comes complete or as kit.
Price: Complete $29.95
Price: Kit form $23.95

T.G.A. LIEGE DERRINGER
Caliber: 451".
Barrel: 2⅜".
Weight: 7 oz. **Length:** 6½" over-all.
Stock: Walnut.
Sights: None.
Features: Removable round, rifled barrel. All metal parts case-hardened. Folding trigger. Introduced 1980. From Trail Guns Armory.
Price: $55.00

CLASSIC ARMS ELGIN CUTLASS PISTOL
Caliber: 44 (.440").
Barrel: 4¼".
Weight: 21 oz. **Length:** 12" over-all.
Stock: Walnut.
Sights: None.
Features: Replica of the pistol used by the U.S. Navy as a boarding weapon. Smoothbore barrel. Available as a kit or finished. From Classic Arms Ltd.
Price: Kit $75.00
Price: Finished $99.95

HOPKINS & ALLEN BOOT PISTOL
Caliber: 36 or 45.
Barrel: 6".
Weight: 42 oz. **Length:** 13" over-all.
Stock: Walnut.
Sights: Silver blade front; rear adj. for e.
Features: Under-hammer design. From Hopkins & Allen.
Price: $69.95

BUCCANEER DOUBLE BARREL PISTOL
Caliber: 44.
Barrel: 9½".
Weight: 40 oz. **Length:** 15½" over-all.
Stock: Walnut, one piece.
Sights: Fixed.
Features: Case hardened and engraved lockplate, solid brass fittings. Percussion or flintlock. Imported by The Armoury. Available as the "Corsair" from Armsport (44 cal. only).
Price: Complete $73.95
Price: Kit form $61.95
Price: Corsair, complete ....$99.50 Kit $86.00

BOUNTY HUNTER PERCUSSION PISTOL
Caliber: 44.
Barrel: 17".
Weight: 3½ lbs. **Length:** 22" over-all.
Stock: Oil stained walnut.
Sights: Fixed.
Features: A Kentucky-style pistol with long barrel. Polish brass furniture, blued barrel, color case hardened lock. Kit or complete. From Hopkins & Allen.
Price: $86.95

Elgin Cutlass

Buccaneer

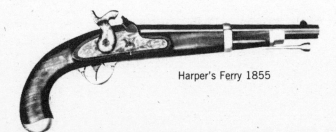

Harper's Ferry 1855

HARPER'S FERRY MODEL 1855 PERCUSSION PISTOL
Caliber: 58.
Barrel: 11¾", rifled.
Weight: 56 oz. **Length:** 18" over-all.
Stock: Walnut.
Sights: Fixed.
Features: Case hardened lock and hammer; brass furniture; blued bbl. Shoulder stock available, priced at $35.00. Imported by Navy Arms.
Price: $200.00
Price: With detachable shoulder stock $245.00

BLACK POWDER SINGLE SHOT PISTOLS—FLINT & PERCUSSION

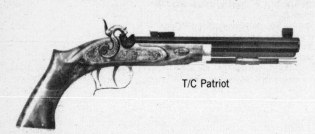

T/C Patriot

THOMPSON/CENTER PATRIOT PERCUSSION PISTOL
Caliber: 45.
Barrel: 9¼".
Weight: 36 oz. **Length:** 16" over-all.
Stock: Walnut.
Sights: Patridge-type. Rear adj. for w. and e.
Features: Hook breech system; double set triggers; coil mainspring. From Thompson/Center Arms.
Price: $155.00

TRADITIONS, INC. PATRIOT PISTOL
Caliber: 45.
Barrel: 9¾", octagon, blued.
Weight: 40 ozs. **Length:** 15½" over-all.
Stock: Selected hardwood.
Sights: Brass blade front, rear adj. for windage.
Features: Color case-hardened lock, early brass trigger, blued trigger guard, adjustable sear engagement, stainless steel nipple. Imported by Traditions, Inc.
Price: Assembled, percussion $92.00
Price: Assembled, flint $97.00
Price: Kit, percussion $81.00
Price: Kit, flint $86.00

> Consult our Directory pages for the location of firms mentioned.

Trophy Winner

TROPHY WINNER PERCUSSION TARGET PISTOL
Caliber: 44.
Barrel: 10" octagonal.
Weight: 42 oz.
Stocks: Walnut.
Sights: Bead front, rear adj. for w. and e.
Features: Engraved scenes on frame sides; brass backstrap and trigger guard; case hardened frame and hammer. Imported by Dixie.
Price: $125.00
Price: Optional 28-ga. shotgun barrel, 10" long $19.95

BLACK POWDER REVOLVERS

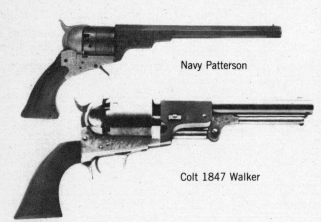

Navy Patterson

Colt 1847 Walker

NAVY ARMS COLT PATTERSON
Caliber: 36, 6-shot.
Barrel: 9".
Weight: 2½ lbs. **Length:** 14" over-all.
Stocks: Walnut.
Sights: Fixed.
Features: Made in a limited edition of 500 standard guns and 50 engraved models. Imported by Navy Arms.
Price: Standard $195.00
Price: Engraved $500.00

COLT 1847 WALKER PERCUSSION REVOLVER
Caliber: 44.
Barrel: 9", 7 groove, RH twist.
Weight: 73 oz.
Stocks: One-piece walnut.
Sights: German silver front sight, hammer notch rear.
Features: Made in U.S. by Colt. Faithful reproduction of the original gun, including markings. Color cased frame, hammer, loading lever and plunger. Blue steel backstrap, brass square-back trigger guard. Blued barrel, cylinder, trigger and wedge. Accessories available. Re-introduced 1979.
Price: $500.95

WALKER 1847 PERCUSSION REVOLVER
Caliber: 44, 6-shot.
Barrel: 9".
Weight: 72 oz. **Length:** 15½" over-all.
Stocks: Walnut.
Sights: Fixed.
Features: Case hardened frame, loading lever and hammer; iron backstrap; brass trigger guard; engraved cylinder. Imported by Sile, Navy Arms, Dixie, Armsport.
Price: . . . .$125.00 to $160.00
Price: Single cased set (Navy Arms) $219.00

Walker 1847

CAUTION: PRICES CHANGE. CHECK AT GUNSHOP.

BLACK POWDER REVOLVERS

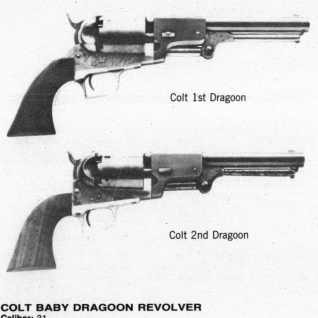

Colt 1st Dragoon

Colt 2nd Dragoon

COLT 1st MODEL DRAGOON
Caliber: 44.
Barrel: 7½", part round, part octagon.
Weight: 66 oz.
Stocks: One piece walnut.
Sights: German silver blade front, hammer notch rear.
Features: First model has oval bolt cuts in cylinder, square-back flared trigger guard, V-type mainspring, short trigger. Ranger and Indian scene on cylinder. Color cased frame, loading lever, plunger and hammer; blue barrel, cylinder, trigger and wedge. Polished brass backstrap and trigger guard. Re-introduced in 1979. From Colt.
Price: $399.95

Colt 2nd Model Dragoon Revolver
Similar to the 1st Model except this model is distinguished by its rectangular bolt cuts in the cylinder, straight square-back trigger guard, short trigger and flat mainspring with roller in hammer.
Price: $399.95

Colt 3rd Model Dragoon Revolver
Similar to the 1st Model except has oval trigger guard, long trigger, flat mainspring and rectangular bolt cuts.
Price: $399.95

COLT BABY DRAGOON REVOLVER
Caliber: 31.
Barrel: 4", 7 groove, RH twist.
Weight: About 21 oz.
Stocks: Varnished walnut.
Sights: Brass pin front, hammer notch rear.
Features: Unfluted cylinder with Ranger and Indian scene; cupped cylinder pin; no grease grooves; one safety pin on cylinder and slot in hammer face; straight (flat) mainspring. Silver backstrap and trigger guard. Re-introduced in 1979. From Colt.
Price: $361.50

> Consult our Directory pages for
> the location of firms mentioned.

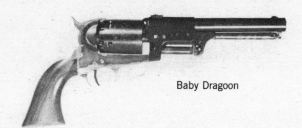

Baby Dragoon

BABY DRAGOON 1848 PERCUSSION REVOLVER
Caliber: 31, 5-shot.
Barrel: 4", 5", 6".
Weight: 24 oz. (6" bbl.). **Length:** 10½" (6" bbl.).
Stocks: Walnut.
Sights: Fixed.
Features: Case hardened frame; safety notches on hammer and safety pin in cylinder; engraved cylinder scene; octagonal bbl. Imported by Sile, F.I.E., Hawes, Dixie.
Price: . . . .$54.95 to $110.00
Price: Kit form (F.I.E. Corp.) $52.50
Price: Fully engraved (F.I.E. Corp.) $60.95

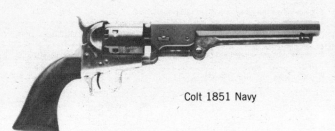

Colt 1851 Navy

COLT 1851 NAVY PERCUSSION REVOLVER
Caliber: 36.
Barrel: 7½", octagonal, 7 groove, LH twist.
Weight: 42 oz.
Stocks: One-piece varnished walnut.
Sights: Brass pin front, hammer notch rear.
Features: Made in U.S. by Colt. Faithful reproduction of the original gun. Color cased frame, loading lever, plunger, hammer and latch. Blue cylinder, trigger, barrel, screws, wedge. Silver plated brass backstrap and square-back trigger guard. Accessories available. Re-introduced in 1979.
Price: $374.50

Lyman 1851 Squareback Navy 36
Same as standard Colt model except 36 cal. only, has square-back trigger guard, nickel plated backstrap, color case hardened frame $149.95
Price: Kit form $109.95

Colt 1861 Navy Percussion Revolver
Similar to 1851 Navy except has round 7½" barrel, rounded trigger guard, German silver blade front sight, "creeping" loading lever.
Price: $374.50

CAUTION: PRICES CHANGE. CHECK AT GUNSHOP.

BLACK POWDER REVOLVERS

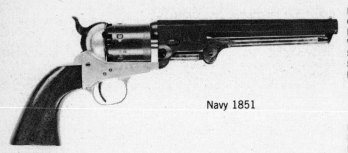

Navy 1851

1851 SHERIFF MODEL PERCUSSION REVOLVER
Caliber: 36, 44, 6-shot.
Barrel: 5".
Weight: 40 oz. **Length:** 10½" over-all.
Stocks: Walnut.
Sights: Fixed.
Features: Brass back strap and trigger guard; engraved navy scene; case hardened frame, hammer, loading lever. Available with brass frame from some importers at slightly lower prices. Imported by Sile, The Armoury, Richland.
Price: Steel frame ....$41.95 to $110.00
Price: Brass frame ....$34.95 to $102.00
Price: Kit, brass or steel frame (Sile) $66.15

ARMY 1851 PERCUSSION REVOLVER
Caliber: 44, 6-shot.
Barrel: 7½".
Weight: 45 oz. **Length:** 13" over-all.
Stocks: Walnut finish.
Sights: Fixed.
Features: 44 caliber version of the 1851 Navy. Imported by Sile, Valor, The Armoury, Richland.
Price: ....$33.50 to $138.00

NEW MODEL 1858 ARMY PERCUSSION REVOLVER
Caliber: 36 or 44, 6-shot.
Barrel: 6½" or 8".
Weight: 40 oz. **Length:** 13½" over-all.
Stocks: Walnut.
Sights: Fixed.
Features: Replica of Remington Model 1858. Also available from some importers as Army Model Belt Revolver in 36 cal., shortened and lightened version of the 44. Target Model (Hawes, Iver Johnson, Navy) has fully adj. target rear sight, target front, 36 or 44 ($74.95-$152.45). Imported by Navy Arms, F.I.E., Valor, Iver Johnson, The Armoury, Shore (44 cal., 8" bbl. only), Richland, Euroarms of America (engraved and plain), Armsport, Hopkins & Allen, Sile.
Price: $49.95
Price: Kit form ....$66.95 to $106.95
Price: Nickel finish (Navy Arms) $140.00
Price: Stainless steel (Euroarms, Navy Arms, Sile) ....$140.00 to $180.00
Price: Target model (Sile, Euroarms, H & A Navy Arms) .$95.95 to $149.95

1860 ARMY PERCUSSION REVOLVER
Caliber: 44, 6-shot.
Barrel: 8".
Weight: 40 oz. **Length:** 13⅝" over-all.
Stocks: Walnut.
Sights: Fixed.
Features: Engraved navy scene on cylinder; brass trigger guard; case hardened frame, loading lever and hammer. Some importers supply pistol cut for detachable shoulder stock, have accessory stock available. Imported by Navy Arms, Shore, The Armoury, Dixie (half-fluted cylinder, not roll engraved), Lyman, Iver Johnson, Richland, Euroarms of America (engraved, burnished steel model), Armsport, Sile.
Price: ....$44.95 to $178.00
Price: Single cased set (Navy Arms) $194.00
1861 Navy: Same as Army except 36 cal., 7½" bbl., wt. 41 oz., cut for stock; round cylinder (fluted avail.), from Navy $130.00
Price: Kit (Lyman) $119.95

NAVY MODEL 1851 PERCUSSION REVOLVER
Caliber: 36 or 44, 6-shot.
Barrel: 7½".
Weight: 42 oz. **Length:** 13" over-all.
Stocks: Walnut finish.
Sights: Fixed.
Features: Brass backstrap and trigger guard; some have engraved cylinder with navy battle scene; case hardened frame, hammer, loading lever. Imported by Shore, (36 cal. only), The Armoury, Navy Arms, Valor, Century, F.I.E., Dixie, (illus.) Richland, Euroarms of America, Kassnar, Sile, Armsport, Hopkins & Allen.
Price: Brass frame ....$31.50 to $119.95
Price: Steel frame ....$40.95 to $121.95
Price: Kit form ....$30.95 to $66.50
Price: Engraved model (F.I.E., Dixie) ....$51.50 to $52.95
Price: Also as "Hartford Pistol," Kit (Richland) . $59.95 Complete ..$79.95
Price: Also as "Hartford Dragoon Buntline" (Hopkins & Allen) $166.95
Price: Navy-Civilian model (Navy Arms) $115.00

1851 NAVY-SHERIFF
Same as 1851 Sheriff model except: 4" barrel, fluted cylinder, belt ring in butt. Imported by Richland, Armoury, Euroarms of America.
Price: ....$50.00 to $114.95

LYMAN 44 NEW MODEL ARMY REVOLVER
Caliber: 44, 6-shot.
Barrel: 8".
Weight: 40 oz. **Length:** 13½" over-all.
Stock: Walnut.
Sights: Fixed.
Features: Replica of 1858 Remington. Brass trigger guard and backstrap, case hardened hammer and trigger. Solid frame with top strap. Heavy duty nipples. From Lyman Products.
Price: $155.95
Price: Kit form $119.95

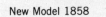
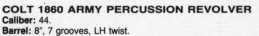

New Model 1858

COLT 1860 ARMY PERCUSSION REVOLVER
Caliber: 44.
Barrel: 8", 7 grooves, LH twist.
Weight: 42 oz.
Stocks: One-piece walnut.
Sights: German silver front sight, hammer notch rear.
Features: Made in U.S. by Colt. Steel backstrap cut for shoulder stock; brass trigger guard. Cylinder has Navy scene. Color case hardened frame, hammer, loading lever. Basically a continuation of production with all original markings, etc. Original-type accessories available. Re-introduced 1979.
Price: $383.95
Price: Fluted cylinder model $406.50

1860 Army

CAUTION: PRICES CHANGE. CHECK AT GUNSHOP.

1861 NAVY MODEL REVOLVER

Caliber: 36, 6-shot.
Barrel: 7½".
Weight: 2½ lbs. **Length:** 13" over-all.
Stocks: One piece smooth walnut.
Sights: Fixed.
Features: Shoots .380" ball. Case-hardened frame, loading lever and hammer. Cut for shoulder stock. Non-fluted cylinder. From Navy Arms, Iver Johnson, Armsport, Euroarms of America.
Price: ....$100.00 to $130.00
Price: With full fluted cyl. ....$100.00 to $104.95
Price: Single cased set (Navy Arms) $191.00

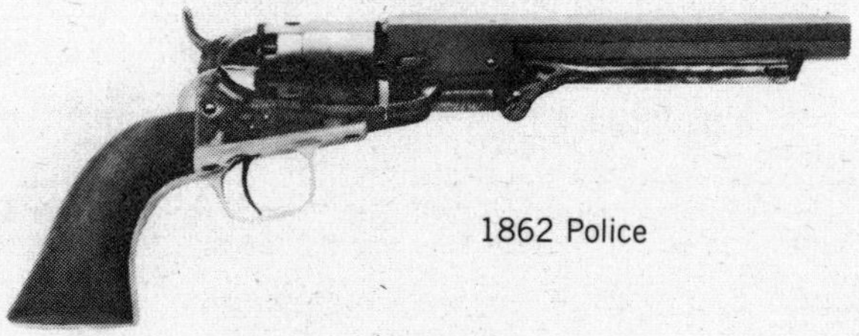

1862 Police

Rogers & Spencer

Spiller & Burr

Dixie Wyatt Earp

NAVY ARMS 1862 LEECH & RIGDON REVOLVER

Caliber: .375"
Barrel: 7½".
Weight: 2 lbs., 10 oz. **Length:** 13½" over-all.
Stocks: Smooth walnut.
Sights: Fixed.
Features: Modern version of the famous Civil War revolver. Brass backstrap and trigger guard. Color case-hardened frame. Copy of the Colt Navy but with round barrel. From Navy Arms.
Price: $125.00

COLT 1862 POCKET NAVY PERCUSSION REVOLVER

Caliber: 36.
Barrel: 5½", octagonal, 7 groove, LH twist.
Weight: 27 oz.
Stocks: One piece varnished walnut.
Sights: Brass pin front, hammer notch rear.
Features: Made in U.S. by Colt. Rebated cylinder, hinged loading lever, silver plated backstrap and trigger guard, color cased frame, hammer, loading lever, plunger and latch, rest blued. Has original-type markings. Re-introduced 1979.
Price: $351.50

Colt 1862 Pocket Police Revolver

Similar to 1862 Pocket Navy except has 5½" round barrel, fluted cylinder, different markings and loading lever. Faithful reproduction of the original gun.
Price: $351.50

1862 POLICE MODEL PERCUSSION REVOLVER

Caliber: 36, 5-shot.
Barrel: 4½", 5½", 6½".
Weight: 26 oz. **Length:** 12" (6½" bbl.).
Stocks: Walnut.
Sights: Fixed.
Features: Half-fluted and rebated cylinder; case hardened frame, loading lever and hammer; brass trigger guard and back strap. Imported by Sile, Navy Arms (5½" only), Euroarms of America.
Price: ....$125.00 to $165.00
Price: Cased with accessories (Navy Arms) $165.00

ROGERS & SPENCER PERCUSSION REVOLVER

Caliber: 44.
Barrel: 7½".
Weight: 47 oz. **Length:** 13¾" over-all.
Stocks: Walnut.
Sights: Cone front, integral groove in frame for rear.
Features: Accurate reproduction of a Civil War design. Solid frame; extra large nipple cut-out on rear of cylinder; loading lever and cylinder easily removed for cleaning. Comes with six spare nipples and wrench/screwdriver. From Euroarms of America, Navy Arms, Dixie.
Price: ....$120.00 to $160.00
Price: Nickel plated $120.00
Price: Kit version $95.00
Price: Target version $200.00

SPILLER & BURR REVOLVER

Caliber: 36.
Barrel: 7", octagon.
Weight: 2½ lbs. **Length:** 12½" over-all.
Stocks: Two-piece walnut.
Sights: Fixed.
Features: Reproduction of the C.S.A. revolver. Brass frame and trigger guard. Also available as a kit. From Dixie, Navy Arms, Richland.
Price: ....$69.95 to $100.00
Price: Kit form ....$39.95 to $65.00

DIXIE "WYATT EARP" REVOLVER

Caliber: 44.
Barrel: 12" octagon.
Weight: 46 oz. **Length:** 18" over-all.
Stock: Two piece walnut.
Sights: Fixed.
Features: Highly polished brass frame, backstrap and trigger guard; blued barrel and cylinder; case hardened hammer, trigger and loading lever. Navy-size shoulder stock ($45.00) will fit with minor fitting. From Dixie Gun Works.
Price: $85.00

BLACK POWDER REVOLVERS

GRISWOLD & GUNNISON PERCUSSION REVOLVER
Caliber: 36, 44, 6-shot.
Barrel: 7½".
Weight: 44 oz. (36 cal.). **Length:** 13" over-all.
Stocks: Walnut.
Sights: Fixed.
Features: Replica of famous Confederate pistol. Brass frame, backstrap and
   trigger guard; case hardened loading lever; rebated cylinder (44 cal. only).
   Imported by Navy Arms.
Price: $125.00
Price: As above from Sile (1851 Confederate) $75.90
Price: Kit (Navy Arms) $70.00

Griswold & Gunnison

RICHLAND 44 BALLISTER REVOLVER
Caliber: 44, 6-shot.
Barrel: 12".
Weight: 2¾ lbs.
Stocks: Two-piece walnut.
Sights: Fixed.
Features: Barrel and cylinder blued, frame and trigger guard are brass; ham-
   mer and loading lever are color case hardened. From Richland Arms.
Price: $78.00

Richland 44 Ballister

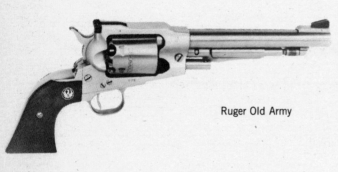

Ruger Old Army

RUGER 44 OLD ARMY PERCUSSION REVOLVER
Caliber: 44, 6-shot. Uses .457" dia. lead bullets.
Barrel: 7½" (6-groove, 16" twist).
Weight: 46 oz. **Length:** 13½" over-all.
Stocks: Smooth walnut.
Sights: Ramp front, rear adj. for w. and e.
Features: Stainless steel standard size nipples, chrome-moly steel cylinder
   and frame, same lockwork as in original Super Blackhawk. Also available in
   stainless steel in very limited quantities. Made in USA. From Sturm, Ruger
   & Co.
Price: Stainless steel $225.00
Price: Blued steel $172.50

BLACK POWDER MUSKETS & RIFLES

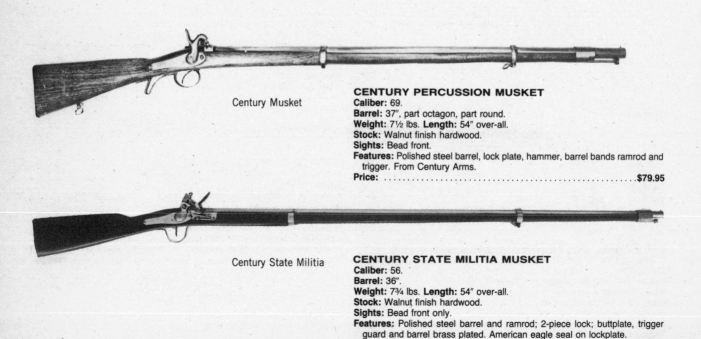

Century Musket

CENTURY PERCUSSION MUSKET
Caliber: 69.
Barrel: 37", part octagon, part round.
Weight: 7½ lbs. **Length:** 54" over-all.
Stock: Walnut finish hardwood.
Sights: Bead front.
Features: Polished steel barrel, lock plate, hammer, barrel bands ramrod and
   trigger. From Century Arms.
Price: $79.95

Century State Militia

CENTURY STATE MILITIA MUSKET
Caliber: 56.
Barrel: 36".
Weight: 7¾ lbs. **Length:** 54" over-all.
Stock: Walnut finish hardwood.
Sights: Bead front only.
Features: Polished steel barrel and ramrod; 2-piece lock; buttplate, trigger
   guard and barrel brass plated. American eagle seal on lockplate.
Price: $74.95

CAUTION: PRICES CHANGE. CHECK AT GUNSHOP.

BLACK POWDER MUSKETS & RIFLES

Dixie Brown Bess

DIXIE SECOND MODEL BROWN BESS
Caliber: 74.
Barrel: 41¾" smoothbore.
Weight: 9½ lbs. **Length:** 57¾".
Stock: Walnut-finished hardwood.
Sights: Fixed.
Features: All metal finished bright. Brass furniture. Lock marked "Tower" and has a crown with "GR" underneath. From Dixie Gun Works.
Price: **$265.00**

CVA Mountain Rifle

CVA MOUNTAIN RIFLE
Caliber: 45, 50.
Barrel: 32", octagon; ¹⁵⁄₁₆" across flats.
Weight: 8 lbs. **Length:** 48" over-all.
Stock: American maple with cheekpiece.
Sights: German silver blade front, screw-adj. rear.
Features: Available in percussion or flintlock. Engraved lock with adj. sear engagement; hooked breech with two barrel tenons; rifled 1-in-66"; double set triggers; German silver patch box, tenon plates, pewter-type nosecap; browned iron furniture.
Price: Either caliber, kit, percussion **$189.95**
Price: Kit, flintlock **$199.95**
Price: Finished rifle, percussion **$269.95**
Price: Finished rifle, flintlock **$284.95**

CVA Big Bore

CVA Big Bore Mountain Rifle
Similar to the standard Mountain Rifle except comes in 54 or 58 cal. only. Barrel flats measure 1" across. Stock does not have a patch box. Introduced 1980.
Price: 54 or 58 cal., complete rifle **$279.95**
Price: 54 or 58 cal., perc. kit **$199.95**
Price: 54 cal. flintlock, kit only **$209.95**

CVA Kentucky

CVA KENTUCKY RIFLE
Caliber: 45 (.451" bore).
Barrel: 32", rifled, octagon (⅞" flats).
Length: 50" over-all.
Stock: Dark polished walnut.
Sights: Brass Kentucky blade type front, dovetail open rear.
Features: Available in either flint or percussion. Stainless steel nipple included. Imported by CVA.
Price: Percussion **$167.95**
Price: Flint **$177.95**
Price: Percussion Kit **$99.95**
Price: Flint Kit **$109.95**

Dixie Kentucky

DIXIE STANDARD KENTUCKY RIFLE
Caliber: 45.
Barrel: 40", six land and grooves, 1 turn in 48".
Weight: 10 lbs. **Length:** 56½".
Stock: Chestnut colored maple.
Sights: Brass blade front, Kentucky-type rear.
Features: Trigger guard, buttplate, patchbox and thimbles are brass. Color case hardened lock. From Dixie Gun Works.
Price: Percussion **$260.00**

TRADITIONS, INC. KENTUCKY RIFLE
Similar to CVA Kentucky Rifle except 33½" blued barrel, weighs 7 lbs., 4 oz., 48" over-all. Choice of one-piece American walnut stock, or two-piece hardwood. Stainless steel nipple (percussion). Imported by Traditions, Inc.
Price: Assembled, percussion, 1-piece stock **$155.00**
Price: As above, 2-piece stock **$147.00**
Price: Assembled, flint, 2-piece stock **$160.00**
Price: Kit, percussion, 1-piece stock **$87.00**
Price: As above, flint **$97.00**
Price: Kit, percussion, 2-piece stock **$79.00**

CAUTION: PRICES CHANGE. CHECK AT GUNSHOP.

BLACK POWDER MUSKETS & RIFLES

Traditions, Inc. Frontier Rifle

Similar to CVA Frontier Rifle except stock of selected hardwood. Bridle, fly, hooked breech, adjustable sear engagement. Hardwood ramrod with brass tips, brass furniture, stainless steel nipple. Imported by Traditions, Inc.

Price: Assembled, percussion **$175.00**
Price: Assembled, flint **$182.00**
Price: Kit, percussion **$125.00**
Price: Kit, flint **$132.00**

DIXIE TENNESSEE MOUNTAIN RIFLE

Caliber: 50.
Barrel: 41½", 6-groove rifling, brown finish.
Length: 56" over-all.
Stock: Walnut, oil finish; Kentucky-style.
Sights: Silver blade front, open buckhorn rear.
Features: Re-creation of the original mountain rifles. Early Schultz lock interchangeable flint or percussion with vent plug or drum and nipple. Tumbler has fly. Double-set triggers. All metal parts browned. From Dixie.

Price: Flint and Percussion, finished rifle **$225.00**
Price: Kit **$175.00**
Price: Left-hand model, flint or perc. **$245.00**

Lyman Trade Rifle

LYMAN TRADE RIFLE

Caliber: 50 or 54.
Barrel: 28" octagon, 1-48" twist.
Weight: 8¾ lbs. **Length:** 45" over-all.
Stock: European walnut.
Sights: Blade front, open rear adj. for w.
Features: Polished brass furniture with blue steel parts. Hook breech, single trigger, coil spring percussion lock. Steel barrel rib and ramrod ferrules. Percussion only. Introduced 1979. From Lyman.

Price: **$224.95**
Price: Kit **$179.95**

CVA Frontier

CVA FRONTIER RIFLE

Caliber: 45 or 50.
Barrel: 28", octagon; ¹⁵⁄₁₆" flats.
Weight: 6 lbs., 14 oz. **Length:** 44" over-all.
Stock: American hardwood.
Sights: Brass blade front, screw-adj. open rear.
Features: Available in flint or percussion. Solid brass nosecap, trigger guard, buttplate, thimbles and wedge plates; blued barrel; color case-hardened lock and hammer. Double set triggers, patented breech plug/bolster, V-type mainspring. Hooked breech. Introduced 1980.

Price: 45 or 50 cal., percussion, complete rifle **$199.95**
Price: 50-Cal. flint, complete rifle **$209.95**
Price: 45 or 50 cal., percussion, kit **$149.95**
Price: 50 cal. flint, kit only **$159.95**

HOPKINS & ALLEN MINUTEMAN RIFLE

Caliber: 36, 45, 50.
Barrel: 39", ¹⁵⁄₁₆" octagon.
Weight: 9½ lbs.
Stock: One piece, American maple.
Sights: Silver blade front, notched Kentucky rear.
Features: Cut-rifled barrel, percussion lock with fly. Authentic Pennsylvania Bedford styling. Available as kit or assembled. Made in U.S.A. Available in flint or percussion lock.

Price: Flint, complete **$289.95**
Price: Percussion, complete **$274.95**

Hopkins & Allen Model 7000 Short Rifle

Same as H&A Minuteman except has 2-piece beech stock without patchbox. Converts easily from flint to percussion. Has 34" barrel, ¹⁵⁄₁₆" diameter. Made in U.S. by H.&A. Kit or finished.

Price: Complete **$131.95**
Price: Kit **$99.95**

PENNSYLVANIA HALF-STOCK PLAINS RIFLE

Caliber: 45 or 50.
Barrel: 32", rifled, ¹⁵⁄₁₆" dia.
Weight: 8½ lbs.
Stock: Walnut.
Sights: Fixed.
Features: Available in flint or percussion. Blued lock and barrel, brass furniture. Offered complete or in kit form. From Hopkins & Allen, The Armory.

Price: Flint **$279.95**
Price: Percussion **$267.95**

HOPKINS & ALLEN DELUXE BUGGY RIFLE

Caliber: 36 or 45.
Barrel: 20", octagonal.
Weight: 6½ lbs. **Length:** 37" over-all.
Stock: American walnut.
Features: A shortened version of the under-hammer Heritage rifle. Blued barrel and receiver, black plastic buttplate.

Price: **$199.95**

KENTUCKY FLINTLOCK RIFLE

Caliber: 44 or 45.
Barrel: 35".
Weight: 7 lbs. **Length:** 50" over-all.
Stock: Walnut stained, brass fittings.
Sights: Fixed.
Features: Available in Carbine model also, 28" bbl. Some variations in detail, finish. Kits also available from some importers. Imported by Navy Arms, The Armoury, Challenger, F.I.E., CVA, Armsport, Hopkins & Allen, Sile, Shore (45-cal. only).

Price: . . . . **$59.95 to $250.00**
Price: Kit form (CVA, Numrich, Hawes, F.I.E., Sile) . . . . . **$72.95 to $171.50**
Price: Deluxe model, flint or percussion (Navy Arms, Sile), about . . **$400.00**

Kentucky Percussion Rifle

Similar to flintlock except percussion lock. Finish and features vary with importer. Imported by Navy Arms, F.I.E. Corp., The Armoury, CVA, Armsport (rifle-shotgun combo), Shore, Sile.

Price: . . . . **$54.95 to $250.00**
Price: Kit form (F.I.E., Sile) **$151.80**
Price: Armsport combo **$295.00**
Price: Deluxe model (Navy Arms) **$375.00**

KENTUCKIAN RIFLE & CARBINE

Caliber: 44.
Barrel: 35" (Rifle), 27½" (Carbine).
Weight: 7 lbs. (Rifle), 5½ lbs. (Carbine). **Length:** 51" (Rifle) over-all, carbine 43".
Stock: Walnut stain.
Sights: Brass blade front, steel V-Ramp rear.
Features: Octagon bbl., case hardened and engraved lock plate. Brass furniture. Imported by Dixie, Euroarms of America.

Price: Rifle or carbine, flint or percussion . . . . **$135.00 to $165.00**

BLACK POWDER MUSKETS & RIFLES

DIXIE PLAINSMAN RIFLE
Caliber: 45 or 50.
Barrel: 32″, octagon.
Weight: 8 lbs. **Length:** 47½″.
Stock: Cherry wood.
Sights: Brass blade front, buckhorn rear.
Features: Bolster-type breech plug with blow-out screw, brass stock furniture.
Price: $205.00

YORK COUNTY RIFLE
Caliber: 45.
Barrel: 36″, rifled, ⅞″ octagon, blue.
Weight: 7½ lbs. **Length:** 51½″ over-all.
Stock: Maple, one piece.
Sights: Blade front, V-notch rear, brass.
Features: Adjustable double-set triggers. Brass trigger guard, patchbox, butt-plate, nosecap and sideplate. Case-hardened lockplate. From Dixie Gun Works.
Price: Percussion $152.95
Price: Flint $162.95

Mowrey A&T

MOWREY ALLEN & THURBER REPLICA
Caliber: 54 or 58.
Barrel: 32″, 8-groove rifling, octagon.
Weight: 10¼ lbs. **Length:** 48″ over-all.
Stock: Walnut with curved brass buttplate.
Sights: Open, adj. for w. & e.
Features: Polished brass furniture, brass fore-end, ramrod. Made by Mowrey, available from Interarms.
Price: Complete $229.00

MOWREY GEORGIA TREE GUN
Caliber: 54, 58.
Barrel: 22″.
Weight: 7¼ lbs. **Length:** 38″ over-all.
Stock: Walnut.
Sights: Blade front, step adj. rear.
Features: Shortened version of Allen & Thurber Special rifle especially suited for tree stand shooting. Made by Mowrey, available from Interarms.
Price: Complete gun $239.00

Mowrey Squirrel Rifle

MOWREY ETHAN ALLEN SQUIRREL RIFLE
Caliber: 32, 36, or 45.
Barrel: 28″, 8-groove rifling, octagon, 1:60 twist.
Weight: 7½ lbs. **Length:** 43″ over-all.
Stock: Curly maple.
Sights: Open, fully adj.
Features: Box-lock action, cut-rifled barrel, hand-rubbed oil finish. Available with either brass or steel furniture, action. Made in U.S.
Price: Complete $229.00
Price: Kit $216.00

Mowrey Plains Rifle

Mowrey Ethan Allen Plains Rifle
Similar to Squirrel Rifle except in 50 or 54 caliber, 32″ barrel, weighs 9½ lbs.
Price: Complete $299.00
Price: Kit $216.00
Price: "Trapper" (same as Plains Rifle except has cherry wood stock with matte oil finish) $263.00

"TEXAS CARBINE" Model 1 of 1000
Caliber: 58, takes .575″ mini-ball or round ball.
Barrel: 24″ octagon, 4-groove.
Weight: 8 lbs. **Length:** 39″ over-all.
Stock: Walnut stock and fore-end, brass fore-end cap.
Sights: Adjustable front and rear.
Features: Model "1 of 1000". Saddle ring with leather thong and Texas seal imbedded in stock. Distributed by Trail Guns Armory.
Price: $250.00

RICHLAND MICHIGAN RIFLE
Caliber: 45, 50.
Barrel: 26″ octagon, ⅞″ flats.
Weight: 5¾ lbs. **Length:** 41⅜″ over-all.
Stock: Hand finished maple.
Sights: Blade front, open fixed rear drift adj. for w.
Features: Color case hardened lock plate; brass patch box, buttplate, trigger guard, fore-end tip and sights; adjustable double set triggers. From Richland Arms.
Price: Percussion $186.00
Price: Flintlock $200.00
Price: Kit form, percussion $144.00
Price: Kit form, flintlock $154.00

THOMPSON/CENTER HAWKEN RIFLE
Caliber: 45, 50 or 54.
Barrel: 28″ octagon, hooked breech.
Stock: American walnut.
Sights: Blade front, rear adj. for w. & e.
Features: Solid brass furniture, double set triggers, button rifled barrel, coil-type main spring. From Thompson/Center Arms.
Price: Percussion Model (45, 50 or 54 cal.) $255.00
Price: Flintlock model (45, 50, or 54 cal. only) $265.00

BLACK POWDER MUSKETS & RIFLES

T/C Renegade

THOMPSON/CENTER RENEGADE RIFLE
Caliber: 50 and 54 plus 56 cal., smoothbore.
Barrel: 26", 1" across the flats.
Weight: 8 lbs.
Stock: American walnut.
Sights: Open hunting (Patridge) style, fully adjustable for w. and e.
Features: Coil spring lock, double set triggers, blued steel trim.
Price: Percussion model $195.00
Price: Flintlock model, 50 and 54 cal. only $200.00
Price: Percussion kit $155.00
Price: Flintlock kit $165.00

T/C Seneca

THOMPSON/CENTER SENECA RIFLE
Caliber: 36, 45.
Barrel: 27".
Weight: 6½ lbs.
Stock: American walnut.
Sights: Open hunting style, square notch rear fully adj. for w. and e.
Features: Coil spring lock, octagon bbl. measures $^{13}/_{16}$" across flats, brass stock furniture.
Price: Rifle $255.00

BUFFALO HUNTER PERCUSSION RIFLE
Caliber: 58.
Barrel: 25½".
Weight: 8 lbs. **Length:** 41½" over-all.
Stock: Walnut finished, hand checkered, brass furniture.
Sights: Fixed.
Features: Designed for primitive weapons hunting. 20 ga. shotgun bbl. also available **$65.00.** Imported by Navy Arms, Dixie.
Price: .... $215.00 to $265.00

SILE HAWKEN HUNTER CARBINE
Caliber: 45, 50, 54.
Barrel: 22", full octagon with hooked breech and hard chrome smooth bore.
Weight: 7 lbs. **Length:** 38" over-all.
Stock: Walnut with checkered p.g. and fore-end, rubber recoil pad.
Sights: Blade front, fully adjustable open rear.
Features: Black oxidized brass hardware, engraved case hardened lock plate, sear fly and coil spring mechanism. Stainless steel nipple. Adjustable double set triggers. From Sile Dist.
Price: Percussion $217.30
Price: Flintlock $227.10
Price: Hawken Super Deluxe Rifle $217.30

Armoury Hawken

ARMOURY R140 HAWKIN RIFLE
Caliber: 45, 50 or 54.
Barrel: 29".
Weight: 8¾" to 9 lbs. **Length:** 45¾" over-all.
Stock: Walnut,, with cheekpiece.
Sights: Dovetail front, fully adjustable rear.
Features: Octagon barrel measures ⅜" across flats; removable breech plug; double set triggers; blued barrel, brass stock fittings, color case hardened percussion lock. From Armsport and The Armoury.
Price: .... $175.00 to $282.00
Price: Kit (Armsport) $210.00

HAWKEN RIFLE
Caliber: 45, 50, 54 or 58.
Barrel: 28", blued, 6-groove rifling.
Weight: 8¾ lbs. **Length:** 44" over-all.
Stock: Walnut finish.
Sights: Blade front, fully adj. rear.
Features: Coil mainspring, double set triggers, polished brass furniture. Also available with chrome plated bore or in flintlock model. Introduced 1977. From Kassnar, Sile, Hawes, Dixie (45 or 50 only, walnut stock), Armsport, Shore (50-cal. only).
Price: .... $175.00 to $252.95
Price: Hard chrome bore, Sile, about $238.95

CVA HAWKEN RIFLE
Caliber: 50 or 54.
Barrel: 28", octagon; 1" across flats.
Weight: 7 lbs. 15 oz. **Length:** 44" over-all.
Stock: Select walnut.
Sights: Beaded blade front, fully adj. open rear.
Features: Fully adj. double set triggers; brass patch box, wedge plates, nose cap, thimbles, trigger guard and buttplate; blued barrel; color case-hardened, engraved lockplate. Percussion or flintlock. Hooked breech. Introduced 1981.
Price: Finished rifle, percussion $249.95
Price: Finished rifle, flint lock $259.95
Price: Kit, percussion $167.95
Price: Kit, flintlock $177.95

Traditions, Inc. Hawken Rifle
Similar to standard Hawken except in 50 or 54 cals. only, walnut stock with fully formed beavertail cheekpiece. Beaded blade front sight, adjustable hunting-type open rear. Color case-hardened lock, bridle, fly, adjustable sear engagement. Stainless steel nipple.
Price: Assembled, percussion $215.00
Price: Assembled, flint $235.00
Price: Kit, percussion .... N.A.
Price: Kit, flint .... N.A.

Armsport Hawken Rifle-Shotgun Combo
Similar to Hawken above except 50-cal. only, with 20 gauge shotgun barrel. From Armsport.
Price: $250.00

CAUTION: PRICES CHANGE. CHECK AT GUNSHOP.

BLACK POWDER MUSKETS & RIFLES

F.I.E. Hawken

F.I.E. DELUXE HAWKEN RIFLE
Caliber: 50.
Barrel: 28".
Weight: 7 lbs. **Length:** 43½" over-all.
Stock: Dark polished walnut.
Sights: Blade front, open read adj. for w.
Features: Brass patchbox, trigger guard, buttplate and furniture; color case hardened lock, rest blued. From F.I.E. Corp.
Price: $214.95
Price: Kit form $189.95
Price: Finished flintlock model $249.95

Ithaca-Navy Hawken

ITHACA-NAVY HAWKEN RIFLE
Caliber: 50 and 54.
Barrel: 32" octagonal, 1-inch dia.
Weight: About 9 lbs.
Stock: Black walnut.
Sights: Blade front, rear adj. for w.
Features: Completely made in U.S. Hooked breech, 1⅞" throw percussion lock. Attached twin thimbles and under-rib. German silver barrel key inlays, Hawken-style toe and buttplates, lock bolt inlays, barrel wedges, entry thimble, trigger guard, ramrod and cleaning jag, nipple and nipple wrench. American made. Introduced 1977. From Navy Arms.
Price: Complete, percussion $395.00
Price: Kit, percussion $275.00
Price: Complete, flint $425.00
Price: Kit, flint $300.00

Richland Wesson

RICHLAND PERCUSSION WESSON RIFLE
Caliber: 50.
Barrel: 28", 1⅛" octagon.
Length: 45" over-all.
Stock: Walnut.
Sights: Blade front, rear adj. for e.
Features: Adjustable double set triggers, color case hardened frame. Introduced 1977. From Richland Arms.
Price: With false muzzle $295.00
Price: Engraved version $412.00

Browning Mountain

JONATHAN BROWNING PERCUSSION MOUNTAIN RIFLE
Caliber: 45, 50 or 54.
Barrel: 30", 1" across flats.
Stock: Traditional half-stock with semi-cheekpiece.
Sights: Blade front, Buckhorn rear screw-adj. for e.
Features: Single set trigger; hooked breech. 45-cal. rifled 1 in 56", 50-cal. rifled 1 in 62", 54-cal. rifled 1 in 66" twist. Offered in choice of browned steel or brass finish on buttplate, trigger guard and complimentary furniture. Hickory ramrod with brass ends. Spare nipple and cleaning jag included. Introduced 1977. From Browning.
Price: Brass or browned furniture, 45, 50 or 54 cal. $449.95

HAWKEN HURRICANE & HUNTER
Caliber: 45 or 50.
Barrel: 28", octagon.
Weight: 6 lbs. **Length:** 44¾" over-all.
Stock: American walnut.
Sights: Blade front, open fixed rear.
Features: American made. Curved buttplate, brass stock furniture. From Navy Arms.
Price: 45 or 50 cal. $225.00
Price: Hawken Hunter (58 cal.) $225.00
Price: Hawken kit $149.95

PARKER-HALE ENFIELD 1853 MUSKET
Caliber: .577".
Barrel: 39", 3-groove cold-forged rifling.
Weight: About 9 lbs. **Length:** 55" over-all.
Stock: Seasoned walnut.
Sights: Fixed front, rear step adj. for elevation.
Features: Three band musket made to original specs from original gauges. Solid brass stock furniture, color hardened lock plate, hammer; blued barrel, trigger. Imported from England by Navy Arms.
Price: $400.00

Consult our Directory pages for the location of firms mentioned.

London Armory Co. 3-Band Musket
Re-creation of the famed London Armory Company Pattern 1853 Enfield Musket. One-piece walnut stock, brass buttplate, trigger guard and nosecap. Lockplate marked "1862 L.A. Co." and with a British crown. Blued Baddeley barrel bands. From Dixie, Euroarms of America.
Price: $280.00
Price: 2-Band rifle $285.00

CAUTION: PRICES CHANGE. CHECK AT GUNSHOP.

BLACK POWDER MUSKETS & RIFLES

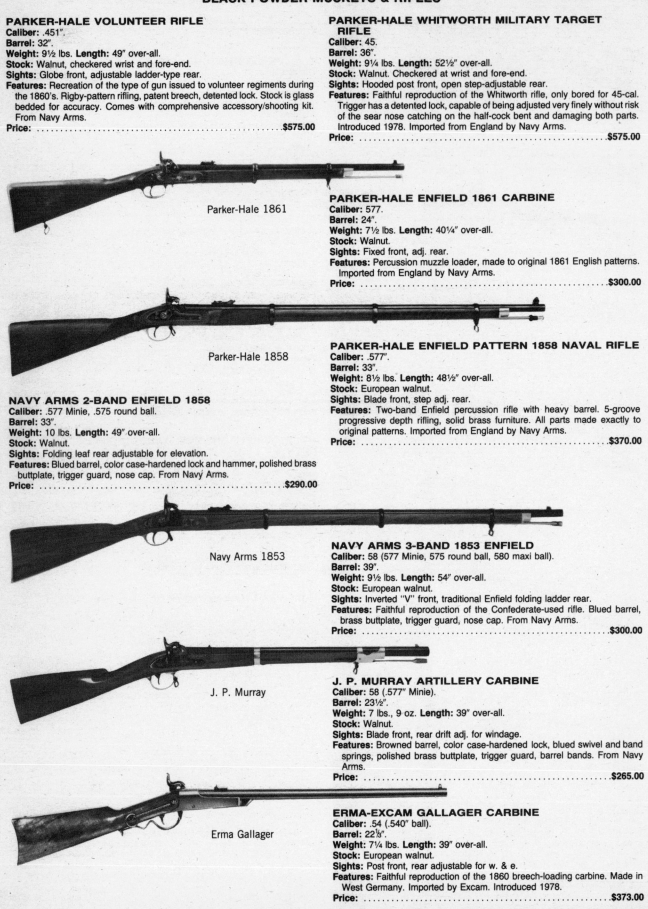

PARKER-HALE VOLUNTEER RIFLE
Caliber: .451″.
Barrel: 32″.
Weight: 9½ lbs. **Length:** 49″ over-all.
Stock: Walnut, checkered wrist and fore-end.
Sights: Globe front, adjustable ladder-type rear.
Features: Recreation of the type of gun issued to volunteer regiments during the 1860's. Rigby-pattern rifling, patent breech, detented lock. Stock is glass bedded for accuracy. Comes with comprehensive accessory/shooting kit. From Navy Arms.
Price: $575.00

Parker-Hale 1861

Parker-Hale 1858

NAVY ARMS 2-BAND ENFIELD 1858
Caliber: .577 Minie, .575 round ball.
Barrel: 33″.
Weight: 10 lbs. **Length:** 49″ over-all.
Stock: Walnut.
Sights: Folding leaf rear adjustable for elevation.
Features: Blued barrel, color case-hardened lock and hammer, polished brass buttplate, trigger guard, nose cap. From Navy Arms.
Price: $290.00

Navy Arms 1853

J. P. Murray

Erma Gallager

PARKER-HALE WHITWORTH MILITARY TARGET RIFLE
Caliber: 45.
Barrel: 36″.
Weight: 9¼ lbs. **Length:** 52½″ over-all.
Stock: Walnut. Checkered at wrist and fore-end.
Sights: Hooded post front, open step-adjustable rear.
Features: Faithful reproduction of the Whitworth rifle, only bored for 45-cal. Trigger has a detented lock, capable of being adjusted very finely without risk of the sear nose catching on the half-cock bent and damaging both parts. Introduced 1978. Imported from England by Navy Arms.
Price: $575.00

PARKER-HALE ENFIELD 1861 CARBINE
Caliber: 577.
Barrel: 24″.
Weight: 7½ lbs. **Length:** 40¼″ over-all.
Stock: Walnut.
Sights: Fixed front, adj. rear.
Features: Percussion muzzle loader, made to original 1861 English patterns. Imported from England by Navy Arms.
Price: $300.00

PARKER-HALE ENFIELD PATTERN 1858 NAVAL RIFLE
Caliber: .577″.
Barrel: 33″.
Weight: 8½ lbs. **Length:** 48½″ over-all.
Stock: European walnut.
Sights: Blade front, step adj. rear.
Features: Two-band Enfield percussion rifle with heavy barrel. 5-groove progressive depth rifling, solid brass furniture. All parts made exactly to original patterns. Imported from England by Navy Arms.
Price: $370.00

NAVY ARMS 3-BAND 1853 ENFIELD
Caliber: 58 (577 Minie, 575 round ball, 580 maxi ball).
Barrel: 39″.
Weight: 9½ lbs. **Length:** 54″ over-all.
Stock: European walnut.
Sights: Inverted "V" front, traditional Enfield folding ladder rear.
Features: Faithful reproduction of the Confederate-used rifle. Blued barrel, brass buttplate, trigger guard, nose cap. From Navy Arms.
Price: $300.00

J. P. MURRAY ARTILLERY CARBINE
Caliber: 58 (.577″ Minie).
Barrel: 23½″.
Weight: 7 lbs., 9 oz. **Length:** 39″ over-all.
Stock: Walnut.
Sights: Blade front, rear drift adj. for windage.
Features: Browned barrel, color case-hardened lock, blued swivel and band springs, polished brass buttplate, trigger guard, barrel bands. From Navy Arms.
Price: $265.00

ERMA-EXCAM GALLAGER CARBINE
Caliber: .54 (.540″ ball).
Barrel: 22⅛″.
Weight: 7¼ lbs. **Length:** 39″ over-all.
Stock: European walnut.
Sights: Post front, rear adjustable for w. & e.
Features: Faithful reproduction of the 1860 breech-loading carbine. Made in West Germany. Imported by Excam. Introduced 1978.
Price: $373.00

CAUTION: PRICES CHANGE. CHECK AT GUNSHOP.

BLACK POWDER MUSKETS & RIFLES

F.I.E. PERCUSSION BERDAN RIFLE
Caliber: 45.
Barrel: 25", rifled, octagon.
Weight: 7 lbs. **Length:** 42¾" over-all.
Stock: Walnut-finished hardwood.
Sights: Brass blade front, adj. open rear.
Features: Double-set triggers; brass trigger guard, patch box and buttplate. From F.I.E. Corp.
Price: $87.95

U.S. M-1862 REMINGTON CONTRACT RIFLE
Caliber: 58.
Barrel: 33".
Weight: 9½ lbs. **Length:** 48½" over-all.
Stock: Walnut, brass furniture.
Sights: Blade front, folding 3-leaf rear.
Features: Re-creation of the 1862 military rifle. Each rifle furnished with two stainless steel nipples. From Euroarms of America.
Price: About $200.00

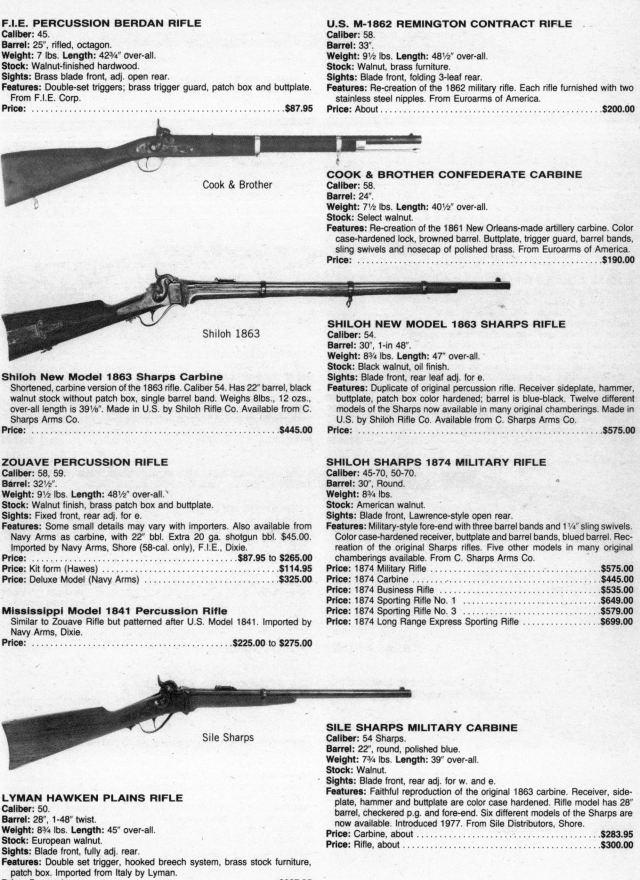

Cook & Brother

COOK & BROTHER CONFEDERATE CARBINE
Caliber: 58.
Barrel: 24".
Weight: 7½ lbs. **Length:** 40½" over-all.
Stock: Select walnut.
Features: Re-creation of the 1861 New Orleans-made artillery carbine. Color case-hardened lock, browned barrel. Buttplate, trigger guard, barrel bands, sling swivels and nosecap of polished brass. From Euroarms of America.
Price: $190.00

Shiloh 1863

Shiloh New Model 1863 Sharps Carbine
Shortened, carbine version of the 1863 rifle. Caliber 54. Has 22" barrel, black walnut stock without patch box, single barrel band. Weighs 8lbs., 12 ozs., over-all length is 39⅛". Made in U.S. by Shiloh Rifle Co. Available from C. Sharps Arms Co.
Price: $445.00

SHILOH NEW MODEL 1863 SHARPS RIFLE
Caliber: 54.
Barrel: 30", 1-in 48".
Weight: 8¾ lbs. **Length:** 47" over-all.
Stock: Black walnut, oil finish.
Sights: Blade front, rear leaf adj. for e.
Features: Duplicate of original percussion rifle. Receiver sideplate, hammer, buttplate, patch box color hardened; barrel is blue-black. Twelve different models of the Sharps now available in many original chamberings. Made in U.S. by Shiloh Rifle Co. Available from C. Sharps Arms Co.
Price: $575.00

ZOUAVE PERCUSSION RIFLE
Caliber: 58, 59.
Barrel: 32½".
Weight: 9½ lbs. **Length:** 48½" over-all.
Stock: Walnut finish, brass patch box and buttplate.
Sights: Fixed front, rear adj. for e.
Features: Some small details may vary with importers. Also available from Navy Arms as carbine, with 22" bbl. Extra 20 ga. shotgun bbl. $45.00. Imported by Navy Arms, Shore (58-cal. only), F.I.E., Dixie.
Price: ....$87.95 to $265.00
Price: Kit form (Hawes) $114.95
Price: Deluxe Model (Navy Arms) $325.00

SHILOH SHARPS 1874 MILITARY RIFLE
Caliber: 45-70, 50-70.
Barrel: 30", Round.
Weight: 8¾ lbs.
Stock: American walnut.
Sights: Blade front, Lawrence-style open rear.
Features: Military-style fore-end with three barrel bands and 1¼" sling swivels. Color case-hardened receiver, buttplate and barrel bands, blued barrel. Recreation of the original Sharps rifles. Five other models in many original chamberings available. From C. Sharps Arms Co.
Price: 1874 Military Rifle $575.00
Price: 1874 Carbine $445.00
Price: 1874 Business Rifle $535.00
Price: 1874 Sporting Rifle No. 1 ....$649.00
Price: 1874 Sporting Rifle No. 3 ....$579.00
Price: 1874 Long Range Express Sporting Rifle $699.00

Mississippi Model 1841 Percussion Rifle
Similar to Zouave Rifle but patterned after U.S. Model 1841. Imported by Navy Arms, Dixie.
Price: ....$225.00 to $275.00

Sile Sharps

SILE SHARPS MILITARY CARBINE
Caliber: 54 Sharps.
Barrel: 22", round, polished blue.
Weight: 7¾ lbs. **Length:** 39" over-all.
Stock: Walnut.
Sights: Blade front, rear adj. for w. and e.
Features: Faithful reproduction of the original 1863 carbine. Receiver, sideplate, hammer and buttplate are color case hardened. Rifle model has 28" barrel, checkered p.g. and fore-end. Six different models of the Sharps are now available. Introduced 1977. From Sile Distributors, Shore.
Price: Carbine, about $283.95
Price: Rifle, about $300.00

LYMAN HAWKEN PLAINS RIFLE
Caliber: 50.
Barrel: 28", 1-48" twist.
Weight: 8¾ lbs. **Length:** 45" over-all.
Stock: European walnut.
Sights: Blade front, fully adj. rear.
Features: Double set trigger, hooked breech system, brass stock furniture, patch box. Imported from Italy by Lyman.
Price: Percussion $237.95
Price: Kit, percussion $189.95

BLACK POWDER MUSKETS & RIFLES

Lyman Great Plains

LYMAN GREAT PLAINS RIFLE
Caliber: 50 or 54 cal.
Barrel: 32″, 1-66″ twist.
Weight: 9 lbs.
Stock: Walnut.
Sights: Steel blade front, buckhorn rear adj. for w. & e.
Features: Browned steel furniture. Coil sring lock, Hawken-style trigger guard and double set triggers. Round thimbles recessed and sweated into rib. Steel wedge plates and toe plates. Introduced 1980. From Lyman.
Price: Percussion $289.95
Price: Flintlock $324.95
Price: Percussion Kit $224.95

REVOLVING PERCUSSION CARBINE
Caliber: 44, 6-shot.
Barrel: 18″, 20″.
Weight: 5 lbs. **Length:** 38″ over-all.
Stock: Walnut, brass buttplate.
Sights: Blade front adj. for w., buckhorn rear adj. for e.
Features: Action based on 1858 Remington revolver. Brass trigger guard. Imported by Navy Arms.
Price: $225.00

KODIAK DOUBLE RIFLE
Caliber: 58 (std.), 50 cal. and 50-cal./12 ga. optional.
Barrel: 28″, 5 grooves, 1-in-48″ twist.
Weight: 9½ lbs. **Length:** 43¼″ over-all.
Stock: Czechoslovakian walnut, hand checkered.
Sights: Adjustable gold bead front, adjustable open rear.
Features: Hooked breech allows interchangeability of barrels, matted rib. Comes with sling and swivels, adjustable powder measure, bullet mould and bullet starter. Engraved lock plates, top tang and trigger guard. Locks and top tang polished, rest browned. From Trail Guns Armory, Inc.
Price: 58 cal. SxS $495.00
Price: 50 cal. SxS $495.00
Price: 50 cal. x 12 ga., 58x12 ....$495.00
Price: Spare barrels, 58 cal. SxS, 50 cal. SxS $267.50
Price: Spare barrels, 50 cal. x 12 ga., 58x12 ....$267.50
Price: Spare barrels, 12 ga. x 12 ga. $160.00

Kodiak Double

MORSE/NAVY RIFLE
Caliber: 45, 50 or 58.
Barrel: 26″, octagonal.
Weight: 6 lbs. (45 cal.). **Length:** 41½″ over-all.
Stock: American walnut, full p.g.
Sights: Blade front, open fixed rear.
Features: Brass action, trigger guard, ramrod pipes. From Navy Arms.
Price: $149.95
Price: Kit $100.00

Yorkshire Rifle

YORKSHIRE RIFLE
Caliber: 45.
Barrel: 36″, rifled, ⅞″ octagon.
Weight: 7½ lbs. **Length:** 51¾″ over-all.
Stock: Select maple.
Sights: Blade front, open U-notch rear.
Features: Adj. double set triggers. Brass front and rear sights, trigger guard, patch box, buttplate and fore-end. Case hardened lock plate. From Richland.
Price: Percussion ....$144.00 to $150.00
Price: Flintlock ....$153.00 to $159.95

BLACK POWDER SHOTGUNS

Mowrey A&T

MOWREY A. & T. 12 GAUGE SHOTGUN
Gauge: 12 ga. only.
Barrel: 32″, octagon.
Weight: 8 lbs. **Length:** 48″ over-all.
Stock: Curly maple, oil finish, brass furniture.
Sights: Bead front.
Features: Available in percussion only. Steel or brass action. Uses standard 12 ga. wadding. Made by Mowrey.
Price: Complete $299.00
Price: Kit form $216.00

SINGLE BARREL PERCUSSION SHOTGUN
Gauge: 12, 20, 28.
Barrel: 28″.
Weight: 4½ lbs. **Length:** 43″ over-all.
Stock: Walnut finish, choice of half or full stock.
Features: Finish and features vary with importer. Imported by Dixie.
Price: ....$32.95 to $59.95

Consult our Directory pages for the location of firms mentioned.

PRICES CHANGE. CHECK AT GUNSHOP.

BLACK POWDER SHOTGUNS

SILE DELUXE DOUBLE BARREL SHOTGUN
Gauge: 12.
Barrel: 28" (Cyl. & Cyl.); hooked breech, hard chrome lining.
Weight: 6 lbs. **Length:** 44½" over-all.
Stock: Walnut, with checkered grip.
Features: Engraved, polished blue and color case-hardened hardware, locks are color case-hardened and engraved. Steel buttplate; brass bead front sight. From sile.
Price: Percussion only $244.40
Price: Confederate Cavalry Model (shortened version of above model with 14" bbl. 30½" o.a.l.) $244.40

EOA MAGNUM CAPE GUN
Gauge: 12.
Barrel: 32", open choked.
Weight: 7½ lbs. **Length:** 47½" over-all.
Stock: European walnut, oil finished.
Features: Classic English-styled single barrel shotgun. Barrel, underrib, thimbles, nosecap, trigger guard and buttplate blued. Lock left in the white with scroll engraving. From Euroarms of America.
Price: $200.00

TRAIL GUNS KODIAK 10 GAUGE DOUBLE
Gauge: 10.
Barrel: 30¾" (Cyl. bore).
Weight: About 9 lbs. **Length:** 47⅛" over-all.
Stock: Walnut, with cheek rest. Checkered wrist and fore-end.
Features: Chrome plated bores; engraved lockplates; brass bead front and middle sights; sling swivels. Introduced 1980. From Trail Guns Armory.
Price: $379.95

> Consult our Directory pages for the location of firms mentioned.

F.I.E. Gallyon

F.I.E. "THE GALLYON" FOWLING PIECE
Gauge: 12.
Barrel: 32" (open choked).
Weight: 7½ lbs.
Stock: European walnut, English style. Hand checkered, satin oil finish.
Sights: Bead front.
Features: Faithful reproduction of an old English fowling piece. Fine scroll engraving on lock, barrel and trigger guard. Steel buttplate. Introduced 1979. From F.I.E. Corp.
Price: $169.95

Morse/Navy

MORSE/NAVY SINGLE BARREL SHOTGUN
Gauge: 12 ga.
Barrel: 26".
Weight: 5 lbs. **Length:** 41½" over-all.
Stock: American walnut, full p.g.
Sights: Front bead.
Features: Brass receiver, black buttplate. From Navy Arms.
Price: $149.95
Price: Kit $100.00

Navy Classic

NAVY CLASSIC DOUBLE BARREL SHOTGUN
Gauge: 12.
Barrel: 28".
Weight: 7 lbs., 12 ozs. **Length:** 45" over-all.
Stock: Walnut.
Features: Color case-hardened lock plates and hammers; hand checkered stock. Imported by Navy Arms.
Price: $325.00
Price: Kit $250.00

Double Barrel

DOUBLE BARREL PERCUSSION SHOTGUN
Gauge: 12.
Barrel: 30" (I.C.& Mod.).
Weight: 6¼ lbs. **Length:** 45" over-all.
Stock: Hand checkered walnut, 14" pull.
Features: Double triggers, light hand engraving. Details vary with importer. Imported by The Armoury, Dixie, Euroarms of America, Hopkins & Allen.
Price: Upland ....$125.00 to $260.00
Price: 10 ga. (Dixie) $315.00

AIR GUNS—HANDGUNS

Guns in this section are powered by: A) disposable CO_2 cylinders, B) hand-pumped compressed air released by trigger action, C) air compressed by a spring-powered piston released by trigger action. Calibers are generally 177 (BB or pellet) and 22 (ball or pellet); a few guns are made in 20 or 25 caliber. Pellet guns are usually rifled, those made for BB's only are smoothbore.

BSA SCORPION AIR PISTOL
Caliber: 177 or 22.
Barrel: 7⅞", rifled.
Weight: 3.6 lbs. **Length:** 15¾" over-all.
Power: Spring-air, barrel cocking.
Stock: Moulded black plastic contoured with thumbrest.
Sights: Interchangeable bead or blade front with hood, open rear adjustable for w. & e.
Features: Muzzle velocity of 510 fps (177) and 380 fps (22). Comes with pellets, oil, targets and steel target holder. Scope and mount optional. Introduced 1980. From Precision Sports.
Price: 177 or 22 cal. $119.95
Price: 1.5x15 scope and mount $39.50

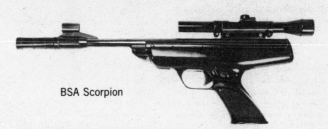

BSA Scorpion

BEEMAN 700 TARGET/SPORT PISTOL
Caliber: 177, single shot.
Barrel: 7", rifled steel.
Weight: 3.1 lbs. **Length:** 16" over-all.
Power: Spring piston.
Stocks: Checkered, wood-grained synthetic.
Sights: Hooded fixed front, micro-click rear with 4 rotating notches.
Features: Adjustable double-pull trigger. Auto. safety. Scope mount available. Velocity 460 fps MV. Shoulder stock and scope available. Imported by Beeman's.
Price: Right hand $150.00
Price: Left hand $117.00

BEEMAN/WEBLEY HURRICANE PISTOL
Caliber: 177 or 22.
Barrel: 8", rifled.
Weight: 2.4 lbs. **Length:** 16⅞₁₆" over-all.
Power: Spring piston.
Stocks: Thumbrest, checkered plastic.
Sights: Hooded front, micro-click rear adj. for w. and e.
Features: Velocity of 470 fps (177-cal.). Single stroke cocking, adjustable trigger pull, manual safety. Scope base included; 1.5x scope $39.95 extra. Shoulder stock available. Introduced 1977. Imported by Beeman's.
Price: $125.00

BEEMAN 800 TARGET/SPORT PISTOL
Caliber: 177, single shot.
Barrel: 7", rifled steel.
Weight: 3.2 lbs. **Length:** 16" over-all.
Power: Spring piston.
Stocks: Checkered, wood-grained synthetic.
Sights: Hooded front with interchangeable inserts, micro click rear with 4 rotating notches.
Features: Velocity 400 fps MV. Advanced recoilless action. Shoulder stock and scope mount available. Imported by Beeman's.
Price: Right hand $185.00
Price: Left hand $187.00

Beeman 800

Beeman 900

BEEMAN 900 MATCH PISTOL
Caliber: 177, single shot.
Barrel: 7".
Weight: 3.3 lbs. **Length:** 16.5" over-all.
Power: Barrel cocking spring piston.
Stocks: Walnut with adjustable palm rest and sliding support plate.
Sights: Adj. post front from 2.5mm to 4.0mm width; adj. rear with interchangeable notches.
Features: Recoilless action; trigger adj. for length of pull, area of contact, travel length, pre-travel weight, pressure point and weight; auto. cocking safety trigger stop; rear sight has three positions; new removeable barrel weights. Shoulder stock and scope/mount available. Imported by Beeman's.
Price: Right hand $425.00
Price: Left hand $499.00

BEEMAN/WEBLEY TEMPEST AIR PISTOL
Caliber: 177 or 22, single shot.
Barrel: 6.75", rifled ordnance steel.
Weight: 32 oz. **Length:** 9" over-all.
Power: Spring piston.
Stocks: Checkered black epoxy with thumbrest.
Sights: Post front; rear has sliding leaf rear adjustable for w. and e.
Features: Adjustable trigger pull, manual safety. Velocity 470 fps (177 cal.). Steel piston in steel liner for maximum performance and durability. Shoulder stock available. Introduced 1979. Imported by Beeman's.
Price: $90.00

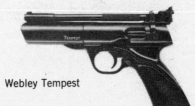

Webley Tempest

CAUTION: PRICES CHANGE. CHECK AT GUNSHOP.

AIR GUNS—HANDGUNS

BEEMAN/WISCHO S-20 STANDARD
Caliber: 177.
Barrel: 7".
Weight: 2 lbs., 2 oz.
Power: Spring piston.
Stock: Walnut.
Sights: Hooded front, open rear adj. for elevation.
Features: Stock suitable for right or left-handed shooters; 450 fps; 24 oz. trigger pull. Introduced 1980. Imported by Beeman's.
Price: $115.00

Wischo S-20

BEEMAN MODEL 850 AIR PISTOL
Caliber: 177, single shot.
Barrel: 7", rifled steel.
Weight: 3.2 lbs. **Length:** 16" over-all.
Power: Spring, barrel cocking.
Stocks: Checkered, wood-grained synthetic.
Sights: Infinite width rotating post front 2.5 to 4mm, micro click rear with 4 rotating notches.
Features: Velocity 490 fps. Advanced recoilless action. Rotating barrel housing for easier cocking. Optional muzzle weight available. Chocie of right- or left-hand grips; can be ambidextrous. Scope mount and shoulder stock available. Introduced 1979. Imported by Beeman's.
Price: Right-hand $215.00
Price: Left-hand $217.00

Consult our Directory pages for the location of firms mentioned.

BEEMAN/FEINWERKBAU MODEL 80 MATCH PISTOL
Caliber: 177, single shot.
Barrel: 7.5".
Weight: 2.8 to 3.2 lbs. (varies with weight selection). **Length:** 16.4" over-all.
Power: Spring piston, single-stroke sidelever cocking.
Stocks: Stippled walnut with adjustable palm shelf.
Sights: Interchangeable-blade front, rear notch micro. adj. for w. and e.
Features: Two-stage trigger adjustable for finger length. Recoilless operation. Interchangeable weights attach to frame, not barrel. Weights may be arranged to suit balance preference. Cocking effort 16 lbs. Muzzle velocity 475-525 fps. Introduced 1978. Imported by Beeman's.
Price: Right-hand $595.00
Price: Left-hand $620.00

Beeman/FWB-80

BENJAMIN SUPER S. S. TARGET PISTOL SERIES 130
Caliber: BB, 22 and 177; single shot.
Barrel: 8"; BB smoothbore; 22 and 177, rifled.
Length: 11". **Weight:** 2 lbs.
Power: Hand pumped.
Features: Bolt action; fingertip safety; adj. power.
Price: M130, BB $50.70
Price: M132, 22 .... $50.70
Price: M137, 177 .... $50.70

Benjamin 130

CROSMAN MODEL 1861 SHILOH REVOLVER
Caliber: 177 pellets or BBs, 6-shot.
Barrel: 6" rifled.
Weight: 2 lbs., 8 oz. **Length:** 12¾" over-all.
Power: CO$_2$ Powerlet.
Stocks: Wood-grained plastic.
Sights: Fixed.
Features: Modeled after the 1861 Remington revolver. Averages 42 shots per CO$_2$ Powerlet. Velocity of 330 to 350 fps with pellets. Introduced 1981.
Price: About $25.00

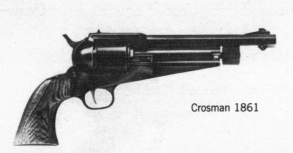
Crosman 1861

CROSMAN MODEL 1322 AIR PISTOL
Caliber: 22, single shot.
Barrel: 8", button rifled.
Length: 13⅝". **Weight:** 37 oz.
Power: Hand pumped.
Sights: Blade front, rear adj. for w. and e.
Features: Moulded plastic grip, hand size pump forearm. Cross bolt safety. Also available in 177 Cal. as **Model 1377.**
Price: About $36.99

CAUTION: PRICES CHANGE. CHECK AT GUNSHOP.

Crosman 454

Crosman 1600

CROSMAN MARK I TARGET PISTOL

Caliber: 22, single shot.
Barrel: 7¼", button rifled.
Length: 11". **Weight:** 42 oz.
Power: Crosman Powerlet CO_2 cylinder.
Features: New system provides same shot-to-shot velocity, adj. from 300- to 400 fps. Checkered thumbrest grips, right or left. Patridge front sight, rear adj. for w. & e. Adj. trigger.
Price: About $43.00

DAISY 179 SIX GUN

Caliber: BB, 12-shot.
Barrel: Steel lined, smoothbore.
Length: 11½". **Weight:** NA
Power: Spring.
Features: Forced feed from under-barrel magazine. Single action, molded wood grained grips.
Price: About $19.50

DAISY MODEL 188 BB/PELLET PISTOL

Caliber: 177.
Barrel: 9.9".
Weight: 1.67 lbs. **Length:** 12" over-all.
Stocks: Die-cast metal; checkered with thumbrest.
Sights: Blade and ramp front, notched rear.
Features: Single shot for pellets, 24-shot for BBs. Spring action with under-barrel cocking lever. Grip and receiver of die-cast metal. Introduced 1979.
Price: About $19.50

CROSMAN 38T TARGET REVOLVER

Caliber: 177, 6-shot.
Barrel: 6", rifled.
Length: 11". **Weight:** 40 oz.
Power: CO_2 Powerlet cylinder.
Features: Double action, revolving cylinder. Adj. rear sight.
Price: About $38.00

Crosman 38C Combat Revolver

Same as 38 Target except 3½" BBL., 36 oz., about $38.00

FEINWERKBAU FWB-65 MKI AIR PISTOL

Caliber: 177.
Barrel: 7½"; fixed bbl. wgt. avail.
Length: 14½" over-all. **Weight:** 42 oz.
Power: Spring, sidelever cocking.
Stocks: Walnut, stippled thumbrest.
Sights: Front, interchangeable post element system, open rear, click adj. for w. & e. and for sighting notch width. Scope mount avail.
Features: Cocking effort 9 lbs. 2-stage trigger, 4 adjustments. Quiet firing, 525 fps. Programs instantly for recoil or recoilless operation. Permanently lubricated. Steel piston ring. Special switch converts trigger from 17.6 oz. pull to 42 oz. let-off. Available from Air Rifle Hdq., Beeman's.
Price: Right-hand ....$485.00 to $624.50

Feinwerkbau Model 65 International Match Pistol

Same as FWB 65 MKI pistol except: new adj. wood grips to meet international regulations, optional 3 oz. barrel sleeve weight. Available from Air Rifle Hdqtrs., Beeman's.
Price: Right-hand $598.50
Price: Left-hand $624.50

CROSMAN 454 BB PISTOL

Caliber: BB, 16-shot.
Length: 11" over-all. **Weight:** 30 oz.
Power: Standard CO_2.
Stocks: Contoured with thumbrest.
Sights: Patridge-type front, fully adj. rear.
Features: Gives about 80 shots per powerlet, slide-action safety, steel barrel, die-cast receiver. Lanyard ring for easy piercing of CO_2 cylinder.
Price: About $28.00

Crosman Model 1600 Air Pistol

Same specifications as Model 454 except has fixed sights, black plastic grips, no lanyard ring.
Price: About $24.00

Crosman Mark II Target Pistol

Same as Mark I except 177 cal., about $43.00

Crosman Mk.1

Daisy 179

Daisy 188

Crosman 38T

FWB-65 Mk.1

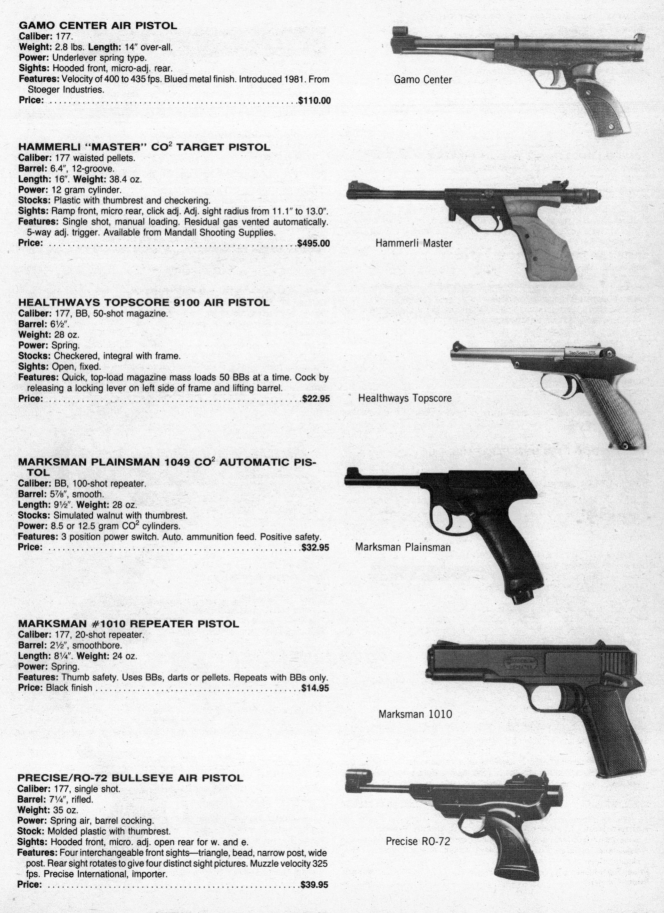

GAMO CENTER AIR PISTOL
Caliber: 177.
Weight: 2.8 lbs. **Length:** 14″ over-all.
Power: Underlever spring type.
Sights: Hooded front, micro-adj. rear.
Features: Velocity of 400 to 435 fps. Blued metal finish. Introduced 1981. From Stoeger Industries.
Price: $110.00

Gamo Center

HAMMERLI "MASTER" CO_2 TARGET PISTOL
Caliber: 177 waisted pellets.
Barrel: 6.4″, 12-groove.
Length: 16″. **Weight:** 38.4 oz.
Power: 12 gram cylinder.
Stocks: Plastic with thumbrest and checkering.
Sights: Ramp front, micro rear, click adj. Adj. sight radius from 11.1″ to 13.0″.
Features: Single shot, manual loading. Residual gas vented automatically. 5-way adj. trigger. Available from Mandall Shooting Supplies.
Price: $495.00

Hammerli Master

HEALTHWAYS TOPSCORE 9100 AIR PISTOL
Caliber: 177, BB, 50-shot magazine.
Barrel: 6½″.
Weight: 28 oz.
Power: Spring.
Stocks: Checkered, integral with frame.
Sights: Open, fixed.
Features: Quick, top-load magazine mass loads 50 BBs at a time. Cock by releasing a locking lever on left side of frame and lifting barrel.
Price: $22.95

Healthways Topscore

MARKSMAN PLAINSMAN 1049 CO_2 AUTOMATIC PIS-TOL
Caliber: BB, 100-shot repeater.
Barrel: 5⅞″, smooth.
Length: 9½″. **Weight:** 28 oz.
Stocks: Simulated walnut with thumbrest.
Power: 8.5 or 12.5 gram CO_2 cylinders.
Features: 3 position power switch. Auto. ammunition feed. Positive safety.
Price: $32.95

Marksman Plainsman

MARKSMAN #1010 REPEATER PISTOL
Caliber: 177, 20-shot repeater.
Barrel: 2½″, smoothbore.
Length: 8¼″. **Weight:** 24 oz.
Power: Spring.
Features: Thumb safety. Uses BBs, darts or pellets. Repeats with BBs only.
Price: Black finish $14.95

Marksman 1010

PRECISE/RO-72 BULLSEYE AIR PISTOL
Caliber: 177, single shot.
Barrel: 7¼″, rifled.
Weight: 35 oz.
Power: Spring air, barrel cocking.
Stock: Molded plastic with thumbrest.
Sights: Hooded front, micro. adj. open rear for w. and e.
Features: Four interchangeable front sights—triangle, bead, narrow post, wide post. Rear sight rotates to give four distinct sight pictures. Muzzle velocity 325 fps. Precise International, importer.
Price: $39.95

Precise RO-72

AIR GUNS—HANDGUNS

POWER LINE MATCH 777 PELLET PISTOL
Caliber: 177, single shot.
Barrel: 9.61" rifled steel.
Weight: 49 ozs. **Length:** 13½" over-all.
Power: Sidelever, single pump pneumatic.
Stocks: Smooth hardwood, fully contoured; right or left hand.
Sights: Blade and ramp front, match-grade open rear with adj. width notch, micro. click adjustments.
Features: Adjustable trigger; manual cross-bolt safety. MV of 360 fps. Comes in foam-filled carrying case and complete cleaning kit, adjustment tool and pellets.
Price: About $183.75

Power Line 777

POWER LINE 717/722 PELLET PISTOLS
Caliber: 177 (Model 717), 22 (Model 722), single shot.
Barrel: 9.61".
Weight: 48 oz. **Length:** 13½" over-all.
Stocks: Molded wood-grain plastic, with thumbrest.
Sights: Blade and ramp front, micro. adjustable notch rear.
Features: Single pump pneumatic pistol. Rifled brass barrel. Cross-bolt trigger block. Muzzle velocity 360 fps (177 cal.), 290 fps (22 cal.). From Daisy. Introduced 1979.
Price: Either model, about $61.50

POWER LINE CO² 1200 CUSTOM TARGET PISTOL
Caliber: BB, 177
Barrel: 10½", smooth
Weight: 30 oz. **Length:** 11¼" over-all.
Power: Daisy CO² cylinder.
Stocks: Contoured, checkered moulded wood-grain plastic.
Sights: Blade ramp front, fully adj. square notch rear.
Features: 60-shot BB reservoir, gravity feed. Cross bolt safety. Velocity of 420-450 fps for more than 100 shots.
Price: About $30.95

Sheridan EB

SHERIDAN MODEL EB CO² PISTOL
Caliber: 20 (5mm).
Barrel: 6½", rifled, rust proof.
Weight: 27 ozs. **Length:** 9" over-all.
Power: 12 gram CO² cylinder.
Stocks: Checkered simulated walnut. Left- or right-handed.
Sights: Blade front, fully adjustable rear.
Features: Turn-bolt single-shot action. Gives about 40 shots at 400 fps per CO² cylinder.
Price: $55.90

POWER LINE MODELS 780 & 790
Caliber: 22 cal. pellet (780), 177 cal. pellet (790), single-shot.
Barrel: 8½", rifled steel.
Weight: 42 oz.
Power: 12 gram CO² cartridge.
Stocks: Simulated walnut, checkered. Thumbrest. Left or right hand.
Sights: Patridge front, fully adj. rear with micro. click windage adjustment.
Features: Pull-bolt action, crossbolt safety. High-low power adjustment.
Price: $61.25

Power Line 780

WALTHER MODEL LP-3
Caliber: 177, single shot.
Barrel: 9⅜", rifled.
Length: 13³⁄₁₆". **Weight:** 45½ oz.
Power: Compressed air, lever cocking.
Features: Recoiless operation, cocking in grip frame. Micro-click rear sight, adj. for w. & e., 4-way adj. trigger. Plastic thumbrest grips. Imported by Interarms.
Price: $450.00

Walther LP-3

WALTHER MODEL LP-53 PISTOL
Caliber: 177, single shot.
Barrel: 9⅜".
Length: 12⅜" over-all. **Weight:** 40.5 oz.
Power: Spring air.
Features: Micrometer rear sight. Interchangeable rear sight blades. Target grips. Bbl. weight available at extra cost. Interarms, Alexandria, Va.
Price: $250.00

Walther Model LP-3 Match Pistol
Same specifications as LP-3 except for grips, frame shape and weight. Has adjustable walnut grips to meet international shooting regulations. Imported by Interarms.
Price: $540.00

WISCHO BSF S-20 CUSTOM MATCH PISTOL
Caliber: 177, single shot.
Barrel: 7" rifled.
Length: 15.8" over-all. **Weight:** 45 oz.
Stocks: Walnut with thumbrest.
Sights: Bead front, rear adj. for e.
Power: Spring piston barrel cocking.
Features: Cocking effort of 17 lbs.; M.V. 450 f.p.s.; adj. trigger. Optional scope and mount available. Detachable aluminum stock. Available from Beemans.
Price: $145.00

WEIHRAUCH HW-70 AIR PISTOL
Caliber: 177, single shot.
Barrel: 6¼", rifled.
Length: 12¾" over-all. **Weight:** 38 oz.
Sights: Hooded post front, square notch rear adj. for w. and e.
Power: Spring, barrel cocking.
Stocks: Plastic, with thumbrest.
Features: Adj. trigger. 24-lb. cocking effort, 410 f.p.s. M.V.; automatic barrel safety. Available from Air Rifle HQ, Beeman's.
Price: . . . . $98.00 to $124.50

CAUTION: PRICES CHANGE. CHECK AT GUNSHOP.

A.R.H./FEINWERKBAU F-12 CX
Caliber: 177.
Barrel: 18¼", rifled.
Weight: 8 lbs., 14 ozs. **Length:** 43½" over-all.
Power: Spring air, single stroke barrel cocking.
Stock: Walnut-finished hardwood, hand-cut checkered p.g., Monte Carlo cheekpiece.
Sights: 2x-6x 1"-tube wide field scope included.
Features: Comes with 1" sling, detachable swivels, filler screws, trigger shoe. Internally accurized for optimum performance. From Air Rifle Headquarters.
Price: $548.50

ARH F-12

A.R.H./WEIRAUCH HW 35 DX
Caliber: 177.
Barrel: 19¼", rifled, hinged-type.
Weight: 9 lbs., 4 ozs. **Length:** 44½" over-all.
Power: Spring air, single stroke barrel cocking.
Stock: Walnut with Monte Carlo cheekpiece, hand-cut checkering, beavertail fore-end and rubber buttplate.
Sights: 2x-6x 1"-tube wide field scope included.
Features: Comes with 1" sling, detachable swivels, filler screws, trigger shoe, automatic safety. Accurized internally for optimum performance. From Air Rifle Headquarters.
Price: $548.50

ARH HW35DX

Anschutz 250

ANSCHUTZ 250 TARGET RIFLE
Caliber: 177, single shot.
Barrel: 18½", rifled, one piece with receiver.
Length: 45". **Weight:** 11 lbs. with sights.
Power: Spring, side-lever cocking, 17 lb. pull.
Features: Recoilless operation. Two-stage adj. trigger. Checkered walnut p.g. stock with Monte Carlo comb & cheekpiece; adj. buttplate; accessory rail. Available from Beeman's.
Price: $598.50

BSA BUCCANEER AIR RIFLE
Caliber: 177 or 22.
Barrel: 18.5", rifled.
Weight: 6 lb. **Length:** 35.5" over-all.
Power: Spring-air, barrel cocking.
Stock: High impact polyurethane, thumbhole design.
Sights: Interchangeable bead or blade front, aperture rear adjustable for windage and elevation.
Features: Adjustable trigger; non-automatic safety; checkered p.g. and fore-end. Comes with targets and steel target holder, oil, pellets. Scope and mounts optional. Introduced 1980. From Precision Sports.
Price: 177 or 22 cal. $139.50
Price: 5x15 scope and mount $39.50

BSA Buccaneer

BSA AIRSPORTER-S AIR RIFLE
Caliber: 177 or 22.
Barrel: 19.5", rifled.
Weight: 8 lbs. **Length:** 44.7" over-all.
Power: Spring air, underlever action.
Stock: Oil-finished walnut, high comb Monte Carlo cheekpiece.
Sights: Ramp front with interchangeable bead and blade, adjustable for height; tangent-type rear adj. for w. & e.
Features: Muzzle velocity of 825 fps (177) and 635 fps (22). Fully adj. trigger. Cylinder is a large diameter, one-piece impact extrusion. Scope and mount optional. Introduced 1980. From Precision Sports.
Price: 177 or 22 cal. $350.00
Price: 4x20 scope and mount $38.50

BSA Airsporter

BSA MERCURY AIR RIFLE
Caliber: 177 or 22.
Barrel: 18.5", rifled.
Weight: 7 lbs. **Length:** 43.5" over-all.
Power: Spring-air, barrel cocking.
Stock: European hardwood. Monte Carlo cheekpiece, ventilated butt pad.
Sights: Adjustable bead/blade front, tangent rear adj. for w. & e.
Features: Muzzle velocity of 700 fps (177) and 550 fps (22). Reversible. "V" and "U" notch rear sight blade. Single stage match-type trigger, adj. for weight of pull and sear engagement. Scope and mount optional. Introduced 1980. From Precision Sports.
Price: 177 or 22 cal. $199.50
Price: 4x20 scope and mount $38.50

BSA Mercury

CAUTION: PRICES CHANGE. CHECK AT GUNSHOP.

AIR GUNS—LONG GUNS

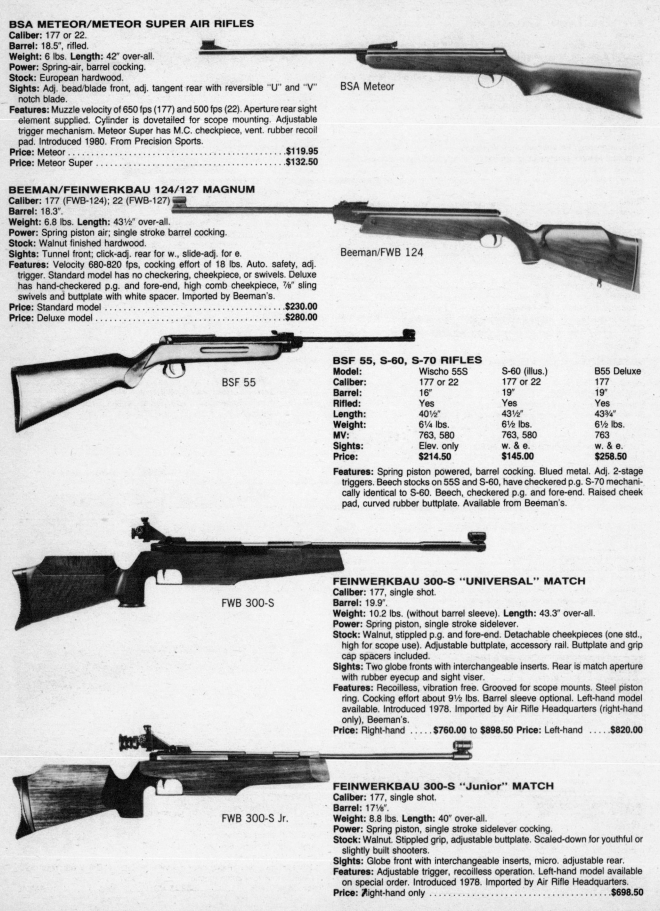

BSA METEOR/METEOR SUPER AIR RIFLES
Caliber: 177 or 22.
Barrel: 18.5″, rifled.
Weight: 6 lbs. **Length:** 42″ over-all.
Power: Spring-air, barrel cocking.
Stock: European hardwood.
Sights: Adj. bead/blade front, adj. tangent rear with reversible "U" and "V" notch blade.
Features: Muzzle velocity of 650 fps (177) and 500 fps (22). Aperture rear sight element supplied. Cylinder is dovetailed for scope mounting. Adjustable trigger mechanism. Meteor Super has M.C. checkpiece, vent. rubber recoil pad. Introduced 1980. From Precision Sports.
Price: Meteor $119.95
Price: Meteor Super $132.50

BSA Meteor

BEEMAN/FEINWERKBAU 124/127 MAGNUM
Caliber: 177 (FWB-124); 22 (FWB-127)
Barrel: 18.3″.
Weight: 6.8 lbs. **Length:** 43½″ over-all.
Power: Spring piston air; single stroke barrel cocking.
Stock: Walnut finished hardwood.
Sights: Tunnel front; click-adj. rear for w., slide-adj. for e.
Features: Velocity 680-820 fps, cocking effort of 18 lbs. Auto. safety, adj. trigger. Standard model has no checkering, cheekpiece, or swivels. Deluxe has hand-checkered p.g. and fore-end, high comb cheekpiece, ⅞″ sling swivels and buttplate with white spacer. Imported by Beeman's.
Price: Standard model $230.00
Price: Deluxe model $280.00

Beeman/FWB 124

BSF 55

BSF 55, S-60, S-70 RIFLES

Model:	Wischo 55S	S-60 (illus.)	B55 Deluxe
Caliber:	177 or 22	177 or 22	177
Barrel:	16″	19″	19″
Rifled:	Yes	Yes	Yes
Length:	40½″	43½″	43¾″
Weight:	6¼ lbs.	6½ lbs.	6½ lbs.
MV:	763, 580	763, 580	763
Sights:	Elev. only	w. & e.	w. & e.
Price:	$214.50	$145.00	$258.50

Features: Spring piston powered, barrel cocking. Blued metal. Adj. 2-stage triggers. Beech stocks on 55S and S-60, have checkered p.g. S-70 mechanically identical to S-60. Beech, checkered p.g. and fore-end. Raised cheek pad, curved rubber buttplate. Available from Beeman's.

FWB 300-S

FEINWERKBAU 300-S "UNIVERSAL" MATCH
Caliber: 177, single shot.
Barrel: 19.9″.
Weight: 10.2 lbs. (without barrel sleeve). **Length:** 43.3″ over-all.
Power: Spring piston, single stroke sidelever.
Stock: Walnut, stippled p.g. and fore-end. Detachable cheekpieces (one std., high for scope use). Adjustable buttplate, accessory rail. Buttplate and grip cap spacers included.
Sights: Two globe fronts with interchangeable inserts. Rear is match aperture with rubber eyecup and sight viser.
Features: Recoilless, vibration free. Grooved for scope mounts. Steel piston ring. Cocking effort about 9½ lbs. Barrel sleeve optional. Left-hand model available. Introduced 1978. Imported by Air Rifle Headquarters (right-hand only), Beeman's.
Price: Right-hand .....$760.00 to $898.50 **Price:** Left-hand $820.00

FWB 300-S Jr.

FEINWERKBAU 300-S "Junior" MATCH
Caliber: 177, single shot.
Barrel: 17⅛″.
Weight: 8.8 lbs. **Length:** 40″ over-all.
Power: Spring piston, single stroke sidelever cocking.
Stock: Walnut. Stippled grip, adjustable buttplate. Scaled-down for youthful or slightly built shooters.
Sights: Globe front with interchangeable inserts, micro. adjustable rear.
Features: Adjustable trigger, recoilless operation. Left-hand model available on special order. Introduced 1978. Imported by Air Rifle Headquarters.
Price: Right-hand only $698.50

CAUTION: PRICES CHANGE. CHECK AT GUNSHOP.

AIR GUNS—LONG GUNS

BEEMAN/WEBLEY OSPREY AIR RIFLE
Caliber: 177 or 22.
Barrel: 18½".
Weight: 7¾ lbs. **Length:** 43¼" over-all.
Power: Spring piston air; one stroke side-lever.
Stock: Walnut; sculptured cheekpiece, Monte Carlo comb,
rubber buttplate.
Sights: Hooded front, micro. click rear adj. for w. & e.
Receiver grooved for aperture sight or scope.
Features: Manual safety plus cocking lever safety to prevent accidental clos-
ing. Steel automotive-type piston rings. Velocity 700 fps (177), 550 fps (22).
Trigger is adjustable from 3 to 8 lbs. Imported by Beeman's Precision Air-
guns.
Price: $260.00

BEEMAN/WEIRAUCH HW60 SMALL BORE RIFLE
Caliber: 22 LR.
Barrel: 26.8".
Weight 10.8 lbs. **Length:** 45.7".
Stock: Walnut, with adj. buttplate.
Sights: Hooded ramp front with inserts, match aperture rear.
Features: Single shot. Adj. match trigger with push-button safety. Stippled
fore-end and pistol grip. Rail with adj. swivel. Left-hand version available.
Introduced 1980. Imported by Beeman's.
Price: $495.00

BEEMAN/WEBLEY VULCAN AIR RIFLE
Caliber: 177 or 22.
Barrel: 17", rifled steel.
Weight: 6.8 lbs. **Length:** 41" over-all.
Power: Spring piston air, barrel cocking.
Stock: Beech with cheekpiece and rubber buttplate.
Sights: Hooded front; micro click rear adj. for w. & e.
Features: Receiver grooved for scope mounting. Manual safety. Trigger ad-
justable down to about 2 lbs. Velocity 800 fps (177), 600 fps (22). Imported
by Beeman's.
Price: $160.00

Webley Osprey

BEEMAN MODEL 400 RECOILLESS MATCH RIFLE
Caliber: 177, single shot.
Barrel: 18.9".
Weight: 10.7 lbs. **Length:** 44½" over-all.
Power: Spring-piston, single-stroke side lever cocking.
Stock: European walnut with full length fore-end accessory rail, curved adjust-
able rubber buttplate, stippled grip.
Sights: Globe front with adjustable aperture and optional standard inserts; rear
aperture sight with micrometer adjustments for w. and e.
Features: Double-acting 2-piston recoilless action—receiver does not move.
Cocking effort 9 lbs. Fully adjustable trigger including length of pull and lateral
angle. Left-hand version with left-hand lever available. Detachable muzzle
weight. Front aperture is unique neoprene O-ring with knurled ring to vary
size. Non-reflective finish. Left-hand version has reversed cocking lever.
Imported by Beeman's.
Price: $585.00
Price: Left-hand model $585.00

> Consult our Directory pages for
> the location of firms mentioned.

BEEMAN Model 100 TARGET RIFLE
Caliber: 177, single shot.
Barrel: 18.7", rifled.
Weight: 6 lbs. **Length:** 42" over-all.
Power: Spring, barrel cocking.
Sights: Hooded front, 4-notch rotating rear micro. adj. for w. & e.
Features: Velocity 660 fps MV. Grooved for scope or peep sights; 17 lbs. single
stroke cocking; adjustable trigger. Imported by Beeman's.
Price: $155.00

Beeman 100

BEEMAN MODEL 250 AIR RIFLE
Caliber: 177 and 22.
Barrel: 20.4".
Weight: 7.7 lbs.
Power: Spring piston.
Sights: Globe front with inserts; micrometer rear.
Features: Velocity of 800-830 fps (177-cal.). Grooved for scope mounts. Auto-
matic safety. Adjustable trigger. Introduced 1980. Imported by Beeman.
Price: $209.00

Beeman 250

Benjamin 3100

BENJAMIN SERIES 3100 SUPER REPEATER RIFLES
Caliber: BB, 100-shot; 22, 85-shot.
Barrel: 23", rifled or smoothbore.
Length: 35". **Weight:** 6¼ lbs.
Power: Hand pumped.
Features: Bolt action. Piggy back full view magazine. Bar V adj. rear sight.
Walnut stock and pump handle.
Price: M3100, BB .... **$62.45** M3120, 22 rifled **$62.45**

AIR GUNS—LONG GUNS

Benjamin 340

BENJAMIN SERIES 340 AIR RIFLE
Caliber: 22 and 177 pellets or BB; single shot.
Barrel: 23", rifled and smoothbore.
Length: 35". **Weight:** 6 lbs.
Power: Hand pumped.
Features: Bolt action, walnut Monte Carlo stock and pump handle. Ramp-type front sight, adj. stepped leaf type rear. Push-pull safety.
Price: M340, BB $62.45
Price: M342, 33 ....$62.45 M347, 177 ....$62.45

Crosman Model 1

CROSMAN MODEL 1 RIFLE
Caliber: 22, single shot.
Barrel: 19", rifled brass.
Weight: 5 lbs., 1 oz. **Length:** 39" over-all.
Power: Pneumatic, variable power.
Stock: Walnut stained American hardwood.
Sights: Blade front, Williams rear with micrometer click settings.
Features: Precision trigger mechanism for light, clean pull. Metal receiver grooved for scope mounting. Bolt action with cross-bolt safety. Muzzle velocities range from 365 (three pumps) to 625 (10 pumps). Introduced 1981.
Price: About $70.00

CROSMAN MODEL 73 SADDLE PAL CO^2
Caliber: 177 pellets or BBs, 16-shot magazine.
Barrel: 18", steel.
Weight: 3 lbs., 3 ozs. **Length:** 34¾" over-all.
Stock: Simulated wood.
Sights: Ramp front, rear adj. for e.
Features: Positive lever safety. Velocity is 425 fps (pellets), 440 fps (BBs). 100 shots per CO^2 cartridge.
Price: About $24.00

CROSMAN MODEL 2200 MAGNUM AIR RIFLE
Caliber: 22, single-shot.
Barrel: 19", rifled steel.
Weight: 4 lbs., 13 ozs. **Length:** 39¾" over-all.
Stock: Full-size, wood-grained plastic with checkered p.g. and fore-end.
Sights: Ramp front, open step-adjustable rear.
Features: Variable pump power—3 pumps give 395 fps, 6 pumps 530 fps, 10 pumps 620 fps (average). Full-size adult air rifle. Has white line spacers at pistol grip and buttplate, nickel plated receiver. Introduced 1978.
Price: About $46.99

CROSMAN MODEL 788 BB SCOUT RIFLE
Caliber: 177, BB.
Barrel: 14", steel.
Weight: 2 lbs. 7 ozs. **Length:** 31" over-all.
Stock: Wood-grained ABS plastic.
Sights: Blade on ramp front, open adj. rear.
Features: Variable pump power—3 pumps give MV of 330 fps, 6 pumps 437 fps, 10 pumps 470 fps (BBs, average). Steel barrel, cross-bolt safety. Introduced 1978.
Price: About $22.00

CROSMAN AMERICAN CLASSIC 766 AIR RIFLE
Caliber: 177 pellets or BBs, 15-shot magazine.
Barrel: 19" rifled.
Weight: About 5 lbs. **Length:** 39½" over-all.
Power: Pump-up, pneumatic.
Stock: Wood-grained checkered ABS plastic.
Features: Three pumps gives about 450 fps, 10 pumps about 700 fps. Cross-bolt safety; concealed reservoir holds over 180 BBs.
Price: About $44.00

> Consult our Directory pages for the location of firms mentioned.

DAISY MODEL 850 PNEUMATIC RIFLE
Caliber: BB or 177, 100-shot BB reservoir.
Barrel: 20.8", rifled steel.
Length: 33⅜" over-all. **Weight:** 4.3 lbs.
Power: Single pump pneumatic.
Stock: Moulded plastic with woodgrain finish.
Sights: Ramp front, fully adjustable open rear.
Features: Shots either BB's or pellets at 520 fps (BB) and 480 fps (pellet). Manual cross-bolt trigger block safety. International 1981.
Price: About $57.95

Daisy 850

Crosman 760

CROSMAN MODEL 760 POWERMASTER
Caliber: 177 pellets or BB, 180 shot.
Barrel: 19½", rifled steel.
Length: 35". **Weight:** 4 lbs., 3 ozs.
Power: Pneumatic, hand pump.
Features: Short stroke, power determined by number of strokes. Walnut finished plastic checkered stock and fore-end. Post front sight and adjustable rear sight. Cross-bolt safety. Scope and mount optional.
Price: About $36.00

AIR GUNS—LONG GUNS

Daisy 1894

DAISY MODEL 840
Caliber: 177 pellet (single-shot) or BB (350-shot).
Barrel: 19″, smoothbore, steel.
Weight: 3¼ lbs. **Length:** 37⅛″ over-all.
Stock: Moulded wood-grain stock and fore-end.
Sights: Ramp front, open, adj. rear.
Features: Single pump pneumatic rifle. Muzzle velocity 325 fps (BB), 300 fps (pellet). Steel buttplate; straight pull bolt action; cross-bolt safety. Fore-end forms pump lever. Introduced 1978.
Price: About **$30.00**

Daisy 845

Daisy 499

DAISY RIFLES
Model:	95	111	105
Caliber:	BB	BB	BB
Barrel:	18″	18″	13½″
Length:	35″	35″	30½
Power:	Spring	Spring	Spring
Capacity:	700	700	450
Price: About	$30.65	$25.50	$20.50

Features: 95 stock is wood, fore-end plastic; 105 and 111 have plastic stocks.

POWER LINE 880 PUMP-UP AIR GUN
Caliber: 177 pellets, BB.
Barrel: Smooth bore, steel.
Length: 37¾″ over-all. **Weight:** 6 lbs.
Power: Spring air.
Stock: Wood grain moulded plastic.
Sights: Ramp front, open rear adj. for e.
Features: Crafted by Daisy. Variable power (velocity and range) increase with pump strokes. 10 strokes for maximum power. 100-shot BB magazine. Cross-bolt trigger safety. Positive cocking valve.
Price: About **$46.50**

Power Line 880

POWER LINE 881 PUMP-UP AIR GUN
Caliber: 177 pellets, BB.
Barrel: Decagon rifled.
Length: 37¾″ over-all. **Weight:** 6 lbs.
Power: Spring air.
Stock: Wood grain moulded plastic with Monte Carlo cheekpiece.
Sights: Ramp front, step-adj. rear for e.
Features: Crafted by Daisy. Accurized version of Model 880. Checkered fore-end and p.g.
Price: About **$56.00**

POWER LINE MODEL 917/922
Caliber: 177 or 22 pellets, 5-shot clip.
Barrel: 20.8″. Decagon rifled brass barrel.
Weight: 5 lbs. **Length:** 37¾″ over-all.
Stock: Molded wood-grained plastic with checkered p.g. and fore-end.
Sights: Ramp front, full adj. open rear.
Features: Muzzle velocity from 285 fps (two pumps) to 555 fps. (ten pumps). Straight pull bolt action. Separate buttplate and grip cap with white spacers. Introduced 1978.
Price: About **$61.95**

Power Line 917

DAISY 1894 SPITTIN' IMAGE CARBINE
Caliber: BB, 40-shot.
Barrel: 17½″, smoothbore.
Length: 38⅜″.
Power: Spring.
Features: Cocks halfway on forward stroke of lever, halfway on return.
Price: About **$39.00**

Daisy Model 845 Target Gun
Special target version of the Model 840. Same as the 840 except comes with globe front sight and No. 5845 Daisy Receiver Sight.
Price: About **$36.00**

DAISY 499 MATCH TARGET
Caliber: BB, single shot.
Barrel: 18″, smoothbore.
Weight: About 4 lbs. **Length:** 36¼″ over-all.
Stock: Stained harwood, Monte Carlo-style. Fore-end has provision for adding extra weight.
Sights: Globe front, peep rear (Daisy No. 5845, fully adj.)
Features: Official model of the NRA-sanctioned Daisy/U.S. Jaycees Shooting Education Program. Introduced 1980.
Price: About **$44.95**

Consult our Directory pages for the location of firms mentioned.

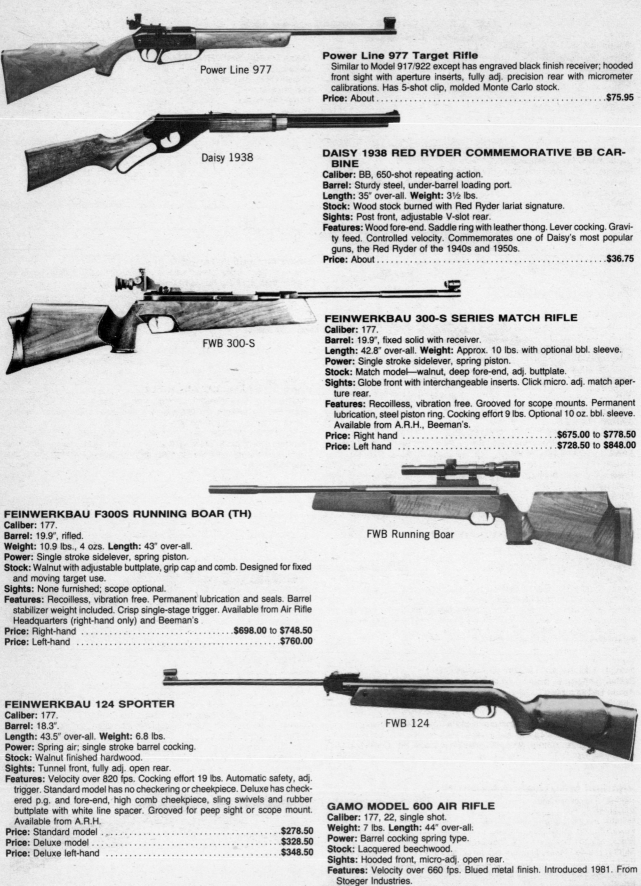

Power Line 977

Power Line 977 Target Rifle
Similar to Model 917/922 except has engraved black finish receiver; hooded front sight with aperture inserts, fully adj. precision rear with micrometer calibrations. Has 5-shot clip, molded Monte Carlo stock.
Price: About **$75.95**

Daisy 1938

DAISY 1938 RED RYDER COMMEMORATIVE BB CAR-BINE
Caliber: BB, 650-shot repeating action.
Barrel: Sturdy steel, under-barrel loading port.
Length: 35″ over-all. **Weight:** 3½ lbs.
Stock: Wood stock burned with Red Ryder lariat signature.
Sights: Post front, adjustable V-slot rear.
Features: Wood fore-end. Saddle ring with leather thong. Lever cocking. Gravity feed. Controlled velocity. Commemorates one of Daisy's most popular guns, the Red Ryder of the 1940s and 1950s.
Price: About **$36.75**

FWB 300-S

FEINWERKBAU 300-S SERIES MATCH RIFLE
Caliber: 177.
Barrel: 19.9″, fixed solid with receiver.
Length: 42.8″ over-all. **Weight:** Approx. 10 lbs. with optional bbl. sleeve.
Power: Single stroke sidelever, spring piston.
Stock: Match model—walnut, deep fore-end, adj. buttplate.
Sights: Globe front with interchangeable inserts. Click micro. adj. match aperture rear.
Features: Recoilless, vibration free. Grooved for scope mounts. Permanent lubrication, steel piston ring. Cocking effort 9 lbs. Optional 10 oz. bbl. sleeve. Available from A.R.H., Beeman's.
Price: Right hand . . . .**$675.00** to **$778.50**
Price: Left hand . . . .**$728.50** to **$848.00**

FEINWERKBAU F300S RUNNING BOAR (TH)
Caliber: 177.
Barrel: 19.9″, rifled.
Weight: 10.9 lbs., 4 ozs. **Length:** 43″ over-all.
Power: Single stroke sidelever, spring piston.
Stock: Walnut with adjustable buttplate, grip cap and comb. Designed for fixed and moving target use.
Sights: None furnished; scope optional.
Features: Recoilless, vibration free. Permanent lubrication and seals. Barrel stabilizer weight included. Crisp single-stage trigger. Available from Air Rifle Headquarters (right-hand only) and Beeman's.
Price: Right-hand . . . .**$698.00** to **$748.50**
Price: Left-hand **$760.00**

FWB Running Boar

FEINWERKBAU 124 SPORTER
Caliber: 177.
Barrel: 18.3″.
Length: 43.5″ over-all. **Weight:** 6.8 lbs.
Power: Spring air; single stroke barrel cocking.
Stock: Walnut finished hardwood.
Sights: Tunnel front, fully adj. open rear.
Features: Velocity over 820 fps. Cocking effort 19 lbs. Automatic safety, adj. trigger. Standard model has no checkering or cheekpiece. Deluxe has checkered p.g. and fore-end, high comb cheekpiece, sling swivels and rubber buttplate with white line spacer. Grooved for peep sight or scope mount. Available from A.R.H.
Price: Standard model **$278.50**
Price: Deluxe model **$328.50**
Price: Deluxe left-hand **$348.50**

FWB 124

GAMO MODEL 600 AIR RIFLE
Caliber: 177, 22, single shot.
Weight: 7 lbs. **Length:** 44″ over-all:
Power: Barrel cocking spring type.
Stock: Lacquered beechwood.
Sights: Hooded front, micro-adj. open rear.
Features: Velocity over 660 fps. Blued metal finish. Introduced 1981. From Stoeger Industries.
Price: **$144.00**

CAUTION: PRICES CHANGE. CHECK AT GUNSHOP.

GAMO GAMATIC AIR RIFLE
Caliber: 177, repeater.
Weight: 6.5 lbs. **Length:** 38" over-all.
Power: Barrel cocking spring type.
Stock: Aluminum buttstock with polymer fore-end.
Sights: Hooded front, micro-adj. rear.
Features: Velocity over 660 fps. Blued metal finish. Introduced 1981. From Stoeger Industries.
Price: $178.00

GAMO 68 AIR RIFLE
Caliber: 177, 22, single shot.
Weight: 6.5 lbs. **Length:** 38" over-all.
Power: Barrel cocking spring type.
Stock: Aluminum buttstock with polymer fore-end.
Sights: Hooded front, micro-adj. rear.
Features: Velocity of 600 fps. Blued metal finish. Introduced 1981. From Stoeger Industries.
Price: $144.00

Gamo Expomatic

GAMO EXPOMATIC AIR RIFLE
Caliber: 177 only, repeater.
Weight: 5.5 lbs. **Length:** 42" over-all.
Power: Barrel cocking spring type.
Stock: Lacquered beechwood.
Sights: Hooded front, micro-adj. rear.
Features: Velocity of 600 fps. Blued metal finish. Introduced 1981. From Stoeger Industries.
Price: $144.00

GAMO CADET AIR RIFLE
Caliber: 177 only.
Weight: 5 lbs. **Length:** 37" over-all.
Power: Barrel cocking spring type.
Stock: Lacquered beechwood.
Sights: Hooded front, micro-adj. open rear.
Features: Velocity of 570 fps. Blued metal finish. Receiver grooved for scope mounting. Introduced 1981. From Industries.
Price: $94.00

Gamo Cadet

GAMO EXPO AIR RIFLE
Caliber: 177, 22..
Weight: 5.5 lbs **Length:** 42" over-all.
Power: Barrel cocking spring type.
Stock: Lacquered beechwood.
Sights: Hooded front, open micro-adj. rear.
Features: Velocity of 600 fps. Blued metal finish. Introduced 1981. From Stoeger.
Price: $110.00

GAMO MODEL 300 AIR RIFLE
Caliber: 22 only, single shot.
Weight: 7 lbs. **Length:** 44" over-all.
Power: Barrel cocking spring type.
Stock: Lacquered beechwood.
Sights: Hooded front, micro-adj. rear.
Features: Velocity of 600 fps. Blued metal finish. Introduced 1981. From Stoeger Industries.
Price: $104.00

Marksman 1741

MARKSMAN 1741 AIR RIFLE
Caliber: 177, 100-shot.
Barrel: 15-½", smoothbore.
Length: 36½". **Weight:** 4 lbs., 2 oz.
Power: Spring, barrel cocking.
Stock: Moulded high-impact ABS plastic.
Sights: Ramp front, open rear adj. for e.
Features: Automatic safety; fixed front, adj. rear sights; shoots 177 cal. BB's pellets and darts. Velocity about 450 fps.
Price: $29.50

NORICA 80-G TARGET RIFLE
Caliber: 177, single shot.
Barrel: 18".
Weight: 6 lbs., 14 ozs. **Length:** 43" over-all.
Power: Barrel cocking, spring type.
Stock: Walnut stained beechwood
Sights: Globe front with interchangeable inserts; rear is adj. for w. and e. and has interchangeable inserts.
Features: Two-stage trigger with provision for adjustments. Stock has hefty pistol grip with black cap, buttplate and beavertail fore-end. Cocking effort is 20 lbs. Imported from Spain by Air Rifle Headquarters. Introduced 1980.
Price: $168.50

NORICA MODEL 73
Caliber: 177, single shot.
Barrel: 17¾".
Weight: 6½ lbs. **Length:** 41½" over-all.
Power: Barrel cocking, spring type.
Stock: Walnut-finished hardwood
Sights: Globe front with interchangeable inserts, open rear adj. for w. and e.
Features: Two-stage trigger with 3 lb. pull. Cocking effort of 18 lbs. Velocity of 637 fps. Rear cylinder is dovetailed for scope mounts. Introduced 1980. Imported from Spain by Air Rifle Headquarters.
Price: $118.50

PRECISE MINUTEMAN® MAGNUM
Caliber: 177, single shot.
Barrel: 19.4", rifle.
Weight: 7¼ lbs. **Length:** 44" over-all.
Power: Spring, under-lever cocking.
Stock: Stained hardwood, with cheek rest.
Sights: Hooded front, open rear adj. for w. and e.
Features: Velocity of 575 fps. Blued finish. Receiver grooved for scope mounting. Precise International, importer.
Price: $99.00

Precise Magnum

AIR GUNS—LONG GUNS

PRECISE MINUTEMAN® MARSHALL
Caliber: 177, single shot.
Barrel: 14" rifled.
Weight: 5½ lbs. **Length:** 37" over-all.
Stock: Stained hardwood.
Sights: Hooded front, open rear adj. for w. and e.
Features: Receiver grooved for scope mounting. Velocity 525 fps. Precise
   International, importer.
Price: $64.95

Precise Marshall

SIG 420

SIG-HAMMERLI MILITARY LOOK 420
Caliber: 177 or 22, single shot.
Barrel: 19" rifled.
Weight: About 7 lbs. **Length:** 44¼" over-all.
Stock: Synthetic stock and handguard.
Sights: Open, fully adj.
Features: Side lever cocking; adjustable trigger; rifled steel barrel. Introduced
   1977. Imported by Mandall Shooting Supplies.
Price: $295.00

SIG 401

SIG-HAMMERLI MODELS 401 & 403 AIR RIFLE
Caliber: 177, single shot.
Weight: 7.8 lbs. **Length:** 44" over-all.
Power: Spring air, sidelever cocking.
Stock: Beechwood.
Sights: Globe front accepts interchangeable inserts; fully adj. open rear (Model
   401) or match aperture rear (Model 403).
Features: Sidelever cocking effort of 20 lbs. Automatic safety. Model 403 has
   a 2-lb. barrel sleeve and adj. buttplate. Fully adj. trigger. Introduced 1980.
   Imported by Great Lakes Airguns, Mandall Shooting Supplies.
Price: Model 401 ....$136.04
Price: Model 403 ....$395.00

Sheridan CO^2

SHERIDAN CO^2 AIR RIFLES
Caliber: 5mm (20 cal.), single shot.
Barrel: 18½", rifled.
Weight: 6 lbs. **Length:** 37" over-all.
Stock: Walnut sporter.
Power: Standard 12.5 gram CO^2 cylinder.
Sights: Open, adj. for w. and e. Optional Sheridan Williams 5D-SH receiver
   sight or Weaver D4 scope.
Features: Bolt action single shot, CO^2 powered. Velocity approx. 514 fps.,
   manual thumb safety. Blue or Silver finish. Left-hand models avail. at same
   prices.
Price: CO^2 Blue Streak $94.05
Price: CO^2 Silver Streak $97.60
Price: CO^2 Blue Streak with receiver sight $109.40
Price: CO^2 Blue Streak with scope $140.00

Sheridan Silver Streak

SHERIDAN BLUE AND SILVER STREAK RIFLES
Caliber: 5mm (20 cal.), single shot.
Barrel: 18½", rifled.
Length: 37". **Weight:** 5 lbs.
Power: Hand pumped (swinging fore-end).
Features: Rustproof barrel and piston tube. Takedown. Thumb safety. Mann-
   licher type walnut stock. Left-hand models same price.
Price: Blue Streak ....$94.05 Silver Streak $97.60
   Sheridan accessories: Intermount, a base for ⅜" Tip-Off scope mounts,
   $11.70; Sheridan-Williams 5DSH receiver sight, **$11.50** Sheridan Pelletrap,
   $17.60; Sheridan 5mm pellets, **$5.35** for 500. Weaver 4 x scope and Intermount installed **$49.00 (extra).**

CAUTION: PRICES CHANGE. CHECK AT GUNSHOP.

Walther LGV

Walther LGR

WALTHER LGV SPECIAL
Caliber: 177, single shot.
Barrel: 16", rifled.
Length: 41⅜". **Weight:** 10¼ lbs.
Power: Spring air (barrel cocking).
Features: Micro. click adj. aperture receiver sight; Adj. trigger. Walnut match stock, adj. buttplate. Double piston provides vibration-free shooting. Easily operated bbl. latch. Removable heavy bbl. sleeve. 5-way adj. trigger. Imported by Interarms.
Price: **$600.00**

WALTHER LGR RIFLE
Caliber: 177, single-shot.
Barrel: 19½", rifled.
Length: 44¼" over-all. **Weight:** 10.2 lbs.
Power: Side lever cocking, compressed air.
Stock: French walnut.
Sights: Replaceable insert hooded front, Walther micro. adjustable rear.
Features: Recoilless operation. Trigger adj. for weight, pull and position. High comb stock with broad stippled fore-end and p.g. Imported by Interarms.
Price: **$750.00**

Walther LGR Match Air Rifle
Same basic specifications as standard LGR except has a high comb stock, sights are mounted on riser blocks. Introduced 1977.
Price: **$850.00**

Weihrauch 30

WEIHRAUCH 30 & 50 SERIES RIFLES

Model:	30S	30M-II	50S	50 M
Caliber:	177	177	177	177
Barrel:	17"	17"	18½"	18½"
Trigger:	adj.	adj.	adj.	adj.
Length:	40"	40"	43½"	43"
Wgt., lbs.:	5½	5½	7	7
Price:	$140.00	$128.50	$150.00	$210.00

Features: All are rifled and spring-operated by single stroke cocking. Post and ramp front sights (50M has globe front with 4 inserts). Open click rear sights, adj. for w. & e. Walnut finished stocks. 30M-II and 50 Deluxe have cheekpiece, wide fore-end, M.C. comb, ⅞" sling swivels. MV of all 660-705 fps. Available from Air Rifle Hdqtrs., Beeman's.

Weihrauch 35

WEIHRAUCH 35 SPORTER RIFLES

Model:	35/S	35L	35EB	35TH
Caliber:	177	177	177 or 22	177
Barrel:	19½"	19½"	19½"	19½"
Length:	45½"	43½"	45½"	44½"
Wgt. lbs.:	7.9	8	8	8.6
Rear sight:	open	open	Open	Open
Front sight:	All with globe and 5 interchangeable inserts.			
Power:	All spring (barrel cocking).			
Price: About	$234.50	$258.50	$284.50	$264.50

Features: Trigger fully adj. and removable. Manual safety. Open rear sight click adj. for w. and e. P.g. high comb stock with beavertail fore-end, walnut finish, except 35E has checkered walnut with standard cheekpiece. 35L has Bavarian cheekpiece stock. Model 35EB with American-styled stock with cheekpiece, white spacers and sling swivels. Model 35TH (Beeman's only) has thumbhole stock. Beeman's does not have Model 35/S. Available from Air Rifle Hdqtrs., Beeman's.

WEIHRAUCH 55 TARGET RIFLES

Model:	55SM	55MM	55T
Caliber:	177	177	177
Barrel:	18½"	18½"	18½"
Length:	43½"	43½"	43½"
Wgt. lbs.:	7.8	7.8	7.8
Rear sight:	All aperture		
Front sight:	All with globe and 4 interchangeable inserts.		
Power:	All springs (barrel cocking). 660-700 fps.		
Price: About	$300.00	$430.00	$400.00

Features: Trigger fully adj. and removable. Micrometer rear sight adj. for w. and e. on all. P.g. high comb stock with beavertail fore-end, walnut finish stock on 55SM. Walnut stock on 55MM, (illus.) Tyrolean stock on 55T. Available from Air Rifle Hdqtrs., Beeman's.

Chokes & Brakes

Choke-Matic
Cutts Compensator

The Cutts Compensator is one of the oldest variable choke devices available. Manufactured by Lyman Gunsight Corporation, it is available with either a steel or aluminum body. A series of vents allows gas to escape upward and downward. For the 12-ga. Comp body, six fixed-choke tubes are available: the Spreader—popular with Skeet shooters; Improved Cylinder; Modified; Full; Superfull, and Magnum Full. Full, Modified and Spreader tubes are available for 12, or 20, and an Adjustable Tube, giving Full through Improved Cylinder chokes, is offered in 12, or 20 gauges. Cutts Compensator, complete with wrench, adaptor and any single tube $54.95; with adjustable tube $69.95. All single choke tubes $14.95 each. No factory installation available.

Dahl Muzzle Blast Controller

Only 1⅞" long by ¾" in diameter, this device is claimed to reduce recoil up to 30%. An outer sleeve, threaded onto the gun muzzle, is threaded on the inside to accept a machined plug which is bored through for bullet passage. Gas behind the bullet is bled off through slots in the plug, swirled through a number of tiny passages while contained by the sleeve, and then vented upward, this final action offsetting muzzle jump without discomfort to the shooter or bystanders. Price is $50.00, installed.

Emsco Choke

E. M. Schacht of Waseca, Minn., offers the Emsco, a small diameter choke which features a precision curve rather than a taper behind the 1½" choking area. 9 settings are available in this 5 oz. attachment. Its removable recoil sleeve can be furnished in dural if desired. Choice of three sight heights. For 12, 16 or 20 gauge. Price installed, $24.95. Not installed, $17.50.

LymanCHOKE Adapter
Upland Tube
Recoil Chamber
Adjustable LymanCHOKE
All Purpose Tube
Long Range Tube

Jet-Away Choke

Arms Ingenuity Corp., makers of the Jet-Away, say that this device controls patterns through partial venting of the powder gases which normally enlarge patterns. The Jet-Away has a series of three slots in the top of the tube and a sliding control sleeve. When the sleeve is in its rearward position, all slots are uncovered, the maximum of gas is vented and patterns are densest. To obtain more open patterns, the sleeve is moved to cover one or more slots. Jet-Away is the only adjustable choke made in 10 gauge. In 10, 12, 16 or 20 gauge only, the Jet-Away is made of aluminum and weighs 3 ozs. Prices (installed), 10 and 12 gauge $80.00; 16 and 20 gauge $60.00.

Lyman CHOKE

The Lyman CHOKE is similar to the Cutts Comp in that it comes with fixed-choke tubes or an adjustable tube, with or without recoil chamber. The adjustable tube version sells for $39.95 with recoil chamber, $33.00 without, in 12 or 20 gauge. Lyman also offers Single-Choke tubes at $14.95. This device may be used with or without a recoil-reduction chamber; cost of the latter is $6.95 extra. Available in 12 or 20 gauge only, no factory installation offered.

Mag-Na-Port

Electrical Discharge Machining works on any firearm except those having shrouded barrels. EDM is a metal-erosion technique using carbon electrodes that control the area to be processed. The Mag-Na-Port venting process utilizes small trapezoidal openings to direct powder gases upward and outward to reduce recoil.

No effect is had on bluing or nickeling outside the Mag-Na-Port area so no refinishing is needed. Cost for the Mag-Na-Port treatment is $45.00 for handguns, $60.00 for rifles, plus transportation both ways, and $1.50 for handling.

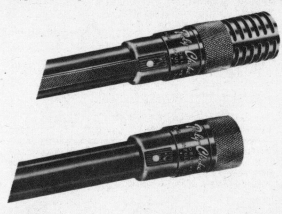

Poly-Choke

The Poly-Choke Co., manufacturers of the original adjustable shotgun choke, now offers two models in 12, 16, 20 and 28 gauge, the Deluxe Ventilated and the Deluxe Standard. Each provides 9 choke settings including Xtra-Full and Slug. The Ventilated model reduces 20% of a shotguns recoil, the company claims, and is priced at $39.95. The Standard model is $37.95.

Pro-Port

A compound ellipsoid muzzle venting process similar to Mag-na-porting, only exclusively applied to shotguns. Like Mag-na-porting, this system reduces felt recoil, muzzle jump, and shooter fatigue. Very helpful for Trap doubles shooters. Pro-Port is a patented process and installation is available in both the U.S. and Canada. Cost for the Pro-Port process is $110.00 for over-unders (both barrels); $80.00 for only the bottom barrel; $80.00 for side-by-sides; and $65.00 for single barrel shotguns. Prices do not include shipping and handling.

Micrometer Receiver Sights

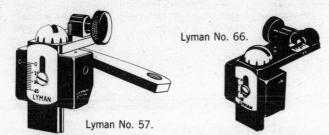

Lyman No. 66.

Lyman No. 57.

LYMAN No. 57
¼-min. clicks. Target or Stayset knobs. Quick release slide, adjustable zero scales. Made for almost all modern rifles. Price **$34.95**

LYMAN No. 66
Fits close to the rear of flat-sided receivers, furnished with target or Stayset knobs. Quick release slide, ¼-min. adj. For most lever or slide action or flat-sided automatic rifles. Price **$34.95**

REDFIELD "PALMA" TARGET SIGHT
Windage and elevation adjustments are ¼-MOA and can be adjusted for "hard" or "soft" feel. Repeatability error limited to .001" per click. Windage latitude 36 MOA, elevation 60 MOA. Mounting arm has three positions, providing ample positioning latitude for other sighting aids such as variable diopter correction, adjustable filters. An insert in the sighting disc block accepts either the standard American sighting disc thread or the European 9.5mm × 1 metric thread. Elevation staff and the sighting disc block have dovetail construction for precise travel. Price **$160.70**

WILLIAMS FP
Internal click adjustments. Positive locks. For virtually all rifles, T/C Contender, plus Win., Rem. and Ithaca shotguns. Price **$28.85**
With Twilight Aperture **$29.70**
With Target Knobs **$34.35**
With Target Knobs & Twilight Aperture **$35.20**
With Square Notched Blade **$30.35**
With Target Knobs & Square Notched Blade **$35.85**

B-SQUARE SMLE (LEE-ENFIELD)
For No. 4 and Jungle carbine. No drilling or tapping required. ³⁄₃₂" disc furnished. Price **$5.95**

BUEHLER
"Little Blue Peep" auxiliary rear sight used with Buehler scope mounts. Price **$3.35**

FREELAND TUBE SIGHT
Uses Unertl 1" micrometer mounts. For 22-cal. target rifles, inc. 52 Win., 37, 40X Rem. and BSA Martini. Price, less peep **$90.00**

WILLIAMS 5-D SIGHT
Low cost sight for shotguns, 22's and the more popular big game rifles. Adjustment for w. and e. Fits most guns without drilling or tapping. Also for Br. SMLE. Price **$16.40**
With Twilight Aperture **$17.25**
Extra Shotgun Aperture **$4.30**

Williams FP.

Williams 5 D.

Redfield "Palma."

WILLIAMS GUIDE
Receiver sight for .30 M1 Car., M1903A3 Springfield, Savage 24's, Savage-Anschutz rifles and Wby. XXII. Utilizes military dovetail; no drilling. Double-dovetail W. adj., sliding dovetail adj. for E. Price **$15.70**
With Twilight Aperture **$16.55**
With Open Sight Blade **$14.50**

Sporting Leaf and Tang Sights

BURRIS SPORTING REAR SIGHT
Made of spring steel, supplied with multi-step elevator for coarse adjustments and notch plate with lock screw for finer adjustments. Price ... **$9.95**

LYMAN No. 16
Middle sight for barrel dovetail slot mounting. Folds flat when scope or peep sight is used. Sight notch plate adjustable for e. White triangle for quick aiming. 3 heights; A—.400" to .500", B—.345" to .445", C—.500" to .600". Price **$7.50**

MARBLE FALSE BASE
New screw-on base for most rifles replaces factory base. ⅜" dovetail slot permits installation of any Marble rear sight. Can be had in sweat-on models also. Price **$3.60**

MARBLE CONTOUR RAMP
For late model Rem. 725, 740, 760, 742 rear sight mounting. ⁹⁄₁₆" between mounting screws. Price **$8.00**

MARBLE FOLDING LEAF
Flat-top or semi-buckhorn style. Folds down when scope or peep sights are used. Reversible plate gives choice of "U" or "V" notch. Adjustable for elevation. Price **$7.20**
Also available with both w. and e. adjustment **$8.40**

MARBLE SPORTING REAR
With white enamel diamond, gives choice of two "U" and two "V" notches of different sizes. Adjustment in height by means of double step elevator and sliding notch piece. For all rifles; screw or dovetail installation. Price**$7.40—$8.40**

Marble's Folding Leaf rear.

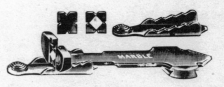

Williams Guide.

Marble's Sporting Rear.

MARBLE SPORTING REAR
Single step elevator. "U" notch with white triangle aiming aid. Lower priced version of double step model. Price **$5.00**

WILLIAMS DOVETAIL OPEN SIGHT
Open rear sight with w. and e. adjustment. Furnished with "U" notch or choice of blades. Slips into dovetail and locks with gib lock. Heights from .281" to .531". Price with blade **$9.00**
Less Blade **$5.90**
Extra Blades **$3.10**

WILLIAMS GUIDE OPEN SIGHT
Open rear sight with w. and e. adjustment. Bases to fit most military and commercial barrels. Choice of square "U" or "V" notch blade, ³⁄₁₆", ¼", ⁵⁄₁₆", or ⅜" high **$10.85**
Extra blades, each **$3.10**
Price, less blade **$7.75**

Front Sights

BURRIS FRONT SIGHTS
Two styles: Patridge, gold bead. Widths are .250", .340", .500" and Mauser .310". .... from **$4.50** to **$5.00**

LYMAN BLADE & DOVETAIL SIGHTS
Made with gold or ivory beads 1⁄16" to 3⁄32" wide and in varying heights for most military and commercial rifles. Price **$6.50**

MARBLE STANDARD
Ivory, red, or gold bead. For all American made rifles. 1⁄16" wide bead with semi-flat face which does not reflect light. Specify type of rifle when ordering. Price **$4.25**

Marble's Standard Blade, Sheard, Contour, Standard.

MARBLE-SHEARD "GOLD"
Shows up well even in darkest timber. Shows same color on different colored objects; sturdily built. Medium bead. Various models for different makes of rifles so specify type of rifle when ordering. Price **$5.25**

MARBLE CONTOURED
Same contour and shape as Marble-Sheard but uses standard 1⁄16" or 3⁄32" bead, ivory, red or gold. Specify rifle type **$4.80**

WILLIAMS GUIDE BEAD SIGHT
Fits all shotguns. 1⁄8" ivory, red or gold bead. Screws into existing sight hole. Various thread sizes and shank lengths **$3.05**

Globe Target Front Sights

Freeland Superior sight with inserts.

FREELAND SUPERIOR
Furnished with six 1" plastic apertures. Available in 4½"-6½" lengths. Made for any target rifle. Price with base **$31.00**
Price with 6 metal insert apertures **$33.00**
Price, front base **$7.40**

FREELAND TWIN SET
Two Freeland Superior or Junior Globe Front Sights, long or short, allow switching from 50 yd. to 100 yd. ranges and back again without changing rear sight adjustment. Sight adjustment compensation is built into the set; just interchange and you're "on" at either range. Set includes 6 plastic apertures. Twin set (long or short) **$45.00**
Price with 6 metal apertures **$49.00**

Freeland Military.

Lyman No. 17A.

FREELAND MILITARY
Short model for use with high-powered rifles where sight must not extend beyond muzzle. Screw-on base; six plastic apertures. Price **$29.00**
Price with 6 metal apertures **$31.00**
Price, front base **$6.40**

LYMAN No. 17A
7 interchangeable inserts which include 4 apertures, one transparent amber and two posts .50" and .100" in width. Price **$13.95**

REDFIELD Nos. 63 and 64
For rifles specially stocked for scopes where metallic sights must be same height as scopes. Instantly detachable to permit use of scope. Two styles and heights of bases. Interchangeable inserts. No. 64 is ¼" higher. With base, Price, ¾43 .... **$29.30 Price:** ¾44 .... **$34.50**

REDFIELD No. 65
1" long, 5⁄8" diameter. Standard dovetail base with 7 aperture or post inserts which are not reversible. For any rifle having standard barrel slot. 13⁄32" height from bottom of base to center of aperture. No. 65NB same as above with narrow base for Win. 64 N.R.A., 70, and Savage 40, 45, and 99 with ramp front sight base. Price **$23.90**

REDFIELD No. 66
Replaces entire removable front sight stud, locked in place by screw in front of barrel band. ¾" from bottom of base to center of aperture. For Spgfld. 1903. Price **$26.20**

REDFIELD No. 68
For Win. 52, heavy barrel, Sav. 19 and 33, and other rifles requiring high front sight. 17⁄32" from bottom of base to center of aperture. Standard dovetail size only. Price **$22.10**

REDFIELD OLYMPIC FRONT
Detachable. 10 inserts—5 steel, sizes .090", .110", .120", .140", .150"; one post insert, size .100"; four celluloid, sizes .090", .110", .120", .140". Celluloid inserts in clear, green, or amber, with or without cross hairs. For practically all rifles and with any type rear sight. Fits all standard Redfield, Lyman, or Fecker scope blocks. With base, Price **$43.60**

REDFIELD INTERNATIONAL SMALLBORE FRONT
Similar to Olympic. Drop-in insertion of eared inserts. Outer sleeve prevents light leakage. Comes complete with 6 clear inserts and 6 skeleton inserts **$46.60**

REDFIELD INTERNATIONAL MILITARY BIG BORE
Same as International Match except tube only 2¼" long. For 30 cal. use. Price **$46.60**

Ramp Sights

LYMAN SCREW-ON RAMP AND SIGHT
Used with 8-40 screws but may also be brazed on. Heights from .10" to .350". Price with sight ..... **$11.90 Price:** Ramp without sight **$8.95**

MARBLE FRONT RAMPS
Available in either screw-on or sweat-on style. 5 heights; 3⁄16", 5⁄16", 3⁄8", 7⁄16", 9⁄16". Standard 3⁄8" dovetail slot. Price **$7.50**
Hoods for above ramps **$1.65**

WILLIAMS SHORTY RAMP
Companion to "Streamlined" ramp, about ½" shorter. Screw-on or sweat-on. It is furnished in 1⁄8", 3⁄16", 9⁄32", and 3⁄8" heights without hood only. Price **$7.70**

Marble sight ramp base.

WILLIAMS STREAMLINED RAMP
Hooded style in screw-on or sweat-on models. Furnished in 9⁄16", 7⁄16", 3⁄8", 5⁄16", 3⁄16" heights. Price with hood **$12.20**
Price without hood **$10.10**

WILLIAMS SHOTGUN RAMP
Designed to elevate the front bead for slug shooting or for guns that shoot high. Diameters to fit most 12, 16, 20 ga. guns. Fastens by screw-clamp, no drilling required. Price, with Williams gold bead **$7.50**
Price, without bead **$5.50**
Price, with Guide Bead **$8.55**

Handgun Sights

BO-MAR DE LUXE
Gives 3⁄8" w. and e. adjustment at 50 yards on Colt Gov't 45, sight radius under 7". For GM and Commander models only. Uses existing dovetail slot. Has shield-type rear blade. Price **$38.00**

BO-MAR LOW PROFILE RIB
Streamlined rib with front and rear sights; 7⅛" sight radius. Brings sight line closer to the bore than standard or extended sight and ramp. Weighs 4 oz. Made for Ruger Mark I Bull Barrel, Colt Gov't 45, Super 38, and Gold Cup 45 and 38. Price **$50.00**
With extended sight and ramp, 8⅛" radius, 5¾ oz. Price **$57.00**
Rib & tuner—inserted in Low Profile Rib—accuracy tuner. Adjustable for barrel positioning. Price **$59.00**

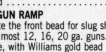

BO-MAR COMBAT RIB
For S&W Model 19 revolver with 4" barrel. Sight radius 5¾"; weight 5½ oz.
Price $50.00

BO-MAR FAST DRAW RIB
Streamlined full length rib with integral Bo-Mar micrometer sight and serrated fast draw sight. For Browning 9mm, S&W 39, Colt Commander 45, Super Auto and 9mm. Price $50.00

BO-MAR WINGED RIB
For S&W 4" and 6" length barrels—K-38 M10, HB 14 and 19. Weight for the 6" model is about 7¼ ozs. Price $58.00

BO-MAR COVER-UP RIB
Adj. rear sight, winged front guards. Fits right over revolver's original front sight. For S&W 4" M-10HB, M-13, M-58, M-64 & 65. Ruger 4" models SDA-34, SDA-84, SS-34, SS-84, GF-34, GF-84. Price $56.00

MICRO
Click adjustable w. and e. rear with plain or undercut front sight in ⅛" widths. Standard model available for 45, Super 38 or Commander autos. Low model for above pistols plus Colt Service Ace. Also for Ruger with 4¾" or 6" barrel. Price for sets.
Price with ramp front sight $35.00
Adjustable rear sight only $24.00
Front ramp only, with blade $14.00

MICRO
All-steel replacement for Ruger single-action and double-action revolvers.
Two styles: MR-44 for square front end of sight leaf $18.00

Omega Maverick Range Finder sight blades.

MMC "BAR CROSS" SIGHT SYSTEM
Provides a quick, clear sight picture in a variety of lighting conditions. Black oxide finish is non-reflective. Front sight has a horizontal white bar with vertical white bar, gives illusion of cross hair in poor light. Fixed rear comes with or without white outline. Various front blades available.
White outline rear sight $14.55
Plain rear $11.40
Ramp Bar Cross front $10.45

MMC COMBAT DESIGN
Available specifically for Colt M1911 and descendants, High Standard autos, Ruger standard autos. Adaptable to other pistols. Some gunsmithing required. Not necessary to replace front sight.
Price, less leaf $22.00
Plain leaf $6.55
White outline leaf $9.60
Extra for satin nickel finish (base only) $7.60

MMC NO. 5
Fully adjustable and replaces the factory sight for S&W M39 and M59. Supplied assembled. ⅛" wide notch, white outline or plain. Not necessary to replace front sight.
Complete, plain $51.75
White outline $54.65
Extra for satin nickel finish (base only) $7.60

Millett Series 100
Replacement front and rear sights, both fixed and adjustable, for Colt, S&W, Ruger, Dan Wesson and Browning handguns. Two interchangeable rear sight leaves, "positive light deflection system," windage and elevation screws have a spring and plunger detent for repeated adjustments. For both revolvers and autos. Prices are for both front and rear sights.
Price: from ....$39.95 to $56.95

OMEGA OUTLINE SIGHT BLADES
Replacement rear sight blades for Colt and Ruger single action guns and the Interarms Virginian Dragoon. Standard Outline available in gold or white notch outline on blue metal.
Price $5.95

OMEGA MAVERICK SIGHT BLADES
Replacement "peep-sight" blades for Colt, Ruger SAs, Virginian Dragoon. Three models available—No. 1, Plain, No. 2, Single Bar, No. 3 Double Bar Rangefinder.
Price, each $6.95

Sight Attachments

FREELAND LENS ADAPTER
Fits 1⅛" O.D. prescription ground lens to all standard tube and receiver sights for shooting without glasses. Price without lens $40.50
Price: Clear lens ground to prescription $20.00
Price: Yellow or green prescription lens $20.00

MERIT ADAPTER FOR GLOBE FRONT SIGHTS
An Iris Shutter Disc with a special adapter for mounting in Lyman or Redfield globe front sights. Price $38.00

MERIT IRIS SHUTTER DISC
Eleven clicks gives 12 different apertures. No. 3 and Master, primarily target types, .022" to .125"; No. 4, ½" dia. hunting type, .025" to .155". Available for all popular sights. The Master Disc, with flexible rubber light shield, is particularly adapted to extension, scope height, and tang sights. All Merit Deluxe models have internal click springs; are hand fitted to minimum tolerance.
Std. Master ....$41.25   Master Deluxe $51.25

MERIT LENS DISC
Similar to Merit Iris Shutter (Model 3 or Master) but incorporates provision for mounting prescription lens integrally. Lens may be obtained locally, or prescription sent to Merit. Sight disc is ⁷⁄₁₆" wide (Mod. 3), or ¾" wide (Master). Lens, ground to prescription, **$19.00** Standard tints, **$23.50.** Model 3 Deluxe. Price $52.50
Master Deluxe $61.25

MERIT OPTICAL ATTACHMENT
For revolver and pistol shooters. Instantly attached by rubber suction cup to regular or shooting glasses. Any aperture .020" to .156". Price, Deluxe (swings aside) $49.50

REDFIELD SURE-X SIGHTING DISC
Eight hole selective aperture. Fits any Redfield target sight. Each click changes aperture .004". Price $18.30

REDFIELD SIGHTING DISCS
Fit all Redfield receiver sights. .046" to .093" aperture. ⅜", ½" and ⅞" O.D. Price, each $4.10

WILLIAMS APERTURES
Standard thread, fits most sights. Regular series ⅜" to ½" O.D., .050" to .125" hole. "Twilight" series has white reflector ring. .093" to .125" inner hole. Price, regular series . **$3.00.** Twilight series $3.15
New wide open ⁵⁄₁₆" aperture for shotguns fits 5-D and Foolproof sights. Price $4.30

Shotgun Sights

ACCURA-SITE
For shooting shotgun slugs. Three models to fit most shotguns—"A" for vent. rib barrels, "B" for solid ribs, "C" for plain barrels. Rear sight has windage and elevation provisions. Easily removed and replaced. Includes front and rear sights.
Price: ....$14.95 to $18.95

FOR DOUBLE BARREL SHOTGUNS (PRESS FIT)
Marble 214—Ivory front bead, ¹¹⁄₆₄" . . . $2.40; 215—same with .080" rear bead and reamers . . . $8.15. Marble 220—Bi-color (gold and ivory) front bead, ¹¹⁄₆₄" and .080 rear bead, with reamers . . $9.25; Marble 221—front bead only . . . $3.50. Marble 223—Ivory rear .080 . . . $2.20. Marble 224—Front sight reamer for 214-221 beads . . . $2.25; Marble 226—Rear sight reamer for 223 ....$1.75

FOR SINGLE OR DB SHOTGUNS (SCREW-ON FIT)
Marble 217—Ivory front bead ¹¹⁄₆₄" . . . $2.65; Marble 216 $5.50 Marble 218—Bi-color front, ¹¹⁄₆₄" . . . $3.85; Marble 219 . . . $6.70 Marble 223T— Ivory rear .080 ....$3.65
Marble Bradley type sights 223BT—⅛", ⁵⁄₆₄" and ¹¹⁄₆₄" long. Gold, Ivory or Red bead $2.50

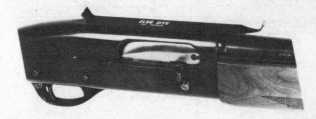

SLUG SITE
A combination V-notch rear and bead front sight made of adhesive-backed formed metal approx. 7" over-all. May be mounted, removed and re-mounted as necessary, using new adhesive from the pack supplied $10.00

SCOPES & MOUNTS
HUNTING, TARGET ■ & VARMINT ■ SCOPES

Maker and Model	Magn.	Field at 100 Yds (feet)	Relative Brightness	Eye Relief (in.)	Length (in.)	Tube Diam. (in.)	W&E Adjustments	Weight (ozs.)	Price	Other Data
American Import Co.										
Dickson 200[1]	4	19	13.7	3.5	11.5	¾	Int.	6	**$ 9.95**	[1]Complete with mount for 22-cal. RF rifles. [2]Standard crosshair reticle, coated lenses. [3]Anodized finish. [4]Wide angle. [5]Wide angle. [6]Post and crosshair, 2 post, tapered post, crosshair and 4-post crosshair all available as options.
Dickson 218 32mm	2½	32	164	3.7	12	1	Int.	9.3	**36.95**	
Dickson 220 32mm[2]	4	29	64	3.6	12	1	Int.	9.1	**34.95**	
Dickson 226 40mm[3]	6	20	44.7	3.7	13	1	Int.	10	**41.50**	
Dickson 228 32mm[4]	4	37	64	3.3	12	1	Int.	10.5	**44.95**	
Dickson 230 40mm[5]	4	37	100	3.8	12.4	1	Int.	12	**52.95**	
Dickson 233 20mm[6]	4	42	25	3	9.8	1	Int.	10.2	**66.95**	
Dickson 240 32mm	3-9	37-12.3	112-13	3	12.8	1	Int.	13.8	**52.95**	
Dickson 242 40mm	3-9	37-12.3	177-19.4	3	12.8	1	Int.	15.2	**55.95**	
Burris										
4x Fullfield[1]	3.8	37	49	3¼	11¼	1	Int.	11	**129.95**	Dot reticle $10 extra. Target knobs $15 extra. ½-minute dot $10 extra. LER=Long Eye Relief—ideal for forward mounting on handguns. Plex or crosshair only. Matte "Safari" finish avail. on 4x, 6x, 2-7x, 3-9x with Plex reticle, $10 extra, [1]3" dot $10 extra. [2]1"-3" dot $10 extra. [3]1"-3" dot $10 extra.
2x-7x Fullfield[2] HiLume	2.5-6.8	50-19	81-22	3¼	11⅞	1	Int.	14	**175.95**	
3x-9x Fullfield[3] HiLume	3.3-8.6	40-15	72-17.6	3¼	12¾	1	Int.	15	**189.95**	
2¾ Fullfield	2.7	53	49	3¼	10½	1	Int.	9	**116.95**	
6x Fullfield	5.8	24	36	3¼	13	1	Int.	12	**139.95**	
1¾-5x Fullfield HiLume	2.5-6.8	70-27	121-25	3¼	10¾	1	Int.	13	**159.95**	
4x-12x Fullfield	4.4-11.8	28-10½	—	3-3¼	15	1	Int.	18	**231.95**	
6x-18x Fullfield	6.5-17.6	17-7.5	—	3-3¾	15.8	1	Int.	18.5	**235.95**	
10x Fullfield	9.8	12½	—	3¼	15	1	Int.	15	**183.95**	
12x Fullfield	11.8	11	—	3¼	15	1	Int.	15	**190.95**	
2x LER	1.7	21	—	10-24	8¾	1	Int.	6.8	**95.85**	
3x LER	2.7	17	—	10-20	8⅞	1	Int.	6.8	**102.95**	
2x-7x Mini	2.5-6.9	32-14	—	3¾	9⅜	1	Int.	10.5	**141.95**	
4x Mini	3.6	24	—	3¾	8¼	1	Int.	7.8	**98.95**	
6x Mini	5.5	17	—	3¾	9	1	Int.	7.8	**106.95**	
8x Mini	7.6	13	—	3¾	9⅞	1	Int.	8.9	**111.95**	
3x-9x Mini	3.6-8.8	25-11	—	3¾	9⅞	1	Int.	11.5	**147.95**	
Bushnell										
Scope Chief VI	4	29	96	3½	12	1	Int.	9.3	**104.95**	All ScopeChief, Banner and Custom models come with Multi-X reticle, with or without BDC (bullet drop compensator) that eliminates hold-over. Prismatic Rangefinger (PRF) on some models. Contact Bushnell for data on full line. Prices include BDC—deduct $5 if not wanted. Add $30 for PRF. BDC feature available in all Banner models, except 2.5x. [1]Wide angle. [2]Complete with mount rings. [3]Equipped with Wind Drift Compensator and Parallax-free adjustment. [4]Parallax focus adjustment. [5]Wide angle. [6]Wide angle. [7]Parallax focus adjustment. [8]Phantoms intended for handgun use. [9]Mount separate.
Scope Chief VI	3-9	35-12.6	267-30	3½-3⅓	12.6	1	Int.	14.3	**169.95**	
Scope Chief VI	2½-8	45-14	247-96	3.7-3.3	11.2	1	Int.	12.1	**144.95**	
Scope Chief VI	1½-4½	73.7-24.5	267-30	3.5-3.5	9.6	1	Int.	9.5	**139.95**	
Custom 22	4	28.4	—	2½	10 5/16	⅞	Int.	5¼	**31.95**	
Custom 22	3-7	29-13.6	28-5	2¼-2½	10	⅞	Int.	6½	**37.95**	
Banner	2½	45	96	3½	10.9	1	Int.	8	**74.95**	
Banner 32mm	4	29	96	3½	12	1	Int.	10	**89.95**	
Banner 40mm	4	37⅓	150	3	12⅓	1	Int.	12	**119.95**	
Banner[1]	6	19½	42	3	13½	1	Int.	10½	**99.95**	
Banner 22[2]	4	27.5	37.5	3	11⅝	1	Int.	8	**42.95**	
Banner Silhouette[3]	10	12	24	3	14½	1	Int.	14.6	**159.95**	
Banner	10	12	24	3	14½	1	Int.	14.6	**129.95**	
Banner[4]	1½-4	63-28	294-41	3½	10½	1	Int.	10.3	**117.95**	
Banner[5]	1¾-4½	71-27	216-33	3	10.2	1	Int.	11½	**132.95**	
Banner 32mm	3-9	39-13	171-19	3½	11.5	1	Int.	11	**127.95**	
Banner 38mm[6]	3-9	43-14.6	241-26½	3	12	1	Int.	14	**154.95**	
Banner 40mm	3-9	35-12.6	267-30	3½	13	1	Int.	13	**169.95**	
Banner[7]	4-12	29-10	150-17	3.2	13½	1	Int.	15½	**149.95**	
Magnum Phantom[8]	1.3	17	441	7-21	7.8	15/16	Int.	5½	**59.95**	
Magnum Phantom[9]	2½	9	100	8-21	9.7	15/16	Int.	6½	**62.95**	
Davis Optical										
Spot Shot 1½"	10.12 15.20 25.30	10-4	—	2	25	.75	Ext.	—	**116.00**	Focus by moving non-rotating obj. lens unit. Ext. mounts included. Recoil spring $3.50 extra.
Spot Shot 1¼"	10,12, 15.20	10-6	—	2	25	.75	Ext.	—	**90.00**	
Fontaine										
4x32 Wide Angle	4	38	64	3.0	11.8	1	Int.	10.0	**104.45**	Non-waterproof also available. Scopes listed have Jennison TCS with Optima system. Extra TCS drums $5.50 ea. Scopes with TCS also avail.
4 x 40 Wide Angle	4	38	100	3.0	12.0	1	Int.	11.6	**115.45**	
3-9 x 32 Wide Angle	3-9	43.5-15	114-12.8	3.3-3.0	12.2	1	Int.	12.0	**156.20**	
3-9 x 40 Wide Angle	3-9	43.5-15	177.3-19.6	3.3-3.0	12.2	1	Int.	12.5	**159.45**	
4 x 32 Standard	4	29	64	3.3	11.7	1	Int.	10.2	**87.95**	
4 x 40 Standard	4	29	100	3.3	13.0	1	Int.	23.0	**93.45**	
3-9 x 32 Standard	3-9	35.3-13.2	114-12.8	3.3-3.0	12.0	1	Int.	11.3	**126.45**	
3-9 x 40 Standard	3-9	35.3-13.2	177.3-19.6	3.3-3.0	12.0	1	Int.	12.7	**134.15**	
Hertel & Reuss										
3-10 x 46 Exclusiv[1]	3-10	32-14	160-21.2	2-3	12.7	26	Int.	18.7	**519.00**	Other models available. Imported by Friedr. Wilh. Heym. [1]Aluminum tube with mounting rail(s). [2]Aluminum tube with mounting rails on middle and objective tubes. [3]Highest luminosity of the H&R scopes. [4]With mounts. [5]Very high luminosity. [6]Focus with right turret. [7]Focus with right turret.
6 x 46 Exclusiv[2]	6	22	59	3-3¼	12.7	26	Int.	14.8	**379.00**	
Macro-Variables[3] 2¾-10 x 46	2¾	35-14	150-21.2	3-4	12.7	26	Int.	14.1	**509.00**	
2-7 x 36	2-7	53-18	150-27	3-4	11.3	26	Int.	12.3	**439.00**	
Fixed Power[4] 4 x KK 22	4	29	23	2½-3½	11.2	22	Int.	7.4	**129.00**	
4 x 36[5]	4	36	81	3¼-4½	11.3	26	Int.	10.2	**319.00**	
6 x 46[6]	6	24	60	3¼-4½	12.7	26	Int.	12.3	**359.00**	
8 x 46[7]	8	20	34	3¼-4½	12.7	26	Int.	12.3		
Jason										
860	4	29	64	3	11.8	1	Int.	9.2	**39.00**	Constantly centered reticles, ballbearing click stops, nitrogen filled tubes, coated lenses. 4-Post crosshair about $3.50 extra on models 860, 861, 864, 865. (continued)
861	3-9	35-13	112-12	3	12.7	1	Int.	10.9	**57.00**	
862	4	19	14	2	11	¾	Int.	5.5	**12.50**	
864	6	19	28	3	11.8	1	Int.	12.2	**41.00**	

CAUTION: PRICES CHANGE. CHECK AT GUNSHOP.

HUNTING, TARGET ■ & VARMINT ■ SCOPES

Maker and Model	Magn.	Field at 100 Yds (feet)	Relative Bright- ness	Eye Relief (in.)	Length (in.)	Tube Diam. (in.)	W&E Adjust- ments	Weight (ozs.)	Price	Other Data
Jason (cont'd.)										
865	3-9	35-13	177-19	3	13	1	Int.	12.2	**60.00**	
869	4	19	25	2	11.4	¾	Int.	6	**16.00**	
873	4	29	100	3	12.7	1	Int.	11.1	**46.00**	
875	3-9	35-13	177-19	3	13	1	Int.	12.2	**61.00**	
877	4	37	100	3	11.6	1	Int.	11.6	**56.00**	
878	3-9	42.5-13.6	112-12	2.7	12.7	1	Int.	12.7	**66.00**	
Kahles										
Helia Super 2/S[1]	2.5	57.2	64	3.15	9.6	1″ or 26mm	Int.	11.3	**252.00**	[1]L Model (Alloy) weighs 10.5 oz. [2]L Model—11 oz. [3]L Model—12.9 oz. [4]L Model—17.8 oz. [5]L Model—10 oz. [6]L Model—10 oz. [7]L Model—12.25 oz. Alloy only. All models except ZF69 avail. in alloy or steel tube. Imported by Del-Sports, Inc.
Helia Super 4/S[2]	4	32.9	60	3.15	11	1″ or 26mm	Int.	12.9	**289.00**	
Helia Super 6/S[3]	6	22.5	49	3.15	12.2	1″ or 26mm	Int.	15.7	**314.00**	
Helia Super 8/S[4]	8	17.4	49	3.15	14	1″ or 26mm	Int.	20.6	**349.00**	
Helia Super 15/S[5]	1.5-4.5	89.6-30	176-19.6	3.15	10	1″ or 26mm	Int.	12.2	**336.00**	
Helia Super 27/S[6]	2.3-7	45.7-21	182-19.5	3.15	11.4	1″ or 26mm	Int.	13.3	**460.00**	
Helia Super 39/S[7]	3-9	36.5-16.4	196-22	3.15	12.6	1″ or 26mm	Int.	16.2	**489.00**	
ZF 69	6	22.5	49	3.15	12.2	26mm	Int.	16.8	**524.00**	
Kassnar										
2x-7x Wide Angle	2-7	49-19	258-21	3-2.7	11	1	Int.	12.8	**94.95**	Other models avail., including ¾″ and ⅞″ tubes for 22-cal. rifles. Contact Kassnar for details. [1]Also in 3x-9x40—$109.95. [2]Also in 4x40—$79.95. [3]Also in 3x-9x40—$89.95.
3x-9x Wide Angle[1]	3-9	42-15	112-13	3-2.7	12.2	1	Int.	13	**99.95**	
4x32 Wide Angle[2]	4	36	64	3.5	12	1	Int.	9.2	**69.95**	
6x40 Wide Angle	6	24	44	3	12.8	1	Int.	12	**84.95**	
1.5x-4x Std.	1.5-4	52-27	177-25	4.4-3	10	1	Int.	9.5	**79.95**	
2x-7x Std.	2-7	42-16	256-21	3.1-3	11	1	Int.	12.5	**84.95**	
3x-9x Std.[3]	3-9	36-13	112-13	3.1-3	12.2	1	Int.	13.5	**87.95**	
4x-12x40 Std.	4-12	27-9.6	100-11	3-2.7	13.5	1	Int.	16	**159.95**	
2.5x32 Std.	2.5	36	164	3.6	12	1	Int.	9.3	**64.95**	
Leupold										
M8-2xEER[1]	1.8	22	—	10-24	8.1	1	Int.	6.8	**134.15**	Constantly centered reticles; in addition to the crosshair, the post, tapered (CPC), post and duplex, and duplex reticles are optional at no extra cost. Dot reticle $14 extra. 2x suitable for handgun and Win. 94. [1]Extended Eye Relief of from 10″ to 24″ for top ejecting arms, muzzleloaders. 50-ft. Focus Adapter for indoor target ranges, $29.50. [2]Also in 10x Silhouette—$236.15. [3]Mounts solidly on action; ¼ MOA clicks; crosshair or dot. [4]With adj. obj.—$264.70. [5]With adj. obj.—$308.55. [6]¼-minute clicks. Comes with sunshade. Crosshair or Dot ($347.95). [7]Duplex, CPC or Dot reticle ($351.75).
M8-4x EER	3.5	7.7	—	10-24	8.4	1	Int.	7.6	**163.70**	
2.5 Compact	2.3	42	—	4.3	8.5	1	Int.	7.4	**143.30**	
4x Compact	3.6	26.5	—	4.1	10.3	1	Int.	8.5	**163.70**	
M8	3	43	45	3.85	10.13	1	Int.	8.25	**152.50**	
M8	4	30	50	3.85	11.50	1	Int.	9.00	**163.70**	
M8	6	18	—	3.85	11.7	1	Int.	10.3	**173.90**	
M8 Adj. Obj.	8	14	32	3.60	12.60	1	Int.	12.75	**233.05**	
M8 Adj. Obj.[2]	10	10	16	3½	13	1	Int.	13¾	**233.05**	
M8 Adj. Obj.	12	9	11	3½	14½	1	Int.	14	**236.15**	
M8 Adj. Obj.[3]	24	4½	—	3½	15¼	1	Int.	15½	**328.95**	
M8 Adj. Obj.[6]	36	3.2	—	3.4	13.9	1	Int.	15.5	**328.95**	
Vari-X II	1-4	70-28	—	4¼-3½	9½	1	Int.	9½	**200.45**	
Vari-X II	2-7	42-18	144-17	3.7-4.12	11.00	1	Int.	10.75	**218.80**	
Vari-X II[4]	3-9	30.5-13	208-23	3.5-4.12	12.60	1	Int.	13.75	**235.10**	
Vari-X III	1½-5	64-23	—	4½-3½	9¾	1	Int.	9¾	**238.15**	
Vari-X III	2½-8	36-12½	—	4¼-3½	11¾	1	Int.	11½	**268.75**	
Vari-X III[5]	3½-10	29½-10½	—	4-3½	12¾	1	Int.	12¾	**281.00**	
Vari-X III[7]	6.5-19.2	5.7	—	3.5	14.2	1	Int.	16	**332.75**	
Lyman										
Lyman 4x	4	30	—	3¼	12	1	Int.	10	**139.95**	Choice of standard CH, tapered post, or tapered post and CH reticles. All-weather reticle caps. All Lyman scopes have Perma-Center reticle which remains in optical center regardless of changes in w&e. Adj. for parallax. [1]⅛ or ¼ MOA clicks. [2]Non-rotating objective lens focusing. ¼ MOA click adjustments. Sunshade, $4.95 extra. Wood cases, $29.95 extra. 5 different dot reticles, $12.50 extra. [3]Standard crosswire, 4 Center-Range reticles. [4]Std. Fine, Extra Fine, 1 Min. Dot, ½-Min. Dot reticles. External adjustment knobs; hand lapped zero repeat w. and e. systems. Choice of 9 reticles.
Variable	1¾-5	47-18	—	3	12¼	1	Int.	12¼	**149.95**	
■ 20x LWBR[1]	20	5.5	—	2¼	17⅛	1	Int.	15¼	**309.95**	
■ All-American[2]	3-9	39-13	—	3¾-3¼	10½	1	Int.	14	**189.95**	
2x-7x Var.	1.9-6.8	49-19	—	3¼	11⅝	1	Int.	10½	**159.95**	
■ 25x LWBR	25	4.8	—	3	17	1	Int.	19	**339.95**	
Metalic Silhouette[3] 6x-SL	6.2	20	—	3¼	13⅞	1	Int.	14¼	**209.95**	
Metallic Silhouette[4] 8x-SL	8.1	14	—	3¼	14⅝	1	Int.	15¼	**219.95**	
Metallic Silhouette 10x-SL	10	12	—	3¼	15⅜	1	Int.	15¼	**229.95**	
Nickel-Fixed										
1 x 12 Supralyt[1]	1	118	144	4	10.6	26mm	Int.	11.3	**269.00**	[1]Steel or aluminum tube, with or without rail mount. [2]Aluminum tube with rail mount. [3]Steel tube, w/o rail. [4]Aluminum tube with rail. Other models available. Imported by Friedr. Wilh. Heym.
2.5 x 20 Supralyt	2.5	49	64	4	10.6	26mm	Int.	11.3	**269.00**	
4 x 20 Supralyt	4	36	25	4	10.6	26mm	Int.	11.3	**269.00**	
4 x 36 Supra	4	23	36	4	11.4	26mm	Int.	13.4	**309.00**	
6 x 36 Supra	6	23	36	4	11.4	26mm	Int.	13.4	**309.00**	
Variables 1.5-6 x 36 Supra[2]	1.5-6	66-25	176-36	4	12.2	30mm	Int.	15.5	**489.00**	
3-10 x 42 Supra[3]	3-10	35-14	81-16	4	12.6	26mm	Int.	18.3	**479.00**	
3-12 x 50 Supra[4]	3-12	31-11	276-17.6	4	14.9	30mm	Int.	21.5	**589.00**	
Redfield										
Traditional 4x¾″	4	24½	27	3½	9⅜	.75	Int.	—	**89.20**	*Accutrac feature avail. on these scopes. Traditionals have round lenses. 4-Plex reticle is standard. [1]"Magnum Proof." Specially designed for magnum and auto pistols. Uses "Double Dovetail" mounts. [2]Mounts solidly. 20x—$341.75; 24x—$353.55. [3]Mounts on receiver. CH or dot. 20x—$308.20, 24x—$317.65.
Traditional 2½x	2½	43	64	3½	10¼	1	Int.	8½	**123.15**	
Traditional 4x	4	28½	56	3½	11⅜	1	Int.	9¾	**139.20**	
Traditional 6x	6	19	—	3½	12½	1	Int.	11½	**160.65**	
Traditional 3x-9x* Royal	3-9	34-11	—	3½-4¼	12½	1	Int.	13	**244.25**	
Traditional 2x-7x*	2-7	42-14	207-23	3½	11¼	1	Int.	12	**191.00**	
Traditional 3x-9x*	3-9	34-11	163-18	3½	12½	1	Int.	13	**210.65**	

(continued)

HUNTING, TARGET ■ & VARMINT ■ SCOPES

Maker and Model	Magn.	Field at 100 Yds (feet)	Relative Bright-ness	Eye Relief (in.)	Length (in.)	Tube Diam. (in.)	W&E Adjust-ments	Weight (ozs.)	Price	Other Data
Redfield (Cont'd.)										
Traditional 8xMS	8	16.6	—	3-3¾	14⅛	1	Int.	17¹/₅	244.60	
Traditional 10xMS	10	12.6	—	3-3¾	14⅛	1	Int.,	17½	255.30	
Traditional 12xMS	12.4	8.1	—	3-3¾	14⅛	1	Int.	17.5	267.80	
Pistol Scopes										
1½xMP[1]	1.5	14	—	19-32	9¹³/₁₆	1	Int.	10.5	128.50	
2½xMP	2.5	9	—	14-24	9¹³/₁₆	1	Int.	10.5	135.65	
4xMP	3.6	9	—	12-22	9¹¹/₁₆	1	Int.	11.1	149.95	
Traditional 4x-12x*	4-12	26-9	112-14	3½	13⅞	1	Int.	14	287.45	
Traditional 6x-18x*	6-18	18-6	50-6	3½	13¹⁵/₁₆	1	Int.	18	317.85	
Low Profile Scopes										
Widefield 2¾xLP	2¾	55½	69	3½	10½	1	Int.	8	166.00	
Widefield 4xLP	3.6	37½	84	3½	11½	1	Int.	10	180.30	
Widefield 6x	6	24	—	3½	12¾	1	Int.	11	196.40	
Widefield 1¾x5xLP	1¾-5	70-27	136-21	3½	10¾	1	Int.	11½	219.60	
Widefield 2x7xLP*	2-7	49-19	144-21	3½	11¾	1	Int.	13	237.45	
Widefield 3x-9xLP*	3-9	39-15	112-18	3½	12½	1	Int.	14	264.25	
3200 Target[2]	16, 20, 24	6½, 4, 3¾	9, 3¼, 2¼	2½	23¼	1	Int.	21	332.80	
6400 Target[3]	16, 20, 24	6½, 5, 4½	5¾, 3½, 2½	3	17	1	Int.	18	298.70	
Sanders										
Bisley 2½x20	2½	42	64	3	10¾	1	Int.	8¼	48.50	Alum. alloy tubes, ¼" adj. coated lenses. Five other scopes are offered; 6x45 at $68.50, 8x45 at $70.50, 2½x7x at $69.50, 3-9x33 at $72.50 and 3-9x40 at $78.50. Rubber lens covers (clear plastic) are $3.50. Write to Sanders for details. Choice of reticles in CH, PCH, 3-post.
Bisley 4x33	4	28	64	3	12	1	Int.	9	52.50	
Bisley 6x40	6	19	45	3	12½	1	Int.	9½	56.50	
Bisley 8x40	8	18	25	3¼	12½	1	Int.	9½	62.50	
Bisley 10x40	10	12½	16	2½	12½	1	Int.	10¼	64.50	
Bisley 5-13x40	5-13	29-10	64-9	3	14	1	Int.	14	86.50	
Southern Precision										
556	3-7	24.5-11.5	43.5-8.1	2.4	12	⅞	Int.	10.3	24.95	
558	4	15.7	13.7	3.7	10.7	¾	Int.	6.1	8.95	
564CW	4	30	64	3.7	12	1	Int.	9.1	29.95	
567DW	6	23.5	44.7	3.1	12.5	1	Int.	10	37.95	
576CW	3-9	35.8-12.7	112.4-13	3.1-2.9	12.8	1	Int.	13.8	45.00	
579DWE	4-12	43-16	100-11.1	3.1-2.5	14.3	1	Int.	16	69.50	
Swarovski										
Habicht 1.5x20 DV SD 1A	1.5	69	—	3⅛	10	26mm	Int.	11.9	435.00	All models steel except LD model light alloy. All-weather scopes. 4x & 6x scopes fitted with centered reticles—7 different designs. NOVA has eyepiece recoil shield to protect face. 5 Year warranty. Spirit Level, add $66. IMPORTER: Strieter Corp.
Habicht 4x32 DV SD 1A	4	30	—	3⅛	11	26mm	Int.	13.3	455.00	
Habicht 4x32 DV LD 1A	4	30	—	3⅛	11	26mm	Int.	11.9	455.00	
NOVA 4x32 DV SD 1A	4	30	—	3⅛	11	26mm	Int.	13.3	570.00	
Habicht 6x42 DV SD 1A	6	20	—	3¼	11	26mm	Int.	15.4	475.00	
NOVA 6x42 DV SD 1A	6	20	—	3¼	12	26mm	Int.	15.4	590.00	
Swift										
Mark I 4x15	4	16.2	—	2.4	11	.75	Int.	4.7	22.00	All Swift Mark I scopes, with the exception of the 4x15, have Quadraplex reticles and are fog-proof and waterproof. The 4x15 has cross-hair reticle and is non-waterproof.
Mark I 4x32	4	29	—	3½	12	1	Int.	9	68.00	
Mark I 4x32 WA	4	37	—	3½	11¾	1	Int.	10½	74.00	
Mark I 4x40 WA	4	35½	—	3¾	12¼	1	Int.	12	86.00	
Mark I 3-9x32	3-9	35¾-12¾	—	3	12¾	1	Int.	13¾	89.50	
Mark I 3-9x40 WA	3-9	42½-13½	—	2¾	12¾	1	Int.	14	99.50	
Mark I 6x40	6	18	—	3¾	13	1	Int.	10	76.00	
Mark I 1½-4½x32	1½-4½	55-22	—	3½	12	1	Int.	13	94.50	
Tasco										
611V Wide Angle	2-6	66-25	100-16	2¾	10	1	Int.	9.5	114.95	Lens covers furnished. Constantly centered reticles. Write the importer, Tasco, for data on complete line. [1]Brass tube for Hawkins, Plaines, Pa. ½-stock, FIE Zouave and Ky. [2]For Savage #72 and Gallagher.
627W	3-9	35-14	177-19	3½	12⅛	1	Int.	13	99.95	
628V Wide Angle	3-9	43.5-15	177-19	3½	12	1	Int.	12¼	149.95	
1860 Tube Sight[1]	4	12½	14	3	32½	¾	Ext.	25	124.95	
1903 Tube Sight[2]	4	14	14	3¾	18½	¾	Ext.	17½	104.95	
Unertl										
■ 1" Target	6, 8, 10	16-10	17.6-6.25	2	21½	.75	Ext.	21	139.00	[1]Dural ¼ MOA click mounts. Hard coated lenses. Non-rotating objective lens focusing. [2]¼ MOA click mounts. [3]With target mounts. [4]With calibrated head. [5]Same as 1" Target but without objective lens focusing. [6]Price with ¼ MOA click mounts. [7]With new Posa mounts. [8]Range focus until near rear of tube. Price is with Posa mounts. Magnum clamp. With standard mounts and clamp ring $231.
■ 1¼" Target[1]	8,10,12,14	12-6	15.2-5	2	25	.75	Ext.	25	183.00	
■ 1½" Target	8,10,12,14, 16,18,20	11.5-3.2	—	2¼	25½	.75	Ext.	31	208.00	
■ 2" Target[2]	8,10,12, 14,16,18, 24,30,36	8	22.6-2.5	2¼	26¼	1	Ext.	44	281.00	
■ Varmint, 1¼∞[3]	6,8,10,12	1-7	28.7-1	2½	19½	.875	Ext.	26	184.00	
■ Ultra Varmint, 2"[4]	8,10 12,15	12.6-7	39.7-11	2½	24	1	Ext.	34	263.00	
■ Small Game[5]	4, 6	25-17	19.4-8.4	2¼	18	.75	Ext.	16	105.00	
■ Vulture[6]	8 10	11.2 10.9	29 18½	3-4 —	15⅝ 16⅛	1	Ext.	15½	202.00	
■ Programmer 200[7]	8,10,12 14,16,18, 20,24,30,36	11.3-4	39-1.9	—	26½	1	Ext.	45	349.00	
■ BV-20[8]	20	8	4.4	4.4	17⅞	1	Ext.	21¼	242.00	
Universal										
UE-4	4	29	64	3½	12	1	Int.	9.1	28.95	*All scopes have alloy tubes, constantly centered reticles, coated lenses. Asterisk denotes quadraplex reticle is avail., otherwise standard crosshair is offered. Write to Universal Sporting Goods for details.
UK-4*	3-9	36-13	112-13	3	12.8	1	Int.	13.8	43.95	
UK*	3-9	36-13	112-13	3	12.8	1	Int.	13.8	42.95	
UL-4	3-9	36-13	177-19	3	12.8	1	Int.	15.2	46.95	
UE40-4	4	29	100	3½	12½	1	Int.	10	30.95	
UD	4	23	25	2	12	⅞	Int.	12	21.95	
UA	4	16	14	4	10,8	¾	Int.	10.8	9.95	
UEW-4 Wide Angle*	4	35	64	3¼	12¼	1	Int.	12	28.95	

CAUTION: PRICES CHANGE. CHECK AT GUNSHOP.

HUNTING, TARGET ■ & VARMINT ■ SCOPES

Maker and Model	Magn.	Field at 100 Yds (feet)	Relative Brightness	Eye Relief (in.)	Length (in.)	Tube Diam. (in.)	W&E Adjustments	Weight (ozs.)	Price	Other Data
Weatherby										
Mark XXII[1]	4	25	50	2½-3½	11¾	⅞	Int.	9¼	57.95	[1]Focuses in top turret. [2]Centered, non-mag-
Premier Standard	2¾	45	212	3½	11¾	1	Int.	12¼	131.95	nifying reticles. Binocular focusing. Lumi-Plex
Premier Standard[2]	4	31	100	3½	12¾	1	Int.	12¼	137.95	$10 extra.
Premier Standard	3-9	43½-14½	177-19	3	12	1	Int.	14¾	142.95	
Premier Wide Angle	4	35¾	100	3	11¾	1	Int.	14	159.95	
Premier Wide Angle	3-9	43½-14¾	177-19	3	12	1	Int.	14¾	179.95	
Weaver										
K1.5	1½	55	—	5¼	9⅜	1	Int.	9¾	95.00	Steel-Lite II (lighter weight, glossy finish) in K, V
K2.5	2.6	38	—	4½	10⅜	1	Int.	10¼	95.00	and Wider View scopes. Crosshair and Dual-X
K3	3.2	34	—	4	10⅝	1	Int.	10¼	103.00	reticle optional on all K and V scopes (except
K4	4.1	27	—	4	11¾	1	Int.	12	112.00	no RF in K1.5, K2.5, K3 and K3W; no post in K8,
K6	5.9	19	—	3⅞	13½	1	Int.	13½	134.00	10, 12; no post or RF in T models). Dot, post and
K8	7.7	15	—	3½	15	1	Int.	15½	153.00	RF $18 extra in T models. [1]Avail. with mount for
K-856[2]	7.7	15	—	3½	15	1	Int.	18.7	210.00	Rem. 1100 or 870, Dual-X reticle. K1.5—$127,
K10F	10	12	—	3½	15¾	1	Int.	16¼	160.00	K2.5—$127. [2]56mm objective gives big 7mm
K12F	11.6	10	—	3½	16	1	Int.	16½	175.00	exit pupil. Excellent for low light conditions.
K3-W	2.9	48	—	3½	11	1	Int.	11	138.00	German post reticle $18 extra. [3]Micro-Trac
K4-W	3.7	38	—	3⅝	11¹³/₁₆	1	Int.	13	144.00	standard on all K and V models. ¼" Graduated
K6-W	6	24	—	3½	13¼	1	Int.	14½	168.00	adjustments. [4]¼-minute adj. [5]¼-minute adj. [6]¼"
M3-9V	3-9	32-11	—	5-3¾	13¼	1	Int.	11¾	81.00	click stops. Crosshair and Dual-X Standard on
M1	4	26	—	4	11⅝	1	Int.	9½	57.00	T models. [7]Features both range determination
M1-SF-TO	4	26	—	4	11⅝	1	Int.	9½	57.00	and trajectory compensation in fixed power.
M34W	4	27	—	2	11⅞	.750	Int.	5½	17.15	[8]Range determination and trajectory compen-
M34	4	25	—	2	11⅝	.750	Int.	5½	13.25	sation are totally independent of variable mag-
V4.5-W	1.6-4.2	74-27	—	4¼-3¾	10⅜	1	Int.	14¼	177.00	nification function. [9]$2.50 extra for Dual-X on
V7-W	2.6-6.9	43-17	—	3⅝-3¾	12⅜	1	Int.	15¼	192.00	V22, D4 or D6. D model prices include N or
V9-W	3.3-9	35-13	—	3⅝	14⅛	1	Int.	18¼	198.00	Tip-Off mount. [10]Projects red dot aiming point.
V9-WF[4]	3.3-9	35-13	—	3⅝	14	1	Int.	18¼	209.00	
V4.5	1.6-4.3	63-24	—	4⅜-3⅞	10⅜	1	Int.	13½	143.00	
V7	2.5-6.7	40-15	—	4-3⅞	12⅜	1	Int.	14½	157.00	
V9	3.3-8.8	31-12	—	3¾	14⅛	1	Int.	17½	176.00	
V9F[3]	3.3-8.8	31-12	—	3¾	14	1	Int.	17½	176.00	
V12F	4.4-11.8	23-9	—	3⅞-4¼	14	1	Int.	17½	188.00	
T6	6	19	—	3½	14¼	1	Int.	17¾	238.00	
T10	10	11	—	3½	15	1	Int.	18	253.00	
T16	16	7	—	3⅝	15¾	1	Int.	18¾	266.00	
T20[5]	20	4.8	—	3¾	18½	1	Int.	20	300.00	
T25	25	4.2	—	3¾	19⅛	1	Int.	20	316.00	
T-30[6]	30	3.3	—	3½	19⅜	1	Int.	21	324.00	
Auto-Comp[7] FX-4	4	27	—	4	11.8	1	Int.	13	149.95	
Auto-Comp[8] VX-9	3.3-8.8	31-12	—	3.8	14.2	1	Int.	18	199.95	
V22[9]	3-5.8	31-16	—	1⅝-2¼	12⅜	.875	Int.	7¾	32.50	
D4	4.2	29	—	2¼	11⅞	.875	Int.	6½	24.50	
D6	6.2	20	—	2¼	12⁵/₁₆	.875	Int.	6¾	27.00	
Qwik-Point[10]	1	—	—	6	—	—	Int.	8	75.00	
Williams										
Twilight Crosshair	2½	32	64	3¾	11¼	1	Int.	8½	89.50	TNT models.
Twilight Crosshair	4	29	64	3½	11¾	1	Int.	9½	95.90	
Twilight Crosshair	2-6	45-17	256-28	3	11½	1	Int.	11½	129.50	
Twilight Crosshair	3-9	36-13	161-18	3	12¾	1	Int.	13½	136.00	

■ Signifies target and/or varmint scope.

Hunting scopes in general are furnished with a choice of reticle—crosshairs, post with crosshairs, tapered or blunt post, or dot crosshairs, etc.

The great majority of target and varmint scopes have medium or fine crosshairs but post or dot reticles may be ordered.

W—Windage   E—Elevation   MOA—Minute of angle or 1" (approx.) at 100 yards, etc.

Redfield's Magnum Proof 1.5x and 2.5x pistol scopes, in conjunction with the Redfield mounting system, have the strength to easily handle the vicious snap of 41 and 44 magnum recoil. This scope/mount system is extremely solid and good looking, too. Each scope weighs 10 ounces and measures 9.82" long.

TELESCOPE MOUNTS

Maker, Model, Type	Adjust.	Scopes	Price	Suitable for
B-Square				[1]All dovetail receivers such as Nylon 66. No drilling or tapping. [2]M-94 Winchester. No drilling or tapping. Clamps on barrel. [3]M-94 Winchester. No drilling or tapping. [4]Instant on and off (with large thumb screw). [5]Ruger Mini-14. Mounts on top of receiver. Gunsmith Drill Jig avail. for guns not drilled—$39.95. [6]Ruger Mini-14. Attaches by replacing bolt stop cover. No gunsmithing and no sight removal. [7]Most popular rifles. [8]Remington 40X, 700 Models. [9]All standard target blocks. [10]Ruger Blackhawk (has bolted rings). [11]T-C Contender, all calibers. Heavy Recoil model. [12]No gunsmithing. Clamps on vent rib barrel. [13]No gunsmithing. Clamps on vent rib barrel. [14]Slides onto receiver. No gunsmithing. Thumb screw clamps. Use with iron sights.
Dovetail Rings[1]	No	1″ scopes.	$19.95	
M-94 Mono-Mount[2]	No	1″, long eye relief such as Leupold M8-2X. Mounts ahead of action.	24.95	
M-94 Side Mount[3]	W&E	All 1″ scopes.	31.95	
AR-15 Mount[4]	W&E	All 1″ scopes.	31.95	
Mini-14 Mount[5] (180 Series)	W&E	All 1″ scopes.	31.95	
Mini-14 Mount[6] (181 & 182 Series)	W&E	All 1″ scopes.	Blue—49.95 Stainless—59.95	
One Piece Base Mounts[7] (Includes B-Square Dovetail Rings)	No	1″ scopes.	24.95	
Target Mounts[8]	W&E	1″ scopes.	31.95	
Target Block Mount[9]	W&E	1″ scopes.	39.95	
Ruger Blackhawk Pistol[10]	No	1″ scopes.	31.95	
T-C Contender Pistol[11]	No	1″ scopes.	31.95	
Dan Wesson Pistol[12]	W&E	1″ scopes.	39.95	
Colt Python Pistol[13]	W&E	1″ scopes.	39.95	
Heckler & Koch M91/M93[14]	No	1″ Scopes.	49.95	
Buehler				[1]Most popular models. [2]Most popular models. [3]Most popular models. [4]Sako dovetail receivers. [5]15 models. [6] No drilling & tapping.
One Piece (T)[1]	W only	1″ split rings, 3 heights. 1″ split rings, 3 heights. 26mm, 2 heights	Complete—49.50 Rings only—69.50 Rings only—36.00	
One Piece Micro Dial (T)[2]	W&E	1″ split rings.	Complete—61.25	
Two Piece (T)[3]	W only	1″ split rings.	Complete—49.50	
Two Piece Dovetail (T)[4]	W only	1″ split rings.	Complete—61.25	
One Piece Pistol (T)[5]	W only	1″ split rings.	Complete—49.50	
One Piece Ruger Mini 14 (T)[6]	W only	1″ split rings.	Complete—61.25	
Burris				[1]Most popular rifles. Universal, rings, mounts fit Burris. Universal, Redfield, Leupold and Browning bases. Comparable prices. [2]Browning Standard 22 Auto rifle. [3]Most popular rifles. [4]Grooved receivers. [5]Universal dovetail; accept Burris, Universal, Redfield, Leupold rings. For Dan Wesson, S&W, Virginian, Ruger Blackhawk, Win. 94. [6]Medium standard front, extension rear, per pair. Low standard front, extension rear, per pair.
Supreme One Piece (T)[1]	W only	1″ split rings, 3 heights.	22.95 1 piece base—15.00	
Trumount Two Piece (T)	W only	1″ split rings, 3 heights.	2 piece base—12.50	
Browning Auto Mount[2]	No	¾″, 1″ split rings.	10.95	
Sight-Thru Mount[3]	No	1″ Split rings.	16.95	
Rings Mounts[4]	No	¾″, 1″ split rings.	¾″ rings—10.95 1″ rings—10.95	
L.E.R. Mount Bases[5]	No	1″ split rings.	12.50	
Extension Rings[6]	No	1″ scopes.	26.95	
Bushnell				[1]Most popular rifles. Includes windage adj. [2]V-block bottoms lock to chrome-moly studs seated into two 6-48 holes. Rem. XP-100. [3]Heavy loads in Colt, S&W, Ruger revolvers, Ruger Hawkeye. [4]M94 Win., center dovetail.
Detachable (T) mounts only[1]	W only	1″ split rings, uses Weaver bases.	Rings—12.50	
22 mount	No	1″ only.	Rings— 5.95	
All Purpose[2]	No	Phantom.	11.95	
Rigid[3]	No	Phantom.	12.95	
94 Win.[4]	No	Phantom.	15.95	
Clearview				[1]All popular rifles including Sav. 99. Uses Weaver bases. [2]Rings have wide oval effect for use of open sights. [3]For 22 rimfire rifles, with grooved receivers or bases. [4]Remington 14, 141, Sears 54, 100, Win. 94, 94-375.
Universal Rings (T)[1]	No	1″ split rings.	18.95	
Mod 101, & 336[2]	No	1″ split rings.	17.95	
Model 104[3]	No	1″ split rings.	10.95	
SM-94[4]	No	1″ split rings.	21.95	
Conetrol				[1]All popular rifles, including metric-drilled foreign guns. Price shown for base, two rings. Matte finish. [2]Gunnur grade has mirror-finished rings, satin-finish base. Price shown for base, two rings. [3]Custum grade has mirror-finished rings and mirror-finished, contoured base. Price shown for base, 2 rings. [4]Win. 94, Krag, older split-bridge Mannlicher-Schoenauer, Mini-14, M-1 Garand, etc. Prices same as above. [5]For all popular guns with integral mounting provision, including Sako, BSA, Ithacagun, Ruger, H&K and many others. Also for grooved-receiver rimfires and air rifles. Prices same as above. [6]For XP-100, T/C Contender, Colt SAA, Ruger Blackhawk, S&W.
Hunter[1]	W only	1″, 26mm, 26.5mm solid or split rings, 3 heights.	39.96	
Gunnur[2]	W only	1″, 26mm, 26.5mm solid or split rings, 3 heights.	49.95	
Custum[3]	W only	1″, 26mm, 26.5mm solid or split rings, 3 heights.	59.91	
One Piece Side Mount[4]	W only	1″, 26mm, 26.5mm solid or split rings, 3 heights.		
Daptar Bases[5]	W only	1″, 26mm, 26.5mm solid or split rings, 3 heights.		
Pistol Bases[6]	W only	1″ scopes.		
Pistol Bases, 3-Ring[7]	W only	1″ scopes.		
EAW				Most popular magazine rifles.
Pivot Mount	W&E	1″ or 26mm.	125.00-135.00	
Griffin & Howe				All popular models (Garand $100; Win. 94 $100). All rings $45.
Standard Double Lever (S).	No	1″ or 26mm split rings.	100.00	
Holden				[1]Most popular rifles including Ruger Mini-14, H&R M700, Win. 94BB and muzzleloaders. Rings have oval holes to permit use of iron sights. [2]For 1″ scopes. [3]For ¾″ or ⅞″ dia. scopes. [4]For 1″ dia. extended eye relief scopes. [5]Fits Redfield and Weaver bases.
Ironsighter Center Fire[1]	No	1″ Split rings.	16.75	
Ironsighter 22 cal. rimfire				
Model #500[2]	No	1″ Split rings.	8.95	
Model #600[3]	No	⅞″ Split rings also fits ¾″.	8.95	
Ironsighter Handguns[4]	No	1″ Split rings.	18.95	
Holden "Straight Shooter"[5] Bullet Drop Compensating Scope Mount	Yes	1″ Split rings.	41.95	

Left, Buehler's new two-piece dovetail mount for Sako rifles.

Clearview SM-94, SM-94-375.

CAUTION: PRICES CHANGE. CHECK AT GUNSHOP.

TELESCOPE MOUNTS

Maker, Model, Type	Adjust.	Scopes	Price	Suitable for
Jaeger				
QD, with windage (S)	W only	1″, 3 heights.	125.00	All popular models.
Jaguar				
QD Dovetail (T)	No	1″, 26mm and 26½mm rings.	23.30	For BSA Monarch rifle (Galef, importer).
Kesselring				
Standard QD (T)	W only	¾″, ⅞″, 1″, 26mm split rings.	29.95	All popular rifles, one or two piece bases. Rem.
See-Em-Under (T)	W only	Same.	35.00	760, 740, Win. 100, 88, Marlin 336, Steyr 22, Sako,
Dovetail (T)	W only	1″, 26mm.	35.00	BRNO, Krico.
Kris Mounts				
Side-Saddle[1]	No	1″, 26mm split rings.	10.98	[1]One-piece mount for Win. 94. [2]Most popular rifles
Two Piece (T)[2]	No	1″, 26mm split rings.	7.98	and Ruger. [3]Blackhawk revolver. Mounts have
One Piece (T)[3]	No	1″, 26mm split rings.	10.98	oval hole to permit use of iron sights.
Kwik-Site				
KS-See-Thru[1]	No	1″	15.95	[1]Most rifles. Allows use of iron sights. [2]22-cal.
KS-22 See-Thru[2]	No	1″	12.95	rifles with grooved receivers. Allows use of iron
KS-W94[3]	Yes	1″	27.95	sights. [3]Model 94, 94 Big Bore. No drilling or tap-
KSM Imperial[4]	No	1″	24.95	ping. [4]Most rifles. One-piece solid construction.
Leupold				
STD (T)[1]	W only	1″ only, 3 heights, Interchangeable with Redfield Jr. and Sr. components.	Rings—26.00 Base—18.00	[1]Most popular rifles. [2]For M8-2x or 4x EER mounting on a Colt Gold Cup N.M. 45.
45 ACP "Gold Cup" Mount[2]	No	1″ split rings.	36.00	
Marlin				
One Piece QD (T)	No	1″ split rings.	7.95	Most Marlin and Glenfield lever actions.
Numrich				
Side Mount	No	1″ split rings.	7.95	M-1 carbine.
Pachmayr				
Lo-Swing (S)[1]	Yes	¾″, ⅞″, 1″, 26mm solid or split loops.	55.00	[1]All popular rifles, including Ruger Mini-14, Browning BBR. Scope swings aside for instant use of iron sights. [2]Adjustable base. Win. 70, 88;
Lo-Swing (T)[2]	Yes	¾″, ⅞″, 1″, 26mm split rings.	55.00	Rem. 721, 722, 725, 740, 760; Mar. 336; Sav. 99. New Model for Colt Sauer.
Parker-Hale				
Roll-Off	No	1″ and 26mm.	15.55	Most popular rifles.
Precise				
40421 (rings only)	No	1″ tube; not over 32mm obj.	7.50	Fits Weaver bases.
40422 (rings only)	No	1″ tube; 40mm obj. scopes.	7.50	
Redfield				
JR-SR (T)[1]	W only	¾″, 1″, 26mm.	Rings—26.50 Bases—17.95-21.10	[1]Low, med. & high, split rings. Reversible extension front rings for 1″. 2-piece bases for Mannlicher-Schoenauer and Sako. Colt Sauer bases $44.50. [2]Split rings for grooved 22's. See-thru
Ring (T)[2]	No	¾″ and 1″.	Rings—59.50 26.30	mounts $23.30. [3]Used with MP scopes for: S&W K or N frame. XP-100, Colt J or I frame. T/C Conten-
Double Dovetail MP[3]	No	1″, split rings.	49.10	der, Colt autos, black powder rifles.
S&K				
Insta-Mount (T) base only[1]	No	Most take S&K or Weaver rings.	15.00-36.00	[1]1903, A3, M1 Carbine, Lee Enfield #3, #4, #5, P14, M1917, M98 Mauser, FN Auto, AR-15, AR-180, M-14, M-1. Bases—M94, 64. [2]Most popular rifles.
Conventional rings and bases[2]	No	1″ split rings.	30.00	For "see through underneath" risers, add $4.15.
Sako				
QD Dovetail	W only	1″ only.	39.95	Sako, or any rifle using Sako action. 3 heights available, Stoeger, importer.
Savage				
No. 40 (S)[1]	No	1″	5.10	[1]For Savage 340, 840, Springfield. [2]For Savage
No. 70[2]	No	1″	5.10	170, 170-C rifles. [3]For 24V, 222, or 30-30.
B-5[3]	No	1″	15.75	
Tasco				
790 and 792 series[1]	Yes	1″ split rings, regular or high.	9.95	[1]Many popular rifles. [2]For 22s with grooved
794[2]	No	Split rings.	9.95	receivers. [3]Most popular rifles. [4]Most popular
795 Quick Peep[3]	No	1″ only.	11.95	rifles.
800L Series (with base)[4]	No	1″ only.	13.95	
Unertl				
Posa (T)[1]	Yes	¾″, ⅞″, 1″ scopes.	Per set 47.00	[1]Unertl target or varmint scopes. [2]Any with regu-
¼ Click (T)[2]	Yes	¾″, 1″ target scopes.	Per set 41.00	lar dovetail scope bases.
Weaver				
Detachable Mount (T & S)[1]	No	¾″, ⅞″, 1″, 26mm.	17.95	[1]Nearly all modern rifles. Extension rings, 1″ $20.95. [2]Same. High or low style mounts. [3]Most
Type N (S)[2]	No	⅞″ scopes only.	9.95	modern big bore rifles. [4]22s with grooved
Pivot Mount (T)[3]	No	1″	22.95	receivers. [5]Same. Adapter for Lee Enfield—$8.75.
Tip-Off (T)[4]	No	¾″, ⅞″.	9.95	[6]⅞″—$11.95. 1″ See-Thru extension—$20.95.
Tip-Off (T)[5]	No	1″, two-piece.	17.95	[7]Colt Officer's Model, Python, Ruger B'hawk,
See-Thru Mount[6]	No	1″ Split rings and ⅞″-tip-off. Fits all top mounts.	17.95	Super B'hawk, Security Six, 22 Autos, Mini-14. No drilling or tapping.
Mount Base System[7]	No	1″	39.95	
Williams				
Offset (S)[1]	No	¾″, ⅞″, 1″ 26mm solid, split or extension rings.	41.60	[1]Most rifles. Br. S.M.L.E. (round rec.) $3.85 extra. [2]Same. [3]Most rifles. [4]Most rifles. [5]Many modern
QC (T)[2]	No	Same.	34.15	rifles. [6]Most popular rifles.
QC (S)[3]	No	Same.	34.15	
Low Sight-Thru[4]	No	1″, ⅞″, sleeves $1.80.	17.75	
Sight-Thru[5]	No	1″, ⅞″, sleeves $1.80.	17.75	
Streamline[6]	No	1″ (bases form rings).	17.75	

(S)—Side Mount (T)—Top Mount 22mm=.866″ 25.4mm=1″1.024″ 26.5mm=1.045″ 30mm=1.81″

Wever's new Mount Base System on the Ruger Mini-14. It also fits many handguns.

Redfield See-Thru mounts.

SPOTTING SCOPES

BAUSCH & LOMB DISCOVERER—15X to 60X zoom, 60mm objective. Constant focus throughout range. Field at 1000 yds. 40 ft. (60X), 156 ft. (15X). Comes with lens caps. Length 17½″, wgt. 48½ oz. **$375.00**
BUSHNELL SPACEMASTER*—60mm objective. Field at 1000 yds., 158′ to 37′. Relative brightness, 5.76. Wgt., 36 oz. Length closed, 11⅝″. Prism focusing, without eyepiece...................................... **$198.00**
    15X, 20X, 25X, 40X and 60X eyepieces, each **$37.00**
    22X wide angle eyepiece **$42.00**
BUSHNELL SPACEMASTER 45°—Same as above except: Wgt., 43 oz., length closed 13″. Eyepiece at 45°, without eyepiece.
    Price:.. **$253.00**
BUSHNELL ZOOM SPACEMASTER—20X-45X zoom. 60mm objective. Field at 1000 yards 120′-72′. Relative brightness 9-1.7. Wgt. 36 oz., length 11⅝″
    Price:.. **$295.00**
BUSHNELL SENTRY*—50mm objective. Field at 1000 yards 120′-45′. Relative brightness 6.25. Wgt., 25½ oz., length 12⅝″, without eyepiece.
    Price:.. **$107.00**
    20X, 32X and 48X eyepieces, each **$32.00**
BUSHNELL ZOOM SPOTTER—40mm objective. 9X-30X var. power.
    Price:.. **$84.50**

Bushnell Zoom Spotter

BUSHNELL COMPETITOR—40mm objective. Prismatic. Field at 1000 yards 140′. Minimum focus 33′. Length 12½″, weight 18½ oz. ... **$79.50**
BUSHNELL TROPHY—16X-36X zoom. Rubber armored, prismatic. 50mm objective. Field at 1000 yards 131′ to 90′. Minimum focus 20′. Length with caps 13⅝″, weight 38 oz.**$236.00** With interchangeable eyepieces—20x, 32x, 48x **$179.00**
BUSHNELL—10x30mm hand telescope. Field 183 ft. at 1000 yards. Weight 11 ozs.; 10″ long. Tripod mount............................... **$24.95**
DICKSON 270—20x to 60x variable, 60mm objective, achromatic coated objective lens, complete with metal table tripod with 5′ vertical and horizontal adjustments. Turret type, 20x, 30x, 40x 60x.
    Price.. **$239.95**
DICKSON 274A—20x to 60x variable zoom. 60mm achromatic coated objective lens, complete with adjustable metal table tripod.
    Price.. **$110.00**
DICKSON 274B—As above but with addition of 4×16 Finder Scope.
    Price.. **$121.95**
HUTSON CHROMATAR 60—63.4mm objective. 22.5X eyepiece at 45°. Wgt. 24 oz. 8″ over-all. 10½ foot field at 100 yards. **$119.00**
    15X or 45X eyepieces, each........................... **$22.00**
SOUTHERN PRECISION MODEL 550—60mm objective and 5 eyepieces from 15X to 60X; folding tripod. 14¾″, Wgt., 4¼ lbs............ **$129.50**
SOUTHERN PRECISION ZOOM MODEL 543—60mm objective, 15X to 50X; folding tripod. 18″, wgt. 4½ lbs. with tripod (included)......... **$119.95**
SOUTHERN PRECISION MODEL 552—80mm objective, 20X. Folding tripod. 13″, wgt. 3 lbs. **$117.50**
SWAROVSKI HABICHT 30x75 IRALIN TELESCOPE—75mm objective, 30X. Field at 1,000 yds. 90ft. Minimum, focusing distance 90 ft. Length: closed 13 in., extended 20½″. Weight: 47 oz. Precise recognition of smallest details even at dusk. Leather or rubber covered.
    Price:.. **$885.00**
Same as above with short range supplement. Minimum focusing distance 24 to 30 ft.
    Price:.. **$920.00**
SWIFT TELEMASTER M841—60mm objective. 15X to 60X variable power. Field at 1000 yards 160 feet (15X) to 40 feet (60X). Wgt. 3.4 lbs. 17.6″ over-all.
    Price:.. **$415.00**
    Tripod for above **$79.95**
    Photo adapter **$19.00**
    Case for above **$57.50**
SWIFT TELEMASTER JR. M842—25-50mm zoom spotting scope. Smaller version of M841 with same features. 14.9″ over-all, wgt. 2.2 lbs. **$255.00**

SWIFT M844 COMMANDO PRISMATIC SPOTTING SCOPE, MK. II—60mm objective. Comes with 20X eyepiece; 15X, 30X, 40X, 50X, 60X available. Built-in sunshade. Field at 1000 yds. with 20X, 120 ft. Length 13.7″, wgt. 2.1 lbs.
    Price:.. **$245.00**
SWIFT M700 SCOUT—9X-30X, 30mm spotting scope. Length 15½″, weighs 2.1 lbs. Field of 204 ft. (9X), 60 ft. (30X).
    Price:.. **$96.00**
TASCO 18T ZOOM—60mm objective. 20X to 60X variable power. Field at 100 yards 9 feet (20X) to 3 feet (60X). Wgt. 4 lbs. 16″ overall ... **$199.95**
TASCO 28T ANGLEVIEW—60mm objective. 25X, resolves to 2 sec. at 100 yds. Rapid focus knob. Table top tripod with adj. elevation leg. Camera tripod adapter, extending sun shade. Wgt., 6 lbs., length 16½″. Complete with lens covers **$399.95**
TASCO 8T SPOTTING 60—60mm objective, 4 par-focal, variable power eye-lenses 15X, 30X, 40X and 60X. Resolves 2.8 sec. at 100 yds. Wgt., 4 lbs., length 16½″. **$299.95**
UNERTL "FORTY-FIVE" SCOPE—20X (single power only, no interchangeable eyepieces). 54mm objective. Field of view at 100 yds. 10 ′10″. Eye relief 1.074″. Has 45° angular eyepiece. Weight about 2 lbs. Over-all length 15¾″. From **$195.00**
UNERTL RIGHT ANGLE—63.5mm objective. 24X. Field at 100 yds., 7 ft. Relative brightness, 6.96. Eye relief, ½″. Wgt., 41 oz. Length closed, 19″. Push-pull and screw-focus eyepiece. 16X and 32X eyepieces $31.00 each.
    Price:.. **$219.00**
UNERTL STRAIGHT PRISMATIC—Same as Unertl Right Angle except: straight eyepiece and wgt. of 40 oz........................... **$185.00**
UNERTL 20X STRAIGHT PRISMATIC—54mm objective. 20X. Field at 100 yds., 8.5 ft. Relative brightness, 6.1. Eye relief, ½″. Wgt., 36 oz. Length closed, 13½″. Complete with lens covers **$155.00**
UNERTL TEAM SCOPE—100mm objective. 15X, 24X, 32X eyepieces. Field at 100 yds. 13 to 7.5 ft. Relative brightness, 39.06 to 9.79. Eye relief, 2″ to 1½″. Weight, 13 lbs. 29⅞″ overall. Metal tripod, yoke and wood carrying case furnished (total weight, 67 lbs.)...................... **$734.00**
WEATHERBY—60mm objective, 20X-45X zoom **$305.95**
    Tripod for above **$65.95**

SCOPE ATTACHMENTS

BUTLER CREEK LENS COVERS—Waterproof, dustproof. Springs open at a touch. Work in all weather. Sizes to fit all scopes. Per pair..... **$10.95**
DAVIS TARGETEER—Objective lens/tube units that attach to front of low power scopes, increase magnification to 8X. 1¼″ lens, **$27.50**, 1½″ lens **$32.50**
HERMANN LONGHORN DUST CAPS—All leather. Connected leather straps, hand made, natural color. For all popular scopes. **$6.50**
LEE TACKHOLE DOTS—Various size dots for most scopes. Price**$16.00**— **$25.00**
W. H. SIEBERT—Converts Lyman, Leupold and Unertl varmint scopes to 15X-36X.. **$40.00**
STORM KING LENS CAPS—A hinged glass-and-rubber protector set (2), made in various sizes for all scopes. May be unhinged or sighted through. Anderson Mfg. Co. Per pair.................................... **$5.45**
    Price: with Haze Cutter **$6.55**
SUPREME LENS COVERS—Hinged protectors for most scope models, front and rear lenses shielded. Butler Creek Corp. Per pair, postpaid.... **$7.95**

SPOTTING SCOPE STANDS

FREELAND OLYMPIC—Bipod adjustable for elevation. All angle mount with padded worm drive clamp. Folding legs. Clamps available for any scope tube size. Gray crinkle finish. Price...................... **$55.00**
    Also 12″, 18″, 24″ extensions................. **$7.00, $10.00, $11.00**
    Zoom head for tripod or bipod........................ **$20.50**

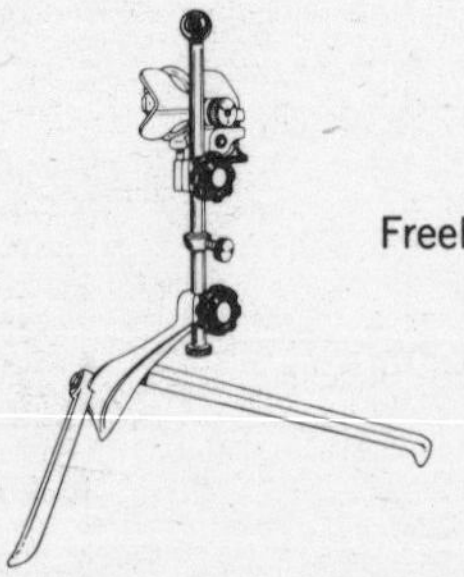

Freeland Regal Bipod

FREELAND REGAL BIPOD—Choice of saddle or zoom head. All adjustment knobs are oversize for easy adjusting. Large "ball" carrying knob. Gray finish.. **$46.00**
    Above with stability weight **$86.50**
FREELAND GALLERY SPECIAL BIPOD—For all shooting positions. Zoom or saddle head. Adjustable for elevation. Comes with bipod base, gallery special head assembly and 12″ extension. Gray finish, saddle head.**$53.00**
    As above with 18″ extension............................ **$55.00**

CAUTION: PRICES CHANGE. CHECK AT GUNSHOP.

ARMS ASSOCIATIONS
IN
AMERICA AND ABROAD

UNITED STATES

ALABAMA

Alabama Gun Collectors Assn.
Dick Boyd, Secy., P.O. Box 5548, Tuscaloosa, AL 35405

ALASKA

Alaska Gun Collectors Assn.
Gene Coppedge, P.O. Box 4-1898, Anchorage, AK 99509

ARIZONA

Arizona Gun Collectors Assn., Inc.
Clay Fobes, Secy., P.O. Box 17061, Tucson, AZ 85731

CALIFORNIA

Burbank Rifle & Revolver Club, Inc.
P.O. Box 6765, Burbank, CA 91510
Calif. Hunters & Gun Owners Assoc.
V. H. Wacker, 2309 Cipriani Blvd., Belmont, CA 94002
Greater Calif. Arms & Collectors Assn.
Donald L. Bullock, 8291 Carburton St., Long Beach, CA 90808
Los Angeles Gun & Ctg. Collectors Assn.
F. H. Ruffra, 20810 Amie Ave., Torrance, CA 90503

COLORADO

Pikes Peak Gun Collectors Guild
Charles Cell, 406 E. Uintah St., Colorado Springs, CO 80903

CONNECTICUT

Antique Arms Coll. Assn. of Conn.
T. N. Reiley, 17 Philip Rd., Manchester, CT 06040
Ye Conn. Gun Guild, Inc.
Robert L. Harris, P.O. Box 8, Cornwall Bridge, CT 06754

FLORIDA

Unified Sportsmen of Florida
P.O. Box 12577, Tallahassee, FL 32308

GEORGIA

Georgia Arms Collectors
Cecil W. Anderson, P.O. Box 218, Conley, GA 30027

HAWAII

Hawaii Historic Arms Assn.
Roy D. Warren, P.O. Box 1733, Honolulu, HI 96806

IDAHO

Idaho State Rifle and Pistol Assn.
Tom Price, 3631 Pineridge Dr., Coeur d'Alene, ID 83814

ILLINOIS

Central Illinois Gun Collectors Assn., Inc.
Joe Richardson, R.R. 3, Jacksonville, IL 62650

Fox Valley Arms Fellowship, Inc.
P.O. Box 301, Palatine, IL 60067
Illinois Deer Hunters Assn.
Terry Jenkins, 5002 Stewart Dr., Decatur, IL 62521
Illinois State Rifle Assn.
224 S. Michigan Ave., Room 200, Chicago, IL 60604
Illinois Gun Collectors Assn.
P.O. Box 1694, Kankakee, IL 60901
Little Fort Gun Collectors Assn.
Ernie Robinson, P.O. Box 194, Gurnee, IL 60031
Mississippi Valley Gun & Cartridge Coll. Assn.
Harold S. Parsons, R.R. No. 2, Alexis, IL 61412
Sauk Trail Gun Collectors
Gordell M. Matson, 3817-22 Ave., Moline, IL 61265
Wabash Valley Gun Collectors Assn., Inc.
Mrs. Betty Baer, 1659 N. Franklin St., Danville, IL 61832

INDIANA

Indiana Sportsmen's Council—Legislative
Maurice Latimer, P.O. Box 93, Bloomington, IN 47402
Indiana State Rifle & Pistol Assn.
Thos. Glancy, P.O. Box 552, Chesterton, IN 46304
Southern Indiana Gun Collectors Assn., Inc.
Harold M. McClary, 509 N. 3rd St., Boonville, IN 47601

IOWA

Central States Gun Collectors Assn.
Avery Giles, 1104 S. 1st Ave., Marshtown, IA 50158

KANSAS

Four State Collectors Assn.
M. G. Wilkinson, 915 E. 10th, Pittsburg, KS 66762
Kansas Cartridge Coll. Assn.
Bob Linder, Box 84, Plainville, KS 67663
Missouri Valley Arms Collectors Assn.
Chas. F. Samuel, Jr., Box 8204, Shawnee Mission, KS 66208

KENTUCKY

Kentuckiana Arms Coll. Assn.
Tony Wilson, Pres., Box 1776, Louisville, KY 40201
Kentucky Gun Collectors Assn., Inc.
J. A. Smith, Box 64, Owensboro, KY 42302

LOUISIANA

Bayou Gun Club
David J. Seibert, Jr., 2820 Ramsey Dr., New Orleans, LA 70114
Ft. Miro Muzzleloaders
Sandra Rushing, P.O. Box 256, Main St., Grayson, LA 71435.

MARYLAND

Baltimore Antique Arms Assn.
Stanley I. Kellert, R.D. 1, Box 256, Lutherville, MD 21093

MASSACHUSETTS

Bay Colony Weapons Collectors Inc.
Ronald B. Santurjian, 47 Homer Rd., Belmont, MA 02178
Massachusetts Arms Collectors
John J. Callan, Jr., P.O. Box 1001, Worcester, MA 01613

MICHIGAN

Royal Oak Historical Arms Collectors, Inc.
Dee Hamal, P.O. Box 202, Royal Oak, MI 48067

MINNESOTA

Minnesota Weapons Coll. Assn., Inc.
Box 662, Hopkins, MN 55343

MISSISSIPPI

Mississippi Gun Collectors Assn.
Mrs. Jack E. Swinney, P.O. Box 1332, Hattiesburg, MS 39401

MISSOURI

Mineral Belt Gun Coll. Assn.
D. F. Saunders, 1110 Cleveland Ave., Monett, MO 65708

MONTANA

Montana Arms Collectors Assn.
Lewis E. Yearout, 308 Riverview Dr. East, Great Falls, MT 59404
The Winchester Arms Coll. Assn.
Lewis E. Yearout, 308 Riverview Dr. East, Great Falls, MT 59404

NEBRASKA

Nebraska Gun & Cartridge Collectors
E. M. Zalud, 710 West 6th St., North Platte, NB 69101

NEW HAMPSHIRE

New Hampshire Arms Collectors Inc.
Frank H. Galeucia, Rte. 28, Box 44, Windham, NH 03087

NEW JERSEY

Englishtown Benchrest Shooters Assn.
Tony Hidalgo, 6 Capp St., Carteret, NJ 07008
Experimental Ballistics Associates
Ed Yard, 110 Kensington, Trenton, NJ 08618
Jersey Shore Antique Arms Collectors
Joe Sisia, P.O. Box 100, Bayville, NJ 08721
New Jersey Arms Collectors Club, Inc.
Angus Laidlaw, 230 Valley Rd., Montclair, NJ 07042

NEW YORK

Hudson-Mohawk Arms Collectors Assn., Inc.
Bennie S. Pisarz, 6 Lamberson St., Dolgeville, NY 13329
Iroquois Arms Collectors Assn.
Dennis Freeman, 12144 McNeeley Rd., Akron, NY 14001
Mid-State Arms Coll. & Shooters Club
Jack Ackerman, 24 S. Mountain Terr., Binghamton, NY 13903
Westchester Arms Collectors Club, Inc.
F. E. Falkenbury, Secy., 79 Hillcrest Rd., Hartsdale, NY 10530

NORTH CAROLINA

Carolina Gun Collectors Assn.
David Blalock, Jr., Rt. 1, Linden, NC 28356

OHIO

Central Ohio Gun and Indian Relic Coll. Assn.
Coyt Stookey, 134 E. Ohio Ave., Washington C.H., OH 43160
Maumee Valley Gun Collectors Assn.
A. Kowalka, 3203 Woodville Rd., Northwood, OH 43619
Ohio Gun Collectors, Assn., Inc.
P.O. Box 300, Mount Gilead, OH 43338
The Stark Gun Collectors, Inc.
Russ McNary, 147 Miles Ave., N.W., Canton, OH 44708

OKLAHOMA

Indian Territory Gun Collectors Assn.
P.O. Box 4491, Tulsa, OK 74104

OREGON

Oregon Cartridge Coll. Assn.
Richard King, 3228 N.W. 60th, Corvallis, OR 97330
Oregon Arms Coll. Assn., Inc.
Ted Dowd, P.O. Box 25103, Portland, OR 97225

PENNSYLVANIA

Presque Isle Gun Coll. Assn.
James Welch, 156 E. 37 St., Erie, PA 16506

SOUTH CAROLINA

Belton Gun Club Inc.
J. K. Phillips, Route 1, Belton SC 29627
South Carolina Arms Coll. Assn.
J. W. McNelley, 3215 Lincoln St., Columbia, SC 29201

SOUTH DAKOTA

Dakota Territory Gun Coll. Assn., Inc.
Curt Carter, Castlewood, SD 57223

TENNESSEE

Memphis Antique Weapons Assn.
Jan Clement, 1886 Lyndale #1, Memphis, TN 38107
Smoky Mountain Gun Coll. Assn., Inc.
M. C. Wiest, P.O. Box 8880, Knoxville, TN 37916
Tennessee Gun Collectors Assn., Inc.
M. H. Parks, 3556 Pleasant Valley Rd., Nashville, TN 37204

TEXAS

Houston Gun Collectors Assn.
P.O. Box 37369, Houston, TX 77036
Texas State Rifle Assn.
Lafe R. Pfeifer, P.O. Drawer 340809, Dallas TX 75234

UTAH

Utah Gun Collectors Assn.
S. Gerald Keogh, 875 20th St., Ogden, UT 84401

VIRGINIA

Virginia Arms Collectors & Assn.
Clinton E. Jones, P.O. Box 333, Mechanicsville, VA 23111

WASHINGTON

Washington Arms Collectors, Inc.
J. Dennis Cook, P.O. Box 7335, Tacoma, WA 98407

WISCONSIN

Great Lakes Arms Coll. Assn., Inc.
E. Warnke, 1811 N. 73rd St. Wauwatosa, WI 53213
Wisconsin Gun Collectors Assn., Inc.
Rob. Zellmer, P.O. Box 181, Sussex, WI 53089

WYOMING

Wyoming Gun Collectors
Bob Funk, Box 1805, Riverton, WY 82501

NATIONAL ORGANIZATIONS

Amateur Trap Shooting Assn.
P.O. Box 458, Vandalia, OH 45377
American Association of Shotgunning
P.O. Box 3351, Reno, NV 89505
American Defense Preparedness Assn.
Rosslyn Center, 1700 N. Moore St., Suite 900, Arlington, VA 22209
American Police Pistol & Rifle Assn.
1100 N.E. 125th St., No. Miami, FL 33161
American Single Shot Rifle Assn.
L. B. Thompson, 987 Jefferson Ave., Salem, OH 44460
American Society of Arms Collectors, Inc.
Robt. F. Rubendunst, 6550 Baywood Lane, Cincinnati, OH 45224
Armor & Arms Club
J. K. Watson, Jr., 25 Broadway, New York, NY 10004
Association of Firearm and Toolmark Examiners
Eugenia A. Bell, Secy., 7857 Esterel Dr., La Jolla, CA 92037
Boone & Crockett Club
205 South Patrick., Alexandria, VA 22314
Cast Bullet Assn., Inc.
Sidney F. Musselman, 5522 Trent St., Chevy Chase, MD 20015
Citizens Committee for the Right to Keep and Bear Arms
Natl. Hq.: Bellefield Office Park, 1601 114, S.E., Suite 151, Bellevue, WA 98004
Contender Collectors Assn.
Fred Schimel, 4302 S. Wisconsin Ave., Stickney, IL 60402
Deer Unlimited of America, Inc.
P.O. Box 509, Clemson, SC 29631
Ducks Unlimited, Inc.
P.O. Box 66300, Chicago, IL 60666
Experimental Ballistics Assoc.
Ed Yard, 110 Kensington, Trenton, NJ 08618
International Benchrest Shooters
Evelyn Richards, 411 N. Wilbur Ave, Sayre, PA 18840
International Cartridge Coll. Assn., Inc.
Victor v. B. Engel, 1211 Walnut St., Williamsport, PA 17701
International Handgun Metallic Silhouette Assoc.
Box 1609, Idaho Falls, ID 83401
Miniature Arms Collectors/Makers Society Ltd.
Joseph J. Macewicz, 104 White Sand Lane, Racine, WI 53402
National Assn. of Federally Licd. Firearms Dealers
Andrew Molchan, 7001 N. Clark St., Chicago, IL 60626
National Automatic Pistol Collectors Assn.
Tom Knox, P.O. Box 15738, Tower Grove Station, St. Louis, MO 63163
National Bench Rest Shooters Assn., Inc.
Stella Buchtel, 5735 Sherwood Forest Dr., Akron, OH 44139
National Deer Hunter Assn.
1415 Fifth St. So., Hopkins, MN 55343
National Muzzle Loading Rifle Assn.
Box 67, Friendship, IN 47021
National Police Officers Assn. of America
609 West Main St., Louisville, KY 40202
National Reloading Mfrs. Assn., Inc.
1221 S.W. Yamhill St., Portland, OR 97205
National Rifle Assn.
1600 Rhode Island Ave., N.W., Washington, DC 20036
National Shooting Sports Fdtn., Inc.
Arnold H. Rohlfing, Exec. Director, 1075 Post Rd., Riverside, CT 06878
National Skeet Shooting Assn.
Ann Myers, P.O. Box 28188, San Antonio, TX 78228
National Wild Turkey Federation, Inc.
P.O. Box 467, Edgefield, SC 29824
North American Edged Weapon Collectors Assn.

John Cox, 2224 Wyandoge Dr., Oakville, Ont. L6L 2T5, Canada
North-South Skirmish Assn., Inc.
John L. Rawls, Route 1, Box 226A, Bentonville, VA 22610
Ruger Collector's Assn., Inc.
Nancy J. Padua, P.O. Box 211, Trumbull, CT 06611
Second Amendment Foundation
Bellefield Office Park, 1601—114th S.E., Suite 157, Bellevue, WA 98004
Southern California Schuetzen Society
Thomas Trevor, 13621 Sherman Way, Van Nuys, CA 91405
SAAMI, Sporting Arms and Ammunition Mfrs. Inst., Inc.
P.O. Box 218, Wallingford, CT 06492
U.S. Revolver Assn.
Stanley A. Sprague, 59 Alvin St., Springfield, MA 01104
Winchester Arms Collectors Assoc.
Lewis E. Yearout, 308 Riverview Dr.,E, Great Falls, MT 59404

AUSTRALIA

Sporting Shooters' Assn. of Australia Inc.
Mr. K. MacLaine, P.O. Box 210, Belgrave, Vict. 3160, Australia

CANADA

ALBERTA

Canadian Historical Arms Society
P.O. Box 901, Edmonton, Alb., Canada T5J 2L8

BRITISH COLUMBIA

B.C. Historical Arms Collectors
Ron Tyson, Box 80583, Burnaby, B.C. Canada V5H 3X9

NEW BRUNSWICK

Canadian Black Powder Federation
Mrs. Janet McConnell, P.O. Box 2876, Moncton, N.B. E1C 8T8, Can.

ONTARIO

Oshawa Antique Gun Coll. Inc.
William A. Vaughan, Box 544, Whitby, Ont. L1N 5V3, Canada

EUROPE

ENGLAND

Arms and Armour Society of London
Joseph G. Rosa, 17 Woodville Gardens, Ruislip, Middlesex HA4 7NB
British Cartridge Collectors Club
Peter F. McGowan, 15 Sandhurst Dr., Ruddington, Nottingham
Historical Breechloading Smallarms Assn.
D. J. Penn, M.A., Imperial War Museum, Lambeth Rd., London SE1 6HZ, England. Journal and newsletter are $8 a yr. seamail; surcharge for airmail.
Muzzle Loaders' Assn. of Great Britain
Membership Records, 12 Frances Rd., Baginton, Coventry, England
National Rifle Assn. (British)
Bisley Camp, Brookwood, Woking, Surrey, GU24 OPB, England

GERMANY (WEST)

Deutscher Schutzenbund
Lahnstrasse, 6200 Wiesbaden-Klarenthal, West Germany

NEW ZEALAND

New Zealand Deerstalkers Assn.
Miss P. A. Howitt P.O. Box 6514, Wellington, New Zealand

SOUTH AFRICA

Historical Firearms Soc. of South Africa
P.O. Box 145, 7725 Newlands, Republic of South Africa
South African Reloaders Assn.
Box 27128, Sunnyside, Pretoria 0132, South Africa

PERIODICAL PUBLICATIONS

Airgun World
10 Sheet St., Windsor, Berks., SL4 1BG, England. $23 for 12 issues. Monthly magazine catering exclusively to the airgun enthusiast.

Alaska Magazine
Alaska Northwest Pub. Co., Box 4-EEE, Anchorage, AK 99509. $18.00 yr. Hunting and fishing articles.

The American Blade*
American Blade Corp., 112 Lee Parkway Dr., Suite 104, Chattanooga, TN 37421. $10.00 yr. Add $6 f. foreign subscription. A magazine for all enthusiasts of the edged blade.

American Field†
222 W. Adams St., Chicago, IL. 60606. $18.00 yr. Field dogs and trials, occasional gun and hunting articles.

American Firearms Industry
Nat'l. Assn. of Federally Licensed Firearms Dealers, 7001 No. Clark St., Chicago, IL 60626. $15 yr. For firearms dealers & distributors.

The American Handgunner
591 Camino de la Reina, San Diego, CA 92108. $9.95 yr. Articles for handgun enthusiasts, collectors and hunters.

The American Hunter (M)
Natl. Rifle Assn., 1600 Rhode Island Ave. N.W., Washington, DC 20036. $15.00 yr. Wide scope of hunting articles.

The American Rifleman (M)
National Rifle Assn., 1600 Rhode Island Ave., N.W., Wash., DC 20036. $15.00 yr. Firearms articles of all kinds.

The American Shotgunner
P.O. Box 3351, Reno, NV 89505. $15.00 yr. Official publ. of the American Assn. of Shotgunning. Industrial shooting, reloading, used gun classifieds. Membership and benefits w. yrly. subscr.

The American West*
Amer. West Publ. Co., P.O. Box 40310, Tucson, AZ 85717. $15.00 yr.

Arms Collecting (Q)
Museum Restoration Service P.O. Drawer 390, Bloomfield, Ont., Canada K0K IG0. $7.50 yr.

Australian Shooters' Journal
Box 1064 G.P.O., Adelaide, SA 5001, Australia. $20 yr. locally; $25 yr. overseas. (U.S. distr.: Blacksmith Corp., P.O. Box 424, Southport, CT 06490; $35 yr., samples $3.50.) Hunting and shooting articles.

Black Powder Times
P.O. Box 842, Mount Vernon, WA 98273. $15.00 for 12 issues. Newspaper for blackpowder activities; test reports.

The Buckskin Report
P. O. 885, Big Timber, MT 59011. $15.00 yr. Articles for the blackpowder shooter.

Deer Unlimited*
P.O. Box 509, Clemson, SC 29631. $12.00 yr.

Deutsches Waffen Journal
Journal-Verlag Schwend GmbH, Postfach 100340, D7170 Schwabisch Hall, Germany. DM48.00 yr. plus DM10.80 postage. Antique and modern arms. German text.

Ducks Unlimited, Inc. (M)
P.O. Box 66300, Chicago, IL 60666.

Enforcement Journal (Q)
Frank J. Schira, editor, Natl. Police Officers Assn., 609 West Main St., Louisville, KY 40202 $6.00 yr.

The Field†
The Harmsworth Press Ltd., Carmelite House, London E.C.4 England. $88.00 yr. Hunting and shooting articles, and all country sports.

Field & Stream
CBS Publications, 1515 Broadway, New York, N.Y. 10036. $9.94 yr. Articles on firearms plus hunting and fishing.

Fur-Fish-Game
A. R. Harding Pub. Co., 2878 E. Main St., Columbus, OH 43209. $7.00 yr. "Gun Rack" column by Don Zutz.

Gray's Sporting Journal*
Gray's Sporting Journal Co., 42 Bay Rd., So. Hamilton, MA 01982. $19.50 f. 4 Issues. Hunting and fishing journals.

Gun Journal*
Charlton Publications, Inc., Charlton Bldg., Derby, CT 06418. $7.50 for six issues. Guns, hunting and shooting articles.

The Gun Report
World Wide Gun Report, Inc., Box 111, Aledo, IL 61231. $20.00 yr. For the gun collector.

The Gunrunner
Div. of Kexco Publ. Co. Ltd., Box 565, Lethbridge, Alb., Canada T1J 3Z4. $6.00 yr Newspaper, listing everything from antiques to artillery.

Gun Week
Hawkeye Publishing, Inc., P. O. Box 411, Station C, Buffalo NY 14209. $12.00 yr. U.S. and possessions; $16.00 yr. other countries. Tabloid paper on guns, hunting, shooting.

Gun World
Gallant Publishing Co., 34249 Camino Capistrano, Capistrano Beach, CA 92624. $12.00 yr. For the hunting, reloading and shooting enthusiast.

Guns & Ammo
Petersen Pub. Co., 8490 Sunset Blvd., Los Angeles, CA 90069. $11.94 yr. Guns, shooting, and technical articles.

Guns
Guns Magazine, 591 Camino de la Reina, San Diego, CA 92108. $11.95 yr. Articles for gun collectors, hunters and shooters.

Guns Review
Ravenhill Pub. Co. Ltd., Box 35, Standard House, Bonhill St., London E.C. 2A 4DA, England. $34.70 USA & Canada yr. For collectors and shooters.

Handloader*
Wolfe Pub. Co. Inc., Box 3030, Prescott, AZ 86302 $13.00 yr. The journal of ammunition reloading.

International Shooting Sport*
Union Internationale de Tir, Bavariaring 21, D-8000 Munich 2, Germany. Europe: (Deutsche Mark) DM39.00 yr., p.p.; outside Europe: DM45.00. For the International target shooter.

The Journal of the Arms & Armour Society (M)
Joseph G. Rosa (Secy.), 17 Woodville Gardens, Ruislip, Middlesex HA4 7NB, England. $16.00 yr. Articles for the historian and collector.

Journal of the Historical Breechloading Smallarms Assn.
Publ. annually, Imperial War Museum, Lambeth Road, London SE1 6HZ, England. $8 yr. Articles for the collector plus mailings of lecture transcripts, short articles on specific arms, reprints, newsletter, etc.; a surcharge is made f. airmail.

Knife World
Knife World Publications, P.O. Box 3395, Knoxville, TN 37917. $8.00 yr., $14.00 2 yrs. Published monthly f. knife enthusiasts and collectors. Articles on custom and factory knives; other knife related interests.

Law and Order
Law and Order Magazine, 5526 N. Elston Ave., Chicago, IL 60630 $11.00 yr. Articles on weapons for law enforcement, etc.

The Lookout(M)
Canadian Black Powder Federation Newsletter, P.O. Box 2876, Postal Sta. "A", Moncton, N.B. E1C 8T8, Canada. 5 issues per yr. w. $10 membership.

MAN Magazine
SA Man (Pty) Ltd., United Building, St. Georges St., Cape Town, Rep. of South Africa. R14 f. 12 issues. Hunting, shooting and knife articles.

Man At Arms*
222 West Exchange St., Providence, RI 02903. $18.00 yr. The magazine of arms collecting-investing, with excellent brief articles for the collector of antique and modern firearms.

Muzzle Blasts (M)
National Muzzle Loading Rifle Assn. P.O. Box 67, Friendship, IN 47021. $14.00 yr. For the black powder shooter.

The Muzzleloader Magazine*
Rebel Publishing Co., Inc., Route 5, Box 347-M, Texarkana, TX 75503. $8.50 U.S., $9.50 foreign yr. The publication for black powder shooters.

National Defense (M)*
American Defense Preparedness Assn., Rosslyn Center, Suite 900, 1700 North Moore St., Arlington, VA 22209. $22.50 yr. Articles on military-related topics, including weapons, materials technology, management and policy.

National Rifle Assn. Journal (British) (Q)
Natl. Rifle Assn. (BR.), Bisley Camp, Brookwood, Woking, Surrey, England. GU24 OPB. $12.00 inc. air postage.

National Wildlife*
Natl. Wildlife Fed., 1412 16th St. N.W., Washington, DC 20036. $9.50 yr. (6 issues); *International Wildlife*, 6 issues, $9.50 yr. Both, $14.50 yr., plus membership benefits. Write to this addr., attn.: Promotion Dept., for the proper information.

New Zealand Wildlife (Q)
New Zealand Deerstalkers Assoc. Inc., P.O. Box 6514, Wellington, N.Z. $5.00 U.S. and Canada, elsewhere on application. Hunting and shooting articles.

Northwestern Sportsman
Box 1208, Big Timber, MT 59011. $10.00 yr.

Outdoor Life
Times Mirror Magazines, Inc., 380 Madison Ave., New York, NY 10017. $11.94 yr. Shooting columns by Jim Carmichel, and others.

Point Blank
Citizens Committee for the Right to Keep and Bear Arms (sent to contributors) 1601 114th S.E., Suite 151, Bellevue, WA 98004

Police Command (M)
1100 NE 125th St., N. Miami, FL 33161

The Police Marksman*
305 So. Lawrence St. Montgomery, AL 36104. $15.00 yr.

Police Times (M)
1100 N.E. 125th St., No. Miami, Fla. 33161.

Popular Mechanics
Hearst Corp., 224 W. 57th St., New York, NY 10019. $9.97 yr., $15.97 Canada and foreign. Hunting, shooting and camping articles.

Precision Shooting
Precision Shooting, Inc., 133 State St., Augusta, ME 04330. $9.00 yr. Journal of the International Benchrest Shooters and target shooting in general.

Rifle*
Wolfe Publishing Co. Inc., Box 3030, Prescott, AZ 86302. $13.00 yr. Journal of the NBRSA. The magazine for shooters.

Rod & Rifle Magazine
Lithographic Serv. Ltd., P. O. Box 38-138, Petone, New Zealand. $10.00 yr. (6 issues) Hunting and shooting articles.

Saga
Gambi Publ., 333 Johnson Ave., Brooklyn, N.Y. 11206. $13.50 yr. U.S.

Second Amendment Reporter
Second Amendment Fdn., Bellefield Off. Pk., 1601—114th St. SE, Suite 157, Bellevue, WA 98004. $15.00 yr. (non-contributors).

Shooter's Journal*
McMullen Publishing Inc., 2145 W. LaPalma, Anaheim, CA 92801 $11.00 yr.

The Shooting Industry
Publisher's Dev. Corp., 591 Camino de la Reina, Suite 200, San Diego, CA 92108. $25.00 yr. To the trade $12.50.

Shooting Magazine
10 Sheet St., Windsor, Berksh., SL4 1BG England. $25.00 for 12 issues. Monthly journal catering mainly to claypigeon shooters.

The Shooting Times & Country Magazine (England) †
10 Sheet St., Windsor, Berkshire SL4 1BG, England. $49.40 yr. (52 issues). Game shooting, wild fowling, hunting, game fishing and firearms articles.

Shooting Times
PJS Publications, News Plaza, P.O. Box 1790, Peoria, IL 61656. $11.95 yr. Guns, shooting, reloading; articles on every gun activity.

The Shotgun News‡
Snell Publishing Co., Box 669, Hastings, NB 68901. $9.50 yr. Sample copy $2.00. Gun ads of all kinds.

Shotgun West
2052 Broadway, Santa Monica, CA 90404. $8.50 yr. Trap, Skeet and international shooting, scores, articles, schedules.

The Sixgunner (M)
Handgun Hunters International, P. O. Box 357 MAG, Bloomingdale, OH 43910

The Skeet Shooting Review
National Skeet Shooting Assn., P.O. Box 28188, San Antonio, TX 78228. $12.00 yr. (Assn. membership of $20.00 includes mag.) Competition results, personality profiles of top Skeet shooters, how-to articles, technical, reloading information.

Sporting Goods Business
Gralla Publications, 1515 Broadway, New York, NY 10036. Trade journal.

The Sporting Goods Dealer
1212 No. Lindbergh Blvd., St. Louis, Mo. 63166. $9.00 yr. The sporting goods trade journal.

Sporting Gun
Bretton Court, Bretton, Peterborough PE3 8DZ, England. £11.30 (airmail £23.50) yr. For the game and clay enthusiasts.

Sports Afield
The Hearst Corp., 250 W. 55th St., New York, N.Y. 10019. $11.97 yr. Grits Gresham on firearms, ammunition and hunting.

Sports Merchandiser
A W.R.C. Smith Publication, 1760 Peachtree Rd. NW, Atlanta, GA 30357. Trade Journal.

TACARMI
Via Volta 60, 20090 Cusago (Milan), Italy. $37.20 yr. Antique and modern guns. (Italian text.)

Trap & Field
1100 Waterway Blvd., Indianapolis, IN 46202. $14.00 yr. Official publ. Amateur Trapshooting Assn. Scores, averages, trapshooting articles.

Turkey Call* (M)
Natl. Wild Turkey Federation, Inc., P.O. Box 467, Edgefield, SC 29824. $12.00 w. membership.

The U.S. Handgunner* (M)
U.S. Revolver Assn., 59 Alvin St., Springfield, MA 01104. $5.00 yr. General handgun and competition articles. Bi-monthly sent to members.

Waterfowler's World*
P.O. Box 38306, Germantown, TN 38138. $12.00 yr.

Wisconsin Sportsman*
Wisconsin Sportsman, Inc., P.O. Box 2266, Oshkosh, WI 54903. $7.50.

* Published bi-monthly † Published weekly ‡ Published twice per month. All others are published monthly.
M Membership requirements; write for details. Q Published Quarterly.

Shooting Sports Booklets & Pamphlets

Basic Pistol Marksmanship—Textbook for basic courses in pistol shooting. 50¢[2]

Basic Rifle Marksmanship—Text for a basic course in shooting the rifle. 50¢[2]

The Cottontail Rabbit—56-page rundown on America's most popular hunting target. Where to find him, how to hunt him, how to help him. Bibliography included. $2 ea.[4]

The Elk—125-page report on the hunting and management of this game animal, more properly called *wapiti*. Extensive biblio. $2 ea.[4]

Fact Pact II—Authoritative and complete study on gun use and ownership. This is a valuable 102-page reference. $2 ea.[1]

For The Young Hunter—A 32-page booklet giving fundamental information on the sport. 50¢ each.[4]

Free Films—Brochure listing outdoor movies available to sportsmen's clubs. Free[1]

Fundamentals of Claybird Shooting—A 39-page booklet explaining the basics of Skeet and trap in non-technical terms. Many diagrams. 25¢[5]

Game, Gunners and Biology—A thumbnail history of American wildlife conservation. $2 ea.[4]

Gray Fox and Squirrels-112-page paperbound illustrated book giving full rundown on the squirrel families named. Extensive bibliography. $2 ea.[4]

Hunting Dogs—An excellent primer on hunting dogs for the novice hunter. 50¢ ea.[4]

The Mallard—80-page semi-technical report on this popular duck. Life cycle, laws and management, hunting—even politics as they affect this bird—are covered. Bibliography. $2 ea.[4]

The Mourning Dove—Illustrated booklet includes life history, conservation and hunting of the mourning dove. $2[4]

NRA Air Gun Training Program—A "self-teaching" precision air rifle and pistol manual.$1[2]

NRA Hunter Safety & Conservation Program Instructor's Manual—Teaching outlined and sources of information for hunter safety and conservation instructor, including exercises and demonstrations. 50¢[2]

NRA Hunter Safety & Conservation Program Student Manual (Revised)—Textbook for use in creating safer hunting environment and explain hunter's involvement in wildlife conservation. 50¢[2]

NRA Illustrated International Shooting Handbook—18 major articles detailing shooting under ISU rules, training methods, etc. NRA, Washington, DC, 1964. $2.50 ea. ($1.50 to NRA members.)[2]

Principles of Game Management—A 25-page booklet surveying in popular manner such subjects as hunting regulations, predator control, game refuges and habitat restoration. Single copies free, 25¢ each in bulk.[4]

The Ring-Necked Pheasant—Popular distillation of much of the technical literature on the "ringneck." 104-page paperbound book, appropriately illustrated. Bibliography included. $2 ea.[2]

Ruffed Grouse, by John Madson—108-page booklet on the life history, management and hunting of *Bonasa umbellus* in its numerous variations. Extensive biblio. $2[4]

Trap or Skeet Fundamentals—Handbooks explaining fundamentals of these two sports, complete with explicit diagrams to start beginners off right. Free.[3]

The White-Tailed Deer—Interesting fact-filled booklet gives life history, conservation and hunting information on this popular game animal. $2[4]

[1]National Shooting Sports Foundation, Inc., 1075 Post Road, Riverside, CT 06878

[2]National Rifle Association of America, 1600 Rhode Island Ave., Washington, DC 20036

[3]Remington Arms Company, Dept. C, Bridgeport, CT 06602

[4]Olin Corp., Conservation Dept., East Alton, IL 62024

[5]Winchester-Western, Shotgun Shooting Promotion, P.O. Box 30-275, New Haven, CT 06511

The Arms Library for

COLLECTOR · HUNTER · SHOOTER · OUTDOORSMAN

A selection of books—old, new and forthcoming—for everyone in the arms field, with a brief description by . . . JOE RILING

NEW BOOKS

(Alphabetically, no categories)

The Airgun Book, by John Walter, Stackpole Books, Harrisburg, Pa., 1981. 320 pp., illus. $19.95.

Provides the airgun enthusiast with a much-needed basic book on his subject.

American Engravers, by C. Roger Bleile, Beinfeld Publishing, Inc., North Hollywood, CA, 1980. 191 pp., illus. $29.95.

A comprehensive overview of those men (and women) who are working in the gun and knife engraving field.

American Knives; The First History and Collector's Guide, by Harold L. Peterson, The Gun Room Press, Highland Park, NJ, 1980. 178 pp., illus. $15.00.

A reprint of this 1958 classic. Covers all types of American knives.

American Police Handgun Training, by Charles R. Skillen and Mason Williams, Charles C. Thomas, Springfield, IL, 1980. 216 pp., illus. $13.00.

Deals comprehensively with all phases of current handgun training procedures in America.

Askins on Pistols and Revolvers, by Col. Charles Askins, NRA Books, Wash., D.C., 1980. 144 pp., illus. Paper covers. $8.95.

A book full of practical advice, shooting tips, technical analysis and stories of guns in action.

Bannerman Catalogue of Military Goods—1927, replica edition, DBI Books, Inc., Northfield, IL, 1981. 384 pp., illus. Paper covers. $12.95.

Fascinating insights into one of the more colorful American arms merchants.

Beretta: The World's Oldest Industrial Dynasty, by Marco Morin and Robert Held, Acquafresca Editrice, Chiasso, Switzerland, 1980. 283 pp., illus. $44.95.

This book covers the guns made by this famous firm 1530 to the present date.

The Black Powder Handgun, by Sam Fadala, DBI Books, Inc., Northfield, IL, 1981. 288 pp., illus. Paper covers. $8.95.

The author covers this oldtime weapon in all its forms: pistol and six-shooter in both small and large bore, target and hunting.

The Book of Shooting for Sport and Skill, edited by Frederick Wilkinson, Crown Publishers Inc., New York, NY, 1980. 348 pp., illus. $19.95.

A comprehensive and practical encyclopedia of gunmanship by a squad of over twenty experts from both sides of the Atlantic.

British Gunmakers; Their Trade Cards, Cases and Equipment 1760-1860, by W. Keith Neal and D. H. L. Back, The Compton Press, Wiltshire, England, 1980. 128 pp., illus. $55.00.

Provides a photographic index of trade cards together with an historical account of the case and its contents.

British Military Pistols 1603-1888, by R. E. Brooker, Jr., Le Magazin Royal Press, Coral Gables, FL, 1978. 139 pp., illus. $20.00.

Covers flintlock and percussion pistols plus cartridge revolvers up to the smokeless powder period.

The Bullet's Flight, by Franklin Mann, Wolfe Publishing Co., Inc., Prescott, AZ, 1980. 391 pp., illus. $22.00.

The ballistics of small arms. A reproduction of Harry Pope's personal copy of this classic with his marginal notes.

Classic Bowie Knives, by Robert Abels, The Gun Room Press, Highland Park, NJ, 1980. 96 pp., illus. $15.00.

A reprint of the classic work on these American knives.

Clyde Baker's Modern Gunsmithing, revised by John E. Traister, Stackpole Books, Harrisburg, Pa., 1981. 530 pp., illus. $19.95.

A revision of the classic work on gunsmithing.

Death in the Silent Places, by Peter Hathaway Capstick, St. Martin's Press, New York, NY, 1981. 243 pp., illus. $13.95.

The author recalls the extraordinary careers of the legendary hunters such as Corbett, Karamojo Bell, Stigand and others.

The Desert Bighorn, edited by Gale Monson and Lowell Sumner, University of Arizona Press, Tucson, AZ, 1980. 392 pp., illus. $27.50.

Life history, ecology and management of the Desert Bighorn.

The Duck-Huntingest Gentlemen, by Keith C. Russell et al, Winchester Press, Tulsa, OK, 1980. 284 pp., illus. $14.95.

A collection of waterfowling stories.

Fighting Knives, by Frederick J. Stephens, Arco Publishing Co., Inc., New York, NY, 1980. 127 pp., illus. $14.95.

An illustrated guide to fighting knives and military survival weapons of the world.

Firearms Assembly 3: The NRA Guide to Rifles and Shotguns, NRA Books, Wash., D.C., 1980. 264 pp., illus. Paper covers. $8.95.

Text and illus. explaining the takedown of 125 rifles and shotguns, domestic and foreign.

Firearms Assembly 4: The NRA Guide to Pistols and Revolvers, NRA Books, Wash., D.C., 1980. 253 pp., illus. Paper covers. $8.95.

Text and illus. explaining the takedown of 124 pistol and revolver models, domestic and foreign.

Firearms in Colonial America: The Impact on History and Technology 1492-1792, by M. L. Brown, Smithsonian Institution Press, Wash., D.C., 1980. 449 pp., illus. $65.00.

An in-depth coverage of the history and technology of firearms in Colonial North America.

The Firearms Price Guide, 2nd Edition, by D. Byron, Crown Publishers, New York, NY, 1981. 448 pp., illus. Paper covers. $9.95.

An essential guide for every collector and dealer.

The .45-70 Springfield, by Albert J. Frasca and Robert H. Hall, Springfield Publishing Co., Northridge, CA, 1980. 380 pp., illus. $39.95.

A carefully researched book on the trapdoor, including all experimental and very rare models.

Gallant Grouse, by Cecil E. and Dorothy Heacox, David McKay Co., Inc., New York, NY, 1981. 171 pp., illus. $14.95.

All about the hunting and natural history of Old Ruff.

German Military Handguns, 1879-1918, by John Walter, Fortress Publications, Inc., Stoney Creek, Ontario, Canada 1980. 80 pp., illus. $18.95.

A fully illustrated study of the principle German handguns of the Second Reich.

Goose Hunting, by Charles L. Cadieux, Stone Wall Press, Inc., Boston, Mass., 1979. 197 pp., illus. $14.00.

Personal stories of goose hunting from Quebec to Mexico.

The Gun Digest, 1982, 36th Edition, edited by Ken Warner, DBI Books, Inc., Northfield, IL, 1981. 448 pp., illus. Paper covers. $11.95.

The world's greatest gun book in its 36th annual edition.

The Gun Digest Book of Firearms Assembly/Disassembly, Part V: Shotguns, by J. B. Wood, DBI Books, Inc., Northfield, IL, 1980. 288 pp., illus. Paper covers. $8.95.

A professional presentation on the disassembly and reassembly of shotguns.

Gun Digest Book of Gunsmithing Tools and Their Uses, by John E. Traister, DBI Books, Inc., Northfield, IL, 1980. 256 pp., illus. Paper covers. $7.95.

The how, when and why of tools for amateur and professional gunsmiths and gun tinkerers.

Gun Digest Book of Modern Gun Values, 3rd Edition, by Jack Lewis, ed. by Harold A. Murtz, DBI Books, Inc., Northfield, IL, 1981. 384 pp., illus. Paper covers. $9.95.

Expanded to include all non-military guns introduced in the U.S. between 1900 and 1978.

Gun Digest Review of Custom Guns, edited by Ken Warner, DBI Books, Inc., Northfield, IL, 1980. 256 pp., illus. Paper covers. $8.95.

An extensive look at the art of custom gun making.

Guns Illustrated, 1982, 14th Edition, edited by Harold A. Murtz, DBI Books, Inc., Northfield, IL, 1981. 288 pp., illus. Paper covers. $9.95.

Technical articles for gun enthusiasts plus a complete illustrated catalog of all current guns, ammo and accessories including specifications and prices.

Guns, Pistols, Revolvers, by Heinrich Muller, St. Martin's Press, New York, NY, 1980. 224 pp., illus. $29.95.

A comprehensive overview of the various types of hand and small arms in use from the 14th to the 19th century.

Hal Swiggett on North American Deer, by Hal Swiggett, Jolex Inc., Oakland, NJ, 1980. 272 pp., illus. Paper covers. $8.95.

Where and how to hunt all species of North American deer.

Hallock's .45 Auto Handbook, by Ken Hallock, The Mihan Co., Oklahoma City, OK, 1981. 178 pp., illus. $11.95.

For gunsmiths, dealers, collectors and serious hobbyists.

Handbook of Metallic Cartridge Reloading, by Edward Matunas, Winchester Press, Tulsa, OK, 1981. 272 pp., illus. $14.95.

Up-to-date, comprehensive loading tables prepared by the four major powder manufacturers.

Handloading, by Bill Davis Jr., NRA Books, Wash., D.C., 1980. 400 pp., illus. Paper covers. $12.95.

A complete update and expansion of the NRA Handloader's Guide.

The History of Winchester Firearms 1866-1980, edited by Duncan Barnes, et al, Winchester Press, Tulsa, OK, 1980. 237 pp., illus. $21.95.

Specifications on all Winchester firearms. Background information on design, manufacture and use.

Hornady Handbook of Cartridge Reloading, Hornady Mfg. Co., Grand Island, NE, 1981, 650 pp., illus. $9.95.

New edition of this famous reloading handbook. Latest loads, ballistic information, etc.

How to Make Your Own Knives, by Jim Mayes, Everest House, New York, NY, 1978. 191 pp., illus. $7.95.

An illustrated step-by-step guide for the sportsman and home hobbyist.

Hunter's Digest, 2nd Edition, edited by Erwin A. Bauer, DBI Books, Inc., Northfield, IL, 1980. 288 pp., illus. Paper covers. $7.95.

The best ways, times and places to hunt the most popular species of large and small game animals of North America.

Hunting the Whitetail Deer, by Norm Nelson, David McKay Co., Inc., New York, NY, 1980. 212 pp., illus., $12.95.

How to bring home North America's No. 1 big-game animal.

Kentucky Knife Traders Manual No. 6, by R. B. Ritchie, Hindman, KY, 1980. 217 pp., illus. Paper covers. $10.00.

Guide for dealers, collectors and traders listing pocketknives and razor values.

Knives '81, edited by Ken Warner, DBI Books, Inc., Northfield, IL, 1981. 192 pp., illus. Paper covers. $5.95.

A new annual guide that will help to define this rapidly growing field.

The Krieghoff Parabellum, by Randall Gibson, Randall Gibson, Midland, TX, 1980. 280 pp., illus. $30.00.

A definitive work on the most desirable model Luger pistol.

Learn Gunsmithing, by John Traister, Winchester Press, Tulsa, OK, 1980. 202 pp., illus. $12.95.

The troubleshooting method of gunsmithing for the home gunsmith and professional alike.

Lyman Cast Bullet Handbook, 3rd Edition, edited by C. Kenneth Ramage, Lyman Publications, Middlefield, CT, 1980. 416 pp., illus. Paper covers. $12.95.

Information on more than 5,000 tested cast bullet loads and 19 pages of trajectory and wind drift tables for cast bullets.

Lyman Centennial Journal 1878-1978, edited by C. Kenneth Ramage and Edward R. Bryant, Lyman Publications, Middlefield, CT, 1980. 222 pp., illus. Paper covers. $10.95.

The history of the Lyman company and its products in both words and pictures.

Modern Firearm Engravings, by Mario Abbiatico, Edizioni Artistiche Italiane, Gardone Valtrompia, Italy, 1980. 284 pp., illus. $65.00.

A much needed work on the art of gun embellishment. English text.

Modern Guns Identification and Values, 3rd Edition, edited by Russell and Steve Quertermous, Collector Books, Paducah, KY, 1981. 432 pp., illus. Paper covers.

A catalog of well over 20,000 guns with important identifying information and facts.

Military Small Arms Ammunition of the World, 1945-1980, by Peter Labbett, Presidio Press, San Rafael, CA, 1980. 128 pp., illus. $18.95.

An up-to-date international guide to the correct identification of ammunition by caliber, type and origin.

The Official 1981 Price Guide to Collector Knives, by James F. Parker and J. Bruce Voyles, House of Collectibles, Orlando, FL, 1981. 533 pp., illus. Paper covers. $9.95.

Buying and selling prices on collector pocket and sheath knives.

The Pennsylvania-Kentucky Rifle, by Henry J. Kauffman, Crown Publishers, New York, NY, 1981. 293 pp., illus. $9.98.

A colorful account of the history and gunsmiths who produced the first American rifle superior to those brought from the Old Country.

Reloading for Shotgunners, edited by Robert S. L. Anderson, DBI Books, Inc., Northfield, IL, 1981. 224 pp., illus. Paper covers. $8.95.

Articles on wildcatting, slug reloading, patterning, skeet and trap loads, etc., as well as extensive load tables.

Revolver Guide, by George C. Nonte Jr., Stoeger Publishing Co., So., Hackensack, NJ, 1980. 288 pp., illus. Paper covers. $8.95.

Complete, fully illustrated guide to selecting, shooting, caring for and collecting revolvers of all types.

Rifles in Colonial America, Volume I, by George Shumway, George Shumway, York, PA, 1980. 352 pp., illus. $49.50.

An extensive photographic study of American longrifles made in the late Colonial period, the Revolutionary period, and the post-Revolutionary period.

Sheep and Sheep Hunting, by Jack O'Connor, Winchester Press, Tulsa, OK, 1980. 308 pp., illus. $12.95.

Memorial edition of the definitive book on the wild sheep.

Shooter's Bible No. 73, 1982 Edition, ed. by R. F. Scott, Stoeger Publ. Co., So. Hackensack, NJ. 1981. 575 pp., illus. Paper covers. $8.95.

Annually published guide to firearms, ammunition and accessories.

Shooting Facts & Fancies, by Gough Thomas, Adam & Charles Black, London, 1980. 280 pp., illus. $21.95.

An enlarged version of the author's Second Gun Book.

Shotgun Digest 2nd Edition, edited by Jack Lewis and Jack Mitchell, DBI Books, Inc., Northfield, IL, 1980. 288 pp., illus. Paper covers. $8.95.

An all-new look at shotguns by a double-barreled team of writers.

The Trophy Hunters, by Col Allison, Murray Books, Ultimo, NSW, Australia, 1979. 240 pp., illus. $20.00.

Action-packed tales of hunting big game trophies around the world—1860 to today.

Still More Single Shot Rifles, by James J. Grant, Pioneer Press, Union City, TN, 1979. 211 pp., illus. $17.50.

A sequel to the author's classic works on single shot rifles.

Turkey Hunting with Charlie Elliott, by Charles Elliott, David McKay Co., Inc., 1979. 275 pp., illus. $14.95.

The old professor tells all about America's big-game bird.

20 Great Trophy Hunts, by John O. Cartier, David McKay Co., Inc., New York, NY, 1981. 320 pp., illus. $17.95.

The cream of outstanding true-life adventure stories.

Uganda Safaris, by Brian Herne, Winchester Press, Tulsa, OK, 1979. 236 pp., illus. $12.95.

The chronicle of a professional hunter's adventures in Africa.

The Winchester Book, by George Madis, Art & Reference House, Lancaster, TX, 1980. 638 pp., illus. $39.50.

A greatly enlarged edition of this most informative book on these prized American arms.

ballistics and handloading

ABC's of Reloading, 2nd Edition, by Dean A. Grennell, DBI Books, Inc., Northfield, IL, 1980. 288 pp., illus. Paper covers. $8.95.

A natural, logical, thorough set of directions on how to prepare shotgun shells, rifle and pistol cases prior to reloading.

American Ammunition and Ballistics, by Edward A. Matunas, Winchester Press, New York, NY, 1979. 288 pp., illus. $13.95.

A complete reference book covering all presently manufactured and much discontinued American rimfire, centerfire, and shotshell ammunition.

Ballistic Science for the Law Enforcement Officer, by Charles G. Wilber, Ph.D., Charles C. Thomas, Springfield, IL, 1977. 309 pp., illus. $30.00.

A scientific study of the ballistics of civilian firearms.

Cartridges of the World 4th Edition, by Frank C. Barnes, DBI Books, Inc., Northfield, IL, 352 pp., illus. Paper covers. $9.95.

Gives the history, dimensions, performance and physical characteristics for more than 1,000 different cartridges.

Cast Bullets, by Col. E. H. Harrison, A publication of the National Rifle Association of America, Washington, DC, 1979. 144 pp., illus. Paper covers. $8.95.

An authoritative guide to bullet casting techniques and ballistics.

The Complete Book of Practical Handloading, by John Wooters, Winchester Press, NY, 1976. 320 pp., illus. $13.95

An up-to-the-minute guide for the rifleman and shotgunner.

Computer for Handloaders, by Homer Powley. A slide rule plus 12 page instruction book for use in finding charge, most efficient powder and velocity for any modern centerfire rifle. $5.50

Firearms Identification, by Dr. J. H. Mathews, Charles C. Thomas, Springfield, IL, 1973 3 vol. set. A massive, carefully researched, authoritative work published as:

Vol. I. **The Laboratory Examination of Small Arms.** . . . 400 pp., illus. $56.75.

Vol. II. **Original Photographs and Other Illustrations of Handguns.** 492 pp., illus. $56.75.

Vol. III. **Data on Rifling Characteristics of Handguns and Rifles.** 730 pp., illus. $88.00.

Firearms Investigation, Identification and Evidence, by J. S. Hatcher, Frank J. Jury and Jac Weller. Stackpole Books, Harrisburg, PA, 1977. 536 pp. illus. $22.50.

Reprint of the 1957 printing of this classic book on forensic ballistics. Indispensable for those interested in firearms identification and criminology.

Game Loads and Practical Ballistics For The American Hunter, by Bob Hagel, Alfred A. Knopf, NY, NY, 1978. 315 pp., illus., hardbound. $12.95.

Everything a hunter needs to know about ballistics and performance of commercial hunting loads.

Handbook for Shooters and Reloaders, by P. O. Ackley, Salt Lake City, UT, 1970. *Vol. 1,* 567 pp., illus. $9.75. *Vol. II,* a new printing with specific new material. 495 pp., illus. $9.75. Both volumes. Paper covers $19.50.

Handloader's Digest, 8th Edition, edited by John T. Amber, DBI Books Inc., Northfield, IL, 1978. 288 pp., illus. Paper covers. $8.95.

This completely new edition contains the latest data on ballistics, maximum loads, new tools, equipment, etc., plus a fully illus. catalog section, current prices and specifications.

Handloader's Digest Bullet and Powder Update, edited by Ken Warner, DBI Books, Inc., Northfield, IL, 1980. 128 pp., illus. Paper covers. $4.95.

An update on the last ed. of "Handloader's Digest" the 8th edition. Included is a round-up piece on new bullets, another on new primers and powders plus five shooters' reports on the various types of bullets.

Handloading for Handgunners, by Geo. C. Nonte, DBI Books, Inc., Northfield, IL, 1978. 288 pp., illus. Paper covers, $7.95.

An expert tells the ins and outs of this specialized facet of reloading.

Handloading for Hunters, by Don Zutz, Winchester Press, NY, 1977. 288 pp., illus. $14.95.

Precise mixes and loads for different types of game and for various hunting situations with rifle and shotgun.

Hodgdon "New" Data Manual No. 23, Hodgdon Powder Co., Shawnee Mission, KS, 1977. 192 pp., illus. $4.95.

New data on Pyrodex and black powder. New section on how to reload for beginners. Information on rifle, pistol, shotgun and lead bullet loads.

The Home Guide to Cartridge Conversions, by Maj. George C. Nonte, Jr., The Gun Room Press, Highland Park, NJ, 1976. 404 pp., illus. $15.00

Revised and updated version of Nonte's definitive work on the alteration of cartridge cases for use in guns for which they were not intended.

Hornady Handbook of Cartridge Reloading, Rifle-Pistol, Vol. 2, by J. W. Hornady, Hornady Mfg. Co., Inc., Grand Island, NB, 1973. 512 pp., illus. $5.95.

A comprehensive guide to handloading and shooting; nearly 100 rifle/pistol cartridge combinations. Thousands of loads.

Lyman Black Powder Handbook, ed. by C. Kenneth Ramage, Lyman Products for Shooters, Middlefield, CT, 1975. 239 pp., illus. Paper covers. $10.95.

The most comprehensive load information ever published for the modern black powder shooter.

Lyman Handbook No. 45. Lyman Gunsight Corp., Middlefield, CT, 1967. $10.95.

Latest edition of a favorite reference for ammunition handloaders, whether novice or veteran.

Lyman Pistol & Revolver Handbook, edited by C. Kenneth Ramage, Lyman Publications, Middlefield, CT, 1978. 280 pp., illus. Paper covers. $6.95.

An extensive reference of load and trajectory data for the handgun.

Lyman Shotshell Handbook 2nd ed., edited by C. Kenneth Ramage, Lyman Gunsight Corp., Middlefield, CT, 1976. 288 pp., illus., paper covers. $6.95.

Devoted exclusively to shotshell reloading, this book considers: gauge, shell length, brand, case, loads, buckshot, etc. plus an excellent reference section. Some color illus.

Metallic Reloading Basics, edited by C. Kenneth Ramage, Lyman Publications, Middlefield, CT, 1976. 60 pp., illus. Paper covers. $1.95.

Provides the beginner with loading data on popular bullet weights within the most popular calibers.

Modern Handloading, by Maj. Geo. C. Nonte. Winchester Press, NY, 1972. 416 pp., illus. $10.00.

Covers all aspects of metallic and shotshell ammunition loading, plus more loads than any book in print; state and Federal laws, reloading tools, glossary.

Nosler Reloading Manual Number One, compiled and edited by Bob Nosler, Nosler Bullets, Inc., Bend, OR, 1976. 234 pp., illus. $5.95.

Provides thorough coverage of powder data, specifically tailored to the well-known Nosler partition and solid base bullet designs in all weights and calibers.

Pet Loads, by Ken Waters, Wolfe Publ. Co., Inc., Prescott, AZ, 1979. Unpaginated. In looseleaf form. $29.50.

A collection of the last 13 years' articles on more than 70 metallic cartridges. Most calibers featured with updated material.

Pocket Manual for Shooters and Reloaders, by P. O. Ackley. publ. by author, Salt Lake City, UT, 1964. 176 pp., illus., spiral bound. $4.95.

Good coverage on standard and wildcat cartridges and related firearms in popular calibers.

Sierra Bullets Reloading Manual, Second Edition, by Robert Hayden et al, The Leisure Group, Inc., Santa Fe Springs, CA, 1978. 700 pp., illus. Loose-leaf binder. $11.95.

Includes all material in the original manual and its supplement updated, plus a new section on loads for competitive shooting.

Small-Caliber Ammunition Identification Guide Volume I: Small Arms Cartridges up to 15mm, by R. T. Huntington, Military Arms Research Service, San Jose, CA, 1978. 204 pp., illus. Paper covers. $9.95.

Covers center-fire military cartridges from 25 ACP to 15mm Besa. Historical employment, weapons used, and a comprehensive section on headstamps.

Small-Caliber Ammunition Identification Guide Volume II: Small Arms Cartridges 20mm to 40mm, by R. T. Huntington, Military Arms Research Service, San Jose, CA, 1978. 165 pp., illus. Paper covers. $9.95.

Identifies the large infantry and aircraft cartridges giving full coverage to Soviet and East Bloc ammunition.

Speer Reloading Manual Number 10, Omark Industries, Inc., Lewiston, ID, 1979. 560 pp., illus. Paper covers. $10.00.

Expanded version with facts, charts, photos, tables, loads and tips.

Why Not Load Your Own? by Col. T. Whelen. A. S. Barnes, New York, 1957, 4th ed., rev. 237 pp., illus, $7.95.

A basic reference on handloading, describing each step, materials and equipment. Loads for popular cartridges are given.

Yours Truly, Harvey Donaldson, by Harvey Donaldson, Wolfe Publ. Co., Inc., Prescott, AZ, 1980. 288 pp., illus. $19.50.

Reprint of the famous columns by Harvey Donaldson which appeared in "Handloader" from May 1966 through December 1972.

COLLECTORS

The Age of Firearms, by Robert Held. Digest Books, Inc., Northfield, IL, 1970. New, fully rev. and corrected ed., paper covers. 192 pp., fully illus. $4.95.

A popular review of firearms since 1475 with accent on their effects on social conditions, and the craft of making functional/artistic arms.

American Boys' Rifles 1890-1945, by Jim Perkins, RTP Publishers, Pittsburg, PA, 1976. 245 pp., illus. $17.50.

The history and products of the arms companies who made rifles for the American boy, 1890-1945.

American, British & Continental Pepperbox Firearms, by Jack Dunlap. H. J. Dunlap, Los Altos, CA, 1964. 279 pp., 665 illus. $19.95.

Comprehensive history of production pepperboxes from early 18th cent. through the cartridge pepperbox. Variations are covered, with much data of value to the collector.

The American Cartridge, by Charles R. Suydam, Borden Publ. Co., Alhambra, CA, rev. ed., 1973. 184 pp., illus. $8.50.

An illus. study of the rimfire cartridge in the U.S.

The American Percussion Revolver, by F. M. Sellers and Sam E. Smith. Museum Restoration Service, Ottawa, Canada, 1970. 200 pp., illus. $20.00.

Antique Firearms, by Frederick Wilkinson, Presidio Press, San Rafael, CA, 1977. 276 pp., illus. $14.95.

Traces the history of firearms from their introduction to 14th century Europe through to the appearance of the modern repeating rifle.

Arms and Armor Annual, Volume I, edited by Robert Held, Digest Books, Inc., Northfield, IL, 1973. 320 pp., illus., paper covers. $9.95.

Thirty outstanding articles by the leading arms and armor historians of the world.

Arms Makers of Maryland, by Daniel D. Hartzler, George Shumway, York, PA, 1975. 200 pp., illus. $35.00.

A thorough study of the gunsmiths of Maryland who worked during the late 18th and early 19th centuries.

Ballard Rifles in the H. J. Nunnemacher Coll., by Eldon G. Wolff. Milwaukee Public Museum, Milwaukee, Wisc., 2nd ed. 1961. Paper, 77 p. plus 4 pp. of charts and 27 plates. $3.50.

A thoroughly authoritative work on all phases of the famous rifles, their parts, patent and manufacturing history.

Basic Documents on U.S. Martial Arms, commentary by Col. B. R. Lewis, reissue by Ray Riling, Phila., Pa., 1956 and 1960.

Rifle Musket Model 1855. The first issue rifle of musket caliber, a muzzle loader equipped with the Maynard Primer, 32 pp. $2.50.

Rifle Musket Model 1863. The Typical Union muzzle-loader of the Civil War, 26 pp. $1.75.

Breech-Loading Rifle Musket Model 1866. The first of our 50 caliber breechloading rifles, 12 pp. $1.75.

Remington Navy Rifle Model 1870. A commercial type breech-loader made at Springfield, 16 pp. $1.75.

Lee Straight Pull Navy Rifle Model 1895. A magazine cartridge arm of 6mm caliber. 23 pp. $1.75.

Breech-Loading Rifle Musket Model 1868. The first 50-70 designed as such. 20 pp. $1.75.

Peabody Breech-Loading Arms (five models)—27 pp. $2.75.

Ward-Burton Rifle Musket 1871—16 pp. $2.50.

Springfield Rifle, Carbine & Army Revolvers (cal. 45) model 1873 including Colt and Smith & Wesson hand arms. 52 pp. $3.00.

U.S. Magazine Rifle and Carbine (cal. 30) Model 1892 (the Krag Rifle) 36 pp. $3.00.

The Breech-Loader in the Service, 1816-1917, by Claud E. Fuller, N. Flayderman, New Milford, Conn., 1965. 381 pp., illus. $14.50.

Revised ed. of a 1933 historical reference on U.S. standard and experimental military shoulder arms. Much patent data, drawings, and photographs of the arms.

A voluminous work that covers handloading—and other things—in great detail. Replete with data for all cartridge types.

California Gunsmiths 1846-1900, by Lawrence P. Sheldon, Far Far West Publ., Fair Oaks, CA, 1977. 289 pp., illus. $29.65.

A study of early California gunsmiths and the firearms they made.

Cartology Savalog, by Gerald Bernstein, Gerald Bernstein, St. Louis, MO, 1976. 177 pp., illus. Paper covers. $8.95.

An infinite variations catalog of small arms ammunition stamps.

Civil War Carbines, by A. F. Lustyik. World Wide Gun Report, Inc., Aledo, ILL, 1962. 63 pp., illus. paper covers, $2.00.

Accurate, interesting summary of most carbines of the Civil War period, in booklet form, with numerous good illus.

Civil War Guns, by William B. Edwards, Castle Books, NY, 1976. 438 pp., illus. $10.00

Describes and records the exciting and sometimes romantic history of forging weapons for war and heroism of the men who used them.

The Collecting of Guns, ed. by Jas. E. Serven. Stackpole Books, Harrisburg, PA, 1964. 272 pp., illus. $5.95.

A new and massive compendium of gun lore for serious collectors by recognized experts. Separate chapters cover major categories and aspects of collecting. Over 600 firearms illus. Handsomely designed, deluxe binding in slip case.

The Collector's Handbook of U.S. Cartridge Revolvers, 1856 to 1899, by W. Barlow Fors, Adams Press, Chicago, IL, 1973. 96 pp., illus. $6.00.

Concise coverage of brand names, patent listings, makers' history, and essentials of collecting.

Colonel Colt, London, by Joseph G. Rosa, Fortress Publ., Inc., Stoney Creek, Ontario, Can., 1976. 208 pp., illus. $26.50.

The history of Colt's London firearms 1851-1857. Details the arms produced in the London armoury.

Colt Firearms from 1836, by James E. Serven, new 8th edition, Stackpole Books, Harrisburg, PA, 1979. 398 pp., illus. $28.95.

Excellent survey of the Colt company and its products. Updated with new SAA production chart and commemorative list.

The Colt Heritage, by R. L. Wilson, Simon & Schuster, 1979. 358 pp., illus. $39.95.

The official history of Colt firearms 1836 to the present.

Colt Peacemaker Dictionary & Encyclopedia Illustrated, by Keith A. Cochran, Colt Collectors Press, Rapid City, SD, 1976. 300 pp., illus. Paper covers, $12.95. Cloth, $15.95.

Over 1300 entries pertaining to everything there is to know about the Colt Peacemaker.

Colt's SAA Post War Models, by George Garton, Beinfield Publishing, Inc., No. Hollywood, CA, 1978. 176 pp. illus. $17.95.

Complete story on these arms including charts, tables and production information.

Colt's Variations of the Old Model Pocket Pistol, 1848 to 1872, by P. L. Shumaker. Borden Publishing Co., Alhambra, CA 1966, a reprint of the 1957 edition. 150 pp., illus. $6.00.

A useful tool for the Colt specialist and a welcome return of a popular source of information that had been long out-of-print.

Confederate Longarms and Pistols, "A Pictorial Study", by Richard Taylor Hill and Edward W. Anthony, Taylor Publishing Co., Dallas, TX, 1978. $29.95.

A reference work identifying over 175 Confederate arms through detailed photography, and a listing of information.

Digest of Patents Relating to Breech-Loading and Magazine Small Arms (1836-1873), by V. D. Stockbridge, WA, 1874. Reprinted 1963 by E. N. Flayderman, Greenwich, Conn. $12.50.

An exhaustive compendium of patent documents on firearms, indexed and classified by breech mechanism types, valuable reference for students and collectors.

Ethan Allen, Gunmaker, by Harold R. Mouillesseaux, Museum Rest. Serv., Ottawa, Ont., Can., 1973. 170 pp., illus. $25.00.

A complete history of Ethan Allen, his arms and his companies.

Fifteen Years in the Hawken Lode, by John D. Baird, The Gun Room Press, Highland Park, NJ, 1976. 120 pp., illus. $15.00.

A collection of thoughts and observations gained from many years of intensive study of the guns from the shop of the Hawken brothers.

'51 Colt Navies, by N. L. Swayze. Gun Hill Publ. Co., Yazoo City, MS, 1967. 243 pp., well illus. $15.00.

The first major effort devoting its entire space to the 1851 Colt Navy revolver. There are 198 photos of models, sub-models, variations, parts, markings, documentary material, etc. Fully indexed.

Firearms of the Confederacy, by Claud R. Fuller & Richard D. Steuart, Quarterman Publ., Inc., Lawrence, MA, 1977. 333 pp., illus. $25.00.

The shoulder arms, pistols and revolvers of the Confederate soldier, including the regular United States Models, the imported arms and those manufactured within the Confederacy.

Flayderman's Guide to Antique American Firearms . . . and Their Values, 2nd Edition, by Norm Flayderman, DBI Books, Inc., Northfield, IL, 1980. 608 pp., illus. Paper covers. $15.95.

All values in this new second edition have been completely brought up-to-date and a number of guns not covered in the first edition have been included.

The 45/70 Trapdoor Springfield Dixie Collection, compiled by Walter Crutcher and Paul Oglesby, Pioneer Press, Union City, TN, 1975. 600 pp., illus. Paper covers. $9.95.

An illustrated listing of the 45-70 Springfields in the Dixie Gun Works Collection. Little known details and technical information is given, plus current values.

Gun Collector's Digest, Volume II, edited by Joseph J. Schroeder, Jr. DBI Books, Inc., Northfield, IL, 1976, 288 pp., illus. Paper covers $7.95.

Comprehensive coverage on guns, gun shows, bayonets, commemoratives, security, gun laws, current Treasury regulations. Includes updated collectors bibliography and gun show directory.

The Gun Collector's Handbook of Values 1980-1981, by C. E. Chapel, Coward, McCann & Geoghegan, Inc., New York, NY, 1980. 462 pp., illus. $16.95.

Thirteenth rev. ed. of the best-known price reference for collectors.

Gun Digest Book of Modern Gun Values, 2nd. Ed., by Jack Lewis, DBI Books, Inc., Northfield, IL, 1978. 288 pp., illus. $7.95.

Revised and updated prices give latest values. Invaluable guide for buying, selling, trading or identifying guns—handguns, rifles and shotguns are covered in separate sections. Feature articles relate to collecting and values.

Gunmarks, by David Byron, Crown Publishers, Inc., New York, NY, 1979. 185 pp., illus. $10.00.

Tradenames, codemarks, and proofs from 1870 to the present.

Gun Traders Guide, 9th Edition, by Paul Wahl, Stoeger Publ. Co., S. Hackensack, NJ, 1978. 256 pp., illus. Paper covers. $9.95.

A fully illustrated and authoritative guide to identification of modern firearms with current market values.

Gunsmiths of Ohio—18th & 19th Centuries: Vol. I, Biographical Data, by Donald A. Hutslar, George Shumway, York, PA, 1973. 444 pp., illus. $35.00.

An important source book, full of information about the old-time gunsmiths of Ohio.

Hall's Breechloaders, by R. T. Huntington, Geo. Shumway, Publ. 1972. 369 pp., illus. Paper, $18.00.

Definitive treatise on John H. Hall and his inspectors. Shows all known models of the Hall rifle, appurtenances and pistol.

Hawken Rifles, The Mountain Man's Choice, by John D. Baird, The Gun Room Press, Highland Park, NJ, 1976. 95 pp., illus. $15.00.

Covers the rifles developed for the Western fur trade. Numerous specimens are described and shown in photographs.

Historical Hartford Hardware, by William W. Dalrymple, Colt Collector Press, Rapid City, SD, 1976. 42 pp., illus. Paper covers. $5.50.

Historically associated Colt revolvers.

A History of the Colt Revolver, by Charles T. Haven and Frank A. Belden, Outlet Books, New York, NY, 1978. 711 pp., illus. $10.95.

A giant of a book packed with information and pictures about the most cherished American revolver.

History of Modern U.S. Military Small Arms Ammunition, Vol. 2, 1940-1945, By F. W. Hackley, W. M. Woodin and E. L. Scranton, The Gun Room Press, Highland Park, NJ, 1976. 300 pp., illus. $25.00.

A unique book covering the entire field of small arms ammunition developed during the critical World War II years.

History of Smith & Wesson, by Roy G. Jinks, Beinfeld Publ., Inc., No. Hollywood, CA, 1977. 290 pp., illus. $15.95.

A record of 125 years of progress and excellence in producing fine products.

The History of Weapons of the American Revolution, by George C. Neuman, Outlet Books, NY, 1976. 373 pp., illus. $6.98.

A new printing of this important and timely work. Traces the history of Revolutionary War weapons of all types.

The Kentucky Rifle, by Merrill Lindsay. Arma Press, NY/The Historical Society of York County, York, PA, 1972. 100 pp., 81 large colored illustrations. $15.

Presents in precise detail and exact color 77 of the finest Kentucky rifles ever assembled in one place. Also describes the conditions which led to the development of this uniquely American arm.

Kentucky Rifle Patchboxes & Barrel Marks, by Roy F. Chandler, Valley View Offset, Duncannon, PA, 1971. 400 pp., $20.00.

Reference work illustrating hundreds of patchboxes, together with the mark or signature of the maker.

Kentucky Rifles and Pistols 1756-1850, compiled by members of the Kentucky Rifle Association, Wash., DC, Golden Age Arms Co., Delaware, OH, 1976. 275 pp., illus. $29.50.

Profusely illustrated with more than 300 examples of rifles and pistols never before published.

The Krag Rifle Story, by Franklin B. Mallory and Ludwig Olson, Springfield Research Service, Silver Spring, MD, 1979. 224 pp., illus. $20.00.

Covers both U.S. and European Krags. Gives a detailed description of U.S. Krag rifles and carbines and extensive data on sights, bayonets, serial numbers, etc.

Krag Rifles, by William S. Brophy, Beinfeld Pub. Inc., No. Hollywood, CA, 1980. 200 pp., illus. $24.95.

The first comprehensive work detailing the evolution and various models, both military and civilian.

Lever Action Magazine Rifles Derived from the Patents of Andrew Burgess, by Samuel L. Maxwell Sr., Samuel L. Maxwell, Bellevue, WA, 1976. 368 pp., illus. $29.95.

The complete story of a group of lever action magazine rifles collectively referred to as the Burgess/Morse, the Kennedy or the Whitney.

Luger: An Illustrated History of the Handguns of Hugo Borchardt and Georg Luger, 1875-1975, by John Walter, Fortress Publ., Inc., Stoney Creek, Ontario, Can., 1977. 256 pp., illus. $27.50.

A full and comprehensive coverage of the world's most famous pistol.

Maine Made Guns and Their Makers, by Dwight B. Demeritt, Main State Museum, Hallowell, ME, 1973. 209 pp., illus. $22.00.

A fine reference work on Maine gunsmiths.

Manhattan Firearms, by Waldo E. Nutter, Stackpole Books, Harrisburg, PA, 1958. 250 pp., illus., in halftone. $10.00.

Complete history of the Manhattan Firearms Mfg. Co., and its products. Excellent specialized reference.

Mauser Bolt Rifles, by Ludwig Olson, F. Brownell & Son, Inc., Montezuma, IA, 1976. 364 pp., illus. $24.95.

The most complete, detailed, authoritative and comprehensive work ever done on Mauser bolt rifles.

Miniature Arms, by Merrill Lindsay. Winchester Press, New York, NY, 1970. 111 pp., illus. $5.95.

A concise study of small-scale replicas of firearms and other weapons of collector interest. Fine color photographs.

M1 Carbine, Design, Development and Production, by Larry Ruth, Desert Publications, Cornville, AZ. 300 pp., illus. Paper covers $14.95.

The complete history of one of the world's most famous and largest produced firearms.

More Single Shot Rifles, by James C. Grant, The Gun Room Press, Highland Park, NJ, 1976. 324 pp., illus. $15.00.

Details the guns made by Frank Wesson, Milt Farrow, Holden, Borchardt, Stevens, Remington, Winchester, Ballard and Peabody-Martini.

The Muzzle-Loading Cap Lock Rifle, by Ned H. Roberts, George Shumway Publisher, York, PA and Track of the Wolf Co., Osseo, MN, 1978. 308 pp., illus. $24.50.

Reprint of the revised and enlarged privately printed edition of this general survey of its subject and of the makers of the rifles.

The NRA Collector's Series, Digest Books, Inc., Northfield, IL, 1971, 84 pp. paper covers $2.95.

Reprint of the three predecessors of *American Rifleman* magazine and the first edition of *American Rifleman*.

The New England Gun, by Merrill Lindsay, David McKay Co., NY, 1976. 155 pp., illus. Paper covers, $12.50. Cloth, $20.00.

A study of more than 250 New England guns, powder horns, swords, and polearms in an exhibition by the New Haven Colony Historical Society.

Simeon North: First Official Pistol Maker of the United States, by S. North and R. North, Rutgers Book Center, Highland Park, NJ, 1972. 207 pp., illus. $7.95.

Exact reprint of the original. Includes chapters on New England pioneer manufacturers and on various arms.

The Northwest Gun, by Charles E. Hanson, Jr., Nebraska State Historical Society, Lincoln, NB, 1976. 85 pp., illus., paper covers. $6.

Number 2 in the Society's "Publications in Anthropology." Historical survey of rifles which figured in the fur trade and settlement of the Northwest.

Paterson Colt Pistol Variations, by R. L. Wilson and R. Phillips, Jackson Arms Co., Dallas, TX, 1979. 250 pp., illus. $35.00.

A tremendous book about the different models and barrel lengths in the Paterson Colt story.

Peacemaker Evolutions & Variations, by Keith A. Cochran, Colt Collectors Press, Rapid City, SD, 1975. 47 pp., illus. Paper covers. $6.50.

Corrects many inaccuracies found in other books on the Peacemaker and gives much new information regarding this famous arm.

Pennsylvania Longrifles of Note, by George Shumway, George Shumway, Publisher, York, PA, 1977. 63 pp., illus. Paper covers. $6.95.

Illustrates and describes samples of guns from a number of Pennsylvania rifle-making schools.

The Plains Rifle, by Charles E. Hanson, Jr., The Gun Room Press, Highland Park, NJ, 1977. 171 pp., illus. $15.00.

Historical survey of popular civilian arms used on the American frontiers, their makers, and their owners.

The Post-War Colt Single-Action Revolvers, by Don Wilkerson, The Single Action Shop, Apple Valley, MN, 1978. 152 pp., illus. $17.95.

Detailed descriptions of 37 variations, plus information on engraved and special models.

The Rare and Valuable Antique Arms, by James E. Serven, Pioneer Press, Union City, TN, 1976. 106 pp., illus. Paper covers. $4.95.

A guide to the collector in deciding which direction his collecting should go, investment value, historic interest, mechanical ingenuity, high art or personal preference.

Remington Arms in American History, by A. Hatch, Rinehart & Co., NY, 1956. 359 pp., illus. $6.50.

Collector's guide with appendix of all Remington arms, ballistics tables, etc.

Samuel Colt's New Model Pocket Pistols; The Story of the 1855 Root Model Revolver, by S. Gerald Keogh, S. G. Keogh, Ogden, UT, 1974. 31 pp., illus., paper covers. $3.50.

Collector's reference on various types of the titled arms, with descriptions, illustrations, and historical data.

Savage Automatic Pistols, by James R. Carr. Publ. by the author, St. Charles, Ill., 1967. A reprint. 129 pp., illus. with numerous photos. $10.00.

Collector's guide to Savage pistols, models 1907-1922, with features, production data, and pictures of each.

Shotgun Shells: Identification, Manufacturers and Checklist for Collectors, by F. H. Steward. B. and P. Associates, St. Louis, Mo., 1969. 101 pp., illus., paper covers. $10.00.

Historical data for the collector.

Small Arms, by Frederick Wilkinson, Hawthorne Books, Inc., New York, 1966. 256 pp., illus. $4.95.

A history of small firearms, techniques of the gunsmith, equipment used by combatants, sportsmen and hunters.

Small Arms of the Sea Services, by Robt. H. Rankin. N. Flayderman & Co., New Milford, CT, 1972. 227 pp., illus. $14.50.

Encyclopedic reference to small arms of the U.S. Navy, Marines and Coast Guard. Covers edged weapons, handguns, long arms and others, from the beginnings.

Smith and Wesson 1857-1945, by Robert J. Neal and Roy J. Jenks. A. S. Barnes and Co., Inc., NYC, 1975. 500 pp., illus. with over 300 photos and 90 radiographs. $25.00.

A long-needed book, especially for knowledgeable enthusiasts and collectors. Covers an investigation of the series of handguns produced by the Smith and Wesson Company.

Southern Derringers of the Mississippi Valley, by Turner Kirkland. Pioneer Press, Tenn., 1971. 80 pp., illus., paper covers. $2.00.

A guide for the collector, and a much-needed study.

Spanish Military Weapons in Colonial America, 1700-1821, by S. B. Brinckerhoff & P. A. Chamberlain. Stackpole Books, Harrisburg, PA, 1972. 160 pp., illus. $14.95.

Spanish arms and armaments described and illustrated in 274 photographic plates. Includes firearms, accoutrements, swords, polearms and cannon.

The Standard Directory of Proof-Marks, ed. by R. A. Steindler, The John Olson Company, Paramus, NJ, 1976. 144 pp., illus. Paper covers. $5.95.

A comprehensive directory of the proof-marks of the world.

Stevens Pistols and Pocket Rifles, by K. L. Cope, Museum Restoration Service, Ottawa, Can., 1971. 104 pp. $12.50.

All are shown, identified, detailed, variations, listings of dates, etc.

The Story of Allen & Wheelock Firearms, by H. H. Thomas, C. J. Krehbiel Co., Cincinnati, OH, 1965. 125 pp., illus. $10.95.

A comphrehensive study of the firearms made by the firm of Allen & Wheelock.

The 36 Calibers of the Colt Single Action Army, by David M. Brown. Publ. by the author at Albuquerque, NM, new reprint 1971. 222 pp., well-illus. $15.00.

Edited by Bev Mann of *Guns Magazine.* This is an unusual approach to the many details of the Colt S.A. Army revolver. Halftone and line drawings of the same models make this of especial interest.

The Trapdoor Springfield, by M. D. Waite and B. D. Ernst, Beinfeld Publ. Co., Inc., No. Hollywood, CA, 1979. 250 pp., illus. $29.95.

The first comprehensive book on the famous standard military rifle of the 1873-92 period.

Underhammer Guns, by H. C. Logan. Stackpole Books, Harrisburg, PA, 1964. 250 pp. illus. $10.00.

A full account of an unusual form of firearm dating back to flintlock days. Both American and foreign specimens are included.

U.S. Cartridges and Their Handguns, by Charles R. Suydam, Beinfeld Publ., Inc., No. Hollywood, CA, 1977. 200 pp., illus. Paper covers. $9.95.

The first book ever showing which gun used what cartridge. A must for the gun and cartridge collector.

U.S. Martial and Semi-Martial Single-Shot Pistols, by C. E. Chapel, Coward-McCann Inc., NYC, 1962. 352 pp., over 150 illus. $10.00.

Describes in detail all single shot martial pistols used by the US armed forces and by military units of the states. A definitive guide.

The Virginia Manufactory of Arms, by Giles Cromwell, University Press of Virginia, Charlottesville, VA, 1975. 205 pp., illus. $25.00.

The only complete history of the Virginia Manufactory of Arms which produced muskets, pistols, swords, and cannon for the state's militia from 1802 through 1821.

Walther Models PP and PPK, 1929-1945, by James L. Rankin, assisted by Gary Green, James L. Rankin, Coral Gables, FL, 1974. 142 pp., illus. $14.00.

Complete coverage on the subject as to finish, proof marks and Nazi Party inscriptions.

Walther Volume II, Engraved, Presentation and Standard Models, by James L. Rankin, J. L. Rankin, Coral Galbes, FL 1977. 112 pp., illus. $17.50.

The new Walther book on embellished versions and standard models. Has 88 photographs, including many color plates.

The Whitney Firearms, by Claud Fuller. Standard Publications, Huntington, W. Va., 1946. 334 pp., many plates and drawings. $25.00.

An authoritative history of all Whitney arms and their maker. Highly recommended. An exclusive with Ray Riling Arms Books Co.

The William M. Locke Collection, compiled by Robert B. Berryman, et al, The Antique Armory, Inc., East Point, GA, 1973. 541 pp., illus. $40.00.

A magnificently produced book illustrated with hundreds of photographs of guns from one of the finest collection of American firearms ever assembled.

Winchester—The Gun That Won the West, by H. F. Williamson. Combat Forces Press, Washington, D.C., 1952. Later eds. by Barnes, NY 494 pp., profusely illus., paper covers. $9.95.

A scholarly and essential economic history of an honored arms company, but the early and modern arms introduced will satisfy all but the exacting collector.

EDGED WEAPONS

The Robert Abels Collection of Bowie Type Knives of American Interest, by Robert Abels, Robert Abels, Hopewell Junction, NY, 1974. 20 pp., illus. Paper covers. $1.95.

A selection of American Bowie-type knives from the collection of Robert Abels.

American Axes, by Henry Kauffman, The Stephen Greene Press, Brattleboro, VT, 1972. 200 pp., illus. $12.50.

A definitive work on the subject. Contains a roster of American axe makers, glossary and notes on the care and use of axes.

The American Bayonet 1176-1964, by Albert N. Hardin, Jr., Albert N. Hardin, Jr., Pennsauken, NJ, 1977. 234 pp., illus. $24.50.

Describes and illustrates over two hundred separate and distinct types of American bayonets from Colonial times to the present day.

American Indian Tomahawks, by Harold L. Peterson, Museum of the American Indian, Heye Foundation, NY, 1965. 142 pp., illus. $10.00.

A brief description of various types and their makers.

American Polearms 1526-1865, by Rodney Hilton Brown, N. Flayderman & Co., New Milford, CT, 1967. 198 pp., illus. $14.50.

The lance, halbred, spontoon, pike and naval boarding weapons used in the American military forces through the Civil War.

American Socket Bayonets 1717-1873, by Donald B. Webster, Jr., Museum Restoration Service, Ontario, Canada, 1964. 47 pp., illus. Paper covers. $2.50.

Helps identify the many variations of the triangular and angular bayonets used by the U.S. Army.

The American Sword, 1775-1945, by Harold L. Peterson, Ray Riling Arms Books, Co., Phila., PA, 1980. 286 pp. plus 60 pp. of illus. $22.50.

1977 reprint of a survey of swords worn by U.S. uniformed forces, plus the rare "American Silver Mounted Swords, (1700-1815)."

The Art of Blacksmithing, by Alex W. Bealer, Funk & Wagnalls, New York, NY, revised edition, 1976. 438 pp., illus. $16.95.

Required reading for anyone who makes knives or is seriously interested in the history of cutlery.

The Arts of the Japanese Sword, by B. W. Robinson, Faber and Faber, London, England, 1978. 218 pp., illus. $33.00.

Detailed information on making blades, chief schools of Japanese swordsmiths, care, cleaning and marks.

Basic Manual of Knife Fighting, by William L. Cassidy, Paladin Press, Boulder, CO, 1978. 41 pp., illus. Paper covers. $4.

A manual presenting the best techniques developed by the experts from 1930 to date.

Bayonets of the World, Volume 1, by Paul Kiesling, Military Collectors Service, Kedichem, Holland, 1973. 278 plates. $19.95.

Covers bayonets up to 515mm in length, includes scabbards, sockets, etc.

Bayonets of the World, Volume 2, by Paul Kiesling, Military Collectors Service, Kedichem, Holland, 1974. 131 pp., illus. $19.95.

Covers bayonets of all types and all countries. Arranged in size starting with 515mm and larger.

Bayonets of the World, Volume 3, by Paul Kiesling, Military Collectors Service, Kedichem, Holland, 1975. 130 pp., illus. $19.95.

Part 3 of this fine series on bayonets of all countries. Includes a cross index reference for all three volumes.

Bayonets of the World, Volume 4, by Paul Kiesling, Military Collectors Service, Kedichem, Holland, 1977. 190 pp., illus. $24.00.

The final volume in this monumental work on bayonets.

The Best of Knife World, Volume I, edited by Knife World Publ., Knoxville, TN, 1980. 92 pp., illus. Paper covers. $3.95.

A collection of articles about knives. Reprinted from monthly issues of Knife World.

Blacksmithing for the Home Craftsman, by Joe Pehoski, Joe Pehoski, Washington, TX, 1973. 44 pp., illus. Paper covers. $2.50.

This informative book is chock-full of drawings and explains how to make your own forge.

Blades and Barrels, by H. Gordon Frost, Wallon Press, El Paso, TX, 1972. 298 pp., illus. $16.95.

The first full scale study about man's attempts to combine an edged weapon with a firearm.

Bowie Knives, by Robert Abels, Robert Abels, NY, 1960. 48 pp., illus. Paper covers. $3.00.

A booklet showing knives, tomahawks, related trade cards and advertisements.

British Cut and Thrust Weapons, by John Wilkinson Latham, Charles E. Tuttle Co., VT, 1971. 112 pp., illus. $7.50.

Well illustrated study tracing the development of edged weapons and their adoption by the British armed forces.

The Complete Book of Knife Fighting, by William L. Cassidy, Paladin Press, Boulder, CO, 1975. 119 pp., illus. $10.95.

Most complete book of knife fighting technique and history with every facet covered.

Custom Knife . . . II, by John Davis Bates, Jr., and James Henry Schippers, Jr., Custom Knife Press, Memphis, TN, 1974. 112 pp., illus. $20.00.

The book of pocket knives and folding hunters. A guide to the 20th century makers' art.

The Cutlery Story: From Stone Age to Steel Age, by Lewis D. Bement, Custom Cutlery Co., Dalton, GA, 1972. 36 pp., illus. Paper covers. $3.50.

A classic booklet about the history, romance, and manufacture of cutlery from the earliest times to modern methods of manufacture.

A Directory of Sheffield: Including the Manufacturers of the Adjacent Villages, a facsimile reprint of the 1707 London edition, Da Capo Press, Inc., NY, 1969. Illus. $11.50.

With the several marks of the cutlers, scissor and edge-tool makers.

Edge of the Anvil, by Jack Andrews, Rodale Press, Emmaus, PA, 1978. 224 pp., illus. $9.95.

A basic blacksmith book.

European Swords and Daggers in the Tower of London, by Arthur Richard Dufty, Her Majesty's Stationery Office, London, England, 1974. 157 pp., illus. $37.50.

An illustrated and descriptive guide to the swords and daggers in the Tower of London Armouries collections.

The Fighting Knife, by W. D. Randall, Jr. and Col. Rex Applegate, W. D. Randall, Orlando, FL, 1975. 60 pp., illus. Paper covers. $2.75.

Manual for the use of Randall-made fighting knives and similar types.

For Knife Lovers Only, by Harry K. McEvoy, Knife World Publ., Knoxville, TN, 1979. 67 pp., illus. Paper covers. $4.95.

A fascinating and unusual approach to the story of knives.

The German Bayonet, by John Walter, Arms and Armour Press, London, England, 1976. 128 pp., illus. $12.50.

A comprehensive illustrated history of regulation patterns, 1871-1945.

A Guide to Handmade Knives, edited by Mel Tappan, The Janus Press, Inc., Los Angeles, CA, 1977. Paper covers. $9.50; Deluxe hardbound. $19.50.

The official directory of the Knifemakers Guild.

Gun Digest Book of Folding Knives, by Jack Lewis and B. R. Hughes, DBI Books, Inc. Northfield, IL, 1977. 288 pp., illus. Paper covers. $7.95.

A cut above any other volume published on pocket or folding knives.

The Gun Digest Book of Knives, by B. R. Hughes and Jack Lewis, DBI Books, Inc., Northfield, IL, 1973. 228 pp., illus. Paper covers. $6.95.

How to collect, buy and care for knives.

The History of the John Russell Cutlery Company, 1833-1936, by Robert L. Merriam et al, The Bete Press, Greenfield, MA, 1976. 120 pp., illus. $12.95.

A complete history of the people, places and events behind legendary American knives such as the Barlow, Green River Knife, Dadley and others.

How to Make Knives, by Richard W. Barney & Robert W. Loveless, Beinfield Publ., Inc., No. Hollywood, CA, 1977. 178 pp., illus. Paper covers. $9.95; Deluxe hardbound. $15.95.

A book filled with drawings, illustrations, diagrams, and 500 how-to-do-it photos.

Introduction to Japanese Swords, by William M. Hawley, William M. Hawley, Hollywood, CA, 1973. 20 pp., illus. Paper covers. $3.95.

Clear concise details of construction that made Japanese swords the world's finest edged weapons.

The Knife Album Price Guide 1976 Edition, by Robert Mayes, Robert Mayes, Middlesboro, KY, 1976. 174 pp. Paper covers. $6.00.

The only book on identification and accurate pricing.

Knife Digest, First Annual Edition, edited by William L. Cassidy, Knife Digest Publ. Co., Berkeley, CA, 1974. 285 pp., illus. Paper covers. $5.95.

The first annual publication ever produced for the knife and edged weapon enthusiast and collector.

Knife Digest, Second Annual Edition, edited by William L. Cassidy, Knife Digest Publ. Co., Berkeley, CA, 1976. 178 pp., illus. Paper covers. $7.95; Cloth. $15.00.

The second annual edition of the internationally known book on blades.

Knife Throwing, Sport . . . Survival . . . Defense, by Blackie Collins, Knife World Publ., Knoxville, TN, 1979. 31 pp., illus. Paper covers. $3.00.

How to select a knife, how to make targets, how to determine range and how to survive with a knife.

Knife Throwing a Practical Guide, by Harry K. McEvoy, Charles E. Tuttle Co., Rutland, VT, 1973. 108 pp., illus. Paper covers. $3.95.

If you want to learn to throw a knife this is the "bible."

Knifecraft: A Comprehensive Step-by-Step Guide to the Art of Knifemaking, by Sid Latham, Stackpole Books, Harrisburg, PA, 1978. 224 pp., illus. $18.95.

An exhaustive volume taking both amateur and accomplished knifecrafter through all the steps in creating a knife.

Knifemakers of Old San Francisco, by Bernard R. Levine, Badger Books, San Francisco, CA, 1978. 240 pp., illus. $12.95.

The story about the knifemakers of San Francisco, the leading cutlers of the old West.

The Knife Makers Who Went West, by Harvey Platts, Longspeak Press, Longmont, CO, 1978. 200 pp., illus. $19.95.

Factual story of an important segment of the American cutlery industry. Primarily about Western knives and the Platts knife makers.

Knives and Knifemakers, by Sid Latham, Winchester Press, NY, 1973. 152 pp., illus. $17.50.

Lists makers and suppliers of knife-making material and equipment.

Light But Efficient, by Albert N. Hardin, Jr. and Robert W. Hedden, Albert N. Hardin, Jr., Pennsauken, NJ, 1973. 103 pp., illus. $7.95.

A study of the M1880 Hunting and M1890 intrenching knives and scabbards.

Marble Knives and Axes, by Konrad F. Schreir, Jr., Beinfeld Publ., Inc., No. Hollywood, CA, 1978. 80 pp., illus. Paper covers. $5.95.

The first work ever on the knives and axes made by this famous old, still-in-business, manufacturer.

The Modern Blacksmith, by Alexander G. Weygers, Van Nostrand Reinhold Co., NY, 1977. 96 pp., illus. $8.95.

Shows how to forge objects out of steel. Use of basic techniques and tools.

Nathan Starr Arms Maker 1776-1845, by James E. Hicks, The Restoration Press, Phoenix, AZ, 1976. 166 pp., illus. $12.95.

Survey of the work of Nathan Starr of Middletown, CT, in producing edged weapons and pole arms for the U.S., 1799-1840, also some firearms.

Naval Swords, by P. G. W. Annis, Stackpole Books, Harrisburg, PA, 1970. 80 pp., illus. $5.50.

British and American naval edged weapons 1660-1815.

A Photographic Supplement of Confederate Swords with Addendum, by William A. Albaugh III, Moss Publications, Orange, VA, 1979. 259 pp., illus. $20.00.

A new updated edition of the classic work on Confederate edged weapons.

Pocket Knife Book 1 & 2—Price Guide, by Roy Ehrhardt, Heart of America Press, Kansas City, MO, 1974. 96 pp., illus. Spiral bound stiff paper covers. $6.95.

Reprints from the pocket knife sections of early manufacturers and sporting goods catalogs.

Pocket Knife Book 3—Price Guide, by Roy and Larry Ehrhardt, Heart of America Press, Kansas City, MO, 1974. Spiral bound stiff paper covers. $6.95.

Compiled from sections of various product sales catalogs of both Winchester and Marble Co. dating from the '20s and '30s.

The Pocketknife Manual, by Blackie Collins, Blackie Collins, Rock Hill, SC, 1976. 102 pp., illus. Paper covers. $5.50.

Building, repairing and refinishing pocketknives.

Practical Blacksmithing, edited by J. Richardson, Outlet Books, NY, 1978. 4 volumes in one, illus. $7.98.

A reprint of the extremely rare, bible of the blacksmith. Covers every aspect of working with iron and steel, from ancient uses to modern.

The Practical Book of Knives, by Ken Warner, Winchester Press, New York, NY, 1976. 224 pp., illus. $12.95.

All about knives for sport and utility.

A Primer of German Military Knives of the Two World Wars, by Gordon A. Hughes, Gordon A. Hughes, Sussex, England, 1976. 20 pp., illus. Paper covers. $4.00.

Detailed line drawings of some 40 trench combat knives of Imperial and Nazi Germany together with sheath variations.

A Primer of Military Knives: European & American, Combat, Trench & Utility Knives, by Gordon Hughes and Barry Jenkins, Brighton, England, 1973. 24 pp., illus. Paper covers. $5.00.

A primer of the knives used in the First and Second World Wars, with line drawings of the weapons and descriptive text.

A Primer of World Bayonets, by John Walter and Gordon Hughes, Brighton, England, 1969. In two volumes. Vol. I, 26 pp.; Vol. 2, 23 pp., illus. Paper covers. $6.50.

Vol. I, common knife and sabre bayonets. Vol. 2, further knife, sabre and socket bayonets.

The Rapier and Small-Sword 1460-1820, by A. V. B. Norman, Arms and Armour Press, London, Eng., 1980. 416 pp., illus. $95.00.

The story of the evolution of the rapier and its successor, the small-sword, by one of the world's great experts on edged weapons.

Rice's Trowel Bayonet, reprinted by Ray Riling Arms Books, Co., Phila., PA, 1968. 8 pp., illus. Paper covers. $3.00.

A facsimile reprint of a rare circular originally published by the U.S. Government in 1875 for the information of U.S. Troops.

The Samurai Sword, by John M. Yumoto, Charles E. Tuttle Co., Rutland, VT, 1958. 191 pp., illus. $9.95.

A must for anyone interested in Japanese blades, and the first book on this subject written in English.

Scottish Swords from the Battlefield at Culloden, by Lord Archibald Campbell, The Mowbray Co., Providence, RI, 1973. 63 pp., illus. $5.00.

A modern reprint of an exceedingly rare 1894 privately printed edition.

Secrets of Modern Knife Fighting, by David E. Steele, Phoenix Press, Arvada, CO, 1974. 149 pp., illus. Paper covers. $9.95; Cloth. $15.00.

Details every facet of employing the knife in combat, including underwater fighting.

The Sheffield Bowie & Pocket-Knife Makers 1825-1925, by Richard Washer, T. A. Vinall, Nottingham, England, 1974. 144 pp., illus. $14.50.

Alphabetical listing of all known makers with their various identification marks and their periods of manufacture.

Step-by-Step Knifemaking, by Davis Boye, Rodale Press, Emmous, PA, 1978. 288 pp., illus. $10.95.

Gives the fundamentals of knifemaking and shows how to make knives either as a hobby or as a business.

Swords and Daggers, by Eduard Wagner, Hamlyn, London, 1975. 253 pp., illus. $10.00.

Traces all types of European cut-and-thrust weapons from ancient times through their development to the twentieth century.

Swords and Other Edged Weapons, by Robert Wilkinson-Latham, Arco Publishing Co., New York, NY, 1978. 227 pp., illus. $8.95.

Traces the history of the "Queen of Weapons" from its earliest forms in the stone age to the military swords of the Twentieth century.

Tomahawks Illustrated, by Robert Kuck, Robert Kuck, New Knoxville, OH, 1977. 112 pp., illus. Paper covers. $8.50.

A pictorial record to provide a reference in selecting and evaluating tomahawks.

U.S. Military Knives, Bayonets and Machetes, Book III, by M. H. Cole, M. H. Cole, Birmingham, AL, 1979. 219 pp., illus. $23.00.

The most complete text ever written on U.S. military knives, bayonets, machetes and bolo's.

GENERAL

Air Gun Digest, by Robert Beeman & Jack Lewis, DBI Books, Inc., Northfield, IL, 1977. 224 pp., illus. Paper covers. $6.95.

Traces the first air, spring air, CO_2 and other types from prototype to current models.

The Album of Gunfighters, by J. Marvin Hunter and Noah H. Rose, Warren Hunter, Helotes, Texas, 1965. 4th printing. 236 pp., wonderfully illus., with spectacular oldtime photos. $30.

For the serious gunfighter fan there is nothing to equal this factual record of the men-behind-the-star and the human targets that they faced.

The American B.B. Gun, by A. T. Dunathan, A. S. Barnes, S. Brunswick, NJ, 1971. 154 pp., illus. $10.00.

Identification reference and a price guide for B.B. guns, plus a brief history and advertising plates.

18 species; their origin, history, range, food, diseases, etc.

Author and Subject Index to the American Rifleman Magazine 1971-1975, by W. R. Burrell, Galesburg, MI, 1973-75. 64 pp., Paper covers. $6.50.

Alphabetical listing by author, title and subject of this famous arms publication.

Beginner's Guide to Guns and Shooting, by Clair F. Rees, DBI Books, Inc., Northfield, IL, 1978. 224 pp., illus. Paper covers. $6.95.

Indispensible to the beginner, and an enlightening review for the seasoned sportsman.

Black Powder Gun Digest, 2nd ed., by Jack Lewis and Robert Springer, DBI Books, Inc., Northfield, IL, 1977. 288 pp., illus. Paper covers. $7.95.

A most comprehensive, authoritative book on black powder rifles, handguns, scatterguns and accessories.

Carbine; The Story of David Marshall "Carbine" Williams, by Ross E. Beard, Jr., The Sandlapper Store, Inc., Lexington, SC, 1977. 315 pp., illus. Deluxe limited edition, numbered and signed by the author and "Carbine." $25.

The story of the man who invented the M1 Carbine and holds 52 other firearms patents.

Carbine Handbook, by Paul Wahl. Arco Publ. Co., N.Y.C., 1964. 80 pp., illus. $6.00. Paperbound, $4.95.

A manual and guide to the U.S. Carbine, cal. .30, M1, with data on its history, operation, repair, ammunition, and shooting.

Colonial Riflemen in the American Revolution, by Joe D. Huddleston, George Shumway Publisher, York, PA, 1978. 70 pp., illus. $18.00.

This study traces the use of the longrifle in the Revolution for the purpose of evaluating what effects it had on the outcome.

The Complete Black Powder Handbook, by Sam Fadala, DBI Books, Inc., Northfield, IL, 1979. 288 pp., illus. Paper covers. $8.95.

Everything you want to know about black powder firearms and their shooting.

Dead Aim, by Lee Echols, Acme Printing Co., San Diego, CA, a reprint, 1972. 116 pp., illus. $6.00.

Nostalgic antics of hell-raising pistol shooters of the 1930s.

Eli Whitney and the Whitney Armory, by Merrill Lindsay, Arma Press, North Branford, CT, 1979. 95 pp., illus. Paper covers. $4.95. Cloth. $9.95.

History of the Whitney Armory 1767-1862, with notes on how to identify Whitney flintlocks.

The Encyclopedia of Infantry Weapons of World War II, by Ian V. Hogg, Harper & Row, New York, NY, 1977. 192 pp., illus. $15.95.

A fully comprehensive and illustrated reference work including every major type of weapon used by every army in the world during World War II.

Encyclopedia of Modern Firearms, Vol. 1, compiled and publ. by Bob Brownell, Montezuma, IA, 1959. 1057 pp. plus index, illus. $50.00. Dist. by Bob Brownell, Montezuma, IA 50171.

Massive accumulation of basic information of nearly all modern arms pertaining to "parts and assembly." Replete with arms photographs, exploded drawings, manufacturers' lists of parts, etc.

The Firearms Dictionary, by R. A. Steindler, Paladin Press, Boulder, CO, 1976. 288 pp., illus. Paper covers, $6.95. Cloth, $12.50.

The basic illustrated reference encyclopedia of gun language. Defines over 1800 English and foreign terms relating to firearms, ammunition, accessories and gun repairing techniques.

Firearms Encyclopedia, by George C. Nonte, Jr., Outdoor Life/Harper & Row, NY, 1973. 341 pp., illus. $17.95.

A to Zed coverage of gun and shooting terms, plus a complete appendix of useful information and an index.

Gun Digest Book of Metallic Silhouette Shooting, by Elgin Gates, DBI Books, Inc., Northfield, IL, 1979. 256 pp., illus. Paper Covers. $6.95.

Examines all aspects of this fast growing sport including history, rules and meets.

Gun Digest Book of Gun Accessories, by Joseph Schroeder and the editors of Gun Digest, DBI Books, Inc., Northfield, IL, 1980. 288 pp., illus. Paper covers. $8.95.

The first single source reference for gun related items ever published.

Gun Digest Book of Modern Gun Values, 2nd ed., by Jack Lewis, DBI Books, Inc., Northfield, IL, 1978. 288 pp., illus. $7.95.

Invaluable guide for buying, selling, trading or identifying guns—handguns, rifles and shotguns are covered in separate sections. Feature articles relate to collecting and values.

Gun Digest Book of Exploded Firearms Drawings 2nd Edition, edited by Harold A. Murtz, DBI Books, Inc., Northfield, IL, 1978. 320 pp., illus. Paper covers. $7.95.

Hundreds of exploded drawings of modern and collector's firearms.

Gun Digest Treasury, 5th Edition, edited by John T. Amber, DBI Books, Inc., Northfield, IL, 1977. 288 pp., illus. Paper covers. $7.95.

The best articles from the first 30 years of Gun Digest.

Gun Talk, edited by Dave Moreton. Winchester Press, NY, 1973. 256 pp., illus. $9.95.

A treasury of original writing by the top gun writers and editors in America. Practical advice about every aspect of the shooting sports.

The Gun That Made the Twenties Roar, by Wm. J. Helmer, rev. and enlarged by George C. Nonte, Jr., The Gun Room Press, Highland Park, NJ, 1977. Over 300 pp., illus. $16.95.

Historical account of John T. Thompson and his invention, the infamous "Tommy Gun."

The Gunfighter, Man or Myth? by Joseph G. Rosa, Oklahoma Press, Norman, OK, 1969. 229 pp., illus., (including weapons). $9.95.

A well-documented work on gunfights and gunfighters of the West and elsewhere. Great treat for all gunfighter buffs.

The Gunfighters, by Dale T. Schoenberger, The Caxton Printers, Ltd., Caldwell, ID, 1971. 207 pp., illus. $12.95.

Startling expose of our foremost Western folk heroes.

The Guns of Harpers Ferry, by S. E. Brown Jr. Virginia Book Co., Berryville, VA, 1968. 157 pp., illus. $20.00.

Catalog of all known firearms produced at the U.S. armory at Harpers Ferry, 1798-1861, with descriptions, illustrations and a history of the operations there.

The Gunsmith in Colonial Virginia, by Harold B. Gill, Jr., University Press of Virginia, Charlottesville, VA, 1975. 200 pp., illus. Paper covers, $7.50; Cloth, $10.00.

The role of the gunsmith in colonial Virginia from the first landing at Jamestown through the Revolution is examined, with special attention to those who lived and worked in Williamsburg.

Hatcher's Notebook, by Maj. Gen. J. S. Hatcher. Stackpole Books, Harrisburg, Pa., 1952. 2nd ed. with four new chapters, 1957. 629 pp., illus. $19.95.

A dependable source of information for gunsmiths, ballisticians, historians, hunters, and collectors.

Home Guide to Muzzle Loaders, by Geo. C. Nonte, Jr., Stackpole Books, Harrisburg, PA, 1974. 219 pp., illus. $6.95.

From the basics of muzzle loading, its ammo, to the differences between the modern and replica muzzle loader, plus how-to-make one.

The Identification and Registration of Firearms, by Vaclav "Jack" Krcma, C. C. Thomas, Springfield, IL, 1971. 173 pp., illus. $21.50.

Analysis of problems and improved techniques of recording firearms data accurately.

Kill or Get Killed, by Col. Rex Applegate, new rev. and enlarged ed., Paladin Press, Boulder, CO, 1976. 421 pp., illus. $15.95.

For police and military forces. Last word on mob control.

Law Enforcement Handgun Digest, 3rd Edition, by Jack Lewis, DBI Books, Inc., Northfield, IL, 1980. 288 pp., illus. Paper covers. $8.95.

Covers such subjects as the philosophy of a firefight, SWAT, weapons, training, combat shooting, etc.

Lyman Muzzleloaders' Handbook, first ed., edited by C. Kenneth Ramage, Lyman Publ., Middlefield, CT, 1976. 248 pp., illus. Paper covers. $10.95.

A complete black powder catalog of all such rifles, pistols, shotguns, kits and accessories available today.

Marksmanship: Secrets of High Scoring from a World Champ, by Gary L. Anderson. Simon & Schuster, NY, 1972. 79 pp. $5.95.

Illus. step-by-step guide to target shooting. Covers equipment, ammunition, breath control, arm position, etc.

Medicolegal Investigation of Gunshot Wounds, by Abdullah Fatteh, J. B. Lippincott Co., Phila., PA, 1977. 272 pp., illus. $22.50.

A much-needed work, clearly written and easily understood, dealing with all aspects of medicolegal investigation of gunshot wounds and deaths.

The 1951 Gun Digest Commemorative 5th Edition, edited by John T. Amber, DBI Books, Inc., Northfield, IL, 1977. 224 pp., illus. Paper covers. $6.95.

A reprint of the classic 5th edition, the first edition edited by John T. Amber.

No Second Place Winner, by Wm. H. Jordan, publ. by the author, Shreveport, LA (Box 4072), 1962. 114 pp., illus. $7.50.

Guns and gear of the peace officer, ably discussed by a U.S. Border Patrolman for over 30 years, and a first-class shooter with handgun, rifle, etc.

Olympic Shooting, by Colonel Jim Crossman, NRA, Washington, DC, 1978. 136 pp., illus. $12.95.

The complete, authoritative history of U.S. participation in the Olympic shooting events from 1896 until the present.

Outdoor Life Gun Data Book, by F. Philip Rice, Harper & Row Publ., Inc., NY, 1975. 480 pp., illus. $11.95.

Packed with formulas, data, and tips essential to the modern hunter, target shooter, gun collector, and all others interested in guns.

The Practical Book of Guns, by Ken Warner, Winchester Press, New York, NY, 1978. 261 pp., illus. $13.95.

A book that delves into the important things about firearms and their use.

E. C. Prudhomme, Master Gun Engraver, A Retrospective Exhibition: 1946-1973, intro. by John T. Amber, The R. W. Norton Art Gallery, Shreveport, LA, 1973. 32 pp., illus., paper covers. $3.50.

Examples of master gun engraving by Jack Prudhomme.

The Quiet Killers II: Silencer Update, by J. David Truby, Paladin Press, Boulder, CO, 1979. 92 p., illus. Paper covers.

A unique and up-to-date addition to your silencer bookshelf.

Sam Colt: Genius, by Robt. F. Hudson, American Archives Publ. Co., Topsfield, MA, 1971. 160 pp., illus. Plastic spiral bound. $6.50.

Historical review of Colt's inventions, including facsimiles of patent papers and other Colt information.

The Shooter's Workbench, by John A. Mosher, Winchester Press, NY, 1977. 256 pp., illus. $12.95.

Accessories the shooting sportsman can build for the range, for the shop, for transport and the field, and for the handloading bench.

Small Arms of the World, 11th Edition, a complete revision of W. H. B. Smith's firearms classic by Edward Clinton Ezell, Stackpole Books, Harrisburg, PA, 1977. 667 pp., illus. $25.00.

A complete revision of this firearms classic now brings all arms enthusiasts up to date on global weapons production and use.

Sporting Arms of the World, by Ray Bearse, Outdoor Life/Harper & Row, N.Y., 1977. 500 pp., illus. $15.95.

A mammoth, up-to-the-minute guide to the sporting world's favorite rifles, shotguns, handguns.

Survival Guns, by Mel Tappan, The Janus Press, Inc., Los Angeles, CA, 1976. 458 pp., illus. Paper covers. $9.95.

A guide to the selection, modification and use of firearms and related devices for defense, food gathering, etc. under conditions of long term survival.

Treatise on Military Small Arms and Ammunition 1888, compiled by Col. J. Bond, R. A. Arms and Armour Press, London, Eng., 1971. 142 pp., illus. $12.50.

Facsimile of the original compiled in 1888 at the School of Musketry, Hythe, and accepted by the British Army as a definitive textbook.

Triggernometry, by Eugene Cunningham. Caxton Printers Lt., Caldwell, ID, 1970. 441 pp., illus. $9.95.

A classic study of famous outlaws and lawmen of the West—their stature as human beings, their exploits and skills in handling firearms. A reprint.

Weapons of the American Revolution, and Accoutrements, by Warren Moore. A & W Books, NY, 1974. 225 pp., fine illus. $15.

Revolutionary era shoulder arms, pistols, edged weapons, and equipment are described and shown in fine drawings and photographs, some in color.

Gunsmithing

The Art of Engraving, by James B. Meek, F. Brownell & Son, Montezuma, IA, 1973. 196 pp., illus. $19.95.

A complete, authoritative, imaginative and detailed study in training for gun engraving. The first book of its kind—and a great one.

Artistry in Arms. The R. W. Norton Gallery, Shreveport, LA., 1970. 42 pp., illus. Paper, $3.50.

The art of gunsmithing and engraving.

Black Powder Gunsmithing, by Ralph T. Walker, DBI Books, Inc., Northfield, IL, 1978. 288 pp., illus. Paper covers. $7.95.

An overview of the entire subject from replica building to the advanced, intricate art of restoration.

Building the Kentucky Pistol, by James R. Johnston, Golden Age Arms Co., Worthington, OH, 1974. 36 pp., illus. Paper covers. $4.00.

A step-by-step guide for building the Kentucky pistol. Illus. with full page line drawings.

Building the Kentucky Rifle, by J. R. Johnston. Golden Age Arms Co., Worthington, OH, 1972. 44 pp., illus. Paper covers. $5.

How to go about it, with text and drawings.

Checkering and Carving of Gun Stocks, by Monte Kennedy. Stackpole Books, Harrisburg, PA, 1962. 175 pp., illus. $17.95.

Rev., enlarged clothbound ed. of a much sought-after, dependable work.

The Complete Rehabilitation of the Flintlock Rifle and Other Works, by T. B. Tryon. Limbo Library, Taos, NM, 1972. 112 pp., illus. Paper covers. $6.95.

A series of articles which first appeared in various issues of the *American Rifleman* in the 1930s.

Do-It-Yourself Gunsmithing, by Jim Carmichel, Outdoor Life-Harper & Row, New York, NY, 1977. 371 pp., illus. $14.95.

The author proves that home gunsmithing is relatively easy and highly satisfying.

Firearms Blueing and Browning, by R. H. Angier. Stackpole Books, Harrisburg, PA, 151 pp., illus. $9.95.

A useful, concise text on chemical coloring methods for the gunsmith and mechanic.

Gun Care and Repair, by Monte Burch, Winchester Press, NY, 1978. 256 pp., illus. $12.95.

Everything the gun owner needs to know about home gunsmithing and firearms maintenance.

Gun Digest Book of Firearms Assembly/Disassembly Part I: Automatic Pistols, by J. B. Wood, DBI Books, Inc., Northfield, IL, 1979. 320 pp., illus. Paper covers. $8.95.

A thoroughly professional presentation on the art of pistol disassembly and reassembly. Covers most modern guns, popular older models, and some of the most complex pistols ever produced.

Gun Digest Book of Firearms Assembly/Disassembly Part II: Revolvers, by J. B. Wood, DBI Books, Inc., Northfield, IL, 1979. 320 pp., illus. Paper covers. $8.95.

How to properly dismantle and reassemble both the revolvers of today and of the past.

The Gun Digest Book of Firearms Assembly/Disassembly Part III: Rimfire Rifles, by J. B. Wood, DBI Books, Inc., Northfield, IL, 1980. 288 pp., illus. Paper covers. $8.95.

A most comprehensive, uniform, and professional presentation available for disassembling and reassembling most rimfire rifles.

The Gun Digest Book of Firearms Assembly/Disassembly Part IV: Centerfire Rifles, by J. B. Wood, DBI Books, Inc., Northfield, IL, 1980. 288 pp., illus. Paper covers. $8.95.

A professional presentation on the assembly and reassembly of centerfire rifles.

The Gun Digest Book of Pistolsmithing, by Jack Mitchell, DBI Books, Inc., Northfield, IL, 1980. 288 pp., illus. Paper covers. $8.95.

An experts guide to the operation of each of the handgun actions with all the major functions of pistolsmithing explained.

Gun Owner's Book of Care, Repair & Improvement, by Roy Dunlap, Outdoor Life-Harper & Row, NY, 1974. 336 pp., illus. $12.95.

A basic guide to repair and maintenance of guns, written for the average firearms owner.

Gunsmith Kinks, by F. R. (Bob) Brownell. F. Brownell & Son., Montezuma, I. 1st ed., 1969. 496 pp., well illus. $9.95.

A widely useful accumulation of shop kinks, short cuts, techniques and pertinent comments by practicing gunsmiths from all over the world.

Gunsmithing, by Roy F. Dunlap. Stackpole Books, Harrisburg, PA, 714 pp., illus. $19.95.

Comprehensive work on conventional techniques, incl. recent advances in the field. Valuable to rifle owners, shooters, and practicing gunsmiths.

Gunsmiths and Gunmakers of Vermont, by Warren R. Horn, The Horn Co., Burlington, VT, 1976. 76 pp., illus. Paper covers. $5.00.

A checklist for collectors, of over 200 craftsmen who lived and worked in Vermont up to and including 1900.

Hobby Gunsmithing, by Ralph Walker, Digest Books, Inc., Northfield, IL, 1972, 320 pp., illus. Paper, $6.95.

Kitchen table gunsmithing for the budding hobbyist.

Home Gun Care & Repair, by P. O. Ackley. Stackpole Books, Harrisburg, PA, 1969. 191 pp., illus. Paper covers. $6.95.

Basic reference for safe tinkering, fixing, and converting rifles, shotguns, handguns.

Home Gunsmithing Digest, 2nd ed., by Robt. Steindler, DBI Books, Inc., Northfield, IL, 1978, 288 pp., very well illus. within stiff decorated paper covers. $7.95.

An unusually beneficial assist for gun owners doing their own repairs, maintenance, etc. Many chapters on tools, techniques and theories.

HOW . . . by L. Cowher, W. Hunley, and L. Johnston. NMLR Assn., IN, 1961. 107 pp., illus. Paper covers. $3.95.

This 1961 rev. ed., enlarged by 3 chapters and additional illustrations, covers the building of a muzzle-loading rifle, target pistol, and powder horn, and tells how to make gunflints.

How to Build Your Own Wheellock Rifle or Pistol, by Georg Lauber, The John Olson Co., Paramus, NJ, 1976. Paper covers. $6.95.

Complete instructions on building these arms.

How to Build Your Own Flintlock Rifle or Pistol, by Georg Lauber, The John Olson Co., Paramus, NJ, 1976. Paper covers. $6.95.

The second in Mr. Lauber's three-volume series on the art and science of building muzzle-loading black powder firearms.

"How to Build Your Own Percussion Rifle or Pistol", by Georg Lauber, The John Olson Co., Paramus, NJ, 1976. Paper covers, $6.95.

The third and final volume of Lauber's set of books on the building of muzzle-loaders.

Lock, Stock and Barrel, by R. H. McCrory. Publ. by author at Bellmore, NY, 1966. Paper covers, 122 pp., illus. $5.00.

A handy and useful work for the collector or the professional with many helpful procedures shown and described on antique gun repair.

The Modern Kentucky Rifle, How to Build Your Own, by R. H. McCrory. McCrory, Wantagh, NY, 1961. 68 pp., illus., paper bound. $5.00.

A workshop manual on how to fabricate a flintlock rifle. Also some information on pistols and percussion locks.

The NRA Gunsmithing Guide, National Rifle Association, Wash., DC, 1971. 336 pp., illus. Paper. $9.95.

Information of the past 15 years from the "American Rifleman," ranging from 03A3 Springfields to Model 92 Winchesters.

Pistolsmithing, by George C. Nonte, Jr., Stackpole Books, Harrisburg, PA, 1974. 560 pp., illus. $17.95.

A single source reference to handgun maintainence, repair, and modification at home, unequaled in value.

Professional Gunsmithing, by W. J. Howe, Stackpole Books, Harrisburg, PA, 1968 reprinting. 526 pp., illus. $24.95.

Textbook on repair and alteration of firearms, with detailed notes on equipment and commercial gunshop operation.

Recreating the American Rifle, by Wm. Buchel & Geo. Shumway, George Shumway, York, PA, 1973. 194 pp. illus. Paper $10.00.

A new edition with additional illustrations showing the workmanship of today's skilled rifle-makers.

Respectfully Yours H. M. Pope, compiled and edited by G. O. Kelver, Brighton, CO, 1976. 266 pp., illus. $16.50.

A compilation of letters from the files of the famous barrelmaker, Harry M. Pope.

The Trade Gun Sketchbook, by Charles E. Hanson, The Fur Press, Chadron, NB, 1979. 48 pp., illus. Paper covers. $4.00.

Complete full-size plans to build seven different trade guns from the Revolution to the Indian Wars and a two-thirds size for your son.

The Trade Rifle Sketchbook, by Charles E. Hanson, The Fur Press, Chadron, NB, 1979. 48 pp., illus. Paper covers. $4.00.

Includes full scale plans for ten rifles made for Indian and mountain men; from 1790 to 1860, plus plans for building three pistols.

Troubleshooting Your Handgun, by J. B. Wood, DBI Books, Inc., Northfield, IL, 1978. 192 pp., illus. Paper covers. $5.95.

A masterful guide on how to avoid trouble and how to operate guns with care.

Troubleshooting Your Rifle and Shotgun, by J. B. Wood, DBI Books, Inc., Northfield, IL, 1978. 192 pp., illus. Paper covers. $5.95.

A gunsmiths advice on how to keep your long guns shooting.

handguns

American Pistol and Revolver Design and Performance, by L. R. Wallack, Winchester Press, NY, 1978. 224 pp., illus. $14.95.

How different types and models of pistols and revolvers work, from trigger pull to bullet impact.

Blue Steel and Gun Leather, by John Bianchi, Beinfeld Publishing, Inc., No. Hollywood, CA, 1978. 200 pp., illus. $9.95.

A complete and comprehensive review of holster uses plus an examination of available products on today's market.

Book of Pistols & Revolvers, by W. H. B. Smith. Stackpole Books, Harrisburg, PA, 1968. 758 pp., profusely illus. $8.95.

Rev. and enlarged, this encyclopedic reference, first publ. in 1946, continues to be the best on its subject.

Colt Automatic Pistols, by Donald B. Bady, Borden Publ. Co., Alhambra, CA, 1974. 368 pp., illus. $15.

The rev. and enlarged ed. of a key work on a fascinating subject. Complete information on every automatic marked with Colt's name.

The Colt .45 Auto Pistol, compiled from U. S. War Dept. Techinical Manuals, and reprinted by Desert Publications, Cornville, AZ, 1978. 80 pp., illus. Paper covers. $4.95.

Covers every facet of this famous pistol from mechanical training, manual of arms, disassembly, repair and replacement of parts.

Combat Handgun Shooting, by James D. Mason, Charles C. Thomas, Springfield, IL, 1976. 256 pp., illus. $27.50.

Discusses in detail the human as well as the mechanical aspects of shooting.

Combat Handguns, edited by Edward C. Ezell, Stackpole Books, Harrisburg, PA, 1980. 288 pp., illus. $19.95.

George Nonte's last great work, edited by Edward C. Ezell. A comprehensive reference volume offering full coverage of automatic handguns vs. revolvers, custom handguns, combat autoloaders and revolvers—domestic and foreign, and combat testing.

Combat Shooting for Police, by Paul B. Weston. Charles C. Thomas, Springfield, IL, 1967. A reprint. 194 pp., illus. $13.95.

First publ. in 1960 this popular self-teaching manual gives basic concepts of defensive fire in every position.

Defensive Handgun Effectiveness, by Carroll E. Peters, Carroll E. Peters, Manchester, TN, 1977. 198 pp., charts and graphs. $10.00.

A systematic approach to the design, evaluation and selection of ammunition for the defensive handgun.

Flattops & Super Blackhawks, by H. W. Ross, Jr., H. W. Ross, Jr., Bridgeville, PA, 1979. 93 pp., illus. Paper covers. $9.75.

An expanded version of the authors book "Ruger Blackhawks" with an extra chapter on Super Blackhawks and the Mag-Na-Ports with serial numbers and approximate production dates.

A Handbook on the Primary Identification of Revolvers & Semi-automatic Pistols, by John T. Millard, Charles C. Thomas, Springfield, IL, 1974. 156 pp., illus. $12.50.

A practical outline on the simple, basic phases of primary firearm identification with particular reference to revolvers and semi-automatic pistols.

Handgun Competition, by Maj. Geo. C. Nonte, Jr., Winchester Press, NY, 1978. 288 pp., illus. $14.95.

A comprehensive source-book covering all aspects of modern competitive pistol and revolver shooting.

High Standard Automatic Pistols 1932-1950, by Charles E. Petty, American Ordnance Publ., Charlotte, NC, 1976. 124 pp., illus. $12.95.

A definitive source of information for the collector of High Standard pistols.

Japanese Hand Guns, by F. E. Leithe, Borden Publ. Co., Alhambra, CA, 1968. Unpaginated, well illus. $9.95.

Identification guide, covering models produced since the late 19th century. Brief text material gives history, descriptions, and markings.

Jeff Cooper on Handguns, by Jeff Cooper, Petersen Publishing Co., Los Angeles, CA, 1979. 96 pp., illus. Paper covers. $2.50.

An expert's guide to handgunning. Technical tips on actions, sights, loads, grips, and holsters.

Know Your 45 Auto Pistols—Models 1911 & A1, by E. J. Hoffschmidt, Blacksmith Corp., Southport, CT, 1974. 58 pp., illus. Paper covers. $4.95.

A concise history of the gun with a wide variety of types and copies illus.

Know Your Walther P.38 Pistols, by E. J. Hoffschmidt, Blacksmith Corp., Southport, CT, 1974. 77 pp., illus. Paper covers. $4.95.

Covers the Walther models, Armee, M.P., H.P., P-38—history and variations.

Know Your Walther P.P. & P.P.K. Pistols, by E. J. Hoffschmidt, Blacksmith Corp., Southport, CT, 1975. 87 pp., illus. Paper covers. $4.95.

A concise history of the guns with a guide to the variety and types.

The Luger Pistol (Pistole Parabellum), by F. A. Datig. Borden Publ. Co., Alhambra, CA, 1962. 328 pp., well illus. $9.50.

An enlarged, rev. ed. of an important reference on the arm, its history and development from 1893 to 1945.

Luger Variations, by Harry E. Jones, Harry E. Jones, Torrance, CA, 1975. 328 pp., 160 full page illus., many in color. $22.50.

A rev. ed. of the book known as "The Luger Collector's Bible."

Lugers at Random, by Charles Kenyon, Jr. Handgun Press, Chicago, IL. 1st ed., 1970. 416 pp., profusely illus. $20.00.

An impressive large side-opening book carrying throughout alternate facing-pages of descriptive text and clear photographs. A new boon to the Luger collector and/or shooter.

Mauser Pocket Pistols 1910-1946, by Roy G. Pender, Collectors Press, Houston, TX, 1971. 307 pp., $13.50.

Comprehensive work covering over 100 variations, including factory boxes and manuals. Over 300 photos. Limited, numbered ed.

The Mauser Self-Loading Pistol, by Belford & Dunlap. Borden Publ. (Alhambra, CA. Over 200 pp., 300 illus., large format. $12.50.

The long-awaited book on the "Broom Handles," covering their incept in 1894 to the end of production. Complete and in detail: pocket pist Chinese and Spanish copies, etc.

The Pistol Guide, by George C. Nonte, Stoeger Publ. Co., So. Hackensa NJ, 1980. 256 pp., illus. Paper covers. $8.95.

A unique and detailed examination of a very specialized type of gun: t autoloading pistol.

Pistol and Revolver Digest 2nd Edition, ed. by Dean A. Grennell & Jack Lew DBI Books, Inc., Northfield, IL, 1979. 288 pp., illus. Paper covers. $7.9

Articles on reloading, maintenance and repairs, handguns for silhouet shooting, handgunning for big game, new developments in handguns a handgun ammo, etc.

Pistol & Revolver Guide, 3rd Ed., by George C. Nonte, Follett Publ. C Chicago, IL, 1975. 224 pp., illus. Paper covers. $6.95.

A new and up-dated ed. of the standard reference work on military ai sporting handguns.

Quick or Dead, by William L. Cassidy, Paladin Press, Boulder, CO, 1978. 1 pp., illus. $10.95.

Close-quarter combat firing, with particular reference to prominei twentieth-century British and American methods of instruction.

Report of Board on Tests of Revolvers and Automatic Pistols. From The *Annu Report* of the Chief of Ordnance, 1907. Reprinted by J. C. Tillinghas Marlow, NH, 1969. 34 pp., 7 plates, paper covers. $5.00.

A comparison of handguns, including Luger, Savage, Col Webley-Fosbery and other makes.

System Mauser, a Pictorial History of the Model 1896 Self-Loading Pistol, b J. W. Breathed, Jr., and J. J. Schroeder, Jr. Handgun Press, Chicago, Il 1967. 273 pp., well illus. 1st limited ed. hardbound. $17.50.

10 Shots Quick, by Daniel K. Stern, Globe Printing Co., San Jose, CA, 196 153 pp., photos. $8.50.

History of Savage-made automatic pistols, models of 1903-1917, wit descriptive data for shooters and collectors.

U.S. Test Trials 1900 Luger, by Michael Reese II, Pioneer Press, Union City TN, 1976. 130 pp., illus. Paper covers. $4.95.

Revised edition containing much additional material on the notabl American Eagle test pieces. Rare illustrations.

The Walther P-38 Pistol, by Maj. Geo. C. Nonte, Paladin Press, Boulder, CC 1975. 90 pp., illus. Paper covers. $5.00.

Covers all facets of the gun—development, history, variations, technica data, practical use, rebuilding, repair and conversion.

The Walther Pistols 1930-1945, by Warren H. Buxton, Warren H. Buxton Los Alamos, NM, 1978. 350 pp., illus. $29.95.

Volume I of a projected 4 volume series "The P.38 Pistol." The historie evolutions, and variations of the Walther P.38 and its predecessors.

hunting

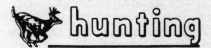

NORTH AMERICA

All About Deer in America, ed. by Robert Elman, Winchester Press, NY, 1976. 256 pp., illus. $10.

Twenty of America's great hunters share the secrets of their hunting success.

All-Season Hunting, by Bob Gilsvik, Winchester Press, NY, 1976. 256 pp., illus. $11.95.

A guide to early-season, late-season and winter hunting in America.

All About Small-Game Hunting in America, ed. by Russell Tinsley, Winchester Press, NY, 1976. 308 pp., illus. $11.95.

Collected advice by the finest small-game experts in the country.

All About Wildfowling in America, by Jerome Knap, Winchester Press, NY, 1977. 256 pp., illus. $11.95.

More than a dozen top writers provide new and controversial ideas on how-to and where-to hunt wildfowl successfully.

The Art of Hunting Big Game in North America, by Jack O'Connor, Random House, NY, 1978. 418 pp., illus. $13.95.

A new revised and updated edition on technique, planning, skill, outfitting, etc.

Art of Successful Deer Hunting, by F. E. Sell, Stackpole Books, Harrisburg, PA, 1971. 192 pp., paper, $3.95.

Illus. re-issue of "The Deer Hunter's Guide." Western hunting lore for rifle and bow-hunter.

The Best of Nash Buckingham, by Nash Buckingham, selected, edited and annotated by George Bird Evans. Winchester Press, NY, 1973. 320 pp. $12.50.

Thirty pieces that represent the very cream of Nash's output on his whole range of outdoor interests—upland shooting, duck hunting, even fishing.

The Big Game Animals of North America, by Jack O'Connor, Outdoor Life, NY, 1977, updated and revised edition. 238 pp., illus. $14.95.

A classic work on North American big game.

Big Game Hunter's Digest, by Tom Brakefield, DBI Books, Inc., Northfield, IL, 1977. 288 pp., illus. Paper covers. $7.95.

A truly complete reference to North American big game hunting.

Bird Hunting Know-How, by D. M. Duffey, Van Nostrand, Princeton, NJ, 1968. 192 pp., illus. $5.95.

Game-getting techniques and sound advice on all aspects of upland bird hunting, plus data on guns and loads.

Black Powder Hunting, by Sam Fadala, Stackpole Books, Harrisburg, PA, 1978. 192 pp., illus. $10.95.

The author demonstrates successful hunting methods using percussion firearms for both small and big game.

Bobwhite Quail Hunting, by Charley Dickey, printed for Stoeger Publ. Co., So. Hackensack, NJ, 1974. 112 pp., illus., paper covers. $2.95.

Habits and habitats, techniques, gear, guns and dogs.

The Bobwhite Quail, its Life and Management, by Walter Rosene. Rutgers University Press, New Brunswick, NJ. 1st ed., 1969. 418 pp., photographs, maps and color plates. $27.50.

An exhaustive study of an important species which has diminished under the impact of changing agricultural and forestry practices.

The Complete Book of Deer Hunting, by Byron W. Dalrymple, Winchester Press, NY, 1973. 247 pp., illus. $12.95.

Practical "how-to" information. Covers the 20 odd North-American subspecies of deer.

The Complete Book of the Wild Turkey, by Roger M. Latham, Stackpole Books, Harrisburg, PA, 1978. 228 pp., illus. $8.95.

A new revised edition of the classic on American wild turkey hunting.

The Complete Guide to Bird Dog Training, by John R. Falk, Winchester Press, NY, 1976. 256 pp., illus. $10.95.

How to choose, raise, train, and care for a bird dog.

Deer Hunting, by R. Smith, Stackpole Books, Harrisburg, PA, 1978. 224 pp., illus. $10.95.

A professional guide leads the hunt for North America's most popular big game animal.

The Dove Shooter's Handbook, by Dan M. Russell, Winchester Press, NY, 1974. 256 pp., illus. $9.95.

A complete guide to America's top game bird—natural history, hunting methods, equipment, conservation and future prospects.

Dove Hunting, by Charley Dickey, Galahad Books, NY, 1976. 112 pp., illus. $6.00.

This indispensable guide for hunters deals with equipment, techniques, types of dove shooting, hunting dogs, etc.

Drummer in the Woods, by Burton L. Spiller, Stackpole Books, Harrisburg, PA, 1980. 240 pp., illus. $12.95.

Twenty-one wonderful stories on grouse shooting by "the Poet Laureate of Grouse."

The Duck Hunter's Handbook, by Bob Hinman, Winchester Press, NY, 1974. 252 pp., illus. $11.95.

Down-to-earth, practical advice on bagging ducks and geese.

Ducks of the Mississippi Flyway, ed. by John McKane. North Star Press, St. Cloud, MN, 1969. 54 pp., illus. Paper covers, $2.98.

A duck hunter's reference. Full color paintings of some 30 species, plus descriptive text.

Expert Advice on Gun Dog Training, ed. by David M. Duffey, Winchester Press, NY, 1977. 256 pp., illus. $11.95.

Eleven top pros talk shop, revealing the techniques and philosophies that account for their consistent success.

A Gallery of Waterfowl and Upland Birds, by Gene Hill, with illustrations by David Maass, Pedersen Prints, Los Angeles, CA, 1978. 132 pp., illus. $39.95. Deluxe bound, signed edition, in slipcase. $250.

Gene Hill at his best. Liberally illustrated with fifty-one full-color reproductions of David Maass' finest paintings.

Getting the Most out of Modern Waterfowling, by John O. Cartier, St. Martin's Press, NY, 1974. 396 pp., illus. $10.95.

The most comprehensive, up-to-date book on waterfowling imaginable.

The Great Arc of the Wild Sheep, by J. L. Clark, Univ. of Oklahoma Press, Norman, Okla., 1978. 247 pp., illus. Paper covers. $8.95.

Every classified variety of wild sheep is discussed, as found in North America, Asia & Europe. Numerous hunting stories by experts are included.

Grizzly Country, by Andy Russell. A. A. Knopf, NYC, 1973, 302 pp., illus. $10.00.

Many-sided view of the grizzly bear and his world, by a noted guide, hunter and naturalist.

Grouse and Woodcock, An Upland Hunter's Book, by Nick Sisley, Stackpole Books, Harrisburg, PA, 1980. 192 pp., illus. $11.95.

Latest field techniques for effective grouse and woodcock hunting.

Handgun Hunting, by Maj. George C. Nonte, Jr. and Lee E. Jurras, Winchester Press, NY, 1975. 245 pp., illus. $10.95.

A book with emphasis on the hunting of readily available game in the U.S. with the handgun.

Hard Hunting, by Patrick Shaughnessy and Diane Swingle, Winchester Press, New York, NY, 1978, $11.95.

A couple explores a no-frills, low-cost, highly successful, adventurous approach to wilderness hunting.

Horns in the High Country, by Andy Russell, Alfred A. Knopf, NY, 1973. 259 pp., illus. $15.00.

A many-sided view of wild sheep and the natural world in which they live.

How to Hunt, by Dave Bowring, Winchester Press, NY, 1978. 256 pp., illus. $10.95.

A basic guide to hunting big game, small game, upland birds, and waterfowl.

How to Measure and Score Big-Game Trophies, by Grancel Fitz, revised edition, David McKay Co., Inc., New York, NY, 1977. 128 pp., illus. $12.50.

The official scoring method used by Boone and Crockett Club and Pope and Young Club. Plus every official scoring chart for all 26 species.

Hunt Close!, by Jerome B. Robinson, Winchester Press, NY, 1978. 224 pp., illus. $12.95.

A realistic guide to training close-working dogs for today's tight cover conditions.

A Hunter's Fireside Book, by Gene Hill Winchester Press, NY, 1972. 192 pp., illus. $11.95

An outdoor book that will appeal to every person who spends time in the field—or who wishes he could.

Hunting the American Wild Turkey, by Dave Harbour, Stackpole Books, Harrisburg, PA, 1975. 256 pp., illus. $9.95.

The techniques and tactics of hunting North America's largest, and most popular, woodland game bird.

Hunting America's Game Animals and Birds, by Robert Elman and George Peper, Winchester Press, NY, 1975. 368 pp., illus. $12.95.

A how-to, where-to, when-to guide—by 40 top experts—covering the continent's big, small, upland game and waterfowl.

Hunting Big-Game Trophies; A North America Guide, by Tom Brakefield, E. P. Dutton & Co., Inc., NY, 1976. 446 pp., illus. $10.95.

Where to go, when to go, camp savvy, animal lore, the hunt, etc.

Hunting Dog Know-How, by D. M. Duffey, Van Nostrand, Princeton, NJ, 1965. 177 pp., illus. $6.95.

Covers selection, breeds, and training of hunting dogs, problems in hunting and field trials.

Hunting for all Seasons, by Alex Kay, A & W Books, NY, 1976. 159 pp., illus. $5.95.

The complete how-to handbook on when and where to bag your quarry, how much gun to use on what game.

Hunting Moments of Truth, by Eric Peper and Jim Rikhoff, Winchester Press, NY, 1973. 208 pp., illus. $8.95.

The world's most experienced hunters recount 22 most memorable occasions.

Hunting with Bow and Arrow, by George Laycock and Erwin Bauer. Arco Publ. Co., Inc., NYC, 1966. $3.95.

A practical guide to archery as a present-day sport. Mentions equipment needed and how to select it. Illus. instructions on how to shoot with ease and accuracy.

Hunting Trophy Deer, by John Wootters, Winchester Press, NY, 1977. 288 pp., illus. $14.95.

One of America's most experienced and respected hunting writers provides all the specialized advice you need to succeed at bagging trophy deer.

Hunting Upland Birds, by Chas. F. Waterman. Winchester Press, NY, 1972. 320 pp., illus. $8.95.

Excellent treatment of game habits and habitat, hunting methods, and management techniques for each of the 18 major North American gamebird species.

Hunting the Uplands with Rifle and Shotgun, by Luther A. Anderson, Winchester Press, NY, 1977. 224 pp., illus. $12.95.

Solid, practical know-how to help make hunting deer and every major species of upland game bird easier and more satisfying.

Hunting Whitetail Deer, by Robert E. Donovan, Winchester Press, NY, 1978. 256 pp., illus. $12.50.

For beginners and experts alike, this book is the key to successful whitetail hunting.

Hunting the Woodlands for Small and Big Game, by Luther A. Anderson, A. S. Barnes & Co., New York, NY, 1980. 256 pp., illus. $12.00.

A comprehensive guide to hunting in the United States. Chapters on firearms, game itself, marksmanship, clothing and equipment.

In Search of the Wild Turkey, by Bob Gooch, Greatlakes Living Press, Ltd., Waukegan, IL, 1978. 182 pp., illus. $9.95.

A state-by-state guide to wild turkey hot spots, with tips on gear and methods for bagging your bird.

The Market Hunter, by David and Jim Kimball, Dillon Press Inc., Minneapolis, MN, 1968. 132 pp., illus. $6.95.

The market hunter, one of the "missing chapters" in American history, is brought to life in this book.

In a simple and entertaining manner the author explains how to live

Modern Hunting with Indian Secrets, by Allan A. Macfarlan. Stackpole Books, Harrisburg, PA, 1971. 222 pp., $10.00.

How to acquire the new-old skills of the Redman, how to apply them to modern hunting.

Modern Turkey Hunting, by James F. Brady, Crown Publ., N.Y.C., NY, 1973. 160 pp., illus. $9.95.

A thorough guide to the habits, habitat, and methods of hunting America's largest game bird.

More Grouse Feathers, by Burton L. Spiller. Crown Publ., NY, 1972. 238 pp., illus. $8.50.

Facsimile of the original Derrydale Press issue of 1938. Guns and dogs, the habits and shooting of grouse, woodcook, ducks, etc. Illus. by Lynn Bogue Hunt.

Mostly Tailfeathers, by Gene Hill, Winchester Press, NY, 1975. 192 pp., illus. $11.95.

An interesting, general book about bird hunting with some stories on fishing.

North American Big Game, ed. by Wm. H. Nesbitt and Jack S. Parker, The Boone and Crockett Club and the National Rifle Association of America, Wash., DC, 8th ed., 1981. 367 pp., illus. $29.50.

The official records book for outstanding native North American big game trophies.

The North American Waterfowler, by Paul S. Bernsen. Superior Publ. Co., Seattle, WA, 1972. 206 pp. Paper covers, $4.95.

The complete inside and outside story of duck and goose shooting. Big and colorful, illus. by Les Kouba.

1001 Hunting Tips, by Robert Elman, Winchester Press, N.Y., NY, 1978. 256 pp., illus. $15.95.

A post-graduate course in big-game hunting, small-game hunting, wildfowling, and hunting upland birds.

The Old Man's Boy Grows Older, by Robert Ruark, Holt, Rinehart and Winston, New York, NY, 1961. 302 pp., illus. $25.00.

A classic by a gib-game hunter and world traveler.

One Man's Wilderness, by Warren Page, Holt, Rinehart and Winston, NY, 1973. 256 pp., illus. $11.50.

A world-known writer and veteran sportsman recounts the joys of a lifetime of global hunting.

Outdoor Life's Deer Hunting Book, by Jack O'Connor, et al, Harper & Row Publ., Inc., NY, 1974. 224 pp., illus. $7.95.

A major new work on deer hunting. Covers every aspect of the sport.

The Outlaw Gunner, by Harry M. Walsh, Tidewater Publishers, Cambridge, MD, 1973. 178 pp., illus. $12.50.

A colorful story of market gunning in both its legal and illegal phases.

The Practical Hunter's Dog Book, by John R. Falk, Winchester Press, NY, 1971. 314 pp., illus. $10.95.

Helps to choose, train and enjoy your gun dog.

The Practical Hunter's Handbook, by Anthony J. Acerrano, Winchester Press, New York, NY, 1978. 224 pp., illus. $11.95.

How the time-pressed hunter can take advantage of every edge his hunting situation affords him.

Practical Pointer Training, by Sherman Webb, Winchester Press, NY 1976. 192 pp., illus. $9.95.

A good bird dog training book that fills the bill.

Ranch Life and the Hunting Trail, by Theodore Roosevelt, Readex Microprint Corp., Dearborn, MI. 1966. 186 pp., With drawings by Frederic Remington. $10.

A facsimile reprint of the original 1899 Century Co. edition. One of the most fascinating books of the West of that day.

Ringneck! Pheasants & Pheasant Hunting, by Ted Janes, Crown Publ., NY, 1975. 120 pp., illus. $8.95.

A thorough study of one of our more popular game birds.

Selected American Game Birds, by David Hagerbaumer and Sam Lehman, The Caxton Printers, Ltd., Caldwell, ID, 1972. The entire text of this book is executed in decorated calligraphy. $30.00.

Twenty-six of David Hagerbaumer's exquisite original watercolors, representing 29 bird species. A must for every book collector and art lover.

Shooting Pictures, by A. B. Frost, with 24 pp. of text by Chas. D. Lanier. Winchester Press, NY, 1972. 12 color plates. Enclosed in a board portfolio. Ed. limited to 750 numbered copies. $75.

Frost's twelve superb 12″ by 16″ pictures have often been called the finest sporting prints published in the U.S. A facsimile of the 1895-6 edition printed on fine paper with superb color fidelity.

Shots at Mule Deer, by Rollo S. Robinson, Winchester Press, New York, NY, 1970. 209 pp., illus. $15.

Description, strategies for bagging it, the correct rifle and cartridge to use.

Small Game Hunting, by Tom Brakefield, J. B. Lippincott Co., Phila., PA, 1978. 244 pp., illus. $10.

Describes where, when, and how to hunt all major small game species from coast to coast.

The Sportsman's Companion, by Lee Wulff. Harper & Row, N.Y.C., 1968. 413 pp., illus. $11.95.

Compendium of writings by various experts on hunting and fishing for American game. A useful reference for the outdoorsman.

Squirrels and Squirrel Hunting, by Bob Gooch. Tidewater Publ., Cambridge, MD, 1973. 148 pp., illus. $6.

A complete book for the squirrel hunter, beginner or old hand. Details methods of hunting, squirrel habitat, management, proper clothing, care of the kill, cleaning and cooking.

Successful Waterfowling, by Zack Taylor, Crown Publ., NY, 1974. 276 pp., illus. $10.95.

The definitive guide to new ways of hunting ducks and geese.

Timberdoodle, by Frank Woolner, Crown Publ., Inc., NY, 1974. 168 pp., illus. $10.95.

A thorough, practical guide to the American woodcock and to woodcock hunting.

Topflight; A Speed Index to Waterfowl, by J. A. Ruthven & Wm. Zimmerman, Moebius Prtg. Co., Milwaukee, WI, 1968. 112 pp. $7.50.

Rapid reference for specie identification. Marginal color band of book directs reader to proper section. 263 full color illustrations of body and feather configurations.

Trouble With Bird Dogs . . . and What to do About Them, by George Bird Evans, Winchester Press, NY, 1976. 288 pp., illus. $12.95.

How to custom-train your dog for specific kinds of hunting.

Turkey Hunter's Guide, by Byron W. Dalrymple, et al, a publication of The National Rifle Association, Washington, DC, 1979. 96 pp., illus. Paper covers. $4.95.

Expert advice on turkey hunting hotspots, guns, guides, and calls.

Upland Bird & Waterfowl Hunting, ed. by Dave Petzal, Simon & Schuster, NY, 1976. 315 pp., illus. $9.95.

A collection of stories by an outstanding panel of knowledgeable experts on the subject.

The Whitetail Deer Hunter's Handbook, by John Weiss, Winchester Press, New York, NY, 1979. 256 pp., illus. $12.95.

Wherever you live, whatever your level of experience, this brand-new handbook will make you a better deer hunter.

Whitetail: Fundamentals and Fine Points for the Hunter, by George Mattis, World Publ. Co. New York, NY, 1976. 273 pp., illus. $9.95.

A manual of shooting and trailing and an education in the private world of the deer.

The Wings of Dawn, by George Reiger, Stein and Day, New York, NY, 1980. 320 pp., illus. $29.95.

The complete book of North American waterfowling.

The Young Shot, by Noel M. Sedgwick, A. & C. Black, London, Eng., 1976. 240 pp., illus. $8.95.

A revised and re-illustrated edition of Sedgwick's original work plus a preface and appendix dealing with changes in law since the first ed.

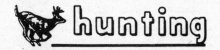

AFRICA/ASIA

African Rifles & Cartridges, by John Taylor, The Gun Room Press, Highland Park, NJ, 1977. 431 pp., illus. $16.95.

Experiences and opinions of a professional ivory hunter in Africa describing his knowledge of numerous arms and cartridges for big game. A reprint.

Big Game Hunting Around the World, by Bert Klineburger and Vernon W. Hurst, Exposition Press, Jericho, NY, 1969. 376 pp., illus. $15.00.

The first book that takes you on a safari all over the world.

Death in the Long Grass, by Peter Hathaway Capstick, St. Martin's Press, New York, NY, 1977. 297 pp., illus. $11.95.

A big game hunter's adventures in the African bush.

Elephant, by D. E. Blunt, Neville Spearman, London, 1971. 260 pp., illus. $25.00.

Reprint, of a rare book, a hunter's account of the ways of an elephant.

Great Game Animals of the World, by Russell B. Aitken. Winchester Press, N.Y, 1969. 192 pp. profusely illus. in monochrome and color. $22.50.

Accounts of man's pursuit of big game in all parts of the world, told in many fine pictures.

Green Hills of Africa, by Ernest Hemingway. Charles Scribner's Sons, NY, 1963. 285 pp. illus. Paper covers, $4.95.

A famous narrative of African big-game hunting, first published in 1935.

Horned Death, by John F. Burger. Standard Publications, Huntington, WV, 1947. 340 pp. illus. $45.00.

Hunting the African cape buffalo.

Jim Corbett's India, ed. by R. E. Hawkins, Oxford University Press, London, England, 1978. 250 pp., illus. $14.95.

A selection of Jim Corbett's writings from 1907 to 1939 taken from his books on hunting and his expeditions.

Rowland Ward's Records of Big Game, 17th ed., comp. by G. A. Best, Rowland Ward Pub., Ltd., 1976. 438 pp., illus. $85.00

New edition of the authoritive record of big game kills in Africa, by species.

Travel & Adventure in Southeast Africa, by F. C. Selous. A & F Press, N.Y.C., 1967. 522 pp. illus. $50.00.

New edition of a famous African hunting book, first published in 1893.

The Accurate Rifle, by Warren Page. Winchester Press, NY, 1973. 256 pp., illus. $11.95.

A masterly discussion. A must for the competitive shooter hoping to win, and highly useful to the practical hunter.

American Rifle Design and Performance, by L. R. Wallack, Winchester Press, NY, 1977. 288 pp., illus. $14.95.

An authoritative, comprehensive guide to how and why every kind of sporting rifle works.

The Bolt Action: A Design Analysis, by Stuart Otteson, ed. by Ken Warner, Winchester Press, NY, 1976. 320 pp., illus. $12.95.

Precise and in-depth descriptions, illustrations, and comparisons of 16 bolt actions. A new approach.

Bolt Action Rifles, by Frank de Haas, ed. by John T. Amber, Editor of Gun Digest. DBI Books, Inc., Northfield, IL, 1971. 320 pp., illus. Paper, $7.95.

The definitive work, covering every major design since the Mauser of 1871.

The Book of the Garand, by Maj.-Gen. J. S. Hatcher, The Gun Room Press, Highland Park, NJ, 1977. 292 pp., illus. $15.00.

A new printing of the standard reference work on the U.S. Army M1 rifle.

The Book of Rifles, by W. H. B. Smith. Stackpole Books, Harrisburg, PA, 1963 (3rd ed.). 656 pp., profusely illus. $7.98.

An encyclopedic reference work on shoulder arms, recently up-dated. Includes rifles of all types, arranged by country of origin.

Carbines Cal. .30 M1, M1A1, M2 and M3, by D. B. McLean. Normount Armament Co., Wickenburg, AZ, 1964. 221 pp., well illus., paperbound. $6.95.

U.S. field manual reprints on these weapons, edited and reorganized.

The Deer Rifle, by L. R. Wallack, Winchester Press, New York, NY, 1978. 256 pp., illus. $12.95.

Everything the deer hunter needs to know to select and use the arms and ammunition appropriate to his needs.

Description and Instructions for the Management of the Gallery-Practice Rifle Caliber .22—Model of 1903. Inco., 1972. 12 pp., 1 plate. Paper, $2.50.

Reprint of 1907 War Dept. pamphlet No. 1925.

Description of Telescopic Musket Sights, Inco., 1972. 10 pp., 4 plates. Paper, $2.50.

Reprint of 1917 War Dept. pamphlet No. 1957, first publ. in 1908.

The First Winchester, by John E. Parsons. Winchester Press, New York, NY, 1977. 207 pp., well illus., $14.95.

This new printing of *The Story of the 1866 Repeating Rifle* (1st publ. 1955) is revised, and additional illustrations included.

A Forgotten Heritage; The Story of a People and the Early American Rifle, by Harry P. Davis, The Gun Room Press, Highland Park, NJ, 1976. 199 pp., illus. $9.95.

Reprint of a very scarce history, originally published in 1941, the Kentucky rifle and the people who used it.

Garand Rifles M1, M1C, M1D, by Donald B. McLean. Normount Armament Co., Wickenburg, AZ, 1968. Over 160 pp., 175 illus., paper wrappers. $6.95.

Covers all facets of the arm: battlefield use, disassembly and maintenance, all details to complete lock-stock-and-barrel repair, plus variations, grenades, ammo., and accessories; plus a section on 7.62mm NATO conventions.

The Golden Age of Single-Shot Rifles, by Edsall James, Pioneer Press, Union City, TN, 1975. 33 pp., illus. Paper covers. $2.75.

A detailed look at all of the fine, high quality sporting single-shot rifles that were once the favorite of target shooters.

The Gun Digest Book of the .22 Rimfire, by John Lachuk, DBI Books, Northfield, IL, 1978. 224 pp., illus. Paper covers. $6.95.

Everything you want to know about the .22 rimfire and the arms that use it.

The Hunting Rifle, by Jack O'Connor. Winchester Press, NY, 1970. 352 pp., illus. $13.95.

An analysis, with wit and wisdom, of contemporary rifles, cartridges, accessories and hunting techniques.

Know Your M1 Garand, by E. J. Hoffschmidt, Blacksmith Corp., Southport, CT, 1975. 84 pp., illus. Paper Covers. $4.95.

Facts about America's most famous infantry weapon. Covers test and experimental models, Japanese and Italian copies, National Match models. WY, 1969. 32 pp., illus., paper covers. $3.00.

The Model 70 Winchester 1937-1964, by Dean H. Whitaker, Taylor Publishing Co., Dallas, TX, 1978. 210 pp., illus. $24.95.

An authoritative reference book on this model. Gives production history, changes, dimensions, specifications on special-order guns, etc.

The M-14 Rifle, facsimile reprint of FM 23-8, Desert Publications, Cornville, AZ. 50 pp., illus. Paper. $4.95.

In this well illustrated and informative reprint, the M-14 and M-14E2 are covered thoroughly.

The Modern Rifle, by Jim Carmichel, Winchester Press, NY, 1975. 320 pp., illus. $12.95.

The most comprehensive, thorough, up-to-date book ever published on today's rifled sporting arms.

100 Years of Shooters and Gunmakers of Single Shot Rifles, by Gerald O. Kelver, Brighton, CO, 1975. 212 pp., illus. Paper covers $10.00.

The Schuetzen rifle, targets and shooters, primers, match rifles, original loadings and much more. With chapters on famous gunsmiths like Harry Pope, Morgan L. Rood and others.

The '03 Springfields, by Clark S. Campbell, Ray Riling Arms Books Co., Phila., PA, 1978. 320 pp., illus. $25.00.

The most authoritative and definitive work on this famous U.S. rifle, the 1903 Springfield and its 30-06 cartridge.

The Pennsylvania Rifle, by Samuel E. Dyke, Sutter House, Lititz, PA, 1975. 61 pp., illus. Paper covers. $3.00.

History and development, from the hunting rifle of the Germans who settled the area. Contains a full listing of all known Lancaster, PA gunsmiths from 1729 through 1815.

Position Rifle Shooting, by Bill Pullum and F. T. Hanenkrat. Winchester Press, NY, 1973. 256 pp., illus. Paper covers, $5.95.

The single most complete statement of rifle shooting principles and techniques, and the means of learning, teaching and using them, ever to appear in print.

The Revolving Rifles, by Edsall James, Pioneer Press, Union City, TN, 1975. 23 pp., illus. Paper covers. $2.50.

Valuable information on revolving cylinder rifles, from the earliest matchlock forms to the latest models of Colt and Remington.

The Rifle Book, by Jack O'Connor, Random House, NY, 1978. 337 pp., illus. $13.95.

The complete book of small game, varmint and big game rifles.

Rifle Guide, by Robert A. Steindler, Stoeger Publishing Co., South Hackensack, NJ, 1978. 304 pp., illus. Paper covers. $7.95.

Complete, fully illustrated guide to selecting, shooting, caring for, and collecting rifles of all types.

Rifles AR15, M16, and M16A1, 5.56 mm, by D. B. McLean. Normount Armament Co., Wickenburg, AZ, 1968. Unpaginated, illus., paper covers. $6.95.

Descriptions, specifications and operation of subject models are set forth in text and picture.

Schuetzen Rifles, History and Loading, by Gerald O. Kelver, Gerald O. Kelver, Publisher, Brighton, CO, 1972. Illus. $7.50.

Reference work on these rifles, their bullets, loading, telescopic sights, accuracy, etc. A limited, numbered ed.

Single Shot Rifles and Actions, by Frank de Haas, ed. by John T. Amber, DBI Books, Northfield, IL, 1969. 352 pp., illus. $8.95.

The definitive book on over 60 single shot rifles and actions. Covers history, parts photos, design and construction, etc.

Sniper Rifles of Two World Wars, by W. H. Tantum IV. Museum Restoration Service, Ottawa, Can., 1967. 32 pp., illus. $2.50.

Monograph on high-accuracy rifles used by troops in world wars I and II and in Korea. Paper wrappers.

The Sporting Rifle and its Projectiles, by Lieut. James Forsyth, The Buckskin Press, Big Timber, MT, 1978. 132 pp., illus. $9.50.

Facsimile reprint of the 1863 edition, one of the most authoritative books ever written on the muzzle-loading round ball sporting rifle.

The .22 Rifle, by Dave Petzal. Winchester Press, NY, 1972. 244 pp., illus. $9.95.

All about the mechanics of the .22 rifle. How to choose the right one, how to choose a place to shoot, what makes a good shot, the basics of small-game hunting.

The American Shotgun, by David F. Butler, Lyman Publ., Middlefield, CT, 1973. 256 pp., illus. Paper covers. $9.95.

A comprehensive history of the American smoothbore's evolution from Colonial times to the present day.

American Shotgun Design and Performance, by L. R. Wallack, Winchester Press, NY, 1977. 184 pp., illus. $14.95.

An expert lucidly recounts the history and development of American shotguns and explains how they work.

The Double Shotgun, by Don Zutz, Winchester Press, New York, NY, 1978. 288 pp., illus. $14.95.

The history and development of the most classic of all sporting arms.

How to be a Winner Shooting Skeet & Trap, by Tom Morton, Tom Morton, Knoxville, MD, 1974. 144 pp., illus. Paper covers. $8.95.

The author explains why championship shooting is more than a physical process.

The Mysteries of Shotgun Patterns, by Geo. G. Oberfell and Chas. E. Thompson, Oklahoma State University Press, Stillwater, OK, Xerox edition, 1978. 328 pp. Paper covers. $20.00.

Shotgun ballistics for the hunter in non-technical language, with information on improving effectiveness in the field.

New England Grouse Shooting, by W. H. Foster, Chas. Scribner's, NY, 193 pp., illus. $25.00.

Many interesting and helpful points on how to hunt grouse.

The Parker Gun, by Larry L. Baer, Beinfeld Publ., Inc., No. Hollywood, CA, 1980. 240 pp., illus. $24.95.

Originally published as two separate volumes. This is the only comprehensive work on the subject of America's most famous shotgun. Included are new material and new photographs.

Pigeon Shooting, by Archie Coates, Andre Deutsch Ltd., London, England, 1975. 142 pp., illus. $10.95.

Helpful and practical advice on every facet of the sport.

The Police Shotgun Manual, by Robert H. Robinson, Charles C. Thomas, Springfield, IL 1973. 153 pp., illus. $15.00.

A complete study and analysis of the most versatile and effective weapon in the police arsenal.

Score Better at Skeet, by Fred Missildine, with Nick Karas. Winchester Press, NY, 1972. 160 pp., illus. $5.95. In paper covers, $2.95.

The long-awaited companion volume to *Score Better at Trap.*

75 Years with the Shotgun, by C. T. (Buck) Buckman, Valley Publ., Fresno, CA, 1974. 141 pp., illus. $7.50.

An expert hunter and trapshooter shares experiences of a lifetime.

The Shotgun Book, by Jack O'Connor, Alfred A. Knopf, New York, NY, 1978. 341 pp., illus. $15. Paper covers, $8.95.

An indispensable book for every shotgunner containing up-to-the-minute authoritative information on every phase of the shotgun.

The Shotgun in Combat, by Tony Lesce, Desert Publications, Cornville, AZ, 1979. 148 pp., illus. Paper covers. $5.95.

A history of the shotgun and its use in combat.

Shotgunner's Guide, by Monte Burch, Winchester Press, New York, NY, 1980. 208 pp., illus. $10.50.

A basic book for the young and old who wants to try shotgunning or who wants to improve his skill.

Shotgunning: The Art and the Science, by Bob Brister, Winchester Press, NY, 1976. 321 pp., illus. $12.95.

Hundreds of specific tips and truly novel techniques to improve the field and target shooting of every shotgunner.

Shotguns & Shooting, by E. S. McCawley, Jr., Van Nostrand Reinhold Co., NY, 1965. 146 pp., illus. Paper covers. $4.95.

Covers the history and development, types of shotguns and ammunition, shotgun shooting, etc.

Skeet Shooting with D. Lee Braun, Robt. Campbell, ed. Grosset & Dunlap, NY, 1967. 160 pp., illus. Paper covers $3.95.

Thorough instructions on the fine points of Skeet shooting.

Trapshooting with D. Lee Braun and the Remington Pros., ed. by R. Campbell. Remington Arms Co., Bridgeport, CT, 1969. 157 pp., well illus., Paper covers. $3.95.

America's masters of the scattergun give the secrets of professional marksmanship.

Wing & Shot, by R. G. Wehle, Country Press, Scottsville, NY, 1967. 190 pp., illus. $12.

Step-by-step account on how to train a fine shooting dog.

The World's Fighting Shotguns, by Thomas F. Swearengen, T. B. N. Enterprises, Alexandria, VA, 1979. 500 pp., illus. $29.95.

The complete military and police reference work from the shotgun's inception to date, with up-to-date developments.

You and the Target, by Kay Ohye, Kay Ohye Enterprises, No. Brunswick, NJ, 1978. 83 pp., illus. Paper covers. $9.95.

All new trapshooting handbook to better scores.

COLLECTORS (BRITISH & OTHERS)

Antique European and American Firearms in the Hermitage Museum, by L. Tarassuk, Arco Pub. Co., NY, 1972. 224 pp., 130 pp. of illus., 54 pp. in full color. $22.50.

Selected from the museum's 2500 firearms dating from the 15th to 19th centuries, including the magnificently decorated Colt rifle and pistols presented by Samuel Colt to Tzars Nicholas 1st and Alexander II.

Antique Pistol Collecting 1400-1860, by James Frith and Ronald Andrews, The Holland Press, London, England, 1978. 122 pp., illus. $45.

A brief resume of the evolution of pistols (mainly English) to the close of the percussion revolver era.

Australian Service Longarms, by Ian D. Skennerton, I. D. Skennerton, Margate, Australia, 1975. 213 pp., illus. $23.50.

A study of the firearms used in Australian service, from the first landing there (1788) to the present day.

The Boxer Cartridge in the British Service, by B. A. Temple, B. A. Temple, Burbank, Australia, 1977. 250 pp., illus. $30.

This work relates the history of the Boxer Cartridge as used by Britain and her colonies from 1866 to the 1930s.

The British Dueling Pistol, by John A. Atkinson, Museum Restoration Service, Bloomfield, Canada, 1978. 108 pp., illus. $20.00.

Enables firearms enthusiasts to trace the origin and development of the English duelling pistol.

Dutch Firearms, by Arne Hoff, ed. by Walter A. Stryker, Philip Wilson Publishers Ltd., Sotheby Parke Bernet Publications, London, England, 1978. 264 pp., illus. $105.00.

An important and essential work of reference for all museums and private collectors.

Dutch Muskets & Pistols, by J. B. Kist, J. P. Puype, and W. Van Der Mark, George Shumway, York, PA, 1974. 176 pp., illus. $25.00.

An illus. history of 17th Century gunmaking in the Low Countries.

English Gunmakers, by DeWitt Bailey and Douglas A. Nie, Arms & Armour Press, London, England, 1978. 128 pp., illus. $15.

The Birmingham and Provincial gun trade in the 18th and 19th century.

English Pistols & Revolvers, by J. N. George. Arco Publ. Co., Inc., N.Y.C., 1962, 256 pp., 28 plates. $24.75.

The 2nd reprinting of a notable work first publ. in 1938. Treats of the historical development and design of English hand firearms from the 17th cent. to the present. A much better book than the former reprint, particularly as to clarity of the tipped-in plates.

Fine Arms from Tula, compiled by Valentin Mavrodin, Harry N. Abrams, Inc. N.Y., NY, 1977. 14 pp. of text plus 137 full color plates. $25.

The fine arms wrought by the artisans of Tula in the 18th and 19th century now in the Hermitage Museum.

Forsyth & Co.—Patent Gunmakers, by W. Keith Neal and D. H. L. Back. G. Bell & Sons, London, 1st ed., 1969. 280 pp., well illus. $20.

An excellent study of the invention and development of the percussion system by the Rev. Alexander Forsyth in the early 19th century. All Forsyth types are covered, plus a diary of events from 1768 to 1852.

French Pistols and Sporting Guns, by A. N. Kennard. Transatlantic Arts, Inc., Levittown, NY, 1972. 63 pp., illus. $3.95.

Traces the technical evolution of French pistols and sporting guns from matchlock to breechloader.

French Military Weapons, 1717-1938, by James E. Hicks. N. Flayderman & Co., New Milford, CT, 1964. 281 pp., profusely illus. $9.50.

A valuable reference work, first publ. 1938 as *Notes on French Ordnance,* this rev. ed. covers hand, shoulder, and edged weapons, ammunition and artillery, with history of various systems.

The Gunsmiths of Canada, by S. James Gooding, Museum Rest. Serv., Ottawa, Ont., Can., 1974. 32 pp., illus. Paper covers. $2.50.

Names, dates and locations for over 800 gunsmiths, plus bibliography.

Handbook of Identification Marks on Canadian Arms, by R. Barrie Manarey, Century Press, Alberta, Can., 1973. 82 pp., illus. Paper covers. $6.00.

Lists over 1000 translations of codes and initials which appear on Canadian arms.

Illustrated British Firearms Patents, 1714-1853, comp. and ed. by Stephen V. Grancsay and Merrill Lindsay, Winchester Press, NY, 1969. Unpaginated. $30.00.

Facsimile of patent documents with a bibliography. Limited, numbered ed. of 1000 bound in 3/4 leather and marbled boards.

The Lee British Service Rifle, from 1880 to 1960, by Robert J. Dynes, Museum Restoration Service, Bloomfield, Ontario, Canada, 1978. 24 pp., illus. Paper covers. $2.50.

The Lyle Orticial Arms and Armour Review, 1980, compiled by Margaret Anderson, Lyle Publications, Selkirkshire, Scotland, 1978. 382 pp., illus. $16.95.

Compiled prices on edged weapons, firearms and militaria from the auctions by Wallis & Wallis. Prices in English pounds and U.S. dollars.

Manual of Pistol and Revolver Cartridges, Volume I, Centerfire Metric Calibers, by Hans A. Erlmeier and Jakob H. Brandt, Journal-Verlag, Weisbaden, Germany, second edition, 1978. 271 pp., illus. $9.95.

A reference work in both German and English text which lists cartridges both by caliber and alphabetically. Contains accurate scale photographs for cartridge identification.

Scottish Arms Makers, by C. E. Whitelaw, ed. by Sarah Barter, Fortress Publ., Inc., Stoney Creek, Ontario, Can., 1977. 338 pp. illus. $44.95.

A bibliographical dictionary of firearms makers, edged weapons and armor working in Scotland from the 14th century to 1870.

A Treatise on the Snider: The British Soldier's Firearm 1866-c. 1880, by Ian D. Skennerton, Ian D. Skennerton, Queensland, Australia, 1977. 181 pp., illus. $23.50.

Development, manufacture and issue of the Snider rifles and carbines for that period.

GENERAL (BRITISH & OTHERS)

Brassey's Infantry Weapons of the World, 2nd Edition, edited by J. I. H. Owen, Brassey's Publishers Ltd., London, England, 1979. 480 pp., illus. $55.00.

Infantry weapons, including infantry support vehicles, and combat aids in current use by the regular and reserve forces of all nations.

Brassey's Infantry Weapons of the World 1950-1975, edited by Maj. Gen. J. I. H. Owen, Bonanza Books, NY, 1977. 323 pp., illus. $7.98.

Infantry weapons and combat aids in current use by the regular and reserve forces of all nations.

The Complete Illustrated Encyclopedia of the World's Firearms, by Ian V. Hogg, A & W Publishers, New York, NY, 1978, 328 pp., illus. $24.95.

Military and civilian firearms from the beginnings to the present day . . . An A-Z directory of makes and makers from 1830.

The Dairy of Colonel Peter Hawker, by Col. P. Hawker, Richmond Publ. Co., Richmond, England, 1971. 759 pp., illus. $25.00.

Reprint of the 1893 ed. covers shooting in every way and how to outwit your opponent!

Firearms Control, by Colin Greenwood, Routledge & Kegan Paul, London (England), 1972. 274 pp. $13.50.

A study of armed crime and firearms control in England and Wales.

A History of Firearms, by Major Hugh B. C. Pollard, Burt Franklin, NY, a facsimile ed. with a new introduction by Joseph R. Riling, 1973. 320 pp., illus. $25.50.

An excellent survey of the development of hand firearms. Lists over 2,000 American and foreign-gunmakers.

The Illustrated Book of Guns and Rifles, edited by Frederick Wilkinson, Hamlyn Publishing Group Ltd., London, England, 1979. 191 pp., illus. $10.98.

A wide-ranging and fascinating study of the longarm weapons of the soldier and sportsman.

Scloppetaria, by Capt. H. Beaufroy, Richmond Publ. Co., Richmond, England, 1971. 251 pp. $18.50.

Reprint of the 1808 edition written under the pseudonym "A Corporal of Riflemen". Covers rifles and rifle shooting, the first such work in English.

Technical Dictionary for Weapon Enthusiasts, Shooters and Hunters, by Gustav Sybertz. Publ. by J. Neumann-Neudamm, 3508 Melsungen, W. Germany, 1969, 164 pp., semi-soft covers. $12.50.

A German-English and English-German dictionary for the sportsman. An excellent handy work.

Your First Gun, by Roderick Willet, Seeley, Service & Co., London, England, 1975. 88 pp., illus. $7.50.

A useful handbook for those about to start shooting, young or old.

HANDGUNS (BRITISH & OTHERS)

The Complete Handgun 1300 to the Present, by Ian V. Hogg and John Batchelor, Exeter Books, New York, NY, 1979. 128 pp., illus. $7.98.

The full story of the handgun from its earliest crude form.

German Pistols and Revolvers 1871-1945, by Ian V. Hogg, A. & W. Books, NY, 1975. 160 pp., illus. $20.00.

Over 160 photos and drawings showing each gun, plus exploded views, markings, firms, patents, mfg. codes, etc.

The Inglis-Browing Hi-Power Pistol, by R. Blake Stevens, Museum Rest. Serv., Ottawa, Can., 1974. 28 pp., illus. Paper Covers. $2.00.

The history of this scarce gun and its variations.

Pistols of the World, by Ian V. Hogg and John Weeks, Arms and Armour Press, London, England, 1978. 304 pp., illus. $24.95.

A comprehensive illustrated encyclopedia of the world's pistols and revolvers from 1870 to the present day.

HUNTING (BRITISH & OTHERS)

The ABC of Shooting, ed. by Colin Willock, Andre Deutsch, Ltd., London, England, 1975. 351 pp., illus. $14.95.

A complete shotgun guide to game and rough shooting, wild fowling, pigeon shooting, deer stalking and clay pigeon shooting.

The Big Shots; Edwardian Shooting Parties, by Jonathan Garnier Rutfer, Debrett's Peerage Ltd., London, England, 1978. 300 pp., illus. $21.95.

Reveals the secrets behind the Imperial, Royal and Noble shooting parties that have been an integral part of upper class English life for so long.

Shooting Game, by Michael Kemp, A & C Black, London, England, 1972. 176 pp., illus. $14.95.

A step-by-step course to successful and enjoyable shooting.

The Young Shot, by Noel M. Sedgwick, A. & C. Black, London, Eng., 1976. 240 pp., illus. $8.95.

A revised and re-illustrated edition of Sedgwick's original work plus a preface and appendix dealing with changes in law since the first ed.

RIFLES (BRITISH & OTHERS)

Pictorial History of the Rifle, by G. W. P. Swenson, Ian Allan Ltd., Shepperton, Surrey, England, 1971. 184 pp., illus. $9.50.

Essentially a picture book, with over 200 rifle illustrations. The text furnishes a concise history of the rifle and its development.

Sir Charles Ross and His Rifle, by Robt. Phillips and J. J. Knap, Museum Restoration Service, Ottawa, Canada, 1969. 32 pp., illus. Paper covers. $2.95.

The story of the man who invented the "Ross Model 1897 Magazine Sporting Rifle," the 1900 under the name of Bennett, and many others.

Small-Bore Target Shooting, by W. H. Fuller, 3rd edition, revised by A. J. Palmer, Barrie & Jenkins, London, England, 1978. 240 pp., illus. $11.95.

Includes an appendix on air rifle shooting, which may become an Olympic Games event in 1980. The complete treatise on the sport of 22 and 177 in competition rifle shooting.

Target Rifle Shooting, by E. G. B. Reynolds & Robin Fulton. Barne & Jenkins, London, Eng., 1972. 200 pp., illus. $11.95.

For the novice and intermerdiate shooter who wants to learn the basics needed to become a rifle marksman.

SHOTGUNS (BRITISH & OTHERS)

The British Shotgun Vol. I, 1850-1870, by I. M. Crudgington and D. J. Baker, Barrie & Jenkins, London, England, 1979. 192 pp., illus. $25.

An attempt to trace, as accurately as is now possible, the evolution of the shotgun during its formative years in Great Britain.

Churchill's Game Shooting, ed. by Macdonald Hastings, Michael Joseph, London, England, 1978, 250 pp., illus. $27.50.

A textbook on the successful use of the modern shotgun.

Gough Thomas's Gun Book, by G. T. Garwood, A. & C. Black, London, England, 1969. 160 pp., illus. $21.95.

Excerpts of articles on the shotgun published in *Shooting Times,* by a noted British authority. Wide-ranging survey of every aspect on the shotgun, its use, behavior, care, and lore.

High Pheasants, by Sir Ralph Payne-Gallwey, Richmond Publ. Co., Richmond, England, 1970. 79 pp. $18.50.

The first and last word on its subject.

The New Wildfowler in the 1970's, by N. M. Sedgwick, et al. Barrie & Jenkins, London, Eng., 1970. 375 pp., illus. $11.50.

A compendium of articles on wildfowling, hunting practices and conservation. An updated reprint.

Rough Shooting, by G. A. Gratten & R. Willett. Faber & Faber, London, Eng., 1968, 242 pp., illus. $17.95.

The art of shooting, dogs and their training, games, rearing and their diseases, proof marks, etc.

Shotgun and Shooter, by Percy Stanbury and G. L. Carlisle, 2nd edition, Barrie & Jenkins, London, England, 1978. 224 pp., illus. $11.95.

Guns, gamekeepers, rough shooting, wildfowling, field trials and decoys.
Shotgun Marksmanship, by Percy Stanbury & G. L. Carlisle, 3rd edition, Barrie & Jenkins, London, England, 1978. 224 pp., illus. $11.95.

This book teaches, through words and photographs, how to become a first-class shot, whether the interest lies in shooting game or in competitive shooting.
Shotguns & Cartridges, by Gough Thomas, A. & C. Black, London, Eng., 1975. 254 pp., illus. $15.00.

A thoroughly revised and updated book on the understanding of modern guns and cartridges for clay pigeon and game shooting.
Successful Shotgun Shooting, by A. A. Montague. Winchester Press, NY, 1970. 160 pp., illus. $8.95.

The work of a superb shot and a great teacher; even the experts can read with profit.

CATALOGS

American Sporting Arms of the 18th & 19th Century, compiled by Herbert G. Houze, Chicago Historical Society, Chicago, IL, 1975. 32 pp., illus. Paper covers. $3.75.

A catalog of the Chicago Historical Society collection of antique sporting and martial firearms.
1909 Baker Gun Catalog, reprinted by Ronald Frodelius, Fayetteville, NY, 1976. 20 pp., illus. Paper covers. $2.95.

A facsimile reprint of a scarce old Baker Arms Co. catalog.
The Browning Superposed, a facsimile reprint by Empire Press, Santa Fe, NM, 1980, 32 pp., illus. Paper covers $6.00.

A facsimile reprint of the 1931 catalog of Browning Arms Co. concerning their superposed models.
Colt 1896 English Price List, a reprint by American Archives, Topsfield, MA, 1976. 16 pp., illus. Paper covers. $3.00.

Illustrates and prices (in English currency) the full Colt line of the period.
Colt Firearms Catalog, 1934, a reprint by Americana Archives, Topsfield, MA, 1976. 40 pp., illus. Paper covers. $4.00.

28 Colt revolvers and automatic pistols are described and illustrated.
Hopkins & Allen Gun Guide and Catalog, (ca. 1913). Wagle Publ., Lake Wales, FA, 1972. 32 pp., illus. Paper covers. $5.00.

Facsimile of the original catalog. Shows the firms rifles, shotguns and pistols, and includes prices. Full color cover painting by Dan Smith.
Marlin Catalog of 1897. A reprint in facsimile by the Rocky Mountain Investment and Antique Co.; Cheyenne, WY, 1969. 192 pp. Well illus., paper covers, $5.00.

All models are covered, cartridges, sights, engraving, accessories, reloading tools, etc.
Marlin Catalog, 1905, Rocky Mountain Investment and Antique Co.; Cheyenne, WY, 1971. 128 pp. Paper, $5.00.

Reprint. Rifles, shotguns, pistols, tools, cartridge information, factory engraving and carving illustrated and described.
Maynard Catalog of 1880, a reprint in facsimile by the Rocky Mountain Investment and Antique Co.; Cheyenne, WY, 1969, 32 pp., illus., paper covers. $3.00.

All models, sights, cartridges, targets etc.
The NRA Collector's Series, Digest Books, Inc., Northfield, IL., 1971, 84 pp. paper covers $2.95.

Reprint of the three predecessors of *American Rifleman* magazine and the first edition of *American Rifleman.*
Parker Brother Gun Catalog, 1869. B. Palmer, Tyler, TX, 1972, 14 pp., illus. Paper covers. $4.

Facsimile of Charles Parker's first issued catalog on "Parker Breech-Loading Shot Guns."
Parker Guns Catalog 1930, a reprint, by Empire Press, Santa Fe, NM, 1979. 32 pp., illus. Paper covers $10.00.

Facsimile reprint showing all models, including the Parker single barrel trap gun.
Rare Selections from Old Gun Catalogs 1888-1919, edited by Joseph J. Schroeder, DBI Books, Inc., Northfield, IL, 1978. 96 pp., illus. Paper covers. $4.95.

Selections from rare old gun catalogs.
Remington Catalog (Price List) of 1885, a reprint in facsimile, by The Rocky Mountain Investment and Antique Co., Cheyenne, WY, 1969. 48 pp., well illus., paper covers. $3.00.

All rifles, handguns, cane gun, sights, cartridges, shotguns, accessories etc. A priced catalog.
E. Remington & Sons, Reduced Price List for 1877, reprinted by Pioneer Press, Union City, TN, 1977. 42 pp., illus. Paper covers. $1.95.

A facsimile reprint showing all models of rifles, shotguns, pistols, etc. manufactured during this period by this firm.
Remington Arms Revised Price-List, 1902. Arthur McKee, Northport, NY, n.d. 64 pp. Paper covers. $4.00.

Reprint, fully illustrated.
Remington Firearms, 1906 Catalog, Arthur McKee, Northport, NY, n.d., 48 pp., illus. Paper covers, $4.00.

Reprint. Guns, parts, ammo., prices, etc.
Savage Arms Co. 1900 Catalog, a facsimile reprint by Sand Pond Gun Shop, Marlow, NH, 1978. 55 pp., illus. Paper covers. $5.

Shows all grades of engraving for the Model 99 Savage, sporting and military rifles, cartridges, sights, and the Savage "Ideal" reloading tools.
Sharps' Rifle Manufacturing Company Catalog, 1859, a facsimile reprint 1976. 16 pp., illus. Paper covers. $3.

Shows the carbine and rifle, the forms for shot and powder tubes, plus cleaning directions.
Sharps' Rifle Manufacturing Company Catalog, 1864, a facsimile reprint 1976. 16 pp., illus. Paper covers. $3.

Illustrates the carbine, sporting rifle and army rifle with bayonet. Complete instructions on use, preparing charges and a manual of arms.

Sharps' Rifle Manufacturing Company Catalog, 1874, a facsimile reprint 1976. 32 pp., illus. Paper covers. $3.

Six different rifles are illustrated, including the famous Creedmore.
Starr Arms Co., 1864 Catalog, a reprint. 1976. 22 pp., illus. Paper covers. $3.

Contains operating and disassembly instruction, trial results and military testimonials.
Thompson Guns: 1929 Commercial Price List and Catalog, published by Auto-Ordnance Corp., Ray Riling Arms Books Co., Phila., PA, 1976. A facsimile reprint. 18 pp., illus., paper covers. $5.

A limited, numbered reprint of the scarce 1929 Catalog on the Thompson, Submachine Gun.
Winchester Repeating Firearms Co. Catalog 1875, facsimile reprint by King & Co., Peoria, IL, 1978. 64 pp., illus. Paper covers. $5.

Exhibiting repeating firearms, rifled muskets, carbines, hunting and target rifles and metallic cartridges manufactured by Winchester Repeating Arms Co.
Winchester Catalog of 1891, a facsimile reprint by the Rocky Mountain Investment and Antique Co., Cheyenne, WY, 1973. 84 pp., well illus., paper covers. $5.00.

All rifles, shotguns, reloading tools and ammunition of the time. A priced catalog.
Winchester Repeating Arms Co. Catalog, February, 1893, facsimile reprint by King & Co., Peoria, IL, 1978, 84 pp., illus. Paper covers. $4.50.

Exhibiting repeating firearms, single shot rifles, rifled muskets, carbines, repeating shotguns, Hotchkiss magazine firearms for military and sporting use.
Winchester Repeating Arms Co. Catalogue No. 58, December, 1896, a facsimile reprint by Empire Press, Santa Fe, NM, 1980. 130 pp., illus. Paper covers. $8.50.

A facsimile reprint of Winchester's 1896 catalog exhibiting repeating rifles, carbines and muskets, etc.
Winchester Repeating Arms Co. Catalog, October, 1897, Highly Finished Arms, a facsimile reprint by Rocky Mountain Investment and Antique Co., Cheyenne, WY, 1970. 28 pp. illus. Paper covers. $7.50.

A facsimile reprint of Winchester's catalog showing artistically ornamented arms.
Winchester Sales Manual 1938, a facsimile reprint by Empire Press, Santa Fe, NM, 1980. 66 pp., illus. Paper covers. $10.00.

A facsimile reprint of the manual given to the sales personnel to familiarize them with the company history and products.

CATALOGS (BRITISH & OTHERS)

Arms of the World—1911, ed. by Joseph J. Schroeder, Jr., Digest Books Inc., Northfield, IL, 1972, 420 pp., profusely illus. $5.95.

Reprint of the Adolph Frank ALFA 21 catalog of 1911 in 4 languages—English, German, French, Spanish.
Boss & Co., Guns, Catalog, 1910, a facsimile reprint by Empire Press, Santa Fe, NM, 1980. 7 pp., illus. Paper covers. $5.00.

A facsimile reprint of this famous British gunmakers 1910 catalog, showing their line of fine shotguns.
E. J. Churchill, Ltd., Catalog 1922, Some Notes on Churchill Best Guns, a facsimile reprint by Empire Press, Santa Fe, NM, 1979, 32 pp., illus. Paper covers. $10.00.

A facsimile reprint of this famous British gunmaker's catalog for 1922, showing their line of deluxe shotguns.
History and Catalog of Holland & Holland Ltd., distributed by Service Armament Co., Ridgefield, NJ, 1977. 144 pp., illus. Paper covers. $35.00.

A folio containing a reprint of the Holland & Holland 72 page catalog of 1912, together with a 72-page book describing the Holland & Holland gun collection and the history of this famous firm of gunmakers.
Holland & Holland Gun & Rifle Makers, a facsimile reprint of the 1924 catalog of Holland & Holland, Ltd., by Empire Press, Santa Fe, NM, 1978. 32 pp., illus. Paper. $7.50.

A fine reproduction of one of this firm's early catalogs.
Lancaster's, The Gun House, facsimile reprint of the 1924 catalog of Charles Lancaster & Co. Ltd., by Empire Press, Santa Fe, NM, 1978, 48 pp., illus. Paper covers. $12.50.

A fine reproduction of a famous English gun manufacturers catalog.
The Original Mauser Automatic Pistol, Model 1930, a reprint by Harold C. Bruffett, Croswell, MI, 1973. 32 pp., illus., paper covers. $2.50.

Facsimile of the 1931 English-text export catalog on the "Broom Handle Mauser."
The "Parabellum" Automatic Pistol, Stoeger Publ. Co., S. Hackensack, NJ, 49 pp. plus three fold out tables. $2.00.

An exact reproduction of the instruction book issued in English by the original Luger manufacturer "Deutsche Waffen and Munitionsfabriken, Berlin."
Purdey Guns & Rifles, facsimile reprint of the 1931 James Purdey & Sons Ltd. catalog, by Empire Press, Santa Fe, NM, 1978. 27 pp., illus. Paper covers. $7.50.

Fine reproduction of one of the most famous of English gun manufacturers catalogs.
1901 John Rigby & Co. Catalog, a facsimile reprint by Empire Press, Santa Fe, NM, 1980, 15 pp., illus. Paper covers. $5.00.

A facsimile reprint of this famous British gunmaker's 1901 catalog.
1932 Rigby Double Rifles, a facsimile reprint by Empire Press, Santa Fe, NM, 1980. 15 pp., illus. Paper covers. $7.50.

A facsimile reprint of the 1932 catalog of John Rigby & Co., London.
Westley Richards Shotguns, 1932, facsimile reprint by Empire Press, Santa Fe, NM, 1980. 50 pp., illus. Paper covers. $15.00.

A facsimile reprint of this great gunmakers 1932 catalog.
James Woodward & Sons Catalog, 1925, a facsimile reprint by Empire Press, Santa Fe, NM, 1979. 20 pp., illus. $7.50.

A facsimile reprint of this famous British gunmaker's 1925 catalog showing complete line of shotguns and rifles.

CATALOGS (KNIVES & EDGED WEAPONS)

Ka-Bar Dependable Pocket Knives, reprinted by Ka-Bar Knives, Olean, NY 1976. Unpaginated. Paper covers. $3.50.

A facsimile reprint of the 1925 Union Cutlery Co. catalog with many illustrations of old Ka-Bar knives.

Presenting America's Aristocracy of Fine Cutlery, reprinted by American Reprints, St. Louis, MO, n.d. 40 pp., illus. Paper covers. $3.50.

Reprints of a W. R. Case & Sons pocket knife catalog.

Remington Cutlery, reprinted by American Reprints, St. Louis, MO, 1969. Unpaginated, illus. Paper covers. $2.50.

A facsimile reprint of a 1936 pocket knife catalog issued by Remington Arms Co.

Russell Green River Works Cutlery, reprinted by Dewey P. Ferguson, Fairborn, OH, 1970. 49 pp. illus. Paper covers. $5.00.

Facsimile reprint of an early pocketknife catalog with a modern pricing guide added.

Schrade Pocket Knives and Price Guide, Catalog 'E' and Supplements, reprinted by A. G. Russell Knife Collectors Club, A. G. Russell, Springdale, AR, 1971. 123 pp., illus. Paper covers. $5.00.

Hundreds of illustrations of Schrade pocket knives with their values.

E. C. Simmons "Keen Kutter" Cutlery and Tools, reprinted by American Reprints Co., St. Louis, MO, 1970. 56 pp., illus. Paper covers. $3.50.

A facsimile reprint of a 1930 E. C. Simmons catalog.

HOW FAR IS FAR?

Experienced shooters are generally knowledgeable about effective shotgun range, but the maximum distance that various sizes of shot will carry is a mystery to many.

Of interest to all shooters, these data are particularly relevant to those selecting sites for gun clubs or for informal clay target shooting.

The figures in the table below apply to all *all* current shotgun gauges; the range determining factor is the size of the shot itself.

Maximum Distance in Yards to Point of Impact

(for leading pellets in shot string)

Shot Size	Max. Distance
BB	386
2	336
3	320
4	303
5	290
6	273
7½	243
8	240
9	223
00 Buck	610
0 Buck	590
1 Buck	567
3 Buck	497
4 Buck	480
Rifled Slugs	817

Farm Woodlots Boon to Wildlife

Time was when a small woodlot was absolutely essential to a farm operation. It meant fencing, rough lumber for construction and fuel for heat and cooking. Many of those needs are now being met in more modern ways. But woodlots, properly managed, can still be a source of income and pleasure to any farm family, according to Clark G. Webster, manager of wildlife management for Remington Arms Company, Inc.

"The landowner with an eye to the future will nurture his woodlands," continues Webster. "The outlook is for an increased need for wood products, and not all the merchantable timber is being produced in forests. Small woodland tracts contribute substantially to the national timber harvest, and they offer multiple values when properly handled.

"The most common mistake in the use of farm woodlands is permitting grazing by livestock. Cattle and timber production don't go together. Little is gained in the form of pasture and much is lost from the standpoint of tree reproduction and use by wildlife. Practically all farmers will be ahead economically if they fence their woodlots and manage such areas for a future wood crop. If loafing shade is needed for cattle, a small portion can be left outside the fence.

"Bearing in mind the interest of the average farmer in wildlife, woodlot management and game management go hand in hand. A protected woods has the understory of shrubs, vines and young trees that spell home-sweet-home to a variety of critters of sporting interest. First off, the cottontail is a common resident of ungrazed woodlands. But when cattle come in the bunnies go out. They need cover and a pastured woods doesn't have it. The same for pheasants and quail. The coppice growth of protected woodlots provides good cover for these game birds as well as yielding a food crop in the form of berries and fruits.

As for songbirds, there's just no comparison in what you'll find in grazed as compared with ungrazed woodlots. Some species of birds are almost confined to a shrub-type environment, and a protected woods will have ten times the number and variety that you'll find in a unit trampled by cows.

"Tree squirrels, of course, are tied to woodland habitat. In most areas they will build leaf nests for make-shift shelter. But in rough weather and for rearing their young, tree hollows make for better survival. Leaving one or two den trees per acre is good squirrel management. And even if it is a minor departure from intensive forest management the pay off, come autumn, makes it worth-while. It will mean better squirrel hunting, the farm boys' delight. And as for yearling squirrels in the frying pan—well, there just isn't anything to come close.

"If you don't have a farm woodlot, maybe you should have one," continues Webster. "Slopes that are inclined to wash with pasturing are best converted to woodland. And various inducements are available which make tree planting attractive economically. Most every county in the nation has a forester standing by to provide technical assistance. Planting stock normally is available from state nurseries at no cost or a very nominal one.

"All in all, a managed timber stand is a good bet for most any farm. It's a way of disposing effectively of problems that appear on steep, gulley-susceptible land. It adds variety to an otherwise monotonous landscape, and offers a place of relaxation and sport. And over the long pull it will represent a source of income which took little or no effort to produce."

Directory of the Arms Trade

AMMUNITION (Commercial)

Alcan Shells, (See: Smith & Wesson Ammunition Co.)
Bingham Ltd., 1775-C Wilwat Dr., Norcross, GA 30093
Cascade Cartridge Inc., (See Omark)
DWM (see RWS)
Dynamit Nobel of America, Inc., 105 Stonehurst Court, Northvale, NJ 07647/201-767-1660 (RWS)
Eclipse Cartridge, Inc., 26407 Golden Valley Rd., Saugus, CA 91350/213-367-1091
Federal Cartridge Co., 2700 Foshay Tower, Minneapolis, MN 55402
Frontier Cartridge Division-Hornady Mfg. Co., Box 1848, Grand Island, NE 68801/308-382-1390
Midway Arms, Inc., R. R. #5, Columbia, MO 65201
Omark Industries, Box 856, Lewiston, ID 83501
Precision Prods. of Wash., Inc., N. 311 Walnut Rd., Spokane, WA 99206 (Exammo)
RWS (see Dynamit Nobel of America)
Remington Arms Co., Bridgeport, Conn. 06602
Service Armament, 689 Bergen Blvd., Ridgefield, N.J. 07657
Smith & Wesson Ammunition Co., 2399 Forman Rd., Rock Creek, OH 44084
Super Vel, Hamilton Rd., Rt. 2, P.O. Box 1398, Fond du Lac, WI 54935/414-921-2652
Velet Cartridge Co., N. 6809 Lincoln, Spokane, WA 99208
Weatherby's, 2781 E. Firestone Blvd., South Gate, Calif. 90280
Winchester-Western, East Alton, Ill. 62024

AMMUNITION (Custom)

American Pistol Bullet, 133 Blue Bell Rd., Greensboro, NC 27406/919-272-6151
Bill Ballard, 830 Miles Ave., Billings, MT 59101 (ctlg. 50¢)
Ballistek, Weapons Systems Div., 3450 Antelope Dr., Lake Havasu City, AZ 86403/602-855-0997
Beal's Bullets, 170 W. Marshall Rd., Lansdowne, PA 19050 (Auto Mag Specialists)
Bell's Gun & Sport Shop, 3309-19 Mannheim Rd., Franklin Park, IL 60131
Brass Extrusion Labs. Ltd., 800 W. Maple Lane, Bensenville, IL 60106
C. W. Cartridge Co., 71 Hackensack St., Wood-Ridge, NJ 07075
Russell Campbell, 219 Leisure Dr., San Antonio, Tex. 78201
Collectors Shotshell Arsenal, E. Tichy, 365 So. Moore, Lakewood, CO 80226
Crown City Arms, P.O. Box 1126, Cortland, NY 13045
Cumberland Arms, Rt. 1, Shafer Rd., Blantons Chapel, Manchester, TN 37355
E. W. Ellis Sport Shop, RFD 1, Box 315, Corinth, NY 12822
Ellwood Epps Northern Ltd., 210 Worthington St. W., North Bay, Ont. PIB 3B4, Canada
Ramon B. Gonzalez, P.O. Box 370, Monticello, NY 12701
Gussert Bullet & Cartridge Co., Inc., P.O. Box 3945, Green Bay, WI 54303
J-4, Inc., 1700 Via Burton, Anaheim, CA 92806 (custom bullets)
Jensen's Custom Ammunition, 5146 E. Pima, Tucson, AZ 85716
R. H. Keeler, 817 "N" St., Port Angeles, WA 98362/206-457-4702
KTW Inc., 710 Foster Park Rd., Lorain, OH 44053 (bullets)
Dean Lincoln, P.O. Box 1886, Farmington, NM 87401
Lomont Precision Bullets, 4421 S. Wayne Ave., Ft. Wayne, IN 46807/219-694-6792 (custom cast bullets only)
Mansfield Gunshop, Box 83, New Boston, N.H. 03070
Numrich Arms Corp., 203 Broadway, W. Hurley, N.Y. 12491
Robert Pomeroy, Morison Ave., Corinth, ME 04427 (custom shells)
Precision Ammunition & Reloading, 122 Hildenboro Square, Agincourt, Ont. M1W 1Y3, Canada
Precision Prods. of Wash., Inc., N. 311 Walnut Rd., Spokane, WA 99206 (Exammo)
Anthony F. Sailer-Ammunition, 707 W. Third St., P.O. Box L, Owen, WI 54460
Sanders Cust. Gun Serv., 2358 Tyler Lane, Louisville, Ky. 40205
Geo. Spence, 202 Main St., Steele, MO 63877/314-695-4926 (box-primed cartridges)
The 3-D Company, Box 142, Doniphan, NB 68832 (reloaded police ammo)

AMMUNITION (Foreign)

K. J. David & Company, P.O. Box 12595, Lake Park, FL 33043
Dynamit Nobel of America, Inc., 105 Stonehurst Court, Northvale, NJ 07647/201-767-1660 (RWS, Geco, Rottweil)
Guilio Fiocchi S.p.A., P.O. Box 236, 22053 Lecco-Belledo, Italy
Hirtenberger Patronen-, Zündhütchen- & Metallwarenfabrik, A.G., Leobersdorfer Str. 33, A2552 Hirtenberg, Austria
Hy-Score Arms Co., 200 Tillary, Brooklyn, N.Y. 11201

Paul Jaeger Inc., 211 Leedom St., Jenkintown, PA 19046/215-884-6920
S. E. Laszlo, 200 Tillary, Brooklyn, N.Y. 11201
NORMA-Precision, 798 Cascadilla St., Ithaca, NY 14850
RWS (Rheinische-Westfälische Sprengstoff) see: Dynamit Nobel of America

AMMUNITION COMPONENTS—BULLETS, POWDER, PRIMERS

The Alberts Corp., P.O. Box 157, Franklin Lakes, NJ 07417/201-337-5848 (Taurus bull.)
Alcan, (see: Smith & Wesson Ammunition Co.)
Ammo-O-Mart Ltd., P.O. Box 125, Hawkesbury, Ont., Canada K6A 2R8 (Curry bullets)
Austin Powder Co. (see Red Diamond Dist. Co.)
Ballistic Prods., Inc., Box 488, 2105 Shaughnessy Circle, Long Lake, MN 55356
Barnes Bullets, P.O. Box 215, American Fork, UT 84003
B.E.L.L., Bell's Gun & Sport Shop, 3309-19 Mannheim Rd., Franklin Pk., IL 60131
Bitterroot Bullet Co., Box 412, Lewiston, ID. 83501. 35¢ (coin or stamps) and #10 SASE for lit.
Brass Extrusion Laboratories, Ltd., 800 W. Maple Lane, Bensenville, IL 60106
CCI, See: Omark Industries
Kenneth E. Clark, 18738 Highway 99, Madera, CA 93637 (Bullets)
Division Lead, 7742 W. 61 Pl., Summit, Ill. 60502
DuPont, Explosives Dept., Wilmington, Del. 19898
Dynamit Nobel of America, Inc., 105 Stonehurst Court, Northvale, NJ 07647/201-767-1660 (RWS percussion caps)
Elk Mountain Shooters Supply Inc., 1719 Marie, Pasco, WA 99301 (Alaskan bullets)
Farmer Bros., 1616-15th St., Eldora, IA 50627/515-858-3651 (Lage wad)
Federal Cartridge Co., 2700 Foshay Tower, Minneapolis, MN 55402 (nickel cases)
Forty Five Ranch Enterprises, 119 S. Main, Miami, OK 74354/918-542-9307
Godfrey Reloading Supply, Hi-Way 67-111, Brighton, IL 62012 (cast bullets)
Lynn Godfrey, see: Elk Mtn. Shooters Supply
Green Bay Bullets, 233 No. Ashland, Green Bay, Wis. 54303 (lead)
Gussert Bullet & Cartridge Co., Inc., P.O. Box 3945, Green Bay, WI 54303
Hardin Specialty Distr., P.O. Box 338, Radcliff, KY 40160 (empty, primed cases)
Hercules Powder Co., 910 Market St., Wilmington, Del. 19899
Hodgdon Powder Co. Inc., 7710 W. 63rd St., Shawnee Mission, KS 66202/913-362-5410
Hornady Mfg. Co., Box 1848, Grand Island, NE 68801/308-382-1390
N. E. House Co., 195 West High St., E. Hampton, CT 06424/203-267-2133 (zinc bases only)
J-4, Inc., 1700 Via Burton, Anaheim, CA 92806 (custom bullets)
Jaro Bullet Co., P.O. Box 6125, Pasadena, TX 77506/713-472-0417
Keel Co., Bullet Metal Div., 327 East "B" St., Wilmington, CA 90744/213-834-2555 (bullet lead)
L. L. F. Die Shop, 1281 Highway 99 North, Eugene, Ore. 97402
Lage Uniwad Co., 1102 Washington St., Eldora, IA 50627
Ljutic Ind., Inc., Box 2117, Yakima, WA 98902 (Mono-wads)
Lomont Precision Bullets, 4421 S. Wayne Ave., Ft. Wayne, IN 46807/219-694-6792 (custom cast bullets)
Lyman Products Corp., Rte. 147, Middlefield, CT 06455
Michael's Antiques, Box 233, Copiague, L.I., NY 11726 (Balle Blondeau)
Miller Trading Co., 20 S. Front St., Wilmington, N.C. 28401
Norma-Precision, 798 Cascadilla St., Ithaca, NY 14850
Nosler Bullets, P.O. Box 688, Beaverton, OR 97005
Omark Industries, Box 856, Lewiston, ID 83501/208-746-2351
The Oster Group, 50 Sims Ave., Providence, RI 02909 (alloys f. casting bull.)
Robert Pomeroy, Morison Ave., East Corinth, ME 04427
Rainel de P.R. Inc., 1353 Boston Post Road, Madison, CT 06443/203-245-0505 (shotshells)
Red Diamond Distributing Co., 1304 Snowdon Dr., Knoxville, TN 37912 (black powder)
Remington-Peters, Bridgeport, Conn. 06602
Sierra Bullets Inc., 10532 Painter Ave., Santa Fe Springs, CA 90670
Smith & Wesson Ammunition Co., 2399 Forman Rd., Rock Creek, OH 44084
Speer Products, Box 856, Lewiston, ID 83501
C. H. Stocking, Rte. 3, Box 195, Hutchinson, Minn. 55350 (17 cal. bullet jackets)
Taracorp Industries, 16th & Cleveland Blvd., Granite City, IL 62040/618-451-4524 (Lawrence Brand lead shot)
Taurus Bullets, (see: Alberts Corp.)
Taylor Bullets, P.O. Box 21254, San Antonio, TX 78221 (cast)
United Cartridge Co., P.O. Box 604, Valley Industrial Park, Casa Grande, AR 85222/602-836-2510 (P.C. wads)

Vitt & Boos, 2178 Nichols Ave., Stratford, CT 06497/203-375-6859
(Aerodynamic shotgun slug, 12-ga-only)
Winchester-Western, 275 Winchester Ave., New Haven, CT 06504
Xelex Ltd., P.O. Box 543, Renfrow, Ont. K7V 4B1, Canada (powder, Curry
bullets)
Zero Bullet Co., P.O. Box 1188, Cullman, AL 35055

ANTIQUE ARMS DEALERS

Robert Abels, 2881 N.E. 33 Ct., Ft. Lauderdale, FL 33306/305-564-6985
(Catalog $1.00)
Beeman Precision Airguns, Inc., 47 Paul Dr., San Rafael, CA
94903/415-472-7121 (airguns only)
Wm. Boggs, 1243 Grandview Ave., Columbus, Ohio 43212
Ellwood Epps Northern Ltd., 210 Worthington St. W., North Bay, Ont. PIB
3B4, Canada
William Fagan, 126 Belleview, Mount Clemens, MI 48043/313-465-4637
N. Flayderman & Co., Squash Hollow, New Milford, Conn. 06776
Fulmer's Antique Firearms, Chet Fulmer, P.O. Box 792, Detroit Lakes, MN
56501/218-847-7712
Garcia National Gun Traders, Inc., 225 S.W. 22nd Ave., Miami, Fla. 33135
Herb Glass, Bullville, NY 10915/914-361-3021
Goergen's Gun Shop, Rte. 2, Box 182BB, Austin, MN 55912/507-433-9280
Goodman's for Guns, 1002 Olive St., St. Louis, MO 63101
Griffin's Guns & Antiques, R.R. 4, Peterborough, Ont., Canada K9J
6X5/705-748-3220
The Gun Shop, 6497 Pearl Rd., Cleveland, OH 44130/216-884-7476
Hansen & Company, 244 Old Post Rd., Southport, CT 06490
Holbrook Arms Museum, 12953 Biscayne Blvd., N. Miami, Fla. 33161
Lew Horton Sports Shop, Inc., 450 Waverly St., Framingham, MA 01701
Jackson Arms, 6209 Hillcrest Ave., Dallas, Tex. 75205
Lever Arms Serv. Ltd., 572 Howe St., Vancouver, B.C., Canada V6C 2E3
Lone Pine Trading Post, Highways 61 and 248, Minnesota City, MN
55959/507-689-2922
Charles W. Moore, R.D. 2, Box 276, Schenevus, NY 12155
Museum of Historical Arms, 1038 Alton Rd., Miami Beach, FL
33139/305-672-7480 (ctlg. $5)
New Orleans Arms Co., 5001 Treasure St., New Orleans, LA
70186/504-944-3371
O.K. Hardware, Westgate Shopping Center, Great Falls, MT 59404
Old West Gun Room, 3509 Carlson Blvd., El Cerrito, Cal. 94530 (write for
list)
Pioneer Guns, 5228 Montgomery, (Cincinnati) Norwood, OH 45212
Martin B. Retting Inc., 11029 Washington, Culver City, Calif. 90230
Ridge Guncraft, Inc., 125 E. Tyrone Rd., Oak Ridge, TN
37830/615-483-4024
S.G. Intl., P.O. Box 702, Hermosa Beach, CA. 90254
San Francisco Gun Exch., 124 Second St., San Francisco, Calif. 94105
Santa Ana Gunroom, P.O. Box 1777, Santa Ana, Calif. 92701
Ward & Van Valkenburg, 114-32nd Ave. N., Fargo, ND 58102
M. C. Wiest, 125 E. Tyrone Rd., Oak Ridge, TN 37830/615-483-4024
J. David Yale, Ltd., 2618 Conowingo Rd., Bel Air, MD 21014/301-838-9479
Lewis Yearout, 308 Riverview Dr. E., Great Falls, MT 59404

BOOKS (ARMS), Publishers and Dealers

Arms & Armour Press, 2-6 Hampstead High Street, London NW3 1QQ,
England
Beinfeld Publishing, Inc., 12767 Saticoy St., No. Hollywood, CA
91605/213-982-3700
Blacksmith Corp., P.O. Box 424, Southport, CT 06490/203-366-0671
Blacktail Mountain Books, 42 First Ave. West, Kalispell, MT
59901/406-257-5573
DBI Books, Inc., One Northfield Plaza, Northfield, IL 60093/312-441-7010
Dove Press, P.O. Box 3882, Enid, OK 73701/405-234-4347
EPCO Publ. Co., 62-19 Cooper Ave., Glendale, NY 11385/212-497-1100
Empire Co., P.O. Box 2902, Santa Fe, NM 87501/505-983-2381
Fairfield Book Co., Inc., P.O. Box 289, Brookfield Center, CT
06805/800-243-1318
Fortress Publications Inc., P.O. Box 241, Stoney Creek, Ont. L8G 3X9,
Canada
Guncraft Books, Div. of Ridge Guncraft, Inc., 125 E. Tyrone Rd., Oak
Ridge, TN 37830/615-483-4024
Gunnerman Books, P.O. Box 4292, Auburn Heights, MI
48057/313-879-2779
Handgun Press, 5832 S. Green, Chicago, IL 60621
Jackson Arms, 6209 Hillcrest Ave., Dallas, TX 75205
Lyman, Route 147, Middlefield, CT 06455
John Olson Co., 294 W. Oakland Ave., Oakland, NJ 07436
Personal Firearms Record Book Co., P.O. Box 2800, Santa Fe, NM
87501/505-983-2381
Ray Riling Arms Books Co., 114 Greenwood Ave., Box 135, Wyncote, PA
19095/215-886-5303
Rutgers Book Center, Mark Aziz, 127 Raritan Ave., Highland Park, NJ
08904
Stackpole Books, Cameron & Kelker Sts., Telegraph Press Bldg.,
Harrisburg, PA 17105
Stoeger Publishing Co., 55 Ruta Court, South Hackensack, NJ 07606
James C. Tillinghast, Box 405, Hancock, NH 03449/603-525-6615
Ken Trotman, 2-6 Hampstead High St., London, NW3 1QQ, England

BULLET & CASE LUBRICANTS

Chopie Mfg. Inc., 531 Copeland, La Crosse, Wis. 54601 (Black-Solve)
Cooper-Woodward, Box 972, Riverside, Cal. 92502 (Perfect Lube)

Corbin Mfg. & Supply Inc., P.O. Box 758, Phoenix, OR
97535/503-826-5211
Green Bay Bullets, 233 N. Ashland, Green Bay, Wis. 54303 (EZE-Size
case lube)
Gussert Bullet & Cartridge Co., Inc., P.O. Box 3945, Green Bay, WI 54303
(Super Lube)
Hodgdon Powder Co., Inc., 7710 W. 63rd St., Shawnee Mission, KS
66202/913-362-5410
Javelina Products, Box 337, San Bernardino, CA 92402/714-882-5847 (Alox
beeswax)
Jet-Aer Corp., 100 Sixth Ave., Paterson, N.J. 07524
LeClear Industries, P.O. Box 484, 1126 Donald Ave., Royal Oak, MI
48068/313-588-1025
Lenz Prod. Co., Box 1226, Sta. C, Canton, O. 44708 (Clenzoil)
Lyman Products Corp., Rte. 147, Middlefield, CT 06455 (Size-Ezy)
Marmel Prods., P.O. Box 97, Utica, MI 48087 (Marvelube, Marvelux)
Micro Ammunition Co., P.O. Box 117, Mesilla Park, NM
88047/505-522-2674 (Micro-Lube)
Mirror Lube, P.O. Box 693, San Juan Capistrano, CA 92675
M&N Bullet Lube, Box 495, Jefferson St., Madras, OR 97741
Pacific Tool Co., P.O. Box 2048, Ordnance Plant Rd., Grand Island, NE
68801/308-384-2308
Precision Ammunition & Rel., 122 Hildenboro Square, Agincourt, Ont. M1W
1Y3, Canada
RCBS, Inc., Box 1919, Oroville, Calif. 95965
SAECO Rel. Inc., P.O. Box 778, Carpinteria, CA 93103
Shooters Accessory Supply (SAS), see Corbin Mfg. & Supply
Tamarack Prods., Inc., Box 224, Barrington, IL 60010 (Bullet lube)
Testing Systems, Inc., 220 Pegasus Ave., Northvale, NJ
07647/201-767-7300

BULLET SWAGE DIES AND TOOLS

C-H Tool & Die Corp., 106 N. Harding St., Owen, WI 54461/715-229-2146
Lester Coats, 416 Simpson St., North Bend, OR 97459 (lead wire cutter)
Corbin Mfg. & Supply Inc., P.O. Box 758, Phoenix, OR
97535/503-826-5211
Hollywood, Whitney Sales Inc., P.O. Box 875, Reseda, CA 91335
Huntington's Die Specialties, P.O. Box 991, Oroville, CA 95965
Independent Machine & Gun Shop, 1416 N. Hayes, Pocatello, ID 83201
(TNT bullet dies)
L.L.F. Die Shop, 1281 Highway 99 North, Eugene, OR 97402
Rorschach Precision Products, P.O. Box 1613, Irving, TX 75060
SAS Dies, see: Corbin Mfg. & Supply
Sport Flite Mfg., Inc., 2520 Industrial Row, Troy, MI 48084/313-280-0648
TNT (see Ind. Mach. & Gun Shop)

CARTRIDGES FOR COLLECTORS

AD Hominem, R.R. 3, Orillia, Ont., Canada L3V 6H3
Antique Arsenal, 365 S. Moore, Lakewood, CO 80226
Cameron's, 16690 W. 11th Ave., Golden, Colo. 80401
Centrefire Sports Dunedin, P.O. Box 1293, 41 Dowling St., Dunedin, New
Zealand
Chas. E. Duffy, Williams Lane, West Hurley, N.Y. 12419
Tom M. Dunn, 1342 So. Poplar, Casper, Wyo. 82601
Ellwood Epps (Orillia) Ltd., Hwy. 11 North, Orillia, Ont. L3V 6H3,
Canada/705-689-5333
Idaho Ammunition Service, 410 21st Ave., Lewiston, ID 83501
San Francisco Gun Exchange, 124 Second St., San Francisco, CA 94105
Perry Spangler, 519 So. Lynch, Flint, Mich. 48503 (list 50¢)
Ernest Tichy, 365 So. Moore, Lakewood, CO 80226
James C. Tillinghast, Box 405, Hancock, NH 03449/603-525-6615 (list 50¢)
Lewis Yearout, 308 Riverview Dr. E., Great Falls, MT 59404

CASES, CABINETS AND RACKS—GUN

Action Co., P.O. Box 528, McKinney, TX 75069
Alco Carrying Cases, 601 W. 26th St., New York, NY 10001/212-675-5820
Allen Co., Inc., 640 Compton St., Broomfield, CO 80020/303-469-1857
Art Jewel Enterprises, Box 819, Berkeley, IL 60163
Morton Booth Co., Box 123, Joplin, Mo. 64801
Boyt Co., Div. of Welsh Sportg. Gds., Box 1108, Iowa Falls, Ia. 50126
Brenik, Inc., 925 W. Chicago Ave., Chicago, IL 60622
Browning, Rt. 4, Box 624-B, Arnold, MO 63010
Cap-Lex Gun Cases, Capitol Plastics of Ohio, Inc., 333 Van Camp Rd.,
Bowling Green, OH 43402
Dara-Nes Inc., P.O. Box 119, East Hampton, CT 06424/203-267-4175
(firearms security chests)
East-Tenn Mills, Inc., 2300 Buffalo Rd., Johnson City, TN 37601 (gun
socks)
Ellwood Epps (Orillia) Ltd., R.R. 3, Hwy. 11 North, Orillia, Ont. L3V 6H3,
Canada/705-689-5333 (custom gun cases)
Norbert Ertel, Box 1150, Des Plaines, IL 60018 (cust. gun cases)
Flambeau Plastics Corp., 801 Lynn, Baraboo, Wis. 53913
Gun-Ho Case Mfg. Co., 110 East 10th St., St. Paul, Minn. 55101
Harbor House Gun Cabinets, 12508 Center St., South Gate, CA 90280
Marvin Huey Gun Cases, Box 98, Reed's Spring, MO 65737/417-538-4233
(handbuilt leath. cases)
Jumbo Sports Prods., P.O. Box 280-Airport Rd., Frederick, MD 21701
Kalispel Metal Prods. (KMP), Box 267, Cusick, WA 99119 (aluminum
boxes)
Kolpin Mfg., Inc., Box 231, Berlin, WI 54923/414-361-0400
Marble Arms Corp., 420 Industrial Park, Gladstone, Mich. 49837
Bill McGuire, 1600 No. Eastmont Ave., East Wenatchee, WA 98801
(custom cases)

W. A. Miller Co., Inc. (Wamco), Mingo Loop, Oguossoc, ME 04964 (wooden handgun cases)
National Sports Div., Medalist Ind., 19 E. McWilliams St., Fond du Lac, WI 54935
Nortex Co., 2821 Main St., Dallas, Tex. 75226 (automobile gun rack)
North American Case, Inc., Industrial Park Rd., Johnstown, PA 15904/814-266-8941
North Star Devices, Inc., P.O. Box 2095, North St., Paul, MN 55109 (GunSlinger portable rack)
Paul-Reed, Inc., P.O. Box 227, Charlevoix, Mich. 49720
Penguin Industries, Inc., Airport Industrial Mall, Coatesville, PA 19320/215-384-6000
Precise, 3 Chestnut, Suffern, NY 10901
Protecto Plastics, Inc., 201 Alpha Rd., Wind Gap, Pa. 18091 (carrying cases)
Provo Steel & Supply Co., P.O. Box 977, Provo, UT 84601 (steel gun cases)
Richland Arms Co., 321 W. Adrian, Blissfield, Mich. 49228
Saf-T-Case Mfg. Co., Inc., P.O. Box 5472, Irving, TX 75062
San Angelo Co. Inc., Box 984, San Angelo, TX 76901
Buddy Schoellkopf, 4949 Joseph Hardin Dr., Dallas, TX 75236
Se-Cur-All Cabinet Co., K-Prods., P.O. Box 2052, Michigan City, IN 46360/219-872-7957
Security Gun Chest, see: Tread Corp.
Stearns Mfg. Co., P.O. Box 1498, St. Cloud, MN 56301
Stowline Inc., 811 So. 1st, Kent, WA 98031
Tread Corp., P.O. Box 13207, 1734 Granby St. N.E., Roanoke, VA 24012 (security gun chest)
Trik Truk, P.O. Box 3760, Kent, WA 98301 (P.U. truck cases)
Weather Shield Sports Equipm. Inc., Rte. #3, Petoskey Rd., Charlevoix, MI 49720
Woodstream Corp., Box 327, Lititz, Pa. 17543
Yield House, Inc., RFD, No. Conway, N.H. 03860

CHOKE DEVICES & RECOIL ABSORBERS

Arms Ingenuity Co., Box 1; 51 Canal St., Weatogue, CT 06089/203-658-5624 (Jet-Away)
C&H Research, 115 Sunnyside Dr., Lewis, KS 67552/316-324-5445 (Mercury recoil suppressor)
Dahl's Gun Shop, 6947 King Ave., Route 4, Billings, MT 59102
Diverter Arms, Inc., P.O. Box 22084, Houston, TX 77027 (shotgun diverter)
Edwards Recoil Reducer, 1104 Milton Rd., Alton, IL 62002/618-462-3257
Emsco Variable Shotgun Chokes, 101 Second Ave., S.E., Waseca, MN 56093/507-835-1481
Griggs Recreational Prods. Inc., P.O. Box 324, Twin Bridges, MT 59754/406-684-5202 (recoil director)
J & K Enterprises, Rte. 1, B.O.B. 202-A, Scappoose, OR 97056 (Mercury recoil absorbers)
Lyman Products Corp., Rte. 147, Middlefield, CT 06455 (Cutts Comp.)
Mag-Na-Port Arms, Inc., 30016 S. River Rd., Mt. Clemens, MI 48043 (muzzle-brake system)
Mag-Na-Port of Canada, 1861 Burrows Ave., Winnipeg, Manitoba R2X 2V6, Canada
Poly-Choke Co., Inc., Box 2496, Hartford, CT 06101
Pro-Port Canada, 1861 Burrows Ave., Winnipeg, Manitoba R2X 2V6, Canada
Pro-Port U.S.A., 30016 South River Rd., Mt. Clemens, MI 48045/313-469-7323

CHRONOGRAPHS AND PRESSURE TOOLS

B-Square Co., Box 11281, Ft. Worth, Tex. 76110
Custom Chronograph Co., Box 1061, Brewster, WA 98812/509-689-2004
Diverter Arms, Inc., P.O. Box 22084, Houston, TX 77027 (press. tool)
Oehler Research, P.O. Box 9135, Austin, Tex. 78756
Sundtek Co., P.O. Box 744, Springfield, Ore. 97477
Telepacific Electronics Co., Inc., P.O. Box 1329, San Marcos, CA 92069/714-744-4415
Tepeco, P.O. Box 502, Moss Point, MS 601-475-7645 (Tepeco Speed-Meter)
M. York, 5508 Griffith Rd., Gaithersburg, MD 20760/301-253-4217 (press. tool)

CLEANING & REFINISHING SUPPLIES

A 'n A Co., Box 571, King of Prussia, PA 19406 (Valet shotgun cleaner)
Armite Labs., 1845 Randolph St., Los Angeles, CA 90001 (pen oiler)
Armoloy Co. of Ft. Worth, 204 E. Daggett St., Ft. Worth, TX 76104
Birchwood-Casey, 7900 Fuller Rd., Eden Prairie, MN 55344/612-927-1733
Bisonite Co., Inc., P.O. Box 84, Kenmore Station, Buffalo, NY 14217
Blue and Gray Prods., Inc., R.D. #6, Box 348, Wellsboro, PA 16901/717-724-1383
Jim Brobst, 299 Poplar St., Hamburg, Pa. 19526 (J-B Compound)
GB Prods. Dept., H & R, Inc., Industrial Rowe, Gardner, MA 01440
Browning Arms, Rt. 4, Box 624-B, Arnold, Mo. 63010
J. M. Bucheimer Co., P.O. Box 280, Airport Rd., Frederick, MD 21701/301-662-5101
Burnishine Prod. Co., 8140 N. Ridgeway, Skokie, Ill. 60076 (Stock Glaze)
Caddie Products Corp., Div. of Jet-Aer, Paterson, NJ 07524 (the Cloth)
Chem-Pak Inc., Winchester, VA 22601 (Gun-Savr. protect. & lubricant)
Chopie Mfg. Inc., 531 Copeland, La Crosse, Wis. 54601 (Black-Solve)
Clenzoil Co., Box 1226, Sta. C, Canton, OH 44708/216-833-9758
Clover Mfg. Co., 139 Woodward Ave., Norwalk, CT 06856 (Clover compound)

Diah Engineering, Co., 5177 Haskell St., La Canada, CA 91011/213-625-2184 (barrel lubricant)
Dri-Slide, Inc., Industrial Park, 1210 Locust St., Fremont, MI 49412
Forty-Five Ranch Enterpr., 119 S. Main St., Miami, OK 74354/918-542-9307
Gun-All Products, Box 244, Dowagiac, Mich. 49047
Frank C. Hoppe Div., Penguin Ind., Inc., Airport Industrial Mall, Coatesville, PA 19320/215-384-6000
J & G Rifle Ranch, Box S 80, Turner, MT 59542
Jet-Aer Corp., 100 Sixth Ave., Paterson, N.J. 07524 (blues & oils)
Kellog's Professional Prods., Inc., P.O. Box 1201, Sandusky, OH 44870
K.W. Kleinendorst, R.D. #1, Box 113B, Hop Bottom, PA 18824/717-289-4687 (rifle clg. cables)
LPS Chemical Prods., Holt Lloyd Corp., 4647 Hugh Howell Rd., Tucker, GA/404-934-7800
LEM Gun Spec., Box 31, College Park, Ga 30337 (Lewis Lead Remover)
Liquid Wrench, Box 10628, Charlotte, N.C. 28201 (pen. oil)
Lynx Line Gun Prods. Div., Protective Coatings, Inc., 20626 Fenkell Ave., Detroit, MI 48223
Marble Arms Co., 420 Industrial Pk., Gladstone, Mich. 49837
Micro Sight Co., 242 Harbor Blvd., Belmont, Ca. 94002 (bedding)
Mirror-Lube, P.O. Box 693, San Juan Capistrano, CA 92675
New Method Mfg. Co., Box 175, Bradford, PA 16701/814-362-6611 (gun blue; Minute Man gun care)
Northern Instruments, Inc., 6680 North Highway 49, Lino Lake, MN 55014 (Stor-Safe rust preventer)
Numrich Arms Co., West Hurley, N.Y. 12491 (44-40 gun blue)
Old World Oil Products, 3827 Queen Ave. No., Minneapolis, MN 55412
Original Mink Oil, Inc., P.O. Box 20191, 10652 N.E. Holman, Portland, OR 97220/503-255-2814
Outers Laboratories, Route 2, Onalaska, WI 54650/608-783-1515 (Gunslick kits)
Radiator Spec. Co., 1400 Independence Blvd., Charlotte, N.C. 28201 (liquid wrench)
Reardon Prod., 103 W. Market St., Morrison, IL 61270 (Dry-Lube)
Rice Gun Coatings, 1521-43rd St., West Palm Beach, FL 33407
Rig Products Co., Div. of Mitann, Inc., 21320 Deering Ct., Canoga Park, CA 91304/213-883-4745
Rusteprufe Labs., Sparta, WI 54656
San/Bar Corp., Break-Free Div., 9999 Muirlands Blvd., Irvine, CA 92714/714-855-9911
Saunders Sptg. Gds., 338 Somerset, No. Plainfield, NJ 07060 (Sav-Bore)
Schultea's Gun String, 67 Burress, Houston, TX 77022 (pocket-size rifle cleaning kit)
Schwab Industries, Inc., 330 Alta Ave., Santa Monica, CA 90402/213-395-6997 (Rust Guardit)
Service Armament, 689 Bergen Blvd., Ridgefield, N. J. 07657 (Parker-Hale)
Silicote Corp., Box 359, Oshkosh, Wis. 54901 (Silicone cloths)
Silver Dollar Guns, P.O. Box 475, 10 Frances St., Franklin, NH 03235 (Silicone oil)
Sportsmen's Labs., Inc., Box 732, Anoka, Minn. 55303 (Gun Life lube)
Taylor & Robbins, Box 164, Rixford, Pa. 16745 (Throat Saver)
Testing Systems, Inc., 220 Pegasus Ave., Northvale, NJ 07647/201-767-7300 (gun lube)
Texas Platers Supply Co., 2453 W. Five Mile Parkway, Dallas, TX 75233 (plating kit)
Totally Dependable Prods., Inc., (TDP Ind.) P.O. Box 277, Zieglerville, PA 19492/215-287-7851
C. S. Van Gorden, 120 Tenth Ave., Eau Claire, Wis. 54701 (Instant Blue)
WD-40 Co., 1061 Cudahy Pl., San Diego, CA 92110
West Coast Secoa, 3915 U S Hwy. 98S, Lakeland, FL 33801 (Teflon coatings)
Williams Gun Sight, 7389 Lapeer Rd., Davison, Mich. 48423 (finish kit)
Winslow Arms Inc., P.O. Box 783, Camden, SC 29020 (refinishing kit)
Wisconsin Platers Supply Co., see: Texas Platers Supply Co.
Woodstream Corp., P.O. Box 327, Lititz, Pa. 17543 (Mask)
Zip Aerosol Prods., 21320 Deering Court, Canoga Park, CA 91304

CUSTOM GUNSMITHS

Ahlman Cust. Gun Shop, R.R. 1, Box 20, Morristown, Minn. 55052
Don Allen, Rte. 4, Timberland, Northfield, MN 55057/507-645-9216
Amrine's Gun Shop, 937 Luna Ave., Ojai, CA 93023
Anderson's Guns, Jim Jares, 706 S. 23rd St., Laramie, WY 82070
Antique Arms, D. F. Saunders, 1110 Cleveland Ave., Monett, MO 65708/417-235-6501 (Hawken copies)
R. J. Anton, 874 Olympic Dr., Waterloo, IA 50701/319-233-3666
John A. Armbrust, John's Gun Shop, 313 E. 11th St., Mishawaka, IN 46544/219-255-0973
Armurier Hiptmayer, P.O. Box 136, Eastman, Que. JOE 1PO, Canada/514-297-2492
Atkinson Gun Co., P.O. Box 512, Prescott, AZ 86301
E. von Atzigen, The Custom Shop, 890 Cochrane Crescent, Peterborough, Ont., K9H 5N3 Canada/705-742-6693
Richard W. Baber, 28 Dudley Ave., Colorado Springs, CO 80909
Bacon Creek Gun Shop, Cumberland Falls Rd., Corbin, Ky. 40701
Bain and Davis Sptg. Gds., 599 W. Las Tunas Dr., San Gabriel, Calif. 41776
Stan Baker, 5303 Roosevelt Way NE, Seattle, WA 98105 (shotgun specialist)
Joe J. Balickie, Rte. 2, Box 56-G, Apex, NC 27502
Barta's, Rte. 1, Box 129-A, Cato, Wis. 54206
Roy L. Bauer, c/o C-D Miller Guns, St. Onge, SD 57779
Bell's Custom Shop, David Norin, 3319 Mannheim Rd., Franklin Park, IL 60131/312-678-1900 (handguns)
Bennett Gun Works, 561 Delaware Ave., Delmar, N.Y. 12054
Irvin L. Benson, Saganaga Lake, Pine Island Camp, Ontario, Canada (via Grand Marais, MN 55604)

Gordon Bess, 708 River St., Canon City, Colo. 81212
Bruce Betts Gunsmith Co., 100 W. Highway 72, Rolla, MO 65401
Al Biesen, 5021 Rosewood, Spokane, WA 99208/509-328-9340
Roger Biesen, W. 2039 Sinto Ave., Spokane, WA 99201
John Bivins, Jr., 200 Wicklow Rd., Winston-Salem, NC 27106
Bob's Gun & Tackle Shop, 746 Granby St., Norfolk, VA 23510/804-627-8311
Boone Mountain Trading Post, 118 Sunrise Rd., Saint Marys, PA 15857/814-834-4879
Victor Bortugno, Atlantic & Pacific Arms Co., 4859 Virginia Beach Blvd., Virginia Beach, VA 23462
Art Bourne, see: Guncraft
Breckheimers, Rte. 69-A, Parish, NY 13131
L. H. Brown, Brown's Rifle Ranch, 1820 Airport Rd., Kalispell, MT 59901
Lenard M. Brownell, Box 25, Wyarno, WY 82845 (Custom rifles)
E. J. Bryant, 3154 Glen St., Eureka, CA 95501
Ted Buckland, 361 Flagler Rd., Nordland, WA 98358/206-385-2142 (ML)
Daved Budin, Main St., Margaretville, NY 12455/914-568-4103
George Bunch, 7735 Garrison Rd., Hyattsville, Md. 20784
Samuel W. Burgess, Sam's Gun Shop, 25 Squam Rd., Rockport, MA 01966/617-546-6839 (bluing repairs)
Leo Bustani, P.O. Box 8125, W. Palm Beach, Fla. 33407
Cache La Poudre Rifleworks, 168 No. College Ave., Ft. Collins, CO 80524/303-482-6913/303-482-6913 (cust. ML)
Cameron's Guns, 16690 W. 11th Ave., Golden, CO 80401
Lou Camilli, 4700 Oahu Dr. N.E., 4700 Oahu Dr. N.E., Albuquerque, NM 87111/505-293-5259 (ML)
Carter Gun Works, 2211 Jefferson Pk. Ave., Charlottesville, VA 22903
Ralph L. Carter, Carter's Gun Shop, 225 G St., Penrose, CO 81240/303-372-6240
R. MacDonald Champlin, P.O. Box 74, Wentworth, NH 03282 (ML rifles and pistols)
Mark Chanlynn, Bighorn Trading Co., 1704-14th St., Boulder, CO 80302
Jim Clark, Custom Gun Shop, 5367 S. 1950 West, Roy, UT 84067
Classic Arms Corp., P.O. Box 8, Palo Alto, CA 94302/415-321-7243
Kenneth E. Clark, 18738 Highway 99, Madera, Calif. 93637
John Corry, P.O. Box 109, Deerfield, IL 60015/312-541-6250 (U.S. agent for Frank E. Malin & Son)
The Country Gun Shoppe Ltd., 251 N. Front St., Monument, CO 80132
Raymond A. Cover, Rt. 1, Box 101A, Mineral Point, MO 63660/314-749-3783
Crest Carving Co., 14849 Dillow St., Westminster, Ca. 92683
Crocker, 1510 - 42nd St., Los Alamos, NM 87544 (rifles)
J. Lynn Crook, Rt. 7, Box 119-A, Lebanon, TN 37087/615-449-1930
Philip R. Crouthamel, 513 E. Baltimore, E. Lansdowne, PA 19050
Curt Crum, c/o Dave Miller, 3131 E. Greenlee Rd., Tucson, AZ 85716/602-326-3117
Jim Cuthbert, 715 S. 5th St., Coos Bay, Ore. 97420
Dahl's Custom Stocks, Rt. 4, Box 558, Schofield Rd., Lake Geneva, WI 53147/414-248-2464
Dahl's Gunshop, 6947 King Ave., Billings, MT 59102
Homer L. Dangler, Box 254, Addison, MI 49220 (Kentucky rifles)
Jack Dever, 8520 N.W. 90, Okla. City, OK 73132
R. H. Devereaux, 475 Trucky St., St. Igance, MI 49781
Dominic DiStefano, 4303 Friar Lane, Colorado Springs, CO 80907
Bill Dowtin, P.O. Box 72, Celina, TX 75009
Charles Duffy, Williams Lane, W. Hurley, N.Y. 12491
David R. Dunlop, Rte. 1, Box 199, Rolla, ND 58367
D. W. Firearms, D. Wayne Schlumbaum, 1821 - 200th S.W., Alderwood Manor, WA 98036
John H. Eaton, 8516 James St., Upper Marlboro, MD 20870
Jere Eggleston, P.O. Box 50238, Columbia, SC 29250/803-799-3402
Elko Arms, Dr. L. Kortz, 28 rue Ecole Moderne, B-7400 Soignies, H.T., Belgium
Bob Emmons, 238 Robson Rd., Grafton, OH 44044
Bill English, 4411 S. W. 100th, Seattle, Wash. 98146
Armas ERBI, S. coop., Avda. Eulogio Estarta, Elgoibar (Guipuzcoa), Spain
Ken Eyster, Heritage Gunsmiths Inc., 6441 Bishop Rd., Centerburg, OH 43011/614-625-6131
N. B. Fashingbauer, P.O. Box 366, Lac Du Flambeau, WI 54538/715-588-7116
Andy Fautheree, P.O. Box 863, Pagosa Springs, CO 81147/303-264-2892 (cust. ML)
Ted Fellowes, Beaver Lodge, 9245-16th Ave., S.W., Seattle, WA 98106/206-763-1698 (muzzleloaders)
Jack First Distributors Inc., 44633 Sierra Highway, Lancaster, CA 93534/805-942-2016
Fischer Sports Center, 221 E. Washington, Ann Arbor, MI 48104/313-769-4166
Marshall F. Fish, Rt. 22 North, Westport, NY 12993
Jerry Fisher, 1244—4th Ave. West, Kalispell, MT 59901/406-755-7093
Flynn's Cust. Guns, P.O. Box 7461, Alexandria, LA 71306/318-445-7130
Larry L. Forster, Box 212, Gwinner, ND 58040
Clark K. Frazier/Matchmate, RFD 1, Rawson, OH 45881
Jay Frazier, Box 8644, Bird Creek, AK 99540
Freeland's Scope Stands, 3737—14th Ave., Rock Island, Ill. 61201
Fredrick Gun Shop, 10 Elson Drive, Riverside, R.I. 02915
R. L. Freshour, P.O. Box 2837, Texas City, TX 77590
Frontier Arms, Inc., 420 E. Riding Club Rd., Cheyenne, Wyo. 82001
Frontier Shop & Gallery, The Depot, Main St., (Box 1805), Riverton, WY 82501/307-856-4498
Fuller Gunshop, Cooper Landing, Alas. 99572
Karl J. Furr, 76 East 350 No., Orem, UT 84057/801-225-2603
Garcia Natl. Gun Traders, Inc., 225 S.W. 22nd Ave., Miami, Fla. 33135
Gentry's, The Bozeman Gunsmith, 218 No. 7th, Bozeman, MT 59715/406-586-1405
Edwin Gillman, R.R. 6, Box 195, Hanover, PA 17331/717-632-1662
Dale Goens, Box 224, Cedar Crest, NM 87008

A. R. Goode, 12845 Catoctin Furnace Rd. Thurmont, MD 21788/301-271-2228
Gordie's Gun Shop, Gordon Mulholland, 1401 Fulton St., Streator, IL 61364/815-672-7202
Charles E. Grace, 10144 Elk Lake Rd., Williamsburg, MI 49690
Roger M. Green, Box 984, Glenrock, WY 82637/307-436-9804
Griffin & Howe, 589 Broadway, New York, N.Y. 10012
H. L. "Pete" Grisel, 61912 Skyline View Dr., Bend, OR 97701/503-389-2649 (rifles)
Karl Guenther, 43-32 160th St., Flushing NY 11372/212-461-7325
Gun City, 504 Main Ave., Bismarck, ND 58501
Guncraft, Inc., 117 W. Pipeline, Hurst, TX 76053/817-268-2887
Guncraft (Kamloops) Ltd., 127 Victoria St., Kamloops, B.C. V2C 1Z4, Canada/604-374-2151
Guncraft (Kelowna) Ltd., 1771 Harvey Ave., Kelowna, B.C. V1Y 6G4, Canada
The Gunshop, R. D. Wallace, 320 Overland Rd., Prescott, AZ 86301
H & R Custom Gun Serv., 68 Passaic Dr., Hewitt, N.J. 07421
H-S Precision, Inc., 112 N. Summit, Prescott, AZ 85302/602-445-0607
Paul Haberly, 2364 N. Neva, Chicago, IL 60635
Martin Hagn, Herzogstandweg 41, 8113 Kochel a. See, W. Germany (s.s. actions & rifles)
Chas. E. Hammans, Box 788, Stuttgart, AR 72160
Harkrader's Cust. Gun Shop, 825 Radford St., Christiansburg, VA 24073
Harp's Gun Repair Shop, 3349 Pio-Nono Circle, Macon, GA 31206 (cust. rifles)
Rob't W. Hart & Son Inc., 401 Montgomery St., Nescopeck, PA 18635 (actions, stocks)
Hal Hartley, 147 Blairs Fork Rd., Lenoir, NC 28645
Hartmann & Weiss KG, Rahlstedter Str. 139, 2000 Hamburg 73, W. Germany
Hubert J. Hecht, Waffen-Hecht, 724-K St., Sacramento, CA 95814/916-448-1177
Edw. O. Hefti, 300 Fairview, College Sta., Tex. 77840
Iver Henriksen, 1211 So. 2nd St. W., Missoula, MT 59801
Wm. Hobaugh, Box M, Philipsburg, MT 59858
Richard Hodgson, 5589 Arapahoe, Unit 104, Boulder, CO 80301
Hoenig Rodman, 6521 Morton Dr., Boise, ID 83705/208-375-1116
Dick Holland, 422 N.E. 6th St., Newport, OR 97365/503-265-7556
Hollingsworth's Guns, Route 1, Box 55B, Alvaton, KY 42122/502-842-3580
Hollis Gun Shop, 917 Rex St., Carlsbad, N.M. 88220
Bill Holmes, Rt. 2, Box 242, Fayetteville, AR 72701/501-521-8958
Huntington's, P.O. Box 991, Oroville, CA 95965
Hyper-Single Precision SS Rifles, 520 E. Beaver, Jenks, OK 74037
Independent Machine & Gun Shop, 1416 N. Hayes, Pocatello, Ida. 83201
Jackson's, Box 416, Selman City, TX 75689
Paul Jaeger, Inc., 211 Leedom St., Jenkintown, PA 19046/215-884-6920
J. J. Jenkins Ent. Inc., 375 Pine Ave. No. 25, Goleta, CA 93017/805-967-1366
Jerry's Gun Shop, 9220 Ogden Ave., Brookfield, Ill. 60513
Neal G. Johnson, 111 Marvin Dr., Hampton, VA 23666/804-838-8091
Bruce Jones, 389 Calla Ave., Imperial Beach, CA 92032
Joseph & Associates, 4810 Riverbend Rd., Boulder, CO 80301/303-332-6720
Jos. Jurjevic, Gunshop, 605 Main St., Marble Falls, TX 78654
John Kaufield Small Arms Eng. Co., 7698 Garden Prairie Rd., Garden Prairie, IL 61038 (restorations)
Ken's Gun Specialties, K. Hunnell, Box 241, Lakeview, AR 72642/501-431-5606
Kennedy Gun Shop, Rte. 12, Box 21, Clarksville, TN 37040/615-647-6043
Monte Kennedy, P.O. Box 214, Kalispell, MT 59901
Kennon's Custom Rifles, 5408 Biffle, Stone Mtn., GA 30083/404-469-9339
Stanley Kenvin, 5 Lakeville Lane, Plainview, NY 11803/516-931-0321
Kesselring Gun Shop, 400 Pacific Hiway No., Burlington, WA 98233/206-724-3113
Don Klein Custom Guns, Box 277, Camp Douglas, WI 54618
K. W. Kleinendorst, R.D. #1, Box 113B, Hop Bottom, PA 18824/717-289-4687
J. Korzinek, RD #2, Box 73, Canton, PA 17724/717-673-8512 (riflesmith) (broch. $1)
L&W Casting Co., 5014 Freeman Rd. E., Puyallup, WA 98371
Sam Lair, 520 E. Beaver, Jenks, OK 74037
Maynard Lambert, Kamas, UT 84036
Harry Lawson Co., 3328 N. Richey Blvd., Tucson, Ariz. 85716
John G. Lawson, (The Sight Shop), 1802 E. Columbia, Tacoma, WA 98404/206-474-5465
LeDel, Inc., Main and Commerce Sts., Cheswold, Del. 19936
Mark Lee, 2323 Emerson Ave., N., Minneapolis, MN 55411/612-521-0673
Bill Leeper, see: Guncraft
Art LeFeuvre, 1003 Hazel Ave., Deerfield, IL 60015/312-945-0073
LeFever Arms Co. Inc., R.D. 1, Lee Center-Stokes Rd., Lee Center, NY 13363/315-337-6722
Leland Firearms Co., 13 Mountain Ave., Llewellyn Park, West Orange, NJ 07052/201-964-7500 (shotguns)
Lenz Firearms Co., 1480 Elkay Dr., Eugene, OR 97404
Al Lind, 7821—76th Ave. S.W., Tacoma, WA 98498
Max J. Lindauer, R.R. 2, Box 27, Washington, MO 63090
Robt. L. Lindsay, J & B Enterprises, 9416 Emory Grove Rd., Gaithersburg, MD 20760/301-948-2941 (services only)
Ljutic Ind., Box 2117, Yakima, WA 98902 (Mono-Wads)
Llanerch Gun Shop, 2800 Township Line, Upper Darby, PA 19082/215-789-5462
Jim Lofland, 2275 Larkin Rd., Boothwyn, PA 19061 (SS rifles)
London Guns, 1528—20th St., Santa Monica, CA 90404
R. J. Maberry, 511 So. K, Midland, Tex. 79701
Harold E. MacFarland, Route #4, Box 1249 Cottonwood, AZ 86326/602-634-5320
Frank E. Malin & Son (see: John Corry)

Monte Mandarino, 4946 Pinewood Drive, Winston Salem, NC 27106 (Penn. rifles)

McCann's Muzzle-Gun Works, 200 Federal City Rd., Pennington, NJ 08354/609-737-1070 (ML)

McCormick's Gun Bluing Service, 609 N.E. 104th Ave., Vancouver, WA 98664

Bill McGuire, 1600 N. Eastmont Ave., East Wenatchee, WA 98801

Monte Mandarino, 4946 Pinewood Dr., Winston-Salem, NC 27106/919-924-1020

Lowell Manley, 3684 Pine St., Deckerville, MI 48427/313-376-3665

Dale Marfell, 107 N. State St., Litchfield, IL 62056

Marquart Precision Co., P.O. Box 1740, Prescott, AZ 86302/602-445-5646

Marsh Al's, Rt. #3, Box 729, Preston, ID 83263

Elwyn H. Martin, Martin's Gun Shop, 937 S. Sheridan Blvd., Lakewood, CO 80226/303-922-2184

Mashburn Arms Co., 1218 N. Pennsylvania, Oklahoma City, OK 73107

Seely Masker, Custom Rifles, 261 Washington Ave., Pleasantville, NY 10570/914-769-2627

Geo. E. Mathews & Son Inc., 10224 S. Paramount Blvd., Downey, CA 90241

Maurer Arms, 2366 Frederick Dr., Cuyahoga Falls, Ohio 44221 (muzzleloaders)

John E. Maxson, Box 332, Dumas, TX 79029/806-935-5990 (high grade rifles)

Eric Meitzner, c/o Don Allen, Inc., Rt. 1, Timberlane, Northfield, MN 55057/507-645-9216

Midwest Firearms & Customizing, 804 E. 2nd, Cameron, MO 64429/816-632-3282

Miller Custom Rifles, 655 Dutton Ave., San Leandro, CA 94577

Miller Gun Works, P.O. Box 7326, Tamuning, Guam 96911

C.D. Miller Guns, Purl St., St. Onge, SD 57779

David Miller Co., 3131 E. Greenlee Rd., Tucson, AZ 85716/602-326-3117 (classic rifles)

Earl Milliron, 1249 N.E. 166th Ave., Portland, Ore. 97230

Wm. Larkin Moore Co., 31360 Via Colinas, Suite 109, Westlake Village, CA 91360/213-889-4160

Larry Mrock, R.F.D. 3, Woodhill-Hooksett Rd., Bow, NH 03301/603-224-4096 (broch. $3)

Clayton N. Nelson, R.R. #3, Box 119, Enid, OK 73701

Bruce Nettestad, R.R. 1, Box 140, Pelican Rapids, MN 56572/701-293-6011

Newman Gunshop, 119 Miller Rd., Agency, IA 52530/515-937-5775

Ted Nicklas, 5504 Hegel Rd., Goodrich, MI 48438/313-797-4493

William J. Nittler, 290 More Drive, Boulder Creek, CA 95006 (shotgun repairs)

Jim Norman, Custom Gunstocks, 11230 Calenda Rd., San Diego, CA 92127/714-487-4173

Nu-Line Guns, 1053 Caulkshill Rd., Harvester, MO 63303/314-441-4500

O'Brien Rifle Co., 324 Tropicana No. 128, Las Vegas, Nev. 89109

Warren E. Offenberger, Star Route, Reno, Oh 45773 (ML)

Vic Olson, 5002 Countryside Dr., Imperial, MO 63052/314-296-8086

Pachmayr Gun Works, 1220 S. Grand Ave., Los Angeles, Calif. 90015

Charles J. Parkinson, 116 Wharncliffe Rd. So., London, Ont., Canada N6J2K3

Paterson Gunsmithing, 438 Main St., Paterson NJ 07501/201-345-4100

Byrd Pearson, 191 No. 2050 W., Provo, UT 84601

John Pell, 410 College Ave., Trinidad, CO 81082

C. R. Pedersen & Son, Ludington, Mich. 49431

Al Petersen, Box 8, Riverhurst, Sask., Canada S0H3P0

A. W. Peterson Gun Shop, 1693 Old Hwy. 441, Mt. Dora, FL 32757 (ML rifles, also)

Eugene T. Plante, Gene's Custom Guns, 3890 Hill Ave., White Bear Lake, MN 55110/612-429-5105

Ready Eddie's Gun Shop, 501 Van Spanje Ave., Michigan City, IN 46360

R. Neal Rice, 5152 Newton, Denver, CO 80221

Ridge Guncraft, Inc., 125 E. Tyrone Rd., Oak Ridge, Tenn. 37830/615-483-4024

Rifle Ranch, Jim Wilkinson, Rte. 5, Prescott, AZ 86301

Rifle Shop, Box M, Philipsburg, MT 59858

Wm. A. Roberts II, Rte. 4, Box 34, Athens, AL 35611 (ML)

W. Rodman, 6521 Morton Dr., Boise, ID 83705

Carl Roth, 4728 Pine Ridge Ave., Cheyenne, WY 82001/307-634-3958 (rust bluing)

Royal Arms, Inc., 10064 Bert Acosta, Santee, Calif. 92071

Murray F. Ruffino, c/o Neal G. Johnson, 111 Marvin Dr., Hampton, VA 23666/804-838-8091

Rush's Old Colonial Forge, 106 Wiltshire Rd., Baltimore, MD 21221 (Ky.-Pa. rifles)

Russell's Rifle Shop, Route 5, Box 92, Georgetown, TX 78626/512-778-5338 (gunsmith services)

Lewis B. Sanchez, Cumberland Knife & Gun Works, 5661 Bragg Blvd., Fayetteville, NC 28303

Sanders Custom Gun Serv., 2358 Tyler Lane, Louisville, Ky. 40205

Sandy's Custom Gunshop, Rte. #1, Box 20, Rockport, IL 62370/217-437-4241

Saratoga Arms Co., 1752 N. Pleasantview Rd., Pottstown, PA 19464/215-323-8326

Roy V. Schaefer, 965 W. Hilliard Lane, Eugene, OR 97404

N.H. Schiffman Cust. Gun Serv., 963 Malibu, Pocatello, ID 83201

SGW, Inc. (formerly Schuetzen Gun Works), 624 Old Pacific Hwy. S.E., Olympia, WA 98503/206-456-3471

Schumaker's Gun Shop, Rte. 4, Box 500, Colville, WA 99114/509-684-4848

Schwartz Custom Guns, 9621 Coleman Rd., Haslett, MI 48840/517-339-8939

Schwarz's Gun Shop, 41-15th St., Wellsburg, WV 26070/304-737-0533

Shaw's, Finest in Guns, 9447 W. Lilac Rd., Escondido, CA 92025/714-728-7070

Shell Shack, 113 E. Main, Laurel, MT 59044

George H. Sheldon, P.O. Box 489, Franklin, NH 03235 (45 autos & M-1 carbines only)

Lynn Shelton Custom rifles, P.O. Box 681, Elk City,, OK 73644

Shilen Rifles, Inc., 205 Metropark Blvd., Ennis, TX 75119

Harold H. Shockley, 204 E. Farmington Rd., Hanna City, IL 61536 (hot bluing & plating)

Shootin' Shop, Inc., 1169 Harlow Rd., Springfield, OR 97477/503-747-0175

Walter Shultz, 1752 N. Pleasantview Rd., Pottstown, PA 19464

Silver Dollar Guns, P.O. Box 475, 10 Frances St., Franklin, NH 03235 (45 autos & M-1 carbines only)

Simmons Gun Spec., 700 Rogers Rd., Olathe, Kans. 66061

Simms Hardware Co., 2801 J St., Sacramento, Calif. 95816

Sklany's Shop, 566 Birch Grove Dr., Kalispell, MT 59901/406-755-4257 (Ferguson rifle)

Skinner's Gun Shop, Box 30, Juneau, Alaska 98801

Markus Skosples, c/o Ziffren Sptg. Gds., 124 E. Third St., Davenport, IA 52801

Jerome F. Slezak, 1290 Marlowe, Lakewood (Cleveland), OH 44107

Small Arms Eng., 7698 Garden Prairie Rd., Garden Prairie, IL 61038 (restorations)

John Smith, 912 Lincoln, Carpentersville, Ill. 60110

Snapp's Gunshop, 6911 E. Washington Rd., Clare, Mich. 48617

Southern Blueing, 6027-B N.W. 31st Ave., Ft. Lauderdale, FL 33309 (blueing)

Southern Penna. Sporting Goods Center, R.D. No. 1, Spring Grove, PA 17362/717-225-5908

Fred D. Speiser, 2229 Dearborn, Missoula, MT 59801

Sport Service Center, 2364 N. Neva, Chicago, IL 60635

Sportsman's Bailiwick, 5306 Broadway, San Antonio, TX 78209

Sportsmens Equip. Co., 915 W. Washington, San Diego, Calif. 92103

Sportsmen's Exchange & Western Gun Traders, Inc., P.O. Box 111, 560 S. "C" St., Oxnard, CA 93030/805-483-1917

George B. Spring, RFD #4, Rt. 82, Salem, CT 06415/203-859-0561

Jess L. Stark, 12051 Stroud, Houston, TX 77072

Ken Starnes, Rt. 1, Box 89-C, Scorggins, TX 75480/214-365-2566

Keith Stegall, Box 696, Gunnison, Colo. 81230

Victor W. Strawbridge, 6 Pineview Dr., Dover Point, Dover, NH 03820/603-742-0013

W. C. Strutz, Rifle Barrels, Inc., P.O. Box 611, Eagle River, WI 54521/715-479-4766

Suter's House of Guns, 332 N. Tejon, Colorado Springs, Colo. 80902

Swanson Custom Firearms, 1051 Broadway, Denver, Colo. 80203

A. D. Swenson's 45 Shop, P.O. Box 606, Fallbrook, CA 92028

T-P Shop, 212 E. Houghton, West Branch, Mich. 48661

Tag Gun Works, 236 Main, Springfield, OR 97477/503-741-4118 (ML)

Talmage Ent., 43197 E. Whittier, Hemet, CA 92343

Taylor & Robbins, Box 164, Rixford, Pa. 16745

James A. Tertin, c/o Gander Mountain, P.O. Box 128 - Hwy. W, Wilmot, WI 53152/414-862-2331

Gordon A. Tibbitts, 1378 Lakewood Circle, Salt Lake City, UT 84117/801-272-4126

Daniel Titus, 872 Penn St., Bryn Mawr, PA 19010/215-525-8829

Tom's Gunshop, 4435 Central, Hot Springs, AR 71901

Todd Trefts, 1290 Story Mill Rd., Bozeman, MT 59715/406-586-6003

Trinko's Gun Serv., 1406 E. Main, Watertown, Wis. 53094

Herb. G. Troester's Accurizing Serv., 2292 W. 1000 North, Vernal, UT 84078/801-789-2158

Dennis A. "Doc" Ulrich, 2511 S. 57th Ave., Cicero, IL 60650

Brent Umberger, Sportsman's Haven, R.R. 4, Cambridge, OH 43725

Upper Missouri Trading Co., Inc., Box 181, Crofton, MO 68730

Chas. VanDyke Gunsmith Service, 201 Gatewood Cir. W., Burleson, TX 76028/817-295-7373 (shotgun & recoil pad specialist)

Milton Van Epps, Rt. 69-A, Parish, NY 13131/313-625-7498

J. W. Van Patten, Box 145, Foster Hill, Milford, Pa. 18337

Vic's Gun Refinishing, 6 Pineview Dr., Dover, NH 03820/603-742-0013

Walker Arms Co., R. 2, Box 73, Selma, AL 36701

Walker Arms Co., 127 N. Main St., Joplin, MO 64801

R. D. Wallace, 320 Overland Rd., Prescott, AZ 86301

R. A. Wardrop, Box 245, 409 E. Marble St., Mechanicsburg, PA 17055

Weatherby's, 2781 Firestone Blvd., South Gate, Calif. 90280

Jerry Wetherbee, 63470 Hamehook Rd., Bend, OR 97701/503-389-6080 (ML)

Cecil Weems,, Box 657, Mineral Wells, TX 76067

Wells Sport Store, 110 N. Summit St., Prescott, Ariz. 86301

R. A. Wells, 3452 N. 1st, Racine, Wis. 53402

Robert G. West, 27211 Huey Lane, Eugene, OR 97402/503-689-6610

Western Gunstocks Mfg. Co., 550 Valencia School Rd., Aptos, CA 95003

Duane Wiebe, P.O. Box 497 Lotus, CA 95651/916-626-6240

M. Wiest & Son, 125 E. Tyrone Rd., Oak Ridge, TN 37830/615-483-4024

Williams Gun Sight Co., 7389 Lapeer Rd., Davison, Mich. 48423

Bob Williams, P.O. Box 143, Boonsboro, MD 21713

Williamson-Pate Gunsmith Service, 117 W. Pipeline, Hurst, TX 76053/817-268-2887

Thomas E. Wilson, 644 Spruce St., Boulder, CO 80302 (restorations)

Robert M. Winter, Box 484, Menno, SD 57045

Stan Wright, Billings Gunsmiths Inc., 421 St. Johns Ave., Billings, MT 59101/406-245-3337

J. David Yale, Ltd., 2618 Conowingo Rd., Bel Air, MD 21014/301-838-9479 (ML work)

Mike Yee, 4700-46th Ave. S.W., Seattle, WA 98116

York County Gun Works, RR 4, Tottenham, Ont., L0G 1W0 Canada (muzzleloaders)

Russ Zeeryp, 1601 Foard Dr., Lynn Ross Manor, Morristown, TN 37814

John G. Zimmerman, 60273 N.W. 31st Ave., Ft. Lauderdale, FL 33309

CUSTOM METALSMITHS

Ted Blackburn, 85 E. 700 South, Springfield, UT 84663 (precision metalwork)
Tom Burgess, 180 McMannamy Draw, Kalispell, MT 59901
Dave Cook, Dave's Gun Shop, 720 Hancock Ave., Hancock, MI 49930
Homer Culver, 1219 N. Stuart, Arlington, VA 22201
John H. Eaton, 8516 James St., Upper Marlboro, MD 20870
Phil Fischer, 2625 N.E. Multnomah, Portland, OR 97232/503-282-7151
Geo. M. Fullmer, 2499 Mavis St., Oakland, CA 94601/415-533-4193 (precise chambering—300 cals.)
Harkrader's Custom Gun Shop, 825 Radford St., Christiansburg, VA 24073
Huntington's, P.O. Box 991, Oroville, CA 95965
Paul Jaeger, Inc., 211 Leedom St., Jenkintown, PA 19046/215-884-6920
Ken Jantz, Rt. 1, Sulphur, OK 73086/405-622-3790
Terry K. Kopp, Highway 13, Lexington, MO 64067/816-259-2083
R. H. Lampert, Rt. 1, Box 61, Guthrie, MN 56451
Mark Lee, 2323 Emerson Ave., N., Minneapolis, MN 55411/612-521-0673
Bruce Nettestad, R.R. 1, Box 140, Pelican Rapids, MN 56572/701-293-6011
Paul's Precision Gunworks, 420 Eldon, Corpus Christi, TX 78412
Dave Talley, Rte. 10, Box 249-B, Easley, SC 29640/803-295-2012
John Vest, 6715 Shasta Way, Klamath Falls, OR 97601/503-884-5585
Herman Waldron, Box 475, Pomeroy, WA 99347
Edward S. Welty, R.D. 2, Box 25, Cheswick, PA 15024
Dick Willis, 141 Shady Creek Rd., Rochester, NY 14623

DECOYS

Carry-Lite, Inc., 5203 W. Clinton Ave., Milwaukee, WI 53223
Custom Purveyors, P.O. Box 886, Fort Lee, NJ 07024
Deeks, Inc., P.O. Box 2309, Salt Lake City, UT 84114
G & H Decoy Mfg. Co., P.O. Box 937, Henryetta, OK 74437
Sports Haven Inc., P.O. Box 88231, Seattle, WA 98188
Tex Wirtz Ent., Inc., 1925 Hubbard St., Chicago, IL 60622
Woodstream Corp., P.O. Box 327, Lititz, PA 17543

ENGRAVERS, ENGRAVING TOOLS

John J. Adams, 47 Brown Ave., Mansfield, MA 02048/617-339-4613
Aurum Etchings, P.O. Box 401059, Garland, TX 75040 (acid engraving)
Paolo Barbetti, c/o Stan's Gunshop, 53103 Roosevelt Way N.E., Seattle, WA 98105/206-522-4575
Joseph C. Bayer, 439 Sunset Ave., Sunset Hill Griggstown, RD 1, Princeton, NJ 08540/201-359-7283
Sid Bell Originals, R.D. 2, Tully, NY 13159
Weldon Bledsoe, 6812 Park Place Dr., Fort Worth, Tex. 76118
Carl Bleile, Box 11285, Cincinnati, OH 45211/513-662-0802
C. Roger Bleile, Box 5112, Cincinnati, OH 45205/513-251-0249
Erich Boessler, Am Vogeltal 3, 8732 Münnerstadt, W. Germany
Henry "Hank" Bonham, 218 Franklin Ave., Seaside Heights, NJ 08751
Bryan Bridges, 6350 E. Paseo San Andres, Tucson, AZ 85710
Burgess Vibrocrafters (BVI), Rt. 83, Grayslake, Ill. 60030
Byron Burgess, 1439 Iris St., San Luis Obispo, CA 93401/805-543-7274
Winston Churchill, Twenty Mile Stream Rd., RFD Box 29B, Proctorsville, VT 05153/802-226-7772
Crocker Engraving, 1510 - 42nd St., Los Alamos, NM 87544
W. Daniel Cullity, 209 Old County Rd., East Sandwich, MA 02537/617-888-1147
Art A. Darakis, RD #2, Box 165D, Fredericksburg, OH 44627/216-695-4271
Tim Davis, 230 S. Main St., Eldorado, OH 45321
James R. DeMunck, 3012 English Rd., Rochester, NY 14616
Gerald R. Desquesnes, P.O. Box 1021, Paris, TX 75460
Ernest Dumoulin-Deleye, 8 rue Florent Boclinville, 4410 Herstal (Vottem), Belgium
Ken Eyster, Heritage Gunsmiths Inc., 6441 Bishop Rd., Centerburg, OH 43011/614-625-6131
John Fanzoi, P.O. Box 25, Ferlach, Austria 9170
Jacqueline Favre, 3212-B Wynn Rd., Suite 214, Las Vegas, NV 89102/702-876-6278
Armi FERLIB, 46 Via Costa, 25063 Gardone V.T. (Brescia), Italy
Heinrich H. Frank, 210 Meadow Rd., Whitefish, MT 59937/406-862-2681
Leonard Francolini, P.O. Box 32, West Granby, CT 06090/203-653-2336
J. R. French, 2633 Quail Valley, Irving TX 75060
GRS Corp., P.O. Box 748, Emporia, KS 66801/316-343-1084 (Gravermeister tool)
Ed F. Giles, 204 Tremont St., Rehoboth, MA 02769
Donald Glaser, 1520 West St., Emporia, Kans. 66801
Eric Gold, Box 1904, Flagstaff, AZ 86002
Daniel Goodwin, P.O. Box 66, Kalispell, MT 59901
Howard V. Grant, P.O. Box 396, Lac Du Flambeau, WI 54538
John Gray, 3923 Richard Dr. NE, Cedar Rapids, IA 52402
Griffin & Howe, 589 Broadway, N.Y., N.Y. 10012
F. R. Gurney Engraving Method Ltd., #2301, 9925 Jasper Ave., Edmonton, Alberta, Can. T5J 2X4/403-426-7474
Bryson J. Gwinnell, 32 Lincoln St., Hartford, CT 06106/203-278-9879
Hand Engravers Supply Co., P.O. Box 3001, Overlook Branch, Dayton, OH 45431/513-426-6762
Frank E. Hendricks, Inc., Rt. 2, Box 189J, San Antonio, TX 78229
Heidemarie Hiptmayer, P.O. Box 136, Eastman, Que. JOE 1PO, Canada/514-297-2492
Ralph W. Ingle, #4 Missing Link, Rossville, GA 30741
Paul Jaeger, Inc., 211 Leedom, Jenkintown, PA 19046/215-884-6920
Bill Johns, 1113 Nightingale, McAllen, TX 78501/512-682-2971
Steven Kamyk, 19 Wilder Ter., West Springfield, MA 01089/413-788-6200
T. J. Kaye, 4745 Dellwood, Beaumont, TX 77706/713-898-0988

Lance Kelly, 1824 Royal Palm Dr., Edgewater, FL 32032/904-423-4933
Jim Kelso, P.O. Box 108, Worcester, VT 05682
Kleinguenther's, P.O. Box 1261, Seguin, TX 78155
E. J. Koevenig, Engraving Service, Box 55 Keystone, SD 57751/605-574-2239
John Kudlas, 622-14th St. S.E., Rochester, MN 55901/507-288-5579
Ben Lane, Jr., 2118 Lipscomb St., Amarillo, TX 79109
Beth Lane, 201 S. Main St., Pontiac, IL 61764
Herb Larsen, 35276 Rockwell Dr., Abbotsford, B.C. V2S 4N4, Canada/604-853-5151
Terry Lazette, R.D. 5, Box 142, Millersburg, OH 44654/216-893-2181
W. Neal Lewis, 9 Bowers Dr., Newnan, GA 30263/404-251-3045
Steve Lindsay, 1212 Tibbals, Holdrege, NE 68949/308-995-4793
London Guns, 1528-20th St., Santa Monica, CA 90404
Ed. J. Machu, Jr., Sportsman's Bailiwick, 5306 Broadway, San Antonio, TX 78209
Lynton S.M. McKenzie, 6940 N. Alvaron, Tucson, AZ 85718/602-299-5090
Wm. H. Mains, 3212-B Wynn Rd., Suite 214, Las Vegas, NV 89102/702-876-6278
Robert E. Maki, P.O. Box 947, Northbrook, IL 60062/312-724-8238
Rudy Marek, Rt. 1, Box 1A, Banks, Ore. 97106
Franz Marktl, P.O. Box 716, Kalispell, MT 59901
S. A. Miller, Miller Gun Works, P.O. Box 7326, Tamuning, Guam 96911
Frank Mittermeier, 3577 E. Tremont Ave., New York, N.Y. 10465
NgraveR Co., 879 Raymond Hill Rd., Oakdale, CT 06370 (engr. tool)
New Orleans Jewelers Supply, 206 Chartres St., New Orleans, LA 70130/504-523-3839 (engr. tool)
Hans Obiltschnig, 12. November Str. 7, 9170 Ferlach, Austria
Warren E. Offenberger, Star Route, Reno, OH 45773
Oker's Engraving, Bell Rd., Bellford Mtn. Hts., P.O. Box 126, Shawnee, CO 80475
Gale Overbey, 612 Azalea Ave., Richmond, VA 23227
Pachmayr Gun Works, Inc., 1220 S. Grand Ave., Los Angeles, CA 90015/213-748-7271
Rex Pedersen, C. R. Pedersen & Son, 2717 S. Pere Marquette, Ludington, MI 49431/616-843-2061
Marcello Pedini, 470 Deer Park Ave., Dix Hills, NY 11746/516-543-6828
Arthur Pitetti, Hawk Hollow Rd., Denver, NY 12421
Jeremy W. Potts, 912 Poplar St., Denver, CO 80220/303-355-5462
Wayne E. Potts, 912 Poplar St., Denver, CO 80220/303-355-5462
Ed Pranger, 1414-7th St., Anacortes, WA 98221/206-293-3488
E. C. Prudhomme, 513 Ricou-Brewster Bldg., Shreveport, LA 71101
Martin Rabeno, Spook Hollow Trading Co., Box 37F, RD #1, Ellenville, NY 12428/914-647-4567
Wayne Reno, c/o Blackhawk Mtn., 1337 Delmar Parkway, Aurora, CO 80010
Jim Riggs, 206 Azalea, Boerne, TX 78006/512-249-8567 (handguns)
Hans Rohner, Box 224, Niwot, CO 80544/303-652-2659
John R. Rohner, Sunshine Canyon, Boulder, CO 80302/303-444-3841
Joe Rundell, 6198 Frances Rd., Clio, MI 48420/313-687-0559
Robert P. Runge, 94 Grove St., Ilion, N.Y. 13357
A. E. Scott, 609 E. Jackson, Pasadena, TX 77506
Shaw-Leibowitz, Rt. 1, Box 421, New Cumberland, WV 26047/304-564-3108 (etchers)
George Sherwood, Box 735, Winchester, OR 97495/503-672-3159
Ben Shostle, The Gun Room, 1201 Burlington Dr., Muncie, IN 47302
Don Simmons, c/o Paul Jaeger, Inc., 211 Leedom St., Jenkintown, PA 19046
W. P. Sinclair, 52 High St., Dilton Marsh, Westbury, Wilshire BA 13 4DY, England
Ron Skaggs, 508 W. Central, Princeton, IL 61536
Russell J. Smith, 231 Springdale Rd., Westfield, Mass. 01085
R. Spinale, 3415 Oakdale Ave., Lorain, OH 44055/216-246-5344
George B. Spring, RFD #4, Rte. 82, Salem, CT 06415/203-859-0561
Robt. Swartley, 2800 Pine St., Napa, Calif. 94559
George W. Thiewes, 1846 Allen Lane, St. Charles, IL 60174/312-584-1383
Anthony Tuscano, 1473 Felton Rd., South Euclid, OH 44121
Robert Valade, Rte. 1, Box 30-A, Cove, OR 97824
John Vest, 6715 Shasta Way, Klamath Falls, OR 97601
Ray Viramontez, 4348 Newberry Ct., Dayton, OH 45432
Louis Vrancken, 30-rue sur le bois, 4531 Argenteau (Liege), Belgium
Vernon G. Wagoner, 2340 East Fox, Mesa, AZ 85203/602-835-1307
Terry Wallace, 385 San Marino, Vallejo, CA 94590
Floyd E. Warren, 1273 St. Rt. 305 N.E. Rt. #3, Cortland, OH 44410
John E. Warren, P.O. Box 72, Eastham, Mass. 02642
Rachel Wells, 110 N. Summit St., Prescott, AZ 86301
Sam Welch, Box 2152, Kodiak, AK 99615
Claus Willig, c/o Paul Jaeger, Inc., 211 Leedom St., Jenkintown, PA 19046
Mel Wood, Star Route, Box 364, Elgin, AZ 85611/602-455-5541

GAME CALLS

Black Duck, 1737 Davis, Whiting, Ind. 46394
Burnham Bros., Box 669, 912 Main St., Marble Falls, TX 78654/512-693-3112
Faulk's, 616 18th St., Lake Charles, La. 70601
Lohman Mfg. Co., P.O. Box 220, Neosho, MO 64850/417-451-4438
Mallardtone Game Calls, 2901 16th St., Moline, IL 61265
Phil. S. Olt Co., Box 550, Pekin, Ill. 61554
Penn's Woods Products, Inc., 19 W. Pittsburgh St., Delmont, Pa. 15626
Scotch Game Call Co., Inc., 60 Main St., Oakfield, NY 14125
Johnny Stewart Game Calls, Box 7954, Waco, TX 76710/817-772-3261
Sure-Shot Game Calls, Inc., P.O. Box 816, Groves, TX 77619
Thomas Game Calls, P.O. Box 336, Winnsboro, TX 75494
Weems Wild Calls, P.O. Box 7261, Ft. Worth, TX 76111/817-531-1051
Tex Wirtz Ent., Inc., 1925 W. Hubbard St., Chicago, Ill. 60622

GUNMAKERS, FERLACH, AUSTRIA

Ludwig Borovnik, Dollichgasse 14, A-9170
Johann Fanzoj, Griesgasse 1, A-9170
Wilfried Glanznig, Werkstr. 9, A-9170
Josef Hambrusch, Gartengasse 2, A-9170
Karl Hauptmann, Bahnhofstr. 5, A-9170
Gottfried Juch, Pfarrhofgasse 2, A-9170
Josef Just, Hauptplatz 18, A-9170
Jakob Koschat, 12.-November-Str. 2, A-9170
Johann Michelitsch, 12.-November-Str. 2, A-9170
Josef Orasche, Lastenstr. 5, A-9170
Komm.-Rat A. Sch. Outschar, Josef-Orgis-Gasse 23, A-9170
Valentin Rosenzopf's Erbe, Griesgasse 2, A-9170
Helmut Scheiring-Düsel, 10.-Oktober-Str. 8, A-9170
R. Franz Schmid, Freibacherstr. 10, A-9170
Anton Sodia, Unterferlach 39, A-9170
Vinzenz Urbas, Neubaugasse 6, A-9170
Benedikt Winkler, Postgasse 1, A-9170
Josef Winkler, Neubaugasse 1, A-9170

GUN PARTS, U. S. AND FOREIGN

Badger Shooter's Supply, Box 397, Owen, WI 54460
Behlert Custom Guns, Inc., 725 Lehigh Ave., Union, NJ 07083 (handgun parts)
Philip R. Crouthamel, 513 E. Baltimore, E. Lansdowne, Pa. 19050
Charles E. Duffy, Williams Lane, West Hurley, N.Y. 12491
Federal Ordnance Inc., 1443 Potrero Ave., So. El Monte, CA 91733/213-350-4161
Jack First Distributors Inc., 44633 Sierra Highway, Lancaster, CA 93534/805-942-2016
Gun-Tec, P.O. Box 8125, W. Palm Beach, FL 33407 (Win. mag. tubing; Win. 92 conversion parts)
Hunter's Haven, Zero Prince St., Alexandria, Va. 22314
Walter H. Lodewick, 2816 N.E. Halsey, Portland, OR 97232
Marsh Al's, Rte. #3, Box 729, Preston, ID 83263 (Contender rifle)
Numrich Arms Co., West Hurley, N.Y. 12491
Pacific Intl. Merch. Corp., 2215 "J" St., Sacramento, CA 95816 (Vega 45 Colt mag.)
Potomac Arms Corp. (see Hunter's Haven)
Martin B. Retting, Inc., 11029 Washington Blvd., Culver City, CA 90230/213-870-1589
Sarco, Inc., 323 Union St., Stirling, NJ 07980
Sherwood Intl. Export Corp., 18714 Parthenia St., Northridge, CA 91324
Simms, 2801 J St., Sacramento, CA 95816
Clifford L. Smires, R.D. 1, Box 100, Columbus, NJ 08022/609-298-3158 (Mauser rifles)
Springfield Sporters Inc., R.D. 1, Penn Run, PA 15765/412-254-2626
N. F. Strebe Gunworks, 4926 Marlboro Pike, S.E., Washington, D.C. 20027
Triple-K Mfg. Co., 568-6th Ave., San Diego, CA 92101 (magazines, gun parts)

GUNS (Foreign)

Abercrombie & Fitch, 2302 Maxwell Lane, Houston, TX 77023 (Ferlib)
Alpha Arms, Inc., 1602 Stemmons, Suite "D," Carrollton, TX 75006/214-245-3115
American Arms International P.O. Box 11717, Salt Lake City, UT 84147/531-0180
Action Arms, 4567 Bermuda, Philadelphia, PA 19124/215-744-3400
AYA (Aguirre y Aranzabal) see: IGI Domino or Wm. L. Moore (Spanish shotguns)
Armoury Inc., Rte. 202, New Preston, CT 06777
Armsport, Inc., 3590 N.W. 49th St., Miami, FL 33142/305-592-7850
Armurier Liegeois-Artisans Reunis (A.L.A.R.), 27, rue Lambert Masset, 4300 Ans, Belgium
Baikal International, 12 Fairview Terrace, Paramus, NJ 07652/201-845-8710 (Russian shotguns)
Pedro Arrizabalaga, Eibar, Spain
Beeman's Precision Airguns, Inc., 47 Paul Dr., San Rafael, CA 94903/415-472-7121 (FWB, Weihrauch firearms)
Benelli Armi, S.p.A., via della Stazione 50, 61029 Urbino, Italy
Beretta U.S.A., 17601 Indian Head Highway, Accokeek, MD 20607/301-283-2191
Britarms, Ltd., Unit 1, Raban's Close, Raban's Lane Industrial Estate, Aylesbury, Bucks., England
Bretton, 21 Rue Clement Forissier, 42-St. Etienne, France
Browning (Gen. Offices), Rt. 1, Morgan, UT 84050/801-876-2711
Browning, (parts & service), Rt. 4, Box 624-B, Arnold, MO. 63010/314-287-6800
Carlo Casartelli, 25062 Concesio (Brescia), Italy
Century Arms Co., 3-5 Federal St., St. Albans, Vt. 05478
Champlin Firearms, Inc., Box 3191, Enid, OK 73701
Ets. Chapuis, 42380 St. Bonnet-le-Chateau, France (see R. Painter)
Connecticut Valley Arms Co., Saybrook Rd., Haddam, CT 06438 (CVA)
Walter Craig, Inc., Box 927-A Selma, AL 36701
Creighton & Warren, P.O. Box 15723, Nashville, TN 37215 (Krieghoff combination guns)
Morton Cundy & Son, Ltd., P.O. Box 315, Lakeside, MT 59922
Charles Daly (see: Outdoor Sports HQ.)
Dikar s. Coop. (see: Connecticut Valley Arms Co.)
Dixie Gun Works, Inc., Hwy 51, South, Union City, TN 38261/901-885-0561 ("Kentucky" rifles)

Dynamit Nobel of America, Inc., 105 Stonehurst Court, Northvale, NJ 07647/201-767-1660 (Rottweil)
Ernest Dumoulin-Deleye, 8 rue Florent Boclinville, 4410 Herstal (Vottem), Belgium
Peter Dyson Ltd., 29-31 Church St., Honley, Huddersfield, Yorkshire HD7 2AH, England (accessories f. antique gun collectors)
Elko Arms, 28 rue Ecole Moderne, 7400 Soignes, Belgium
Euroarms of America, Inc., P.O. Box 3277, 1501 Lenoir Dr., Winchester, VA 22601/703-661-1863 (ML)
Excam Inc., 4480 E. 11 Ave., P.O. Box 3483, Hialeah, FL 33013
Famars, Abbiatico & Salvinelli, Via Cinelli 29, Gardone V.T. (Brescia), Italy 25063
J. Fanzoj, P.O. Box 25, Ferlach, Austria 9170
Armi FERLIB, 46 Via Costa, 25063 Gardone V.T. (Brescia), Italy
Ferlach (Austria) of North America, 2320 S.W. 57th Ave., Miami, FL 33155/305-266-3030
Firearms Center Inc. (FCI), 308 Leisure Lane, Victoria, TX 77901
Firearms Imp. & Exp. Corp., (F.I.E.), P.O. Box 4866, Hialeah Lakes, Hialeah, FL 33014/305-685-5966
Flaig's Lodge, Millvale, Pa. 15209
Auguste Francotte & Cie, S.A., 61 Mont St. Martin, 4000 Liege, Belgium
Freeland's Scope Stands, Inc., 3737 14th Ave., Rock Island, Ill. 61201
J. L. Galef & Son, Inc., 85 Chambers, New York, N.Y. 10007
Renato Gamba, S.p.A., Gardone V.T. (Brescia), Italy (See: Steyr Daimler Puch of America Corp.)
Armas Garbi, Urki #12, Eibar (Guipuzcoa) Spain (shotguns, see W. L. Moore)
Gastinne Renette, 39 Ave. F.D. Roosevelt, 75008 Paris, France
Georges Granger, 66 Cours Fauriel, 42 St. Etienne, France
Hawes National Corp., 15424 Cabrito Rd., Van Nuys, CA 91406
Healthways, Box 45055, Los Angeles, Calif. 90061
Gil Hebard Guns, Box 1, Knoxville, IL 61448 (Hammerli)
Heckler & Koch Inc., 933 N. Kenmore St., Suite 218, Arlington, VA 22201
A. D. Heller, Inc., Box 56, 2322 Grand Ave., Baldwin, NY 11510
Heym, Friedr. Wilh., Box 861, Bolton, Ont. L0P 1A0, Canada
Hunting World, 16 E. 53d St., New York, NY 10022
IGI Domino Corp., 200 Madison Ave., New York, NY 10016/212-889-4889 (AYA, Breda)
Incor, Inc., P.O. Box 132, Addison, TX 75001/214-931-3500 (Cosmi auto shotg.)
Interarmco, see: Interarms (Walther)
Interarms Ltd., 10 Prince St., Alexandria, Va. 22313 (Mauser, Valmet M-62/S)
International Distr., Inc., 7290 S.W. 42nd St., Miami, FL 33155 (Taurus rev.)
Italguns, Via Voltabo, 20090 Cusago (Milano), Italy
Paul Jaeger Inc., 211 Leedom St., Jenkintown, PA 19046/215-884-6920
Jana Intl. Co., Box 1107, Denver, Colo. 80201 (Parker-Hale)
Jenkins Imports Corp., 462 Stanford Pl., Santa Barbara, CA 93111/805-967-5092 (Gebrüder Merkel)
Kassnar Imports, 5480 Linglestown Rd., Harrisburg, PA 17110
Kawaguchiya Firearms, c/o La Paloma Marketing, 4500 E. Speedway Blvd., Suite 93, Tucson, AZ 85712/602-881-4750
Kleinguenther's, P.O. Box 1261, Seguin, TX 78155
Knight & Knight, 5930 S.W. 48 St., Miami, FL 33155 (made-to-order only)
L. A. Distributors, 4 Centre Market Pl., New York, N.Y. 10013
La Paloma Marketing, 4500 E. Speedway Blvd., Suite 93, Tucson, AZ 85712/602-881-4750 (K.F.C. shotguns)
S. E. Laszlo, 200 Tillary St., Brooklyn, N.Y. 11201
Lever Arms Serv. Ltd., 572 Howe St., Vancouver, B.C., Canada V6C 2E3
Liberty Arms Organization, Box 306, Montrose, Calif. 91020
Mandall Shtg. Suppl. 7150 East 4th St., Scottsdale, AZ 85252/602-945-2553
Mannlicher (See: Steyr Daimler Puch of Amer.)
Manu-Arm, B.P. No. 8, Veauche 42340, France
Manufrance, 100-Cours Fauriel, 42 St. Etienne, France
Mendi s. coop. (see: Connecticut Valley Arms Co.)
Merkuria, FTC, Argentinska 38, 17005 Prague 7, Czechoslovakia (BRNO)
Mitchell Arms Corp., 116 East 16th St., Costa Mesa, CA 92627/714-548-7701 (Uberti pistols)
Moore Supply Co., 3000 So. Main, Salt Lake City, UT 84115/801-487-1671 (Nikko)
Wm. Larkin Moore, 31360 Via Colinas, Suite 109, Westlake Village, CA 91360/213-889-4160 (AYA, Garbi, Ferlib, Piotti, Lightwood)
Navy Arms Co., 689 Bergen Blvd., Ridgefield, N.J. 07657
NIKKO (see: Moore Supply)
Outdoor Sports Headquarters, Inc., 2290 Arbor Blvd., Dayton, OH 45439/513-294-2811 (Charles Daly shotguns)
P.M. Air Services, Ltd., P.O. Box 1573, Costa Mesa, CA 92626
Pachmayr Gun Works, 1220 S. Grand Ave., Los Angeles, CA 90015
Pacific Intl. Merch. Corp., 2215 "J" St., Sacramento, CA 95816
Rob. Painter, 2901 Oakhurst Ave., Austin, TX 78703 (Chapuis)
Parker-Hale, Bisleyworks, Golden Hillock Rd., Sparbrook, Birmingham B11 2PZ, England
Ed Paul Sptg. Goods, 172 Flatbush Ave., Brooklyn, N.Y. 11217 (Premier)
Picard-Fayolle, 42-rue du Vernay, 42100 Saint Etienne, France
Pragotrade, a Div. of Molokov Canada, Inc., 307 Humberline Dr., Rexdale, Ont. M9W 5V1, Canada/416-675-1322
Precise, 3 Chestnut, Suffern, NY 10901
Precision Sports, 798 Cascadilla St., Ithaca, NY 14850/607-273-2993
Premier Shotguns, 172 Flatbush Ave., Brooklyn N.Y. 11217
Leonard Puccinelli Co., 11 Belle Ave., San Anselmo, CA 94960/415-456-1666 (I.A.B., Rizzini, Bernardelli shotguns of Italy)
Quantetics Corp., Imp.-Exp. Div., 582 Somerset St. W., Ottawa, Ont. K1R 5K2 Canada/613-237-0242 (Unique pistols-Can. only)
RG Industries, Inc., 2485 N.W. 20th St., Miami, FL 33142 (Erma)

L. Joseph Rahn, Inc., First Natl. Bldg., Room 502, 201 S. Main St., Ann Arbor, MI 48104 (Garbi, Astra shotguns)
Ravizza Caccia Pesca Sport, s.p.a., Via Volta 60, 20090 Cusago, Italy
Richland Arms Co., 321 W. Adrian St., Blissfield, Mich. 49228
F.lli Rizzini, 25060 Magno di Gardone V.T., (Bs.) Italy
Rottweil, see: Dynamit Nobel of America
Ruko Sporting Goods Inc., 195 Sugg Rd., Buffalo, NY 14225 (Tikka)
Victor Sarasqueta, S.A., P.O. Box 25, 3 Victor Sarasqueta St., Eibar, Spain
Sarco, Inc., 323 Union St., Stirling, NJ 07980/201-647-3800
Savage Arms Corp., Westfield, Mass. 01085 (Anschutz)
W. C. Scott & Co. (British shotguns), see: Griffin & Howe
Security Arms Co., See: Heckler & Koch
Service Armament, 689 Bergen Blvd., Ridgefield, N.J. 07657 (Greener Harpoon Gun)
Sherwood Intl. Export Corp., 18714 Parthenia St., Northridge, CA 91324
Shore Galleries, Inc., 3318 W. Devon Ave., Chicago, IL 60645
Shotguns of Ulm, P.O. Box 253, Milltown, NJ 08850/201-297-0573
Sile Distributors, 7 Centre Market Pl., New York, 10013
Simmons Spec., Inc., 700 Rogers Rd., Olathe, Kans. 66061
Sloan's Sprtg. Goods, Inc., 10 South St., Ridgefield, CT 06877
Franz Sodia Jagdgewehrfabrik, Schulhausgasse 14, 9170 Ferlach, (Kärnten) Austria
Solersport, 23629 7th Ave. West, Bothell, WA 98011/206-483-9607 (Unique)
Steyr-Daimler-Puch of America Corp., 85 Metro Way, Secaucus, NJ 07094/201-865-4330
Stoeger Industries, 55 Ruta Ct., S. Hackensack, NJ 07606/201-440-2700
Tradewinds, Inc., P.O. Box 1191, Tacoma, Wash. 98401
Uberti, Aldo & Co., Via G. Carducci 41 or 39, Ponte Zanano (Brescia), Italy
Ignacio Ugartechea, Apartado 21, Eibar, Spain
Valmet Sporting Arms Div., 7 Westchester Plaza, Elmsford, NY 10523/914-347-4440
Valor Imp. Corp., 5555 N.W. 36th Ave., Miami, FL 33142 10020/212-765-4660 (Valmet)
Ventura Imports, P.O. Box 2782, Seal Beach, CA 90740 (European shotguns)
Verney-Carron, B.P. 88, 17 Cours Fauriel, 42010 St. Etienne Cedex, France
Waffen-Frankonia, Box 6780, 87 Wurzburg 1, W. Germany
Weatherby's, 2781 Firestone Blvd., So. Gate, Calif. 90280 (Sauer)
World Public Safety, 5855 Green Valley Circle, Suite 103, Culver City, CA 90230/213-670-4693 (Leader auto rifle)
Fabio Zanotti di Stefano, Via XXV Aprile 1, 25063 Gardone V.T. (Brescia) Italy
Zavodi Crvena Zastava, 29 Novembra St., No. 12, Belgrade, Yugosl.
Antonio Zoli & Co., 39 Via Zanardelli, 25063 Gardone V.T., Brescia, Italy

GUNS & GUN PARTS, REPLICA AND ANTIQUE

Antique Gun Parts, Inc., 1118 S. Braddock Ave., Pittsburgh, PA 15218 (ML)
Armoury Inc., Rte. 202, New Preston, CT 06777
Artistic Arms, Inc., Box 23, Hoagland, IN 46745 (Sharps-Borchardt replica)
Bob's Place, Box 283J, Clinton, IA 52732 (obsolete Winchester parts only)
Carter Gun Works, 2211 Jefferson Pk. Ave., Charlottesville, Va. 22903
Darr Tool Co., P.O. Box 778, Carpinteria, CA 93013 (S.S. items)
Dixie Gun Works, Inc., Hwy 51, South, Union City, TN 38261/901-885-0561
Federal Ordnance Inc., 1443 Portrero Ave., So. El Monte, CA 91733/213-350-4161
Fred Goodwin, Goodwin's Gun Shop, Sherman Mills, ME 04776/207-365-4451 (antique guns & parts)
The House of Muskets, Inc., P.O. Box 900, Pagosa Springs, CO 81147/303-264-2892 (ML guns)
Log Cabin Sport Shop, 8010 Lafayette Rd., Lodi, OH 44254/216-948-1082 (ctlg. $3)
Edw. E. Lucas, 32 Garfield Ave., East Brunswick, NJ 08816/201-251-5526 (45/70 Springfield parts)
Lyman Products Corp., Middlefield, CT 06455
Tommy Munsch Gunsmithing, Rt. 2, Box 248, Little Falls, MN 56345/612-632-5835 (parts list $1.50; oth. inq. SASE)
Numrich Arms Co., West Hurley, N.Y. 12491
Replica Models, Inc., 610 Franklin St., Alexandria, VA 22314
S&S Firearms, 88-21 Aubrey Ave., Glendale, N.Y. 11227
Sarco, Inc., 323 Union St., Stirling, NJ 07980/201-647-3800
C. H. Stoppler, 1426 Walton Ave., New York, NY 10452 (miniature guns)
Upper Missouri Trading Co., 3rd & Harold Sts., Crofton, NB 68730
C. H. Weisz, Box 311, Arlington, VA 22210
W. H. Wescombe, P.O. Box 488, Glencoe, CA 95232 (Rem. R.B. parts)

GUNS (Pellet)

Air Rifle Hq., 247 Court St., Grantsville, W. Va. 26147
Beeman's Precision Airguns, 47 Paul Dr., San Rafael, CA 94903/415-472-7121
Benjamin Air Rifle Co., 1525 So. 8th St., Louis, Mo. 63104
Crosman Airguns, 980 Turk Hill Rd., Fairport, NY 14450/716-223-6000
Daisy Mfg. Co., Rogers, Ark. 72756 (also Feinwerkbau)
K. J. David & Co., P.O. Box 12595, Lake Park, FL 33403/305-844-5124
J. L. Galef & Son, Inc., 85 Chambers St., New York, N.Y. 10007 (B.S.A.)
Great Lakes Airguns, 6175 So. Park Ave., Hamburg, NY 14075/716-648-6666
Harrington & Richardson Arms Co., Industrial Rowe, Gardner, MA 01440 (Webley)
Healthways, Box 45055, Los Angeles, Calif. 90061
Gil Hebard Guns, Box 1, Knoxville, Ill. 61448
Hy-Score Arms Co., 200 Tillary St., Brooklyn, N.Y. 11201
Interarms, 10 Prince, Alexandria, Va. 22313 (Walther)

LARC International, P.O. Box 34007, Coral Gables, FL 33134
Marksman Products, P.O. Box 2983, Torrance, CA 90509
Power Line (see: Daisy Mfg. Co.)
Precise, 3 Chestnut, Suffern, NY 10901
Precision Sports, 798 Cascadilla St., Ithaca, NY 14850/607-273-2993 (B.S.A.)
Service Armament, 689 Bergen Blvd., Ridgefield, N.J. 07657 (Webley)
Sheridan Products, Inc., 3205 Sheridan, Racine, Wis. 53403
Smith & Wesson, 2100 Roosevelt Ave., Springfield, MA 01104
Target Airgun Supply, 11552 Knott St., Suite 3, Garden Grove, CA 92641

GUNS, SURPLUS—PARTS AND AMMUNITION

Can Am Enterprises, Canfield, Ont. NOA 1CO, Canada/416-772-3633 (Enfield rifles)
Century Arms, Inc., 3-5 Federal St., St. Albans, Vt. 05478
Walter Craig, Inc., Box 927-A, Selma, AL 36701
Eastern Firearms Co., 790 S. Arroyo Pkwy., Pasadena, Calif. 91105
Garcia National Gun Traders, 225 S.W. 22nd, Miami, Fla. 33135
Hunter's Lodge, 200 S. Union, Alexandria, Va. 22313
Lever Arms Serv. Ltd., 572 Howe St., Vancouver, B.C., Canada V6C 2E3
Pacific Intl. Merch. Corp., 2215 "J" St., Sacramento, CA 95816
Plainfield Ordnance Co., Box 447, Dunellen, N.J. 08812
Sarco, Inc., 323 Union St., Stirling, NJ 07980/201-647-3800
Service Armament Co., 689 Bergen Blvd., Ridgefield, N.J. 07657
Sherwood Intl. Export Corp., 18714 Parthenia St., Northridge, CA 91324
Springfield Sporters Inc., R.D. 1, Penn Run, PA 15765/412-254-2626

GUNS, U.S.-made

AMT (Arcadia Machine & Tool), 11666 McBean Dr., El Monte, CA 91732
A. R. Sales Co., 9624 Alpaca St., South El Monte, CA 91733 (Mark IV sporter)
Accuracy Systems, Inc., 2105 S. Hardy Dr., Tempe, AZ 85282
American Derringer Corp., P.O. Box 8983, Waco, TX 76710/817-662-6187
ArmaLite, 118 E. 16th St., Costa Mesa, Calif. 92627
Armament Systems and Procedures, Inc., Box 356, Appleton, WI 54912/414-731-8893 (ASP pistol)
Arminex, 2210 Wilshire Blvd., Suite 658, Santa Monica, CA 90403 (Excalibur s.a. pistol)
Artistic Arms, Inc., Box 23, Hoagland, IN 46745 (Sharps-Borchardt)
Auto-Ordnance Corp., Box ZG, West Hurley, NY 12491
Bauer Firearms, 34750 Klein Ave., Fraser, MI 48026
Brown Precision Co., P.O. Box 270W; 7786 Molinos Ave. Los Molinos, CA 96055/916-384-2506 (High Country rifle)
Browning (Gen. Offices), Rt. 1, Morgan, UT 84050/801-876-2711
Browning (Parts & Service), Rt. 4, Box 624-B, Arnold, MO 63010/314-287-6800
Buffalo Arms Inc., 10 Tonawanda St., Tonawanda, NY 14150/716-693-7970
Bushmaster Firearms Co., 309 Cumberland Ave., Portland, ME 04101/207-775-3339 (police handgun)
CB Arms, Inc., 65 Hathaway Court, Pittsburgh, PA 15235/412-795-4621 (Double Deuce h'gun)
Challanger Mfg. Corp., 118 Pearl St., Mt. Vernon, NY 10550 (Hopkins & Allen)
Champlin Firearms, Inc., Box 3191, Enid, Okla. 73701
Charter Arms Corp., 430 Sniffens Ln., Stratford, CT 06497
Colt, 150 Huyshope Ave., Hartford, CT 06102
Commando Arms, Inc., Box 10214, Knoxville, Tenn. 37919
Coonan Arms, Inc., 570 S. Fairview, St. Paul, MN 55116/612-699-5639 (357 Mag. Autom.)
Crown City Arms, P.O. Box 1126, Cortland, NY 13045 (45 auto handgun)
Cumberland Arms, Rt. 1, Shafer Rd., Blanton Chapel, Manchester, TN 37355
Day Arms Corp., 2412 S.W. Loop 410, San Antonio, TX 78227
Leonard Day & Co., 316 Burts Pits Rd., Northampton, MA 01060 (ML)
Demro Products Inc., 345 Progress Dr., Manchester, CT 06040/203-649-4444
Detonics 45 Associates, 2500 Seattle Tower, Seattle, WA 98101 (auto pistol)
Dornaus & Dixon Enterprises, Inc., 16718 Judy Way, Cerritos, CA 90701/213-926-7004 (Bren-Ten)
DuBiel Arms Co., 1724 Baker Rd., Sherman, TX 75090/214-893-7313
EE-DA-How Long Rifles, Inc., 3318 Camrose Lane, Boise, ID 83705
El Dorado Arms, 35 Gilpin Ave., Happauge, NY 11787/516-234-0212
Excalibur (see: Arminex)
FTL Marketing Corp., 12521-3 Oxnard St., No. Hollywood, CA 91601/213-985-2939
Falling Block Works, P.O. Box 22, Troy, MI 48084
Firearms Imp. & Exp. Corp., P.O. Box 4866, Hialeah Lakes, Hialeah, FL 33014/305-685-5966 (FIE)
Freedom Arms Co., Freedom, WY 83120 (mini revolver, Casull rev.)
Golden Age Arms Co., 14 W. Winter St., Delaware, OH 43015
Franklin C. Green, 530 W. Oak Grove Rd., Montrose, CO 81401/303-249-7003 (Green Free Pistol)
Harrington & Richardson, Industrial Rowe, Gardner, MA 01440
A. D. Heller, Inc., Box 268, Grand Ave., Baldwin, NY 11510
High Standard Sporting Firearms, 31 Prestige Park Circle, East Hartford, CT 06108
Holmes Firearms Corp., Rte. 6, Box 242, Fayetteville, AR 72701
Hopkins & Allen Arms, P.O. Box 198, Elmwood Park, NJ 07407/201-794-1800
Hyper-Single Precision SS Rifles, 520 E. Beaver, Jenks, OK 74037
Ithaca Gun Co., Ithaca, N.Y. 14850
Iver Johnson Arms Inc., P.O. Box 251, Middlesex, NJ 08846
J & R carbine, (see: PJK Inc.)

Paul Jaeger, Inc., 211 Leedom St., Jenkintown, PA 19046
Kimber of Oregon, Inc., 9039 S.E. Jannsen Rd., Clackamas, OR
  97015/503-656-1704
H. Koon, Inc., 12523 Valley Branch, Dallas, TX/214-243-8124
L.E.S., 2301 Davis St., North Chicago, IL 60064/312-473-9484
Ljutic Ind.; Inc., P.O. Box 2117, Yakima, WA 98902 (Mono-Gun)
Ljutic Intl., 101 Carmel Dr., Suite 120, Carmel, IN 46032/317-848-5051
M & N Distributors, 23535 Telo St., Torrance, CA 90505/213-530-9000
  (Budischowsky)
MS Safari Arms, P.O. Box 23370, Phoenix, AZ 85062/602-269-7283
Marlin Firearms Co., 100 Kenna Dr., New Haven, Conn. 06473
Merrill Co., 704 E. Commonwealth, Fullerton, CA 92631/714-879-8922
O. F. Mossberg & Sons, Inc., 7 Grasso St., No. Haven, Conn. 06473
Mowrey Gun Works, Box 28, Iowa Park TX 76367
Navy Arms Co., 689 Bergen Blvd., Ridgefield, N.J. 07657
North American Arms, 310 West 700 S., Provo, UT 84601/801-375-8074
North Star Arms, R.2, Box 74A, Ortonville, MN 56278 (The Plainsman)
Numrich Arms Corp., W. Hurley, N.Y. 12491
ODI, Inc., 1244A Greenwood Ave., Midland Park, NJ 07432/201-444-4557
PJK, Inc., 1527 Royal Oak Dr., Bradbury, Ca 91010 (J&R Carbine)
Plainfield Machine Co., Inc., Box 447, Dunellen, N.J. 08812
Plainfield Inc., 292 Vail Ave., Piscataway, NJ 08854
R G Industries, 2485 N.W. 20th SE., Miami, FL 33142
Raven Arms, 1300 Bixby Dr., Industry, CA 91745
Remington Arms Co., Bridgeport, Conn. 06602
Rock Pistol Mfg., Inc., 704 E. Commonwealth, Fullerton, CA
  92631/714-870-8530 (Merrill pistol, etc.)
Ruger (see Sturm, Ruger & Co.)
Savage Arms Corp., Westfield, Mass. 01085
Sceptre, Inc., P.O. Box 1282, Marietta, GA 30061/404-428-5513
Sears, Roebuck & Co., 825 S. St. Louis, Chicago, Ill. 60607
Semmerling Corp., P.O. Box 400, Newton, MA 02160
Sharps Rifle Co., 3428 Shakertown Rd., Dayton, OH 45430
Shiloh Products, 37 Potter St., Farmingdale, NY 11735 (Sharps)
Smith & Wesson, Inc., 2100 Roosevelt Ave., Springfield, MA 01101
Springfield Armory, 111 E. Exchange St., Geneseo, IL 61254
Sterling Arms Corp., 211 Grand St.,, Lockport, NY 14094/716-434-6631
Sturm, Ruger & Co., Southport, Conn. 06490
Thompson-Center Arms, Box 2405, Rochester, N.H. 03867
Trail Guns Armory, 1634 E. Main St., League City, TX 77573
  (muzzleloaders)
Universal Firearms, 3740 E. 10th Ct., Hialeah, FL 33013
Ward's, 619 W. Chicago, Chicago, Ill. 60607 (Western Field brand)
Weatherby's, 2781 E. Firestone Blvd., South Gate, Calif. 90280
Dan Wesson Arms, 293 So. Main St., Monson, Mass. 01057
Wichita Arms, 333 Lulu, Wichita, KS 67211/316-265-0661
Wildey Firearms Co., Inc., P.O. Box 4264, New Windsor, NY
  12250/203-272-7215
Wilkinson Arms, 803 N. Glendora Ave, Covina, CA 91724 (Diane 25 ACP
  auto pistol)
Winchester Repeating Arms Co., New Haven, Conn. 06504

GUNSMITHS, CUSTOM (see Custom Gunsmiths)

GUNSMITHS, HANDGUN (see Pistolsmiths)

GUNSMITH SCHOOLS

Colorado School of Trades, 1545 Hoyt, Lakewood, CO 80215
Lassen Community College, P.O. Box 3000, Susanville, CA 96130
Modern Gun Repair School Inc., 4225 N. Brown Ave., Scottsdale, AZ
  85252
Montgomery Technical Institute, P.O. Drawer 487, Troy, NC
  27371/919-572-3691
Murray State College, Tishomingo, OK 73460
North American School of Firearms, 4401 Birch St., Newport Beach, CA
  92663 (correspondence)
Oregon Institute of Technology, Small Arms Dept., Klamath Falls, OR
  97601
Penn. Gunsmith School, 812 Ohio River Blvd., Avalon, Pittsburgh, PA
  15202
Police Sciences Institute, 4401 Birch St., Newport Beach, CA
  92660/714-546-7360 (General Law Enforcement Course)
Trinidad State Junior College, 600 Prospect, Trinidad, CO
  81082/303-846-5631
Yavapai College, 1100 East Sheldon St., Prescott, AZ 86301/602-445-7300

GUNSMITH SUPPLIES, TOOLS, SERVICES

Albright Prod. Co., P.O. Box 1144, Portola, CA 96122 (trap buttplates)
Alley Supply Co., Carson Valley Industrial Park, Gardnerville, NV 89410
Ametek, Hunter Spring Div., One Spring Ave., Hatfield, PA
  19440/215-822-2971 (trigger gauge)
Anderson Mfg. Co., Union Gap Sta. P.O. Box 3120, Yakima WA
  98903/509-453-2349 (tang safe)
Armite Labs., 1845 Randolph St., Los Angeles, Cal. 90001 (pen oiler)
B-Square Co., Box 11281, Ft. Worth, Tex. 76110
Jim Baiar, 490 Halfmoon Rd., Columbia Falls, MT 59912 (hex screws)
Behlert Custom Guns, Inc., 725 Lehigh Ave., Union, NJ 07083
Al Biesen, W. 2039 Sinto Ave., Spokane, WA 99201 (grip caps, buttplates)
Bonanza Sports Mfg. Co., 412 Western Ave., Faribault, Minn. 55021
Briganti Custom Gun-Smithing, P.O. Box 56, Highland Mills, NY
  10930/914-928-9816 (cold rust bluing, hand polishing, metal work)
Brookstone Co., 125 Vose Farm Rd., Peterborough, NH 03458

Bob Brownell's, Main & Third, Montezuma, Ia. 50171
Lenard M. Brownell, Box 25, Wyarno, WY 82845/307-737-2468 (cust. grip
  caps, bolt handle, etc.)
W. E. Brownell, 1852 Alessandro Trail, Vista, Calif. 92083 (checkering
  tools)
Burgess Vibrocrafters, Inc. (BVI), Rte. 83, Grayslake, Ill. 60030
M. H. Canjar, 500 E. 45th, Denver, Colo. 80216 (triggers, etc.)
Chapman Mfg. Co., Rte. 17 at Saw Mill Rd., Durham, CT 06422
Chase Chemical Corp., 3527 Smallman St., Pittsburgh, PA 15201 (Chubb
  Multigauge)
Chubb (see Chase Chem. Co.)
Chicago Wheel & Mfg. Co., 1101 W. Monroe St., Chicago, Ill. 60607
  (Handee grinders)
Christy Gun Works, 875-57th St., Sacramento, Calif. 95819
Classic Arms Corp., P.O. Box 8, Palo Alto, CA 94302/415-321-7243
  (floorplates, grip caps)
Clover Mfg. Co., 139 Woodward Ave., Norwalk, CT 06856 (Clover
  compound)
Clymer Mfg. Co., Inc., 14241 W. 11 Mile Rd., Oak Park, MI
  48237/313-541-5533 (reamers)
A. Constantine & Son, Inc., 2050 Eastchester Rd., Bronx, N.Y. 10461
  (wood)
Dave Cook, 720 Hancock Ave., Hancock, MI 49930 (metalsmithing only)
Cougar & Hunter, G 6398 W. Pierson Rd., Flushing, Mich. 48433 (scope
  jigs)
Dayton-Traister Co., 9322 - 900th West, P.O. Box 593, Oak Harbor, WA
  98277/206-675-5375 (triggers)
Delta Arms Sporting Goods, Highway 82 West, Indianola, MS
  38751/601-887-5566 (Lightwood/England)
Dem-Bart Checkering Tools, Inc., 6807 Hiway #2, Snohomish, WA
  98290/206-568-7536
Dremel Mfg. Co., 4915-21st St., Racine, WI 53406 (grinders)
Chas. E. Duffy, Williams Lane, West Hurley, N.Y. 12491
Peter Dyson Ltd., 29-31 Church St., Honley, Huddersfield, Yorksh. HD7
  2AH, England (accessories f. antique gun coll.)
E-Z Tool Co., P.O. Box 3186, 25 N.W. 44th Ave., Des Moines, Ia. 50313
  (lathe taper attachment)
Edmund Scientific Co., 101 E. Glouster Pike, Barrington, N.J. 08007
F. K. Elliott, Box 785, Ramona, Calif. 92065 (reamers)
Emco-Lux, 2050 Fairwood Ave.; P.O. Box 07861 Columbus, OH
  43207/614-445-8328
Forster Products, Inc., 82 E. Lanark Ave., Lanark, IL 61046/815-493-6360
Keith Francis Inc., 1020 W. Catching Slough Rd., Coos Bay, OR
  97420/503-269-2021 (reamers)
G. R. S. Corp., P.O. Box 748, Emporia, KS 66801/316-343-1084
  (Gravermeister)
Gager Gage and Tool Co., 27509 Industrial Blvd., Hayward, CA 94545
  (speedlock triggers f. Rem. 1100 & 870 pumps)
Gilmore Pattern Works, P.O. Box 50234, Tulsa, OK 74150/918-245-7614
  (wagner safe-T-Planer)
Glendo Corp., P.O. Box 1153, Emporia, KS 66801/316-343-1084
  (Accu-Finish tool)
Gold Lode, Inc., 181 Gary Ave., Wheaton, IL 60187 (gold inlay kit)
Gopher Shooter's Supply, Box 278, Faribault, MN 55021 (screwdrivers,
  etc.)
Grace Metal Prod., 115 Ames St., Elk Rapids, MI 49629 (screw drivers,
  drifts)
Gunline Tools Inc., 719 No. East St., Anaheim, CA 92805
Gun-Tec, P.O. Box 8125, W. Palm Beach, FL 33407
Half Moon Rifle Shop, 490 Halfmoon Rd., Columbia Falls, MT 59912 (hex
  screws)
Paul Jaeger Inc., 211 Leedom St., Jenkintown, PA. 19046
Jeffredo Gunsight Co., 1629 Via Monserate, Fallbrook, CA 92028 (trap
  buttplate)
Jerrow's Inletting Service, 452 5th Ave., E.N., Kalispell, MT 59901
Johns Rifle Shop, 25 NW 44th Ave., Des Moines, IA 50313/515-288-8680
K&D Grinding Co., P.O. Box 1766, Alexandria, LA 71301/318-487-0823
  (cust. tools f. pistolsmiths)
Kasenit Co., Inc., 3 King St., Mahwah, NJ 07430/201-529-3663 (surface
  hrdng. comp.)
J. Korzinek, RD #2, Box 73, Canton, PA 17724/717-673-8512 (stainl. steel
  bluing; broch. #1)
John G. Lawson, (The Sight Shop), 1802 E. Columbia Ave., Tacoma, WA
  98404/206-474-5465
Lea Mfg. Co., 237 E. Aurora St., Waterbury, Conn. 06720
Lightwood (Fieldsport) Ltd., Britannia Rd., Banbury, Oxfordsh. OX16 8TD,
  England
Lock's Phila. Gun Exch., 6700 Rowland Ave., Philadelphia, Pa. 19149
John McClure, 4549 Alamo Dr., San Diego, CA 92115 (electric checkering
  tool)
Marker Machine Co., Box 426, Charleston, Ill. 61920
Michaels of Oregon Co., P.O. Box 13010, Portland, OR
  97213/503-255-6890
Viggo Miller, P.O. Box 4181, Omaha, Neb. 68104 (trigger attachment)
Miller Single Trigger Mfg. Co., R.D. 1, Box 99, Millersburg, PA
  17061/717-692-3704
Frank Mittermeier, 3577 E. Tremont, N.Y., N.Y. 10465
Moderntools, 1671 W. McNab Rd., Ft. Lauderdale, FL 33309/305-979-3900
N&J Sales, Lime Kiln Rd., Northford, Conn. 06472 (screwdrivers)
Karl A. Neise, Inc., 1671 W. McNab Rd., Ft. Lauderdale, FL
  33309/305-979-3900
Palmgren Prods., Chicago Tool & Eng. Co., 8383 South Chicago Ave.,
  Chicago, IL 60167 (vises, etc.)
Panavise Prods., Inc., 2850 E. 29th St., Long Beach, CA
  90806/213-595-7621
C. R. Pedersen & Son, 2717 S. Pere Marquette, Ludington, MI
  49431/616-843-2061

Pilkington Gun Co., P.O. Box 2284, University Sta., Enid, OK 73701/405-242-0025 (Q.D. scope mt.)
Richland Arms Co., 321 W. Adrian St., Blissfield, Mich. 49228
Riley's Supply Co., 121 No. Main St., Avilla, Ind. 46710 (Niedner buttplates, caps)
A. G. Russell, 1705 Hiway 71N, Springdale, AR 72764 (Arkansas oilstones)
Schaffner Mfg. Co., Emsworth, Pittsburgh, Pa. 15202 (polishing kits)
SGW, Inc. (formerly Schuetzen Gun Works), 624 Old Pacific Hwy. S.E., Olympia, WA 98503/206-456-3471
Shaw's, 9447 W. Lilac Rd., Escondido, CA 92025/714-728-7070
Shooters Specialty Shop, 5146 E. Pima, Tucson, AZ 85712/602-325-3346
Southern Blueing, 6027-B N.W. 31st Ave., Ft. Lauderdale, FL 33309 (gun blueing & repairs)
L. S. Starrett Co., 121 Crescent St. Athol, MA 01331/617-249-3551
Texas Platers Supply Co., 2453 W. Five Mile Parkway, Dallas, TX 75233 (plating kit)
Timney Mfg. Co., 2847 E. Siesta Lane, Phoenix, AZ 85024
Stan de Treville, Box 33021, San Diego, Calif. 92103 (checkering patterns)
Twin City Steel Treating Co., Inc., 1114 S. 3rd, Minneapolis, Minn. 55415 (heat treating)
Will-Burt Co., 169 So. Main, Orrville, OH 44667 (vises)
Williams Gun Sight Co., 7389 Lapeer Rd., Davison, Mich. 48423
Wilson Arms Co., 63 Leetes Island Rd., Branford, CT 06405
Wisconsin Platers Supply Co., see: Texas Platers
W. C. Wolff Co., Box 232, Ardmore, PA 19003 (springs)
Woodcraft Supply Corp., 313 Montvale, Woburn, MA 01801

HANDGUN ACCESSORIES

A. R. Sales Co., P.O. Box 3192, South El Monte, CA 91733
Baramie Corp., 6250 E. 7 Mile Rd., Detroit, MI 48234 (Hip-Grip)
Bar-Sto Precision Machine, 633 S. Victory Blvd., Burbank, CA 91502
Behlert Custom Guns, Inc., 725 Lehigh Ave., Union, NJ 07083
Belt Slide, Inc., 1301 Brushy Bend Dr., Round Lake, TX 78664
Bingham Ltd., 1775-C Wilwat Dr., Norcross, GA 30093 (magazines)
C'Arco, P.O. Box 308, Highland, CA 92346 (Ransom Rest)
Central Specialties Co., 6030 Northwest Hwy., Chicago, Ill. 60631
D&E Magazines Mgf., P.O. Box 4579, Downey, CA 90241 (clips)
Bill Dyer, 503 Midwest Bldg., Oklahoma City, Okla. 73102 (grip caps)
Essex Arms, Box 345, Phaerring St., Island Pond, VT 05846 (45 Auto frames)
R. S. Frielich, 211 East 21st St., New York, NY 10010/212-777-4477 (cases)
Laka Tool Co., 62 Kinkel St., Westbury, L.I., NY 11590 (stainless steel 45 Auto parts)
Lee's Red Ramps, 7252 E. Ave. U-3, Littlerock, CA 93543 (illuminated sights)
Lee Precision Inc., 4275 Hwy. U, Hartford, WI 53027 (pistol rest holders)
Kent Lomont, 4421 So. Wayne Ave., Ft. Wayne, IN 46807/219-694-6792 (Auto Mag only)
Los Gatos Grip & Specialty Co., P.O. Box 1850, Los Gatos, CA 95030 (custom-made)
Mascot rib sights (see: Travis R. Strahan)
Mellmark Mfg. Co., P.O. Box 139, Turlock, CA 95380 (pistol safe)
W. A. Miller Co., Inc., Mingo Loop, Oguossoc, ME 04964 (cases)
No-Sho Mfg. Co., 10727 Glenfield Ct., Houston, TX 77096
Harry Owen, See: Sport Specialties
Pachmayr, 1220 S. Grand, Los Angeles, Calif. 90015 (cases)
Pacific Intl. Mchdsg. Corp., 2215 "J" St., Sacramento, CA 95818 (Vega 45 Colt comb. mag.)
Platt Luggage, Inc., 2301 S. Prairie, Chicago, Ill. 60616 (cases)
Sile Distributors, 7 Centre Market Pl., New York, NY 10013
Sport Specialties, (Harry Owen), Box 5337, Hacienda Hts., CA 91745/213-968-5806 (.22 rimfire adapters; insert bbls. f. T-C Cont.)
Sportsmen's Equipment Co., 415 W. Washington, San Diego, Calif. 92103
Travis R. Strahan, Rt. 7, Townsend Circle, Ringgold, GA 30736/404-937-4495 (Mascot rib sights)
M. Tyler, 1326 W. Britton, Oklahoma City, Okla. 73114 (grip adaptor)
Whitney Sales, Inc., P.O. Box 875, Reseda, CA 91335
Dave Woodruff, Box 5, Bear, DE 19701 (relining and conversions)

HANDGUN GRIPS

Art Jewel Enterprises, Box 819, Berkeley, IL 60163
Beeman's Precision Airguns, Inc., 47 Paul Dr., San Rafael, CA 94903/415-472-7121 (airguns only)
Bingham Ltd., 1775-C Wilwat Dr., Norcross, GA 30093
Fitz, 653 N. Hagar St., San Fernando, CA 91340
Gateway Shooters' Supply, Inc., 10145-103rd St., Jacksonville, FL 32210 (Rogers grips)
The Gunshop, R. D. Wallace, 320 Overland Rd., Prescott, AZ 86301
Herrett's, Box 741, Twin Falls, Ida. 83301
Hogue Combat Grips, P.O. Box 460, Morro Bay, CA 93442 (Monogrip)
Paul Jones Munitions Systems, see: Fitz Co.
Russ Maloni, 24 Ellis Dr., West Falls, NY 14170/716-652-7131
Mershon Co., Inc., 1230 S. Grand Ave., Los Angeles, Calif. 90015
Millett Industries, 16131 Gothard St., Huntington Beach, CA 92647/714-842-5575 (custom)
Monogrip, see: Hogue
Mustang Custom Pistol Grips, 1334 E. Katella Ave., Anaheim, CA 92805/714-978-7474
Robert H. Newell, 55 Coyote, Los Alamos, NM 87544 (custom)
Rogers Grips (see: Gateway Shooters' Supply)
A. Jack Rosenberg & Sons, 12229 Cox Lane, Dallas, TX 75234/214-241-6302 (Ajax)
Russwood, 24 Ellis Dr., West Falls, NY 14170/716-652-7131 (cust. exotic woods)

Jean St. Henri, 6525 Dume Dr., Malibu, CA 90265 (custom)
Schiermeier Custom Handgun Stocks, 306 No. 1st St., Kent, WA 98031/206-854-5358
Sile Dist., 7 Centre Market Pl., New York, N.Y. 10013
Southern Gun Exchange, Inc., 4311 Northeast Expressway, Atlanta (Doraville), GA 30340 (Outrider brand)
Sports Inc., P.O. Box 683, Park Ridge, IL 60068 (Franzite)

HEARING PROTECTORS

AO Safety Prods., Div. of American Optical Corp., 14 Mechanic St., Southbridge, MA 01550 (ear valve)
Bausch & Lomb, 635 St. Paul St., Rochester, N.Y. 14602
David Clark Co., Inc., 360 Franklin St., Worcester, MA 01604
Norton Co., Safety Prods. Div., 16624 Edwards Rd., Cerritos, CA 90701 (Lee-Sonic ear valve)
Safety Direct, 23 Snider Way, Sparks, NV 89431 (Silencio)
Smith & Wesson, 2100 Roosevelt Ave., Springfield, MA 01101
Willson Safety Prods Div., P.O. Box 622, Reading, PA 19603 (Ray-O-Vac)

HOLSTERS & LEATHER GOODS

Alessi Custom Concealment Holsters, 2465 Niagara Falls Blvd., Tonawanda, NY 14150/716-691-5615
American Sales & Mfg. Co., P.O. Box 677, Laredo, Tex. 78040
Andy Anderson, P.O. Box 225, North Hollywood, CA 91603 (Gunfighter Custom Holsters)
Arizona Prods. & Sales. Box 13144, Phoenix, AZ 85002
Armament Systems & Procedures, Inc., P.O. Box 356, Appleton, WI 54912/414-731-8893 (ASP)
Beeman Precision Airguns, Inc., 47 Paul Dr., San Rafael, CA 94903/415-472-7121 (airguns only)
Bianchi Holster Co., 100 Calle Cortez, Temecula, CA 92390
Ted Blocker Custom Holsters, Box 821, Rosemead, CA 91770/213-442-5772
Edward H. Bohlin, 931 N. Highland Ave., Hollywood, CA 90038/213-463-4888
Bo-Mar Tool & Mfg. Co., P.O. Box 168, Carthage, TX 75633/214-693-5220
Boyt Co., Div. of Welch Sptg., Box 1108, Iowa Falls, Ia. 51026
Brauer Bros. Mfg. Co., 817 N. 17th, St. Louis, Mo. 63106
Browning, Rt. 4, Box 624-B, Arnold, MO 63010
J. M. Bucheimer Co., P.O. Box 280, Airport Rd., Frederick, MD 21701/301-662-5101
Cathey Enterprises, Inc., 9516 Neils Thompson Dr., Austin, TX 78758
Chace Leather Prods., Longhorn Div., 507 Alden St., Fall River, MA 02722/617-678-7556
Cobra Ltd., 1865 New Highway, Farmingdale, NY 11735/516-752-8544
Colt's, 150 Huyshope Ave., Hartford, Conn. 06102
Custom Guns & Leather, 27317 Novi Rd., Novi, MI 48050
Daisy Mfg. Co., Rogers, Ark. 72756
G. Wm. Davis, P.O. Box 446, Arcadia, CA 91006
Eugene DeMayo & Sons, Inc., 2795 Third Ave., Bronx, N.Y. 10455
Ellwood Epps Northern Ltd., 210 Worthington St. W., North Bay, Ont. PIB 3B4, Canada (custom made)
The Eutaw Co., Box 608, U.S. Highway 176W, Holly Hill, SC 29059
Goerg Ent., P.O. Box 531, Renton, WA 98056/206-883-1529
Gunfighter (See Anderson)
Hoyt Holster Co., P.O. Box 69, Coupeville, WA 98239
Don Hume, Box 351, Miami, Okla. 74354
The Hunter Corp., 3300 W. 71st Ave., Westminster, CO 80030/303-427-4626
Jackass Leather Co., 7383 N. Rogers Ave., Chicago, IL 60626/312-338-2800
John's Custom Leather, 525 S. Liberty St., Blairsville, PA 15717/412-459-6802
Jumbo Sports Prods., P.O. Box 280, Airport Rd., Frederick, MD 21701
Kirkpatrick Leather, Box 3150, Laredo, TX 89041
Kolpin Mfg., Inc., P.O. Box 231, Berlin, WI 54923/414-361-0400
Morris Lawing, 150 Garland Ct., Charlotte, NC 28202/704-375-1740
Lawman Leather, Inc., P.O. Box 4772, Scottsdale, AZ 85258
George Lawrence Co., 306 S. W. First Ave., Portland, OR 97204
Leathercrafters, 710 S. Washington, Alexandria, VA 22314
Liberty Leather, P.O. Box 306, Montrose, CA 91020/213-248-0618
Mixson Leathercraft Inc., 1950 W. 84th St., Hialeah, FL 33014/305-820-5190
Nordac Mfg. Corp., Rt. 12, Box 124, Fredericksburg, VA 22401/703-752-2552
Kenneth L. Null-Custom Concealment Holsters, R.D. #5, Box 197, Hanover, PA 17331 (see Seventrees)
Arvo Ojala, 3960 S.E. 1st, Gresham, OR 97030
Old West Inc. Leath. Prods., P.O. Box 2030, Chula Vista, CA 92012/714-429-8050
Pioneer Products, 1033 W. Amity Rd., Boise, ID 83705/208-345-2003
Pony Express Sport Shop Inc., 17460 Ventura Blvd., Encino, CA 91316
Red Head Brand Corp., 4949 Joseph Hardin Dr., Dallas, TX 75236/214-333-4141
Rickenbacker's, P.O. Box 532, State Ave., Holly Hill, SC 29059
Rogers Holsters, 1736 St. Johns Bluff Rd., Jacksonville, FL 32216/904-641-9434
Roy's Custom Leather Goods, Hwy. 1325 & Rawhide Rd., Magnolia, AR 71753/501-234-1599
Safariland Leather Products, 1941 So. Walker Ave., Monrovia, CA 91016/213-357-7902
Safety Speed Holster, Inc., 910 So. Vail, Montebello, Calif. 90640
Buddy Schoellkopf Products Inc., 4949 Joseph Hardin Dr., Dallas, TX 75236

Seventrees Systems Ltd., R.D. 5, Box 197, Hanover, PA 17331/717-632-6873 (see NULL)
Sile Distr., 7 Centre Market Pl., New York, N.Y. 10013
Smith & Wesson, 2100 Roosevelt Ave., Springfield, MA 01101
Robert A. Strong Co., 105 Maplewood Ave., Gloucester, MA 01930/617-281-3300
Torel, Inc., 1053 N. South St., Yoakum, TX 77995 (gun slings)
Triple-K Mfg. Co., 568 Sixth Ave., San Diego, CA 92101
Universal Leathergoods, Inc., 6573 E. 21st Pl., Tulsa, OK 74124
Viking Leathercraft, P.O. Box 203, Chula Vista, CA 92012/714-423-8991
Whitco, Box 1712, Brownsville, Tex. 78520 (Hide-A-Way)

HUNTING AND CAMP GEAR, CLOTHING, ETC.

Bob Allen Sportswear, P.O. Box 477, Des Moines, IA 50302
Eddie Bauer, 15010 NE 36th St., Redmond, WA 98052
L. L. Bean, Freeport, Me. 04032
Bear Archery R.R. 4, 4600 Southwest 41st Blvd., Gainesville, FL 32601/904-376-2327 (Himalayan backpack)
Bell Fatigue Co., P.O. Box 3484, Augusta, GA 30904 (camouflage suits)
Bernzomatic Corp., 740 Driving Pk. Ave., Rochester, N.Y. 14613 (stoves & lanterns)
Big Beam, Teledyne Co., 290 E. Prairie St., Crystal Lake, Ill. 60014 (lamp)
Browning, Rte. 1, Morgan, Utah 84050
Camouflage Mfg. Co., P.O. Box 5437, Pine Bluff, AR 71601
Camp Trails, P.O. Box 14500, Phoenix, Ariz. 85031 (packs only)
Camp Ways, 12915 S. Spring St., Los Angeles, CA 90061
Challanger Mfg. Co., Box 550, Jamaica, N.Y. 11431 (glow safe)
Chippewa Shoe Co., 925 First Ave., Chippewa Falls, WI 54729/715-723-5571 (boots)
Cobra, Box 167, Brady, TX 76825 (Cobra 3-in-1 light)
Coleman Co., Inc., 250 N. St. Francis, Wichita, Kans. 67201
Converse Rubber Co., 55 Fordham Rd., Wilmington, MA 01887 (boots)
Dana Safety Heater, J. L. Galef & Son, Inc., 85 Chamber St., N.Y. N.Y. 10007
Danner Shoe Mfg. Co., 5188 S.E. International Way, Milwaukie, OR 97222/503-653-2920 (boots)
DEER-ME Prod. Co., Box 345, Anoka, Minn. 55303 (tree steps)
Dunham Co., P.O. Box 813, Brattleboro, VT 05301/802-254-2316 (boots)
Durango Boot Div., U.S. Industry, 1810 Columbia Ave., Franklin, TN 37064/615-794-1556
Freeman Ind., Inc., 100 Marblehead Rd., Tuckahoe, N.Y. 10707 (Trak-Kit)
French Dressing Inc., 1942 E. 11th St., Tacoma, WA 98421/206-627-1095 (boots)
Game-Winner, Inc., 500 Peachtree Cain Tower, 229 Peachtree, N.E., Atlanta, GA 30303/404-588-0401 (camouflage suits)
Gander Mountain, Inc., Box 248, Wilmot, Wis. 53192
Georgia Boot Div., U.S. Industry, 1810 Columbia Ave., Franklin, TN 37064/615-794-1556
Gokey, 94 E. 4th St., St. Paul, Minn. 55101
Gun Club Sportswear, Box 477, Des Moines, Ia. 50302
Gun-Ho Case Mfg. Co., 110 E. 10th St., St. Paul, Minn. 55101
Joseph M. Herman Shoe Co., Inc., Millis, MA 02054 (boots)
Himalayan Industries, P.O. Box 5668, Pine Bluff, AR 71601
Bob Hinman Outfitters, 1217 W. Glen, Peoria, IL 61614
Hunting World, 16 E. 53rd St., New York, NY 10022
Jung Shoe Mfg. Co., 620 S. 8th St., Sheboygan, WI 53081/414-458-3483 (boots)
Kelty Pack, In., Box 3645, Glendale, Calif. 91201
Laacke & Joys, 1432 N. Water St., Milwaukee, WI 53202 (Wildwood prods.)
La Crosse Rubber Mills Co., P.O. Box 1328, La Crosse, WI 54601/608-782-3020 (boots)
Peter Limmer & Sons Inc., Box 66, Intervale, NH 03845 (boots)
Marathon Rubber Prods. Co. Inc., 510 Sherman St., Wausau, WI 54401 (rain gear)
Marble Arms Corp., 420 Industrial Park, Gladstone, Mich. 49837
National Sports, 19 E. McWilliams St., Fond du Lac, WI 54935
Nimrod & Wayfarer Trailers, 500 Ford Blvd., Hamilton, O. 45011
Charles F. Orvis Co., Manchester, Vt. 05254 (fishing gear)
PGB Assoc., 310 E. 46th St., Suite 3E, New York, NY 10017/212-867-9560
Prime Leather Finishes Co., 205 S. Second St., Milwaukee, WI 53204 (leath. waterproofer; Boot n' Saddle Soap)
Quabaug Rubber Co./Vibram U.S.A., 17 School St. N. Brookfield, MA 01535/617-867-7731 (boots)
Quoddy Moccasins, Div. R. G. Barry Corp., 67 Minot Ave., Auburn, ME 04210/207-784-3555
Ranger Mfg. Co., Inc., P.O. Box 3676, Augusta, GA 30904
Ranger Rubber Co., 1100 E. Main St., Endicott, NY 13760/607-757-4260 (boots)
Red Ball, c/o Uniroyal Inc., World Hq., Middlebury, CT 06749 (boots)
Red Head Brand Corp., 4949 Joseph Hardin Dr., Dallas, TX 75236/214-333-4141
Red Wing Shoe Co., Rte. 2, Red Wing, Minn. 55066
Refrigiwear, Inc., 71 Inip Dr., Inwood, L.I., N.Y. 11696
Reliance Prod. Ltd., 1830 Dublin Ave., Winnipeg 21, Man. R3H 0H3 Can. (tent peg)
Royal Sports Clothing, Washington, IN 47501
W. R. Russell Moccasin Co., 285 S.W. Franklin, Berlin, WI 54923
Buddy Schoellkopf Prods Inc., 4949 Joseph Hardin Dr., Dallas, TX 75236
Servus Rubber Co., 1136 2nd St., Rock Island, Ill. 61201 (footwear)
The Ski Hut-Trailwise, 1615 University Ave., P.O. Box 309, Berkeley, CA 94710
Stearns Mfg. Co., P.O. Box 1498, St. Cloud, MN 56301
Sterno Inc., 300 Park Ave., New York, NY 10022 (camp stoves)
Teledyne Co., Big Beam, 290 E. Prairie St., Crystal Lake, IL 60014

10-X Mfg. Co., 316 So. Lexington Ave., Cheyenne, WY 82001/307-635-9192
Thermos Div., KST Co., Norwich, Conn. 06361 (Pop Tent)
Norm Thompson, 1805 N.W. Thurman St., Portland, Ore. 97209
Utica Duxbak Corp., 1745 S. Acoma St., Denver, CO 80223/303-778-0324
Waffen-Frankonia, Box 6780, 87 Wurzburg 1, W. Germany
Weinbrenner Shoe Corp., Polk St., Merrill, WI 54452
Wenzel Co., 1280 Research Blvd., St. Louis, MO 63132
Wolverine Boots & Shoes Div., Woverine World Wide, 9341 Courtland Dr., Rockford, MI 49351/616-866-1561 (footwear)
Woods Bag & Canvas Co., Ltd., 90 River St., P.O. Box 407, Ogdensburg, NY 13669/315-393-3520
Woodstream Corp., Box 327, Lititz, Pa. 17543 (Hunter Seat)
Woolrich Woolen Mills, Woolrich, Pa. 17779
Yankee Mechanics, RFD No. 1, Concord, NH 03301/603-225-3181 (hand winches)

KNIVES AND KNIFEMAKER'S SUPPLIES—FACTORY and MAIL ORDER

Alcas Cutlery Corp., Olean, NY 14760/716-372-3111 (Cutco)
Atlanta Cutlery, Box 839, Conyers, GA 30207/404-922-3700 (mail order, supplies)
Bali-Song Inc., 3039 Roswell St., Los Angeles, CA 90085/213-258-7021
L. L. Bean, 386 Main St., Freeport, ME 04032/207-865-3111 (mail order)
Benchmark Knives, P.O. Box 998, Gastonia, NC 28052/704-867-6394
Bladesmith, P.O. Box 743, Orange, CA 92666 (supplies)
Boker, The Cooper Group, P.O. Box 728, Apex, NC 27502/919-362-7510
Bowen Knife Co., P.O. Box Drawer 590, Blackshear, GA 31516/912-449-4794
Browne and Pharr Inc., 1775-I Wilwat Dr., Norcross, GA 30091/404-447-9285
Browning, Rt. 1, Morgan, UT 84050/801-876-2711
Buck Knives, Inc., P.O. Box 1267; 1717 Magnolia Ave., El Cajon, CA 92022/714-449-1100
Camillus Cutlery Co., Main St., Camillus, NY 13031/315-672-8111 (Sword Brand)
W. R. Case & Sons Cutlery Co., 20 Russell Blvd., Bradford, PA 16701/814-368-4123
Charter Arms Corp., 430 Sniffens Lane, Stratford, CT 06497/203-377-8080 (Skatchet)
Chicago Cutlery Co., 441 Bonner Rd., Wauconda, IL 60084/312-526-2144
E. Christopher Firearms, State Rte. 123 and Ferry Rd., Miamitown, OH 45041/513-353-1321 (supplies)
Collins Brothers Div. (belt-buckle knife), see: Bowen Knife Co.
Colonial Knife Co., P.O. Box 3327, Providence, RI 02909/401-421-1600 (Master Brand)
Custom Purveyors, (Ted Devlet), P.O. Box 886, Fort Lee, NJ 07024/201-886-0196 (mail order)
Dixie Gun Works, Inc., P.O. Box 130, Union City, TN 38261/901-885-0700 (supplies)
Eze-Lap Diamond Prods., Box 2229, 15164 Weststate St., Westminster, CA 92683/714-847-1555 (knife sharpeners)
Gerber Legendary Blades, 14200 S.W. 72nd St., Portland, OR 99223/503-639-6161
Golden Age Arms Co., 14 W. Winter St., Delaware, OH 43015/614-369-6513 (supplies)
Gutmann Cutlery Co., Inc., 900 S. Columbus Ave., Mt. Vernon, NY 10550/914-699-4044
H & B Forge Co., Rte. 2, Box 24, Shiloh, OH 44878/419-896-3435 (throwing knives, tomahawks)
Russell Harrington Cutlery, Inc., Subs. of Hyde Mfg. Co., 44 River St., Southbridge, MA 01550/617-764-4371 (Dexter, Green River Works)
J.A. Henckels Zwillingswerk, Inc., 1 Westchester Plaza, Elmsford, NY 10523/914-592-7370
Imperial Knife Associated Companies, 1776 Broadway, New York, NY 10019/212-757-1814
Indian Ridge Traders, Box 869, Royal Oak, MI 48068/313-399-6034 (mostly blades)
Jet-Aer Corp., 100 Sixth Ave., Paterson, NJ 07524/201-278-8300
KA-BAR Cutlery Inc., 5777 Grant Ave., Cleveland, OH 44105/216-271-4000
KaBar Knives, Collectors Division, 434 No. 9th St., Olean, NY 14760/716-372-5611
Keene Corp., Cutting Serv. Div., 1569 Tower Grove Ave., St. Louis, MO 63110/314-771-1550
Kershaw Cutlery Co., 6024 Jean Rd., Suite D. Lake Oswego, OR 97034/503-636-0111
Knife and Gun Supplies, P.O. Box 13522, Arlington, TX 76013/817-261-0569
Koval Knives, P.O. Box 14130, Columbus, OH 43214/614-888-6486 (supplies)
Lakota Corp., 30916 Agoura Rd., Suite 311, Westlake Village, CA 91361/213-889-7177
Lamson & Goodnow Mfg. Co., Shelburne Falls, MA 03170/413-625-6331
Al Mar Knives, Inc., 5861 S.W. Benfield Ct., Lake Oswego, OR 97034/503-639-8554
Marble Arms Corp., 420 Industrial Park, Gladstone, MI 49837/906-425-3710
Marttiini Knives, Box 38866, Chicago, IL 60648/312-470-0233
Matthews Cutlery, P.O. Box 33095, Decatur, GA 30033/404-636-7923 (mail order)
R. Murphy Co., Inc., 13 Groton-Harvard Rd., Ayer, MA 01432/617-772-3481 (StaySharp)
Nordic Knives, 1643-C-Z Copenhagen Dr., Solvang, CA 93463 (mail order)
Normark Corp., 1710 E. 78th St., Minneapolis, MN 55423/612-869-3291
Olsen Knife Co., Inc., 7 Joy St., Howard City, MI 49329/616-937-4373
Ontario Knife Co., Subs. of Servotronics, Inc., P.O. Box 145, Franklinville, NY 14737/716-676-5527 (Old Hickory)

Parker Cutlery, 6928 Lee Highway, Chattanooga, TN 37415/615-894-1782

Plaza Cutlery Inc., 3333 Bristol, #161, Costa Mesa, CA 92626/714-549-3932 (mail order)

Queen Cutlery Co., P.O. Box 500, Franklinville, NY 14737/716-676-5540

R&C Knives and Such, P.O. Box 32631, San Jose, CA 95152/408-923-5728 (mail order)

Randall-Made Knives, Box 1988, Orlando, FL 32802/305-855-8075 (ctlg. $1)

Rigid Knives, P.O. Box 816, Hwy. 290E, Lake Hamilton, AR 71951/501-525-1377

A.G. Russell, 1705 Hiwy. 71 N., Springdale, AR 72764/501-751-7341

Bob Sanders, 2358 Tyler Lane, Louisville, KY 40205 (Bahco steel)

San Diego Knives, 2785 Kurtz No. 8, San Diego, CA 92110/714-297-4530 (mail order)

Schrade Cutlery Corp., 1776 Broadway, New York, NY 10019/212-757-1814

Bob Schrimsher, Custom Knifemaker's Supply, P.O. Box 308, Emory, TX 75440/214-328-2453

Paul Sheffield, P.O. Box 141, Deland, FL 32720/904-736-9356 (supplies)

Smith & Wesson, 2100 Roosevelt Ave., Springfield, MA 01101/413-781-8300

Jesse W. Smith Saddlery, E. 3024 Sprague, Spokane, WA 99201 (sheathmakers)

Swiss Army Knives, Inc., P.O. Box 846, Shelton, CT 06484/203-929-6391 (Victorinox; folding)

Tekna, 3549 Haven Ave., Menlo Park, CA 94025/415-365-5112

Thompson/Center, P.O. Box 2405, Rochester, NH 03867/603-332-2394

tommer—Bordein Corp., 220 N. River St., Delano, MN 55328/612-972-3901

Tru-Balance Knife Co., 2115 Tremond Blvd., Grand Rapids, MI 49504/616-453-3679

Utica Cutlery Co., 820 Noyes St., Utica, NY 13503/315-733-4663 (Kutmaster)

Valor Corp., 5555 N.W. 36th Ave., Miami, FL 33142

Washington Forge, Inc., Englishtown, NJ 07727/201-446-7777 (Carriage House)

Wenoka Cutlery Co., 85 North Ave., Natick, MA 01760/617-453-3679

Western Cutlery Co., 1800 Pike Rd., Longmont, CO 80501/303-772-5900 (Westmark)

Walt Whinnery, Walts Cust. Leather, 1947 Meadow Creek Dr., Louisville, KY 40281/502-458-4351 (sheathmaker)

Wilkinson Sword, 1316 W. Main St., Richmond, VA 23220/804-353-1812

J. Wolfe's Knife Works, Box 1056, Larkspur, CA 94939 (supplies)

Wyoming Knife Co., 3700 E. 20th, Casper, WY 82601/307-265-7437

LABELS, BOXES, CARTRIDGE HOLDERS

Milton Brynin, 214 E. Third St., Mount Vernon, NY 10710/914-667-6549 (cartridge box labels)

E-Z Loader, Del Rey Products, P.O. Box 91561, Los Angeles, CA 90009

Jasco, J. A. Somers Co., P.O. Box 49751, Los Angeles, CA 90049 (cartridge box labels)

Peterson Label Co., P.O. Box 186, Redding Ridge, CT 06876 (cartridge box labels; Targ-Dots)

N. H. Schiffman, 963 Malibu, Pocatello, ID 83201 (cartridge carrier)

LOAD TESTING and PRODUCT TESTING, CHRONOGRAPHING, BALLISTIC STUDIES

Hutton Rifle Ranch, 1802 S. Oak Park Dr., Rolling Hills, Tucson, AZ 85710

Kent Lomont, 4421 S. Wayne Ave., Ft. Wayne, IN 46807/219-694-6792 (handguns, handgun ammunition)

Plum City Ballistics Range, Rte. 1, Box 29A, Plum City, WI 54761

Russell's Rifle Shop, Rte. 5, Box 92, Georgetown, TX 78626/512-778-5338 (load testing and chronographing to 300 yds.)

John M. Tovey, 4710 - 104th Lane NE, Circle Pines, MN 55014

H. P. White Laboratory, Inc., 3114 Scarboro Rd., Street, MD 21154/301-838-6550

MISCELLANEOUS

Accurizing Service, Herbert G. Troester, 2292 W. 1000 North, Vernal, UT 84078/801-789-2158

Activator, B.M.F. Activator, Inc., 3705 Broadway, Houston, TX 77017/713-645-6726

Adapters, Sage Industries, P.O. Box 2248, Hemet, CA 92343 (12-ga. shotgun; 38 S&W blank)

Adhesive Flannel, Forest City Prod., 722 Bolivar, Cleveland, OH 44115

Adjusta-Targ, Inc., 1817 Thackeray N.W., Massillon, OH 44646

Archery, Bear, R.R. 4, 4600 Southwest 41st Blvd., Gainesville, FL 32601/904-376-2327

Arms Restoration, J. J. Jenkins Ent. Inc., 375 Pine Ave. No. 25, Goleta, CA 93017/805-967-1366

Barrel Band Swivels, Phil Judd, 83 E. Park St., Butte, Mont. 59701

Bedding Kit, Bisonite Co., P.O. Box 84, Kenmore Station, Buffalo, NY 14217

Bedding Kit, Fenwal, Inc., Resins Systems Div., 400 Main St., Ashland, MA 01721

Belt Buckles, Adina Silversmiths Corp., P.O. Box 348, 3195 Tucker Rd., Cornwell Heights, PA 19020/215-639-7246

Belt Buckles, Bergamot Brass Works, 42 N. Wisconsin, Darien, WI 53114

Belt Buckles, Just Brass Inc., 21 Filmore Place, Freeport, NY 11520 (ctlg. $2)

Belt Buckles, Sports Style Associates, 148 Hendrickson Ave., Lynbrook, NY 11563/516-599-5080

Belt Buckles, Pilgrim Pewter Inc., R.D. 2, Tully, NY 13159/607-842-6431

Benchrest & Accuracy Shooters Equipment, Bob Pease Accuracy, P.O. Box 787, Zipp Road, New Braunfels, TX 78130/512-625-134

Bootdryers, Baekgaard Ltd., 1855 Janke Dr., Northbrook, Ill. 60062

Breech Plug Wrench, Swaine Machine, 195 O'Connell, Providence, R.I. 02905

Cannons, South Bend Replicas Inc., 61650 Oak Rd., S. Bend, IN 46614/219-289-4500 (ctlg. $4)

Cannons, A & K Mfg. Co., Inc., 1651 N. Nancy Rose Ave., Tucson, AZ 85712 (replicas)

Cartridge Adapters, Sport Specialties, Harry Owen, Box 5337, Hacienda Hts., CA 91745/213-968-5806

Case Gauge, Plum City Ballistics Range, Rte. 1, Box 29A, Plum City, WI 54761/715-647-2539

Chrome Brl. Lining, Marker Mach. Co., Box 426, Charleston, Ill. 61920

Clips, D&E Magazines Mfg., P.O. Box 4579, Downey, CA 90241 (handgun and rifle)

CO_2 Cartridges, Nittan U.S.A. Inc., 4901 Morena Blvd., Suite 307, San Diego, CA 92117/714-272-6113

Deer Drag, D&H Prods. Co., Inc., P.O. Box 22, Glenshaw, PA 15116/412-443-2190

Dryer, Thermo-Electric, Golden-Rod, Buenger Enterprises, Box 5286, Oxnard, CA 93030/805-985-9596

E-Z Loader, Del Rey Prod., P.O. Box 91561, Los Angeles, CA 90009

Ear-Valv, Sigma Eng. Co., 16624 Edwards Rd., Cerritos, CA 90701 (Lee-Sonic)

Flares, Colt Industries, Huyshope Ave., Hartford, Conn. 06102

Flares, Smith & Wesson Chemical Co., 2399 Forman Rd., Rock Creek, OH 44084

Game Hoist, Cam Gear Ind., P.O. Box 1002, Kalispell, MT 59901 (Sportsmaster 500 pocket hoist)

Game Hoist, Precise, 3 Chestnut, Suffern, NY 10901

Game Scent, Buck Stop Lure Co., Inc., 3015 Grow Rd. N.W., Stanton, MI 48888/517-762-5091

Game Scent, Pete Rickard, Box 1250, Cobleskill, NY 12043 (Indian Buck lure)

Gas Pistol, Penguin Ind., Inc., Airport Industrial Mall, Coatesville, PA 19320/215-384-6000

Golden-Rod, Buenger Enterprises, P.O. Box 5286, Oxnard, CA 93030 (Thermo-Electric Dryers)

Grip Caps, Classic Arms Corp., P.O. Box 8, Palo Alto, CA 94302/415-321-7243

Grip caps, Knickerbocker Enterprises, 16199 S. Maple Ln. Rd., Oregon City, OR 97045

Grip Caps, Philip D. Letiecq, AQ 18 Wagon Box Rd., P.O. Box 251, Story, WY 82842/307-683-2817

Gun Bedding Kit, Fenwal, Inc., Resins System Div., 400 Main St., Ashland, MA 01721/617-881-2000

Gun Jewelry, Sid Bell Originals, R.D. 2, Tully, NY 13159/607-842-6431

Gun Jewelry, Pilgrim Pewter Inc., R.D. 2, Tully, NY 13159

Gun Jewelry, Al Popper, 614 Turnpike St., Stoughton, Mass. 02072

Gun Jewelry, Sports Style Assoc., 148 Hendricks Ave., Lynbrook, NY 11563

Gun Record Book, B. J. Co., Bridge St., Bluffton, SC 29910

Gun Sling, Kwikfire, Wayne Prods. Co., P.O. Box 247, Camp Hill, PA 17011

Gun Slings, Torel, Inc., 1053 N. South St., Yoakum, TX 77995

Hollow Pointer, Goerg Ent., P.O. Box 531, Renton, WA 98056/206-883-1529

Hugger Hooks, Roman Products, 4363 Loveland St., Golden, CO 80401/303-279-6959

Insect Repellent, Armor, Div. of Buck Stop, Inc., 3015 Grow Rd., Stanton, Mich. 48888

Insert Barrels, Sport Specialties, H. Owen, Box 5337, Hacienda Hts., CA 91745/213-968-5806

Light Load, Jacob & Tiffin Inc., P.O. Box 547, Clanton, AL 35045

Locks, Gun, Bor-Lok Prods., 105 5th St., Arbuckle, CA 95912

Locks, Gun, Master Lock Co., 2600 N. 32nd St., Milwaukee, WI 53245

Miniature Cannons, A & K Mfg. Co., 5146 E. Pima, Tucson, AZ 85712 (ctlg. $1)

Miniature Cannons, Karl J. Furr, 76 East-350 North, Orem, UT 84057 (replicas)

Miniature Guns, Charles H. Stoppler, 5 Minerva Place, New York, NY 10468

Monte Carlo Pad, Frank A. Hoppe Div., Penguin Ind., Airport Industrial Mall, Coatesville, PA 19320/215-384-6000

Muzzle Rest, Meadow Industries, Dept. 50, Forest, VA 24551/804-525-2567

Muzzle-Top, Allen Assoc., 7502 Limekiln, Philadelphia, PA 19150 (plastic gun muzzle cap)

Patterning Data, Whits Shooting Stuff, P.O. Box 1340, Cody, WY 82414

Pell Remover, A. Edw. Terpening, 838 E. Darlington Rd., Tarpon Springs, FL 33589

Powderhorns, Kirk Olson, Ft. Woolsey Guns, P.O. Box 2122, Prescott, AZ 86302/602-778-3035

Practice Ammunition, Hoffman Prods., P.O. Box 853, Lake Forest, IL 60045

Pressure Testg. Machine, M. York, 5508 Griffith Rd., Gaithersburg, MD 20760/301-253-4217

Ransom Handgun Rests, C'Arco, P.O. Box 308, Highland, CA 92346

Retriev-R-Trainer, Scientific Prods. Corp., 426 Swann Ave., Alexandria, VA 22301

Rifle Magazines, Butler Creek Corp., Box GG, Jackson Hole, WY 83001/307-733-3599 (30-rd. Mini-14)

Rifle Slings, Bianchi Leather Prods., 100 Calle Cortez, Temecula, CA 92390,714-676-5621

Rifle Slings, Chace Leather Prods., Longhorn Div., 507 Alden St., Fall River, MA 02722/617-678-7556

Rifle Slings, John's Cust. Leather, 525 S. Liberty St., Blairsville, PA 15717/412-459-6802

RIG, NRA Scoring Plug, Rig Prod. Co., Div. of Mittan, Inc., 21320 Deering Ct., Canoga Park, CA 91304/213-883-4700
Rubber Cheekpiece, W. H. Lodewick, 2816 N. E. Halsey, Portland, Ore. 97232
Saddle Rings, Studs, Fred Goodwin, Sherman Mills, ME 04776
Safeties, Williams Gun Sight Co., 7389 Lapeer Rd., Davison, Mich. 48423
Salute Cannons, Naval Co., R.D. 2, 4747 Cold Spring Creamery Rd., Doylestown, PA 18901
Sav-Bore, Saunders Sptg. Gds., 338 Somerset St., N. Plainfield, NJ 07060
Scrimshaw Engraving, C. Milton Barringer, 217-2nd Isle N., Port Richey, FL 33568
Sharpening Stones, Russell's Arkansas Oilstones, 1705 Hiway 71N., Springdale, AR 72764
Shell Shrinker Mfg. Co., P.O. Box 462, Fillmore, CA 93015
Shooter's Porta Bench, Centrum Industries, Inc., 443 Century, S.W., Grand Rapids, MI 49503/616-454-9424
Shooters Rubber Stamps, Craft Haven, 828 N. 70th, Lincoln, NE 68505/402-466-5739
Shooting Coats, 10-X Mfg. Co., 316 So. Lexington Ave., Cheyenne, WY 82001/307-635-9192
Shooting Glasses, Willson Safety Prods. Division, P.O. Box 622, Reading, PA 19603
Shooting Ranges, Kory Shooting Equipment, 233 S. Wacker, Sears Tower, Suite 7130, Chicago, IL 60606
Shotgun Sight, bi-ocular, Trius Prod., Box 25, Cleves, O. 45002
Shotshell Adapter, PC Co., 5942 Secor Rd., Toledo, OH 43623 (Plummer 410 converter)
Single Shot Action, John Foote, Foote-Shephard Inc., P.O. Box 6473, Marietta, GA 30065
Snap Caps, Edwards Recoil Reducer, 1104 Milton Rd., Alton, IL 62002/618-462-3257
Sportsman's Chair, Custom Purveyors, P.O. Box 886, Fort Lee, NJ 07024
Springfield Safety Pin, B-Square Co., P.O. Box 11281, Ft. Worth, Tex. 76110
Springs, W. Wolff Co., Box 232, Ardmore, Pa. 19003
Stock pad, variable, Meadow Industries, Dept. 50, Forest, VA 24551/804-525-2567
Supersound, Edmund Scientific Co., 101 E. Gloucester Pike, Barrington, NJ 08007 (safety device)
Swivels, Michaels, P.O. Box 13010, Portland, OR 97213/503-255-6890
Swivels, Sile Dist., 7 Centre Market Pl., New York, N.Y. 10013
Swivels, Williams Gun Sight Co., 7389 Lapeer Rd., Davison, Mich. 48423
Tear Gas Pistol, Casady Eng. Associates, 560 Alaska Ave., Torrance, CA 90503
Tree Stand, Advanced Hunting Equipment Inc., P.O. Box 1277, Cumming, GA 30130/404-887-1171 (tree-lounge)
Tree Stand, Climbing, Amacker Prods., P.O. Box 1432; 1011 Beech St., Tallulah, LA 71282/318-574-4907
Trophies, Blackinton & Co., 140 Commonwealth, Attleboro Falls, Mass. 02763
Trophies, F. H. Noble & Co., 888 Tower Rd., Mundelein, IL 60060
World Hunting Info., Jack Atcheson & Sons, Inc., 3210 Ottawa St., Butte, MT 59701
World Hunting Info., J/B Adventures & Safaris, Inc., 800 E. Girard, Suite 603, Denver, CO 80231/303-696-0261
World Hunting Info., Klineburger, 12 & East Pine, Seattle, WA 98122/206-329-1600
World Hunting Info., Wayne Preston, Inc., 3444 Northhaven Rd., Dallas, TX 75229

MUZZLE-LOADING GUNS, BARRELS OR EQUIPMENT

A&K Mfg. C., Inc., 1651 N. Nancy Rose Ave., Tucson, AZ 85712 (ctlg. $1)
Luther Adkins, Box 281, Shelbyville, IN 47176/317-392-3795 (breech plugs)
Anderson Mfg. Co., Union Gap Sta. P.O. Box 3120, Yakima WA 98903/509-453-2349
Armoury, Inc., Rte. 202, New Preston, CT 06777
Beaver Lodge, 9245 16th Ave. S.W., Seattle, WA 98106
John Bivins, Jr., 200 Wicklow Rd., Winston-Salem, NC 27106
Blackhawk SAA East, C2274, Loves Park, IL 61131
Blackhawk SAA Mtn., 1337 Delmar Parkway, Aurora, CO 80010
Blackhawk SAA West, Box 285, Hiawatha, KS 66434
Blue and Gray Prods., Inc., 817 E. Main St., Bradford, PA 16701
Ted Buckland, 361 Flagler Rd., Nordland, WA 98358/206-385-2142 (custom only)
G. S. Bunch, 7735 Garrison, Hyattsville, Md. 20784 (flask repair)
Butler Creek Corp., Box GG, Jackson Hole, WY 83001/307-733-3599 (poly & maxi patch)
Cache La Poudre Rifleworks, 168 N. College, Ft. Collins, CO 80521/303-482-6913 (custom muzzleloaders)
Challanger Mfg. Co., 118 Pearl St., Mt. Vernon, NY 10550
R. MacDonald Champlin, P.O. Box 74, Wentworth, NH 03282 (custom muzzleloaders)
Chopie Mfg. Inc., 531 Copeland Ave., LaCrosse, WI 54601 (nipple wrenches)
Connecticut Valley Arms Co. (CVA), Saybrook Rd., Haddam, CT 06438 (kits also)
Earl T. Cureton, Rte. 2, Box 388, Willoughby Rd., Bulls Gap, TN 37711 (powder horns)
DJ Inc., 1310 S. Park Rd., Fairdale, KY 40118
Leonard Day & Co., 316 Burt Pits Rd., Northampton, MA 10160
Dixie Gun Works, Inc., P.O. Box 130, Union City, TN 38261
EMF Co., Inc., 2911 W. Olive Ave., Burbank, CA 91505/213-843-7777
Eagle Arms Co., 136 Westward Ho Dr., Northlake, IL 60164/312-562-2708
Euroarms of America, Inc., P.O. Box 3277, 1501 Lenoir Dr., Winchester, VA 22601/703-662-1863

The Eutaw Co., Box 608, U.S. Highway 176W, Holly Hill, SC 29059 (accessories)
Excam, Inc., 4480 E. 11th Ave., Hialeah, FL 33012
Andy Fautheree, P.O. Box 863, Pagosa Springs, CO 81147/303-264-2892 (cust. ML)
Ted Fellowes, Beaver Lodge, 9245 16th Ave. S.W., Seattle, Wash. 98106
Firearms Imp. & Exp. Corp., (F.I.E.), P.O. Box 4866, Hialeah Lakes, Hialeah, FL 33014/305-685-5966
Marshall F. Fish, Rt. 22 N., Westport, NY 12993 (antique ML repairs)
The Flintlock Muzzle Loading Gun Shop, 1238 "G" So. Beach Blvd., Anaheim, CA 92804/714-821-6655
Clark K. Frazier/Matchmate, RFD. 1, Rawson, OH 45881
C. R. & D. E. Getz, Box 88, Beavertown, PA 17813 (barrels)
Golden Age Arms Co., 14 W. Winter St., Delaware, OH 43015 (ctlg. $2.50)
A. R. Goode, 12845 Catoctin Furnace Rd., Thurmont, MD 21788/301-271-2228 (ML rifle bbls.)
Guncraft Inc., 117 W. Pipeline, Hurst, TX 76053/817-268-2887
Harper's Ferry Arms Co., 256 E. Broadway, Hopewell, VA 23860 (guns)
Hopkins & Allen, P.O. Box 198, Elmwood Park, NJ 07407/201-794-1800
The House of Muskets, Inc., P.O. Box 900, Pagosa Springs, CO 81147/303-264-2892 (ML bbls. & supplies)
International Arms, 23239 Doremus Ave., St. Clair Shores, MI 48080
JJJJ Ranch, Wm. Large, Rte. 1, State Route 243, Ironton, Ohio 45638/614-532-5298
Jerry's Gun Shop, 9220 Ogden Ave., Brookfield, IL 60513/312-485-5200
Kern's Gun Shop, 319 E. Main St., Ligonier, PA 15658/412-238-7651 (ctlg. $1.50)
Art LeFeuvre, 1003 Hazel Ave., Deerfield, IL 60015/312-945-0073 (antique gun restoring)
Les' Gun Shop (Les Bauska), 105-9th West, P.O. Box 511, Kalispell, MT 59901/406-755-2635
Lever Arms Serv. Ltd., 572 Howe St., Vancouver, BC V6C 2E3, Canada
Log Cabin Sport Shop, 8010 Lafayette Rd., Lodi, OH 44254/216-948-1082 (ctlg. $3)
Loven Firearms Corp., Del Mar Dr., Brookfield, CT 06804
Lyman Products Corp., Rte. 147, Middlefield, CT 06455
McCann's Muzzle-Gun Works, 200 Federal City Rd., Pennington, NJ 08354/609-737-1707
McKeown's Guns, R.R. 4, Pekin, IL 61554/309-347-3559 (E-Z load rev. stand)
Judson E. Mariotti, Beauty Hill Rd., Barrington, NH 03825 (brass bullet mould)
Maurer Arms, 2366 Frederick Dr., Cuyahoga Falls, OH 44221 (cust. muzzleloaders)
Michigan Arms Corp., 479 W. 14 Mile Rd., Clawson, MI 48017
Mountain State Muzzleloading Supplies, Box 154-1, Williamstown, WV 26187
Mowrey Gun Works, FM 368, Box 28, Iowa Park, TX 76367/817-592-2331
Muzzleloaders Etc., Inc., Jim Westberg, 9901 Lyndale Ave. S., Bloomington, MN 55420
Numrich Corp., W. Hurley, N.Y. 12491 (powder flasks)
Kirk Olson, Ft. Woolsey Guns, P.O. Box 2122, Prescott, AZ 86302/602-778-3035 (powderhorns)
Ox-Yoke Originals, 130 Griffin Rd., West Suffield, CT 06093 (dry lubr. patches)
Orrin L. Parsons, Jr., Central Maine Muzzle-Loading & Gunsmithing, RFD #1, Box 787, Madison, ME 04950
A. W. Peterson Gun Shop, 1693 Old Hwy. 441 N., Mt. Dora, FL 32757 (ML guns)
Richland Arms, 321 W. Adrian St., Blissfield, MI 49228
Rush's Old Colonial Forge, 106 Wiltshire Rd., Baltimore, MD 21221
Salish House, Inc., P.O. Box 383, Lakeside, MT 55922/406-844-3625
H. M. Schoeller, 569 So. Braddock Ave., Pittsburgh, Pa. 15221
Sharon Rifle Barrel Co., P.O. Box 106, Kalispell, MT 59901
Shiloh Products, 37 Potter St., Farmingdale, NY 11735 (4-cavity mould)
Shore Galleries, Inc., 3318 W. Devon Ave., Chicago, IL 60645/312-676-2900
Sile Distributors, 7 Centre Market Pl., New York, NY 10013
C. E. Siler Locks, Rt. 6, Box 5, Candler, NC 28715 (flint locks)
Ken Steggles, 17 Bell Lane, Byfield, Near Daventry, Northants NN11 6US, England (accessories)
Tag Gun Works, 236 Main, Springfield, OR 97477/503-741-4118 (supplies)
T.E.S. Firearms, Inc., 2200 Bott St., Colorado Springs, CO 80904/303-475-1167 (underhammer target rifle)
Ten-Ring Precision, Inc., 1449 Blue Crest Lane, San Antonio, TX 78232/512-494-3063
Upper Missouri Trading Co., 3rd and Harold Sts., Crofton, NB 68730
R. Watts, 826 Springdale Rd., Atlanta, GA 30306 (ML rifles)
W. H. Wescomb, P.O. Box 488, Glencoe, CA 95232 (parts)
Thos. F. White, 5801 Westchester Ct., Worthington, O. 43085 (powder horn)
Williamson-Pate Gunsmith Serv., 117 W. Pipeline, Hurst, TX 76053/817-268-2887
York County Gun Works, R.R. #4, Tottenham, Ont. L0G 1W0, Canada (locks)

PISTOLSMITHS

Allen Assoc., 7502 Limekiln Pike, Philadelphia, PA 19150 (speed-cock lever for 45 ACP)
Bain and Davis Sptg. Gds., 559 W. Las Tunas Dr., San Gabriel, Cal. 91776
Lee Baker, 7252 East Ave. U-3, Littlerock, CA 93543/805-944-4487
Bar-Sto Precision Machine, 633 So. Victory Blvd., Burbank, CA 91502 (S.S. bbls. f. 45 Acp)
Behlert Custom Guns, Inc., 725 Lehigh Ave., Union, NJ 07083 (short actions)

F. Bob Chow, Gun Shop, 3185 Mission, San Francisco, Calif. 94110
Brown Custom Guns, Inc., Steven N. Brown, 8810 Rocky Ridge Rd., Indianapolis, IN 46217/317-881-2771 aft. 5 PM
J.E. Clark, Rte. 2, Box 22A, Keithville, LA 71047
Custom Gun Shop, 725 Lehigh Ave., Union, NJ 07083
Davis Co., 2793 Del Monte St., West Sacramento, CA 95691/916-372-6789
Day Arms Corp., 2412 S.W. Loop 410, San Antonio, TX 78227
Dominic DiStefano, 4303 Friar Lane, Colorado Springs, CO 80907/303-599-3366 (accurizing)
Dan Dwyer, 915 W. Washington, San Diego, Calif. 92103
Ken Eversull Gunsmith, Inc., P.O. Box 1766, Alexandria, LA 71301/318-442-0569
Giles' 45 Shop, 8614 Tarpon Springs Rd., Odessa, FL 33556/813-920-5366
The Gunshop, R. D. Wallace, 320 Overland Rd., Prescott, AZ 86301
Gil Hebard Guns, Box 1, Knoxville, Ill. 61448
Paul Jaeger, Inc., 211 Leedom St., Jenkintown, PA 19046/215-884-6920
Lee E. Jurras & Assoc., Inc., P.O. Drawer F, Hagerman, NM 88232
Kart Sptg. Arms Corp., RD 2, Box 929-Broad Ave., Riverhead, NY 11901 (handgun conversions)
Lenz Firearms Co., 1480 Elkay Dr., Eugene, OR 97404
Kent Lomont, 4421 So. Wayne Ave., Ft. Wayne, IN 46807/219-694-6792 (Auto Mag only)
Mag-Na-Port Arms, Inc., 30016 S. River Rd., Mt. Clemens, MI 48043/313-469-6727
Robert A. McGrew, 3315 Michigan Ave., Colorado Springs, CO 80910/303-636-1940
Rudolf Marent, 9711 Tiltree, Houston, TX 77075 (Hammerli)
Nu-Line Guns, 1053 Caulks Hill Rd., Harvester, MO 63303/314-447-4501
Pachmayr Gun Works, 1220 S. Grand Ave., Los Angeles, Calif. 90015
L. W. Seecamp Co., Inc., Box 255, New Haven, CT 06502 (DA Colt auto conversions)
Silver Dollar Guns, P.O. Box 475, 10 Frances St., Franklin, NH 03235 (45 ACP)
Spokhandguns Inc., E. J. Christensen, East 1911 Sprague Ave., Spokane, WA 99202/509-534-4112
Sportsmens Equipmt. Co., 915 W. Washington, San Diego, Calif. 92103
Irving O. Stone, Jr., 633 S. Victory Blvd., Burbank, CA 91502
Victor W. Strawbridge, 6 Pineview Dr., Dover Pt., Dover, NH 03820
A. D. Swenson's 45 Shop, P.O. Box 606, Fallbrook, CA 92028
Trapper Gun, 18717 East 14 Mile Rd., Fraser, MI 48026/313-792-0134
Dennis A. "Doc" Ulrich, 2511 S. 57th Ave., Cicero, IL 60650
Vic's Gun Refinishing, 6 Pineview Dr., Dover, NH 03820
Walters Industries, 6226 Park Lane, Dallas, TX 75225
Dave Woodruff, Box 5, Bear, DE 19701

REBORING AND RERIFLING

P.O. Ackley (see: Dennis M. Bellm Gunsmithing, Inc.)
Atkinson Gun Co., P.O. Box 512, Prescott, AZ 86301
Bain & Davis Sptg. Gds., 559 W. Las Tunas Dr., San Gabriel, Calif. 91776
Dennis M. Bellm Gunsmithing Inc., 2376 So. Redwood Rd., Salt Lake City, UT 84119/801-974-0697; price list $3.
Larry L. Forster, Box 212, Gwinner, ND 58040/701-678-2475
H-S Precision, Inc., 112 N. Summit, Prescott, AZ 85302/602-445-0607
Bruce Jones, 389 Calla Ave., Imperial Beach, CA 92032
Les' Gun Shop, (Les Bauska), 105-9th West, P.O. Box 511, Kalispell, MT 59901/406-755-2635
Morgan's Cust. Reboring, 707 Union Ave., Grants Pass, OR 97526
Nu-Line Guns, 1053 Caulks Hill Rd., Harvester, MO 63303/314-441-4500 (handguns)
Al Petersen, Box 8, Riverhurst, Saskatchewan, Canada S0H3P0
Randy Redman, 3015 So. Illinois, Caldwell, ID 83605/208-454-9435
SGW, Inc. (formerly Schuetzen Gun Works), 624 Old Pacific Hwy. S.E., Olympia, WA 98503/206-456-3471
Sharon Gun Specialties, 14587 Peaceful Valley Rd., Sonora, CA 95370
Siegrist Gun Shop, 2689 McLean Rd., Whittemore, MI 48770
Snapp's Gunshop, 6911 E. Washington Rd., Clare, Mich. 48617
J. W. Van Patten, Box 145, Foster Hill, Milford, Pa. 18337
Robt. G. West, 27211 Huey Lane, Eugene, OR 97402

RELOADING TOOLS AND ACCESSORIES

Advance Car Mover Co., Inc., P.O. Box 1181, Appleton, WI 54911 (bottom pour lead casting ladles)
Anderson Mfg. Co., Royal, IA 51357 (Shotshell Trimmers)
Aurands, 229 E. 3rd St., Lewistown, Pa. 17044
B-Square Eng. Co., Box 11281, Ft. Worth, Tex. 76110
Bill Ballard, 830 Miles Ave., Billings, MT 59101 (ctlg. 50¢)
Ballistic Prods., P.O. Box 488, 2105 Shaughnessy Circle, Long Lake, MN 55356/612-473-1550
Bear Reloaders Inc., 2110 1st Natl. Tower, Akron, OH 44308/216-253-4039
Belding & Mull, P.O. Box 428, 100 N. 4th St., Philipsburg, PA 16866/814-342-0607
Berdon Machine Co., Box 483, Hobart, WA 98025/206-392-1866 (metallic press)
Blackhawk SAA East, C2274 POB, Loves Park, Ill. 61131/812-633-7784
Blackhawk SAA Mtn., Richard Miller, 1337 Delmar Parkway, Aurora, CO 80010/303-366-3659
Blackhawk SAA West, Box 285, Hiawatha, KS 66434
Bonanza Sports, Inc., 412 Western Ave., Faribault, Minn. 55021
Gene Bowlin, Rt. 1, Box 890, Snyder, TX 79549/915-573-2323 (arbor press)
Brown Precision Co., 5869 Indian Ave., San Jose, Calif. 95123 (Little Wiggler)
A. V. Bryant, 72 Whiting Rd., E. Hartford, CT 06118 (Nutmeg Universal Press)
C-H Tool & Die Corp., 106 N. Harding St., Owen, WI 54461/715-229-2146

Central Products f. Shooters, 435 Route 18, East Brunswick, NJ 08816 (neck turning tool)
Camdex, Inc., 2228 Fourteen Mile Rd., Warren, MI 48092/313-977-1620
Carbide Die & Mfg. Co., Box 226, Covina, CA 91724
Carter Gun Works, 2211 Jefferson Pk. Ave., Charlottesville, Va. 22903
Cascade Cartridge, Inc., (See Omark)
Catco-Ambush, Inc., P.O. Box 300, Corte Madera, CA 94926 (paper bullet patches)
Chevron Case Master, R.R. 1, Ottawa, IL 61350
Lester Coats, 416 Simpson St., No. Bend, Ore. 97459 (core cutter)
Container Development Corp., 424 Montgomery St., Watertown, WI 53094
Continental Kite & Key Co., Box 40, Broomall, PA 19008 (primer pocket cleaner)
Cooper-Woodward, Box 972, Riverside, Calif. 92502 (Perfect Lube)
Corbin Mfg. & Supply Inc., P.O. Box 758, Phoenix, OR 97535/503-826-5211
Custom Products, 686 Baldwin St., Meadville, PA 16335/814-724-7045 (decapping tool, dies, etc.)
J. Dewey Mfg. Co., 186 Skyview Dr., Southbury, CT 06488/203-264-3064
Dillon Precision Prods., Inc., 7755 E. Gelding Dr., Suite 106, Scottsdale, AZ 85260/602-948-8009
Diverter Arms, Inc., P.O. Box 22084, Houston, TX 77027 (bullet puller)
Division Lead Co., 7742 W. 61st Pl., Summit, Ill. 60502
Eagle Products Co., 1520 Adelia Ave., So. El Monte, Cal. 91733
Edmisten Co. Inc., P.O. Box 1293, Hwy. 105, Boone, NC 28607/704-264-1490
Efemes Enterprises, P.O. Box 122M, Bay Shore, NY 11706 (Berdan decapper)
W. H. English, 4411 S. W. 100th, Seattle, Wash. 98146 (Paktool)
Farmer Bros., 1616-15th St., Eldora, IA 50627 (Lage)
Fitz, 653 N. Hagar St., San Fernando, CA 91340 (Fitz Flipper)
Flambeau Plastics, 801 Lynn, Baraboo, Wis. 53913
Forster Products Inc., 82 E. Lanark Ave., Lanark, Ill. 61046
Geo. M. Fullmer, 2499 Mavis St., Oakland, CA 94601 (seating die)
Gene's Gun Shop, Rt. 1, Box 890, Snyder, TX 79549/915-573-2323 (arbor press)
Goerg Enterprises, P.O. Box 531, Renton, WA 98056/206-833-1529
Gopher Shooter's Supply, Box 278, Faribault, MN 55021
The Gun Clinic, 81 Kale St., Mahtomedi, Minn. 55115
Hart Products, Rob. W. Hart & Son Inc., 401 Montgomery St., Nescopeck, PA 18635
Henriksen Tool Co., Inc., P.O. Box 668, Phoenix, OR 97535
Hensley & Gibbs, Box 10, Murphy, Ore. 97533
Richard Hoch, The Gun Shop, 62778 Spring Creek Rd., Montrose, CO 81401/303-249-3625 (custom schuetzen bullet moulds)
Hoffman Prods., P.O. Box 853, Lake Forest, IL 60045 (spl. gallery load press)
Hollywood Reloading, (see: Whitney Sales, Inc.)
Hornady (see: Pacific)
Hulme Firearm Serv., Box 83, Millbrae, Calif. 94030 (Star case feeder)
Independent Mach. & Gun Shop, 1416 N. Hayes, Pocatello, Ida. 83201
Ivy Armament, P.O. Box 10, Greendale, WI 53129
JASCO, Box 49751, Los Angeles, Calif. 90049
J & G Rifle Ranch, Box S80, Turner, MT 59542 (case tumblers)
Javelina Products, Box 337, San Bernardino, Cal. 92402 (Alox beeswax)
Neil Jones, 686 Baldwin St., Meadville, PA 16335 (decapping tool, dies)
Paul Jones Munitions Systems, see: Fitz Co.
Kexplore, P.O. Box 22084, Houston, TX 77027/713-789-6943
Kuharsky Bros. (see Modern Industries)
Lac-Cum Bullet Puller, Star Route, Box 240, Apollo, PA 15613/412-478-1794
Lage Uniwad Co., 1102 N. Washington St., Eldora, IA 50627 (Universal Shotshell Wad)
Lee Custom Engineering, Inc., see: Mequon Reloading Corp.
Lee Precision, Inc., 4275 Hwy. U, Hartford, WI 53027
Lewisystems, Menasha Corp., 426 Montgomery St., Watertown, WI 53094
L. L. F. Die Shop, 1281 Highway 99 N., Eugene, Ore. 97402
Dean Lincoln, P.O. Box 1886, Farmington, NM 87401 (mould)
Ljutic Industries, 918 N. 5th Ave., Yakima, Wash. 98902
Lock's Phila. Gun Exch., 6700 Rowland, Philadelphia, Pa. 19149
Lyman Products Corp., Rte. 147, Middlefield, CT 06455
McKillen & Heyer Inc., 37603 Arlington Dr., Box 627, Willoughby, OH 44094/216-942-2491 (case gauge)
Paul McLean, 2670 Lakeshore Blvd., W., Toronto 14, Ont., Canada (Universal Cartridge Holder)
MEC, Inc. (see: Mayville Eng. Co.)
MTM Molded Prod., 5680 Webster St., Dayton, OH 45414
Magma Eng. Co., P.O. Box 881, Chandler, AZ 85224
Judson E. Mariotti, Beauty Hill Rd., Barrington, NH 03825 (brass bullet mould)
Marmel Prods., P.O. Box 97, Utica, MI 48087 (Marvelube, Marvelux)
Marquart Precision Co., P.O. Box 1740, Prescott, AZ 86302/602-445-5646 (precision case-neck turning tool)
Mayville Eng. Co., 715 South St., Mayville, WI 53050/414-387-4500 (shotshell loader)
Mequon Reloading Corp., P.O. Box 253, Mequon, WI 53092/414-673-3060
Merit Gun Slight Co., P.O. Box 995, Sequim, WA 98382
Modern Industries, Inc., 613 W-11, Erie, PA 16501 (primer pocket cleaner)
Multi-Scale Charge Ltd., 3269 Niagara Falls Blvd., North Tonawanda, NY 14120
Normington Co., Box 6, Rathdrum, ID 83858 (powder baffles)
NorthEast Industrial Inc., 2516 Wyoming, El Paso, TX 79903/915-532-8344 (bullet mould)
Ohaus Scale, (see: RCBS)
Omark Industries, Box 856, Lewiston, ID 83501/208-746-2351
P&P Tool Co., 125 W. Market St., Morrison, IL 61270/815-772-7618 (12-ga. shot wad)

Pacific Tool Co., P.O. Box 2048, Ordnance Plant Rd., Grand Island, NE 68801/308-384-2308
Pak-Tool Co., 4411 S.W. 100th, Seattle, WA 98146
Ferris Pindell, R.R. 3, Box 205, Connersville, IN 47331 (bullet spinner)
Plum City Ballistics Range, Rte. 1, Box 29A, Plum City, WI 54761
Ponsness-Warren, Inc., P.O. Box 8, Rathdrum, ID 83858
Marian Powley, Petra Lane, R.R.I, Eldridge, IA 52748/319-285-9214
Precise Alloys Inc., 69 Kinkel St., Westbury, NY 11590 (chilled lead shot; bullet wire)
Quinetics Corp., P.O. Box 29007, San Antonio, TX 78229/516-684-8561 (kinetic bullet puller)
RCBS, Inc., Box 1919, Oroville, CA 95965/916-533-5191
Redding Inc., 114 Starr Rd., Cortland, NY 13045
Reloaders Equipment Co., 4680 High St., Ecorse, MI 48229 (bullet puller)
Remco, 1404 Whitesboro St., Utica, NY 13502 (shot caps)
Rifle Ranch, Rte. 5, Prescott, Ariz. 86301
Rochester Lead Works, 76 Anderson Ave., Rochester, NY 14608/716-442-8500 (leadwire)
Rorschach Precision Prods., P.O. Box 1613, Irving, Tex. 75060
Rotex Mfg. Co. (see Texan)
SAECO Rel. Inc., P.O. Box 778, Carpinteria, Calif. 93013
SSK Industries, Rt. 1, Della Drive, Bloomingdale, OH 43910 (primer tool)
Sandia Die & Cartridge Co., Rte. 5, Box 5400, Albuquerque, NM 87123
Shassere, (Box 35865, Houston, TX 77096/713-780-7041 (cartridge case caddy/loading block)
Shiloh Products, 37 Potter St., Farmingdale, NY 11735 (4-cavity bullet mould)
Shooters Accessory Supply, see: Corbin Mfg. & Supply
Sil's Gun Prod., 490 Sylvan Dr., Washington, Pa. 15301 (K-spinner)
Jerry Simmons, 715 Middlebury St., Goshen, Ind. 46526/219-533-8546 (Pope de- & recapper)
Smith & Wesson Ammunition Co., Inc., 2399 Forman Rd., Rock Creek, OH 44084
J. A. Somers Co., P.O. Box 49751, Los Angeles, CA 90049 (Jasco)
Sport Flite Mfg., Inc., 2520 Industrial Row, Troy, MI 48084/313-280-0648 (swaging dies)
Star Machine, 418 10th Ave., San Diego, CA 92101
T.E.S., Inc., 2200 Bott St., Colorado Springs, CO 80904/303-475-1167 (Vibra-Tek)
T&T Products, Inc., 6330 Hwy. 14 East, Rochester, MN 55901 (Meyer shotgun slugs)
Texan Reloaders, Inc., 444 Cip St., Watseka, IL 60970/815-432-5065
Trico Plastics, 590 S. Vincent Ave., Azusa, CA 91702
WAMADET, Silver Springs, Goodleigh, Barnstaple, Devon, England
Walker Mfg. Inc., 8296 So. Channel, Harsen's Island, MI 48028 (Berdan decapper)
Wammes Guns Inc., 236 N. Hayes St., Bellefontaine, OH 43311 (Jim's powder baffles)
Weatherby, Inc., 2781 Firestone Blvd., South Gate, Calif. 90280
Webster Scale Mfg. Co., Box 188, Sebring, Fla. 33870
Whits Shooting Stuff, P.O. Box 1340, Cody, WY 82414
Whitney Sales, Inc., P.O. 875, Reseda, CA 91335 (Hollywood)
L. E. Wilson, Inc., P.O. Box 324, 404 Pioneer Ave., Cashmere, WA 98815
Xelex, Ltd., P.O. Box 543, Renfrow K7V 4B1, Canada (powder)
Zenith Enterprises, 361 Flagler Rd., Nordland, WA 98358

RESTS—BENCH, PORTABLE, ETC.

B-Square Co., P.O. Box 11281, Ft. Worth, TX 76109/817-923-0964 (handgun)
Bausch & Lomb, 635 St. Paul St., Rochester, NY 14602 (rifle rest)
Jim Brobst, 299 Poplar St., Hamburg, PA 19526 (bench rest pedestal)
C'Arco, P.O. Box 2043, San Bernardino, CA 92401 (Ransom handgun rest)
Cravener's Gun Shop, 1627 - 5th Ave., Ford City, PA 16226 (portable)
Decker Shooting Products, 1729 Laguna Ave., Schofield, WI 54476 (rifle rests)
The Gun Case, 11035 Maplefield, El Monte, Cal. 91733
Harris Inc., Barlow, KY 42024
Rob. W. Hart & Son, 401 Montgomery St., Nescopeck, Pa. 18635
Tony Hidalgo, 6 Capp St., Carteret, NJ 07008 (shooters stools)
North Star Devices, Inc., P.O. Box 2095, North St. Paul, MN 55109 (Gun Slinger)
Progressive Prods., Inc., P.O. Box 41, Holmen, WI 54636 (Sandbagger rifle rest)
Rec. Prods., Res., Inc., 158 Franklin Ave., Ridgewood, N.J. 07450 (Butts Pipod)
Suter's, 332 Tejon, Colorado Springs, CO 80902
Tuller & Co., Basil Tuller 29 Germania, Galeton, PA 16922/814-435-2442 (Protector sandbags)
Turkey Creek Enterprises, Rt. 1, Box 10, Red Oak, CA 74563/918-754-2884 (portable shooting rest)
Wichita Arms, 333 Lulu, Wichita, KS 67211

RIFLE BARREL MAKERS

P.O. Ackley Rifle Barrels (see: David M. Bellm Gunsmithing Inc.)
Atkinson Gun Co., P.O. Box 512, Prescott, AZ 86301
Jim Baiar, 490 Halfmoon Rd., Columbia Falls, MT 59912/406-892-4409
Dennis M. Bellm Gunsmithing Inc., 2376 So. Redwood Rd., Salt Lake City, UT 84119/801-974-0697; price list $3
Ralph L. Carter, Carter's Gun Shop, 225 G St., Penrose, CO 81240/303-372-6240
Christy Gun Works, 875 57th St., Sacramento, Calif. 95819
Clerke Prods., 2219 Main St., Santa Monica, Calif. 90405
Cuthbert Gun Shop, 715 So. 5th, Coos Bay, Ore. 97420

B. W. Darr, Saeco-Darr Rifle Co., Ltd., P.O. Box 778, Carpinteria, CA 93013
Charles P. Donnelly & Son, Siskiyou Gun Works, 405 Kubli Rd., Grants Pass, OR 97526/503-846-6604
Douglas Barrels, Inc., 5504 Big Tyler Rd., Charleston, W. Va. 25312
Douglas Jackalope Gun & Sport Shop, Inc., 1048 S. 5th St., Douglas, WY 82633
Federal Firearms Co., Inc., Box 145, 145 Thoms Run Rd., Oakdale, PA 15071/412-221-0300
C. R. & D. E. Getz, Box 88, Beavertown, PA 17813
A. R. Goode, 12845 Catoctin Furnace Rd., Thurmont, MD 21788/301-271-2228
Half Moon Rifle Shop, 490 Halfmoon Rd., Columbia Falls, MT 59912/406-892-4409
H-S Precision, Inc., 112 N. Summit, Prescott, AZ 85302/602-445-0607
Hart Rifle Barrels, Inc., RD 2, Lafayette, N.Y. 13084
Wm. H. Hobaugh, Box M, Philipsburg, MT 59858
Huntington Precision Arms Inc., David R. Huntington, 670 So. 300 West, Heber City, UT 84032/801-654-2953
Kogot, John Pell, 410 College Ave., Trinidad, CO 81082/303-846-9006 (custom octagon)
Les' Gun Shop, (Les Bauska), 105-9th West, P.O. Box 511, Kalispell, MT 59901/406-755-2635
Marquart Precision Co., P.O. Box 1740, Prescott, AZ 86302/602-445-5646
Nu-Line Guns, 1053 Caulkshill Rd., Harvester, MO 63303/314-441-4500
Numrich Arms, W. Hurley, N.Y. 12491
Al Petersen, The Rifle Ranch, Box 8, Riverhurst, Sask., Canada SOH3PO
Sanders Cust. Gun Serv., 2358 Tyler Lane, Louisville, Ky. 40205
SGW, Inc., D. A. Schuetz, 624 Old Pacific Hwy. S.E., Olympia, WA 98503/206-456-3471
Sharon Gun Specialties, 14587 Peaceful Valley Rd., Sonora, CA 95370/209-532-4139
E. R. Shaw, Inc., Prestley & Thomas Run Rd., Bridgeville, PA 15017/412-221-3636
Ed Shilen Rifles, Inc., 205 Metropark Blvd., Ennis, TX 75119
W. C. Strutz, Rifle Barrels, Inc., P.O. Box 611, Eagle River, WI 54521/715-479-4766
Titus Barrel & Gun Co., R.F.D. #1, Box 23, Heber City, UT 84032
Bob Williams, P.O. Box 143, Boonsboro, MD 21713
Wilson Arms, 63 Leetes Island Rd., Branford, CT 06405

SCOPES, MOUNTS, ACCESSORIES, OPTICAL EQUIPMENT

Aimpoint U.S.A., 201 Elden St., Suite 103, Herndon, VA 22070/703-471-6828 (electronic sight)
The American Import Co., 1167 Mission, San Francisco, CA 94103/415-863-1506
Anderson Mfg. Co., Union Gap Sta. P.O. Box 3120, Yakima, WA 98903/509-453-2349 (lens cap)
Armsport, Inc., 3590 N.W. 49th St., Miami, FL 33122/305-592-7850
B-Square Co., Box 11281, Ft. Worth, TX 76109 (Mini-14 mount)
Bausch & Lomb, Inc., 1400 Goodman St., Rochester, NY 14602/716-338-6000
Beeman's Precision Airguns, Inc., 47 Paul Dr., San Rafael, CA 94903/415-472-7121
Bennett, 561 Delaware, Delmar, N.Y. 12054 (mounting wrench)
Lenard M. Brownell, Box 25, Wyarno, WY 82845/307-737-2468 (cust. mounts)
Browning Arms, Rt. 4, Box 624-B, Arnold, Mo. 63010
Maynard P. Buehler, Inc., 17 Orinda Highway, Orinda, CA 94563/415-254-3201 (mounts)
Burris Co. Inc., 331 E. 8th St., Box 1747, Greeley, CO 80631/303-356-1670
Bushnell Optical Co., 2828 E. Foothill Blvd., Pasadena, Calif. 91107
Butler Creek Corp., Box GG, Jackson Hole, WY 83001 (lens caps)
Kenneth Clark, 18738 Highway 99, Madera, Calif. 93637
Clearview Mfg. Co., Inc., 20821 Grand River Ave., Detroit, MI 48219 (mounts)
Colt's, Hartford, Conn. 06102
Compass Instr. & Optical Co., Inc., 104 E 25th St., New York, N.Y. 10010
Conetrol Scope Mounts, Hwy 123 South, Seguin, TX 78155
D&H Prods. Co., Inc., P.O. Box 22, Glenshaw, PA 15116/412-443-2190 (lens covers)
Davis Optical Co., P.O. Box 6, Winchester, Ind. 47934
Del-Sports Inc., Main St., Margaretville, NY 12455/914-586-4103 (Kahles)
Eder Instrument Co., 5115 N. Ravenswood, Chicago, IL 60640 (borescope)
Flaig's, Babcock Blvd., Millvale, Pa. 15209
Fontaine Ind., Inc., 11552 Knott St., Suite 2, Garden Grove, CA 92641/714-892-4473
Freeland's Scope Stands, Inc. 3734 14th, Rock Island, Ill. 61201
Griffin & Howe, Inc., 589 Broadway, New York, N.Y. 10012
H&H Assoc., P.O. Box 447, Strathmore, CA 93267 (target adj. knobs)
H. J. Hermann Leather Co., Rt. 1, Skiatook, OK 74070 (lens caps)
Friedr. Wilh. HEYM, Box 861, Bolton, Ont. Canada IOP 1AO (Nickel; Hertel & Reuss scopes)
J. B. Holden Co., 295 W. Pearl, Plymouth, MI 48170
The Hutson Corp., 105 Century Dr. No., Mansfield, TX 76063/817-477-3421
Hy-Score Arms Corp., 200 Tillary St., Brooklyn, N.Y. 11201
Import Scope Repair Co., P.O. Box 2633, Durango, CO 81301/303-563-9307
Interarms, 10 Prince St., Alexandria, VA 22313
Paul Jaeger, Inc., 211 Leedom St., Jenkintown, PA 19046
Jana Intl. Co., Box 1107, Denver, Colo. 80201
Jason Empire Inc., 9200 Cody, P.O. Box 12370, Overland Park, KS 66212/913-888-0220
Jennison TCS (see Fontaine Ind., Inc.)
Kahles of America, Div. of Del-Sports, Inc. Main St., Margaretville, NY 12455/914-586-4103

Kesselring Gun Shop, 400 Pacific Hiway No., Burlington, WA 98283/206-724-3113
Kris Mounts, 108 Lehigh St., Johnstown, PA 15905
Kuharsky Bros. (see Modern Industries)
Kwik-Site, 5555 Treadwell, Wayne, MI 48185 (rings, mounts only)
S. E. Laszlo House of Imports, 200 Tillary St., Brooklyn, NY 11201
Leatherwood Bros., Rte. 1, Box 111, Stephenville, TX 76401
T. K. Lee, 2830 S. 19th St., Off. #4, Birmingham, AL 35209 (reticles)
E. Leitz, Inc., Rockleigh, N.J. 07647
Leupold & Stevens Inc., P.O. Box 688, Beaverton, Ore. 97075
Jake Levin and Son, Inc., 9200 Cody, Overland Park, KS 66214
W. H. Lodewick, 2816 N.E. Halsey, Portland, OR 97232 (scope safeties)
Lyman Products Corp., Route 147, Middlefield, CT 06455
Mandall Shooting Supplies, 7150 E. 4th St., Scottsdale, AZ 85252
Marble Arms Co., 420 Industrial Park, Gladstone, MI 49837
Marlin Firearms Co., 100 Kenna Dr., New Haven, Conn. 06473
Robert Medaris, P.O. Box 309, Mira Loma, CA 91752/714-685-5666 (side mount f. H&K 91 & 93)
Millett Industries, 16131 Gothard St., Hungtington Beach, CA 92647/714-842-5575 (mounts)
Modern Industries, Inc., 613 W-11, Erie, PA 16501
O. F. Mossberg & Sons, Inc., 7 Grasso Ave., North Haven, Conn. 06473
Nite-Site, Inc., P.O. Box O, Rosemount, MN 55068/612-890-7631
Normark Corp., 1710 E. 78th St., Minneapolis, Minn. 55423 (Singlepoint)
Numrich Arms, West Hurley, N.Y. 12491
Nydar, see: Swain Nelson Co.
PEM's Mounts, 6063 Waterloo, Atwater, PA 44201
Pachmayr Gun Works, 1220 S. Grand Ave., Los Angeles, CA 90015/213-748-7271
Pilkington Gun Co., P.O. Box 2284, University Sta., Enid, OK 73701/405-242-0025 (Q.D. mt.)
Precise, 3 Chestnut, Suffern, NY 10901
Ranging Inc., 90 Lincoln Rd. North, East Rochester, NY 14445/716-385-1250
Ray-O-Vac, Willson Prod. Div., P.O. Box 622, Reading, PA 19603 (shooting glasses)
Redfield Gun Sight Co., 5800 E. Jewell Ave., Denver, CO 80222/303-757-6411
S & K Mfg. Co., Box 247, Pittsfield, Pa. 16340 (Insta-mount)
Sanders Cust. Gun Serv., 2358 Tyler Lane, Louisville, Ky. 40205 (MSW)
Savage Arms, Westfield, Mass. 01085
Sears, Roebuck & Co., 825 S. St. Louis, Chicago, Ill. 60607
Sherwood Intl. Export Corp., 18714 Parthenia St., Northridge, CA 91324 (mounts)
W. H. Siebert, 22720 S.E. 56th Pl., Issaquah, WA 98027
Singlepoint (see Normark)
Southern Precision Inst. Co., 3419 E. Commerce St., San Antonio, TX 78219
Spacetron Inc., Box 84, Broadview, IL 60155 (bore lamp)
Stoeger Industries, 55 Ruta Ct., S. Hackensack, NJ 07606/201-440-2700
Strieter Corp., 2100 - 18th St., Rock Island, IL 61201/309-794-9800 (Swarovski, Habicht)
Supreme Lens Covers, Box GG, Jackson Hole, WY 83001 (lens caps)
Swain Nelson Co., Box 45, 92 Park Dr., Glenview, IL 60025 (shotgun sight)
Swift Instruments, Inc., 952 Dorchester Ave., Boston, Mass. 02125
Tasco, 1075 N.W. 71st, Miami, Fla. 33138
Ted's Sight Aligner, Box 1073, Scottsdale, AZ 85252
Thompson-Center Arms, P.O. Box 2405, Rochester, N.H. 03867 (handgun scope)
Tradewinds, Inc., Box 1191, Tacoma, Wash. 98401
John Unertl Optical Co., 3551-5 East St., Pittsburgh, Pa. 15214
United Binocular Co., 9043 S. Western Ave., Chicago, Ill. 60620
Verano Corp., Box 270, Glendora, CA 91740
Vissing (see: Supreme Lens Covers)
Wasp Shooting Systems, Box 241, Lakeview, AR 72642/501-431-5606 (mtg. system f. Ruger Mini-14 only)
Weatherby's, 2781 Firestone, South Gate, Calif. 90280
W. R. Weaver Co., 7125 Industrial Ave., El Paso, Tex. 79915
Wide View Scope Mount Corp., 26110 Michigan Ave., Inkster, MI 48141
Williams Gun Sight Co., 7389 Lapeer Rd., Davison, Mich. 48423
Boyd Williams Inc., 8701-14 Mile Rd. (M-57), Cedar Springs, MI 49319 (BR)
Willrich Precision Instrument Co., 95 Cedar Lane, Englewood, NJ 07631/201-567-1411 (borescope)
Carl Zeiss Inc., 444 Fifth Ave., New York, N.Y. 10018 (Hensoldt)

SIGHTS, METALLIC

Accura-Site Co., Inc., Box 193, Neenah, WI 54956
B-Square Eng. Co., Box 11281, Ft. Worth, Tex. 76110
Beeman's Precision Airguns, Inc., 47 Paul Dr., San Rafael, CA 94903/415-472-7121 (airguns only)
Behlert Custom Sights, Inc., 725 Lehigh Ave., Union, NJ 07083
Bo-Mar Tool & Mfg. Co., Box 168, Carthage, Tex. 75633
Maynard P. Buehler, Inc., 17 Orinda Highway, Orinda, CA 94563/415-254-3201
Christy Gun Works, 875 57th St., Sacramento, Calif. 95819
Jim Day, 902 N. Bowonen Lane, Florence, SD 29501 (Chaba)
Freeland's Scope Stands, Inc., 3734-14th Ave., Rock Island, Ill. 61201
Paul T. Haberly, 2364 N. Neva, Chicago, IL 60635
Paul Jaeger, Inc., 211 Leedom St., Jenkintown, PA 19046
Lee's Red Ramps, 7252 E. Ave. U-3, Littlerock, CA 93543/805-944-4487 (illuminated sights)
Jim Lofland, 2275 Larkin Rd., Boothwyn, PA 19061
Lyman Products Corp., Rte. 147, Middlefield, Conn. 06455
Marble Arms Corp., 420 Industrial Park, Gladstone, Mich. 49837
Merit Gunsight Co., P.O. Box 995, Sequim, WA 98382
Micro Sight Co., 242 Harbor Blvd., Belmont, Calif. 94002

Millet Industries, 16131 Gothard St., Huntington Beach, CA 92647/714-842-5575
Miniature Machine Co., 210 E. Poplar, Deming, NM 88030/505-546-2151
Modern Industries, Inc., 613 W-11, Erie, PA 16501
C. R. Pedersen & Son, 2717 S. Pere Marquette, Ludington, MI 49431/616-843-2061
Poly Choke Co., Inc., P.O. Box 2496, Hartford, CT 06101/203-289-2743
Redfield Gun Sight Co., 5800 E. Jewell St., Denver, Colo. 80222
S&M Tang Sights, P.O. Box 1338, West Babylon, NY 11704
Schwarz's Gun Shop, 41 - 15th St., Wellsburg, W. Va. 26070
Simmons Gun Specialties, Inc., 700 Rodgers Rd., Olathe, Kans. 66061
Slug Site Co., Whitetail Wilds, Lake Hubert, MN 56469
Sport Service Center, 2364 N. Neva, Chicago, IL 60635
Tradewinds, Inc., Box 1191, Tacoma, WA 98401
Wichita Arms, 333 Lulu, Wichita, KS 67211/316-265-0661
Williams Gun Sight Co., 7389 Lapeer Rd., Davison, Mich. 48423

STOCKS (Commercial and Custom)

Adams Custom Gun Stocks, 13461 Quito Rd., Saratoga, CA 95070
Ahlman's Inc., R.R. 1, Box 20, Morristown, MN 55052
Don Allen, Rte. 4, Northfield, MN 55057/507-645-9216 (blanks)
Anderson's Guns, Jim Jares, 706 S. 23rd St., Laramie, WY 82070
R. J. Anton, 874 Olympic Dr., Waterloo, IA 50701/319-233-3666
Jim Baiar, 490 Halfmoon Rd., Columbia Falls, MT 59912
Joe J. Balickie, Custom Stocks, Rte. 2, Box 56-G, Apex, NC 27502
Bartas, Rte. 1, Box 129-A, Cato, Wis. 54206
Donald Bartlett, 16111 S.E. 229th Pl., Kent, WA 98031/206-630-2190 (cust.)
Beeman's Precision Airguns, Inc., 47 Paul Dr., San Rafael, CA 94903/415-472-7121 (airguns only)
John Bianchi, 100 Calle Cortez, Temecula, CA 92390 (U. S. carbines)
Al Biesen, West 2039 Sinto Ave., Spokane, Wash. 99201
Stephen L. Billeb, Box 219, Philipsburg, MT 59858/406-859-3919
E. C. Bishop & Son Inc., Box 7, Warsaw, Mo. 65355
John M. Boltin, P.O. Box 1122, No. Myrtle Beach, SC 29582
Border Gun Shop, Garry Simmons, 2760 Tucson Hiway, Nogales, AZ 85621/602-281-0045 (spl. silueta stocks, complete rifles)
Garnet D. Brawley, 8931 Stanwin Ave., Arleta, CA 91331/213-767-0742 (cust.)
Brown Precision Co., P.O. Box 270W; 7786 Molinos Ave., Los Molinos, CA 96055/916-384-2506
Lenard M. Brownell, Box 25, Wyarno, WY 82845
E. J. Bryant, 3154 Glen St., Eureka, CA 95501
Jack Burres, 10333 San Fernando Road, Pacoima, CA 91331 (English, Claro, Bastogne Paradox walnut blanks only)
Calico Hardwoods, Inc., 1648 Airport Blvd., Windsor, CA 95492/707-546-4045 (blanks)
Dick Campbell, 365 W. Oxford Ave., Englewood, CO 80110
Winston Churchill, Twenty Mile Stream Rd., Rt.1, Box 29B, Proctorsville, VT 05153
Crane Creek Gun Stock Co., 25 Shephard Terr., Madison, WI 53705
Reggie Cubriel, 15502 Purple Sage, San Antonio, TX 78255/512-695-8401 (cust. stockm.)
Dahl's Custom Stocks, Rt. 4, Box 558, Schofield Rd., Lake Geneva, WI 53147/414-248-2464 (Martin Dahl)
Jack Dever, 8520 N.W. 90, Oklahoma City, OK 73132
Charles De Veto, 1087 Irene Rd., Lyndhurst, O. 44124
Gary Duncan, 1118 Canterbury, Enid, OK 73701 (blanks only)
David A. Dunlop, Rte. 1, Box 199, Rolla, ND 58367
Jere Eggleston, P.O. Box 50238, Columbia, SC 29250/803-799-3402 (cust.)
Bob Emmons, 238 Robson Road, Grafton, OH 44044 (custom)
Reinhart Fajen, Box 338, Warsaw, MO 65355/814-438-5111
N. B. Fashingbauer, P.O. Box 366, Lac Du Flambeau, WI 54538/715-588-7116
Ted Fellowes, Beaver Lodge, 9245 16th Ave. S. W., Seattle, Wash. 98106
Phil Fischer, 2625 N.E. Multnomah, Portland, OR 97232/503-282-7151 (cust.)
Clyde E. Fischer, Rt. 1, Box 170-M, Victoria, Tex. 77901
Jerry Fisher, 1244-4th Ave. W., Kalispell, MT 59901/406-755-7093
Flaig's Lodge, Millvale, Pa. 15209
Donald E. Folks, 205 W. Lincoln St., Pontiac, IL 61764/815-844-7901 (cust.)
Larry L. Forster, Box 212, Gwinner, ND 58040
Freeland's Scope Stands, Inc., 3734 14th Ave., Rock Island, Ill. 61201
Dale Goens, Box 224, Cedar Crest, N.M. 87008
Gary Goudy, 263 Hedge Rd., Menlo Park, CA 94025/415-322-1338 (cust.)
Gould's Myrtlewood, 1692 N. Dogwood, Coquille, Ore. 97423 (gun blanks)
Charles E. Grace, 10144 Elk Lake Rd., Williamsburg, MI 49690
Rolf R. Gruning, 315 Busby Dr., San Antonio, Tex. 78209
Karl Guenther, 43-32 160th St., Flushing, NY 11372/212-461-7325
Guncraft, Inc., 117 W. Pipeline, Hurst, TX 76053/817-268-2887
The Gunshop, R. D. Wallace, 320 Overland Rd., Prescott, AZ 86301 (custom)
Half Moon Rifle Shop, 490 Halfmoon Rd., Columbia Falls, MT 59912
Harper's Custom Stocks, 928 Lombrano St., San Antonio, Tex. 78207
Harris Gun Stocks, Inc., 12 Lake St., Richfield Springs, N.Y. 13439
Hal Hartley, 147 Blairsfork Rd., Lenoir, NC 28645
Hayes Gunstock Service Co., 914 E. Turner St., Clearwater, Fla. 33516
Hubert J. Hecht, Waffen-Hecht, Sacramento, CA 95814/916-448-1177
Edward O. Hefti, 300 Fairview, College Sta., Tex. 77840
Klaus Hiptmayer, P.O. Box 136, Eastman, Que., JOE 1PO Canada/514-297-2492
Richard Hodgson, 5589 Arapahoe, Unit 104, Boulder, CO 80301
Hollis Gun Shop, 917 Rex St., Carlsbad, N.M. 88220
Henry Houser, Ozark Custom Carving, 117 Main St., Warsaw, MO 65355
Jackson's, Box 416, Selman City, Tex. 75689 (blanks)
Paul Jaeger, Inc., 211 Leedom St., Jenkintown, PA 19046/215-884-6920

Johnson Wood Products, R.R. #1, Strawberry Point, IA 52076/319-933-4930 (blanks)
Monte Kennedy, P.O. Box 214, Kalispell, MT 59901
Don Klein, Box 277, Camp Douglas, WI 54618
LeFever Arms Co., Inc., R.D. 1, Lee Center-Stokes Rd., Lee Center, NY 13363/315-337-6422
Lenz Firearms Co., 1480 Elkay Dr., Eugene, OR 97404
Stanley Kenvin, 5 Lakeville Lane, Plainview, NY 11803/516-931-0321 (custom)
Philip D. Letiecq, AQ 18 Wagon Box Rd., P.O. Box 251, Story, WY 82842/307-683-2817
Al Lind, 7821 76th Ave. S.W., Tacoma, WA 98498 (cust. stockm.)
Bill McGuire, 1600 N. Eastmont Ave., East Wenatchee, WA 98801
Gale McMillan, 28638 N. 42 St., Box 7870 - Cave Creek Stage, Phoenix, AZ 85020/602-585-4684
Maurer Arms, 2366 Frederick Dr., Cuyahoga Falls, OH 44221
John E. Maxson, Box 332, Dumas, TX 79029/806-935-5990 (custom)
Leonard Mews, Spring Rd., Box 242, Hortonville, WI 54944
Robt. U. Milhoan & Son, Rt. 3, Elizabeth, W. Va. 26143
C. D. Miller Guns, Purl St., St. Onge, SD 57779
Milliron Custom Guns & Stocks, 1249 N.E. 166th Ave., Portland, OR 97230/503-252-3725
Nelsen's Gun Shop, 501 S. Wilson, Olympia, Wash. 98501
Bruce Nettestad, R.R. 1, Box 140, Pelican Rapids, MN 56572/701-293-6011 (cust.)
Oakley and Merkley, Box 2446, Sacramento, CA 95811 (blanks)
Jim Norman, Custom Gunstocks, 11230 Calenda Road, San Diego, CA 92127/714-487-4173
Maurice Ottmar, Box 657, 113 E. Fir, Coulee City, WA 99115
Pachmayr Gun Works, 1220 S. Grand Ave., Los Angeles, CA 90015 (blanks and custom jobs)
Paulsen Gunstocks, Rte. 71, Box 11, Chinook, MT 59523 (blanks)
Peterson Mach. Carving, Box 1065, Sun Valley, Calif. 91352
R. Neal Rice, 5152 Newton, Denver, CO 80221
Richards Micro-Fit Stocks, P.O. Box 1066, Sun Valley, CA. 91352 (thumbhole)
Carl Roth, Jr., 4728 Pineridge Ave., Cheyenne, Wy. 82001
Matt Row, Lock, Stock 'N Barrel, 8972 East Huntington Dr., San Gabriel, CA 91775/213-287-0051
Royal Arms, Inc., 10064 Bert Acosta Ct., Santee, Calif. 92071
Sanders Cust. Gun Serv., 2358 Tyler Lane, Louisville, Ky. 40205 (blanks)
Saratoga Arms Co., 1752 N. Pleasantview Rd., Pottstown, PA 19464/215-323-8386
Roy Schaefer, 965 W. Hilliard Lane, Eugene, OR 97404 (blanks)
Shaw's, The Finest in Guns, 9447 W. Lilac Rd., Escondido, CA 92025/714-728-7070
Hank Shows, The Best, 1202 N. State, Ukaih, CA 95482
Walter Shultz, 1752 N. Pleasantview Rd., Pottstown, PA 19464
Sile Dist., 7 Centre Market Pl., New York, N.Y. 10013
Six Enterprises, 6564 Hidden Creek Dr., San Jose, CA 95120 (fiberglass)
Ed Sowers, 8331 DeCelis Pl., Sepulveda, CA 91343 (hydro-coil gunstocks)
Fred D. Speiser, 2229 Dearborn, Missoula, MT 59801
Sport Service Center, 2364 N. Neva, Chicago, IL 60635/312-889-1114 (custom)
Sportsmen's Equip. Co., 915 W. Washington, San Diego, Calif. 92103 (carbine conversions)
Keith Stegall, Box 696, Gunnison, Colo. 81230
Stinehour Rifles, Box 84, Cragsmoor, N.Y. 12420
Surf N' Sea, Inc., 62-595 Kam Hwy., Box 268, Haleiwa, HI 96712 (custom gunstocks blanks)
Swanson Cust. Firearms, 1051 Broadway, Denver, Colo. 80203
Talmage Enterpr., 43197 E. Whittier, Hemet, CA 92343
Brent L. Umberger, Sportsman's Haven, R.R. 4, Cambridge, OH 43725
John Vest, 6715 Shasta Way, Klamath Falls, OR 97601/503-884-5585 (classic rifles)
Weatherby's, 2781 Firestone, South Gate, Calif. 90280
Cecil Weems, Box 657, Mineral Wells, TX 76067
FrankR. Wells, 4025 N. Sabino Canyon Rd., Tucson, AZ 85715/602-887-3559 (custom stocks)
Western Gunstocks Mfg. Co., 550 ValenciaSchool Rd., Aptos, CA 95003
Duane Wiebe, P.O. Box 497, Lotus, CA 95651
Bob Williams, P.O. Box 143, Boonsboro, MD 21713
Williamson-Pate Gunsmith Service, 117 W. Pipeline, Hurst, TX 76053/817-268-2887
Robert M. Winter, Box 484, Menno, S.D. 57045
Mike Yee, 4700-46th Ave. S.W., Seattle, WA 98116
Russell R. Zeeryp, 1601 Foard Dr., Lynn Ross Manor, Morristown, TN 37814

TARGETS, BULLET & CLAYBIRD TRAPS

Beeman's Precision Airguns, Inc., 47 Paul Dr., San Rafael, CA 94903/415-472-7121 (airgun targets, silhouettes and traps)
Caswell Equipment Co., Inc., 1221 Marshall St. N.E., Minneapolis, MN 55413/612-379-2000
Detroit Bullet Trap Co., 2233 N. Palmer Dr., Schaumburg, Ill. 60195/312-397-4070
Electro Ballistic Lab., 616 Junipero Serva Blvd., Stanford, CA 94305 (Electronic Trap Boy)
Ellwood Epps Northern Ltd., 210 Worthington St. W., North Bay, Ont. PIB 3B4, Canada (hand traps)
Gopher Shooter's Supply, Box 278, Faribault, MN 55021 (Lok-A-Leg target holders)
Kory Shooting Equipment, 233 S. Wacker, Sears Tower/Suite 7130, Chicago, IL 60606 (electric ranges)
Laporte S.A., B.P. 212, 06603 Antibes, France (claybird traps)
Laporte Equipment Inc., 70 rue Martin St., Granby, Queb. J2G 8B3, Canada (claybird traps)

MCM (Mathalienne de Construction Mecanique), P.O. Box 18, 17160 Matha, France (claybird traps)
Millard F. Lerch, Box 163, 10842 Front St., Mokena, Ill. 60448 (bullet target)
National Target Co., 4960 Wyaconda Rd., Rockville, MD 20852
Outers Laboratories, Inc., Rte. 2 Onalaska, WI 54650/608-783-1515 (claybird traps)
Peterson Label Co., P.O. Box 1869, Redding Ridge, CT 06876/203-938-2349 (paste-ons; Targ-Dots)
Professional Tape Co., 355 E. Burlington Rd., Riverside, Ill. 60546 (Time Labels)
Recreation Prods. Res. Inc., 158 Franklin Ave., Ridgewood, NJ 07450 (Butts bullet trap)
Remington Arms Co., Bridgeport, Conn. 06602 (claybird traps)
Reproductions West, Box 6765, Burbank, CA 91510 (silhouette targets)
Rocky Mountain Target Co., P.O. Box 700, Black Hawk, SD 57718/605-787-5946 (Data-Targ)
Scientific Prod. Corp., 426 Swann Ave., Alexandria, VA 22301 (Targeteer)
Sheridan Products, Inc., 3205 Sheridan, Racine, Wis. 53403 (traps)
South West Metallic Silhouettes, P.O. Box 476, Uvalde, TX 78801
Time Products Co. (See Prof. Tape Co.)
Trius Prod., Box 25, Cleves, O. 45002 (claybird, can thrower)
Winchester-Western, New Haven, Conn. 06504 (claybird traps)

TAXIDERMY

Jack Atcheson & Sons, Inc., 3210 Ottawa St., Butte, MT 59701
Dough's Taxidermy Studio, Doug Domedion, 2027 Lockport-Olcott Rd., Burt, NY 14028/716-625-8377 (deer head specialist)
Jonas Bros., Inc., 1037 Broadway, Denver, CO 80203 (catlg. $2)
Knopp Taxidermy Studios, N. 6715 Division St., Spokane, WA 99208
Kulis Freeze-Dry Taxidermy, 725 Broadway Ave., Bedford, OH 44146
Mark D. Parker, 1233 Sherman Dr., Longmont, CO 80501/303-772-0214

TRAP & SKEET SHOOTERS EQUIP.

D&H Prods. Co., Inc., P.O. Box 22, Glenshaw, PA 15116/412-443-2190 (snap shell)
Griggs Recreational Prods. Inc., 200 S. Main, Twin Bridges, MT 59754/406-684-5202 (recoil redirector)
Laporte S.A., B.P. 212, Pont de la Brague, 06603 Antibes, France (traps, claybird)
Laporte Equipment Inc., 70 rue Martin St., Granby, Queb. J2G 8B3, Canada (claybird traps)
MCM (Mathalienne de Construction de Mecanique), P.O. Box 18, 17160 Matha, France (claybird traps)
Wm. J. Mittler, 290 Moore Dr., Boulder Creek, CA 95006 (shotgun choke specialist)
Multi-Gauge Enterprises, 433 W. Foothill Blvd., Monrovia, CA 91061 (shotgun specialists)
William J. Nittler, 290 More Dr., Boulder Creek, CA 95006 (shotgun repairs)
Herb Orre, Box 56, Phillipsburg, OH 45354 (shotgun specialist)
Outers Laboratories, Inc., Route 2, Onalaska, WI 54650/608-783-1515 (trap, claybird)
Purbaugh Sporting Goods, 433 W. Foothill Blvd., Monrovia, CA 91016 (shotgun barrel inserts)
Remington Arms Co., Bridgeport, CT 06602 (trap, claybird)
Super Pigeon Corp., P.O. Box 428, Princeton, MN 55371 (claybird target)
Trius Products, Box 25, Cleves, OH 45002 (can thrower; trap, claybird)
Daniel Titus, 119 Morlyn Ave., Bryn Mawr, PA 19010 (hull bag)
Winchester-Western, New Haven, CT 06504 (trap, claybird)

TRIGGERS, RELATED EQUIP.

Ametek, Hunter Spring Div., One Spring Ave., Hatfield, PA 19440/215-822-2971 (trigger gauge)
M. H. Canjar Co., 500 E. 45th Ave., Denver, CO 80216 (triggers)
Central Specialties Co., 6030 Northwest Hwy., Chicago, IL 60631/312-774-5000 (trigger lock)
Custom Products, 686 Baldwin St., Meadville, PA 16335/814-724-7045 (trigger guard)
Dayton-Traister Co., 9322-900th West, P.O. Box 593, Oak Harbor, WA 98277/206-675-5375 (triggers)
Electronic Trigger Systems, (Franklin C. Green), 530 W. Oak Grove Rd., Montrose, CO 81401
Flaig's, Babcock Blvd. & Thompson Run Rd., Millvale, PA 15209 (trigger shoe)
Gager Gage & Tool Co., 27509 Industrial Blvd., Hayward, CA 94545 (speedlock triggers f. Rem. 1100 and 870 shotguns)
Franklin C. Green, See Electronic Trigg. System
Bill Holmes, Rt. 2, Box 242, Fayetteville, AR 72701/501-521-8958 (trigger release)
Michaels of Oregon Co., P.O. Box 13010, Portland, OR 97213/503-255-6890 (trigger guards)
Miller Single Trigger Mfg. Co., R.D. 1, Box 99, Millersburg, PA 17061/717-692-3704
Viggo Miller, P.O. Box 4181, Omaha, NB 68104 (trigger attachment)
Ohaus Corp., 29 Hanover Rd., Florham Park, NJ 07932 (trigger pull gauge)
Pachmayr Gun Works, 1220 S. Grand Ave., Los Angeles, CA 90015 (trigger shoe)
Pacific Tool Co., P.O. Box 2048, Ordnance Plant Rd., Grand Island, NE 68801 (trigger shoe)
Richland Arms Co., 321 W. Adrian St., Blissfield, MI 49228 (trigger pull gauge)
Sport Service Center, 2364 N. Neva, Chicago, IL 60635 (release triggers)
Timney Mfg. Co., 2847 E. Siesta Lane, Phoenix, AZ 85024 (triggers)
Melvin Tyler, 1326 W. Britton Ave., Oklahoma City, OK 73114 (trigger shoe)
Williams Gun Sight Co., 7389 Lapeer Rd., Davison, MI 48423 (trigger shoe)